# ALA World Encyclopedia of Library and Information Services

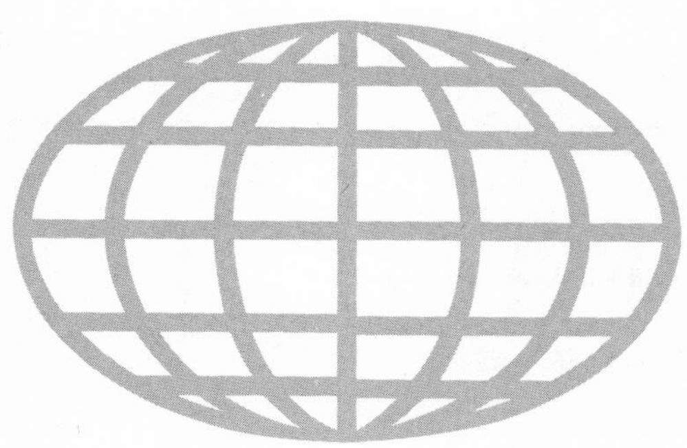

AMERICAN LIBRARY ASSOCIATION
*Chicago 1980*

| | |
|---|---|
| ROBERT WEDGEWORTH | *Editor* |
| DONALD E. STEWART | *Managing Editor* |
| JOEL M. LEE | *Associate Editor* |
| MARILYN LITVIN | *Assistant Editor* |

| | |
|---|---|
| CAROL RANEY KELM | *Indexing Editor* |
| BARBARA CLEARY | *Contributing Editor for Production* |
| CAROL SCHALK | *Contributing Editor* |
| SARAH ELIZABETH HOW | *Contributing Picture Editor* |
| HARRIETT BANNER | *Production Manager and Designer* |
| VLADIMIR REICHL | *Typographic Artist* |
| KEITH MICHAEL FIELS, JOHN ATKINSON, NORA DELL | *Picture Researchers* |
| EILEEN BRAUN, JANE LAGEN, KEITH R. SCHLESINGER | *Contributing Editorial Researchers* |
| ROBERT J. BERAN | *Proofreader* |

---

**Library of Congress Cataloging in Publication Data**
Main entry under title:

ALA world encyclopedia of library and information services.

Editor: R. Wedgeworth.
Includes index.
1. Library science—Dictionaries. 2. Information science—Dictionaries. I. Wedgeworth, Robert. II. American Library Association. III. Title: World encyclopedia of library and information services.
Z1006.A18 020.3 80-10912
ISBN 0-8389-0305-3


*Printed in the United States of America*

# Editor's Preface

The idea of an *ALA World Encyclopedia of Library and Information Services* stems directly from the responsibility of a professional field to *inform* and *educate* its students, its practitioners, and the public about the interests and activities of the field. Efforts to fulfill this responsibility in the latter half of the 20th century have been severely hampered by the extraordinary growth and development of all fields of knowledge. Since understanding the significance of rapid, and sometimes dramatic, change requires periodic review and synthesis, the emergence of the idea upon which this work is based was inevitable.

The need for current information about the field of library and information services was addressed earlier by Donald E. Stewart, Managing Editor, and by the Editor when we created *The ALA Yearbook,* first published in 1976. This annual review of information about library events, activities, and personalities reached its fourth volume in 1979. When the initial discussions of an *ALA Encyclopedia* began in 1976, there was a clear realization that the *Yearbook* alone could not provide a proper historical context for many of the topics it covers. Background information essential for the comprehension of current issues and problems could not be provided in the *Yearbook* and usually did not appear in the literature that it summarized.

From its inception the editors of the *Yearbook* sought an international perspective, but defining the breadth and scope of such coverage demands knowledge of the history as well as the present status and condition of libraries, archives, and other information services in many countries. For these basic reasons, an *ALA Encyclopedia* was conceived to provide an ordered synthesis of library and information services as they have developed throughout the world but with emphasis on North America. An editorial plan for the *Encyclopedia* was proposed to the ALA Publishing Committee and to a selected group of advisers for review in late 1977. Their comments resulted in a revised plan that guided the development of this work.

Several previously published works were helpful in planning this volume. Fritz Milkau's *Handbuch der Bibliothekswissenschaft* is one of the most comprehensive and scholarly encyclopedias of libraries ever published. Although much of its information about the history of libraries in ancient times is without equal, its topical arrangement and the lack of an English language translation render it less than accessible to many readers.

The *Encyclopedia of Library and Information Science,* edited by Kent, Lancour, and Daily, now in its 27th volume, is the most comprehensive current encyclopedia in the field. It is a work of very broad scope, covering technical, historical, and philosophical topics. Nevertheless, it has been affected by the dramatic growth and development of the field since its inception, resulting in some lack of comparability between information in earlier and later volumes. The *Dictionary of American Library Biography,* which consists of scholarly biographies of significant figures in the U.S. library world who are no longer living, set a high standard for the selection and presentation of biographical data quite useful in developing biographies for the *ALA Encyclopedia.*

An important distinction of the *ALA Encyclopedia* as it takes it place among earlier works is that, although initially conceived as a basic companion to the *ALA Yearbook,* the *ALA Encyclopedia* is an entirely new work. It is comparable in style but much broader in scope than the *Yearbook.* In one convenient volume, the *ALA Encyclopedia* seeks to explain fundamental ideas, record historical events and activities, and portray those personalities, living and dead, who have shaped the field.

The editorial plan for the *ALA Encyclopedia* consists of six basic categories of articles:

(1) There are structured articles about the status and condition of libraries with accompanying statistics provided by the contributor for 162 countries in the world. In addition other articles cover the history and role of libraries from ancient times to the present.

(2) Nine articles cover the major types of institutions that deliver library and information services. These articles were directed by a principal contributor, in most cases with a team of contributors who wrote comprehensive articles exploring the purpose, characteristic services, clientele, and patterns of governance, finance, and administration of the institutions. They represent an editorial approach to comparative librarianship, in an attempt to discern commonalities and differences in these institutions and their practices as they exist in many countries.

(3) Twenty-five articles explore the principles and practices of librarianship and information management, explaining and analyzing the fundamental processes and basic types of services to the many different client groups.

(4) Ten articles cover the field of education and research from early apprenticeship to formal library education.
(5) Twenty-eight articles describe the activities of significant international organizations, agencies, and associations not covered under individual countries.
(6) One hundred seventy-two biographical subjects from different places of the world and from different times were selected for inclusion from nominations made by the international advisory group. Among the editors' criteria for inclusion are: foundation of an important library, or a primary role in a major library's growth, development, and influence; author of seminal writings of great impact and lasting influence; leadership in the profession, including activity in professional associations; significant activity as a library educator; contribution to the theory of librarianship in any of the field's components; exemplary role as a practitioner, within any part of the profession; publisher of related books and periodicals; and leadership in important national and international bibliographic enterprises.

The articles, which are alphabetically arranged, vary in length from several hundred to more than a thousand words, providing enough space to treat significant aspects of each topic. One hundred forty-four statistical tables and 300 illustrations enliven and enrich the text.

Two editorial features merit special mention. Before determining the list of articles that would comprise this work, a complete outline of the fields of knowledge was constructed to guide the editors and advisers in initial planning. This approach made it possible to determine the breadth and scope of coverage for each historical topic and technical issue and ensured even geographic representation. It also provided a map that set the scope and limits of each article and that proved useful when provided to contributors. The editors believe the result is a work that achieves a maximum of coherence with a minimum of duplication. The *Outline* is presented in the following pages not only as a table of contents but also as a contribution toward a better understanding of the organization of knowledge in library and information services. The editors are aware that this is only one possible ordering of the topics covered, but it may have special significance for the reader seeking a systematic overview or the student pursuing a course of study.

The articles are complemented by an innovative *Parallel Index* that runs in the margins parallel to the articles in the text. It expands access to the full resources of the 700,000-word volume, while supplementing the articles with additional information. Published in conventional format as the last element of the *ALA Encyclopedia,* it would occupy about 32 pages; it conserves paper and printing, therefore, while bringing together all related index citations and text articles.

The appearance of these references alongside the text may also stimulate interest in articles not initially sought by the reader but likely to provide relevant additional information on the topic of immediate interest. The *Parallel Index* arrangement, as far as the editors are aware, is the first of its kind in comparable reference works. Readers' comments are welcome.

No work of this kind could be accomplished without the collaboration of many colleagues around the world. Thirty-three editorial advisers participated, and 363 authors from about 145 countries contributed articles. The editors acknowledge with appreciation the difficulties many contributors had to overcome in order to meet the relatively tight publishing schedule. In several cases manuscripts were hand delivered for all or a part of the journey in order to obviate the problems of international mail. To obtain information which was otherwise unavailable, one contributor even ventured into an area where local hostilities were in progress. Selected for their knowledge, experience, and professional or scholarly achievements, they lend impressive authority to the *ALA Encyclopedia.*

This work represents a milestone in the collaborative work of the Editor and Managing Editor, who received invaluable assistance from Associate Editor, Joel M. Lee; Assistant Editor, Marilyn Litvin; Indexer, Carol Kelm; and many others.

If, as the editors believe, the *ALA World Encyclopedia of Library and Information Services* offers timely, accurate, comprehensive, and authoritative information in its field, that is more than adequate reason to commend it to librarians, students, public officials, and other readers interested in library and information services. If it, further, proves to be a successful instrument of education, the dedicated efforts of advisers, contributing editors, staff, and contributors will be appropriately rewarded.

ROBERT WEDGEWORTH
*Editor*

*ALA Headquarters*
*Chicago, Illinois*
*January 2, 1980*

# Contents

# Advisers

## General Advisers

**Simeon Babasanya Aje**
Director, National Library of Nigeria, Lagos.

**Joseph Becker**
President, Becker and Hayes, Los Angeles, California.

**Rebecca T. Bingham**
Director of Media Services, Jefferson County Public Schools, Louisville, Kentucky.

**George S. Bobinski**
Professor and Dean, School of Information and Library Studies, State University of New York at Buffalo, Buffalo, New York.

**Shirley Echelman**
Executive Director, Medical Library Association, Chicago, Illinois.

**Kenneth C. Harrison**
City Librarian of Westminster, London, England.

**Edward Gailon Holley**
Dean, School of Library Science, University of North Carolina at Chapel Hill, Chapel Hill, North Carolina.

**Dan Lacy**
Senior Vice-President, McGraw-Hill Book Co., New York, New York.

**Herman Liebaers**
Grand Marshal of the Court of Belgium, Royal Library, Brussels, Belgium.

**Carol A. Nemeyer**
Associate Librarian for National Programs, Library of Congress, Washington, D.C.

**Marietta Daniels Shepard**
former Chief, Library Development Program, Organization of American States, Bedford, Pennsylvania.

**Robert Vosper**
Professor, Graduate School of Library and Information Science, University of California at Los Angeles, Los Angeles, California.

**Alfred Wagner**
Archivdirector, Bundesarchiv, Koblenz, Federal Republic of Germany.

## Regional Advisers

**Hedwig Anuar**
Director, National Library, Singapore. *Asia*

**Amadou Alassane Bousso**
Ecole de Bibliothecaires, Dakar, Senegal. *Africa*

**Averill M. B. Edwards**
Chief Selection Librarian, National Library of Australia, Canberra. *Australia*

**Mohamed Mohamed El Hadi**
Professor of Management Information Systems, National Institute of Management Development, Cairo, Egypt. *Africa*

**Josephine Riss Fang**
Professor, School of Library Science, Simmons College, Boston, Massachusetts. *Asia*

**Juan R. Freudenthal**
Professor, School of Library Science, Simmons College, Boston, Massachusetts. *Ibero-America*

**Richard K. Gardner**
Professor, Graduate School of Library and Information Science, University of California, Los Angeles. *Western Europe*

**William Vernon Jackson**
Professor, Graduate School of Library Science, University of Texas, Austin, Texas. *Ibero-America*

**Ezekiel Enock Kaungamno**
Director, Tanzania Library Service, Dar es Salaam, Tanzania. *Africa*

**R. Brian Land**
Director, Legislative Library of Ontario, Toronto, Ontario. *Canada*

**William Arthur Munford**
Director-General, National Library for the Blind, Bredbury, Stockport, England *Western Europe*

**John Ndegwa**
University Librarian, University of Nairobi Library, Nairobi, Kenya. *Africa*

**L. H. Ofosu-Appiah**
Director, Encyclopaedia Africana Project, Accra, Ghana. *Africa*

**Hans Panofsky**
Curator of Africana, Northwestern University Library, Evanston, Illinois. *Africa*

**Vladimir Popov**
Deputy Director, "Cyril and Methodius" National Library, Sofia, Bulgaria. *Eastern Europe*

**Luwarsih Pringgoadisurjo**
Director, National Scientific Documentation Center (PDIN-LIPI), Jakarta, Indonesia. *Asia*

**Warren Tsuneishi**
Director for Area Studies, Library of Congress, Washington, D.C. *Asia*

**Natalya Tyulina**
former General Director, The United Nations Library, New York, New York. *Eastern Europe*

**Margreet Wijnstroom**
Secretary General, International Federation of Library Associations and Institutions, The Hague, Netherlands. *Western Europe*

**Celia R. Zaher**
Unesco, Paris, France. *Ibero-America*

# Contributors

**Shirley L. Aaron**
Assistant Professor, School of Library Science, Florida State University. *School Libraries: Library Cooperation*

**K. I. Abramov**
Professor, Moscow Institute of Culture, Moscow. *Lev Naumovich Tropovsky*

**Ermelinda Acerenza**
Director, University School of Library Science, Montevideo. *Uruguay*

**Thomas Adams**
John Carter Brown Library, Brown University, Providence, Rhode Island. *Benjamin Franklin*

**Julio Aguirre-Quintero**
Library Consultant, Bogotá, Colombia. *Bolivia*

**Simeon Babasanya Aje**
Director, National Library of Nigeria, Lagos. *Nigeria; F. Adetowun Ogunsheye*

**A. K. M. Shamsul Alam**
Associate Professor and Chairman, Department of Library Science, University of Dacca, Dacca. *Bangladesh*

**Mohammed M. Aman**
Dean, School of Library Science, University of Wisconsin-Milwaukee, Milwaukee, Wisconsin. *Egypt, Arab Republic of*

**Margaret E. Anderson**
Associate Professor, Faculty of Library Science, University of Toronto, Canada. *George Herbert Locke*

**Hedwig Anuar**
Director, National Library, Singapore. *Singapore*

**Arie Arad**
Deputy Director, Israel State Archives, Jerusalem, Israel. *Archives: Technical Aspects*

**C. Wesley Armstrong**
Director of Libraries, University of Liberia, Monrovia. *Liberia*

**Augusta Baker**
Former Coordinator of Children's Services, New York Public Library, Columbia, South Carolina. *Anne Carroll Moore*

**F. W. G. Baker,**
Executive Secretary, International Council of Scientific Unions, Paris. *International Council of Scientific Unions*

**John P. Baker**
Chief, Conservation Division, The New York Public Library, The Research Libraries, New York, New York. *Conservation and Preservation of Library Materials*

**Leigh R. Baker**
Deputy Librarian, Papua New Guinea University of Technology, Lae. *Papua New Guinea*

**Kenneth G. B. Bakewell**
Principal Lecturer, Department of Library and Information Studies, Liverpool Polytechnic, Liverpool, England. *Shiyali Ramamrita Ranganathan*

**Lygia Maria F. C. Ballantyne**
Library of Congress Contract Representative, Port-au-Prince. *Haiti*

**E. Bejide Bankole**
University Librarian, University of Lagos, Lagos, Nigeria. *Standing Conference of African University Librarians*

**Peggy Barber**
Director, Public Information Office, American Library Association, Chicago, Illinois. *Public Relations*

**Daniel W. Barthell**
Head, Search Section, Northwestern University Library, Evanston, Illinois. *Honduras*

**Toni Carbo Bearman**
Special Projects Consultant, INSPEC, Institution of Electrical Engineers, London, England. *Indexing and Abstracting*

**S. H. van den Berg**
Department of Education, School Library Service, Windhoek. *Namibia*

**Russell E. Bidlack**
Dean and Professor, School of Library Science, University of Michigan, Ann Arbor, Michigan. *Accreditation; Rudolph H. Gjelsness*

**Judy Yvonne Blackman**
Senior Librarian, Public Library, Bridgetown. *Barbados*

**George S. Bobinski**
Professor and Dean, School of Information and Library Studies, State University of New York at Buffalo, Amherst, New York. *Andrew Carnegie; Poland*

**Norbert Bonnici**
Research Assistant, Bibliographic Services Division, the British Library London, England. *Malta*

**Richard W. Boss**
Management Consultant, Information Systems Consultants Inc., Boston, Massachusetts. *Circulation Systems*

**Marie Elizabeth Bouscarle**
Librarian, University Library, Libreville. *Gabon*

**Naomi C. Broering**
Medical Center Librarian, Georgetown University Medical Center, Washington, D.C. *Medical Libraries: Laws and Legislation*

**Barry S. Brook**
Executive Officer, Ph.D. Program in Music, Graduate School of the City University of New York, New York, New York. *International Association of Music Libraries*

**Gloria Primm Brown**
Program Associate, Carnegie Corporation of New York, New York, New York. *Frederick Paul Keppel*

**Kenneth R. Brown**
Secretary General, International Federation for Documentation, The Hague, Netherlands. *International Federation for Documentation*

**Robert E. Brundin**
Associate Professor, Faculty of Library Science, The University of Alberta, Edmonton, Alberta, Canada. *Justin Winsor*

**Harrison Bryan**
Librarian, University of Sydney, Sydney. *Australia*

**Charles A. Bunge**
Director, University of Wisconsin-Madison Library School, Madison, Wisconsin. *Reference Services*

**Redmond A. Burke**
Associate Professor, Department of Library Science, University of Wisconsin-Oshkosh, Oshkosh, Wisconsin. *Saint Benedict; Cassiodorus*

**Clifford A. Burmester**
Former Assistant National Librarian, National Library of Australia, Canberra. *Sir John Ferguson; Edward Augustus Petherick*

**Henry Cummings Campbell**
Director, Urban Libraries Study Project, Toronto Public Libraries, Toronto, Ontario, Canada. *Public Libraries: Purposes and Objectives*

**Keva Valencia Campbell**
Assistant Archivist, Public Records Office, Nassau. *Bahamas*

**Luisa Cárdenas Perez**
Director, Education Library, Ministry of Education, Managua. *Nicaragua*

**Michael Carpenter**
Library Consultant, Los Angeles, California. *Seymour Lubetzky*

**Ray L. Carpenter**
Associate Professor, School of Library Science, University of North Carolina

at Chapel Hill, Chapel Hill, North Carolina. *Italy*

**Jane Robins Carter**
Associate Professor, Graduate School of Library Science, Louisiana State University, Baton Rouge, Louisiana. *Library Education, Curriculum in*

**Genevieve M. Casey**
Professor, Division of Library Science, Wayne State University, Detroit, Michigan. *Public Libraries: Collections*

**Robert J. Casey**
Deputy Librarian, Dublin. Dublin Corporation Central Library, Dublin. *Ireland*

**Edwin Castagna**
Former Director, Enoch Pratt Free Library, Baltimore, Maryland. *Joseph Wheeler*

**Cordelia Cavalcanti**
Brasilia, Brazil. *Maria Louisa Monteiro da Cunha*

**Roderick Cave**
Professor of Librarianship, Victoria University of Wellington, Wellington, New Zealand. *Andrew Maunsell*

**Rosemarie Chaït**
Research Attaché, National Library of Algeria, Algiers. *Algeria*

**Peter Nkangafack Chateh**
University Librarian, University of Yaoundé, Yaoundé. *Cameroon*

**Marc Chauveinc**
Director, Bibliothèque Nationale, Paris. *France*

**Mary K. Chelton**
Assistant Professor, Graduate School of Library and Information Studies, Rutgers University, New Brunswick, New Jersey. *Margaret Clara Scoggin*

**Elin B. Christianson**
Library Consultant, Hobart, Indiana. *Special Libraries*

**Jean-Pierre Clavel**
Director, Canton and University Library of Lausanne, Lausanne. *Switzerland*

**Paul E. Cohen**
Reference Librarian, Columbia University, New York, New York. *Isadore Gilbert Mudge*

**John Y. Cole**
Executive Director, The Center for the Book, Library of Congress, Washington, D.C. *Archibald MacLeish; George Herbert Putnam; Ainsworth Rand Spofford*

**Jean Ellen Coleman**
Director, Office for Library Service to the Disadvantaged, American Library Association, Chicago, Illinois. *Joyce Lilieth Robinson*

**John P. Comaromi**
Associate Professor, Graduate School of Library and Information Science, University of California at Los Angeles, Los Angeles, California. *Melvil Dewey*

**Charles William Conaway**
Assistant Professor, School of Library Science, Florida State University, Tallahassee, Florida. *Iceland*

**Michael G. Cook**
University Archivist and Lecturer in Archival Studies, University of Liverpool, Liverpool, England. *Archives: Professional Training*

**Jeannette Fernández de Criado**
Head Librarian, American School, San Salvador. *El Salvador*

**Timothy J. Crist**
Editor, Wing S.T.C. Revision, Yale University Library, New Haven, Connecticut. *Donald Goddard Wing*

**Maria Manuela Cruzeiro**
Director, National Library of Lisbon, Lisbon, Portugal. *Cape Verde; Guinea-Bissau; Portugal*

**Frank Kurt Cylke**
Director, National Library Service for the Blind and Physically Handicapped, Library of Congress, Washington, D.C. *Handicapped, Services to*

**Doris Cruger Dale**
Professor, Department of Curriculum, Instruction and Media, Southern Illinois University, Carbondale, Illinois. *Sarah Comley Norris Bogle*

**Phyllis I. Dalton**
Library Consultant, Sacramento, California. *Institutionalized, Services to*

**Evelyn H. Daniel**
Associate Professor, School of Information Studies, Syracuse University, Syracuse, New York. *School Libraries: Measurement and Evaluation*

**J. Periam Danton**
Professor Emeritus, School of Library and Information Studies, University of California at Berkeley, Berkeley, California. *Austria*

**Donald G. Davis, Jr.**
Associate Professor, Graduate School of Library Science, University of Texas at Austin, Austin, Texas. *Mary Wright Plummer*

**Anthony Debons**
Professor and Vice Chairman, Interdisciplinary Department of Information Science, University of Pittsburgh, Pittsburgh, Pennsylvania. *North Atlantic Treaty Organization*

**Andrew N. DeHeer**
Director, Research Library on African Affairs, Accra, Ghana. *Evelyn Evans*

**Rafael R. Delgado**
Director, General Library, University of Puerto Rico, Río Piedras. *Puerto Rico*

**Ellen Gay Detlefsen**
Associate Professor, Graduate School of Library and Information Sciences, University of Pittsburgh, Pittsburgh, Pennsylvania. *Library Education, Curriculum in*

**Uthai Dhutiyabhodhi**
President, Thai Libraries Association, Bangkok. *Thailand.*

**Oumar Diouwara**
Head Librarian, National Library, Nouakchott. *Mauritania*

**Keith Doms**
Director, Free Library of Philadelphia, Philadelphia, Pennsylvania. *Ralph Munn*

**Henry Dua-Agyemang**
Sub-Librarian, Balme Library, University of Ghana, Legon, Accra. *Ghana*

**Michel Duchein**
Inspector General of the Archives of France, Paris, France. *Archives: Legislative Foundations*

**Winifred E. Duncan**
Director, Bureau of Libraries, Chicago Public Schools, Chicago, Illinois. *School Libraries: Collections*

**Domingos van Dúnem**
Director, National Library of Angola, Luanda. *Angola*

**W. Lyle Eberhart**
Assistant Superintendent, Division for Library Services, Wisconsin Department of Public Instruction, Madison, Wisconsin. *State Library Agencies*

**Johanna Eggert**
Department Chief, Deutsches Institut für Normung and ISO/TC 46-Documentation Secretariat, Berlin, Federal Republic of Germany. *International Organization for Standardization*

**Mohamed Mohamed El Hadi**
Director, Management Information Center, National Institute of Management Development, Cairo, Egypt. *Bahrain; El Sayed Mahmoud El Sheniti; Iraq; Jordan; Kuwait; Oman; Qatar; Saudi Arabia; Syria; United Arab Emirates; Yemen (Aden); Yemen (S'Ana)*

**Roger H. Ellis**
Secretary, Royal Commission on Historical Manuscripts, London, England. *Sir Hilary Jenkinson*

**Hipólito Escolar-Sobrino**
Director, National Library, Madrid. *Spain*

**John R. Turner Ettlinger**
Associate Professor, School of Library Service, Dalhousie University, Halifax, Nova Scotia, Canada. *Middle Ages, Libraries in the*

**Frank B. Evans**
Paris, France. *Archives: Internal Processing; Theodore R. Schellenberg*

**Jürgen Eyssen**
Library Director, Stadtbibliothek, Hanover, Federal Republic of Germany. *International Association of Metropolitan Cities Libraries*

**Elaine Fain**
Assistant Professor, School of Library Science, University of Wisconsin-Milwaukee, Milwaukee, Wisconsin. *Mary Eileen Ahern*

**Josephine Riss Fang**
Professor, School of Library Science, Simmons College, Boston, Massachusetts. *China, People's Republic of*

**E. A. Fenelonov**
Deputy Director, the Lenin State Library, Moscow. *Ogan Stepanovich Chubarian*

**Meyer H. Fishbein**
Director, Military Archives Division, National Archives and Records Service,

Washington, D.C. *Archives: Current Records Management*

**Alice E. Fite**
Executive Secretary, American Association of School Librarians, American Library Association, Chicago, Illinois. *School Libraries: Cooperation*

**Richard Fitzsimmons**
Director of the Library, Worthington Scranton Campus, Pennsylvania State University, Dunmore, Pennsylvania. *Joshua Ballinger Lippincott*

**Marisol Floren**
Bibliographer, Fondo para el Avance de las Ciencias Sociales, *Dominican Republic*

**Georgij Polikarpovich Fonotov**
Deputy Chief, Library Directorate, U.S.S.R. Ministry of Culture, Moscow. *Nadezhda Konstantinovna Krupskaya*

**Edson Nery da Fonseca**
Professor, University of Brasília, Brasília. *Brazil; Rubens Borba de Moraes*

**Vincent Forshaw**
Director, Lesotho National Library Service, Maseru. *Lesotho*

**Douglas John Foskett**
Director of Central Library Services, University of London, London, England. *Sir Frank Francis*

**Barbara Foster**
Assistant Professor, Hunter College Library, New York, New York. *Netherlands Antilles*

**Sir Frank C. Francis**
Former Director and Principal Librarian, British Museum, London, England. *Donald John Urquhart*

**Bernard M. Franckowiak**
Associate Professor, School of Librarianship, University of Washington, Washington. *School Libraries: Federal and State Administration, Governance, and Finance*

**C. Pippa Fray**
Secretary, Commonwealth Library Association, Kingston, Jamaica. *Commonwealth Library Association*

**Ruth S. Freitag**
Associate Chief Bibliographer, Library of Congress, Washington, D.C. *National Bibliographies*

**Yoshiko Moriya de Freundorfer**
Director, School of Library Science, National University of Asunción, Asunción. *Paraguay*

**Stephen E. Furth**
Manhasset, New York. *Hans Peter Luhn*

**Ervin J. Gaines**
Director, Cleveland Public Library, Cleveland, Ohio. *William Howard Brett; Public Libraries: Finance and Administration*

**Ahmed M. Gallal**
General Director, Garyounis University Libraries, Benghazi. *Libya*

**Budd L. Gambee**
Professor, School of Library Science, University of North Carolina at Chapel Hill, Chapel Hill, North Carolina. *Caroline Maria Hewins*

**Carmen Esteva de Garcia Moreno**
Assistant Director of Libraries, Secretariat of Public Education, Mexico City. *Mexico*

**Barbara Gates**
Head, Catalog Department, Brown University Library, Providence, Rhode Island. *Minnie Earl Sears*

**Mary V. Gaver**
Professor Emeritus, Graduate School of Library Service, Rutgers University, Danville, Virginia. *Ralph Robert Shaw*

**Stanley Gillam**
Librarian, The London Library, London, England. *Thomas Carlyle*

**Marion Gilroy**
Associate Professor Emeritus, School of Librarianship, University of British Columbia, Vancouver, British Columbia, Canada. *Elizabeth Homer Morton*

**Margaret Knox Goggin**
Professor, Graduate School of Librarianship and Information Management, University of Denver, Denver, Colorado. *Certification*

**Charles Goodrum**
Former Chief, Office of Planning and Development, Library of Congress, Alexandria, Virginia. *National Libraries*

**Henry Alfred Ian Goonetileke**
Librarian, University of Peradeniya, Peradeniya. *Sri Lanka*

**Martha Gorman**
Consultant, Boulder, Colorado. *Colombia, Ecuador, Peru*

**Else Granheim**
Director, Directorate for Public and School Libraries, Oslo. *Norway*

**Chandler B. Grannis**
Contributing Editor, *Publishers Weekly*, New York, New York. *Daniel Melcher*

**Hans G. Gravenhorst**
Director, Institute of Library Science, University of Buenos Aires. *Argentina*

**D. E. Gray**
Webridge, Surrey, England. *International Association of Agricultural Librarians and Documentalists*

**Belver C. Griffith**
Professor, School of Library and Information Science, Drexel University, Philadelphia, Pennsylvania. *Eugene Garfield*

**Hans W. Groenewegen**
Former Systems Analyst, International Nuclear Information System, Vienna, Austria. *International Atomic Energy Association*

**Laurel A. Grotzinger**
Dean and Chief Research Officer, The Graduate College, Western Michigan University, Kalamazoo, Michigan. *Adelaide Rosalie Hasse; Katherine Lucinda Sharp*

**Aida Kassantini Hafez**
Acting Head Librarian, Beirut University College, Beirut. *Lebanon*

**Alfred D. Hagle**
Public Resources Officer, National Library Service for the Blind and Physically Handicapped, Library of Congress, Washington, D.C. *Handicapped, Services to*

**Robert E. Handloff**
Doctoral Candidate, Northwestern University, Evanston, Illinois. *Ivory Coast*

**Genevieve Sue Hariki**
National Center for Documentation, Rabat. *Morocco*

**Michael H. Harris**
Professor, College of Library Science, University of Kentucky, Lexington, Kentucky. *United States*

**Kenneth C. Harrison**
City Librarian of Westminster, London, England. *Douglas John Foskett; Lionel R. McColvin; William Charles Berwick Sayers; United Kingdom*

**Virginia Haviland**
Chief, Children's Literature Center, Library of Congress, Washington, D.C. *International Board on Books for Young People*

**Robert M. Hayes**
Dean, Graduate School of Library and Information Science, University of California at Los Angeles, Los Angeles, California. *Information Science Education*

**John B. Hench**
Research and Publication Officer, American Antiquarian Society, Worcester, Massachusetts. *John Franklin Jameson; Waldo Gifford Leland*

**Donald D. Hendricks**
Director of the Library, University of New Orleans, New Orleans, Louisiana. *J. Pierpont Morgan*

**Dan Henke**
Professor of Law and Director of the Hastings Legal Information Center, University of California, San Francisco, California. *Law Libraries: Services to Users*

**Joe A. Hewitt**
Associate University Librarian, Technical Services, University of North Carolina at Chapel Hill, Chapel Hill, North Carolina. *Frederick Wilfreid Lancaster*

**Doralyn J. Hickey**
Professor, School of Library and Information Sciences, North Texas State University, Denton, Texas. *Cataloguing; Paul Shaner Dunkin*

**H. van der Hoeven**
Librarian, Royal Library, The Hague. *Netherlands*

**Harold Holdsworth**
Librarian, University of the South Pacific Library, Suva. *Fiji*

**Edward Gailon Holley**
Dean, School of Library Science, The University of North Carolina at Chapel Hill, Chapel Hill, North Carolina. *Lester Eugene Asheim; Charles Evans*

**Oliver W. Holmes**
Former Executive Director, National Historical Publications and Records Commission, Washington, D.C. *Philip May Hamer*

**Virginia H. Holtz**
Director, Middleton Health Sciences Library, University of Wisconsin-Madison, Madison, Wisconsin. *Medical Libraries: Measurement and Evaluation*

## List of Contributors

**Norman Horrocks**
Director, School of Library Service, Dalhousie University, Halifax, Nova Scotia, Canada. *Library Education, Comparative*

**Kenneth W. Humphreys**
Librarian, European University Institute, Florence, Italy. *Ligue des Bibliothèques Européenes de Recherche*

**Kenneth E. Ingram**
University Librarian, University of the West Indies, Kingston, Jamaica. *Association of Caribbean University and Research Libraries*

**Toshio Iwasaru**
Professor of Library Science, Kansai University, Kyoto, Japan. *Keitaro Amano; Fujio Mamiya*

**Sidney L. Jackson**
Professor of Library Science, Kent State University, Kent, Ohio (deceased). *Alexandrian Library; Byzantine Libraries; Egypt (Ancient); Greece (Ancient); Near East (Ancient); Rome*

**William Vernon Jackson**
Professor, Graduate School of Library Science, University of Texas, Austin, Texas. *Seminar on the Acquisition of Latin American Library Materials*

**Roger F. Jacobs**
Law Librarian, Supreme Court of the United States, Washington, D.C. *Law Libraries: Law and Legislation*

**J. Myron Jacobstein**
Professor of Law and Law Librarian, Stanford University Law School Library, Stanford, California. *Law Libraries: Library Cooperation*

**Louis Sydney Jean-François**
Head Librarian, Mauritius Institute, Beau-Bassin. *Mauritius*

**Norman Johnson**
Librarian and Secretary, National Free Library Service, Bulawayo. *Zimbabwe Rhodesia*

**H. G. Jones**
Curator, North Carolina Collection, University of North Carolina at Chapel Hill, Chapel Hill, North Carolina. *Ronald Diggs Wimberly Connor*

**Alma T. Jordan**
Librarian, University of the West Indies, St. Augustine, Trinidad. *Trinidad and Tobago*

**E. J. Josey**
Chief, Bureau of Specialist Library Services, New York State Education Department, Albany, New York. *Eliza Atkins Gleason*

**Gladys M. Jusu-Sheriff**
Librarian, Fourah Bay College, University of Sierra Leone, Freetown. *Sierra Leone*

**Ivan L. Kaldor**
Dean, School of Library and Information Science. State University of New York, College of Arts and Sciences, Geneseo, New York. *Hungary*

**Margaret Kaltenbach**
Associate Professor Emeritus, Case Western Reserve University, Cleveland, Ohio. *Jesse Hauk Shera*

**Lai-Bing Kan**
University Librarian, The Chinese University of Hong Kong, Kowloon. *Hong Kong*

**David Kaser**
Professor, Graduate Library School, Indiana University, Bloomington, Indiana. *Frederick Gridley Kilgour; Keyes DeWitt Metcalf*

**Neal K. Kaske**
Research Scientist, OCLC, Inc., Columbus, Ohio. *Library and Information Science Research*

**Ezekiel Enock Kaungamno**
Director, Tanzania Library Service, Dar es Salaam. *Tanzania*

**Igor I. Kavass**
Director, Vanderbilt University Legal Information Center, Nashville, Tennessee. *International Association of Law Libraries*

**Dhan G. Keswani**
Legon, Accra, Ghana. *Jeremias Mama Akita*

**M. T. Khafagy**
Director, Department of Documentation and Information (DDI), ALECSO, Dokki, Giza, Egypt. *Arab League Educational, Cultural, and Scientific Organization*

**Sha'ban Khalifa**
Assistant Professor, Department of Library Science and Archives, Cairo University, Giza. *Egypt, Arab Republic of*

**Anis Khurshid**
Professor of Library Science, University of Karachi, Karachi. *Pakistan*

**Harry Mayanja Kibirige**
Doctoral Candidate, University of Pittsburgh, Pittsburgh, Pennsylvania. *Uganda*

**Mary E. Kingsbury**
Associate Professor, School of Library Science, University of North Carolina at Chapel Hill, Chapel Hill, North Carolina. *Effie Louise Power*

**Firmin Kinigi**
Chief Librarian, University of Burundi, Bujumbura. *Burundi*

**Preben Kirkegaard**
Rector, The Royal School of Librarianship, Copenhagen. *Denmark*

**Philip A. Knachel**
Associate Director, Folger Shakespeare Library, Washington, D.C. *Henry Clay Folger*

**Helena Kolářová**
Head, Department of Libraries, Ministry of Culture of the Slovak Socialist Republic, Bratislava. *Czechoslovakia*

**Alpha Oumar Konare**
Minister of Arts and Culture, Bamako. *Mali*

**Cecile E. Kramer**
Northwestern University School of Medicine, Chicago, Illinois. *Medical Libraries: Collections*

**Joe W. Kraus**
Director, Illinois State University Library, Bloomington, Illinois. *Robert Bingham Downs*

**Miroslav Krek**
Lecturer in Bibliography, Brandeis University, Waltham, Massachusetts. *Islamic Libraries*

**Larba Ali Krissiamba**
Chief, Interafrican Committee for Hydraulic Studies, Documentation Center, Ouagadougou. *Upper Volta*

**D. W. Krummel**
Professor of Library Science, University of Illinois, Urbana, Illinois. *Conrad Gesner*

**N. H. Kulkarnee**
Assistant Director of Archives, National Archives of India, Janpath, New Delhi, India. *Sri Nandan Prasad*

**Anant Ramachandra Kulkarni**
Professor and Head, Department of History, University of Poona, Poona, India. *Vishwanath Kashinath Rajwade*

**A. W. Z. Kuzwayo**
Librarian, University College of Swaziland, Kwaluseni. *Swaziland*

**Luc Kwanten**
Curator, Far Eastern Library, University of Chicago, Chicago, Illinois. *Bhutan; Tibet*

**Alex Ladenson**
Consultant, The Chicago Public Library, Chicago, Illinois. *William Frederick Poole; Public Library Legislation in the United States*

**Fanny Lalande Isnarde**
Editor, Cameroon Imprint, Douala, Cameroon. *Congo; French Cultural Center Libraries; Guinea*

**F. Wilfrid Lancaster**
Professor, Graduate School of Library Science, University of Illinois, Urbana, Illinois. *Cyril W. Cleverdon*

**Charles T. Laugher**
Archivist, Dalhousie University, Halifax, Nova Scotia, Canada. *Thomas Bray*

**Betty V. LeBus**
Visiting Law Librarian and Professor of Law, University of Wyoming, Laramie, Wyoming. *Law Libraries: Measurement and Evaluation*

**Pongsoon Lee**
Director of Libraries, Ewha Womans University, Seoul. *Korea, Republic of*

**Antje Bultmann Lemke**
Professor, School of Information Studies, Syracuse University, Syracuse, New York. *Library Education, Specialization in*

**Tze-chung Li**
Professor, Rosary College Graduate School of Library Science, River Forest, Illinois; Former Director, National Central Library, Taipei. *China, Republic of (Taiwan)*

**Herman Liebaers**
Grand Marshall of the Court of Belgium, Royal Library, Brussels, Belgium. *Margarita Ivanovna Rudomino*

**Patricia Pui Huen Lim**
Librarian, Institute of Southeast Asian Studies, Singapore, Singapore. *Congress of Southeast Asian Librarians*

**Emma Linares**
Consultant, Buenos Aires, Argentina. *Carlos Victor Penna; Josefa Emilia Sabor*

**Max Liniger-Goumaz**
Professor, École Supérieure de

Commerce, Lausanne, Switzerland. *Equatorial Guinea*

**R. W. Lont**
Department of Librarianship, Ministry of Education and Community Development, Paramaribo. *Suriname*

**John G. Lorenz**
Executive Director, Association of Research Libraries, Washington, D.C. *Lawrence Quincy Mumford*

**Jean E. Lowrie**
Director, School of Librarianship, Western Michigan University, Kalamazoo, Michigan. *International Association of School Librarianship; School Libraries: Purpose*

**Richard A. Lyders**
Executive Director, Houston Academy of Medicine, Texas Medical Center Library, Houston, Texas. *Medical Libraries: Administration, Governance, and Finance*

**Beverly P. Lynch**
University Librarian, University of Illinois at Chicago Circle, Chicago, Illinois. *Academic Libraries: Purposes, Goals, and Objectives*

**Mary Jo Lynch**
Director, Office for Research, American Library Association, Chicago, Illinois. *Public Libraries: Services to Users; Constance Mabel Winchell*

**Rodrick Mabomba**
Director, Malawi National Library Service, Blantyre. *Malawi*

**Elfrieda B. McCauley**
Coordinator of Media Services, Greenwich Public Schools, Greenwich, Connecticut. *School Libraries: Services to Users*

**Donald R. McCoy**
University Distinguished Professor of History, University of Kansas, Lawrence, Kansas. *Solon Justus Buck; Wayne Clayton Grover*

**Mary Lynn McCree**
Manuscript Librarian, University of Illinois at Chicago Circle, Chicago, Illinois. *Ernst Posner*

**Stanley McElderry**
Director, University of Chicago Library, Chicago, Illinois. *Herman Howe Fussler*

**Neil McHugh**
Doctoral Candidate, Northwestern University, Evanston, Illinois. *Benin; Chad*

**Brian K. McKeon**
City Librarian, Wellington Public Library, Wellington. *New Zealand*

**Donald Bruce McKeon**
Tallahassee, Florida. *Jacque-Charles Brunet*

**Haynes McMullen**
Professor, School of Library Science, University of North Carolina at Chapel Hill, Chapel Hill, North Carolina. *Richard Rogers Bowker*

**Marie A. McNamara**
Former Consultant, Bureau of Libraries, Chicago Public Schools, Wilmette, Illinois. *School Libraries: Collections*

**S. G. Malshe**
Director of Postgraduate Studies, S.N.D.T. Women's University, Bombay, India. *Anant Kākbā Priolkar*

**K. A. Manley**
Assistant Librarian, University of London Institute of Historical Research, London, England. *Edward Williams Byron Nicholson*

**Julius J. Marke**
Professor of Law and Law Librarian, New York University School of Law, New York, New York. *Law Libraries: Purpose*

**A. P. Marshall**
Professor of Library Services, Eastern Michigan University, Ypsilanti, Michigan. *Virginia Lacy Jones*

**David J. Martz, Jr.**
Coordinator of Research Collections, Colonial Williamsburg Foundation, Williamsburg, Virginia. *Peter Force*

**Morris Matza**
Comisión Coordinadora SINASBI, National Library, Caracas. *Venezuela*

**Ruby S. May**
Associate Director, Regional Medical Library, Library of the Health Sciences, University of Illinois at the Medical Center, Chicago, Illinois. *Medical Libraries: Library Cooperation*

**Jean Médioni**
Associate Director, Bibliothèque Canton and University Library of Lausanne, Lausanne. *Switzerland*

**Victor Ubaldo Mendieta Ortiz**
University of Panama, El Dorado. *Panama*

**Francis L. Miksa**
Associate Professor, Graduate School of Library Science, Louisiana State University, Baton Rouge, Louisiana. *Charles Ammi Cutter; John Eaton*

**Marion A. Milczewski**
Professor Emeritus, University of Washington School of Librarianship, Seattle, Washington. *Carl Hastings Milam*

**Arthur H. Miller, Jr.**
College Librarian, Lake Forest College, Lake Forest, Illinois. *Collection Development*

**Marilyn L. Miller**
Associate Professor, School of Library Science, University of North Carolina at Chapel Hill, Chapel Hill, North Carolina. *May Hill Arbuthnot; Children's Services*

**Betty Milum**
Reference Librarian, Ohio State University, Lima, Ohio. *Luther Evans*

**Thornton W. Mitchell**
North Carolina State Archivist, Raleigh, North Carolina. *Margaret Cross Norton*

**Margaret E. Monroe**
Professor of Library Science, University of Wisconsin-Madison, Madison, Wisconsin. *Adult Services; Douglas Waples*

**Nick Moore**
Project Officer, Research and Development Department, the British Library, London, England. *Public Libraries: Library Cooperation*

**René Moraga-Neira**
Librarian, Santiago. *Chile*

**William Arthur Munford**
Director-General, National Library for the Blind, Bredbury, Stockport, England. *George Birkbeck; James Duff Brown; Edward Edwards; John Passmore Edwards; John Young Walker MacAlister*

**Reuben Musiker**
University Librarian, University of the Witwatersrand, Johannesburg. *South Africa*

**John Ndegwa**
University Librarian, University of Nairobi, Nairobi. *Kenya*

**Diane M. Nelson**
Cataloguer, Museum of Fine Arts, Boston, Massachusetts. *Li Ta-Chao*

**Robert B. Nelson**
President, Magazine Supply House, Boston, Massachusetts. *Li Ta-chao*

**Sally P. C. N'Jie**
Chief Librarian, National Library of The Gambia, Banjul. *The Gambia*

**Qasim Osman Nur**
University of Khartoum, Khartoum. *Sudan*

**Eli M. Oboler**
University Librarian, Idaho State University, Pocatello, Idaho. *Censorship and Intellectual Freedom*

**Wilhelm C.W. Odelberg**
Head Librarian, Stockholm University with The Royal Swedish Academy of Sciences, Stockholm, Sweden. *Scandinavian Association of Research Libraries*

**Felicia Adetowun Ogunsheye**
Professor of Library Studies, University of Ibadan, Ibadan, Nigeria. *Simeon Babasanya Aje*

**James G. Ollé**
Lecturer, Department of Library and Information Studies, University of Technology, Loughborough, England. *Louis Stanley Jast; Gabriel Naudé; Sir Anthony Panizzi; Ernest Albert Savage*

**Robert W. Oram**
Director, Central University Libraries, Southern Methodist University, Dallas, Texas. *Circulation Systems*

**Guillermo Palma R.**
Librarian, Instituto de Nutricion de Centro America y Panama (INCAP), Guatemala City. *Guatemala*

**Rita Pankhurst**
Chief Librarian, City of London Polytechnic, London, England. *Ethiopia*

**Nicholas C. Pano**
Associate Professor of History, Western Illinois University, Macomb, Illinois. *Albania*

**Anne Pellowski**
Director, Information Center on Children's Cultures, U.S. Committee for UNICEF, New York, New York. *UNICEF*

**Verna E. Penn**
Chief Librarian, Public Library, Road Town, Tortola. *British Virgin Islands*

**Trudy Huskamp Peterson**
Archivist, National Archives and Records Service, Washington, D.C. *Archives: Education and Research*

## List of Contributors

**Günther Pflug**
Generaldirektor, Deutsche Bibliothek, Frankfurt am Main. *Germany, Federal Republic of*

**Ursula G. Picache**
Professor and Dean, Institute of Library Science, University of the Philippines, Quezon City. *Philippines*

**Patricia Barbara Pieterse**
Senior Librarian, Administration Library, Windhoek. *Namibia*

**Harold T. Pinkett**
Chief, Legislative and Natural Resources Branch, National Archives and Records Service, Washington, D.C. *Archives: Services to Users*

**Irwin H. Pizer**
University Librarian, University of Illinois at the Medical Center, Chicago, Illinois. *Medical Libraries: Purpose*

**Peter Andrews Poole**
Director, Center for International Studies, Old Dominion University, Norfolk, Virginia. *Laos*

**Angela I. Popescu-Brădiceni**
Director, Biblioteca Centrală de Stat, Bucharest. *Romania*

**Vladimir Popov**
Deputy Director, "Cyril and Methodius" National Library, Sofia. *Bulgaria*

**Alain-Michel Poutou**
Librarian, University of Bangui, Bangui. *Central African Republic*

**Luella Powers, O.P.**
Professor Emeritus, Rosary College Graduate School of Library Science, River Forest, Illinois. *Carleton Bruns Joeckel*

**Luwarsih Pringgoadisurjo**
Director, National Scientific Documentation Center (PDIN-LIPI), Jakarta. *Indonesia*

**T. S. Rajagopalan**
Documentation Specialist, Mogadiscio. *Somalia*

**T. N. Rajan**
Scientist, Indian National Scientific Documentation Centre, New Delhi, India. *B. S. Kesavan*

**H. Kay Raseroka**
Senior Assistant Librarian, University Library, University College of Botswana, Gaborone. *Botswana*

**Juliette R. Ratsimandrava**
Secretary Generale, Office du Livre Malagasy, Antananarivo. *Madagascar*

**Sheila G. Ray**
Senior Lecturer, City of Birmingham Polytechnic, Birmingham, England. *Young Adult Services*

**W. Boyd Rayward**
Dean, Graduate Library School, University of Chicago, Chicago, Illinois. *International Library and Bibliographic Organizations; John Wallace Metcalfe; Paul-Marie-Ghislain Otlet*

**Paulina M. Retana**
Chief Librarian, Technological Institute of Costa Rica, Cartago. *Costa Rica*

**James B. Rhoads**
Former Archivist of the United States, National Archives and Records Service, Washington, D.C. *International Council on Archives*

**Morris Rieger**
Counselor to the President and Chairman, Committee on Archival Development, International Council on Archives, Bethesda, Maryland. *Archives: Nature, Goals, Principles*

**Constance Rinehart**
Professor, School of Library Science, University of Michigan, Ann Arbor, Michigan. *Margaret Mann*

**David D. Roberson**
Senior Filtration Engineer, James River Paper Company, Richmond, Virginia. *William James Barrow*

**Jean Claude Roda**
Director, Central Library of Prêt des Yvehries, Versailles, France. *Seychelles*

**Frank Bradway Rogers**
Librarian Emeritus, University of Colorado Medical Center, Denver, Colorado. *John Shaw Billings*

**Samuel Rothstein**
Professor, School of Librarianship, University of British Columbia, Vancouver, British Columbia. *Canada; Elizabeth Homer Morton*

**James E. Rush**
Division Director, Research and Development Division, OCLC, Inc., Columbus, Ohio. *Library and Information Science Research*

**Paul Saenger**
Bibliographer of Historical Studies, Northwestern University, Evanston, Illinois. *Renaissance Libraries*

**William Saffady**
State University of New York at Albany, Albany, New York. *Micrographics*

**Armando Samper**
Director General Emeritus, Inter-American Institute of Agricultural Sciences, Bogotá, Colombia. *Daniel Samper Ortega*

**Diane Gail Saunders**
Government Archivist, Public Records Office, Nassau. *Bahamas*

**C. James Schmidt**
University Librarian, Brown University, *Academic Libraries: Administration, Governance, and Finance*

**Hans G. Schulte-Albert**
Associate Professor, School of Library and Information Science, University of Western Ontario, London, Ontario, Canada. *Gottfried Wilhelm Leibniz*

**Mortimer D. Schwartz**
Professor and Associate Dean for the Law Library, University of California at Davis, Davis, California. *Law Libraries: Administration, Governance, and Finance*

**Edith Scott**
Chief Instructor, Cataloging Instruction Office, Library of Congress, Washington, D.C. *James Christian Meinich Hanson; Charles Martel*

**Vasilii Vasilievich Serov**
Head, Library Directorate, the U.S.S.R. Ministry of Culture, Moscow. *Union of Soviet Socialist Republics*

**Emmanuel Serugendo**
Librarian National University of Rwanda, Butare. *Rwanda*

**Shmuel Sever**
Director of the Library and Library Studies, University of Haifa, Haifa. *Israel*

**Russell Shank**
University Librarian and Professor, University of California at Los Angeles, Los Angeles, California. *Charles Coffin Jewett*

**Nasser Sharify**
Dean and Professor, Graduate School of Library and Information Science, Pratt Institute, Brooklyn, New York. *Iran*

**Spencer G. Shaw**
Professor of Librarianship, School of Librarianship, University of Washington, Seattle, Washington. *Augusta Baker*

**Marietta Daniels Shepard**
Former Chief, Library Development Program, Organization of American States, Bedford, Pennsylvania. *Organization of American States*

**Jesse H. Shera**
Dean Emeritus, Case Western Reserve University, Cleveland, Ohio. *Pierce Butler; Librarianship, Philosophy of*

**Gerald R. Shields**
Assistant Dean and Associate Professor, School of Information and Library Studies, State University of New York at Buffalo, Amherst, New York. *David Horace Clift*

**Ritva A. H. Sievänen-Allen**
Librarian, Central Medical Library, Helsinki. *Finland*

**Donald B. Simpson**
Executive Director, Bibliographical Center for Research, Denver, Colorado. *Bibliographic Networks*

**Mary I. A. L. Skiffington**
Head Librarian, Bermuda Library, Hamilton. *Bermuda*

**A. E. Skinner**
Chemistry Librarian, The University of Texas at Austin, Austin, Texas. *Halsey William Wilson*

**Elaine Sloan**
Associate University Librarian, University of California at Berkeley, Berkeley, California. *Academic Libraries: Library Cooperation*

**Geoffrey Smith**
County Librarian, Quorn, Leicestershire, England. *Frederick A. Thorpe*

**Wilfred Irvin Smith**
Dominion Archivist, Public Archives of Canada, Ottawa, Ontario, Canada. *Archives: Management*

**Soemartini**
Director, National Archives of Indonesia, Jakarta, Indonesia. *Harsya Wardhana Bachtiar*

**Jutta Sørenson**
Lecturer, Royal School of Librarianship, Copenhagen, Denmark. *Derek William Austin*

**Claud Glenn Sparks**
Dean, Graduate School of Library

Science, The University of Texas at Austin, Austin, Texas. *William Warner Bishop*

**Carl M. Spaulding**
Consultant, Sunnyvale, California. *Micrographics*

**Francis F. Spreitzer**
University of Southern California, Los Angeles, California. *Reprography*

**David H. Stam**
The Andrew W. Mellon Director of The Research Libraries, The New York Public Library, New York, New York. *Scholarly and Research Services*

**Garland L. Standrod**
Information Outputs Coordinator, Agency for International Assistance, Washington, D.C. *Nepal*

**Costas D. Stephanou**
President, Cyprus Library Association, Nicosia. *Cyprus*

**Yvonne Veronica Stephenson**
Chief Librarian, University of Guyana Library, Georgetown. *Guyana*

**Gordon Stevenson**
Associate Professor, State University of New York at Albany, Albany, New York. *Karl Dziatzko*

**Elizabeth W. Stone**
Chair, Graduate Department of Library and Information Science, The Catholic University of America, Washington, D.C. *Continuing Professional Education in Librarianship*

**Reinaldo José Suárez**
Technical Information Department, National Commission for Atomic Energy, Buenos Aires. *Argentina; Domingo Faustino Sarmiento; Aurelio Zlatko Tanodi*

**Peggy Sullivan**
Assistant Commissioner for Extension Services, The Chicago Public Library, Chicago, Illinois. *Extension Services*

**F. William Summers**
Dean, College of Librarianship, University of South Carolina Columbia, South Carolina. *Francis St. John*

**Thein Swe**
Chief Bibliographer, Louisana State University, Baton Rouge, Louisiana. *Burma*

**Richard J. Talbot**
Director of Libraries, University of Massachusetts at Amherst, Amherst, Massachusetts. *Academic Libraries: Measurement and Evaluation*

**Sönmez Taner**
Information Specialist, Türdok, Scientific and Technical Research Council of Turkey, Ankara. *Turkey*

**G. Thomas Tanselle**
Vice President, John Simon Guggenheim Memorial Foundation, New York, New York. *Frederick Gershom Melcher*

**Ruth W. Tarbox**
Chicago, Illinois. *Mildred Leona Batchelder*

**Betty W. Taylor**
Professor of Law, Director, Law Library, University of Florida, Gainesville, Florida. *Law Libraries: Collections*

**Farideh Tehrani**
Doctoral Student, School of Library Service, Columbia University, New York, New York. *Iran*

**Björn V. Tell**
University Librarian, Lund University, Lund. *Sweden*

**Katherine Thanopoulo**
President, Greek Library Association, Athens. *Greece*

**Leila Theresa Thomas**
Director, Jamaica Library Service, Kingston. *Jamaica*

**Dennis V. Thomison**
Associate Professor, School of Library Science, University of Southern California, Los Angeles, California. *Theresa Hubbell West Elmendorf*

**James C. Thompson**
Assistant Librarian for Technical Services, Milton S. Eisenhower Library, The Johns Hopkins University, Baltimore, Maryland. *Acquisitions*

**Jacques J. Tocatlian**
Director General, General Information Programme (PGI), Unesco, Paris, France. *Unesco*

**Martha V. Tomé**
Senior Specialist, Information, Comunication and Cultural Diffusion, Organization of American States, *Jorge Aguayo; Carmen Rovira*

**Helen Welch Tuttle**
Former Assistant University Librarian for Technical Services, Princeton University Library, Princeton, New Jersey. *William Shepherd Dix*

**H. Ungerer**
Commission of the European Communities, Luxembourg. *Euronet*

**John de Belfort Urquidi**
Regional Activities Consultant, International Federation of Library Associations & Institutions, The Hague, Netherlands. *Afghanistan*

**Willy Vanderpÿpen**
Assistant Librarian, Royal Library, Brussels. *Belgium*

**Marie Gabrielle Veaux**
Documentalist, Archives of Senegal, Dakar. *Senegal*

**Lawrence Gordon Vernon**
Chief Librarian, National Library Service, Belize City. *Belize*

**Ernesto de la Torre Villar**
Austin, Texas. *María Teresa Chávez Campomanes; Juana Manrique de Lara*

**Rose L. Vormelker**
Adjunct Professor, Kent State University, Cleveland, Ohio. *John Cotton Dana*

**Robert Vosper**
Professor, Graduate School of Library and Information Science, University of California at Los Angeles, Los Angeles, California. *Herman Liebaers*

**Frederick H. Wagman**
Professor and Director Emeritus, University Library, University of Michigan, Ann Arbor, Michigan. *Verner Warren Clapp*

**Ruth W. Waldrop**
Executive Secretary, Alabama Library Association, University, Alabama. *School Libraries: Laws and Legislation*

**William D. Walker**
Director, Medical Library Center of New York, New York, New York. *Medical Libraries: Services to Users*

**Clyde C. Walton**
Director of Libraries, University of Colorado, Boulder, Colorado. *Academic Libraries: Laws and Legislation*

**Chi Wang**
Head, Chinese and Korean Section, Library of Congress, Washington, D.C. *Yuan T'ung Li*

**Ruth Warncke**
Former Deputy Executive Director, American Library Association, Chicago, Illinois. *Helen Elizabeth Haines*

**Frances A. Weaver**
Assistant University Archivist, University of North Carolina at Chapel Hill, Chapel Hill, North Carolina. *Louis Round Wilson*

**William H. Webb**
Collection Development Librarian, University of California at San Diego, San Diego, California. *Academic Libraries: Collections*

**Theodore F. Welch**
Assistant University Librarian for Development and Lecturer in Japanese, Northwestern University, Evanston, Illinois. *Japan*

**Hans H. Wellisch**
Associate Professor, College of Library and Information Services, University of Maryland, College Park, Maryland. *Classification*

**Leonard Wertheimer**
Languages Coordinator, Metropolitan Toronto Library Board, Toronto, Ontario, Canada. *Bilingual and Ethnic Groups, Services to*

**Ines Wesley-Tanaskovic**
Professor of Information Science, Medical Academy of Belgrade, Belgrade. *Yugoslavia*

**Herbert S. White**
Professor and Director, Research Center for Library and Information Science, Graduate Library School, Indiana University, Bloomington, Indiana. *Mortimer Taube*

**John Kremers Whitmore**
Program Officer, Center for South and Southeast Asian Studies, University of Michigan, Ann Arbor, Michigan. *Vietnam*

**Wayne A. Wiegand**
Assistant Professor, College of Library Science, University of Kentucky, Lexington, Kentucky. *United States*

**D.E.K. Wijasuriya**
Deputy Director General, National Library of Malaysia, Kuala Lumpur. *Malaysia*

**Margreet Wijnstroom**
Secretary General, International Federation of Library Associations and Institutions, The Hague, Netherlands,

## List of Contributors

*International Federation of Library Associations and Institutions*

**Alice E. Wilcox**
Minitex (Minnesota Interlibrary Telecommunications Exchange), Minneapolis, Minnesota. *Resource Sharing*

**Billy R. Wilkinson**
Associate University Librarian, University of Illinois at Chicago Circle, Chicago, Illinois. *Academic Libraries: Services to Users*

**Alexander Wilson**
Director, Reference Division, British Library, London. *Public Libraries: Library Cooperation*

**Howard W. Winger**
Professor, Graduate Library School, University of Chicago, Chicago, Illinois. *Leon Carnovsky*

**Francis J. Witty**
Professor, School of Arts and Sciences, Catholic University of America, Washington, D.C. *Jean-Paul Bignon*

**Irene Wood**
Editor, Nonprint Materials, *Booklist*, American Library Association, Chicago, Illinois. *Audiovisual Services*

**Pat A. Woodrum**
Director, Tulsa City-County Library, Tulsa, Oklahoma. *Allie Beth Martin*

**H. Curtis Wright**
Professor of Library and Information Sciences, Brigham Young University, Provo, Utah. *Assurbanipal; Callimachus*

**Margaret Wright**
Sub-Librarian, John Rylands University Library, Manchester, England. *Alfred William Pollard*

**Arthur P. Young**
Assistant Dean for Public Services, University of Alabama Library, University, Alabama. *Ernest Cushing Richardson; Arthur Fremont Rider*

---

*Addendum*

**R. K. Das Gupta**
Director, National Library of India, Calcutta, *India*

# Outline of Contents

This *Outline* is organized under five principal divisions.

*Part One,* on *Libraries in Society,* covers the history and role of libraries from ancient times to the present. In addition to nine major articles on historical periods, 162 articles cover libraries and librarianship in the countries of the world. All Part One articles are organized according to the following outline: national libraries, academic libraries, public libraries, school libraries and media centers, special and other libraries, and library associations. The articles appear in alphabetical order in the text. Most articles include comprehensive statistical tables prepared by authorities expressly for this work. Biographies appear in the *Outline* under major headings according to period and place.

*Part Two,* on *The Library as an Institution,* comprises nine major articles on the principal types of libraries and archives; most have been coordinated by a Principal Contributor. Articles emphasize North America but examples and generalizations are also drawn from various systems in other sections of the world.

*Part Three,* on *Theory and Practice of Librarianship,* deals with the heart of librarianship. Twenty-five articles bring together under broad titles the principles and practices of librarianship and information management.

*Part Four,* on *Education and Research,* in ten major articles covers librarianship, information science, and archival administration. The articles treat the fundamentals of curriculum content and issues in research and education.

*Part Five,* on *International Library, Information, and Bibliographical Organizations,* comprises 28 articles that describe the growth and development of international information systems and enumerate the key organizations on the international level.

## PART ONE: The Library in Society



*Note: Throughout this *Outline,* all entries set in capitals are titles of articles.

## PART TWO: The Library as an Institution



## PART THREE: Theory and Practice of Librarianship

## Outline of Contents

## PART FOUR: Education and Research



## PART FIVE: International Library, Information, and Bibliographic Organizations

# Academic Libraries

PURPOSES, GOALS, AND OBJECTIVES

Academic libraries reflect the development of the colleges and universities of which they are a part. These libraries, integral parts of the institutions they serve, design their collections and services to meet the instructional programs of the particular institution. The program of the academic library varies depending upon whether the institution is a doctoral-granting research institution, a comprehensive university or college that offers a liberal arts program as well as several other programs such as engineering or business administration, a liberal arts college, a two-year college or institute, or a specialized institute such as a theological school, or a medical school, law or other professional school.

The basic assumption governing the growth and development of all academic libraries is that the library plays a role of central and critical importance in the instructional and scholarly life of the college or university. In his 1966 report to the American Council on Education, *An Assessment of Quality in Graduate Education,* Allan M. Cartter wrote,

> The library is the heart of the university; no other single non-human factor is as closely related to the quality of graduate education. A few universities with poor library resources have achieved considerable strength in several departments, in some cases because laboratory facilities may be more important in a particular field than the library, and in other cases because the universities are located close to other great library collections such as the Library of Congress and the New York Public Library. But institutions strong in all areas invariably have major national research libraries.

Of the some 2,800 institutions of higher education in the United States, about 200 are doctoral-granting research universities. Most of the universities originally were founded as colleges, and almost without exception each university library developed into a great central li-

University Library, Graz

*Main reading room of the University Library, Graz, Austria.*



The marginal references in **bold-face** type, which parallel the articles of the Encyclopedia, cite **page numbers** in this volume.

brary out of the original college library, adding to it specialized libraries serving the professional schools. The libraries in the universities offer services that facilitate the use of recorded information in all formats. The records that enable access to the collections are designed to be complete, consistent, and in conformity with national bibliographic standards. The collections in university libraries include all those materials necessary for direct support of the university's instructional programs at both the graduate and undergraduate levels. The collections also are designed to be comprehensive so as to support the scholarly efforts of the students and faculty members. With the continued growth of knowledge and the rapid increase in the scholarly literature that results from such growth, no university library now is able to possess in its collections all of the recorded information that faculty members and students may need as they pursue their research. University libraries have designed formal and informal arrangements for the sharing of resources. Many developments at the national and international levels are aimed at providing access to library resources regardless of where those resources might be located. The primary goal of every university library remains, however, to offer to those who may be said to constitute the library's primary clientele—the faculty, students, and academic staff of the university—collections of broad scope and depth and specialized and in-depth assistance in the use of the library's resources. The university library seeks to attain the level of self-sufficiency that is essential to the health and vigor of the university and its academic programs. The library also makes available to its clientele, through various cooperative programs, the resources and collections of other libraries.

The European pattern of a university composed of separate colleges or faculties has been influential in many nations, although to a lesser extent in the U.S., where universities often grew out of individual colleges. Within the former structure, each college, faculty, or department might possess its own library, usually dedicated to a particular subject and often administered independently of other libraries on campus. There has been a strong trend, however, toward centralization of university library administration in the U.S.; departmental libraries are often united within a single administrative structure, with various services performed centrally.

There are about 1,500 liberal arts colleges and comprehensive colleges and universities in the United States. The libraries in these institutions are expected to meet the full curricular needs of the undergraduate student and to provide for the students' requirements in each field in which the institution offers a Masters degree. The college library makes available the standard works representing the heritage of the civilization and the works that will enable the faculty members to keep apprised of the latest advances in their fields. Unlike research libraries, which are required to keep and maintain retrospective holdings, the college library tends to weed its collections regularly and systematically.

The two-year or junior college played a minor role in American higher education until about 1910. By the end of the 1970's, over 1,000 two-year colleges existed in the United States. The libraries in these institutions sometimes are called learning resources centers, reflecting the nature of the collections and the types of services provided. Books, periodicals, films, videotapes, pictures, models, kits, and realia form the collections. A much greater emphasis is placed upon the nonprint materials in the libraries serving the two-year institutions than in other academic libraries. These institutions often serve to prepare students for later baccalaureate study in a university or function as centers for technical training in a variety of fields. Styled often as community colleges, they may offer in addition to training for work as technicians preparatory

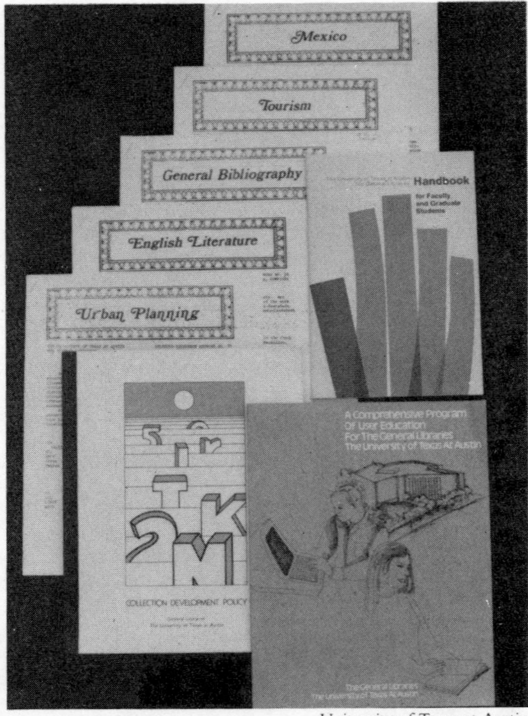


University of Texas at Austin

*Publications of the General Libraries, University of Texas at Austin.*

courses for additional higher education. The subjects taught, in some instances reflect the community's particular needs for trained personnel in certain fields. The library resources in these institutions are designed to support immediate curricular needs.

In other countries universities are similarly complemented by institutions for the training of skilled personnel in specific fields. Most evident are schools for training teachers.

**Historical Background.** The development of higher education in the United States, although influenced by the English and German traditions, is peculiarly American. From the beginning—1636, which marks the founding of Harvard College—colleges proliferated. In 1900, 977 institutions of higher education existed in the United States, but 80 percent of those colleges founded before the Civil War had not survived. Rapid growth in numbers of schools meant that only a few colleges could offer the academic leadership needed or the financial security required of a quality educational program. Before 1900 American colleges resembled more the secondary schools of Europe than the European universities. Generally the libraries in these colleges reflected the same low quality, although the library was considered an important part, if not a central part, of every college. Among the nine American colleges established before the revolution, eight had libraries by 1800.

Unlike Harvard College, which grew and developed into one of the premier universities of the world, most American institutions of higher education have remained colleges. The Harvard College Library started with a collection of books variously estimated as from 260 to 370 volumes bequeathed to the college by John Harvard. It grew to 226,650 volumes in 1876 and 901,000 in 1900. Now a research library of the first rank, Harvard University Library has over 10,000,000 volumes. The collections of Harvard, like those of other major university and independent research libraries, are available to Harvard students and scholars. The collections of most research libraries are so rich, however, that the purpose of the library includes extending the use of its collections to the broad community of scholars outside the institution. Although some university libraries in the United States are being described as great national resources, none fulfills the role of a national library as do many of the university libraries of Europe or other regions of the world.

The collections of the great American university libraries such as Harvard, Yale, and the universities of Illinois, Michigan, and California are prominent and impressive. Also impressive are the rare book collections, the special collections and manuscript collections of some American college libraries: Oberlin has a fine collection on slavery; Amherst College has special collections of Robert Frost and Emily Dickinson; and Bowdoin's collections of Nathaniel Hawthorne and Henry Wadsworth Longfellow are well-known, as are the important collections held by Smith College and Wellesley College of books and manuscripts relating to women.

Until the middle of the 1800's academic libraries in the United States, and the collections within them, owed much of their existence to private donors. There was little in the way of systematic collection development. In his 1850 Annual Report, Charles C. Jewett, the Librarian of the Smithsonian Institution, had this to say:

> College libraries . . . are frequently the chance aggregations of the gifts of charity; too many of them discarded, as well nigh worthless, from the shelves of the donors. This is not true of all our college libraries; for among them are a few of the choicest and most valuable collections in the country, selected with care and competent learning, purchased with economy, and guarded with prudence, though ever available to those who wish to use them aright.

The academic library today still receives materials by gift, but the library now relies upon purchase as the major source of its materials, with gifts and exchange of materials being relatively minor sources. Collection development is a major component of academic library administration.

Much of the impetus for improvement and change in academic libraries in the United States has been provided by private foundations. In 1928 the Carnegie Corporation of New York, seeking a program to encourage the integration of the library into the educational program of the liberal arts college, sponsored several studies of college libraries. Among these studies was a survey of the American college library by William Randall, which described major inadequacies in the book collections of college libraries in their funding, staffing, and physical facilities. His study prompted the Carnegie Corporation to award 83 grants, for a total of $1,011,000, to college libraries for the improvement of their book collections.

**Standards.** Randall and the librarians advising the Carnegie Corporation sought but found no reliable standards for college libraries or definite and comprehensive statistics. So they prepared sets of standards of their own. These efforts led to further work on library standards. The *Standards for College Libraries* were published by the American Library Association in 1959 and were reviewed and revised in 1975. *Standards for Junior College Libraries* were published by the American Library Association in 1960; they were reviewed, revised, and published as *Guidelines for Two-Year College Learning Resources Programs* in 1972. *Standards for University Libraries,* prepared jointly by the Association of College and Research Libraries, a division of ALA, and by the Association of Research Libraries, were published in 1978. Each of these standards addresses the essential questions of the adequacy of library collections, services, staff, physical facilities, finance, and governance, placed in the context of the educational program and objectives of the individual institution being served by the library.

The development and application of standards for academic libraries in the United States, first promoted by the Carnegie Corporation and interested librarians, has become a major activity of the ALA and other organizations. The adoption of the standards and the voluntary use of them in the evaluation of American academic libraries have led to significant improvement in the quality of collections and services in many academic libraries. Standards have influenced the library standards developed internationally by Unesco and have led to the consideration of library standards by various groups within the International Federation of Library Associations and Institutions (IFLA). They have also influenced the development of library standards in other countries. Often the standards are developed and adopted by Ministries of Education, as in Japan, for instance. The application of the standards may become a requirement for academic institutions, not a voluntary application, as in the United States, and may be included in national legislation concerning academic institutions.

Academic librarians have sought better and more objective methods of measurement and evaluation of library services than the expert opinion reflected in the standards. Much of the early work emphasized size of collections, staff, and budget as indicators of quality. More recently, sophisticated techniques have been applied to academic libraries to assist librarians and others in the assessment of the quality of library programs.

**Support and Governance.** Grouping institutions of higher education in the United States commonly is done according to whether the college or university is funded by private or public moneys. About half of the American institutions of higher education are supported by private moneys. Many of these institutions were founded by religious groups and continue to be denominational. The constitutional requirement of the separation of church and state has prohibited the use of public funds for direct support of private colleges and universities. Public colleges and universities are supported principally by local and state taxes, and only in comparatively recent years have

University of Washington Libraries, Seattle

*Library of the University of Washington, Seattle, in 1896—6,780 titles in the attic of the school's only building.*

any federal moneys been provided for support of higher education in the United States. The advent of federal support has not brought governmental control of colleges and universities to any degree approaching that of the European, African, Asian, or South American colleges and universities. While most colleges and universities in the U.S. remain independent and autonomous, local and state boards of higher education have begun to exert greater influence. A trend leading to larger units of governance seemed likely to continue and likely to influence academic and research libraries.

The Higher Education Facilities Act, passed by the Congress in 1963, provided for the first time in the United States federal moneys for the construction of library buildings. Grants were made available on a matching basis to both public and private institutions of higher education. This act successfully addressed the important church-state issue and anticipated the passage in 1965 of the Higher Education Act, which contained provisions for libraries regardless of how they were supported.

**Facilities and Growth.** Between 1967 and 1975, 674 academic library building projects were completed in the United States at a cost of $1,900,000,000. Many of these projects were funded partially from federal funds authorized under the Higher Education Facilities Act. The stimulus of the Act led to the rehousing of a majority of college and university libraries. Private foundations and donors have made many major contributions to the constructions of academic library buildings in the United States and continue to do so.

The academic library buildings constructed in the United States since World War II show a marked change in architectural style from earlier buildings. Modular planning was accepted, and a shift occurred from fixed-function buildings to buildings with functional flexibility. More space was assigned to operations than had been seen as necessary in earlier construction. Many of these changes were proposed as early as the 1930's, when a number of elements were proposed as being important to the design of the successful academic library building: functional and flexible interiors, elimination of interior-bearing walls, open-shelf arrangements, subject arrangements for books, and comfortable furniture. All of these proposals are reflected in academic libraries built since World War II.

Growth in size of collection, staff, and budget required new and additional library space. The predictions of Fremont Rider and others that an academic library's collection would double every 15 years have been fairly accurate. New library buildings and additions to buildings built between 1950 and 1970 were designed to allow space for 20 years of additional growth, but by the beginning of the 1970's it was clear that there would be insufficient money either in the short term or the long term to build all the new academic library buildings needed to match an indefinitely growing number of books.

In the United Kingdom the University Grants Committee, in its Atkinson Report, sought to establish criteria by which the scale, nature, and relative priority of capital projects might be judged. It also proposed a principle of a "self-renewing library of limited growth"; new acquisitions of library materials would be possible only if offset by the same number of withdrawals. German librarians sought models to be used in the design of large cooperative storage facilities. In the United States academic librarians explored more intensively ways to cooperate with one another, seeking to reduce the need for more space and larger budgets while supporting the basic purpose of the library, which is to provide the students and scholars with the materials they need.

Cooperative ventures have taken two major directions. The first centers on bibliographic access and emphasizes the development of standards for bibliographic control and the automation of bibliographic records. The second seeks to design programs of direct access to materials not held by the library supporting the studies of the student or scholar. The Center for Research Libraries in Chicago, the British Library Lending Division at Boston Spa, and the proposed National Periodicals Center in the United States are manifestations of this direction. The private foundations in the United States, including the Carnegie Corporation of New York, the Council on Library Resources, the W. K. Kellogg Foundation, and the Andrew W. Mellon Foundation have been active in support of these ventures.

All of these activities are designed to support the academic and research libraries in the United States and abroad in their efforts to serve the student and the scholar. Specific services and aspects of collection development are described in sections that follow. Also included are detailed descriptions of the administration, governance, and finance of academic libraries, the measurement and evaluation of these libraries, cooperation among academic and research libraries, and the laws and legislation pertaining to academic libraries.

**REFERENCES**

William Warner Bishop, *Carnegie Corporation and College Libraries 1929–1938* (1938).

Keyes D. Metcalf, *Planning Academic and Research Library Buildings* (1965).

William M. Randall, *The College Library: A Descriptive Study of the Libraries in Four-Year Liberal Arts Colleges in the United States* (1932).

Fremont Rider, *The Scholar and the Future of the Research Library* (1944).

Louis Shores, *Origins of the American College Library, 1638–1800* (1935).

BEVERLY P. LYNCH

*Helsinki University Library, built in 1844, also serves as the National Library of Finland.*

Library Association of Finland

SERVICES FOR USERS

The primary functions of academic libraries are to fulfill both the needs of the instructional programs of their parent institutions and the research needs of students, faculty, other staff members, and nonaffiliated persons. The many and varied services designed by academic libraries to serve their clienteles have developed over many years.

After first gathering a reference collection exclusively for the on-site use of officers and faculty of the academic institution, the library next allowed use by undergraduate students. Wayne S. Yenawine, writing in *Library Trends* (1957), succinctly described the developing service:

In the pre-Civil War Library, the librarian, or some one working directly under his surveillance, determined from discussion with the borrower what was needed from the library collection, charged it to the borrower, and cleared the borrower when he returned the material. Circulation service was the sole reader service. Inherent in the situation was the opportunity for the librarian to know the borrower's need. The librarian also knew his resources, and was thus able to fulfill the need within the limits of materials available and of his own competence.

Services have continued to develop into the myriad of activities now found in most academic libraries. In addition to the original "sole" service—circulation of materials, including interlibrary loans, the following other major services are: (1) reference/information services, including bibliographic instruction; (2) all technical processes with their objective of delivery of services for users; and (3) provision of space and facilities.

**Circulation Services.** Contemporary circulation librarians may take as their archetype Professor Otis Robinson, Librarian, University of Rochester. In the 1876 Bureau of Education Report *Public Libraries in the United States,* he stressed that a college library is for the use of students, and wrote:

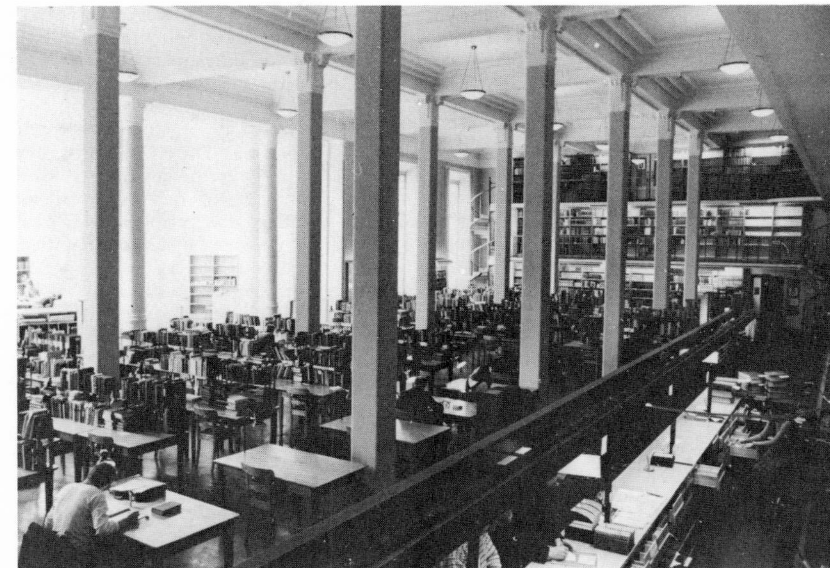

University Library of Uppsala

*First reading room, University Library of Uppsala, Sweden.*

Foto Estudio Callado

*Reading room in the library of the Universidad Católica Madre y Maestra in Santiago, Dominican Republic.*

*Periodicals reading room, Central Library, Chulalongkorn University, Thailand.*

Chulalongkorn University

Among the first of the privileges to be granted to students is that of carrying books to their rooms, to be used there. To this there are many and serious objections which, I learn, are allowed to prevail at several colleges of good standing, viz, the books are worn out; some are never returned; they are not in the library when wanted for consultation. These and other similar objections might have been forcible when books were rare enough to be a luxury. It was doubtless wise, then, to regard the preservation of a library as the chief end of its administration. But now the chief end is its use. If properly used, the wearing out of the good books is the best possible indication.

With this major philosophical shift from conservator to purveyor, American academic librarians have loaned countless volumes to users and have devised record systems to control the daily flux and flow. Manual systems of ledgers and card files formed the first circulation records. By the mid-1970's automated systems were available. Successful automated installations were made in different types and sizes of libraries. However, in both the U.S. and other countries, manual systems are still predominant. It will take a continuing and substantial reduction in costs before most small academic libraries can afford automated systems.

Academic libraries have also extended borrowing privileges to unaffiliated persons. The most formal, if not the earliest, method of serving the unaffiliated is the American Library Association Code for Interlibrary Loans. Building on the European medieval idea of the community of scholars in which each member felt the responsibility to make his own or others' works available to a serious fellow scholar, American librarians in 1917 formally codified the lending of unusual volumes not available in the requesting library. This interlibrary loan system, as it was designed and has developed, did place restrictions on the kinds of materials lent to other libraries (e.g., manuscripts, rare books, current issues of magazines and newspapers, and low cost in-print volumes were excluded). The system excluded interlibrary lending to undergraduate students, reserving this particular service for faculty members and graduate students.

Perhaps learning from their users, who have developed their own informal means of access to the holdings of libraries with which they are not affiliated, contemporary academic libraries have designed simple, but effective, reciprocal borrowing plans. At the present stage of development, reciprocal borrowing plans are usually parochial (i.e., a small number of academic libraries lend directly, upon presentation of proper identification, to all students and faculty of those nearby institutions who have joined in the plan). Reciprocal borrowing, like interlibrary loan, accounts for only a very small portion of the total circulation in all libraries who participate. The development of automated on-line bibliographic systems will probably lead to an even greater and more extensive direct sharing of resources, no longer tied to a part of or one city but expanded to the state or region.

No matter how rapid, sophisticated, and universal circulation services in academic libraries become in the future, it must be remembered that this service rests on a manual system of the exact shelving of thousands or millions of individual books and other library materials. The training and supervision of shelving staff and the maintenance of an accurate and continuous shelf reading program will always play a large and essential part in this most basic user service.

**Reference/Information Services.** A public librarian, Samuel Green of the Worchester Free Library, made the first formal proposal in the U.S. for a program of assistance to readers, as distinguished from occasional aid, in his paper "The Desirableness of Establishing Personal Intercourse and Relations between Librarians and Readers in Popular Libraries," read at the historic 1876 national conference of librarians, but it was Melvil Dewey, the dynamic Librarian at Columbia, who appointed in 1884 the first full-time reference librarians, George Baker and William G. Baker, as members of the reference department. It is clear that "reference department" meant organized personal assistance, because in answer to a questionnaire in 1885, Columbia responded that two reference librarians were on the staff specially to aid inquirers.

Dewey, ever the prophetic voice, called in 1901 for subject specialization in academic library service in an article in *The Library:*

> In this limited number of great libraries the comparatively modern notion of the reference librarian is bound to develop into what I think we may wisely call the "library faculty." One man cannot possibly do the reference work for a large library from lack of time, and no man since Humboldt presumes to be a specialist on all subjects. A process of evolution is inevitable. As demand and income warrant we shall have reference librarians each limited to history, science, art, sociology, law, medicine, education, or some other topic till we shall have in the library, as in the university, a company of men each an authority in his own field. Such a corps is obviously best named a Faculty, and for a library, equipped with such a staff of specialists I propose the name of "faculty library" . . . . It is certain that reference work must be closely divided if it is to be of high value.

Louis Kaplan for the period 1876–93 and Samuel Rothstein for 1850–1950 recorded the growth and development of reference services in academic libraries. Rothstein is particularly thorough, describing the practices as well as the policies and theories of service. After presenting the conservative (minimal assistance or only guidance), the moderate (compromise between the extremes), and the liberal (full information service) theories of reference service and the continuing professional debate over them, Rothstein concludes that assistance on the scale of the librarian as a collaborator in the research process was not common through 1940. The chief problem was the heterogeneous nature of the demands placed on the library, making it hard to differentiate between services for scholars and the more numerous general users. In larger libraries, with thousands of general readers, the great service load often resulted in limited capacity for offering more than only minimal aid.

The academic library community in the United States has come to place considerable emphasis on two services. One is bibliographic or library instruction, generally regarded as teaching the identification and use of information resources to members of the academic community by librarians in a formal classroom setting. The other is on-line computer searching of bibliographic/natural language data bases.

These are only two of the many activities in academic reference/information services. One-on-one, in-person reference assistance, compilation of bibliographies, supervision of professional and nonprofessional staff members, telephone information service, care of periodicals or government publications or curriculum materials, interlibrary borrowing or lending, or one of the other assigned professional, administrative, or clerical tasks are among the responsibilities of the reference/information staff. Robert Balay, reference librarian at Yale, observed, "It would appear that reference work consists of whatever it is that reference departments do" (*The ALA Yearbook,* 1978).

The profession has strongly believed it was wrong to identify reference work as only what goes on in a reference room. Although questions of specialization versus nonspecialization of staff and of centralization or decentralization have concerned academic librarianship (divisional plans, specialized documents departments, reference services in separate undergraduate libraries, etc.), and there has been some description of library systems that provide reference/information services to supplement those offered in the local unit, the profession still is lacking in basic knowledge about users, their information needs, and the uses to which information is put.

**Technical Services.** The technical processes (searching, ordering, receiving, cataloguing, and processing of all library materials for use) have always been a primary service performed in academic libraries. In supporting the instructional and research needs of their students and faculty, academic librarians have attempted to provide maximum access to the collections. In earlier decades staff in technical departments often were accused of a lack of the proper service attitude and a failure to recognize the real purpose of the organization. During the 1960's and 1970's these accusations diminished as the service aspects of the technical processes became predominant. For whatever reasons—the brightest librarians entering the profession were attracted to the intellectual problems of controlling and gaining access to knowledge, computerization in technical services was a great attraction, or for some other reason—much creative activity is occurring. Frederick Kilgour predicted well in 1966:

> The computer, then, will radically change library procedures, particularly those involved in the production of the information store so necessary to reference librarians. In addition, the computer will facilitate the reference librarians' and the users' use of the information store. [*Proceedings . . . Conference, Columbia,* March 30–April 1, 1966, ALA (1967)].

**Space and Facilities for Users.** The academic library building itself may be the most important service for users. The provision of an environment in which the use of library materials for instruction and research can flourish is surely a major goal for academic librarians. American academic librarians, as well as their colleagues in Canada, Great Britain, Japan, Scandinavia, and other countries, engaged in truly successful expansions of facilities in the 1960's and early 1970's.

Not only were central or main academic libraries newly designed but at many larger U.S. institutions, since 1948, when the Lamont Library at Harvard College was opened, until the mid-1970's, separate undergraduate libraries were built, or old main buildings renovated, for undergraduate use. Canada and Great Britain have also designed facilities especially for undergraduates.

In addition to separate branch libraries, special reading rooms in the central building (e.g., for documents, maps, rare books, curriculum materials, manuscripts, microforms, audiovisual materials, or other special types of materials or subject matter) were developed. American libraries were influenced by German research universities. Professors wished to meet their students where the most important books and journals were available; at first, this was the professor's own private library, then the seminar library. During the late 19th and early 20th centuries, the essential works of a discipline could be contained in one's own library or in the seminar library—whether it was in a special room near the university, as in Germany, or in the central university library building, as in the U.S. With the great expansion of scholarly publishing in the mid-20th century, seminar libraries and their progeny—the branch, departmental, collegiate, and institute libraries—have found it impossible to acquire all the essential materials of their disciplines. The development of interdisciplinary studies has also brought into question the elaborate system of separate decentralized collections. These libraries do provide the basic services of seats for study (of one's own material or of library material) and the storage of and access to the collections as well as other services. They vary widely in quality and sophistication. The integration of separate units into a total service plan benefitting the largest number of users is a matter for the review of each academic institution. Recent progress in automation will make the problems of bibliographic control and lack of knowledge of the holdings of branch libraries fade; in contrast, however, current and future economic constraints may not allow for any duplication of holdings. Local conditions, as well as local politics, provide the appropriate answers.

**The Future.** After reviewing the current scene of user services in academic librarianship, there is one certainty—and it will hold true for the future. Stanley McElderry observed:

> What appears to characterize the current stage of development is the application of more rigorous methods of analysis of problems and a more critical assessment of various alternatives. We still face the need for a better understanding of the library as an instrument of instruction and research and the definition of the most efficient and effective way to meet readers' requirements [*College and Research Libraries* (September 1976)].

*Slide room at Ernest Stevenson Bird Library, Syracuse University, Syracuse, New York.* Syracuse University Archives

Although academic librarians have for years attempted to measure use and to study the effects of library use on the performance of students, little progress has been made. Usually the units of measurement have not been more sophisticated than the number of items loaned, interlibrary loans and receipts, or information questions asked or answered and have been limited to a single library. Some studies of library use, such as those of Allen Kent and colleagues, have used more sophisticated techniques. Although the results of users' studies may be controversial, the 1980's will demand such research.

In tracing the development of services for users of academic libraries, one notices the small, but significant, changes in the use of prepositions and terminology. The early writers always discussed services *to* patrons or *to* officers and students. *Reference work* became *reference service* and then *reference/information service.* Later the literature shows concern about services *for* readers or *for* users. It is not too much to read into this language a change in attitude from paternalism to service. It may be hoped that library services will be carried one preposition further as the 21st century is approached. It should be librarians *with* students and faculty—librarians really in touch and truly working *with* the users.

This should be possible because of the substantial progress recently made in the use of computers in libraries. In 1969 Frederick Kilgour wrote in *Library Trends*:

> Fortunately for users, the electronic digital computer has immense potential for individual treatment of people and events. One major ultimate goal of computerization of college libraries must be the recapturing of humanization lost when libraries grew beyond the stage of having a staff of a single librarian familiar with all materials in the collection and able to interpret those

materials personally for each user. To be sure, this goal may not be achieved until the end of the century, but it may not be achieved even then if it is not defined and established now.

Perhaps the ill-defined reference/information services can join with the better defined (even minutely defined) circulation and technical services at one of the many computer terminals now (or soon to be) in evidence about academic library buildings. The academic librarian will be *with* the user at the terminal, coming full circle to the "sole reader service" in Wayne S. Yenawine's phrase; the "recapturing of humanization," lost when academic libraries grew so rapidly, will be happening.

**REFERENCES**

Robert Balay and Christine Andrew, "Use of the Reference Service in a Large Academic Library," *College and University Libraries* (1975).

Louis Kaplan, *The Growth of Reference Service in the United States from 1876 to 1893* (ACRL, 1952).

Stanley McElderry, "Readers and Resources: Public Services in Academic and Research Libraries, 1876–1976," *College and Research Libraries* (1976).

Samuel Rothstein, *The Development of Reference Services* (ACRL, 1955).

BILLY R. WILKINSON

COLLECTIONS

Librarians today may take for granted the collection development activities that occur in the typical academic library. A brief review of American library history, however, reveals that the academic library today bears little or no resemblance to the library of 200 or even 100 years ago. Nowhere is this change more visible than in the role of librarians in collecting materials.

Three aspects of this development deserve attention: (a) the changed role of the librarian; (b) the change in clientele, to include undergraduate students as library users; and (c) the role of growth in the development of the academic library.

In addition, a balanced view of collection development in academic libraries must address five key features of collection management: (a) the philosophy of collection development; (b) budgets; (c) approval plans; (d) serials; (e) deselection.

**Role of Librarians.** A cursory glance at American academic library history reveals a marked change in the role of college and university librarians. While our forebears believed that the library was the centerpiece of higher learning, they certainly did not take many of the actions that today would be considered appropriate in fulfillment of such a lofty sentiment. Although Yale University dates its founding from the donation of 40 books for the library in 1701, no other library programs seem to have followed as an immediate consequence. Time and again library history indicates that individual professors are charged to be "keepers" of the books. Librarianship was not perceived to be a full-time job; indeed even presidents of the colleges often served as "keepers." A part-time professor or president, however, seems preferable to what happened in the mid-19th century at Columbia University. It seems incredible that Stephen Weeks, the Assistant Librarian at Columbia for 30 years, was also the janitor of the college; Melvil Dewey raised him to the rank of Head of the Shelf Department in 1883. Indeed it was only in Dewey's time that professionalization of the librarian's functions occurred. Library collection development may place its origin from this period in history when library tasks became functionally specialized.

The university or college faculty originally acquired the books needed for their own study and were thus the first library book selectors. But as specialization developed by the end of the 19th century, librarians gradually assumed the selection function. However, it was only in the mid-20th century that "chief bibliographers" or "collection development librarians" began to assume the commanding role in book selection.

Of course this is not to suggest that the faculty have no role in collection development. On the contrary, in 1898 Daniel Coit Gilman, who served as Librarian at Yale and then President of Johns Hopkins and the University of California, pointed out that "good libraries are built up" only by the "joint action" of the bibliographer and faculty researcher. More recently, Robert B. Downs, long the Librarian at the University of Illinois, warned in a 1966 *Library Trends* article,

> It is not an uncommon practice in college and university libraries for the staff to abdicate responsibility to the faculty for book collection and collection development. Laboring under the delusion that only scholarly specialists are competent to decide what materials are worth adding, the librarian assigns practically all funds to teaching departments, and treats his acquisition staff as order clerks. The consequences may well be disastrous.

Thus we see the development, very gradually taking place, of librarians working together with the faculty to develop the collection.

What was lacking in earlier years, however, was a commitment to serving students, and the changed focus of clientele is an important factor in the history of collection development.

**Students as Library Users.** The original conception of a university library was as a storehouse of books for the faculty. Students were often denied access to it entirely or, at best, could enter the library only three to five hours per week. The Harvard Library Laws, for example, did not allow lower-division undergraduates to borrow books until 1765, and then only from the small collection of books deemed appropriate for the undergraduates. As a consequence of such restrictions, there grew up in the 18th century "society" libraries—collections of current-interest books and magazines. These student-run collections provided resources for debates and literary societies, as well as popular literature, and were the main source of reading for the typical student. The size of these society libraries was often impressive, sometimes rivaling, in numbers at least, the collections in the university library. In 1876, in the heyday of these libraries, just before most of them merged into the larger campus library, many colleges in the U.S. had significant numbers of volumes in these society libraries. Dartmouth society libraries, for example, held 27,000 volumes—compared with only 25,550 in the college library. At the University of North Carolina at Chapel Hill, the totals were 13,813 society library volumes compared with only 8,392 in the University's main library. These were the exceptions, and other colleges had proportionately smaller society library collections, but overall the society libraries accounted for nearly half a million volumes—nearly 20 percent of all the books in academic libraries in 1876.

In the last quarter of the 19th century, the majority of society libraries gradually merged with the larger campus libraries, a result, in part, of their very size and success. *Poole's Index to Periodical Literature* grew to some extent out of William Frederick Poole's desire to exploit as fully as possible the resources of his society library at Yale.

There is a benchmark here. By 1900 academic library collections had come nearly universally to be seen as places for students as well as for faculty. Yet the pace was slow; only with the great expansion of higher education in the early 1960's do we see the maturation of the idea of a separately housed undergraduate library for students, with a collection designed primarily for students rather than for the faculty researcher.

The success of an idea, however, often brings with it yet one more problem. With student access to library resources assured today, the very size and complexity of the contemporary academic library itself tends to ward off all but the most intrepid beginning scholar. Students more than ever need a helping hand to guide them to the library's resources. A movement toward comprehensive library instruction had been organized by the 1970's, but most practitioners would agree that much still needs to be done to help both students and faculty utilize the library's resources to the fullest extent.

**Importance of Growth.** Collection development as a separate functional operation in academic libraries is largely the result of growth: growth in numbers of published books and serials, bibliographic systems, and networks.

The statistics of sheer size are numbing: in 1850 only one American college library, Harvard, had more than 25,000 volumes. In 1876 only 14 of 71 principal college libraries had more than 25,000 volumes. By 1900 the 21 largest libraries held a median of only 88,000 volumes, with Harvard owning 575,000 volumes, followed by Chicago, Columbia, and Yale each with slightly more than 300,000 volumes. In 1920 the 23 largest libraries held a median of 300,000 volumes. But by 1962 the 63 academic libraries belonging to the Association of Research Libraries (ARL) held a median of 1,406,639 volumes. And by 1976, the 94 university ARL members held a median of 1,592,582 volumes. Thus in the first 75 years of this century, U.S. university libraries increased their median size five times over. If we accept as reliable the figure of 2,304,561 volumes in 356 college libraries to represent virtually all the academic library collections in the U.S. in 1876, then the aggregate figure 100 years later is truly astounding: in 1976 there were 193,550,258 volumes available to American college students at only 94 out of nearly 3,000 libraries—an 80-fold increase.

Yet these numbers only begin to describe the impact of increased publishing activity worldwide. The consequence was perhaps predictable. Today the average large university library adds some 75,000 volumes to its collection annually. One hundred years ago the median annual addition to the top two dozen libraries was fewer than 500 volumes, a 150-fold increase.

Such enormous increases in size and annual additions have led to the growth of a variety of bibliographic systems used to describe the vast bibliographic riches in today's academic library. The card catalogue has been with us for about 100 years; it was a quantum advance over the cumbersome accessions register books it replaced. Today the on-line bibliographic networks (OCLC, RLIN, and others) bid fair to replace the card catalogue. Just as the dictionary catalogue in card form enabled librarians and scholars to know what was in the collection (and not just where it might be located in the library), so the on-line catalogue allows users to see not only what one library has but what dozens of other libraries have—another quantum leap ahead.

Such access to information inevitably leads to cooperative activities. Late in the 19th century, Daniel Coit Gilman pointed with pride to the cooperative network of libraries in the city of Baltimore—the Peabody, Johns Hopkins, the Enoch Pratt, and others—holding such an ideal up for others to emulate. Each library supplied the primary needs of its local constituency but gave access to the others as well, so that 300,000 volumes were thus available to the student in Baltimore. "The principle of differentiation works admirably because each foundation considers the needs of its own clients, and supplies them as far as possible, and all are thus satisfied," Gilman wrote. By the end of the 1970's over 5,000,000 different titles were on-line in OCLC, and the collection development librarian might cast a longing glance toward cooperation once again, in hope that Gilman's "principle of differentiation" will work admirably this time to save the day against the impossible flood of literature.

Having seen the gradual development of the collecting function as a part of the increasing specialization and professionalization of the librarian's role, in the context of a century of dramatic growth, we can now summarize the essential features of collection development as now performed in academic libraries.

**Collection- versus User-Centered Philosophy.** These two approaches to collection development are not mutually exclusive; rather, a well-rounded philosophy of collection development may be described as a spectrum, with the collection-centered approach at one end and the user-centered approach at the other. The collection-centered philosophy asks, "Which are the key books (journals, reports, etc.) needed to make this a complete collection sufficient to enable the researcher to grasp the complete literature of the subject?" The user-centered philosophy; on the other hand, asks, "Which books (journals, reports, etc.) does Professor X or Student Q need?" The first approach emphasizes wholeness, completeness, the integrity of the collection; the second emphasizes the "who-ness," the satisfaction, the specific needs of the specific user. The one tends toward primary concern for the collection; the other, for the user.

The user-centered approach, however, seems to offer greater possibilities for coping with the enormous size and complexity of the literature of science and human endeavor today. No library, not even one with millions of volumes, can hope to have everything, a fact that has long been recognized. So librarians charged with developing the collection should naturally select their targets with care, bringing into the library only those materials that are needed by the library's clientele. To succeed at this, the librarian must develop a sensitivity to the library's user that will enable the library staff to marshal its considerable energies toward the fulfillment of its patrons' wants.

**Budgetary Controls.** Because academic libraries no longer rely on gifts, which had been the usual manner of acquiring books prior to the mid-19th century, book budgets are crucial to the library's success in meeting the needs of its faculty and students. In 1978, 80 U.S. academic libraries spent more than a million dollars each on materials, with two dozen of them spending in excess of $2,000,000 each. Enormous as such sums may seem, most librarians insist that their book budgets are inadequate. In part this is because the librarian is faced with the impossible task of dividing up the funds into ever smaller allocations to satisfy ever greater specific collecting needs and demands.

Some have responded by putting their faith in allocation formulas, of which there have been and will continue to be a variety. Many academic administrators have welcomed formulas as a way of arbitrating faculty pressures. The Clapp-Jordan formula, the Washington revision of it, the Voigt California formula, and the 1975 Association of College and Research Libraries *Standards* are only a few among the more prominent attempts at arriving at dollar amounts for allocating materials budgets in an academic library.

The Clapp-Jordan formula, the first to be widely recognized, focused on the quantity of library volumes judged to be adequate in order to support a specific number of students, faculty, and degree programs. The Washington model is a serious attempt to fit the Clapp-Jordan formula to five academic libraries in the state of Washington by utilizing a variety of allocation criteria, including staffing and processing costs. The Voigt model is an annual acquisitions rate model that has been used for the allocation of total dollar/volume amounts at the nine campuses of the University of California. The ACRL *Stan-*

*dards for College Libraries* proposes "Formula A"—which is merely a revision of the basic elements in the Clapp-Jordan formula but with the added notion of a quality grading based on the percentage of fulfillment of the quantitative criteria.

These formulas apply, however, only in the most gross and aggregated way to a library's total materials budget; the really difficult part is in dividing up the money to satisfy competing local subject-related interests. The result is that a large majority of library materials budgets are allocated to subject fields on a historical basis: "How much did the Psychology Department spend last year?" The loudest squeakers generally get the most grease in such a situation.

And yet, that is not an entirely bad way to divide up the pie. Appropriate user influence is desirable; the key lies in responding appropriately to *in*appropriate influence. Moreover, in those libraries that do use a formula to divide up the book budget, there is usually a small reserve of "flexible money" somewhere so that the librarian will have funds to respond to faculty pressures or unforeseen circumstances. It is fair to say that collection development librarians throughout the country perceive the allocation of book funds to be a never-ending source of discomfiture and debate. No simple solution appears possible.

**Approval and Gathering Plans.** Budgetary controls are so difficult to devise and enforce in part because of the complexity of acquiring library materials. Another reason lies in the inherent cross-disciplinary nature of a large portion of the literature of most subjects. Nowhere is this more evident than in the operations of various approval and gathering plans. The benefits accrued from schemes whereby a book jobber supplies a specified range of publications for librarians to screen and "approve" for purchase are so overwhelming that few administrators are willing to forgo them entirely. Speed of delivery, completeness of coverage, and work simplification are measurable benefits. On the other hand, most persons involved in collection development share an uneasy feeling that their approval plan is missing too large a fraction of wanted titles or is providing too many marginal publications. Unfortunately there is no simple solution; a jobber (and the firm's computer) cannot possibly deal with all the vagaries of campus programs, desires, and personalities. The collection development librarian does that, and—if he or she is doing a good job—does it infinitely better than an off-campus jobber. Rather, approval plans work best when they are limited to the most common, basic kinds of books; the librarian should thus be able to concentrate his or her highly skilled professional energies on selecting specific titles needed from the broad range of publications not adequately available in an approval plan.

A second type of gathering plan is the so-called "blanket-order" or standing-order plan. In such an arrangement—and there are many varieties—the librarian tells the publisher or vendor that all publications on a particular subject or by a particular author, in a specific series, or from a particular publisher are to be shipped to the library. In most cases, the vendor requires such arrangements to be on a "firm order only" basis. Despite the variety of possibilities in this type of gathering plan, the collection development librarian generally breathes more easily and with some degree of assurance that all the desired titles in such carefully defined and specific areas will indeed automatically arrive.

A third type of gathering plan is the cooperative plan of acquisitions. The Farmington Plan is an example: some 60 American libraries agreed to acquire and catalogue selected current publications from up to 16 foreign countries. In the P.L. 480 program up to two dozen American libraries receive the publications of eight countries through the Library of Congress, which administers the U.S. counterpart funds in foreign currencies to purchase the books. These plans are based on the willingness of a number of collection developers to agree to collect intensively and cooperatively in specific countries, so that at least one copy of the bulk of a nation's published output will be collected and housed in at least one American library. Noble as such a goal may be, it flies in the face of economic reality. The Farmington Plan lasted for 25 years until its demise in 1978. For even when such materials come free to the library, as in the P.L. 480 program, there are large continuing costs for processing and housing them. Few libraries are able and willing to afford such programs, particularly when there is very little apparent direct benefit to the campus.

**Serials.** The major issue facing most collection development officers since the early 1970's has been the problem of serials—their costs, their use, and the ideal ratio of serials to nonserials in a collection. Perhaps nowhere has inflation been more apparent than in the cost of periodicals, particularly for the expensive scientific and technical journals. The average U.S. periodical cost $8.66 in 1969; this jumped to $24.59 by 1977, a 184 percent increase. Library book budgets have not kept pace with such an enormous cost spiral.

As an ever greater percentage of library funds goes to purchase the serial literature, at the expense of the monographic literature, collection developers must ask: "Who needs this serial?" And the answers do not come back very clearly.

There is an old myth in library lore that says that the sciences need serial literature more than the social sciences and humanities, but this is simply not true. First, a comparison of the numbers of monographic works published in the U.S. shows that medicine, for example, had 1,818 new titles published in 1978, whereas all of literature had only 1,029. Technology titles outpaced history titles 1,294 to 1,147; science titles numbered 1,811 versus art books totaling only 1,056—again a differential exceeding 50 percent. Differences of such magnitude cannot be waved away as publishing quirks. Second, the practical workaday experience of librarians in touch with their faculty and students confirms the view that the serial literature is just as important to the English student as to the biologist. If there is a difference, it is only in the degree to which the scientific literature is better and more widely indexed and abstracted.

Thus when the serials input significantly exceeds the monographic input in a discipline, the librarian shudders, knowing that there is an imbalance in the collection and that the users of that collection are not being well served. Unfortunately, such knowledge is often not the springboard for corrective action; librarians simply do not have a simple formula for the "ideal" ratio of serials to nonserials. Such a ratio will vary according to both the subject discipline and the interests and needs on each campus. One can only suggest that if 90 percent of the materials budget in a subject goes for serials, then the monographic end of the literature spectrum is probably being unduly squeezed. The difficulty in acting on such knowledge, of course, lies in trying to reduce the number of serial subscriptions, an inherently more difficult challenge because it confronts what "is" (an ongoing journal subscription) with what "might be" (a monograph not yet in the library and perhaps not yet even published).

**Deselection.** There is yet one further aspect of collection development in academic libraries that deserves analysis, weeding—or as some prefer, deselection. The term "deselection" may be preferred in academic libraries because it connotes more accurately those highly professional activities in collection development programs that focus on keeping the collection "live," useful, and accessible. The term "weeding" does not do justice to the full concept of such collection management and is, besides, freighted with pejorative connotations.

Deselection is an integral part of the family of collection development activities, although in most large academic libraries it is a poor stepsister. It is not usually considered to be a part of the regular workload of librarians, and indeed, such activity goes against the instincts of most librarians. Yet few will argue with the fact that libraries cannot—indeed, should not—grow forever larger and larger without limit. Note the radically different premise of deselection from the recent discussions of "zero-growth."

And yet, what could be more natural? The typical large academic library may have 30 or 40 people working in acquisitions but not one single person whose job it is to discard materials. Common sense, practical experience, and philosophical conviction are hard pressed to force a change in the operations link between income and outgo, primarily because deselection *is* so difficult, time consuming, and, yes, negative. Yet an understanding of the living, organic nature of librarianship should compel acceptance of the need and desirability for removing waste products from the information stream with every bit as much attention to grand design and to detail as the acquisition of new material.

The problem of deselection is usually wrongfully identified as being *what* to discard. Seen from such a perspective, it is no wonder that collection managers throw up their hands in despair over the sheer enormity of the undertaking. But the problem of deselection really ought to be viewed in terms of process: *How* are we going to discard? *Who* are we going to involve in the process? *What* will be the criteria for making the collection more usable for more people for a longer period of time? Seen in this light, deselection can become more organic to the entire library program, and not just as an aberration or an afterthought.

**The U.S. Emphasis.** The uniqueness of the American academic library experience is surprising; one might have expected that the British traditions of Oxford and Cambridge would have had more impact on American library collecting habits, or the German graduate school model imported to the U.S. would have brought a concomitant highly decentralized library collection system. That neither of these patterns prevailed attests to both the ingenuity and the different climate of academic endeavor in the U.S. collection development, consequently, is more consciously "worked at" in U.S. academic libraries and its problems more widely discussed. The issues and problems associated with it are central to the core of professional librarianship. It is safe to say that collection concerns will not fade away but will continue to engage even more intensively the creative imagination of the best minds in the profession for the foreseeable future.

WILLIAM H. WEBB

## ADMINISTRATION, GOVERNANCE, AND FINANCE

Patterns of organization, governance, and finance for academic libraries in the United States are tending to be more diverse and less uniform than was the case prior to 1970. A dual organizational pattern common since World War II still predominates—all library activities are described as either reader services or technical services, with each of these services having within it functional- and/or format-based departments. But many variations can be found in library organization. Columbia University Libraries underwent a major organizational change in 1973, organizing its activities into a resources group, a services group, and a technical support group; it provides a widely publicized example of change in organizational patterns in academic libraries. Other patterns, such as a subject divisional plan initiated at the University of Colorado, although not new, continue to be effective. Some of the new patterns of organization are similar in that reader services are no longer grouped under a single manager. The major departure from the dual organizational pattern is based on the reality in many academic libraries that the responsibilities of the public services director have become too extensive. The effect of automation on library activities also has influenced administrative structure. Another characteristic of new patterns of organization is that libraries have relatively flatter structures, with fewer levels in the administrative hierarchy.

Whether a university library should be centralized or not continues to be debated. Columbia has a highly dispersed library system, typical of many of the larger and older universities, while the library of the State University of New York at Albany is at the other extreme—a completely centralized library facility with no branches. The Brown University Library system is moderately decentralized with five units, three of which are integrated organizationally. The unique feature of the Brown organizational design is that functional responsibilities transcend locations. For example, the reference and the circulation functions are headed by managers who are responsible for these functions in all five locations. This contrasts with the usual pattern of all functions at a single location being the responsibility of a manager who is the person who is in charge at that site. Whether departmental libraries should be separated from the central libraries continues to be an issue of concern, more so in countries such as West Germany and Austria, where decentralization is the predominant pattern of organization, than in the United States.

**Key Issues.** The issues faced in designing the organization of academic libraries are not new, but additional insights have been provided by research in the 1960's and '70's. The issues include accountability, autonomy and professionalization, optimal use of staff, response to change, technology, and participation in decision making. Some issues can be posed as questions: Does a library manager coordinate or control? Does this differ by organizational level and/or size, and if so, how? Do some designs centralize authority or decision making more than others? What are the effective limits on the number of persons a manager can coordinate or control? Do some designs enhance utilization of staff? Are some designs more responsive to change? What designs maximize autonomy and professionalism? How has or will technology affect the organization of libraries? Are some designs more hospitable to participatory decision making than others?

Among these issues accountability, in its myriad forms, has had the greatest impact on the recent patterns of organizational design of academic libraries in the United States. In the area of personnel, formal grievance procedures instituted within the college and university, collective-bargaining agreements, equal-opportunity policies and reporting requirements imposed by the federal government, and other formalized institutional procedures have led to the creation in many academic libraries of administrative units whose sole function is to deal with personnel matters.

In financial matters, accounting and audit standards imposed by the institution and growing demands for data supportive of budget are resulting in the appointments of business managers and budget officers in academic libraries of all sizes in the United States. The growth in the size and importance of institutional research and the data produced in these activities have had a corresponding effect on academic libraries, both because libraries have to produce more data for more institutional reports and because there are more reports requiring analysis and response.

The cumulative effect of all accountability devices has been to increase the number of administrative staff positions in academic libraries. This is especially true in public institutions and in libraries where the administration has consciously attempted to buffer heads of operating units—e.g., technical services, public services, acquisitions, cataloguing, reference, serials, etc.—from the encroachment of this administrative workload in order to allow these managers to focus more time and energy on operational and service issues.

**Governance.** Nowhere is the increased variation in patterns of organization among United States academic libraries more apparent than in their governance structures. As librarians seek greater participation in the decision-making process, and as faculty status for academic librarians has become more prevalent, structures have been created to accommodate these changes. In turn, linkages have had to be devised between the collegial governance structure and the formal administrative structure. Some libraries include representation from the library staff in the regular administrative staff meetings. Others have eliminated administrative staff meetings and replaced them with collegially based groups. Variations in these governance arrangements are due as much to personalities and individual styles as to campus tradition, personal preferences, or imagination. For instance, there may be major differences in governance on the same campus among its schools, colleges, and divisions, as well as among departments or units within a school, college, or division. Thus librarians looking for a mode of library governance will make a studied selection from among several alternatives.

The similarities and differences are quite clear among the published models of governance for academic libraries. The most noticeable difference is one of scope. One governance structure may be derived from a need to create formal mechanisms to select, appoint, retain, promote, and evaluate members of the library staff; another structure may be established and authorized to undertake a wider range of activities. Differences of detail are apparent in the committee structures, the method of selection of committee members and chairs, and the role of the head librarian (e.g., presiding officer, ex-officio member of standing committees). The fundamental issue in the internal governance of academic libraries in the United States is the evolution of consensus about which issues are appropriately decided by the administration, which are decided in the forum of the whole (i.e., the entire staff of librarians), and which issues are appropriately resolved within organizational units, such as reference, collection development, public services, and technical services.

Most academic libraries in the United States have faculty library committees designed to advise the librarian on matters pertaining to the budget and to the collections. These committees seldom are involved in any issues of internal governance; indeed, most members of such committees would deem involvement in such matters as an inappropriate intrusion by outsiders into the internal affairs of another academic unit, in much the same way that faculty in the arts and sciences, for example, stay out of the affairs of the faculties in professional schools (which is not to suggest that faculties do not have strong opinions about one another).

In the United States, as in other countries of the world, the academic library remains a unit of the college or university of which it is a part. Although cooperative agreements and contractual arrangements with other institutions are increasing, and governance of these arrangements is complex, the organizational structure, governance, and financial affairs of the library remain based in those of the institution. The role of the national government in relation to academic libraries in England and Europe, by contrast, is much stronger, and governance patterns and structures are influenced accordingly.

**Finance.** In the 1950's and 1960's libraries in the United States received substantial increases in financial resources. By the 1970's budgetary increases were fewer and smaller, and some institutions experienced decreases. The most notable characteristic of the 1970's, however, was the uneven pattern across the country. Academic libraries in northeastern states experienced reductions in base budgets, while those in the Southeast and Southwest received substantial increases. In the Midwest adjacent states had opposite experiences: academic libraries in one might receive an increase in resources, while in another state libraries suffered a reduction in base budget.

Because of the declining birthrate, the typical college-age cohort in the U.S. is becoming a smaller proportion of the total population. There is also some evidence that the percentage of this population that attends college may decline. Thus colleges and universities will be competing for a smaller group of traditional students, as well as reaching into other age groups for potential students. An effect of these demographic factors on finance will be to lower enrollments and to make enrollment-based formulas less workable for budgeting. Beyond the issue of formulas, however, lies the larger question of the level of funding for higher education and its libraries in the 1980's and beyond. It is probable that institutional budgets measured on a per-student basis will continue to rise, albeit more slowly. From the expenditure perspective, labor-intensive education will become even more so as personnel costs increase faster than capital costs. Thus, if institutional expenditures become more labor intensive, as personnel costs rise faster than budgets, expenditures in less labor-intensive areas—like libraries—are likely to suffer.

In the decades ahead academic libraries will begin to receive income from a greater variety of funding sources. Some institutions have long dealt with endowments, alumni, individual donors, foundations, and federal and state government agencies. These sources of revenue will become even more common in more libraries, and added to these will be such others as service fees (interlibrary loans, courtesy borrowing privileges, data base search charges, photocopy and other vending machines), grants from consortia, or cooperative agreements. For librarians at publicly funded institutions this diversity will allow more flexibility than has been possible in the past when nearly all of a library's income derived from appropriated funds.

The 1980's and '90's will also see a continuation of the development and application of new management tools. Since the mid-1960's academic libraries have adopted various approaches and techniques—such as operations research, performance standards, management by objectives, program budgeting, and zero-based budgeting—to identify with more precision their goals and their progress toward meeting those goals.

The expectation for the balance of the 20th century is for greater variety in the organizational patterns, governance styles, administrative methods, and financial circumstances of academic libraries in the United States than was the case in the two and a half decades following World War II. This in turn reflects more variety within the nation not only in economic and demographic trends but also in educational, social, and cultural attitudes and institutions.

C. JAMES SCHMIDT

MEASUREMENT AND EVALUATION

Traditionally library administrators have relied on library surveys or crude rules of thumb to measure and evaluate academic libraries. Library surveys are easily the most popular form of library evaluation. Since Louis Round Wilson designed the first academic library survey to be conducted by an outside team in 1939, the elements of that survey have not changed. They are

1. Are the library's collections adequate to support the objectives of the university?
2. Is the staff sufficient and does it have the appropriate training to carry out the library's programs?
3. Are the library's materials organized effectively?

4. How adequate is the physical equipment and plant?
5. What kind of administrative relationships exist between the library, the faculty, the administration?
6. Is the library adequately financed?
7. Does the library engage in cooperative ventures with other libraries in the state and region?

A library survey is intended to provide an authoritative assessment of a library. It is based on easily gathered, "countable" data, on which the judgment of the authoritative surveyors is to be based. Such techniques are not to be despised; they are commonly employed in academia and elsewhere. But they are inevitably Delphic or prescriptive. They have little empirical foundation, and their credibility largely depends on the prestige of the surveyors. Very often this is what is wanted by academic or even governmental administrators. So these surveys are likely to continue to be performed although they provide, because of their weak empirical foundations, a very uncertain guide for library management.

Examples of rules of thumb that library administrators or surveyors employ are: (1) the library should receive 6 percent of the institutional budget; and (2) its own budget should be divided into 30 percent for acquisitions, 60 percent for personnel and 10 percent for everything else. Such measures really beg the question of measurement because they fail to define total amounts of money. Consequently, librarians have fallen back on comparative measures, and in those cases where they have failed to obtain the kind of institutional support they thought necessary, they have attempted to clothe their comparisons in the form of standards, preferably quantitative standards.

**Quantitative Standards.** The history of the effort to develop quantitative standards for libraries is long and complicated, but the most obvious reason for developing them has never been better stated than by Verner W. Clapp and Robert T. Jordan: "When . . . standardizing authorities omit or refuse to set standards in quantitative terms, the budgeting and appropriating authorities, who cannot avoid quantitative bases for their decisions, are compelled to adopt measures which, though perhaps having the virtue of simplicity, may be essentially irrelevant." This was written in 1965; yet libraries are not much closer to developing adequate quantitative standards by the end of the 1970's than they were then.

The problem is multifaceted, but it tends to resolve itself into three issues: (1) whether quantitative standards for libraries can be created at all; (2) the difficulty of obtaining adequate data; and (3) the necessity to reconceptualize the meaning of library measures to change their focus from a consideration of inputs to a consideration of outputs; that is, from additions to services and collections to measures of performance.

The resistance to the development of quantitative standards on the part of many librarians is based partly on the inadequacy of the data currently available and partly on the fear that crude general measures will be unthinkingly applied. Typically, what tends to be a minimal standard for librarians and scholars is a sufficient standard for budget officers. The libraries of the larger, wealthier, private academic institutions and some public institutions would tend to be above any threshold level of minimal adequacy, and the application of minimum standards to them would weaken their efforts to continue to provide the services and collections to which their users have become accustomed.

It cannot be denied that presently available data are inadequate. Herman Fussler, for example, observes in his 1973 report *Research Libraries and Technology* "Libraries, like universities, tend to have very inadequate analytical data on their own operations and performance. Such data, especially as they relate to costs and system responses to user needs, are critically important in any effort to improve a library's efficiency and responsiveness." Others have criticized the poor quality of library record keeping and have challenged the utility of present library data collection, observing that it fails to measure performance or effectiveness.

In fact, the most generally used academic library formula, the Washington State formula, which has been adopted in most respects by the American Library Association as its standard for college libraries, is statistically imperfect and generally inapplicable. It suffers from what statisticians call multicollinearity, i.e., the explanatory variables used in the formula cannot be isolated, so their effects overlap in ways that defy analysis. While it seems to provide results that in many cases appear acceptable, it is a defective instrument, the use of which cannot be extrapolated to the whole universe of academic libraries. Efforts to apply the formula widely demonstrate a very broad range of variability in the results obtained, so broad that its predictive value is nil. Librarians who seek quantitative standards are then faced with a dilemma. Quantitative measures are needed to analyze what libraries are and to provide a basis for communication about them, but neither presently available formulas nor existing data are completely useful for such analyses.

**Comparative and Internal Measures.** Two kinds of measures are necessary: a comparison between similar institutions, and a yardstick or set of yardsticks for internal measures. The first is necessary to orient the evaluation within the universe of academic libraries. It is a common habit in higher education to compare one institution with another, and libraries are usually one of the features of such comparisons. The inadequacy of comparative data is troublesome, and the counting methods used by most libraries might better be replaced by standardized sampling methods that would be both easier and cheaper to apply. Nevertheless, the Higher Educational General Information Survey data and the Association of Research Libraries data do provide some basis for comparison despite the limitations of the data, especially if the comparisons are carefully selected so that like institution is compared with like on such indexes as size of student body, expenditure per student, similarity of program, etc.

Once this comparison is made, simple inspection of the data thus isolated, aided by rankings, ranges, averages, and medians, can provide useful insights for the experienced library manager. Beyond this, a further reduction of data into ratios can occur. Some of those that provide useful insights into library operations are:

1. The ratio of professional to nonprofessional staff
2. Expenditure for library materials as a percent of total library operating expenditures
3. Ratio of salary expenditures to library material expenditures

Most academic libraries appear to have a ratio of one professional to two nonprofessional staff members. They expend 30 percent of their total budget on library materials and twice as much on salaries. But these figures are not static. They have meaning only in relation to a comparison group. They are not benchmarks at which every institution should aim, but they do provide a relative standard, a background against which a library can begin to be evaluated, always provided that like is being compared with like.

A more extended form of ratio analysis is Allan M. Cartter's Library Resources Index, which is an average of three indexes: total volumes held, volumes added, and periodicals received. This index represents an effort to define a library factor that can be correlated with other institutional factors. In fact, in 1963 when Cartter applied this technique to universities, he found a high correlation between excellence of graduate schools and a high position of the parent institution's library on the index.

Baumol and Marcus extended the comparative analysis of libraries by the use of regression techniques. This provides a more synthetic form of data reduction and enables the analyst to inspect the interaction of a number of variables. Given the easy availability of computer programs to perform regression, this should become more widely used. It remains dependent, however, on the collection of suitable and accurate data. The equations Baumol and Marcus derived predict total staff, professional staff, volumes added, cost of volumes added, and total library operating costs. But they do so largely on the basis of the total number of volumes a library holds, expenditures per student, and number of volumes added. These are not necessarily the most useful variables that can be derived, nor do they measure all one would like to know.

As a statistical technique, regression analysis is an advance over simple ratios, but regression analysis cannot provide more information than the data possess. It cannot eliminate the double inadequacy in most library data: inaccuracy of what is counted and failure to measure what is most relevant. There are no precise measures for how and why people use libraries. Library staff only dimly understand what it is they are trying to measure. This is true both for relative comparative measures and for what are coming to be known as performance measures. As the name implies, performance measures attempt to determine how well a library performs. Can it deliver a particular item when needed? How fast can it do so? And so forth. Performance measures could provide the librarian with a completely new kind of measure—a feedback response mechanism that would permit a standard of performance to be set, a means of comparison to determine adherence to the standard, and a method for correcting performance if it fails to meet the standard.

Every organization, especially difficult-to-manage public service organizations, would like such measures, provided they are cost beneficial to apply. Libraries do not have them yet, but they could be developed. The failure to develop them is probably attributable to the benign environment in which libraries used to exist. This environment is changing, however; socioeconomic and sociotechnological changes are rapidly reshaping the world in which we live. Different modes of information delivery compel a reevaluation of traditional mechanisms for information storage and retrieval. These new modes of delivery challenge the existence of traditional libraries and compete for the funds that support them.

**Future Trends and Goals.** Changes in social objectives and economic conditions have produced a decline in the financial resources available to the parent institutions of academic libraries. Public support for higher education is eroding, and those who predicted a depression in higher education because of the decline in the numbers of college-age youth seemed to be right at the end of the 1970's. Higher education faces a crisis in the 1980's, and every facet of its operations is being subjected to searching scrutiny. Each must justify its existence in terms of its contribution to institutional objectives.

Libraries are not exempt from this examination. The typical library budget is so large a part of the institutional budget that it continually attracts administrative attention every time inflation moves upward or revenue downward. The persistent pressure of inflation makes each library less and less able to maintain its collections, especially its serials collections. The buying power of library funds has been dramatically reduced. Librarians are driven to ask for more funds in an effort to maintain what they have, while administrators increasingly regard libraries as a bottomless pit that can consume all the resources at their disposal.

The pace of inflation in library materials continues to mount at a rate that is variously estimated to be in excess of 20 percent per year. No parent institution can sustain such a rate of growth; each must set a limit on the fraction of its total budget it devotes to the library. That fraction seldom exceeds 6 percent of the total institutional budget and is frequently less. When the parent institution is unable to raise its total budget to keep pace with the rise in the general price level, it is all the more unable to meet library demands. These two trends—the inflation of library materials at a rate greater than the general price level and the inability of most institutions to increase their budgets at the same rate as the general price level—are on a collision course. Everywhere the increase in library budgets is meeting a ceiling, a limit that the parent institution must impose. All this is familiar, but what seems to be misunderstood is that these trends will provoke a fundamental change in what libraries can be. Basically, libraries can continue to reduce their collections gradually, satisfying fewer and fewer of the demands levied upon them, or they can attempt to redefine their roles, to shift their emphasis from collecting materials to providing information.

The situation demands a redefinition of what academic libraries are. Without such a redefinition it is increasingly difficult to say what is to be measured or evaluated. It is common to remark that libraries are the intellectual heart of the college or the university. Most libraries that have established objectives attempt to translate this idea into practice by defining their principal goals as the support of the educational and research needs of the parent institution. To achieve these goals the library may further specify such objectives as the collecting of that fraction of the world's output of printed literature that supports those goals, or having enough seats for 25 percent of the student population, or providing reference service for 80 hours a week, and so on. But the real goals of libraries, at least from the administration's perspective, are not fully describable in this way. Many institutions use their libraries as a magnet to attract other publics: summer visitors, scholars of note, potential donors who may contribute to more than the library itself. All of these purposes make it difficult to establish any uniform standard that can be applied to libraries in general. Consequently, the application to libraries of empirical measurement techniques is still in its infancy. Relatively few practitioners employ them. The literature shows only the hesitant beginnings of such applications. There is no generally accepted set of empirical standards by which libraries can be judged, no agreed-upon body of techniques yet available.

There is a need to redefine academic libraries in ways that are appropriate to the present and future and to distinguish in that definition, to whatever extent possible, various institutional purposes. Once this is done, an effort can be made to obtain more adequate data in order to develop predictive models based on causal factors. Academic librarians have no more pressing need than the development of quantitative measures. Without them they cannot fully understand and therefore cannot adequately manage the libraries in their charge. What is needed is a collective effort to learn basic statistical techniques and to begin to apply them in libraries. Not only can the shared experience that this effort implies gradually produce the needed data, but the data will shape decisions that can redefine and perfect the academic library itself.

**REFERENCES**

William J. Baumol and Matityahu Marcus, *Economics of Academic Libraries* (1973), an examination of the available economic data on college and university libraries using and explaining regression analysis.

Verner W. Clapp and Robert T. Jordan, "Quantitative Criteria for Adequacy of Academic Library Collections," *College and Research Libraries* (1965).

F. W. Lancaster, *The Measurement and Evaluation of Library Services* (1977), a comprehensive review and summary of research efforts on the measurement and evaluation of libraries.

R. Marvin McInnis, "The Formula Approach to Library Size: An Empirical Study of Its Efficacy in Evaluating Research Libraries," *College and Research Libraries* (1972), an analysis of the Clapp-Jordan formula.

RICHARD J. TALBOT

LIBRARY COOPERATION

Cooperation, simply defined as voluntarily joining together for mutual benefit, has long been a goal of the academic library community in the United States. Academic libraries have participated in local, statewide, national, and international cooperative programs. During recent decades the impetus for academic library cooperation has come not only from the academic community itself but also from governmental agencies and private foundations that have provided financial support for various cooperative programs. In addition, the dramatic advances in computer and communications capabilities have supplied the technological means to accomplish some long-hoped-for goals. Although "cooperation" and "network" have frequently been used synonymously, many cooperative efforts preceded the development of the telecommunications capabilities that underlie present-day library networks.

Cooperative programs in academic libraries range from informal, local activities to formal, complex agreements. Cooperative programs vary in scope from those that affect one aspect of library operations or services to those that impact broadly upon library operations and services and that may affect governance. Most cooperative programs are directed toward the achievement of one or more of three major goals: (1) improving bibliographic access to library materials; (2) improving physical access to library materials; and (3) engaging in cooperative collection development.

**Bibliographic Access.** To a large extent the availability of bibliographic information about collections is a prerequisite for other forms of cooperative activities in libraries. Unless there is adequate bibliographic information, agreements to deliver materials or to join in cooperative collection development programs can be little more than lofty goals. It is not surprising, therefore, that some of the earliest efforts in academic library cooperation, and some of the most innovative present-day techniques, involve sharing bibliographic information in order to improve bibliographic access to collections.

The standardization of bibliographic data has improved steadily since 1901, when the Library of Congress began printing its catalogue cards and making them available to others. Although the United States, unlike many other countries, has no national library to provide bibliographic services, the Library of Congress, the nation's largest library, has assumed de facto bibliographic leadership, especially for the academic and research library community. The Library's efforts in the standardization of bibliographic description have led to the development of the machine-readable format for cataloguing, the MARC II format, and to the encouragement, development, and adoption of international bibliographic standards. The UNIMARC format is now used by the Library of Congress in the international exchange of machine-readable data with the national libraries of Australia, Canada, France, Norway, and the United Kingdom.

In 1974 the Council on Library Resources, Inc. initiated a program to provide a reliable and authoritative serials data base to meet the needs of library patrons, other users of information, and the developing national and international bibliographic networks. The CONSER (Conversion of Serials) project, in which the Library of Congress, the National Agricultural Library, the National Library of Medicine, and other research libraries now are participating, will provide an on-line machine-readable core data base of bibliographic information available for use on the international, national, regional, and local levels.

As early as the turn of the century, union lists were produced, containing the combined holdings of several institutions. The first such regional list in the U.S. was created at the California State Library. The number of union lists has increased; they continue to be produced, aided by the use of machine-readable data and the standardization of bibliographic description in the MARC II format.

Cooperative cataloguing, another early interest of academic libraries, has been assisted markedly by the utilization of computer technology. The most successful effort is OCLC, Inc., originally formed by a consortium of Ohio academic libraries in 1967 and now a national network serving over 1,800 libraries of all types. OCLC's central on-line data base in Columbus, Ohio, contains over 5,000,000 records. These records, essentially cataloguing records created by member libraries, serve as a major bibliographic tool in the acquisitions, cataloguing, and interlibrary loan operations of member libraries. OCLC has made a major impact on the operations of all academic libraries and has provided incomparable assistance to the efforts of academic library cooperation.

Other computer-based bibliographic utilities that serve academic libraries include the Research Libraries Information Network (RLIN), the Washington Library Network (WLN), and the University of Toronto Library Automation Systems (UTLAS). RLIN, previously known as BALLOTS, was developed at Stanford University. In 1978 it was selected to be the machine-based cataloguing system of the Research Libraries Group (RLG). RLG, a consortium formed in 1973 by Yale, Harvard, New York Public Library, and Columbia, addresses major issues facing research libraries, including collection development and management, shared resources, preservation and bibliographic control. After the adoption of BALLOTS, Harvard withdrew from the consortium and membership was extended to all research universities. By the fall of 1979, membership increased to 11, including Michigan, Princeton, Dartmouth, University of Pennsylvania, Rutgers, Stanford, Brigham Young and Colorado State University.

WLN was originally designed to serve all types of libraries in the state of Washington. It has recently established working agreements in Idaho, Oregon and California.

UTLAS is the largest catalogue support system in the world outside the United States and the United Kingdom and is used by over 100 academic and public libraries in Canada.

These bibliographic utilities permit participating libraries to produce catalogue cards or store bibliographic information that is fitted to their local needs. Earlier attempts to provide cooperative bibliographic and processing systems, such as those in Colorado, Massachusetts, New Jersey, and Maryland, were less successful. The earlier efforts stressed centralized standards and uniform products; later directions emphasized decentralization and responsiveness to individual library needs.

**Physical Access.** Interlibrary lending is the most long-standing example of academic library cooperation. The first interlibrary loan code was formulated by the American Library Association in 1917. Although interlibrary lending is widespread among academic libraries, it accounts for only 1 percent of recorded transactions in academic libraries. The cost of an interlibrary loan, however, is many times the cost of an internal transaction. For years these costs were borne by the lending libraries, but in the late 1960's, owing to increasing financial pressures, several of the largest academic libraries in the United

States initiated fees for interlibrary loans. Although most academic libraries still do not charge for an interlibrary loan, the high cost and inefficiency of the interlibrary lending system have been of growing concern to academic librarians.

Some statewide networks and regional networks have facilitated direct access to books and journals held in various libraries. MINITEX, the Minnesota Interlibrary Telecommunications Exchange, provides journal articles and other materials from the collections at the University of Minnesota to all types of libraries in Minnesota and North and South Dakota. CLASS, the California Library Authority for Systems and Services, offers an array of bibliographic, educational, and information services to California libraries. The Illinois Regional Library Council enables patrons to use directly the collections of all types of libraries in the Chicago metropolitan area. State networks developed through federal moneys provided by the Library Services and Construction Act first were established as public library networks. Direct borrowing and interlibrary lending were encouraged and made possible among public libraries. Many of the states now are converting the public library systems to multitype library systems in which the academic libraries play important roles.

Recognition of the need for more efficient and effective access to materials, especially journal literature, has led in recent years to the development of plans for a National Periodical Center. This effort has been led by the National Commission for Libraries and Information Services, the Library of Congress, and the Council for Library Resources. Many supporters of the National Periodical Center in the United States look upon the British Library Lending Division (BLLD) as a model. The BLLD has developed an excellent system for delivery of materials to requesting libraries. The service extends not only throughout Great Britain but to other nations as well.

The Interlibrary Loan Code and the proposed National Periodical Center are examples of formal, national programs. Many local agreements have been designed to improve access to materials. Such agreements frequently involve delivery of materials between libraries by vans or similar vehicles, reciprocal borrowing agreements that permit users from one institution to have direct access to library materials of another, photocopy service, and other special delivery or communications services such as telefacsimile.

**Cooperative Collection Development.** Academic librarians, even in the largest and wealthiest libraries, are increasingly aware of their inability to build comprehensive collections. Academic administrators and funding agencies, discouraged by the "bottomless pit" aspect of academic libraries, have supported cooperative collection development programs. There have been several national efforts in the U.S. The Farmington Plan, initiated in 1945, distributed collection responsibilities for current foreign research materials among approximately 60 academic libraries. It ended in 1972, in part, because of the success of both the National Program for Acquisitions and Cataloging (NPAC) and of Public Law 480 programs. Both of these projects were managed by the Library of Congress. Several hundred academic libraries have participated in these programs designed to acquire and catalogue foreign materials. In specialized areas the Latin American Cooperative Acquisitions Program (LACAP) and the Center for Chinese Research Materials have been leaders in acquiring specialized materials for academic libraries.

It appears that the most effective cooperative collection development arrangements are the local, informal agreements made among libraries that have compatible or well-recognized strengths and weaknesses. The formal agreement between the libraries of Duke University and the University of North Carolina, for example, has been in existence since 1931 and has been successful in defining collection development responsibilities for each library. Cooperation between Duke and North Carolina includes not only agreement about collection responsibilities but also delivery of materials and reciprocal borrowing. A similar program between the libraries of the University of California at Berkeley and Stanford University, supported by a grant from the Sloan and Mellon foundations, was initiated in 1976. Both libraries strengthened and formalized existing informal arrangements and began a major effort to formulate a joint collection development policy statement.

A frequently cited example of formal cooperative collection development is the Center for Research Libraries. The Center had its origins in 1949 as the Midwest Interlibrary Center, designed to be a central storage facility for little-used materials deposited by members. Now with a nationwide membership, the Center acquires by gift, deposit, and purchase infrequently used items of research value, such as foreign dissertations, newspapers, the publications of foreign governments, and journals. It therefore serves as a supplement to the collecting activities of member libraries, enabling a library *not* to purchase for its own collections some infrequently used item but to borrow the item directly from the Center. The Universal Serials and Book Exchange (USBE) is another organization that acquires and makes available infrequently used materials.

Informal consultations among libraries frequently take place with regard to the purchase of expensive items. The University of California formalized this consultation process, and 3 percent of the materials budget of the University of California libraries is allocated to a shared purchasing program. Representatives of each of the nine University of California libraries participate in developing guidelines and in the individual selection decisions.

Academic libraries participate in many kinds of cooperative programs that are designed to increase the services and expand the collections available to users. The machine-readable data base programs already have had great impact upon the operations and services of academic libraries. More is expected in the future as the standardization of bibliographic records is extended, the size of the data bases grows, and the world's serials output is placed under bibliographic control. The influence of various cooperative agreements upon the autonomy of the academic library will lead to a reduction in the autonomy of the library. The benefit of greater service to the library user will outweigh the cost. Libraries will strive for more cooperation, not less, in the future.

**REFERENCES**

Beth A. Hamilton and William B. Ernst, Jr., editors, *Multitype Library Cooperation* (1977).

Allen Kent and Thomas J. Galvin, editors, *The Structure and Governance of Library Networks* (1979).

Susan K. Martin, *Library Networks, 1978–79* (1978).

Michael M. Reynolds, editor, *Reader in Library Cooperation* (1972).

ELAINE SLOAN

LAWS AND LEGISLATION

Although there is no large body of federal legislation which deals exclusively with academic libraries, there are two legislative acts which continue to affect directly many academic libraries in the United States: the Library Services and Construction Act (LSCA) and the Higher Education Act (HEA) of 1965. Many other statutes in part affect academic libraries, as, for example, the Occupational Safety and Health Act (OSHA) of 1970, which regulates working and safety conditions, the variety of statutes and acts concerning civil rights, equal opportunity and affirmative action in hiring and personnel administration, the postal regulations generally and the special library postage rate in particular, the 1976 revision of the Copyright Act, and the many programs authorized through the National Endowment for the Humanities. Legislation affecting the Library of Congress, the National Library of Medicine, and the National Agricultural Library in turn may affect academic libraries, because they serve this significant constituency.

Academic librarians generally appear to support the principles that motivated the affirmative action programs and OSHA but are often irritated and frustrated by local interpretations which create overly elaborate, lengthy routines and procedures. Copyright revision was of major concern to most academic librarians, but by 1980 it appeared that the new statute has been less difficult to comply with than had been anticipated. Although additional record keeping is required, most academic librarians have been able to handle this matter without too much difficulty; many are accumulating data which may be useful in considering possible revision, as the act will be reviewed after it has been in effect for five years.

At the state level, legislation establishing and directing the activities of the state library agency, or creating personnel classification systems in state colleges and universities, or regulating union organization activities, or establishing penalties for the theft or mutilation of library materials—all these and hundreds of other state legislative acts affect academic libraries. Not the least of these are the annual appropriations bills which fund state-supported academic libraries. Of more general application have been the series of statutes which established library systems in the individual states, in which academic libraries have come to participate along with other types of libraries.

One of the earliest federal acts concerning academic libraries was a resolution passed in the second session of the 13th Congress, on December 27, 1813. This resolution brought together a series of earlier special acts providing for the printing and distribution of the public journals of the House and Senate. Included were provisions for distributing government publications to colleges and universities. Resolutions adopted in 1857–61 formed the basis for the present Federal Depository Library System. In 1895 the General Printing Act further detailed document distribution, and 1962 amendments established the Regional Depository System. While the present provisions of Title 44 of the U.S. Code do not specifically identify academic libraries as such as depositories, many academic libraries have been so designated (as provided in the statutes) by their local Representative or U.S. Senator.

Other federal legislation in the decade of the 1960's was more directly related to academic libraries. The Academic Facilities Act of 1963 funded construction of academic buildings, including libraries, at both public and private institutions of higher education. The Vocational Education Act (1963) provided for funding the acquisition of vocational and technical material for colleges in order to encourage vocational education. Similarly, the 1965 Medical Library Assistance and Hospital Construction Act provided funding for the development of medical libraries and their collections.

The purpose of Title III of the Library Services and Construction Act is to "establish and maintain local, regional, State or interstate cooperative networks and for the coordination of informational services of school, public, academic, and special libraries and information centers, permitting the user of any one type of library to draw on all libraries and information centers." Academic libraries have benefitted both indirectly and directly as networks have been developed and expanded and as resource centers have been identified and strengthened. For example, the University of Illinois at Urbana-Champaign and Southern Illinois University at Carbondale have received LSCA funds after being designated resource centers in ILLINET, the Illinois Library and Information Network.

**Higher Education Act of 1965.** By far the most important of the federal acts was the Higher Education Act, passed in 1965 and subsequently amended. It is possible to view the Higher Education Act as a barometer which indicates the general status of libraries as they are viewed in Washington; the financial aid made available to libraries reflects not only the general political climate but also the ebb and flow of competing social forces. The Higher Education Act of 1965 was comprehensive in scope and designed to assist all areas of higher education—including libraries—by providing through its various sections (Titles) general funds for purposes to be decided by the granting agency. The section of specific interest to libraries is Title II: College Library Assistance and Library Training and Research; it is administered through the Commissioner of Education. A review of the evolution of funding programs under Title II mirrors with some degree of accuracy the developments, problems, and attempted solutions faced by academic libraries in the past 15 years in their efforts to acquire, process, and disseminate research materials for their users.

Specifically, Title II provides grants for: (1) acquisition of books, periodicals, and other library materials by colleges and universities; (2) training of all types of librarians; (3) research and demonstration projects, including the development of new ways of processing, storing, and distributing information; and (4) aiding the Library of Congress to acquire and catalogue additional scholarly materials.

Under the section of Title II authorizing funds for the purchase of library materials, several types of grants were available. The most widely known of these was the *basic* grant of up to $5,000 for the purchase of all types of library material—books, periodicals, phonograph records, audiovisual materials, magnetic tapes, or other library-related resources. These funds were available to institutions of higher education if acquisitions budgets and total library budgets met certain criteria designed to ensure continuing financial support on the part of the institution (maintenance-of-effort). Also, the requesting institution was required to provide matching funds of the grant money requested. Second, *supplemental* grants were offered which could equal $10 per full-time equivalent student enrolled at the institution. Justification for these funds depended upon the "inadequacy" of the library's collections and did not require matching funding from the institution. Finally, a category of *special purpose* grants existed for awards to libraries on an individual need basis, requiring the requesting library to document adequately its special need, and also to illustrate how the grant would expand the quality of the educational resources of the institution. Moreover, other such grants could be requested for the purpose of meeting specific national or regional library needs or for establishing or strengthening joint-use facilities or other cooperative enterprises.

In addition to strengthening funding for acquisitions, the intent of the legislation was to improve "inadequate" academic libraries with funding to raise the level of their collections and further to support those institutions which could offer programs to build regional areas of strength or promote cooperation among academic libraries. In this respect, Title II seems to have been the precursor of cooperative and networking ideas now considered to be absolutely essential in day-to-day library operations.

Part B of Title II authorized the Commissioner of Education to make grants for research projects and demonstrations which would assist in the development of libraries and the training of librarians. Funding was aimed

| | College Library Resources | Library Career Training | Research and Demonstration | Strengthening Research Library Resources |
|---|---|---|---|---|
| 1966 | 10 | 1 | — | — |
| 1967 | 25 | 3.75 | 3.55 | — |
| 1968 | 24.5 | 8.25 | 3.55 | — |
| 1969 | 25 | 8.25 | 3 | — |
| 1970 | 9.8 | 4 | 2.17 | — |
| 1971 | 9.9 | 3.9 | 2.17 | — |
| 1972 | 11 | 2 | 2 | — |
| 1973 | 7.15 | 3.57 | 1.78 | — |
| 1974 | 5.7 | 2.85 | 1.42 | — |
| 1975 | 5.97 | 2 | 1 | — |
| 1976 | 8.47 | .5 | 1 | — |
| 1977 | 6.97 | 2 | 1 | — |
| 1978 | 6.97 | 2 | 1 | 5 |
| 1979 | 6.97 | 2 | 1 | 6 |

HEA Title II Funding (In Millions of Dollars)

at encouraging librarians to develop new programs and innovative teaching strategies designed to cope with the dynamic changes being experienced in libraries. Funding was also available to make use of new technology to handle the production and dissemination of information. Part C of the legislation indirectly assisted academic libraries by authorizing Title II funds to be transferred by the Commissioner of Education to the Librarian of Congress to acquire scholarly material and to provide prompt cataloguing for those materials. Again, there was an emphasis on expanding cooperative efforts among academic and research libraries.

There have been amendments to Title II over the years which have provided for a wider range of requests from libraries. The Education Amendments of 1972 allowed considerations to be made for institutions which could not meet the maintenance-of-effort requirement. Other changes made it possible for both public and private institutions to apply for grants if their primary function was the provision of library and information services to higher education on a formal, cooperative basis. Perhaps the most significant amendment of 1972 was the elimination of the matching funds requirement for basic grant requests.

Examples of grants approved under Part B of Title II in 1973 also show a broadening scope and an awareness of social concerns. Almost two million dollars were awarded for projects involving studies to provide educational and library materials and services to economically disadvantaged groups or to those groups which had not been successful in traditional higher education settings. Successful applicants for these funds included colleges, universities, school districts, community colleges, and agencies serving ethnic or other specialized groups.

Amendments to Part C of Title II in 1976 allowed for significant grants to be awarded to major research libraries. It is noteworthy that the definition of "research library" was broadened to achieve the effect of opening collections to a wider range of users, whether the library itself was a public, university, state, or independent library; the thrust was that the library make a contribution to scholarly research and open its collections and services to researchers or scholars not affiliated with that institution. Moreover, consideration of grant requests for these funds had to take into account a regional balance in the distribution of awards to ensure geographical equity in the disbursement of federal dollars.

Although Title II is only one piece of legislation affecting academic libraries in recent years, it has surely had the greatest impact in the development of library resources. It is also noteworthy that Title II has paralleled activities in the academic and nonacademic library communities with its emphasis on cooperative library activities and regional strengthening of resources. As those resources have become more expensive, and comprehensive coverage of bibliographical areas becomes increasingly more difficult at individual libraries, cooperative efforts involving library staff, collection building, and information dissemination have been encouraged. While federal funding has not allowed individual libraries to achieve comprehensive collections to meet student and research needs in all areas, the Higher Education Act of 1965 has provided a framework for realistic library programs at a critical time in academic library history.

The evolution of the provisions of Title II of the Higher Education Act, the Library Services and Construction Act, and other federal, state, and local legislation, document governmental efforts to recognize the importance of the development of academic and research libraries, while at the same time recognize the necessity of cooperative and equitable programs for the acquisition and dissemination of information. These statutes have been of immeasurable importance in the growth of American academic libraries.

CLYDE C. WALTON

**ACCREDITATION 299, 320**
archivists **53**
information science **251**

## Accreditation

Accreditation of educational institutions and programs, based on peer evaluation and judgment, developed as an American alternative to the European pattern of control of education by a government agency or the church. No provision was made in the U.S. Constitution for national involvement in education, and only in New York was there a State Board of Regents that was required to report annually to the Legislature on every college in the state.

Introduced late in the 19th century with the creation of the New England Association of Colleges and Secondary Schools, the concept of accreditation spread first to other regions of the United States and then to subject disciplines as professional associations assumed responsibility for monitoring educational programs in their respective fields. Initially, the purpose of accreditation was to improve communication between postsecondary educational institutions and secondary schools in order that students entering college might arrive with more nearly equal academic preparation. Closely allied with this purpose was the goal of standardizing the quality and measurement of learning experiences so that credits earned in one institution could be transferred to another with the assurance that the student's prior education would meet the expectations of the host school.

Another factor in the accrediting movement has been of such increasing importance that it sometimes overshadows the initial primary purposes. This is the social demand that accreditation should protect the public against incompetent and/or poorly educated graduates of educational institutions. While the health professions come most immediately to mind, the same principle applies to all professionals, including librarians. Professional self-regulation in this country begins with the accreditation of professional schools and educational programs. In no sense, however, may an association use accreditation as a device to limit access to the profession in order to reduce competition for jobs. A common misconception is that accreditation should constitute a device to control the number and the geographical distribution of educational programs within a profession. The granting of accreditation to a program signifies that that program meets or exceeds the quality expressed in the written standards for that area of study and thus meets its responsibilities to its constituency.

Accreditation falls into two categories: "general or institutional" and "specialized or programmatic." There is much overlapping, of course, as illustrated by the fact that every library education program currently accredited in the United States exists in an institution that is recognized by one of the six regional accrediting associations. In fact, regional accreditation of the institution is a prerequisite for even the consideration of a program in library education in the United States. However, because the Canadian Library Association many years ago arranged with the American Library Association to accredit programs in Canadian library schools, this requirement does not apply in Canada, where regional accreditation does not exist.

During the early decades of the 20th century, as more and more professional associations assumed responsibility for monitoring educational programs in their fields, it was inevitable that this power to accredit would become a matter of dispute among associations. Furthermore, because much of the cost of accreditation must be borne by the institution or program seeking accreditation, university and college administrators became increasingly concerned with the number of professional associations demanding the right to accredit. In 1949 the National Commission on Accrediting (NCA), supported by some 640 institutions of higher education, was created not only to determine which professional associations would have the power to accredit educational programs but also to monitor the procedures and standards used by these associations. After 1949 no university president would permit an accrediting group on the campus unless that group had been approved by the NCA.

In 1964, in response to a growing concern for "regionalism" in the accrediting process, the accrediting commissions of the six regional associations in the United States were brought together under the Federation of Regional Accrediting Commissions of Higher Education (FRACHE). The goal of FRACHE was to assure "quality education" on a nationwide basis.

In 1975 the National Commission on Accrediting merged with the Federation of Regional Accrediting Commissions of Higher Education to form the Council on Postsecondary Accreditation (COPA). A nongovernmental and nonprofit body, COPA's purpose is to foster and facilitate the roles of both institutional and specialized accrediting agencies in promoting and ensuring the quality and diversity of American postsecondary education. It is now COPA that recognizes agencies that accredit educational programs in various fields and reviews those agencies periodically. COPA receives a portion of its financial support from the accrediting bodies that it recognizes.

The concept of accreditation developed in the United States because the founders had deliberately avoided the imposition of government control of education. It is ironic that when, beginning in the 1950's, the provision of federal aid to higher education introduced the question of institutional eligibility for aid, the U.S. Commissioner of Education turned to the accrediting bodies to help determine that eligibility. Today, like other accrediting agencies, the ALA Committee on Accreditation (COA) is recognized by the Office of Education (OE) as the accrediting agency for programs in library education leading to the first professional degree. As with the Council on Postsecondary Accreditation, so with OE's Division of Eligibility and Agency Evaluation, the COA must undergo periodic review of its procedures and practices in order to retain its authority in the accreditation arena.

Accreditation in library education had its beginning in 1924 when the American Library Association created a Board of Education for Librarianship (BEL). This action was prompted by the publication one year earlier of the famous "Williamson Report," in which a distressingly bleak picture had been painted of the 15 library schools then in existence. Because accreditation decisions in the area of professional education must be based upon standards that have been endorsed by members of the profession, the ALA Council in 1925 approved a document entitled *Minimum Standards for Library Schools*. Like the standards for other professional schools of the time, these 1925 standards were quantitative in nature; they prescribed, for example, a minimum number of faculty members, minimum requirements for admission, and a model curriculum. New standards were adopted in 1933 that, in keeping with accreditation trends, tended to be qualitative rather than quantitative in nature. Whereas the 1925 standards had provided for four types of library schools (from the junior undergraduate school to the advanced graduate school), those of 1933 recognized only three. When in 1948 a number of major schools abandoned the fifth-year bachelor's degree in library science in favor of the master's as the first professional degree, work was begun on a new set of standards, which appeared in 1951. These standards pertained only to the first professional degree in librarianship, however, the so-called fifth-year degree. Library *schools* would no longer be accredited by the ALA; only their programs that lead to the first professional degree.

In 1956, with a general reorganization of the ALA, the COA was created to replace the Board of Education for Librarianship. It is to this committee that the Association delegates its authority in all accreditation matters. While there exists an appeal procedure through which COA decisions can be challenged before ALA's Executive Board (on grounds of procedure but not peer judgment), the Board has authority only to sustain the Committee or to direct that the Committee review the action in question. The ALA Constitution provides a mechanism for replacing the membership of a committee if it is determined that its affairs were conducted in an irresponsible manner.

The 1951 standards remained in effect for 20 years. Considering the changes in the library profession and in library education that occurred during those two decades, it is difficult in retrospect to understand how the document continued to be applied. The answer can be found in the fact that the 1951 standards were qualitative in nature—requirements expressed in quantitative terms had been avoided. Nevertheless, by the late 1960's the document was embarrassingly out-of-date.

In 1969, supported by a substantial grant from the

H. W. Wilson Foundation, Inc., COA appointed a ten-member subcommittee to draft new standards. Those standards were developed after a period of open discussion, and after early drafts had been published for comments from the library community.

The six standards in the 1972 documents differ from earlier requirements in that the first and overriding standard requires that a school establish clearly defined goals and specific objectives for the program for which accreditation is sought. The interpretation of the five remaining standards depends on what the school determines to be its goals and program objectives. The latter five standards treat curriculum; faculty; students; governance, administration, and finance; and physical resources and facilities.

Between January 1, 1973, and July 1976, all but 1 of the 58 library education programs previously accredited by the ALA were visited and evaluated by the COA. (One school requested that it be removed from the accredited list until its new two-year program could be evaluated.) Three previously accredited programs were denied reaccreditation under the 1972 standards, while 10 new programs achieved ALA accreditation for the first time. Of this total of 64 (1978) accredited programs, 6 were in Canada.

The three schools that lost their accreditation were revisited by the COA in 1978, and accreditation was restored to each during the Midwinter Meeting of the ALA in 1979. Likewise, the school that had earlier declined a visit until its two-year program could become effective was evaluated favorably at the same ALA meeting. Meanwhile, a previously accredited program was dropped by its university in 1978. As of January 1979, therefore, 67 library education programs appeared on the ALA's accredited list, seven of which were in Canada.

Despite serious concern in Canada over the appropriateness of accreditation of Canadian library education programs through the American Library Association, the arrangement has continued under the 1972 standards. It should be noted that a Canadian always sits on the COA, and, when a Canadian program is visited, at least one member of the visiting team is a Canadian, and the Canadian Library Association may send an observer.

As a standing committee of the American Library Association, the COA consists of 12 members appointed by the Executive Board. Appointments are for two years, with a second two-year term permitted. Each year one member is appointed by the Executive Board to serve as Chair. The Association's president-elect nominates individuals to fill approaching vacancies. Broad representation on the Committee is sought among practicing librarians and library educators, including two lay members to represent the public interest. The Committee's formal charge is "to be responsible for the execution of the accreditation program of the American Library Association, and to develop and formulate standards of education for librarianship for the approval of the Council."

Extensive documentation has been prepared by the COA for its own guidance in making accreditation decisions and to assist library schools in their preparation for accreditation visits. The two major documents of this nature are the *Manual of Procedures for Evaluation Visits under Standards for Accreditation, 1972* and the *Self-Study: A Guide to the Process and to the Preparation of a Report for the Committee on Accreditation.* Both of these documents were extensively revised in 1977.

Before a site visit for either initial accreditation or reaccreditation, a library school is required to conduct a detailed self-study on which a report is then submitted to the Committee well in advance of the visitation. An annual report is required in October from each library school with an accredited program, the acceptance of which constitutes continued accreditation for that program for the next year. Schools are revisited by a COA team every five to eight years. A site visit lasts four days, and the typical visiting team consists of four members. Special visits may be arranged to reexamine an accredited program on the initiative of either the school or the COA. The membership of a visiting team must be approved by the school, and potential site visitors are required to identify any programs in which they would find themselves in conflict of interest.

While the Committee on Accreditation has been delegated authority to make all decisions regarding accreditation, it is impossible for its 12 members to constitute the total membership of each visiting team. Many outside persons having a thorough knowledge of and keen interest in library education are called upon to assist the COA. Between 1973 and 1976, 101 individuals participated as team members. At least one current or recent COA member serves on each team, though not necessarily as its chair. The team's charge is to examine on site the program for which accreditation is sought, to prepare a detailed report that is both factual and evaluative, and to recommend an accreditation decision to the COA. The Committee must reach such a decision only by formal vote after considering all evidence, including that submitted by the school in response to the team's report. The school being visited covers the costs incurred in the accrediting process.

With the completion of the first round of accreditation visits under the 1972 standards, a detailed questionnaire was sent to each of the 67 schools visited, seeking their reactions to the entire process. All but five schools responded, and while there were some criticisms (most having to do with the performance of individual team members) and while a few schools tended to oppose accreditation, the general response was favorable. The 1972 standards have become widely accepted, even by the severest critics of accreditation, as has ALA's accreditation process. This conclusion was confirmed in a study made by the Task Force on Accreditation Issues of the Association of American Library Schools (AALS) in 1977.

For over 50 years, responsibility for accreditation of American programs in library education has been held by the American Library Association. It is publicly recognized by the Council on Postsecondary Accreditation as the sole agency having this authority. Through the years some library educators have questioned whether ALA is indeed the appropriate organization for this purpose, arguing that library education is of too little concern to ALA's membership, of which at least 90 percent are practicing librarians. It has been argued by some that the AALS, nearly all of whose members are actively engaged in library education, would be a more appropriate agency. This argument, however, has tended to ignore the fact that AALS would first have to convince the 36-member COPA Board that AALS is the appropriate body for this purpose. AALS would have to explain why the ALA membership, itself composed largely of graduates of library schools and employers of the schools' products, should not have the major voice in requiring that library education programs meet standards agreed upon by the library profession. Most practicing librarians and library educators believe that library education should be the concern of the entire library profession. The largest organization representing the entire library profession is the ALA. Each member, through annual dues, helps to pay for—and therefore has a stake in—the accreditation process.

The support of a succession of ALA presidents, coupled with that of the Executive Director, to the Association's accreditation role has been remarkably strong. ALA's Council, to whom COA makes regular reports and which has final authority on the content of its Standards for Accreditation, has demonstrated a keen interest in and support of the Committee's work. Library educators themselves, according to the results of the 1977 survey by the COA and by the AALS Task Force, strongly support ALA's responsibility for accreditation.

A possible role of the American Society for Information Science (ASIS) in accreditation has been a subject of debate among members of that association, and an ASIS Subcommittee on Accreditation and Alternatives was appointed to look into the matter. That subcommittee's chair, Charles H. Davis, recommended during the 1977 annual meeting of ASIS that while the Society might someday consider a certification program for information scientists, ASIS should not become directly involved in accrediting educational programs. Recognizing the growing alliance between library science and information science, ALA's Committee on Accreditation has been sensitive to the need for recognized authorities in information science among its members and on its site visits.

While the COA always has before it matters of controversy and debate—such as the frequency of site visits, the implementation of its recommendations to individual schools, and the readiness of new programs for accreditation visits—the current overarching questions of accreditation in library education can be identified as: (1) Should ALA expand its responsibility in accreditation to include programs other than those leading to the first professional degree, such as doctoral programs? (2) How broad, or how narrow, should be ALA's interpretation of library education? The answers to these questions must come from the collective thinking of a group much larger than the Committee on Accreditation.

**REFERENCES**

Russell E. Bidlack, "Accreditation," in *The ALA Yearbook* (ALA, 1976.)

*The ALA Accreditation Process, 1973–76: A Survey of Library Schools Whose Programs Were Accredited under the 1972 Standards, 1973–76* (ALA, 1977).

"Standards for Accreditation, 1972," in *The Administrative Aspects of Education for Librarianship: A Symposium,* edited by Mary B. Cassata and Herman L. Totten (1975).

Edward G. Holley and Muriel Howick, "The Accreditation Process: What the Task Force Learned," *Journal of Education for Librarianship* (1977).

William K. Seldon and Harry V. Porter, *Accreditation: Its Purposes and Uses* (Council on Postsecondary Accreditation, 1977).

RUSSELL E. BIDLACK

# Acquisitions

The term *acquisitions* is commonly used to designate several facets of library work that focus on the techniques of acquiring library materials. The acquisitions librarian serves, in effect, as the purchasing agent for bibliographic materials, supplying the needs of those involved in collection development and of the library patron. The acquisitions department thereby functions as the link between the library (and its users) and the book trade; it must necessarily be responsive to changes in the trade as well as to developments in library practice and must balance the requirements and standards of both professions.

**Acquisitions and the Book Trade.** Book trade, as used here, encompasses the publishing and distribution of books, serials, and other materials of interest to libraries. It underwent substantial alteration in the 1970's, with the promise of future change. The effects of this process on libraries have been profound.

Library acquisitions typically involves several differentiated sets of procedures, according to the nature of the materials and their availability from the book trade. Major areas of concern include monographs and other materials ordered on a one-time basis, serials, rare materials including out-of-print works and manuscripts, government publications, and publications of all types from less developed areas of the world.

*Monographs.* Until recently, U.S. and European libraries purchased most of their books and serials directly from publishers and, to some extent, from local booksellers. Some booksellers offered their services to libraries as wholesalers, on the domestic or export level, and a few bookselling firms arose without retail connections. Such European firms as B. H. Blackwell, Otto Harrassowitz, Martinus Nijhoff, Marcel Blancheteau, and Mario Casalini—many of them also publishers—have provided U.S. libraries with European publications of all kinds. European libraries, on the other hand, have traditionally ordered their foreign publications from European booksellers. Direct publisher ordering remained the predominant practice for purchasing domestic materials, however, abetted by the fact that publishing in the United States and Europe had been for many decades a stable business, controlled to a large extent by family-owned firms.

In the 1960's this pattern began to change markedly, partly in response to the cornucopia provided to educational institutions during that period. With monographic and subscription orders rising, libraries turned increasingly to booksellers in order to free themselves from the burdensome paperwork required by direct ordering from a multitude of individual publishers and also to take advantage of booksellers' library discounts. Many new wholesalers entered the field, including Richard Abel & Co., an American academic wholesaler that by the early 1970's had become the world's major academic bookseller. Abel pioneered the library approval plan, supplying new books to hundreds of institutions according to individual computer-processed subject profiles—an expanded variation of the long-familiar publisher's blanket ordering plans.

The preference of many librarians for third-party ordering was reinforced by changes in the publishing world. Mergers and acquisition by foreign investors, combined with increasing financial instability in the early

University of Chicago Library

*Serials require the maintenance of voluminous and complex record files, as these files on 40,000 subscriptions at the University of Chicago Library demonstrate.*

to mid-1970's and a pronounced trend toward shorter print runs, often rendered U.S. trade bibliographies, such as *Books in Print,* obsolete even before they appeared. In addition, publishers' standards for order fulfillment, reporting, and accounting deteriorated during this period. Such trends have made it overwhelmingly advantageous for the library to delegate what are often ordering problems to the bookseller, who has the advantages of scale and leverage in dealing with publishers.

With the falling away of library purchasing power in the mid- to late 1970's, library unit orders declined, to the detriment more of the bookseller than of the publisher, whose retail sales have continued to advance. The bankruptcy of Richard Abel & Co. in 1974–75 foreshadowed a decreased interest in approval plans, which have continued to maintain a firm but limited customer base, primarily among large academic libraries (often limited to university press publications) and large public library systems (usually restricted to a few types of material). Several major U.S. and some European booksellers have also failed, and there have been a number of international consolidations of booksellers, the most notable involving the acquisition of the Abel assets by England's Blackwell companies.

*Serials.* While monographs continue to represent the bulk of a library's new unit orders, serials command an increasing proportion of the library budget, owing to a proliferation of titles and continued inflation in subscription prices. In addition, the advantage of timeliness that the journal holds over the monograph has made the former less easily expendable in many libraries.

The use of subscription agents as third-party suppliers of serials has expanded for reasons similar to those affecting monograph wholesalers, though only more recently and still to a lesser extent. European libraries tend to order serials (foreign and domestic) from general domestic booksellers, while American libraries prefer specialized serial subscription agents for U.S. titles. Subscription agents offer relief from the labor intensive procedures of ordering and payment (and, more recently, of claiming missing issues), and provide computer-generated management information that would otherwise be beyond the reach of most libraries.

Exchange agreements with other libraries have traditionally provided many of the more obscure or hard-to-get serial titles, including those originating in countries whose output has been unavailable through conventional booksellers. Exchange, however, is diminishing as a source for serials as personnel become less available to handle this labor intensive process for acquiring what are often marginal titles. The Universal Serials and Book Exchange (USBE) in Washington, D.C., continues to provide inexpensive access to selected issues and many complete back runs of journals from various countries. Increasingly, photocopying of individual journal articles offers an economic alternative to the maintenance of large numbers of little-used subscriptions, in spite of increased royalties necessitated by recent changes in copyright law.

*Rare Materials.* The out-of-print book trade in the U.S. and Europe continued to decline in scope and activity in the 1970's, particularly in the United Kingdom. Given the effects of financing in higher education and the decreased status of the humanities in universities, the market for older works has been inexorably diminished during the last decade and shows no signs of rejuvenation. A large proportion of rare books—now most often considered to be those published prior to 1850—are already placed in academic or private collections; more recent books, which would ordinarily be the trade's major commodity, are succumbing with increasing rapidity to the acid content of their paper and bindings. Thus, the current depressed state of the antiquarian book trade may become a permanent reality. Libraries maintaining specialized o.p. searching staffs are few, though the prevalence of short print runs allows most new books to go out-of-print quickly.

Major institutions continue to acquire retrospectively in special areas but depend increasingly on interlibrary loan and other resource-sharing methods for access to older titles. Rare books and manuscripts maintain their popularity as donated items, but libraries have all but disappeared from the auction market.

*Government and Third World Publications.* The problems inherent in acquiring government publications, particularly those of the U.S., are analogous in many ways to those facing the would-be purchaser of materials from less developed countries: lack of bibliographic control, slowness of delivery, unusual business practices, and a dearth of reliable vendors. These peculiarities have induced many libraries to gather the various functions of collection building into separate area (or documents) departments. This is especially true for regions publishing predominantly in non-Roman alphabets. Since bookselling in the third world tends to be less predictable and reliable than elsewhere, libraries continue to utilize blanket order plans from third world booksellers as a way of compensating for the lack of adequate national bibliography and new book information.

In the U.S., the Farmington Plan and its successors have helped alleviate many of the purchasing problems of the major research libraries (and also their cataloguing arrearages) by providing for the division of responsibility in much foreign collecting among participating libraries. Arrangements with booksellers or national centers in the countries involved result in automatic shipment of new publications to U.S. libraries. Major centers for area studies still depend heavily on buying trips and exchanges with foreign libraries. Other libraries are increasingly willing to rely on these centers, and on such institutions as the Center for Research Libraries and the British Library Lending Division, for provision of third world publications.

*Relationship with the Book Trade* The acquisitions librarian faces the uncommon necessity of adhering to the standards and recognizing the interests not only of the employing institution but also of the firms, mainly booksellers, from which the library obtains its bibliographic materials. The librarian, as purchaser, holds all the cards in dealing with suppliers and has on occasion abused this position by imposing unreasonable demands. More significantly, librarians have failed to recognize the realities of commercial practice to which the bookseller is subject. Slowness of payment is the worst example of this tendency; the bankruptcy of Richard Abel & Co., at the hands of a number of uncompromising publishers when the firm had much of its assets tied up in unpaid library invoices, helped shock the library community into a higher level of awareness of the library's vested interest in the continuity of the book trade. Increased attention was paid to these issues in the late 1970's.

**Acquisitions Work.** The basic operations of an acquisitions department include ordering materials, checking in receipts, following up on nonreceipts, and paying invoices. Preorder searching and fund accounting are also assigned to the acquisitions departments of many libraries, as are various levels of physical processing, including ownership marking and the insertion of magnetic security triggers. The relationship of acquisitions to collection development varies greatly, as does that between acquisitions and other areas of technical services such as cataloguing; these relationships are changing rapidly as processing becomes increasingly automated.

At present, however, acquisitions procedures are manual in most libraries. Requests for purchase, received from a variety of sources, are subjected to a preorder searching process to verify and complete the bibliographic information given, ascertain whether the books are already owned, and provide some degree of control over the selection process. The resultant data are ordinarily used to generate three-by-five-inch order slips from multipart business forms, copies of which serve as purchase orders, report forms, temporary catalogue and shelflist slips, financial vouchers, and archival records. This format is dictated primarily by the multiple uses of the copies in card catalogue drawers. In turn, the book trade has become accustomed to it in preference to all alternatives. Even highly automated acquisitions departments have generally been forced to use their data bases at some point in the process to generate three-by-five-inch slips. Most acquisitions work is devoted to the creation, filing, retrieval, sorting, and annotation of these slips—a fact that will change only as integrated processing data bases become more common.

Serials work involves the additional check-in activity of recurring receipts. The distinct characteristics of this type of recordkeeping mandate a different file structure, and the great variations among serials have made the automation of this procedure difficult. Manual serials records are almost invariably kept on removable check-in cards in sliding drawer files and indicate bibliographic information along with receipt, claiming, and payment data. A number of individual libraries produce automated reports of various serials activities, generally through a batch process, and a few have created on-line check-in and other files.

**Automation.** Early attempts at library automation were aimed primarily at acquisitions work, including serials processing, because these are the most labor intensive and paperbound processing activities. Except in a few pioneering institutions, however, little has been accomplished. A few booksellers have instituted automated ordering systems (both on-line and batch), and a number of libraries support one or more of the individual acquisitions functions with data processing or printing equipment. But the ideal of a completely on-line integrated data base, free of printed files, has not been reached, primarily because of the necessity of coordinating with manual files serving other library functions. Instead, most of the progress in library automation (outside of circulation) has been achieved in the areas of data base searching and the production of cards for the still-manual catalogue. However, with the automation of the catalogue itself now receiving a high priority, it appears that the automation of acquisitions data bases and functions in major libraries may be at hand—but that these developments will follow naturally from catalogue automation, rather than the reverse.

Many current attempts at the automation of library procedures (including most circulation systems) utilize abbreviated record formats, each unique to its own system; this renders them largely incompatible with other systems. Most automated catalogue data bases are being designed around the MARC (Machine-Readable Cataloging) record format and its local variations. MARC records are more complex and hence more expensive to handle than the abbreviated records, which suffice for stand-alone circulation and acquisitions systems, but the costs associated with record manipulation continue to drop, and the advantage of the abbreviated record is losing much of its significance. The development costs of a MARC-based on-line catalogue (for public as well as staff use) will be substantial, but when it has been accomplished, the expansion of the catalogue system into acquisitions and serials control will follow with comparative ease.

Of equal significance are developments in automated communication between libraries and the book trade as well as within the book trade itself. Several of the larger publishers and booksellers in the U.S., the United Kingdom, and West Germany are equipped to transmit and receive orders and financial information in machine readable form; a standard communications format is being established for such transmissions. A large number of British retail booksellers have contracted for "teleordering" service through a national switching center connected to the Whitaker firm's data base. An American affiliate of the software firm that designed the British system has now replicated it in the U.S. for a large retail wholesaler; this system is MARC based and thus potentially compatible with library data bases.

Smaller U.S. booksellers have expressed the fear that direct order transmission from library to publisher (or channeled through a network or a large automated bookseller) would make it impossible for nonautomated firms to compete effectively. This fear remains unresolved, though it appears that the capacity to receive machine readable orders may enable otherwise paper-based firms to remain viable. The handling of the books themselves is subject to only limited mechanization, and the expense of the personal services traditionally provided by booksellers cannot safely be eliminated through automation, as the experiences of several of the largest booksellers have shown.

These developments will have an impact on the basic nature of acquisitions work. With preorder searching, order generation and transmission, and checking-in all performed at computer terminals, and with cataloguing for most receipts available on-line—usually through the same terminals—many of the functions of cataloguing will be performed most economically at the point of receipt of the materials. A trend in this direction is already evident in some libraries with integrated on-line processing systems, such as that at the University of Chicago. If the operative distinction among the various technical services areas up to now has been the difference in recordkeeping procedures and requirements, the implementation of integrated data bases can be expected to eliminate this distinction and hence induce a reordering of departmental structures. This will occur individually in libraries with local operating systems and in smaller libraries through their networks.

**REFERENCES**

American Library Association, *Acquisitions Guidelines*, vol. 1: *Guidelines for Handling Library Orders for In-Print Monographic Publications*, vol. 2: *Guidelines for Handling Library Orders for Serials and Periodicals*, vol. 3: *Guidelines for Handling Library Orders for Microforms*, a series of brief outlines of standard library practice in the acquisition of certain materials, including some discussion of the responsibilities of libraries to publishers and vice-versa.

Stephen Ford, *The Acquisition of Library Materials*, rev. ed. (ALA, 1978), a general but thorough guide to acquisitions procedures.

Ted Grieder, *Acquisitions: Where, What, and How* (1978), treats the practical aspects of acquisitions work (both clerical and professional) in an academic library.

*Library Acquisitions: Practice and Theory*, quarterly, is the only journal devoted exclusively to acquisitions work.

Daniel Melcher, with Margaret Saul, *Melcher on Acquisitions* (ALA, 1971); though somewhat out of date, this provocative book remains an essential starting place for the new acquisitions librarian. In remarkably few words, Melcher identifies the really important facets of acquisitions work and dismisses much of the costly and redundant labors that some librarians impose upon themselves.

JAMES THOMPSON

## Adult Services

Adult services, as a basic phase of the public library's public service program, has distinguished itself from children's services and young adult services and represents the total direct service program made available to adults in the community served by the public library. In this perspective adult services has included responsibility for: selection of the library's resources (both broadly and for special publics); concern for the public's access to that collection (through such services as exhibits, displays, bibliographic guides, telephone reference); provision of assistance to users of the collection (through information, advisory, and group services); the activation of use of the collection within its appropriate community (through such services as selective dissemination of information, book talks, publicity); and for the stimulation of potential users to the awareness of the relevance of library resources and services to their particular needs (through such services as community-wide programming, talks, and programs in community organizations and agencies). It is in this broad perspective that adult services coordinators in large municipal public libraries have developed programs of adult services since 1945.

Adult services as a field has, however, been separated from reference and information services in the thinking of a large portion of the profession. The American Library Association's reorganization in 1956 designated the Reference Service Division as separate and distinct from the Adult Services Division, with the information functions of libraries disassociated from the educational, cultural, and recreational functions by this policy decision. This choice reflected the profession's predominant view at that time. Reference librarians had typically—from the 1930's through the 1950's—rejected educational roles for themselves and had often decried them for public libraries as a whole. Only in the 1970's did a certain illogic in this position become recognized broadly enough to allow a fusion of the ALA's two divisions into the single Reference and Adult Services Division.

In a sense adult services as a field is a designation kept purely for public libraries (either including or excluding the reference functions). Although academic libraries serve adults, as do school libraries and most special libraries (historical, governmental, industrial, research), the particular designation of "adult services" has not been meaningful in the organization of service in these types of libraries. Further, in special libraries, the separation of direct public services into "reference" and "other" categories serves no vital purpose: all service tends to be thought of as information service. Academic libraries tend, on the whole, to use the term "public services" to include both information and instructional services and thus distinguish only between all kinds of direct service to the user and the selection and technical services that prepare the collection for use.

There is a final distinction to be drawn in conceptualizing the field of adult services. While adult service librarians of the 1950's and 1960's probably thought of adult services as the total broad program composed of diverse modes of service to users, it is realistic to recognize that in the late 1970's "adult services" is beginning to take on—even for the adult service specialist—an application more directly to the specific activities requiring the fullest implementation of the adult services model: service to special users, or information and referral (I and R), or literacy programs.

The term "adult services" was coined in the mid-1940's. Adult services, however, have provided the structure for the public library's direct service to the user, and has been the term under which three decades of important development of public library public service have taken place.

**Evolution.** From earliest times the function of the retrieval of resources has gone hand-in-hand with the storage of resources as the work of the librarian. Even Gabriel Naudé's early treatise, *Advice on Establishing a Library* (1627), included comment on assistance to library users: it would be "in vain" for a librarian to go to great expense for books "who does not intend to devote them to public use." But Samuel Swett Green's paper in the U.S. Bureau of Education's centenary publication, *Public Libraries in the United States of America* (1876), is generally acknowledged as the first detailed description of public librarians' personal assistance to readers. Public librarianship in the United States became fully aware of its public service functions during the 1880's and 1890's, and phrases like "teaching force," "molding community reading," and "a people's university" were uncontested in description of public libraries during this period. While the philosophy was congenial to the times, the practice of such levels of educational assistance was only gradually evolved. Recreational functions of the public library's collection were widely acknowledged in the 1890's, whether supported or deplored, and probably represented a major phase of the public library's activities before 1900.

In this same period of the late 19th century, information and bibliographic services began to emerge in the context of reference services as bibliographic indexes and reference tools were developed. The separation of reference services from the other services to adults was made clearly by 1910, with full-time reference specialists appointed to serve the student, business, and other groups of serious library users.

Children's services evolved at the turn of the century under the leadership of several public librarians devoting their full time to establishing such services in major city libraries, and young adult services developed as a parallel special service in the 1920's and 1930's, again with full-time specialists guiding the development of these services in the major metropolitan public libraries.

Thus public services in public libraries by the 1920's were comprised of reference services, services to children, and services to young people; the remaining services typically were captioned "circulation services." It was out of circulation services that innovative services to adults developed in the 1920's, as Jennie M. Flexner's text on *Circulation Work in Public Libraries* (1927) well documents. Circulation services to adults comprised the activities that

Dallas Public Library

*GED (General Educational Development) tutoring classes are offered in several branches of the Dallas Public Library for adults who are working for high school diplomas.*

carried out the educational, cultural, and recreational functions of the public library until the adult services field was formalized in the mid-1940's.

From the beginning of the 20th century, "library extension" provided the subrubric under which lectures, concerts, English literacy classes for foreign born, and individual reading programs were provided to adults by public libraries. Just as reference services had been contested in the 1870's, so these innovative adult services were challenged and debated for the first quarter century. It was this very "library extension" program, however, provided to soldiers and sailors during World War I, that brought national recognition to the American Library Association and laid the groundwork for the development of the library adult education movement with the leadership of adult educators like Lyman Bryson and the support of Frederick P. Keppel of the Carnegie Corporation of New York from 1923 to the late 1930's. Library adult education provided the environment for the development of particular models of adult services: reading guidance, programming services to community organizations, and library-sponsored discussion programs. Each was introduced in its own decade (the 1920's, 1930's, and 1940's) in the context of "adult education," and each having developed its own technique and rationale in the incubator provided by the adult education movement survived to become a fundamental mode for public library adult services.

The term "adult services" came into use in the mid-1940's, when "adult education" was increasingly recognized as a philosophy, rather than a set of specific services, and when the services it had generated were recognized as generic in librarianship. The New York Public Library established its first Office of Adult Services in 1946, and other major public libraries adopted similar structural coordination for services to adults at about this time.

The formal structuring of adult services within the organization of the public library gave it a place in library planning and in budget support and assured the continuity important to the growth of evaluated programs of service to adults. Central "offices" and system "coordinators" provided expertise throughout library systems, and the influence of talented specialists now had proper channels of influence for the exercise of leadership throughout the systems. Full-time adult service specialists were privileged to develop the individual, group, and community services needed by their adult publics. Adult services could be more than a way station for the novice librarian moving up to neighborhood library administration; now there developed specialist positions that made a career orientation for the adult services librarian realistic in the major metropolitan public libraries. When, in the late 1950's, the New York State Legislature passed a law permitting and funding federated public library systems, thus leading the way in system development, adult service coordinator positions suddenly multiplied, and the field of adult services came quickly into its own on a national scale.

The American Library Association's nurture of adult services under the concept of "library adult education" had a continuous history from the Enlarged Program at the end of World War I through the lectures and discussion groups of the People's Institute collaboratively developed in the New York Public Library in the late 1920's; the Keppel/Carnegie support of ALA projects such as the planned reading programs "Reading with a Purpose"; the work of the renowned Subcommittee on Readable Books that initiated new forms in published books for the layman in the 1930's; ALA's collaboration with the Ford Foundation's Fund for Adult Education in the 1950's stressing discussion of public issues, political philosophy, and humanities classics; its sponsorship of research and development in adult services performance and community analysis in the 1950's and 1960's. For a generation the American Library Association, in cyclical ups and downs, provided the status, the funds, the consulting expertise, the training in workshops and conference programs that brought adult services to maturity on a national scale. The names of John Chancellor and of Grace T. Stevenson are outstanding among those of a number of ALA leaders whose work in the field of adult services gave it the professional status needed in its developing years.

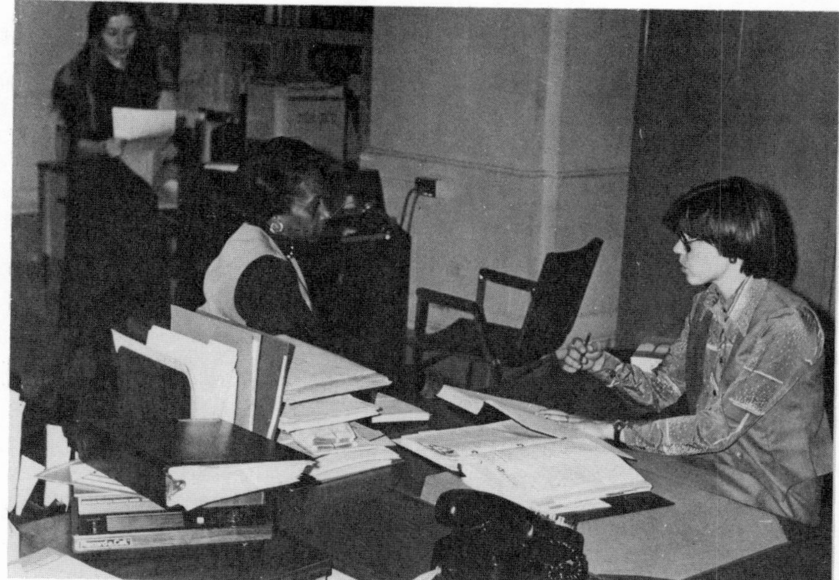

Free Library of Philadelphia

*The Free Library of Philadelphia's Lifelong Learning Center assists adults in career and educational planning. Counselors use both traditional library resources and a computerized information bank.*

The ALA committees and boards supervising adult services projects were complemented by a growing membership structure for adult services. The Adult Education Section of the Public Library Association in the early 1950's was transformed in 1957 into the Adult Services Division, reflecting a vigorous leadership group in this field. It was not until 1972 with the merger of the Reference Services Division with the Adult Services Division that the dominance of the information function over the educational, cultural, and recreational functions was again reasserted strongly in the ALA structure.

The preparation of public librarians for the work of adult services has taken place both in formal library education programs and in a sustained series of workshops and institutes funded by foundations and by the U.S. Office of Education since the late 1940's. The inspired teaching of Miriam Tompkins for 30 years, at Emory University and then at Columbia University, was probably a greater influence during the 1930's and 1940's than any other single educational factor in building the cadre of adult service specialists who gave leadership to the field. The early curriculum focused on reading interests of adults and later expanded to include planning reader services, community study, and special modes of public services to adults.

On the other hand, staff training in major public library systems provided significant dissemination of adult services skills and understanding throughout the nation as staff who benefited from this training in major libraries moved to other public library positions throughout the country. Such staff training included attitude development, skills training, and knowledge sharing. Often staff training was built around the learning needed to carry out staff projects in adult services. Never as successful as reference and information services in its institutionalization in formal library education curriculums, adult services has developed its educational preparation in the staff training programs of major public library systems. Only a handful of library schools in the 1970's offered more than a single course designed specifically for adult services preparation.

**Structure.** The structure of adult services is viewed here in terms of (1) its user orientation, (2) the four major functions its service programs involve, and (3) its method for planning, evaluation, and redirection.

*User Orientation*. The internal structure of adult services relates directly to the structure of the broad field of public services. Analysis of the dimensions of public services has been rudimentary and scattered until, in the 1970's, a sustained focus on community analysis and on information-seeking behavior studies developed. This convergence on understanding the needs and interests of the community (library users and nonusers alike) is a prime element in the structure of adult services. From roots in library adult education and throughout development since the 1940's, adult services have been user oriented and have been a major force in a greater user orientation in public services. The 1950's and 1960's saw the pioneer work of the ALA Library-Community Project centering on community analysis as a basis for adult service programs.

Within the context of community analysis, attention to "special publics" has been an organizing principle for the planning of adult services, from its work with labor and with foreign-born groups at the beginning of the 20th century, through its work with the unemployed during the Depression and with leaders of community organizations in the affluence after World War II, and continuing through the surge of "outreach" programs to the illiterate, ethnic minorities, and the physically and mentally handicapped in the 1960's. Lowell A. Martin emphasized structuring adult services around "distinct groups and interests" in *Library Response to Urban Change* (1969), echoing the attention to "special publics" in the ALA *Minimum Standards for Public Library Systems, 1966*. The New York Public Library's Branch Library System in the late 1970's required annual time commitments from all branch staff for the study of the community, the identification of special publics, and the development of library-community contacts to be sustained in the development of services. The "special publics" approach to community analysis provides a logical, effective access to understanding the needs and interests of library users and potential users.

The adult service response to community needs and interests has been viewed as utilizing four major functions: information, instruction, guidance, and stimulation. Samuel Rothstein, in "Reference Service, the New Dimension in Librarianship," *College and Research Libraries* (January 1961), has identified the first three traditional functions of information, instruction, and guidance. The library's fourth function, stimulation of the public's awareness of the relevance of library resources to their specific needs and interests, achieved its clearest visibility in the public library outreach programs of the 1960's, as described in Margaret E. Monroe, "Reader Services to the Disadvantaged in Inner Cities," *Advances in Librarianship* (1971). Within this function, adult service librarians developed programs of "reading readiness" as well as designing publicity and providing personal interpretation to groups and individuals. At the broadest community level the stimulation function must include the maintenance of the community climate for the use of information, ideas, and creative experience, which the library's resources represent. This is accomplished in part by interactive planning for services between the library and the community; the Illinois State Library's series of public invitational conferences on intellectual resources in the early 1970's provides a brilliant example. Short of interactive planning of services, adult service librarians have used public programs on public issues and social problems as the vehicle for bringing library resources of information and opinion to bear on critical matters requiring community thinking and decision making. Programs sponsored in the late 1970's by the National Endowment for the Humanities well illustrate this adult service model. The 50 years of library adult education and adult services have documented that the value of the function of stimulation is as vital to adults as it has proven in the fields of children's and young adult services.

*Planning*. Planning and evaluation of library services gained a fresh emphasis and has focused on the formulation of public library goals and objectives during the 1970's. Public services have traditionally been developed on a readiness-to-serve basis, but as measurable objectives set targets for measurable service activity, librarians find it essential to develop programs to activate users in the areas of the target objectives. Adult service librarians find this activation of users congenial to their traditional style: cosponsored programs, interactive planning with target groups of users, publicity, and personal interpretation of services to organizations, groups, and neighborhoods are typical of adult service approaches to planning and activating programs. Evaluation of adult services is being challenged to new design, relying not solely on the measures of library inputs (hours of service, number of reading lists prepared, or group programs organized) or of library outputs (numbers of users of services, etc.) but also on measurement of the library's impact on the problems, needs, or interests of the community that each particular service was designed to reach. The preliminary and pioneering work of Richard H. Orr, Vern M. Pings, Edwin E. Olson, and Irwin H. Pizer, "Development of Methodologic Tools for Planning and Managing Library Services," *Bulletin of Medical Library Association* (1968), suggests a valuable broad-scale approach to the evaluation of adult services through the use of inventories. The work of Ernest DeProspo and Ellen Altman (*Performance Measures for Public Libraries* [1973] and *A Data Gathering and Instructional Manual for Performance Measures* [1976]) seeks to establish public library norms and is one significant approach to the evaluation of adult services. *The Disadvantaged and Library Effectiveness* (1972) by Claire E. Lipsman is another, more case-oriented approach that deserves additional development.

The models for adult services have undergone major transformations in the decades of the 1960's and 1970's in response to new publics, new needs and interests, new resources, new technologies. Appraisal of new services against the library's established policies or the library's stated objectives has been common practice. The fluid nature of the community and the uniqueness of each individual user's situation force flexibility, adaptation, and change on the models of adult services. The diverse emerging patterns of service are to be expected and welcomed but equally to be analyzed and critically reviewed. (See Kathleen Heim and Margaret E. Monroe, editors, "Emerging Patterns of Community Service," *Library Trends* [October 1979].)

*Literacy*. The adult service models for literacy have undergone a revolution between ALA's publication of Bernice MacDonald's *Literacy Activities in Public Libraries* in 1966 and its publication of three volumes on literacy by Helen Huguenor Lyman based on her five-year research project: *Library Materials in Service to the Adult New Reader* (1973), *Reading and the Adult New Reader* (1976), and *Literacy and the Nation's Libraries* (1977). MacDonald's 1966 report of services to adult illiterates focused on the need for reading skills and the lack of suitable materials. The model of service to illiterates that emerged included reading instruction by volunteers in the library, collections of materials for teachers and learner, and a growing collection of "supplementary reading" that would create a bridge to regular reading habits. Outreach workers from the library were seen as important in community contacts, bringing library materials where they were needed as well as providing new readers with access to the library. Programs of films and book talks to teachers and new readers were proposed, and collaborative planning with other community agencies was viewed as essential.

From July 1967 through May 1972 Lyman pursued a creative study of library materials for the adult new reader. Not only were formats, readability levels, and subject interests explored but the cultural backgrounds and value systems inherent in the materials were tested. It became clear that the usefulness of materials with adult new literates rose markedly when the reader's backgrounds and values were shared as background of the materials he was engaged in reading. Detailed knowledge of readers, then, became essential for librarians. Further, the definition of literacy underwent change in this five-year period, and by 1977 (11 years after the MacDonald report) it was clear that library literacy efforts must include not only reading in the sense of taking words meaningfully from the printed page but skills in interpreting driving manuals, in completing income tax forms, in everyday mathematical computation, in use of mass media, and in gaining access to the community resources for survival, for comfort in living in the community as a citizen, as well as for participating in the neighborhood as a social environment. Lyman captioned her model of literacy services in 1976 an "active reading development program." This program had the comprehensiveness of interactive community planning, broad and diverse collection of materials in all media formats, individual information and guidance services, extensive group programs to enrich living experience and stimulate intellectual curiosity, recruitment and training of volunteer staff, work with community agencies, extended resource centers outside the library, published evaluations of resources, and long-range plans and evaluation of service. This model is based on the needs of the "special public" and assumes the large percentage of illiterates in major cities justifies a distinctively adapted service for special publics and common backgrounds and needs. The programs at the Langston Hughes Branch of the Queens Borough Public Library (Jamaica, New York) in 1970 and the experimental programs developed by Barss, Reitzel and Associates for their study in 1970 were the concrete examples fulfilling this model of the "active reading development program." It is important to note that not only had user needs been recognized in greater depth; library resources had become more abundant, the experience of the Appalachian Adult Education Center had contributed its model, research had contributed insight, and the professional values of each researcher had entered into the equation that led to the model for adult services to new literates. The emergence of such new models of adult service then needs the critical evaluation of tested experience.

Similar winnowing of the strengths of Information and Referral Services are now under way across the U.S. The humanizing of information delivery for those whose lives are in crisis and for whom the power of information is as yet untried is a critical service. Experiments with new models in Memphis, Detroit, Tulsa, Dallas, and New York were under test at the close of the 1970's. Manfred Kochen's *Information for the Community* (ALA, 1976) brings together some useful critique and appreciation of this new model of service.

Theoretical frameworks for adult services are needed against which to test new service models as they emerge. "Trial and error" has been the standard procedure, which becomes commendable only if failures are closely scrutinized to see why they did not work. Joseph C. Donohue's analysis of failure in "The Public Information Center Project" (Kochen, cited above) suggests the kind of critique to which public library adult service must increasingly subject itself.

MARGARET E. MONROE

# Afghanistan

Afghanistan, a republic in central South Asia, is bordered by the U.S.S.R. on the north, Iran on the west, Pakistan on the east and south, and by China and by Jammu and Kashmir in two areas of the northeast. Pop. (1977 est.) 20,882,000; area 653,000 sq.km. The official languages are Dari Persian and Pashto. It is a peasant-tribal society composed of various ethnic groups (Pashtuns, Tadjiks, Hazaras, Uzbeks, Baluchs, Turkoman, Kirghiz, among others), with a 90 to 95 percent nonliterate population. Political stability has been uncertain; a coup d'etat occurred on April 27, 1978.

**National Library.** There is no national library in Afghanistan, but some functions of one are performed by certain institutions, such as the Kabul University Library, the Ministry of Education Reference Library, and the Public Library of the Ministry of Information and Culture/Kabul. A national bibliography is issued irregularly by the Kabul University Library. Leaders of the former regime expressed the desire to transform the Public Library into a national library.

**Academic Libraries.** The most important and largest library in Afghanistan is the Kabul University Library. Kabul University (Kabul Pohantun) was founded in 1932. Small faculty libraries came into existence but were accessible only to faculty members. In 1967 an Indiana University team reorganized the structure of the university system, and the present library was organized at that time. (Betty White, an American librarian, is remembered for organizing the present University Library.) Its present collection totals 130,000 volumes, arranged by the Library of Congress Classification. It holds special collections dealing with material on Afghanistan and Islamic civilization.

In 13 teacher training institutions in Afghanistan high school graduates are given one to two years of training and then sent to the provinces in a program to eradicate the high illiteracy rate. All the provincial teacher training institutions have small libraries numbering at the most 500 books. These small collections are augmented regularly by small gifts of books from foreign philanthropic and cultural organizations.

Most of these collections, largely in English, are entrusted to teachers untrained in librarianship. The three teacher training institutions in Kabul fare much better. The Higher Teacher's College, a two-year institution for the training of college-level teachers, has a library of approximately 10,000 volumes with a professionally trained librarian. The Academy for Teacher Education and the Dar'ul Mo'alamein training schools have libraries of approximately 1,000 volumes. These libraries suffer from the fact that the greater portion of the collections is in English, a language not usually known by the students.

**Public Libraries.** The Public Library of the Ministry of Information and Culture, usually referred to as the Kabul Public Library, is in the central part of the city facing Zarnegar Park. The Library has its own Reading Garden, a pleasant plane tree grove with reading benches along the public paths, quite popular with Kabul students who use the area as an outdoor reading-study room. Its collection numbers 120,000 volumes; a large portion is in English. Relatively recently a special effort has been made to increase the books in the two national tongues, Pashtu and Dari (Afghan Persian). There is a Children's Section, an Afghan room housing material pertaining to Afghanistan, and a periodical room containing a complete collection of Afghan periodical publications. The Library is under the direct jurisdiction of the Ministry of Information and Culture. It has 1 professional librarian, 4 subprofessional, and 15 other staff members including *tawildars* (store keepers), errand boys, and tea makers (tea is the national drink consumed throughout the day). Not all

**Libraries in Afghanistan (1976)**

| Type | Number | Volumes in collections | Annual expenditures (afghani) | Population served | Professional staff | All staff (total) |
|---|---|---|---|---|---|---|
| Academic | 14 | 140,000 | [a] | 8,600 | 4 | 30 |
| Public | 1 | 120,000 | [a] | 450,000 | 1 | 25 |
| School | 4 | 30,000 | [a] | 3,000 | 0 | 5[b] |
| Special[c] | 5 | 150,000 | [a] | 3,000 | 4 | 24 |
| Total | 25 | 440,000 | | | 9 | 84 |

[a]Not available. The budget, usually determined by the School Director, varies by school and year.
[b]Part-time.
[c]Includes Embassy Libraries open to the general public.

Sources: Louis Dupree, *Afghanistan* (1973); Survey of Progress, Department of Statistics, Ministry of Planning (1977).

books circulate, but all may be used on the premises. The present Library is housed in a two-story building, which was formerly a private mansion, and has five branches. It was envisaged that the Library would evolve into the National Library, but legislation on this subject had not been presented by the late 1970's.

**School Libraries.** In Kabul, Habiba High School, subsidized at one time by the Americans, has a library with a collection of 5,000 books, supervised by a teacher. The Isteqlal Lycée, subsidized by the French government, has a library of approximately 10,000 volumes in French. The "Russian" Polytechnique Institute has a library, but it is not open to the public. It has approximately 10,000 volumes on science and technology. The "German" High School, subsidized to some extent by the West German government, also has a library, primarily in German. None of the unsubsidized high schools has a library, but by 1978 the Afghan government was planning to install a library in all high schools in the future. In elementary schools libraries are practically nonexistent, though a few have small collections of 50 to 100 books, usually administered by a *tawildar,* who discourages lending since he is held financially responsible for all books lost. There is no government assistance to libraries at the elementary school level.

**Special Libraries.** The Historical Society of Afghanistan Library, in the Shar-e-Nau section of the city, has a collection of approximately 40,000 volumes. This specialized collection deals exclusively with anthropology, ethnology, prehistory, archaeology, genealogy, history, and folklore of Afghanistan. It has a staff of five and contains all publications of the Délégation Archéologique Française en Afghanistan (DAFA). DAFA had been in Afghanistan for over 40 years by the end of the 1970's and excavated sites at Ai Khanoum and Hadda.

**Other Libraries.** The Ministry of Education Reference Library and Book Distribution Center in Kabul holds 20,000 books on education, open to teachers and employees of the Ministry. It acts as a central cataloguing agency for books distributed to schools, providing in 1977 some 40,000 books to teacher training institutions and some high schools. The open-shelf libraries of the British Council, American Center, and French Cultural Center are used by students needing materials and study centers; a fee is usually charged at these libraries.

**Associations.** The Anjuman Ketab-khana-e-Afghanistan (Afghanistan Library Association) was organized in 1971 by a former Kabul University Librarian, Abdul Rasul Rahim, and has a membership of about 50. The promotion of literacy and libraries in Afghanistan is its basic objective; it works to improve the status of librarians and to lobby for a national library system and for a School of Library Science within Kabul University. It sponsors training workshops and seminars for teacher-librarians in the teacher training schools and irregularly publishes the *Afghan National Bibliography*.

JOHN DE BELFORT URQUIDI

# Aguayo, Jorge
(1903– )

Jorge Aguayo is considered the founding father of modern library procedure and library education in Cuba. He also contributed to the library development in other parts of Latin America, to furthering library cooperation through the Pan American Union and the American Library Association, and to scholarship in Spanish-language classification.

Born in Havana, Cuba, on December 4, 1903, Aguayo received his early schooling in the capital. At the University of Havana he received degrees in Civil Law in 1925 and in Diplomatic and Consular Law in 1927. After nine years of diplomatic service, Aguayo's interest in books and learning led him to enter the library field.

ALA

*Jorge Aguayo*

In 1937 he began a long and fruitful association with the General Library of the University of Havana, serving as Assistant Director until 1959, when he assumed the post of Director. Aguayo immediately undertook the cataloguing and classification of the book collection according to U.S. models. The Rockefeller Foundation awarded him a one-year fellowship to study at Columbia University's Library School in 1941, and Aguayo took a concentrated curriculum with emphasis on cataloguing problems and university administration. In the years following his return to the University of Havana, the General Library pioneered in the use of fundamental tools such as the dictionary catalogue with subject headings translated and adapted from the Sears and Library of Congress lists, the Dewey Decimal System, the ALA cataloguing rules, the use of Library of Congress printed cards, the establishment of a separate reference collection, and many other services previously unknown to Cuban library users. The results of Aguayo's work are summarized in three manuals written in the 1940's: *Reglas para la ordenación del catálogo diccionario de la Biblioteca General de la Universidad* (Havana, 1940); *Manual práctico de clasificación y catalogación de bibliotecas* (Havana, 1943; 2nd ed., 1951); and *Modelos de fichas* (Havana, 1942; 2nd ed., 1949). The latter two have been used as textbooks by a number of Latin American library schools.

In 1940 Aguayo and three associates initiated the teaching of library science at the Havana Lyceum. All four served as Cuba's first professional faculty of library science, offering a variety of courses lasting three and six months. In 1946 the formal teaching of library science began with the establishment of Cursos de Técnica Bibliotecaria at the Summer School of the University of Havana under Aguayo's direction. He served as Director of the summer courses until 1952 and assumed the professorship of cataloguing and classification in the University's School of Librarianship from its founding in 1950 until his departure from Cuba in 1960.

Aguayo's involvement in library development in individual Latin American countries and the region as a whole went hand in hand with his ambitious program in Cuba. In 1944 the U.S. State Department, the ALA, and the Rockefeller Foundation invited him to teach the first library science course in Peru after a fire destroyed the National Library in Lima. In 1947 he accepted an offer to attend the First Assembly of Librarians of the Americas. He served as a consultant to the Regional Conference of National Commissions of the Western World, held in Havana in 1950, and to the Conference on Development of Public Library Services in São Paulo in 1951. He was President of the first Cuban Library Workshop in 1953.

Aguayo served as a prominent spokesman for Latin American librarians on cataloguing matters within the American Library Association. He was a member of the Canadian and Latin American Subcommittee of the ALA's Special Committee on Dewey Classification from 1944 to 1947. He then served on the ALA's Standing Committee on Cooperation With Latin American Catalogers and Classifiers from 1953 to 1958.

After the Castro revolution in 1960, Aguayo went to the United States and worked for a brief time at Syracuse University as bibliographer in charge of the Farmington Plan for Uruguay, Paraguay, and Argentina. In 1962 he became the Branch Librarian of the Pan American Union (PAU) and served as the Head Librarian of the PAU's central Columbus Library from 1968 until 1973. During that time he was also consultant to the Spanish translation of the Anglo-American Cataloging Rules (1970) and together with Carmen Rovira compiled the PAU-sponsored *Lista de Encabezamientos de Materia para Bibliotecas* (1967), a milestone work that served libraries throughout the Spanish-speaking world as the basic subject heading list. Aguayo was named Editor and Director of the translation into Spanish of the 18th edition of the Dewey Decimal Classification System.

Aguayo wrote more than 50 articles on a variety of library subjects, published in journals in the United States, Peru, Cuba, Bolivia, and Argentina. In addition, he served as Contributing Editor to *Libri,* 1949–50. Aguayo also translated into Spanish *The University Library, Its Organization, Administration and Function,* by Louis R. Wilson and Maurice F. Tauber.

MARTHA TOMÉ

## Ahern, Mary Eileen
(1860–1938)

ALA

*Mary Eileen Ahern*

Mary Eileen Ahern was the Editor of the journal *Public Libraries* (later just *Libraries*) from its beginning in 1896 to its demise in 1931. In its editorial pages, one can find Ahern's ideas about the public library movement, ideas that she believed in and fought for throughout her career. "There is only one solution of all social problems," she proclaimed in the opening issue, "—an increase in intelligence, a gradual education of the people." "The public library," Ahern went on to say in the same editorial, "is the broadest of teachers, one may almost say the only free teacher. It is the most liberal of schools, it is the only real people's college." She frequently reminded her readers that a librarian "must assert himself as a teacher on all proper occasions."

Born in Indiana on October 1, 1860, Ahern was the daughter of Irish immigrants, William and Mary O'Neil Ahern. She attended high school and normal college in Indiana, taught in public schools in various small Indiana towns, and became Assistant State Librarian of Indiana in 1889. While in that office, she helped organize the Indiana Library Association, served as its first Secretary and was later President. She was elected State Librarian by the Indiana Legislature in 1893, but the job ended in 1895 after the Democrats, who had supported her, lost the elections of 1894. Aware that the State Librarian's job was a political football, Ahern mounted a campaign to take the State Library away from the Legislature and assign it to an independent Library Board. According to her own recollections in a 1932 letter, she believed that the new legislature might welcome the opportunity to appear to be "progressive." During that fall of 1894 and until her position ended, she made special efforts to provide library materials and services to all the newly elected legislators. Each time she delivered materials and was told, "It's too bad that you cannot stay on here," she brought up her proposal for an independent library board and an independent state librarian. As it turned out, an independent library board was out of the question politically because of the opposition of a school man with whom Ahern had crossed swords in the past. She did manage, however, to promote a compromise in which the State Library was transferred from the Legislature to the State Board of Education. Part of that compromise was that Ahern would not seek reappointment as State Librarian, but she had already decided in any case to enroll in library school.

Ahern attended the library school at the Armour Institute of Technology in Chicago in 1895–96. It was during her time there that she was offered the editorship of *Public Libraries,* a new journal sponsored and financed by the Library Bureau. The journal was subsequently taken over by the Illinois Library Association, an organization in which Ahern took an active part. A missionary for state and local library association organization and activity, she constantly urged her readers to get involved in the library movement. She was three times elected President of the Illinois Library Association (1908, 1909, and 1915), served on the ALA Council for many years, attended every ALA conference from 1893 to 1931, and was named a Charter

Member of the American Library Institute. She was also Secretary for many years of the Library Department of the National Education Association, an organization whose formation she had heralded in the pages of *Public Libraries*. Other organizations to which she belonged were the Chicago Library Club, the Chicago Women's Club, and the Women's City Club of Chicago.

The relationship between the schools and the public libraries, library training in the normal schools, the role of the school library, and the teaching function of the public librarian were topics with which Ahern was constantly concerned. She wrote on these subjects in *Public Libraries,* gave talks before library associations and civic groups, and contributed articles and reports to other publications. The school, the church, and the library were—in Ahern's view—linked together in a great mission: the education of the American people. She was an enthusiastic supporter of Andrew Carnegie's public library philanthropy. In the high-minded manner so characteristic of public librarians of her period, Ahern emphasized educational work, deplored the vulgarity of the popular newspaper press, and worried about the problems American public libraries experienced because of the publication of so many indelicate French novels.

Ahern gave up the editorship of *Public Libraries* in 1931; she was over 70 years of age, and her eyesight had become too poor for her to be able to continue in editorial work. In the last issue of *Libraries* (which the Illinois Library Association decided to end, rather than continue it without Ahern), many colleagues paid tribute to Ahern and the journal. All agreed that *Public Libraries* had been a voice for small public libraries and had provided an important forum for the more practical aspects of library work. "The loan desk and the field trip," commented Frank K. Walter, Librarian of the University of Minnesota, "have been nearer her heart than the private study or the complicated problem of bibliographical research."

Even after retirement, Ahern continued to travel and to take a keen interest in library affairs. She died on May 22, 1938.

ELAINE FAIN

## Aje, Simeon B.

(1927– )

Simeon Babasanya Aje, Director of the National Library of Nigeria, contributed to professional development through IFLA and Unesco activities.

Aje was born on June 11, 1927, in Ondo State, Nigeria. He attended primary schools in his hometown, Ijurun, and Ijero in Ekiti from 1935 to 1941 and attended Christ's School, Ado-Ekiti, from 1942 to 1945, after which he took the Cambridge School Certificate and a Nigerian teachers examination in 1948. From 1946 to 1954 Aje was a teacher in primary and secondary schools in the old Western Region.

He became a teacher/librarian in the Iwo District Council from 1955 to 1956. In 1957 he moved to the Western Regional Library and obtained leave and a scholarship to study at Loughborough College in England. At Loughborough Aje successfully completed the Great Britain Associateship of the Library Association Examination and obtained the Fellowship of the Library Association in 1959. Before returning to Nigeria, Aje was an Assistant Librarian at the National Central Library London (January–April 1960) and a Cataloguer at the British National Bibliography later in the year. He returned to his post as Librarian with the Western Regional Library and became Senior Librarian at that library in 1967.

Aje went to the U.S. for postgraduate professional education in 1962 at the University of Chicago Graduate School of Library Science, where he obtained an M.A. in 1963. During his stay in Chicago, Aje was also Social Science and Documents Librarian and Head of the Modern Languages Library at the University of Chicago Libraries. He returned as a Librarian in Western Regional Library services in 1964 and became Senior Librarian in 1967. In his post as Regional School Librarian, he was instrumental in promoting school library service and ran training programs for library assistants in primary and secondary schools. In the same year, Aje was appointed Principal Librarian in the National Library of Nigeria, in Lagos. He was Acting Deputy Director from May 1967 to November 1969 and was appointed Deputy Director, 1969–70. Aje became Director of the National Library in September 1971.

As Director of the Library, Aje contributed significantly to the development of librarianship at the national level. He initiated considerable expansion of the National Library services to the state with the establishment of branches located in the states. He also initiated the process for recognition of the profession of librarianship and the establishment of a decree establishing a register of librarians. Aje also introduced the application of national standards in bibliographical description and the use of standard book numbers and standard serial numbers. He continued the publication of the *National Bibliography of Nigeria,* which was taken over in 1970 from the University of Ibadan Library.

Aje also made available his wealth of professional experience in the area of library education and training in Nigeria. He was a Visiting Lecturer at the University of Ibadan from 1960 to 1968 and 1968 to 1976 and Associate Lecturer from 1977. He helped to develop programs and courses on the National Library and on national bibliographic control.

Aje became well known in professional library circles in Britain, Europe, the U.S., and Eastern Europe. He served as a regular member at IFLA and attended Council meetings from 1971. He served as a member of various IFLA-connected committees. Aje also contributed to the work of Unesco through membership in various conferences and councils.

As Director and President of the Nigerian Library Association, Aje influenced the acceptance of library boards and the establishment of state libraries as an essential service to the Nigerian public. He contributed in no small measure to the national public image of the librarian and put Nigeria on the international librarianship map.

Aje wrote *A Biography of Dr. Albert Schweitzer* in Yoruba and prepared a Yoruba translation of Chinua Achebe's *Things Fall Apart,* and he contributed to the library professional literature.

F. A. OGUNSHEYE

**Ajman:** *see* article United Arab Emirates

## Akita Jeremias Mama

(1921– )

During the three decades of his stewardship of the National Archives of Ghana (1949–76), J. M. Akita, more than any other single individual, shaped the development of the archival profession in his country in particular and Africa in general. He attacked almost all the problems that confront the modern archivists and invariably found happy and logical solutions.

Born on May 11, 1921, in Teshi, Accra, Akita had his initial schooling in Ghana. He then proceeded to the Queen's College, Cambridge, in 1945 and graduated in 1948. He did a year's training in Archives Administration at the School of Librarianship and Archives, University of London. Back in Ghana in 1949, he became Chief Archivist of Ghana, a post he held till his retirement in 1976.

His most signal service to Ghana was the founding of the National Archives. He started concentrating the records that were lying about scattered in the government offices, corridors, and attics. At the same time he drew up plans for a new archival building. The construction work, which started in 1959, was completed by 1962. Akita went on to establish regional archival offices in Kumasi (1959) and in Cape Coast (1964), for which permanent buildings were constructed later. He also made building plans for other regional archives offices at various administrative capitals of Ghana.

To give his archival establishments legitimacy and security, he was instrumental in piloting an archival law through the then colonial legislature in 1955. The law envisages taking over all record groups and documents, both historical and administrative, and also those of the future. The procedures of evaluation and appraisal of records before their transfer to the National Archives have also been clearly enunciated.

Akita was elected a member of the Executive Committee of the International Council on Archives from 1968 to 1976. In recognition of his contributions to the International Council on Archives, he was made an honorary member for life of the Council.

When the question of establishment of a Unesco-sponsored training center for Archivists for Anglophone countries of Africa was mooted in 1967, Akita was naturally closely associated with the project. He was in no small measure responsible for the location of the Centre at the Department of Library and Archival Studies of the University of Ghana in 1975. On retirement from the National Archives in 1976, he was invited to head the center. He thereafter worked as Senior Lecturer and Acting Director of the training center.

Akita's professional knowledge and extensive travels made him uniquely qualified to write on archival and ancillary problems, and he wrote numerous articles in professional journals.

Akita shared his specialized skills generously with the neighboring countries. He was appointed Archival Adviser by the Commonwealth Secretariat to the UN Institute for Namibia in Lusaka, Zambia, in 1977, and he drew up a report on the establishment of an archival service in the future Namibia. In 1978 Unesco sent him on a consultancy mission to Uganda to prepare short- and long-term plans for the development of archival services there.

D. G. KESWANI

# Albania

Albania, a people's republic, lies in the Balkan Peninsula in southeastern Europe, bordered by Yugoslavia on the north and east, Greece on the south, and the Adriatic Sea on the west. Pop. (1979 official) 2,594,600; area 28,748 sq.km. The official language is Albanian.

**National Library.** The National Library of the People's Socialist Republic of Albania, situated in the capital city, Tiranë, was established on December 10, 1922. It is the nation's major research library and the depository for all books published in the country. The Library provides cataloguing and limited interlibrary loan services for the district public libraries and academic libraries outside Tiranë. In 1973 the Library had exchange agreements with 350 libraries in 69 countries.

There was only minimal growth in the Library's holdings in the pre-World War II period. Between 1922 and 1938 its book collections increased from 6,000 to 12,000 volumes. A more rapid expansion of its holdings occurred following the establishment of the present regime in 1944. As a consequence of the confiscation of the major private libraries in the country, 51,128 books were added to the Library's collections during 1944–45. The bulk of the Library's subsequent acquisitions have resulted from purchases and exchanges. The Library's book holdings totaled 89,000 volumes in 1947, 156,000 in 1954, 450,000 in 1967, 630,000 in 1972, and 800,000 in 1979.

The most noteworthy holdings of the Library are books and manuscripts dealing with Albanian history, language, literature, folklore, and ethnography. It possesses either an original or copy of virtually every book published in the Albanian language. Its book and manuscript Albanological collections are considered to be the most extensive and important in the world. It also has relatively strong holdings in the history and culture of the other Balkan countries.

The National Library publishes *Bibliografia Kombëtare e R.P.S. të Shqipërisë, Artikujt e periodikut shqip* [The National Bibliography of the PSR of Albania, Albania Periodical Articles] (1961–). This monthly lists the contents of Albanian periodicals. It also publishes *Bibliografia Kombëtare e R.P.S. të Shqipërise, Libri shqip* [The National Bibliography of the PSR of Albania, Albanian Books] (1960–). This quarterly lists, with brief annotations, books published in Albania.

**Academic Libraries.** The major academic library is that of Tiranë State University, founded in 1957. In the mid-1970's its book collections numbered approximately 400,000 volumes, and its periodical holdings consisted of about 30,000 volumes. Other important academic libraries in the mid-1970's were those of the Higher Agricultural Institute in Tiranë (70,000 volumes) and the Higher Pedagogical Institute in Shkoder (60,000 volumes).

**Public Libraries.** In 1938 there were only 5 public libraries in Albania, with total holdings of 25,000 volumes. By 1950 there were 12 public libraries with 202,000 volumes, and in 1972 there were 42 public libraries with 2,223,000 volumes. The largest public libraries were found in the cities of Shkoder (160,000 volumes), Korcë (90,000 volumes), and Elbasan (60,000 volumes). Next to the National Library, the Shkoder Public Library has the richest holdings of works on Albanology and Balkanology. It also contains a valuable collection of 19th-century



**Libraries in Albania (1976)**

| Type | Number | Volumes in collections | Annual expenditures (lek) | Population served | Professional staff | All staff (total) |
|---|---|---|---|---|---|---|
| National | 1 | 800,000[a] | N.A. | 300,000 | N.A. | N.A. |
| Academic | N.A. | N.A. | N.A. | 25,000 | N.A. | N.A. |
| Public | 42[b] | 2,223,000[b] | N.A. | 2,500,000 | N.A. | N.A. |
| School | N.A. | N.A. | N.A. | 650,000 | N.A. | N.A. |
| Special | N.A. | N.A. | N.A. | N.A. | N.A. | N.A. |
| Total | 3,276 | | | | | |

[a]1979.
[b]1972.

manuscript materials that are important for the study of the development of the Albanian nationalist movement.

**Other Libraries.** In 1976 there were 3,276 libraries in Albania. Aside from the public and academic libraries, these were mainly found in houses of culture, cultural hearths, and schools. In 1976 there were 478 houses of culture and 1,447 cultural hearths in the country; it appears that the majority of the libraries in these latter institutions are small (under 1,000 books) and that their holdings consist almost entirely of contemporary Albanian literature, textbooks and instructional manuals, ideological materials, and Albanian periodicals.

NICHOLAS C. PANO

# Alexandrian Library

The Eastern Mediterranean coast and the Near East generally were divided after the death of Alexander the Great (323 B.C.) among his generals, who, along with many of their associates and successors, were educated individuals. Committed to maintaining Greek culture, which they regarded as justification for their rule over other peoples, they stressed a well-rounded education called *paideia;* by 323 B.C. the written word was vital to it. When faced with a foreign cultural tradition, despite whatever merits it had, the occupying Greek community felt obliged to demonstrate the superiority of its own. Such was the purpose of the Museum and the libraries in Alexandria, Egypt, initiated by Ptolemy I Soter with the help of the Athenian scholar Demetrius of Phaleron.

The collections seem to have been developed on the principle that the library should have a proper copy of every title in Greek; before long that objective was enriched with efforts to acquire translations of significant works in other languages, such as the Hebrew Torah. The procurement process embraced not only the standard dealings with book collectors and book dealers but also the practice notorious in the days of Ptolemy III Euergetes (as related by Galen) of obliging ships dropping anchor in the harbor to yield their books so that copies could be made for the library. There is some evidence of the existence of a rapid-copying shop to do the royal bidding, and Galen also notes that the books copied were identified as being "from the ships." Assembled were not only classic and other literary materials but also cookbooks, magic books, and oddities. A case can certainly be made for regarding the Alexandrian Library as the national library of Greek Egypt, not dominated by the publications or commitments of any one school of philosophy as had been common in the scholarly collections in Greece.

According to the most informative witness—the 12th-century Byzantine savant John Tzetzes, whose reports were critically reviewed by modern authority Rudolf Blum—the library in the Brucheion founded by Ptolemy I Soter was enlarged most significantly by his son, Ptolemy II Philadelphus. Demetrius of Phaleron was brought from Athens in the early 3rd century B.C. to develop the collection in Greek tragic and comic poetry, a responsibility that also included preparation of scholarly correct editions. Maintenance of the collections and supervision of library service soon became tasks of equal importance and were placed in the hands of Zenodotus of Ephesus—a Homer scholar and initially junior to Demetrius. Zenodotus seems to have been the first, around 291 B.C., to have been designated Director (*bibliophylax*), at a time when cataloguing and translation were recognized as part of the library routine under the beneficent eye of Ptolemy II Philadelphus.

Just as Zenodotus apparently made his mark first as a textual critic and then as an administrator, the cataloguing achievements of Callimachus, 25 years his junior, evidently enhanced the luster of his literary skills in about 250 B.C. His high repute may have facilitated the appointment of his fellow-Cyrenian, Eratosthenes, scholar in several fields and celebrated by posterity as a geographer as the next Director. During the ensuing century the library continued to be managed by a succession of persons distinguished in science, Fellows of the Museum as it were. After 145 B.C. the record is silent.

When the first of several catastrophes struck, the fire at the Alexandria docks in 47 B.C. during Caesar's invasion, the Brucheion and its "daughter" library (possibly built for overflow), the Serapeum, held jointly some 532,800 rolls. The normal papyrus roll constituting a book was about 20 feet long unrolled, 10 to 12 inches high. Such a roll would contain, for instance, Plato's *Symposium* inscribed on 56 "pages" of 36 lines apiece, each line being 3.4 inches long. Quite a few papyrus rolls had writing on both sides. They were probably arranged in subject groups and utilized only on the premises. There is no proof of that arrangement or of how anything was located; available data are scattered and frequently incomplete. From the *Pinakes* of Callimachus it is known that subject, descriptive, and even evaluative features had been developed rather elaborately. Other surviving testimony is much more limited; notable is the inscribed catalogue found on Rhodes, taken to be the library of a gymnasium of the 2nd century B.C. In this catalogue the writers' names are in alphabetical order, but what order (if any) prescribes the listing of individual titles is not clear.

Information on architecture or furnishings does not exist beyond what archaeologists and chroniclers estimate on the basis of reputations and remnants of other Hellenistic library sites. Strabo the geographer visited Egypt about 24 years after the Brucheion fire and later mentioned the Museum's area with seats for discussion and mess hall for the scholarly staff, but he said nothing of books or library activities. From other sources, like archaeological studies at Pergamum, it can be deduced that the large central area originally provided for sacred or prestige purposes gradually disappeared from libraries; by the time of the Romans all was practical, and libraries comprised a group of moderate size rooms.

Alexandrian science continued during the Roman Empire and perhaps utilized the library as before. Not very clear is the possible relationship between the library and the university developed in Alexandria by the Neoplatonists. Only too obvious, unfortunately, is the record of damage in the later 4th century, a by-product of religious conflict that went as far as street riots. By the time the Christians were finished fighting the pagans and each other, there was not a great deal left for the Islamic conquerors of the mid-7th century to maltreat.

Yet the legacy of the Alexandrian Library was very substantial. For lack of surviving records one cannot produce details, but doubtless many writings of classical Greece and some other cultures were initially preserved for posterity by finding a home in that great repository. Indeed, the scholars hammering out the practices of textual criticism had to be working with numerous copies of many a work. And it is reasonable to assume that, with so much activity for unknown legions of scribes, there must have been considerable standardization of copying and manuscript handling, produced by supervision if not by formal instruction. We have very few precise comments by visitors and no official reports, but there are enough allusions in ancient and early medieval writings to indicate that word about many features, from architecture to the cataloguing implied by Callimachus' *Pinakes,* circulated rather widely. Moreover, for many who had no tangible data there was inspiration in the idea of the physically imposing, comprehensive scholar-library, an inspiration still voiced in Renaissance writings.

To a limited degree, the development of these traditions owed something identifiable to other Hellenistic Age libraries. The Attalids began in the latter half of the 3rd century B.C. to enhance their capital of Pergamum (now in northwestern Turkey, a few miles inland from Lesbos), with attractive installations including a library. The archaeological testimony is scanty, but the literary traditions do touch on the fate of Aristotle's books on the one hand and the misadventures of the Alexandrian Library on the other. Perhaps the clearest record is the statement by late 1st century B.C. scholar Dionysius of Halicarnassus, working in Rome, that in preparing a biography he had used the *pinakes* of both Callimachus and Pergamum.

Other scholarly collections may have been established in the last two centuries of the Roman Republic in the Hellenistic East, because at least three turn up regularly in the histories of Roman conquest as war booty: at Pella, Macedonia, taken by Aemilius Paulus after the battle of Pydna in 168 B.C. at Athens, whence about 86 B.C. Sulla carried off "Aristotle's Library"; and at Sinope, on the Black Sea, after Lucullus defeated Mithridates in 70 B.C. Scraps of archaeological and literary evidence indicate that there were founded also during that epoch, if not earlier, numerous secondary schools *gymnasia* teaching the seven liberal arts and a few medical schools and law schools; all have been thought likely to have had book collections, but proof is rare.

The institutions built during the Roman Empire have understandably left more traces, and certain features, like housing in a temple, can be attributed at least partly to the influence of Egypt and the ancient East. One cannot assume, however, that the numerous libraries established all over the Empire were shaped decisively, let alone exclusively, by Hellenistic models; Roman and local influences were present as well.

SIDNEY L. JACKSON

## Algeria

Algeria, a republic in northern Africa, is bordered by the Mediterranean Sea on the north, Tunisia and Libya on the east, Niger, Mali, and Mauritania on the south, and the Spanish Sahara and Morocco on the west. Pop. (1977 est.) 17,270,000; area 2,322,164 sq.km. The official languages are Arabic and French.

**National Library.** Founded in 1835, the National Library is Algeria's oldest cultural establishment, for which the Ministry of Information and Culture is responsible. In spite of the encyclopedic character of its collection, the humanities predominate. There are an important collection on the Maghreb (Algeria, Tunisia, Morocco), 3,000 manuscripts mainly in Arabic, 150 microfilms, a record library with 3,000 recordings, a collection of musical scores, and a loan library of 20,000 works.

In 1958 the Library owned 400,000 books and 1,200 periodicals; by 1966 the collection had grown to 600,000 books; and by 1976, 700,000, mainly in French, 150,000 additional works in Arabic, and 1,504 periodicals in many languages. The Library enjoys copyright privilege, has a department responsible for publication exchanges, and is part of an interlibrary loan system.

**Academic Library.** The most important academic library is the Central Library of the University of Algiers, founded in 1879. It lost 112,500 books in a fire at the end of the Algerian War in 1962, but it was rebuilt and inaugurated in 1968. The University Library of Algiers heads the libraries of the different departments and those of the numerous institutes. Its collection includes literature, law, the sciences, medicine, and pharmacology. In 1976 the collection included 600,000 works, 1,500 periodicals, and 12,326 works in Arabic, either on microfilm or on microfiche. The university libraries of Oran, Constantine, and Annaba were founded more recently.

B. Ben

*Façade of the National Library of Algeria, originally established in 1835 under the Ministry of Information and Culture.*

**Public Library.** Since independence, Algeria has opened many local libraries throughout its 31 *wilayete (départements)*. These libraries, together with those of local groups and cultural centers, are under the Ministry of Information through the prefect *(walis)*. The most important is in Algiers (founded in 1951). In 1976 its collection included 68,182 books and 30 periodicals.

**School Libraries.** Very few elementary schools and high schools owned a small library for their students and teachers at the end of the 1970's. Only the *hautes-écoles*, of university level, are served by their own libraries.

**Special Library.** Almost every ministry, national company, bank, and other institution owns either a library or a documentation center for its specific needs. According to the first national census, conducted in 1975 and 1976, there were 300 throughout Algeria.

There were no Algerian library associations at the end of the 1970's.

R. CHAIT

## Amano, Keitaro

(1901– )

Keitaro Amano is recognized by many as the creator of modern bibliography in Japan. Born in November 1901 in Kyoto, Amano took a position in the Law Library of Kyoto University in 1922. In 1927 he published *Hosei, Keizai, Shakai Ronbun Soran* ("Index of Articles on Law, Politics, Economics, and Sociology"), which showed at once his brilliant ability as a bibliographer. It was followed by *Honpo Shoshi no Shoshi* ("A Bibliography of Japanese Bibliographies"; 1933), which won him a leading position in the Japanese bibliographical world.

In 1948 Amano moved to the Kansai University Library, where he took an active part in the processing work as the head of the Technical Service Division. In the meantime, he compiled a great variety of bibliographies; among them were "A Bibliography of Dr. Hajime Kawakami" (1956), "Bibliography of the Classical Economics" (1961–64), "Index of All Contents of Journals" (1966), and "A Bibliography of Max Weber in Japan" (1969). Articles collected in his *Shoshi Sakuin Ronko* ("A

Study on Bibliography and Index"; 1979) represent his deep knowledge of the subjects.

Also an excellent cataloguing theorist, Amano wrote many books and articles on cataloguing, including *Yosho-Mokuroku no Tsukurikata* ("Guide to Cataloguing Books in European Languages"; 1949) and *Yosho-Mokurokuho Nyumon* ("Introduction to Cataloguing Books in European Languages"; 1951). In 1959 he represented Japan at the Preliminary Meeting of the International Cataloguing Conference held in London under the auspices of IFLA.

After he retired from the Kansai University Library in 1967, he served as a professor of the Social Science Department, Toyo University. After returning to his home town, Kyoto, in 1971, when he retired from Toyo University, he worked on his life work, *Nihon Shoshi no Shoshi* ("A Japan Bibliography of Bibliographies"), the completely revised and augmented edition of *Honpo Shoshi no Shoshi,* published in 1933. The first volume, "Part Generalia," was published in 1973.

A detailed chronology and comprehensive list (as of 1970) of his works are appended at the end of the book issued in honor of his 70th birthday, *Toshokan-gaku to sono Shuhen* ("On and around Library Science"; 1971).

TOSHIO IWASARU

# Angola

Angola, a people's republic in southwestern Africa, is bordered by Zaire on the north and northeast, Zambia on the east, Namibia on the south, and the Atlantic Ocean on the west. Pop. (1978 est.) 6,831,000; area 1,246,700 sq.km. The official languages are Portuguese and various Bantu languages.

**National Library.** Angola gained its independence on November 11, 1975, and in May 1977 the National Department of Libraries was created, with the task of forming a national network of libraries, archives, and documentation centers. (Academic and school libraries, of the Ministry of Education, were excluded.) In that reorganization of the information community, the National Central Library in Luanda was founded, taking advantage of the collection and facilities of the former National Library (1968), a part of the National Library of Lisbon, Portugal. Its collection was formed in part from materials outside the areas of specialties of the Library of the National Museum of Angola and the Institute for Scientific Investigation of Angola, and also included the Library of Education of the Provincial Secretariat of Education. Legal deposit functioned from Lisbon, which distributed materials through the national libraries of its provinces. The National Central Library was enriched by the recovery of various private and official libraries that had been abandoned. In 1978 a statute was approved to organize and regulate the National Department of Libraries and establishing the National Central Library, and in 1979 a legal deposit law was passed. The Library's collection is composed of 45,000 works (1978), not counting the recovery of manuscripts and documents dispersed in other countries and that can be considered part of the national heritage.

The national network also extends its sphere to cover archives and documentation centers, with the exception of those in history, which are the charges of the National Department of Museums and Monuments (1979).

**Academic Libraries.** The University of Angola maintains a General Library, which also serves as a center for documentation and as the National Center for Scientific Investigation. The Library's holdings are divided into special collections and are distributed in the cities of Luanda, Lubango, and Huambo. Individual departments of Biology, Botany, Geology, and Human Sciences maintain their own specialized collections. Taken together, the several university libraries contain several thousand volumes.

**Public Libraries.** In 1973 only 19 public libraries existed in Angola, to serve a literate population estimated at 1,000,000. Of these, by far the largest was the Municipal Library in Luanda, containing 14,600 volumes. After independence the National Department of Libraries moved, in keeping with the MPLA-Labor Party's literacy campaign, to extend the network of libraries to the rural areas, further expanded by the creation of committees of party militants functioning in such production units as farms and factories. Through these efforts people's libraries had been established in 56 locations by 1978, serving a literate population of more than 2,500,000 (plus a student population of 2,000,000).

**School Libraries.** Thirty-four school libraries functioned in 1974 and are under the direction of the Ministry of Education.

**Special Libraries.** Under the direction of the National Department of Libraries, Angola's special libraries are administratively linked to the different ministries they serve, such as Agriculture, Industry and Energy, Justice, and Petroleum. The largest, in Huambo, Luanda, and Lubango, specialize in agriculture and animal husbandry. Others are in localities throughout the country and numbered 30 libraries in 1978.

DOMINGOS VAN-DÚNEM

# Anuar, Hedwig

(1928– )

Hedwig (Aroozoo) Anuar, Singapore librarian and administrator whose contributions did much to promote and shape the development of Singapore libraries, was born in the Malaysian town of Johor Bahrti on November 19, 1928. In 1937 the Aroozoo family moved to Singapore, where Hedwig continued her education and graduated from the University of Malaya in 1951 with first class honors. She joined the University of Malaya Library in 1952 and was awarded an Inter-University Council Fellowship to study at the Northwestern Polytechnic in London. She obtained the Associateship of the Library Association (U.K.) in 1956 and the Fellowship two years later. She returned to the University of Malaya Library at its new campus in Kuala Lumpur, was assigned to the National Library of Singapore, and eventually became its Director in 1965, a position she held thereafter.

The Library has its beginnings in colonial Singapore as the Raffles Library, a subscription library serving a largely expatriate and English reading public. It became the Raffles National Library in 1957 but was unable to break into a new pattern of service until 1962, when the New Zealand government brought A. Priscilla Taylor and J. R. Cole to Singapore as library consultants under the Colombo Plan. Taylor subsequently stayed on as Director until 1964 to do the initial planning and lay the groundwork for the development of the National Library. Under Hedwig Anuar's directorship, these plans were realized and further extended.

The National Library system serves a total registered membership of 322,440. Book collections amount to more than 1,000,000 volumes and include material in all four official languages—English, Chinese, Malay, and Tamil. In 1978 more than 3,000,000 loans were recorded. Extension services were first provided through mobile libraries that still call at 11 service points. The present policy, however, prefers the establishment of branch libraries housed in attractive new buildings in Queenstown (1970), Toa Payoh (1974), and Marine Parade (1978).

National bibliographical activities include the publication of the *Singapore National Bibliography* (1967– )

and the *Singapore Periodicals Index* (1969–70–). The National Library acts as the Singapore center for regional projects such as the International Serials Data System (ISDS) and the National Libraries and Documentation Center, Southeast Asia Consortium (NLDC-SEA). It is also responsible for the continuation of the *Masterlist of Southeast Asian Microforms* (Singapore University Press, 1978).

For the Library Association of Malaysia, in 1968, she spent three months traveling all over Malaysia. Out of the survey grew her report, *Blueprint for Public Library Development in Malaysia* (1968), which was accepted as the basis for the development of public library services in Malaysia. She served the Library Association of Singapore in many capacities, including the office of President. She chaired the LAS Joint Standing Committee on Library Cooperation and Bibliographical Services, 1965–75, and continued as the Vice-Chairman of its successor, the Committee on Bibliographical and Library Cooperation.

Other positions include Director (concurrent), National Archives and Records Centre, 1969–78, and Honorary Secretary, National Book Development Council of Singapore, from 1965. Her career and interests involve her in many aspects of library development as well as library-related fields. She brought an intellectual quality and sense of vision to her work at the National Library and to other interests that proved unique.

LIM PUI HUEN

# Arab League Educational, Cultural and Scientific Organization

The Arab League Educational, Cultural and Scientific Organization (ALECSO) was established on July 25, 1970, after the first meeting of the Organization's General Conference in Cairo. It plays an active role in the development and promotion of information services in the Arab region through the work of the Information Department of ALECSO. At the beginning this work was planned to include collecting selected documents; facilitating the exchange of information; supporting the research work of other departments of ALECSO; publishing journals, newsletters, guides, bulletins, and bibliographies; holding meetings, seminars, and conferences; and preparing statistics related to the fields served by ALECSO.

Four main activities took place in 1971 that paved the way for the Information Department of ALECSO to fulfill its goals. The first was a Seminar on Promoting Library Services in the Arab World, held in Damascus in October 1971. The second was the Seminar on Cultural Statistics held in Khartoum in December 1971. The third was the formulation of several questionnaires covering the fields of education, culture, and science to collect relevant data related to those fields in the Arab world. Fourth, great effort was exerted to encourage the Arab states to apply legal deposit laws to their national libraries or other institutions with similar functions and roles.

As a result of those efforts, the Information Department carried out several projects in 1972–73, including (1) the preparation of guides and directories containing available data on information institutions, publishing houses, and periodicals in the Arab region; (2) issuing annual bulletins on Arab publications and educational statistics, a periodical entitled *The Arab Culture Magazine,* and a newsletter in Arabic and English; (3) holding a conference on the development of information services in the Arab region, the First Arab Bibliographical Conference (Riyadh, 1973), and a seminar on the Circulation of the Arabic Book (Doha, Qatar, 1972); and (4) organizing three-month training courses for librarians and documentation officers in the Arab world.

In 1974 ALECSO moved to a further stage. The programs and projects to be implemented in 1974–75 were planned to cover four major areas of activities: (1) developing technical, traditional, and mechanized tools used in information; (2) providing advanced bibliographical services in the fields covered by ALECSO; (3) raising the standards of personnel through training courses; and (4) collecting and publishing basic information on the Arab states in the fields of interest to ALECSO. Several projects were initiated, including the *Bibliographical Guide to Reference Books in the Arab World;* a subject bibliography; new issues of the bulletins of statistics, Arab publications, *Arab Culture,* and the *ALECSO Newsletter;* organizing training courses; and holding the first seminar on the use of computers in bibliographical works. The recommendations of the Riyadh were carried out through a manual of Arab cataloguers, including Arabization of ISBD; a list of unified entries of Arab authors; studies on Arabic amendments to the Dewey Decimal Classification System; and experiments with an Arab classification system for Islamic disciplines. An experimental study was conducted on the rules to be adopted in preparing and using an Arab subject heading list. A model part of this list related to Islamic disciplines was produced and tried in some specialized libraries in the Arab states.

According to the results of the previous programs and the evaluation of the work achieved through them, ALECSO planned projects for 1976–77 that included a meeting on mechanical techniques in the field of information, held in Cairo in November 1976, and the Second Arab Bibliographical Conference in Baghdad in 1977. Several studies on information sciences and the application of modern techniques were published in Arabic. A subject bibliography in education was prepared covering Arab specialized periodicals, and a bibliographical guide to Arab works in library science and documentation was also compiled. Training courses were continued, and a meeting of Arab experts in educational statistics was held in Baghdad in 1977. This latter meeting played an important role in developing the annual bulletin of educational statistics.

In 1978 the new information program included preparing the draft Arabic subject heading list, the Arabization of the modified edition of ISBD, and a manual containing models for the application of the Arabized rules. A guide of Arab works in social sciences and anthropology and a guide to documentation centers were also prepared, along with a new bulletin, the *Arab Journal of Information Sciences.*

A new program began in 1978 to build a data base starting with statistics and bibliographical information. ALECSO hoped to build up and establish an Arab Information Network.

M. T. KHAFAGY

# Arbuthnot, May Hill

(1884–1969)

May Hill Arbuthnot was not a librarian, but because of her contributions to education, as teacher, lecturer, children's literature specialist, reading consultant, and writer, children's librarianship in the United States is richer. In recognition of her efforts on behalf of literature and libraries for children, the Children's Services Division (now Association for Library Service to Children) of the American Library Association established in 1969 the May Hill Arbuthnot Honor Lectureship, sponsored by Scott, Foresman and Company.

Born in Mason City, Iowa, on August 27, 1884, May Hill Arbuthnot received a baccalaureate degree from the

University of Chicago in 1922 and her Master's degree from Columbia University in 1924. In 1927 she joined the faculty at Western Reserve University, Cleveland, Ohio (now Case Western Reserve University), from which she retired in 1949 as Associate Professor. Her teaching interests were in the general fields of nursery school and elementary education and the special field of children's literature. Her contributions in these areas were substantial. During her early years at Western Reserve she was a pioneer in the nursery school movement. In 1929, she opened the University Nursery School, which became a successful model of a laboratory for teachers, doctors, nurses, parents, and other adults concerned with child development. Thousands of American children learned to read from the "Basic Curriculum Readers," which she wrote with William Scott Gray in 1951. Many of these children undoubtedly remember those readers as the "Dick and Jane" books.

Arbuthnot was a popular teacher on children's literature. A sought-after speaker throughout the country on children's books and reading, she spoke out firmly on topics related to the evaluation and selection of good books to meet children's developmental needs and reading tastes. In her 1969 acknowledgment of the Honor Lectureship, she remembered "that long stretch of years when I was dashing from one end of the country to the other, bringing children and books together by way of the spoken word." She also offered her opinion that "a forthright, vigorous lecture can set fire to a piece of literature that had failed to come to life from the printed page."

She wrote extensively about children's books. For ten years she was Review Editor of children's books for *Childhood Education* and later for the *Elementary English* (now *Language Arts*). In 1947 the first edition of her exhaustive textbook for children's literature courses, *Children and Books,* was published by Scott, Foresman and Company; she provided historical background on the development of children's literature, giving many examples of the best books of each genre and type, selections from illustrators, and advice on developing a child's reading tastes. While her textbook emphasized excellence in its approach to selecting and using books with children, she also stated as a cautionary, "Two facts we need to keep constantly before us: a book is a good book for children only when they enjoy it; a book is a poor book for children, when adults rate it a classic, if children are unable to read it or are bored by its content." This text, which was in its fifth edition in 1979, was reorganized and rewritten by Zena Sutherland.

Her other books include many anthologies in which she brought together, by genre, excellent examples of fine children's literature and provided advice on its selection and use with children. Those anthologies, all published by Scott, Foresman, include *Time for Poetry,* with Shelton L. Root, Jr. (3rd ed., 1968); *Time for Stories of the Past and Present,* with Dorothy M. Broderick (1968); *Time for Biography,* with Dorothy M. Broderick (1969); *Time for Old Magic* (1970); *Time for New Magic,* with Mark Taylor (1971); and *Time for Discovery,* with Evelyn Wenzel (1971). *The Anthology of Children's Literature* (4th ed. rev., 1976, by Zena Sutherland); a bibliography, *Children's Books Too Good to Miss,* now in its sixth edition (1971); and *Children's Reading in the Home* (1969) are still used in college courses and by others concerned with children's reading.

Arbuthnot's honors included the Constance Lindsay Skinner Award (1959) and the Regina Medal (1964) from the Catholic Library Association.

Three months before Arbuthnot died October 2, 1969, in Cleveland, the May Hill Arbuthnot Honor Lectureship was announced providing for the annual selection of an outstanding author, critic, librarian, historian, or teacher of children's literature to prepare and give a lecture in the United States "which shall be a significant contribution to the field of children's literature." The lecture is presented annually, usually in April, and is subsequently published in an issue of *Top of the News.* By the end of the 1970's, 11 scholars, critics, editors, and authors from nine countries had been selected to present lectures in cities throughout the United States. (For lecturers, see *The ALA Yearbook,* 1976– , "Awards" and "Biographies.").

MARILYN L. MILLER

# Archives

NATURE, GOALS, PRINCIPLES

**Nature of Archives.** Archives constitute one of the world's primary information sources. They arise and grow uniquely out of the activities of any kind of operative entity, be it an organization or institution, a family or even an individual. Since their archives are a component of such entities' records, the latter must first be defined. *Records* are the sum total of all documentary materials—regardless of their physical form or characteristics—created or received, and maintained, by an organization or other entity in connection with the transaction of its business and with such other activities as it is engaged in. An entity's records are the whole, the universe, from which its archives are selected. *Archives,* then, are a greater or lesser fraction of the records of an organization, institution, or other entity that has been selected for permanent preservation because it is considered to possess an enduring value warranting such preservation.

Physically, a wide variety of media have been used for record keeping during the course of human history. In the past these have included cuneiform tablets, papyrus, palm leaves, and parchment; in modern times most records consist of the paper documentation of various kinds that has evolved from the medieval parchments—the so-called "textual" records—but, in addition, many nontextual documentary forms have been brought into being by the new technologies of the 19th and particularly the 20th centuries: still photographs, motion picture films, videotapes, sound recordings, magnetic tapes, and related machine-readable forms. All of these, regardless of their special physical characteristics, are considered to be records, and therefore potentially archives, if used by an organization or other operative entity for record-keeping purposes.

**Types of Archival Agencies.** The term *archives* refers not only to records of archival quality or value but also to the agencies—generally public or private institutions or branches of institutions—that are responsible for selecting, preserving, and making available archival materials. These agencies, as a rule, correspond to and serve the various types of record-creating and record-keeping organizations. Chief among the latter are public bodies, governmental agencies at every level (national or federal, regional, state or provincial, and local), attached to which, in a pattern that varies according to the structure of government in the different countries, are the public archival agencies. The federal-level National Archives and Records Service and the 50 independent state archives in the United States, and the Archives de France, a centralized system encompassing both the Archives Nationales and the archives services of all of the departments, are examples.

Nonpublic archival agencies consist mainly of the "institutional archives," those that are attached to and provide archival services for business firms, trade unions, universities, scientific and philanthropic organizations, religious bodies, and other institutions, both profit and nonprofit. Related to these are archival agencies, unasso-

National Archives of Zimbabwe Rhodesia

*The reading room of the National Archives of Zimbabwe Rhodesia in Salisbury provides workspace for researchers.*



ciated with particular creating institutions, that serve as custodians of the archives of classes of such institutions, e.g., businesses, unions, churches. Archives of institutions are also to be found among the manuscript holdings of public or private libraries and historical societies. Family and personal archives are usually maintained informally by the families concerned but, when more or less prominent people are involved, are often deposited in and administered by libraries and historical societies as "papers" or manuscript collections. Similarly, such papers may find their way to public or private archival agencies attached to organizations with which the families or individuals have been connected.

**Purposes and Functions.** Among archival agencies those serving public organizations were the first to emerge in recent centuries and still make up the predominant category. Today, as in the past, the overriding purpose of these public archival agencies is to identify the relatively small proportion of government records having permanent archival value, and to effect their regular transfer to archival custody, so they may be preserved for future use. Such preservation and use, on the major scale involved, are justified by the density of information contained in the archival sources, which are valuable alike (1) to the government entities that initially produced them as evidence of their origin, organization, policies, programs, and principal operations over time and for long-term legal, financial, and other administrative purposes; (2) to private individuals and unofficial bodies in order to safeguard rights of various kinds and to assist in meeting their obligations; and (3) to scholars working in the fields of history, the other humanities, and the social sciences primarily, but also in the physical sciences, in pursuing their researches.

Having developed programs for the systematic acquisition of records of archival quality, based upon the application of professionally determined evaluation or appraisal standards, the archival agency provides for their physical preservation under the best possible conditions; perfects their organization and arrangement; describes them in guides, inventories, lists, and other finding aids designed to open them to potential users; and, finally, makes them available for consultation—either directly by the provision of microcopies, or through the medium of publication, originally by letterpress exclusively but later in microform as well—by the government itself and by the scholarly and general public.

Since World War II public archival agencies, led by those in the United States, have increasingly expanded their function to the closely interconnected field of records management. Here the archival agency establishes standards of good practice with respect to the creation, organization, maintenance, and retrieval of the current records of government as well as to their eventual retirement or disposition when they cease to be current by transfer to archival custody or by disposal (i.e., destruction); and seek to promote the adoption of these standards by government bodies. Although the involvement of archival agencies in records management was initially motivated by the need to facilitate the transfer to them of the permanently valuable archival core of government records, there has been the concomitant result of more efficient and effective administration of government that is also vitally important.

Institutional archives of all kinds have the same basic purposes and functions as public archival agencies, although they generally operate on a smaller scale and are usually little, if at all, involved in the records management practices of the organizations they serve. Similarly, archival agencies, including archives, libraries and historical societies, unassociated with the organizations, families, and individuals that created the archives they had, play no record management role, and their appraisal standards are predominantly concerned with considerations of research value. Otherwise, however, they share the essential purposes and functions of other archival agencies.

**Basic Principles and Terminology.** A key characteristic of archives, as of the records from which they have been selected, is their *organicity.* This refers to the underlying fact that they are not collected, in the usual sense of the term, by the originating organization or other entity but rather grow naturally—are created or received—out of its own activities and operations. Thus, the individual units that make up an organization's archives do not exist independently but instead are integrated within an overall structure of documentation that is essential to their significance.

The organicity common to all archival documentation leads logically to the fundamental principle of *provenance,* or *respect des fonds* in its original French formulation. This concept, which at bottom implies "belonging," holds that since the archives of a given organization belong to and constitute an organic whole, they must not be intermingled with those of any other

National Photography Collection, Public Archives of Canada

*The enormous volume of governmental records creates special challenges in housing, processing, and using public archives.*

organization. For the same reason, the corollary principle of *respect for original order* (or the "registry principle") requires that the archives of an organization should be maintained in their original internal structural pattern, and in their original filing arrangement (as in European registry offices), in order to preserve intact the close interrelationships between the individual component units. Otherwise, the meaning of the substantive informational content that they share as an organic whole would be seriously impaired or even destroyed. The implications of these principles for archival arrangement and classification on the one hand, and for archival description (i.e., the preparation of finding aids) on the other, are most important; they have resulted in practices in these areas that are fundamentally different from analogous library practices, which are typically concerned with discrete items.

For purposes of control within the archival agency, all of the records, and the archives subsequently selected therefrom, of an organization compose its *fonds* (a classic French term used widely in Europe) or, in Anglo-Saxon parlance, its *record group* or *archives group*. (While there exist certain technical differences between the fonds and the record/archives group concepts, they are essentially comparable.) The contents of a record/archives group normally subdivide into *subgroups,* corresponding to the primary subordinate administrative branches of the organizations concerned. Where an organization has inherited records of a predecessor organization, these would also form a subgroup. There may be other special situations within a given record/archives group that call for the recognition of subgroups.

The primary physical unit within the record/archives group and its constituent subgroups is the *document,* a single item on which information is recorded that may take one of many varied forms, such as a letter or memorandum, a report, the minutes of a meeting, a map or chart, a photograph, a sound recording, or a reel of microfilm or magnetic tape. Documents rarely exist alone; in a manner characteristic of the process of organic growth to which the records of organizations are subject, the individual document tends to be associated, more often than not, with other related documents in *file units* (e.g., the folder, the dossier or case file, the bound volume in earlier centuries), which themselves are grouped in series.

As the basic archival grouping for all purposes, particularly for arrangement and description as well as reference control purposes, the *series* is of paramount importance. It consists of a body of file units, multi-document and/or single document in nature, which are interdependently linked together (1) in accordance with a particular filing scheme or other filing system of any kind, or (2) because they concern a particular function, activity, or subject, have a particular physical character, or share a mutual relationship arising out of their creation, accumulation, or use. Within the record/archives group and its subgroups, the pattern of association of the constituent series reflects the hierarchical structure of the originating organization.

Against this background the following sections deal with the principal functional aspects of archives administration, preceded by a discussion of their legislative foundations. The functional aspects covered are: current records management, records retirement, and appraisal; internal processing: arrangement and description; services to users; archives management; technical aspects (buildings, custodial services, and technical services); and professional training for archivists.

**REFERENCES**

Frank B. Evans, Donald F. Harrison, and Edwin A. Thompson, compilers, "A Basic Glossary for Archivists, Manuscript Curators, and Records Managers," *American Archivist* (July 1974).

Sir Hilary Jenkinson, *A Manual of Archive Administration,* 2nd edition (1965).

T. R. Schellenberg, *Modern Archives: Principles and Techniques* (1956).

MORRIS RIEGER

LEGISLATIVE FOUNDATIONS

**What is Archival Legislation?** Archival legislation is probably as old and universal as archives themselves. Since archives are, according to a Unesco definition, "all noncurrent records of an institution or organization (those no longer needed in the conduct of current business) that are or should be preserved because of their permanent value," their preservation and use have long been regulated by the public powers. We know of the existence of laws on the subject as early as ancient Greece and the Roman Empire. In medieval Europe even the Popes and their Councils issued regulations on church archives, with threats of excommunication for offenders.

But the idea of comprehensive, systematic legislation on the whole matter of the conservation and use of archives is comparatively recent. The first country to conceive of it was France, in 1789–96, as a consequence of the French Revolution. Even now several countries throughout the world (especially developing countries) have no general archival legislation but only partial regulations of limited scope. Such differences from country to country can be explained by the fact that archives are closely linked with the entire legal, administrative, and socioeconomic system of each country. For example, in England and other countries with Anglo-Saxon legal traditions, documents derive legal value from the fact that they are kept in a public archival repository, whereas this is not the case in countries of Latin culture; legislation thus varies on this point. Another difference in the scope of archival laws is whether they are concerned with archives only after they have been transferred from the agency where they originated or also deal with the management of current records; the American and Canadian records management legislation has no equivalent in many countries. For all these reasons, it would be unrealistic to propose an "ideal" model for archival legislation. Many parts of a Russian or Chinese archival law would be meaningless in the U.S. or in Japan, while many requirements, useful in industrialized countries would be useless in developing ones.

**Public and Private Archives.** In the eyes of the legislator, the distinction between public and private (i.e., "nonpublic") archives is fundamental. Unfortunately, there is no consensus of definition in this matter. Definitions differ widely from one country to another, according to differences in socioeconomic and political systems. In socialist countries private ownership of archives is strictly limited to personal and family papers, whereas in other countries most business, society, trade union, university and school, hospital, church, and other institutional archives are largely considered private archives, with many variations from one country to another.

In nonsocialist countries one of the main points of uncertainty is the legal status of papers of heads of state, ministers, and senior public servants. A certain amount of confusion is inevitable between the private, personal correspondence and official papers of these individuals. In some countries the law enables the government to seize the papers of deceased or dismissed ministers and senior public servants, but this is seldom fully implemented, except for top-ranking army officers and diplomats.

The designation "public" applies to the legal status of these archives and not necessarily to their accessibility. Some public archives may not be accessible to the public (e.g., "security-classified" diplomatic or military records), while some private archives may be freely open to inspection. Nor do "private" archives always become public when they are given, bequeathed, or sold to the state or to public institutions. In many countries they retain their private status even when they are public property, the distinction between private and public archives being more in their origin than in their actual ownership.

Public archives are universally declared to be imprescriptible (i.e., not subject to claims or the assertion of customary rights by private parties) and inalienable. They can never cease to be public property, and they can be destroyed only according to official regulations. In some countries, such as the U.S., the legal designation of "archives" is even limited to documents that have a permanent value, while in some others, such as France, it applies to all documents, whether of permanent or temporary value. (There the distinction made between "records" and "archives," in the section Archives: Nature, Purposes, Principles, does not exist.)

As to private archives (which in the U.S. are frequently referred to as manuscript collections or papers), the law really began to be interested in them, with a few exceptions, only at the end of the 19th century and the beginning of the 20th. Even now there is no legal protection for them in some countries, but generally there are at least laws prohibiting the exportation of private archives of historical interest and giving to the government a right of preemption should they be sold.

**Administrative Organization of Public Archives.** Always a matter of legislative concern, the organization of public archives is closely related with the administrative system of each country. In countries with a centralized system, such as France, Italy, Spain, or the Scandinavian countries, archives also are generally centralized under one supreme authority (or a limited number of authorities). In such cases there is an integrated hierarchy of national (central), regional (provincial, departmental, district, etc.), and local archives, as well as of specialized archives such as audiovisual, scientific, literary, diplomatic, military, and educational archives, all subordinate to a central governmental office.

On the other hand, in noncentralized countries, especially in countries with a federal constitution such as the U.S., Brazil, the Federal Republic of Germany, Switzerland, and Yugoslavia, each level of archival responsibility is independent of every other level (e.g., the national/federal and the state levels in the U.S.). For this reason it is very difficult to compare archival organization, for example, in France and the U.S., as in the first case there are laws and regulations applicable to the whole of archives in the country, while in the latter case separate federal and state laws and regulations exist.

In the past, archives and libraries were often confused with each other and placed under one single authority. In the 20th century advanced countries became aware of the basic differences that exist between archives and libraries and consequently created separate organizations for each of them. This was not the case everywhere, however, and in a number of countries there still remains a confusion that is highly prejudicial both to archives and to libraries, since the nature and use of the holdings of each, and the requirements for their administration, are significantly different.

The governmental authority under which archives are placed will also differ from one country to another. In the U.S. the National Archives and Records Service is part of the General Services Administration; in the U.S.S.R. the General Directorate of State Archives depends directly on the Council of Ministers; in England the Public Record Office is under the Lord Chancellor; in France, Italy, and some other countries archives are a responsibility of the Minister of Culture; elsewhere they belong to other ministries such as Education, Interior, or Justice, or they come directly under the authority of the President or the Prime Minister. No system can be said to be ideal, but it seems that, at least in developing countries, only placement at the highest level of authority can give to the archival administration a sufficient degree of legal and administrative effectiveness.

**Accessibility of Public Archives.** Public access to archives is a relatively modern concern; it is linked with the progress of both democracy and objective historical research. The French law of 1794, which opened all public archives to public investigation, was, for a long time, nothing more than window dressing. The duration of the period during which access is restricted has been steadily diminishing. The term has come to be, in most countries, from 30 to 50 years, with special provisions to ensure the protection of individual privacy and state security. In several countries there are no time restrictions at all on access to public archives, except for certain categories and bodies of archives for which limited access is deemed a public necessity. However, despite an evident (but not universal) trend toward liberalization, access to public archives is still restricted in many countries, either by specific laws and regulations (especially when the searcher is a foreigner) or by sheer inertia and bureaucratic red tape.

**Basic Elements of Archival Legislation.** This broad survey of archival legislation and its background throughout the world enables us now to define what basic elements should figure in any archival legislation, regardless of the national political, administrative, and/or socioeconomic systems involved:

(a) Definitions of archives (and of records where the distinction is relevant), both public and private, and of the nation's responsibility concerning their preservation for legal, administrative, evidential, and research needs. Special emphasis, where necessary, should be put on the distinction between archives, libraries, and documentation centers.

(b) Definitions of the organization and functions of public archival agencies, whether centralized or not, including their right to inspect public archives and records wherever they are located, to establish standards (preferably mandatory) of good current records management practice, and to operate intermediate records centers for the storage and maintenance of noncurrent records.

(c) Provisions granting to the archival agency the sole power and responsibility to appraise the value of public records for purposes of disposition (either destruction or preservation).

(d) Provisions governing the controlled destruction of noncurrent public records that have been appraised as lacking further value.

(e) Provisions governing (i) the transfer of noncurrent public records, selected as permanently valuable in the appraisal process, to the custody of archival repositories, and (ii) their subsequent arrangement and description.

(f) Standards for access to public records.

(g) Definitions of the duties and responsibilities of record managers and archivists, and the requirements for their professional training.

(h) Provisions for the protection of private archives having historical interest.

MICHEL DUCHEIN

CURRENT RECORDS MANAGEMENT

Before the Great Depression records management was limited, with rare exceptions, to systems for controlling correspondence and devising methods of classifying centralized files. Chief clerks, then the administrative officers of most governmental agencies, and corporate secretaries or comptrollers in business and other private organizations rarely concerned themselves with the disposition, i.e., the retirement, of noncurrent records. Though World War I had generated large volumes of records in most national governments, the problems of disposition were barely perceived. Filing operations were delegated to poorly paid clerks, and the cost of space for files was not deemed sufficiently high to justify managerial attention.

The public officials and archivists who were influential in establishing modern archives in France, England, Germany, Holland, and several other European countries had scant conceptions of records retirement and neglected any systematic approach to the appraisal of records values. Retirement was limited to the transfer of very old records to the archives. As these records had been produced when documentation was relatively scarce, archivists were inclined to accept all that were offered by the departments. Even records relating to housekeeping activities (personnel management, supplies, and minor fiscal operations) were accepted for preservation. By the latter half of the 19th century, however, small quantities of routine records were being culled from accessions. This weeding operation was not given much professional attention until World War I. During the war, waste paper was used for the manufacture of bullets, and occasionally important records were reduced to pulp without any opportunity for archival intervention. This loss alerted European archivists to the problem of preserving recent records; nonetheless, they failed to develop an appropriate methodology.

One exception to this neglect of systematic records retirement appeared in Poland in the early 1930's. As a result of the country's partition in the late 18th century, old and valuable Polish records were in the custody of Austria, Germany, and the U.S.S.R. Archivists, in order to establish a prestigious institution, were compelled to concentrate on providing for the preservation of valuable recent records. It was thus Poland that pioneered in developing a theoretical approach to appraisal and retirement by scheduling records disposition, i.e., the itemization of discrete bodies of records, each accompanied by specific retention or disposal recommendations. The other European nations did not adopt similar programs until the end of World War II.

Theodore F. Welch

*Entrance to the Yomei Bunko, Kyoto, containing historical records of the Fujiwara-Konoye families.*

In the United States, railroads, banks, and insurance companies were among the first to try to rationalize records programs. They produced relatively large accumulations of records, many required for a number of years for administrative needs and regulatory compliance. Railroads led the reforms at the turn of the century because of the need to manage effectively information about real estate, right-of-way, rolling stock, train movements, and the administration of extensive networks. Furthermore, the Interstate Commerce Commission issued regulations concerning the maintenance of their varied records. Thus, by World War I railroads had adopted prescribed filing systems and designated records for permanent or long-term retention. Banks and insurance companies instituted similar procedures and practices in the years immediately after the war. With the exception of a few railroads these firms did not, however, establish institutional archival units like those emerging in Europe between 1901 and 1930.

**The U.S. National Archives.** When the U.S. National Archives began operations in 1935, the Archivist of the United States recruited, in addition to a managerial and an advisory staff, persons deemed qualified to appraise records for permanent preservation. These appraisers were selected on the basis of some experience with manuscript materials but, more importantly, on subject matter expertise; for example, scholars who specialized in diplomatic and military history and in the westward movement were delegated responsibility for appraising noncurrent records of the defense agencies, the Department of State, and the Department of the Interior, respectively. These archivists (Deputy Examiners) found that the records were in a chaotic state. Trivial materials were intermixed with records required to conduct essential public business, to protect the rights of individuals, and to serve scholarly research needs. Storage areas were inadequate for efficient access to records; some lacked even elemental fire protection.

To avoid uneconomical large-scale weeding operations, the appraisers had to accept or reject massive files of both temporary and permanent records. As the National Archives Building was empty, they could, in good conscience, lean heavily in the direction of conservation. They nevertheless deplored the state of records management and provided some counsel for reforms.

Enabling legislation authorized the Archivist of the United States to submit to Congress proposals by agencies for the destruction of specific bodies of noncurrent records that he deemed unworthy of permanent preservation by the federal government. The task of reviewing the proposals was delegated to the Special Examiners. The Deputy and Special Examiners thus gained considerable experience in past and current records management methods. While most agencies lacked any systematic control over their documentation, the departments of State, War, Navy, and the Treasury had developed classification schemes for some logical arrangement of their records. They had not yet devised rational systems for retiring or destroying records, though units with certain archival functions had been established.

With the start of World War II in 1939 the national archivists took an increasingly active role in advising agencies about reforms. They were especially effective in first the War and Navy departments and, later, in the war regulatory agencies. Some of the leading archivists actually transferred to records management positions in these agencies after they demonstrated how to organize files for more efficient access and how to rid files of records that were no longer needed for administrative purposes. They formed the nucleus of the records management profession that was to develop during and after the war.

These professional records managers worked in close association with their colleagues in the National Archives in developing efficient methods of providing for the orderly retirement of records. Together they successfully petitioned Congress in 1943 to authorize the National Archives to process agency recommendations for scheduling disposal of records after specific periods of time or after the occurrence of specific events. Two years later Congress authorized the National Archives itself to propose to Congress the disposal of records common to all or several agencies (General Records Schedules). The 1950's saw the emergence of the comprehensive records control schedule by means of which agencies or major subdivisions of agencies proposed the retirement of all of their records, either by disposal or by transfer to archives custody. In 1970 Congress transferred to its Administrator of General Services the authority to approve requests for disposal of records. The Administrator, in turn, delegated the responsibility to the Archivist of the United States.

**Growth of the Profession.** During this period, about 1943 to 1970, the records management profession expanded greatly its responsibility for generally controlling records and communication channels.

The Hoover Commission of 1948 gave considerable attention to efficient means for reducing the costs of managing records. It proposed centralizing responsibility for developing records management standards. Agencies

*A 1968 warehouse fire at the Oklahoma Department of Libraries challenged archivists with smoke and water damaged records. Separate leaves had to be dried, and records repacked for storage.*

Oklahoma Department of Libraries

would be required to appoint records management staffs to implement the standards. The recommendations led in 1950 to the incorporation of the National Archives into the National Archives and Records Service (NARS) within the newly established General Services Administration. NARS was delegated the centralized responsibility for records management recommended by the Commission.

This broad mandate led to the expansion of records management from simply developing filing techniques and retiring records to the management of mail, reports, forms, reprography, and correspondence. To facilitate records retirement NARS organized Regional Records Centers based upon agency-controlled centers established during World War II for the temporary storage of noncurrent records. While the records in the centers remained under the legal custody of the creating agencies, reference service and the destruction of disposable records were carried out by center personnel. The centers also facilitated transferring to the National Archives the records designated for permanent preservation.

As records managers and archivists became familiar with the rapidly changing technology for processing information, they promoted the use of various microfilm techniques and the use of electronic devices. They were thus in the forefront of the emerging information revolution. Some, in fact, are now designated information managers rather than paperwork or records managers.

Most of the information-oriented efforts of these managers concerned miniaturization of records. Roll microfilm had been the leading form of miniaturization for storage of records, but in the 1970's they experimented with and increasingly used microfiche and computer output microfilm (COM). Though there was an initial separation between managers of records and of automated equipment, some are cooperating to deal with the massive quantities of information in machine-readable form and in the resultant increases in hard copy documentation and printouts. Like other types of records, machine-readable records and their by-products are being scheduled for preservation or disposal.

These innovations had significant domestic and foreign spinoffs. The several states developed similar programs, and numerous foreign governments sent archivists and records managers to the United States to study techniques for managing current and noncurrent records. Most states and many foreign governments organized records centers, adapted to their special needs. The practice of scheduling the disposal of valueless records, as well as the transfer of permanent records to the archives, became common first in the industrialized nations and more recently in developing nations. Many private organizations, like businesses, labor unions, universities, and churches, have to a greater or lesser extent developed similar records management and archival programs.

For the most part, public archives in other countries and private institutions generally do not differentiate between records managers and archivists. There, records management is still limited largely to advising on file management and retirement methods. In most private institutions, on the one hand, the records managers serve as archivists to the degree that they store records that are deemed of sufficient value for preservation as long as the organization exists. In certain foreign countries, on the other hand, archivists have become directly involved in making decisions about the disposition of public records. The activity common to all these organizations, and which is now recognized as essential to efficient operations of agencies and for preservation of resources for research, is the retirement/disposition process whereby a valuable core of records is selected for permanent retention and the remainder is eventually destroyed.

**Appraisal.** In their initial experience in appraising records the founders of the National Archives benefitted to some extent by the theories and practices of senior archivists elsewhere. The Polish archivist who recommended scheduling as a retirement technique, Gustaw Kalenski, also wrote of a selection process based on the values of records for continuity in government and for scholarly and other research. German archivists emphasized records that are required as evidence of the origin and administration of major governmental activities (evidential values). Other records deserve preservation for secondary purposes, that is, for the information of substantial value they contain for studies about people, places, events, and things (informational values).

The Archivist of the state of Illinois in the 1930's, Margaret Cross Norton, stressed the legal value of certain records as an essential element in selecting records for permanent preservation. Her emphasis on legal values was a direct extension of Germanic concerns about evidential values of basic records. About the same time Sir Hilary Jenkinson, Keeper of the Public Record Office in London, averred that records must have remained in unbroken official custody to assure their legal and evidential values. He also asserted that archivists should not intervene in records management and that archives should simply accept or reject the noncurrent records offered by administrative agencies.

While these views were helpful in developing their appraisal policies, the archivists in the National Archives decided that new concepts were desirable or necessary. The long neglect of records had left them in a poor state, and the frequent alienation of important documentation led these archivists to the conclusion that unbroken custody was secondary to the need to bring valuable records under archival control. While they agreed that archivists are obligated to preserve records that document important governmental policies and decisions, they became more concerned about the value of records for research in history and the other humanities, the social sciences, and, to a lesser extent, the physical sciences. While the identification of records having evidential value for the history of governmental or private organizations is based on specific and concrete criteria, the appraisal of records for their informational values depends on subjective judgments about the likelihood of important research use of them in the future.

Records having evidential value may be classified, in the main, as follows: (1) those that show the origin and organization of agencies and their programs; (2) delegations of authority; (3) regulatory materials; (4) minutes of meetings and other records that document policy determinations; (5) documentation on the allocation of resources; and (6) selected records that deal with the procedures and the general administration of basic functions. It should be noted that these kinds of records can also be used for research on topics other than the history of the agency; for example, regulatory materials may provide valuable information about business operations, and policy records of the Department of State may be sources for research on foreign countries, as well as on U.S. relations with them.

Few concrete criteria for selecting records of informational value have evolved. Basically, archivists seek records containing unique data for research on important topics. Within reason, they should be convinced that researchers will eventually avail themselves of the records. Generally speaking, to judge informational values appraisal archivists must, by extensive study, master broad subject matter fields and familiarize themselves with related research needs and trends. In many countries they must have the concurrence of leading academicians before approving disposal.

While all records by their nature contain information of some evidential and informational value, (i.e., value, topics), more often than not, may be of such marginal interest that the costly preservation of the records involved is unwarranted. Furthermore, the preservation of records relating to minor subjects would so burden researchers as to impede research on significant ones. American and, increasingly, other archivists use aggregate techniques to deal with massive accumulations of records. They judge the values of each series or file on the basis of the total content. Among voluminous records on minor topics there may be some documents of interest. Seeking them would normally not be cost-effective, but records of certain agencies are so significant that an effort to find key documents is justified. In the case of large subject-classified central files, it is often possible to eliminate by class most housekeeping records and other papers that concern minor transactions.

A leading problem in appraisal involves decisions regarding voluminous case files, also known as dossiers in France and as single-instance files in England. Many such files contain unique information for demographic, social, economic, and genealogical research. For research other than that which requires data about all individuals, institutions, or places documented in the series, archivists have used sampling techniques. This methodology assumes that the preservation of significant, typical, or random case files will provide sufficient information on the most important research topics to which the series relates. For functionally significant programs that generate quite routine documentation in the form of case files, appraisers have authorized the retention of another type of sample—a procedural one consisting of only a few cases to illustrate the performance of program operations.

The information and computer revolution has greatly increased pressures on archivists for the preservation of source documents for social, economic, and political research. Before the widespread use of electronic media, detailed research about individuals, institutions, and phenomena generally in large numbers was impeded by the slowness and tedium of manual tabulations. But with computers, researchers can easily undertake the kind of research involving voluminous data that had not been envisioned during the early years of the 20th century.

Social and economic data of great variety are now being recorded in machine-readable form. The electronic media used for the purpose have the advantage of miniaturizing the information and of providing it to researchers in a mode susceptible of rapid, efficient manipulation. Evaluation of these media for permanent preservation, or disposal by erasure of the media, is conducted in Canada, Sweden, the United Kingdom, and the United States according to the same standards as for conventional records—that is, that records should have sufficient evidential or informational value to justify permanent retention.

**REFERENCES**


M. H. Fishbein, "Appraisal of Twentieth Century Records," *Illinois Libraries* (February 1970), explains to non-archivists the principles of appraisal.

Gustaw Kalenski, "Record Selection," *American Archivist* (January 1976), edited by M. H. Fishbein, from *Archivwum Dawynch* (1934), a seminal essay by a Polish archivist.

P. Lewinson, "Archival Sampling," *American Archivist* (October 1957), the first and still best explanation of sampling techniques.

Thornton W. Mitchell; editor, *Norton on Archives: The Writings of Margaret Cross Norton on Archival and Records Management* (1975), includes two essays that explain the administrative and legal values of archives and the role of records managers in retiring records.

Theodore R. Schellenberg, *The Appraisal of Modern Records,* National Archives Bulletin No. 8 (1956), the standard archival text on appraisal principles and techniques.


MEYER H. FISHBEIN

## INTERNAL PROCESSING: ARRANGEMENT AND DESCRIPTION

The theory and practice of archival arrangement and description are of relatively recent origin. Historically, neither the volume, complexity, nor use of archives posed particular problems for either their custodians or their users. When no longer needed for the conduct of current business, most older documents, such as charters or treaties, were maintained in a basic chronological arrangement, while other noncurrent records, such as accounts and correspondence, tended to be maintained in the order in which they were transferred to the treasuries and strong-rooms that served as archival repositories. Archives were conceived of primarily as "arsenals of law" for their parent institutions, and no general principles were needed to govern their arrangement.

During the 18th century, however, the holdings of archival repositories were subjected to a variety of reorganizations. In accordance with the predominant ideas of the Age of Reason, the merits of chronological, subject matter, and geographical arrangement of all documents were vigorously debated, and archives were frequently rearranged with no regard for their organic structure or functional relationships. With the development of the historical sciences, archives had come to be regarded primarily as "arsenals of history," and their custodians, intending to facilitate their use for historical research, adopted various schemes derived chiefly from library experience. Individual dossiers and documents were removed from the series in which they had originally been filed as part of administrative transactions (and for which they furnished the evidence) and were artificially rearranged, usually under specific subject headings.

The results of this policy were disastrous for many archives. The removal of documents and files from the organizational and functional context in which they were created or received, and from the administrative context in which they had been maintained and used, not only obscured or compromised the official and legal character of the records but also destroyed the context necessary for their evaluation and effective use as historical sources. In addition, such rearrangement rendered useless or seriously impaired the value of already existing finding aids, such as indexes and lists, and required that the archival repository undertake the expensive and time-consuming preparation of new and detailed classification schemes and indexes in order to locate and retrieve the incidental subject content that was the focus of many of the new systems. During the last half of the 19th century, however, the unfortunate consequences of artificial subject arrangement, as well as the development of a fuller understanding of the nature and character of archives, led to the formulation of the two basic principles that today are universally recognized as the sole appropriate basis for the arrangement of archives: the principle of provenance, or "respect des fonds," and the principle of respect for original order, or the "registry princple." (See *Archives:* "Archives: Nature, Purposes, Principles" for definitions of these principles.)

**Arrangement.** Because the arrangement and description of archives are so closely related to the administrative structures and procedures and the record-keeping systems of the institutions in which they originated, and because these vary so greatly from country to country and historically within the same country, even a brief account for each country would require a treatise far beyond the scope of this article. The following summary is therefore limited to current arrangement/description practice in the United States and, to a lesser extent, in Canada.

*The Record Group.* In modern archival practice the function of arrangement refers to the process and the results of organizing archives in accordance with the principle of provenance and the principle of respect for original order at as many as necessary of the following levels: repository, record group (or comparable control unit), subgroup(s), series, file unit, and document. The process is intended to achieve physical (or administrative) control and basic identification of the total holdings of a repository, and usually also includes the packing of arranged archives into containers and the labeling and shelving of the containers. This summary of the function assumes a general archival repository that receives the permanently valuable noncurrent records of many different administrative units or offices of a parent institution, for example, a government. Although hierarchically the repository level precedes the record group level, in practice the record group level must be given priority in arrangement. The process then proceeds from the repository level down to the individual item or document level.

Arrangement at the record group level consists of allocating new accessions of records on the basis of provenance to existing record groups, or (upon accession transformed into archives) related by their provenance. However, in establishing a record group, the concept of provenance, though fundamental, may be modified by other pragmatic considerations, particularly the administrative history, the complexity, and the volume of the records involved. In the U.S. National Archives, for example, all archives of the Department of State, on the grounds of common provenance, could theoretically be established as a single record group, but their considerable volume and complexity would serve to impede effective arrangement, description, and reference service. Thus these records have been divided into a number of record groups generally corresponding to the former bureaus of the Department, which exercised considerable autonomy in their operations. The records of the office of the head of the Department, the records of other units concerned with matters such as finance and personnel that affected the Department as a whole, and, in some cases, the records of predecessor agencies that had been incorporated into central files are then usually allocated to a separate "general" record group for the entire Department.

A further modification of the record group concept is the "collective" record group. To avoid creating an unmanageable number of record groups, the records of a number of small or short-lived, though separate, agencies that have an administrative or functional relationship (such as records of district courts or claims commissions) are assigned to a single record group. Within such a record group the records of each constituent agency form a separate and distinct subgroup. Under the record group concept, any particular body of records can belong to only one record group, and except for subgroups or series consisting predominantly of cartographic, audiovisual, machine-readable, or other special physical types, an effort is made to keep together in the stack areas all records belonging to the same record group.

The value and flexibility of the record group concept have been demonstrated by its adaptation not only to the complex archives of governments at every level and for every period, but also to the archives of a wide range of private institutions and organizations and to the holdings of manuscript repositories, including artificially constituted collections (those that did not grow organically, as do archives in the true sense). Although broadly defined, the concept, when consistently applied, enables a repository to establish effective control over documentary materials of every type received from many different agencies, offices, and other sources.

*The Repository*. Once a decision has been made at the record group level, the records constituting that group are then allocated to an appropriate custodial unit for placement within the stacks of the repository. This is arrangement at the repository level, which necessarily will vary with the type of repository, and within the same repository, with the growth in the volume and character of its holdings. Allocation of record groups to custodial units may be made initially on the basis of a distinction between public records and nonpublic manuscripts (including personal papers), or it may be based, in a public repository, upon broad functional or hierarchical divisions. Legislative and judicial archives are frequently maintained separately from those of executive agencies; diplomatic and military archives are frequently maintained as separate units; and county and municipal record groups are generally separate from the records of state agencies in a state archival repository. Another basic division may be made between "open" and "closed" record groups, the latter consisting of the records of discontinued agencies to which no further accessions are expected. As indicated above, separate custodial units are generally established for significant holdings of cartographic, audiovisual, and machine-readable records. Other basic considerations that play a part in arrangement at the repository level include the size and physical layout of the stack areas, the number and type of personnel needed to work with certain bodies of records, the degree of security required for particular holdings, and the character and frequency of reference and research use of certain record groups.

*Subgroups*. The third level of arrangement is that of subgroups within each record group. The subgroup concept is intended to distinguish between and to control the records of all primary subordinate offices or other administrative units that together constitute the record group, including any records of predecessor agencies. Each subgroup, in turn, is divided into as many levels as are necessary to accommodate the successive subordinate organizational units that make up the administrative hierarchy of the subgroup. For example, a bureau may be divided into divisions, each of which has several branches, each of which has several sections, etc. The typical arrangement of subgroups is thus bv administrative structure—the hierarchy of the offices of origin of the records—but where successive reorganizations or the consolidation of records series between offices obscures hierarchical origins, subgroups, and subordinate levels therein may be established in terms of functional, geographical, or chronological relationships, or, if necessary, on the basis of the physical forms of the records.

*The Series*. Arrangement at the series level then takes place within the framework of subgroups within each record group. A series in the archival sense consists of documents in file units that normally are already structured or arranged, by the office that originated, maintained, and used them, in accordance with a filing system, or that were otherwise maintained as a collective unit by that office because they relate to a particular function or subject, result from the same activity, have a particular form, or because of some other unifying relationship arising out of their creation, receipt, or use. Their hierarchical provenance ordinarily determines the specific subgroups within which series are included, but in cases where subgroups have been formed on nonhierarchical bases (see above), the subgroup position of affected series varies accordingly. Since modern decentralized record-keeping systems do not establish a set order of series within agencies or their individual offices, the archivist, on the basis of study of the administrative history, structure, and functions of the institution concerned, and also on the basis of study of the records themselves, must give to the series a meaningful physical order within the subgroup structure.

There is thus no one perfect or correct arrangement sequence for all series, but generally within each subgroup level, series relating to policy formulation and program direction are placed before series documenting program execution, and series of program or substantive records are placed before series of housekeeping or facilitative records. Particular attention is given to the functions of the organization corresponding to the subgroup: as far as possible the series are grouped according to the logical order of those functions and, with respect to each function, according to the logical sequence of actions taken to carry it out. However, regarding older records, which tend to provide more centralized and general coverage of the organization's functions and actions, it may be necessary to group and arrange series in accordance with major breaks in the filing system or according to chronological periods. In each case agency-created indexes or other finding aids are placed close to and usually precede the series to which they apply. Arrangement at the series level is thus intended to facilitate the use of archives while at the same time preserving their integrity within the organizational and functional context out of which they emerged.

*File Units.* Once the series have been arranged within the subgroup structure of a particular record group, arrangement then proceeds to the file unit level. Since most series are already arranged in accordance with filing systems used by the originating agencies, arrangement at this level usually consists of simply verifying the correct placement of each file unit within that system and of correcting obvious misfiles. Only where there is no original arrangement, or where it has been irretrievably lost, or where it cannot be reconstructed without an excessive expenditure of time, is the archivist justified in imposing a new internal arrangement on the series, and in such cases a full explanation of what has been done and the reasons for it should be included in the appropriate finding aid to inform and assist the users of the records.

*Documents.* The final level of arrangement is the document level. This involves the checking, and the correction of their placement when necessary, of the individual documents, enclosures, and annexes, and of the individual pieces of paper making up multipage documents, that collectively constitute the file unit. Because of the volume of modern archives, arrangement at this level remains an ideal rather than actual practice in most major repositories. It is a necessary preliminary, however, for series involved in microfilming or other photoduplication.

The above summary of the sequence of actions involved in arrangement eventually culminates in the transfer of the records from temporary to permanent containers, which are then labeled with the designations of the appropriate record group, subgroups, series, and contents, and finally are shelved. Control down to at least the series level must first be achieved before descriptive work is possible, since finding aids must refer to specific units in an established arrangement and the series is the basic unit of description.

**Description.** The theory and practice of archival description—the process of establishing intellectual control over holdings through the preparation of what are collectively called finding aids—is less developed than that of arrangement. In addition to the finding aids prepared for their own use by the offices of origin—which are properly part of the records and are accessioned and maintained with them—archival repositories produce a wide variety of published and unpublished finding aids that exhibit a lack of general agreement on either terminology or descriptive methodology. Published finding aids generally include guides and catalogues, inventories and registers, special lists, calendars, and indexes. In addition to such published finding aids most archival repositories also prepare unpublished checklists, accession and location registers, and box and shelf lists. Finally, there are appraisal reports, record and manuscript group registration statements, and, for machine-readable records, software documentation, which serve incidentally as finding aids. In recent years, however, there has been a trend toward the development of three basic types of published finding aids in which an increasing uniformity of descriptive practice may be discerned. The three types are inventories (registers for manuscript groups and collections), guides, and what may be called detailed lists.

*Inventories.* Just as the record group level provides the critical key to the collective arrangement of archives, the inventory is the basic finding aid in their collective description. An inventory is prepared for each record group, or major subgroup thereof, in which the unit of entry is the series. An introduction defines the limits of the record group and provides a general description of the structure and functions of the agencies and offices whose records are involved and of the characteristics and general contents of the records themselves. The body of the inventory or register consists of individual series entries organized within the framework of the subgroups within the record group. Since the terms used by offices of origin to identify their "files" are usually meaningless to anyone outside that office, archivists must devise series titles that not only are unique but will also convey the maximum information to the user about the type of records that constitute the series, the functions and activities they reflect or to which they relate, the inclusive dates within which the series was created, and its quantity. Under each series title there is usually a brief descriptive paragraph that indicates the arrangement of the constituent file units, any gaps in the series, further details of importance on the functions and activities that produced or are documented by the series, an indication of the major subject content of the records, and an indication of any restrictions on access and use. Inventories and registers frequently include in an appendix indexes, lists, or file titles or headings relating to particular series that would facilitate their use.

*Guides.* When holdings have been placed under basic intellectual control through a series of inventories or registers, the repository is then in a position to prepare and publish a general guide to its holdings. Such a guide reflects arrangement at the repository level, and the basic unit of entry is the record group. The administrative history, structure, and functions of the particular agency that corresponds to each record group are summarized, and the records that constitute the record group are collectively characterized in terms of physical types and forms, inclusive dates, quantity, and general subject content. Emphasis is also placed on organizational and functional relationships between record groups in order to provide a general orientation to the scope and character of the total holdings of the repository. For the same reason attention is directed to any restrictions on access or use of the records, and the entries also contain bibliographical data on published finding aids and relevant documentary or other publications.

In addition to repository guides, the term *guide* is also used to refer to finding aids that describe the holdings of one or more repositories relating to a particular geographical region, chronological period, or historical event, or to holdings of a particular physical type, such as cartographic or audiovisual. Although they are also called guides, finding aids that briefly describe the holdings of all repositories on the national, regional, or state level might more appropriately be termed directories.

*Detailed Lists.* The third type of finding aid, detailed lists of various kinds such as catalogues, calendars, and indexes, is usually prepared for records whose historical significance or research value and use justify the time and expense involved in their preparation. They may describe individual file units or documents from more than one record group, subgroup, or series that relate to particular subjects, but they are usually confined to the contents of single series or subseries. Such detailed lists are of particular value in assisting users of series whose original arrangement is unknown or that lacked any original arrangement. It should be noted, however, that microfilm publication has largely superseded the calendaring of archives.

As in the arrangement of archives, the principle of provenance remains the basis for all archival descriptive work. Faced with the wealth of major and peripheral subject content in modern public and institutional archives, obviously unable to foresee all future research trends and interests, and lacking the staff and budget necessary to create special subject-oriented finding aids to serve even the present range of research interests, the archivist places primary reliance and emphasis upon the structure and functions of the creating agencies in the closely related tasks of collectively arranging and describing archival holdings. In so doing he preserves the integrity of archives and protects their official and legal character. He also makes it possible for any present or future researcher on any subject to use archives effectively, because the experience of both archival repositories and users attests that knowledge of the organization and functions of their originating agencies serves as the best guide to the widely varied subject content of archives.

**REFERENCES**

Frank B. Evans, "Modern Methods of Arrangement of Archives in the United States," *American Archivist* (1966).

David B. Gracy II, *Archives and Manuscripts: Arrangement and Description* (1977).

Oliver W. Holmes, "Archival Arrangement—Five Different Operations at Five Different Levels," *American Archivist* (1964).

National Archives, *The Control of Records at the Record Group Level,* Staff Information Circular 15 (1950).

———, *The Preparation of Preliminary Inventories,* Staff Information Circular 14 (1950).

T. R. Schellenberg, *The Management of Archives* (1965).

———, *Principles of Arrangement,* Staff Information Paper 18 (1951).

FRANK B. EVANS

SERVICES TO USERS

**Types of Service.** The fundamental purpose of archival work is to preserve permanently valuable records and make them available for use. Together, the activities involved in providing access to records constitute the archival institution's reference service, which consists of furnishing records for use in search rooms, providing information from or concerning records, making copies of records, lending records to certain users, and exhibiting records. Complementing these direct reference services is the provision of indirect access by means of documentary publication.

*Search Rooms.* In the search rooms of archival repositories, which are analogous to library "reading rooms," inquirers are able to examine records under the supervision of repository staff members. The inquirers are usually asked to complete an identification form giving their names and addresses and the purposes of their examination of the records. If necessary, repository personnel can advise inquirers about records that seem pertinent to their research, and explain to them how the records are arranged, and what guides, inventories, lists, or other finding aids are available. They can also make recommendations concerning information that should be included in footnotes or other references to records being examined, and indicate what facilities exist for reproduction of records. Search room regulations governing the use of records typically require that their arrangement be left undisturbed; that they not be mutilated or destroyed by improper handling; that users avoid any actions likely to damage them, such as smoking, eating, or drinking; and that they be returned to search room attendants after their use. There are also regulations to prevent theft of records by requiring examination of objects carried out of the search room. These security measures, however, are often accompanied by increasingly liberal arrangements for the use of search room facilities during hours when repository stack areas are closed.

*Information Services.* On a limited basis, archivists provide information from the records in response to written and oral inquiries. They often furnish specific facts, such as the date or place of an event and the names of principal participants. More extensive information may be furnished for administrative and legal purposes to the agencies that created the records and as a courtesy to high-ranking public officials. Efforts are made to keep written replies reasonably concise and responsive to the inquiries, and replies to recurrent types of inquiries are often made by form letters or by use of standard wording.

Information about records may also be provided orally or in writing, and inquirers are encouraged to seek such information before visiting archival search rooms. If their requests involve consultation of large bodies of records, they are informed of the titles of the pertinent record groups or other subdivisions of the records and of the inclusive dates and quantities thereof. Often such information can be furnished by supplying copies of published finding aids or reproductions of pertinent pages of finding aids. Archivists may feel obliged to furnish more information to inquirers engaged in major research that will be useful to the general public. In supplying any information from or concerning records they strive to make factual statements and to avoid interpretation.

*Copying.* Photoreproduction has increasingly expanded the availability of records for research and other uses. Reproduction services often make it unnecessary for archivists to cull information from records and for inquirers to transcribe or take detailed notes on them. These services generally provide electrostatic, photostatic, or microphotographic copies of records at nominal cost. Electrostatic and photostatic methods are especially useful for furnishing full-size paper copies and reproducing selected records from scattered file locations. Such copies offer advantages in that they can be easily read; arranged, like research notes, in various ways; and examined together with related sources of information. Photographic and diazo prints of nontextual (i.e., other than conventional paper documents) records are also furnished by an increasing number of archival repositories. Microphotography is generally preferred and used for the reproduction of a great quantity of records arranged in sequence. This process produces copies that are less expensive per item than full-size paper copies and have the great advantage of compactness. Such copies, however, require the use of reading devices. In recent years copies of sound recordings and machine-readable records are increasingly being made, in keeping with the growth of these forms among archival holdings.

In the United States the copyright status of records, as defined under the Copyright Law of 1976, determines whether or how copies of them can be made in reference service. Records of the U.S. government, with some exceptions, have no copyright protection and can be freely reproduced by archival repositories. Such reproductions can also be authenticated, if required. Copyrighted materials that have found their way into the custody of public repositories can be reproduced in limited quantities for research purposes, provided there is no contrary agreement with the copyright holders. Such copies must carry a notice of the copyright status of the originals. This arrangement is supported by the accepted legal rule of "fair use," whereby certain uses are not considered an infringement of copyright.

*Lending.* The lending of records by archival repositories takes place only under special circumstances. Normally it occurs when organizations that created the records, or their successors, need them for administrative or legal purposes or exceptionally when such organizations give related organizations official permission to use them. Regulations usually provide that requests for loans be made only by specific officials of the creating organization, and for relatively short periods. Archivists oppose the lending of records in fragile condition and normally, in such cases, will provide photocopies instead. Records in public archival repositories may be lent to nongovernment organizations for exhibit purposes only under what are considered to be fully protective conditions. Loans are not made to individuals outside of repositories. Some American state archival agencies have established a network of regional archival repositories, usually at state universities, where state records may be sent on loan to be used for research purposes. Archival loans are also made in response to subpoenas but, as far as possible, certified photocopies are furnished instead.

*Exhibits.* Exhibiting records is still another way of making them available to users. Archival repositories plan both long-term and short-term exhibits as an important part of their public "outreach" programs. The National Archives Building in Washington, for example, has on permanent display the three fundamental charters of the United States, the Declaration of Independence, the Constitution, and its first ten amendments (Bill of Rights). This repository also mounts temporary exhibits, celebrating the anniversary of historical events in American history or documenting unusual national or international developments. In general, exhibits enable archival institutions to publicize their holdings and develop popular appreciation of historical records as cultural resources.

Documentary publication is an extension of reference service because it disseminates in published form a part of the holdings of archival institutions. Originally, publication was by letterpress exclusively, the contents consisting of documents of importance selected from larger bodies of archives or manuscripts. Since World War II there has developed the concept of complete publication of these larger bodies in order to preclude the danger of subjectivity in selection. A concomitant development has been the adoption of microfilming as an alternative, and far less costly, means of publication by the national archives of such countries as the U.S., Canada, the U.K., and Spain. Microfilm publication involves the preparation of a master negative microcopy of the concerned body of records, usually a series, within which is incorporated an extensive editorial apparatus analogous to that to be found in the conventional letterpress publication. Upon receipt of orders, positive prints are run off. In recent decades it has been U.S. National Archives policy to publish by microfilm all of the principal series in its custody for worldwide sale through a periodically updated catalogue.

**Policies Governing Service.** The use of records in the several types of archival reference service described above is controlled by access policies that vary nationally and, to some extent, within nations. As indicated in *Archives: Legislative Foundations,* p. , the basic closed period has been considerably reduced over the years to the current level of 30 to 50 years. For this development much credit is due to the International Council on Archives, whose 1966 and 1968 Congresses in particular made strong recommendations for such liberalization of access. Also under the stimulus of ICA, archivists in many countries are working to ensure access for foreigners on equal terms with nationals.

In making records available to a growing variety of users, archivists must consider two competing rights: the right to know and the right to privacy. In the United States the first right is protected by a national Freedom of Information Act (1966, amended in 1974), which provides free public access to information in the records of federal executive agencies except for specified categories exempted from disclosure, primarily relating to national defense and foreign policy secrets, confidential commercial and financial data, investigations, personal affairs, and other matters specifically restricted by law.

Similarly, Canadian national government records more than 30 years old are open to the public unless they fall into specifically exempted areas, such as records whose release would constitute a breach of faith with a foreign government, be contrary to law, violate individual privacy, or be harmful to national security. The 30-year rule for access to public records has also been adopted in Great Britain, with exempted records similar to those in Canada. Many U.S. states have enacted "sunshine" or open record laws, which make information in state records more liberally available to the public.

The Federal Privacy Act of 1974 limits access to records relating to individuals in the federal agencies generally but does not apply to the holdings of the National Archives. However, with respect to the latter, the right of privacy is upheld by certain of the exempted categories in the Freedom of Information Act, as well as restrictions imposed by the Archivist of the United States. These restrictions deny general access to records less than 75 years old containing information concerning the physical or mental health or medical or psychiatric treatment of individuals and records concerning investigations of persons or groups of persons by investigative authorities of the federal executive branch. Efforts to protect privacy are also being made by archivists in administering nonfederal records containing personal data on such matters as medical treatment, legal representation, labor management relations, and welfare benefits. Similar concern for protection of privacy is evident in regulations of the Public Record Office of Great Britain, which restrict access to certain records less than 75 years old, such as land revenue records concerning confidential transactions with private individuals and certain classes of police records. Also exemplifying this concern is the regulation of the Public Archives of Canada providing that personnel records may be used for research only 90 years after the birth of the individual involved.

**Trends in Service.** Archival reference service makes records available for several principal purposes. For the creators of the records, or their successors, it furnishes information needed to show administrative or legal precedents and fiscal accountability. For citizens it provides

*A doctoral dissertation takes shape as a graduate student works with manuscript materials.*

Texas State Library, Archives Division

documentary evidence often essential for the protection of various rights. For the researcher, official and academic alike, it supplies data extensively used in all branches of learning—traditionally history and the other humanities; increasingly the social sciences; and, to a more limited extent, the physical sciences as well. Reference for these purposes constitutes by far the greatest part of all reference service, and the records involved are preponderantly in the custody of public archival institutions.

These government sources have long been used in the writing of political, diplomatic, and military history, since they were early recognized as basic for the purpose. As government functions and activities have expanded, especially in the 20th century, in various ways that touch closely the day-to-day life of the people and the operations of the national economy, government records have become more highly valued and more greatly used for research not only in social and economic history but also in political science, economics, sociology, anthropology, geography, and other social sciences. These studies have in recent decades been facilitated by the development of automation and automated records processes, symbolized by the computer and the machine-readable record. Increased use of public records has also been stimulated in recent years by mass media presentations of genealogical subjects, such as Alex Haley's *Roots* (1976), emphasizing the value of these records as sources for personal and family history.

Reference service in nongovernment archival repositories also supports important research. In such repositories records of educational, religious, business, labor, professional, civic, and other organizations are being relied upon increasingly for social scientific studies (of, for example, intellectual trends, population characteristics, urban and industrial life, and humanitarian causes) in a way similar to the expanded and unconventional use of public records today.

Archival repositories customarily maintain certain statistics on the quantity and performance of reference service. In providing records to the search room, on loan, for reproduction, or for exhibit, the unit employed for reporting purposes is an item such as a single document, folder, bound volume, roll of microfilm, or archival container. In furnishing written information from or concerning records, the unit is the transmitting letter or report. In supplying oral information the unit is the telephone call or personal conference. In most archival repositories statistics of reference service tend to show increases year after year. At the U.S. National Archives, for example, since about 1940 total units of reference service have increased annually from a few thousand to more than 2,000,000. The increases result largely from expanded and diversified holdings of repositories, liberalization of access to them, and publicity given to their subject matter and value by publications, archives-sponsored scholarly conferences, and other informational methods. This trend seems likely to continue, since there is a growing appreciation of archives not only as cultural resources but also as major components of national and international information systems.

**REFERENCES**

Robert L. Clark, Jr., editor, *Archive-Library Relations* (1976), a seminal work dealing with the joint interests of the library and archival professions; includes treatment of these interests in reference service and in handling issues of copyright, literary property rights, and access.

Sue E. Holbert, *Archives and Manuscripts: Reference and Access* (1977), a publication in the "basic" manual series" of the Society of American Archivists explaining principles and practices in providing access to records and manuscripts, types of reference service, and legal problems in access and use of these materials; especially useful for archivists in small and medium-size repositories.

Ernst Posner, *American State Archives* (1964), a critical survey of practices in American state archival repositories that includes a brief description of prevailing reference service activities and recommendation of desirable standards in these activities.

Alfred Wagner, "The Policy of Access to Archives: From Restriction to Liberalization," *Unesco Bulletin for Libraries* (1970), a useful historical summary of access policies followed by public archives in the western world with special attention to the efforts of the International Council on Archives since 1966 to liberalize these policies.

HAROLD T. PINKETT

TECHNICAL ASPECTS

The technical aspects of archives administration help to fulfill the main obligation of the archivist: to preserve, for posterity, archival material and to make it available for use by the administration, by the scientific community, and by the public. These aspects are necessarily based on the nature of archival materials and on the functions served by archives. Archival materials—stores of information now predominantly recorded on paper—accumulate, organically, within an administration or other organization as a by-product of its activities. Consequently documents are physically heterogeneous and exist either uniquely or in only a few copies each. Unlike modern books issued in planned editions and prepared by professionals, documents accumulate over time with little control over their physically diverse properties. Moreover, the modern media increasingly introduced by administrations, such as the various audiovisual forms and the magnetic tapes associated with automated data processing (ADP), bring about even greater diversity.

Archives must serve their parent administrations as well as the scholarly and general publics, and thus have to absorb materials for both their administrative and legal values on the one hand and their informational values on the other. Since materials possessing such values are being created constantly and must be preserved permanently by archival institutions, the potential for the latter's physical expansion is unlimited.

The uniqueness of records, the diversity of forms, the duties to the administration and the public, and the unlimited growth—all leave their mark on the technical aspects of the profession and particularly on archival buildings and facilities, conservation of materials, microphotography, and automation.

**Archival Buildings and Equipment.** The need to provide suitable housing for archives has played an important role in the establishment and design of archival buildings. This need is evident in the report of the parliamentary committee of 1836 in Britain as well as in the discussions leading to the establishment of the U.S. National Archives in 1934. The main purposes of an archival building are: to provide safe storage for an ever-increasing amount of valuable material, to keep the material indefinitely, and to make it available for use.

Safety and security considerations, as well as the prospect of unlimited growth, have in the 20th century led to a clear-cut separation between storage space and public reading rooms. Modern archives should be planned with an eye to expansion or decentralization. The need for expansion as well as the high cost of urban properties tends to drive archives to the urban periphery (as in the case of the Public Record Office in Britain). The developed countries may have to choose between separating the urban service areas from the extraurban storage areas and decentralizing the archives themselves. In both cases, transportation and communication problems will have to be solved.

Storage specifications are dictated by the need to store vast amounts of material and to protect it from damage, natural or man-caused. In some countries the tendency is to build underground storage facilities, probably as a result of World War II experience (e.g., the Riksarkivet in Oslo and the National Archives in Tokyo). This necessitates artificial lighting and air conditioning and thus larger expenditure. It also makes construction dependent on soil conditions. In other countries construction is both above and below ground. Some of the underground specifications are also applicable to above-ground construction, namely artificial lighting and climate control.

It is now widely recognized that control of temperature, humidity, and radiation is most important for inhibiting deterioration due to factors inherent in the documents, while filtering of the air is necessary to protect against pollution. Temperatures of 10°–14° C and 40 percent relative humidity are believed to be optimal conditions for most kinds of archival material. These conditions are, however, unsuitable for humans, and material kept under these conditions has to be preconditioned before it is transferred to reading-room environments. The accepted compromise is, therefore, 18°–20° C and about 50 percent relative humidity. Dust, aerosol, and hydrosol filtering should be introduced in most regions. In some countries, mostly tropical, the air-conditioning systems are used for fumigation. Light should be free from ultraviolet rays, since they are harmful to paper (and to other polymers). The issue of incandescent versus fluorescent lighting is still undecided; safety and economy of both are still under discussion.

Fire protection is a cardinal problem of planning. To facilitate isolation of fires and to enhance asphyxiation, storage areas are divided into compartments no larger than 200 square meters (about 2,000 square feet) and no higher than 2.4 meters (about 8 feet). Electrical wiring, switches, and outlets should be reinforced (the European term is "Panzer"); metal fuse boards with automatic fuses are preferable. Fire detection and alarm systems are considered essential, and a direct alarm connection to a fire station is desirable. Water-sprinkler extinguishing systems are not recommended since water may cause considerable damage to archival material. Automatic extinguishing systems employing nontoxic gases, aerosols, and hydrosols (Freon, BCF, etc.) are gradually being introduced.

Efficient use of storage space leads to rectangular compartments with shelves usually running parallel to the long side of the rectangle. Internal planning depends on shelf size and aisle size. Though bodies of archives are heterogeneous, and many still consist of large series of bound volumes in various sizes, most modern archival material is loose and boxed in containers, usually of standard cardboard, corrugated cardboard, and lately of plastics. The size of such containers varies, ranging from about 30 by 40 by 28 centimeters (about 12 by 16 by 10 inches, or a volume of about 1 cubic foot) to one-third that amount. This requires a shelf size of around 80 centimeters (32 inches) deep and a length of some multiple of 35 centimeters (13 inches). Aisle width runs from 80 centimeters for side aisles to 100 centimeters (3 feet) for main aisles. Mobile stacks or compact stacks (known as "compactus") are becoming widely used, and although they are considerably more expensive than stationary shelves, they save space up to almost 50 percent. Floor load is around 700 kilograms per square meter (145 pounds per square foot) for stationary stacks and as high as 1,000 kilograms per square meter (about 200 pounds per square foot) for mobile or compact stacks. All shelving nowadays is metal and is rustfree or properly protected.

Since archival materials sometimes include extremely valuable documents and classified papers, most institutions therefore have vaults for protection against fire and theft. The large amounts of nonpaper documentation, such as tapes, films, microforms, and sound recordings, call for metal cans, small boxes, racks, air conditioning, and other special facilities.

Many archival institutions place documents on exhibition. This poses the specially complex problem of preserving documents while making them accessible to the public. One of the most elaborately protected exhibits is the American Declaration of Independence and the Constitution at the National Archives in Washington; it is displayed in a case that is simultaneously a vault and an elevator.

While reading rooms (also known as "search" rooms) in archives are not essentially different from those in libraries, they have certain requirements of their own: readers' desks should be large enough to accommodate archives and records; special research rooms for researchers working on long-term projects are needed; more room for micro-readers is required; and space for playing sound recordings and for viewing films should be provided. Appropriate facilities must eventually be made available for use of the growing accumulation of machine-readable records on magnetic tapes.

Record centers, an American invention of the late 1940's, are, in their essence, physically similar to archives buildings. However, they are generally smaller than the latter because they do not require as much reading room space and, given their function of accepting materials for limited periods only, are not meant to expand indefinitely. A typical feature of record centers is the loading platform needed for receiving (and sending out) large consignments of records. Adjacent to the loading platforms are usually rooms for the cleaning and fumigation, the primary arrangement, and the boxing and labeling of records. These features have all been inherited from the modern archives building.

**Conservation of Archival Material.** Conservation comprises *preservation,* preventive measures, and *restoration,* remedial measures. Preservation starts with the arrival of records at the archives. Unlike books, usually bought in new condition, records are deposited in the archives after years of frequent handling. Preliminary treatment (dry cleaning and fumigation) is necessary before transferring them to the stacks. Other preventive measures have been discussed above.

Document conservation presents some problems not encountered in book conservation. For instance, black printing ink, used in books, has remained virtually unchanged since the invention of printing. Documents, on the other hand, were first written with india ink (similar in stability to printing ink), then with ferrous ink—a stable material whose acidity, however, weakened the paper and even corroded it. The 20th century brought unstable and washable fountain-pen inks, and in the 1940's the ball-point pen was introduced. The typewriter (patented in 1714 and put on the market in 1874) and carbon paper produced additional forms of unstable writing found in documents. Other features contributing to the problems of documentary conservation are paper clips, seals, and rubber stamps and the most recent nuisance, adhesive tapes used for repairs.

In the 1930's the process of silking (to prevent documentary damage or to stabilize it once it has occurred) gave way to lamination by cellulose acetate, first practiced on a large scale by the U.S. National Archives. Yellowing and brittleness of the first laminates led to William J. Barrow's work, which resulted in the recognition of the importance of paper acidity and the necessity of deacidification. In the 1950's polyethylene was introduced for lamination in Eastern Europe, and in the 1960's Kathpalia initiated "cold lamination" (by cellulose acetate and acetone) in India. Lamination raised the problem of the reversibility of restoration where required. It is still a controversial issue, as are some new techniques that have been developed, such as encapsulation, introduced in the 1970's.

The vulnerability of modern inks encouraged research into nonaqueous deacidification, such as Bains-Cope's barium hydroxide in methanol. Gaseous deacidification by ammonia has been practiced in Germany since the 1950's but is not widely accepted since it is considered unstable. Various vapor-phase-deacidification methods have been rejected, either because of unsatisfactory results or because of toxicity (e.g., cyclohexilamine-carbonate). While experimentation goes on, the important problem of nonliquid deacidification has not yet been solved satisfactorily.

Paper casting, introduced in the 1960's, is not suitable for documents with unstable inks. The only way to reduce damage to ink is to fix it, the most popular fixer being soluble nylon sprayed on the document. The results of such fixing, however, are not altogether satisfactory.

The International Council on Archives, through its Conservation Committee, is trying to set standards for archival conservation and to help train archival conservators.

**Microphotography.** Microphotography is used in archives for a number of purposes: (1) Security copies: copying of the most valuable documents to insure against loss or destruction. These copies are usually deposited in vaults, preferably separate from the main storage area. (2) Supplementary material: copying records in other custody, mainly in foreign countries, of interest to the copying institution; this is especially important for countries formerly under colonial rule. (3) Publication: microphotography is considered, nowadays, the cheapest way to publish documents, especially in limited editions (see Archives: Reference Services). (4) Preservation: microcopies of documents in bad physical condition are substituted in reference service for the originals, thus protecting the originals from further damage.

Microforms present special preservation problems. The silver halide films, although the most durable of photographic materials (if properly processed), are not durable enough on the archival time-scale; periodic film-to-film copying is considered essential for long-term preservation until more lasting materials are introduced. Past problems concerning the admissibility of microcopies as legal evidence of the existence of the originals have been solved in most countries.

The earlier notion that microphotography automatically solves archival space problems, once widely believed, is now regarded more skeptically since the cost of filming is often greater than that of storing the originals, even for a long period.

The International Council on Archives' Microfilm Committee is concerned with the archival aspects of microfilming and publishes a bulletin on the subject.

**Computers and Archives.** Archives are affected by the "electronic revolution" in two ways. Being themselves information systems, archives first use the new tool for more efficient information retrieval. Many archives employ automated techniques for the registration and indexing of archival material, though on-line systems are still rare in archives' reading rooms.

Second, since automation has penetrated into administration, records are increasingly kept on magnetic media, and archives have to preserve the valuable part of such records. Machine-readable archives present some serious problems—tapes are extremely unstable, and even when kept under optimal conditions (i.e., complete environmental control, dust control, and protection from magnetic fields), they do not last more than about 15 years. Regular recopying procedures are therefore essential. It is hoped that Computer Output Microfilm (COM) and Computer Input Microfilm (CIM) may ease the problem to some extent.

In order to make effective use of the magnetic media, it is necessary to preserve, together with them, the complete documentation associated with their creation. The International Council on Archives Committee is guiding archivists in these subjects by conducting seminars, publishing manuals, and issuing a bulletin.

**REFERENCES**

Yash Pal Kathpalia, *Conservation and Restoration of Archives: A Survey of Facilities* (Unesco, 1978).

Louis A. Simon, "Some Observations on Planning Archives Buildings," in *Building and Equipment for Archives,* Bulletin of the National Archives no. 6 (1944).

A. ARAD

ARCHIVES MANAGEMENT

Archives management is a subject that has been virtually ignored in archival literature, but there is some evidence that its importance is beginning to be recognized. Management is the utilization of human, financial, and material resources to perform the functions for which an organization exists. Indeed, good management is particularly important for archives. Because of the traditionally low priority given to archives in the allocation of public funds, it is necessary to make the most effective use of the resources available, and, if additional resources are required, the justification should be documented and presented in a manner that will convince legislators, budget officials, and the general public that such expenditures will produce measurable benefits to the community that is served.

While archives are universal in the sense that all human activity produces them, there exist a wide variety of archival institutions concerned with different types of archives: government archives (national, state, municipal); the archives of businesses, universities, and other corporate bodies; and specialized archives for particular subject-matter areas (labor, immigration, science) or particular physical types of archival material (films, sound recordings). The place of archives in an administrative structure varies even for similar types of archives. For example, some state archives are a part of a government department, while others are a part of state libraries or historical societies. Whatever the place of an archives in an administrative structure, it is desirable that it have a distinct identity, with a separate budget, staff, accommodation, and direct relationships with creators of records; and that the director have authority to control the complete operations of the archives and its available resources.

The main functions of management are planning, evaluation, organization, staffing, and external relations.

**Planning.** While the general objectives of archives are formulated in legislation, they are not precise enough to meet planning needs. Long-term plans should include objectives and goals to be achieved in, for example, a period of five years. For each year operational plans should have precise targets and the allocation of precise resources that can be translated into an operating budget. While managers are subject to constraints such as regulations and management systems that apply to an entire government jurisdiction or other organization of which the archival institution is a part, they have the primary responsibility for the definition of objectives for the archives and the development of the plans to meet them. The approval of long-term plans implies a commitment of the resources that are necessary to attain them, and annual budgets as stages in the implementation of an approved plan are more likely to be adopted than if they were based on ad hoc increments to programs antedating the plan. Planning is a cooperative exercise in which all concerned managers should participate, but the particular objectives and plans of subunits should be in the context of a comprehensive plan for the institution as a whole. Factors that are important in archival planning are: the requirements for services to users; necessary accommodation, including space for expansion; the emphasis on conservation; the adaptation of technology to archival operations; and the commitment of a rational allocation of resources that will ensure the execution of all archival operations.

**Evaluation.** Plans are based on priorities at a point in time and on the information that is available at that time. Even if the elements in the plan are valid and conditions that affect its implementation do not change, it is essential to be able to assess and measure the progress in achieving the objectives for which the plan was developed. This requires performance measurement, based on quantifiable indicators that will indicate production or work accomplished. On the basis of information obtained by monitoring implementation, of changing priorities, and of other modifications arising from the allocation of resources, plans must be evaluated periodically and appropriate changes made in objectives and programs. To use the example of conservation, if all the resources called for in a particular year are not provided, if production is more or less than was projected, or if technological innovations affect the original program, these factors, considered in the evaluation of the program, will result in the revision of the original plans. Management control, then, requires a plan, the measurement of activity, the comparison of actual to planned activity, analysis of results, and corrective action. Important elements in evaluation are the promotion of economy, efficiency (the ratio of input to output), effectiveness (the extent to which the objectives are achieved), and the quality and level of service (which user surveys should test).

It is recognized that statistics are essential for planning, organizing, directing, and controlling. Most archives compile statistics for their own purposes on holdings, accessions, arrangement and description, reproduction, and reference services. But they tend to lag behind libraries in the standardization of statistics (which is necessary for comparison with similar activities in other institutions) and in using statistical data for planning purposes. For example, a plan for protective microfilming should take into consideration all the elements in the program and their costs. Although the quantity of material and salaries of the different types of staff involved are known, it is difficult to project the cost of such a program without information concerning time norms for prefilming preparation of material and microfilming rates. The use of statistical information is necessary not only in the costing of programs and decisions on various options but also in planning every aspect of an archival service from accommodation to reference services, establishing priorities, ensuring the most effective utilization of available resources, and justifying additional resources.

**Organization.** While libraries and archives have, in the words of Robert L. Clark, Jr., a common purpose "to collect, maintain and make available the written and graphic record of man's intellect and experience," differences in the origin and nature of the sources with which they are concerned impose differences in organization and methodology. Since archives are the official records of a corporate body, the relationship between the originating body and the archival institution is an essential concern of archives management. Indeed, archives are not collected but are accumulated, as records, through a process of creation or reception by the originating body. The doctrine of continuous custody (between the originating body and the archival institution that serves it), which has been put forward by Sir Hilary Jenkinson, a former Director of the English Public Record Office, has been extended, particularly in North America, to the concept of the integrated records/archives life cycle that encompasses the entire existence of records from creation to permanent preservation of their valuable nucleus as archives and destruction of the valueless remainder. Under the general direction of the chief archivist there are two distinct major operational units in the archival institution, one for current records management and retirement, and the other for archival operations, each with appropriate subdivisions. Separate units also exist for conservation, reprography, and general administration. There are two basic elements in records management operations: advisory services to originating departments, and services for records centers, intermediate repositories housing noncurrent records prior to their destruction upon expiration of residual values, or to transfer of their valuable segments to the archival institution.

Several factors, including the unique nature of archival materials, the principle of respect des fonds, and the need for knowledge of the content of records, affect the organization of internal archival operations. While libraries are usually organized on functional lines with divisions and separate staff for accessioning, cataloguing, and reference, it is not unusual for individual archivists to be involved in all functions with respect to particular bodies of archives: appraisal, acquisition, arrangement, description, reference, and even the preparation of publications and exhibitions. Subdivisions are usually established on the basis of broad subject-matter areas—e.g., foreign or military affairs—deriving from the functions of the originating bodies, or of significant chronological periods, or a combination of both. When an archival institution, in addition to receiving the official records of its parent body, accepts related corporate or personal records from external sources, these records should be maintained in a separate section or division. Other special units are required for nontextual types of archival materials—machine-readable archives, maps, photographs, films, and sound recordings. Special units are required for conservation and reprography. The institution should also have its own archival reference library.

No special organization is required for basic administrative functions such as personnel, financial, and materials management. Arrangements depend to some extent on the degree of autonomy of individual institutions, which ranges from separate archives departments, with all the staff required for administration, to archives divisions within a government department or library that provides administrative services for the archives as well as its other components. These services, however, must be responsive to the special requirements of archives with regard to specialized staff and training, special accommodation and equipment, and the essential purposes of the archival institution: preservation and service to the public.

**Staffing.** The most important resources in archival operations are human. Since these operations are labor intensive in nature, a major proportion of a budget (perhaps 75 percent) is for salaries. One could gain the impression from publications relating to archival functions that most of these functions are carried out uniformly by professional archivists. On the contrary, the fact is that in any archival organization that has a staff of more than one there is a degree of specialization that increases with its size and scope. Indeed, the operations of an archival institution require a variety of specialized skills, and an important task of its management is the recruitment and allocation of personnel possessing these skills—at the appropriate levels and in the appropriate numbers—in order to ensure the collective achievement of the objectives of the institution.

For statistical as well as functional purposes the archival staff usually comprises professional, professional support, clerical, technical, and administrative categories. While in North America the qualifications of a professional archivist are not as precise as in European countries, which typically have uniform preappointment training, a minimum educational qualification is a university degree, usually in history or a related field. Professional functions require a combination of academic knowledge, professional skills, and the exercise of judgment. To make the most effective use of staff, a "professional support" category (the archives assistant), between the professional and clerical categories, is most important. A proportion of two professional, one professional support, and three clerical positions has been suggested as most suitable for archival operations. As mentioned earlier, specialists are required to deal with such record media as maps, photographs, film, and machine-readable archives. It is advisable, however, to train professional archivists to work in the first and last of these media areas rather than to recruit the corresponding media specialists, i.e., cartographers and computer programmers. The reason is that substantive archival considerations are more important in these areas than are technical ones. On the other hand, conservation and reprography are entirely technical support areas for which trained technical specialists are essential. Similarly technical specialists are needed in such areas of administration as financial and personnel management. But in all of these areas it is indispensable that senior management direct all operations, approve policies, set priorities, and ensure the maintenance of acceptable standards. Staff requirements should be identified in the context of the budgetary cycle.

**External Relations.** A former Archivist of the United States, Robert H. Bahmer, insisted that one of the most important functions of archival management is the interpreting of the archives to "a variety of publics." This is more than public relations in the conventional sense. An archives does not operate in isolation, and the effectiveness of its operations depends to a considerable extent on the quality of its relationships with many elements in society. The archival manager should miss no opportunity to interpret "archival work to the public as a necessary factor in an enlightened society" through speeches, interviews, conferences, publications, etc.

A number of specific "publics" require special attention. One is the authority from which the financial resources supporting the archives are obtained, usually a legislature, and particularly the responsible minister. Another is the officialdom throughout the records-creating departments responsible for the management of records there; still another, in the case of archival institutions that accession materials from the private sector, is the body of donors, potential donors, or friends of potential donors. The users of archives and their professional associations make up another important public with which close relationships must be maintained. Among them are the historians concerning whom a great deal has been said and written, but the support and approval of many other bodies of users, in academic and nonacademic fields alike, is also vital. Close connections must be cultivated as well with related institutions such as libraries and historical societies, and with national and international professional archives associations.

W. I. SMITH

PROFESSIONAL TRAINING

Professional training for archivists in the strict and formal sense began in Western Europe in the first half of the 19th century. Five types or traditions have developed.

**The European Tradition.** Here the training offered was originally based mainly on the historical auxiliary sciences, in particular paleography and diplomatics (generally relating to the study, deciphering, and authentication of old historical documents and manuscripts), which during the 19th century and after were among the central disciplines of "scientific" history. The first formal training schools for archivists were the École Nationale des Chartes in Paris and the Bayerische Archivschule München (Munich), both founded in 1821. These were followed during the next half-century by eminent schools in many European countries, such as the Institut für Österreichische Geschichtsforschung, Vienna, founded in 1854. Some of the leading institutes of this period no longer exist, but all those remaining were radically reorganized in the period immediately after World War II, at which time a number of new schools were set up. Today virtually all European countries have a center of some type in which the archivists for their national archives services at least (if not for other institutions) are trained. The older traditions are still carried on to a certain extent by most of the countries of Central and Eastern Europe, for example by the State Institute of History and Archives at Moscow.

The training schools of the European tradition are usually either autonomous institutes, financed by government (like the French École des Chartes), or are attached to principal archives services (like the Archivschule Marburg, West Germany), or are associated with the historical faculty of a university (like the Institute of History and Archivistics, Nicholas Copernicus University, Torun, Poland). Among these training schools a distinction is possible between those in which students are already staff members of the national archives services, or in which successful graduates are guaranteed appointments in those services on completion of the course, and those in which the students compete in an open job market. A distinction is also possible between those schools that take students at about the age of 18 years, on completion of their secondary school education, and those that take students on completion of their university education. The former courses are naturally longer than the latter, usually three to four years as opposed to one to two years, but there are great variations from country to country both in the length and the weight of courses, practical requirements, etc. The most extreme case of prolonged training is found in Germany, where students are recruited at the postdoctoral stage and then given another two years of training. Such students will be at least 27 years old before starting employment. The average starting age in most European countries, however, would be 22 or 23.

Relatively little attention was given until recent years to professional subjects, as distinct from the historical sciences, so much so that in France the National Archives has had to institute a second training course, known as the Stage Technique International des Archives. This course must be attended by all its new staff members and may be attended by external and foreign students also. It has had a potent influence in disseminating professional standards and knowledge in many countries.

**Italo-Hispanic Tradition.** The second of the main traditions in archival training may be termed the Italo-Hispanic. In Italy there are no fewer than 17 government-financed schools of archivistics, paleography, and diplomatics, one in each province. Together, these turn out more than 3,000 students per year, only a tiny proportion of whom actually become archivists. In Spain, and even more in Latin America, there is a similar phenomenon. In the latter continent there are at least 18 archival schools or courses in 12 countries, most of them attached to universities. Particularly notable is the Interamerican Center for Archival Development at the Escuela Nacional de Archiveros in Córdoba, Argentina, which acts as a regional training school. Most courses in this tradition offer first degrees in archival science or in librarianship and archival science. In the Spanish and Portuguese traditions, a close link is maintained between archival and library training; indeed it is difficult to differentiate them in such schools as that of the Faculty of Letters, University of Coimbra (Portugal), or the School of Documentalists, National Library of Spain, Madrid. In these first-degree courses, a large number of the students do not intend to follow an archival career.

**British Tradition.** A third model is provided by the British tradition. Here there is no specialization until the student has taken his first degree, usually at the age of 21, by which time he or she has completed his general education. At this point he may be recruited into an established archives service and trained by apprenticeship in-house or, more usually, will follow a one-year postgraduate course leading to a Diploma in Archive Administration. These courses are offered by four universities (Liverpool, London, Oxford, and Wales). They concentrate on technical and professional subjects, give practical instruction, and can be closely associated with historical researchers and research methodology. Small numbers of students (6-20) are normal. A similar pattern of training may be seen elsewhere in the world where the British tradition in education is important, particularly in the Commonwealth countries in Africa, Asia, and Australasia.

**North America.** In the U.S. and Canada there is no universally established method of initial training. The Society of American Archivists issues an *Education Directory,* periodically updated, which lists courses and institutes in archival subjects. The 1976 issue lists 17 multi-course offerings, 23 single-course offerings, and 9 institutes and internships at universities, archival institutions, or historical societies. None of these courses constitutes a full-time specialized training program, and many of them are not accredited academically. Normally locally based archivists provide the teaching staff. Professionals in North America complain about the inability of the region to establish either a professional training institute on the European model, or a regular full-time course on the British model, but despite this the U.S. has achieved a flexible and economic system, which makes maximum use of the teaching potential of practicing archivists and local archives services and which can respond quickly to local demand. In many cases the academic and professional standing of these courses is high, and they have made substantial contributions to the theory and practice of archives administration. The courses held at the American University, Washington, D.C., are associated with the name of the world-famous archivist, Ernst Posner, who taught during the period 1939–61. The development of short, comprehensive summer institutes—often held in library schools, open to all comers, and a very characteristic feature of North American training methods—is associated initially with Posner and later with T. R. Schellenberg (who taught 1963–70). In recent years the Society of American Archivists has promoted studies of training requirements and is seeking to develop systems of accreditation of training programs and of certification of qualified archivists.

**The Third World.** In the third world there has been a natural tendency to continue the traditions of the former imperial countries. This is particularly true in Latin America. But the 1970's saw the emergence of the regional training school movement, sponsored in large part by Unesco and the International Council on Archives. In Senegal (University of Dakar), the regional school for French-speaking tropical African countries runs a two-year course to train archives assistants; students at a higher level must seek training overseas, mainly in Europe. Archivists for English-speaking countries in tropical Africa are trained in a one-year postgraduate program at the University of Ghana. A similar program for Southeast Asia, first mooted in 1968 and formally recommended by a 1973 regional conference for establishment in Kuala Lumpur, Malaysia, has not yet been realized. In South Asia the Indian national training school at New Delhi caters to students from the region as a whole, while Iraq has set up a training center in Baghdad that performs the same function for the Arab countries. As noted above, regional training for Latin America is offered at a center in Argentina sponsored by the Organization of American States. The centers in Senegal and Ghana are associated with university library schools, as would be that proposed for Malaysia; the Argentine center is also within a university structure, while the Indian school is attached to the National Archives.

**World Problems.** Despite the variety of these traditions, no country or region has yet achieved a system of archival training that meets with general approval. There is a widespread feeling that existing facilities are inadequate and, at least in part, inappropriate. In particular, even when established training schools produce a sufficient number of trained archivists to staff the public, government-supported archives services, they frequently do not attempt to serve the archives services in the private sector. The curriculum is frequently directed toward old-fashioned and inappropriate goals, i.e., biased toward the teaching of historical sciences at the expense of professional subjects, modern methodology, and practical training. Where courses are attached to library schools, there are complaints that library subjects predominate unduly.

Worldwide, there are at present approximately 126 archival training schools or courses, and these provide some 3,000 student places (excluding the Italians mentioned above). Since the world's practicing body of archivists numbers some 7,000, and there is by a recent computation an immediate developmental need for the training of another 6,000, an apparent shortage of student places exists in the immediate future but not in the long term. However, this calculation is upset by the fact that many, indeed the majority, of the student places available in the larger schools are given to general students who do not intend to enter the profession. Additionally, there is a serious imbalance from region to region: Latin America is oversupplied with schools of indifferent reputation, and the remaining countries of the third world are seriously undersupplied. For them, the places available in the training schools of the third world itself, plus those of the developed countries of Europe, North America, and Australasia, amount only to about 25 professional and 40 sub-professional trainees per year—about enough to supply the archival needs of one large country.

An important characteristic of archival training schools is the wide variety of subjects that must be taught. There are three main subject areas: professional studies (archives administration, records management, managerial and administrative studies, research methodology); auxiliary historical or interpretative sciences; and administrative or institutional history. It is probable that a complete course of training that limits itself strictly to these subjects and does not include any element of general education or languages would require about eight professors. To render a teaching body of this size possible, there would have to be a student enrollment of 80–100, but so large a training school would exceed the requirements of most countries and would demand a considerable investment. Hence there exists the problem of providing professional training to a student body of beginning archivists that typically numbers only between 10 and 30.

Consequently, most specialized archival training schools are associated with larger institutions. These are usually of one of three kinds: a large archives service, such as that to which the West German Archivschule Marburg is attached; a school of historical studies at a university; or a library school. There is much debate within the profession as to the relative merits of association with each of these. Schools dependent on archival services are probably the most effective in terms of teaching practical skills, and they can provide, better than others, for periods of supervised practical laboratory work. But few national or other archives services have the standing or the resources to undertake this work (although many larger archives systems do in fact offer training programs, and these are not usually strictly limited to their own novice staff members). Archives schools associated with historical studies have the advantage that archivists trained there may easily become, in their professional practice, members of the research communities of their countries. In the exercise of his or her professional skills an archivist should represent research interests, in the world of administration, and should apply his or her knowledge of research methodology and of research findings to the basic archival function of appraisal. The main drawback of the association of archival training with historical studies, however, is the tendency of the archivists so trained to withdraw from active administration and from involvement in the fundamental day-to-day professional, as opposed to scholarly, functions of the archival institution.

The tendency today, and one that was given powerful backing by the leading theorist of archival science, T. R. Schellenberg, is to associate archival with library training. This has been done in the most recently established archival schools, in Senegal, Ghana, and Australia (University of New South Wales, Sydney). The benefits to be obtained from this association are considerable, and particularly so since the likely future development of technology in both archives and libraries is likely to increase the area of common skills. Conservation, reprography, computer technology, and documentation services are important fields in which both professions are operating increasingly. However, there are and will remain considerable differences in methodology inherent in the different media with which archivists and librarians work, and so far no attempt to devise common curricula for training has been practicable. Apart from technical areas shared with the librarian, such as conservation, reprography, and automation, archival training courses that are situated within library schools will still have to maintain a distinct syllabus and teaching staff and inculcate a distinct professional ethos.

**Technical Training.** So far only peripheral mention has been made of the technical fields of conservation, reprography, and automation with the fundamentals of which the professional archivist must be familiar if he is to plan and administer the technical aspects of archival programs and operations. The degree of attention professional training schools give these subjects varies considerably, but generally speaking it can be described as inadequate. Similarly facilities for training the actual practitioners—the technicians themselves—are inadequate as well; most technicians either learn on the job or receive prior training in a nonarchival setting. In recognition of this deficiency initiatives are being taken, both in the archivally-advanced countries and in the developing world, to provide improved technical training. In particular, concrete efforts are being made to organize technical training centers on the third world regional level.

**REFERENCES**

Statistical data are from a report by Michael Cook, *The Education and Training of Archivists,* made to the Unesco meeting of experts on . . . archival training programs, November 1979.

Frank B. Evans, "Post-Appointment Archival Training: A Proposed Solution for a Basic Problem," *American Archivist* (1977), surveys history and problems of training in the U.S. and proposes solutions.

"La formation des archivistes en Europe." *Archives et Biliothèques de Belgique* (1975); articles on archival training in East and West Germany, Spain, Austria, Holland, Italy, Britain, and the Vatican; in German, Spanish, English, and Italian.

Charles Kecskemeti, *La formation professionnelle des archivistes: liste des écoles et des cours de formation professionnelle d'archivistes,* Conseil International des Archives/Unesco (1966); the only published survey and analysis of training schools to date; in French.

Morris Rieger, "The Regional Training Center Movement," *American Archivist* (1972); background to development of the third world schools.

MICHAEL COOK

## Archives: Education and Research

Training to be an archivist is like training to be struck by lightning, remarked J. Franklin Jameson, one of the early leaders of the archival profession. The growth of U.S. archives is a 20th-century phenomenon, and professional training remains a vexing problem. Archivists have argued for decades over the relative merits of preappointment and postappointment training, the values of short-term institutes and graduate degree programs, and the relationship between training in archival practices and training in the correlative fields of history and library science. The Society of American Archivists (SAA) adopted guidelines in 1977 for a standard curriculum in graduate programs of archival education and in the late 1970's was considering a proposal to approve formally those graduate programs that meet SAA-approved criteria. The impact of those developments, however, has not been fully felt by individual archivists and archival institutions.

Although some historical and antiquarian societies existed during the early and mid-19th century, the modern archival institutions, and with them the archival profession, are a direct result of the interest in "scientific" history that developed late in the century. This type of historical scholarship depended on access to original source materials, and proponents of the new method urged that archives be established to preserve, protect, and make available permanently valuable historical materials. Consequently, in 1899 the young American Historical Association (AHA) established a Public Archives Commission to locate and publish guides to source materials. In 1909 the Association sponsored the first Conference of Archivists.

Those historians in the forefront of this movement for archival institutions were familiar with archives and archival training in Europe. On the Continent training often took place in a university or institute affiliated with an archival institution. This preappointment training usually culminated in an examination, and only those persons who passed were appointed to archival positions in state archives. History, historical methods, and such auxiliary subjects as paleography, sigillography (the study of seals), and diplomatics (the study of documents) were emphasized. In England and Scandinavia the Continental models of preappointment training had not gained vogue by the end of the 19th century; instead, the archival institutions hired university graduates and gave them postappointment training that varied greatly in content, aim, and efficiency.

Drawing on the Continental experience, Waldo Gifford Leland, historian and archival proponent, told the 1909 Conference of Archivists that archivists should have historical and legal training. He proposed that university history departments and library schools introduce courses on archives, but no such courses developed from his initial proposal. During the next quarter-century, Leland and other historians devoted themselves to the task of establishing a national archives. The National Archives eventually was founded in 1934, employing the largest number of archivists on the North American continent and inaugurating a need for programs to train archivists. Two years later the Conference of Archivists, which had been a feature of AHA conventions since 1909, split from AHA and became an independent organization, the Society of American Archivists. The Society quickly established a Committee on the Training of Archivists, composed of five academic historians and chaired by Samuel Flagg Bemis. The report of that committee reaffirmed the need for historical training for archivists, rejected librarianship as an appropriate background, and suggested that specialized courses in archives be "grafted on" to graduate programs in history in "first-class" American universities.

This report profoundly affected the nascent profession's psyche but negligibly affected its practice. Solon J. Buck did teach an archives course at Columbia in 1938–39, but the University was uninterested in continuing the program. In 1941 the first major program in archives was established by Buck and Ernst Posner at American University in Washington, D.C. Posner had been trained in the German archival tradition; he attempted to institute a similar program at American University.

Soon it was clear to Posner that a single graduate program could not supply trained archivists in sufficient numbers to meet staffing needs of growing archival institutions. Furthermore, it was apparent that institutions would continue to employ untrained persons and then would either train them within the institution or seek a source of external short-term training in archival theory. To meet this need, Posner began, in 1945, a summer institute in archival administration and preservation. He secured the cooperation of the National Archives, the Maryland Hall of Records, and, later, the Library of Congress. The program was designed to meet the instructional needs of persons without formal training who were already employed by archival institutions. With modifications, this institute has been offered one or more times each year, while sponsorship has shifted from the university to the National Archives.

European training was thus brought to the United States: the Continental practice of preappointment academic training was reflected in the formal American University credit offerings, while the British practice of postappointment training was reflected in the short-term institute. During the 1950's and 1960's both models spread beyond American University programs. The Colorado State Archives and the University of Denver began offering both academic courses and a summer institute; Wayne State University developed an academic program; by 1979 more than 30 colleges and universities offered two or more courses in archives administration. Many additional schools offered single courses in archives, and a half dozen short-term institutes provided additional educational alternatives.

The expansion of graduate programs in archives education fostered a debate that was part of the larger, unresolved controversy over the relative merits of preappointment or postappointment training. This time the issue was whether the most appropriate university preappointment archival training was in history departments or in schools of library science. (Given the small numbers of students, independent archival departments seemed unrealistic.) The debate was especially heated in the mid-1960's; as of 1979 it had not been resolved. Archival courses continue to be offered in history departments, library schools, and, increasingly, in joint programs carried by both departments. In addition, some courses, especially those related to records management, are offered in public administration departments, and at least one college has introduced a course of archival studies for undergraduates.

A series of moves to develop some nationwide standards for archival education began in the 1970's. In March 1973 ten teachers of archives courses attended a two-day meeting sponsored by the Society of American Archivists and prepared draft guidelines for credit courses and institutes. They were approved by the Council of the Society and were published for comment by the membership. Next the Society's Committee on Education and Training produced curriculum standards for multicourse programs of archival education that would lead to a minor or concentration in a graduate degree program. Those guidelines were adopted by the Council.

The Committee next broadened its scope to include professional development. Proposals called for approved programs of archival education in graduate schools, certification of individual archivists, and guidelines on the practicum required by the approved curriculum. In addition, an ad hoc committee of the Society developed a plan to certify archival institutions. A second ad hoc committee was writing a code of ethics for the profession at the end of the 1970's. These proposals form the structure of the continuing debate on the nature and character of the archival profession.

With these moves the Society has focused strongly on graduate archival education. While it may appear that the historic debate over preappointment and postappointment training has been *tacitly* resolved, this is not the case. Major archival institutions continue to conduct postappointment training for their new employees. Members of religious orders, employees of various businesses and institutions, and staffs of local governments continue to find themselves suddenly saddled with records management and archival responsibilities for which they are unprepared. Grant-giving institutions continue to require at least short-term archival training for persons employed in an archival capacity on grant-supported projects. All these persons need appropriate postappointment training. University archival education programs are not yet the sole answer to the profession's training needs.

The resolution of the preappointment or postappointment training debate may come not from educational institutions or teachers of archives courses but rather from employers. Job listings for archivists most often specify that the applicant hold either an M.L.S. or a graduate degree in history. However, if employers begin to require an academic degree with a minor or concentration in archives, the market for preappointment training will grow and the market for postappointment training will decline.

As techniques and practices in archival administration evolve, they will continue to diverge from the practices of both the library and the historical professions. The archivist, the librarian, and the historian all must confront such technological developments as the hologram and the digital audio recording, but each will react in terms of his or her profession's doctrine and administrative needs. Persons trained in one discipline may find it increasingly difficult to transfer into one of the other two. Even within the archival area, divisions are surfacing. For example, records management developed from archivists' concerns for the entire life cycle of records, but records management is now a highly specialized field with its own independent certification program, making it difficult for archivists to shift into that area.

Employment opportunities in archives are never great, compared with the positions available annually in libraries or academia. While new archives are being established and staffs are expanding, the developments are slow and small. Archival work does not offer a solution to the employment crisis in either the history or library fields.

Pre- and postappointment training; education in history departments or schools of library science: the old issues are not resolved. And yet the profession has moved very far in the last few years. It is estimated that over half the membership of the Society of American Archivists in 1978 had joined since 1975; the basic questions of who an archivist is, what an archivist knows, and what standards an archivist upholds are being debated in the controversies over certification, approval of graduate programs, adoption of a code of ethics, and measurement of the practices of individual archival institutions. These debates will have a direct impact on archival education, its curricula, its locus, its goals. And perhaps in the aftermath of these debates the old questions on archival training will be answered for this generation.

**REFERENCES**

Samuel Flagg Bemis, "The Training of Archivists in the United States," *American Archivist* (1939).
Solon J. Buck, "The Training of American Archivists," *American Archivist* (1947).
Frank B. Evans, "Educational Needs for Work in Archival and Manuscript Depositories," *Indian Archives* (1972).
"Postappointment Archival Training: A Proposed Solution for a Basic Problem," *American Archivist* (1977).
H. G. Jones, "Archival Training in American Universities, 1938–68," *American Archivist* (1968).
Waldo G. Leland, "American Archival Problems," AHA *Annual Report* (1909).
Ernst Posner, *Archives and the Public Interest,* edited by Ken Munden (1967).
Theodore R. Schellenberg, "Archival Training in Library Schools," *American Archivist* (1968).
Society of American Archivists, *Education Directory* (1978).
"Archives Education Guidelines Approved," *SAA Newsletter* (1977).
"Board for Archival Certification Proposed," *SAA Newsletter* (1978).
"Program for Archival Certification," *SAA Newsletter* (1977).
"Report of Committee on Institutional Evaluation," *SAA Newsletter* (1978).

TRUDY HUSKAMP PETERSON

# Argentina

Argentina, a federal republic and the second largest country of South America, is bounded by Chile on the west, the Atlantic Ocean and Uruguay on the east, Brazil on the northeast, and Bolivia and Paraguay on the north. Pop. (1978 est.) 26,393,000; area 2,776,900 sq.km. The official language is Spanish.

**National Library.** In 1810 the government's junta of the Revolution of May established the public library of Buenos Aires on September 7, 1810, and announced that it would be inaugurated March 16, 1812. On August 29, 1884, the library was nationalized, and from September 9 it was called the National Library. The first collection was based on the libraries of the Colegio San Carlos, Major and Minor Library of Córdoba (belonging to the Jesuits), the private collections of Bishop Manuel de Azamor y Ramírez, General Manuel Belgrano, and others given as donations. The public was also asked for donations in funds and books.

Materials are received through the legal deposit, and books are acquired by purchase and trade. Donations—requested and spontaneous—are accepted. It holds approximately 1,800,000 volumes, 20,000 musical compositions, 10,000 magazines, 6,000 dailies, and 5,000 maps. Among special collections are some works belonging to General José de San Martín, donated by his son-in-law. The library owns the manuscripts of Rubén Darío and other notable writers. Well-known persons of Argentine letters served as Directors at one time or another: Manuel Moreno, Carlos Tejedor, José Mármol, Vicente G. Quesada, José A. Wilde, Paul Groussac, Gustavo A. Martinez Zuviría, Jorge Luis Borges, Vicente Sierra, and José Edmundo Clemente.

**Academic Libraries.** In 23 universities, according to a 1976 guide to university libraries, the library total is 195. They are coordinated by the Council of Librarians of the National Argentine Universities. The Council's program embraces professional organization, interlibrary loan, newspapers, exchange, collective cataloguing and a catalogue of university publications, user preparation, microfilming of articles, and so on.

The Institute of Library Sciences of the University of Buenos Aires was founded in 1941. Its objective is to coordinate the libraries of the University of Buenos Aires through the Council of Librarians, as the University does not have a central library. The principal tool it possesses is its centralized catalogue, containing in its 900,000 entries the largest bibliographic collection in the country, covering about 3,000,000 volumes. From 1970 the Institute also compiled the catalogue of the libraries of the national universities of the Interior, another important source of information. Four times a year it publishes an *Information Bulletin.*

**Public Libraries.** Under a law of September 23, 1870, passed during the tenure of President D. F. Sarmiento, an original coordinating organism was established as the Commission Protector of Popular Libraries, now known as the Office of Popular Libraries. Sometimes the libraries act as school libraries. The total is approximately 2,500, distributed throughout the length and breadth of the country. Some, such as San Fernando, are a hundred years old, and their principal contribution is to collect material relative to the history of the locality in which they operate, principally diaries and magazines.

**School Libraries.** No one organism coordinates the activities of school libraries, nor is there common action between school and library. The government of the province of Buenos Aires, for example, reports a total of 178 units in a register required under a government rule of 1963. A guide was edited, in collaboration with the Provincial Center of Educational Information, bringing the information contained in the register up to date; it covers

ALA

*The Bernardino Rivadavia Public Library in Bahia Blanca, Argentina.*

not only Buenos Aires Province but others as well (United Nations, Latin American Center of Economic and Social Documentation, *Directory of Information Units for Development: Argentina: Educational Sector,* Santiago, Chile, 1978).

**Special Libraries.** Special libraries consist of those associated with private or official institutions: banks, ministries, national institutes, state enterprises, and others such as the National Commission on Atomic Energy and the National Institute of Industrial Technology. Most are grouped under the Argentine Association of Libraries and Scientific and Technical Centers of Information, with headquarters in Buenos Aires.

A collective catalogue lists the periodicals received by special libraries and the university libraries, registered by the Argentine Center for Scientific and Technological Information (CAICYT), which depends on the National Council of Scientific and Technical Investigations (CONICET), making it relatively easy to obtain copies of the material that might interest readers, maintaining contact with the libraries integrated into the system by means of telecommunications. These libraries conform to international standards whether referring to agriculture, cattle breeding, or nuclear technology.

**Associations.** The Association of Graduate Librarians of the Argentine Republic (ABGRA) deals mostly with professional matters concerning documentation, information, and teaching, including continuous education for librarians at a postgraduate level. The Association was founded in Buenos Aires November 5, 1953, as the Association of Librarians of the Federal Capital. It can be considered a virtual continuation of the Center for Library Studies of the Argentine Social Museum, established October 12, 1943, relinquishing its purpose upon the establishment of ABGRA. It is a member of IFLA. Members must be professional librarians, a titled conferred only by authorities designed to do so. There are approximately 600 members. It issued a *Bulletin* (suspended, the last issue dated April 1975). It also produces occasional documents, minutes of national meetings, and other items. A new review, *Library Sciences and Documentation,* went to press in 1979. An annual national meeting of librarians was first held in Buenos Aires in 1962. Annual meetings were held regularly thereafter. The first Ibero-American meeting was held in Buenos Aires, August 14–23, 1974.

HANS GRAVENHORST
REINALDO J. SUÁREZ

# Asheim, Lester E(ugene)

(1914–  )

Lester Asheim contributed to librarianship in many ways, through writing, teaching, and work with the American Library Association. He helped to define the principles of book selection, to establish criteria for library education and personnel, and to foster communication among librarians all over the world. Asheim was born in Spokane, Washington, on January 22, 1914. Except for a short period in Idaho, he grew up in Seattle, where he received from the University of Washington an A.B. in English in 1936, along with a Phi Beta Kappa key; a B.A. in Librarianship in 1937; and an M.A. in American Literature in 1941. Asheim began library work as a page in the Seattle Public Library, and from 1937 to 1941 he served as Junior Reference Assistant at the University of Washington while he continued his work on his Master's degree.

For the year 1941–42, Asheim served as Librarian of the Prison Library at McNeill Island, Washington. During World War II he served for three years in the U.S. Army Signal Intelligence Corps, chiefly in Alaska.

Upon his return to civilian life in 1945, Asheim organized a library for the Federal Public Housing Authority in Seattle. Taking advantage of a fellowship and the G.I. Bill, he enrolled at the Graduate Library School (GLS) of the University of Chicago, from which he received a Ph.D. degree in 1949. His doctoral dissertation, *From Book to Film: A Comparative Analysis of the Content of Novels and the Films Based on Them,* combined his interest in literature and nonprint media, an interest that he maintained throughout his career. His dissertation was published in an edited version in four installments of *Hollywood Quarterly* (1951) and *The Quarterly of Film, Radio and Television* (1951–52).

At the GLS Asheim's talents were early recognized. He assisted Bernard Berelson in writing *The Library's Public: A Report of the Public Library Inquiry* (1949) and then edited the papers of the GLS conference on the Inquiry, *A Forum on the Public Library Inquiry* (1949). This was only the first of a number of GLS conference volumes for which he was to serve as Editor, including *The Core of Education for Librarianship* (1954), *The Future of the Book* (1955), *New Directions in Public Library Development* (1957), *Persistent Issues in American Librarianship* (1961), and *Differentiating the Media* (1975).

Asheim was appointed Assistant Professor at the GLS, 1948–52; Dean of Students, 1951–52; and Dean and Associate Professor, 1952–61. During the decade of his deanship he continued to study library education, but his most important work was probably his now classic article "Not Censorship but Selection" (1956), which has been widely reprinted. In 1957 he published *The Humanities and the Public Library,* which has been widely used in library schools as a guide to selection and use of humanities materials.

In 1961 Asheim became Director of the International Relations Office (IRO) of the American Library Association. In his five years in that post he visited 44 countries and shared his experience in American librarianship with students and practicing librarians throughout the world. One result of his IRO activities was an invitation to deliver the Phineas Lawrence Windsor Lectures at the University of Illinois. These lectures, subsequently published as *Librarianship in the Developing Countries* (1966), were a major contribution to the study of comparative librarianship and brought him the Scarecrow Press Award for "an outstanding contribution to library literature" in 1968. In 1966 Asheim resigned his IRO post to accept the directorship of ALA's new Office for Library Education. The rapid expansion of libraries during the period of the Great Society programs placed serious strains on library education, which was urged to produce not only more librarians but also better trained librarians. Much of Asheim's work was concentrated on the development of a statement defining the titles, basic requirements, and responsibilities of library personnel—both professional and supportive. His statement on "Library Education and Manpower" (often known as the Asheim Paper or Statement) was adopted as the official policy of the American Library Association on June 30, 1970. In the spring of 1976 that document, without substantive change, was renamed "Library Education and Personnel Utilization" and remains the major position on personnel development of the American library community.

While Director of the ALA Office of Library Education, Asheim continued to write and speak on library education and other topics. He had earlier chaired ALA's Committee on Accreditation and over the years frequently served as a consultant for library education programs. In 1976–77 he was President of the Library Education Division of ALA.

In 1971 Asheim returned to the University of Chicago as Professor in the Graduate Library School and in 1972 became the Editor of the *Library Quarterly,* the major scholarly journal in American librarianship, a post he held for the next three years.

University of North Carolina

*Lester Eugene Asheim*

On January 1, 1975, Asheim became William Rand Kenan, Jr., Professor of Library Science at the University of North Carolina at Chapel Hill, a position he still holds. In honor of his 65th birthday, colleagues presented him with a Festschrift, *As Much to Learn as to Teach* (1979). As is apparent from the topics treated in this series of essays—such as intellectual freedom, library service to the public, library education, professional associations, international and comparative librarianship, and mass communications—Lester Asheim showed interest in many areas of librarianship, and to most he has made significant contributions. Many testify that this diligent researcher and writer is an excellent teacher and a delightful colleague.

Asheim was selected as the 1973 recipient of the Beta Phi Mu Award for Distinguished Service to Education for Librarianship. At the ALA Centennial Conference he was awarded the Joseph W. Lippincott Award for distinguished service to the profession of librarianship. The University of Washington School of Librarianship gave him its Distinguished Alumnus Award in 1966 and the Illinois Library Association its Intellectual Freedom Award the same year. He was named a member of the Advisory Committee to the Center for the Book at the Library of Congress in 1978.

**REFERENCE**

Joel M. Lee and Beth A. Hamilton, editors, *As Much to Learn as to Teach: Essays in Honor of Lester Asheim* (1979), includes biographical information and a bibliography of Asheim's writings.

EDWARD G. HOLLEY

## Association of Caribbean University Research and Institutional Libraries

The Association of Caribbean University Research and Institutional Libraries (ACURIL) was inaugurated at a meeting of some 40 delegates from university and research institute libraries in the Caribbean region and 30 observers from other libraries within and outside the region, convened in Puerto Rico, June 1969, under the sponsorship of the Association of Caribbean Universities and Research Institutes (UNICA) to promote regional library cooperation. The arrangements for the meeting were made by the University of Puerto Rico General Library. Among those principally responsible for this meeting were Alma Jordan, then Deputy Librarian of the University of the West Indies Library at Saint Augustine, Trinidad, and Albertina Peréz de Rosa, Chief of the Department of Latin American Studies and Exchange, Jose M. Lázaro Library, University of Puerto Rico, Río Piedras. The former was elected first President and the latter first Vice-President of the Association.

The objects of the Association as set forth in its constitution and bylaws are "to facilitate the development and use of libraries and the identification of library collections in support of the whole range of intellectual and educational endeavour throughout the Caribbean area, to strengthen the profession of librarianship in the region and to promote co-operative library activities in pursuit of these objectives."

Membership, formerly open only to qualified university and research libraries and archives, has subsequently been extended to all qualified libraries that have an institutional basis. Member institutions must be situated within the area of the Caribbean archipelago, the mainland countries, or those states of the U.S. that border on the Caribbean Sea or Gulf of Mexico. Associate membership is open to libraries and archives with interests or collections pertinent to the Caribbean area but outside the region. Personal membership is open to staff members holding professional posts in member institutions and to library school faculty members in the area. Neither of the last two categories of membership may vote. In 1978 the membership of the Association stood at 77 institutional members, 1 associate member, and 47 personal members.

The affairs of the Association are managed by an Executive Council composed of representatives of member institutions; it includes among its officers a President, Vice-President, Secretary, and Treasurer who are elected annually. They are assisted by a small secretariat staffed by a part-time General Secretary and Assistant Treasurer, who are located in Puerto Rico, where the association has its headquarters.

The Association holds an Annual Meeting, usually in November, at which administrative sessions are joined with a conference or workshop on a predetermined theme. Continuity of the Association's work is achieved through the efforts of a number of standing committees, appointed by the Executive Council, to deal with acquisitions, bibliography, constitution and bylaws, indexing, library education, microfilming, personnel, planning and research, public relations, publications, in addition to annually constituted committees on nominations and resolutions. The committees on acquisitions and indexing are further subdivided into committees on English-speaking and Spanish-speaking areas.

The Association publishes a bilingual quarterly newsletter entitled *ACURIL Carta Informativa/Newsletter* and has begun to issue the proceedings of its annual conferences, of which the documents of the fourth annual conference have been published to date, under the title *Personnel Management of Libraries in the Caribbean/La Administración de Personal Bibliotecario en el Caribe* (San Juan, 1975). The papers of the first and second conferences of the Association have been published in English by the American Library Association under the title *Research Library Cooperation in the Caribbean,* edited by Alma Jordan (Chicago, 1973).

The Association is an affiliate of the Association of Caribbean Universities and Research Institutes (UNICA).

K. E. INGRAM

## Assurbanipal

### (fl. 7th century B.C.)

Assurbanipal (Ashurbanipal), King of Assyria, warrior, administrator, and pragmatic librarian, assembled a "Library of Congress" at Nineveh. He personifies Assyrian civilization, the peak of an older Mesopotamian culture that nourished successive civilizations from the Sumerians through the Chaldeans. After Babylon fell to Cyrus the Great in 539 B.C., this complex culture was combined with its Egyptian counterpart by Persian foreigners who created a comprehensive synthesis of cultural influences from all the near eastern civilizations. The combined influence of the Persian cultural synthesis has been enormous. Mitigated somewhat in Hellenistic times, it nevertheless affected Alexandrian civilization, overwhelmed the Greco-Roman tradition in late antiquity, and sustained the Middle Ages for nearly a thousand years. It has also created the ambivalence of modern thought by confronting humanism with theological presuppositions.

The Sumerians were cultural innovators who pioneered the Mesopotamian tradition and invented its form of writing. Subsequent innovations were largely confined to military, administrative, and artistic improvements. The tradition went through a long period of cultural stagnation under the Old Babylonians. It was preserved, organized, and consolidated by the Assyrians,

*Assurbanipal* British Museum

whose originality was confined to administrative and military matters. The Chaldeans, who tried to revive the Old Babylonian culture, substantially altered the tradition itself. It was further diluted by the Persians, who ended its political existence, and by the Greeks, who resented its otherworldliness; but its cultural influence has never been completely lost.

The Assyrians were bristling warlords with a flair for culture. They were a pragmatic people who made war as brutal and effective as possible. They created centralized government on a large scale, the first sprawling empire to rule the world with iron laws. The bureaucratic machinery they created survived the wreckage of their empire to rise again in the Persian Empire, where it served as a model for the Roman Empire, the precursor of Western administrative procedures. Poets and scholars were sponsored by the early kings of Ur, Isin, Larsa, and Babylon; Tiglath-Pileser I, Sargon II, and Esarhaddon were addicted to Babylonian literature, and Assurbanipal systematically rescued the whole inheritance of the past. Virtually everything we know of Mesopotamian history derives from the cultural interests of these kings and their attendants.

Assurbanipal, the last important king of Assyria (7th century B.C.), helped create both its Golden Age of literature and its sudden destruction. He organized coteries of scribes, sending them all over the empire to find and copy Sumero-Babylonian documents, and even learned the scribal art himself, in order to assemble the Assyrian "Library of Congress" at Nineveh. The resulting library operation represents the basic content, and possibly the complete corpus, of the Mesopotamian scribal tradition. But it does not represent the realities of librarianship for several reasons.

Assurbanipal was first of all a warrior, then an administrator, and finally a librarian. Like most imperialists, he was overly pragmatic, preferring to manage things and people rather than ideas. Accordingly, he reduced librarianship to housekeeping routines for ordering clay tablets in the only library of Mesopotamia. The literatures of Sumer and Old Babylon were thus preserved by "the Assyrian gift for arranging and systematizing," not by any "marked advance in thought." There was no contemporary literature or science because the Assyrians were better consumers than producers of information. Their only original contributions were archival grist for the future historians of Assyria, but the Assyrians themselves were not concerned with "scholarly accuracy" or with "the truth."

Assurbanipal was the first ultrapragmatic librarian to exhibit "a complete absence of any speculative or reasoning effort." Not ability, mind you, but *effort.* When his bibliographical methods arrived in Alexandria, the Greeks simply accepted them as folksy procedures for running a library and turned to substantive issues—like inventing the higher and lower criticisms for managing the literary tradition itself. Thus, they avoided the unresolved problems of bibliographic organization and control, which passed through the Romans to Western Europe. The resultant utter lack of Greek influence in bibliographical matters is essentially what is wrong with librarianship today: it has never been able to get Assurbanipal off its back.

The weary Assurbanipal cried out: "Why has sickness, woe of heart, misery and destruction bound me? In the land is battle, in the house is intrigue; they are never taken from my side. Destruction and an evil word are lined up against me; ill of heart and ill of body have bowed down my form. With 'Alack' and 'Alas' I end my day; [even] on the day of the city god, the feast day, I am destroyed. Death is bringing upon me my end, I am oppressed; in want and sorrow I grieve day and night. I wail: 'O God, give this to those who do not fear the gods; may I see thy light! How long, O God, wilt thou do this unto me? As one who fears not god or goddess have I been afflicted" (Olmstead, *History of Assyria,* 414, adding: this is "far indeed . . . from the hero . . . who brought in the millennial dawn!").

H CURTIS WRIGHT

## Audiovisual Services

**Technology.** The audiovisual resources of libraries embrace a wide variety and sophistication of formats and related equipment, each of which has distinctive characteristics, applications, and advantages as conveyors of information. The types generally found in most libraries include sound recordings, slides, filmstrips, transparencies, flat pictures, photographs, prints, realia, films, and video.

*Sound Recordings.* These include 33⅓-rpm phonodiscs, reel-to-reel tapes, and cassette tapes, all of which are used for the playback reproduction of a variety of musical and spoken-word compositions. The long-playing phonodisc from the 1950's is perhaps the primary and most common format in libraries, with its wide representation of classical, jazz, folk, and popular music titles and plays, poetry, speeches, foreign language instruction, self-improvement, and children's material. The appearance in the 1960's of the permanently encased tape cassette with its small size and relative durability and the increasing availability of material in this format (enhanced by the

Dolby feature for finer music reproductions) have spurred many libraries to invest in sizable cassette collections, either as adjunct to their phonodiscs or as their sole audio resource. Most cassette collections have proved extremely popular. Especially appealing in the reel-to-reel tape, and to a lesser extent in the cassette, are the recording capabilities that allow elementary or high school students to provide their own audio material for a report or enable public libraries to capture local events or participate in oral history projects. All audio formats are of particular interest to libraries serving the physically and visually disabled or other patrons unable to use traditional print resources.

*Slides.* The cost, quality, wide availability of subjects, and flexibility of arrangement have made two-inch-by-two-inch 35-mm transparent slides a popular library resource. Either with notes or with synchronized audiotape accompaniment, individual slides or slide programs give added fidelity to works of art and to studies of nature, some of the most common subjects of slides. In addition to the wide-ranging topics of commercially produced slide programs, the slide-tape format lends itself to local production in school and academic libraries for specific curriculum needs and in public libraries for a variety of program topics.

*Filmstrips.* Less flexible than slides in their fixed arrangement of visuals are filmstrips, either captioned, with accompanying notes, or with synchronized accompanying audio phonodisc or tape. This medium offers a more easily stored and used progression of still images that is especially suitable for single-concept educational needs or for independent learning experiences and thus is quite popular in schools and in a growing number of college libraries. Although primarily directed to the school market with its curriculum-related topics, filmstrips concerned with children's stories and subjects of a general educational nature, such as vocational information or child care, can be applicable for public library collections as well.

Photographs, prints, art reproductions, and flat pictures are available in libraries for study, display, and circulation, according to the functions and clientele of a particular library. Their use primarily by individuals has been enhanced by the opaque projector, which reproduces them for audience viewing or classroom presentation.

Acetate transparencies are useful in instructional situations for projecting written material for an audience or class, as the printed matter may be preprinted, added while a lecture is in process, or overlayed to show developmental progress.

*Realia.* Toys, games, sculpture, models, three-dimensional art, and a range of other tangible objects that are designed to be handled, used, and studied rather than being exhibited in display cases come under the heading of realia, which in some extreme instances has come to include such library-circulated items as jigsaw puzzles, automotive repair tools, and live pets.

*Motion Pictures.* The most prominent and widely available motion picture format in libraries is the 16-mm film, which includes theatrical feature films transferred from the commercial 35-mm stock, as well as educational films, which range from independent and television documentaries on issues of social concern, to live-action or animated narratives for both children and adults, to personal and experimental cinema for more esoteric tastes and audiences. Increasingly used in the post-World War II decades, 16-mm films have been popular, if expensive, components of public library programs and are accepted and useful elements in the educational process in schools and colleges. Their appeal and value stem from their compelling union of motion and sound, increasingly sophisticated special effects and photographic techniques, and wide range of content matter.

The difficulties inherent in the expense of both the 16-mm films themselves and the required projectors have been offset to some extent by the arrival in the early 1970's of the 8-mm format, which cuts down in size of film stock, expense, equipment, and administration. Hailed especially in schools as ideal small group or individual teaching tools, these compact, easy-to-use-and-circulate "paperback" films have also been popular in public libraries, many of whose patrons have their own 8-mm home movie projectors. The difficulties with this format, however, lie in the varying versions of 8-mm films and the incompatibility of equipment, as first silent and then sound 8-mm films became available both in reel-to-reel formats or as "single concept" film loops requiring several different types of hardware. The arrival of the Super 8 format, which has a larger frame and gives a 60 percent larger image, rendered standard 8-mm equipment unusable for either the Super 8 open-reel or cartridge versions. While there is a dual-8 projector that can handle both standard and Super 8 formats, the general lack of standardization of format, incompatibility of equipment, decreases in new, or newly transferred from 16-mm, film software, along with some diminishing of public library patron interest, have soured the early promise of 8-mm film.

*Video.* Much of the compactness and relative cheapness that appealed in 8-mm have been offset by the appearance of video technology, which grew tremendously in the late 1970's and changes rapidly. Developed in the early 1970's for electronic reproduction and instant playback of visual images, videotape is available in a variety of formats, two of which have traditionally been of greatest interest to libraries: the half-inch open-reel format used by schools, public libraries, and community groups for recording and production; and three-quarter-inch cassettes that play back a variety of prerecorded, commercially available programs for easy-to-use classroom and public library applications.

The appearance in the mid-1970's of the half-inch cassette home video recording systems and the ensuing arrival of the heralded videodisc are developments that affect libraries, since consumer acceptance of these newer home video formats will influence library investment in yet another, incompatible video format or may encourage libraries to take a plunge into video for the first time. The two vying half-inch cassette formats (Beta and VHS) are incompatible, but recent trends indicate that the VHS format is the one preferred in the consumer market, thus pointing a way to libraries for the half-inch equipment and software in which to invest. The two major videodisc systems (laser or mechanical stylus) are also incompatible, but the relative inexpensiveness of the phonodisc-like software and the random access, freeze-frame, and computer-link-up capabilities of the emerging videodisc technology are making the videodisc an increasingly attractive format for many types of libraries, which will feel the impact of consumer acceptance of this format in the range and amount of educational and entertainment software that will be made available at attractive prices.

**Services.** How audiovisual resources are used depends, of course, on the philosophy and standards of service that guide libraries in providing information to their patrons.

*Schools.* Elementary and secondary schools have been in the forefront of accepting audiovisual resources as integral to their educational mission and to their library services. Although at the end of World War II audiovisual services were a distinctly separate aspect of the educational process, there was a call for unity of print and nonbook resources in instruction in the 1950's and 1960's. While the topic caused much debate, the approach gained increasing acceptance as educators and librarians saw how it could enhance tht total educational process. The 1969 *Standards for School Media Programs*—jointly published by ALA's American Association of School Librarians (AASL) and Department of Audiovisual Instruction (DAVI), the forerunner of the Association for Educational Communications and Technology (AECT)—boldly called for such a fully integrated media program, a position reemphasized in the 1975 revision *Media Programs: District and School* (AASL and AECT). Now, almost universally accepted in both attitude and practice, the inclusion of audiovisual resources or educational technology in the school library media center gives credence to the firm belief that open access to nonbook material is a vital support of the curriculum and that it offers a broad range of learning experiences toward individualized instruction for personalized learning. Great Britain and the Scandinavian countries are among those nations that are following this trend and are utilizing a full range of educational technology in the instructional process and library center.

With a strong systematic and scientific rationale for use in the school media center, audiovisual resources are evident as a student retreats to an individual carrel to view a single-concept 8-mm film loop, or as a group of students share a filmstrip presentation via multiple sets of headphones, or as another individual checks out a cassette player for use at home. Such activities are typical of school districts like the Los Alamitos (California) School District, winner of the 1977 School Library Media Program of the Year (sponsored by AASL and Encyclopaedia Britannica). The school district credits its success to the involvement and integration of the school media centers with the instructional process. While some not so enlightened schools may be reluctant to embrace the use and production of media so fervently, elementary and high school students themselves reared in the electronic age are eager and willing forces toward achieving this goal.

*Academic Libraries.* Slower to respond to the impetus of audiovisual materials than school libraries, libraries in institutions of higher education nevertheless have felt the influence of the schools' call for the use of audiovisual materials in instruction and as a part of a traditional library collection. Two-year institutions, possibly because of their relatively recent development, goals and purposes different from those of four-year schools, and closeness to the secondary schools' philosophy and clientele, have more openly embraced audiovisual materials in their instructional programs and materials collections. The nature of the two-year curriculum—with its inclusion of vocational, adult, and remedial education courses, its community orientation, and the diversity of its student population—encourages a broad view of educational process and requires more flexibility in instructional approaches and methods than traditional four-year institutions. Geared to instructional and individual needs, learning resource centers in two-year institutions encompass both traditional print material and newer media in centers that provide sophisticated audiovisual production facilities and that integrate the diverse materials, even to intershelving them, in an approach that determines collection size and budgetary allowance as a "bibliographic unit" rather than as a book or a film.

Pioneering in this effort in the mid-1960's were Miami-Dade Community College in Florida and Orange Coast College in California. The College of DuPage in Illinois provides a fine example of the congenial intershelving of traditional print resources with all of their audiovisual acquisitions except film.

The 1972 *Guidelines for Two-Year College Learning Resources Programs* and the 1979 *Statement on Quantitative Standards for Two-Year Learning Resources Programs* (ALA's Association of College and Research Libraries, American Association of Community and Junior Colleges, and Association for Educational Communications and Technology) offer diagnostic, descriptive, and quantitative guidelines for learning resource centers that are an integral part of the instructional system with collections geared to the needs of the institution, faculty, and students and with programs that facilitate and improve learning through the provision of a variety of readily accessible services and materials.

ALA

*Record listening facilities were among the first audiovisual services provided library users. Here, an early user of the Hill School, Pennsylvania, listens to recorded music.*

Far more cautiously, four-year college and university libraries have grown to acknowledge the worth of audiovisual materials in meeting the requirements for general reference and curriculum support that the traditional library has fulfilled. Nonprint materials have been present in varying degrees in colleges and universities since the early years of this century, but their use had been viewed as distinctly separate from the library. Most visible have been the university film-rental libraries and the film extension services, which have grown in number and importance from their inception in the 1920's. When interest spurred development of further audiovisual services, they were usually housed with the film rental library. Indeed, on many campuses today the only nonprint media are provided by these agencies. University of California Extension Media Services and Pennsylvania State Audio Visual Services are among the 50 leading film-rental libraries of the Consortium of University Film Centers that have built up large and influential film collections for on-campus as well as extension services use.

Collections of slides and art prints in the art department and of recordings in the music department are traditional examples of instructional adjuncts that were not accorded room in the library. One reason is that college and university faculty have been skeptical of audiovisual media and have not considered them part of the educational process. In the early 1970's, however, there began a trend toward incorporating media in academic libraries, notably in undergraduate libraries. Such centers as the undergraduate libraries at the University of Washington, University of Maryland, and the University of Tennessee at Knoxville have facilities that are similar to the learning resource centers of two-year colleges. The prevalent attitude is that of acquisition of information regardless of the format.

The 1968 *Guidelines for Audio-Visual Services in Academic Libraries* (Audiovisual Committee, Association of

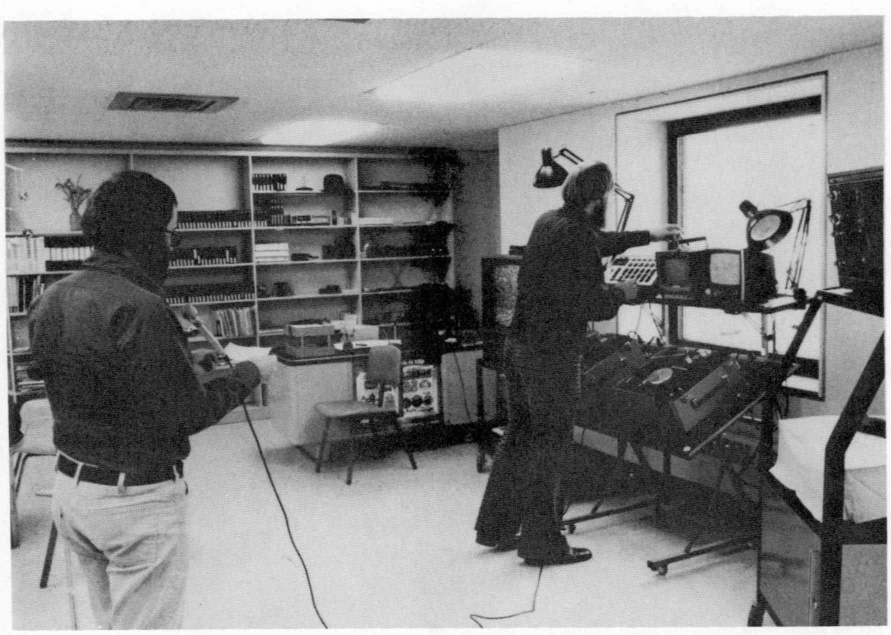

St. Paul Public Library

*Editing room at the St. Paul Public Library's Video Communications Center. The Center allows library users to check out equipment and offers training in production.*

College and Research Libraries) gives welcome credibility to the rich potential of audiovisual resources in libraries, addressing materials selection, budget, housing, and personnel. While acknowledging the existence of separate housing of audiovisual resources, the guidelines state a preference for combined facilities and advise that similar types of material be shelved together. Revision of these guidelines, in process, will undoubtedly provide a firmer philosophical outlook toward the admission of nonprint resources in library collections, since the audiovisual guidelines will be incorporated in ACRL's overall standards for four-year institutions.

Similar interest in the richness and diversity of audiovisual resources is being shown in academic institutions in Australia, Great Britain, and other nations that are becoming extremely active in incorporating nonprint media into academic library collections.

As librarians recognize and develop the newer media as part of traditional library and educational services, they will be aided and encouraged by the cultural, social, and technological forces in society that are forging an innovative approach to education and the provision of information. Of special note in this regard is Britain's Open University home study curriculum, combining print material with radio and television broadcasts, which inspired in the early and mid-1970's such similar programs as those at Empire State College of the State University of New York, the Free University of Iran, and the Open University of Venezuela.

*Special Libraries.* Audiovisual services in special libraries are highlighted by health sciences libraries, which in the late 1960's and 1970's have supplemented their traditional print collections for research with a wide range of nonprint media for individual student learning and continuing education. Following the lead of school media specialists, medical and other health sciences librarians have recognized the advantage of individualized, self-paced instruction and the effectiveness of various types of media in maximizing teaching and learning time. For example, audiotapes enable students to hear the sounds of a heartbeat, slides can provide high-resolution documentation of a rare physical condition, while film and video can demonstrate complete surgical procedures. To this end health sciences libraries, such as the IRC Building Health Sciences Center at the University of British Columbia in Vancouver and the Fleishmann Teaching and Learning Center at Stanford University in California, have impressive floor plans that include individual and group study areas and storage and production facilities geared to the diverse media employed in medical instruction and with special attention to easy access to some of the most favored resources—slides, audio, and video.

Continuing education is currently of specialized interest and concern to health care professionals who seek to cope with and disseminate new research information in rapidly changing and highly specialized areas of medicine. Video technology is ideal for such information sharing, as shown by the American Hospital Association and several other professional health associations, which in 1979 produced two-way television panel discussions on various topics of health care that were transmitted by RCA satellite and picked up by cable systems in 600 hospitals throughout the U.S. Utilization of videotaped case studies within the panel presentation, and interaction between panel participants and viewers who telephoned in their specific questions for the speakers, proved to be an intriguing use of media in a vital area of specialized information services.

*Public Libraries.* From the turn of the century, in the form of recordings, flat pictures, and even films, audiovisual materials have been part of library collections in North America. Since 1945, however, the interest in and collection of nonbook resources, including films, sound recordings, video, slides, filmstrips, and realia, have significantly affected library services within the library, as librarians specializing in children's, young adult, and adult services have selected and programmed nonprint media for the needs and interests of their particular clientele, and outside the library, as librarians have devised new programs and services to extend its resources to such patrons as the shut-ins, senior citizens, the disadvantaged, and other groups not reached by traditional means.

The amount and variety of audiovisual media libraries acquire depend on their size and other considerations, but all public libraries have access to a range of media, especially the more expensive formats of film through state library agencies, film cooperatives such as the Missouri Libraries Film Cooperative, or regional film resources such as those in Ontario that centralize their film resources in 14 public library systems for use by local communities. The 1975 *Guidelines for Audiovisual Materials and Services for Large Public Libraries* and the *Recommendations for Audiovisual Materials and Services for Small and Medium Sized Public Libraries* (Public Library Association Audiovisual Committee) argue for the validity of nonprint resources in libraries and urge the freely accessible provision of audiovisual resources to library patrons. To that end descriptive and quantitative standards are detailed for administrative responsibilities, materials, services, staffing, and physical facilities.

Public libraries in Scandinavia, Australia, and Great Britain have also incorporated audiovisual resources in their collections and services, from the comfortable listening center in a Danish library to the spectacular public library at the Georges Pompidou Center in Paris, where patrons enjoy free access to a fine slide collection and to a film collection transferred to the video format. In the U.S. an interesting example of public library use of media is found at the Library and Museum of the Performing Arts, part of the New York Public Library, where listening stations, slide programs, and rear screen projection of film loops exist happily and attractively among books and sheet music in a total learning environment for both children and adults.

Some of the most intriguing and innovative use of nonprint media in U.S. public libraries has arisen with the advent of video technology. The Chicago Public Library and the City Colleges of Chicago, for instance, in the mid-1970's initiated a joint external degree and independent study program comprised of college-produced videocassettes available for student viewing at library branches. Port Washington (New York) Public Library has been one of the pioneering institutions for community-access video, taping community meetings and interviews with artists whose work has been exhibited at the Library and training local citizens in video production.

The linking of a library's video equipment and materials with the commercial broadband cable television systems available in many communities has allowed many public libraries to explore their potential as information resource centers. Producing their own programs, often in conjunction with community groups, specifically directed to the needs and interests of the local citizenry or as advertisement for these libraries' own services, has been a stimulative and satisfying experience for such libraries as the one in Pocatello, Idaho, which traveled to local migrant-labor camps to produce Spanish-language programs, and the one in Everett, Washington, which cablecasts local author interviews.

Many other libraries around the nation have become involved in video and cable in small or large projects and successful or disappointing experiences, but the medium remains an intriguing avenue of exploration for libraries that are becoming increasingly comfortable with new media.

**Organizations.** Institutional guidance for the selection and use of audiovisual materials and hardware is found in the U.S. in such noteworthy organizations as the Association for Educational Communications and Technology, Educational Film Library Association, various divisions of ALA, Film Library Information Council, Health Education Media Association, and National Medical Audiovisual Center. The Association for Media Technology in Education in Canada, the Council for Educational Technology for the United Kingdom, and Unesco are among the host of national and international groups concerned with the study, production, and dissemination of audiovisual resources in various library and educational settings.

**Issues.** The bibliographic control of nonprint materials has been an issue of continuing concern to librarians attempting to locate and access needed information for their collections. Several approaches to this problem include Project Mediabase, a joint effort of AECT and the National Commission on Libraries and Information Science, which during the 1970's attempted to assess the goals, objectives, and functional specifications for bibliographic control of nonprint media. The Learning Materials Recording Study has a similar goal for the bibliographic control of audiovisual materials in Great Britain.

The National Information Center for Educational Media (NICEM) has since 1964 built a computerized data bank to provide bibliographic information on nonprint materials supplied by the Library of Congress, media producers, and media centers and libraries for the production and dissemination of yearly indexes listing a wide range of nonprint formats.

On a global level, the International Federation of Library Associations and Institutions has established an International Standard Bibliographic Description (nonbook material)—ISBD (NBM)—program, which adds specific requirements for the description and identification of nonbook materials to its long-term goal of universal bibliographic control through international communication of bibliographic data, achieved by means of international standards for bibliographic description.

Since 1972 the MAchine Readable Cataloging (MARC) system of tagging and coordinating bibliographic data in machine-readable form has included nonprint formats, the most recent of which is for videotape. Of interest to health sciences libraries is AVLINE, which is the National Library of Medicine's subject-accessed computerized data base for reviewed audiovisual materials in health sciences, begun in 1975.

Given impetus by the Library of Congress's entry into the cataloguing of nonbook materials, the inadequate provisions for the handling of such media in the 1967 *Anglo-American Cataloging Rules* (ALA) were addressed by American, Canadian, and British groups and dealt with by a 1975 publication revising chapter 12 of the rules to improve the handling of principal audiovisual media and newer educational media, as well as instructional aids. This revision remains generally intact in the second edition of the rules, published in 1978, which attempts to integrate the cataloguing of nonprint materials throughout the rules while giving specific guidelines for description and forms of entry for any kind of nonprint material.

Attempts to provide identification of audiovisual materials and review sources that have evaluated them are the *International Index to Multi-Media Information* and its supplement *Film and Video Review Index* and *Media Review Digest*.

Once audiovisual materials have been identified and selected, the equally vexing problems of their physical control appear. The nature of their nonbook formats, the lack of standardization of packaging among such formats as sound filmstrip sets, and the problems of multiple components in such materials as slide-tape presentations often make handling and shelving a problem. The philosophy of service regarding open or restricted access, the expense and technical intricacies of audiovisual materials, and the circulation policies regarding various audiovisual formats and hardware are aspects that also must be considered. The actual intershelving of audiovisual materials with print resources has always been a point of controversy. Generally, some libraries with smaller collections, such as school media centers and community college learning resource centers, are willing to accommodate nonprint items on their shelves; public libraries have been reluctant to intershelve, while the size of collections in college and university libraries makes intershelving impractical.

Because of the technical nature of audiovisual materials necessitating restricted access, and in some cases trained operators for the required equipment, and because of the powerful medium of expression of such formats as 16-mm films, the problem of censorship of nonprint materials is a troubling and unique one that faces librarians attempting to assure freedom of information to their patrons.

Although much activity and many developments in audiovisual services in libraries were spurred by the Library Services and Construction Act of 1964, federal funding dwindled during the 1970's, and tightening of local funds, as in the case of California's Proposition 13 tax revolt, has been felt by libraries. Because of the expense of nonprint media and because of a lack of understanding of the worth of audiovisual resources in total library information services, school, public, and academic libraries have felt this fiscal restraint and financial pinch severely in the area of audiovisual materials. While the rapidly changing technology of the 1970's and 1980's makes such new formats as the videodisc increasingly attractive, decreases in budgets, staff, and administrative support make it difficult to utilize audiovisual resources and electronic technology in improving and expanding library services.

Increased reliance on multitype library cooperation and such ventures as cooperative film circuits will be the pattern for the coming decades, while new video formats, personal computers, and satellite communications will have an impact on the selection and utilization of nonprint media in libraries of the not-so-distant future.

**REFERENCES**

James W. Brown, editor, *Educational Media Yearbook 1978* (1978), and earlier years.

James W. Brown, *New Media in Public Libraries: A Survey of Current Practices* (1976).

Margaret Chisholm, *Reader in Media, Technology and Libraries* (1975).

Seth Goldstein, *Video in Libraries: A Status Report, 1977–78* (1977).

Pearce S. Grove, *Nonprint Media in Academic Libraries* (1975).

Warren B. Hicks and Alma M. Tillin, *Managing Multimedia Libraries* (1977).

IRENE WOOD

## Austin, Derek William
(1921–     )

Derek Austin made significant contributions to the field of indexing, through his work with the Classification Research Group and the development of the PRECIS (PREserved Context Index System). He was born in London on August 11, 1921. He started his library career in 1938, joining the staff of his local public library directly from grammar school. He spent most of the period 1941–46 on army service in India, Burma, China (with a commando unit), and Germany. After being demobilized he applied for an ex-serviceman's grant to study at Loughborough Library School and achieved the Associateship of the Library Association in 1948, passed the LA Final examination (with honors) in 1949, and was elected a Fellow of the Library Association in 1950.

Most of his early career was spent in public libraries (Enfield, Hertfordshire, and Tottenham), usually in the capacity of reference librarian, readers' adviser, or subject specialist. Service of this kind, requiring a constant use of indexes as tools for relating queries to answers, is a necessary background, Austin became convinced, for anyone who intends to produce an index or attempts to design an indexing system.

He became involved in index production when he joined the staff of the *British National Bibliography* as a Subject Editor in 1963. He was seconded from *BNB* in 1967 to work on the NATO-supported research, directed by the Classification Research Group (London), into a new library classification based on faceted principles. Although the CRG classification had not materialized when the NATO funds ran out, Austin came to consider that such an innovation was no longer necessary. The general principles of subject analysis formulated during that research were the critical starting point for his later research into subject indexing.

The need for a fresh approach to indexing arose when the editors of *BNB* decided that all its issues from the start of 1971 should be produced by computer from MARC records. With just over a year to go, Austin was appointed to lead a team with the task of designing a new subject index. The goal was a controlled-language, precoordinated indexing system conceived from the outset with the computer in mind. The system had to satisfy the following main criteria: (1) all index entries, and their supporting cross-references, should be generated, filed, and printed entirely by the computer; (2) the indexer would prepare only an input string of terms and coded instructions, which would then be manipulated by standard algorithms into index entries under any selected term; and (3) all entries should be meaningful and equally coextensive, and the mechanical generation of entries should not entail any loss of information, nor any distortion of the subject. All these goals were achieved by PRECIS (PREserved Context Index System)—a name that has become almost a synonym for Derek Austin.

Although Austin's work on classificatory theory formed a necessary basis for his later ideas on indexing, PRECIS has taken the concept of subject analysis and concept organization in a new direction: away from relative significance as the organizing principle and toward general linguistic principles and an order of terms in index entries which is directly concerned with the clear expression of meaning. Thus, an explanation of PRECIS mainly calls for reference to grammatical categories and general logical relations.

It is, perhaps, typical of Derek Austin that he continued to be surprised by the spreading use of PRECIS and by its impact on the general approach to subject organization. Although PRECIS is still a relatively young system (what might be called the definitive version for the English language was adopted by *BNB* in 1974), it is now employed by a number of indexing agencies in Britain, Australia, and Canada, and experimental indexes are being produced in several other countries. The logic on which the system is based, and on which the production of meaningful entries depends, appears to be language-independent, and the system has been applied successfully in a range of European languages.

Austin's current research is concerned with program extensions for the use of PRECIS in different natural languages and with the potential of PRECIS as a translingual switching system, i.e., a system which will allow the computer to translate index data from one language into another.

In the course of his researches, Austin necessarily had to reexamine many facets of the total indexing operation. Several of the techniques developed originally for PRECIS are capable of standing in isolation, and many indexers who have no intention of adopting PRECIS have nevertheless benefited from a study of its approach to concept analysis, the treatment of compound terms, and the construction of a machine-held thesaurus. The general applicability of these techniques is mentioned only occasionally in Austin's own writing on PRECIS, but they appear, nevertheless, in two documents that would otherwise, by their very nature, remain anonymous; Austin was the principal author of a Draft International Standard on techniques for document analysis and of the current British Standard on the construction of a monolingual thesaurus.

In 1976 Austin received the first Ranganathan Award presented by the FID for original contributions to classification (defined in its widest sense). This was followed by the Margaret Mann Citation for 1978.

**REFERENCES**

Hans Wellisch, editor, *The PRECIS Index System: Principles, Applications, and Prospects* (1977).

Derek Austin, *PRECIS: A Manual . . .* (London, 1974).

JUTTA SØRENSEN

## Australia

Australia, a federal parliamentary state, is an island continent between the Pacific and Indian oceans. It includes six states: New South Wales, Victoria, Queensland, South Australia, Tasmania, and Western Australia. Pop. (1978 est.) 14,212,900; area 7,682,300 sq.km. The official language is English.

**National Library.** The National Library of Australia was established in 1902 as the library of the infant Parliament of the Commonwealth of Australia, but in 1907 the Parliamentary Library Committee recommended that the library should develop along the lines of the Library of Congress.

In an Australian library world dominated by the six state libraries of the former colonies, and especially by those of New South Wales and Victoria, this statement of intent went quite unnoticed, or at most was not taken very seriously. Nevertheless, over the next half century the Commonwealth Parliamentary Library did develop a national role in addition to its direct responsibility to the legislature and undertook also the development of the national archives. From 1923 the title "Commonwealth National Library" came into use for this tripartite activity, and in 1927 the Library moved from its temporary location in Melbourne to the new national capital, Canberra.

In 1960, on the recommendation of a Commonwealth Government Committee of Enquiry, the Paton Committee, the three functions were separated, the National Library of Australia being distinguished, as a separate institution, from the Parliamentary Library and the Archives. From that time increasingly, and especially with the great advantage since 1968 of a major building, the Library has assumed a proper position of national leadership, resting in large part on its provision of national bibliographical services, of which the most significant are regular publication of the national bibliography (*Australian National Bibliography,* ANB), maintenance of the *National Union Catalogue of Monographs* (NUCOM), maintenance of one of the two National Union Catalogues of Serial Holdings (*Serials in Australian Libraries, Social Sciences and Humanities,* SALSSAH), and provision of central cataloguing services including AMRS (the Australian MARC Record Service).

The Library has made continuous efforts to establish a coordinated national plan for library and information services, but those efforts have been largely frustrated by inability to attract increased national funding. A limited degree of resource sharing has been promoted, however, with the support of other major libraries in some subject fields. Examples are the life sciences, centered on MEDLINE, and a general computerized literature searching service, AUSINET, which provides local access to some major overseas data bases. The Library's collections and services have been reorganized as a series of subject agglomerations whose names, such as ANSTEL (Australian National Scientific and Technological Library) and ANHUL (Australian National Humanities Library), indicate the same general philosophy.

The Library's holdings were estimated in 1976 at 1,626,000 volumes, together with extensive collections in microform and of films, records, and other nonbook materials. Significant collections and strengths in various fields are described in a *Guide to the Collections* published by the Library.

**State Libraries.** The decentralized form of Australian federalism perpetuates the importance of the central libraries of the constituent states. However, the development of the National Library and the rapid growth of academic libraries since the mid-1950's have reduced the relative contribution of the state libraries to the bibliographical resources of the nation and, as a group, they have shifted their emphasis increasingly away from research collecting to the coordination and supplementation of public library services within their respective states. Nevertheless, there remains inevitably a continuing need to define areas of collecting vis à vis the National Library, especially in relation to Australiana, as highlighted by the fact that, for historical reasons, the world's leading collection in this field is probably still the Mitchell Library within the State Library of New South Wales.

**Academic Libraries.** A major library phenomenon of recent years has been the multiplication and expansion of academic libraries in Australia, due to the injection of massive Commonwealth funding into universities, colleges of advanced education (the alternative form of tertiary institution), and institutes of technical and further education. Federal funding of universities began in earnest as a result of the report of the Murray Committee, set up by the Commonwealth government in 1957. At that time there were nine universities or university colleges, the libraries of which had a total stock of 1,500,000 volumes, employed 269 staff, and accounted for a combined expenditure of almost $1,000,000. By 1977 there were 19 universities, and the comparative figures were 10,800,000 volumes, 2,226 staff, and more than $38,000,000 expenditure. This rapid growth has shifted the balance of the nation's research collections away from the public library sphere. The oldest and largest of the university libraries, the University of Sydney Library, with more than 2,000,000 volumes, has the largest collection of any library in Australia and perhaps in the Southern Hemisphere.

Robert Wedgeworth

*The children's library in the Waverly Public Library in Sydney, Australia. A Commonwealth Committee of Inquiry reported in 1976 that public library service reached 93 percent of Australia's population.*

Colleges of Advanced Education resulted from the recommendations of the Martin Committee (1965) that Australia should develop a binary system of tertiary education, offering a more practically oriented alternative to universities. There were 83 colleges in 1977, including many former teacher training institutions. Generous federal funding had revolutionized the libraries of these institutions, but many of them still fell short of the interim standards set in 1969 for their development by the library subcommittee of the Commission of Advanced Education, the government body coordinating the funding and growth of the colleges. The largest college library, that of the Western Australian Institute of Technology, held 338,000 volumes in 1976.

Technical and further education libraries, based on the collections of former technical colleges, were also the subject of a government inquiry in the 1970's and have received a measure of Commonwealth financial support. As a group, however, they still fall far short of being able to meet the needs of their parent institutions.

**Public Libraries.** The provision of direct library service to the public is largely the responsibility of local government authorities in each of the six states. In the Australian Capital Territory, however, the Canberra Public Library Service is a branch of the National Library of Australia.

In every state local government expenditure on libraries is supplemented by state subsidy. The form of the subsidy varies considerably from state to state, producing a corresponding variation in the degree to which local library services are integrated on a statewide basis. At one extreme, in Tasmania, local public libraries either are, or are likely to become, completely absorbed by the State Library. At the other, in New South Wales, municipal and shire councils retain the fullest measure of autonomy, simply receiving state subsidy for library activities that commend themselves to the state authority. In Western Australia subsidy is provided through the provision of bookstock from a single state collection. An array of intermediate positions is adopted by the other three states. In general there is a substantial trend toward the greater integration of services and toward increasingly active participation by the state authority—in practice, the state library.

Public libraries date effectively from the passage of the first State Library Act (New South Wales, 1939), which was the outcome of community action following the recommendations of a Carnegie-funded survey of Australian libraries (the Munn-Pitt Report) undertaken in 1934. Though there has been rapid development over this 40-year period, a Commonwealth Committee of Inquiry into Public Libraries reported in 1976 (the Horton Report) that there were grave inadequacies still in completeness of coverage and in the level of service provided and that only the provision of federal funding could arrest a continuing deterioration in the situation. By late 1979 there had still been no official response to this report. The Horton Committee found that some kind of public library service is available to 93 percent of the population and that all the libraries involved had a total bookstock of some 13,980,000 volumes (1975).

**Special Libraries.** The most important groups of special libraries are the libraries of the Commonwealth and state parliaments, the libraries of Commonwealth and state departments and instrumentalities, and the libraries of business and industry. Parliamentary libraries present a fairly wide range, in both function and resources. The Commonwealth Parliamentary Library has been liberally supported in the 1970's and has been able to provide legislative research services of high quality, in addition to maintaining more conventional reference service. Within their greater financial limitations, the state parliamentary libraries are developing in the same direction.

Unique among the second group of special libraries is the library service of the Commonwealth Scientific and Industrial Research Organization (CSIRO). CSIRO's nationwide network of some 60 or more branch libraries attached to various laboratories and divisions provides considerable support to library services generally, and the Organization's outward looking and cooperative attitude is typified by its continued publication of the older and more significant of the two national union lists of serials, *Scientific Serials in Australian Libraries* (SSAL). For some time it appeared that CSIRO might develop as a national science library but, following the report of a committee set up by the Council of the National Library, the Scientific and Technological Information Services Enquiry Committee (STISEC), in 1972, the National Library itself moved more positively into this area.

Libraries of business and industry vary greatly in size and sophistication. An example of a well-developed special library is that of Australian Consolidated Industries, which provides computer-based SDI and current awareness services to members of the firm. An estimate of 800 significant special libraries in 1978 is probably not inaccurate, though a business recession from 1975 saw many closures of such services.

**School Libraries.** This is a field in which, again, federal assistance in the 1970's brought about very notable improvements. Commonwealth funding has been most effective in relation to secondary schooling, which benefited from a dramatic improvement in facilities, resources, and staffing. The problem was of such vast dimensions, however, that it would be generally agreed that there are still very many inadequate school libraries. Federal funding extends to both public and private schools.

**Libraries in Australia (1976)**

| Type | Number | Volumes in collections | Annual expenditures (dollar) | Population served | Professional staff | All staff (total) |
|---|---|---|---|---|---|---|
| National[a] | 1 | 1,600,000 | A$10,800,000 | 14,000,000 | 140 | 670 |
| State[b] | 6 | 3,676,000 | N.A. | 14,000,000 | 574 | 1,490 |
| Academic | | | | | | |
| Universities | 18 | 10,878,000 | A$38,343,000 | 165,000 | 567 | 2,226 |
| Colleges of Advanced Education[c] | 59 | 3,787,000 | A$20,148,000 | 161,000 | 361 | 1,306 |
| Technical and Further Education[d] | 110 | 800,000 | N.A. | 760,000 | N.A. | N.A. |
| Public[e] | 550 | 13,980,000 | A$49,800,000 | 12,466,000 | 648 | 3,026 |
| School[f] | 3,200 | N.A. | N.A. | 1,200,000 | N.A. | N.A. |
| Special[g] | 754 | 5,829,000 | N.A. | N.A. | N.A. | 2,380 |
| Total | 4,698 | | | | | |

[a]The National Library has as one of its activities the Canberra Public Library Service; stock, staff, and operational figures for this service have been transferred to Public Libraries. Figures are for 1975–76.

[b]Several state libraries have staff dedicated to public library support, and some directly operate regional library services. Figures for both these operations have been transferred to Public Libraries. Figures are for 1975.

[c]Colleges of Advanced Education are described as "equal to but different from" universities. There are 83 such colleges, but only 59 are recorded in statistical source.

[d]Technical and further education institutions offer trade and other courses largely at postprimary level but some at postsecondary level. Only 40,000 of some 738,000 students are enrolled full-time.

[e]Figures are for 1975. The count is of library services and not of service points. It includes the public library service provided by the National Library and similar services (and staff) provided by some state libraries. Figures are for 1975.

[f]Those libraries that provide a standard acceptable to the Australian Schools Commission.

[g]Figures are for 1975. Volume count is misleadingly small. Statistical source quotes number of volumes for monographs only.

Sources: National Library of Australia, *Annual report;* Australia, Committee of Inquiry into Public Libraries, *Report* (1976); Australia, Schools Commission, *Report for the Triennium 1976–78;* Library Association of Australia, Special Libraries Section, *Directory of Special Libraries in Australia* (1976); Australian Advisory Council on Bibliographical Services, *The Work of AACOBS* (1976).

**Associations.** The Library Association of Australia (LAA) was established in 1949 in direct succession to the Australian Institute of Librarians, founded in 1937 as an outcome of the Munn-Pitt survey. The Association, incorporated by Royal Charter in 1963, welcomes all interested in libraries but also provides for professional membership. It conducted examinations in librarianship from 1944 and has an active program of accreditation of library schools. The Australian School Libraries Association (ASLA) is a federation of state associations of school librarians. Though there is no formal link between ASLA and the LAA, there is a joint standing committee to facilitate cooperation. The Australian Advisory Council on Bibliographical Services (AACOBS) is a unique voluntary association of representatives of all major library, archive, and information services throughout the country. It provides a mechanism for day-to-day consultation and cooperation and a device for the expression of group criticism and advice to governments, both federal and state, and to the National Library. The National Library funds a secretariat and supports the activities of five working parties of AACOBS: on bibliography, information resources, user needs, research and development, and systems and communications. AACOBS is committed to the enunciation of a policy on information, for which it hopes to secure Commonwealth government endorsement, and to the setting out at least of guidelines for national planning in relation to library and information services.

**REFERENCES**

John Balnaves and P. Biskup, *Australian Libraries,* 2nd ed. (1975), is a standard work.

Harrison Bryan and G. Greenwood, editors, *Design for Diversity: Library Services for Higher Education and Research in Australia* (1977), is a major work with historical and other detail not found elsewhere.

HARRISON BRYAN

## Austria

Austria, a federal republic in central Europe, is bounded on the west by Switzerland and Liechtenstein, on the east by Hungary, on the north by the Federal Republic of Germany and Czechoslovakia, and on the south by Italy and Yugoslavia. Pop. (1977 est.) 7,518,300; area 83,860 sq.km. The official language is German.

**National Library.** The National Library (Die Österreichische Nationalbibliothek), formerly the Wiener Hofbibliothek (Viennese Court Library), is the largest and most important in Austria; its beginnings trace back to the 14th century. The first full-time librarian, Hugo Blotius, was appointed in 1575, and by 1591 the collection contained about 9,000 volumes. Following the end of the monarchy and the dissolution of the Austro-Hungarian Empire in 1918, the Library became the property of the Republic, which it has served in steadily expanding ways.

The collection of printed works totals nearly 2,300,000 volumes, but the Library's special collections are its particular glory. These include manuscripts (around 30,000, plus 130,000 autographs and nearly 8,000 incunabula), maps (190,000, 40,000 volumes, 130 globes), music (34,000 volumes of manuscripts and 85,000 printed works), papyrus (100,000 pieces), portraits (approximately 800,000), photographs (600,000), and theater (52,000 printed works, 5,300 theatrical manuscripts, 60,000 autographs, 260,000 sheets, 84,000 drawings, over 300,000 film and theater photographs, and 840 stage models). Together, they make the Library one of the world's great scholarly resources.

The Library is the seat of the Union Catalogue of Foreign Periodicals (ZAZ); the Austrian national bibliography, biweekly from 1949; international exchange and interlibrary loan; the Association of Austrian Librarians (Vereinigung Österreichischer Bibliothekare), founded in 1896; the Austrian Institute for Library Research (Österreichisches Institut für Bibliotheksforschung); a union catalogue of all new foreign acquisitions by Austrian research libraries (Büchernachweisstelle); and the final stage of professional education for state research libraries. By copyright law the Library receives two copies of every book and four copies of every newspaper and periodical edited or printed in Austria.

The Library occupies a large section of the former court complex. In 1966 a part of the new imperial palace (Neue Hofburg) was added and drastically remodeled to make modern main reading, reference, and periodical rooms; catalogue and loan areas; and offices. None attempts to match in dazzling elegance the 18th-century Prunksaal (State Hall), noted for its magnificent baroque interior.

**Academic Libraries.** In Austria the institutions of higher education include 4 full universities, at Graz, Inns-

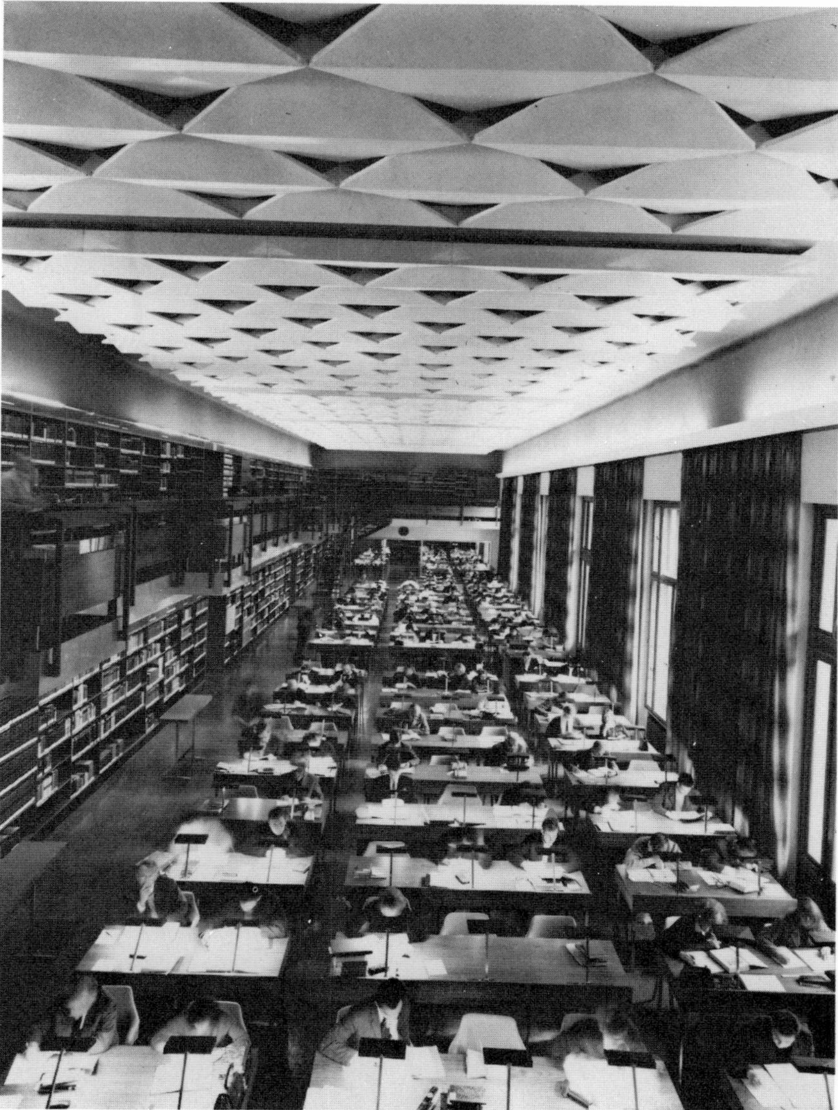

Österreichische Nationalbibliothek

*The modernized main reading room in the National Library of Austria, which traces its beginnings to the 14th century and which was formerly the Viennese Court Library.*

bruck, Salzburg, and Vienna; 2 general technical universities; at Graz and Vienna; 12 technical universities and academies for the study of one or more special fields such as educational sciences, social sciences, design, music, art, commerce, mining, agriculture, or veterinary medicine; and numerous pedagogical academies. The oldest largest, and most important academic library is that of the University of Vienna, which celebrated its 600th anniversary in 1965. The collection numbers around 2,000,000 volumes, to which are added about the same number in the independent libraries of the various faculties, academic institutes, and seminars. The inclusive holdings of the other three university libraries range from 500,000 to 1,000,000 volumes.

**Public Libraries.** Each of Austria's nine provinces (Bundesländer) has a central library that acts as a regional collecting agency, is a copyright deposit for books and periodicals published in the province, and is open for general public use. Where no provincial library (Landesbibliothek) as such exists, these functions are assumed by other institutions, such as a provincial museum or archive.

There are, in addition, more than 400 libraries serving towns and cities. The largest is the system in the capital, which has over 50 branches, bookmobiles, and a collection of some 400,000 volumes. (Vienna's population at about 1,650,000 is well over one-fifth of the country's total). During the 1960's and 1970's a large number of modern public library buildings were built, in the capital and elsewhere.

**School Libraries.** There are over 6,000, varying greatly, as in most countries, in size and quantity of stock.

**Special Libraries.** A score are maintained to serve the Parliament (Nationalrat), the ministries, the Patent Office, the postal and telegraph system, the national airline and railways, and other governmental agencies. Some of these, such as the libraries of the Ministry of Defense (about 600,000 volumes), the Ministries of Science, Research, and Education (285,000 volumes), and the Federal Chancellery (400,000 volumes), are especially important collections. The nongovernmental Chamber of Commerce and that of workers, as well as the larger industrial and commercial establishments, also have special libraries. One of the most modern and accessible special libraries is that of the International Atomic Energy Commission in Vienna.

**Monastic Libraries.** A special bibliographical resource and treasure is found in Austria's oldest libraries, those of more than a hundred monasteries and abbeys, of which Admont (1074), Altenburg (1144), Göttweig (1072), Heiligenkreuz (1135), Klosterneuburg (1106), Kremsmünster (777), Melk (1089), Saint Florian (1071), Saint Peter, Salzburg (690), and Zwettl (1138) are among the best known. The importance of the libraries lies not in their size (from 25,000 to 180,000 volumes) but rather in their holdings of pre-Gutenberg manuscripts (800–1,800), incunabula (700–1,000), and 16th- and 17th-century books. Modern reference and bibliographical works are generally available for the scholar's use. Some of the libraries, perhaps most notably those of Admont, Altenburg, Göttweig, Melk, Saint Florian, and Zwettl, are housed in magnificent baroque rooms.

**Associations.** The Association of Austrian Librarians had a membership of some 800 academic, scholarly, and research librarians in 1979. The proceedings of its meetings appear in the journal *Biblos*. The Association of Austrian Public Libraries (Verband Österreichischer Volks-büchereien) had a membership of around 350 libraries, having a total of 2,000 branches and combined holdings of over 4,000,000 volumes. The proceedings of its meetings, as well as other matters of interest to public and school librarians, are published in *Erwachsenenbildung* (formerly *Neue Volksbildung*), under the aegis of the Ministry of Education.

**REFERENCES**

J. Periam Danton, "Austria: Its Libraries and Librarianship," *Libri* (1966); now out of date as to statistics, but the most general, comprehensive account in English.

Josef Hofinger, "Developments in Austrian University Libraries," *Library Trends* (1964).

J. PERIAM DANTON

## Bachtiar, Harsya W(ardhana)
(1934– )

Harsya Wardhana Bachtiar, Indonesian archivist, educator, sociologist, anthropologist, and historian, was Dean of the Faculty of Letters, University of Indonesia, 1969–75. Concerned about the importance of the acquisition, storage, and accessibility of information, upon assuming the position of Dean, he immediately involved himself actively in programs to increase the capacity of library, documentation, and archival centers in Indonesia to provide improved services.

Born in Bandung, Indonesia, on May 3, 1934, he studied at the Faculty of Social and Political Science, University of Amsterdam, 1953–55; College of Arts and Sciences, and then Graduate School of Arts and Sciences, Cornell University, 1955–59; and later in the Graduate

**Libraries in Austria (1974)**

| Type | Number | Volumes in collections | Annual expenditures (schilling) | Population served | Professional staff | All staff (total) |
|---|---|---|---|---|---|---|
| National | 1 | 2,237,000 | AS 50,642,000 | N.A. | 127 | 256 |
| Academic | 742[a] | 9,563,000 | N.A. | N.A. | 253 | 569[b] 313[c] |
| Public | 426 | 4,364,000 | 106,656,000 | 7,500,000 | 358[b] 273[c] | 441[b] 718[c] |
| School | 6,244 | 11,000,000 | N.A. | N.A. | N.A. | N.A. |
| Special | 512 | 7,384,000 | N.A. | N.A. | N.A. | N.A. |
| Total | 7,925 | 34,548,000 | | | | |

[a]Administrative units; includes, therefore, the libraries of faculties, institutes, seminars, and research units in the institutions.
[b]Full-time.
[c]Part-time.

Source: Unesco, *Statistical Yearbook* (1977).

School of Arts and Sciences, Harvard University, 1963–67. He earned a Ph.D. in Sociology from Harvard with a dissertation on "The Formation of the Indonesian Nation." He lectured at the Faculty of Letters, University of Indonesia, from 1959, becoming a full Professor of Sociology and Social History in 1976.

He served as Acting Director of the National Institute of Economic and Social Research (LEKNAS), Indonesian Institute of Science (LIPI), 1969–75. On the national level, he took an active part in the development of higher education and research in the social sciences as Coordinator of the Consortium of Social Sciences and Humanities, an advisory body to the Minister of Education and Culture, Republic of Indonesia, 1971–75, and then, among others, as Executive Secretary of the Interdisciplinary Consortium, one of 11 consortia maintained to assist the Director General of Higher Education. He served as a member of various official Indonesian delegations, such as the delegation to the annual conferences of the Southeast Asian Ministers of Education Organization (SEAMEO) at Kuala Lumpur, 1971, Saigon, 1972, and Vientiane, 1973, the delegation to the UNESCO General Conference in Paris, 1974, when he was elected Vice-Chairman of Commission V (Social Science, Humanities, and Culture), and in Nairobi, 1976. From 1975 he also served as Chairman of the Indonesian Steering Committee, Dutch-Indonesian Cooperation for the Promotion of Indonesia Studies.

He participated in many conferences on archives and worked closely with the Director of the National Archives of the Republic of Indonesia, particularly in matters of archival professional training, archival cooperation among Southeast Asian countries, archival cooperation between Indonesia and the Netherlands, and oral history.

Among his many publications is a *Directory of Social Scientists in Indonesia* (Jakarta, 1976).

SOEMARTINI

# Bahamas

An independent state off the southeast coast of the United States in the Atlantic Ocean, the Bahamas comprises 700 islands of which only about 30 are inhabited. The islands basically parallel Cuba's north coast. Pop. (1978 est.) 226,000; area 13,864 sq.km. The official language is English.

**National Library.** There was no national library in the Bahamas in early 1979, but in February 1972 a committee was appointed by the government for the purpose of raising funds to establish a Public Library Service. When established, this library will maintain a national union catalogue, national bibliography, national and international loan service, and a strong local history collection. Arrangements will be made for the library to become the official depository for all government and other publications of the Bahamas, as well as for copyrighted works. It will also possess audiovisual material and equipment, periodicals, and microforms and will include a high percentage of children's materials.

The national library will open with a minimum of 440,000 volumes (or 2 volumes per capita), with an increase of 100,000 over a 20-year period, according to plans in 1979.

**Academic Libraries.** The College of the Bahamas Library is the principal academic library in the Bahamas. It was established in 1975 and incorporated the Bahamas Teachers' College Library (now defunct), the Technical College Library, and the San Salvador Teachers' College Library. Its general collection numbers 25,000 volumes and three special collections and includes Bahamian, African, and West Indian works; materials on teaching practice; and theses by students.

**Table 2. Archives in the Bahamas (1970)**

| | |
|---|---|
| Number | 1 |
| Holdings | 1,400 linear feet |
| Annual expenditures | B$220,000 |
| Professional staff | 5 |
| All Staff (total) | 24 |

Source: Archives Annual Report.

**Public Libraries.** There are five public libraries in Nassau and some 32 in the Family Islands (those outside Nassau). The public libraries operate as independent units under their respective Boards of Trustees, as provided by the Nassau Public Library Act (1847) and the Out Island Public Library Act (1909). The public libraries were included in the portfolio of the Minister of Education and Culture from 1964.

**School Libraries.** The majority of the schools in the Bahamas (both government and private) possess a library; comparative information and statistics on their collections were not available in 1979.

**Other Libraries.** The Ranfurly Out Island Library, founded in Nassau in 1954, is a branch of an international charitable and voluntary organization with headquarters in London and branches in 63 countries. It is a nonsectarian and nonracial organization, primarily interested in building up school libraries. It sends free boxes of both adults' and children's books to Family (Out) Island headteachers, who make them available to the community. Approximately 200,000 volumes were donated in some 25 years. Some government departments have libraries within their agencies that serve the department and the Public Service (e.g., the Department of Statistics and the Public Service Training Centre).

**REFERENCES**

Enid Baa and Mary Heneghan, *Report to the National Library Committee on the Proposal for Establishing a Public Library Service in the Bahama Islands* (1973).

D. G. Reid, *Bahamas—Public Library Service* (Unesco, 1973).

Ministry of Education and Culture, Bahamas, *Annual Report 1970–1971*.

D. GAIL SAUNDERS;
KEVA CAMPBELL

**Table 1. Libraries in the Bahamas (1970)**

| Type | Number | Volumes in collections | Annual expenditures (Bahamian dollar) | Population served | Professional staff | All staff (total) |
|---|---|---|---|---|---|---|
| Academic | 1 | 25,000 | B$30,000 | 1,650 | 2 | 12 |
| Public | 37 | 56,509 | B$111,000 | 200,000 | 4 | 79 |
| School | N.A. | N.A. | N.A. | N.A. | N.A. | N.A. |
| Special | N.A. | N.A. | N.A. | N.A. | N.A. | N.A. |

## Bahrain

Bahrain, an independent monarchy in the Middle East, lies in the Persian Gulf between Saudi Arabia and the Qatar Peninsula. Pop. (1978 est.) 277,600; area 662 sq.km. The official language is Arabic.

Bahrain does not possess a national library. Only seven Arabic books were produced in the country in 1975 according to the Arab League Educational, Cultural, and Scientific Organization. Depository regulations, a national bibliography, and bibliographical services are not found in the country.

Two college libraries are attached to the Teachers Training Colleges for men and women. There are no statistics available on the book collections in these libraries, but their holdings are considered to be the largest in Bahrain.

There are two public libraries in the towns of Manamah and Isa. The central Public Library at Manamah, the older and larger, was established in 1946 as the Educational Library, and its services were directed to the personnel, teachers, and students of the Directorate of Education. It is open to the public and offers library services to schools and institutions throughout the country.

Moderate-sized book collections are found in the primary, intermediate, secondary, and technical schools in Bahrain. Professional staff and procedures are negligible.

The Directorate of Educational Planning of the Ministry of Education administers a documentation center, which aims at offering documentation services to the Ministry.

MOHAMED M. EL HADI

## Baker, Augusta
(1911- )

Augusta Baker, distinguished librarian, administrator, educator, author, raconteur, and folklorist, won a preeminent place in library service to children. She was born April 1, 1911, in Baltimore, Maryland, and received a Bachelor of Arts in Education from the State University of New York in 1933 and a Bachelor of Science in Library Science from the same institution in 1935. For the period 1937–74 Baker was a staff member of the New York Public Library, where her career was marked with notable contributions in service to children in the areas of administration, collection development, programs, and services.

As a children's librarian in the Countee Cullen Regional Branch from 1937 to 1953, she pioneered in the momentous task of bringing to the children of Harlem a knowledge of and appreciation for their cultural heritage and background. Working closely with Arthur Schomburg, whose unique collections of materials relating to the black experience were housed in the Branch Library and with certain Harlem women interested in black culture, she established the James Weldon Johnson Memorial Collection for children because of Johnson's interest in the children and the Library. Enriching experiences for children and adults were made possible and augmented through her programs of storytelling, concerts, reading clubs, visits of school classes, and guest appearances of eminent Negro artists, writers, dramatists, and other specialists from various professions.

Entering into the administration of library service to children in the New York Public Library, Augusta Baker served as Assistant Coordinator and Storytelling Specialist from 1953 to 1961. Her established reputation as a storyteller and folklorist enabled her to continue the great tradition of the Library in utilizing the art form of storytelling in bringing together children and books. Creative and gifted, she shared her talents with others within and outside the Library through inspired instruction and guidance.

Administratively, she furthered the work of library service to children with the renowned Coordinator of the Children's Department, Frances Lander Spain. Recognized as an authority in the field of black literature for children, Baker continued her research in the area with a Dutton-Macrae Award, given to her in 1953 by the American Library Association. Her subsequent publication, *Books about Negro Life for Children* (1963), was a landmark and became a prototype for several revised editions under the new title, *The Black Experience in Children's Books*. During this same year she accepted an invitation to organize children's library service for the Trinidad Public Library, Port of Spain, Trinidad. She began a teaching career in 1955 as a Visiting Lecturer in the Columbia University School of Library Service.

The year 1961 was significant for the New York Public Library when Augusta Baker was appointed Coordinator of Children's Services. Recognizing her strengths as an administrator imbued with a practical idealism and dedicated to the advancement of library service to children, the library's administrators established a precedent for large urban library systems by elevating a member of an ethnic minority group to a high-level, policymaking position. Extending the traditional boundaries of service in the Library's 82 branches and six bookmobiles in Manhattan, the Bronx, and Staten Island, Baker expanded the children's collections to include recordings and cassettes; she enlarged the annual bibliography of children's books to include special juvenile materials. Utilizing the media of television and radio, she initiated the series of weekly broadcasts "The World of Children's Literature" on WNYC in 1971 and moderated the television program "It's Fun to Read." She served as a consultant and bibliographer of materials for the television program "Sesame Street."

Baker's influence as a librarian, storyteller, and an authority in materials for children is national and international in scope. She lectured or taught in many universities including Rutgers (1965–67) and Syracuse (1955–60) universities, Texas Women's University (1975), and the universities of Nevada, Southern Florida, and Washington. She lectured before the Australian Library Association in 1973 and participated in conferences of the International Board on Books for Young People (IBBY). Active in the ALA from 1953, she served as Councillor (1965–68, 1968–72), President of the Association for Library Service to Children (1967–68), Chairperson, Newbery-Caldecott Awards Committee (1966), and on the ALA Executive Board (1968–72). She was a member of the Hans Christian Andersen Award Committee (1974–78), and she was representative to UNICEF for the ALA/IBBY. Recognizing her many years of service, ALA extended to her its highest award of Honorary Membership in 1975.

Other professional affiliations include membership in the New York Library Association, the Women's National Book Association, and the New York Folklore Society. Augusta Baker was a delegate to the 1970 White House Conference on Children. She also served as a consultant to the Council on Library Resources, the Teen Age Book Club of the Scholastic Book Service, and the *Children's Digest* magazine. She has been a member of the Advisory Board, Center for the Study of Children's Literature, Simmons College, Boston, Massachusetts, and Co-chairperson for the Friends of (New York Public Library) Children's Services.

She is the recipient of numerous awards and honors, including the *Parent's Magazine* Medal Award (1966) "for outstanding service to the nation's children"; the ALA Grolier Award (1968) "for outstanding achievement in guiding and stimulating the reading of children and young people"; and the Clarence Day Award (1974) "for leadership given to the world of children's books." She also received the Distinguished Alumni Award, State University of New York, Albany. In 1978 Baker received the Honorary Doctor of Letters from Saint John's University, Queens, New York.

Among the publications she edited are *Talking Tree* (1955), *Golden Lynx* (1960), *Young Years* (1960), and *Readings for Children* (New York Library Association, 1964). She wrote *The Black Experience in Children's Books* (New York Public Library, 1971) and was co-author with Ellin Green of *Storytelling: Art and Technique* (1977). She wrote other articles and reviews for professional periodicals and the press.

SPENCER G. SHAW

## Bangladesh

Bangladesh, a people's republic, consists of territory that was until 1972 East Pakistan (the old province of East Bengal and the Sylhet district of Assam). Pop. (1978 est.) 84,655,000; area 143,998 sq.km. The official language is Bengali. The country is crossed by a network of navigable rivers including the Ganges, the Jamuna, the Padma, the Meghna, the Surma, and the Karnaphuli, which flow into the Bay of Bengal. Libraries in Bangladesh suffered great losses during its war for independence.

**National Library.** The National Library of Bangladesh, in the capital city of Dacca, operated in a rented building in 1979. It had three sections, two of which were fully functioning. Compiling bibliographies of all books and periodicals published in the country and received under the copyright law, it has been publishing the Bangladesh National Bibliography since 1972. It also indexed the articles of all the newspapers published in Dacca by language and subject up to 1975. Regular reference and loan services are not provided because of lack of accommodation. On January 21, 1978, the foundation of the new permanent building was laid at Agar Gaon, Sher-e-Banglanagar, Dacca. The Library's collection totaled 203,000 volumes, including bound volumes of periodicals.

*National Bibliography of Bangladesh 1973–76* covers all publications of Bangladesh and about Bangladesh. It includes annotation where necessary. An index to periodicals of all newspapers published in Dacca up to 1976 is published by the National Library.

**Academic Libraries.** There are six university libraries: Dacca (1921), Rajshahi (1953), Chittagong (1966), Jahangirnagar (1970), Bangladesh University of Engineering and Technology (1962), and Mymensingh Agricultural University (1966), all of which have modern libraries with trained librarians.

With 400 staff members, the libraries serve 29,700 students and teachers with over 670,000 books, including over 5,400 periodicals. The Dacca University library, the oldest and largest, has 2,000 valuable manuscripts in Bengali, Sanskrit, Pali, Urdu, Persian, and Arabic languages. Current collections are not sufficient to meet the required needs of the total university population.

Bangladesh's 373 colleges have a few libraries with trained librarians; many college libraries have rare collections in Oriental languages. Fifty government-owned colleges have modern libraries with trained librarians and have some 750,000 volumes including periodicals.

**Public Libraries.** The public library movement dates back to the mid-19th century. In 1854 four public libraries in important district headquarters were established. There are 128 public libraries, but most have collections that do not exceed 2,000 volumes. They are poorly stocked and staffed. With the library movement's growth, a few libraries have provided excellent services; notable is the Jessore Public Library (1854), which has a community delivery service using mail and rickshaw transport besides other usual library services. Government public libraries at Dacca, Chittagong, Khulna, and Rajshahi have been set up on modern lines. The Bangladesh Central Public Library, established in 1953, has a collection of 75,000 volumes and many periodicals. The Library has also a children's section. This library is the nerve center of all public libraries in Bangladesh. The Chittagong Public Library, established in 1963, has 28,000 volumes; Khulna Public Library (1964) has 44,970 volumes besides a number of periodicals. Other important ones that are privately financed and managed but also government aided include Bogra Woodburn Public Library (1854), 15,000 volumes; Khawja Nazimuddin Hall Public Library, Dinajpur (1931), 25,621 volumes; Kushtia Public Library, 6,500 volumes; Barisal Public Library (1854), 10,000 volumes) Shere Bangla Public Library, Faridpur (1950), 12,000 volumes; Jessore Public Library (1854), 16,000 volumes; Chittagong Public Library (1860), 13,000 volumes; Muslim Institute, Mymensingh (1931), 11,000 volumes; Noakhali Public Library (1897), 7,000 volumes; Ananda Govinha Public Library, Pabna, 12,000 volumes; Rangpur Public Library (1950), 11,500 volumes; Central Muslim Sahitya Sangsad, Sylhet (1941), 22,000 volumes; Birchand Public Library, 14,500 volumes; Tangail Public Library (1957), 8,000 volumes; Jamalpur Public Library, 5,000 volumes; Chittagong Hill Tracts Public Library, 7,000 volumes; and Patuakhali Public Library, 7,000 volumes.

**School Libraries.** In government primary schools, numbering 3,615, organized libraries are nonexistent, although there are such teaching materials as charts, maps, globes, and textbooks. Private schools, numbering 4,148, have libraries, but they are unorganized. There are 2,562 junior high schools, of which 5 are government and the rest are private. Library services are poor. Only a few have libraries with untrained personnel. Secondary

**Table 1. Libraries in Bangladesh (1976)**

| Type | Number | Volumes in collections | Annual expenditures (taka) | Population served | Professional staff | All staff (total) |
|---|---|---|---|---|---|---|
| National | 1 | 20,300 | Tk 618,000 | (whole country) | 14 | 22 |
| Academic | 379 | N.A. | N.A. | N.A. | N.A. | N.A. |
| Public | 124 | N.A. | N.A. | N.A. | N.A. | N.A. |
| School | 16,784[a] | N.A. | N.A. | N.A. | N.A. | N.A. |
| Special | 102 | N.A. | N.A. | N.A. | N.A. | N.A. |

[a]Number of schools.

Sources: Ministry of Education, *Statistical Profile of Education in Bangladesh* (1978); Ministry of Sports and Culture; university annual reports.

schools have libraries, but again they are unorganized. A teacher usually serves as librarian. There are 6,469 secondary schools, 147 of which are government run. Many schools have libraries with good collections but no trained librarian. A marked change is taking place, however, with government pilot and model schools. All have standard libraries with trained librarians. As of 1979 there were no separate allocations of funds for them. Only a yearly grant is given to these libraries for purchasing books.

**Table 2. Archives in Bangladesh (1976)**

| | |
|---|---|
| Number | 1 |
| Holdings | 7,050 linear feet |
| Professional staff | 12 |
| All staff (total) | 20 |

**Special Libraries.** Government departments, research organizations, and the like have special libraries, totaling more than 100. Most are found in Dacca and other important district towns. Since most were established during the 1960's, they were planned more efficiently than the older public and college libraries. Special libraries are staffed by trained librarians, whose aim is to collect, organize, catalogue, digest, and supply necessary material in order to stimulate production and scientific advancement. The Bangladesh National Scientific Documentation Center is notable in this regard. BANSDOC is also the UNISIST national focal point of Bangladesh. It has been selected as the national input center for AGRIS. It regularly publishes abstracts of all scientific and technological materials and provides subject bibliographies and other materials to research workers.

bar association libraries 298

Bangladesh Institute of Development Studies (BIDS) has a fairly large library, with 50,000 books, 10,000 microfilms, 10,000 documents, and 800 current periodicals covering social science, demography, and other subjects. The center has a staff of 20 that perform current awareness on a weekly basis; selective dissemination of information service (SDI); abstracting, indexing, and bibliographic services; document supply service; and the preparing of directories. The Bangladesh National Medical Library was established in 1974. Its main function is to procure medical journals, particularly recent ones for support of research programs and patient care. It also serves as a nerve center of eight other medical college libraries in the country. The two other leading medical libraries are the library of the International Centre for Diarreal Diseases and Research (founded 1962) and the library of the Institute of Postgraduate Medicine and Research (1966).

*The headquarters of the Public Library in Bridgetown, Barbados, has seven branches and serves 70 percent of the country's schools with three mobile libraries.*

Barbados Government Information Service

Several libraries in research organizations perform documentation work, for example, Rice Research Institute Library, Jute Research Institute Library, Fuel Research Institute Library, Institute of Business Administration, Bangladesh Studies (Rajshahi), Varendra Research Library (Rajshahi), Institute of Education and Research Library, Asiatic Society Library, Bangla Academy Library, Bangladesh Shisho Academy, Shilpa Kala Academy, Bangladesh Council for Scientific and Research Library, Atomic Energy Centre Library, National Institute of Public Administration Library, and Bangladesh Education Extension and Research Institute Library.

**Foreign Mission Libraries.** These are valuable in the dissemination of information in Bangladesh. University and college students and citizens use them. The British Council Library, on the Dacca University campus, gives maximum services to students and teachers. The American Center Library also gives the same services besides its normal programs. These institutions serve a dual purpose: as cultural ambassadors and as institutions promoting the idea of free public library services in Bangladesh.

A. K. M. SHAMSUL ALAM

# Barbados

Barbados, an independent state of the southern Caribbean Sea, is the easternmost island of the West Indies, Pop. (1978 est.) 253,100; area 430 sq. km. The official language is English.

Subscription libraries existed from the 18th century, and the act to establish the Public Library and Museum was passed as early as 1847. However, today the development of library services is still uneven and patchy. Academic and public libraries are reasonably well established, but much needs to be done in the areas of special and school libraries. One promising feature is that recognition for professionally qualified staff has gained acceptance, with the government assuming greater responsibility since the 1960's.

**National and Public Library.** The Public Library consists of a Headquarters, seven branches, and three mobile libraries. Its services are available free to all residents from age six, and it offers the usual services to users. Its stock includes an excellent West Indiana reference collection. This Library is de facto the National Library. It has legal deposit status and from 1975 published the *National Bibliography of Barbados*. It advises the government on all aspects of library policy and has been in the forefront for training of librarians.

**Academic Libraries.** The University of the West Indies (Cave Hill Campus) group of libraries comprise the major academic libraries. These are the Main Library (1963), the Law Library (1971), the Library, Institute of Social and Economic Research (Eastern Caribbean) (1962), and the Library of the School of Education (1973). Together their stock totals about 117,000 volumes, exclusive of periodicals and nonbook materials. The Law Library has begun to play a crucial role in shaping West Indian jurisprudence and should eventually develop into a center of paramount importance.

The other academic library of note is that of the Barbados Community College, which was still in its infancy in 1978, but it is hoped that its stock eventually will be about 55,000. Other libraries with important collections are the Medical Library of the Queen Elizabeth Hospital, the Erdiston Teachers' Training College Library, and that of the Samuel Jackman Prescod Polytechnic.

**School Libraries.** In theory, each public school has a library; in reality, however, there are only two libraries worthy of note. (No comprehensive information was available on the status of private schools.) In an effort to remedy the situation, the Public Library has been operat-

**Libraries in Barbados (1976)**

| Type | Number | Volumes in collections: Books | Volumes in collections: Periodicals | Annual expenditures (Barbados dollar) | Population served | Professional staff | All staff (total)[a] |
|---|---|---|---|---|---|---|---|
| National and Public | 8 and 3 mobile units | 206,556[b] | 208 | $455,061[c] $470,321[d] | c. 250,000 | 11 | 60 |
| Academic | 8 | 143,336 | 2,018 | | 3,300 | 13 | 40 |
| School | 20 plus a public library school library mobile service | 26,194[e] | N.A. | $16,750[f] | 61,921[g] | 1 | c. 30 |
| Special | 24 | 66,125[h] | 887 | $182,303[i] | N.A. | 5 | c. 30 |
| Archives | 1 | N.A. | N.A. | $98,847[c] $102,764[d] | N.A. | 4 | 15 |
| Total | 64 | | | $1,780,957 | | 30 | 175 |

[a]Figures exclude janitorial staff.
[b]Figures as of March 1976.
[c]Financial year April 1975–March 1976.
[d]Financial year April 1976–March 1977.
[e]Figures for public library school service only.
[f]Figures for 10 schools only.
[g]Figures as of December 1975.
[h]Figures for 17 libraries.
[i]Figures for 14 libraries.

ing a mobile service to over 70 percent of the schools since 1968.

**Special Libraries.** Although this area needs further development, there are four special libraries that must be noted. They are the Caribbean Meteorological Institute Library (1967) and Caribbean Development Bank Library (1970), both regional organizations; Christian Action for Development in the Caribbean (CADEC) Documentation Service (1971), a division of the Caribbean Conference of Churches; and the Library of the Central Bank of Barbados (1974). They all have important collections and are well organized.

**Association.** The Library Association of Barbados is the sole professional organization.

JUDY BLACKMAN

# Barrow, William J(ames)

(1904–1967)

William J. Barrow's research into the factors that cause paper to deteriorate resulted in the development of processes to restore and preserve precious library and archival materials. His work forms the basis for the increasing attention to the conservation and preservation of library resources.

Barrow was born December 11, 1904, in Brunswick County, Virginia, the son of a rural physician. After graduation from Randolph-Macon Academy in 1923, he attended Randolph-Macon College. For a time he was employed by a relative's company that manufactured overalls, but when the business faltered he turned his attention elsewhere.

In 1932 he became interested in document preservation and began to study bookbinding and the preservation techniques then in use at the Library of Congress. The Virginia State Library gave him workshop space and document restoration assignments.

During the late 1930's Barrow operated a shop at the Mariners Museum in Newport News, Virginia, where he developed the first practical roller-type laminator for the lamination of weakened and disintegrating documents, using the cellulose acetate film that had been approved for the purpose by the National Bureau of Standards. In this laminator the document and the acetate film were preheated together and fed through the nip of two synchronously driven steel rolls. Not long after, Barrow began to add strong long-fibered tissue to his laminates, which made them stronger without sacrificing legibility. The acetate filled the interstices of the tissue in such a way that there was little light scattering, and the added layers were quite transparent.

In 1940 Barrow was back at the Virginia State Library operating a restoration shop and speculating on the causes of deterioration. It seemed likely that degradation of the paper would continue even after lamination if it were not stopped. Concluding that the major cause was acidity in the paper itself, he completed by the end of 1945 the development of a deacidification process in which solutions of calcium hydroxide and calcium and/or magnesium bicarbonate are used to neutralize acidity. Subsequent events have substantiated his judgment that paper acidity is the most important single cause of paper deterioration. Barrow now had the means of greatly reducing paper's rate of deterioration and restoring integrity and strength to those already damaged. His laminators and techniques have since been obtained by more than 30 institutions throughout the world.

Barrow recognized early that much of his restoration work was on papers manufactured after 1875 and that many papers, much older, had no need of it. This was often ascribed to the use in modern papers of wood pulp, which came into fairly common use about that time, while some blamed it on an increasingly polluted industrial atmosphere. In 1957, with the sponsorship of the Virginia State Library and the support of the Council on Library Resources, he undertook a testing program involving papers from 500 books published between 1900 and 1949. Although it is true that the early wood pulps were not as good as they could have been and that atmospheric pollution is a deteriorative factor, this study showed that the poor condition of most of the papers examined was caused by acidity resulting from the use of alum-rosin sizing in their manufacture.

With the continued involvement of CLR and VSL and the advice of A. L. Rothschild and other paper industry people, Barrow planned a series of experiments, begun in the laboratories of the Herty Foundation in Savannah, Georgia, to determine if modern methods and materials could be used to make an affordable long-lasting paper. This work culminated in December 1959 in the production of such a paper at Standard Paper Manufacturing Company in Richmond. Only chemical wood pulps were used; Aquapel sizing, which is compatible with mild alkalinity, replaced alum and rosin, and calcium carbonate was added to ensure that the paper would remain alkaline for many years.

Barrow then published tentative specifications for long-life paper, setting minimum performance at high but demonstrably attainable levels. At that time only his paper met those criteria, but in 1972 eight commercially available papers were identified that could meet similar requirements. Such papers have the physical strength to withstand handling and use (durability) and the chemical stability that makes their deterioration very slow (permanence).

In 1961 the Council on Library Resources under the leadership of Verner W. Clapp, who was always interested and involved in Barrow's research, provided a grant that made possible the establishment of the W. J. Barrow Research Laboratory in the Virginia Historical Society Building. There Barrow studied polyvinyl acetate binding adhesives and defined the properties required for long useful life. Testing equipment was designed, and experimental work for the development of library binding performance standards was performed for the American Library Association. One study resulted in better catalogue card stock. Archival materials are protected from the migration of impurities by the acid-free file folders developed there. Barrow's test facilities and experience were brought to bear in the selection of paper for the ALA National Union Catalog.

Barrow believed the two physical tests most relevant to printing and records paper durability were folding endurance and tear resistance. Extensive testing of a variety of papers at many temperatures showed that these two properties usually decline according to a predictable pattern and that the rate of decline is related to temperature in a specific and consistent way. This work gives credibility to predictions of paper's useful life at natural temperatures, which are based on test results from oven-aged samples. The research was also the basis of his suggestion that materials of great lasting value should be stored at low temperature.

The results of Barrow's research and the techniques he developed were reported in a number of publications. The restoration process is described in *The Barrow Method of Restoring Deteriorated Documents* (1965), and the research into the structure and materials of books was published in the five-part *Permanence/Durability of the Book* (1963–65). These and other publications form the basis for contemporary practice in restoration of deteriorating print materials.

Barrow died August 25, 1967. The Laboratory continued its research until 1977. The Restoration Shop in the Virginia State Library was still in operation at the end of the 1970's, managed by his wife, Ruth Gibbs Barrow.

DAVID D. ROBERSON

ALA

*Mildred Leona Batchelder*

## Batchelder, Mildred Leona
(1901– )

In July 1966 the Grolier Award was presented to Mildred Leona Batchelder, the citation praising her years of "devoted attention to children's reading and books for younger readers. Throughout her career she has emphasized the values of selectivity in books. . . . Her influence has been an international one, reaching children's and school librarians, and through them the children from coast to coast in America and also in foreign lands where she has lectured and traveled. Her judgment, her knowledge, her wit, her persuasive leadership have made her a national figure in the world of books."

Batchelder was born September 7, 1901, in Lynn, Massachusetts. She received a B.A. degree from Mt. Holyoke College in 1922 and a B.L.S. from New York State Library School, Albany, in 1924.

Her professional career began as Head of the Children's Department, Omaha Public Library, Nebraska (1924–27), and continued as Children's Librarian, State Teachers College, Saint Cloud, Minnesota (1927–28). She was Elementary and Intermediate School Librarian at the Haven School in Evanston, Illinois (1928–36).

In 1936 she joined the headquarters staff of the American Library Association as School Library Specialist, becoming Chief of the School and Children's Library Division in 1938. In 1946 she was named Acting Chief, Department of Information and Advisory Service, and a year later became Chief of that department, a position she held until 1949, when a headquarters reorganization took place. Batchelder then became Executive Secretary of the Division of Libraries for Children and Young People (DLCYP), which included the School Librarians Section. When the School Libraries Section achieved division status in 1951, Batchelder became half-time Executive Secretary for the DLCYP and half-time Special Assistant to the ALA Executive Secretary on Special Membership Promotion. She held those positions until 1954, when the DLCYP executive secretaryship was made a full-time position. With reorganization in 1957 she became the Executive Secretary of the Children's Services Division (CSD) and the Young Adult Services Division (YASD); she retired from that position in 1966.

As an ALA staff member she served, at various times, as liaison to the Committee on Intellectual Freedom, the Audio-Visual Committee, the Joint ALA-National Education Association Committee, and the Joint ALA-Children's Book Council Committee.

During 30 years of service on the ALA staff Batchelder made many significant contributions to the profession. At her retirement the Executive Director of ALA commented on her "rare ability to see opportunities for service, to devise new ways of getting a job done, and to enlist the enthusiastic support of other people."

The development, growth, and accomplishments of the organizational units she worked with are evidence of her skill as a leader. A division president described her as "a catalyst of magical proportions." Many programs and projects begun under her direction continue today, including the Frederic G. Melcher Scholarship and the divisional journal *Top of the News.* Special activities initiated and carried out under her guidance included "The Lively Art of Picture Books," a film commissioned by CSD; the exhibit "The Children's World" at the Seattle Century 21 Exposition in 1962; and the children's library in Library/USA at the New York World Fair in 1964–65.

Batchelder initiated working relationships with many people and organizations outside the library profession in the U.S. and abroad that continue to benefit libraries and librarians today. In 1960 the first edition of *Let's Read Together,* a family reading list, was published by ALA, the work of a Special Committee of the National Congress of Parents and Teachers and the Children's Services Division.

She represented ALA at the White House Conference on Children and Youth in 1950 and 1960 and participated in the planning. An active member of the Council of National Organizations for Children and Youth (CNOCY), she served as its Secretary and was a member of the National Committee on Children and Youth (NCOCY).

At a ceremony in 1966 held during the annual National 4-H Club Conference in Washington, D.C., Batchelder was one of seven leaders in business, education, and industry commended for outstanding contributions to 4-H Club work.

Batchelder's interest in the promotion of children's reading and good books for young readers extended beyond national boundaries. She held that children's books can be an aid to international understanding and has worked for this in numerous ways. In 1949 the International Youth Library was established in Munich by Jella Lepman. The U.S. portion of the funds given during the launching of this unique project was a Rockefeller Foundation Grant, administered 1949–57 by the CSD Office.

She recognized the need for thoughtful selection of books to be translated, and a list of 100 children's books published from 1930 to 1954 "recommended for translation" was prepared by CSD in 1955 and distributed to Unesco, USIA, library contacts in other countries, publishers, and others. Annual lists were prepared from 1955.

During a five-month sabbatical in 1964 Batchelder visited 11 European countries and studied the translation of children's books as an aid to international understanding. She wrote later, "To know the classic stories of a country creates a climate, an attitude for understanding the people for whom that literature is a heritage. . . . Interchange of children's books between countries, through translation, influences communication between the people of those countries, and if the books chosen are worthy books, the resulting communication may be deeper, richer, more sympathetic, more enduring. I accept and believe these assumptions."

Recognizing Batchelder's concern about the selection of books of quality for translation and the responsibility for integrity in translation, CSD established the Mildred L. Batchelder Award in 1966; the first award was given in 1968. A citation to an American publisher, the award is intended to encourage international exchange of quality children's books by recognizing publishers of such books in translation.

The Constance Lindsay Skinner Award of the Women's National Book Association was given to Batchelder in 1967. She retired in 1966.

RUTH TARBOX

# Belgium

Belgium, a constitutional monarchy of Europe, is bounded by the North Sea on the northwest, the Netherlands on the north, the Federal Republic of Germany and Luxembourg on the east, and France on the south and southwest. Pop. (1978 est.) 9,837,500; area 30,521 sq.km. Languages are Dutch, French, and German. The ethnic groups are Flemings of the northern provinces (speaking Dutch), Walloons of the southern provinces (French), and a small German-speaking population in the southeast. The capital, Brussels, is officially bilingual (Dutch and French).

**National Library.** The National Library in Brussels (Koninklijke Bibliotheek Albert I; Bibliothèque Royale Albert Ier) originated from the 15th-century library of the Burgundian dukes and was established as the Royal Library of Belgium in 1837. It performs the twofold function of a national library and a central research library. The act of Parliament instituting the Copyright Deposit (April 8, 1965), obligating each Belgian publisher to deposit one copy of each work, enables it to operate as a national library. On the basis of the deposit copies, the monthly issues of the Belgian Bibliography *(Belgische Bibliografie; Bibliographie de Belgique)* are published. As a central research library, the Royal Library in Brussels has a number of specialized divisions and documentation centers: the prints division, the division of manuscripts, of precious works, of music, the numismatic collection, and the collection of maps. The documentation centers are the National Center for Scientific and Technical Documentation, the Center for American Studies, the Center for African Documentation, and the Documentation Center for Tropical Agriculture and Rural Developmental Works. In 1977 the Royal Library held about 3,000,000 volumes, 41,000 precious works, 70,000 maps, 37,000 manuscripts, 700,000 prints, and 180,000 coins and medals. Circulation amounted to 400,000. Although the Royal Library is a library of attendance—all documents can be used for reference only—it participates in the interlibrary loan cooperation with Belgian and foreign research libraries.

**Academic Libraries.** The six great universities in Belgium all have a general academic library, each of them possessing a fairly extensive collection. The universities of Ghent and Liège are state universities founded in 1816. The central library of the University of Liège contains 1,650,000 volumes, that in Ghent 2,000,000 volumes and 5,060 manuscripts. The Catholic University of Louvain, founded in 1425, the oldest university in Belgium, was split into two separate, autonomous universities in 1968: the Katholieke Universiteit Leuven (KUL) and the Université Catholique de Louvain. Since 1970 the original library has also been split. The Dutch section possesses 900,000 volumes, the French section 1,300,000.

The Free University of Brussels was established in 1834. Since 1970 this institution has been split into two autonomic universities. The library of the Dutch section, the Vrije Universiteit Brussel, contains 160,000 volumes; the French section, the Université Libre de Bruxelles, 1,247,000.

Apart from the six complete universities in Belgium, there exist also a number of college institutions with one or more integral or partial faculties. Antwerp has three such centers. The Universitaire Faculteiten Sint-Ignatius (the University Faculties Saint Ignatius) were founded in 1852. The disciplines taught are philosophy and arts, social and political sciences, law, and economics. The Rijksuniversitair Centrum Antwerpen (Antwerp State University) was established in 1965 and specializes in applied economics and exact sciences. In the two university institutions mentioned previously, only the first study-cycle is taught (two years of "candidatures"). In the Universitaire Instelling Antwerpen (Antwerp University Institution), founded in 1971, the second study-cycle (two years of "licentiate" studies) and the third study-cycle (doctorial studies) are taught in the following disciplines: sciences, medicine, philosophy and arts, law, and social and political sciences. The number of volumes in the specialized libraries of the three institutions amounts to 700,000.

A department of the faculties of medicine, exact sciences, law, and philosophy and arts of the KUL was founded in 1965 in Courtray (first cycle). Its library possesses 56,000 volumes. From 1968–69 economics was taught in the Limburgs Universitair Centrum (Limburg University Center) in Diepenbeek near Hasselt (three cycles). From 1971–72 the first study-cycle of sciences and medicine could also be followed there. The library of that university possesses 30,000 volumes. The Facultés Universitaires Saint Louis (the University Faculties Saint Louis), founded in 1858, specializes in philosophy and arts, law and economics, and social and political sciences (first study-cycle). The library contains 100,000 volumes.

The library of the Universitaire Faculteiten Sint Aloysius (University Faculties Saint Aloysius), where from 1968 the first study-cycles in law, philosophy and arts, and economics were taught, has 36,000 volumes. Mons has three university institutions: the Université de l'Etat à Mons (the State University Mons), founded in 1965, offering lectures in sciences, applied economics, psychology, and pedagogy; the Faculté Polytechnique de Mons (the Mons Polytechnic Faculty), founded in 1837 and specializing in applied sciences; and the Faculté Universitaire Catholique de Mons (the Mons Catholic University Faculty), founded in 1965 and specializing in economics. Volumes in the libraries of the three colleges in Mons total 400,000. The Facultés Universitaires Notre Dame de la Paix in Namur, founded in 1831, teaches philosophy and arts, law, economics, exact sciences, and medicine. The library possesses an extensive collection of 700,000 volumes.

The Faculté de Sciences Agronomiques de l'Etat (the State Faculty of Agronomic Sciences) in Gembloux, established in 1947, has 32,000 volumes. The Faculté de Théologie Protestante de Bruxelles (the Faculty of Protestant Theology of Brussels), founded in 1942, possesses the same number of volumes.

Many university colleges are institutions of a comparatively recent date, and their libraries, more than others, employ the modern and economical library techniques. In applications of modern automation they are unrivaled.

**Public Libraries.** As is the case with Belgian librarianship viewed as a whole, Belgian public librarianship is not well organized. Considerable improvement was anticipated, however, under two decrees that passed both the Dutch and French Councils of Culture in 1978. Up to that time all public libraries in Belgium came under the "Law Destrée" (1921), which did not effectively deal with the obligation to establish public libraries, the definition of such institutions, their financial support, and their general organization. The two decrees of 1978, however, defined a logical structure that meets contemporary demands for local public libraries. Their activities and operations are coordinated by central public libraries. A national center of public libraries (in both Flanders and Wallonia) studies problems concerning the public library and provides for some special (noncommercial) central services. The decree promulgated by the Dutch Council of Culture requires the municipalities to establish public libraries. This obligation is less rigidly formulated in the decree of the French Council of Culture (the king *can* put the municipalities under an obligation to establish public libraries). The subsidization is satisfactory. The method used for the shelving of books in public libraries is nearly always the open-access sytem. Works are arranged in classified order, usually UDC in French libraries; in Dutch libraries a specific system is in use (SISO system—system for the arrangement of the classified catalogue in public libraries). The important public libraries have special departments: record library, media center, a center for pictures, and even a department of toys.

The Statistics on Belgian public libraries in the mid-1970's compared with those of the mid-1960's clearly show that the "importance" of public libraries has increased by about 50 percent during the decade. From 1965 to 1975 the total number of public libraries did not change significantly—1,389 Dutch libraries in 1975 (1,377 in 1965) and 2,591 French libraries in 1975 (2,729 in 1965). There were, however, substantial increases in the total number of volumes (21,199,750 in 1975; 14,648,389 in 1965) and in circulation (38,023,017, 1975; 23,079,850, 1965). Though the number of institutions was slightly reduced, as increasing public interest was demonstrated: the number of readers was augmented by 50 percent (1,593,566 in 1975; 1,037,946 in 1965). The growth of population amounted to only 3 percent. The number of circulations increased by about 65 percent, and the growth of the collections amounted to about 45 percent. The increasing interest in public libraries is more strongly marked among Dutch-speaking Belgians than among French-speaking Belgians.

**School Libraries.** School librarianship in Belgium was little developed at the end of the 1970's. On the level of secondary education, hardly any school had a librarian. At best there were a few class libraries set up by the teacher of a subject speciality. On the level of higher, nonuniversity education are some important libraries that are often administered by a librarian. Most of them are inadequately catalogued, however. The Royal Conservatory in Brussels, for instance, possesses a significant library containing 650,000 volumes, but it was not adequately staffed for cataloguing.

**Special Libraries.** The ministry departments in Belgium have libraries containing documents related to the specific sphere that lies within the ministry's competence. The Ministry of Economic Affairs, for instance, possesses an important collection of 630,000 volumes (Fonds Quetelet). This library takes a leading position in Belgium in automation. The parliamentary library, containing 1,500,000 volumes on law and social and political sciences, possesses a significant collection of documents of several European parliaments.

Various research institutions are often equipped with well-organized libraries. The Royal Institute of Natural Sciences of Belgium, for example, possesses about 800,000 volumes.

Libraries of business companies are often well-structured centers of documentation. The best example can be found in the library and documentation service of Agfa-Geevaert in Mortsel, where books and articles in the field of photography and related sciences are abstracted.

Some cities also have a "city-library," operating independently of the public libraries. Usually they are very old, humanistic, books-preserving libraries that somewhat perform the function of a "national library" in their own region. The city-library of Antwerp, for example, which was founded in 1607, possesses 650,000 volumes.

**Associations.** Belgium has a great number of associations of librarians and libraries. The Vereniging van Archivarissen en Bibliothecarissen van België—Association des archivistes et bibliothécaires de Belgique (the Belgian Association of Archivists and Librarians), founded in 1907, groups all persons who perform a scientific function in a record office or library. The Association publishes *Archief- en Bibliotheekwezen in België—Archives et Bibliothèques en Belgique.*

The Vlaamse Vereniging van Bibliotheek-, Archief-, en Documentatiepersoneel (the Flemish Society of the Archive-, Library-, and Documentation Staff) was founded in 1921 and assembles the staff of libraries and archives in Flanders. Its organ is *Bibliotheekgids.* The monthly publication *Bibinfo* contains up-to-date information on the society and on the activities outside the society itself.

The Katholiek Centrum voor Lektuurinformatie en Bibliotheekvoorziening (the Catholic Center for Reading-Information and Library-Supplies) publishes criticism in its monthly annotated bibliographical review *Boekengids en Jeugdboekengids.* Its monthly publication *Openbaar* includes general information.

The Nationaal Bibliotheekfonds (National Funds of Libraries) groups Flemish socialist libraries and librarians and publishes criticism in *Lektuurgids.*

Librarians belonging to the French-speaking part of the country are chiefly grouped in three associations: the Association Nationale des Bibliothécaires d'Expression Française (the National Association of French-speaking Librarians), the Association des Bibliothécaires-Documentalistes de l'Institut Supérieur d'Etudes Sociales de l'Etat (the Association of Librarian-Documentalists of the Higher State Institution for Social Studies), and the Association Professionelle des Bibliothécaires et Documentalistes (the Professional Association of Librarians and Documentalists).

The Belgische Vereniging voor Documentatie (the Belgian Society for Documentation) serves Belgian documentalists. Steps were being taken at the end of the 1970's to rationalize the wide fabric of associations in each language community. The three French associations cited here planned to unify in the Association des Bibliothécaires, Archivistes, et Documentalistes (Association of Librarians, Archivists, and Documentalists). Dutch-speaking librarians, archivists, and documentalists were considering a similar merger.

The Vlaamse Bibliotheek Centrale (the Flemish Library-Center) is a central service that provides a large assortment of library-technical and bibliographical material.

WILLY VANDERPIJPEN

# Belize

Belize, a colony of Great Britain, lies on the east coast of the Yúcatan Peninsula in Central America. It is bounded by Mexico on the north and northwest, Guatemala on the west and south, and the Caribbean Sea on the east. Pop. (1977 est.) 129,800; area 22,965 sq.km. The official language is English.

**National and Public Library.** Library services in Belize revolve around the National Library Service, which in 1960 came under the direction of the Minister of Education. As early as 1825 a library service existed, and between that time and 1902 there were seven libraries and reading rooms. The Jubilee Library, from which the public library concept commenced in Belize, opened in 1935 with assistance from the Carnegie Corporation of New York. The central government undertook to provide an annual subvention for the library service. A statutory library board administers the service. The Services' bookstock totals 100,000.

The main lending library, which is also the headquarters of the National Library Service, is in the Bliss Institute in Belize City and offers some 20,000 volumes in English and Spanish. A national collection comprises about 1,500 volumes and includes books primarily on Belize or by Belizeans, a West Indian collection, and a Central American Collection including works on the Maya civilization.

There are 77 service points or sublibraries throughout the country, administered by a staff of 2 professional librarians, 16 paraprofessionals, and a bookbinder, along with a host of voluntary part-time workers in the villages. A bookmobile service was being introduced during 1979. Other sections of the Service include a children's library and a reference library. The National Library Service will extend full library services to all government and government-supported schools, various departments, and institutions, so that it can in time attain the true status of a national library.

Membership at any service point of the National Library Service is free. Any child who is able to read may join a library and on reaching age 16 can register as a member of the adult library. Members total 21,000, of which the majority are children; books issued average 80,000 annually.

**Academic Library.** The University of the West Indies maintains a university center in Belize. Its library consists of some 2,500 volumes and other printed material.

**School Libraries.** A school library program is operated by the National Library Service on behalf of the Education Department. Through this system some schools outside of Belize City receive 50 books at a time to be exchanged and circulated periodically. All secondary schools offer a fair standard of library service to their students, maintaining some 2,000 volumes in each school.

**Table 1. Libraries in Belize (1978)**

| Type | Number | Volumes in collections | Annual expenditures (dollar) | Population served | Professional staff | All staff (total) |
|---|---|---|---|---|---|---|
| Academic | 1 | 2,500 | N.A. | NA. | N.A. | 1 |
| Public | 1 | 100,000 | $129,000 | 150,000 | 2 | 31 |
| School | 200 | 30,000 | N.A. | 38,000 | N.A. | N.A. |
| Special | 16 | 10,000 | N.A. | 5,000 | N.A. | 16 |

**Table 2. Archives in Belize (1978)**

| | |
|---|---|
| Number | 1 |
| Holdings | 1,010,000 cubic inches |
| Annual expenditures | $14,458 |
| Professional staff | 1 |
| All staff | 3 |

Source: National Archivist.

**Special Libraries.** All departments and ministries of government have collections of printed material, and many private industrial firms also have libraries.

L. G. VERNON

# Benedict, St.

(*c.* 480—*c.* 546)

Saint Benedict, Abbot of the monastery at Monte Cassino who is considered the father of Western monasticism, made his main contribution through the constitution of monasticism, the Benedictine Rule, written at Monte Cassino (c. 530—540). It became the most influential factor in the spread of Western monasticism. He also made provisions for the care of books, and it is difficult to overestimate his contributions to reading.

In the 6th century A.D. all was in a state of civil war, confusion, and looting, on the decline of the Roman Empire. Benedict provided the will, the means, and the men to bring some degree of cultural order out of chaos. After spending 35 years at Subiaco, he founded a monastery at Monte Cassino, about 70 miles southeast of Rome. The Rule of Benedict rapidly circulated among all European monasteries with far-reaching cultural influence and has been practiced for 14 centuries.

In the period of Eastern monasticism, the individual monk's career was largely of a solitary kind, whereas under the Benedictine Rule the labors of the community were determined not only for its collective good but likewise for service to the world at large. Monasticism was no longer regarded so much as a life of austerity but as one of service, philanthropy, and Christian charity. The main occupations of the monks were the work of God, devotion, and physical labor. Benedict made special provision in his Rule for the illiterate but imposed the obligation of devotional reading upon the literate monks.

Reading was not so much an intellectual activity as a means to the contemplation of God and self-improvement in the life of grace. As a remedy for idleness, the life of the monk was to be devoted to physical labor and the study of sacred subjects. The Rule added:

> From Easter to the Calends of October, . . . From the fourth hour until close upon the sixth let them apply themselves to reading.

The Rule mentioned the siesta following the sixth hour, important to Italians during the hot season of the year. Those who preferred to read were encouraged to do so, but in a low voice. After the seasonal labors in the fields were concluded in October, work was concentrated inside the monastery. The Rule canceled siestas and set out changes in the manual labor and in the time for reading. From morning until the close of the second hour, the monks were to devote their time to reading.

During the third and final period, the Lenten season, the Rule made some changes in the daily schedule and paid special attention to a systematic program of additional reading. Benedict reflected a certain severity when communal ownership did not permit personal property ("neither a book, nor tablets, nor a pen . . ."), but in no way did he intend privation for any monk. Provisions were to be made for an adequate collection of manuscript codices so that each monk could have one for his personal reading. Though Benedict was silent on intellectual study or scribal work, the reading requirements of his Rule necessitated a monastic book collection that was essentially spiritual. The monastic library was to have sufficient books for the ceremonial distribution of books at the beginning of Lent.

The reading program discouraged skipping through pages or reading at random in a perfunctory manner. The Rule did not prescribe a definite time for loans, nor did it seem to imply that the book must be completely read by the close of Lent. But certain disciplinary measures were established to encourage individuals who felt little attraction for deciphering or other distractions. Surely some preferred working in the field to reading sermons or biblical commentators. These points are carefully detailed in the following passage:

> Let one or two seniors be deputed to go round the monastery at the hours when the brethren are engaged in reading, and see that there be no slothful brother . . . not applying himself to his reading.

On Sundays the monks did only essential work such as kitchen duty. The most desirable use of time was to be spent in reading books of devotion, but monks who found the task too difficult were to be assigned other duties so they would not be idle. Bible reading was mentioned several times in the Rule. Benedict also recommended biblical commentaries of the Church Fathers to help the monks devotionally. This was an impressive list for monks of the 6th century, and latitude on the selection of other books was also expressed in the Rule: "or something else that may edify the hearers," for those public readings were to be held every evening.

The monks assembled in the oratory at stated hours of the day and night for choral recitation of the Divine Office. The service was fixed in its general outlines, and the recitation of the psalms was its main substance.

The Rule set forth Benedict's program for beginners in the monastic life. Only the final chapter of it opens up horizons beyond the elementary reading program for monks aspiring to the advanced stages of perfect life. For such members of the monastic community he intended that his Rule would be complemented by a range of books that were the special heritage of monastic ideals and that would bring his followers to the summit of Christian perfection. Among prescribed books were the *Rule* of Saint Basil, John Cassian's *Conferences* and *Institutes,* an author from Gaul who wrote around 435, and the "Lives of the Fathers"; that is to say, the biographies of Anthony of Egypt, Pachomius, and Macarius of Alexandria.

**The Rule of Silence and the Use of Sign Language.** It was the monastic idea that silence was golden. Benedict laid down rules on the subject and, for the most part, only three hours of speaking time was allowed in each day. This severe rule was mitigated by the provision that a brother could read aloud from a "common book." Singing was differentiated from speaking and thus allowed, provided the singer not sit too near a silent reader. Such restraints were, in practice, softened somewhat. An elaborate code of signs to allow silent communication was developed, for example; it was essentially the same for all monasteries and indispensable to the monk who used the library in a silent hour. Examples follow.

> If one wants a book, he shall make the general sign, *i.e.,* extend his hand in a movement of turning the leaves of a book. For the sign of a missal, make the same movement adding the sign of the fingers as though flying. For the sign of a tract, lay one hand on the abdomen and the other across the mouth. For the sign of a sequence or hymn, raise the hand bent and, moving it away from the breast, invert it so that what was before up shall be under. For a book containing a lesson for Sundays and feast days make the sign of a book, add the sign of reading, and, clenching the fist, place the arm over the shoulder, imitating the action of him that carries a burden, on account of the size of the book.

The books called for above are strictly liturgical. For a secular author like Ovid, the sign was different. For such pagan authors, after making the general sign, "Scratch your ear with your finger, even as a dog when itching does with his foot, for pagans may be compared with such an animal." It is not necessary to read library catalogues to infer that monkish ears itched often.

**REFERENCES**

*The Rule of Saint Benedict,* translated by Dom Justin McCann (1961), best English translation.

E. C. Butler, *Benedictine Monachism,* 2nd ed. (1961).

L. J. Daly, *Benedictine Monasticism* (1961).

Jean Decarreaux, *Monks and Civilization,* translated by Charlotte Haldane (1964).

REDMOND A. BURKE

# Benin

Benin, a people's republic in West Africa, is bordered by Togo on the west, Upper Volta on the northwest, Niger on the northeast, Nigeria on the east, and the Gulf of Guinea on the south. Pop. (1978 est.) 3,341,000; area 112,600 sq.km. The official language is French.

**National Library.** The Bibliothèque nationale was established in the capital, Porto Novo, in 1961 and was reorganized in 1975. Under the jurisdiction of the Ministry of Youth, Popular Culture, and Sports, it houses 1,500 volumes and over 20 periodicals.

**Academic Libraries.** The University of Benin Library, founded in 1970, is housed in two buildings, one on the Abomey-Calavi campus and serving the departments of Letters, Linguistics, and Social Sciences; Law and Economics; Physical Sciences; and Agronomy; the other in Cotonou to serve the Department of Medical and Para-Medical Studies. In the early 1970's, the collection grew from 9,000 to some 24,000 books, theses, and brochures. Also within the university system, the Centre de Formation administrative et de Perfectionnement handles 1,000 works and 100 periodicals in its documentation center (Cotonou).

The teacher training colleges for women (Abomey) and men (Parakou) and the Ecole pastorale évangelique (Porto Novo) furnish basic libraries in the relevant fields.

**Libraries in Benin (1976)**

| Type | Number | Volumes in collections | Annual expenditures (franc) | Population served | Professional staff | All staff (total) |
|---|---|---|---|---|---|---|
| National | 1 | 1,500 | | | | |
| Academic | 5 | 25,000 | N.A. | N.A. | N.A. | N.A. |
| Public | N.A. | N.A. | N.A. | 2,000 | N.A. | N.A. |
| School | N.A. | N.A. | N.A. | N.A. | N.A. | N.A. |
| Special | 9 | 10,500 | N.A. | N.A. | N.A. | N.A. |

Sources: *Annuaire 1971–2* and *1974–5,* Université du Bénin (ex-Dahomey); Dominique Zidouemba (ed.), *Directory of Documentation, Libraries and Archives Services in Africa* (Unesco, Paris, 1977); Hans M. Zell (ed.), *The African Book World and Press —A Directory,* Hans Zell Publishers, Oxford (1977).

**Public Libraries.** A Central Library Service under the Ministry of Youth, Popular Culture, and Sports has established provincial libraries at Abomey, Natitingou, Ouidah, Parakou, and Porto Novo.

**Special Libraries.** There are a number of research libraries associated with government agencies and institutes that are responsible for the study of society, education, agriculture, industry, and mining in Benin. The Institut de Recherches appliquées du Bénin, in Porto Novo, supplanted the local branch of IFAN (Institut français d'Afrique noire) in 1961 and offers a collection of 8,500 works as well as an information service. It published *Etudes dahoméennes* from 1963 to 1970. Libraries specializing in agriculture and textiles are those of Niaouli's Institut de Recherches agronomiques tropicales et des Cultures vivrières (established 1970) and Cotonou's Institut de Recherches du Coton et des Textiles exotiques (1970). ORSTOM (Office de la Recherche scientifique et technique Outre-Mer) maintains a center in Cotonou. Other libraries serve the Chamber of Commerce, research institutes in education and palm oil, the Laboratoire d'Agropédologie, the Ministry of Rural Development, and the mining and geology division of the Ministry of Industry, Commerce, and Tourism.

**Associations.** Benin is a member of the Association internationale pour le Développement de la Documentation, des Bibliothèques et des Archives en Afrique (AIDBA). There was no evidence of any formal library association within the country at the end of the 1970's.

NEIL MCHUGH

# Bermuda

Bermuda is a self-governing colony of the United Kingdom and comprises a group of islands in the western part of the North Atlantic Ocean. Pop. (1977 est.) 56,900; area 46 sq.km. The official language is English.

**National and Public Library.** The Bermuda Library provides both national and public library services, including legal deposit. Opened in 1839, it now functions under the Bermuda Library Act 1946 as amended. Headquarters are at Par-la-Ville in Hamilton, the capital city, with the Junior Library a few blocks away and small branches at St. George's and Somerset. Reference services are free to all, and on April 1, 1979, lending services became free to all, residents and visitors alike. A free mailing service has operated since 1855. As of March 1977 total bookstock stood at 131,450; annual cricculation was 190,640. Total membership still represents only some 10 percent of Bermuda's 56,500 residents, giving cause for concern.

Phonograph records, a telescope, and slides with a projector may be borrowed, and a talking-books service is provided. The Bermuda Library Concert Hour may be heard weekly over radio, and the Junior Library holds regular story hours and film shows; seasonal and special programs are also presented.

The Bermudiana collection includes all available books and other materials of local interest; there is a nearly complete file of the *Royal Gazette* newspaper. A national bibliography and a subject index exist on five-

**Table 1. Libraries in Bermuda (1976)**

| Type | Number | Volumes in collections | Annual expenditures (dollar) | Population served | Professional staff | All staff (total) |
|---|---|---|---|---|---|---|
| National and Public | 1 | 131,450 | $BDA 257,360 | 56,500 | 5 | 16 plus 6 part-time |
| Academic | 1 | 10,000 | $BDA 16,195 | 2,011 | N.A. | 1 |
| School | 39[a] | 73,200 | $BDA 33,550 | 12,200 | 3[b] | 39 |
| Special | 7 + 50[a] | N.A. | N.A. | N.A. | 2[c] | 5 plus numerous part-time |
| Total | 48 + 50 | | | | | |

[a]Depends upon the definition of *library*. Some schools have well-developed, separately housed libraries, others only small classroom collections. There are only seven special libraries as such but many important small collections even when only a few shelves in a corner.
[b]These are teachers with formal school library training, not fully qualified professional librarians.
[c]One of these is an audiovisual officer, not a librarian.

Sources: The Head Librarian; *Annual Report of Ministry of Education 1975–76; Annual Statistics of the Bermuda Library 1976–77; Estimates of Revenue and Expenditure 1976–77* (Bermuda government).

by-three-inch cards. Microfilm and photocopy services are offered. A union list of serials was in preparation in the late 1970's.

**Academic Libraries.** Bermuda does not have a university, but undergraduate extension students are served by the Bermuda Library, the libraries of the Bermuda College, and the Naval Air Station. The College Library stocks 12,000 volumes and 150 periodicals and is geared to the courses offered by the departments of Academic Studies, Commerce and Technology, and Hotel Technology.

**Table 2. Archives in Bermuda (1976)**

| | |
|---|---|
| Number | 1 |
| Holdings | 244 linear meters (Archives) |
| Annual expenditures | $73,035 |
| Professional staff | 1 |
| All staff (total) | 4 |

Sources: *The Archivist; Annual Report of Ministry of Education 1975–76; Estimates of Revenue and Expenditure 1976–77* (Bermuda government).

**School Libraries.** There are libraries in all government secondary schools and most primary schools, although some of the latter are still only classroom collections. Standards of the Library Association (U.K.) in accommodation and stock are attempted, but there is a need for trained personnel. Library service in private schools is comparable.

**Special Libraries.** Among the larger and more formally organized libraries in government departments are those of the Supreme Court, Education, Agriculture and Fisheries, Health and Social Services, and the Hospital. The E. L. Mark Memorial Library at the Bermuda Biological Station provides research facilities in marine and environmental sciences; it has a stock of 13,000 volumes and 250 current periodicals. Larger professional and business office libraries specialize in such areas as banking, accounting, insurance, and oil and gas.

Bermuda boasts a number of significant private libraries and some rare book collectors. Community organizations such as churches and youth centers also maintain small collections.

**Association.** A Library Association of Bermuda was in the process of formation in 1979.

MARY SKIFFINGTON

# Bhutan

In the Himalayan chain, Bhutan is bounded by China on the north and India on the south. Its population, primarily of Tibetan extraction, is estimated at about 1,262,000; the area is approximately 46,100 sq.km. Its remoteness and near inaccessibility kept Bhutan for many years outside the mainstream of cultural and political developments in the world. Only comparatively recently, under the administration of the Wangchuk dynasty, were steps taken to bring Bhutan into the 20th century. In the 1960's Bhutan was estimated to have a 95 percent illiteracy rate.

No libraries other than Tibetan monastic libraries existed in Bhutan until, in the early 1960's, with support of the Indian government, the Bhutanese ruler, Druk Gyalpo Jigme Dorji Wangchuk, initiated the creation of elementary and high schools in the country, an effort continued by his successor, Druk Gyalpo Jigme Sinye Wangchuk. In 1966 the country had a total of 36 schools with an enrollment of 2,500 students; in 1976 there were 100 schools with 16,000 students enrolled. There were also plans to create a university center, along the lines of a U.S. community college, in Thimpu, the country's capital. Most of the schools are in the three principal cities, Thimpu, Paro, and Phun Tsoling.

No detailed statistics of any kind dealing with libraries had been published by the end of the 1970's. The education budget does not provide a breakdown for the acquisition of library materials. It is doubtful, however, that significant numbers of books—other than basic ones for support of classes—are acquired. In 1975 a decision was made to use English as the principal language until 1985, when it would be replaced by Dzongkha, the national language and a Tibetan dialect.

By the end of the 1970's there were no plans to create a national library, although a deliberate effort was being made to collect the country's archives in the former royal palace in Pharo.

LUC KWANTEN

# Bibliographic Networks

The definition of a bibliographic network has become more elusive in recent years rather than more clear-cut, as might be expected. A profession such as librarianship tends to define its terminology to suit its own needs. While this was possible for a time, the massive infusion of technology into the library networking process has meant that librarianship's definitions of certain words held in common with other disciplines have had to undergo modification and refinement. This phenomenon was made particularly necessary by the technologists involved with computer science, systems analysis, and communications networking who, in dealing with computers, are accustomed to precision and clear, simple, and direct statements. The generalizations of less precise professions are rejected rapidly by these practitioners.

Earlier definitions of a bibliographic network, as illustrated by R. C. Swank's paper at the 1970 Airlie House Conference on Interlibrary Communications and Information Networks, have been reexamined and redetailed into highly specific areas of endeavor and, as can be anticipated, into the direct opposite of specificity—simplistic, generalized overusage. Swank's definition summarizes the thoughts of several others into six main characteristics for an information (i.e., bibliographic) network: (1) information resources; (2) readers or users; (3) schemes for the intellectual organization of documents, or data; (4) methods for the delivery of resources; (5) formal organization; and (6) bidirectional telecommunications.

Greater specificity had been obtained by 1978, as can be seen in the variety of definitions contained in the Library of Congress Network Development Office's *Network Planning Paper Number 2: A Glossary for Library Networking,* which was prepared by Dataflow Systems Inc. Here one sees no definition for a bibliographic or for an information network; rather, one sees defined the bibliographic service center, the bibliographic utility, the multitype network, the national library network, the network coordinating agency, etc. Network is simply defined as (1) "two or more organizations engaged in a common pattern of information exchange through telecommunications links, for some common objectives," and (2) "an interconnected or interrelated group of nodes."

Despite the clarity of the definitions contained in the publication cited, common usage has incorporated the term "bibliographic network" into the everyday usage and vocabulary. Therefore, when one hears, "network," one cannot be sure what is meant, as the additional topical areas related to bibliographic networks cited below will demonstrate. Further points to be considered include types of networks, criteria for network products and services, types of network governance structures, sources of network funding, and the needs of network users.

**Functions.** By the late 1970's in the United States, two discernible networking functions had emerged with identifiable organizations clustering around the two types. The first is the bibliographic utility, a term quite unsatisfactory to some librarians but reasonably useful to others. The Dataflow Systems *Glossary* (1978) defines a bibliographic utility as "an organization that maintains online bibliographic data bases, enabling it to offer computer-based support to any interested users . . . and provide a standard interface through which bibliographic service centers . . . may gain access to the . . . network." Examples of organizations that are generally thought to fit this definition and carry out this role are OCLC, Inc., Research Libraries Information Network (RLIN), Washington Library Network, and the Library of Congress.

The second type of networking function is carried out by the bibliographic service center, which Dataflow Systems defines as "an organization that serves as a broker or distributor of computer-based bibliographic processing services. A service center gains access . . . through the facilities of a bibliographic utility." Examples of this type of organization are the New England Library Information Network (NELINET), the Southeast Library Network (SOLINET), and the Bibliographical Center for Research (BCR). For a time it appeared as if these two functional organizational types would remain relatively identifiable. The identification is complicated, however, by the latter's acquiring the computer hardware to carry out functional tasks not dissimilar in many respects to the activities of the former. The communications minicomputer of NELINET and the magnetic-tape processing minicomputer of SOLINET (both of which have substantially greater capabilities) are two visible examples.

Because the developing bibliographic network process and configuration in the United States is highly dynamic, it remains to be seen whether competition or cooperation will take the dominant position. One might expect to see a hierarchical-distributed network result in which each of the entities carried out functions serving the needs of the whole. However, struggles over territory, arising out of special interest and business practice, could result in stiff competition. While a reasonable amount of competition can strengthen the ability of the competitors to serve the needs of their users, an all-out life-and-death struggle could be highly self-defeating in furthering the goals of librarianship as a profession.

**Types and Structures.** A bibliographic network is often more easily described than defined by using several categories, each of which has a number of possible characteristics. The first of these categories is functional type: cooperative acquisitions, shared cataloguing, interlibrary loan, etc. Another category is organizational type: a single type of library only (e.g., public libraries), more than one type of library, etc. A third category is structural type: government entity, nonprofit private corporation, public corporation, interstate compact, for-profit corporation, etc. By drawing a simple matrix, one can partially define a network in fairly exacting terms and, with caution, effect some limited but useful functional comparisons among networks.

Bibliographic networks can be self-perpetuating in that the need for the network and the support that its participants give it continue indefinitely. Or the network can be self-destructing in that once the stated objectives are achieved, the network goes out of operation. Bibliographic networks can be either institutionally based, in which the basic members are individual libraries, or they can be state based, where a state's libraries may be represented by the state library agency, which coordinates the network activities within a state. In the latter illustration, the state-based regional network tends to be either a loosely held or tightly held confederation of statewide networks. Since funding is always a critical question for library networking activities, and the main channel for federal funds to libraries is through the state library agency, the statewide network or state-based regional network may be able to deal more easily with funding problems than other types of networks. The real question in structure is whether a statewide network has the depth and breadth of resources, has the ability to establish the best possible vendor contracts, and has the quantity of libraries, in type and size, to support a highly effective network operation. In larger states the answer often favors the statewide network.

If the statewide network can offer services to libraries and if funding is coming to libraries through the state library agencies, then what advantages do state-based regional networks provide over statewide networks? Largely this can be answered by two points: (1) in some aspects of networking (e.g., telecommunications, training, vendor group discounts) an economy of scale is achieved by having a larger group with which to work; and (2) in some states the size of the user population and the quantity and quality of resources available are not sufficient to support a large-scale networking effort in that one state alone.

**Services and Benefits.** Networks can offer a number of effective services to their libraries, ranging, for example, from regional or statewide distribution of shared cataloguing systems to on-line searching of information-retrieval data bases to document delivery. It is possible for structure to influence the services that a network can offer. Computerized networks' ability to provide information retrieval or shared cataloguing services is irrespective of the size of the network, although the larger the network, the greater the unit savings as a general rule. Other services such as the delivery of documents seem to be more successful in smaller network environments because geographical proximity is an asset to this type of service.

The values of networking are the subject of controversy. Networks have the potential to reduce costs through the economy of scale phenomenon, through resource sharing, and through astute and successful network management. Networks demonstrating economic success (i.e., self-supporting) tend to price their services on a formula that allows individual libraries to purchase

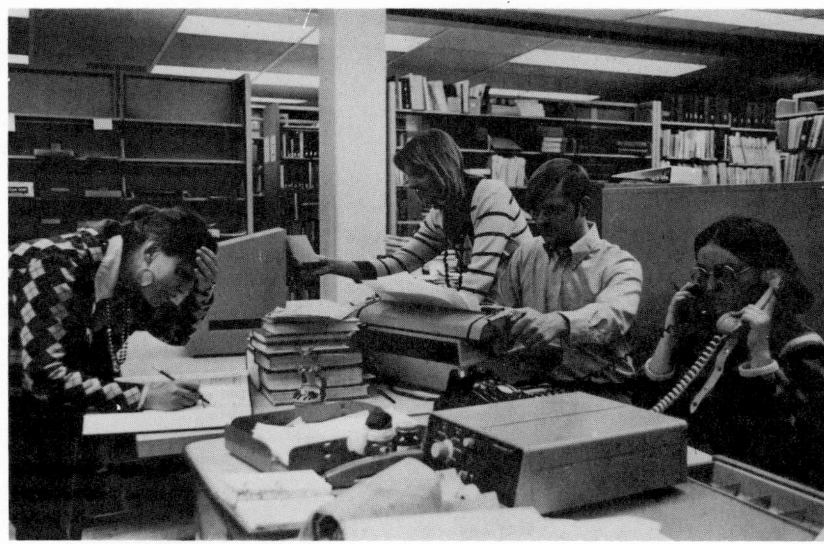

New Orleans Public Library

*The staff of SEALLINC, Southeast Louisiana Library Network Cooperative—a network providing a variety of library services in Louisiana. Headquarters is in the New Orleans Public Library.*

services from the network for less cost than the library would pay by going directly to the vendor, which means that the network must purchase from the vendor for less than the network charges the individual library. The unsubsidized network must capture its overhead recovery in that margin.

Networks usually provide more than just a monetary savings to their participants. They also provide leadership in achieving the objectives of their participants and a forum for their members to discuss issues and develop strategies to tackle library problems. Networks tend to pursue and attain progress on philosophical questions within the profession.

The number of bibliographic networks falling into the patterns cited above have proliferated to a prodigious number. At all levels, in all structural patterns, and with all product and service offerings, there are literally hundreds. The outstanding example of a largely successful computerized bibliographic network is OCLC, Inc. OCLC, itself a bibliographic network of the bibliographic utility functional type, contracts with more than 20 other networks of the bibliographic service-center type. The commercial data-base vendors, such as Lockheed Retrieval Services, SDC Search Services, and Bibliographic Retrieval Services, can also be considered bibliographic networks.

**Key Concerns.** Above all, a bibliographic network concerns itself with fulfillment of the user needs and of system requirements, because only if these needs are met will there be continuing use of the networking facilities. The following are 16 major points of bibliographic network concern as viewed by users in the local libraries:

*Ease of Access.* Before network facilities can be used, many administrative arrangements must be understood and learned. User documentation or procedure manuals exist in a variety of formats, with different degrees of detail. Assistance to users may often not be available when needed. Improvement of uniformity, simplicity of operation, and standardization in this area are required.

*Ease of Use and Operation.* Messages between the system and the user should be unambiguous and should indicate what action is required by each party. System actions depending on requests from the user should be well documented and easy to find in the documentation of all concerned.

*One-Point Contact.* In order to facilitate easy access, efficient operation, and support of the network user, it is desirable to have a one-point contact, at which the user may make arrangements for services, obtain the latest information on types of services, availability, and prices, and obtain advice and consultation on how to solve operational problems of access procedures, identification, and other details.

*Terminology.* The emergence of the new network technology has brought computer technologists and libraries face to face. The technical language used to describe, specify, and measure systems and system performance reflects this diversity and, as a consequence, the terminology used today is often confusing to users.

*User Assistance.* There are several forms of assistance users require. Certain information can be conveniently disseminated "on-line," upon user request, at sign-on or sign-off, or at other times. Other types of information can be handled in tutorials regarding systems operation or applications, new product announcements, system changes, documentation changes, or status reports on operating conditions. Other assistance resources can be developed as part of the overall network development, including human professional assistance in systems analysis, training for use of services, or general consultation in a specialty available at the network resource center.

*Consultation.* Human communications are often neglected in the design of automated information systems; yet there is a great need for human intellectual support to all potential users. Highly individualized assistance may be required by a local user in adapting to new programs. Since consultation by its nature is a human communications process, it is best done in direct person-to-person contact, but various "hot-line" arrangements have been successful where a large geographic area has to be covered.

*Orientation and Training.* Certain orientation and training activities are required periodically for all echelons of all participating organizations. These may range from short concise briefings on network objectives, status, or current problem areas for top-level library managers to detailed, specific courses in operational aspects or procedures for staff. Timing of such efforts is of importance and needs to be considered in the overall planning of introduction of services or the development of new capabilities.

*Documentation.* Documentation in various forms is required for hardware, software, and system services procedures. It is required for system operations, maintenance, orientation, and training, as well as for all management functions. Documentation will vary in level of detail, from general networkwide policy and procedures statements to details regarding network access methods, log-in procedures, identification, passwords, and emergency procedures.

Examples of documentation pertaining to the network are operations and maintenance manuals, policy and procedures manuals, directories, reference manuals, and training documentation. Some material for general orientation and public relations purposes will be required.

*Equipment Design.* Equipment design must accommodate all user and system requirements to provide a useful and efficient system. Especially for interactive users, many of the user and system requirements are only approximated by many present-day terminals, which in the case of teletypewriter types were designed for different purposes and in a different technological environment. Development of low-cost, state-of-the-art terminals is being pursued, and positive results of these efforts will enhance networking applications for libraries.

*User Feedback.* Interactive capacities have given the user a greater capability to influence an ongoing information-handling process. This communication between the user and the system can also be used to elicit responses that can provide valuable information to management on system usage, system performance, and system utility. Such feedback can also be gained as part of the consultation process; user replies can be translated into new policies and operational procedures.

*Information Control.* Users have certain requirements for keeping their files, data, and routines restricted to their own use or may want to keep usage restricted to persons authorized by them. Users may wish to restrict access on a file basis or on a partial-file basis. Various data-management systems provide such capabilities, but not all systems are flexible enough to accommodate all user requirements.

*Reliability.* A national network must run on a precise schedule, and its computer systems must be available when scheduled. Technical performance criteria, such as mean time between failures and mean time to repair, are available for hardware components, and overall systems criteria can be developed for availability and reliability and must be specified. System reliability is an important ingredient contributing to user confidence; only a trouble-free performance record will ensure continuity of use of the system. Another related factor is system stability, which ensures not only that the system remains operational within specified conditions and times but also that its characteristics remain unaltered.

*Product Quality.* Hardware quality control has become a specialized branch of information science and has made great progress over the years. Software quality control, in contrast, is still in the developing stage. In a national network formal mechanisms have to be established for classification of software malfunctions and reporting, evaluating, and correcting errors.

*Network Continuity*. The network must be so organized that various components can be planned and added at various times based on growth requirements. Older-generation machines can be shifted to different system tasks, while new-generation machines take over the tasks of the older machines. Purchased last-generation machines may be obtainable at less cost per operation than newer machines, at least for certain classes of problems. Thus, with increased demand for service both machines can remain in operation.

A network should be able to accommodate addition or removal of equipment or system features without subjecting the users to major inconvenience. Furthermore, elimination of any user node must not affect the rest of the network as far as operations at other nodes are concerned. Similarly, organizational and financial provisions must be made to minimize a crippling loss of revenue and of operations funded through revenue and to provide operational compensating mechanisms to continue service.

*Network Performance Criteria*. Various echelons of network management need to be apprised of the "state of well being" of the network at times when major decisions have to be made. No widely recognized general concepts of network status and performance have been developed yet to suit this need.

*Standards*. Successful operation of various components of the network requires standards for description of systems operation and performance, for system measurements, and for evaluation criteria to permit service evaluation and comparisons.

**REFERENCES**

Susan K. Martin, *Library Networks, 1978–79* (1978).

Raynard C. Swank, "Interlibrary Cooperation, Interlibrary Communications, and Information Networks—Explanation and Definition," in Joseph Becker, editor, *Interlibrary Communications and Information Networks* (ALA, 1972).

DONALD B. SIMPSON

## Bignon, Jean-Paul
(1662–1743)

Jean-Paul Bignon, who oversaw the Royal Library during the reign of Louis XV, was born at Paris, September 19, 1662, to a family prominent in public affairs and closely associated with the management of the Bibliothèque du Roi. His early formal education was received at the College of Harcourt, where Bossuet directed his thesis in philosophy. Since his cultural tastes seemed to point toward the priesthood, he began his sacerdotal studies at the Séminaire de S. Magloire. In 1684 he was received as a priest into the Congregation of the Oratory, where, in the same year, he published his first work, a life of a Father Levêque of the same order. Seeking a retreat where he could pursue the primary sources for his literary and historical studies, the Abbé Bignon retired first to a country manor, but because of its lack of resources he returned to Paris, where he found a suitable residence and library in the Maison de S. Honoré. In 1691 he left the Oratory so that he could pursue his scholarly interests completely. In that year he was appointed to the Académie Royale des Inscriptions et Belles-Lettres. Ten years later he was named Conseiller d'État, although he continued both his scholarly and priestly activities, even acquiring a reputation for his occasional sermons.

His extensive studies, of course, led him to acquire a sizable library; thus, it is not surprising that in 1718 he was appointed by Louis XV to oversee the Royal Library. His accession to this prestigious position seems to have introduced a new golden age into the history of the collection. Shortly after his appointment he saw to it—like Naudé with the Bibliothèque Mazarine—that the Library was opened to the public (1720). Thus, as Hessel observes, the leading scholars of the Enlightenment were able to utilize the collection for their studies. Under the Abbé's direction the Library was divided into five sections: printed books, manuscripts, genealogical titles, engravings, and medals, and the holdings were significantly enlarged. During his administration the 6,645 manuscripts acquired by Colbert, along with the Louvre and Fontainebleau collections, were added. Following the precedent of Colbert, he acquired books and manuscripts through the diplomatic corps on an even larger scale than did his predecessors. In 1739 he supervised the initial publication of the printed catalogue, which was completed ten years after his death, in six folio volumes. His four-volume catalogue of Oriental, Greek, and Latin manuscripts (1739–44) prefigured similar undertakings of the late 19th and early 20th centuries. During his term as *Bibliothècaire du Roi* he continued his wide-ranging studies, producing an extended commentary on the *Bibliotheca* of Apollodorus, a primary source for the study of Greek mythology. His personal life seems to have been austere; rising at 4:00 A.M. to pursue his scholarly interests until 8:00 A.M., he then went to his regular duties as librarian and academician. In 1741, about to enter his 80th year, he began to suffer from a violent abdominal disorder and surmised that death was close at hand. Accordingly he had his Royal Library position transferred to his nephew, Jérôme Bignon. The Abbé's health steadily deteriorated and, on March 14, 1743, he died, having lived over 80 years. To the day of his death, according to Fréret, he retained his "reason, not to mention the sweetness and equanimity that he had displayed" throughout his life.

FRANCIS J. WITTY

## Bilingual and Ethnic Groups, Services to

While the meaning of *bilingual* is adequately conveyed in this article through the paragraphs dealing with it, the same may not be assumed about "ethnic." It has already become a platitude to say apologetically, "After all, everybody is an ethnic." But in some contexts in which the word appears, it often means *they* as against *we*, and *they* are people with one or more of such characteristics as coming from another country, speaking another language, or having a different color and a different way of life.

Lubomyr Wynar gives for America the following definition:

> The difference between the non-ethnic American and the ethnic American is that while the former has lost the link with his past heritage, the latter has chosen to retain it, to take pride in it, and to enrich it, by adding to it American created cultural forms ("History of Services to Ethnic Communities," *Catholic Library World*, 1977).

For the purpose of this article, ethnicity is in most cases identified with a language different from that of the majority in any one country, but the realities of the demands on libraries and services given by them do not permit a rigid interpretation. It has seemed necessary, for instance, to recognize the existence of Afro-American culture and black librarianship among speakers of En-

California State Library

*Chinese library reading room of central California, Fresno, c. 1910.*

glish; similarly, West Indians, who are white and black and in-between and who, as immigrants in Canada and Britain ask for specialized service, are also treated in this article.

In Europe and North America, libraries, originally and for a long time, provided their services solely in the official language or languages of their own countries, and providing for other language groups was an acknowledged concern in relatively few countries. On the assumption that all citizens should know the national language, such service as was provided seldom went beyond a small collection of "foreign" books. An understanding that the responsibility to provide library service equally to all involves going beyond the official languages developed only recently. In examining the services offered today, a distinction has been made, therefore, between countries where a mixed population goes back far into history (the established multilingual countries) and those where the traditional composition of population was changed by immigration or influx of migrant workers in more recent years.

**Established Multilingual Countries.** In Europe most of the countries with more than one language group have been created over the centuries by wars and their peace agreements. The degree of cultural and language amalgamation varies considerably and so consequently do their libraries' services, as the following examples illustrate.

*Belgium.* In Belgium live two culturally, linguistically different groups who are also territorially separated, the Dutch-speaking Flemings in the north and the French-speaking Walloons in the south, with both languages spoken only in Brussels; this strict division is also followed in the libraries.

*Switzerland.* Less rigidity is exercised in Switzerland, where in different areas French, German, Italian, and Romansch are spoken. In each area public libraries, while organized for service to the dominant group, also provide a reasonable quantity of books in the other languages.

*South Africa.* Two official languages, Afrikaans and English, are taught in schools and are used equally in all spheres of life. Library personnel must be bilingual in them as a condition of employment in most if not all provincial and municipal institutions, and the collections reflect, of course, language policy as well as reading needs. There are also about eight other large language groups, both African and Asian, in South Africa, but they are regarded as "nonofficial."

*Finland.* Finland is an example of how the foreign language of a larger and dominant nation persists even after political ties have been broken. Besides the Finnish language, Swedish is spoken and read by a large minority, and, accordingly, public libraries in large centers, such as Helsinki, provide material in both languages.

*Yugoslavia.* Yugoslavia is inhabited by many ethnic and linguistic groups, each residing mainly within a well-defined area and therefore not presenting communication problems. It is normal practice for a large library in an area where several languages are spoken to provide some material in those languages, even for minority groups.

*North America.* In North America the history of bilingualism is of more recent date. Canada is often described as a bilingual country, but the description is not entirely accurate, since French is spoken primarily in the province of Quebec. The Official Languages Act accords equal status to English and French in Parliament and in the federal civil service. Public libraries, while intent on meeting the needs of the majority groups in their environment, also provide books in the other language. Many libraries in the English-speaking provinces consider it a patriotic as well as a cultural duty to promote the reading of French, especially works by French Canadian authors.

Although the U.S. is officially unilingual, cultural pluralism has been a fact for a long time. Until comparatively recently concerns with ethnicity, bilingual personnel, and foreign books were mainly, though not exclusively, directed to the Spanish-speaking, and when one speaks of bilingualism in the U.S. today, one thinks of Spanish as the "other" language. It predominates in the Southwest, where it has always been a feature of the linguistic map. During the 1940's public libraries in the U.S. were inevitably affected by bilingual education, if not by the sheer presence of ethnic groups. Progress in the provision of services to the Spanish-speaking was reported in successive issues of *The ALA Yearbook.* Development was stimulated with funds from the Library Services and Construction Act.

The need of Chicanos and other Spanish-speaking groups for service in their own language resulted in the demand for and eventually the creation of library positions for bilingual personnel, and libraries frequently owe their success to their Spanish-speaking staff. Library services to the Spanish-speaking, Afro-American, and American Indian populations have had a continuous period of growth, which is well documented in library literature. The same is not true of other ethnic groups.

**Multinational Minorities after World War II.** World War II and its aftermath caused massive demographic changes in many countries and presented libraries with new and difficult tasks. Two variants of the population movement are clearly distinguishable and should be treated separately because they impinge somewhat differently on the functions of libraries. They are the migrant workers, more common in Europe, and the immigrants who move to a country to live there permanently.

*Migrant workers.* These workers have had profound impact in many central and western European countries. When the postwar expansion of industry in Germany, Belgium, Switzerland, Denmark, and Sweden—to name the countries most affected—depleted the reservoir of indigenous labor, workmen were recruited from the southern European countries, notably Yugoslavia, Italy, Greece, Spain, Turkey, and Algeria.

The theory was that the *Gastarbeiter* (guest workers)

would stay a few years in the host country and then return home. This theory also served as an excuse for withholding cultural, educational, and some social services from them. Contrary to expectations, it turned out that though a certain number of workers went home when their contracts expired, others arrived to take their place, and a growing number remained when immigration regulations permitted. Eventually libraries took notice of the new challenge, for which most if not all were largely unprepared. The newcomers did not at first know the indigenous languages, were in many cases illiterate, and were in most cases ignorant or distrustful of the public library as an institution. Libraries, on the other hand, usually lacked bilingual or multilingual staff and lacked books in foreign languages and the means of getting them. Faced with such difficulties, they had to look for good reasons for providing materials and services for foreign readers, and they had to instill motivation in staffs.

The support for special services was not, however, difficult to justify. Migrant workers contributed to the national wealth not only through their work but also through taxes and therefore had a claim on public services. In the interest of general economic and social welfare, it was important to help them adapt to prevailing circumstances; through knowledge of the national language the newcomers could not only better understand their daily work and the living conditions but also improve their vocational knowledge and their participation as citizens. Furthermore, it was unavoidable that families followed or were started by the workers. Children who went to school and were taught in the indigenous language could become estranged from their parents. When the time came to return to their home country, both old and young might have become completely assimilated and unable to resume, or, in the case of children born abroad, unable to enter into the prevailing way of life there.

*Immigrants.* Immigrants must be considered in the majority of cases as permanent additions to a nation, although again exceptions are possible. The types of immigrants—and consequently the role of libraries—differ from country to country, and from one period to another. The largest group of immigrants to Great Britain arrived after the war from countries of the Commonwealth—India, Pakistan, the West Indies—but that immigration had virtually stopped by the late 1970's. Immigrants to France come from northern and western Africa and usually have at least some speaking knowledge of English and French. The United States has always attracted immigrants from Europe and to a lesser degree from Asia. Canada has accepted immigrants from non-English, non-French backgrounds for 300 years. Recently many West Indians have immigrated to Canada. Only after World War II did Australia relax its preference for white immigrants.

BEGINNINGS

In North America at the turn of the 19th century, honest attempts were made by librarians to provide books to immigrants in non-English languages. The ALA established in 1917 the Committee on Work for the Foreign Born, which published in 1929 a special handbook, *Reading Services for the Foreign Born.* In 1948 the Committee was renamed Committee on Intercultural Relations and nothing more was heard of it. At the same time, the long and honorific history of services to ethnic groups, as exemplified by the public libraries of Cleveland, Detroit, and New York, showed signs of stagnation. Wynar and C. B. Joeckel cite as reasons declining immigration, better-educated immigrants with greater demands on library material, and declining circulation. The emphasis then shifted to the "disadvantaged"; i.e., the Afro-Americans, Spanish-Americans, and the American Indians. The influx of immigrants after World War II, greater in Canada

Arthur Plotnik

*Student interest in ethnic studies is sustained at the University of New Mexico Library, Albuquerque.*

than in the U.S., revived consciousness of the centuries-old ties between the Old and the New World.

The so-called melting-pot theory never reached fruition; immigrant communities were transformed into American ethnic communities in the U.S., while in Canada the government declared a policy of multiculturalism, i.e., one nation based on cultural pluralism.

U.S. libraries began in the 1970's to concern themselves with ethnic reading needs once more, a decade after their Canadian counterparts. When Congress passed the Educational Amendment of 1972, which provided for an Ethnic Heritage Studies Program, it noted that "in a multiethnic society a greater understanding of the contribution of one's own heritage and those of one's fellow citizens can contribute to a more harmonious, patriotic, and committed populace."

More and more public libraries provide funds, either from their own budget or out of special grants, for the selection and purchase of books in *community* languages. (This term is preferred to *foreign,* which is imprecise and also offensive to many ethnic citizens.) Encouraging signs of deepening concern for the objectives as much as for the difficulties have been noted in the literature as well as in personal communications to the author from many countries. Even so, the difficulties are enormous: problems of selection and bibliographic aids; problems of acquisition from faraway countries; problems of processing; and, finally, problems of promoting the resources to the intended user groups. Library associations in Britain, France, Germany, and Sweden, among others, are grappling with the problem. In 1975 the American Library Association's Public Library Association constituted a Multilingual Services Committee, which met for the first time during ALA's Midwinter Meeting in Chicago in 1978.

LIBRARY SERVICES IN INDIVIDUAL LIBRARIES

**Objectives and Standards.** Even before the practi-

Chicago Public Library

*An innovative library program at the Chicago Public Library's Chinatown Branch included a series of Chinese cooking classes.*

cal problems are tackled, philosophy for service should be stated and goals set. It is not enough merely to start a "foreign" or "multilingual" collection; some thought must be given to general library objectives, reading habits of the target groups, and the extent to which special (and invariably costly) resources for minority readers should be developed. Are they to be helped in order to assimilate? This would entail their need to receive language manuals and books descriptive of their new country. Are they to be helped to maintain and hand down their cultural traditions through judiciously selected works by their national authors? Or will the whole point be "books in your language," irrespective of author and content? Other issues include literacy of new citizens and attitudes toward institutions such as libraries, toward book buying, and toward book borrowing habits, and personal preference for or against retention of the mother tongue.

*Selection.* The implication for careful selection is obvious. It is difficult, if not impossible, to plan a complete, effective service to minority groups from scratch. Census figures are inadequate guides; one has to proceed by educated guesses, trial and error.

Standards for bibliographic records and book reviewing and reporting vary considerably from country to country. As a general rule, however, one feature is almost universal: most of them are written in the language of the country of production. Knowledge of that language is, to say the least, helpful in order to consider titles for ordering. Failing that, one has to rely on booksellers at home and abroad or, worse, restrict purchases to translations of easily identified titles.

Booklists are relatively easy to obtain from publishers and booksellers; occasionally they are annotated. Critical reviews can often be found in literary or general magazines, but it is doubtful, given the language problem, whether the average library would subscribe to them except for the use of their ethnic readers. The ALA *Booklist* carries annotated lists of foreign books with addresses of some appropriate booksellers in the U.S. Some libraries issue acquisition lists at regular or irregular intervals, with or without annotations in English and vernacular (Cumberland County Library System, New York Public Library, Cleveland Public Libraries, and others). A comprehensive guide to selection aids and suppliers was published in 1979 by the Canadian Library Association and K. G. Saur as *Books in Other Languages.*

The frequently asked question "How many volumes?" is more difficult to answer. It depends on many factors, such as number of readers, rate of adoption of the host country's language, rate of retention of their own language, and limit on book stock imposed by budget or library policy. IFLA standards recommend distinction between national minorities with fixed residence who should have "adequate quantity of their national literature" and nonresident groups, who should have service when they number at least 500. It is suggested that for a population of 2,000, 1 volume per migrant worker is appropriate; for over 2,000, 1 for 10. There should be a minimum of 100 volumes.

*Acquisition.* It is axiomatic that the best source of supply is in the country of production, and the source gets poorer in direct proportion to distance from that country. Immigrants, unless heavily concentrated in a particular area or town, do not offer a lucrative market for bookshops, but those shops that do exist have stocks that are usually limited in quality and quantity; nevertheless, librarians should not bypass them entirely. An alert and knowledgeable bookseller can provide valuable guidance on books and take orders for transmission to publishers abroad, who often are not equipped to deal with customers from other countries.

Conversely, many librarians cannot deal with booksellers and publishers in foreign countries and in foreign languages. The languages problem can be aggravated by unusual local commercial practices concerning, for example, terms of payment or means of conveyance. In some countries publishing is carried on by many small enterprises, each of which sells only its own product. Only a capable jobber on the spot or a staff member on a buying trip can ensure timely purchase, for the press runs are usually limited and there is no reprinting. By far the best, reliable, and under ideal circumstances even the most economical way to purchase foreign books in other languages is to buy them personally in the country of publication; an adequate volume of ordering is necessary to justify the expense of a buying trip. This suggests cooperation on regional, national, and international levels.

*Processing.* Books in foreign languages, often also in different scripts, find most librarians unprepared. The difficulty begins when checking the bill against the consignment, especially when the bill is in a different language *and* in a non-Roman script. When non-Roman material is catalogued and classified, the standard aids for checking authors and authorities and for interpreting content are often inadequate or unavailable.

*Staff.* Mere knowledge of a language is not in itself sufficient qualification; of course, it is important when assisting those ethnic users who do not as yet speak the language of the country. In order to select books, a good education and cultural background is essential. This does not mean that the staff member must be a native of the country whose cultural heritage is to be promoted, but it helps. In the promotion of books and contact with users, the employment of members of ethnic groups is useful and frequently recommended.

**Cooperation, Coordination, Networks.** If ever words like these can be justified, it is in the realm of book service in community languages, since the unit cost is invariably higher because of the smaller number of copies per title ordered and processed. Because book-producing countries have had to adjust to higher costs for paper and rising wages, inexpensive books are no longer to be had. It is therefore to the advantage of library systems to have a central acquisition system to relieve the individual library of the difficult tasks of book selection, ordering, and cataloguing. Foremost among such organizations is the Swedish Bibliotekstjänst at Lund, a state enterprise founded in 1951. In response to the large numbers of migrant workers from southern and southeastern Europe,

Swedish public libraries were confronted with the task of providing reading material. Bibliotekstjänst obtains books from appropriate countries by sending staff members regularly on buying trips, where they also advise or instruct reliable booksellers or publishers, and attend book fairs.

**Successful Projects.** The Birmingham (England) Public Library administers a central collection of books in Indian and Pakistani languages which are lent in batches on a fee basis to libraries throughout Great Britain.

Since 1975 an imaginative project has been operating in Canada. While many libraries in large cities have paid attention to the needs of ethnic groups and have built up substantial collections in various languages since the 1950's, the smaller towns and communities have been less successful. Much of the population remained unserved except by interlibrary loans (and then only if adequate bibliographic data were at hand). In order to remedy this situation the National Library of Canada established the Multilingual Biblioservice, a department staffed and equipped to purchase books in some 25 languages for rotating loans throughout the country. These features can be usefully adapted to requirements in other countries.

In Australia the Victoria government granted some money in 1974 for a rotating collection of books for migrants residing in the western suburbs of Melbourne, the Westfund Project. The Project was very successful, creating an awareness of the minorities' need for books in their languages. Monash University, in Clayton, Victoria, gives courses on library service to migrants. In 1978 the Ethnic Affairs Commission of New South Wales published a report, *Library Service to Ethnic Groups,* which in part recommended the expansion of existing services and the setting up of a cooperative acquisition and processing unit.

**Service to Children.** Children of ethnocultural minorities present a somewhat different task to libraries. Again, there is a distinction between children of migrant workers and those of immigrants or their descendants and between children arriving in the host country at preschool age or at schoolgoing age. In the latter case, learning of language, culture, and way of life comes easily, more so than for children who during the primary years of growth are confined to their home, where that knowledge is inadequate.

It normally happens that the children receive a good education in the country where their parents work but are then expected to return with their parents to their home country when the work contract expires. It is essential, then, that they be educated in their native tongue and learn about the history and culture of their native country in order to ease social and psychological problems that might be faced by the children in the host country or at their repatriation. An additional reason for all children, whether temporary or permanent residents, to retain language and feeling of identity of their ethnic group is the need to prevent estrangement between parent and children, which can and does occur very easily when children assimilate completely into the society of the host country while their parents alone retain language and way of life to which they have been accustomed.

Awareness of the need for library services to ethnic and cultural minorities in many countries has led to earnest investigation of ethnicity, of acquisition problems, and in many cases to the development of interesting projects. Given the uncertainty of human mobility in the future and the inevitable consequences of acculturation, the possibility and desirability of long-term plans cannot be taken for granted. For the present, however, most libraries have still much inducement for developing, even creating, a useful service to ethnic groups.

**REFERENCES**

John D. Buenker and Nicholas C. Burckel, *Immigration and Ethnicity: A Guide to Information Sources* (1977).

Eric Clough and Jacqueline Quarmby, *A Public Library Service for Ethnic Minorities in Great Britain* (1978).

Monteria Hightower, "Serving Our Ethnic Publics," *PLA Newsletter* (1976).

W. F. Mackey, *Bilingualism as a World Problem* (1967).

Silva Simsova, "Marginal Man," *Journal of Librarianship* (1974).

Lubomyr Wynar, "History of Services to Ethnic Communities," *Catholic Library World* (1977).

Marie F. Zielinska, "Multiculturalism and Library Services to Ethnic Communities," *Unesco Bulletin for Libraries* (1978).

Christobel Mattingley, "Ethnic Connections," *Australian Library Journal* (1976).

LEONARD WERTHEIMER

## Billings, John Shaw
(1838–1913)

ALA

*John Shaw Billings*

John Shaw Billings, physician and librarian, was active in many fields and played a leading role in most of them. He made significant contributions in hospital design and construction, in the public hygiene and sanitation movement, in the reform of medical education, and in the development of vital statistics. His most enduring accomplishments were in the field of librarianship and bibliography, as the creator of two great U.S. research libraries —what became the National Library of Medicine and the New York Public Library. Billings was born in Switzerland County, Indiana, on April 12, 1838. His family moved to Rhode Island in 1843 and returned in 1848 to Allensville, Indiana, where his father, James Billings, ran a country store and served as postmaster and shoemaker. The young Billings attended a country school for three months each winter and read everything he could lay his hands on; by the age of eight he had read the Bible through verse by verse and had finished *Pilgrim's Progress, Plutarch's Lives, Robinson Crusoe,* and *The Deerslayer.* With the help of a grammar, a dictionary, and the local clergyman, he taught himself Latin and a little Greek and managed to pass the entrance examination for the subfreshman class at Miami University, Oxford, Ohio, in the fall of 1852. Miami was a typical western college of the period, with a small faculty and student body, a fixed and limited curriculum, a religiously oriented administration, and a library of 8,000 volumes that was open on Sundays from 9 A.M. to 12 noon. Billings graduated in 1857, second in his class.

He then spent an interim year as a tutor and as a lecturer with a traveling lantern show, saving his earnings to enter the Medical College of Ohio at Cincinnati in 1858. "In those days," he said later, "they taught us medicine as you teach boys to swim, by throwing them in the water." He attended a course of lectures for five months and then attended the identical course of lectures for another five months in the following year, graduating with his M.D. degree in 1860. He said that he practically lived in the dissecting room and in the clinics; when he wrote his thesis on the *Surgical Treatment of Epilepsy*, he found that even after ransacking public and private libraries in Cincinnati and searching in the libraries of Philadelphia and New York, he was unable to make a complete survey of the pertinent literature. This experience formed the kernel of his resolve to try to establish a fairly complete medical library, with catalogues and indexes to match, should the opportunity appear.

After graduation he stayed on at the school—one of a faculty of nine—as demonstrator of anatomy. On the April day in 1861 when the guns fired on Fort Sumter, Billings was celebrating his 23rd birthday. In September 1861 he went to Washington and took the three-day examination for admission to the Medical Corps of the Army; he passed first on the list and was immediately hired as a contract surgeon until his commissioning as First Lieutenant and Assistant Surgeon in April 1862. He was placed in charge of Cliffburne Hospital, which he set up in an old cavalry barracks on the hill above Georgetown. In August 1862 he was transferred to Philadelphia as Executive Officer of the West Philadelphia Hospital, and on September 3, 1862, he married Katherine Mary Stevens of Washington. In March 1863 he reported for duty with the Army of the Potomac; by May he was performing field surgery at Chancellorsville; in July he joined the 7th Regiment of the Second Division, V Corps, at Gettysburg; and in August he was in New York City in the aftermath of the Draft Riots. He eventually was reassigned to hospital duty on Bedloe's Island, and in February 1864 he was given command of an extraordinary secret expedition to Haiti to rescue some 371 survivors of a group of freed slaves who had been resettled there and swindled in the process. The rescue was successful, and by the end of March Billings had been reassigned as Acting Medical Inspector of the Army of the Potomac. In August he was reassigned to duties in Washington, and in December 1864 he was transferred to the Surgeon General's Office.

The war over, Billings settled down to a routine of office duties involving "arid drudgery among invoices and receipts, requisitions and bills of lading, treasury drafts and auditor's decisions. His days were filled with routine office work, with questions of bookkeeping and pecuniary responsibility." He also began to study German and undertook to teach himself something about microscopy, eventually publishing four papers on fungi between 1869 and 1872. In 1869–70 he was detailed to the Secretary of the Treasury to conduct a survey of the Marine Hospital Service, and he prepared a reorganization plan that set the Service, later renamed the Public Health Service, on a new course. During the period 1870–75 he prepared long reports on army hospitals and army hygiene. Beginning in 1875, he became closely involved in the development of the new Johns Hopkins Hospital and Medical School. Billings's plans were chosen for the new Hospital, which was begun in 1877 and opened in 1889. He arranged the curriculum of the school and was instrumental in bringing Welch and Osler to the faculty. Shuttling by train back and forth to Baltimore, he gave his advice and delivered his lectures in the history of medicine—which he also was repeating in Boston, New York, and abroad.

Billings served as Vice-President of the National Board of Health in 1879, and in that year surveyed and reported on the sanitary condition of Memphis following that summer's devastating yellow fever epidemic. In 1880 he served as President of the American Public Health Association and began his long consulting association with the U.S. Census Bureau, stressing the need for collecting morbidity as well as mortality statistics and striving for standardized reporting. In that capacity he suggested to Herman Hollerith the desirability of developing a mechanical tabulating machine. In the decade or so after 1880 Billings published dozens of papers on vital statistics, on sanitation and sewage disposal, and on heating and ventilation. He also found time to be President of the Philosophical Society of Washington in 1886, Treasurer of the National Academy of Sciences from 1887 to 1898, and Treasurer of the Cosmos Club, 1878–79, and its President, 1886–87.

The wonder is that in the midst of all these activities his major task for the 30 years from 1865 to 1895 was directing the Library of the Surgeon General's Office, which he organized and developed into the foremost medical library in the world. For a staff Billings had a dozen civilian employees, most of them former army hospital stewards; they were dependable and reliable, if not learned, and Billings trained them in the rudiments of bibliographic procedure. Exchanges were instituted with medical societies and institutions; begging letters were written to private individuals at home and abroad; and duplicates were amassed for exchanging. Reference services were not neglected; Billings and his small staff answered in a typical year about 2,000 inquiries. He also instituted an interlibrary loan system; physicians were required to make a deposit before borrowing books. And the collections kept growing—1,800 volumes in 1865, 6,000 volumes in 1868, 50,000 titles in the three-volume catalogue of 1873–74.

In 1876 Billings published the renowned *Specimen Fasciculus of a Catalogue of the National Medical Library*. The title itself is noteworthy; "National Medical Library" appeared in large, bold type. (The letterheads of the Library at this time bore the same legend, foreshadowing the transformation to the National Library of Medicine in 1956.) The *Specimen* set forth in dictionary order both books and periodical articles; the books were listed by author and by subject, the periodical articles by subject only, in a single alphabet. On this model the first volume of the great *Index-Catalogue of the Library of the Surgeon General's Office* appeared in 1880; the first series in its 16 volumes was completed in 1895, having listed 300,000 books and pamphlets and 500,000 periodical articles during that period.

The bibliographic workflow was arranged so that library clerks copied out titles on cards, which then went to Billings and to Robert Fletcher, his assistant from 1876, who penciled a single appropriate subject rubric across the top of each card. Those cards dealing with current materials were utilized, beginning in 1879, as the substance of the *Index Medicus,* "A Monthly Classified Record of the Current Medical Literature of the World," published by Frederick Leypoldt. Thus Billings provided both a bibliographic service for current awareness, the *Index Medicus*, and a service designed primarily for retrospective search, the *Index-Catalogue,* from the same data base.

From 1876 to 1896 Billings made eight European trips. In 1884 he received the degree of LL.D. from the University of Edinburgh, in 1889 the degree of D.C.L. from Oxford, in 1892 an honorary M.D. from Dublin. Especially noteworthy are the address he gave at the 7th International Medical Congress, London, 1881, on "Our Medical Literature," and his address before the British Medical Association in 1886, "Medicine in the United States, and Its Relations to Co-operative Investigation."

In 1895 Billings retired from the Army and went to Philadelphia to become Professor of Hygiene at the University of Pennsylvania and Director of its laboratory of hygiene, which he had opened in 1892. In November 1895 a great banquet in his honor was held, at which his English and American friends presented him with a check for $10,000 and the Surgeon General announced that Billings's portrait was to be painted and hung at the Library. Just at that time he was offered the directorship of the New York Public Library, which had been formed earlier that year through a merging of the Astor Library, the Lenox Library, and the Tilden Trust. Billings remained in Philadelphia through spring 1896, then went to London as a delegate to the Royal Society's International Conference on a Catalogue of Scientific Literature, and when he returned at the end of summer, he settled in New York, where he was to remain for the last 17 years of his life as Director of the New York Public Library.

In its emergent and as yet indeterminate state, the

New York Public Library presented some heavy challenges. Billings set to work. He drew up a classification scheme; he reorganized the chaotic cataloguing situation and brought in a system that was much like that of the *Index-Catalogue,* with periodical articles carded among the books. He set up two miles of temporary wooden shelving in the Astor building and installed artificial lighting in both buildings. He successfully bargained for a site for a new building on the land occupied by the old Croton Reservoir at Fifth Avenue and 42nd Street. The cornerstone of the new building was laid in 1902, and it opened to the public in May 1911. The staff was augmented and reorganized; the collections grew from 500,000 volumes in 1901 to over 1,000,000 in 1913, while the 40 branch libraries that Billings established held another million volumes.

In 1902 Billings was President of the American Library Association. From the founding of the Carnegie Institution of Washington in 1902 Billings served on its Executive Committee and from 1903 on as Chairman of its Board of Trustees. Between 1905 and 1908 Billings was engaged in drawing up plans for the Peter Bent Brigham Hospital in Boston.

On March 11, 1913, Billings died in New York City in his 75th year. He was buried at Arlington National Cemetery.

**REFERENCES**

Fielding H. Garrison, *John Shaw Billings, a Memoir* (1915).

Harry M. Lydenberg, *John Shaw Billings, Creator of The National Medical Library and Its Catalogue, First Director of the New York Public Library* (ALA, 1924).

Dorothy Schullian and Frank B. Rogers, "The National Library of Medicine," *Library Quarterly* (1958).

*Selected Papers of John Shaw Billings,* compiled, with a life of Billings, by Frank Bradway Rogers (1965); contains a bibliography of Billings.

FRANK BRADWAY ROGERS

## Birkbeck, George

(1776–1841)

George Birkbeck was a "founding father" of the Mechanics' Institutes, which were the closest predecessors of public libraries in Britain. He was born at Settle, North Yorkshire, on January 10, 1776. He came of a Quaker banking family but, having decided on a scientific career, was trained in what was then the only satisfactory medium, medicine. By the time he received his degree at the University of Edinburgh in 1799, he had rubbed shoulders with Walter Scott, Francis Jeffrey, and many of the other great literary figures then associated with "the Athens of the North." At the age of 23 he was appointed Professor of Natural Philosophy at the Glasgow Institution and began to lecture there on physics and chemistry.

The Glasgow Institution, which had been founded as a rival to the University of Glasgow, was functioning at the beginning of the 19th century as a kind of early technical college. Birkbeck was impressed by the keen interest in scientific and technical matters displayed by some of the mechanics, or skilled and semiskilled manual workers employed to make his medical apparatus, and he organized an evening class in elementary science for them. He moved to London, however, in 1804 and established himself there, not as a scientist, but as a medical man in general practice. That practice was soon fashionable and successful and included many of his distinguished neighbors, including the Grotes, the Mills, and the Ricardos. In the meantime, his class at the Glasgow Institution was kept going by his successor, Andrew Ure. It continued to flourish, and its members built up a small scientific library; in 1823 it was reestablished as a semiautonomous association, the Mechanics Class of the Glasgow Institution, which by head and tail abbreviation became known as the Mechanics' Institute. Birkbeck continued to be keenly interested and supported the movement to establish a similar institution in central London despite being earlier of the opinion that the lower standards of elementary education ill prepared the student for mechanics' classes. The London Mechanics' Institute, of which Birkbeck became and remained President until his death on December 1, 1841, started classes and began to accumulate a small scientific library in temporary premises. It then built its own new headquarters, but these proved much too ambitious for its finances, since its only income, apart from the gifts of a few wealthy benefactors, was from the small subscriptions of its members. Birkbeck himself lent nearly £4,000 toward the building fund. Thus, the library grew slowly and was heavily dependent on gifts.

The mechanics' institute movement spread rapidly; by the middle 1830's institutes had been established in many large and other somewhat smaller provincial towns, including Manchester, Liverpool, Newcastle-upon-Tyne, Birmingham; in Dundee, Scotland; and in other London districts. The classes and library facilities, however limited, began to appeal more to middle-class than to working-class people. Subjects such as English grammar, elementary mathematics, and foreign languages soon were included in the London Institute's curriculum. Birkbeck continued his interest in the national expansion and visited many of the provincial institutes. By the time of his death there were still more MI's even in the smallest towns and villages throughout the country. It was abundantly obvious, of course, that if those in the larger towns found financial viability difficult, the situation elsewhere was nearly hopeless. Dickens satirized one of the small MI's in his *Uncommercial Traveller.*

Despite the MI's continuing problems, influential people in addition to Birkbeck continued to interest themselves in them, notably Lord Brougham and his Society for the Diffusion of Useful Knowledge. The Society

Courtesy of The Newberry Library

*George Birkbeck*

was responsible for the publication of *A Manual for Mechanics Institutes* in 1839, which was especially interesting and revealing because following a careful survey of existing institutes, it included a model building plan with two rooms for a library. The library was to be systematically arranged and catalogued and satisfactorily administered with the aid of a model code of rules and regulations. Several paragraphs were devoted to the bookstock, and in these the risks of relying on gifts were suitably emphasized and the risks to readers relying on "miscellaneous perusal of books" suitably underlined. The fiction problem raised its ugly head as it has continued to do during the succeeding century and a half; the manual expressed the view that persistent novel reading was "an abuse of the library of a M.I." The select list of recommended subjects, authors, and titles appended nevertheless included some fiction, although no works by the questionable if standard 18th-century novelists such as Fielding, Richardson, Smollett, and Sterne. The nonfiction subjects and authors included were heavy, although a few lighter books on such perennially popular subjects as disasters at sea had managed to creep in. The MI's had always sought most assiduously to exclude any political or religious books that might be regarded as in any way controversial; most of their libraries must have been extremely dull places.

The available evidence suggests that by 1850, the beginning of the rate-supported public library movement in Britain, only a small number of MI's had been able to build up bookstocks likely to attract many readers. There were happy exceptions; the Brontë sisters, for example, made good use of the library of nearly 2,000 volumes accumulated by the Keighley MI. Some of these MI's, with or without their bookstocks, were taken over by the early public libraries, and the debt of the latter to the former should not be underestimated. Birkbeck's own pioneer institute in central London, popularly known as the Birkbeck Institute, grew finally, after a long period of stagnation, into Birkbeck College of the University of London. It has continued to provide evening classes and lectures, supported by a good library, for several generations of students employed during normal working time.

**REFERENCES**

T. Kelly, *George Birkbeck: Pioneer of Adult Education* (1957).

W. A. Munford, "George Birkbeck and Mechanics' Institutes" in C. B. Oldman and others, *English Libraries 1800–1850: Three Lectures Delivered at University College, London* (1958).

W. A. MUNFORD

## Bishop, William Warner
(1871–1955)

ALA

*William Warner Bishop*

Through his writings and speeches, William Warner Bishop furthered the adoption of enlightened practices in libraries and promoted ideals of technical performance, new in the early part of the 20th century but now taken for granted. He promoted international intellectual cooperation and, as an articulate advocate of cooperative and specialized acquisitions, union catalogues, and other forms of cooperation, he led his contemporaries in thinking of library adequacy for research on a regional and national basis.

Bishop was born on July 20, 1871, in Hannibal, Missouri. When his father, William Melancthon Bishop, died in 1878, his mother, Harriette Anna Warner Bishop, returned to her native Detroit with young Warner and his two sisters. Bishop attended the University of Michigan, where he earned the A.B. degree in Classics in 1892 and the Master's degree a year later. He taught one year at Missouri Wesleyan College and one year at the Academy of Northwestern University before spending three years as Instructor of Greek and Assistant Librarian at Garrett Biblical Institute in Chicago.

A year at the American School of Classical Studies in Rome (1898–99) was followed by service as Librarian and Latin teacher at the Polytechnic Preparatory School in Brooklyn (1899–1902) and five years at Princeton, first as Cataloguer (1902–05) and then as Reference Librarian (1905–07). At Princeton he began to mature professionally, laying foundations under the tutelage of Head Librarian Ernest Cushing Richardson for his later prominence in national and international library affairs. His professional growth continued (1907–15) during service as Superintendent of the Reading Room at the Library of Congress, ably administered then by Herbert Putnam.

From 1915 until he retired in 1941, Bishop was Director of Libraries at the University of Michigan. During his administration the library grew into one of the largest and best selected research collections in the country. His efforts in promoting library education culminated in 1926 in the formation of the Department of Library Science, which he administered as Chairman until 1941. A thorough scholar himself, Bishop insisted on a scholarly approach to education for librarianship at Michigan and elsewhere.

Bishop joined the American Library Association in 1896. He was Chairman of the Cataloging Section (1906–07) and of the College and Reference Section (1908–09; 1917–18); for five years beginning in 1912 he served on Council. These, along with some committee work, were his major ALA activities until he was elected President for 1918–19, the fifth academic librarian to serve in that capacity since formation of the organization in 1876. During his tenure the ALA War Service received much of his attention, but the end of World War I came during his year in office; the net effect of Bishop's presidency was a strong effort to set the stage for postwar organizational change and progress.

Having served as President comparatively early in his career, before the age of 50, Bishop had many years left to provide leadership in the ALA as a knowledgeable senior statesman. Chief among his assignments were those related to the international affairs of the organization, and for over two decades he played a multifaceted role in that realm. He was active in the 1920's on the Executive Board (as Chairman of the Subcommittee on Foreign Affairs), on the Committee on Library Cooperation with Other Countries, and in the planning groups concerned with the celebration in 1926 of ALA's 50th anniversary. He was Chairman of the Committee on International Relations (1926–34) and a committee member (1935–37), then consultant to the ALA Board on International Relations from 1942 to 1949. From 1928 to 1945 he was ALA's first representative in the International Federation of Library Associations, serving as President of IFLA (1931–36). He gave stimulating, responsible leadership to IFLA, both in the formation and conduct of the organization itself and in the action taken on matters that came before it for consideration.

Bishop saw in the entire area of international intellectual cooperation an opportunity and duty to influence library development worldwide, to diminish the influence of nationalism in the library field, to promote the pursuit of knowledge, and to advance research in the world at large. He did not, therefore, limit his efforts to ALA assignments with international import. At the request of League of Nations officials, he served on their Library Planning Committee (1928–37). As a frequent adviser to the Carnegie Endowment for International Peace, the Carnegie Corporation, and the Rockefeller Foundation, he took part in a number of the international projects sponsored by those organizations in the 1920's, 1930's, and early 1940's. One of the most significant and interesting of his foundation activities resulted in his being the principal adviser to the Vatican Library in its reorganization and modernization, financed by the Carnegie Endowment for International Peace. Under his general direction, during the years 1927–34, bibliographic records for the Vatican Library were planned and initiated, which opened its great manuscript and printed-book collections for modern scholarship.

Throughout the United States significant improvements resulted from his work as Chairman of several advisory groups formed by the Carnegie Corporation to help selected college libraries by gifts of suitable books and by endowment of several college librarianships. From 1928 through 1943, Bishop headed advisory groups concerned with four-year liberal arts colleges, junior colleges, teachers colleges, colleges for Negroes, state colleges, and technological colleges. In all, 302 grants totaling $2,600,000 were made. Out of the project grew the first qualitative standards for libraries in four-year colleges and junior colleges, as well as lists to be used for selection of basic books for collections in them. The body of doctrine on college libraries, inadequate in the literature of librarianship, was substantially increased. The books distributed under Bishop's guidance no doubt helped to raise standards of teaching in many institutions, to promote the development of reading habits among college students, and to inform college administrators of the real signifiicance of their institutional libraries.

Bishop married Finie Murfree Burton of Louisville, Kentucky, in 1905. They had one son, William Warner Bishop, Jr., born in 1906. Bishop died on February 19, 1955.

**REFERENCES**

Claud Glenn Sparks, "William Warner Bishop: A Biography," Ph.D. dissertation, University of Michigan, 1967. Includes complete bibliographies of sources of information about Bishop and of Bishop's writings.

*William Warner Bishop: A Tribute* (1941).

CLAUD GLENN SPARKS

# Bodley, Sir Thomas

(1545–1613)

Thomas Bodley, English diplomat, was the founder of the Bodleian Library of Oxford University. He was the son of John Bodley, a Protestant who fled to Germany and Switzerland during the Counter-Reformation of Queen Mary I. The family lived among other Protestant refugees until 1558, when they returned to London. In 1559 Bodley entered Magdalen College, Oxford, where he was tutored by Lawrence Humphrey, another former Protestant refugee. Bodley earned his B.A. in 1563 and left for Merton College, where he was elected Fellow and began lecturing in Greek and natural philosophy. In 1566 he received his M.A. degree and was elected a Proctor, a chief university administrative officer elected annually by colleges in rotation. He also acted as Deputy Public Orator.

Bodley's ambition was to be in state service, so he left Oxford in 1576 to become fluent in foreign languages. He traveled in Italy, France, and Germany for four years, then returned to England to accept an appointment at Court. Beginning in 1585 he was in the diplomatic service on missions to Denmark, Germany, and France, and in 1588 he became English Resident in the United Provinces. He retired in 1596 after gaining a high reputation for his service in Holland.

In 1598 Bodley wrote to the Vice-Chancellor of Oxford to explain his plan for restoring the former public library to use by the university. He rarely visited Oxford

Bodleian Library

Sir Thomas Bodley

during his project but kept a detailed correspondence with Librarian Thomas James, beginning in December 1599; they discussed among other details, the chaining of books and combating woodworms as well as more general topics such as classification and cataloguing. He also corresponded on questions of building and furnishing. Bodley acquired books through his public service contacts, including men such as the Earl of Dorset, Sir Walter Raleigh, Lord Hunsdon, and Lord Southampton, who contributed money for their purchase. The Earl of Essex contributed the Bishop of Faro's library, which he had seized in 1596 when he landed the English army in Portugal. Notable antiquarians and collectors, such as William Camden, Sir Robert Cotton, and Lord Lumley, gave gifts of manuscripts. Others were received from ecclesiastical bodies, among them the Chapters of Exeter and Windsor.

The Library was also furnished with standing presses of a medieval pattern, similar to those in Merton College Library. (They are still in use.) By 1602 the original library room had been refurnished and housed books by major Protestant writers. On November 8, 1602, it opened to serve the University.

Bodley's great success in acquiring books for the Library led to a need for expansion. The year 1610 marked the opening of the Arts End extension, which Bodley supervised and financed. He also saw that there would be further need for book storage room, so he urged the University to restore the lecture rooms adjacent to the Library. Upon his death in 1613, Bodley left his fortune to the Library and for building the storage extensions that he had proposed. The top floor of the Schools Quadrangle was the first to be completed, in 1620. It now contains the main series of reading rooms.

Bodley wrote in his autobiography of the elements that made the establishment of the Library possible: knowledge of literature, ability to finance the project, friends for assistance, and the leisure in which to work.

Having all of these elements under his control, Thomas Bodley established the Bodleian Library of Oxford University on a strong foundation that has allowed it to continue as a strong center of learning and research.

## Bogle, Sarah Comly Norris
(1870–1932)

Sarah Bogle, Assistant Secretary of the American Library Association from 1920 to 1931, was an influential figure in the activities of the ALA, in library development overseas, and in the growth of library education. She was born in Milton, Pennsylvania, on November 17, 1870, to John Armstrong Bogle, a chemical engineer, and Emma Ridgway Norris Bogle. Harrison Craver, in a tribute to her at the 1932 annual conference of the American Library Association in New Orleans, described her education as "the typical training then in vogue for women of leisure." This consisted of attendance at Miss Stevens' School in Germantown, Pennsylvania, and extensive foreign travel. She attended Drexel Institute Library School in Philadelphia, receiving a certificate of proficiency in 1904; that year she joined the American Library Association.

She began her library career as Librarian at Juniata College in Huntingdon, Pennsylvania, where she remained for three years. After another year of study she became a branch librarian for the Queens Borough Public Library. In spring 1909 she was invited by Craver to join the staff of the Carnegie Library of Pittsburgh, where she spent the next ten years, first in a branch library, then as the Principal of the library school and as the chief children's librarian.

In 1920 she joined the staff of the ALA in Chicago and soon became Assistant Secretary to Carl Hastings Milam. Her work at Headquarters reflected her previous interests in library education and library services for children. Her writings also reflected these interests; of the 16 articles written by her and indexed in the first two compilations of *Library Literature* (1921–32 and 1933–35), over half express her thoughts and experiences in library education and her work as Secretary to the Temporary Library Training Board and its successor, the Board of Education for Librarianship. Sample titles are: "A Survey of the Library School Situation in the Southern States," "Training for Negro Librarians," "Trends and Tendencies in Education for Librarianship," and "Education of School Librarians in America." Two articles reflect her interest in children's library services: "The Child and the Book," and "A Conception of the Children's Librarian." Three relate her experiences as Director of the Paris Library School and her interest in the library movement in France: "The Fascination of the New Library Movement in France," "Library Development in France," and "The Future of the Paris Library School."

She traveled extensively, attending 18 ALA annual conferences and many state library association conferences, as well as library meetings abroad, such as those of the British Library Association and the British Institute of Adult Education. Besides her interest in library development in France, she conducted a survey of library needs for the Virgin Islands under a Carnegie Corporation grant in 1929 and represented ALA at the meetings of the International Library Committee in Stockholm in 1930.

At Headquarters she was second in command to Milam and remained loyal to him and ALA. She had a special competence in supervising staff and dealing with people. Harold Brigham called her the "balance wheel" and the "power behind the throne." Milam called her his "tower of strength." Emily Danton said: "They were a great team during the twenties. Her vision and her personal connections, antedating her service at headquarters, must never be forgotten. She knew her way around in international relationships and she did much to help her younger chief gain background in these aspects of his work. They supplemented each other in many ways, and both were highly stimulating to their associates."

Her special interests at ALA included the selection of staff, work with foundations, especially the Carnegie Corporation, education for librarianship, and the direction of the Paris Library School. In addition there was the daily routine of work at Headquarters. Miss Bogle, speaking to the members of the Illinois Library Association in October 1925, said:

> What about the daily routine: the mail, letters, one from a principal of a school in Tennessee asking for information concerning the organization of a library; a letter asking about libraries in jail and penitentiaries; plans for a library building; the usual letters asking about placements, Committee appointments and a telegram from the Carnegie Corporation granting a renewal of the appropriation of $158,000 of 1925—this means a continuation of the activities of the last year and some new ones.

Everett Fontaine, ALA publishing officer, described her as a grande dame—a large woman, erect, well-groomed, with perfectly set blond-gray hair, and with a velvet or beaded band high up on her throat. She lived with her mother and took a taxi to work, carrying a briefcase filled with whodunits. She was a Republican and an Episcopalian.

She served on the ALA Council (1917–20) and was a member of many library and educational groups including the Association of American Library Schools (she was President, 1917–18), the Keystone State Library Association, the Pennsylvania Library Association, the Illinois Library Association, the Illinois Chapter of the Special Libraries Association, the American Library Institute, the American Woman's Association, the American Association for Adult Education, the National Education Association, and the Chicago Library Club (President, 1922–23).

She died on January 11, 1932, in White Plains, New York, and was buried in Milton, Pennsylvania.

She was not replaced at ALA until 1944 because of Depression-era budgets. In 1951 she was selected by *Library Journal* for a "Library Hall of Fame for the 75th Anniversary" of the American Library Association, one of 13 women included with the 40 librarians selected.

ALA

*Sarah Comly Norris Bogle*

**REFERENCES**

Harrison Warwick Craver, "Sarah C. N. Bogle: An Appreciation," *ALA Bulletin* (1932).

Emily Miller Danton, "Mr. ALA: Carl Hastings Milam," *ALA Bulletin* (1959).

Peggy A. Sullivan, *Carl H. Milam and the American Library Association* (1976).

ALA Archives, University of Illinois at Urbana.

DORIS CRUGER DALE

# Bolivia

Bolivia, a republic in central South America, is bounded by Brazil on the north and east, Paraguay on the southeast, Argentina on the south, and Chile and Peru on the southwest and west. Pop. (1978 est.) 4,886,700; area 1,098,581 sq.km. The official language is Spanish.

**National Library.** The National Library—founded on June 23, 1821, by Mariscal Andrés de Santa Cruz and reorganized in 1938—is in Sucre, the official capital of the country (La Paz is the political capital). The main part of the collection is made up of 19th-century publications. The National Archive, founded in 1883, is at the National Library. The National Depository Library is in La Paz and functions as the legal depository.

**Academic Libraries.** Libraries are located in all ten Bolivian universities. During the colonial period the most important academic library was at the Universidad San Francisco Javier, founded in Sucre in 1624, which housed the Colonial Academy, founded in 1776, which provided much of the intellectual stimulus for the independence of Latin America.

The most important academic library is at the Universidad Mayor de San Andrés, with 150,000 volumes and a complete collection of the country's leading newspapers. Collections in the other university libraries range from 10,000 to 35,000 volumes, with strengths in the humanities and the social sciences. Cataloguing in all the academic libraries is deficient as a result of the almost complete lack of library school graduates in the country.

**Public and School Libraries.** In 1968 the Book Bank (Banco de Libro) was created to organize public and school libraries throughout the country. The Organization of American States began in 1976 to provide technical assistance to the Book Bank in its effort to establish a National Technical Processes Center in La Paz. From November 1976, 55 branches of the Book Bank were founded throughout the country, with pilot centers in Sucre, Tarija, Cobija, and Trinidad. The branches serve both students and the general public. Book Bank branches are in each town's House of Culture, and cooperation between the local community and the Bolivian Institute of Culture is a necessary link in providing Book Bank services. Collections in the branches range from 800 to 1,500 volumes.

The largest public library in Bolivia is the Municipal Library in La Paz, founded in 1838 by Mariscal Andrés de Santa Cruz, with current holdings of 90,000 volumes. The Municipal Library has set up 12 branches in the poorer sections of the city. Another branch serves as a

**Table 1. Libraries in Bolivia (1976)**

| Type | Number | Volumes in collections | Annual expenditures (peso) | Population served | Professional staff | All staff (total) |
|---|---|---|---|---|---|---|
| National | 1 | 80,000 | 61,000,000 | 60,000 | 1 | 10 |
| Academic | 9 | 390,000 | | 107,000 | 3 | 100 |
| Public and School | 70 | 345,000 | | 1,000,000 | 2 | 72 |
| Special | 15 | 450,000 | | 75,000 | 3 | 48 |
| Total | 95 | 1,265,000 | | | 9 | 320 |

Source: Universidad Boliviana, *Catalogo General*, La Paz.

*The Municipal Library of La Paz, Bolivia, (extreme left) was founded in 1838 and is the country's largest public library.*

Arthur Plotnik

special library for the students at the Medical School at the Universidad Mayor de San Andrés, and a "bibliobus" (book bus) serves the schools in zones without libraries.

A unique aspect of Bolivia's municipal library system is a procedure whereby bookstores pay their municipal taxes with books selected by staff of the municipal library in amounts equal in value to what the stores would have otherwise paid in taxes.

**Table 2. Archives in Bolivia (1976)**

| | |
|---|---|
| Number | 9 |
| Holdings | 1,800 linear meters |
| Professional staff | 2 |
| All staff (total) | 38 |

Source: Director of the Archives of La Paz.

**Special Libraries.** Most of Bolivia's special libraries are located in La Paz. Libraries are found in the Documentation Center, Ministry of Mines and Hydrocarbons; Documentation Center, National Office of Standards and Technology, Ministry of Industry and Tourism; Military School; and the Central Bank.

**Association.** The Bolivian Association of Librarians is headquartered in La Paz. Its members include both practicing librarians and students enrolled in the country's only library school, at the Universidad Mayor de San Andrés.

JULIO AGUIRRE QUINTERO

## Botswana

Botswana, a republic of southern Africa, is surrounded by South Africa on the south and southeast, South West Africa on the north and west, Zambia on the north, and Rhodesia on the east and northeast. Pop. (1978 est.) 766,000; area 576,000 sq.km. The official languages are English and Setswana.

**National Library.** The Botswana National Library Service (BNLS) is both the national library and the national public library service and is headquartered in the capital, Gaborone. It was established by the National Library Service in 1967 and officially opened on April 8, 1968. BNLS is an administrative, planning, and advisory center and a clearinghouse for all matters connected with the development of library services in Botswana; it consists of three sections. (1) The Administrative, Secretarial, and Clerical Section is responsible for general administration, including the control finance for the library system. (2) The Technical Services Section is the acquisition and technical processing center. Through legal deposit locally published materials are obtained and form entries for the triennial *National Bibliography of Botswana* (NABOB), published materials are obtained and form entries for the triannual National Bibliography of Botswana (NABOB), first published in 1969. (3) The External Services Section is responsible for all relationships with all types of libraries outside the headquarters. It operates a mobile library service to villages around Gaborone (with plans to extend the service to other parts of the country), provides a postal lending service, and runs branch libraries and library centers throughout the country. A branch library is owned and staffed by the BNLS; buildings and staff of a library center are provided by another agency, with BNLS providing stock, equipment, and supplies. Of 12 branch libraries, 4 are headed by professionals. BNLS represents the country at various international conferences.

**Academic Libraries.** The University College library was established in July 1971 as a branch of the then University of Botswana, Lesotho, and Swaziland. The initial stock of 2,000 volumes and 50 periodical titles served 67 students and 11 lecturing staff in the first two years of a four-year program. By 1976 the College library supported a fully operational undergraduate program in the basic humanities, sciences, and education. Its collection consisted of 29,522 volumes and 454 periodical titles for use by 778 readers and 86 lecturing staff, in contrast to 24,720 volumes and 300 periodical titles to 633 readers and 73 staff in 1973.

**Table 2. Archives in Botswana (1976)**

| | |
|---|---|
| Number | 1 |
| Holdings | N.A. |
| Annual expenditures | R1,800[a] |
| Professional staff | 1 |
| All staff | 5 |

[a]Materials Fund only.

Source: J. A. V. Rose, Report on the National Archives for the period April 1975 to March 1976 (Gaborone: Government Printer).

**School Libraries.** School libraries were at a developing stage in the 1970's, with library facilities in schools varying from those that were at planning stages to those that were well stocked and organized. It was intended that each secondary school library should have a minimum of 10,000 volumes. A survey carried out in 1972 indicated that most of those schools responding had from 2,000 to 3,000 volumes. The recurrent budget is allocated by the Ministry of Education at the rate of three pula per student. Capital projects for buildings, equipment, and initial bookstock were allocated at 200,000 pula and phased at an estimate of 40,000 pula a year. In most secondary schools there is no provision for full-time school librarians. Schools assign responsibility for the library to a teacher who is given a lighter teaching load to provide time to spend on library work. Student library assistants usually perform simple routine tasks. While it was planned that the BNLS would eventually provide staff to

**Table 1. Libraries in Botswana (1976)**

| Type | Number | Volumes in collections | Annual expenditures (South African rand) (Botswana pula) | Population served | Professional staff | All staff (total) |
|---|---|---|---|---|---|---|
| National and Public[a] | 8 | 61,315 | R60,836 | 700,000[b] | 8 | 22 |
| Academic | 1 | 29,522 | P18,000 | 700 | 6 | 15 |
| School[c] | 9 | 2,400[d] | N.A. | 5,564 | 2 | N.A. |
| Special | 21 | N.A. | N.A. | N.A. | N.A. | N.A. |

[a]1973 figures.
[b]Estimated rate of illiteracy 80%. Actual registered borrowers total 15,780.
[c]Secondary schools only.
[d]Average per school

secondary schools and teacher training colleges, it acted in an advisory capacity to those institutions in the late 1970's.

An experimental "book box" service has been inaugurated in some areas to cater to primary schools. Branch library staff are responsible for book selection, supply, advice, and supervision, while teachers are responsible for operating the book box scheme.

**Special Libraries.** Most special libraries are in Gaborone in government departments. They acquire such current materials as reports, journals, and research papers and usually have a small reference collection. They are used mainly by staff within the department. Of the 21 established special libraries, 7 are well developed, though most do not have trained library personnel and thus must depend on the cooperation of the BNLS for assistance and advice.

**REFERENCE**

S. M. Made, "Reading—Library Facilities in Botswana," F.L.A. thesis, University of Botswana, Lesotho, and Swaziland, Luyengo (1977).

KAY RASEROKA

## Bousso, Amadou Alassane
(1933– )

Amadou Allassane Bousso initiated and organized formal library education in Senegal and worked for professional training and support in other African countries. He was born in 1933 at Kanel in the Senegal Valley to a family with a tradition of Islamic learning. His postprimary education was at the Ponty school, the one full teacher training school for the whole of French West Africa, from which he was graduated in 1956. He then taught in primary and secondary schools in the Dakar area and attended Dakar University, where he took a degree in literature.

He was appointed counterpart to the Unesco expert in charge of setting up EBAD (Ecole de Bibliothècaire, Archivistes et Documentalistes de Dakar) in 1962. The school was intended to address the need for trained librarians in former French colonies of Africa; before independence, none had been trained locally or overseas. It first took as students existing library personnel, most of whom had certificates for four years of secondary school education, which was the level Africans were usually allowed to reach, and some younger trainees with full secondary schooling. The first program crammed training into one school year. Bousso participated in a number of international meetings and traveled extensively in other countries, persuading a number of governments to send students to the school and urging them to organize the profession of librarianship so that the graduates could find suitable posts on returning home. His work proved difficult since library support by various governments often lagged.

EBAD in 1979 offered a two-year course and annually enrolled 50 or more pupils with full secondary education. It became part of Dakar University, was housed in handsome new buildings, and, more important, had a full-time staff of 11 teachers at the end of the 1970's. It planned to offer a Master's degree course.

F. LALANDE ISNARD

## Bowker, Richard Rogers
(1848–1933)

Richard Rogers Bowker, Publisher and Editor of *Library Journal* and *Publishers' Weekly*, was noted as a friend of libraries and political reformer. He was born September 4, 1848, in Salem, Massachusetts, to proper and prosperous parents, Daniel and Theresa Maria (Savory) Bowker. The panic of 1857 brought business reverses to his father, who was never really successful afterward despite a move to New York City and several attempts to start again. Before Rogers was 20, he provided the main financial support for his mother, father, and younger sister, Carolyn.

Bowker enrolled as a student at the Free Academy in New York City in 1863, which became the City College of New York before he graduated in 1868. He had an excellent academic record and formed several lasting friendships. For a while he operated single-handedly one of the first student newspapers in the country and was influential in establishing one of the earliest student government organizations. Neither of these enterprises found favor with the college administration; when Bowker helped start a chapter of Phi Beta Kappa, the President of the College prevented the young activist's membership.

Bowker's experience in operating the student newspaper led directly into one of his several careers. While he was still in college, he reported some events for the New York *Evening Mail* and began working full-time for that paper on the day after his commencement. He became Literary Editor of the *Mail* in 1870; as one of the many pieces he wrote for outside papers and periodicals, he contributed a series of articles reviewing American literature in 1871 that appeared early in 1872 in Frederick Leypoldt's *Publishers' and Stationers' Weekly Trade Circular* and in the third edition of Leypoldt's *Annual American Catalogue*. The *Weekly Trade Circular* became *Publishers' Weekly* in 1873 with Bowker as part-time Assistant; in 1875 he began to work on it full-time and bought it from Leypoldt in 1878. He owned *PW* until his death, exercising varying degrees of editorial control through the years, and was listed as its Editor for most of his life.

In his early years Bowker was intensely interested in the contemporary literary scene. Since many authors and publishers were his friends, he was deemed the perfect choice when the Harper firm needed a representative in London to make contacts with British authors and to launch a transatlantic version of *Harper's Magazine*. He spent two happy and successful years in England, from 1880 to 1882, but wished to come home for many reasons; he missed his family, his friends, and the chance to take part in liberal political movements.

One of his favorite causes was closely related to his work in the book world: the movement for international copyright. Bowker's innate sense of fairness and his lifelong habit of expressing his convictions through actions made it natural for him to support this cause through the pages of *Publishers' Weekly*, through his position as Chairman of the Executive Committee of the American Copyright League, and through continual efforts at personal persuasion. He was perhaps as influential as any other single individual in obtaining the copyright acts in 1891 and 1909.

It is difficult to determine when Bowker first became interested in libraries. Leypoldt's *Publishers' and Stationers' Weekly Trade Circular* had carried some news of libraries before Bowker's association with the firm, and *Publishers' Weekly* continued this practice after Bowker became a member of its staff. He joined Leypoldt and Melvil Dewey in the establishment in 1876 of the *Library Journal* and in the planning that preceded the meeting in that same year at which the American Library Association was formed.

The *Library Journal* lost money regularly in the early years, partly because Dewey, its Editor, had struck a hard financial bargain, demanding 20 percent of gross receipts from subscriptions and advertisements. Publishing the periodical was a great nuisance to Leypoldt and Bowker because Dewey was dilatory and careless. Bowker, how-

ALA

*Richard Rogers Bowker*

ever, continued to support the library movement, keeping the *Library Journal* alive after Dewey's departure in 1881 and Leypoldt's death in 1884. Bowker wrote editorials and articles for *LJ* throughout his life; they were always informative, positive in tone, and sometimes quite laudatory of good works. Typical of the articles are "The Work of the Nineteenth-Century Librarian for the Librarian of the Twentieth" (September–October 1883), in which he saw the librarian as a liberator rather than a keeper of books; "The Formation and Organization of Public Libraries" (March 1887), in which he demonstrated a good knowledge of library legislation and suggested some practical ways to start a public library; "Making the Most of the Small Library" (March 1915), practical advice on the operation of a public library too small to hire a professional librarian; and "Women in the Library Profession," a three-part article in 1920, in which he pointed out gains made by women in the profession and discussed the contributions of a number of leading women librarians.

Bowker's friendship for libraries was expressed in another way: he was an active member of the ALA, serving on the Council for more than 20 years and as Chairman of the Committee on Public Documents for some time. He refused the presidency of the Association three times, believing that a librarian should hold the post, but was made Honorary President when he was in his 70's.

He promoted the welfare of several individual libraries in a number of ways. He was one of the two people who were most influential in persuading President McKinley to appoint Herbert Putnam as Librarian of Congress and later gave several thousand dollars to the LC Trust Fund. In Brooklyn, where he lived for many years, he worked hard in the movement that culminated in the formation of the Brooklyn Public Library in 1902; he then served as one of its trustees until his death. He was also President of the Library Association in Stockbridge, Massachusetts, where his summer home was located, from 1904 until 1928. He wrote articles for the *Library Journal* about the work of public library trustees.

Of course, Bowker's bibliographic work also helped libraries. He carried on Leypoldt's *Publishers' Weekly* and *American Catalogue* and inaugurated a few bibliographic enterprises of his own, most notably three features added to the *American Catalogue* that he felt were needed by librarians: a list of federal government publications (1885), a list of society publications (1885), and a list of state publications (1891). But Bowker was not the innovative bibliographer that Leypoldt had been, nor was he in his later years as inventive and as quick to sense the needs of librarians as was his younger rival, H. W. Wilson.

Perhaps Bowker did not change or develop his bibliographical work further because throughout his life his basic interests had been broadly humanitarian, not bookish or bibliographic, and he directed much of his tremendous energy into fighting bravely and intelligently for almost every liberal cause. He was a part of a small group of men who founded the "Mugwumps," a liberal group in the Republican Party, though he may not have been, as some have said, *the* founder of that movement. He fought against corrupt politicians and for civil service. A supporter of tariff reform, he felt that existing U.S. tariffs protected special interests at the expense of the public. His concern for the welfare of mankind in general led him to oppose imperialistic and militaristic tendencies in the government. He also worked for the benefit of minorities within the United States. He wrote articles strongly advocating the establishment of settlement houses, vigorously opposed tendencies toward anti-Semitism in his alma mater, City College, gave generously to colleges for blacks, and opposed the persecution of conscientious objectors during World War I.

Bowker held liberal, humanitarian views about the conduct of business and put them into practice. He believed that owners and managers should voluntarily hold down profits and should show concern for their employees and for consumers. He accepted the position as Executive Officer of the Edison Electric Illuminating Company in New York in 1890 partly in order to put his ideas about the proper conduct of a business into practice on a larger scale than he could at the *Publishers' Weekly* office. For a while he was successful, managing to reduce the cost of electricity to consumers while raising wages and paying a fair return to stockholders, but he resigned in 1899 when a group of stock manipulators, planning to establish a monopoly, managed to gain control of the company.

When Bowker left Edison, he was beginning to have serious eye trouble, and he became completely blind in a few years. His failing sight would have prevented him from giving close personal supervision to the development of new bibliographic or indexing services, a situation that may have prevented the diversification of the Bowker Company's services during his later life.

Around the time Bowker was adjusting to the loss of his eyesight, he surprised his friends by marrying Alice Mitchell on New Year's Day, 1902, when he was 53 and she was 38. The couple had known each other for several years.

Although Bowker had lost his sight, his general health was good, and his concern for other human beings was undiminished; for many years he wrote and spoke in favor of a variety of causes. He remained active until November 12, 1933, when he died, after a short illness, at the age of 85. At the time of his death, Herbert Putnam surely expressed the feeling of librarians when he wrote in the special December 1, 1933, issue of *Library Journal,* "Our profession has had no friend who, without the professional obligation, has aided so greatly to define its aims, maintain its dignity, and promote its fellowship."

**REFERENCES**

E. M. Fleming, *R. R. Bowker, Militant Liberal* (1952), is an excellent book-length biography of Bowker. The largest depository of his manuscripts is in the New York Public Library; others are listed in the bibliography of the Fleming volume.

HAYNES McMULLEN

## Bradford, Samuel Clement
(1878–1948)

Samuel Clement Bradford was a supporter of moves to improve the control of scientific and technical information and contributed to the development of the field of documentation. He was born in London, England, on January 10, 1878. He trained as a chemist, and a former colleague related that Bradford obtained his degree by study at night school and his doctorate by research in his office in the Science Museum Library. He was fond of roses, and sandwiched between his many writings on chemistry and documentation was a book on the science of roses.

He joined the staff of the Science Museum in 1899 and worked in its library from 1901 until his retirement in 1938, becoming Assistant Keeper in 1922, Deputy Keeper in 1925, and Keeper in 1930. During his tenure he devoted his vision and energy to turning the Science Museum Library into the National Science Library. D. J. Urquhart observed that his great achievement was that he managed to change a small scientific library into the largest collection of scientific literature in Europe.

Bradford enthusiastically supported the adoption of the Universal Decimal Classification (UDC) throughout the world, with a view to the production of a world bibliography, and Bradford is well remembered for his advocacy of UDC as superior to any other system of classification and to alphabetical systems. He introduced UDC into the Science Library and was a keen supporter of the International Institute of Bibliography, later to become the International Federation for Documentation (FID). It was largely to further the use of UDC that in 1927 Bradford formed, with Professor A. F. C. Pollard, the British Society for International Bibliography (BSIB) as the British Committee of FID, and BSIB became one of the main channels of communication about UDC in Britain. He edited the *Proceedings of the British Society for International Bibliography* from its inception in 1939 until the amalgamation of BSIB with Aslib (then the Association of Special Libraries and Information Bureaux) in 1948. He followed Pollard as President of BSIB in 1945 and was elected a Vice-President of FID and Chairman of its International Committee on Classification in 1947.

One of the reasons for Bradford's strong support of UDC was his concern that the scientific literature should be fully documented and well organized. In *Documentation* (1948), he refers to experiments conducted at the Science Library that showed that less than half the useful papers published were being covered by abstracting journals. He then investigated the manner in which articles on one subject would often appear in periodicals not primarily concerned with that subject. He deduced a common pattern in this "bibliographical scatter," which led to the formulation of Bradford's "Law of scatter." "Bradford's Law" has received a great deal of attention from writers on scientific documentation—too much, according to Bradford's successor, Urquhart, who wrote, "Bradford's Law . . . was but a small element in his propaganda war," and suggested that "Bradford would be appalled by the academic discussion which has taken place about his law. He was interested in much more practical things."

Bradford published 35 contributions to documentation, but he also wrote many papers on chemistry and other scientific subjects. He will be best remembered by librarians as a writer for the collection of essays published as *Documentation,* which Margaret Egan, reviewing the book in *Library Quarterly* (1950), said "should be useful in directing the attention of American librarians to the importance of bibliographic control in some form and the need for further investigation of this neglected aspect of librarianship." The conclusion to her review showed that Bradford was human and that he did not always practice what he preached: "One cannot conclude, however, without expressing surprise that Mr. Bradford, who argues so convincingly for more adequate indexing services, should be so inconsiderate as to give us this book without an index, organized according to either the UDC or even the abhorred concealed classification of subject headings." It is interesting that an index *was* provided for the reprint, published five years after Bradford's death, to which Egan and Jesse Shera contributed a 35-page introductory essay calling for librarianship and documentation to be regarded as a unity.

Urquhart remarks that Bradford seemed to him at first "a very fussy man." The official support given to the National Lending Library for Science and Technology (now incorporated in the British Library Lending Division) owed a great deal to the pioneering propaganda efforts of Bradford, and Urquhart observes, "That to me is how Bradford should be remembered—as one who sought to convince others of the importance of scientific information and who did a great deal despite the odds against him to make scientific information available. The fussy little man I once met was really a giant in disguise."

**REFERENCES**

E. M. R. Ditmas, "Dr. S. C. Bradford," *Journal of Documentation* (1948).

D. J. Urquhart, "S. C. Bradford," *Journal of Documentation* (1977).

M. Gosset, "S. C. Bradford, Keeper of the Science Museum Library 1925–1937," *Journal of Documentation* (1977).

K. G. B. BAKEWELL

## Bray, Thomas (1658–1730) BRAY, THOMAS 576

Because of his own activities, and those of the societies he founded, Thomas Bray was one of the greatest single cultural influences at work in the American colonies during the 18th century. He was born in Marton, Shropshire, England, in 1658. Edward Lewis, Vicar of the nearby town of Chirbury, noticed Bray's aptitude for learning and made available his notable collection of chained books. Through Lewis's influence, Bray's parents sent him to Oswestry Grammar School. He matriculated at All Souls College, Oxford, in 1674 as a *puer pauper,* supporting himself through service to the fellows, and receiving his Bachelor of Arts degree in 1678. He later took Bachelor of Divinity and Doctor of Divinity degrees from Magdalen College.

Bray's first appointment was to a parish near Bridgnorth, Warwickshire, in 1681. A few months later he was asked to preach the annual assize sermon. One of the members of the congregation was Simon, Lord Digby. Impressed with the young priest's presentation, he convinced his brother, William, to offer Bray the parish of Over Whitacre. In 1690 William presented Bray with the living at Sheldon, which he continued to hold until his death, although an appointed curate actually served the parish for over 25 years while Bray labored in London on his various schemes.

Through his friendship with the Digbys, Bray came to the notice of Bishop Compton of London, who had been concerned for some time with the lack of spiritual leadership in the colonies. He had appointed James Blair as Commissary of Virginia in 1689, and in 1696 he offered Bray the position in Maryland.

Bray, who was concerned with the intellectual as well as the spiritual life of the colonists, developed a scheme to provide libraries for all the parishes of Maryland, and agreed to accept the position if Compton would support his plan. With Compton's approval, he began collecting books and interviewing missionaries for service in the colony. He was so successful that Governor Nicholson suggested Compton appoint Bray Commissary for New York, Pennsylvania, and New England as well.

At the start, Bray's primary concern was for Maryland, but as he began to hear from ministers in the New World about the lack of books in other colonies, he expanded his plan to provide libraries for each of the colonies. By 1697, 16 libraries had been established in Maryland and 7 in the other colonies, and plans were under way for 6 more.

In his *Bibliothecae Americanae Quatripartidiae,* Bray outlined his colonial library system. In the major city of each colony, a large provincial library would be established. The second type, the parochial library, would be established in each parish. Third, the layman's library would be comprised of certain religious books that would be loaned by the minister, and a number of tracts would be given free to the people.

When he presented his final report on the libraries to the Society for the Propagation of the Gospel in Foreign Parts in 1704, Bray could claim the establishment of provincial libraries in Boston, New York, Philadelphia, Annapolis, Charleston, and Bath, North Carolina. He had provided 29 parochial libraries for Maryland and at least one such library in each of the other colonies, as well as providing over 35,000 volumes for the layman's libraries in all the colonies.

Some of Bray's library ideas were surprisingly modern. In his *Memorial to the Clergy of Maryland,* published in 1700, he outlined two ideas for increasing and preserving the libraries. First, each library would provide a catalogue of its collection to the others so that they might exercise a primitive system of interlibrary loan. Second, a small annual subscription would be assessed on the borrowers to enlarge the collections.

Given his personal involvement in library establishment, it is certain that had Bray been able to return to America, he would have promoted their growth and development. Because he could not return, they were left to struggle on their own. Without support and encouragement from the colonists, they gradually diminished as an intellectual force in the life of the people.

In addition to providing libraries and missionaries for the colonies, Bray steered a bill for the establishment of the Church of England in Maryland through Parliament. At the same time, in order to further his library plans, he founded the Society for the Promotion of Christian Knowledge, the Society for the Propagation of the Gospel in Foreign Parts, and the Bray Associates. The Act of Establishment of the Church remained in force throughout the colonial period, and the societies still exist today, active in missionary enterprise, publishing, and education.

Bray died in London on February 15, 1730. Although Bray had the satisfaction of seeing legislative protection given to libraries in three colonies during his lifetime, he failed in his attempts to secure public support for their growth and continued development. Despite his concern, it would be nearly a century and a half before the support necessary for the development of the library as a public institution would develop. Had he lived in the 19th century, Bray would have been one of the driving forces in that development.

**REFERENCES**

Charles T. Laugher, *Thomas Bray's Grand Design* (ALA, 1973).

Henry Thompson, *Thomas Bray* (1954).

CHARLES T. LAUGHER

## Brazil



Brazil, a federal republic, is the largest country in South America. It is bordered on the north, east, and south by every South American country except Chile and Ecuador; the Atlantic Ocean borders on the west. Pop. (1977 est.) 113,208,500; area 8,512,000 sq.km. The official language is Portuguese.

**National Libraries.** Brazil has two national libraries: the National Agricultural Library in Brasília was established at the end of 1978; the other is much older, and like many national libraries originated as a royal library and is made up of many collections.

When Portugal was invaded by Napoleon's armies under the command of Junot in 1807, the Portuguese King, Don João VI, transferred the royal court to Brazil and settled in Rio de Janeiro in 1808. During that year various centers of higher education, together with the Royal Press, were established. The Royal Library was founded in 1810 with a collection of books and manuscripts that had been brought from Portugal and numbered more than 60,000 volumes. When Don João VI returned to Portugal, leaving his son Don Pedro as Prince Regent of Brazil, the cultural and educational institutions, including the Library, remained in Rio de Janeiro.

In 1822 the Portuguese Prince Regent himself, guided by José Bonifácio de Andrade e Silva, declared Brazil's independence, and the Library became the property of the Brazilian government. In 1825 it became known as the Imperial and Public Library; since 1878 its official title has been the National Library of Rio de Janeiro. When the last emperor, the scholarly Don Pedro II, left Brazil after the proclamation of the Republic, he donated his personal collection of some 50,000 volumes to the National Library.

Throughout its history the National Library has enriched its holdings and has undergone various reforms to adapt itself to the advances in library science. A recent reform began in 1971 with the appointment of the General Director—the first professional librarian to occupy the post—required by a law of June 1962 that regulates the profession of librarianship. In 1974 the National Library had holdings of approximately 3,600,000 volumes, 600,000 manuscripts, 30,950 periodicals, 100,000 musical scores, 200,000 iconographic pieces, and 60,000 volumes of rare books. Since 1971 its problems—some of them chronic—have been defined and technical problem-solving projects have been launched. The Library has received financial aid for these projects from government agencies, Unesco, and the Ford Foundation. The Library receives, as the legal depository in Brazil since 1847, all publications printed in the country and issues semiannually, in its *Boletim Bibliográfico,* the current national bibliography. Recent volumes of the *Boletim Bibliográfico* are computer-produced through an agreement between the National Library and the Center for Informatics of the Ministry of Education and Culture (CIMEC). The National Library also acts as the Brazilian agency for the International Standard Book Number (ISBN).

**Academic Libraries.** Higher education in Brazil began rather late in comparison with other Latin American countries; students usually attended the University of Coimbra or French universities. It was only during the second decade of the 19th century that schools of higher education were founded in Brazil: two Law Schools (in São Paulo and Olinda), two Schools of Medicine (Rio de Janeiro and Bahia), and one Polytechnic School (Bahia). The first university was created by the federal government in Rio de Janeiro in 1920. In 1934 São Paulo established the first state university. In 1979 there were 57 universities and 803 independent colleges. Almost without exception their library collections and technical processes are decentralized, with undesirable duplication arising from such a system.

The University of Brasília, maintained by a foundation, was established in 1962 and has only one centralized library, thus avoiding the duplication that occurs in the majority of the other libraries. The library possesses 350,000 volumes and 6,500 periodicals and is open to the public 23 hours a day. In 1976, 882,412 persons used the library services during 347 days. Its modern building was constructed with funds from the Interamerican Development Bank at a cost of $1,500,000 and with a capacity of 1,000,000 volumes. The example of the University of Brasília has been a model for newer institutions, such as the Federal University of Paraíba, which have centralized library administration and collections.

**Public Libraries.** Even before the Royal Library opened to the public in 1814, a public library was inaugurated in the state of Bahia in 1811, modeled along the lines of the subscription public libraries that arose in the United States and in England in the 18th century. The first state to follow the example of Bahia was Maranhão, where a public library was founded in 1829 and opened in 1831. It was only in the second half of the 19th century that other public libraries were established in the states of Sergipe (1851), Pernambuco (1852), Espírito Santo (1855), Paraná (1857), Paraíba (1858), Alagoas (1865), Ceará (1867), Amazonas and Rio Grande do Sul (1871), Rio de Janeiro (1873), Pará (1894), and Santa Catarina (1895).

The other public libraries in the country were founded in the 20th century; all are state libraries with the exception of the Municipal Library of São Paulo, founded in 1925. This public library—today called the Mario de Andrade Library, in honor of one of the greatest Brazilian authors—is worthy of mention, because after its reform in 1942 it became one of the best libraries of its kind in Latin America. Recognizing this, Unesco chose São Paulo in October 1951 as the site of the Conference on the Development of Public Library Services in Latin America. The reorganization of the Municipal Library of São Paulo was accomplished by the faculty members and students of an American oriented course in library science sponsored by the College of Sociology and Political Science. This framework also influenced the reorganization of the old public libraries in the states of Maranhão (1947) and Paraná (1954); they are considered among the best of their kind in Brazil.

In 1977 the National Book Institute began the National System of Public Libraries, comprising the states of Pernambuco, Minas Gerais, Ceará, Rio Grande do Sul, and the Federal District. In 1978 the states of Pará, Bahia, São Paulo, Rio de Janeiro, and Espírito Santo joined the system. The system was created through a pilot project in Pernambuco with financial support from Unesco.

**School Libraries.** The first libraries in Brazil were school libraries, maintained by the Jesuit fathers in the schools they founded in São Vicente (1550), Rio de Janeiro (1567), and Bahia (1568). The most important was that of the latter, which had European librarians; one of them was the famous preacher and Portuguese-Brazilian author Father Antônio Vieira. Another important school library was that of the Seminary of Olinda, founded by Bishop Azeredo Coutinho in 1798, which not only educated future priests but also admitted the lay elite. This practice was consistent with the spirit of the Enlightenment and the reform of public education carried out by the Marquis of Pombal in Portugal. Unfortunately, the traditions of the Jesuits and of the later Seminary of Olinda did not continue. Thus, in Brazil there were no adequate school libraries in the educational system at the end of the 1970's.

**Special Libraries.** Some of the most important special libraries in the country are in the universities since they are connected with schools of medicine, engineering, and agronomy. Worthy of mention is the Regional Library of Medicine (BIREME), which is a Latin American subsystem of the National Library of Medicine of the United States. BIREME is maintained in São Paulo by the São Paulo School of Medicine, in cooperation with the World Health Organization and the Pan American Health Organization. With subcenters in several Brazilian universities, it maintains an efficient biomedical information system. The Oswaldo Cruz Institute Library, maintained by the Federal University of Rio de Janeiro, possesses the country's largest collection of periodicals in the biomedical sciences.

In the agricultural sciences there is a national system for agricultural information administered by the Brazilian Agency for Technical Assistance and Rural Extension (EMBRATER); it is a component of such international systems as the International Information System for the Agricultural Sciences and Technology (AGRIS). Begun in 1975, under an agreement between the Ministry of Agriculture and FAO, this system gave rise to the founding of the National Agricultural Library (BINAGRI) at the end of 1978. It also introduced SDI (Selective Dissemination of Information) services to Brazil. The special libraries form a network coordinated by the Brazilian Institute for Information in Science and Technology (IBICT), which maintains, among other services, a national union catalogue of books (only in cards) and periodicals (in both cards and book form).

**Associations.** The São Paulo Librarians Association, founded in 1938, was the first in the country. There are 14 librarians' associations, most of them at the state level, and the one municipal association is in São Paulo. In 1959, on the occasion of the Second Brazilian Congress of Library Science and Documentation, the Brazilian Federation of Librarians' Associations (FEBAB) was founded, with headquarters in São Paulo. FEBAB works through permanent commissions for public and school libraries, documentation in agriculture, biomedical sciences, law, and technology, and technical processes. At Belo Hori-

Antonio Miranda

*The Municipal Public Library of Maringá in Paraná, Brazil.*

**Table 1. Libraries in Brazil (1974)**

| Type | Number | Volumes in collections | Annual expenditures (cruzeiro) | Population served | Professional staff | All staff (total) |
|---|---|---|---|---|---|---|
| National | 1 | 3,574,623 | Cr$10,122,000[a] | 94,714 | 154 | 360 |
| Academic | 613 | 9,771,558 | N.A. | 6,365,659 | N.A. | 3,604 |
| Public | 2,333 | 13,894,006 | N.A. | 13,240,561 | N.A. | 6,859 |
| School | N.A. | N.A. | N.A. | N.A. | N.A. | N.A. |
| Special | 572 | 10,513,012 | N.A. | 3,745,259 | N.A. | 2,534 |
| Total | 3,519 | 37,753,199 | | 23,446,193 | | 13,357 |

[a]Salaries excluded.

Source: *Anuário Estatístico do Brasil* (1977; Rio de Janeiro: Fundação IBGE, 1978); Director of the National Library of Rio de Janeiro.

*William Howard Brett* ALA

**Table 2. Archives in Brazil (1974)**

| | |
|---|---|
| Number | 2,395 (a National System of Archives (SINAR) was created only in 1978) |
| Holdings | 11,000 linear meters |
| Annual expenditure | Cr$23,812,000 |
| Professional staff | 21 |
| All staff (total) | 190 |

Source: Director of the National Archive in Rio de Janeiro.

zonte in 1967 the Brazilian Association of Schools of Library Science and Documentation (ABEBD) was founded to work toward the improvement of library education.

The first national congress of librarians was held in Recife in July 1954; others have followed through the 10th in Curitiba (1979). Only the acts of the 8th and 9th congresses are published.

Library science and documentation in Brazil are served by four primary publications: *Ciência da Informação* (IBICT, 1972–, semiannual); *Revista da Escola de Biblioteconomia da UFMG* (Federal University of Minas Gerais, 1972–, semiannual); *Revista Brasileira de Biblioteconomia e Documentação* (FEBAB, 1973–, quarterly); and *Revista de Biblioteconomia de Brasília* (Federal District Librarians' Association and Department of Library Science of the University of Brasília, 1973–, semiannual). There is an additional irregular publication, the *Bibliografia Brasileira de Documentação,* published by IBICT. The first volume, covering the period 1811–1960, was published in 1960; volume 2, covering the period from 1960 to 1970, was published in 1973. *Quem é quem na biblioteconomia e documentação no Brasil* ("Brazilian Who's Who in Library Science and Documentation") was published by IBICT in 1970.

**REFERENCE**

Edson Nery da Fonseca, *A biblioteconomia brasileira no contexto mundial* (Rio de Janeiro, 1979).

EDSON NERY DA FONSECA

## Brett, William Howard
(1846–1918)

William Howard Brett, librarian of the Cleveland Public Library and library educator, was born in Braceville, Ohio, on July 1, 1846. Shortly after his birth the family moved to the banks of the Mahoning River in Warren, where as a boy he frequented the bookshop of William Porter, who by example and counsel influenced Brett's choice of career. Brett attended public schools in Warren and became the school librarian in the Warren High School at the age of 14. He enlisted and fought with Ohio infantry in the Civil War before entering the University of Michigan and later Western Reserve University, but he was forced by poverty to abandon his academic studies.

Brett settled in Cleveland. He worked for a Cleveland bookdealer, Cobb and Andrews Company, and expanded his acquaintanceship among bibliophiles, including John Griswold White, who was instrumental in appointing Brett Librarian of the Cleveland Public Library in 1884.

Brett soon distinguished himself for his contributions to cataloguing in the traditions set by Cutter and Dewey. By 1890 he was developing the concept of the open-shelf library, which led among other things to his being invited to London to deliver a paper on his ideas of free access to library collections.

Brett continued to grow and expand in almost every aspect of librarianship. Andrew Carnegie depended much on Brett's advice during the most fruitful years of the steel magnate's philanthropy. Brett was expert in building design. He published the first issue of his *Cumulative Index to the Selected List of Periodicals* in 1896, a publication that after several metamorphoses became the familiar *Reader's Guide to Periodical Literature.* In the same year he was elected President of the American Library Association.

Brett campaigned vigorously for libraries for children and established an alcove for juvenile books in the Cleveland Public Library. Under his leadership the first branch libraries were opened in Cleveland.

Staff training came to occupy a large place in the thinking of Brett, and he came to realize the importance of specialized education to the work of librarians. His interest in this direction developed eventually into a plan for a library school at Western Reserve University, where in 1904 he was present at the birth of that school. He was its first dean even as he remained head of the public library.

During the last years before his death in 1918, Brett developed plans for the main library building on Superior Avenue, which, although not opened until 1925, bears the imprint of his thought.

Few librarians, even among that remarkable group who were his contemporaries, displayed more virtuosity or made more contributions to disparate parts of the profession than William Howard Brett.

**REFERENCE**

Linda A. Eastman, *Portrait of a Librarian: William Howard Brett* (1940).

ERVIN J. GAINES

## British Virgin Islands

The British Virgin Islands, a colony of Great Britain, in the Caribbean Sea, together with the U.S. Virgin Islands, form a 100-km. arc east of Puerto Rico to the Anegada Passage, which connects the Atlantic Ocean and the Caribbean Sea. The British islands comprise 4 larger and 32 smaller islands on the north and east of the arc. Pop. (1977 est.) 12,000; area 153 sq.km. The official language is English.

In lieu of an official national library, the Virgin Islands Public Library provides nationwide service. Established in 1943, it provides free library services to rural and out-island communities, in addition to the capital, Road Town, as required under the Library Legislation of 1973. Such services include a reference department at the main library, two independent branch libraries, a bookmobile system, a parcel post book-delivery project, and administration of all school libraries. More than half of the Islands' population are registered library members. The Library's collection amounts to 27,000 volumes and a selection of audiovisual materials.

The National Archives were housed and managed in 1979 by the Government's Legal Department, but much consideration was directed toward combining libraries, museums, and the Archives into one national information network.

The Virgin Islands Public Library's main branch houses a special academic collection based on the syllabus of the University of the West Indies. The Library also established "minilibraries" in government departments. It provides a current awareness service to library members in various academic and professional disciplines and publishes a Union Catalogue of government reports with annual supplements and five-year cumulations.

School libraries in the Islands are funded by British Overseas Development Aid (BODA). Ten primary school libraries with modest initial collections were established with BODA in the 1970's. The Comprehensive

**Table 1. Libraries in the Virgin Islands (1976)**

| Type | Number | Volumes in collections | Annual expenditures (pound) | Population served | Professional staff | All staff (total) |
|---|---|---|---|---|---|---|
| Public | 3 | 21,672 | 7,733 | 10,800 | 1 | 7 |
| School[a] | 1 | 2,000 | N.A. | 800 | 1 | N.A. |
| Total | | 23,672 | | 11,600 | 2 | 7 |

[a]Collections of the other ten school libraries are modest, about 200 each. They are not included here.

**Table 2. Archives in the Virgin Islands (1976)**

| | |
|---|---|
| Number | 1 |
| Holdings | 20 cubic meters |
| Annual expenditures | U.S. $1,000 |
| All staff | 1[a] |

[a]Unqualified with six months' practical training; part-time (also legal secretary).

Source: Public Library Report, 1976. Archives Files—Archivist medium.

Secondary School in Road Town also received a BODA grant for the purchase of West Indian publications for its library.

**Association.** A Friends of the Library Association promotes the growth and development of the public libraries. A full-fledged library association did not exist at the end of the 1970's.

VERNA PENN

# Brown, James Duff
(1862–1914)

From about 1890 until 1914 the best-known initials in British librarianship were those of J. D. B., James Duff Brown. Brown was a library pioneer of outstanding importance.

Brown was born November 6, 1862, in Edinburgh into a working class family that was unusually musical and in which books counted for much. He was educated at an excellent normal school but only up to the age of 12, when he was apprenticed to a local bookselling firm. Moving with his family in 1876 to Glasgow, he found temporary employment there with another bookseller but began his real library career at the age of 16 when appointed to a junior post in the Mitchell Library. That library, named after its founder, Stephen Mitchell, a Glasgow tobacco magnate, had opened its doors for the first time only one year before Brown joined its staff. Its founder had endowed it with the then very large sum of £70,000 to enable it to be established and to function as a large public library. Its origins were therefore comparable with those of the New York Public Library and, like its American counterpart, it provided an outstanding reference service that did not originally form part of a normal municipal system.

J. D. B. spent ten formative years at the Mitchell and saw its bookstock increase to 80,000—a period of growth that provided good bibliographical training for a young librarian. In 1888 he was appointed the first Librarian of Clerkenwell, one of the increasing number of London parishes that were adopting the Public Libraries Acts and initiating municipal libraries. Brown's early years at Clerkenwell established him as an apparently orthodox but unusually gifted librarian of the period, but in 1894 he became a pioneer by converting his library to "safeguarded open access."

Prior to this date British public libraries, unlike many American ones, had not admitted readers to the shelves; books were requested at counters and fetched for readers by members of the staff. Although J. D. B. manifested throughout his life a marked antipathy to American library methods and indeed to American librarianship generally, there can be little doubt that his attendance at the ALA Congress at Chicago (1893) and visits to many libraries in the eastern states prepared the way for "open access." It remained a highly controversial issue for many years following 1894, although after 1920 British public libraries remaining "closed" could be safely regarded as extremely old-fashioned.

In 1905 J. D. B. moved from Clerkenwell, or rather from the Metropolitan Borough of Finsbury, into which his London parish had been recently absorbed, and became Borough Librarian of next-door Islington. His years at Clerkenwell/Finsbury had been very happy—an exceptional librarian being supported and encouraged by an understanding, progressive, and forward-looking committee. Although by contrast his governing body at Islington proved obstructive, unsympathetic, and parsimonious, J. D. B., struggling with every conceivable discouragement, built up a public library service that was regarded at the time as a model.

Despite the excellence of the two municipal library systems for which J. D. B. was successively responsible and for which, to avoid using the much disliked Dewey Decimal, he created no fewer than three systems of "Brown" classification, much of his reputation was gained outside London, mostly as journalist and author. He was the main public library contributor to MacAlister's *The Library* from 1890, and when it became clear that the Library Association would be discontinuing its recognition as the "official organ" and instead establishing its own *Library Association Record,* he ensured his own continuing independence by founding another monthly magazine, *The Library World;* the first number appeared in 1898.

This new journal not only provided a useful medium in which many librarians began and continued their journalistic careers but also enabled J. D. B. himself to write and print his own material, which he could subsequently revise and use in one or other of his many books. The best known of these was his *Manual of Library Economy.* This should have provided British librarianship, and particularly British public librarianship, with its basic textbook. The second and substantially revised edition of 1907 assuredly did; the first edition of 1903 was excessively opinionated. The third (1920) and subsequent editions were edited and rewritten by W. C. Berwick Sayers and others.

Other notable books by J. D. B. were his *Subject Classification* (first edition, 1906; second edition, 1914; third edition [by J. D. Stewart], 1939); *Library Classification and Cataloguing* (1912), the successor to his *Manual of Library Classification and Shelf Arrangement* of 1898; *The Small Library: A Guide to the Collection and Care of Books* (1907); and *Manual of Practical Bibliography* (1906) based primarily on lectures delivered at the pioneer school of li-

Library Association

*James Duff Brown*

brarianship at the London School of Economics). J. D. B. was always a keen advocate of better education and better opportunities for young librarians and was also largely responsible for beginning the system of correspondence courses or classes upon which most British librarians depended for their professional studies until at least the later 1930's.

Brown's membership in a musical family had lifelong influence. He published *Biographical Dictionary of Musicians* (1886) and *British Musical Biography* (1897) and edited *Characteristic Songs and Dances of All Nations* (1901). This special musical interest also manifested itself in his keen desire to encourage and improve the provision of music and musical literature in public libraries, early symbolized by his *Guide to the Formation of a Music Library* (1893).

He exercised profound influence on British public library thinking during his lifetime and long after his death on February 26, 1914. That influence had at least two shortcomings; it stimulated irrational prejudice against the methods of American librarianship and against the methods of types of British librarianship other than the municipal. He was a keen admirer of the pioneer work of Edward Edwards (1812–86), the great British librarian of the mid-19th century, and ranks with him as one of the makers of modern British librarianship.

**REFERENCE**

W. A. Munford, *James Duff Brown 1862–1914: Portrait of a Library Pioneer* (1968).

W. A. MUNFORD

## Brunet, Jacques-Charles
(1780–1867)

A bookseller and bibliographer, Jacques-Charles Brunet was born November 2, 1780, the son of Thomas Brunet, in Paris, where he would spend virtually his entire life. His formal education was scanty even by the standards of his day and was terminated by the revolutionary events of 1792; thereafter he was self-educated.

His private life and work in bibliography and classification are so entwined that to separate them is to falsify them. He never married, and his close friends were few; although created Chevalier of the Legion of Honor in 1845, he functioned largely outside the literary and political worlds. The sole biography devoted to Brunet was done for an antiquarian book exposition in 1960—a pastiche of obituaries and contemporary literary commentaries.

Brunet's current reputation is founded upon two complementary aspects of his bibliographical work: he was a pioneer in library classification from literary warrant and, more concretely, his massive, meticulously detailed, and often charming rare-book bibliography (each edition expanded its predecessor) is a mainstay of rare-book librarians and dealers.

To supplement this work and provide an ordering for lesser works, Brunet conceived a classification set forth most fully in the final volume of his *Manuel du libraire et de l'amateur de livres.* This scheme, reportedly based upon the commerce-tested logic of the successful bookseller, was taken up and used with various modifications by numerous libraries. The entire scheme, along with Brunet's historical introduction (a somewhat biased history of cataloguing), was made available for the first time in English in 1976.

The most salient feature of Brunet's scheme is its a posteriori character; in contrast to most of his predecessors, he eschewed a priori theoretical structures and founded his arrangements on pragmatism. Although the weighting of the divisions (Theology: 7.3 percent; Jurisprudence: 3 percent; Arts and Sciences: 22.7 percent; Literature: 28.2 percent; History: 38.8 percent) is quite inappropriate today and reflects the tastes of his classically educated clientele, its principle that a library's content and purpose should govern its arrangement was a forerunner of modern library classification for use.

The first known direct use of the Brunet scheme in the United States was at Harvard College in 1830. At various times, it was also used by the Saint Louis Mercantile Library, the Philadelphia Library, and others.

Among Brunet's publications, his *Manuel* perpetuates his name (a reprint edition is currently available); his remaining production consisted chiefly of contemporary articles. He was perhaps the last of the individual polyhistors to work alone on such massive works of bibliography. The last expansion of his *Manuel* was completed after his death by his friends P. Deschamps and Gustave Brunet.

He passed away peacefully in his own armchair on November 17, 1867, in his 87th year, surrounded by the books that had been the friends of his life.

**REFERENCE**

D. B. McKeon, *The Classification System of Jacques-Charles Brunet* (Louisiana State University Graduate School of Library Science Occasional Papers no. 1, 1976).

DONALD BRUCE McKEON

## Buck, Solon Justus
(1884–1962)

Solon Justus Buck, Archivist of the United States and writer, achieved outstanding success as a scholar, teacher, archivist, and historical adminstrator. He was born in Berlin, Wisconsin, August 16, 1884. Buck received B.A. and M.A. degrees from the University of Wisconsin in 1904 and 1905 and took a Ph.D. at Harvard University in 1911.

A leading protégé of the eminent historian Frederick Jackson Turner, Buck early reached prominence as a publishing scholar. In quick succession he produced *The Granger Movement* (1913), *Illinois in 1818* (1917), and *Agrarian Crusade* (1920), all of which were widely and favorably noted. Although Buck taught at Indiana University in 1908–09 and indeed was an outstanding teacher during much of his life, his career was basically that of a historical administrator. During 1910–14 he was a Research Associate at the University of Illinois on the "Illinois Centennial History" project. From 1914 to 1931 Buck served as Superintendent of the Minnesota Historical Society, transforming that institution into a model state historical society, greatly expanding and professionalizing its library and manuscripts collections, launching a journal, editing other historical publications, and promoting the formation of county historical societies. He also found time to become the prime fund raiser for the American Historical Association, to publish *Stories of Early Minnesota* (1925) with his wife, Elizabeth, whom he had married in 1919, and to serve as Professor of History at the University of Minnesota. During 1931–35 Buck served as Director of the Western Pennsylvania Historical Survey and Professor at the University of Pittsburgh. From this period came Solon and Elizabeth Buck's *The Planting of Civilization in Western Pennsylvania* (1939).

In 1935 Buck became one of the four chief assistant administrators of the new National Archives. His title was Director of Publications, but that belied the scope of his activities. He had found a new stage upon which to act out his career and took full advantage of it. He became the chief envoy of the National Archives to historical associations, especially as Treasurer of the American Historical Association (1936–57) and as representative in 1938 to the International Committee of Historical Sciences. He was one of the founders of the Society of American Archivists in 1936 and was active in the formation of

Solon Justus Buck

Records of the National Archives

the American Documentation Institute. At Columbia University in 1938 he inaugurated the first professional course in archival administration in the United States; he refined this instruction at the American University in 1939, so that it became the model for archival courses offered over the country during the following generation. Among the many other successful projects he initiated or headed at the National Archives was the Finding Mediums Committee of 1940–41, the report of which greatly changed archival administration with its recommendations for organizing archives on the basis of record groups and for providing a variety of guides to them, most notably the preliminary inventory. Ironically, as Secretary of the National Historical Publications Commission (NHPC), his most visible job at the Archives, Buck was unable to make any significant progress.

As a result of Buck's imaginative and usually successful work at the National Archives, President Franklin D. Roosevelt appointed him to head the agency as Archivist of the United States in 1941. Buck's work during his almost seven years in that position was often brilliant, though mixed in results. Despite severe shortages of staff and equipment, he expanded the services of the National Archives. Buck plunged his agency into the work of records management, resulting in more efficient and economical government control over its burgeoning records. One by-product of this was the Archives's role in developing the new records management profession and in encouraging archivists to take a broader view of their work. Buck also played the leading role in founding the International Council on Archives (1948). In addition to his continuing interest in archival training and professional organization, he found a variety of war-related research, technical, and consulting tasks for archivists to perform. He forwarded the earlier programs of his agency, especially the accessioning of older federal archives, the microfilming program, the *Federal Register,* and the Franklin D. Roosevelt Library.

Buck's frequent experiments with reorganizing the National Archives made the agency more efficient but at the cost of considerable staff unhappiness and congressional criticism. Although he made the Archives into a more nearly perfect servant of the state, it was at the price of the agency's becoming too acquiescent in restrictions on the private use of federal records. Buck's authoritarian leadership and his sometimes abrasive personality, moreover, contributed to problems among his staff and with Congress. In effect, this jeopardized the appropriations for the support of the National Archives. By 1948 it was clear that Buck—tired, aging, and having recently suffered serious illness—was unlikely to improve his staff's morale and to gain appropriations for new programs.

Buck resigned that year as Archivist of the United States and accepted the position of Chief of the Manuscripts Division of the Library of Congress. Three years later he became Assistant Librarian, a job he held until his retirement in 1954. Although his vitality was gone, he functioned satisfactorily at the Library of Congress, performing a number of administrative and intellectual tasks as an elder statesman of research and information management, including membership on the reinvigorated NHPC. He served as Acting Director of the Minnesota Historical Society in 1954–55 and occasionally as a consultant to the Library of Congress.

In recognition of Buck's services, the University of Minnesota conferred an honorary LL.D. degree upon him in 1954. He has throughout his career been an officer in a variety of historical, archival, and research organizations, serving as President of the Mississippi Valley Historical Association, the Agricultural History Society, and the Society of American Archivists. In addition to his several books, he was the author of numerous historical and archival articles. His was a remarkably broad career. Buck died in Washington, D.C., May 25, 1962.

**REFERENCES**


Donald R. McCoy, *The National Archives: America's Ministry of Documents, 1934–1968* (1978).

Theodore C. Blegen, "Solon Justus Buck—Scholar—Administrator," *The American Archivist* (1960).

Ernst Posner, "Solon Justus Buck—Archivist," *The American Archivist* (1960).


DONALD R. MCCOY

# Bulgaria



Bulgaria, a people's republic in southeastern Europe, lies on the eastern Balkan Peninsula. It is surrounded by the Black Sea on the east, Romania on the north, Turkey and Greece on the south, and Yugoslavia on the west. Pop. (1977 est.) 8,785,700; area 110,912 sq.km. The official language is Bulgarian.

The first Bulgarian state was created in 681, in the northeastern part of the Balkan Peninsula. It rapidly developed and expanded. In the second half of the 10th century it already was one of the mightiest states in Europe. After the acceptance of Christianity as the official religion in A.D. 864 and following the introduction of the Cyrillic alphabet (A.D. 893), invented by the learned brothers Cyril and Methodius, Bulgaria experienced a period known as the Golden Age of Bulgarian Literature. Two great cultural centers emerged: one in the capital, Preslav, the other in the region of Ochrid. In those areas evolved the so-called Preslav Literary School and Ochrid Literary School sponsored by the Bulgarian sovereigns.

The first Bulgarian libraries of significance were created at those centers of medieval culture. One of them, perhaps the largest of all, was established in the King's palace under the direct supervision of King Simeon. It contained a large collection of old Greek and Byzantine manuscripts and all Bulgarian writings produced at the time. The literature created in the 10th century spread to other countries, especially to Russia (Kiev), thus fostering its cultural development.

After the liberation of Bulgaria from Byzantine domination, which lasted for almost two centuries (1018–1186), Bulgaria experienced a new period of cultural revival and expansion, reaching a climax in the 14th century during the reign of King Ivan Alexander. A flourishing literary school emerged in the capital, Tărnovo, and several major libraries were established in the King's palace, at the Patriarchate of the Bulgarian Orthodox Church, at monasteries and churches, and in the palaces of feudal rulers.

During the five centuries of Ottoman domination (1393–1878), all Bulgarian libraries were destroyed, with the exception of the libraries of some 300 monasteries. The monastic librarians preserved the literary heritage of

Bulgaria, copied Bulgarian manuscript books, and translated foreign books and compiled historical chronicles. The most important were those of the Rila, the Bachkovo, and the Zograph monasteries.

The first Bulgarian public libraries within the Ottoman Empire began to appear after 1840 during the renaissance of Bulgarian culture and politics. They were school libraries and libraries of the so-called *chitalishta* ("reading clubs"), and they rapidly increased in number. Thanks to them, Bulgarian writings and cultural traditions have been preserved.

After liberation from Ottoman domination (1878), public libraries played an important role in assisting the nation's education and were the most important cultural centers in the country. Research libraries also began to appear, the first being the Library of the Bulgarian Literary Society (which developed into the Bulgarian Academy of Sciences) and the National Library. The revolutionary changes after World War II gave a strong impetus to the development of libraries.

**National Library.** The Cyril and Methodius National Library possesses a complete collection of the national production of printed materials, an important selection of foreign publications in all fields, and the largest collection of foreign periodicals, about 8,000 current titles. It has a full collection of UN publications and the basic publications of other international organizations. Its basic holdings are over 1,500,000 library units. In addition, it has a large collection of Bulgarian and foreign manuscripts, old and rare books, and historical documents. It maintains the current bibliographic registration for all Bulgarian publications and publishes the national bibliography. In addition, the National Library is a very active bibliographic information center and functions as a research institute in the fields of library science and in bibliography. As a methodological center for help and guidance, it coordinates the variety of activities of the country's library system.

**Academic Libraries.** Twenty-seven academic libraries at universities and other institutions of higher education hold more than 2,400,000 volumes. The largest libraries are at Sofia University and the Central Medical Library at the Higher Medical Institute in Sofia.

**Public Libraries.** "Chitalishta" libraries, those in village or town reading clubs or houses of culture, number about 4,000. Each town or village community has one, and it serves the entire population free of charge. The second largest group consists of over 1,500 libraries organized at industrial and trade enterprises and public agencies, which serve their staffs. They are sponsored and guided by trade unions. District libraries, 27 in all, assumed the functions of research libraries, and there are city and town libraries.

**Special Libraries.** More than 700 special scientific libraries are organized in academies of sciences, other research institutes, learned societies, industrial enterprises, business firms, museums, and editorial boards, with total holdings of 6,100,000 volumes. The most important are the Library of the Bulgarian Academy of Sciences (with a central library and over 40 branch libraries), the Central Agricultural Library (heading a network of specialized agricultural libraries), and the Central Technical Library (coordinating the work of specialized technical libraries).

**School Libraries.** Every school in Bulgaria has its own library. There are more than 3,500 school libraries with total holdings of 13,300,000 volumes (of which 60 to 70 percent are children's books). About 80 percent of the country's enrolled students are registered readers of the school libraries. They are directed by the Ministry of Education and guided by the Committee on Culture; the school libraries are part of the Unified Library System of the country.

**Association.** In the absence of a library association, the Cyril and Methodius National Library has assumed the functions of such an association. The National Library is a member of IFLA and other international organizations.

VLADIMIR POPOV

## Burma

Burma, a republic of Southeast Asia, is bounded by China on the north, Thailand and Laos on the east, the Bay of Bengal and Bangladesh on the west, and India on the northwest. To the southwest and south lie the Gulf of Martaban and the Andaman Sea. Pop. (1978 est.) 33,550,000; area 676,577 sq.km. The official language is Burmese.

**National Libraries.** There are two national libraries in Burma, one in the capital city, Rangoon, the other in Mandalay. Their combined strength approximated 100,000 volumes at the end of the 1970's, with about a third of the materials in English. The library in Rangoon provides author and title indexes to leading Burmese periodicals from their dates of publication. The strength of holdings lies predominantly in primary source materials on Colonial Burma; however, both libraries receive books and periodicals under the Press Registration Act of 1962 and are thus depository libraries. In addition to periodicals and newspapers, the libraries also contain several thousand books in manuscript form. Although open access is not allowed, spacious reading rooms are available. The rate of acquisition exceeds several thousand titles a year and is primarily reflective of the quantity of publications in Burma. The history of Burma's national libraries may be traced to the 11th century A.D., when the Pitaka Taik, or library housing King Anawrahta's collection of scriptures in palm-leaf manuscript form, was constructed. Burma also has its National Archives, whose holdings include the entire run of the *Burma Gazette*.

**Libraries in Bulgaria (1976)**

| Type | Number | Volumes in collections | Annual expenditures (lev) | Population served[a] | Professional staff | All staff (total) |
|---|---|---|---|---|---|---|
| National | 1 | 920,635 | 1,228,410 | 22,670 | 249 | 380 |
| Academic | 27 | 2,494,715 | 1,254,456 | 87,117 | 316 | N.A. |
| Public | 5,961 | 40,313,253 | 12,045,544 | 2,265,607 | 2,990 | N.A. |
| School | 3,714 | 13,300,000 | 2,004,984 | 829,017 | 553 | N.A. |
| Special | 704 | 6,118,558 | 3,756,240 | 233,744 | 845 | N.A. |
| Total | 10,407 | 62,373,462 | 20,289,634 | | 4,953 | |

[a]Registered readers only.

Source: *Bibliotekite v Bulgaria 1976* (Sofia: National Library, 1978).

**Academic Libraries.** Major academic libraries are those of Rangoon University, Mandalay University, and Moulmein College. At Rangoon the Central Universities Library is responsible for acquisition of foreign materials except for medical literature, acquired by the Department of Medicine Research Library. The libraries conduct literature searches, maintain union catalogues of holdings on campuses, and prepare and publish bibliographies. A notable activity is the library orientation program at Rangoon Institute of Technology, where library training has also been incorporated into the curriculum. A major research library is the library of the Central Research Institute, which completed a Union List of Scientific Serials covering some 20 libraries. The library has an exchange program with the British Library Lending Division. Burma's academic libraries are decentralized; there are several departmental and institute libraries such as the library of the Institute of Veterinary Science. Decentralization appeared to be giving way to attempts at centralization in the late 1970's.

**Public Libraries.** Three or four major State Libraries provide the bulk of library service to the general populace. Perhaps the most outstanding public library is the Sarpay Beikman, or "House of Literature" Institute Library, which has its own publishing house and which administers reading rooms in numerous Burmese villages. The bulk of Burma's domestic interlibrary loan activities are carried out by this library.

**Special Libraries.** Special libraries are found within the industries and institutes of various ministries. Plans in 1979 called for a National Science Library that would combine, at least administratively, science libraries among the respective ministries. A special library of significance is the Research Library of Buddhistic Studies, whose holdings are world reknowned.

Burma's libraries receive high-level government understanding and available support but are faced with the common problem of a shortage of funds.

**REFERENCES**

G. Miller, "Notes on Libraries in Burma," *International Library Review* (July 1978), an excellent and up-to-date overview.

G. Raymond Nunn, "Libraries in Burma," *International Library Review* (October 1975), emphasizes activities of libraries in Burma.

THEIN SWE

# Burundi

Burundi, a republic in central eastern Africa, is bordered by Rwanda on the north, Tanzania on the east and south, Lake Tanganyika on the southwest, and Zaire on the west. Pop. (1978 est.) 4,068,000; area 27,834 sq.km. The official languages are Kirundi and French.

**Academic Libraries.** Burundi's library resources are primarily concentrated in the Université Officielle and a few smaller, usually government-supported schools. All institutions of higher learning along with their library holdings are in the capital city of Bujumbura.

The Official University's library system consists of a Central Library and five independent departmental libraries. Aggregate holdings of all facilities amount to about 70,000 titles, 670 periodicals (approximately 290 of which are kept fully up to date), and 100 microfiches. The Central Library's collection of over 33,000 volumes covers all major subjects and is utilized by 1,650 students and 240 faculty.

The staff of 36, trained in France and Senegal, generally maintains an acquisition rate of 3,000 titles a year through expenditure of funds provided, gifts, and exchanges with foreign universities. Departmental libraries are provided for administrative and economic sciences, letters and humanities, medicine, psychology and education, and physical sciences. A library was in preparation for the Department of Agriculture in 1979.

In addition to those at the Official University, libraries are maintained at the Theological College of Bujumbura, the Military High Institute, and the École Normale Supérieure du Burundi; only the last, a college for teachers, possesses a collection in the range of 10,000 volumes, which serves to emphasize the central importance of Burundi's single university among academic libraries.

**Public Libraries.** The Ministry of Education maintains a single public library facility in the capital city of Bujumbura. It maintains a collection of approximately 26,000 volumes. As with academic libraries, no services or supplies exist outside the capital.

**Special Libraries.** A number of government-supported institutes and government departments maintain important technical and historical collections. The Institut des Sciences Agronomiques du Burundi (Burundi Institute of Agronomy) maintains a 1,500-volume collection on scientific agriculture in the capital and four field stations in other parts of the country. The Institute library supports services vital to Burundi's future growth and prosperity. The Laboratoire de Recherches Vétérinaires in Bujumbura provides access to 200 volumes on animal husbandry and health care, topics closely related to the future success of agriculture. The Ministry of Economy and Finance's Department of Geology and Mines possesses a 100-volume library that provides valuable information on another important factor in Burundi's future development. Historical materials and recorded folklore are available at the Institut Burundi d'Information et de Documentation in the capital.

Also in Bujumbura are two foreign libraries contained within cultural missions. The French Cultural Center (Alliance Française) contains over 1,500 volumes; the American Cultural Center maintains a 3,000-volume collection. Both libraries are available to any citizen, although in practice only those living in the capital have an opportunity to utilize them.

FIRMIN KINIGI

# Butler, Pierce
(1886–1953)

Pierce Butler, library educator and scholar, was not concerned with the technology of librarianship, which he left to others, but with its philosophy, the basic principles that give it unity and cohesiveness. He was a historian and humanist, though he did not discredit the contribution that science has made to our culture and could make to librarianship. This point of view was the central theme of Butler's major course on the history of scholarship and of his *Introduction to Library Science* (1933).

The work begins with an introductory essay on the nature of science followed by an analysis of three major problem areas in librarianship—the sociological, the psychological, and the historical. The book concludes with a summary chapter on "Practical Considerations." In the literature of librarianship, which is characterized mainly by its ephemera, Butler's little volume stands out as a true landmark in the development of library thought. Almost 50 years after its publication Butler's *Introduction* is still read by students and practitioners alike.

Pierce Butler was born December 19, 1886, at Clarendon Hills, Illinois. As a child he suffered a severe attack of scarlet fever that left him with seriously impaired hearing. (As a teacher he began every class session with the ceremony of setting out the large Columbia no. 6 dry-cell battery that powered his hearing aid, a procedure that often was accompanied by, "Wait 'till I get my antenna up.") He received a Ph.B. from Dickinson College in 1906, taught for one year at the Virginia Military Academy, and from 1907 to 1909 studied at the Union Theological Seminary. The following year he returned to Dickinson for an A.M., and he received the B.D. from the Hartford Theological Seminary that same year. He was also a Fellow in Medieval History at Hartford, and in 1912 he was awarded the Ph.D.

For a period of time prior to the invitation to join the Newberry Library staff in 1916, he had a clerical position in the offices of the Burlington Railroad. For the first year at Newberry he was a Reference Assistant, but his rise was rapid. Within a year he was promoted to Head of the Order Department and Bibliographer and Custodian of the John Wing Foundation on the History of Typography and the Printed Book. He continued in those capacities until his resignation in 1931. While at the Newberry he published a checklist of its holdings of books printed in the 15th century, issued in revised form in 1924. In 1926 he married Ruth Lapham, who was the Newberry's Curator of the Ayer Collection on the American Indian and a productive scholar in her own right.

In 1928 Butler was appointed part-time lecturer on the history of books and printing at Chicago's Graduate Library School and liked to boast that he taught the first class at the opening of the school. In 1931, at the insistance of Douglas Waples and William Randall, he joined the full-time faculty of the School; this was during the period when Waples was acting Dean. The remainder of Butler's professional life was spent at the GLS, until his retirement in 1952.

Butler's books are relatively few in number, the *Check List,* the *Introduction,* and *The Origin of Printing in Europe* (1940). In his unorthodox study of printing, he espoused the belief that Gutenberg was not the inventor of printing from movable type but that the technology was the product of many men working in various cities beginning as early as the 1440's. Butler saw Gutenberg as a shadowy figure whose primacy in the printing craft was the result of myth and the tendency of earlier generations to attribute innovation to a single figure who had caught the popular imagination.

His little pamphlet *Scholarship and Civilization,* "Published as Proof" by the University of Chicago in 1944, is a synopsis of his course on the history of scholarship and a tantalizing essay—tantalizing because it shows what a major work on that subject the pamphlet could have been had he but persisted in carrying it to completion. It still remains valuable to all who would seek insight into the sociological and anthropological relationships to the development of the library. One gains from it a deepening understanding of the origins of the library and its intellectual roots.

At the time of his death he was working on a treatment of the management and administration of rare book collections, a subject on which he was well qualified to speak. He wrote many articles on librarianship and its philosophy and was a popular speaker. He was an excellent raconteur and always enjoyed a good story.

During his Chicago years he made an impression on cultural thought and the philosophy of librarianship that, as he confessed, exceeded his expectations. He was convinced that it was his role to recognize and interpret the social history of the library in terms that would validate it for our own age. Thus he linked the philosophical approach to the intellectual and technical problems of librarianship. "I wrote my *Introduction,*" he said, "to persuade my professional colleagues to be more scientific. Now I have to struggle to keep them from being too damned scientific." Because he had strong convictions, and prejudices, he attracted both loyalty and antagonism, though even those who disagreed sharply with him at almost every philosophical level respected him for his scholarship and his erudition.

Erudite Pierce Butler certainly was. His breadth of knowledge was little short of phenomenal—a true polyhistor of the 20th century. William Randall of the Chicago faculty once showed this writer a super-intelligence test, a thousand or more questions on a wide variety of subjects. The test had been validated by a number of prominent scholars and intellectuals in public life, of whom very few scored better than the low 90's; of the entire list, Butler missed only two.

Pierce Butler was a superior teacher, as many who attended his classes, or were privileged to study under his direction, were aware. The other teachers at Chicago's Graduate Library School taught students how to *be* librarians, and they taught well. However, Butler taught what librarianship *could be.* In his favorite course on the history of scholarship he gave students, almost without their knowing it, an intellectual heritage to which many have returned as experience has reinforced its significance.

Though he was the kindest and most gentle of men, he did not suffer fools gladly but taught always for the "top" of the class. "The better I like a dissertation, the harder I criticize it," he once told one of his students. "Most of the students are doing the best they can and I can't do much to help them, but anyone who writes as well as you, can write even better, and I intend to see that you do."

Within the library profession, Butler was as controversial a figure as was his intellectual antagonist, Douglas Waples. Many librarians insisted that, though his *Introduction* was beautifully written, they could not understand what he was talking about and, moreover, he had never attended a library school. Admittedly, he could be dogmatic and had his prejudices, which might not always have been rational. With many eminent scholars he shared the schizophrenia of liberalism in his field of specialization and conservatism in most everything else. Politically he was a confirmed Republican, on a faculty that otherwise was unanimously Democratic, while teaching a student body that in the 1930's was overwhelmingly dedicated to Roosevelt and the New Deal.

His favorite political story, which he told on more than one occasion, related to a new deacon—Butler was an Episcopalian deacon himself—who was being introduced to a venerable and quite deaf member of the congregation. "Eh? eh? What's that you say, he's a New Dealer?" "No, no, no. He's our new *deacon.* He's the son of a bishop." "Yeah, I know," came the response; "They all are."

He liked people and, despite the handicap of defective hearing, enjoyed a fruitful social life. He reveled in an audience and was at his best on a public platform. He loved all animals, especially dogs. His was, indeed, a complex personality, and he merits a serious intellectual biography that will interpret him to the present generation and establish his contribution to the philosophy of librarianship.

The writer's own association with him was marked by frequent arguments. These discussions were often heated but never acrimonious, and were always suffused with mutual respect and the warmth of friendship. At the end of the summer quarter of 1952, when Butler was retiring and the writer was leaving Chicago for another academic post, he finally burst out, "Pierce, before we part company I do hope you will realize that I *am* on your side. I, too, am a humanist despite my defense of science." "Oh, I know that, Shera; I know that," he replied, "but I sometimes feel about you as I do about Bob Hutchins; your heart is in the right place, but you are forever saying things that give aid and comfort to the enemy."

Less than a year later, on March 28, 1953, he died in an automobile crash while returning from the dedication of a new library building in Winston Salem, North Carolina.

JESSE H. SHERA

## Byzantine Libraries

Knowledge of the Byzantine libraries is scattered and uncertain. Because of turbulent political change and major fires and even earthquakes, there is hardly any archaeological evidence pertaining to the major centers. The student is heavily dependent upon inferences from such literary testimony as the 5th-century writings of Stobaeus (John of Stobi, Macedonia), the 9th-century "Library" of Patriarch Photius, the 10th-century encyclopedic miscellany known to the admiring West as Suidas, and the massive collection of quotations presented in poetic form by John Tzetzes in the 12th century. Some direct documentation, mainly theological, is extant in either the original locations or Western research collections, in the form of Greek codices from the Byzantine era, presumably used for study and argumentation in the churches and monasteries of the Near East, Egypt, Greece, and the Aegean islands.

The outstanding library was reportedly the imperial collection in Constantinople (capital of the Eastern Empire, 395–1453); it was founded in 353 and favored administratively by such steps as were ordered in 372 by Emperor Valens, incorporated in the Theodosian Code. It may have held 100,000 "volumes," the largest assemblage at that time known to Western records; most, if not all, were apparently consumed in the fire of 475(?). There are references to higher studies in the 6th and 7th centuries with tantalizingly unclear hints of book collections. It is indeed known that in the years 607–10 the Patriarch of Constantinople built a library in his palace—burned in 780. Further, it is plausible that library support existed during the 8th century despite the discouragements of the Iconoclasts because a renaissance flowered in the 9th century. In any case, Benedictine-like copying began in 789 at the Constantinople abbey directed by reformer Theodore of Studium.

The "Library" of Patriarch Photius helps to illuminate the question of what reading matter was apparently available to career men and able women of privilege in 9th-century Constantinople and the Eastern Empire, although not such particulars as where one obtained a desired book or whether it could be borrowed. Concerning Stobaeus, for example, Photius reports the author's stated purpose, the contents of the 208 chapters organized into four books, and the numerous philosophers, poets, orators, historians, kings, and generals from whom he has drawn his material. The list of "philosophers" includes Aristotle, Euclid, and Zoroaster; among the poets are Homer and Sappho. The last list, more varied, includes orator Demosthenes, physician Hippocrates, and historian Thucydides. Photius recommends Stobaeus's encyclopedia as "obviously" a great help for those who have read the writings referred to, as a painless way for others to get acquainted with their essential contributions, and as a bag from which a speaker or writer can pull an apt quotation. R. Henry, who edited Photius (Paris, 1960), can vouch for Photius's care with attributions and copying from some 300 texts but withholds any assurance as to what the Patriarch read in the original and what was picked up in anthologies. Nor is there a shred of evidence to date as to contacts between Photius and any library.

Hellenic culture continued to be promoted in both the new imperial schools at the capital and several established elsewhere. Considering the centralization that so sharply differentiated Byzantine civilization from Western conditions, benefit likely flowed from the advances at the imperial court. The 10th century was marked by the broad interests of Constantine Porphyrogenitus (i.e., "of the breed of Porphyry," influential promoter of Aristotle); the 11th by Constantine Monomachos, reorganizer of the university, and the philosopher Michael Psellos; and the 12th by several dictionary and encyclopedia compilers and by Princess Anna Comnena, who reputedly took good advantage of her opportunities in learning.

The Crusaders arrived in the early 13th century. Driving out the existing regime, they also wrecked its libraries on some infamous days in 1204. The defeated retired to Nicaea and assembled, among other things, a new library. By 1263 they were able to return to Constantinople, where they remained for two centuries. When the Turks ended Christian domination in 1453, the Greek manuscript treasures, with their remarkable illumination and bindings, had long since migrated westward. The copying still conducted in the East had settled in monasteries like those at Patmos and Mount Athos; around 1200, at least, many libraries of the North Aegean borrowed liturgical items from Patmos. Fame for book wealth was to be rebuilt in later Istanbul, whose Suleiman Library would cherish thousands of Arabic, Persian, and Turkish codices.

**REFERENCES**


S. K. Padover, "Byzantine Libraries," in J. W. Thompson, *Medieval Libraries* (1939).

*Handbuch der Bibliothekswesen* III-1 (1955).


SIDNEY L. JACKSON

## Callimachus

(fl. 3rd century B.C.)

A critical biography of Callimachus cannot be written, as surprisingly little is known of his life. He rose from the obscurity of schoolteaching to become the lynchpin of Hellenistic poetry in its Golden Age (290–240 B.C.). Although he never became its director, he worked as a bio-bibliographer at the Alexandrian Library, where he compiled the *Pinakes,* a *catalogue raisonné* of Greek literature in 120 volumes. Beyond that we know only a few details, mostly of his childhood.

Homer and Callimachus represent the traditional and modern viewpoints of ancient Greece. The traditional culture, which prevailed from Homer through Aristotle, was born of the Greek oral past; it was created in the absence of writing and maintained against the encroachments of literacy as long as possible. But Callimachus, less than 20 years after Aristotle, stood on the threshold of a new age whose culture was created by the book. The oral and literary cultures of Greece thus found expression in the two differing poetries of Homer and Callimachus.

Homer produced poetry spontaneously in live performances before a native audience; his was an oral art addressed to the ear, a matter of arranging preestablished musical formulas without fishing for the right word or adjusting it to the meter. Callimachus, however, composed poetry in the study, carefully selecting his words and working them into a few impeccable lines each day. He strove for technical perfection, regarding the ideal poem as a tiny jewel to be cut, polished, and admired by experts, and addressed an esoteric audience of educated connoisseurs in the artificial climate of Alexandria. He always looked things up before rehashing them.

Callimachus, finally, should not be regarded as the patron saint of cataloguers, even though he completed the bibliographical projects initiated by Zenodotus, which culminated in the higher and lower criticisms and in exegesis. The result of his work was a massive catalogue, the *Pinakes,* based on the *pinax,* the annotated list underlying all antiquarian writing in the 5th century B.C. It contained much more information than a library catalogue, providing for each writer a brief biographical sketch and a list of his works, including lost ones. Any doubts about the authenticity of the book were also noted, and it was apparently arranged according to large categories such as epic, oratory, and history. Not merely a library catalogue, the

*Pinakes* was actually a critical inventory of Greek literature, the first scientific literary history, attempting no less than a complete record of all Greek literature as it then existed.

Despite the availability of Oriental cataloguing techniques, Callimachus had no real model for his immense project because his bibliographical aims were typically Western: he wanted to make the *ideas* of Greek literature available for the use of scholars. The Orient, on the other hand, which regarded books as *things*, had invented a complicated system of cataloguing for keeping track of them, but it focused not on scholarship but on descriptive notes and parallel glossaries, which served only the practical needs of the archives, libraries, and schools of temples. These conflicting aims have created permanent bibliographical ambivalence. Do cataloguers deal primarily with the physical "body" of a book, or with its metaphysical "spirit" as a complex of meanings? Should they perpetuate the ancient cataloguing practices devised for managing things, or invent new procedures capable of managing ideas? The *Pinakes* of Callimachus constitutes an experiment that failed, for its influence on libraries is difficult to trace beyond the Byzantine period. But the work does raise for the Western cataloguer the bothersome question of bibliography as bookology—an issue that helps to explain, at least partially, why the problems of bibliographic organization and control continue unresolved.

**REFERENCES**

K. J. McKay, *The Poet at Play: Kallimachos, the Bath of Pallas* (1962).

H. Curtis Wright, *The Oral Antecedents of Greek Librarianship* (1978).

H. CURTIS WRIGHT

# Cambodia

Cambodia, or the Khmer Republic (officially Kampuchea), is a republic of Southeast Asia in the southwest part of the Indochinese Peninsula. It is bounded on the southwest by the Gulf of Thailand, on the east and southeast by Vietnam, on the west and northwest by Thailand, and on the northeast by Laos. Pop. (1977 est.) 8,580,000; area 181,035 sq. km. The official language is Khmer; French is widely spoken.

During the four-year period of Communist rule (1975–79), and after the Vietnamese conquest of Cambodia in 1979, library services were reportedly effectively eliminated. There was no evidence that any were functioning in 1979. The University of Phnom Penh was reported totally inactive in April 1979. Several public and university libraries, as well as collections in museums and temples, have been destroyed. The libraries described here were those in operation before 1975.

The Archives et Bibliothèque Nationales, founded in 1923 in Phnom Penh, is a national deposit library, which housed more than 31,000 volumes. An ordinance of 1956 required publishers to deposit five copies of all works published there. Printers were obliged to deposit three copies. No law required that every administrative document be forwarded to the National Archives, although a decree of 1918 required public departments to deposit such documents periodically. Some departments did not deposit their documents.

There is no national bibliography in Cambodia, although the National Library and National Archives compiled catalogues of their holdings, including books, pamphlets, official publications, university dissertations and theses, maps, atlases, and standards.

A national exchange center, the Bibliothèque centrale in Phnom Penh, was created in 1972 to collect works in all fields of knowledge and to establish contacts with foreign libraries. An exchange system was developed among the university libraries, which included the Université des Beaux-Arts, the Université de Phnom Penh, the Université Bouddhique, the Université des Sciences Agronomiques, and the Université Technique, all in Phnom Penh.

The Bibliothèque de l'Institut Bouddhique, founded in 1923 in Phnom Penh, housed books and manuscripts in French, English, Thai, Burmese, Singhalese, Chinese, Tibetan, and Mongolian, as well as documents in Khmer and Pali on Khmer folklore and Buddhism. The library built a collection of about 40,000 volumes and 16,200 manuscripts on palm leaves.

The Institut national de la statistique et des recherches économiques, founded in 1963 in Phnom Penh under the Ministère du Plan, became a documentation center holding more than 300 volumes. The Institut compiled national and international statistical and economic data and published the *Bulletin trimestriel de statistique, Annuaire statistique,* and the *Comptes économiques*.

The library of the Association des écrivains khmers, founded in 1962 in Phnom Penh, housed 4,525 volumes. The Association was created to aid writers and promote literature in the Khmer language; it published a monthly literary review. There was no official library association, although a governmental department, the Office national de planification et de développement des bibliothèques, was established in 1975 to coordinate library and archival activity within Cambodia.

PETER A. POOLE; STAFF

# Cameroon

Cameroon, a republic in western Africa, is bounded on the southwest by the Gulf of Guinea (part of the Atlantic Ocean), on the south by Gabon and Equatorial Guinea, on the southeast by the Congo, on the east by the Central African Empire, on the northeast by Chad, and on the northwest by Nigeria. Pop. (1978 est.) 7,980,700; area 465,054 sq.km. The official languages are English and French.

**National Library.** Until November 1977 the Cameroon National Library was attached to the National Archives in a single department (headed by the same person), established by a decree issued August 17, 1966. By the provisions of another decree issued November 3, 1977, the National Library became attached to the Department of Culture in the Ministry of Information and Culture.

On November 20, 1978, the President issued a new decree, restructuring the Ministry of Information and Culture, and with it—under Article 48—the National Library became part of the Department of Cultural Affairs, with three subsections: Acquisition and Legal Deposit, Classification and Cataloguing, and History of Cameroon and National Bibliography. The holdings of the Archives and Library in 1973 numbered about 5,000 books and 700 files.

**Academic Libraries.** The largest is that of the University of Yaoundé. It was established in 1966, bringing together a number of small book depots scattered over the campus. It did not comprise a large collection; in 1973 it totaled 52,000 books, 620 serials, 17 maps, 207 slides, 12 tapes, and 88 microfilms. In 1977 the book collection had increased to 65,000, but the number of serial holdings had changed nominally. There was no special collection at the end of the 1970's.

Two libraries existed on the campus until 1974: the Library of African History, with holdings of 4,000, and the Centre de Recherches et de Documentation Africaine, with 500 books. The latter was mainly intended to serve law and economics research Fellows.

Six specialized libraries belong to the Colleges or Schools of the University, including the University Centre for Health Sciences; the School of Agriculture; the

School of International Relations; the School of Journalism; the Higher Teacher's College, Ecole Normale Supérieure; and the School of Engineering.

**Public Libraries.** Most of the public library services in Yaoundé and Douala are provided by cultural centers attached to embassies. In Yaoundé there are four main ones: the British Council Library, the American Cultural Centre Library, the French Cultural Centre Library, and the German Cultural Centre Library. These serve about 15 percent of the population. Many of them are understaffed and hold between 5,000 and 19,000 volumes. Some of them also provide children's sections and hold films, records, and tapes.

**School Libraries.** As of 1978 there was no legislation on school libraries and no systematic organization of them. Most secondary schools, however, have either a library or at least a reading room with some books. The Cameroon Association of Librarians makes efforts to encourage the establishment of libraries in all institutions of learning.

**Special Library.** The most important special library in the country is that of the former Office de la Recherche Scientifique et Technique d'Outre-Mer (ORSTOM), now in the Human Sciences Institute in the National Research Institute. It was created in 1949 as Institut de Recherche Camerounaise; on the eve of its transformation in 1973, its library held 10,000 books, 691 serials, and 1,198 microfilms. Except for the University Library, that library is the most active in research.

**Association.** In July 1975 the Cameroon Association of Librarians, Archivists, Documentalists, and Museum Technicians (ABADCAM) was founded. The main aims of the Association are encouraging the establishment of libraries at all levels in the country and promoting the training of personnel for libraries, archives, museums, and documentation centers. It had 40 members in 1978.

PETER NKANGAFACK CHATEH

# Canada

In Canada, as in any other country, library development has depended on the interaction of five main factors: geography, demography, economics, political and governmental organization, and history. To this list must be added a special factor of profound importance—the influence of the United States. Directly or indirectly, Canadian libraries have largely patterned themselves on United States counterparts; at the same time, the indigenous factors noted above have made for significant differences from those models. As a result Canadian libraries are recognizably "American," but they are "American with a difference."

In the context for Canadian library service, the most easily discernible element is geography—and its corollaries, settlement and communications. Canada is the second largest country in the world (area: 9,976,139 sq.km.), but only 7 percent of the land is arable, and the climate is severe. Accordingly, the entire population is only 23,500,000 (1978 est.), and the vast majority live within a 4,000-mile-long corridor extending some 200 miles north of the U.S. border. This combination of distance, formidable terrain, and harsh climate has meant that access is a perennial problem, particularly for those living outside the cities. The effect for libraries is that Canada has experienced unusual difficulty in providing service for all its inhabitants. Conversely, Canada has learned to be more than ordinarily resourceful in finding solutions for problems of library outreach. Indeed, in some instances, such as the development of regional libraries or service to native peoples in the far North, it has made innovations of world interest.

This same example of regional libraries may also serve to illustrate the way in which political and historical factors have produced distinctively Canadian problems and responses. In Great Britain and the U.S., the county library had proved to be an effective means of serving people in smaller towns and rural areas. In Canada the county did not exist as a unit of government in most regions, and where it did it was too small to serve as a practicable basis of operation. In the province of British Columbia, therefore, pioneering librarians had to invent "a special and suitable library district," which was a combination of school districts and small municipalities cooperating specifically for regional library purposes.

Actually, British Columbia's version of the regional library is only one of many in Canada. The diversity reflects two more central facts of Canadian life: the profound linguistic, cultural, and economic differences between the various parts of Canada and the federal form of government. The differences between French-speaking and English-speaking Canada are well known; what is less well known is that the differences *within* these two blocs are nearly as great as those between them. Some Canadian historians have thus found it reasonable to speak of "five or even ten Canadas." A familiar metaphor describes Canada as a "mosaic" in contrast with the idea of the U.S. "melting pot."

Given the diversity imposed by geography, language, history, and socioeconomic conditions, Canada inevitably began and has continued as a federation rather than a unitary state. Under the British North America Act, powers are divided among the national government (which also governs the Yukon and Northwest Territories) and ten provincial governments. Libraries fall mainly within provincial jurisdiction and therefore reflect the differing interests, conditions, and capacities of the provinces.

The result is a pattern of markedly uneven library development; Canada is unable to plan and enact countrywide measures for library improvement. In such vital areas as research, cooperation, and maintenance of standards, the progress of Canadian librarianship is largely dependent on extragovernmental action.

Fortunately for Canadian libraries, if the factors of geography, demography, and constitutional framework have made for difficulties, there have been more than compensating advantages in the socioeconomic sphere. The country's abundance of natural resources and considerable technological advancement have combined to produce a standard of living that has long been among the highest in the world. The Canadian people have had the means and willingness to give generous support to educational and cultural enterprises, and this disposition has been markedly enhanced by the growing Canadian nationalism of the last 20 years. Thus Canadian libraries of all types have, compared with other countries, enjoyed keen public interest and excellent financial backing. In buildings, equipment, advanced technological methodology, and extent of use, they rank very high by world standards. Their collections, though seldom notable for rarities or scholarly distinction, warrant a very favorable rating when measured by more utilitarian considerations. Perhaps most important, Canada's affluence and concern for educational standards have placed the practice of librarianship on a high professional level. Most Canadian libraries require, as a minimum qualification for positions of professional responsibility, a Master of Library Science degree, representing six years of university education. This is probably the longest preparation demanded anywhere in the world for the first professional degree in librarianship.

Beginning as cultural colonies of Britain and France, coming later under very strong American influence, Canadian libraries have matured into their own distinctive amalgam of borrowed and indigenous characteristics. Though they are still visibly "American," the relationship of Canadian libraries to those of the United States is now not so much a matter of following as of proceeding along parallel lines. Canadian librarianship has acquired maturity, its own identity, and quite often a position of leadership.

NATIONAL LIBRARIES

**The National Library of Canada.** Although the idea of a national library was espoused by Canada's first Prime Minister, Sir John A. Macdonald, as early as 1883, the National Library of Canada was not actually established until 1953 and did not occupy permanent quarters until 1967. The long delay is probably chiefly attributable to the lack of a strong sense of national cultural consciousness. It was customary and convenient to draw upon the collections of U.S. university libraries and upon the bibliographical services of the Library of Congress. Moreover, in the absence of a national library association, there was no organization prepared to exert sustained pressure for the creation of a national library.

Shortly after its formation in 1946, the Canadian Library Association, in conjunction with other groups, presented a brief urging the establishment of a bibliographic center as the first step toward a national library. The government responded by appointing W. Kaye Lamb as Dominion Archivist with the specific additional responsibility of preparing the way for a national library. In 1950 the Canadian Bibliographic Centre was formed under Lamb's direction, and work began on the preparation of the national bibliography (*Canadiana*) and the National Union Catalogue. Finally, with the passage of the National Library Act in 1952, the National Library of Canada at last came into being, with Lamb serving in the dual role of National Librarian and Dominion Archivist.

Operating in temporary quarters, the National Library staff began developing collections, drawing initially on a large quantity of material transferred from the Library of Parliament. The enactment of the legal deposit requirement brought in current Canadian publications, and a purchasing program, relatively small but carefully designed to avoid unwarranted duplication with other libraries' holdings, added significant older and foreign publications.

Lamb retired in 1968 and was succeeded as National Librarian by Guy Sylvestre. A separate appointment was made to the directorship of the Dominion Archives, the two positions having by now grown too large in responsibilities to be held by the same person. There followed a period of very rapid expansion and change for the National Library. In 1969 a new National Library Act came into force; it extended the powers of the National Library to coordinate the work of all federal government libraries and to assume a role of leadership in establishing a network of bibliographic systems and services for the nation. The National Library was to be, in Sylvestre's phrase, "the prime mover."

In the next six years no fewer than 14 new divisions and service units were added, and the National Library conducted or sponsored extensive studies on federal government libraries, the National Union Catalogue, and automation. By 1976 the period of rapid growth had come to an end. It was an appropriate time to review the role, services, and objectives of the Library, and a large-scale study was undertaken toward that end. In-house research and briefs from "outside" bodies such as the Canadian Library Association indicated that the National Library, for all its recent progress, still had serious limitations. The main problems were that it provided too little direct service to the libraries of Canada and that it lacked a "presence" outside of Ottawa. The National Library was not yet, as had originally been hoped for, the Canadian "libraries' library."

**Canada Institute for Scientific and Technical Information (CISTI).** Although no longer called the National Science Library, CISTI does in fact serve as such, thereby enabling the National Library to concentrate its efforts in the humanities and social sciences. The history of the national science library service goes back to 1924 when the National Research Council of Canada (NRC) formed its library with the express intention of serving not only the NRC staff but also scientific workers elsewhere in Canada. Under the direction of Madge Gill and later of Jack Brown, an impressive collection was developed, and services, such as the publication of a national union list of scientific serials, were provided. The NRC was de facto a national library, and its status as such was legally recognized in 1966 when it was officially named the National Science Library. To avoid unwarranted duplication a formal agreement was made in 1959 with the National Library to indicate the division of responsibilities between them.

In addition to serving as the principal "backstop" collection of materials in its field (readily available through an efficient photocopying and interlibrary loan

*The National Library of Canada in Ottawa was established with the passage of the National Library Act of 1952, but did not occupy its present permanent quarters until 1967.*

The National Library of Canada

service), the Library made a notable contribution, which attracted international attention, in the development of an automated STI (scientific and technical information) service. Its CAN/SDI Service provided subscribers with inexpensive batch delivery of bibliographic citations based on searches of machine-readable data bases. The companion on-line service (CAN/OLE) is available through terminals in various parts of the country.

In 1974, on the occasion of the dedication of the impressive new building of the National Science Library, the NRC announced a reorganization of its information services. The National Science Library was to be amalgamated with the NRC's longstanding Technical Information Service, providing advice, information, and field assistance to Canadian industry, so as to constitute the Canada Institute for Scientific and Technical Information.

CISTI continues to carry on the various activities of its two predecessor units, including the operation of a Resource Centre for the Health Sciences. It also holds responsibility, formally assigned by the federal government to the NRC, for developing a national network of scientific and technical information. An advisory body (ABSTI: Advisory Board for Scientific and Technical Information) provides CISTI with proposals and consumer reactions for the latter purpose.

**The Library of Parliament.** The Library of Parliament, which in various antecedent forms goes back as far as 1792, was the major national collection until the establishment of the National Library and served as a quasi-national library. It carried responsibility for acquiring and storing copyright deposit materials and was the agent for international exchange agreements. Its collections were of a scope going well beyond the needs of the legislators.

Since the inception of the National Library, some 250,000 seldom-used volumes have been transferred to that institution, and the latter also took over responsibilities for deposit and exchange. The Library of Parliament became primarily a legislative reference service, offering in-depth assistance to the House and Senate. Its collections, however, are still so extensive and of such general scholarly importance as to warrant ranking the Library of Parliament as a national rather than a departmental library.

**La Bibliothèque Nationale du Québec.** Established under a Quebec law of 1968, the BNQ, as the name implies, is based on the assumption that culturally the people of Quebec constitute a nation. The BNQ accordingly goes well beyond the usual scope of a provincial library. With collections derived originally from its predecessor library—the Bibliothèque Saint-Sulpice—the BNQ undertakes to acquire all materials relating to Quebec and French Canada (it has the right of legal deposit for Quebec imprints). It issues a bibliography of current publications *(Bibliographie du Québec);* maintains a union catalogue of all important holdings in the province; publishes a Quebec periodical index; and provides reference, interlibrary loan, and bibliographic services. It also operates an extensive program of international exchanges, notably with the Bibliothèque Nationale de France.

ACADEMIC LIBRARIES

In Canada, unlike the U.S., "academic libraries" are more or less synonymous with the libraries of publicly supported universities. With the exception of the two-year community colleges, which are a recent though increasingly important addition to Canadian education, there are very few undergraduate institutions in Canada and almost none that are really private in respect of governance and funding. This situation reflects the historical development of higher education in Canada. Although some older institutions (all in Eastern Canada) go back to the first half of the 19th century, 20 out of the 58 major degree-granting institutions (1976) were not founded until after World War II, and the others acquired their present character and dimensions only within the three decades of the 1950's, '60's, and '70's. The creation or marked expansion of facilities required funding on a scale that only provincial governments could command, and these wanted multipurpose institutions that would offer professional and graduate studies as well as undergraduate programs.

Metropolitan Toronto Library

*The five-story Metropolitan Toronto Library opened in 1977, the largest library in North America with seating for 1,300 patrons.*

Most of the growth and change in Canadian higher education was concentrated in the 1960's. A combination of affluence and substantial population increase swelled enrollments. Perhaps more important, the need to produce highly trained people for the Canadian economy and the desire to cast off "cultural colonialism" led the universities to establish programs of specialization and research. Before World War II it was generally assumed that Canadians wanting to do advanced studies would go abroad (mainly to the U.S.); later Canada sought to become self-sufficient academically.

Not surprisingly, the development of the Canadian university libraries closely paralleled that of the parent institutions. As late as 1949 only McGill University Library had over 500,000 volumes, and only two others had over 300,000. As the institutions changed, in effect, from colleges to universities, their libraries were forced to expand at a rate wholly unprecedented for them and impressive by any standard. Alerted by such persuasive and well-timed studies as the Williams Report (1962) to the severe inadequacy of existing holdings, Canadian universities supported their libraries in a program of simultaneous collection, at an intensive level, of both older materials and current publications. At Queen's University, for example, the acquisitions budget grew from $20,788 in 1947 to just about $1,000,000 in 1966, and this rise was by no means exceptional. In the ten-year period from 1961 to 1971, total Canadian academic library holdings increased from some 7,000,000 volumes to over 24,000,000.

The growth in collections was only the most dramatic of the changes that transformed Canadian university libraries in the 1960's. The percentage of institutional budgets devoted to the library averaged (median) over 7.5 percent, nearly twice the percentage usually obtained in the larger American university libraries. This degree of support enabled the libraries to multiply service outlets, double and triple their staffs, and put up imposing new buildings. Homemade or antiquated classification schemes were replaced by the use of the Library of Congress classification, and the same impetus for modernization led to a surprisingly early and widespread use of automation. Canadian university libraries such as Toronto, Laval, and British Columbia could well claim continential and even world significance for their leadership in this area.

As in the United States the "golden years" for Canadian university libraries ended with the 1960's, but the

*The Library of Parliament in Ottawa primarily serves as a legislative reference service, but also houses extensive scholarly collections.*

The National Film Board of Canada

fall-off was not felt so severely in Canada. "Steady-state budgets" (which, of course, in the light of rapid inflation meant a considerable reduction in purchasing power) led to sizable declines in the rate of acquisition, but staff losses were modest, and they were almost entirely in the non-professional ranks.

Even so, it would be fair to say that many of the new developments of the 1970's reflected a sense of mounting economic difficulty. Concern over their financial position led the support staff to unionize, while the librarians tended to join with their teaching colleagues in some form of collective bargaining. Both groups also sought greater power in administration, and staff participation in management became the norm rather than the exception.

For their part, the directors of Canadian libraries looked increasingly to cooperation as a means of effecting economies in acquisitions and processing. While libraries were not able to achieve "rationalization of collecting" on any large scale, such cooperative groups as OULCS (Ontario Universities Library Cooperative System) and TRIUL (Tri-University Libraries, British Columbia) could point to successes in interavailability of borrowing rights, interuniversity transit, and shared cataloguing. The biggest success came right at the end of the decade when the University of Toronto Library Automation System (UTLAS) began to supply a large number of university libraries with on-line cataloguing that was faster and cheaper than they could furnish on their own.

UTLAS, a highly sophisticated catalogue support system, may also be taken as an indicator of the maturity Canadian university libraries had reached by the end of the 1970's. With no less than seven Canadian institutions as members of the Association of Research Libraries (the University of Toronto Library actually leading the ARL statistics in 1973–74 in six of ten categories), with rates of circulation consistently higher than American norms, and with buildings such as the Sedgewick Undergraduate Library (UBC) and the Robarts Research Library (Toronto) attracting international attention, Canadian university libraries were no longer the "poor relations" of 30 years ago.

**College Libraries.** In Canada the term "college libraries" has taken on a new connotation. There are now only a very few colleges in the traditional sense of four-year, degree-granting institutions. There are, however, some 145 non-degree-granting institutions that offer postsecondary programs. These programs, usually of two or three years' length, cover three main areas: academic courses designed for university transfer, technical and vocational programs, and continuing education programs with special reference to the needs of the local community. In Quebec these institutions are known as CEGEPs (collèges d'enseignement général et professionel), in Ontario as CAATs (colleges of applied arts and technology), and elsewhere as community colleges or technical institutes. The Quebec and Ontario colleges do not offer university transfer courses.

The Canadian "college" is essentially a product of the last 15 years, the great majority being founded since 1965. Typically the colleges were organized in haste and used improvised community facilities. Their libraries reflect that sense of haste and improvisation. Although they have grown very rapidly, they have still not been able to catch up to the demands imposed by booming college enrollments.

The Canadian college libraries are, however, much more than just newish, developing academic libraries. They offer several distinctive features. The emphasis on audiovisual materials is noteworthy. College librarians have stressed bibliographic instruction since so many students (especially immigrants and returning older students) often have little idea of how to use a library. The college librarians have also tended to work more closely with the teaching faculty than has usually been true in the university libraries and nearly always have full faculty status. Finally, the college libraries have frequently offered borrowing privileges to the local community, thus constituting a useful link between the general public and with academe.

## PUBLIC LIBRARIES

The British North America Act of 1867, which is in effect Canada's constitution, assigned jurisdiction over education to the provinces. Libraries, without being actually mentioned in the BNA Act, were assumed to be covered by that provision; hence public libraries in Canada have been established and are governed under the legislation of ten different provinces and two territories. While provincial governments thus have, legally, the ultimate controlling power over public libraries, their actual participation and influence in the development of Canadian public libraries was until recently rather small. No province has enacted mandatory legislation requiring the provision of public library service. Few provinces have promulgated public library standards, and even fewer have made serious efforts to enforce their observance. The financial support rendered by provincial governments, while considerably larger recently, has with few exceptions accounted for only a minor share of public library funding.

What happened, in effect, was that the provincial governments, while responsible for the overall enabling legislation, left the operation and financing of the public libraries in the hands of local authorities—boards of trustees appointed by municipal councils. The development of public libraries in Canada has thus been very much a matter of local initiative, local control, and local support. Canadian public libraries are as various as the interests, character, and capacity of the communities they serve.

Paradoxically, the differences among Canadian public libraries are not as great as the complete lack of centralized direction would suggest. There are indeed substantial variations depending on whether communities are rich or poor, rural or urban, new or old, Anglophone or Francophone. Still, the settlers in one part of Canada usually came from another and brought with them familiar patterns of organization. Some British precedents (notably the mechanics' institutes) and the strongly influential American pattern were known to all. Moreover, schooling itself, both in level and kind, was remarkably similar from province to province.

**Trends.** The result is that one can distinguish several large-scale themes or trends that have dominated the history of Canadian public libraries. Until after World War II library extension was probably the chief concern; then the majority of Canada's rural population had no public library service. The extension movement was spurred by provincial development agencies such as the Public Library Commission of British Columbia and was usually achieved by some form of regional library organization. For the towns and smaller cities the problem was that the population and tax base were too small to permit more than minimal service; a "larger unit" than the individual municipality had to be found. In the metropolitan areas—such as Toronto, Winnipeg, and Vancouver—coordination and cooperation as between the various governmental units was the problem; "systems," whether "federated" as in the case of the Greater Vancouver Library Federation or "unified" as in the case of the Metropolitan Toronto Library Board, were seen as the answer. And everywhere in Canada, as the inadequacy of local support and initiative became apparent, the role of the senior governments became progressively more important. Provincial government agencies eventually gave substantial grants, employed field workers and consultants, and in several provinces, notably Saskatchewan, provided a whole array of direct services such as centralized processing and backup collections.

The most notable instance of the intervention of a provincial government was in Quebec, where since 1960 the whole public library scene has been virtually transformed. The percentage of the population served by public libraries increased from some 20 percent in 1959 to over 60 percent by 1974, and per capita support rose by nearly 500 percent in the same period.

While no other province could show the extent or speed of improvement so dramatically demonstrated in Quebec, the 1960's brought very considerable progress everywhere. From 1961 to 1971 book stocks increased by 63 percent, the number of personnel by about 50 percent, and operating expenditures by just over 100 percent. The most visible part of the transformation was in the many new or remodeled library buildings, of which that of the Metropolitan Toronto Library (1977) attracted world attention for its size and design.

In the latter half of the 1970's Canadian public libraries seemed to be resting on a high plateau. They had escaped some of the problems that had beset the large cities of the United States—deteriorating "cores," declining circulations, and actual cuts in funds. Still, Canadian public libraries had plenty of problems to contend with: budgetary pressures, learning to adapt to the unionization of staff, the effects of large-scale immigration on service demands and capabilities, and the longstanding but still unsuccessful attempt to secure federal funding. The traditional structure, based on local control and local support, still dominated the Canadian public library scene and was serving reasonably well, but strains were showing, and major changes were clearly inescapable.

### SCHOOL LIBRARIES

Canadian school libraries range from modern, even lavishly equipped, media centers to ragbag collections in the back of a classroom; the school librarian may have a Master's degree in Library Science or (far more frequently) no library training whatsoever. The unevenness derives from a central fact of Canadian education. Coming as education does under provincial jurisdiction, there is no unified national policy. Each province sets its own policy, and indeed within each province there is much variation arising from the very considerable autonomy held by the boards of the school districts.

Some generalizations are, however, reasonably accurate. Before the end of World War II, centralized school libraries were uncommon outside the larger cities. The function of the school library was mainly to supply "good reading" as a supplement to the teaching program in English literature and to serve as a study hall. In a textbook-centered, prescribed curriculum, the library was a marginal element in the Canadian school, and its facilities, staff, and collections all reflected that fact.

In the 1950's and especially in the 1960's, many Canadian schools adopted a "child-centered" approach that gave greater emphasis and opportunity to individual

**Table 1. Libraries in Canada (1976–77)**

| Type | Number | Volumes in collections | Annual expenditures (Canadian dollar) | Population served | Professional staff | All staff (total) |
|---|---|---|---|---|---|---|
| University | 77[a] | 37,490,416 | $142,568,366 | 367,821[b] | 1,582[c] | 6,688[c] |
| "Colleges"[d] | 145 | 6,110,316 | $25,857,969 | 211,277[b] | 351[c] | 1,391[c] |
| Public[e] | 754 | 37,533,848 | $176,344,698 | 22,992,000 | 1,607[c] | N.A. |
| School[f] | 8,692 | 49,412,275 | $24,956,624[g] | 3,371,026 | 2,948[h] | N.A. |
| Special[i] | 1,098 | N.A. | N.A. | N.A. | 600[j] | N.A. |

[a]Includes parent universities only; 110 with affiliated colleges.
[b]Includes full-time enrollment only.
[c]Includes full-time staff only; does not include part-time positions filled in full-time equivalents.
[d]The category covers non-degree-granting institutions of various kinds, usually offering two-year programs.
[e]The statistics are for 1976.
[f]Includes centralized school libraries only; excludes Quebec.
[g]Includes expenditures on materials only; excludes staff costs.
[h]Includes personnel with training in school librarianship.
[i]The statistics are for 1976.
[j]Estimate based on data given in Beryl L. Anderson, "Special Libraries in Canada," in *Canadian Libraries in Their Changing Environment* (1977).

Sources: The Culture Sub-Division, Education, Science, and Culture Division of Statistics Canada (1978); *A.L.A. Yearbook, 1978;* Beryl L. Anderson, "Special Libraries in Canada," in *Canadian Libraries in Their Changing Environment* (1977).

*Top left, exhibit in the Public Archives Center of the National Library, titled "Into the Silent Land: Survey Photography in the Canadian West 1858–1900."*
*Top, the Winnipeg Public Library, Manitoba. Canadian metropolitan libraries continue to be locally funded, as attempts to attain federal funding have been unsuccessful.*
*Left, interior of the Metropolitan Toronto Library, which attracted world attention for its size and design upon completion in 1977.*
*Bottom, The Public Archives Record Center of Canada in Ottawa.*

(Top left and bottom) Pierre De Mentionner, Public Archives of Canada
(Top) Gerry Cairns
(Left) Metropolitan Toronto Library

learning. Under this plan the school library became important as the learning laboratory and chief means of independent study. With concomitant expansion of collections to include much more audiovisual material, many school libraries changed character and name to become variously known as learning resource centers, materials resource centers, or instructional materials centers.

Another factor for progress was the employment by provincial departments of education of supervisors or consultants specifically to plan and oversee the development of school libraries on the provincial level. By 1974 only two provinces had failed to make such appointments. Much the same kind of approach was taken in the wealthier areas at the district level, where "school district librarians" provided advisory, coordinating, and centralized technical services in assistance of the individual school libraries.

Nevertheless, as the 1970's neared their end, problems were still more apparent than progress. *Statistics Canada* data for 1976–77 indicated that (excluding Quebec) centralized libraries existed in only 71.3 percent of elementary and secondary schools. (Such schools did, however, enroll 85.43 percent of the pupils; clearly, the larger schools were very likely by now to have centralized libraries.) Even more disturbing, of those schools that did have centralized libraries only 6.2 percent were staffed by persons with a library science degree; another 34 percent had staff with some training in school librarianship. Obviously, a qualified librarian was not yet considered an indispensable part of the Canadian school library.

With a tightening economic squeeze affecting school funding in every province and libraries still frequently regarded as something of a "frill," Canadian school librarians of the late 1970's felt hard pressed. In fact, however, there were almost no closures or dismissals. While yet far indeed from achieving the goals set forth in the *Standards,* Canadian school libraries were well enough established to be proof against considerable adversity.

**Table 2. Canadian School Libraries**[a]

| | 1958–59 | 1966–67 | 1976–77[b] |
|---|---|---|---|
| Percentage of schools with centralized libraries | 35.8 | 44.1 | 71.7 |
| Books per pupil in centralized school libraries | 4.2 | 5.0 | 14.6 |

[a]Based on Dominion Bureau of Statistics, *Survey of Libraries, part 2: Academic Libraries, 1958–59,* tables 14 and 16; *Survey of Libraries, part 2: Academic Libraries, 1966–67,* tables 17 and 19; Statistics Canada, *Centralized School Libraries, 1976–77* (unpublished data).
[b]Excludes Quebec.

*The National Library of Quebec, established in 1968, houses acquisitions relating to Quebec and to French Canada.*

SPECIAL LIBRARIES

Although the existence of special libraries in Canada can be traced back as far as 1725, their chief development has been very recent. Beryl L. Anderson's definitive study, "Special Libraries in Canada," in *Canadian Libraries in Their Changing Environment* (1977), indicates that 75 percent of Canadian special libraries have been established since World War II and perhaps as many as half the total number from 1968 to 1978.

A "branch plant economy" that historically characterized Canada probably accounts for the late development of special libraries. With so many Canadian firms being subsidiaries of foreign companies, the research operations and head offices of these firms were often not in Canada, suggesting lack of need for special library services in Canada itself. Much the same considerations account for the fact that the great majority of special libraries which have been established in Canada are located in Ottawa, Toronto, and Montreal—the headquarters cities for Canadian government, industry, and finance.

From 1968 to 1978 the combination of population increases, industrialization, emphasis on economic nationalism, and regional development (notably the concentration of oil companies in Alberta) has made for an unprecedented demand for special library services. Special libraries are the growth sector in contemporary Canadian librarianship.

Predictably, however, Canadian special libraries are still rather small. Anderson indicates that as of 1970, 85 percent had under 5,000 sq.ft. of space, and only about half had budgets of over $50,000. In 1975 over one-half had under 10,000 volumes; more significantly, only just

**Table 3. Archives in Canada (1976–77)**

| | |
|---|---|
| Number reporting | 64 |
| Collection size | 21 archives reported collection size of less than 10,000 items; 12 reported size of 10,000 to 100,000; and 17 reported size of more than 100,000. |
| Annual expenditures (46 archives reporting) | $12,676,932 |
| Full-time professional staff (41 archives reporting) | 336 |
| Other full-time staff | 53 |

Source: Unpublished data furnished by the Culture Sub-Division, Education, Science, and Culture Division of Statistics Canada (1978).

over one-half had more than one full-time staff member and then usually not more than two. It is important to note, nevertheless, that those one-person libraries were likely to be under professional direction as the 1970's ended. In 1975, 59 percent of the special libraries reporting indicated that they had professional full-time staff; in 1970 the comparable figure was 44 percent. It is very likely that Canadian special libraries have registered substantial increases in quality and range of service.

Other noteworthy trends of the last decade are the countrywide spread of special libraries (they are now to be found in some numbers outside of the "Ottawa-Montreal-Toronto triangle"), the rapid growth in the number of free-lance librarians ("special librarians without a library"), the employment of librarians by many law firms, and the formation of several associations specifically to serve the needs of Canadian special librarians. While the latter continue to belong to such American organizations as the Special Libraries Association, which has chapters in Montreal and Toronto, the Medical Library Association, and the American Association of Law Libraries, they have also started organizations of their own. The establishment and growth of the Association of Canadian Map Libraries (1967), the Association of Parliamentary Librarians in Canada (1975), the Canadian Association for Information Science (1970), the Canadian Association of Law Libraries (1960), the Canadian Association of Music Libraries (1972), the Canadian Association of Special Libraries and Information Services (1972), and the Canadian Health Libraries Association (1976)—to name only those associations of national scope—testify to the expansion and increasingly professional character of special libraries in Canada.

LIBRARY ASSOCIATIONS

*The Directory of Library Associations in Canada* (1978) lists no fewer than 137 library associations as still active in Canada. The very high number (for a population of 23,000,000) reflects the diversity and regionalism that have characterized Canadian library development. No fewer than 117 of these associations have been established since 1960, which is also revealing; it shows how recent and rapid that development has been.

The senior library associations in Canada are all provincial organizations. The Ontario Library Association, the oldest, was founded in 1900; the British Columbia Library Association began in 1911, and by 1936 there were provincial or regional associations in every area of the country. The national library association—the Canadian Library Association/Association Canadienne des Bibliothèques (CLA)—was, however, not formed until 1946. Until that time Canadian librarians wishing to meet together on a national basis used to do so by meeting at the American Library Association conferences.

**Canadian Library Association and ASTED.** With an increasing sense of national identity (and much greater ease in communication through air travel), Canadian librarians have tended to make the CLA their principal medium for furthering professional interests. Since 1968, however, CLA no longer presumes to be bilingual; in an amicable recognition of linguistic, cultural, and political realities, CLA left the representation of Francophone librarians to the national French-speaking library association, ASTED (Association pour l'avancement des sciences et des techniques de la documentation). ASTED is itself a reorganization (1973) of the older Francophone association ACBLF (Association canadienne des bibliothécaires de langue française), which in turn was originally a Catholic association. The changes of association name and outlook thus represent almost a capsule history of the development of librarianship in French Canada.

The Canadian Library Association (4,500 members in 1979) resembles the American Library Association in its breadth of activities and complexity of organization. There are major divisions—almost autonomous associations—for the different types of library and many committees to represent special interests. CLA maintains an active publications program and serves as spokesman for librarians' concerns in respect of public relations and politics. The lobbying function is, however, far more limited in the CLA than in the ALA, and the same is true for the Canadian provincial library associations, as compared with their state association counterparts in the U.S. The Canadian governmental system does not allow much opportunity for direct political pressure by smaller groups.

The national, provincial, and regional associations are "open" in the sense that anyone may belong, though the great majority of members are in fact professional librarians. The associations thus act as "umbrella" organizations, trying simultaneously and not wholly successfully to work for both the advancement of libraries and the self-interest of librarians.

**Professional Associations.** A type of association quite prominent in Canada but not known widely elsewhere in North America—the professional librarians' association, limiting membership to those holding stated professional qualifications—undertook the representation of self-interests of librarians. The Institute of Professional Librarians of Ontario (IPLO) was the largest and most influential of such purely professional groups; others were established in British Columbia, Alberta, and Quebec. Of these only the Corporation des bibliothécaires professionels de Québec/Corporation of Professional Librarians of Quebec and the Institute of Victoria Librarians (British Columbia) survive. They lacked sufficient numbers and failed to secure licensing powers. Unions and faculty associations, moreover, were increasingly seen as the most effective vehicles for protecting librarians' selfinterests.

**Association Role.** With their small memberships and inadequate funding, Canadian library associations seldom have had achievements to match their aims. Nevertheless, they serve an absolutely vital function in Canadian librarianship. In a country of marked regional and cultural diversity and where librarians work largely in comparative isolation from each other, the library associations serve as indispensable means of communication and informal continuing education.

**REFERENCES**

F. Dolores Donnelly, *The National Library of Canada* (1973).

Loraine Spencer Garry and Carl Garry, editors, *Canadian Libraries in Their Changing Environment* (1977).

*Librarianship in Canada, 1946 to 1967: Essays in Honour of Elizabeth Homer Morton,* edited by Bruce Peel (1968).

SAMUEL ROTHSTEIN

## Cape Verde

Cape Verde, an independent African republic, is an island archipelago in the Atlantic Ocean approximately 620 km. off Africa's west coast. Pop. (1978 est.) 311,000; area 4,033 sq.km. The official language is Portuguese.

**National Library.** Cape Verde gained its independence from Portugal in July 1975. A National Library, with headquarters in the capital of Praia, was established to play an important role in coordinating educational activities and directing new initiatives. Coordination is especially crucial because the nation is distributed among a collection of small islands. The Library was to evaluate the relative importance of various islands in the allocation of buildings, equipment, and personnel.

**Public Libraries.** Facilities open to the general public were restricted at the end of the 1970's to the nation's two major cities; both the capital of Praia on the island of

Santiago and Mindelo on the island of Sao Vicente operate relatively small libraries.

**School Libraries.** Libraries in the public schools provide the broadest coverage in library service to the islands. Fifteen school libraries are found in all the major islands of the archipelago.

**Special Libraries.** The Government Statistics Service maintains a technical library for the use of government administrators. The Service's library serves as a center for documentation, maintaining census and other statistical records.

MARIA MANUELA CRUZEIRO

*Thomas Carlyle*

Courtesy of The Newberry Library

## Carlyle, Thomas
(1795–1881)

Thomas Carlyle was responsible for founding the London Library. He was born at Ecclefechan, Dumfriesshire, Scotland, on December 4, 1795. He entered Edinburgh University in 1809 and studied mathematics, of which subject he became a teacher. Later on he also read law at Edinburgh, but it is as a historian and essayist that he is best remembered today.

Carlyle moved to London in 1834, but two years earlier he had written in his journal: "What a sad want I am in of libraries, of books to gather facts from! Why is there not a Majesty's library in every county town? There is a Majesty's gaol and gallows in every one." This cry from the heart came almost 20 years before the Public Libraries Act of 1850 was passed. Carlyle's only source of books in London was the British Museum, but to one who was extremely sensitive to physical discomforts, the Museum was an unfriendly place and its principal librarian, Sir Anthony Panizzi, totally unhelpful. Moreover, the journey from Chelsea to Bloomsbury was tedious, the Museum closed at five in the afternoon, and books could not be taken away.

Carlyle, therefore, decided to explore the possibility of forming a library containing the sort of books that would be useful to him and that he could take home. He canvassed his many influential friends and acquaintances, called a public meeting, and formed a committee. The London Library opened its doors on May 3, 1841, with 500 subscribers and 3,000 books.

The Earl of Clarendon was elected President, and he persuaded the Prince Consort to become patron of the Library, which has enjoyed the privilege of royal patronage ever since. Once the Library was on its feet, Carlyle took little interest in its day-to-day affairs, although he was greatly concerned about finding the right librarian. Eventually he secured the election of John George Cochrane, already 60 years of age and with no library experience, although he had recently compiled the catalogue of the Scott library at Abbotsford. After 11 years in office Cochrane died, and Carlyle, who in the intervening years had seldom attended committee meetings, once more entered the fray. There were more than 200 candidates for the vacant post. Gladstone, who was on the Library Committee, supported the application of Neapolitan emigré Giacomo Lacaita, but Carlyle was determined that he should not be appointed. In the end he had his way. The Committee chose William Bodham Donne, who received 16 votes, while Lacaita received only 4.

Carlyle's final appearance in the Committee Room took place five years later when Donne resigned and the question of a successor arose, but no record remains of the discussions that took place. Carlyle remained on the Committee until 1870, when on the death of the President, the Earl of Clarendon, he was invited to fill the vacancy. He accepted on the strict understanding that he must never be asked to preside, and he remained in office until his death in 1881.

**REFERENCES**

Frederic Harrison, editor, *Carlyle and the London Library* (1907).

Simon Nowell-Smith, *Carlyle and the London Library,* in *English Libraries 1800–1850* (1958).

STANLEY GILLAM



## Carnegie, Andrew
(1835–1919)

ALA

*Andrew Carnegie*

Andrew Carnegie, often referred to as the "Patron Saint of Libraries," made new library buildings available to hundreds of communities all over the world. He donated $56,162,622 for the construction of 2,509 library buildings throughout the English-speaking parts of the world. More than $41,000,000 of this amount was given for the erection of 1,679 public library buildings in 1,412 communities of the United States. Another $4,283,000 was given toward the construction of 108 academic library buildings in the U.S. After 1911 library grants were made by the Carnegie Corporation rather than by Andrew Carnegie personally, although he was president of the Corporation until his death in 1919.

This library philanthropy was actually only a small part of Carnegie's benefactions. More than $333,000,000 (90 percent of his fortune) was spent by the "Steel King" for what he termed "the improvement of mankind." The range of Carnegie's philanthropy was great and included the Simplified Spelling Board, more than 7,000 church organs, the Carnegie Hero Fund, the Carnegie Institute in Pittsburgh, the Carnegie Institution of Washington, the Foundation for the Advancement of Teaching, and the Carnegie Endowment for International Peace.

Andrew Carnegie was born in a weaver's cottage on November 25, 1835, in Dunfermline, Scotland. Because of the rapid industrialization of the textile trade, his father was forced to sell out his business, Carnegie's formal education came to an end, and the family moved to the United States in 1846. They settled in Allegheny, Pennsylvania, a suburb of Pittsburgh. Carnegie's first job, at the age of 13, was that of a bobbin boy for $1.20 per week. After one year he became a messenger boy for a local telegraph company, where he taught himself the art of telegraphy and met important people. Carnegie eventually worked his way up in the Pennsylvania Railroad, made many wise investments, and built up the Carnegie Steel Company until it was sold to J. P. Morgan in 1901 for nearly $500,000,000. Then at the age of 66—healthy, alert, and keenly interested in politics and literature—Carnegie retired to devote the rest of his life to philanthropy and to securing international peace. He had married Louise Whitfield in 1887, and their daughter, Margaret, was born in 1897. Bronchial pneumonia caused his death on August 11, 1919.

A memorandum found among Carnegie's papers after his death revealed that as early as 1868, at the age of 33, he made plans to use the surplus of his income for the benefit of others. But it was not until 1889 that he formally declared his philosophy of the trusteeship of wealth or, as it came to be called, the Gospel of Wealth.

In his first essay on the subject, "Wealth," Carnegie declared that wealthy men were to live without extravagance, provide moderately for the legitimate needs of their dependents, and then consider all the remainder as surplus funds that they as trustees should distribute in their lifetime for the best promotion of welfare and happiness of the common man. The main consideration was to help those who would help themselves—but only to assist and never or rarely to do all, because neither the individual nor the group was improved simply by almsgiving.

In his second essay, entitled "The Best Fields for Philanthropy," Carnegie lists seven fields to which the wealthy could devote their surplus in the following order: universities, libraries, medical centers, public parks, meeting and concert halls, public baths, and churches. The best gift that could be given to a community was a free library, "provided the community will accept and maintain it as a public institution, as much a part of the city property as its public schools, and, indeed, an adjunct to these."

Why did Andrew Carnegie select libraries to be among his first and foremost benefactions? One reason was given by a personal friend of the philanthropist who said that all of Carnegie's gifts were dedicated to causes and movements with which he was personally concerned. Libraries and books seemed to be of special concern to Carnegie. His father had led his fellow weavers in Dunfermline to pool their contributions for the purchase of books and delegated one of their number to read aloud while the others worked. This collection became the first circulating library in town. It was to Dunfermline that Carnegie gave his first library in 1881.

While Carnegie was still a working boy in Pittsburgh, a Colonel Anderson of Allegheny established in 1850 the J. Anderson Library of Allegheny City to furnish reading matter for the mechanics and workingmen in the trades. Young Andrew wrote a letter to the newspaper requesting that the library be opened to all working boys, and he was invited to use it. In later years he recalled awaiting Saturday afternoons with intense longing, "and it was when reveling in the treasures which he opened to us that I resolved, if ever wealth came to me, that other poor boys might receive opportunities similar to those for which we were indebted to that noble man."

Carnegie's confidence in the value of free libraries as a wise object of philanthropy may also have been stimulated by earlier and contemporary library philanthropists. He praised Ezra Cornell for beginning the distribution of his wealth by establishing a public library in Ithaca, New York, in 1857. He also had a high regard for Enoch Pratt's gift to Baltimore of $1,000,000 with a requirement that the city pay 5 percent of this sum annually to the library trustees for the support of the main library and branches.

Perhaps Carnegie's library philanthropy was also influenced by his business background. He once told an audience that far from being a philanthropist he was making the best bargains of his life. For instance, when he gave money to a city for library buildings, he succeeded in obtaining a pledge that the city would furnish sites and maintain the libraries forever. The city's investment was greater than his. "This was not philanthropy but a clever stroke of business." To all of these motivations must be added one with which Andrew Carnegie was frequently charged. His accusers claimed that he built libraries as monuments of himself for posterity.

The procedure for obtaining a Carnegie public library building grant was fairly simple. A community in need of a library structure had to have its mayor and council promise to provide a site. The city pledged to support the new library through local taxation in an annual amount that would be at least 10 percent of the sum given for the library building. That sum was usually based on about $2 per capita of local population.

The importance of Carnegie public library philanthropy lies in its perfect timing, coming in the best possible period—during the height of library expansion in the United States. Beginning in the 1890's, states began to play active roles in organizing public libraries in each community. The need for library buildings was desperate, and Carnegie's gifts helped to fill the void. The provision of new buildings created an avid interest in and enthusiasm for libraries in their early, crucial years of development. Carnegie dramatized the value of libraries and stimulated other philanthropists to provide library benefactions.

More importantly, Carnegie's philanthropy widened the acceptance of the principle of local government responsibility for the public library. The method of giving was not perfect; poor sites were often selected, and the 10 percent support pledge was sometimes broken or more often not surpassed. Nevertheless, it was a wise provision, placing indirect pressure on government and the public to accept the organization and maintenance of the public library as a governmental service.

Actually, about two-thirds of the communities receiving funds for one or more Carnegie library buildings already had a free public library or were in the process of organizing one when the Carnegie gift was offered. To be sure, many had just been organized or were being organized as a result of the stimulation of Carnegie benefactions and with the hope of obtaining new buildings. The incentive of Carnegie's gifts was enough to accelerate the library movement to a stampede. Some 188 public libraries in 1876 grew to 3,873 by 1923.

Andrew Carnegie's philanthropy continued to benefit public libraries and librarianship long after the formal termination of building grants. This extended library philanthropy is still in evidence today; in many ways it is even more important than the original bequest of Carnegie buildings, which ended after World War I.

In 1918 the Corporation asked Charles C. Williamson to make a study of library training. His report recommended that librarians should receive their education in a university rather than in a training school sponsored by public libraries and other agencies. Williamson also recommended the establishment of a graduate library school for advanced study, a national accrediting and certification system for library schools, and numerous fellowships. His study was a monumental work that resulted in a complete revision of the curriculum in library schools.

A Carnegie Corporation-sponsored study in 1924 by William S. Learned centered on the role of the library as a medium for spreading information. It called for expanded services to be provided by the American Library Association and for local and regional experiments and demonstrations leading to better ways of getting books to the people.

In 1926 the Corporation embarked on a ten-year Library Service Program, for which the trustees approved $5,000,000 in financial support. The aim of this program was to strengthen the library profession by supporting the activities of the ALA, by improving training opportunities, and by support for certain centralized library services and projects.

Andrew Carnegie had already provided $100,000 in endowment funds to the ALA in 1902, and the Corporation gave $549,500 for the general support of the Association from 1924 to 1926; in 1926 it added $2,000,000 in endowment funds. During this period the Corporation also provided financial assistance to the Library of Congress and to bibliographic centers and regional catalogues such as those at the Denver and Philadelphia public libraries.

Gifts for the endowment and support of library schools and the establishment of the first graduate library school at the University of Chicago totaled $3,359,550. Fellowships for library training and the sponsorship of conferences, studies, and publications were also provided.

The Corporation also provided funds for several demonstrations of methods and techniques for bringing books to people of all ages who were living in rural areas far from the major population centers.

Following World War II, the Corporation provided $212,170 to the Social Science Research Council for the Public Library Inquiry. The idea of a study of the library's actual and potential contribution to American society was suggested by the ALA. The appraisal was made in sociological, cultural, and human terms.

Again, financial assistance from the Carnegie Corporation helped the ALA in 1956 to formulate and publish what popularly became known as the Public Library Standards. The Public Library Inquiry discovered the failings of the public libraries, and the Standards presented what they should be doing by setting up minimum guidelines for good service. Public libraries were urged to cooperate, federate, or consolidate into library systems for better library service. The Corporation's financial support of demonstration centers for extension of library service in rural areas, of the Public Library Inquiry, and of the Standards was an important factor in bringing about federal aid for public libraries beginning in 1956.

Carnegie's benefactions have, in truth, played a major role in American public library development and have had a significant impact in all areas of American librarianship as well as those throughout the English-speaking world.

**REFERENCES**

George Bobinski, *Carnegie Libraries: Their History and Impact on American Public Library Development* (ALA, 1969), contains extensive bibliography.

Andrew Carnegie, *Autobiography of Andrew Carnegie* (1920).

Carnegie Corporation of New York, *Carnegie Corporation Library Program, 1911–1961* (1963).

Burton Hendrick, *The Life of Andrew Carnegie* (1932).

GEORGE S. BOBINSKI

## Carnovsky, Leon
(1903–1975)

Leon Carnovsky, a member of the faculty of the Graduate Library School of the University of Chicago, excelled in teaching, writing, editing, and service to the profession of librarianship. He was born to Isaac and Jennie Stillman Carnovsky in St. Louis, Missouri, on November 28, 1903. Appointed Instructor at Chicago in 1932, he advanced to the rank of Professor in 1944. He continued active service until 1971 when as Professor Emeritus he moved to his retirement home in Oakland, California. He died there on December 6, 1975.

From early boyhood, his parents fostered his intellectual interests. His father had been a Talmudic scholar before emigrating from Lithuania, and his mother also came from a rabbinical family. In Saint Louis they ran a small grocery store, which provided for them and their seven children, and they encouraged Leon to frequent the public library. After high school he worked for two years as a secretary, then entered the University of Missouri. Graduating with an A.B. in philosophy in 1927, he entered the training school of the St. Louis Public Library, going on in 1928 to become Assistant to the Librarian at Washington University. In 1929 he received a fellowship in the newly established Graduate Library School at the University of Chicago, where he earned his Ph.D. in 1932, the same year he joined the faculty.

As a teacher he conducted courses in the library and society, research methods, public libraries, comparative librarianship, and education for librarianship. His lectures, logical and coherent, were presented in a vibrant and resonant voice. He exerted a warm and dynamic presence within and without the classroom, and large numbers of his students regarded him as a confidant and friend. Foreign students were particularly drawn to him. He was both rigorous and skillful in directing theses and dissertations, and he was exceptionally adept at eliciting publishable papers from members of his classes.

His bibliography of published writings includes more than 160 items. Clearly and gracefully written, the quality matches the quantity; the range is far-reaching. Lester Asheim described the scope of this writing in a memorial tribute rendered Carnovsky in 1976:

> His doctoral dissertation was only one of his many contributions to the seminal studies of reading that marked the early years of GLS's innovative research program. His many library surveys, and studies of public libraries, became guides to action, as well as models for other professional appraisals. His writings on intellectual freedom, which anticipated by many years the themes which are now watchwords on this always contemporary issue, led to his chairmanship of ALA's Committee on Intellectual Freedom and subsequently built upon that experience. His long list of writings on library education cover developments from the early defensive days . . . through his chairmanship of the ALA's Committee on Accreditation, and after. His studies and reports on aspects of international librarianship reflect his foreign travels, as a Fulbright Fellow and on assignments for ALA, Unesco, and the American government.

Through 18 years, from 1943 to 1961, Carnovsky edited *The Library Quarterly*. In this work he maintained a standard of content and style that made the *Quarterly* the leading learned journal in its field, a model for both creative and careful editing. The work absorbed a huge amount of his energy and concentration. He devoted detailed attention to every phase of the publication process, from judging and editing manuscripts to proofreading and surveying the subscription list. Equally well edited were the many conference volumes he planned and prepared for the Graduate Library School.

His many library surveys and consultations throughout the world strongly represent his service to the profession. A notable example of their influence is his *Report of a Programme for Library Education in Israel,* prepared for Unesco in 1957, which led to the founding of the library school at Hebrew University. Also active in library associations, he was President of the Association of American Library Schools (1942–43) and Chairman of the ALA Committee on Intellectual Freedom (1944) and of the Committee on Accreditation (1963–65). He received the Melvil Dewey Medal in 1962 "for creative professional achievement of a high order," the Beta Phi Mu Award in 1971 for "distinguished service to education for librarianship," and the Joseph W. Lippincott Award in 1975 for "distinguished service in the profession of librarianship."

In personal appearance Carnovsky was of medium height with a muscular frame, had a ruddy complexion, wore thick-lensed glasses, and was bald from his early years on. He enjoyed swimming, hiking, and fishing. He was a connoisseur of music, the ballet, drama, literature, and fine food. Carnovsky married Marian Satterthwaite, a librarian and author of a book on public libraries, in August 1939. She died in January 1965. In June 1967 he

ALA

*Leon Carnovsky*

married Ruth French Strout, a colleague on the Graduate Library School faculty. His homes were distinguished by their genial hospitality.

**REFERENCES**

"The Brothers Carnovsky: A Profile, a Monologue," *University of Chicago Magazine* 7 (January/February 1970); his brother, Morris, gained public notice as a distinguished actor.

William Converse Haygood, "Leon Carnovsky: A Sketch," *Library Quarterly* (October 1968).

Frederick A. Schlipf, "Leon Carnovsky: A Bibliography," *Library Quarterly* (October 1968).

HOWARD W. WINGER

CASSIODORUS 374

# Cassiodorus

(*c.* 485–after 580)

Flavius Cassiodorus Senator, writer and monk, was noted for his direction of his library at Vivarium. He was born in southern Italy around 485 and died after 580. Though his contemporaries called him Senator, later writers refer to him as Cassiodorus. From the scholarship displayed in his writings it can be inferred that he received the customary liberal arts training for public service. Besides giving orations, he found time while in public service at Ravenna to produce a number of writings: *A History of the Goths,* his *Chronicle,* and several other treatises.

The Gothic kingdom virtually came to a close in 540, when the royal city Ravenna fell before the onslaught of Belisarius. About the same time, and possibly as a result of it, Cassiodorus relinquished his position. He first proposed to Pope Agapetus the creation of a university at Rome on the pattern of the schools of Alexandria and of Nisibus in Syria, a plan that had to be abandoned because of unfavorable conditions. Evidently it caused the Pope to create a library in Rome.

Cassiodorus then returned to southern Italy, where he found time to establish and govern a monastery. The sacred retreat established by Cassiodorus was by no means a cheerless prison. At the estate of Cassiodorus, Squillace, overlooking a beautiful bay, it included luxuries and various attractions, such as elaborate baths and fishponds. From the latter extravagance the monastery derived its name; it was called *Vivarium,* or the fish pond. Cassiodorus's ideal was complete literacy among the monks, for reading was basic to education. The written word was an instrument to develop one's individual perfection and in leading to a deeper understanding of the Bible. His *Introduction to Divine and Secular Readings* outlined the general monastic educational program. Devotional reading naturally held the highest place and comprised the content of the first of two books. The goal was a thorough knowledge of the Bible, and because the Psalms were recited in common, the Psalter was to be memorized. The total number of 1,399 lines is divided as follows:

| Subject | Number of lines | Percent of total |
|---|---|---|
| logic (dialectics) | 517 | 37 |
| rhetoric | 238 | 17 |
| arithmetic | 221 | 16 |
| music | 197 | 14 |
| astronomy | 105 | 7.5 |
| grammar | 70 | 5 |
| geometry | 51 | 3.5 |

The proportion of emphasis probably reflects the chiefly literary content that constituted the curriculum of schools of his day.

Special provisions were made for those not intellectually gifted to follow the regular liberal arts program of study. It would be sufficient for them to study the outlines and usefulness of the seven liberal arts. For them Cassiodorus recommended practical training on the material needs of the monastery, including a reading program of such selected writers as Gargilius Martial, Columella, and Emilianus on the cultivation of farms, gardens, bees, birds and fish and the study of herbs.

These two books constituted training in the correct understanding of the Bible, an art in which the liberal arts led the way. Cassiodorus drew up his study program to develop methods in appreciation of the Bible: how to read it, how to understand it, how to interpret it in the light of recommended commentators, how to treat the manuscript text, and how to edit and transcribe it so that authentic writings could be preserved intact and passed on to coming generations. The last portion of the first book treated the techniques of literary transcriptions.

Cassiodorus saw the possibility of including intellectual labor within the sphere of monastic duties. Under his direction the multiplication, translation, and correction of manuscript texts was to become part of the daily routine of qualified monks. The Writing Place was equipped with mechanical devices such as a sundial and a water clock to indicate the hours for the convenience of copyists, editors, and binders. It was lighted by self-filling lamps so that not even a cloudy day or nightfall should interrupt their tasks. Through his methodical directives, Cassiodorus made available for copyists a guidebook with rules for scribal work.

In addition to furnishing practical rules, he provided complete bibliographical references to allied fields in the reproduction of manuscripts. He recommended some knowledge of geography, abbreviations, and other secular studies as an aid to correct reading and understanding of handwritten texts. And because correctness of spelling was of high importance, he reminded them of the standard works and of his own separate book on the subject, *De Orthographia.* Some monks were trained for more advanced work in the Writing Room. Since not all the monks could read Greek, some undertook Latin translations. Questions of textual criticism were reserved for emendators *(notarii),* who compared variant copies and added rubric notes and punctuation marks.

The craft of bookbinding was viewed as important to manuscript book production. Cassiodorus equipped a staff of binders to attire the books or, as he phrased it, "wedding garments for the heavenly feast," for the external decoration was intended to express the beauty of its content. Those assigned to the Bindery were provided with a Manual of Sample Bindings to assist them in selecting appropriate bindings.

Though our knowledge of the library collection at Vivarium is limited, a key to the reconstruction of its holdings is to be found in his Manual. Cassiodorus referred to 123 authors, including the Greek classical writers such as Aristotle, Homer, Hippocrates, Dioscorides, Euclid, Archimedes, Galen, Plato, Ennius, Terence, Lucretius, Varro, Cicero, Virgil, Horace Columellam Fortunatius, Valerius Probus, Seneca, Pliny, Quintilian, and Macrobius. Some of the manuscript books that lined the shelves of the library at Vivarium are extant; these are listed by D. M. Cappuyns. The library was arranged in nine bookcases with all Greek books put together in the eighth case. The classification scheme was based upon subject matter rather than authors. Several works on the same subject were sometimes bound together in a single volume.

**REFERENCES**

D. M. Cappuyns, "Cassiodore," *Dictionaire d'Histoire et Geographie Ecclesiastiques* (1948), vol. 2, pp. 1349–1408, excellent for identification and location of books housed in the Library of Cassiodorus.

Cassiodorus, *Institutiones,* edited by R. A. B. Mynors (1937).

L. W. Jones, *Cassiodorus Senator: An Introduction to Divine and Human Readings* (1946), superb introduction to Cassiodorus in English and a translation of his *Institutes.* REDMOND A. BURKE

# Cataloguing

Although it is sometimes assumed by library users that librarians can immediately recall what items are in the collections and where they may be located, such a memory feat has seldom been deemed adequate for good service. Curators even of ancient libraries are known to have prepared at least rudimentary lists of their holdings, if only to serve as a device for checking to determine whether the collection was complete. In addition, perhaps to demonstrate the strength of the library as well as to aid in locating particular materials, descriptions of basic information about those materials were gradually compiled. These catalogues, which served principally as inventory and finding lists, usually offered some indication of the title or *incipit* (first words of the text) of a work, its author (if known), the extent of the work (such as the number of scrolls or tablets required to transcribe it), its location in the library, its provenance (history of ownership), and perhaps the name of the scribe who copied it.

Defining "cataloguing" as the production of lists of library holdings serves to distinguish the discipline from the more general one called "bibliography." While bibliographers attempt to identify all items relevant to a particular field, produced in a given nation, or issued during a period of time, cataloguers direct their attention to the contents of a particular repository. The separation of bibliography from cataloguing came, however, largely after the development of printing from movable type. During the 20th century there has been something of a trend toward the reintegration of the two disciplines, especially since the impact of modern technology and the development of comprehensive library collections, particularly at the national level, have combined to transform some large catalogues into major bibliographies.

**Types of Catalogues.** Over the centuries various types of library catalogues were devised, with formats and arrangements dictated mainly by the context that they were designed to serve. Broad groupings of materials by their form (such as literature or music) or by the discipline represented (such as philosophy, religion, or science) suggested the organizing principles for certain catalogues, while others emphasized such characteristics as authorship of the works and specific topics covered. The amount of detail in the description of materials and the order in which descriptive elements were presented differed, however, sometimes quite markedly from library to library.

Even the cultural setting of the library influenced to some degree the kinds of lists that appeared. European catalogues, for example, tended especially in the wake of the Renaissance to focus upon personal authorship as the leading element for each entry and to utilize the Roman alphabet as the principle of arrangement. In contrast, many of the catalogues in the Orient used the title of the work as the key element and arranged the descriptions according to the number of strokes in the initial characters of that title.

*Subject Organization.* Catalogues organized according to subject or topic have proved to be popular, especially when only fragmentary or inconsistently developed subject bibliographies were available. Such catalogues have the distinct advantage of revealing materials immediately accessible to library users, whereas bibliographies identify but often do not locate the items listed.

One form of subject catalogue called "classified" or "classed" gained popularity especially in Europe. Although many subject catalogues, particularly those in card form, are arranged alphabetically according to the words or phrases chosen to express the topics of the material, classed catalogues are organized according to symbols representing a logical, usually hierarchical, system that moves from general classes to specific subclasses in an orderly fashion. To make use of such a catalogue, a person must either identify quickly the classification pattern or consult an index that leads to relevant sections. One strength of the classed catalogue is its ability to display a variety of materials either broadly or more specifically pertinent to a field of interest, without forcing its user to move back and forth among unrelated entries. A weakness, however, is that no general classification system can fully anticipate the unusual juxtapositions of topics library users sometimes require.

One effort to make the classed catalogue easier to consult eventuated in the development of the "alphabetico-classed" list. In it, materials are categorized first by general discipline, then further by classes, and finally by specific subject. The general disciplines are not arranged by logic, however, but alphabetically by the words designating them; then classes are alphabetically arranged under the name of the discipline, as are subjects under the names of the classes. This system requires some understanding of the hierarchical relationships but has the advantage of showing the subjects in a more directly visible manner than the symbols of a classification system can.

*Dictionary Catalogue.* A popular 20th-century catalogue is the "dictionary" list, in which all types of entries are arranged alphabetically. Such a catalogue generally relies upon a unit of descriptive information about each item in the collection; the unit is then reproduced as many times as required to provide access under the names of persons, names of groups, titles of the work, and subject and form headings related to the item catalogued. Dictionary catalogues thus obviate the need for a separate index. Although this arrangement came to be a dominant one in the United States, its value has come into question because of the increased size and complexity of the card files in which it was ordinarily used.

In an effort to simplify the dictionary card file, a number of libraries constructed a "divided catalogue," in which various types of entries were separated according to their function. Some placed author and title entries in one section with subject entries in another; others found a threefold division into author (or name), title, and subject files to be more desirable. These patterns have been retained in many of the contemporary catalogues issued in book form as well.

**Forms of Catalogues.** Any discussion of catalogue arrangement is necessarily linked with a consideration of the form in which that arrangement is displayed. One ancient library is reported to have inscribed its catalogue on the walls of its building. More commonly, the catalogue has been recorded in a form similar to that of the library materials themselves: on a clay tablet, on a scroll, or in a book ("codex"). After the invention of movable type, most catalogues were issued in printed form. During the 19th century, however, many libraries began to shift from these expensive printed "book catalogues" to a more easily updated loose-leaf format (including sheaf catalogues and guard books). The proliferation of materials made possible by technological advancements required the construction of catalogues flexible enough to respond to the rapid growth of library collections. At first the solution was to interleave printed catalogues with blank sheets on which new items could be entered or to utilize unbound copies into which new pages could be inserted. Subsequently cards, eventually standardized to 7.5 × 12.5 centimeters (3 × 5 inches), became the dominant format for the early 20th-century catalogues.

Improvements in photographic and printing tech-

Carnegie Library of Pittsburgh

*Catalogue card production in 1907: a library assistant works the press.*

*Cataloguing Department, Main Library, University of Pittsburgh, in the 1920's.*

University of Pittsburgh Archives

niques, followed by the invention of electrostatic duplication processes, made the production of cards easier and faster. Particularly in the United States, centralized services permitted many libraries to benefit from the cataloguing work performed by one library or commercial organization. These same techniques, however, also encouraged the reintroduction of the book catalogue, since photolithography provided a flexible and relatively inexpensive means of reproducing cataloguing data.

More recently available are data processing and computer-based systems that can display cataloguing data in a wide variety of formats and arrangements, limited only by the imagination of the cataloguers and the financial resources available. Contemporary cataloguing staffs are producing lists both in advance and on demand, utilizing systems ranging from the traditional typing—or even handwriting—of catalogue data all the way to the automatic reproduction of information compiled by a national library or bibliographic service in advance of the publication of the material. The output of systems using Cataloging-in-Publication techniques (CIP) may be viewed in card form, on typed or printed pages, in loose-leaf or bound volumes, on microfilm or microfiche, or on a television console or a teletypewriter connected with a computer.

This almost unlimited variety of catalogue formats has also stimulated experimentation with new configurations of data. The card catalogue in dictionary form, once considered the epitome, has given way to a new model: a catalogue that exists as a series of electronic codes suitable for computer manipulation and that can be printed in whole or in part "on demand" (at the time of perceived need) in accord with the requirements of a particular library user.

**Standardization.** While catalogue librarians have regularly been concerned about the arrangement, format, and production techniques of their lists, they have also moved to devise systems that can assure some uniformity in the recording of cataloguing data. Standardization of the data elements—their order, extent, and punctuation style—has been seen as a way to enable one library to construct records usable by a variety of others and permit the library user to obtain information from several facilities without having to learn the cataloguing peculiarities of each. Standardization may, however, produce undesirable consequences if it obscures the special purposes of some libraries by requiring them to conform to a procedure detrimental or irrelevant to the needs of their clientele. Further, an inflexible adherence to established rules and procedures may impede the effective cataloguing of new types of materials because they cannot easily be related to previously discerned patterns. The tension between the values of uniformity, on the one hand, and those of spontaneity and flexibility, on the other, continues to occasion much debate among cataloguers.

Attempts to standardize cataloguing procedures became particularly important as library collections began to grow rapidly. Not surprisingly, many of the efforts to devise cataloguing rules originated in large research libraries and national repositories. Almost all of the resulting codifications provide guidance in the description of materials (the recording of such data as name of author, title, edition, place of publication, publisher, date, physical extent and characteristics, and series connection), selection of entry points (names of persons or groups, titles, and series, among others), and regularization of forms in which entries are listed (authority work). Some also offer patterns for subject analysis and the physical construction of the cataloguing medium.

**Cataloguing Codes.** Although some cataloguing codes have been created essentially as internal documents, many of the influential rule books have been published and adopted by a group of libraries. Such noted works as the 1791 *Instruction pour procéder à la confection du catalogue . . .* issued from Paris for those libraries taken over during the French Revolution, the "91 Rules" of Antonio Panizzi designed in the 1830's for the printed book collection of the British Museum, and the "Prussian Instructions" of 1908 set the stage for further efforts.

*Anglo-American Cataloguing Rules.* The contributions in the United States of such imaginative thinkers as Charles C. Jewett, Melvil Dewey, and Charles A. Cutter led the way to the cooperative development of the first Anglo-American rules, published as *Catalog Rules: Author and Title Entries* in 1908 under the auspices of the American Library Association and the Library Association of Britain. Although the effects of World War II prevented much meaningful cooperation in the production of the preliminary second edition in 1941 (issued as *A.L.A. Catalog Rules*) or the 1949 *A.L.A. Cataloging Rules for Author and Title Entries,* with its companion volume, *Rules for Descriptive Cataloging in the Library of Congress,* Anglo-American efforts were again stimulated in the compilation of what came to be known as the *Anglo-American Cataloging Rules* (AACR) of 1967.

At the international level, a seminal conference was sponsored in 1961 by the International Federation of Library Associations (IFLA) to try to achieve some compromise among differences, particularly between the Anglo-American and German traditions. The results of this International Conference on Cataloguing Principles held in Paris seemed to bode well for increased cataloguing uniformity, but an American review of the consequences for the card files in large libraries caused dissension. Lack of agreement concerning especially the rules for the formation of corporate entry headings finally resulted in the publication of two versions of AACR: the North American text and the British text.

AACR was adopted in North America in partial fashion, following the principle of "superimposition" used by the Library of Congress; under this principle only entries established and materials described after 1967 conformed to AACR. The North American text also perpetuated entry of certain institutions and governmental bodies under the name of the place in which they are located, while the British text supported entry directly under the name of the body.

Stimulated by the International Meeting of Cataloguing Experts (Copenhagen, 1969), IFLA, through its Cataloguing Secretariat, promulgated a new approach to descriptive cataloguing called International Standard Bibliographic Description (ISBD). This development in concert with the increased utilization of computer-based systems in many national libraries (*e.g.,* the Library of Congress Machine-Readable Cataloging System: MARC) suggested that AACR might be revised to bring the two texts together and introduce the ISBD as a coordinating principle for the description of all types of library materials, produced anywhere in the world.

*AACR 2.* The publication of the new edition of the *Anglo-American Cataloguing Rules* in December 1978 occasioned something of a crisis in many libraries. AACR 2 represented a break with traditional entry patterns and heading forms. Its implementation in numerous countries then using AACR was expected to force the closing (or "freezing") of many large card files and the opening of machine-based cataloguing systems. Further international cooperation extends the concept of "shared cataloguing," whereby one country can use the lists of another without significant alteration. A universal MARC (UNIMARC) program is being created along with the design of an international "authority" system so that access points to library materials can be understood and, if necessary, translated from one language or national practice to another.

Amid the advancements in standardization and technology, the basic intent of cataloguing has not essentially changed. Though arrangements and formats may vary, catalogues exist to provide library clientele with useful lists of available materials and library staff with a means for evaluating and controlling local collections.

Buffalo and Erie County Public Library

*In the 1970's, cataloguers at the Buffalo and Erie County Public Library use OCLC data.*

*Microfiche catalogue at the State University of New York at Albany.* Arthur Plotnik

**REFERENCES**

Dorothy Anderson, *Universal Bibliographic Control: A Long Term Policy, A Plan for Action* (1974), the basic statement of the UBC program of IFLA.

Paul S. Dunkin, *Cataloging U.S.A.* (1969), a sometimes irreverent historical view of the American cataloguing traditions.

Kathryn Luther Henderson, " 'Treated with a Degree of Uniformity and Common Sense': Descriptive Cataloging in the United States, 1876–1975," *Library Trends* (1976), a detailed recounting of American cataloguing history, with some reference to the international scene.

*Library Catalogs: Changing Dimensions* (1964), the 28th Annual Conference of the Graduate Library School, University of Chicago, August 5–7, 1963, edited by Ruth French Strout, papers reviewing the function of the catalogue in the United States and Europe.

*Prospects for Change in Bibliographic Control* (1977), Proceedings of the 38th Annual Conference of the Graduate Library School, University of Chicago, November 8–9, 1976, edited by Abraham Bookstein, Herman H. Fussler, and Helen F. Schmierer, papers considering cataloguing as part of national and international efforts toward achievement of bibliographic uniformity.

Mary Ellen Soper and Benjamin F. Page, editors, "Trends in Bibliographic Control: International Issues," *Library Trends* (1977), articles surveying cataloguing and bibliographic systems from a variety of perspectives.

*Toward a Better Cataloging Code* (1957), papers presented before the 21st Annual Conference of the Graduate Library School, University of Chicago, June 13–15, 1956, edited by Ruth French Strout, contributions from American and British cataloguing experts, treating the history and development of cataloguing codes and particularly the Anglo-American tradition.

DORALYN J. HICKEY

# Censorship and Intellectual Freedom

CENSORSHIP

Censorship is the conscious effort by an individual, group, or government agency—legal or extralegal—to prevent access to whatever is available to be read, seen, or heard. The motivations—covert or overt—for censorship are as diverse as its means of manifestation but may be generalized as being usually based on the professed attempt to protect or maintain particular standards of morality, to guard the national security, or to assure only a one-sided presentation of volatile social, political, or economic issues. It is a social phenomenon that has existed as long as recorded history and that is as widespread as civilization, appearing to some extent in all cultures. Censorship of *reading* materials is the chief consideration of this article.

**History.** The first official "censors" were those Roman officials (from the 5th century B.C. on) who bore that title, one of whose responsibilities was to guard the morals of Roman citizens. They went well beyond the policing of reading materials to check on citizens' private and public activities, but through the ages the original censors' comparatively minor interest in policing the individual's thinking has developed into what is now a nearly universal tendency for a paternalistic government to shield its citizens from possible harm, whether moral or otherwise.

The Judeo-Christian ethic has been somewhat in conflict in the areas of censorship, particularly in areas relating to sexual activity, its description and portrayal. The utter frankness of the Old Testament bears witness to the basic Jewish belief in freedom of speech; the Gospels' section of the New Testament is just about equally frank. The Pauline epistles, however, were the beginning of what still today persists as a basic Christian attitude in favor of concealment and prudishness in regard to sexual matters, of veneration for asceticism and chastity.

The most significant impetus for censorship in the Western world came with the invention of printing in the 15th century and the consequent wide promulgation of reading matter of all sorts. As long as the potential audience was severely limited, as it was before Gutenberg, there was little call for the censor's services. Fra Girolamo Savonarola, leader in Florentine religious life during the latter part of the 15th century, was responsible for the Burning of the Vanities during the Carnival of 1497, which culminated in the destruction of thousands of so-called lewd books and pictures. The Council of Trent, which provided basic rules for the Catholic Church, called in 1564 for the censorship of books on "lascivious or obscene subjects," in its rule number seven. It set up the *Index of Prohibited Books*, which served until the mid-1950's as a standard for theological censors and barred such writers as Voltaire, Zola, Balzac, and Montaigne from the consideration of the devout.

The Reformation did not end theologically-based censorship. The Protestants' emphasis was on works considered heretical and revolutionary. George Haven Putnam states that "it was considered to be the right and duty of the Church, and of the State, under the influence of the Church, to supervise and control the production of the printing press and the reading of the people."

The beginnings of censorship in the U.S. were as diverse as the origins of the colonies that later became states. Massachusetts and most of the other New England colonies (except Rhode Island, where Roger Williams's broad view of toleration prevailed) carefully scanned reading matter for possible unorthodoxy or immorality, but Virginia and most of the other southern colonies were quite permissive.

The First Amendment to the U.S. Constitution has served as the principal barrier to governmental censorship since it was added in 1791 as part of the Bill of Rights. It explicitly forbids Congress to make any laws that abridge freedom of speech or press, but the individual states still retained the right to censor as one of the powers reserved to the states, until 1925, under *Gitlow* v. *New York*.

The first United States obscenity prosecution (a successful one) was against an art dealer in Philadelphia in 1815 for displaying "a certain lewd, wicked, scandalous, infamous, and obscene painting." In 1821 the Massachusetts Supreme Court found an American edition of *Fanny Hill* to be obscene. Various state antiobscenity laws were passed in the early 19th century, but it was not until 1836 that the first federal censorship law was proposed. Favored by Andrew Jackson, it was opposed by Senators Clay, Webster, and Calhoun; it would have barred antislavery materials from the mails. It failed to get congressional support.

Anthony Comstock, self-styled "Roundsman of the Lord," and his Society for the Suppression of Vice succeeded in lobbying through Congress in 1873 the federal law, which still is in force, on the mailing of "obscene or crime-inciting matter" (Title 18, chapter 71). The states that did already have antiobscenity laws followed with more stringent "Comstock laws" on their own, very soon thereafter. Through the years that followed, the censor, in general, prevailed, with some minor setbacks.

After many years of congressional agitation about the need for reconsideration of the Comstock Law, Congress finally approved the establishment of a Presidential Commission on Obscenity and Pornography. Its 1970 report recommended the repeal of all existing federal legislation prohibiting or interfering with "consensual distribution of 'obscene' material by adults." They went further, to recommend the repeal of all state and local antiobscenity legislation except that which was concerned with minors. President Richard Nixon rejected the Commission's conclusions out of hand; the U.S. Senate voted 60–5 to reject the Commission's findings and recommendations. Despite objections in some quarters to its methodology and conclusions, its ten volumes of technical reports still stand as a unique statement of expert research into a most perplexing social issue.

The U.S. Supreme Court has made a succession of occasionally contradictory decisions on the right to publish, distribute, read, and view presumably "obscene" matter. In the case of *Chaplinsky* v. *New Hampshire* (1942), the Court unanimously ruled that "there are certain well-defined and narrowly limited classes of speech, the prevention and punishment of which has never been thought to cause any Constitutional problems. These include the lewd and obscene, the profane, the libelous, and the insulting or 'fighting' words . . . such utterances are no essential part of any exposition of ideas, and are of such slight social value as a step to truth that any benefit that may be derived from them is clearly outweighed by the social interest in order and morality."

But in *Butler* v. *Michigan* (1957) the Supreme Court for the very first time agreed that the state could not "reduce the adult population of Michigan to reading only what is fit for children." This ruling led directly to so-called variable obscenity statutes in most states, which distinguish between the offensive or criminal character of reading or viewing matter intended for adults, as compared with those aimed at youth. In a way, this may have presaged the current "G-PG-R-X" rating system for motion pictures.

The landmark case of *Roth* v. *United* States (1957) combined with *Butler* to stop almost all lawsuits involving adults and obscenity-reading or viewing—a halt that lasted nearly 20 years. By stating that "*all* ideas having even the slightest redeeming social importance . . . have . . . full protection," this decision effectively staved off the censor. Interestingly, the mere fact that a public library purchased one particular book was used to prove "redeeming social importance" in one of the cases defended under *Roth*. In *Miller* v. *California,* the Court majority dropped the *Roth* and *Memoirs* criteria and changed to a consideration of "whether the work, taken as a whole, lacks serious literary, artistic, political, or scientific value," a much more difficult standard for defendants to reach. Justice Douglas, in his dissent in *Paris Adult Theatre I* v. *Slaton,* said, "What we do today is rather ominous as respects librarians. The net now designed by the Court is so finely meshed that taken literally it could result in raids on libraries." Justice Douglas's forebodings have not proven generally true; in at least a dozen states, librarians are specifically exempted from obscenity worries relating to adults.

**The Librarian as/and the Censor.** An American Library Association President, Joseph Nelson Larned, used the occasion of his 1893 inaugural address to state what librarians—particularly public librarians—were supposed to be doing: "To judge books with adequate knowledge and sufficient hospitality of mind; to exercise a just choice among them without offensive censorship; to defend his shelves against the endless siege of vulgar literature, and yet not waste his strength on the resistance—these are generally the crucial demands made on every librarian." Three well-researched books—Marjorie Fiske's *Book Selection and Censorship* (1959), Charles H. Busha's *Freedom versus Suppression and Censorship* (1972), and Michael Pope's *Sex and the Undecided Librarian* (1974)—suggest one of the chief groups of censors in America is composed of fearful, timid librarians who do not wait for outside censorship but practice it themselves. Busha's study of "a stratified random sample of public librarians in . . . Illinois, Indiana, Michigan, Ohio, and Wisconsin" revealed, via an opinion questionnaire, that, for example, 14 percent, if offered a gift copy of a report of the latest annual Soviet Communist Party Congress, were not willing to accept it; another 21 percent would not agree to purchase "right wing" publications such as the *Blue Book of the John Birch Society*. Perhaps the most interesting, even significant, finding of Busha's study was that "the data show a marked disparity between the attitudes of many librarians toward intellectual freedom as a concept and their attitudes toward censorship as an activity." He notes, "The attitudes of the public librarians . . . were predominantly not sympathetic toward censorship and . . . only 22 percent . . . were strongly opposed to censorship practices." Perhaps most important was Busha's conclusion that "the attitudes of the remaining 64 percent of Midwestern public librarians were somewhat neutral, neither highly favorable nor unfavorable toward censorship."

The earlier comparable study by California librarian Marjorie Fiske revealed that "nearly two-thirds of all librarians who have a say in book selection reported instances where the controversiality of a book or an author resulted in a decision not to buy." But "nearly one-half of the librarians interviewed . . . expressed unequivocal freedom-to-read convictions." Fiske's study, incidentally, included school librarians, who were in general less likely to practice self-censorship than their colleagues in public libraries.

Michael Pope's "study of librarians' opinions on sexually oriented literature" is based on 718 school, college, and public librarians' replies to questionnaires, from all 50 states. Pope found that "librarians with more extensive educational backgrounds are less restrictive than those with less formal preparation," that "female librarians are more restrictive than males," and that, in general, the older the librarian, the more likely he or she is to be on the censorious side. Finally, Pope says that "it is too easy for librarians to label materials which do not coincide with their personal predilections as 'not appropriate.' " The profession as a whole, however, is doing all it can to counter the censor. Through the years the American Library Association has been a leader in anticensorship efforts, not least for its publications in this field. The ALA's Office for Intellectual Freedom has prepared an *Intellectual Freedom Manual* (1974) for librarians, trustees, and others interested in the topic. Included are the official policies and documents of the association that are concerned with intellectual freedom, along with authoritative, brief, but comprehensive chapters on such topics as "Library Bill of Rights," "Before the Censor Comes: Essential Preparations," and "Assistance from ALA." Some other ALA publications include Robert B. Downs's collection of readings *The First Freedom: Liberty and Justice in the World of Books and Reading* (1960); Everett Moore's reports and comments on actual library censorship cases, *Issues of Freedom in American Libraries; Freedom of Inquiry* (1964); and David K. Berninghausen's *The Flight from Reason* (1975).

**The Etiology of Censorship.** The etiology of censorship is certainly far from understood. Since censorship is clearly a universal and probably permanent social phenomenon, it would be helpful to those who must deal with it to understand its causes, but, like many other social phenomena, censorship is not something that seems to follow any particular "natural" laws; it is far too complex to inspire or present readily ascertainable explanations. *The Fear of the Word* (1973), by Eli Oboler, attempts to come to some understanding of sex-related censorship; the origins of political, theological, and social censorship await even the beginnings of study.

The urge to censor is based on many motives, but one of the most common is the belief that the individual or group doing the censoring has a better knowledge of what is good for others than does the would-be reader, listener, or viewer. Some New York Jews in the 1930's tried to have Shakespeare's *Merchant of Venice* removed from school libraries and curricula as anti-Semitic; some religious fundamentalists in Kanawha, West Virginia, in the late 1970's successfully opposed the inclusion of pro-evolutionary theory materials in their schools; a large group of ALA members tried in 1977 to force ALA to withdraw from circulation an ALA-sponsored intellectual freedom movie, *The Speaker,* because it purportedly helped those who believe in the genetic intellectual inferiority of blacks. All of these—and many, many more—claimed that the possible evil consequences of the materials they attacked were far beyond the possible negative consequences of denial of freedom of speech. Clearly, this is a dilemma without simple answers.

There has been some research in the field of antipornography. Some researchers for the U.S. Commission on Obscenity and Pornography in the early 1970's offer a theory based on their analysis of the "natural histories" of two antipornography crusades. They see antipornography groups as being composed of those who suffer what they call "status discontent," which occurs "when the individual's power is less than he expects as someone who has pledged to an usually prestigious style of life." This suggests that the censors act not really for the improvement of society's moral level but to gain social recognition they otherwise could not possibly achieve.

INTELLECTUAL FREEDOM

Intellectual freedom is the antithesis of censorship. Broadly considered, it is both an idea and an ideal, limited by cultural taboos, conventional morality, and the basic survival needs of both society and the individual. When tightly constrained, it boils over in such manifestations as underground organizations and publishing, the alternative press, and political pamphlets.

Intellectual freedom begins in the human mind but is conveyed through public discourse and the media. It is an integral, fundamental component of democracy and an essential revelation of the human spirit. It exists wherever and whenever the human mind is free to go beyond the routine and stereotyped to the original and creative.

The ALA Office for Intellectual Freedom, in its *Intellectual Freedom Manual,* defined intellectual freedom as "the right of any person to believe whatever he wants on any subject, and to express his beliefs or ideas in whatever ways he thinks appropriate," as well as "the right of unrestricted access to all information and ideas regardless of the medium of communication used." Simply put, intellectual freedom means both freedom of expression and access to the ideas that are expressed. The 1948 United Nations Universal Declaration of the Rights of Man includes the statement, "Everyone has the right to freedom of opinion and expression; this right includes freedom to hold opinions without interference and to seek, receive, and impart information and ideas through any media regardless of frontiers."

**World Survey.** Since 1973 Freedom House, an independent group concerned with the status of freedom around the world, has issued an annual "Comparative Survey of Freedom." As part of this report, the Survey assesses political censorship, which they define as that "applied in defense of a ruling party or its politicians." According to the 1978 Freedom House Survey, Denmark and Australia exemplify the highest level of freedom of speech, where a great variety of media and freedom of expression are "both possible and evident." Venezuela, India, West Germany, and Italy are on the next level, described as countries where "non-government papers exist and engage in criticism, but are under periodic threats of censorship," while Colombia and Turkey exemplify a third level, with suppression of publications a common event. Guatemala and Nigeria are in a fourth group, with comparatively broad, but still limited, press freedoms, while Brazil and the Philippines are on a fifth level, government-controlled media. Sixth-rated states include Burma and the U.S.S.R.; there the rights of the state are legally given priority (as explicitly stated in the Soviet Constitution) over the rights of other groups or individuals. Albania and the former Central African Empire were cited as examples of states where *no* public internal criticism was allowed.

There is a different kind of censorship in Great Britain. Legal censorship of theatrical performances was a system of national prior censorship, operated by the Lord Chamberlain, an official of the royal household, from 1843 until passage of the "Act to Abolish Censorship of the Theatre" in 1968. (Local jurisdictions still may refuse to give theatrical licenses.) The Public Libraries and Museums Act of 1964 does not permit barring items from public libraries on political grounds or because of the social unconventionality or "low" moral tone of works concerned. The Obscene Publication Act 1959 (as modified by a provision in the Criminal Justices Act 1967) requires that either the Director of Public Prosecution or a Constable (similar to a county sheriff in the U.S.) can cause a warrant for search and forfeiture of "obscene" items in a bookstore. Perhaps the greatest variance from U.S. procedure and rules occurs with prosecutions under the Official Secrets Acts 1911, 1920, and 1939 (all modifications of the Official Secrets Act 1889), which has been officially criticized in Parliament as having "a tendency . . . to be used for the purpose of muzzling criticism or restraining the passage of information, outside the strict realm of security."

**Intellectual Freedom and U.S. Law.** The United States has never officially approved governmental control of political expression except for the Alien and Sedition Acts of 1798 (voided by Jefferson a few years later) and to some extent during the various wars. The Civil War in particular brought censorship under federal auspices but not so blatantly as during World War I, when the Espionage Act of 1917 and the 1918 Sedition Act attempted to stop criticism of the government's war activities.

Although in *Schenck* v. *United States* (1919) Justice Oliver Wendell Holmes backed the conviction of a Socialist for sending out draft-resistance leaflets, he also promulgated the still-prevailing "clear and present danger" theory to justify his opinion. In *Abrams* v. *United States* (1919) a Holmes-Brandeis dissent, however, disagreed with the majority opinion (prohibiting the printing and distributing of leaflets against American intervention on the side of the White armies in the Russian Revolution). They said, "We should be eternally vigilant against attempts to check the expression of opinions that we loathe and believe to be fraught with death, unless they so imminently threaten immediate interference with the lawful and pressing purposes of the law that an immediate check is required to save the country."

The plea of national security has been the main argument, historically, for political censorship. Oscillating between the majority view in *Abrams* (that speech cannot be permitted if it shows a "tendency" to produce dangerous actions) and the minority opinion ("clear and present danger" as the only justification for political censorship), there have been many varying Supreme Court decisions on these matters since then.

**The Library and Intellectual Freedom.** In the 1930s the American Library Association began to take positive measures to defend intellectual freedom. A nationwide wave of censorship of Steinbeck's *Grapes of Wrath* was followed by the adoption in 1939 of the "Library's Bill of Rights"; in 1948 a completely revised Library Bill of Rights was adopted by the ALA Council. With various revisions and interpretations (in 1951, 1961, and 1967) the Library Bill of Rights—again under revision in 1979–80—remains the official statement of ALA policy and belief on intellectual freedom and censorship.

The Intellectual Freedom Committee, founded in 1940, states and clarifies policy; the Office for Intellectual Freedom, established in December 1967, coordinates and conducts the ALA's activities related to intellectual freedom. It issues two regular publications, a bimonthly *Newsletter on Intellectual Freedom* and a monthly *OIF Memorandum* (the latter directed principally to state intellectual freedom committees). The *Newsletter* is the national medium that centralizes and publishes information on individual censorship cases, intellectual freedom achievements, and pertinent judicial decisions.

The so-called "legal arm" of the ALA-IFC (although neither legally nor officially a part of ALA) is the Freedom to Read Foundation (FTRF), established in 1969. Throughout its existence the FTRF (whose membership includes both librarians and nonlibrarians) has served as the means of providing funds to those involved in anti-censorship litigation and by direct or indirect (via amicus curiae briefs) involvement in freedom of the press or of speech litigation. R. Kathleen Molz said in her review of the first decade of the FTRF, "We . . . add the weight of our small but determined mallet in eroding punitive enactments that treat all of us as children."

The major non-library-related American organizations that fight for intellectual freedom are the American Civil Liberties Union, the Association of American Publishers, the National Education Association, the National Council of Teachers of English, and the American Association of University Professors. Through the years the ACLU has led nationally in this endeavor, although occasionally their efforts have resulted in disagreements within the organization.

The publicly supported library that develops and adheres to a written, explicit, and publicly known materials selection and public-room use policy (at the very minimum, in consonance with the Library Bill of Rights) has really very little to fear from censorship. The library's governing group—whether a board of trustees, school board, or college board—must, of course, also be aware of the basic importance of protecting the intellectual freedom of the institution.

**Key Issues in the 1970's.** Harriet F. Pilpel has described today's censorship as conveniently being subsumed under a handy acronym, RSVP (*R*eligion and *R*ace, *S*ex, *V*iolence, and *P*olitics). Of all these varieties of censorship, the most common, today or yesterday, is that based on hatred of "otherness," the desire to impose a narrow ethnic or religious view. The 1970's saw frequent attacks on school textbooks and library selections that differ from a local mind-set relative to "creationism" versus "evolutionism," or "values" education opposed to rote learning.

During the 1970's U.S. high school librarians were the principal objects of censorial attack; most of the court decisions favored the librarians. For example, in *Minarcini* v. *Strangsville City School District* (6th Cir., 1976), the verdict stated that a library is "a mighty resource in the free marketplace of ideas . . . specially dedicated to broad dissemination of ideas . . . a forum for silent speech."

In an eloquent decision in the case *Right to Read Defense Committee* v. *School Committee* (Mass., 1978), Judge Joseph Tauro ruled that "if this work may be removed by a committee hostile to its language and theme, then the precedent is set for removal of any other work. The prospect of successive school committees [equivalent to school boards in other jurisdictions] 'sanitizing' the school library of views divergent from their own is alarming, whether they do it book by book or one page at a time." He concluded, "The most effective antidote to the poison of mindless orthodoxy is ready access to a broad sweep of ideas and philosophies. There is no danger in such exposure. The danger is in mind control."

But in 1979 two conflicting decisions were delivered: in a Nashua, New Hampshire, case involving the removal of a feminist periodical, *Ms.*, from the school library, a U.S. District Court judge ruled that the school board "could not place conditions on the use of the library related solely to the social or political tastes of Board members"; in a New York case involving the Island Trees School Board's removal of certain books as "anti-American, anti-Christian, anti-Semitic and just plain filthy," the U.S. District Court judge ruled that such removal "fell within the broad range of discretion to educational officials who are elected by the community." The Island Trees case will eventually go to the U.S. Supreme Court for ultimate decision.

In 1820 a leading German librarian, Friedrich Adolph Ebert, wrote a little study on *The Training of the Librarian* that summarized very well what the librarian's attitude should be toward his obligations as book selector. Ebert said, "He must, while not oblivious to the phenomena of his time, never incline to servile one-sidedness nor obscure his judgment by yielding to tendencies and prejudices which are local and contemporary." If the librarian follows this high standard, it seems very likely that Ebert's prediction—that he would then be classed as one "who desires to work for posterity . . . [and] stand above his contemporaries"—will come true.

During the rest of this century the most likely library technology and systems developments—networking, automation, and miniaturization—all will have implications for intellectual freedom. As always, the library will be affected by *whatever* societal changes develop (in the struggle for individual privacy, for example). But the library will fulfill its unique and vital obligations to society only if it adheres to the basic principles of intellectual freedom.

**REFERENCES**

Lester Asheim, "Not Censorship but Selection," *Wilson Library Bulletin* (1953).

LeRoy Charles Merritt, *Book Selection and Intellectual Freedom* (1970).

Eli M. Oboler, *Defending Intellectual Freedom: The Librarian and the Censor* (1980).

ELI M. OBOLER

# Central African Republic

The Central African Republic, a former territory of French Equatorial Africa, is bounded by Chad on the north, the Sudan on the east, the Congo and Zaire on the south, and Cameroon on the west. Pop. (1978 est.) about 2,000,000; area 622,000 sq.km. The official language is French. The national language is Sango.

**National Library.** The Central African Republic did not have a National Library as of the end of the 1970's, but plans were under way to create one. A Public Library, upon completion, was to serve as a national library.

**University Library.** The University of Bangui, the only university in the country, comprises four schools and five institutes, one of which is in M'baïki (107 kilometers southwest of Bangui). The University Library (24,000 volumes) did not have a building to house its collection in 1979. The library is divided into five smaller libraries for the School of Law and Economics, the School of Arts and Human Sciences, the School of Sciences, the School of Health Science, and the University Institute of Agricultural Technology of M'baïki. A new building was projected that would hold 100 places for the 1,000 students enrolled at the University of Bangui.

**Public Library.** Public libraries existed only in an embryonic stage of development, but they offered the principal library service available in the country. In Bangui the library of the French Cultural Center, with 12,000 volumes, began operation in 1966. The library of the American Cultural Center, which consisted of only 1,000 books in 1979, closed its library in 1972 and gave its funds to the University of Bangui and to the secondary schools; it was reopened in February 1979.

Libraries of Youth Centers, found in the highly populated areas of Bangui, are supported by the Ministry of

National Education, Youth, Sports, Arts, Culture, and Scientific Research with the help of the French and American Cultural Centers. At the provincial level are libraries of Youth Centers in 16 chief residences of the prefectures of the country. They are funded by the Ministry of National Education, Youth, Sports, Arts, Culture, and Scientific Research, the American and French Cultural Centers, and the municipalities they serve. Libraries are also maintained by evangelical missions.

**School Libraries.** School Libraries, poorly developed in the Central African Republic, are limited in service to the distribution of school books to students. Two training centers in Bangui offer libraries with a reading room—the National School of Administration and Magistracy with 9,000 volumes and the School of Education for Primary and Higher Education, which in 1979 was in the process of becoming a university institute. Certain high schools of Bangui and the provinces began to establish small reading rooms for their students.

**Special Libraries.** Bangui, the seat of several international organizations, houses libraries of the African and Mauritian Communal Organization (OCAM) and the Customs and Economic Union of Central Africa (UDEAC). The Supreme Court also has quite a library at its disposal. Research institutes offer documentation services.

**Associations.** There was no library association in 1979. Two Central Africans with degrees in library science worked at the University of Bangui; teachers served as librarians in the high schools. Few graduate librarians and archivists were available.

ALAIN-MICHEL POUTOU



## Certification of Librarians

One of the major characteristics of any profession is the concern exhibited by its members for the quality of the services provided its clientele. This responsibility for the work of the profession is exhibited in every field by the setting of standards of quality for those practicing in the field and by the establishment of some means by which those entering it can be measured. Several types of credentialling have been developed to fulfill this responsibility.

Educational credentials may take the form of accreditation, whereby a governmental or other specially constituted agency recognizes the ability of an educational institution or program to satisfy certain criteria. In this way quality of the educational preparation is equated with a measure of the quality of the services that can be rendered by the profession. In some professions practitioners are required to obtain a license that legally certifies that they may practice, thus making it illegal for anyone not so licensed to practice that profession.

The third method is certification. Certification has been defined by the Organization for Economic Cooperation and Development as "a process or act by which individuals are awarded educational credentials after successfully fulfilling a set of prescribed requirements at a certain educational level," attesting to the fact that those "individuals have acquired a minimum set of qualifications for pursuing a particular occupation or profession."

Certification requirements have been adopted in the United States and many other countries for those entering such professions as public school teaching, medicine, accounting, law, social work, nursing, as well as librarianship. In each the specification of certain formal educational requirements and entry level qualifications certifies to the public that the persons have attained a certain accepted code of behavior, a recognizable level of knowledge and job responsibility, and standards of acceptable service performance within that profession. Certification should guarantee to "society an adequate supply of practitioners who are, and who remain available at reasonable cost, competent to carry out a certain range of tasks."

Certification provides employers with objective selection criteria by which to identify those with minimal qualification for the professional positions to be filled and thus allows for less biased and less disciminatory hiring. It provides a clear path toward employment in the profession and protects the professional from competition by the substandard or unqualified person. The professional therefore can have a reasonable sense of job security.

Certification in the field of librarianship generally has been applied to the school library media field, public libraries, and some selected special library areas, with few applications to academic libraries. Requirements for certification are the results of the efforts of librarians working through their professional associations and in cooperation with other agencies, and it is the librarians and their associations who monitor the process, revise, and redesign it.

Certification of librarians may be mandated by state law, may be permitted by state law but not required, or may be a voluntary plan executed by a professional organization or agency. As a general rule certification of school library media personnel is required by law; public librarians' certification may be required, permitted, or voluntary, while special librarians are certified through voluntary professional activity.

**School Librarians/Media Specialists.** School librarians, as a part of the teaching personnel of a school system, are certified first as teachers, with library or media certification as an added special competency endorsement. Thus they share the long established tradition of teacher certification with its legislative authorization carried out through rules and regulations specified by the departments of education in each state. Mandatory certification for libraries, as for teachers, is now accepted in every state in the United States, although the specific requirements vary widely from state to state.

The names or titles of the certificates awarded those performing the library functions in the school systems varies. While some states have retained the "Teacher-Librarian" and "School Librarian" certificates, others have such titles as: Librarian/Media Specialist, Educational Media Specialist, Career Library Media Specialist, Education Media Generalist, Media Professional and Media Specialist, School Media Specialist (Library) and School Media Specialist (Educational Communications), Library Specialist and Audiovisual Specialist, and Learning Resources Specialist. Despite this variety of titles, the trend is to have one track for those who manage the library/media center, as evidenced by the decreasing number of states with both library and audiovisual certification positions.

As varied as the titles of the certificated positions are the requirements in credit hours and in courses and competencies. Credit hours range from 6 quarter hours to 60 quarter hours, with 18–27 hours as average for the first or minimal certification for grades K through 12. Only six states retained separate certification for Elementary Librarians and Secondary Librarians, and most states recognize the need for the same quality and quantity of educational preparation for both levels. As certification requirements are revised, the trend is to require more hours of preparation, with the Master's degree becoming common as the necessary credential.

The knowledge and skills specified as requirements for certification, although varied, generally encompass administration, cataloguing and classification, production and design of media, reference, selection, and evaluation of resources for children and youth. Field work or a practicum is a frequent added requirement. In about one-fifth of the states the competency concept is being used as a certification requirement, although there seems to be no pattern or generally accepted mode for acting on competency-based credentials. Consistent with the requirements for teacher recertification, library/media personnel must renew their certificates with evidence of continuing education participation during a specified period of time.

The American Association of School Librarians, a division of the American Library Association, has led school media personnel in a study of certification trends and practices toward the goal of producing a certification model to be used as guidelines for those planning state certification design, assessing candidates for certification, and identifying areas of competencies for certification. This much-discussed model was issued in 1976 and is providing guidance to those working in this active area.

**Public Librarians.** Certification of public librarians in the U.S. can be traced back to a 1911 California law requiring certification of the head librarian of county libraries and to a similar requirement for county librarians in Texas in 1919. Since that time some form of certification for some classes of librarians has been adopted by some 33 states. Certification plans may be voluntary under sponsorship of the state library association and generally administered by the association; they may be permissive, that is, specified by law but not made compulsory; or they may be mandatory with certification required by state law.

Most of the mandatory and permissive certification legislation is similar in requiring evidence of a four-year college degree and a degree from a library school whose program is accredited by the American Library Association. The right to present equivalencies for these two educational requirements is provided for in the law or regulations of most states but is exercised relatively few times. Equivalent education for those coming from an educational system outside the United States may be assessed under the "exception clause" through analysis of personal records. Those candidates from nonaccredited programs or from a variety of work/study combinations may have the opportunity in some states to take an examination covering the content of the credited equivalency.

The certification requirement may be applied selectively to certain positions or generally to all professionals. Some states include professional staffs of all public libraries serving a population above some set figure; others certify chief librarians only in any library supported in part or in whole by public funds; and others apply certification to heads of county libraries only. County law librarians are generally exempt in all states, while individual states may identify unique exemptions.

Within each state types of certification may range from temporary to provisional to professional graduate or may be categorized under lettered or numbered series depending upon education and experience. Within an atmosphere of rediscussion, review, and revision, the trend is toward eliminating provisional categories and raising certification standards.

**Special Certifications.** Medical librarianship has led the way toward special certification in a library specialty. As early as 1948 the Medical Library Association adopted a Code of Training and Certification of Medical Librarians, based upon models in existence in the medical and health professions. This voluntary certification, developed and implemented by the professional association itself rather than by an outside authority, provided for three grades or levels of certification in a system whose goal was to aid in improving medical librarianship through basic standards for education and training and by certifying qualified librarians.

Grade I required a fifth-year library degree from an ALA-accredited school with a course in medical librarianship approved by the Medical Library Association. For

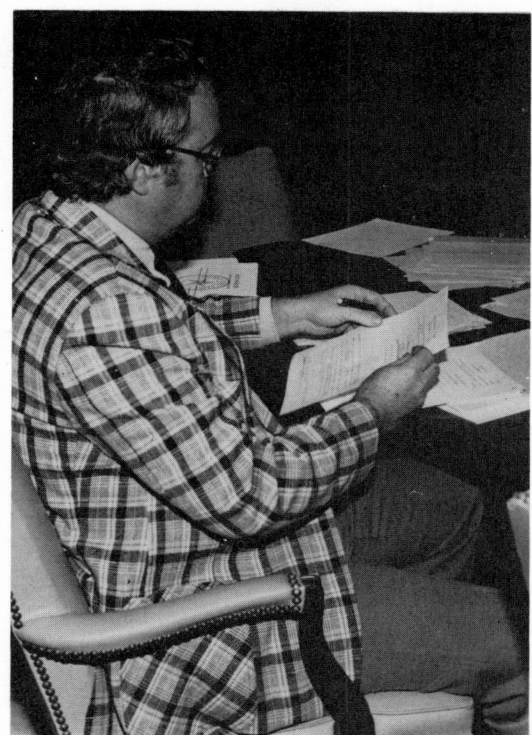

Texas State Library

*Harold Billings examines documents submitted by applicants for County Librarian Certificates. As director of General Libraries at the University of Texas at Austin, he is ex-officio secretary of the Texas Board of County Library Examiners.*

Grade II the candidate took an internship in a medical library approved for this type of training capability. Hampered by the limited number of opportunities for interns that the medical library field could accommodate in any year, the Association revised the requirements for this grade by substituting a Master's degree in an appropriate subject field coupled with one year of experience in a medical library. Grade III required participation in a two-year program of advanced study in library science and medicine leading to a degree. Two revisions to the qualifications for this grade expanded the education to a doctorate in librarianship or in any appropriate subject field while retaining the five years of experience in a medical library. This code, with revisions, remained in effect from 1949 to 1977, certifying over 3,200 individuals on a voluntary basis.

During the last years of the Code, members of the Medical Library Association developed a new code to add to the basic requirements of education and experience, a competency-based examination for all and a provision for recertification at the end of every five years. Adopted in 1974, the new Code was implemented in 1978 when the first examinations were given.

The American Association of Law Libraries adopted a voluntary plan to certify law librarians who are members of the Association and who have fulfilled the educational and experiential requirements it has set forth. Category I requires a graduate degree in Library Science from an ALA-accredited program and an accredited law degree or admission to the Bar and two years of professional library experience, one-half of which must be in a law library. This represents the preferred certification standard for all law librarians and the goal of the Association as the necessary preparation for the practicing professional. Category II specifies a law degree from an approved law school or admission to the Bar and four years of library experience, while Category III requires a graduate library degree and from six to ten years of professional library experience depending upon the accreditation status of the degree program. As a type of "grandfather clause," Category IV provides for certification after 20 years of responsible professional law library experience and outstanding contribution to the profession.

Other special library professionals may have or may be developing special voluntary certification plans.

**Other Countries.** Outside North America similar criteria are applied in those countries where formal certification of librarians is found. The completion of certain courses or of a prescribed study and training program, successful performance on examinations, and a period of work experience or internship are criteria that may be used in formulating certification requirements. In some countries certification is mandatory for professional-level employment. Various grades of certification, reflecting graduated requirements for education, experience, or examination, may determine the level at which librarians are employed.

Administration of certification also varies, with the responsibility held by professional associations, governmental agencies, or academic bodies. In Great Britain, for example, the Library Association has administered standards for training and certification of librarians, but this pattern is currently under revision.

**Trends.** Trends in certification for librarianship as in other professions point toward the gradual elimination of alternative, nonformal paths to entry into the field of practice. Substitution of experience for education is being eliminated, and certification through formal graduate education is becoming the common rule. Certification for life is being reexamined, with the alternative of a renewable certificate that would include a continuing education component gaining a growing number of advocates.

MARGARET KNOX GOGGIN



# Chad

Chad, a republic in central western Africa, is bordered by Libya on the north, Sudan on the east, the Central African Republic on the south, and Cameroon, Nigeria, and Niger on the west. Pop. (1978 est.) 4,285,000; area 1,284,000 sq.km. The official language is French.

**Academic Libraries.** The library of the University of Chad, in N'Djaména, was founded with the university itself in 1971 and consists of three collections: the central university library with just over 9,000 volumes; the library of the Institut universitaire des Sciences, in Farcha, which offers some 1,500 volumes relating to the physical and biological sciences, and the collection of the Institut universitaire des Techniques de l'Elevage with its 500 volumes and 20 periodicals.

**Public Libraries.** While there is no centralized and uniform system of public libraries, most of the major towns have at least one library, falling within one of several classifications. Cultural Centers are in Abéché, Am Timan, Ati, Biltine, Doba, Fianga, and Oum Hadjer. Mission libraries with general collections number about 30 throughout the country. Five other larger libraries are particularly noteworthy: the Municipal Library of Sarh, the library established by the Alliance Française in Moundou, the American Cultural Center (a bilingual collection in English and French), the Libyan Cultural Center (Arabic), and the French Cultural Center (the largest collection in Chad—some 24,847 volumes in 1975 with a lending rate of 8,000 per month) in the capital. The French Cultural Center also offers a film collection.

**Table 2. Archives in Chad (1976)**

| | |
|---|---|
| Number | 1 (one) |
| Holdings | 250 cubic meters |

Source: C. Gut, *Creation d'un service national d'archives: décembre 1972–févvier 1973,* Unesco (Paris, 1973).

**Special Libraries.** The Institut National pour les Sciences Humaines, primarily a research institution, was founded in 1961 and has a library of some 3,000 volumes and 3,000 documents relating to Chadian ethnology, archaeology, geography, history, and linguistics. A similar range of subject matter is covered in the collection of the Bibliothèque Afrique et Tchad of the Archdiocese of N'Djaména.

Materials on problems of development are housed in the library of the Centre d'Etude et de Formation pour le Développement (CEFOD). The Centre de Documentation Pédagogique, founded in 1962, offers materials on education in French and Arabic. Other small library collections are those of the Institut d'Elévage et de Médecine Vétérinaire du Pays Tropicaux (in Farcha), the Central Hospital, and the Chadian branch of the Office de la Recherche Scientifique et Technique Outre-Mer (ORSTOM).

NEIL McHUGH

# Chavez Campomanes, Maria Teresa

(1890– )

Mexican library educator Maria Teresa Chavez contributed significantly to the education of Mexican librarians, the improvement of teaching methods, and steps toward the goal of making libraries an extension of the classroom.

Born in Puebla de los Ángeles, Mexico, on August 1, 1890, Maria Teresa Chavez studied at the School for Librarians in Mexico City under the direction of Emilio Baz, and she traveled to the United States for further study, eventually graduating from Pratt Institute; she did postgraduate work in library science in Detroit and at Columbia. Later she was employed in the New York Public Library and the Library of Congress in Washington.

Upon her return from the U.S., she continued to

**Table 1. Libraries in Chad (1976)**

| Type | Number | Volumes in collections | Annual expenditures (franc) | Population served | Professional staff | All staff (total) |
|---|---|---|---|---|---|---|
| National | N.A. | N.A. | N.A. | N.A. | N.A. | N.A. |
| Academic | 1 | 11,000 | N.A. | 655 | N.A. | N.A. |
| Public | c. 42 | N.A. | N.A. | c. 400,000 | N.A. | N.A. |
| School | N.A. | N.A. | N.A. | N.A. | N.A. | N.A. |
| Special | c. 7 | N.A. | N.A. | c. 250,000 | N.A. | N.A. |

Sources: France, Service des Etudes et Questions Internationales, *Tchad: Donneés Statistiques* (Paris, 1976); *The World of Learning 1976–1977.*

Maria Teresa Chavez Campomanes

Mexican Library Association

study Spanish literature in the Faculty of Philosophy and Letters of the National University. She received the degree of Doctor of Literature in 1953 with a thesis on books that became a classic. She was Director of the Franklin Library and Subdirector (later Director) of the Library of Mexico from its establishment under José Vasconcelos, a philosopher. The progress of that library was due in great measure to her perseverance, and she became one of the few to serve the body of youth of the metropolis with vigor and efficiency.

She came to be regarded as the very foundation of teaching at the National School of Archivists and Librarians of the Secretariat of Education and a similar school of the Faculty of Philosophy and Letters of the National University. The great majority of Mexican librarians learned at her side, gaining as much from her teaching as from the effective manuals of classification and cataloguing that she wrote. As a teacher, she was a model of clarity and patience. She was named Teacher Emeritus of the Secretariat of Education and won wide respect as one of the most distinguished women of Mexico.

ERNESTO DE LA TORRE VILLAR

## Children's Services

Children in many countries throughout the world are served by two major library systems: one in the schools and one designated as public—whether administered and housed separately from the public library system for adults or as an integral physical part of the system. The two systems usually complement each other philosophically, and collections in the two systems will usually overlap. Unique mission statements, however, shape the differences in services, collection development, programming, and access. The school library, now often called the school media center in some Western countries, ideally serves the child's initial instructional and basic curricular needs for learning materials, while the public library seeks to serve the child's broader and highly individualized need for materials to serve educational, recreational, and personal developmental needs.

**History.** The history of library service to children differs in each country of the world. The need to provide books to support a rising rate of literacy, the desire to enhance the social and intellectual welfare of the children, and the demands of the children themselves, however, all have broad universal bases in the history of library service to children. In the United States, for instance, library service to children is little more than 100 years old. Philanthropic, educational, and religious efforts in the 19th century resulted in the establishment of social libraries, mercantile and apprentice libraries, Sunday school libraries, and short-lived efforts in several states to establish school district libraries to provide books for both children and adults. These libraries were not necessarily the forerunners of library services for children but were important in that they provided reading materials. They also alerted champions of the young, who were concerned for the social welfare of children, that tax-supported, organized library facilities and services were essential for children as well as for adults.

The earliest public libraries in the United States served children by placing collections in the schools. By 1891 Samuel S. Green could affirm "that almost all public libraries are trying in one way and another to be of assistance to schools." The early cooperation was mostly with the grammar school (grades 7–9) and the high school, so younger children were left out. Teachers usually were issued a special card for the borrowing of a specified number of books for a specified loan period, after which time books could usually be exchanged. Collections were kept in individual classrooms or housed in a central location to which children came by class at appointed times to check out books.

Slowly, however, public libraries began providing facilities for the children. Champions within the libraries began to speak out for children's needs and rights to books. Gradually, seating space was provided; small collections of specially selected materials were made available; and attempts to provide programs, clubs, and other programming activities were successful in attracting the attention of children.

The first half of the 20th century in the United States saw children's work in public libraries develop as a vital and important part of total library operation and service. Children's work was established on a departmental basis in most libraries of any size and was becoming a part of branch library service as well. Criteria were being developed to evaluate children's literature, and the identification and production of bibliographical aids were established as a responsibility of children's librarians. Individual methods of reading guidance were being developed and described in the literature by a growing, talented, and dedicated new generation of children's librarians. An important signal to the future lay in the efforts by forward-looking librarians to develop relationships with community agencies interested in the education, social welfare, and guidance of youth.

Libraries serving children in elementary schools were not to develop in substantial numbers in the United States until the 1960's. The substantial increase in numbers that did occur was a result mainly of tremendous national efforts made by professional organizations and community

Children's library, with its own separate entrance, attached to Japan's Osaka Municipal Library.

Theodore F. Welch

groups, and an outpouring of federal funds aimed at providing better educational opportunities for the so-called educationally disadvantaged and at increasing the quantities of materials available to all children. Prior to the 1960's public libraries in many communities were providing major book service to schools through liberal check-out privileges for teachers, revolving school collections, and bookmobile stops at or very close to schools. That decade saw also the end of many of these relationships as the school library became philosophically and financially stronger. The pendulum swings, and the late 1970's, with its changing economic conditions, saw a redefinition and reshaping of patterns of library service to children.

The development of children's services in other countries has been uneven for many reasons. In the Netherlands the idea of a special library for children is relatively new. The first real children's library was opened in Amsterdam in 1912; prior to this, books were being collected and loaned to children through small libraries attached to schools and churches. Children's departments in public libraries are now commonly found throughout the country. In both East and West Germany efforts are being made at all levels of government to improve library service. Aftering being disrupted by war and suffering wholesale destruction of materials, both countries have made serious commitments to public library service to children.

Independent children's libraries began to be developed in the U.S.S.R. early in the 20th century. Government statistics report 8,000 independent libraries for children under the Ministry of Culture and 156,000 school libraries under the Ministry of Education. Once independent administratively as well as physically, children's libraries are now as a rule integrated administratively into general networks or systems of public libraries. Children's library needs are also served through organized programs in Pioneer Palaces, trade union libraries, and libraries in state nurseries and kindergartens.

In the Far Eastern countries, library service to children has developed very slowly, and little has appeared in English about library development in these countries. In Japan, for instance, statistics published in 1978 report only 1,133 public libraries. However, children's service has been developing as a very active part of public library service throughout the country. One alternative to public library service to children is the home library movement. Started in 1958 by Momoko Ishi, author-translator of children's books, the idea has spread widely in reaction to the slow pace of development of public service.

**Library Services to Children.** Traditional library services to children are based on the provision and use of a special collection of books. The basic collection will include quantities of picture books, classics, modern favorites, folk and fairy tales, and informational books for the general use of the hobbyist, the interested, or the child needing material for a school assignment. Using this collection, librarians have served children through story-hour programs and other reading guidance activities for both parents and children. They have provided school-related services by helping with reference questions, teaching students how to use the library and its resources, and assisting children in locating needed information in adult departments or other agencies. Children are voracious users of information, and for many of them the children's department is but a beginning point in their search.

Recently newer services have begun to be described widely in the literature. Preschool and early-early childhood programs (one's and two's) that have been popular in libraries of all sizes need toys, realia, and games for their success. Craft and hobby programs, audiovisual programs, drama, music, dance materials, resource speakers, and participatory activities, meeting places for children who have no other place to meet after school, literacy development activities, special services for the handicapped, bilingual, multiethnic, and multicultural collections and programming, and programming for adults (discussed later in this article) are typical of the variety of services offered through children's departments.

**Programming for Children.** It is through programming that services are implemented. Margaret Kimmel states the rationale for library programming for children this way: "If children's service goes beyond housing materials, if indeed, it is to provide an opportunity for an individual child to go beyond what he thinks he wants to what he might want, stimulating, effective programs should be developed as a basic part of a library's service. And the program must be regularly evaluated and revised, because the program itself is a service, not an end." Amy Kellman gives three reasons for doing programs: (1) because they give the library visibility; (2) because they stimulate the use of materials in the library; and

> (3) the third reason . . . defies evaluation; if this is romantic, unscientific and unbusinesslike, so be it. Librarians do not know if the dancer brought in to move and talk to children in the intimate and comfortable setting of the library will touch the individual child or not. They do know that they are providing an experience the child might not have had otherwise. Expanding a child's world contributes positively to the quality of his or her life. It may be years before the impact of that program is felt. However, there is enough testimonial literature from successful adults about the effects of seeing an artist, hearing someone speak or reading a book as a young child to know that such programming is worth pursuing.

Indeed, children's work in public libraries is not based on a body of serious research. Circulation statistics consistently indicate that children's borrowing accounts for the lion's share of circulation in many libraries. This fact, added to experience with children's attendance and performance at programs, the enthusiasm of parents, faith in the efficacy of establishing sound patterns in reading, social education, and the like, has formed the basis for the belief of children's librarians that their work on the behalf of children is of value.

The competence and the creativity of the librarian shape library services to children, but when considering programming and related activities specifically, one soon recognizes that budget, space, and availability of resources and type of community must also be taken into consideration. Availability of total resources is linked to size of community, so a general review of kinds of programs and opportunities by size of library will provide a brief look at the programming aspect of library service to children.

**Services in Small Public Libraries.** Experts differ on what characterizes a small public library. Elizabeth Gross's 1963 study *Children's Services in Public Libraries* defined small libraries as those serving populations under 35,000. Bridget Lamont has defined them as serving fewer than 20,000 or even 10,000. In describing programming services to children in these smallest of public libraries, Lamont notes that there are several ways these services are provided: "(1) by a professionally trained children's librarian with para-professional or clerical support staff; (2) by a professionally trained librarian who is the library director and works in every service area as needed, but who delegates certain tasks to para-professional staff members on a daily basis; or more commonly (3) by a librarian who is not professionally trained and who works in all areas." Programming in the smallest of libraries relies on the traditional services of the public library: story hours, films, puppet shows, and summer reading clubs.

While programming is often uneven in quality and quantity in these smallest of libraries, standards of excellence can be attained. Improved consultant service, system development, and the increasing availability of qualified staff and volunteers in small communities, as huge urban areas lose their attractiveness in highly developed countries, all may have favorable impact on service and programming for children in small communities.

**Medium-Sized Public Libraries.** The medium-sized public library has been defined as one serving a population of between 25,000 and 150,000. In this library, still small by sprawling urban standards, children still can have access to a total library collection relatively unimpeded by bureaucracy and spatial relationships. Medium-sized libraries will have at least one children's librarian who has completed some professional preparation through either formal course work or continuing education activities. With the attention of increased professional staff, more specialized programs in depth and variety can be provided to a broader audience. Programs in the park, storytelling festivals, cooking classes, filmmaking, dinner theater, and hobby clubs can be planned. The variety is endless.

It is in the medium-sized library that we can begin to see libraries working with other agencies interested in the social welfare of children. Capitalizing on the availability of professional children's librarians, public libraries can be seen working with schools, museums, arts and special interests groups, institutionalized children, and recreational agencies.

**Large Public Libraries.** The potential and challenges of library service to children increase as the size of library systems increases. Sheer numbers of children to be served, new audiences for the library represented in changing populations, the variety of ethnic groups residing in large metropolitan areas, and the problems of communicating the availability of services all place pressures on program planning. Serving the nonuser in the emphasis on community outreach has brought increased pressure to expand the programming that has always existed in agencies and locations outside the physical walls of the library. The development of the school library in the 1960's in the United States, for example, resulted in new programming and a special emphasis on serving the youngest child who had no instant access to materials and facilities in a school facility. Service to special children, the poor, the bilingual, the educationally disadvantaged, has assumed new dimensions in urban areas and has tested the creative mettle of many urban children's librarians. The results of these efforts are seen in a growing collection of bibliographies of bilingual materials, literacy programs, programs to promote intercultural understanding and general expansion of the recognition by children's librarians of the informational and esthetic potential of audiovisual resources.

Similar programming can be found throughout the world. Collections of materials in the children's rooms contain material similar to American collections: picture books, easy readers, fiction, nonfiction, books of folk and fairy tales, and other imaginative literature. Many favorite books of U.S. children can be found in translation in these collections. In Japan's Mother's and Children's rooms, many special activities are provided. Musical evenings, children's library helpers clubs, storytelling, and talks to parents about children's books are available. In the Netherlands outreach to children, especially the disadvantaged and those with reading problems, is now a focal point.

In the two Germanies also, children's programming will include story hours, displays, book talks, readers' advisory services, and instruction in library use. Special weeks, like Children's Book Week in the U.S., are also observed. In East Germany there is Soviet Book Week. In the U.S.S.R. one of the notable library events in all Soviet children's libraries is the annual Week of Children's Books held during the spring vacation. The week is full of activities planned to make reading attractive to children, to bring authors and children together, and to call attention of the general public to the problems and concerns related to children's reading and the activities and programs available in libraries. Book exhibits, discussions, conferences, literary matinees and evenings, meetings with writers and journalists, meetings with artists, excursions to printing shops, and showing of films round out a week that concludes with a big festival of books.

In many countries one can find special centers, institutes, or study groups for the study and dissemination of information about children's literature and library service. The Center of Children's Literature in East Germany, the Study Group for Children's and Juvenile Literature in West Germany, and the Study-Centre for Children's Libraries in the Netherlands are examples of such study centers.

**Children's Library Personnel.** Traditionally, the hallmarks of good professional children's librarians have been the same: respect for children, knowledge of their growth and developmental characteristics, and competence in applying their knowledge of their chosen profession. Professional literature the world over indicates that children's librarians have taken these requirements seriously. In countries with larger numbers of children's librarians, programming has been creative and highly developed. Children's librarians everywhere have accepted their responsibility to know materials, especially literature for children.

However, children's library leaders have begun to define more carefully the role and function of the professionally educated children's specialist in the increasingly complex library establishment in which children's services are provided. The contemporary children's librarian must be prepared to work in a world of management-by-objectives, budgets, computers, staff development, and decision-making processes. The contemporary children's librarian must be intimately concerned with all aspects of the school or total library operation for every other department in the organization, governance decision, or major change in environment, economics, or public attitude impacts library service to children. So, in addition to children's literature and storytelling, would-be children's librarians are urged to expand their knowledge of the fields of management and administration, information science, and the application of technology to library organization and to the collection, storage, retrieval, and dissemination of information. They are urged to demonstrate competence in budgeting, program evaluation, and the application of sound principles of management and decision making.

Children's librarians are further urged to become more alert to the needs of special children: the handicapped, the gifted, the educationally disadvantaged, and the reluctant readers.

In a 21st-century library world dominated by technology and a multiplicity of information systems and networks, we may see a marked relationship between the survival of basic children's services and the ability of the children's librarian to talk in terms of community goals and objectives, statistics, research, and the effect of materials on human development.

Subsequently, increasing responsibility for management, budget decisions, and program evaluation, coupled with a shortage of professionally educated staff, for whatever reason, will spur reanalysis of position descriptions for children's services. In libraries where this analysis has already taken place, paraprofessionals are emerging as an important part of the staffing of many programming activities. Consideration and examination of the roles and functions of the professional librarian, the generalist, and the paraprofessional will occur more often in the future in children's library services.

**Materials Collections.** Earlier an overview was provided of the types of print material needed in a children's collection. Added to this are appropriate reference materials, periodicals, and a range of audiovisual materials including audio and video recordings, filmstrips, and film. The children's collection is a highly specialized one, but the children's librarians who build that collection work with the same kinds of problems and decisions that face selectors of materials for adults.

For instance, the oft-discussed information explosion has not bypassed materials for children. In the 1960's and '70's librarians have been inundated with an almost overwhelming abundance of material. There are a variety of reasons for the explosion of publishing for children. The increased availability of funds is a major reason; federal funding for schools and public libraries in the United States encouraged publishers and producers to accelerate the numbers of book titles published. Federal, state, and local emphasis on the teaching of reading in the schools and on appropriately designed programs for the teaching of the educationally disadvantaged, the provision of bilingual materials, and the changes in curriculum for children with special learning, physical, and mental needs have all had a tremendous impact on the types and quantities of materials for children. Strong interest in the education of young children has provided complete new ranges and types of materials for library collections to house. Liberal viewpoints of what can and should be published for children, rapidly expanding school curricula, and emphasis on individualized learning have also contributed to the increased responsibility of the librarian in collection development. Of no less importance is the ongoing dialogue among librarians themselves about the role of the library in providing mostly books of highest quality, as opposed to providing a wide range of books that meet a wide range of abilities, motivation, and interest in the children who want to read.

Added to the difficulties of building a print collection is the proliferation of problems caused by the variety of audiovisual formats now available to collection developers. Children's librarians in public libraries have not been as quick as their colleagues in the schools to add audiovisual media to their collections. However, the availability of varieties of formats and of quality presentations are finally being recognized by many children's librarians in public libraries as important considerations in the unprecedented growth of fine materials for children. As they and other forward-thinking librarians grow more comfortable in evaluating and selecting audiovisual media for children and in using the necessary hardware, these collections will expand. More important, as these librarians learn more about how children learn, especially young and educationally disadvantaged children, and as they observe the preferences of individual children for individual media depending on what they need or want from the media, collections will expand in quality.

*Children watch chicks hatch at Woodson Regional Library, Chicago, part of a farm study project planned with the assistance of the University of Illinois 4-H Cooperative Extension Service.*

Phil Moloitis

**Trends and Issues.** As indicated earlier, public library service to children has not been an area of rigorous research. School librarians can point to a growing body of research in that field and in related areas of education, learning theory, and psychology to support the development of media programs and the importance of a librarian to the instructional program. Much of this research is applicable or useful to the work of the public children's librarian, but there have been few attempts to use it, build on it, or conduct research related to public library service patterns and the role of the children's specialist. In the United States far more research has been completed in the area of materials than in any other aspect of library work with children. One study of research in children's services found only 14 studies on public libraries published from 1960 through fall 1972; another shows that in approximately the same period of time, ten times that number of studies were published on subjects related to materials. This imbalance should shift as the demands for programs and services based on data become more pronounced and as children's librarians learn to collect, analyze, and interpret data. Staff development programs organized to teach research techniques, more doctoral dissertations, more children's specialists on library education faculties, and increased leadership by professional associations will help develop a more positive attitude toward the necessity of developing a body of research data.

Cooperation between school and public libraries serving children is both an issue of debate and a current trend. No one disputes the need, in a world of shrinking resources, for intense cooperative efforts among agencies that serve the same individual with related services. Electronic communication media will solve some problems, as networking patterns develop, but librarians serving youth will be forced politically and economically to share information about their patrons and about their programs. Sharing of resources, facilities, and staff competencies will probably follow as concern for the user overrides fear of loss of autonomy and territory.

Several trends in book publishing for children will continue to develop as serious issues for children's librarians and to have adverse effects on materials services. Rising costs, new formats, and the growing emphasis on paperbacks is one set of factors that children's librarians must deal with. Rising production costs, especially of picture books, will surely diminish the flood of new titles. Paperbacks may take up the slack in some areas of the collection but do not provide the total answer. For instance, an issue of great concern in the late 1970's relates to the increasing unavailability of desired materials. Standards and "old favorite" titles are disappearing from publishers' in-print stocks. Costs of warehousing, the need for subsidiary sales, and the cost of the luxury of allowing a book to win a child audience are playing havoc with collection development in many libraries. Continued elusiveness of a system of bibliographic control that works equally well for a wide variety of media plagues children's librarians.

Library Association

Mime time in the weekly story period, Shard End Library, Birmingham, England.

Detroit Public Library

*Sculptor Samuel Cashwan's "Tom Thumb Relates His Adventures" decorates the Children's Library of the Detroit Public Library.*

A trend toward providing services and programs for adults is apparent in children's departments. The adults using children's services include parents, teachers and workers at early childhood education centers, college students, and various professional workers from community agencies and service organizations. Artists, dramatists, writers and producers of other media, and adults seeking beginning-level information on a subject help make up a large group of adults who turn to the children's collection and to the expertise of the children's librarian for materials and reference service. Specialized collections on parenting programs, on children's books and reading, and on other topics related to child growth, development, and education are becoming part of programming in many children's departments.

Last, but not least, is the issue of access to information by children. Advocates of children's rights identify several issues related to access. The successful efforts of special-interest groups to bring pressure on school boards, administrators, and school librarians are of concern. Of no less concern is what has been styled the self-censorship by librarians and that has been documented repeatedly. The result of severe budget cutting in communities where there are no working plans for resource sharing is an adverse effect on children's access to materials. A recent study by a committee of ALA's Association of Library Service to Children reveals that discriminatory interpretation of the Interlibrary Loan Code is often used against the young and may be used against adult scholars seeking children's materials. Restrictive age rules for use of the adult department will deter many children from easy access. As noted earlier, children are voracious users of information, and for many of them the children's department or the elementary school library media center is but the beginning in their search for materials.

**REFERENCES**

Joan Foster, editor, *Reader in Children's Librarianship* (1978).

Amy Kellman, "Services of Medium Sized Public Libraries," in Selma K. Richardson, editor, *Children's Services of Public Libraries* (1978).

Margaret M. Kimmell, "Library—Program—Storehouse?" *Top of the News* (1975).

Bridget L. Lamont, "Services of Small Public Libraries," in Richardson, *Children's Services.*

Harriet G. Long, *Public Library Service to Children: Foundation and Development* (1969).

MARILYN L. MILLER

## Chile

Chile is on the southern Pacific coast of South America. Comprising about 750,000 sq.km. in its continential zone and claiming 1,250,000 sq.km. in Antarctica, it is bounded by Peru, Bolivia, and Argentina. Pop. (1978 est.) 10,847,600. The inhabitants are distributed chiefly in the 4,270 km. of long and narrow borderland between the Andes Mountains and the Pacific Ocean. About one-third of the population live in the capital city, Santiago.

**National Library.** This library was founded on August 19, 1813, during the first years of Chile's independence; its basic collection consisted of 8,000 volumes that belonged to the ancient colonial library of the Jesuits and had been preserved in the University of San Felipe until they were transferred to the National Library. Ten years later its holdings had increased to 12,000 volumes. By 1978 its collection totaled some 1,800,000 volumes. One of the most important sources for increasing the collection has been legal deposit, established in 1825. In that year a decree obliged the printers to place in the National Library one copy of any book or pamphlet printed in Santiago. Legal deposit is fulfilled by delivery of 15 copies to the National Library by the publishing companies of Chile.

The National Library has been distinguished for its outstanding collection of Chilean literature. In the late 1970's it continued as a center for legal deposit and the international exchange of publications. It publishes the *Yearbook of the Chilean Press (Anuario de la prensa chilena)*, which started in 1877 and is the most important national bibliography.

**Academic Libraries.** There are eight universities: three in Santiago—University of Chile, Catholic University of Chile, and State Technical University; two in Valparaiso—Federico Santa María Technical University and Catholic University of Valparaíso; one in Antofagasta—Northern University; one in Concepción—University of Concepción; and one in Valdiva—Austral University. The three universities of Santiago also have important branches in other cities; every major city has its own regional university.

The library services of the universities are, together with the special libraries, the best organized in Chile. This is due to several factors. First a library school was founded at the University of Chile in 1946 in order to train personnel in service and provide professional librarians for academic and special libraries. In addition, the university authorities understood the need for good library services to support the research and studies of faculty and students. Finally, important contributions were made by foundations, institutions, and foreign governments to aid the formation and development of several university libraries.

*The Regional Center for Demographic Training and Research in Latin America (CELADE) in Santiago, Chile, provides intensive training in the techniques of demographic analysis and research and is funded by 12 Latin American nations.*



**Public Libraries.** The library services provided by the public and school libraries traditionally have been poor. Isolated efforts had been made to create public libraries, but only a few operated as such and were well organized.

The public library system is administered by a Department of Libraries, Archives and Museums within the Ministry of Education. Up to 1976 there were 56 public libraries belonging to or under the supervision of the department. In 1977 the government initiated a National Plan for Libraries to create more public libraries. In order to finance the plan a significant amount of money collected from sales tax on books, newspapers, and magazines was assigned to the effort. By 1978 there were 152 public libraries, including 80 municipal libraries. The plan also provides for the creation of new libraries through agreements with municipalities, private societies, community centers, and other institutions interested in meeting the information needs of patrons living in their areas of service. The National Plan for Libraries provides books and technical assistance, the institutions a facility and personnel.

Three municipal libraries in Santiago deserve special mention. Created in the late 1950's, they serve three sizable areas of population belonging to the municipalities of Providencia, Nuñoa, and Las Condes. They come closest to the North American standards for small public libraries and have served as models to several other municipal libraries in other regions of the country.

**School Libraries.** A decree of June 18, 1813, stated that every school should have funds for books to serve students. Another decree, of December 1, 1863, ordered that in every major city a local library would be established in the main public school. Despite the evidence of the legal documents that from the beginning of Chile's independence government authorities understood the importance of the library in the school, they proved only written promises and good wishes. In 1962, according to figures published in a 1964 report, only 259 out of 5,831 schools had library facilities. In 1976 there were 7,845 schools, but only 295 had some kind of library service.

School libraries in Chile can be classified as those in public schools that possess a small book collection and offer a few hours of library services and those that have a well-rounded book collection with at least one person, or even a professional, in charge of the library. In 1976 the Ministry of Education approved and designed a national system of school libraries, and at the end of the 1970's plans were made to start a program to create new school libraries throughout the country.

**Special Libraries.** These libraries are generally well organized and have enough bibliographical and human resources to offer good library service to their patrons in government, national and international organizations, professional and learned societies, industry, banks, and binational institutes. The increase of this type of library has been dramatic. In 1962 there were 62 special libraries in Chile. By 1978 there were 225 special libraries, excluding the special libraries in universities. Among the most notable special libraries are the following: the National Congress Library, the Chilean North American Institute, the Economic Commission for Latin America Library, the Copper Corporation Library, and the Central Bank of Chile Library.

**Libraries in Chile (1976)**

| Type | Number | Volumes in collections | Annual expenditures | Population served | Professional staff | All staff (total) |
|---|---|---|---|---|---|---|
| National | 1 | 1,800,000 | N.A. | N.A. | 31 | 133[a] |
| Academic | 179 | 2,869,481 | N.A. | 147,049 | 456 | 1,080[b] |
| Public | 152 | 197,600 | N.A. | N.A. | 37 | 264[a] |
| School | 295 | 261,253 | N.A. | 2,498,676 | 51 | N.A. |
| Special | 229 | 1,474,781 | N.A. | N.A. | 223 | 862[b] |
| Total | 856 | 6,603,115 | | | 798 | |

[a]1977. [b]1978.

**Library Associations.** The Association of Librarians was created in 1953 to unite and represent the librarians of the country and to participate in the creation and development of libraries. That association ceased when a 1969 law created the Colegio de Bibliotecarios de Chile. By law only those registered in the Colegio de Bibliotecarios, which represents librarians, are authorized to practice librarianship, and only those graduated from accredited library schools of the Chilean universities can be registered with the Colegio. In November 1978 1,213 librarians were registered.

**REFERENCE**

Juan Rothschild Feudenthal, "Development and Current Status of Bibliographic Organization in Chile" (Ph.D. dissertation, University of Michigan, 1972).

RENÉ MORAGA-NEIRA

# China, People's Republic of

China, a people's republic in eastern Asia, is bordered by the Mongolian People's Republic on the north, the U.S.S.R. and South Korea on the northeast, the Yellow Sea and East China Sea on the east, South China Sea on the southeast, Vietnam, Burma, Laos, India, Bhutan, Sikkim, and Nepal on the south, Pakistan on the southwest, and Afghanistan and the U.S.S.R. on the west. Pop. (1978 est.) 960,000,000; area 9,561,000 sq.km. The official language is Chinese.

## EARLY HISTORY

The earliest records of Chinese writings were found inscribed on animal bones and tortoise shells kept in the royal archives of the Shang Dynasty, about 1500 B.C., although recent archaeological discoveries and explorations may indicate even earlier origins. Inscriptions were also made on shells, bronze, stone, pottery, jade, and clay; later, as forerunners of the Chinese book, they were made on bamboo, wooden slips, and silk rolls. Paper was discovered in China in the early 2nd century and extensively used by the 4th. Ink was used from the 1st and 2nd centuries A.D. together with the well-developed Chinese brush. Woodblock printing is believed to have developed from similar techniques using seals; the earliest examples are from A.D. 757 in the form of a religious spell. An example of block-printed books dates from A.D. 868.

The long tradition of official archives collecting documents began during the Chou Dynasty (*c.* 1030–256 B.C.). When China became unified under the Ch'in Dynasty (221–207 B.C.), writing was standardized and censorship of literature was introduced. Many books were ordered burned in 213 B.C. Under the Han Dynasty (202 B.C.–A.D. 220), a systematic effort was made to recover all previously written works and gather them in the first centralized imperial library to be used by scholars. The collection was catalogued and described by Liu Hsiang (80–8 B.C.), and a classification scheme was later developed by Liu Hsin (d. A.D. 23), his son. Despite political turbulences in the ensuing centuries, all books were transcribed on paper from about the 4th century. A standard classification scheme, which was used for the next 15 centuries, was introduced by Hsun Hsu (A.D. 231–289), a curator of the imperial library. Buddhist literature flourished, particularly during the Sui Dynasty (590–618).

The T'ang emperors (618–907) greatly furthered literature and libraries. During that period block printing was utilized by Feng Tao (882–954), who made the Confucian classics and their commentaries available to scholars. The number of books increased considerably. In spite of continuous military disruption, literature continued to grow under the Sung Dynasty (960–1279), and great encyclopedias and annotated catalogues were compiled, while printing developed into a high art. Imperial as well as private libraries grew rapidly. Further progress occurred under the Ming Dynasty (1368–1644), when all existing literature was copied by 1408 into 11,095 handwritten folio volumes, of which fewer than 400 have survived. Many imperial and private libraries were built during that period. The Manchus founded the Ch'ing Dynasty (1644–1912) and strongly supported Chinese literature. The so-called Four Treasure Library was compiled in 1782 and consisted of 3,500 titles in 36,000 handwritten volumes. Of the seven sets produced, only four exist today.

## MODERN HISTORY

In 1909 the Capital Library, later known as the National Library, was established in Peking. In 1912 the Republic of China was formed under Sun Yat-sen. In the midst of cultural and political changes, various institutions of higher education were founded from 1912 to 1949, when the People's Republic of China was created. Library de-



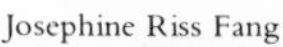
Josephine Riss Fang

*Beijing (Peking) University Library opened this new building in 1975. It is the largest academic library in the country, housing nearly 4,000,000 volumes.*

velopment was geared toward the socialist construction of the country, buttressed by various decrees. The Cultural Revolution in the late 1960's initiated changes in formal education and cultural life and affected library development. After the death of Mao Tse-tung (Mao Zedong) in 1976, the country officially moved toward modernization, and library support for this goal was emphasized. Numerous libraries are being constructed during this period of expansion, to handle the growth of available Chinese and foreign publications and to accommodate increasing readership.

**The National Library of Beijing (Peking).** Founded in 1910 as the Capital Library of Peking and formally opened to the public in 1912, the National Library of Beijing changed its name and location several times until it finally moved to its present place west of Peihai Park in 1931. Its collection began some 700 years ago and includes the Imperial Library of Southern Sung Dynasty (1127–1279) and the Imperial Library of the Ming Dynasty (1368–1644).

Directly under the State Administrative Bureau of Museums and Archaeological Data, the Library fulfills a leadership role in library activities throughout the country as the largest and most important library. It serves as depository library for all publications in China. Besides providing specialized services to leading departments of the Party, the government, the Army, and research institutes, the Library sees its general task as raising the people's cultural and scientific level. Various bibliographies and indexes on specialized topics are compiled, and exhibits and lectures are sponsored. The Library is organized in broad departments: the Party Committee, Library Services, Building Development, General Administration, Acquisition, Cataloguing, Readers Services, Study Room for Marxism-Leninism and Mao Tse-tung Thought, Reference and Research Services, Periodicals, Newspapers and Serials, Rare Books and Special Collections, and Unified Cataloguing. It provides in-house services through 15 reading rooms with a seating capacity of 700 and reprographic services with copying and microfilming. Through its cataloguing of Chinese books, it supplies over 3,000 libraries with printed cards, over 6,850,000 of which were issued in 1977. During 1977 the Library carried out international exchange programs with some 2,000 libraries in 119 countries. As member of the Regional Libraries Coordinating Group of Beijing (Peking) it cooperates with 17 libraries of all types to develop resource sharing, union catalogues, and training programs for the staff.

The National Library's collection totaled over 9,500,000 volumes in 1978. The collection consists of 5,000,000 books (60 percent Chinese, 40 percent foreign), 3,500,000 volumes of periodicals (20 percent Chinese, 80 percent foreign), 60,000 volumes of bound newspapers (50 percent Chinese, 50 percent foreign), 140,000 volumes of other materials, documents, and the like (25 percent Chinese, 75 percent foreign), and 560,000 volumes in the Special Collection with valuable rare books and manuscripts from the various dynasties and Chinese revolutionary documents. In 1978, 10,000 Chinese and foreign periodicals were subscribed to (80 percent in the natural sciences and technology, 20 percent in the social sciences).

**Academic Libraries.** Academic libraries are under the jurisdiction of the Ministry of Higher Education. The comprehensive universities have large general libraries in addition to departmental libraries. The largest libraries in Beijing (Peking) are the Peking University (1975; 3,700,000 volumes, including the Department of Library Science), Tsinghua University (over 2,000,000 volumes), and Normal University (2,000,000 volumes). Of the 400 universities in China, other prominent libraries are those of Nankai University (1,000,000 volumes) in Tientsin, Fudan (Futan) University (*c.* 1,600,000) in Shanghai, Gaodung (Chiao-tung) Universities in Shanghai and Sian, Nanking University (2,000,000), Zhongshan (Chungshan) University (2,000,000) in Guangzhou (Kwangchow), and particularly the fast-growing Wuhan University (1,800,000) with its Department of Library and Information Science. The so-called Revolutionary Committees, which have administered the libraries since the Cultural Revolution, are gradually being displaced by professional administrators.

**Public Libraries.** Public libraries are under the jurisdiction of the Ministry of Culture: the State Administrative Bureau for Museums and Archaeological Data, which is directly under the State Council. China has a hierarchical network of public libraries: they range from provincial, district, county, commune, and production brigades in the countryside to municipal, district, neighborhood, and street levels in the cities, with technical (but not administrative) assistance given from the higher to the lower levels. The National Library of Peking is set apart as being directly under the State Bureau. Provincial libraries have been established in 27 provinces except Tibet and Hebei (Hopei). They are under the cultural bureaus of their provinces. Besides taking care of the rare book collections of their provinces, they assist the lower-level libraries throughout their province in their work. Some important libraries are the Nanking Library (4,700,000 items) for Jiangsu (Kiangsu) Province, Wuhan Library (1,800,000, including 400,000 classical books) for Hubei (Hopei) Province and with a new building under construction in the late 1970's, and the Provincial Library of Yunnan Province (1,600,000) in Kunming (opened 1975), whose collection reflects the interests and study of the 22 national minorities in the province. The most famous municipal library is the Shanghai Library (6,500,000), the largest public library in China and renowned for its collection of 1,500,000 classical Chinese books.

**School Libraries.** Libraries attached to elementary and secondary schools are under the jurisdiction of the Ministry of Education. They may range from a small reading room to a sizable collection headed by professional staff and assisted by the students themselves. An example is the Nankai Middle School in Tientsin (Tianjing), whose collection of 100,000 volumes serves a high school with the five upper grades and whose most famous alumnus was Premier Chou En-lai (Zhou Enlai). Services to children are carried out as part of the public libraries programs as well as through reading rooms in the so-called Children's Palaces, which serve as recreational and educational activity centers after school hours.

**Special Libraries.** Libraries of various government agencies and institutions are under the jurisdiction of their appropriate agencies. There are two types of libraries in this category in China: (1) the libraries of the Academy of Science, both that of the Natural Sciences and that of the Social Sciences, with their specialized institutes, and (2) the special libraries for various departments, such as geology, medicine, agriculture, steel industries, and others. The Academy of Science Library in Beijing is a major research library, with over 2,600,000 books and technical reports in its collection with emphasis on the theoretical aspects of science and technology, carrying out exchanges with 1,400 institutions from 77 countries in 1978, and giving technical assistance to its over 130 Research Institute Libraries throughout China.

Although partly functioning as academic libraries, the libraries of the Central Institute of Nationalities in Beijing and the libraries of the nine similar institutes established in the provinces can be regarded as special libraries, since they focus on some of the 50 minority nationalities of China, their language, culture, and education.

**Libraries in the People's Republic of China (1976)**

| Type | Number | Volumes in collections | Annual expenditures (yuan) | Population served | Professional staff | All staff (total) |
|---|---|---|---|---|---|---|
| National | 1 | 9,500,000 | N.A. | over 900,000,000 | about 200 | 697 |
| Academic | c. 800 | 50,000,000 | N.A. | over 2,000,000 | N.A. | N.A. |
| Public | c. 400 (major ones) | 35,000,000 | N.A. | over 900,000,000 | N.A. | N.A. |
| School | c. 1,000 | 20,000,000 | N.A. | 300,000,000 | N.A. | N.A. |
| Special | c. 300 | 40,000,000 | N.A. | 300,000,000 | N.A. | N.A. |

Sources: National Library of Beijing (Peking) (1978); *World of Learning 1978–79*. Except for the National Library of Beijing, all statistics are highly speculative, since no official statistics on libraries in China have been released.

**Associations.** After the Cultural Revolution, no professional associations existed in China. In late 1978, however, the government gave permission for the reestablishment of a national library association. Before that, regional groups had formed, including all types of libraries as well as representatives of the Hsinhua (Xinhua) Book Agency, which supplies libraries with Chinese and foreign publications. Such groups exist in Peking, Shanghai, Szechwan (Sichuan), Kwangtung (Guandong), and Tientsin (Tianjing).

**REFERENCES**

Current information on Chinese publications was not yet available through a national bibliography by the end of the 1970's. The Xinhua Book Agency publishes announcements for internal use only, to be sent to libraries in China, and most of the major libraries publish lists of their acquisitions in journal form. Some information on library development and planning is published in articles in the journals published by universities; e.g., in numbers 5 and 6, 1978, of the Journal of Wuhan University (in Chinese). The Chinese-language newspaper *Guang Ming Ribao* published an editorial on the development of academic library services on September 19, 1978.

For further information see Josephine Riss Fang, *China's Libraries on the New Long March* (1980).

JOSEPHINE RISS FANG

# China, Republic of (Taiwan)

Taiwan, an island in eastern Asia off the southeast coast of the People's Republic of China, became the seat of Nationalist China in 1949 and is formally the Republic of China. Pop. (1978 est.) 16,978,200; area 35,981 sq.km. The country comprises the islands of Taiwan (Formosa), Penghu (Pescadores), Quemoy, and others.

**National Libraries.** Two national libraries are in the capital city, Taipei: the National Central Library and the National Central Library Taiwan Branch. The National Central Library was established in Nanking in 1934, moved to Taiwan in 1948 before the Communists took over mainland China, and resumed its operation in 1955. The National Central Library Taiwan Branch, formerly the Provincial Taipei Library, was merged with the National Central Library in 1973, but it more or less maintained its independent status. The Branch—like the National Central Library—is directly responsible to the Ministry of Education.

In addition to its routine library functions, the National Central Library functions as a library of libraries. It is a legal deposit; it is charged with the development of nationwide librarianship; it serves as an official organ for international exchange of publications; it engages in programs of library training; and it plays a significant role in bibliographic services and control.

The two national libraries have a collection of about 1,000,000 volumes. The most precious is the rare books collection of the National Central Library totaling about 140,000 volumes, of which 281 titles are Sung (960–1279) imprints. Collections of significance at the National Central Library Taiwan Branch include some 25,000 volumes of books on Taiwan in many languages and periodicals and newspapers published in Taiwan during the past decades.

**Academic Libraries.** There are 9 universities, 15 colleges, and 88 junior colleges with an estimated combined collection of 8,600,000 volumes. Three academic libraries have collections of over 400,000 each: National Taiwan University, National Chengchi University, and National Taiwan Normal University. The National Taiwan University is the only institution with a library collection of over 1,000,000. Special collections of the National Taiwan University consist of the *Wu-shi-shan-fang* collection, *Ku-bo* collection on Chinese drama, *Kao Lin-wei*'s collection of block printing. *Tan-hsin* documents, and *An-li-ta-she* cultivation documents. The National Chengchi University is noted for its collections in the social sciences and U.S. government documents.

**School Libraries.** The school system in Taiwan

**Libraries in Republic of China (1976)**

| Type | Number | Volumes in collections | Annual expenditures (dollars) | Population served | Professional staff | All staff (total) |
|---|---|---|---|---|---|---|
| National | 2 | 1,000,000 | NT $ 139,617,000 | 16,800,000 | 65 | 189 |
| Academic | 112 | 8,600,000 | 133,300,000 | 308,583 | 631 | 1,191 |
| Public | 20 | 1,370,000 | 57,324,000 | 16,800,000 | 218 | 478 |
| School | 2,405 (schools) | N.A. | N.A. | 3,882,645 | N.A. | N.A. |
| Special | 101 | 3,700,000 | NT $ 63,340,000 | 240,000 | 323 | 564 |
| Total | 2,640 | | | | | |

Source: National Central Library, Taipei (supplied by Periodical Librarian, Rui-lan Ku Wu)

consists of primary schools, mainly government operated, and secondary schools, which include junior high, senior high, and vocational schools. There are over 2,400 schools, but not every school has a library or a reading room. Fewer than 500 schools had separate rooms for book collections at the end of the 1970's. At the secondary level, some 300 schools had collections of over 10,000 volumes each, and 10 had over 40,000 volumes.

**Public Libraries.** The Regulation Governing Public Libraries in Provinces and Municipalities of 1952 as amended requires that a public library must be established in each province, municipality (under the Executive Yuan), or *hsien* (county). There were 20 public libraries at the level of province, municipality (under the Executive Yuan), and *hsien* with a total collection of over 1,370,000 volumes. Among the public libraries, the Taipei City (under the Executive Yuan) Library has a fairly large budget and the largest collections. It planned to establish one branch library in each of its 16 *chu* (districts).

In general, circulation is low and reference services stagnant; in some libraries these are nonexistent. One feature of public libraries is its stress on social education. Many libraries have moved toward the goal of being a center of education for children and adults. Various programs have been sponsored for this purpose, such as adult reading improvement, children's reading improvement, Chinese calligraphy, children's painting, high school mathematics, adult English courses, and the study of the thought of founding fathers.

**Special Libraries.** About 50 special and research libraries have collections of over 15,000 volumes each. Chun-shan Institute of Science and Technology, Taiwan Forestry Bureau, Taiwan Sugar Corporation Research Institute, and Industrial Technology Research Institute are some of the special libraries offering fine collections in the fields of science and technology. Three special libraries deserve particular attention. The Academia Sinica, founded at Nanking in 1928, is the highest research institution under the President of the Republic of China. It has ten departmental libraries. Some of its libraries have the best collections in their subject fields. Collections of archives of past dynasties, bamboo tablets of the Han Dynasty, oracle bones, and local history are unique. The National Palace Museum has one of the largest collections of archives, and its collection of rare books is second only to the National Central Library. The Science and Technology Information Center was created in 1968.

**Library Association.** The Library Association of China was incorporated in 1953 with 184 individual members and 20 institutional members. In 1978 it had 1,130 individual members and 116 institutional members. Membership is open to everyone who has studied library science or is interested in library work. The highest organ of the Association is the membership meeting. It elects the Board of Directors and Board of Supervisors. The Board in turn elect their Standing Directors and one Standing Supervisor, respectively. The Association is run by the Standing Directors, but the daily business is taken care of by an Executive Secretary appointed by the Board of Directors. Professional activities of the Association are carried on through committees. Major accomplishments include summer workshops to train library workers and the formulation of library standards, released from 1961 to 1964. The Association also publishes *Bulletin of the Library Association of China,* an annual from 1954, and a quarterly, *Library Association of China Newsletter,* from 1975.

TZE-CHUNG LI

# Chubarian, Ogan Stepanovich

(1908–1976)

Ogan Chubarian was a specialist in library science who greatly stimulated the development of library science and practice in the U.S.S.R. through his many-sided scientific, pedagogical, and administrative activities. He was born in Rostov-on-Don on October 8, 1908, and received professional training at Advanced Bibliographic Courses, which functioned at the State Book Chamber of the R.S.F.S.R. Chubarian prepared a candidate dissertation on "The Technical Book in Russia during the Reign of Peter the Great." He was granted a Doctor's degree for his monograph "General Library Science." Chubarian began his career as a rank and file librarian and in 1963 became one of the senior officers of the National Library of the Soviet Union. He published over a hundred works dealing with different problems of librarianship, bibliography, and bibliology. "General Library Science," one of his most important works, gives contemporary interpretations of the role of librarianship in Soviet society. This work formulates and reveals in detail the main principles of library development in the U.S.S.R.: the state character of librarianship, the availability of libraries for all, planned organization of the library network, centralization, and the drawing of representatives of the population into the work of libraries and their management.

Chubarian was the first Soviet library specialist to cover the essence and place of library science in the general system of sciences from a Marxist standpoint.

Many works by Chubarian were devoted to the study of current problems of library development and the activities of libraries, such as problems of centralization of librarianship, cooperation of libraries and information centers, surveys of readership, development of national libraries of the Union republics, and acquisitions.

Chubarian laid stress on the common goals and tasks of libraries that should not be ignored by any library institution regardless of its specific character.

Chubarian gave much of his time and effort to bibliography; he advocated the recommendatory bibliography as an efficient instrument in the guidance of reading. His idea that library and bibliographic activities should be carried out in close cooperation represents one of the leading concepts in defining the role of Soviet libraries.

In his studies theoretical propositions and pragmatic conclusions interlace, and the examination of problems is closely connected with the practice and tasks of libraries.

For many years he guided the activities of important Soviet library institutions such as the Moscow State Institute of Culture, the State Public Technical and Scientific Library, and the State Lenin Library. He was also Vice-Chairman of the Council for Coordination of Research in Library Science and Bibliography attached to the U.S.S.R. Ministry of Culture.

He was one of the founders of two periodicals—*Sovetskoye bibliotekovedeniye* ("Soviet Library Science") and *Nauchniye i tekhnicheskiye biblioteki SSSR* ("Scientific and Technical Libraries of the U.S.S.R."), which greatly stimulated research in the field.

He had many pupils, whom he helped to write dissertations and become library specialists. He also directed many important surveys, and it was through his efforts that the following studies were published: *The Soviet Reader* (1968), *The Book and Reading in the Life of Towns* (1973), and *The Book and Reading in the Life of the Soviet Village* (1978).

He edited many collections of articles such as *Lenin and Contemporary Problems of Library Science, History of Librarianship in the U.S.S.R.: Documents and Materials,* and *Problems of Sociology and Psychology of Reading,* and a *Dictionary of Library Terms.*

O. S. Chubarian did much in the way of acquainting foreign librarians with the state of library science and practice in the Soviet Union. He persistently endeavored to develop the exchange of information on problems of library development; he took part in the organization of many international conferences, discussions, and joint research projects and the development of international book exchange. He participated in many IFLA sessions and worked on a number of reports. In 1966 he was elected Chairman of the IFLA Bibliographic Committee, and later he headed the Committee on Library Science.

His works have been translated into many foreign languages. The U.S.S.R. Ministry of Culture and party and state authorities of the country frequently invited him to act as adviser when important documents concerning librarianship were drawn up.

Chubarian was granted the title of Professor and the honorary title "Merited Worker of Culture of the R.S.F.S.R." He was also granted state awards and a Library in Artashat in the Armenian S.S.R. was named after him. He died in Moskow on January 7, 1976.

E. A. FENELONOV

# Circulation Systems

During the last 150 years, one of the continuing problems in librarianship has been to find an inexpensive, yet efficient, system to provide the proper control of a collection. The early literature shows that a primary consideration was almost complete control, that is, to know where the book was at any given time, who had it, whether the use was legitimate, what the user's past and present reading habits were, and to be able to judge the influence of the circulated book on the collection, as well as deduce a number of statistics. It became apparent that maintaining a circulation system was expensive, in staff or user time or both as well as in equipment and supplies. The next step, therefore, was to sacrifice control for simplification. It became cheaper to use various standardized systems that could be installed with a minimum of training for staff and patrons. Furthermore, these systems often had commercially available supplies. But because standardization is often limiting, there was a tendency to tamper with a system to make it fit local needs. One system or type of system might not fit different types of libraries or even the same type of library with differing demands. A mechanical system suitable for a public library, which usually aimed toward a simple, fast system, was not adaptable for an academic or special library, which needed readily available information on the books in circulation. Later, when automated systems allowed libraries to regain a larger measure of control, it was ironic that some of this information could not be collected on an individual basis because of protection of privacy and because the cost was often more immediately expensive. It is recognized that manual systems in many instances prove still superior to available automated systems.

Although at least 40 qualities of a circulation system have been identified, these aspects can be summarized into a few important points. An ideal system should be convenient for both user and library, have fast charging and discharging, handle renewals simply, incorporate a method of obtaining overdues, handle "holds" or "saves" or academic course reserves, provide sufficient statistical information, maintain a flexible loan period, generate accurate and legible records, prevent forgery, provide for expansion, and routinize daily work. The search for these qualities has often brought about discontent with the system in use, but, at the same time, there has been a reluctance to change, out of fear that a new system would not prove to be more efficient and less expensive.

## HISTORICAL DEVELOPMENT

The history of circulation systems has been a slow movement toward obtaining the benefits listed above. This progress was marked by the strong feeling that if an element of control was given up in favor of simplicity, the collection would deteriorate, and the librarian would be found wanting by the trustees of the collection. Most libraries before and during the 19th century felt that there was a need to protect the book, and in rare book rooms and specialized reference collections there was and is still this need. But the protective feeling about circulation was extended to other, more public institutions, if indeed the book was allowed outside the building at all. As late as the mid-1800's, some academic institutions did not freely circulate their books to students but only to faculty, who could be kept under better control or were thought more responsible. The need to protect public collections resulted in involved record keeping that today seems cumbersome but that was then considered the correct way of handling materials. These records gave the librarian who was entrusted with keeping the inventory a written method to indicate that care had been taken. Not only was the book charged out to a registered and therefore bona-fide borrower, but also the borrower's past use of materials was often noted, so that infractions could be screened closely and proper steps taken to monitor future use. With the exception of small institutional libraries whose clientele changes constantly, it is now difficult to tell from library records how many books are charged out to one borrower or what books he or she has used in the past; if that information is available through the computer, there are limitations on its use. Statistics generated are broad aggregates, since concern for privacy has eliminated a borrower's past records, once so much a part of readers' services. One substitute for that record has been a user's profile, obtained through interview or questionnaire.

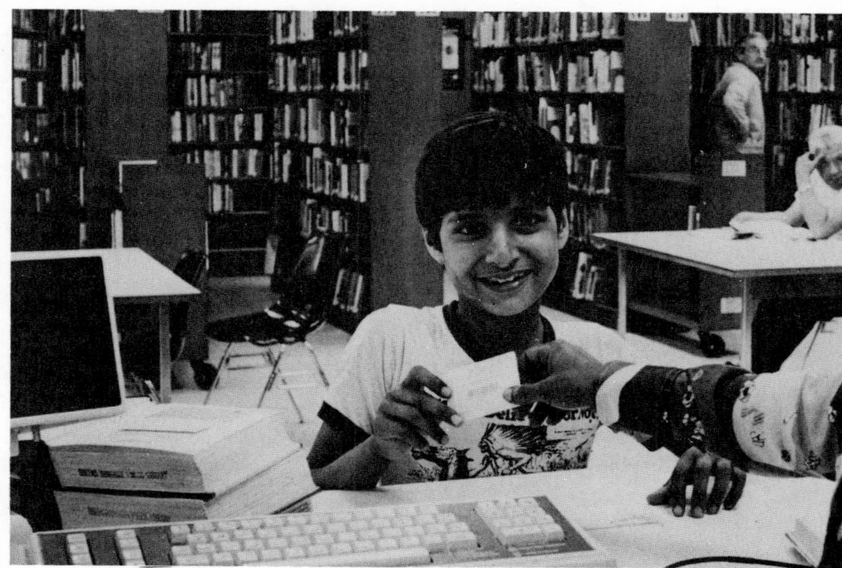

Queens Borough Public Library

*Laminated card with individual bar code, part of the computerized circulation system in the Queens Borough Public Library.*



**Manual Systems.** The earliest systems depended on handwritten records, which took the forms developed by business firms, such as the day book and ledger sheet. In the day book each day's transactions were entered on a page or pages, including information on author, title, and borrower's name. Gradually a ledger system evolved in which the daily record was moved to a set of sheets, eliminating a search through the day book for each item. The ledger sheet could be filed in a variety of ways, such as by call numbers, but the usual way was to number a page, which became the registration number of the borrower who had his or her transactions duly recorded with the call number and the date due set in columns. The book's return was noted through the date's being entered in another column or the record's being crossed through. The book also had to indicate the page of the ledger so that the

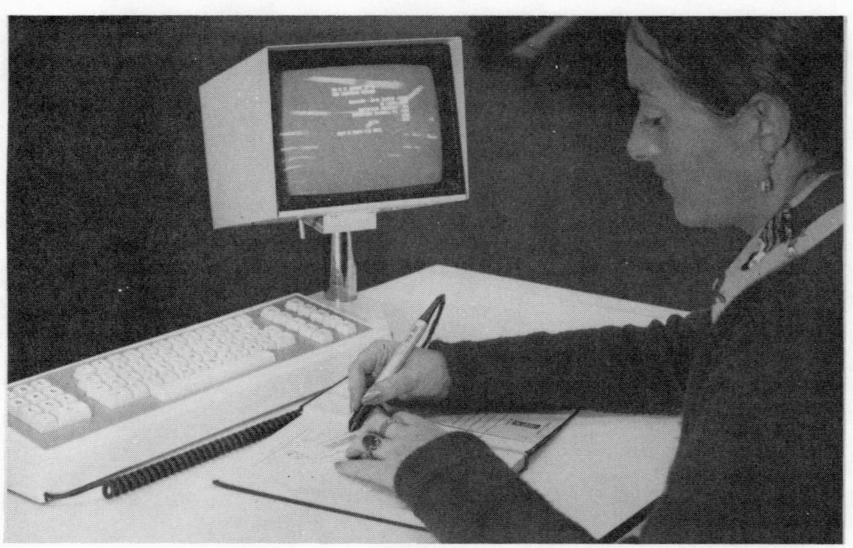

Guelph University

*Circulation attendant at Guelph University Library, Ontario, Canada, scans a patron's badge to charge out a book.*

discharge could take place. At first the ledger served as simply a borrower's record; later librarians began to recognize its use as an aid to collection development. There were some disadvantages—overdue notices required a search through the records, and legibility was also a problem, despite the attempt to train employees in a library hand. Entry in a ledger forced the patron to wait while each transaction was made, a problem that was common to all handwritten systems. Despite these problems, the ledger proved to be one of the most popular systems until the middle of the 19th century. In fact, ledgers are still in use today, mainly in small collections.

Often small libraries used a "dummy" system in which a wooden block (or a sheet of paper or a card) was substituted for the book on the shelf with a record of the borrower's name on this paper-covered dummy. This system was predicated on small use and sufficient time for the borrower to wait in order to charge and discharge the book. Dummies used today substitute for books shelved in special locations.

Growth of a collection brought the temporary-slip system, in which the borrower filled out his or her name and address and registration number. The slip was destroyed or used as a receipt when the book was returned. The slip could be filed by date due, by the borrower's name or number, or by call number. In some libraries where control of all of these elements was felt necessary, slips in duplicate or triplicate were made of the original and stored in separately maintained files that required careful discharging. Carbon paper was often used to avoid copying errors; however, some libraries employed students or clerks to rewrite the additional slips. While in general this duplication of handmade records has gone out of favor, some special nonautomated libraries use such methods if they need to have an immediate circulation record by patron and by book (as in the case when a user is forced to clear his records before leaving an organization or when a book is in demand by another patron). The smaller the library, the more likely such a system will be used, although even here the margin of error is great. The McBee Key-Sort System is a variant of the temporary slip, but the card need be filed in only one place, since the edge punch allows multiple uses.

The permanent slip or card was an obvious outgrowth of the slip system. Each book had its own card prepared ahead of time with call number, author, and title. The card was then stored in a pocket or other retaining device in the book itself. The registration number or name and address were written on the card, which was then filed by date due. It had the advantage of avoiding copying errors plus giving a permanent record of use of the item. A highly effective device, it is still in use in many libraries, since it can easily be adapted through various mechanical or photographic devices into a rapid charging system. It has remained a standby of public libraries and of course-reserve systems in academic libraries where the simple writing of the name and address or student identification number allows books to be charged for quick, short-term loans. Some academic libraries that had used automated systems for course reserves have reverted to this card as less expensive and more easily managed. The rapid charging and discharging are benefits, though legibility and forgery are sometimes problems. Overdues are automatic, since the charges left in the date-due file are easily identified. Both temporary slips and permanent cards are substitutes for dummies, but they are kept together at the circulation desk and can thus be searched by the staff without their going to the shelves.

A variant of the permanent card system is the Browne System, employing a reader's pocket holding the book card with the date due stamped on it. The reader's pocket was then filed by call number or author behind the date due. While the system seemed simplicity itself, the number of books the reader could take out was limited unless he was liberally supplied with reader's pockets. Filing the unused reader's pockets was felt by some to present a space problem. The Browne System was succeeded by the Newark System, which could be expanded through mechanical devices such as the Bro-Dart and Gaylord charging machines.

By the late 19th century, several firms were selling the supplies and equipment required by the various systems, although none was actually marketing complete systems. Each library could develop its own forms and supplies, but it soon became evident that buying these supplies from commercial firms was often cheaper and helped standardize a system.

British and continental libraries (aside from large research libraries) generally went through the same evolution as U.S. libraries. In some instances European libraries were quicker to adapt to mechanical systems, and automated systems are often more sophisticated and in wider use than in U.S. libraries. In British libraries there was also a more dedicated attempt to eliminate any participation by the borrower, hence the widespread use of the Browne System (often called the Brown System after its British advocate). Also favored in Britain was the Token System, which is rather like the coat claim system used in hotels and restaurants. The disadvantages of having no record of the borrower or of books out on loan discouraged the use of this type of system in the U.S.

ROBERT W. ORAM

MODERN SYSTEMS

**Mechanical Systems.** The development of a mechanical circulation system by the Newark Public Library in 1900 was a major advance. Several firms subsequently developed and marketed variations of the Newark machine, among them Gaylord Brothers and the Demco Educational Corporation. The improved and electrified Newark System remains one of the most popular circulation systems ever used, with over 7,500 units in libraries in 1978. In this system, borrowers' names and due dates are maintained on the book cards by imprinting that information from embossed borrower cards along with one of four standard due dates recorded in the machine. The book cards are filed by author or call number under the due dates. When the books are returned, the due dates on the date-due slips indicate to the library staff where to find the book cards. Book cards remaining in the file past their due dates are easily identified as overdue; overdue notices can then be prepared after the borrowers have been identified by number in the patron registration file. One variation introduced in the 1960's eliminated the look up in the registration file; the plastic borrower cards are embossed with the name, address, and number of the patron. Since this information remains on the book cards, the library achieves a saving in staff time, although patron anonymity is sacrificed. Most libraries lease charging machines of this type.

The Bro-Dart Company marketed a similar unit for more than a decade by the end of the 1970's, the Sysdac System; special tape is imprinted with the names and addresses of the borrowers using the embossed borrower cards. The tape is attached to the book cards with one end protruding from the right side of the cards in one of four positions corresponding to the selected due date. The book cards are filed in a special V-tray in alphabetical or call-number order. Libraries have the option of bending the tape back and filing by due date as in the Gaylord and Demco systems. When items are returned, the book cards are pulled, the tape is removed, and the book cards are put back in the books. The anonymity of the patron is assured without burdening the library staff. An advantage is that it eliminates book card replacement costs, though other costs are higher than those of the Gaylord and Demco systems.

A system originally designed for records control in business and industry has been adapted to libraries, the McBee Key-Sort System. A single preprinted prepunched card is made out by the patron, including author, title, and call number as well as the patron's name and identification number. The edges of the cards contain prepunched holes that represent patron status categories and due dates. The appropriate holes are notched, by hand punch or machine, before the cards are filed by call number. Overdues are identified by inserting a needle through the hole representing the due date selected and lifting a large number of cards. The notched overdues will fall out. Staff labor is reduced, but patrons have to do a great deal of writing. Illegible records may prevent accurate identification of all borrowers with overdue materials.

Photographic charging is another commercial system adapted for libraries. The principal vendor is the Eastman Kodak Company. Its Recordak Starfile Microfilmer RV-1 is a 16-mm camera with a tray specifically designed for libraries. Three compartments accommodate the patron identification card and two stacks of transaction cards, one for each of two standard due dates. The book card is placed on one of the two stacks of transaction cards, and a photographic record is made. The transaction cards are filed in the books. The discharge involves removing the transaction cards from the books and filing them in the return file. The returned transaction cards are sorted periodically and a list of overdues produced for checking against the microfilm record. Overdue notices are written from the film. The Brodac system by Bro-Dart is similar, but the record of the transaction consists of thermographic copies on three-by-four-inch slips. They are filed in transaction number order with the records for returned items removed so that the balance may be used to prepare overdue notices.

Photocharging systems cost from $1,200 to $1,900 per unit. They have usually been installed in public libraries with very high circulation volumes, enabling them to avoid the problems associated with borrower files, book card files, and the pulling and slipping of hundreds of thousands of book cards a year. Basic collection control is accomplished, but the current status of materials cannot be determined.

**Automated Systems.** Automation of circulation began in the 1940's, but only a small number of libraries had installed systems by 1970. The systems were developed by the libraries themselves using equipment available from IBM, Mohawk, and other computer hardware vendors. Virtually all installations were batch processing systems, with fast, reliable collection of data, elimination of filing, and automatic printing of notices. Almost all of these systems have been upgraded to on-line systems.

From the very beginning it was felt by such pioneers as Ralph Parker that an automated circulation system should be the end result of a total system; that is, the final phase of the processing chain. Most batch systems certainly were considered to be temporary and would be revamped when the integrated schemes were finished. That the complete system never developed up to this time probably was due to the expense and complexity of complete integration, and, therefore, separate circulation systems continued to function. The bibliographic utilities such as OCLC planned total systems, but work on the circulation aspects was postponed or in favor of the more intricate acquisitions or interlibrary loan function.

Commercial firms such as CLSI are working from a circulation system back into full inventory control, but the problem for most systems was that it seemed too slow, too expensive to manipulate the full MARC record on a rapid basis. In fact, the planners of most early circulation systems made a conscious decision that the short form of entry would be used.

On-line systems offer immediate access to all files by a variety of approaches. These systems offer libraries an opportunity to go beyond collection control to a variety of services and management information programs. Among the features of most such systems are: (1) quick determination of what titles are in the library's collection and where they are located; (2) quick determination of what is currently in circulation and when it is/was due back; (3) quick determination of what notices have been sent to patrons with materials charged out and what action is due next; (4) quick determination of what titles are being held for patrons, for whom they are held, and after what date they are no longer wanted; (5) provision of management information on the utilization of the collection to aid staff in scheduling, collection weeding, storage, and selection; and (6) capability to adjust to dramatic changes in circulation volume with minimum investment in new staff or equipment.

The earliest on-line systems were developed by libraries, but the great majority of those now in use have been purchased from vendors who have developed turn-key systems. CLSI pioneered turn-key, on-line systems in 1973. They had installed over a hundred systems by 1978, over 80 percent of the turn-key systems in use. The early systems were attractive because they handled high volumes of circulation very well, but surveys of librarians emphasize the service improvements they make possible. Improvements made by CLSI and by other vendors, among them DataPhase and Gaylord, came to offer libraries full inventory control, rather than a record of that which is absent from the library. Charges and discharges can be performed in two seconds or less; holds are easily placed; notices are processed automatically; and a variety of statistics are generated.

System characteristics change rapidly, and *Library Technology Reports* commissioned studies of the available systems in 1975, 1977, and 1978 and planned periodic updates. Vendors of circulation systems are developing new functions to augment the circulation function. Acquisitions systems and on-line catalogues were in the plans of at least five of the ten U.S. vendors active in the late 1970's.

The trend appeared to be toward the development of integrated library systems with the various library functions controlled by a single minicomputer with the capacity for a search of book jobbers' data bases for bibliographic and price verification, electronic order placement, on-line access to a cataloguing network, and subsequent circulation control of the newly added items. Long-term planning in some libraries called for security control, word processing, and numerous other activities to be performed from any one of the in-house system's terminals.

These trends appear to be influencing how libraries convert their records into the circulation file. Abbreviated records are being replaced by full MARC records or MARC compatible records. Partial conversions are less common, while complete conversions using commercial services or large data bases from networks or book jobbers are being conducted. Networking or electronically connecting the library systems of several libraries was another trend well established by the late 1970's.

Circulation systems of the future will not be merely a series of data collection activities for collection control but an integral element of the total management system of a library.

**REFERENCES**

"Circulation Systems," in *Library Technology Reports* (ALA, 1965– ).

George Fry and Associates, Inc., *Study of Circulation Control Systems* (ALA, 1961).

H. T. Geer, *Charging Systems* (ALA, 1955).

L. H. Kirkwood, *Charging Systems* (1961).

RICHARD W. BOSS

## Clapp, Verner Warren
(1901–1972)

One of the most influential and productive librarians of his generation, Verner Warren Clapp was born on June 3, 1901, in Johannesburg, Union of South Africa. His father, George Herbert Clapp, was a native of New Hampshire who had gone to Johannesburg on business. His mother, May Sybil Helms, was of Danish descent. The Clapps met in Johannesburg and were married there in 1898 but left Johannesburg for Poughkeepsie, New York, in 1905, after the Boer War. Verner attended the public schools in Poughkeepsie and earned the A.B. degree at Trinity College in Hartford, Connecticut, where he captained the track team, joined Sigma Nu fraternity, and was elected to Phi Beta Kappa. Following his graduation in 1922, he joined his parents in Washington, D.C., where they then lived, and found temporary summer employment cataloguing manuscripts at the Library of Congress. In the fall he left the Library to study philosophy at Harvard, but at the close of the academic year he decided to return to the Library of Congress and was employed as a reference librarian in the main reading room. His great energy, intelligence, and wide-ranging interests impressed his superiors, and in 1928, when the Library's Congressional Unit was organized, he was placed in charge. At that time he also met Dorothy Devereux Ladd; they were married on August 24, 1929, and had three children, Nancy Priest, Verner Warren, and Judith Ladd. In Dorothy he had found a kindred spirit who shared many of his diverse interests and who matched him in spirit.

In 1931 Clapp was promoted to the post of Special Assistant to the Superintendent of the Reading Rooms. Six years later he became Assistant Superintendent of the Reading Rooms and was given additional responsibility for the Division for the Blind. Under his administration the production of braille and talking books was increased, and regional libraries were established to improve services to the blind.

In 1940, shortly after Archibald MacLeish's appointment as Librarian, the Library of Congress was reorganized and a Department of Administrative Services was established. Clapp became its first Director and undertook a reform of the Library's fiscal management. When the United States entered World War II, he was given responsibility for the evacuation to Fort Knox of the nation's cherished documents—the Declaration of Independence, the Constitution of the United States, and the Articles of Confederation—and, also, the copy of the Magna Carta, which the British Government had sent to the Library of Congress for safekeeping.

After helping plan the organization of an Acquisitions Department in 1943, Clapp was named its first Director. With his usual vigor and vision he revamped the Library's acquisitions program to make it more comprehensive and responsive to the new and increased informational needs of the government. His contributions during this period were not limited to development of the Library's collections, however. His ideas were influential in the organization of the Library's Reference Department, in the shaping of its personnel policies, in proposals for the revision of the Copyright Act, in efforts to develop interlibrary cooperation in microfilming, and in various other areas of library activity.

Immediately after World War II, Clapp entered into a new period of noteworthy and varied activity. During the war years the flow of publications to the United States from Germany and other countries of Europe had been cut off. With the cessation of hostilities, Clapp helped plan, and was made responsible for, a vast undertaking, the Cooperative Acquisitions Project, which involved the procurement of some 2,000,000 European publications for the Library of Congress and 112 other American research libraries and the distribution of these publications on an equitable basis. Additionally, in 1946 his talent for diplomacy was tested in successful negotiations in Berlin with representatives of the U.S.S.R. to effect the release of books and journal issues that had been ordered before the war by U.S. libraries and were being held in storage in East Germany. In 1945 and 1946 he was given the assignment of collecting and making useful disposition of a vast quantity of books published in special wartime editions for the use of the military. Even finding temporary storage for these publications was a monumental task, but the project was carried out to the satisfaction of all concerned. The books were distributed to colleges and universities whose rapidly increasing enrollments were creating a demand for scarce teaching materials.

Of quite a different order was his assignment in 1945 to organize a library and provide a reference service for the United Nations Conference at San Francisco; he did so with great skill, working under extreme pressure. The United Nations turned to him on numerous occasions thereafter for advice on UN library matters, and from 1959 to 1962 he served, with three other librarians, as a consultant to the Director General of the United Nations and the architects employed for the project in the planning of the United Nations Library building.

In 1947 the Librarian of Congress decided to appoint a deputy, and it was no surprise to anyone in the profession when, on March 5 of that year, Clapp was named Chief Assistant Librarian of Congress. Before he had been in that position a year, he was asked to chair a United States Library Mission to Japan to assist in the establishment of a National Diet Library. In two months he and Charles Harvey Brown, Director of the library of Iowa State College, produced a plan for the organization and services of the proposed library as well as drafts of the legislation needed for its implementation. Their ideas were accepted, and the necessary legislation was enacted promptly by the Diet. At the celebration of the 20th anniversary of the National Diet Library in 1968, he was honored by Japan with the Order of the Sacred Treasure.

When Luther Harris Evans resigned as Librarian of Congress to become Director General of Unesco, Clapp assumed the duties of Acting Librarian and served in that capacity from July 4, 1953, until September 1954.

Over the years of its existence the Ford Foundation

Arthur Plotnik

*Verner Warner Clapp*

had been the recipient of numerous grant requests from research libraries. In 1955 it requested Louis B. Wright, Director of the Folger Library, Leonard Carmichael, Secretary of the Smithsonian Institution, and L. Quincy Mumford, Librarian of Congress, to call a meeting of librarians and scholars to advise it on how it might assist in the solution of library problems. Two conferences were held at the Folger Library that year on the problems of research libraries and the possibility of using new scientific and technological developments in solving them. At the second meeting it was decided that a new and independent organization was needed. In September 1956 the Council on Library Resources, Inc., was established with a $5,000,000 grant from the Ford Foundation, and, on the advice of many librarians and others whose opinions had been solicited, Verner Clapp was persuaded to serve as President. He threw himself into the work of the Council with all the energy and enthusiasm he had displayed throughout his career for every venture that engaged his interest. Under his direction the Council sponsored a variety of highly productive projects. Among many other undertakings, it supported: the study that stimulated the automation of the Library of Congress; the preliminary work that led to the mechanization of the production of the *Index Medicus;* the work of the Barrow Laboratory on the deterioration of book paper, the development of a formula for "permanent/durable" paper, an aerosol process for the deacidification of deteriorating books, and performance standards for library binding; development of the *National Union Catalog of Manuscript Collections;* the third edition of *The Union List of Serials;* production by the American Historical Association of a *Guide to Photocopied Historical Manuscripts;* the establishment of the *National Register of Microform Masters;* the planning and introduction of Cataloging in Publication; the production of the International Inventory of Musical Sources; a system for searching statute law by computer; the American Library Association's Library Technology Project and the book-selection service through the journal *Choice,* and *Books for College Libraries.* In addition, Clapp was quick to assist, through Council grants, various national and international library conferences, as well as cooperative library undertakings, surveys, studies, and extensions of worthwhile existing programs. Council support made possible the first publication of a scientific journal exclusively in microform and the production of such notable publications as Keyes Metcalf's *Planning Academic and Research Library Buildings* and Robert Hayes and Joseph Becker's *Handbook of Data Processing for Libraries.* In 1967 Clapp retired from the presidency of the Council on Library Resources but continued until 1972 to give the Council, as a full-time consultant, the benefit of his long experience and encyclopedic knowledge.

The range of Clapp's interests is exemplified by the many varied organizations in which he maintained membership: the American Antiquarian Society; the American Association for the Advancement of Science; the American and Canadian Bibliographic Societies; the American Institute of Graphic Art; the American, Canadian, and District of Columbia Library Associations; the Abstracting Board of the International Council of Scientific Unions; the National Microfilm Association; and the Special Libraries Association.

He was also a member of the National Advisory Commission on Libraries and the Science Information Council. For 18 years he served as a Director of the Forest Press, Inc., and, for the last 12 years of his life, as its President. He was a Trustee of the Lake Placid Club Education Foundation from 1955 until his death in 1972. It is not entirely coincidental, perhaps, that one of the most important contributors to librarianship since Melvil Dewey should have had such close affiliation with projects that continued Dewey's work.

Clapp served during his career on many committees and published extensively. His writings, always lucid and lively, exhibit an astonishing range of knowledge. They number more than 200 but represent only a fraction of the subjects that engaged his interest.

Few librarians have been as honored as he in their lifetimes, nor have many been so nobly eulogized in death. The American Library Association awarded him the Lippincott Award and the Melvil Dewey Medal and made him an Honorary Life Member. The Special Libraries Association gave him a Special Citation, and the Association of Research Libraries, at the time of his retirement from the Council on Library Resources, honored him with a citation for his "selfless dedication to the cause of librarianship and the service of scholarship," his service "to the United Nations and to foreign governments, to library organizations" and "to scholarly associations." It called him "an honored spokesman for the library profession" who had exerted "a more beneficent influence on research librarianship" than any other man of our time, and it named him the "Librarian's Librarian." Verner Warren Clapp died on June 15, 1972, in Virginia. At his retirement from the Library of Congress Mumford said of Clapp, "His contributions to the Library of Congress and to the library world are so varied and numerous that one is staggered at the knowledge that a single person in his lifetime could accomplish this and at the same time manage to be a loving husband, father, and friend." At the memorial tribute to him held in the Coolidge Auditorium of the Library of Congress on June 20, 1972, David C. Mearns, the former Assistant Librarian of Congress and Honorary Consultant in the Humanities, said of him, "Verner was . . . indomitable, exuberant, prodigious, passionate, inexhaustible, a polymath, and a fellow of infinite zest. . . . He was generous with his patience, with his counsel, with his consideration. . . . his friends were legion; his admirers a mighty host."

FREDERICK H. WAGMAN

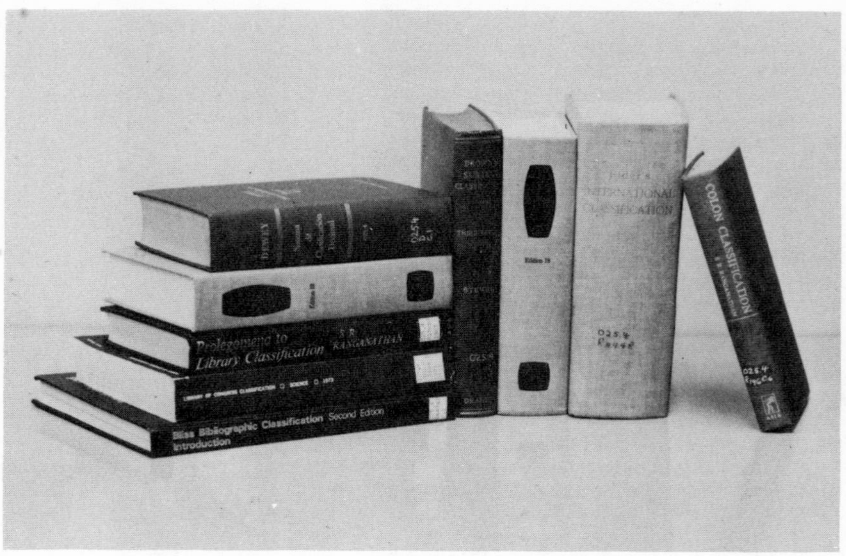


Arthur Plotnik

*Some key publications in classification.*



# Classification

The book of Genesis tells us that the world was created out of chaos when "God divided the light from the darkness." Thus, the idea of classification, literally "the making of classes," is shown to be the origin and essence of the world we live in. The ability to classify is indeed a fundamental faculty without which no living organism can function. We must, for example, distinguish between edible and inedible things, or animals that are (or may be) dangerous to us and those that are not. Everyone goes through life constantly making distinctions between things that are like and those that are unlike while at the same time also grouping them into larger containing classes or into smaller subclasses and perceiving relationships between different classes. The farmer keeps cattle, horses, and poultry apart, but together he thinks of them as his livestock, and each class of animals may at times have to be further subdivided into milch and beef cows, riding and draft horses, and chickens, turkeys, and geese. The mechanic sorts his fasteners into nuts and bolts and puts each of these into separate bins according to shape, size, threading, and so on. Even very young children keep round marbles separate from square blocks and know that both belong to the things called toys.

Ever since human knowledge has been recorded in durable form and collected in repositories, the need has been felt to arrange the resulting documents in such a manner that records with the same or similar characteristics could be found together. A collection of documents is thus deemed to be a library only when they are arranged in a systematic pattern. In a larger sense all arrangements of documents, whether by author, title, subject, or physical form, are based on some kind of classification, but in a more restricted sense only the systematic arrangement of documents (or their surrogates) by *subject* is commonly understood to be the purpose of library classification.

It is important to distinguish between three different but interrelated meanings of the term *classification* in library practice: in its most literal and basic sense it is the act of *classifying* or *the making of a classification scheme* (the resulting scheme often being called a classification for short); second, it is the act of *classing* or the assignment of class marks to documents so as to indicate their subject content; third, it is the resulting *physical arrangement* of documents (books and so forth) on shelves or the related (but not necessarily identical) arrangement of document surrogates (catalogue entries) in a classified subject catalogue.

The first of these, the making of a classification scheme, is obviously the fundamental one, the others being dependent on it. It has been defined by the International Federation for Documentation (FID) as follows:

> By classification is meant any method creating relations, generic or other, between individual semantic units, regardless of the degree of hierarchy contained in the systems and of whether those systems will be applied in connection with traditional or more or less mechanized methods of document searching.

A classification scheme consists generally of three interrelated parts: (1) A *schedule* or *table* listing the classes in a sequence perceived by the makers of the scheme as the most logical or useful one, normally subdivided in hierarchical order from the most general to the most specific topics. The phrase "relations, generic or other" in the FID definition means that a classification scheme may show not only hierarchic (genus-species) relations but also others—such as whole-part, agent-action, associative, or coordinated ones—and it may even use alphabetical subdivision; e.g., for names of persons or objects. Recurrent features, such as place names, time periods, or forms of presentation that are applicable throughout all or most of a scheme, may be listed separately in *auxiliary schedules.* (2) A *notation* that mechanizes the order of schedules by means of symbols, consisting of digits, letters, or a combination of both; other marks, such as mathematical symbols or punctuation marks, may also be used, although these do not have a universally agreed-upon and known order. (3) An *alphabetical index* that lists subjects by their names and synonyms and shows distributed aspects (their relationship to other subjects), in each case indicating through the notation their place in the schedules. Traditional classification schemes were arranged almost entirely on enumerative hierarchical principles, resulting in fixed "pigeonholes" for preconceived subjects. Modern classification schemes are both hierarchical and synthetic, providing for individual "facets" or aspects of subjects that can be combined at will to express the subject content of a document, thus avoiding the rigidity of older schemes and readily accommodating even entirely new subjects and relationships.

**Early Library Classifications.** The clay tablets found in one of the world's oldest libraries, the large royal archives of Assurbanipal (7th century B.C.), contained a catalogue that divided the works into several main classes (Grammar, History, Law, Natural history, Geography, Mathematics, Astronomy, Magic, Religion, Legends), each being subdivided into several subclasses. No actual classification scheme from Greek and Roman libraries has survived, but the catalogue of the great Alexandrian library, the *Pinakes* ("tables") compiled by Callimachus (3rd century B.C.), is reported to have been classified into Poets, Lawmakers, Philosophers, Historians, Rhetoricians, and Miscellaneous writers; further subdivisions were by form, subject, and time. The libraries of China at the end of the Western Han period (1st century A.D.) were classified into seven large groups: Encyclopedias, the Six arts, Philosophy, Poems and songs, Military art, Soothsaying, and Medicine. During the later Wei and Tsin dynasties (3rd to 5th centuries) a system was designed that survived practically unchanged until the 20th century. It consisted of four main classes (retaining several of the older classes as subdivisions): (1) Classics; (2) Philosophy, Military art, Mathematics, Theology; (3) History, Government, Miscellanea; (4) Literature.

**Medieval Library Classifications.** The early monastic libraries were so small that they had no need for a classification, but later it became common practice to divide the holdings of such libraries into three large groups, namely Theological works, Classical authors of antiquity, and Contemporary authors on the Seven arts. The latter were also the backbone of classification in the university libraries, where books were arranged according to the classical division of the curriculum into the Trivium (Grammar, Rhetoric, Logic) and the Quadrivium (Arithmetic, Geometry, Music, Astronomy).

**Philosophical and Pragmatic Classifications.** Since the Renaissance two main types of classifications can be distinguished: those that are based on a philosophical scheme or an ideal order of knowledge and those that aim merely at a practical arrangement of books on shelves. Outstanding among the former is the Swiss polyhistor Conrad Gesner's *Pandectarum . . . libri xxi,* the classified part of his *Bibliotheca universalis* that listed most learned books known at the time (1548). The system arranged books according to their subjects by 20 major classes, each with a number of subdivisions. Gesner's scheme marked the beginning of modern library classification and served as a model for the arrangement of many libraries until the end of the 18th century. Another philosophical scheme was contained in Francis Bacon's *Advancement of Learning* (1605), dividing human knowledge into History (Memory), Poesy (Imagination), and Philosophy (Reason); though it was not intended for library use, it influenced many later classifiers, including Jefferson and Dewey. A practical scheme, first developed in the mid-17th century by the Paris booksellers and ascribed to Ismael Bouilleau, was further elaborated by the French bibliographer Jacques-Charles Brunet in the early 19th century; the scheme was quite simple and had only five main classes—Theology, Jurisprudence, Sciences and Arts, Literature, and History—each with a moderate number of subdivisions. It is still used in part by the Bibliothèque Nationale and some other large French libraries; an adaptation of the scheme is used in the library of the British Museum (now part of the British Library).

A classification scheme that combined both philosophical principles of arrangement with practical applicability was designed in the 1840's by the German Orientalist and librarian A. A. E. Schleiermacher for the court library at Darmstadt. It comprised 25 main classes (A/Z) with some 13,000 subdivisions, making it the most detailed scheme of the 19th century. It was remarkably modern in its use of auxiliary tables for recurrent geographical (and some other) features, and it had a fully developed relative index. The scheme was used in some German national and university libraries well into the 20th century.

**The Dewey Decimal Classification (DDC).** Melvil Dewey designed his scheme for the small library at Amherst College in 1873 and first published it in 1876. It grew from a slim booklet containing less than 1,000 subdivisions on 12 pages (at the time criticized as excessively detailed!) and an alphabetical index of 18 pages to a three-volume work of more than 3,400 pages, comprising Schedules for several thousands of classes and their subdivisions, supplemented by an array of seven auxiliary Tables, and a comprehensive Relative Index. It had gone through 19 full and 11 abridged editions by the end of the 1970's. It has been translated into several dozen languages, including seven in non-Roman scripts, and it is used in thousands of libraries of all kinds throughout the world. It is also used for the arrangement of a number of national bibliographies.

The success of DDC is due to several features. It has a simple notation that is independent of language or script based on the principle of decimal fractions that are infinitely expandable "horizontally"; i.e., for further subdivision of an existing class (whereas "vertical" expansion, i.e., intercalation of a new subject into an existing hierarchy, is not always possible). The notation also has mnemonic features and is made flexible through the use of standard subdivisions for Forms, Areas, Literatures, Languages, Racial, ethnic, and national groups, Languages, and Persons which are applicable throughout the schedules (though not for all numbers). The principle of number building allows subdivision of one basic number by all or part of another, thus indicating certain aspects or relationships between subjects, while at the same time not burdening the schedules with an excessive number of subdivisions. These last two features are Dewey's most important contribution, and they formed the nucleus for the later development of faceted classifications. Finally, and perhaps most important, the DDC is backed by its own organization and by the Library of Congress, thus assuring its continued existence and revision to keep the scheme up to date.

Among the shortcomings of the scheme are: its sequence of main classes, reflecting the world outlook of the late 19th century; the allocation of only one main class each to science and technology, resulting in overcrowding and long notations as well as a separation of the basic sciences from their technological applications; the separation of history from social sciences; the separation of political geography from other geographical topics; and the strict adherence to the principle of "integrity of numbers," which often prevents the restructuring of old schedules to accommodate new topics and sometimes even the proper application of general facets. To a certain extent, the latter deficiency has been remedied by the introduction of so-called Phoenix schedules, which are completely redesigned sections of the scheme.

In the U.S. the DDC is used almost exclusively for shelf classification of books, mainly in school, public, and small college libraries. Some subject bibliographies, notably the *American Book Publishing Record,* are also classified by DDC. The Library of Congress provides DDC numbers for the majority of books for which cards are printed, and these are also available in the MARC data base. In the U.K. and several European countries and in many Asian and African libraries the DDC is widely used not only for shelf classification but also for the construction of classified subject catalogues and bibliographies, in which the detailed (and sometimes long) notations made possible by number building can be used to much better advantage than as mere call numbers on the spines of books.

**The Universal Decimal Classification (UDC).** In the 1890's two Belgian lawyers, Paul Otlet and Henri LaFontaine, conceived the idea of a worldwide bibliography on cards of all recorded knowledge, not only in book form but also in articles, reports, patents, and so on. To achieve this end they needed a highly specific classification. The DDC had by then become known in Europe, and the two men considered it suitable for their project, although it was not sufficiently detailed. In 1895 they asked for and received Dewey's permission to adopt, translate, and further develop his scheme (then in its fifth edition). Otlet and LaFontaine thereupon proceeded to translate the schedules into French, make some changes in religion, the social sciences, and technology, and thus develop with the help of subject specialists the *Classification décimale universelle* (for some time known as the "Brussels Expansion").

Although the UDC was and still is based on the DDC, it differs from it in several respects. The basic structure of ten main classes and most of the first 1,000 three-digit codes were retained (except for final 0's, which were dropped), but a much larger number of sometimes very minute subdivisions were introduced. Dewey's form and place auxiliaries were expanded to "general auxiliaries" expressing also aspects of language, race, nationality, time, and point-of-view (and later also persons and materials), while "special" auxiliaries applicable to certain classes only were designed for other recurrent features.

**"Classification System for Chinese Libraries"** 149

***Classification, Theoretical and Practical*** 482

***Classified Catalogue of the Sudan Collection*** 548

***Classroom Libraries for Public Schools*** 190

All auxiliaries were indicated by means of mathematical symbols or punctuation marks. Finally, the colon sign was introduced to link two or more UDC codes so as to indicate relationships, a device that makes the notation highly flexible: A document on "Use of computers in hospital management" is classed as 362.1:658.3:519.68 (Hospitals: Personnel management: Computers); each of the three codes can be used as an access point.

The full UDC tables were first published in French in 1905 under the title *Manuel du répertoire bibliographique universel,* followed later by full editions in German, English, Russian, Spanish, Japanese, and eight other languages. These full editions contain about 150,000 subdivisions. Medium editions (about 30 percent of the full tables) exist in English, German, French, Japanese, and 13 other languages. Abridged editions (about 10–15 percent of the full tables) exist in 17 languages and 5 different scripts. In addition there are special editions for certain subject fields in which the codes for the special subjects are given in full, while codes for fringe subjects are listed only in abbreviated form.

Whereas the idea of a worldwide bibliography had to be abandoned in the 1920's as impractical, the UDC was rapidly adopted throughout the world by many libraries, abstracting services, and journals, especially for scientific and technical subjects, and it is still a widely used general system of classification, with an estimated 100,000 institutional and individual users. The U.S. is the only major country in which the UDC has not had much success, though several specialist subject bibliographies, a large abstracting service, and several libraries use the system. In the Soviet Union, on the other hand, the UDC has been made mandatory since 1963 for all scientific and technical libraries, as well as for abstracting services, foremost among them *Referativnyi Zhurnal;* all scientific and technical books also carry a UDC number. In Eastern European countries the UDC is consequently also widely used, and it has also long since been employed in Japanese documentation.

Although the basic structure of the UDC still follows DDC's ten main classes (except for class 4, which is presently empty, Language having been amalgamated with Literature in class 8), it is no longer fully compatible with the DDC notation because many subjects are now classed by codes that are quite different. The responsibility for the revision and development of the UDC lies with the FID in the Hague, working through committees of specialists or interested individuals. *Extensions and Corrections* are published semiannually, each issue containing many hundreds of new, corrected, or deleted codes, thus keeping the scheme continuously up to date. Due to its highly faceted structure and largely expressive notation, the UDC is the only one of the large general classification schemes that has been used successfully in computerized information retrieval, and it has also been employed as a switching language between subject heading lists and thesauri.

**The Expansive Classification (EC).** While Dewey conceived the DDC in the tradition of the pragmatic classifications, his older colleague Charles Ammi Cutter designed a scheme in the 1880's and 1890's that was influenced by the then current philosophy of "evolutionary order in nature." The EC consisted of seven different but related schemes (the last of which remained unfinished). The first was rather broad, comprising only seven classes, each subsequent "expansion" being more finely subdivided and intended to be used by increasingly larger libraries. The notation of main classes consisted of letters, while auxiliary tables used digits; a full stop was also used as a notational device. Unfortunately, EC's notation had to be extended throughout the seven expansions, necessitating constant reclassification when a library grew and wished to move from one expansion to the next. Only a small number of American libraries ever used the scheme. Within ten years of the death of its inventor in 1903, attempts to keep it up to date failed, so that it was soon almost entirely abandoned. Its importance lies in the fact that both Cutter's notation and his ideas of an order of subjects suggested by a scientific consensus had a decisive influence on two other American schemes, namely that of the Library of Congress and Bliss's Bibliographic Classification.

**The Library of Congress Classification (LC).** When the Library of Congress moved into its present main building in 1897, it needed a new classification scheme since the one originally devised by Thomas Jefferson (which was an adaptation of the Baconian scheme) had become inadequate. In 1899 the DDC was considered, but Dewey could not agree to some major changes that were required by the Library. The Library then decided to design its own scheme, taking many features from Cutter's EC but essentially producing a pragmatic system primarily based on its own holdings and tailored to the design of the building. The LC is in fact not one system but a loosely coordinated series of 21 special classifications, each with its own structure, notation, auxiliary tables, and index, occupying 34 volumes with a total of more than 10,600 pages. One class, P (Language and Literature), occupies more than 3,200 pages (30 percent of the whole scheme), whereas all of science and technology constitutes only 13 percent; Class K (Law) is still incomplete.

The notation is mixed, consisting of one or two letters for main classes followed by ordinal numbers up to a maximum of four digits for subdivisions. Gaps are left between numbers for future expansion, but where these have been filled, decimal subdivision, generally by one or two digits.
Beyond (or instead of) decimal subdivision, further subdivision of a subject is alphabetical, often by the English name of a subject expressed by Cutter numbers (a letter plus one or more digits); this feature results in dispersion of closely related subjects. No use is made of synthesis or mnemonics. Where geographical, historical, or form subdivisions are necessary, they are specially developed for each subject without regard to similar subdivisions in the same or in other classes.

Revision of the schedules is carried out individually for each class; whole blocks of numbers may be canceled, the subjects classed there moved to an entirely different schedule, and the former numbers used for different subjects. Sometimes added subjects are arbitrarily inserted just where a vacant number exists and without regard to collocation of related subjects.

Several hundred American libraries have switched from DDC to LC since the 1960's, primarily because of the administrative advantages of centralized classification and the universal availability of LC class marks on cards and on MARC (whereas DDC class marks are assigned by the Library of Congress only to entries for certain categories of books). A few university libraries outside the United States have also adopted LC for similar reasons, though they often make their own adaptations and expansions for topics not covered by the scheme at all or not in sufficient detail.

**The Bibliographic Classification (BC).** Henry Evelyn Bliss, the most eminent of American classification theorists, devoted a lifetime to the design of a scheme that would reflect the "scientific consensus" on the order of things and ideas. It was considered by many to be far superior to all other general schemes both in structure and notation, but by the time it was published by the H. W. Wilson Co. (1935–53), most American libraries had already been classified by either DDC or LC and could not or would not change to a new and unproven system. Only about a hundred libraries in the U.K. adopted the

BC. The scheme consists of 26 main classes (A/Z) and an "anterior class" (1/9) for form subdivisions that are applicable throughout the schedules. A characteristic feature is the provision of alternative locations or treatments for many subjects, depending on the point of view of the book or the needs of a particular library. Thus, a book on economic history may be classed under History at LG or under Economics at T3. The notation makes use of all letters of the alphabet up to four capital letters and also uses lowercase letters for geographical subdivisions and digits for forms, which results in very compact class marks; e.g., BOV3 History of broadcasting, or JCAe Educational research in England.

After Bliss's death in 1955 upkeep and revision of the BC ceased for almost 15 years, and several libraries abandoned the scheme. In the 1970's it was revived in England under the editorship of Jack Mills; the first new schedules began to appear in 1976, and the complete scheme was to be published in 20 parts through 1980. The revised BC is in fact a new classification built upon the scheme of Bliss but with a modern faceted structure and a much improved notation. Whether it will meet with more success than the original BC remains to be seen.

**The Colon Classification (CC).** This is the last of the great universal schemes to be designed by one person. The Indian mathematician-turned-librarian S. R. Ranganathan published the first version of his CC in 1933. It constituted an almost complete break with traditional methods of classifying, relying on an analytico-synthetic approach. Instead of enumerating classes of things and ideas and their ever more minute subdivisions, the CC lists only general properties and characteristics, or "facets," whose class marks can be combined to express exactly the subject of a document. It thus abandoned the method of creating fixed "pigeonholes" for preconceived and precoordinated subjects that had bedeviled earlier classification schemes. The backbone of the scheme is formed by 43 main classes (denoted by one or two capital letters and two Greek letters), roughly corresponding to traditional disciplines but not extensively subdivided. All detail is provided by the facets, which are combined according to the formula PMEST, where P stands for Personality (generally the primary or central aspect of a subject), E for Energy (any kind of action or process and their results), M for Material, S for Space (=Place), and T for Time. Each facet is set off from others by different punctuation marks (originally only the colon sign from which the scheme takes its name and which was itself adopted from the UDC). When constructing a class mark, not all facets may have to be used, whereas others may appear more than once. Thus, a work on "Attempts to eradicate poverty in Scotland in the 1940's" would first of all be put into main class Y Sociology, because it deals with a social phenomenon. Analyzing the subject, we find that it is concerned with Poverty, :434 in the E facet and its Eradication, :64, also in E; Scotland is .563 in S, and the 1940's are 'N4 in facet T, so that the complete class mark becomes

Y : 434 : 64 .563 'N4
(P E 2E S T)

(In this case, no Material facet is involved, but 2 Energy facets are used.) The alphabetical index to the scheme is also constructed along new lines, the "chain-indexing" principle invented by Ranganathan.

Though the seeds of generally applicable facets were sown by Dewey, and the idea was further developed in the UDC, it was fully applied and systematized only in the CC, which is now in its seventh edition, prepared by the Documentation Research and Training Centre in Bangalore, India. Schedules for specific topics not dealt with in sufficient detail in the general scheme are also published from time to time. Although the CC is used in relatively few libraries in its homeland, and in fewer still elsewhere, its underlying theory has had a major impact on classification. Since the 1950's, the structure and revision policy of all existing or newly devised classification schemes (with the exception of the LC) have been more or less affected by Ranganathan's ideas.

**The Bibliothecal-Bibliographic Classification (BBK).** A new classification system for the libraries of the U.S.S.R., the BBK, was elaborated by the Lenin Library in Moscow and published in 30 volumes from 1960 to 1968. An abridged edition in six volumes was published in 1970–75, and a one-volume abridgment for very small libraries appeared in 1975. The BBK consists of 21 main classes, each of which is indicated by one of the 28 letters of the Russian Cyrillic alphabet. First is Marxism-Leninism, followed by the Sciences, Technology (eight classes), Agriculture, Medicine, Social Sciences (seven classes), Literature, Art, Religion, Philosophy, and Generalia. The 21 classes are further subdivided into a total of about 45,000 main headings. The notation is mixed, the letter of the main class being followed by digits expressed in decimal fractions, with points after every three digits. General auxiliary tables are provided for geographical areas and for other facets, most of which are modeled on those in the UDC (though the notation is different). Each class has its own index, and there is as yet no general index. Most class marks are enumerative and they are often precoordinated (similar to LC), but some combinations are possible.

The BBK has been made mandatory in Soviet general and university libraries and those dealing primarily with the social sciences. It has also been introduced in other Eastern European countries and in the German Democratic Republic, where it is used for the classified arrangement of the *Deutsche Nationalbibliographie.* Further development of the BBK (which is still partially incomplete) and revision will probably be carried out by the Lenin Library, though there is as yet no central BBK office formally charged with the task.

**Modern Chinese Classification Schemes.** In the early years of the 20th century the classification scheme used for almost 2,000 years proved to be unsuitable for modern Chinese literature. DDC began to be used by some libraries in 1907, and during the 1920's LC was also tried. Neither scheme proved to be adequate for Chinese topics, and local adaptations were made. After the establishment of the People's Republic of China, an entirely new general classification scheme was designed, the first version of which was published in 1953. It had 17 main classes with many subdivisions, the first of which in each class was always devoted to the Marxistic-Leninistic and Maoist view of a subject. The notation used only Arabic digits. A revised version, *Zhongguo Tushu Ziliao Fenlei Fa* [Chung-kuo to shu tzu liao fen lei fa, in Wade-Giles transcription] ("Classification System for Chinese Libraries"), appeared in 1975, now with 22 main classes notated by one or two Roman uppercase letters, subdivisions with a decimal numerical notation, general auxiliaries using lowercase Roman letters, and special auxiliaries expressed by hyphens and digits (e.g., −0). An example from the schedules is

| | |
|---|---|
| T | Technology |
| TF | Metallurgy |
| TF 111 | Production methods |
| TF 111.522 | By electrolysis of molten salts |

While the new Chinese scheme is modeled on Western ones (especially the UDC) and uses Roman letters and Arabic digits, its index follows traditional Chinese methods, the logograms expressing the name of each subject being arranged by number of strokes.

**The Broad System of Ordering (BSO).** The most recent general classification scheme is one commissioned by Unesco in 1971 and elaborated by FID as a "roof classification." It was first published by FID in 1978 and is intended to be used as a "switching language" between existing classification systems, thesauri, and other information-retrieval systems, centers, or organizations, not in order to supplant any of these, but to make them utually compatible on a general level. As its name implies, it is quite general, providing only about 4,000 not very detailed subdivisions, most of which can be freely combined according to modern principles of faceted classification. BSO features an entirely new system of notation based on digits that are used in groups of millesimal and centesimal fractions, separated by commas, thus ensuring a maximum of hospitality and flexibility in a pattern of 3,2,2 digits. The scheme has only three general facets, namely, Types of information sources (roughly corresponding to form auxiliaries in other schemes), Time, and Place or Location. Within each subject field, the details are arranged in the following facet pattern:

Main subject
- Tools or equipment for operation
- Operations (activities by people)
- Processes, interactions
- Parts, subsystems of objects, or products
- Objects of study, products, total systems.

For example:

| | |
|---|---|
| 716 | Building construction & services |
| ,10,30 | Building materials |
| ,30 | Building construction work |
| ,37 | Timber construction |
| ,40 | Parts of buildings |
| ,45 | Walls |
| ,50 | Engineering services & installations |
| ,52 | Heating |
| ,70 | Finishing & decorating |

(Only a few of the subdivisions in the schedule are shown in this example.) Complex subjects can be expressed by combinations of class marks from different parts of the scheme, separated by a hyphen, e.g., "Environmental aspects of building construction" is 716-390, where 390 is Environment.

Although the BSO was not designed for classification of books in libraries, it could very well be employed for broad shelf classification, which is all that is needed in many open-shelf browsing collections. Whether it will also achieve its stated goal as an international switching language will depend more on strong organizational backing than on the inherent merits of the scheme.

**Research on Classification.** In 1952 a Classification Research Group (CRG) was founded in England to study the theoretical foundations of classification. The members of the CRG subsequently constructed several special classification schemes, and some members were also instrumental in the design of the BSO. Similar research groups were founded in other countries during the 1960's, and their work attracted much interest also on the part of philosophers and linguists, resulting in several international study conferences. The FID also has a standing Committee on Classification Research (FID/CR), mainly concerned with maintaining a register of current research on classification, the education and exchange of classification researchers, the organization of annual meetings, and the publication of research reports.

**REFERENCES**

"Classification: Theory and Practice," *Drexel Library Quarterly* (1974).

Ingetraut Dahlberg, "Major Developments in Classification," *Advances in Librarianship* (1977).

Douglas J. Foskett, *Classification and Indexing in the Social Sciences* (1974).

Leo La Montagne, *American Library Classification* (1961).

W. C. Berwick Sayers, *A Manual of Classification for Librarians,* 5th ed., rev. by Arthur Maltby (1975).

E. I. Shamurin, "History of Library and Bibliographical Classification" (Moscow, 1955–59). In Russian. there is a German translation: *Geschichte der bibliothekarisch-bibliographischen Klassifikation* (Munich, 1967–68).

Brian C. Vickery, *Faceted Classification: A Guide to Construction and Use of Special Schemes* (1960).

HANS H. WELLISCH

## Cleverdon, Cyril W.

(1914–  )

Cyril Cleverdon is best known for his work in information retrieval. He was born in Bristol, September 9, 1914, and served on the staff of Bristol Public Libraries from 1932 to 1938. From 1938 to 1946 he was the Librarian of the Engine Division of the Bristol Aeroplane Co. Ltd. In 1946 he was appointed Librarian of the College of Aeronautics at Cranfield (later the Cranfield Institute of Technology), where he remained until his retirement in 1978. In 1976–78 he also served there as Professor of Information Transfer Studies. He later became Executive Secretary of the European Association of Information Services (EUSIDIC).

Cleverdon has been a leader in the evaluation of information systems. In 1957 the National Science Foundation awarded a grant to Aslib for an evaluation of indexing systems, to be undertaken under Cleverdon's direction at the College of Aeronautics. Thus began the Aslib Cranfield Research Project. "Cranfield 1," 1957–62, compared the performance of four index languages: UDC, alphabetical subject catalogue, Uniterms, and a special faceted classification. The study was large, involving 18,000 documents and 1,200 search topics. The twin measures of recall ratio and precision ratio assumed major significance for the first time in the experiments. In comparing the systems, many performance variables were studied, including type of document, indexing time, qualifications of the indexers, and the number of index terms assigned. The results indicated surprisingly little difference in the performance of the systems. Human errors in indexing and searching were more serious than failures due to file organization. Cleverdon concluded that specificity of vocabulary and exhaustivity of indexing are much more important than file organization as factors affecting the performance of information systems.

Cranfield 1 was important because it revealed which factors importantly affect the performance of retrieval systems and which do not. It also developed methodologies that could be applied successfully to evaluation of experimental, prototype, and fully operating information systems. The Cranfield techniques were subsequently used in the evaluation of a number of operating systems, including the extensive evaluation of MEDLARS conducted in the period 1966 to 1968.

The second stage of the studies ("Cranfield 2") began in 1963. The major objective was to investigate the components of index languages and their effects on the performance of retrieval systems. In Cranfield 2 the various index language devices were each evaluated according to their effect on the recall and precision of a retrieval system. Altogether 29 index languages, consisting of various combinations of the several devices, were evaluated, using a test collection of 1,400 documents and 221 test searches. The results again were rather unexpected because the index languages that performed best were natural-language systems based on words occurring in document texts.

Cleverdon is the author of many reports and journal articles in the field of information retrieval, the most important being the detailed reports on the two phases of the Cranfield studies: *Report on Testing and Analysis of an Investigation into the Comparative Efficiency of Indexing Systems* (College of Aeronautics, 1962) and *Factors Determining the Performance of Index Languages* (ASLIB Cranfield Research Project, 1966), the latter written with Jack Mills and E. Michael Keen.

Cleverdon served on the Council of Aslib for most of the period from 1952 to 1967 and was its Chairman in 1958, 1975, and 1976. He became a Fellow of the Library Association, an Honorary Fellow of the Institute of Information Scientists, and an Honorary Member of ASLIB.

Cleverdon's contributions were widely recognized in the United States, Europe, and elsewhere. He received the Professional Award of the Special Libraries Association in 1962 and the Award of Merit of the American Society for Information Science in 1971.

F. W. LANCASTER

## Clift, David Horace

(1907–1973)

David H. Clift served as the chief executive of the American Library Association from 1951 to 1972. He led the association in expanding its membership and program and in organizing its headquarters.

Born on June 16, 1907, in the bluegrass hills of Washington, Kentucky, the eldest of six children, Clift was a reader all his life. He loved books and went out of his way to be involved with them. By the time he had finished high school in 1925, he had decided to attend the University of Kentucky in Lexington. He saved money by boarding with friends of the family while taking any part-time job he could find. By his junior year he had won a student assistant job in the university library. Using that experience as a springboard, he was able to obtain summer work in the Lexington Public Library.

He knew where he wanted to go by then. At that time the evolving library profession offered a fifth-year Bachelor's degree. Clift secured a loan from the Masonic Order of DeMolay and went to New York City in 1930 to attend the famous Columbia University School of Library Service. He found part-time work in the university library until he finished his degree in mid-1931.

Instead of returning to Kentucky during the Great Depression, he stayed in New York, working in the famous "reference" Room 315 of the New York Public Library. He was among many famous librarians to emerge from the same room; Keyes D. Metcalf, L. Quincy Mumford, Robert B. Downs, and Ed Freehafer are just a few of the people with whom he worked. He married Eleanore Flynn, a children's librarian for the Brooklyn Public Library. Their six years in the New York system were happy ones for both of them, but Clift could not resist the blandishments of Charles C. Williamson, Director of the Columbia University Library, and Clift joined him as his assistant at Columbia in 1937. For the next five years he sharpened his personnel skills and managerial talent; it was there that Frederick G. Kilgour came to know Clift and appreciate his quiet and sure way with organization and personnel supervision.

In 1942 Clift was drafted into the Army and assigned as an orderly in a hospital. He was soon transferred into the Office of Strategic Services (OSS), where intelligence-gathering activity was growing under the Interdepartmental Committee for the Acquisition of Foreign Acquisitions. Clift became the Deputy to the Executive Director—who happened to be Frederick G. Kilgour. Clift soon found himself supervising a staff of 140 people.

Following his honorable discharge in 1945, Clift became Associate Librarian at Yale. There he became a Fellow of Trumbull College and developed for the library a position classification and pay plan that was an admired model for academic librarians.

*David Horace Clift*

During this period he led a delegation of the Library of Congress Mission to Germany (1945–46) and served as President of the Connecticut Library Association (1950–51).

Clift became Executive Secretary of the American Library Association in September 1951. He moved into the crowded old McCormick Mansion on Huron Street in Chicago, which had been serving as headquarters for the Association for far too long. The membership was 19,701 and the general funds budget was $191,129. The outlook was bleak, but Clift's strong points were administration, personnel work, and subtlety. When once asked what he felt was required of an association executive, he replied that it was to administer the policies decided by membership and leave the leadership to those elected by the membership. He went to work on reorganizing headquarters staff and creating an equitable pay plan that enabled ALA to recruit some of the most able and dedicated people in the field.

But it was his dealings with the professional leadership that contributed to his long tenure as ALA chief. He was able to encourage consensus and compromise, thus avoiding some of the divisive in-fighting that had marked some previous headquarters administrations. When Clift retired in 1972 as Executive Director of ALA, the membership stood at 30,592 and the general funds budget was $2,262,971. During his 20 years of service some $15 million in grants came to ALA, making possible the establishment of national library standards and advances in professional library education. Among other achievements were advances in making a place for libraries in schools. *Choice* was founded as a review medium for undergraduate collection development, under the auspices of the Association for College and Research Colleges, an ALA division. The official *ALA Bulletin* changed from a journal primarily of record to a lively magazine called *American Libraries*. A series of nationwide adult education programs were conducted in libraries, and goals set for public library service. New emphasis was placed on the defense of intellectual freedom in library service. Further, the ALA Washington Office emerged as an important agency, resulting in the successful involvement of the federal government in support and assistance programs for libraries.

David H. Clift, who retired in 1972, was returning from a European trip collecting data for a study on comparative librarianship when he died on October 12, 1973. Grace Stevenson, his long-time associate at ALA, said of Clift, "He was never selling a bill of goods—or himself—just libraries."

GERALD R. SHIELDS

# Collection Development

The term "collection development" describes a cluster of functions which, together, shape the holdings of materials in a library: funding, self-study and evaluation, selection, weeding, and maintenance. This article focuses on the shaping and management of the collection, the decision-related aspects of the process, rather than on techniques of acquisitions or preservation. Also beyond the scope of this discussion are censorship, media, and resource sharing.

## EVOLUTION OF THE CONCEPT

Discussions of functions relating to library collections center traditionally on the techniques of materials selection and collection building. Certainly the challenges of collection building and selection are important; they dominate the work of librarians today in the U.S. and in many other parts of the world. But the decade of the 1970's brought new challenges. New initiatives and major shifts altered the collecting patterns which had characterized modern librarianship for more than a century.

When libraries are just getting started, selection is a dominant concern, for scarce purchase funds have to be directed where they will have the most impact. At this point, differences of opinions about whether to buy the books patrsons demand or to choose carefully from the first materials which will challenge the individual are paramount. As the library and the environment in which it functions progress, more and more demands will be placed on the library, and selection (accompanied by the implication that much is not selected) yields to a broader task of collection building. Collecting becomes less exclusive and more inclusive, as selectors seek to plan ahead for an apparently continuing expansion of demands on the collection. At some point either the materials approach meeting the needs of the users, theoretically, or the limits to the means of further collection building are reached. Under this new circumstance, the task of the collection librarian is broadened again to seek answers to new questions: How well does the collection meet the needs of current (rather than future or past) users? How large does the collection need to be? How best can the collection be maintained? During the 1970's, these new questions came to dominate the thinking of collection librarians.

## ENVIRONMENT

Decisions about selection, maintenance, and weeding of collections are determined by a wide range of factors. These factors can be grouped as follows: (1) support, or the means available to acquire and maintain a collection (most often, funding); (2) the quantity of materials available for acquisition; (3) the accessibility of other collections; and (4) the needs of the library's user clientele. For the developed Western countries, in about 1970, major shifts in the funding and information situations led librarians to put new emphasis on access to other collections through resource sharing, and to a comprehensive review of user needs. This section will consider the background for understanding the recent substantial shift in approach toward library collections.

**Support.** An analysis of the means of obtaining materials for libraries, and the relation of these to public policy, highlights the social foundation of library collecting. Selection, especially, and also collection building assume the chief means of acquisition to be purchase. It is useful to keep in mind such other sources as gifts, deposits, and copying. Certainly the backbone of the great modern national collections is deposit. Great research libraries have been built on gifts of collections and to a lesser extent by exchanges. The monastic libraries were built by copying from borrowed texts. Each of these means survives today, often less frequently as dominant collecting vehicles, but nearly always significant. After World War II, for example, the National Library of the Philippines was rebuilt through copying resources which were available in Chicago's Newberry Library. More recently, the Genealogical Society of the Church of Latter Day Saints has amassed great quantities of copies of early records through an international program of microfilming, for access and preservation. But most library collecting is done through purchase and can be a reflection of public policy, directly or indirectly.

Public policy provides for library collections in four major ways: tax authority, direct appropriation, tax incentives and exemptions, and copyright deposit requirements. A key element of the modern library movement has been the passage into law of these means of support. The history of library legislation has shown a growing commitment to the values of libraries, learning, and book collections. This commitment is an aspect of broader historical trends.

**Cultural, Social, and Political Determinants.** A very brief history of library collecting cannot overlook the point that the modern state's commitment to collecting is the successor to earlier forms of patronage. The copying carried out for the monastic collections reflects the central role of the medieval Church in the preservation and management of information, learning, and knowledge. The Church's partner in patronage was the aristocracy. Hierarchical religious and governmental institutions fostered centralized collections of limited access for the purpose of preserving those institutions. The social changes and reforms which began with the Renaissance and the Reformation and included the Age of Revolutions dramatically altered the means of distributing and collecting information. By the mid-19th century, radicals and progressive conservatives were united in working for means to create an informed and educated electorate, to make aristocrats of the masses in order to preserve institutions and culture. Library collections were one of the key means of achieving these ends, and for over a century they have prospered as the trend toward social equality has continued. Along with the rise of democracy, the growth of capitalism and technology created new demands for libraries. In the quarter century after World War II, rapid growth of technology and Western influence in the world led to specialization and to an information explosion.

**Recent Changes.** The transition from the 1960's to the 1970's demonstrated how much the collecting of library materials was tied to external factors, national and international social or political trends, and library responses. Around the world, the post-World War II era of librarianship had seen broad expansion, the recovery from Depression austerity and from war, the reaching of new publics, and a new and firmer partnership with technology. The economy was expanding while inflation was moderate or—by late 1970's criteria—nonexistent. The new American world role brought new collection building demands in the U.S. and creative responses to those demands. But as the 1960's drew to a close, the environment shifted dramatically. The American optimism of the early 1960's was reversed, and a critical mass of new circumstances arose with significance for the planning and management of collections of library materials.

*Emergence of New Subject Demands.* Building throughout the 1960's was a worldwide interest in scientific and technical subjects. Later, social topics (independence, ethnicity, radicalism, feminism) in quick succession generated demand on limited library resources. By the 1970's, alternative technologies, psychological topics, and interest in careers and business caused additional expansion of library collecting scope for public and educational libraries. The 1979 White House Conference on Libraries and Information Science articulated dramatically the broad range of new and emerging user demands. Increased specialization was characteristic of books and users. At the end of the 1970's, the typical university press run for a new title was about as large as at the beginning of the century, even though the number of titles had grown tremendously.

*Information Explosion.* Reflecting the increase in specialization and the expanded learning of the post-Sputnik Western world, there was a marked growth in journal literature, book publication, and the production of government documents. By the 1970's, this was followed by the expansion of index and abstract sources, made possible in part by computer technology. By the late 1970's, much of this new access capability was available, directly or indirectly, to a great number of patrons in on-line data bases.

*Energy.* The shortage of energy and the premium to be paid for it caused major reallocations of funds, inevitably diverting moneys away from collection building and creating intense pressure to limit collection growth by resorting to storage, deaccessioning, and resource sharing. Conversely, the resulting redistribution of wealth stimulated collecting in new, energy-rich regions—to support rapid economic development efforts.

*Funding Constraints.* Beginning in the late 1960's, academic libraries encountered slowed growth of budgets and even budget decline as institutions reached their income limits and as graduate enrollments dropped. The first crunch, around 1970, was felt in slashed library budgets, leaving permanent gaps in many American research and high technology collections. By the late 1970's, academic librarians were preparing, as well, for a decline in undergraduate enrollments. Public librarians met taxpayer resistance and even revolt, as in the Jarvis-Gann Proposition 13 in California, which reduced property taxes. Corporate special libraries struggled in the face of uneven profits throughout the 1970's.

*Inflation.* The cost of books and periodicals rose more rapidly than the costs of many other goods during the 1970's. Periodicals rose most strikingly and claimed greater and greater shares of library materials budgets. High interest rates penalized publishers and jobbers who carried large inventories. The results were short press runs and growing numbers of sought-for out-of-print titles. Thus, many books which had been "selected" never became a part of the library collection. Currency values experienced major readjustments and had grave consequences for library collections, particularly in English-speaking countries. Series published in Germany quickly went beyond the reach of all but the largest and strongest collections, for example.

**Library Response.** As the basic social conditions around library collecting changed from the 1960's to the 1970's, the professional response took two main directions, toward resource sharing and toward improved management skills for the functions relating to collecting. These new thrusts were reactions to changes from outside the environment.

*Resource sharing.* Related closely to the development of resource sharing was the effort on the part of librarians and those who depend most on libraries to affect public policy so as to provide adequate funds to meet the increased costs and new demands and to cover the broader range of materials. When those who form public policy and the library community had worked together long enough to understand each other's limitations, proposals for resource sharing began to emerge. On state, local, and consortium levels concrete projects began to emerge which would affect the collecting environment of individual libraries profoundly. Linking mechanisms between libraries developed: most notably union card catalogues (to be succeeded by microform and by on-line circulation and bibliographic data bases) and new specialized locating tools.

The idea of cooperative collecting, long a hope of the profession and more recently a panacea grasped onto by some funding sources, has been almost totally impractical in the absence of effective bibliographic control. The new linking mechanisms, though, have opened the way to new serious consideration of the potential and problems of this idea. Nevertheless, the problem of bibliographic control has been less complex for periodicals, where the task is broken up between the location devices (union lists, etc.) and the indexes. A limited amount of effort could create a holdings list of journal titles so that articles found in indexes could be traced easily in remote locations. The 1970's saw libraries responding to spiraling journal costs both by creating union lists and by turning to centers for periodical servicing. The largest scaled example is the British Library Lending Division in Boston Spa, England. Materials available here were accessible internationally within days.

In the U.S. the importance of Chicago's Center for Research Libraries grew as member research libraries came to call on this central source for more and more less frequently needed titles. Also in Chicago the Periodical Bank of the Associated Colleges of the Midwest showed in the late 1960's and early 1970's that smaller academic and other libraries could meet their journal needs by relying on a central, dedicated collection of more frequently called-for titles which still might be beyond the needs of each individual library. The idea was successfully demonstrated in Illinois's North Surburban Library System, where the Central Serials Service provides a comprehensive backup to public libraries. Plans for a National Periodicals Center were under discussion in the late 1970's.

*Management Methods.* As the quantity of materials, the demands, and the funds for collecting all went out of synchronization to a significant degree, the skills needed to make collecting decisions began to proliferate. The bibliographer, or person knowledgeable about developments in a particular field or fields, needed to be familiar with the collections of nearby libraries as well. Also, limited funds required that nothing be purchased that was not needed by the user clientele. Those who provided the funds and those who called on the library began to hold the library accountable in new ways. The response has been to develop a new range of quantitative and qualitative tools for collection development: needs assessment, planning, and evaluation.

CURRENT PRACTICE

The tasks of selection and building, supplemented by the relatively newer emphasis on collection maintenance and weeding, depend on the results of self-study.

**Managing the Collection.** Functions relating to planning and managing collections today have roles equal in importance to those held almost exclusively by selecting and collection building functions a few years ago. In the recent literature librarians have turned much of their attention to the means available to organize scarce resources in new ways to meet demands. Of course, the idea of self-study is not new. John Cotton Dana's *Library Primer* (1899), which sums up a generation of library thought, begins by discussing what good a library does, generally. Later on, when treating selection, Dana's chapter is subtitled "Fitting the Library to Its Owners." A number of principal factors are considered: proximity to other libraries, broadly stated purposes, funds available and projected, and the characteristics of the user public (level of education, use habits or patterns, etc.). In this most recent period old wisdom has gained new sophistication. As indicated above, librarians have been able to redefine the "proximity" of other libraries through new linking devices. In addition, they have given greater attention to analyzing the characteristics of the user public. Another of Dana's chapters, one on general library policy, begins by admonishing "Remember always (1) that the public owns its public library, and (2) that no useless lumber is more useless than unused books." Current collecting practice can be seen as seeking to create effective tools to pursue these two guidelines.

*Needs Assessment.* What are the needs of those who place demands on the library? This is not a new question, but a century ago there appears to have been more consensus about this than is found today. Once again Dana illustrates the nature and tenor of discussion earlier:

> Don't buy a novel simply because it is popular. If you follow that line you will end with the cheapest kind of stuff. Some librarians pretend that they must buy to please the public taste; that they can't use their own judgment in selecting books for a library. . . . Why these librarians don't supply the Police Gazette is difficult to understand. 'The public' would like it—some of them. . . . The silly, the weak, the sloppy, the wishy-washy novel, the sickly love story, the belated tract, the crude hodge-podge of stilted conversation, impossible incident, and moral platitude or moral posh for children—these are not needed.

Dana's *Primer* summed up a generation of experience, and in the preface he traces the roots of his material back to the report *Public Libraries in the United States of America,* published by the U.S. Bureau of Education in 1876, particularly an article by Poole. But the report contained a variety of articles and a diversity of views. F. B. Perkins spoke strongly in favor of supplying the books that people wanted to read, rather than collecting those things people *should* want to read. And Cutter thought there would be money enough to buy only perfect books when people themselves had been perfected.

In the 1970's the issue once again was a vital one. A study at the University of Pittsburgh found that many of the books acquired and housed in the university's library never were used. In rebuttal of these findings, Jasper Shad (in "Pittsburgh University Studies of Collection Usage: A Symposium," *Journal of Academic Librarianship,* 1979) reiterated Dana's earlier conviction: "In the last analysis, need, not use, should determine what libraries contain."

In general, needs assessment has encompassed the whole range of factors. The need to know the users well, the "owners," has prompted community analysis projects to take place in many areas to aid in public library programming. What people want, certainly, is a factor, and surveys of the most popular young adult literature have been carried out by many public libraries. Academic libraries have placed new emphasis on liaison with faculty and students. Curricular demands are related to collection goals. Daniel Gore and Richard Trueswell, also, have suggested that academic (particularly undergraduate) users often want the same books at the same time.

*Planning.* As librarians have measured needs against funds for collecting, they have added a range of strategies, many beyond collecting. In response to the perceived clustering of demands, some academic libraries (such as Northwestern University's) have set up "core collections," not unrelated to the undergraduate collections set up before the great period of expansion. In some cases, loan periods have been shortened to provide better turnover. At this same time, U.S. public libraries found themselves serving more and more part-time and commuting postsecondary students, and operations of public and academic libraries became more similar.

For collections, short funds and better cooperative prospects led to more formal collecting policies. Larger collections, following leadership from Stanford librarians, sought to articulate the level of collecting intensity in various fields. This process generated internal consensus on collecting issues and provided a framework for effective cooperative collecting.

Large public library systems and cooperative systems tended to define quite carefully levels of collecting in units of the whole, dividing subject and sophistication responsibility.

*Evaluation.* The key issues of collection development today are: How well does the collection meet the needs of users? How large does the collection need to be?

When needs are ascertained and profiled, they can serve to gauge collection quality. Qualitative tools, standard lists and bibliographies, provide a useful measure for most types of libraries. Needs—by type of clientele, by type of material, or by subject—can be compared to actual holdings. If deficiencies are found, collections can be upgraded. Public libraries can rely on lists of recommended titles, from landmarks such as the *A.L.A. Catalog* to more specialized lists appearing in *Library Journal* and elsewhere. *Magazines for Libraries,* as well as the titles indexed in the *Readers' Guide,* provides direction in choosing periodicals.

The American Library Association issues lists of *Basic Book Collections* for various levels of school libraries and, for colleges, it provides *Books for College Libraries.* Research and special libraries can use either comprehensive tools *(Ulrich's International Periodicals Directory* or the *Library of Congress Catalog; Books: Subjects,* for example) or specialized bibliographies. The availability of the latter improved in the 1970's, partly owing to computer assistance. Still another tool in highly specialized areas is citation checking, to determine whether or not research or a monograph could have been done in the collection under study.

The consideration of optimum size for the collection has also been the topic of study. Is the collection large enough to meet reasonable needs, but not so large as to impede other library and/or institutional functions?

Size standards set in the 1960's and 1970's for academic libraries reflect projections tied to the recommendations implied by lists such as *Books for College Libraries.* The Clapp-Jordan formula prescribed size goals, with other variables factored in; a smaller collection could be assumed to be unable to meet some needs. But studies by Richard Trueswell and another at the University of Pittsburgh suggest that not all of the books bought or on hand were being used. Particularly in light of current resource sharing capabilities, collection growth could be seen as counterproductive—in some cases—to collection and institutional effectiveness.

In the face of the range of issues, a comprehensive approach to building consensus on collecting policy is necessary. The introduction of management techniques to gain an overview has been noticed. A recent major leadership effort of the Association of Research Libraries' Office of Management Studies has been the creation of a package of self-study and analysis tools, a key component of which has been the Collection Analysis Project (CAP). Aimed first at large, but later also at small, academic libraries, CAP provides carefully designed and tested modules for considering a wide range of issues relating to collection development: goals setting, allocation, resource sharing, staffing, etc. The process enables the library staff and the community it serves and to which it is accountable to take stock of the library's situation in light of the profound changes which have taken place in the environment of the library.

Periodic evaluation will tend to restructure the formal or informal collecting policy of the library. From this will come efforts in selecting new materials, maintaining needed materials, and removing less vital items.

**Selection.** The collecting policy will result in procedures for selecting materials—who will make the final decision, how funds will be allocated, how items will be identified, etc. Who decides on particular titles will depend on the size and type of library and other factors. For Dana, it is clear that the librarian should select. The tendency in academic libraries has been away from faculty and toward the librarians, as the scale has increased.

In 1899 Dana offered a guide for allocations. While specific percentages are given, local considerations are seen as the controlling factors. As quantitative tools for evaluating need and collection effectiveness improve, librarians may find themselves looking more and more at allocation—the directing of resources. The emergence of approval plans in larger libraries in the 1960's reflected this need, and these plans are still important in the operation of many libraries.

The task of selecting individual titles, guided by careful planning and evaluation, must reflect a balance of need versus want. Review media exist at all levels and inevitably reflect more potential user needs than can be accommodated. In some subject areas, large or small, a library may want all of the material—on the local nuclear plant struggle or on the pet topic of Professor X. Selection implies that some titles are "bad." And reviewers confirm that. Will the user, tracing a citation, accept this judgment? How many ILL requests result from decisions not to buy "bad" books?

Censorship is the dark side of ferreting out bad books. It is the librarian's function to maintain a pluralistic outlook on all large and small matters—political, ideological, and academic. Thus, librarians have led the movement to establish racial and nonsexist balance in library collections. This reflects the fundamental social roots of library collecting.

The searching out of new material is at a premium, especially with today's rapid changes. The selector must be widely read. In high technology situations, recourse to on-line searching will supplement traditional sources. The challenge often will be to make items available before they are obsolete.

**Weeding.** During the austerity of the 1930's and under the growth pressures of the 1960's the task of weeding collections—for disposal or storage—gained importance. But the combined pressures of the 1970's—funding, continued collection growth, and energy—have confronted growing and mature libraries with stubbornly inelastic buildings. Resource sharing makes direct access to marginal items less compelling. And, finally, the Trueswell and Pittsburgh studies question the utility of larger collections. In some cases, the failure to weed judiciously puts at jeopardy the library's mission to its users.

Choosing items for removal from the collection is not an inexpensive process. The decision making and record keeping are labor intensive—excluding mention of the physical work involved. Community consensus on policy and on particulars is essential to the task. The involvement of users often builds a sense of common purpose.

Storage is costly in capital, in labor, and in utility. Movable stacks are ideal for high technology collections in the plush surroundings of corporate high rises. Storage requires a large commitment for entry to the program. Microform storage provides the alternative of greater compactness and more potential for incremental growth. Both of these means of storage place special physical demands: movable shelving, with the accompanying density of volumes, brings a heavy weight to bear on the structure of the library and may involve electrical power; microfilm requires expensive viewing, copying, and storage equipment and, according to standards, cannot be stored at over 70° F. These arrangements, along with remote storage, necessitate delay or inconvenience for the user. How substantial this is, along with cost and lack of access to other collections, will determine the value of storage over disposal.

The decision to store or dispose of an item should rest on a clear consensus of need and purpose, both for the task and for the item in question. Reference to standard lists and to union catalogues should provide guidance on important items. More than one person or viewpoint should be represented in the process.

**Maintenance.** Careful selection and weeding based on a comprehensive planning and evaluation process will result in a detailed and quite accurate profile of those elements of the collection that are essential to the library's users. At some point the librarian necessarily comes to the conclusion about some item or another that "This I want to keep!" Alas, this may be the hardest choice of all to implement. Many materials will be on paper and in bindings that defy preservation, and this may represent as much as two-thirds of the circulation of a liberal arts college library, for example. Climate control in its ideal form exists in no known library and is approached in only a few. Many collection librarians, then, face the certainty of some materials wearing out physically long before they cease to be of value intellectually. In addition, many of the libraries that were designed well in terms of climate create other preservation problems. In the open-stack idealism of the 1950's and 1960's, many libraries were built in ways that make security for materials difficult, and books are stolen or mutilated as a result. Decay and abuse, especially in light of emerging cries to keep on hand those most-called-for items, place another encumbrance on limited materials budgets as needed items are identified and replaced.

**Comprehensive Collecting: Whose Responsibility?** *Changing Collection Profiles.* Collections of the 1960's may have reflected the goals of academic researchers or standard qualitative guides more than in 1980. New additions more and more reflect current demand. The "core collection" concept from Trueswell's circulation use study findings will tend to prevail, formally or informally, in many types of libraries. At the same time, subject specialties and subject special collections will continue to flourish. The current strength in this area is seen in the greatly expanded fifth edition of Lee Ash's *Subject Collections* (1979). Resource sharing capabilities allow even relatively small libraries to pursue without guilt special local interests which result in demand from and the orientation of the primary clientele. The rising cost of journals, combined with the access promise of on-line systems, signals continuing pressure to keep down the size of the book collection. But resource sharing also makes available journal materials, and early experience suggests that the copyright changes implemented in 1978 will have little or no real effect on the availability of articles from outside. Thus, books and journals can be acquired to a greater extent than previously around current, primarily local, considerations of need and use. This observation is a very relative one, certainly. Princeton will be blissfully unaware of the existence of the Monoxide Gardens branch. But Princeton will be taking more notice of Penn, Yale, and the New York Public, it can be assumed.

At the same time that libraries will tend to be developing core collections and special and subject collections, their bibliographic holdings will grow in size and sophistication. The advent of computer-generated bibliographic tools coincides with the emergence of location tools. When an item can be obtained for research purposes even

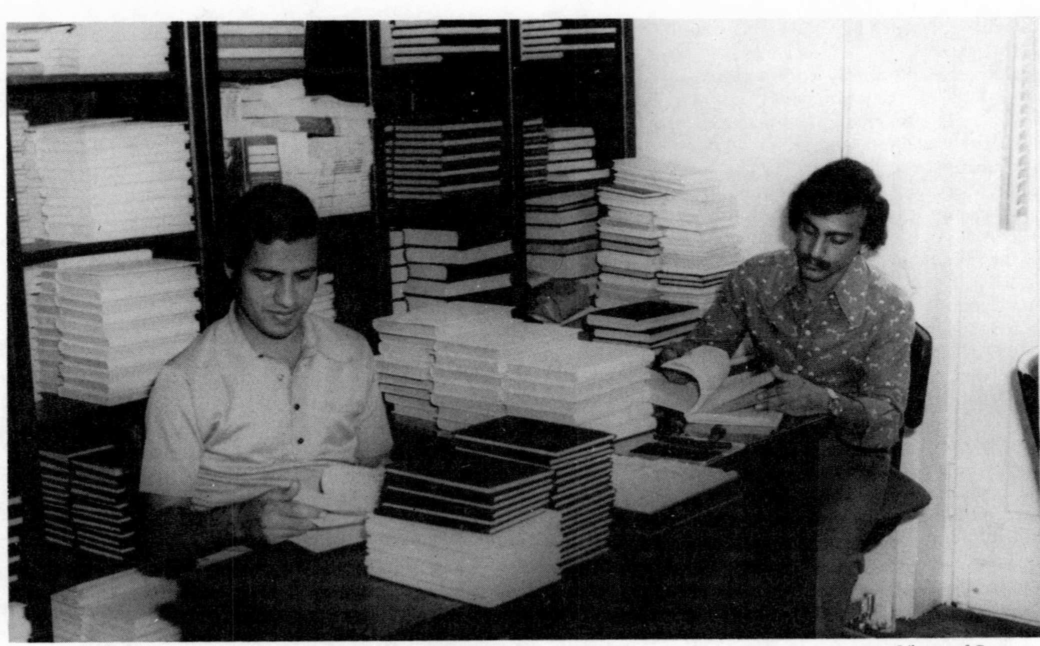

*Copies of books purchased at the Library of Congress Field Office in Cairo are sent to participants in LC's Middle East Program.*

Library of Congress

if it is held at a distance, a new premium is placed on knowing that the specialized item even exists. Since Sputnik in the late 1950's, research literature has grown tremendously. In the late 1970's index and abstract tools showed signs of adjusting to the increase. Tools that became unwieldly split or changed format; the most recent phenomenon was on-line access. Tools which had become prohibitively expensive for smaller libraries now are available on-line. In addition, more specialized and focused access sources have emerged. The result is an increased share or allotment of collection budgets for new tools, overall. But there have been some countertrends. On-line access has permitted the dropping of some hard copy subscriptions and the passing-up of expensive cumulations. Still, the increased emphasis in all types of libraries on knowing what exists, not just what is on hand, has altered allocation and collecting patterns.

*National and International Challenges.* At a time when large and small libraries are carefully scrutinizing their collecting policies with pressure to limit or reduce commitments, the issue of a collecting policy for the nation emerges. At the end of the 1970's consideration of a U.S. National Periodicals Center was a focal point of discussion. Who will be responsible for seeing that everything is to be collected and maintained somewhere? If this requires centralized decision making, does it require a centralized operation? How much can we afford to service hypothetical, "elite" requests in an era of broadly based heavy demand and fading prospects for funding?

Research libraries worked hard to address these issues in the 1960's and 1970's. Individually and, more recently, collectively, the independent research libraries have defined their missions more around their collections and less around demand. Libraries such as the Huntington, the Newberry, the American Antiquarian Society, and the New York Public now function as national resources for scholarship and learning—building and preserving great collections and, when possible, attracting researchers who will address these libraries' priorities. In countless humanities and historical fields these independent libraries in particular act as "libraries of record" along with the Library of Congress and the largest academic libraries to preserve for the nation our aggregate patrimony of culture and learning. Recently, this essential mission has gained public support and acceptance in the Title II-C program to encourage research collection development. The grants have been few and small each year, but the recognition by the shapers of public policy is significant. Most recently Title II-B funding for all large and small academic libraries, which extends back to the 1960's, has yielded to this new priority. And in a real sense, the assumption of an absolute collecting responsibility by a very small number of great libraries frees smaller libraries in the thousands to pursue collecting goals more locally based. The independent research library movement, then, is the foundation on which rests the intellectual and financial solvency of the emerging national network in the U.S.

The prospect of telefacsimile transmission in the reasonable future points toward greater international cooperative collecting. Already the Center for Research Libraries relies on Boston Spa for many journal titles. Growing cooperation and trust at the level of the International Federation of Library Associations and Institutions and in preparing the Anglo-American cataloguing codes point to continued mutual activities. As progress in the area of bibliographic control is made, formal international collecting can follow.

**REFERENCES**

Mary Carter Duncan and Wallace John Bonk, *Building Library Collections,* 3rd ed. (1969), a public library perspective, with a good historical foundation.

Daniel Gore, editor, *Farewell to Alexandria: Solutions to Space, Growth, and Performance Problems of Libraries* (1976).

F. Wilfrid Lancaster, *The Measurement and Evaluation of Library Services* (1977), a sound review of the literature of use studies, especially in Chapter 5, "Evaluation of the Collection." "Resources in [Year]." Published annually in the Summer issue of *Library Resources & Technical Services.*

University of Pittsburgh, Graduate School of Library Science, *A Cost-Benefit Model of Some Critical Library Operations in Terms of Use of Materials* (1978). For a summary, see Thomas J. Galvin and Allen Kent, "Use of a University Library Collection," *Library Journal* (1977).

ARTHUR H. MILLER, JR.

## Colombia

Colombia, a republic in northwestern South America, is bounded by the Caribbean Sea on the north, Venezuela and Brazil on the east, Peru and Ecuador on the south, the Pacific Ocean on the west, and Panama on the northwest. Pop. (1978 est.) 25,867,500; area 1,138,914 sq.km. The official language is Spanish.

**National Libraries.** The Biblioteca Nacional was founded in 1777 in the capital, Bogotá. In 1979 its collection totaled nearly half a million volumes. Legal deposit was considered necessary as early as 1886; a law of 1946 regulates the system, and although the law has never been strictly enforced, the collection grew considerably. An extensive renovation was completed in 1978, coinciding with the nation's bicentennial celebration. It publishes the *Anuario Bibliográfico Colombiano*.

The Luis Ángel Arango Library, founded and funded by the Banco de la República, the National Bank of Colombia, complements the National Library with a full collection of Colombian publications from 1950, and the Hemeroteca Nacional, or National Periodical Publications Collection, assures the control of and access to Colombian periodical publications. Both libraries have closed collections, and neither permits circulation—even on interlibrary loan.

**Academic Libraries.** Ninety-eight academic libraries vary greatly in size, quality, and services. In public and private universities and technical training institutes, they employ a total of about 800 professional and nonprofessional staff, and their potential users number 215,000 students and professors. The Instituto Colombiano para el Fomento de la Educación Superior (ICFES; Colombian Institute for the Promotion of Higher Education) supervises the Colombian Academic Library Network, which attempts to coordinate the services offered as well as the technical aspects of these libraries on a national level. ICFES also prepares a number of very useful information tools, such as the Collective Catalogue of Periodical Publications in Colombia, Index of Periodical Publications in Spanish, National Thesis Catalogue, and the Master List of Approved Subject Headings in Spanish. The cooperative automation of academic card catalogues was one of the more ambitious projects under way in 1979.

It is difficult to single out the most notable university library among eight to ten in principal urban centers. The National University's Library in Bogotá is perhaps the most extensive, with a total collection of some 150,000 volumes divided among a Central Library and nine special collections. The Central Library was one of the few academic libraries in Colombia that had open stacks in the late 1970's, but serious theft problems threatened to force a change.

The majority of academic libraries permit direct circulation to users. Large reserve collections are common and the use of microformats still minimal. There are widespread security problems. Few university libraries enjoy budgets that would permit them to serve their institutions adequately. The majority of professional Colombian librarians work in academic libraries.

**Public Libraries.** The Instituto Colombiano de Cultura (COLCULTURA) (Colombian Cultural Institute) is the government agency most directly involved in promoting the creation and upgrading of the approximately 200 public libraries in Colombia, the majority of which were founded between 1973 and 1977. Excluding those several founded much earlier and in the principal cities, such as the Biblioteca Pública Piloto (Pilot Public Library) in Medellín, Colombian public libraries are fledgling attempts, tempered by local problems, which are closely related to the local school or literacy program, especially in rural areas. All have serious financial problems, lack trained personnel, have inadequate collections, and offer relatively few services. Enthusiasm and support have been shown on the local level; many joint projects by banks and city, county, or state governments were creating new public libraries at the end of the 1970's.

Although public libraries have been formally given a high priority by the Colombian government since 1973, academic and special libraries employ the great majority of trained professionals and generally enjoy more favorable conditions than school and public libraries.

**School Libraries.** The National Ministry of Education promotes and coordinates public school libraries. Various other institutions, most notably the Centro Regional para el Fomento del Libro en América Latina y el Caribe (CERLAL) (the Unesco Regional Office for the Promotion of Books in Latin America and the Caribbean) and the Instituto Colombiano para el Bienestar Familiar (ICBF) (Colombian Institute for Family Welfare) also participate in the national effort to upgrade existing school libraries and promote the creation of new ones in the many schools without them, through training programs for paraprofessionals, funding, and research. A program to create school libraries in strategically located cooperative centers, managed by trained teachers, has high priority within the Ministry of Education and received much needed outside funding. These libraries are being founded within the planned context of a national school library system and are considered essential for the success of many educational reforms.

Although the national curriculum for secondary education includes a library unit, the libraries themselves have been unable to take full advantage of this opportunity due to a serious lack of resources. A great effort is being made to assure the relevance of the collection and services to the school curriculum. Because the curriculum is standard in all public schools, collections tend to be sufficiently homogeneous to permit centralized processing within the offices of the Ministry of Education. The work of the Ministry, however, is limited to public schools. One of the major objectives of this long-range program is to promote reading in general and create an interest in research at this level of the educational system. Other activities are aimed at the parents of schoolchildren and at elementary and secondary schoolteachers.

Although great efforts have been made since 1968, school libraries are still painfully inadequate a decade later. Many students are forced to use the National Library, the Luis Ángel Arango Library, or local university libraries, or do without library service.

**Special Libraries.** The approximately 300 special libraries and information centers in Colombia, which cover varied humanistic, scientific, and technical fields, are perhaps the most favored in financial support and prestige. The Fondo Colombiano de Investigaciones Científicas y Proyectos Especiales "Francisco José de Caldas" (COLCIENCIAS) (Colombian Institute for Scientific Research and Special Projects) loosely coordinates these centers through the Sistema Nacional de Información (SNI) (National Information Network), founded in 1973. Subsystems in the areas of agriculture, health sciences, marine studies, education, industry, ecology, and natural resources have been set up to facilitate further use of these specialized centers located mainly in the three principal cities of Bogotá, Medellín, and Cali. In addition to establishing national policy and priorities, COLCIENCIAS also provides a technical reference service, a research-in-progress information center, interlibrary loan, and reprography agreements with major international centers and coordinates the National Technical Committee. The Servicio Nacional de Aprendizaje (SENA) (National Apprenticeship Service) has recently created a Technical Information Network with specialized information centers in such industrial fields as metalworking, welding, and small scale industrial development.

There is a tendency in special libraries to hire subject specialists rather than trained librarians. Indexing, as opposed to the use of classification schemes, is coming into greater use, and collections are dominated by non-Spanish language materials. Open collections and a greater emphasis on services predominate. Since 1960 there has been extensive growth in special libraries; 60 percent have been founded since 1960, and half of these since 1970. Many are recognized throughout Latin America and participate actively in international information programs, such as AGRINTER and UNISIST.

**Associations.** The principal professional association in Colombia is Asociación Colombiana de Bibliotecarios (ASCOLBI) (Colombian Association of Librarians), founded in 1958. Under a reorganization of 1976, ASCOLBI has a national Board of Directors, four regional chapters, and approximately 200 members. The *Carta del Bibliotecario* constitutes the country's major professional periodical. ASCOLBI supported legislation that would regulate the profession.

A paraprofessionals' organization, ASBIAC, and the National Association of Archivists are also active. Colombia participates in FID and IFLA.

MARTHA GORMAN

## Commonwealth Library Association

The Commonwealth Library Association (COMLA) was founded at the instigation of the Commonwealth Foundation, an autonomous body primarily devoted to fostering professional development throughout the British Commonwealth. Following a preliminary meeting in London, England, in 1971, COMLA was formally inaugurated in Lagos, Nigeria, in November 1972, with 20 national library associations as Founder Members. As of March 1979 national membership stood at 48. At the Lagos meeting it was decided to locate the Secretariat in Jamaica.

The Commonwealth Library Association is intended to help improve libraries in the Commonwealth, to maintain and strengthen links between librarians of the various countries, to support and encourage library associations in the individual countries, to promote the status and education of librarians and the recognition of their qualifications, to initiate research projects, and to further the technical development of libraries in the Commonwealth.

The Council of the Association met in Nigeria (1972), Jamaica (1975), and Fiji (1979), while meetings of the Executive Committee were held in Lagos (1972), London (1974, 1977), Kingston (1975, 1976), and Fiji (1979).

COMLA was co-host to a Planning Meeting for National Bibliographies in the English-speaking Caribbean in Jamaica early in 1974. In November of that year COMLA funded a library workshop in Malta sponsored by the Malta Library Association with assistance from the Liverpool Polytechnic Department of Library Studies. In 1977 a COMLA Asian Regional Workshop on Research Methodology in Librarianship was held in Singapore. A Seminar on Reciprocity of Qualifications and Training for Librarianship was held in Jamaica in 1975 immediately after COMLA Council II. In 1976 and 1978 COMLA Canada/Caribbean Regional meetings were held in Jamaica.

During 1974 and 1975 the President, K. C. Harrison, with financial help from the British Council, toured the West Indies and East and Southeast Asia. As a Commonwealth Foundation Lecturer he visited East Africa. Early in 1974 the Secretary, Pippa Fray, toured West Africa, the Mediterranean, the United Kingdom, and Canada.

There are two categories of membership of COMLA, Full and Affiliated. Full members, restricted to one per Commonwealth country, are normally national library associations. Where no national library association exists, membership may be vested in some other national institution representing the library profession. Affiliated membership is open to organizations concerned with library and information science or archives, individual libraries, and similar institutions in the Commonwealth. Non-Commonwealth institutions may be Subscribers but are not eligible for membership.

COMLA is governed by a Council consisting of all the Full members, up to five representatives of the Affiliated membership, and the Immediate Past President. The Executive Committee is elected by the Council and must include one member from each region (Africa, the Americas and Caribbean, Asia, Europe, South Pacific) plus the Immediate Past President (ex-officio). The officers are the President, Vice-President, and Honorary Treasurer. The Secretary, who must be a professional librarian, is appointed by Council. Ad hoc Working Parties are set up as needed. The Working Parties on Reciprocity of Qualifications and on Attachments, Internships, and Exchanges of Library Staffs both produced reports and were then disbanded.

COMLA's main sources of funds are triennial grants from the Commonwealth Foundation, grants from the Commonwealth Fund for Technical Cooperation, and membership subscriptions. Subscriptions have been kept very low, and the effectiveness of the Commonwealth Foundation's generous grants has been drastically eroded by inflation. As a result, the programs envisaged when COMLA was first launched have had to be curtailed. Increased membership, though welcomed, has complicated matters as the cost of travel for Council members far exceeds the income from their subscriptions. Plans for restructuring on a regional basis to streamline administration and reduce travel costs are being considered.

Under its Attachments and Internships Scheme COMLA has made grants to the library associations of Fiji, Guyana, Jamaica, and Papua New Guinea to enable members to travel abroad for study and practical experience and to assist the President of the International Association of School Librarianship to attend its 1977 annual conference in Australia. In 1976 the Regional Representative for Africa presented a draft proposal for a pilot project on rural library development, which has been approved in principle.

*COMLA Newsletter* is published quarterly. Workshop and working party reports are published occasionally.

COMLA belongs to IFLA and FID. Regionally COMLA is a member of ACURIL (Association of Caribbean University Research and Institutional Libraries) and has close relations with SCECSAL (Standing Conference of East, Central, and Southern African Librarians), CONSAL (Conference of Southeast Asian Librarians), and SCOPAL (Standing Conference of Pacific Librarians).

**REFERENCES**

K. C. Harrison, "COMLA," *IFLA Annual* (1974).
Norman Tett and John Chadwick, *Professional Organizations in the Commonwealth,* revised edition (1976).

C. PIPPA FRAY

## Congo, People's Republic of the

The People's Republic of the Congo (République Populaire du Congo; not to be confused with Zaire, formerly Belgian Congo) was, up to 1960, a French colony as part of French Equatorial Africa. Located on the equator, the country is bounded by the Central African Republic on the north, Zaire on the east and south, Angola on the

**Libraries in the Congo (1976)**

| Type | Number | Volumes in collections | Annual expenditure (estimate) (cfa franc) | Professional staff | All staff (total) |
|---|---|---|---|---|---|
| National | 1 | 10,000 | 10,000,000 | 6 | 20 |
| Academic | 1 | 90,000 | 25,000,000 | 6 | 20 |
| School | N.A. | | | | |
| Special | 20 | between 50,000 and 100,000 | N.A. | N.A. | N.A. |
| Public | 2 (French) | 30,000 | 10,000,000 | 1 | 6 |

Sources: Françoise Mbot, *Inventaire des bibliothèques et centres de documentation en Afrique Centrale;* local inquiries.

southwest, the Atlantic Ocean and Gabon on the west, and Cameroon on the northwest. Its total population was estimated at more than 1,400,000 in 1978; about 300,000 live in or around the capital, Brazzaville, a town founded in 1884 and developed mostly after it was reached by a railroad in 1934. Area 342,000 sq.km. The official language is French; Bantu dialects are spoken.

Under colonial rule Brazzaville was the seat of the Governor of the whole French Equatorial Africa, with a comparatively important Archives and Library. The Archives were transferred to France (Aix en Provence) at the time of independence.

**National Library.** The Direction des Services de Bibliothèques, d'Archives et de Documentation, organized in 1971, supervises the National Library, Archives and Documentation Center. It has no authority over the university library or special libraries of the government ministries. Since its founding in 1971, the Bibliothèque Nationale Populaire has been designated the depository library. Extension work and readers services are considered important, the "popular" part of the name being taken seriously by its Director. Lacking a new building, the Library did most of its work outside through the libraries in schools and other institutions. The National Documentation Center began work in 1978. It issues mimeographed bulletins, which list both foreign and national periodicals.

**Academic Libraries.** The Bibliothèque Universitaire is the oldest and most important library in the country. It received at least part of the library of the central government when it was founded (1959) as Bibliothèque de la Fondation pour l'Enseignement supérieur en Afrique Centrale. It is divided into three sections, each housed with the department of the university it serves, all of them in Brazzaville: (1) Bibliothèque Centrale (Law and Letters), 50,000 volumes, 400 current periodicals; (2) Bibliothèque des Sciences 20,000 volumes, 120 current periodicals; (3) Sciences de l'Education, 20,000 volumes, 25 current periodicals.

**Special Libraries.** Apart from the National Documentation Center, several ministries, hospitals, and other institutions have small libraries, usually without professional staff, often with very limited resources. Among those with more than about 1,000 volumes and with trained staff may be noted Centre de Documentation Economique, founded in 1967, and the Institut de Recherche Pedagogique, founded in 1966 with help from Unesco. ORSTOM, a French research organization (Office pour la recherche Scientifique Outre Mer), runs research programs for the Congolese government. Its two libraries had good resources but no professional librarian in 1979. ORSTOM Brazzaville covers soils, water, plants, and health (15,000 volumes) and ORSTOM Pointe Noire sea and fishes (1,500 volumes).

The World Health Organization has a regional office in Brazzaville; its library was founded in 1963 (20,000 volumes).

**Public Libraries.** There is no proper public library. The French Ministère de la Coopération runs Cultural Centers that, among other activities (movies, exhibitions, theater), run libraries open to the public. The Cultural Center Library in Brazzaville stocked 20,000 volumes (5,000 for children); the Pointe Noire Cultural Center Library, 7,000 volumes (2,000 for children).

FANNY LALANDE ISNARD

# Congress of Southeast Asian Librarians

The Congress of Southeast Asian Librarians (CONSAL) was founded at the First Conference of Southeast Asian Librarians in Singapore, August 14–16, 1970. Sponsored by the Library Association of Malaysia and the Library Association of Singapore, the Conference was attended by delegates from Cambodia, Indonesia, Malaysia, Philippines, Singapore, Thailand, and Vietnam, as well as observers from other countries. The conference theme was regional cooperation, and the delegates resolved to establish a regional library organization to facilitate such cooperation. Its aims are (1) to establish and strengthen relations among librarians, libraries, library schools, library associations, and related organizations in the region; (2) to promote cooperation in the fields of librarianship, library education, documentation, and related activities in the region; and (3) to cooperate with other regional and international organizations and institutions in the fields of librarianship, library education, documentation, and related activities.

The constitution envisaged a loosely structured organization. CONSAL would meet at least once in three years; the CONSAL Committee was based in the host country with a mandate to carry out the resolutions of the preceding conference. While there were no formal memberships or suscriptions, the Committee had the authority to raise funds for its activities. The Chairman is nominated by the succeeding host country and endorsed by the delegates present, but the remaining Committee members are nominated by the respective library associations.

CONSAL II was held in Manila, December 10–14, 1973, with library education as its theme. CONSAL III, in Jakarta, December 1–5, 1975, focused on integrated library and documentation services and changed the organization's name to the "Congress" of Southeast Asian Librarians. CONSAL IV in Bangkok, June 5–9, 1978, discussed the development of national information services. CONSAL V was planned for Kuala Lumpur in 1981.

In addition to the main sessions during CONSAL IV, a number of smaller meetings were held for the first time on the formation of an Agricultural Information Society for Asia (AISA), International Information System for the Agricultural Sciences and Technology (AGRIS), International Serials Data System in Southeast Asia

North Carolina State Archives
*Connor*

(ISDSSEA), Unesco Bibliography on Malay Culture, International Standard Book Number (ISBN), and National Libraries and Documentation Center in Southeast Asia Consortium (NLDC-SEA Consortium).

By CONSAL IV, it was felt that CONSAL ought to be placed on a firmer footing. While its aims and basic structure remained unchanged, the constitution was revised to provide for national membership comprising national library associations and national and other libraries and related organizations within the member countries and for associate membership comprising libraries and related organizations of nonmember countries, as well as individuals interested in the objectives of CONSAL. Membership rates were set, the duties and powers of the Executive Board defined, and affiliation with other regional bodies made possible CONSAL still had no permanent secretariat in 1978, but it was expected that a rotating secretariat would be attached to the current Chairman. At that time the secretariat was at National Library of Malaysia.

CONSAL's closest relationship is with its archival counterpart, the Southeast Asian Regional Branch of the International Council on Archives (SARBICA). Together they have successfully completed a major project to compile a *Masterlist of Southeast Asian Microforms* (Singapore, 1978). Another continuing joint program is the Regional Microfilm Clearing-House, which publishes the semiannual *Southeast Asia Microfilms Newsletter,* distributed by the SARBICA Secretariat in Kuala Lumpur.

CONSAL has no official relationship to Unesco, but its members are involved in a number of Unesco projects such as ISDS. Other members are involved in the Food and Agriculture Organization's project, AGRIS. AISA was formed during CONSAL IV, and other special library groups are likely to follow. CONSAL thus provides a means of professional contact and generates a climate conducive to cooperative activities. In this way, it has fulfilled the hopes of its founders—to act as a focus and catalyst for library development and cooperation in Southeast Asia.

LIM PUI HUEN

## Connor, Robert Digges Wimberly

(1878–1950)

Robert Digges Wimberly Connor, historian and the first Archivist of the U.S., was born in Wilson, North Carolina, September 26, 1878, one of 12 children of Henry Groves and Kate (Whitfield) Connor. He attended the local public schools and in 1899 received a Ph.B. from the University of North Carolina at Chapel Hill. For four years he was engaged in public school work; then from 1904 to 1907 he served as Secretary of the state educational campaign committee. In 1903 Connor was appointed by Governor Charles B. Aycock to membership on the newly created North Carolina Historical Commission; for four years he served as the Commission's unpaid Secretary.

In 1906 Connor published a booklet, *A State Library and Department of Archives and Records,* an ambitious plan for the revitalization of the State Library and the establishment of a state archival agency. In response to his prodding, the General Assembly the following year broadened the authority of the Historical Commission and gave it an increased appropriation. Thereupon Connor accepted the salaried secretaryship and during the next 14 years developed one of the nation's outstanding state historical agencies. In addition, he was Secretary of the North Carolina Teachers Assembly for six years, President of the North Carolina Literary and Historical Association for a year and its Secretary for seven, member of the University of North Carolina's Board of Trustees for seven years and its Secretary for five, President of the General Alumni Association of the University from 1917 to 1921, and member of the National Board of Historical Service during World War I.

After a leave of absence to study at Columbia University in 1920–21, Connor resigned from the Historical Commission to accept the Kenan Professorship in History and Government at the University of North Carolina, where his lectures, characterized by their clarity and wit, made him an unusually popular teacher.

In 1934, with the strong endorsement of the American Historical Association, Connor was appointed the first Archivist of the United States by President Franklin D. Roosevelt. His tasks were monumental: the National Archives building was unfinished; a 150-year backlog of public records crowded offices throughout the federal government; and there were only a few persons acquainted with European archival principles in the entire country. For the next six years Connor presided over the completion and occupation of the new building, the organization and training of a large staff, and the establishment of policies and procedures for the transfer, repair, arrangement, description, and use of the nation's archives. He gathered around him other historians of high standing, encouraged the formation in 1936 of the Society of American Archivists (SAA), and insisted that the National Archives share its growing expertise with records custodians at the state level. He also worked closely with the President in establishing the Franklin D. Roosevelt Library, the first of a number of similar archival institutions administered by the National Archives.

Connor resigned as Archivist in 1941 and returned to Chapel Hill as Craige Professor of Jurisprudence and History, but he maintained his interest in archival administration, serving as President of the SAA in 1941–43 and as Chairman of the North Carolina Historical Commission and its successor, the Executive Board of the State Department of Archives and History, from 1942 until his death.

Connor's most notable published work was his two-volume history, *North Carolina: Rebuilding an Ancient Commonwealth, 1584–1925* (1929). Among other books were *History of North Carolina: The Colonial and Revolutionary Periods, 1584–1783* (1919); *The Life and Speeches of Charles Brantley Aycock* (1912); *Race Elements in the White Population of North Carolina* (1920); and *The Story of the United States, for Young People* (1916). *The North Carolina Manual 1913,* which he compiled, was for 60 years a standard reference work.

He died February 25, 1950, and was buried in the Chapel Hill Cemetery. The Historical Society of North Carolina presents each year the Robert D. W. Connor Award for the best article published in the *North Carolina Historical Review.*

H. G. JONES

## Conservation and Preservation of Library Materials

Conservation of library materials is part of a broader concern that is sometimes referred to as the conservation of cultural property. Some authorities trace the beginnings of conservation to the Age of Enlightenment and the discoveries of Pompeii and Herculaneum. Others claim that conservation is as old as civilization itself and is rooted in the idea that mankind learns from what has gone before, and that the evidence of earlier times is important and worth saving. Libraries, particularly research libraries and other institutions whose collections serve an archival function, play a primary role in collecting and preserving the written record, although not everything worth preserving is collected by libraries, nor do they preserve everything they collect. Indeed, *Scholarly Communication: The Report of the National Enquiry* (1979) warns that thousands of books have already been lost and hundreds of thousands more are so fragile that their next use will be their last.

Although librarians and archivists often consider themselves conservators, for whom "to collect" implies "to preserve for the future," this view in itself fails to provide a convincing rationale for conservation. The danger of destruction threatens not only library and archive collections but also the works of knowledge and scholarship that they support and generate. Conservation is an indispensable link in scholarly communication and assures access now and in the future to the resources that libraries collect.

*Conservation* and *preservation* are often used interchangeably in current parlance, and there seems to be no clearcut distinction between the two terms. *Preservation* seems more specific and object-oriented, whereas *conservation* is a broader concept that embraces preservation as well as protection, maintenance, and restoration in its meaning. It also carries a connotation of official policy and perhaps for that reason is the preferred term to describe the entire constellation of administrative and technical activities that bear on collections management in libraries, museums, and archives.

Conservation touches other aspects of library administration at several points. In part, it was recognition of this that led the Library of Congress to establish in 1967 a Preservation Office under the supervision of an Assistant Director, bringing most of the functions pertaining to the maintenance and protection of the collections under one administrative unit. Following LC's lead, the Research Libraries of the New York Public Library established a Conservation Division in 1972, with a broad mandate that included the binding, repair, and preservation microrecording programs, environmental monitoring, emergency planning, cooperative programs with other libraries and with micropublishing and reprinting firms, preparation of materials for exhibition, and, to some extent, collection maintenance. Other major research libraries in the United States, including those of Columbia University and the University of California at Berkeley, have since followed this pattern of administrative development.

Conservation of library and archival materials was not viewed as a matter of great urgency in the U.S. until the early 1960's, although the concern of individual librarians and, from time to time, the American Library Association can be traced to the closing decade of the 19th century. In England, John Murray called the attention of the reading public to "the present state of the wretched compound called *Paper*" as early as 1823. In 1919 the French mycologist Pierre Sée selected for the subject of his dissertation a study of the fungi that attack paper.

Perhaps the greatest influence on the future development of the field within the U.S. was William J. Barrow's assertion, based on his investigations as reported in *Deterioration of Book Stock: Causes and Remedies: Two Studies on the Permanence of Book Paper* (1959), that most library books printed in the first half of the 20th century will be in an unusable condition in the next century. Important and sudden stimulus to the conservation movement came from two disasters that occurred in 1966—a fire at the library of the Jewish Theological Seminary in New York City that consumed 70,000 volumes and damaged an additional 150,000; and the flood of the Arno River in Florence, Italy, that inundated a million volumes stored in the cellar and ground floor of the Biblioteca Nazionale Centrale, including 150,000 volumes of the Magliabecchiana Collection, gathered during the 17th century by Florentine scholars to create Italy's first public library. These events, vivid reminders of the vulnerability of books, particularly books that are also cultural artifacts, contributed to the development of emergency salvage techniques for water-damaged materials and methods of physical restoration and jolted many libraries into action in such areas as planning for disaster preparedness and recovery.

**Characteristics.** Some of the more important characteristics of the library conservation field at its present stage of development may be summarized as follows: (1) the field is highly technical and is concerned with such complicated issues as the chemistry of materials, the monitoring of environmental systems, and the design of book structures; (2) the ethical and philosophical framework within which conservation decisions must be made is not well developed; (3) the problems of library conservation are highly diverse as a result of the wide range of physical formats found in library collections and the difficulty of distinguishing materials of an artifactual nature from materials that are of value solely for their intellectual content; (4) the need for conservation of library and archival collections is both massive and urgent; (5) conservation is expensive—the traditional approaches of microfilming and physical treatment are frighteningly costly, given the quantity of material that needs preservation; (6) library conservation is a developing field—there were no comprehensive training programs at the close of the 1970's; the literature of the field is of varying quality; there are few standards, and numerous technical questions demand solution; (7) conservation is an interdisciplinary enterprise and demands close cooperation of the library profession, the conservation profession, the suppliers of materials and services, and the scientific community.

**Nature and Extent of Deterioration.** Present-day collections are largely composed of books printed on unstable paper, and libraries will continue to acquire significant works printed on poor paper.

Scientists have defined deterioration as a process of transition from a higher to a lower energy level. Cellulose, the principal component of most library materials, is remarkably stable in its pure form, but when conditions are right, it tends to break down into simpler molecules, returning eventually to carbon dioxide. Natural oxidation is accelerated by two other chemical reactions—hydrolytic attack on cellulose fibers by acid in the paper itself, and photochemical degradation caused by light and other forms of radiant energy. Environmental factors, such as the polluted air present in most urban centers, widely fluctuating levels of temperature and relative humidity, and biological factors—mold, vermin, insects, and man himself—also contribute to the deterioration process.

Edwin Williams stated the matter succinctly when he said that the topic might be dealt with in a single sentence that would read, "Everything in library collections is deteriorating today, was deteriorating yesterday, and will continue to deteriorate tomorrow although we ought to retard the process." His presentation, entitled "Deterioration of Library Collections Today," is in *Deterioration and Preservation of Library Materials* (1970), a volume issued by the University of Chicago Press that includes other papers presented at a 1969 conference. The volume has since become the bible of the library conservation profession.

**Preventive Conservation.** Preventive conservation—that is, action taken *before* damage has occurred that will retard further deterioration—has emerged as a basic concept within the field. The single most effective measure that libraries can take to slow the deterioration process is to reduce the temperature in book-storage areas. The higher the temperature, the greater the rate of chemical reaction accelerates; conversely, paper scientists generally agree that for every ten degrees Celsius the storage temperature can be reduced, the life of the paper can be approximately doubled.

There are immediate steps that libraries can take to prolong the useful life of their collections. Smaller libraries with limited funds and small staffs can identify brittle

*Sequential steps in preserving the typescript of Richard Wright's* Native Son:

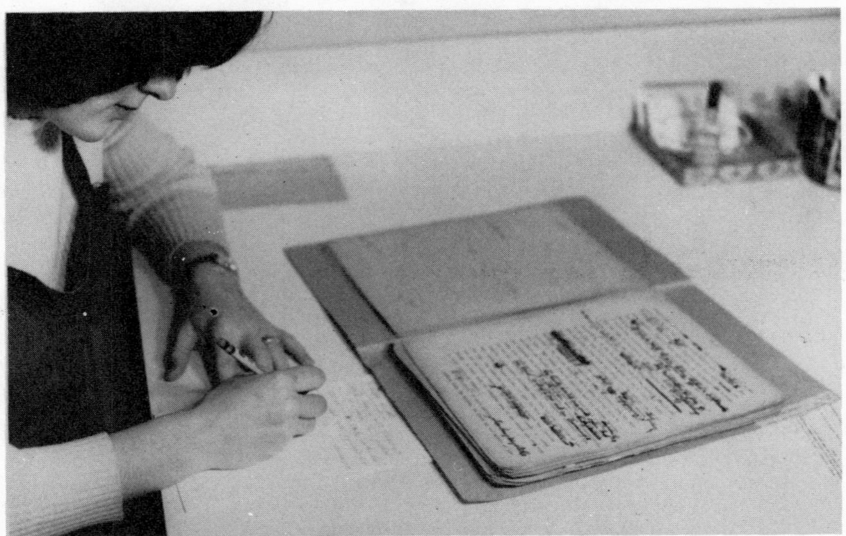

*(1) Examining and documenting the condition of the untreated leaves.*

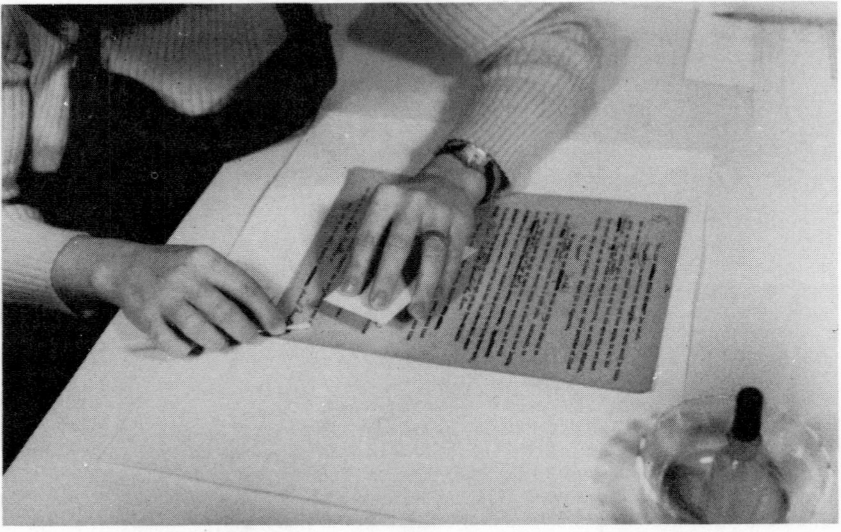

*(2) Testing the stability of the inks in order to determine the most appropriate deacidification treatment.*

books that are too poor to rebind and insert them into acid-free paper wrappers until such time as the titles can be repaired or replaced. Flat paper objects such as manuscripts and prints can be interleaved with acid-free tissue paper available from conservation supply houses and stored in archival-quality folders and boxes. Extremely fragile paper objects in single-leaf formats can be placed in envelopes of polyester film available in the U.S. under the trade name Mylar. Volumes can be cleaned and a program of minor repairs begun using procedures such as those described in Carolyn Horton's *Cleaning and Preserving Bindings* (ALA, 1969).

In large libraries faced with massive deterioration problems, a phased preservation program can be developed, doing the simplest, least expensive steps first and leaving costlier, more complex tasks until later. A key element is the need to undertake administrative planning *before* embarking on a course of action. Initial steps should include inspecting the physical storage facilities to identify particular problems, conducting a spot survey of the collections to determine more precisely the extent of deterioration and the various formats of material needing treatment (e.g., books, photographs, posters, scrapbooks, clippings, etc.), framing a realistic plan of action tailored to the budgetary and staffing realities of the particular institution, and planning a disaster preparedness and recovery program. In the early planning stage, it is usually not advisable to establish a restoration facility and a physical treatment program involving sophisticated procedures even if funding is available.

Easiest of all, the librarian in charge of conservation can read. The literature of the field is already large and is growing rapidly. An excellent series of articles was begun in the May 1, 1979, issue of *Library Journal* under the editorial guidance of Pamela W. Darling, Head of the Preservation Department of Columbia University Libraries. A useful annotated reading list is "Selected References in the Literature of Conservation" (*Preservation Leaflet* No. 1), available free from LC's Office of Preservation in Washington, D.C.

**Training.** Within the field of library conservation, considerable educational effort is needed in four areas of training: programs for new and practicing librarians, archivists, and curators; programs for training professional conservators in the treatment of books and materials in other formats traditionally collected by libraries; programs for the education of conservation administrators; and programs for training hand bookbinders and other conservation technicians.

About a dozen library schools in the U.S. offer courses on conservation and preservation of library materials for academic credit; a pamphlet available from ALA's Resources and Technical Services Division, entitled *Preservation Training Flyer,* is an important source of information.

Outside the limited number of conservation facilities that occasionally have openings for qualified apprentices, there are few training centers in the U.S. that offer intensive programs for conservation technicians. The Camberwell School of Arts and Crafts in London, England, offers full-time courses of one and two years' duration in hand bookbinding, book restoration, paper conservation, and print and drawings conservation.

Academic degree-granting institutions in the U.S. offering graduate programs for museum conservators are extremely limited, and there is none that has specialized programs for training library and archive conservators. An important directory that lists training centers throughout the world in all areas of conservation is the *ICCROM International Index in Conservation* (1978), published by the International Centre for the Study of the Preservation and Restoration of Cultural Property in Rome.

The possibility of establishing a one-year training program for conservation administrators and a two-year program for library and archive conservators based at Columbia University's School of Library Service was being investigated at the close of the 1970's by Paul N. Banks, Conservator of the Newberry Library, Chicago.

**Research Centers.** Despite growing awareness in the 1960's and 1970's of the magnitude of the preservation problem, expenditures for basic and applied research have been disturbingly small. The high cost of staffing and equipping a research facility has obliged most libraries to place their emphasis on physical preservation treatment rather than on analysis and research. Such laboratories as do exist are usually with a museum or other organization caring for a wide variety of cultural properties.

The *Report of the Study Committee on Scientific Support* (1979) of the National Conservation Advisory Council asserts that both the number and sizes of conservation laboratories in the U.S. are inadequate to serve the needs of the nation's many thousands of public and private museums, libraries and archives, and historic sites. Of 12 laboratories conducting research (1979), only half are involved to any appreciable extent with analytic or treatment research on paper, leather, and other materials that compose objects collected by libraries.

The Preservation Research and Testing Office of the Library of Congress, the only facility in the U.S. devoted exclusively to problems of library preservation, has made significant advances in the search for a method of gaseous deacidification of books. The laboratory, staffed by 13 scientists and technicians, developed promising techniques for improved means of protecting or supporting fragile documents without resorting to lamination. (The W. J. Barrow Research Laboratory in Richmond, Virginia, which conducted research and published several important works including *Permanence/Durability of the Book,* vols. 1–7 (1963–74), was closed in 1977.)

Although the number of restoration workshops outside the U.S. has increased considerably in the 1960's and 1970's, growth of research facilities has been slow. In India important conservation services were developed at the National Archives and the National Museum, both in New Delhi. Facilities in Europe include, in the U.S.S.R., research laboratories at the Academy of Sciences in Leningrad and the laboratory of the Lenin State Library in Moscow. In England a laboratory was established in the British Museum in the late 1950's and has conducted some research on conservation of graphic art materials in the intervening years. France has a Center of Research on the Conservation of Graphic Documents, in the Library of the Museum of Natural History in Paris. The central facility provides analytical and technical services to several agencies and departments of the French government, including the Bibliothèque Nationale and the Archives Nationales. Two important facilities in Italy, both in Rome, are the Istituto Centrale di Patalogia del Libro, founded in 1938, and the International Centre for the Study of the Preservation and the Restoration of Cultural Property (ICCROM), established under the auspices of Unesco.

An Institute for the Conservation of Cultural Material was established in Australia in 1976. National planning in that country calls for construction of conservation laboratories in a new building of the Australian War Memorial Museum in Canberra (scheduled for completion in 1979). The laboratories are expected to play a leading role in the development of conservation resources and services throughout Australia, Southeast Asia, and Oceania.

In 1972 the government of Canada established the Canadian Conservation Institute (CCI) in Ottawa within the National Museums of Canada. The Institute has produced several useful publications that deal with various aspects of environmental monitoring and analysis. Fiscal and personnel restraints forced a reevaluation of priorities, however, so it was uncertain at the end of the 1970's whether Canadian libraries and archives would benefit directly or indirectly from the research services of the central laboratories. A second development involving applied research in Canada was the selection of Richard D. Smith's Nonacqueous Book Deacidification System by the Public Archives of Canada for a pilot trial in 1974. The system became operative in 1977 and is described, together with other leading processes of mass deacidification, in John C. Williams's *Preservation of Paper and Textiles of Artistic and Historic Value* (1977).

Laboratories in other countries are rare, but in several there are individual researchers working either in restoration facilities in libraries, archives, and museums or in close cooperation with them.

*(3) A single leaf, deacidified, mended, and encapsulated in stable polyester film (Mylar) preparatory to being placed in a post binding.*

*(4) The completed volume.*

*(5) The project completed: bound volumes of the encapsulated leaves preserved for scholarly research.*

Schomburg Center for Research in Black Culture, New York Public Library

**REFERENCES**
John P. Baker and Marguerite C. Soroka, editors, *Library Conservation: Preservation in Perspective* (1978).
George M. Cunha, *Conservation of Library Materials,* 2nd ed. (1971–72).
Peter Waters, *Procedures for Salvage of Water-Damaged Library Materials,* 2nd ed. (1979).

JOHN P. BAKER

## Continuing Professional Education

Maintenance of knowledge, growth in skill, and development of competencies for performing roles in the work environment are all critical aspects of belonging to a profession. Consider the criteria for professionalism as summarized by the School Library Manpower Project:

> Professionalism is the conduct of qualified people who share responsibilities for rendering a service; for engaging in continued study; and for maintaining high standards of achievement and practice within the principles, structure and content of a body of knowledge (ALA, 1970).

The elements of continuing library/information/media education were identified in a comprehensive study by Stone, Patrick, and Conroy, *Continuing Library and Information Science Education* (1974). They may be summarized into a definition as the formal, or informal, lifelong learning, or training, that updates, refreshes, or upgrades knowledge, skills, or competencies of library/information/media personnel, enabling them better to perform their roles in the profession; it does not include general education for academic credentials or preparation for job entry. It allows for diversification to a new area within the profession and assumes that the individual carries the basic responsibility for self-directed learning and development.

Although continuing professional education (CPE) occurs after entrance into the profession, it directly supports professionalism. It provides a way for practitioners to be lifelong learners, maintain an awareness of research and current trends, and relate new knowledge to their own roles in the profession. It is a method to improve and maintain lifelong competency.

Despite the close relationship between professionalism and CPE, continuing education has been until recently essentially a peripheral activity in librarianship. The profession's responsibility for continuing education was brought sharply into focus in 1965 by Samuel Rothstein in his 1975 *Library Journal* article, "Nobody's Baby: A Brief Sermon on Continuing Professional Education," in which he made a plea for the baby's adoption. Since then the issue has been one of increasing attention throughout the profession, to the point that Conroy was led to characterize the situation in 1978 in this way: "Now, the dilemma is no longer that learning for library personnel is nobody's baby, but rather that it is considered to be everybody's baby."

In spite of increased interest, research, and a continuing stream of recommendations, the goal of providing quality continuing education opportunities to all practitioners has not yet been attained. Progress is being made, but there is little evidence to show that CPE receives adequate attention when priorities are set, financial resources allocated, or cooperative programs developed.

**The Need for CPE.** Over the past 25 years there have been revolutionary changes in procedures and tools for recording, processing, and disseminating information, which stem in part from increasing recognition of the economic, military, and social value of information—a recognition that has spurred demands for more timely and comprehensive information services in every field. Another reason for change has been the spectacular growth of computer systems and of microform, publication, and communication technologies. These developments have been steadily changing the technological bases and operational patterns in library and information service activities. Because these changes affect every professional practice to some degree, continuing education can be seen as even more important.

A major concern of continuing education is obsolescence stemming from technological and societal change. Within a few years of one's preparation to enter the profession, the practitioner can find skills obsolete. In order to maintain job competence, all professional personnel need to acquire new knowledge after receiving their degrees; professional education cannot be considered terminated at any point. There are three types of obsolescent individuals: (1) persons who have not kept up with new knowledge and techniques in their field; (2) those who are overspecialized, having kept up only with their own very narrow field and having lost contact with major trends and changes; and (3) those persons who move from one career pattern to another, more distantly related one, so that their training is no longer closely integrated with their work.

By the late 1970's continuing professional development was becoming no longer only a "desirable" thing but rather something considered critical and essential to the profession. The National Commission on Libraries and Information Science highlights as a priority one of its *Goals for Action* (1975): "To achieve a technological upgrading of libraries and information centers will require new approaches to recruitment, personnel development, continuing education, technical training, trustee orientation and other matters relating to human resources." As it has developed, CPE is a complex field with a wide array of target groups, varying methods of producing and delivering learning opportunities by a large and diverse group of providers, many ways for giving credit or recognition, and different means for acquiring financial support.

**Target Groups.** The dominant focus in continuing education should be on service to the public. Its goals therefore are (1) quality library and information service to all and (2) maintenance of the competence of practitioners.

In order to achieve these goals, the respondents taking part in the study by Stone et al., sponsored by the National Commission on Libraries and Information Science, were asked for whom continuing education should be provided by the profession. Eighty-eight percent of those queried believed that continuing education should be provided to *all* levels of personnel, including both professional and supportive. This is a distinctive feature in library and information science, as many other professions concentrate only on continuing education for professionals. The inclusion of support staffs and those associated with libraries makes the continuing education responsibilities of the profession much more difficult and comprehensive than those assumed by many other professions.

Within the category "all personnel" respondents were asked to rank all target groups in order of priority for consideration. The overall ranking indicates that first priority should be provided to librarians with Master's degrees in library or information science; second, to those librarians without the MLS degree; third to paraprofessionals (library associates); fourth to technical information specialists without MLS degrees; fifth to library technicians (technical assistants); sixth to library trustees; and seventh to clerical staff.

**Providers and Delivery Systems.** There is now a separate group of learning opportunities available in the field that proclaim assistance to practitioners. The providers of these continuing education opportunities are chiefly academic library education programs, library associations, state library agencies, and employing libraries. A major issue is the role that each of these should play in CPE so that there will be less overlap in coverage, no gaps in content, and more cooperation in planning and implementing programs. The 1970's have seen the formulation of outlines of responsibilities for the providers of CPE; the 1980's will lead to greater collaboration and cooperative efforts among providers.

Generally, the continuing education literature assumes that the individual carries the basic responsibility for lifelong learning and continuing education but that various elements in the profession share the responsibility of providing quality programs that are easily accessible to practitioners. The employer has the responsibility both of providing opportunities for continuing education and of ensuring a job structure that encourages employees to keep up-to-date.

*Associations and Institutions.* Professional societies are expected to identify needs in the field and coming trends; provide continuing education through conference programs, workshops, and publications (17 ALA units addressed the issue of CPE in 1979); and identify resources of help to their members. They are also expected to set standards and guidelines for continuing education; for example, Lester Asheim included three strong points on continuing education when drafting the American Library Association's 1970 "Manpower" policy, now titled "Library Education and Personnel Utilization":

31. Continuing education is essential for all library personnel, professional and supportive, whether they remain within a position category or are preparing to move into a higher one. Continuing education opportunities include both formal and informal learning situations, and need not be limited to library subjects or the offerings of library schools.
32. The "continuing education" which leads to eligibility for Senior Librarian or Specialist positions may take any forms suggested directly above so long as the additional education and experience are relevant to the responsibilities of the assignment.
33. Library administrators must accept responsibility for providing support and opportunities (in forms of leaves, sabbaticals, and released time) for the continuing education of their staffs.

Another example is the 1972 position paper, "The Role of the Association of American Library Schools in Continuing Education," which is based on four key assumptions:

> (1) that the continuing education of librarians is one of the most important problems facing library education today; (2) that in spite of the undeniably good job which is being done by some library schools, there is a great need for coordination and expanded programming in post-graduate continuing library education in order to meet the needs of practicing librarians; (3) that the library schools have a responsibility to develop programs which will (a) enable graduate librarians to continue their lifelong professional development and (b) meet the needs of the profession by lessening the gap that exists between available knowledge, concepts, and technology and their application in library practice; and (4) that continuing library education is a national problem for which the best solutions can only be found through coordinated and vigorous national planning involving at a minimum five cooperating components: the library schools, the library associations, the libraries, the state and regional library agencies, and individual librarians.

Still another example is provided by the Medical Library Association, which began its continuing education efforts in 1957 with national seminars. By the end of the 1970's it had a full-scale national program directed by a full-time Director of Medical Library Education. Prominent within the profession, MLA advocated certification for librarians and developed a certification system for medical librarians. In December 1977 MLA took a major step with the publication of an *Examination Booklet.* In addition to graduation from an ALA-accredited library school program, requirements for certification include a passing grade on a competency-based examination and two years of post-Master's experience in a health sciences library.

Academic institutions are expected to help professionals by providing educational opportunities from which individuals can select those opportunities best suited to their needs. During the 1970's there was increased interest on the part of graduate library schools in the development of continuing education; in October 1978, 56 percent of the 57 ALA-accredited library schools in the United States offer post-Master's specialist or certificate programs; this compares with 50 percent for 1977. Only one library school (Columbia) offered such a program in 1961.

State library agencies have a responsibility for the improvement of the quality of library services in their states. The 1970 *Standards for Library Functions at the State Level* of the American Association of State Libraries say, "The state library agency should promote and provide a program of continuing education for library personnel at all levels, as well as for trustees." The document suggests that the achievement of this goal may be attained through cooperation with library schools, professional associations and sponsoring meetings and workshops.

*CLENE.* In regional hearings conducted in 1972 by the National Commission on Libraries and Information Science, one concern was the availability of continuing education for the development and maintenance of the competencies needed to delivery library and information services to the nation. Subsequently, in 1973, the Commission funded a study to recommend a nationwide program for continuing education that culminated in the Stone report cited earlier. It made recommendations that led to the formation in July 1975 of the Continuing Library Education Network and Exchange (CLENE).

Activities carried out by CLENE since its formation have included an annual directory of continuing education opportunities in library/media/information science; monthly updates of current programs published as the *Continuing Education Communicator;* periodic directories of human resources available in the field of CPE; a quarterly newsletter on continuing education activities within and without the profession, the *CLENExchange;* publication of *Concept Papers* dealing with major issues in continuing education; and development of proposals to gain financial support for programs. In 1976 and 1978 CLENE received federal grants to provide two Institutes to train state library agency personnel in implementing and strengthening statewide systems of continuing education. One Institute placed special emphasis on cooperative planning for continuing education in the state between state library agency personnel, library associations, and library education programs. A major product of the 1978–79 Institute was the development of CE Resource Packages—"an exchange of documents" that makes available on loan resource materials in areas of concern to continuing education planners.

Two other major issues that have been addressed by CLENE through federal funding have been the development of a model recognition system for personnel engaged in continuing education and the development of a prototype home-study program as a way of breaking down the barriers of geographic isolation or other factors. Overall, CLENE is a special service and resource facility that makes continuing education opportunities available to the entire library/information/media community. It develops and promotes a coordinated and concentrated continuing education program throughout the nation. It is the only association that has as its chief mission quality continuing education for library/information/media personnel.

**Credit and Recognition.** The professional's real reward for participation in continuing education should be intellectual stimulation and an improved ability to serve the needs of users. This does not preclude the importance of public recognition for participation in continuing education programs or the need to demonstrate accountability to the public for participation in lifelong learning activities. In order to give recognition for participation in the noncredit nontraditional forms of learning prevalent in today's professions, the Continuing Education Unit (CEU) was developed as a uniform measure to assist in the accumulation and exchange of standardized information about participation in continuing education activities. The CEU is defined as "ten contact hours of participation in an organized continuing education activity under responsible sponsorship, capable direction and qualified instruction."

Since 1976 associations, state library agencies, and universities have started to use the CEU as a way of giving credit for various types of nontraditional learning experiences, and it is anticipated that the trend will continue.

In 1978 the South Dakota State Library was authorized by the state to give CEU's as a form of credit for workshop attendance in keeping with South Dakota's State Plan for the Continuing Education Unit (1975). In the summer of 1978, the Michigan Department of Education State Library Services established a recognition system, based on awarding and recording CEU's. In October 1978 the Wisconsin Association of Public Libraries adopted a recognition system for public library personnel, based on earning a required number of academic credits, CEU's, or contact hours for self-guided learning.

Concurrently, CLENE has been working on the presentation of a recognition system to the profession as a whole that includes the use of the CEU, the academic credit, and contact hours relative to independent learning. The concern of CLENE is that a compatible system be developed that can be used on a nationwide basis. This would (1) facilitate the recognition of participation in continuing education in all parts of the country and different types of libraries; (2) provide employees with a commonly understood record of continuing education activities; and (3) facilitate the review of the records of individuals whose continuing education activities take place in more than one state, institution, or association.

**Trends.** Continuing professional education is an essential element in the maintenance of professional skills, the application of knowledge, and competence in practice. Increasing attention has been given to CPE throughout the profession, leading to an unprecedented and explosive growth of continuing education opportunities. As a result there are now many opportunities available that proclaim assistance to practitioners, but experience shows that many lack quality, and loud and persistent complaints have come for some type of quality criteria for these continuing education opportunities. It seems only logical that this now-separable segment of curriculum development should be the subject of the same type of systematic evaluation and appraisal that has been developed for the Master's program. There is no process operating nationally to evaluate and approve continuing education programs. CLENE sees this as an important and serious gap in the profession and views this deficiency as an opportunity for leadership by proposing to the profession (1) the development of criteria of quality for continuing education programs; (2) the establishment of a voluntary system for approving programs; and (3) the provision of recognition to those providers who meet the criteria.

Current programs suggest that future CPE efforts will focus to a greater extent on procedures by which individual professionals can assess their own needs and carry out learning activities in response to an evaluation of the way they are fulfilling their roles in the work place. Debate has also begun concerning the question of legally mandated CPE. In librarianship, as in other professions, a fundamental issue is the degree to which CPE changes knowledge, how much changed knowledge affects competence, and how much competence affects actual practice.

**REFERENCES**

Barbara Conroy, *Library Staff Development and Continuing Education: Principles and Practices* (1978); the author presents unusually full and comprehensive definitions of and distinctions between staff development and continuing education.

Malcolm S. Knowles, "Model for Assessing Continuing Education Needs for a Profession," *Proceedings of First CLENE Assembly: January 23–24, 1976;* this is a practical model presented by Knowles for librarians to assess their competency development.

National Task Force on the Continuing Education Unit, *The Continuing Education Criteria and Guidelines* (1974; rev. ed. 1979), the authoritative source of all subsequent serious studies of the Continuing Education Unit (CEU).

Elizabeth W. Stone, "Continuing Education for Librarians in the United States," in *Advances in Librarianship* (1978), includes an extensive bibliography.

Elizabeth W. Stone, Ruth Patrick, and Barbara Conroy, *Continuing Library and Information Science Education,* Final Report to NCLIS (1974).

ELIZABETH W. STONE

## Costa Rica

Costa Rica, a republic of Central America, lies between the Pacific Ocean and the Caribbean Sea, bounded by Nicaragua on the north and Panama on the southeast. Pop. (1977 est.) 2,070,600; area 50,898 sq.km. The official language is Spanish.

**National Library.** The National Library is in San José, the capital city of Costa Rica. Under a law enacted in 1910, it became the depository for the national bibliography. Access to the collection is permitted only in the Library. Loans of materialal for home use are seldom approved. The Library maintains an interlibrary loan service with several institutions. Its collection totals 302,000 volumes and 5,800 periodicals.

**Academic Libraries.** The principal academic library is in the Carlos Monge Alfaro Library of the University of Costa Rica. The oldest academic library in Costa Rica (created in 1946), it has one of the largest collections of any library in the country (300,000 volumes). The University also has three branch or regional libraries with a general collection of 90,000 volumes. The library of the National University has special collections in education, marine science, and veterinary medicine. The library of the Costa Rican Institute of Technology has a collection of 20,000 volumes on science and technology as well as on other subjects.

**Public Libraries.** A law enacted in 1890 established the first public libraries; however, most of the libraries are without trained professionals and are handicapped by inferior facilities and collections (most with fewer than 5,000 volumes). Costa Rica had 18 public libraries

**Table 1. Libraries in Costa Rica (1976)**

| Type | Number | Volumes in collections | Annual expenditures (colón) | Population served | Professional staff | All staff (total) |
|---|---|---|---|---|---|---|
| National | 1 | 302,000 | ¢ 5,000,000 | 215,500 | 7 | 93 |
| Academic | 4 | 500,000 | ¢11,500,000 | 53,000 | 62 | 232 |
| Public | 18 | 707,000 | ¢ 1[a] | 254,500 | 0 | 31 |
| School | 175 | 1,700,000 | ¢ 400,000 | 140,000 | 51 | 180 |
| Special | 21 | 142,000 | ¢ 750,000 | N.A. | 14 | 58 |
| Total | 219 | 3,451,000 | ¢17,650,001 | | 134 | 594 |

[a]Budget is included in National Library total.

**Table 2. Archives in Costa Rica (1976)**

| | |
|---|---|
| Number | 1 |
| Holdings | 7,500 linear meters |
| Annual expenditures | ¢ 2,225 |
| Professional staff | 13 |
| All staff (total) | 52 |

Source: Congreso Nacional de Bibliotecología, Documentación e Información, 1 (San José, 1977).

throughout the country in 1979. Library materials are available for use only in the library. Students make up most of the library users. Activities are coordinated by a National Library Director.

**School Libraries.** School libraries were created in 1893 by a presidential resolution. In 1975 a new program called the Development Plan for the School Library System was created. Its goal is to increase efficiency in school library services by working together to achieve common objectives. A cataloguing center has been created to catalogue all of the materials of the libraries of the system.

**Special Libraries.** The Library of the Centro Agronómico Tropical de Investigación y Enseñanza (CATIE) provides agricultural information. The Oficina del Café maintains a collection on the cultivation and marketing of coffee. The Instituto Costarricense de Electricidad (ICE) has a library with information on electrification and telecommunication. Health science information is provided through five hospital libraries. The Instituto Centroamericano de Administración Pública (ICAP) has a library collection that emphasizes public administration.

**Associations.** Colegio de Bibliotecarios de Costa Rica was created in 1971. There is also the Asociación Costarricense de Bibliotecarios.

PAULINA RETANA ACEVEDO

# Cuba

Cuba, a socialist republic in the Caribbean, occupies the largest island in the Greater Antilles of the West Indies. The Cuban archipelago consists of several thousand small islands, islets, and cays. Pop. (1978 est.) 9,648,900; area 110,922 sq.km., including the Cuban archipelago. The official language is Spanish.

**National Library.** The Biblioteca Nacional "José Martí" (National Library) was established on October 18, 1901, in Havana, by order of the Military Governor. It functions as a central library for an extensive network of public libraries and arranges for lending services for the country's public and special libraries. More than 530,000 volumes are housed there. In addition, the National Library holds nearly 57,000 nonbook items, including more than 20,000 maps of Cuba and the rest of the world, as well as drawings, engravings, records, and printed music. It also holds a special collection of Cuban manuscripts by and about famous Cubans, which is under the direction of the Cuban Bibliography Department. This department is also responsible for the annual national bibliography, the *Bibliografía Cubana,* which first appeared in 1938. The national bibliography includes books and pamphlets published in Cuba, books by Cubans that were published outside Cuba, official publications, films, records, exhibition catalogues, posters, postage stamp issues, and periodicals that appeared for the first time that year. The National Library also publishes the *Revista de la Biblioteca Nacional José Martí,* devoted to historical and literary research; the *Anuario Martiano;* the annual *Indice General de Publicaciones Periódicas Cubanas,* abstracts of periodical articles published that year; *La Polillita,* a monthly publication on children's literature; and the *Boletin Bibliotecas,* which deals with questions related to librarianship.

Special departments within the National Library have been established in the visual arts and music; Library Extension and Juvenile departments have also been created. The library extension program sponsors the operation of small libraries in factories and other places of work and runs technical training programs. The Juvenile Department, established for children and adolescents, has an extensive collection exceeding 18,000 volumes. In an effort to encourage children to read, the Juvenile Department sponsors story recitals throughout the country. Literacy is currently at 95 percent, as compared with the prerevolution rate of 25 percent. The Library has also established a Department of Scientific and Technical Infor-

ALA

*The Havana University Library, originally founded in 1728, is now in this building which was erected in 1937.*

mation, which is responsible for the production of a union catalogue of scientific and technical journals. It lists more than 18,500 journals and indicates which of the 120 or so libraries hold such journals.

During the 1960's and 1970's major emphasis has been placed upon book publishing in Cuba. Children's book publishing there is subsidized totally by the state. Statistics from the Ministry of Culture estimated that 36,000,000 copies of 1,500 titles were published in 1978. Before 1959 there were no publishing houses in Cuba.

**Academic Libraries.** There are four major universities in Cuba, with university branches in each of the provinces. They are the Universidad de la Habana, founded in 1728 and reorganized in 1863, 1943, and 1962; the Universidad de Oriente, founded in Santiago in 1947; the Universidad Central de Las Villas, founded in 1948 in Santa Clara, Las Villas; and the Universidad Ignacio Agramonte, founded in 1974 in Camagüey as a branch of the University of Havana.

The Havana University Library holds 202,881 volumes and many scholarly journals and Cuban periodicals. In addition, there are many specialized libraries connected with the University's faculties (technology, medicine, sciences, agriculture, and humanities) and its research institutes. The university library at Las Villas holds approximately 75,000 volumes, and the library at Santiago 118,000 volumes.

The library of the Pre-University Institute of Education, founded in 1894, in Zulueta y San José, holds 32,000 volumes and an extensive newspaper collection. The Institute owns some rare works dating back to the early 17th century.

**Public Libraries.** The network of public libraries in Cuba is directed by the National Library Administration, under the National Council of Culture, with headquarters in the National Library. In the early 1970's library service was made available for the first time to small towns, including minilibraries, without professional staff, in several rural areas. The local branch of the National Library in Nueva Gerona, the Julio A. Mello Biblioteca, houses about 15,000 volumes, including an extensive reference collection.

Every public library with a children's department receives one free copy of every work published for juveniles. There are more than 190 children's library branches throughout Cuba, with about six in Havana. In addition, small reading rooms in parks provide library materials to the public. This is administered through the park system rather than the local library system.

**Special Libraries.** There are many research libraries in Cuba affiliated with the Academy of Sciences (Academia de Ciencias de la República de Cuba). The Institute for Scientific and Technical Documentation and Information (IDICT—Instituto de Documentación e Información Científica y Técnica), which is part of the Academy of Sciences of Cuba, coordinates research in the area of scientific information handling and provides assistance in information services development and mechanization and automation of information management. IDICT also participates in the training of specialists in scientific and technical information and provides published, as well as unpublished, documentation to individual and institutional users. Certain units within this information network coordinate national information subsystems and offer information services on a national scale. There are also specialized units that provide scientific and technical information primarily to personnel working in a particular subject area. These include the Agricultural Information and Documentation Center (CIDA—Centro de Información y Documentación Agropecuario) of the Ministry of Agriculture and the National Medical Science Information Center (Centro Nacional de Información de las Ciencias Medicas) of the Ministry of Public Health. These centers or units, each at its own level of development and with its own subject specialization, exist within the majority of the centralized offices of the government. In addition, many professional associations and government offices have important special collections.

**Associations.** Cuba did not have an active library association at the close of the 1970's. Two former library associations, the Asociación Cubana de Bibliotecarios and the Colegio Nacional de Bibliotecarios Universitarios, were not active.

STAFF

## Cunha, Maria Luisa Monteiro da
(1908– )

Librarian and Brazilian cataloguing specialist active in national and international library activities, Maria Luisa Monteiro da Cunha was born in Santos (São Paulo) on September 14, 1908. She received a Bachelor's degree in Dentistry (1928); later, she registered at the Library School of the Fundação Escola de Sociologia e Política (São Paulo) and received in 1940 a Bachelor's degree in Library Science. She won a special scholarship granted by the American Library Association and, during the academic year of 1946–47, studied at Columbia University School of Library Service. She prepared a term paper that, translated into Portuguese, contributed to the development of cataloguing practice in Brazil. She represented Columbia University at the First Conference of Librarians of the Americas (Washington, D.C., 1947). From 1942 to 1949 she worked at the São Paulo Municipal Public Library. She was Director of the University of São Paulo Central Library from 1949 to 1970 and of the Documentation and Library Division from 1970 to 1978. In 1965 she was appointed one of the members of a Special Committee nominated to study the creation and organization of an Institute devoted to the professional teaching of communication media including journalism, theater, the movies, radio, television, librarianship, documentation, and public relations. The Committee activities resulted in the Communications and Arts School. A member of its Faculty from 1967 to 1972, she gave courses on librarianship and cataloguing. Cunha became an active member of specialized committees, mainly the Brazilian Committee on Library Technical Services. She was one of the members of the Working Group on Coordination of Cataloguing Principles (created in 1959 by IFLA under a grant from the Council on Library Resources) for the organization and follow-up of the International Conference on Cataloguing Principles (Paris, 1961). She participated in the 1st Seminar on University Libraries (Monticello, Illinois, 1961), the International Meeting of Cataloguing Experts (Copenhagen, 1969), and the Revision Meeting for International Standard Bibliographic Description-M (Grenoble, 1973). Brazil came to rely heavily on her expert advice. From 1954 she was an invited participant at Brazilian library conferences. In 1973 she received a gold medal from the Seventh Brazilian Documentation and Librarianship Congress (Belém, Pará).

She wrote *Treatment of Brazilian and Portuguese names* (Paris, IFLA, 1961), *Formación profesional* (1965), *Controle bibliográfico universal* (Brasília, 1975), and *Bibliotecas universitárias em sistemas nacionais de informação* (Porto Alegre, 1977).

CORDELIA R. CAVALCANTI

## Cutter, Charles Ammi
(1837–1903)

One of the most important of all contributors to U.S. librarianship, Charles Ammi Cutter was born on March

*Charles Ammi Cutter*

ALA

14, 1837, in Boston. He lived with his grandfather and his three aunts in West Cambridge, Massachusetts, where he was raised in a strong Unitarian religious atmosphere. He was sent to the Hopkins Classical School, a school designed to prepare young men for Harvard College. By ten he had also become acquainted with the West Cambridge town library as both a patron and an occasional assistant to his aunt, Charlotte Cutter, who served as its Librarian from 1849 to 1851.

Cutter enrolled in the fall of 1851 at Harvard College, where he applied himself diligently to his studies, winning several prizes and subsequently graduating third in his class. He studied French literature, science, and mathematics with great interest and was thoroughly exposed to the mental philosophy of Scottish Common Sense Realism through the teaching of Francis Bowen. His interest in scientific studies was such that for a semester after he graduated in 1855 he attended the Lawrence Scientific School as a special student in mathematics.

Cutter was ambivalent about pursuing a scientific career, however, and in the fall of 1856 he enrolled in the Harvard Divinity School, again distinguishing himself in scholarship by winning the Bowdoin prize dissertation competition in 1857. Although his course of studies trained him for the Unitarian ministry, the experience that had the most influence on him while in the Divinity School was his tenure as the School's student librarian for the period 1857–59. He not only discharged his regular duties but also directed the writing of a new catalogue and the complete rearrangement of the books on the shelves. His work as a librarian also brought him into contact with Ezra Abbot, the College Library's cataloguer. This relationship was significant, not only for the personal influence that Abbot had over Cutter, but also because several months after Cutter graduated from the School in 1859, Abbot successfully obtained Cutter's appointment as his assistant in the College Library. Thus, on May 11, 1860, Cutter formally entered the career that would occupy him throughout the remainder of his life.

Cutter's years at the Harvard College Library from 1860 to the end of 1868 were formative in several ways. He experienced first-hand the growth and administrative problems of a large academic library, then under the direction of John Langdon Sibley. He learned from Abbot a systematic approach to the organization of knowledge in catalogue form, the chief characteristic of which was its basis in the classificatory theory that was inherent in the Scottish realists' view of mental processes. He also learned the techniques of cataloguing, for he not only helped Abbot to plan the alphabetico-classed card catalogue that bears Abbot's name but also assumed supervisory control over the project.

In May 1863 Cutter married Sarah Fayerweather Appleton, and by the summer of 1868 three sons had been born to them. His growing family responsibilities made it necessary for him to supplement his regular wages through a variety of special projects. These included assisting Joseph Sabin as a bibliographer on the *Bibliotheca Americana;* working as a part-time cataloguer at the Boston Public Library (1866–68), where he came into personal contact with Charles Coffin Jewett; indexing scholarly books in preparation for their publication; and writing reviews and articles for the *North American Review* and for the *Nation.* He was able to dispense with much of that activity, however, when he accepted the position of Librarian of the prestigious Boston Athenaeum on January 1, 1869.

**Years of Success, 1869–80.** The years from 1869 to 1880 were for Cutter ones of great success and undoubted personal satisfaction. His work at the Athenaeum consisted of a thoroughgoing and continuous systematization of the library's programs. His ideal, gained from his scientific and philosophical training, was that all elements and processes of the library should together form an integrated whole that efficiently reached stated goals at the most reasonable cost—much like a finely tuned machine. In carefully reaching toward that systematization, Cutter captured not only the confidence of his trustees but also the admiration of the new but advancing profession of librarianship.

The confidence and admiration that he gained was due in no small part to his special accomplishments; the most notable were in the realm of cataloguing. He planned and published between 1869 and 1882 a monumental five-volume dictionary catalogue of the Athenaeum's collections that was not only a testament to his ideals of systematization but also so artfully executed and convenient to use that it brought general esteem to both Cutter and the library. Moreover, Cutter presented both the theory and procedures he used in making the catalogue to the wider library world in the form of an essay, "Library Catalogues," and his *Rules for a Printed Dictionary Catalogue,* both important parts of the Bureau of Education's important special report of 1876, *Public Libraries in the United States of America, Their History, Condition, and Management.* The *Rules* were afterward published in three more editions, the last and most notable issued posthumously in 1904. The second of his accomplishments consisted of his classification work; by the end of 1880 he had circulated the first copies of his author tables, later published in three separate formats (a two-figure author table, 1887; the *Cutter-Sanborn Three-Figure Author Table,* 1896; and Cutter's own three-figure expansion of his earlier two-figure table, 1901). By 1880 Cutter had also worked out the general plan and had circulated the first schedules of his "Boston Athenaeum Classification."

Concurrent with the foregoing activities and accomplishments, Cutter also took part directly in the formal rise of the library profession. He worked closely with Melvil Dewey and others in the establishment of the American Library Association in 1876. Preferring the shadows more than the limelight, he became one of ALA's most active committee workers, chairing the very important Cooperation Committee from its inception in 1877. His literary contributions also increased in number. Though he was shy and somewhat reticent in public, he was able in his writing to express with great logic and clarity, as well as with occasional sharpness, the forcefulness of his views. His writings included major articles and reviews on library matters in the *Library Journal;* many literary pieces in the *Nation,* notable for their pithiness and wit; and the bibliography columns that he compiled and edited for the *Library Journal.* Finally, Cutter also joined with Dewey and others in 1879 in the formation of the Readers' and Writers' Economy, a speculative business venture of Dewey's designed to profit from the new commercial market arising with the growing library field.

But the venture proved to be short-lived and engendered a financial imbroglio that cast a pallor over an otherwise bright and energetic period.

**ALA Leadership from 1881.** One important result of the financial imbroglio of 1880 was the realignment of some of the ALA leadership responsibilities. For example, Dewey—the forceful if unofficial leader of the ALA—relinquished his editorship of the *Library Journal,* which Cutter then assumed in January 1881 and eventually continued until late in 1893. Cutter also worked on most of the Association's important new committees during the following decade and, from 1887 to 1889, served as its President. But Cutter, along with others, represented an essentially conservative approach to professional library leadership. He was content to view the meetings of the ALA and the pages of the *Journal* as a forum in which librarians shared their insights, debated their differences, and gained general inspiration. Colleagues could then apply to their own situation whatever techniques seemed appropriate. Dewey, however, represented a rising bureaucratic spirit who saw the future of the profession in the exercise of its organizational power; the formation of explicit standards; centralized control of library processes, methods, and leadership where possible; and simple, pragmatic solutions to library programs. From his vantage point in New York, Dewey offered an increasingly attractive alternative to the regular leadership of the profession. The force with which he presented his program not only brought him the presidency of the Association twice during the early 1890's but also changed the character of the Association and its general purposes.

Cutter's response to the changes taking place, especially after 1885, was ambivalent. On the one hand, he agreed with Dewey in many matters, particularly those related to classification and education. And because of his good-natured humor, his patience, and the esteem in which others held his judgment, he was able to play a mediating role, defending Dewey's work and standing between Dewey and others who opposed him. On the other hand, Cutter found himself increasingly uncomfortable with Dewey's tendency to oversimplify library problems and their solutions and with his emphasis on the exercise of organizational power to achieve what were clearly Dewey's own goals. By the early 1890's Cutter was taking decided stands against some of Dewey's measures and in the editorials of the *Journal* increasingly emphasized the more conservative interpretation of the role of the Association. But he recognized that the ALA was changing dramatically and, as bewildering as it may have appeared, accepted it as inevitable.

Changes in the Association during that period were paralleled by changes at the Athenaeum. Cutter finished the dictionary catalogue and began the arduous task of applying his classification scheme to the Athenaeum's collections. The latter dragged on for ten years, however, and its cost and disruption brought criticism from Athenaeum members. Furthermore, the Board of Trustees of the Athenaeum underwent a significant turnover in membership during the mid-1880's. The new members, bringing with them a growing sense of protectiveness against outsiders, criticized Cutter's openness in administration and willingness to use the Athenaeum for what they considered expensive experiments on behalf of the wider library world. In 1892 the conflict over administration priorities broke into the open when Cutter was unofficially censured by the trustees. Cutter began to search for another library position, but his search was unsuccessful. In April 1893 he resigned his Athenaeum post and traveled to Europe for a rest. He returned in the summer to attend the Columbian Exposition library meetings, but his subsequent search for a new position was likewise unsuccessful. In October 1893, he again returned to Europe, severing most of his ties with the American library scene until the following summer.

**Forbes Library, 1894–1903.** While in Europe, Cutter was contacted by the trustees of the new Forbes Library in Northampton, Massachusetts, for the purpose of purchasing books for their library. After subsequent negotiations, he returned to the Forbes in August 1894 as its first Librarian. Cutter's accomplishments during the next ten years were considerable; he increased the Forbes collections to nearly 90,000 carefully selected volumes, built large circulating collections of art reproductions and music, and began a medical collection for the area's physicians, a children's section within the Library, and a branch library system for the area surrounding Northampton. But the administration of the Forbes brought him grief as well, for while generous funds were available for purchases and building needs, severe limitations were constantly imposed on the funds necessary for the administration of the Library. As a result, Cutter was unable to hire highly trained assistants, and those he trained himself regularly left the Forbes for better paying positions elsewhere. This factor made it impossible, for example, to catalogue and classify the collection in any more than a rudimentary manner.

The application of the shelf classification was of great concern to Cutter. During the late 1880's, he had remodeled his Boston Athenaeum classification into his much better known *Expansive Classification.* By 1893 he had published the first six expansions of the scheme. Believing it to be the best arranged and most adaptable classification available, he hoped that it might overtake Dewey's Decimal Classification as the scheme most used by all libraries. To that end he promoted his classification scheme tirelessly, presenting its merits whenever he could. In 1897 this effort took him as far as the International Conference of Librarians in London and the Institut Internationale de Bibliographie in Brussels. But his inability to apply it fully to the Forbes and the enormous work of singlehandedly editing it, supervising its printing, promoting it, and distributing it slowed to a snail's pace his progress on the seventh and final expansion. At his death it remained unfinished, although its use as a fundamental pattern for the Library of Congress's classification extended its influence immeasurably.

Cutter's last years brought, as a result, a mixture of accomplishments and frustrations. Given to selfless labor on behalf of libraries, he constantly took on arduous projects. Between 1901 and early 1903, besides his Forbes work, he participated without reserve in the demanding work of the catalogue code revision committee of ALA, addressed local library groups, and lectured at library schools. He died in New Hampshire on September 6, 1903.

**REFERENCES**

W. P. Cutter, *Charles Ammi Cutter* (1931).

W. E. Foster, "Charles Ammi *Cutter: A Memorial Sketch," Library Journal* (1903).

Francis L. Miksa, editor, *Charles Ammi Cutter: Library Systematizer* (1977).

FRANCIS L. MIKSA

# Cyprus

Cyprus, an island in the eastern Mediterranean Sea, lies 65 km. south of Turkey. Pop. (1978 est.) 700,000; area 9,251 sq.km. The official languages are Greek and Turkish.

The history of Cyprus goes back to the 6th millennium B.C. with remains of Neolithic settlements. In ancient and classical times, Cyprus shared Greek culture, and libraries can be traced back to those times. The earliest were attached to the temples and kept archives, such as the sanctuary of Aphrodite at Paphos, the temple of Apollo at Curium, and the temple of Cybele at Soli.

The earliest known public library (Bibliophylakion) in Cyprus was in the city state of Soli; a man called Apollonius was in charge. Nicocrates the Cypriot is also mentioned for his famous private library.

During the Christian period Cyprus was among the first places to be converted to Christianity, and with the spread of Christian literature one can assume that libraries were created, and books were kept in churches and monasteries. No trace of such a library is found, but there are many codices and manuscripts from Cyprus related to the Christian era in several major libraries abroad (including the Vatican, Paris, and Venice).

In the Frankish period (1191–1571) there were libraries in the court of Lusignan kings and in churches, monasteries, and abbeys. During the Turkish occupation (1571–1878) nearly all works of art were destroyed, and the cathedrals of Saint Sophia in Nicosia and Saint Nicolas in Famagusta were converted to mosques. The books kept in churches and other places were destroyed. Only a few books were saved in isolated small churches and monasteries.

After 1821 a small library was formed by the Archbishopric in Nicosia, where all books saved from ancient collections in various monasteries and bishoprics were collected. The library of the Archbishopric of Cyprus originates from those collections.

At the beginning of the 19th century a small library known as the Library of Sultan Mahmut II was set up by the Ottoman government with Turkish, Arabic, and Persian works. Originally housed in a medieval building behind Saint Sophia Cathedral, it is now at Evkaf.

After the cession of Cyprus to England in July 1878, there was an increase in book imports, mainly from Greece and England. New libraries were started, mainly in government offices. In July 1878 operation of the first printing press was begun by a Greek Cypriot at Larnaca.

In 1887 a legal deposit law was passed, and a depository set up in the office of the Chief Secretary. Two copies of each book were also sent to the Keeper of the Department of Printed Books at the British Museum. Since independence in 1960, three copies have been kept in the Public Information Office of the Ministry of Interior, Nicosia.

Nearly all libraries in Cyprus, except those mentioned above, started functioning after 1927, mainly after independence in 1960.

In July 1974 Turkey invaded Cyprus and occupied 40 percent of its territory. Many library collections were either damaged or access to them lost in the ensuing fighting. The library service has since faced many difficulties, including a reduced stock of books and library facilities. The situation is gradually improving as library facilities and stocks are replaced.

**National and Public Libraries.** There is no national library in Cyprus. The Public Library of Nicosia, established in 1927 and transferred to Nicosia Municipality in 1936, has its own building in the center of Nicosia. It was closed in 1953 but reopened in 1977. Also housed in the same building is the library of the Ministry of Education (1960). These two libraries are run by the same Library Committee and Administration and serve as a central library where books printed in Cyprus are kept. The Library of the Ministry of Education serves every citizen of Cyprus. Patrons can borrow books personally or by mail. The two libraries have about 50,000 volumes of bound books and periodicals, mainly in Greek and English.

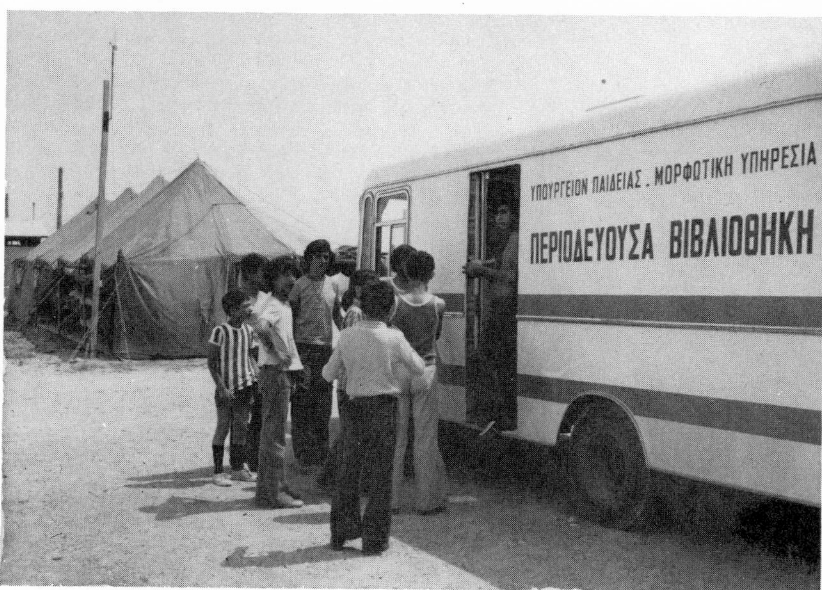

Public Information Office, Nicosia, Cyprus

*A mobile library visiting a refugee camp near Nicosia, Cyprus. Three mobile units serve about 40,000 people in the districts of Nicosia and Larnoca.*

In the main towns of Cyprus there are public libraries in special buildings run by the municipalities. There are also 110 communal libraries in large villages, run by the Cultural Service of the Ministry of Education. The Ministry of Education also runs three mobile units serving about 40,000 people in the districts of Nicosia and Larnaca.

There is no national bibliography. Since 1960 the Cyprus bibliographical bulletin has been published by C. D. Stephanou. It records the publications of Cyprus in the original language and is classified according to Dewey Decimal Classification.

**Academic Libraries.** Cyprus, with many students studying abroad, has no central university of its own. The country's six tertiary institutions of higher education are the Pedagogical Academy (College of Education), the Higher Technical Institute, the Forestry College, the School of Nursing and Midwifery, the Hotel Catering Institute, and the Psychiatric School of Nursing. All these institutions have libraries of about 40,000 volumes.

**School Libraries.** All 439 primary schools of Cyprus have their own lending libraries of varying size. All 91 secondary schools have libraries ranging from 3,000 to

**Libraries in Cyprus (1978)**

| Type | Number | Volumes in collections | Annual expenditures (pound) | Population served | Professional staff | All staff (total) |
|---|---|---|---|---|---|---|
| Academic | 6 | 40,000 | N.A. | 1,455 | 2 | 7 |
| Public | 114 | 100,000 | N.A. | 350,000 | 2 | 114 |
| School[a] | 91 | 273,000 | N.A. | 50,000 | N.A. | 93 |
| Special | 15 | 50,000 | N.A. | N.A. | N.A. | 15 |
| Total | 226 | 463,000 | | | | 229 |

[a]Excludes elementary schools.

40,000 volumes. School libraries are run by librarians or teacher-librarians. All are supported by the Ministry of Education, which contributes an allowance, according to the number of pupils, for the purchase of books.

**Special Libraries.** All ministries and special departments have specialized libraries. Mention can be made of the library of the Archaeological Museum with an excellent collection on Cyprus's archaeology, the Cyprus Research Centre with a fine collection on Cyprus's history and folklore, and the library of the Productivity Centre. The Library of the Archbishopric, with its fine collections in theology, also has many rare codices and manuscripts. The Public Record Office Library, which opened in 1972, houses all public records and archives of Cyprus.

**Association.** The Cyprus Library Association was founded in 1962. It is a member of IFLA and COMLA.

COSTAS D. STEPHANOU

# Czechoslovakia

Czechoslovakia, a socialist republic in central Europe, is bounded by the German Federal Republic on the west, the German Democratic Republic on the northwest, Poland on the northeast, Hungary on the southeast, the U.S.S.R on the east, and Austria on the southwest. Pop. (1978 est.) 15,138,000; area 127,877 sq.mi. The official languages are Czech and Slovak.

The system of libraries in Czechoslovakia consists of two independent systems—the Czech and the Slovak. Organization structure of the whole system and its management were determined under the Library Act of 1959. According to their functional purpose or specialization, libraries are loosely incorporated in the national systems. On principle, the services of the libraries are provided free of charge. The national systems are headed by central libraries that function as national libraries.

**National Libraries.** *State Library of the Czech Socialist Republic, Prague.* Origins of this library date back to 1348. Its activities comprise the functions of both the Czech national and central library and the general research library.

The Library serves as the national center of research and methodology, interlibrary lending service on the international scale, and Unesco and UN depository library. The Library publishes the Czech national bibliography in four basic series covering books, periodicals, articles, and printed music. It also provides research and lending services to specialists. As the oldest depository library, with the right to receive legal depository copies, it has vast collections (4,750,000 units in 1977); among them are unique collections of manuscripts, incunabula and rare printed items, printed music, and various special collections.

*Matica slovenská, Martin.* Founded in 1863, the Slovak national and central library is charged with care and protection of historical collections, and it is a center for bibliography and methodology, education, and theory of libraries and research.

The Library serves also as the central library publishing house and fills the function of the central museum and archives of literature. It is a depository for legal deposit copies of the whole country and the national center for interlibrary lending service. Publishing activities include the Slovak national bibliography in four basic series—books, periodicals, articles, and printed music. In 1977 computer technology was introduced. The Library provides research and lending services to specialists. Collections of Matica slovenská (3,865,000 units in 1977) include manuscripts, incunabula and rare printed items, archival collection (1,400,000 units), printed music, posters, postcards, and special recordings.

**Academic Libraries.** These are specialized libraries attached to the research centers and institutes of the Czechoslovak and Slovak Academy of Science. Their library, bibliographic, documentary, research, and other types of activities are oriented to support scientific research and education of research workers. The central library in the Czech Socialist Republic is the Basic Library–Science Information Center of the Czechoslovak Academy of Science, founded in 1786 (810,000 volumes in 1977). It is the specialized information center for social sciences. In Slovakia the same functions are executed by the Central Library of the Slovak Academy of Sciences in Bratislava, founded in 1942 (440,000 volumes in 1977).

**Public Libraries.** These provide educational and cultural services as well as services for specialists in a region. They are open to the public and are used by more than 50 percent of inhabitants in rural and more than 70 percent of inhabitants in urban areas. In 1975 their collections were comprised of 28 percent nonfiction, 47.4 percent fiction, and 24.6 percent literature for children and youth. Sixty percent of library lendings in the CSSR were by public libraries (regional, municipal, district, and local). According to the Library Act of 1959, regional and district public libraries are the center of methodology, bibliography, information, and interlibrary lending services.

**Research Libraries.** Libraries are either universal or specialized, with central or regional functions. They provide bibliographic and information services to specialists in science, research, management, and education. The most important research libraries are the University Library in Bratislava (general collection 1,550,000 volumes in 1977), the Center of Scientific, Technological, and Economic Information–the State Technical Library in Prague (specialized collection of 1,500,000 volumes in 1977), the Slovak Technical Library in Bratislava (specialized collection of 2,220,000 volumes in 1977), the Library of the National Museum in Prague (specialized historical collection of 1,550,000 volumes in 1977), the State Scientific Library in Brno (universal collection—3,875,000 volumes in 1977), the State Scientific Library in Košice (universal collection—1,700,000 in 1977). Specialized services are provided also by central agricultural and forestry libraries in Prague, Nitra, and Zvolen and by central libraries of biological and medical sciences, peda-

**Libraries in Czechoslovakia (1975)**

| Type | Number | Volumes in collections | Population served[a] | All staff (total) |
|---|---|---|---|---|
| National | 2 | 6,932,326 | 40,610 | 896 |
| Academic | 125 | 3,600,000 | 52,000 | 594 |
| Public | 13,056 | 41,700,000 | 2,224,000 | 4,577 |
| Research | 15 | 13,767,674 | 169,390 | 1,076 |
| Others | 31,794 | 84,000,000 | 3,514,000 | 1,558 |
| Total | 44,992 | 150,000,000 | | 8,701 |

[a]Registered readers.

gogic, and economic libraries in Bratislava and Prague.

**Others.** University libraries operate within the national library systems. They form a part of the university and have appropriate specializations, school and pedagogic libraries for the needs of education (functioning at primary and secondary schools), technical, agricultural, and medical libraries (at the factories and appropriate institutions), special libraries of museums, galleries, and archives, and trade union libraries, which are considered to have an educational role.

**Organizations.** The Central Library Council of the CSR (Ministry of Culture) is an advisory and coordinating body. Its aim is "to follow and evaluate the activity of the library system in the CSR, to consider the conception of development and the long-term plans of activity of the national library system according to the needs of society, to coordinate the activity of the respective networks, to supervise the advancement of political and professional development of library workers, their social appreciation and adequate remuneration." The Council cooperates with international library associations and is a member of IFLA. Members of the Council are executives and experts in the field of librarianship and information science. In Slovakia the same functions are executed by the Slovak Library Council.

The Association of Slovak Librarians and Informatists is a voluntary organization of librarians, bibliographers, and information workers, residing in Bratislava with two branch offices in Banská Bystrica and Košice. It was founded in 1968 and had 2,100 members in 1978. The Association is concerned with the advancement of the specialization and with state cultural and scientific policy in the field of libraries, bibliography and information science, and international cooperation of libraries. The Association organizes conferences, meetings, courses, and other events and publishes specialized materials. It is a national member of IFLA. The bodies of the Association are the General Assembly (convened every three years), the Committee and the Board, the Control Commission, the Secretariat, and sections on library services (committees for public libraries, children's and school libraries, research libraries, university libraries, historical collections), on bibliography, and on information. The Association publishes the Bulletin of the Association, library and information manuals, and proceedings of conferences and meetings.

HELENA KOLÁŘOVÁ

Jan Tachezy

*The catalogue room in the Prague University Library.*

ALA

*John Cotton Dana*

## Dana, John Cotton
(1856–1929)

John Cotton Dana, public librarian for four decades, notable for his innovations in offering and promoting library services and public education, was a leader of the library profession who served as President, and sometimes critic, of ALA and was an organizer and President of the Special Libraries Association.

Born on August 19, 1856, in Woodstock, Vermont, Dana spent his early life in Woodstock, where he was reared in a home in which education and reading were emphasized. He received an introduction to business there also, working in his father's general store "on the green," a store originally opened by his grandfather in 1802. He maintained strong ties with Woodstock throughout his life and spent many summer vacations there. In 1874 Dana entered Dartmouth College. There he made a good academic record and was elected to Phi Beta Kappa in 1878.

In June 1878 he returned home and began the study of law in the firm of French and Southgate in Woodstock. In addition to his study of law, he found time to read widely from the classics, biography, travel, and metaphysics. Less than two years later, threatened with tuberculosis, he sought a higher and drier climate. One of his college friends, Frank Wadleigh Gove, had gone to Colorado in 1879 and had become a deputy United States land and mineral surveyor in the mining section of the state. Dana joined him at Rico, Colorado, in 1880 and continued his study of law there. He was admitted to the Colorado bar later that year. Mostly, however, he worked with Gove as a surveyor until 1882.

Dana returned to Woodstock for a brief time before moving to New York City. There he lived with his brother Charles, a doctor, while he continued his study of law and also did some tutoring. Dana passed the New York State Bar examinations in May 1883. About the same time health problems surfaced again, and in March 1884 he went to Fergus Falls, Minnesota, where another college friend, William D. Parkinson, lived. From there he moved to Ashby, Minnesota, where he practiced law and in July 1884 became Editor, for a short time, of the local newspaper, the *Avalanche*. After a few months he returned to Colorado and again engaged in work as a surveyor and later as construction superintendent for the Colorado Midland Railroad, living in construction camp tents a good deal of the time. He also began to make public appearances as a lecturer on religious and social questions. For one month he occupied the pulpit in a Unitarian church, and there he met Adine Rowena Waggener, a native of Russellville, Kentucky, whom he married in November 1888.

For a while after marriage the couple lived on a Colorado ranch, where Dana began to write articles for publication on a variety of subjects including travel and educational and sociological matters. He also wrote letters to the editors of newspapers. An article entitled "The Public School," critical of the public school system in the United States, was published in the *Denver Arbitrator* for February 16, 1889, and attracted wide attention. To a degree it may well have been this very article that was responsible for Dana's eventual entrance into the library profession. Other influences, however, may have played a part also. Aaron Gove, Superintendent of the Denver Public School system, was Frank Wadleigh Gove's brother. For some time he and his Board had hoped to establish a library for the high school that could be open to the public and function as a public library too. The tax leveled for educational purposes in Colorado included a provision that made this plan legal. Dana's article in the *Denver Arbitrator* spurred Gove on to proceed toward accomplishment of that hope. Gove made the recommendation to his Board to vote for the establishment of the library to serve the school and the public and to appoint John Cotton Dana as the Librarian. It was so voted. Dana accepted, and in 1889 began his career in librarianship that lasted four decades.

**Denver.** Dana began at once to organize the Denver Public Library, gather a staff, acquire materials in books, magazines, newspapers, and pamphlets, supplementing the 2,000 books in the school library, which he inherited upon his appointment, and to initiate service. Most significant of all, he began to advertise it. His idea about libraries was to get them used. He sent notices about the new library to the editors of every newspaper published in Colorado and to national educational and religious journals, and he made personal visits to many of the editors. He sought their cooperation and help in making the services, planned for everyone, known and specifically indicated to them how he was sure the library could be of use to them too.

Advertising a library had not been the custom in the profession, and Dana's first moves in that direction were frowned upon by many in it. Other libraries were giving many of the services Dana inaugurated for Denver, but publicizing and advertising them was Dana's unique contribution. He also sought a sharing of experiences from fellow librarians.

He proceeded at once to issue a monthly library bulletin entitled *Books* (the first issue was dated October 1889); he invited educational and civic leaders to give lectures in the public library open to the public; he gave many talks himself before business, educational, and other professional groups, many of which have been published. He followed William Howard Brett's innovative policy of open access to shelves. In 1894 Dana opened the very first children's room in a public library—a room with suitable furniture, decoration, and a supply of children's literature for their enjoyment, information, and personal development.

His library flourished. Its resources and use, as determined by circulation figures, grew significantly. Visitors numbered 1,000 daily. He assembled a collection of business books and related materials and placed it in the Chamber of Commerce, thus becoming one of the entrepreneurs, among librarians, attempting to provide service for the business community. A special collection of medical books was developed in cooperation with the Colorado Medical Library Association that later formed the nucleus of the Denver Medical Library.

With all this he also started a library training class for his staff. As procedures and forms became established, he took great pains to put them in writing for frequent review. Some of these became part of a book, the *Public Library Handbook,* in 1893. He took an active part in professional associations as a member and also officer, being elected President of the Colorado Library Association in 1895 and Chairman of its Convention Committee for the forthcoming conference of the American Library Association to be held in Cleveland the next year.

Dana began to look elsewhere for an opportunity to pursue his vocation. A controversy had arisen concerning his policy of providing library materials on both sides of the free silver matter, a policy Dana defended earnestly; the School Board was criticized by Denver's Chamber of Commerce for using part of its tax appropriation to finance the business library there, even though the action was definitely within the law. Dana became the Librarian of the City Library of Springfield, Massachusetts, effective January 1, 1898.

**Springfield.** The City Library of Springfield, Massachusetts, was already established with a collection over four times larger than the one Dana left in Denver and a staff already organized and at work. Dana saw possibilities for making the library better known in the community and more usable and inviting physically. He put into effect policies found successful in Denver, such as providing easier access to the shelves and a special corner for children's books and removing all devices—bars, gates, or anything else—that deterred direct contact of the public with the library staff. Because the library building was on a hill, and access to the entrance necessitated climbing flights of stairs up that hill, he had an elevator installed. He also started library training classes to provide qualified assistants for the library. The interest shown in his classes prompted him to invite the librarians in that northwestern part of the state to a meeting to discuss mutual library problems. An outgrowth of these sessions was the organization of the Western Massachusetts Library Club.

Dana wrote a series of articles entitled "A Library Primer," which were published in the first six issues of *Public Libraries* in 1896. Later he revised, rewrote, and extended the original draft for publication in book form. He included additional material selected from many sources, written by other library pioneers, for *A Library Primer* (same title as his 1893 book), published in 1899.

Dana resigned his post in Springfield on December 18, 1901, to become Librarian of the Free Public Library of Newark, New Jersey, succeeding his friend and fellow Dartmouth graduate, Frank P. Hill.

**Newark.** Dana joined the Free Public Library of Newark, New Jersey, as Librarian, on January 15, 1902, and remained there the rest of his life. The new building had been completed the year before. The resources for reference and lending were comprehensive. The staff was capable, qualified, and interested. Beatrice Winser, who had been Assistant Librarian under Hill, and who was appointed Acting Librarian when Hill left, had administered the Library capably for seven months. Dana with Winser as Assistant Librarian formed a dynamic team. He did much writing, planned policies, edited Newark library publications, e.g., *The Newarker, The Library,* prepared broadsides, gave numerous talks to alert the public on the contribution the Library could and did make to the social structure of the community, and directed preparation of various book lists. He provided new activities for the Library, such as the hospital library service, a special collection of foreign language books for the immigrants coming to the city, and branch libraries. All of these developments provided news items for the newspapers, business, professional, and other journals, and gave Dana opportunities to keep the library in the public eye. He was spectacularly successful in doing so.

Always searching for new ways to make the Library more meaningful, he became deeply involved in museums. His philosophy, expressed in one of the Library's booklists, was, "Libraries and museums exist to furnish the knowledge that leads to understanding." Though there were no museums in Newark, he saw possibilities in creating some museum activities within the Library, e.g., preparing exhibits that could be displayed there, and proceeded to borrow materials from citizens of Newark, from department stores, and from other museums for that purpose. He organized exhibits on American art and on science.

On April 29, 1909, the Newark Museum Association was formed with Dana as its Secretary. Almost four years later he was appointed the Association's first Director, holding that position as well as his Library post until his death. In this capacity he began to see his dream of a museum building and museum service for Newark come true. And so it did, but not without controversy over location, disputes, and other delays.

Finally, on March 17, 1926, the Newark Museum of Art, Science, and Industry, near the Library, was opened.

Perhaps Dana's most famous contribution to the library profession was establishment of what became the Business Library of the Newark Public Library. He had been aware of the possibilities of library service to the business community in Denver and in Springfield and initiated services there, working with business groups such as Chambers of Commerce and with community business leaders. But the information needs of business were not very clearly defined at that time, and very little printed documentation of what was defined was available to libraries. In Newark he was fortunate in recognizing a member of his staff, Sarah B. Ball, who shared his enthusiasm for seeking ways to make the Library of genuine use to business. She was the Librarian of Branch No. 1, opened in October 1904 and located in Newark's business district. In reporting to him of the use being made of the branch by businessmen, she suggested a change of name to Business Men's Library and began collecting as much material as could be found on anything relating to business. No one could have been happier about this than Dana. The Business Men's Library flourished largely because of the tremendous dedication and enthusiasm of Ball, who had the wholehearted support of Dana and Richard C. Jenkinson, one of the Trustees, and also because the "flood" of business print had started from the presses.

At the Business Men's Library emphasis was put on providing exact information needed—specific facts and figures. Lists of book and periodical references for specific business subjects were issued frequently, and a regular bulletin entitled "Business Literature" had subscribers throughout the country. The Library became a model for other public libraries seeking to extend similar services for their communities.

Dana's work as Librarian of the Denver Public Library brought him to the attention of members of the American Library Association, some of whom stopped on the way to a San Francisco convention to meet Dana and see the Denver Public Library. The visit led to his first ALA Conference, and in 1895 he became its President-Elect.

His concern with some of the country's and world's great problems made a number of the ALA's topics for discussion seem puerile to him, and he was soon in controversy with some of its members and officers. Dana, however, was willing and anxious to identify with library and education associations as a member even when he differed with them or was actively opposed to some of their activities. He was elected or appointed to many committees of national, state, and local organizations: President of the American Library Association, 1895–96; member of its Council, 1896–1902; President of the New Jersey Library Association, 1904–05 and 1910–11. He also became President of the Special Libraries Association, which he helped organize, 1909–10.

The group whose efforts finally resulted in the formation of the Special Libraries Association had started really with Sarah B. Ball and Anna Sears, Librarian of the Merchants' Association of New York. They had invited librarians doing special library research work outside public libraries, as well as those specializing in business information and other specialties within public libraries, to meet together informally while they were in attendance at ALA meetings. When this was brought to Dana's attention, he started the action that brought together about 56 librarians working in fields of law, insurance, chambers of commerce, engineering, public utilities, museums, municipal research, and others.

Largely through Dana's help this group organized themselves into the Special Libraries Association, a name suggested by Dana.

Dana hoped to get the new Association under the umbrella of the ALA, and his failure to accomplish this because of reluctance, or misunderstanding on both sides, increased his dissatisfaction with the ALA. He remained an active member of the Association, however, and continued vocal in his criticism when he disagreed in its decisions.

Shortly before his death on July 21, 1929, he wrote to Matthew S. Dudgeon of the Milwaukee Public Library:

> I have been for years, now and then, the down-right critic of the A.L.A. During these same years I hope I have been of assistance to A.L.A. in all its good work. My criticism is what I'm remembered for, I assume, and I cannot help feeling that I have been, not infrequently, unfairly judged concerning it (Chalmers Hadley, *John Cotton Dana—A Sketch,* ALA, 1943).

Dana had many interests in his life—politics, education, business, art, music, printing; in fact, anything that affected mankind concerned him.

**Publications.** Dana was a prolific writer and speaker. Many of his talks and addresses were printed in library, business, and other professional journals, often in more than one. A comprehensive list, chronologically arranged, compiled by Hazel Johnson and Beatrice Winser, was published with Hazel Johnson's article on Dana in *The Library Quarterly* (1937). *Literature of Libraries in the Seventeenth and Eighteenth Centuries* (1906–07), edited by J. C. Dana and Henry W. Kent, was reprinted in 1967 by the Scarecrow Reprint Corporation, Metuchen, New Jersey.

His family's Elm Tree Press in his home in Woodstock, Vermont, operated mainly by two of his brothers, was used frequently to print works written or edited by him or in collaboration with others. Edmund Lester Pearson's *The Old Librarian's Almanack* (1909) was printed there for many years, as were Dana's translations of 17th- and 18th-century classics on librarianship.

Newark recognized him as "the First Citizen of Newark" and celebrated the 100th anniversary of his birth with a Centennial Convocation of October 17, 1956.

Dana's philosophical approach to librarianship is best revealed in his book *Suggestions,* published by F. W. Faxon in 1921. It consists of extracts from his papers and essays. They were selected by him to help the beginner in library work look at the profession with fresh interest and make it seem deserving of careful thought. They contain those nuggets of thought that, through the years, have been quoted over and over again on such subjects as reading, books, and business.

ROSE L. VORMELKER

## Denmark

Denmark, a constitutional monarchy, lies between two bodies of water—the North and Baltic seas—in north central Europe. Denmark includes the greater part of the Jutland Peninsula and approximately 100 offshore islands in the Kattegat and Skagerrak straits. Pop. (1978 est.) 5,099,000; area 43,075 sq.km. The official language is Danish.

**National Library.** The National Library of Denmark, in the capital city of Copenhagen, is the Royal Library and can be traced back to the 16th century, when the King founded his private library in the Castle of Copenhagen. From the early days the Royal Library has felt the duty to serve as the Danish national library, including the obligation to establish and maintain a national bibliography. Danish publications have been provided through legal deposit from 1697, and the modern legal deposit act was passed in 1927. In addition to these functions the Royal Library has subject responsibility within the national research library network in the fields of humanities, theology, and social sciences and acts as the main library of the University of Copenhagen in these disciplines.

Among the Library's principal departments is the Danish Department, which holds the most complete collection of Danish imprints in existence as well as all material printed outside Denmark that deals with Denmark and translations of Danish works into foreign languages. The Manuscript Collection, the Department of Maps and Prints, the Department of Oriental Manuscripts, the Collection of Judaica, the Rare Book Department, and the Foreign Department all possess rich collections. The Royal Library's collection totaled 1,800,000 volumes in 1975 and 2,100,000 in 1977; to these holdings can be added manuscripts, recordings, musical scores, maps, prints, and other materials.

**Academic and Research Libraries.** The principal academic libraries in Denmark include the University Library in Copenhagen; founded in 1482, it is divided into two sections, one for the humanities and one for science and medicine. Another important library is the State and University Library of Aarhus, which has the function of a library serving the University of Aarhus and other educational institutions in the Aarhus region and is a focal point in the national interlibrary lending system, providing specialized literature to public libraries. This general library was established in 1902; its general collection numbered 1,400,000 volumes in 1977.

The present network of research libraries is to a great extent based on a library reform of 1926, which introduced a scheme of subject specialization among libraries. The National Technological Library of Denmark and the Danish Veterinary and Agricultural Library are examples of major research libraries with nationwide subject responsibilities. The research library network also includes the university libraries in Odense, Roskilde, and Aalborg founded in the 1960's and 1970's. Its central bodies are the Office of the National Librarian, set up in 1943 to promote cooperation between the various units of the research library system, and the National Advisory Council of Danish Research Libraries, created in 1970 to deal with a variety of issues relating to the structure, policy, planning, and technology in the research library field.

**Public Libraries.** The Public Libraries Act of 1964, slightly amended in 1975, constitutes the basis of the public library system in Denmark. According to this Act each municipality, either alone or in association with other municipalities, is required to maintain a public library including a department for children. The underlying basic principle is that all citizens should be given equal access to libraries. In January 1975 there were 251 autonomous public library units in 275 municipalities. State grants to public libraries amount to 20 percent of the operating expenses of individual public library systems. In addition, 3.25 percent of the total grant monies is retained as a sum set aside for undertakings for the benefit of all the nation's libraries. A revision of the Library Act based on the work of a Library Commission appointed in 1976 was scheduled for the parliamentary session 1979–80.

**School Libraries.** In Denmark the term *school libraries* generally refers to those in primary schools. Primary school libraries are required by the Public Libraries Act and subsidized by state grants up to 15 percent of the school library's running expenses. Libraries in secondary schools are an emerging type of library that expanded gradually during the mid-1970's, but they lack the legislative basis of primary school libraries. School libraries are developing into media centers offering a wide range of learning resources and audiovisual aids. As a result of this growth a new bill on school libraries was envisaged by 1978.

**Special Libraries.** Special libraries in Denmark form a heterogeneous group ranging from libraries in museums, independent research institutions, university institutes, technical schools, and teacher training colleges to commercial firms. Many libraries in this category are small and often staffed by nonprofessionals.

**Table 1. Archives in Denmark (1976)**

| | | |
|---|---|---|
| Number | Principal archives: 1 | Provincial archives: 4 |
| Holdings | 150,000 shelf meters | |
| Annual expenditures | D.kr. 17,600,000 | |
| Professional staff | 50 | |
| All staff (total) | 200 | |

Source: Rigsarkivet (The National Archive).

**Table 2. Libraries in Denmark (1976)**

| Type | Number | Volumes in collections | Annual expenditures (krone) | Population served | Professional staff | All staff (total) |
|---|---|---|---|---|---|---|
| National | 1 | 2,100,000 | D.kr. 42,612,034 | N.A. | 117 | 338 |
| Academic | 29[a] | 6,054,631 | D.kr. 118,189,222 | N.A. | 372 | 553 |
| Public | 251 | 22,941,074[b] | D.kr. 654,900,000 | 5,065,197 | 1,565 | 4,305[c] |
| School | 1,835[d] | 12,275,409 | D.kr. 163,700,000 | 745,665 | 2,825 | N.A. |
| Special | N.A. | N.A. | N.A. | N.A. | N.A. | N.A. |

[a]Also included are some major special libraries that act as research libraries.
[b]AV-materials: gramophone records: 801,207
cassettes: 94,978
[c]Part-time served libraries not included.
[d]Refers only to primary school libraries.

Sources: Biblioteksårbog 1975–76; Skolebiblioteksårbog 1976–77; Bibliotekstilsynet, Årsberetning 1975–76 and 1976–77.

**Associations.** The following are the major library associations in Denmark: the Library Bureau (assists Danish libraries in carrying out work in bibliography and library service), the Danish Library Association, the Danish Research Library Association, the Librarians' Union (the trade union for public librarians and librarians employed at research and academic libraries).

**REFERENCES**

Palle Birkelund, "Some Remarks on Danish University Libraries," *LIBER Bulletin* (1973).

*Scandinavian Public Library Quarterly* (1974). Special issue including articles on Danish public libraries.

Arne Holst, Keld Irgens, and Jørgen Tølløse, editors, *School Libraries in Denmark* (1974).

Leif Thorsen, *Public Libraries in Denmark* (Copenhagen, 1972).

PREBEN KIRKEGAARD

Royal Library of Denmark

*The Royal Library serves as Denmark's national library and traces its beginnings to the 16th century. It also serves as the main library of the University of Copenhagen for the humanities, theology, and social sciences.*

*Melvil Dewey*

ALA

# Dewey, Melvil

(1851–1931)

At an early age Melvil Dewey concluded that knowledge was better than ignorance, that education was the surest means to knowledge, and that beyond schooling reading was the surest means to an education—to reach understanding one needed only diligence and a book. He also concluded that he would have to see to it that the best means to bring person and book together be found and employed. Librarianship did not exist when Dewey set out on his self-assigned task. To be sure, there were libraries and people worked in them, but no unified body of purpose and practice (which we call librarianship) existed to guide them.

From 1873 to 1906 he was to devise and construct almost singlehandedly the forms and substance of librarianship (Charles Ammi Cutter providing the other hand on occasion). To achieve what he did Dewey had to play many roles:

*organizer:* of the ALA and other professional associations; of a classification scheme (the Dewey Decimal Classification); and of a library school.

*advocate:* for professionalism in librarianship; for the education of its members; for an equal role for women.

*standardizer:* of supplies, equipment, tools, methods, education.

*librarian:* of one of the first modern university libraries (Columbia); of the foremost state library of its day (New York).

*teacher:* through editing and writing for *Library Journal* and *Library Notes;* through the establishment of apprentice programs and a library school; through promoting the role of the college library in academic pursuits; through pursuing always the role of the library as the "People's University"; and through inspiration and example.

Melville Louis Kossuth Dewey was born on December 10, 1851, in Adams Center, New York, to Joel and Eliza Dewey. He gathered his early education in bits and pieces, entering Amherst College in 1870. While there he launched his career in librarianship, the first step being to examine exemplary libraries of the Northeast in order to determine the methods libraries should use in carrying out their roles. This quest led him to his most lasting achievement in librarianship.

Libraries normally arranged their collections by the fixed location method—a book's physical location was fixed on a specific shelf in a specific range. Dewey pondered the inevitable costs of such a system: works on the same subject did not shelve near each other, and when a library grew beyond its four walls, its collection had to be renumbered on book and in catalogue—an expensive business. (Two cornerstones of Dewey's lifelong activities were his concerns for time and cost.) To prevent the unwanted effects of fixed location Dewey conceived relative location, using decimal fractions to number the contents of books rather than the physical book. That stroke of genius led to the Dewey Decimal Classification, published in 1876, in its 19th edition at the end of the 1970's and the most widely used library classification in the world. From it was to stem the Universal Decimal Classification, also widely used, and itself one of the bases of information science through S. C. Bradford's *Documentation* (1948).

The year 1876 saw Dewey lay other foundations for the profession. (1) He was the motive force in bringing together the Conference of Librarians in Philadelphia at which the American Library Association was born (and dominated by him for 30 years). (2) By approaching Frederick Leypoldt and Richard R. Bowker on the need for a journal in librarianship, Dewey assured the future publication of the *Library Journal* and subsequently helped direct it for its first five years (1876–81). (3) He established the Library Burea, a firm that took major steps toward standardization in supplies, equipment, and library methods.

Dewey moved to Boston in 1876 and for six years cultivated his slowly growing garden. During this time the DDC was being developed toward the epochal second edition; the Library Bureau was founded; he contributed greatly to the modernization of the profession through the *Library Journal*. He also suggested, and with Cutter and Justin Winsor guided, the abortive but brilliant idea of cataloguing data accompanying a book—title-slip registry. We have the idea in practice today—the justly appreciated Cataloging-in-Publication. Dewey had taken that idea originally from one suggested by Natale Battezzati in 1871—colored catalogue cards would accompany a book to booksellers so that they could compile various catalogues of their inventory and better serve their patrons. Dewey's borrowing here is a good example of his capacity to recognize a useful idea when he saw one and to meld it with other ideas to produce a method or tool that, though not original in its parts, was new in its totality. Predictably, some resented this capability as much as Dewey's originality.

On October 26, 1878, Dewey married Annie Godfrey, his companion and adviser for the next half century and mother to his only child, Godfrey Dewey (1887–1977), himself important in librarianship (primarily in his association with the DDC). He also contributed to the success of the 1932 Winter Olympics in Lake Placid, New York.

In 1883 Columbia College offered Dewey the opportunity to develop its library. In doing so he epitomized the schism between scholar and librarian that lasts to this day in strongly centralized academic libraries. Dewey believed—and convinced Columbia's administration—that the library is the heart of the college. His belief led to the growth of the central library that gathers as many books (and therefore as much power) to itself as it can. Many scholars believe, on the other hand, that books in their specialty (preferably just down the hall) promote the scholarship of a faculty that in turn is the heart of a college. The Columbia faculty waited as Dewey combined the diverse subject collections and integrated them through the DDC, created a classed catalogue, extended library service to other users, initiated instruction of users through the reference department, and formulated strict and often restrictive rules for the use of the library. When, in the establishment of a library school at Columbia, 17 of the 20 students to matriculate in the first class in 1887 were women, Dewey's critics saw the chance to rid themselves of the pest in the library. Late in 1888 the trustees voted to suspend him from his duties in the Library but not in the School.

His work done at Columbia, Dewey moved to the next opportunity awaiting him. After being impressed by Dewey's views on the educational role of the library delivered in a speech before them, and being in need of a state librarian, the Regents of the University of the State of New York offered him the post. They were so impressed by his vigor and accomplishments that they also offered him the responsibilities of another vacant post—thus he became both Secretary and Treasurer of the Board, as well as Director of the State Library.

If there was one aspect of life that Dewey loved more than work, it was power. His new positions gave him power and the means to gain more. He used power not primarily for personal gain (except to the extent that he equated himself with his projects) but to further the role of the library as the "People's University." Every action Dewey took furthered the library's role in the schools, colleges, cities, states, and national library (the Library of Congress) of the United States.

One of Dewey's first acts at Albany was to obtain permission for the transfer of his library school from Columbia to the State Library. There instruction and supervision could be given the students for the work they did in the Library, thus maintaining the means to develop a unified profession through standard methods and a cadre of people to convey them, as well as facilitating the development of the collection and services of the State Library.

While at Albany, Dewey continued to develop the purposes and methods of the profession. (1) Just as he had founded the New York Library Club in 1885, he now was the prime mover in establishing the New York Library Association in 1890, the first of the state associations and the model for those to come. (2) The State Library became a reference center and "collection of last resort." (3) He instituted special collections and services for medicine, the blind, women, children, individuals with an interest in social matters and concerns, and even traveling libraries to provide support to libraries about the state and to carry libraries to people otherwise without access to books. He also proposed bookmobiles ("book-wagons") for the isolated, especially farmers. (4) He extended acquisitions to materials other than books; pictures, slides, and other media began to flow into the Library. (5) He advocated depository libraries for seldom used books, centralized cataloguing by the Library of Congress, national library status for the Library of Congress to which the nation's libraries could turn for guidance. (6) He pioneered and advocated the use in libraries of such new equipment as the typewriter and the telephone. (7) He served in many professional offices, among them as President of the Association of State Librarians from 1889 to 1892 and as President of ALA in 1890 and 1892–93. For ALA he was instrumental in the success of an excellent library exhibit at the World's Columbian Exposition of 1893. (8) And with his able lieutenants—Walter Stanley Biscoe, Evelyn May Seymour, and Dorcas Fellows—he developed the DDC through its sixth edition. With them he was instrumental in producing the *A.L.A. Catalog: 8,000 Volumes for a Popular Library, with Notes* (1904), yet another standardized and standardizing tool for the profession.

Many of his dreams achieved and many dawning, the profession now well on its way to success in bringing education to the people who cherished and sought it, Dewey was forced to resign his positions as Director of the State Library, the Home Education Department, and the Library School. He had lost a power struggle with Andrew S. Draper, a man who admired neither Dewey nor his views and who had become his superior in 1904. The ostensible cause for his resignation on January 1, 1906, was the flap over the anti-Semitism of the Lake Placid Club, an organization that Dewey had been instrumental in founding and guiding. The actual cause, however, was that Draper sought to strengthen the position of schools at the expense of libraries regardless of the role Dewey wanted them to fulfill. Dewey had to leave or be discredited. Though he did not bring on the adverse criticism himself, Draper did let the criticism take its course, and Dewey was forced to leave.

Dewey was a visionary. Capable of perseverance and extreme dedication, he cared more for results than the particular means and not only was willing to adopt readily new materials and methods but also expected such things to change continually. (Note his attitude toward books and other media for communicating ideas to people and his adoption of the typewriter, the telephone, and other mechanical improvements. He would have equally easily adopted the computer if he were working now. It is important to note that he would have used mechanical means for his ends—he did not adapt his ends to suit the exigencies of the means, a response seen too often in today's library world.) In his writings and speeches he advocated virtually every process that librarianship has come to or is coming to: standardization and cooperation in cataloguing (he envisioned networking); standardization of cataloguing rules (the rules not to be changed unless overwhelming improvement results); the Library of Congress to be the national library; centralized storage; and "fee for service" activities.

Dewey stood for the needs of the user above all; these included the need for information, education, and recreation. Libraries, though they change in nature, should tell the news, answer what and how and why, tell a story, and sing a song.

Scholars of library history have not truly grasped the nature of Melvil Dewey. They refer to him as being complex, charismatic, and any of a host of other terms that tell us little about anyone. The matter is not so complex: Dewey was simply a genius confident in his capacity, a demon for work, and one who took pleasure in acquiring and using power. Those who would be leaders resented or hated him; those who would follow admired or adored him. He was a master politician despite his abrasive nature; rarely did he not bring people to do what he wanted them to do—the battles he lost (Columbia, Albany) were to overwhelming odds. Nor did he accept defeat or frustration ungraciously. He did not like to lose, but he was too smart to let it show; there would always be another day. But after January 1, 1906, there was not another day.

Though Dewey never fully left his work in librarianship, his semiretirement to the Lake Placid Club removed from librarianship its strongest advocate, its most original designer, and its most effective organizer. Perhaps his leaving was not so great a loss as it was a shame; his work may have been done. One may believe, however, that had he continued, libraries would have become more central to education than they were to come to be. Dewey knew that knowing was better than not knowing, that any means to knowledge were good means if they produced enlightened leaders and citizens, and that the profession had to work hard and together to bring knowledge through books or other media. Where we work hard and together, Dewey lives.

**REFERENCE**

The only biography of Dewey worth consulting is Sarah K. Vann's in *Melvil Dewey, His Enduring Presence in Librarianship* (1978), from which for this article most of the facts of Dewey's life have been drawn. The book presenting the full impact of Dewey upon librarianship and other undertakings has not been written.

JOHN P. COMAROMI

# Dix, William Shepherd

(1910–1978)

William S. Dix, Librarian of Princeton University from 1953 until 1975, did not have a library science degree, but he *became* a librarian by *being* one. His character and scholarship fitted him peculiarly to bridge the gap between the user and the library. With a lineage traced back to William the Conqueror, he matched the tradition of gentleman with a strong sensitiveness to each individual's needs. He was honored widely for contributions to library and academic communities. Born on November 19, 1910, in Winchester, Virginia, Dix grew up in Berryville, Virginia, and Hagerstown, Maryland. In 1931 he graduated with honors from the University of Virginia and took his M.A. in English there the following year.

He began his career in the Darlington School for Boys in Rome, Georgia, as a teacher of English from 1932 to 1939 and went on to teach at Western Reserve University and Williams College before going to Harvard in 1944 on the staff of the wartime Radio Research Laboratory. When the Laboratory was disbanded in 1946, he taught for one year at Harvard and completed his Ph.D. in American Literature at the University of Chicago.

In 1947 Dix became an English instructor at Rice Institute (now Rice University) in Houston and the next year accepted the additional assignment of directing the school's library. He was an Associate Professor of English and Librarian when he left Rice in 1953 to head the Princeton University Library. He was Princeton's 22nd Librarian and had served 22 years when he retired in 1975.

The considerable Dix activities outside his daily obligations were apparent early. During his two years at Western Reserve he became Director of the Committee on Private Research. His book, *The Amateur Spirit in Scholarship* (Western Reserve University Press, 1942), describes the work of that body, whose purpose was to promote amateur activities in scholarly and creative research.

During the Princeton years, he served the campus, the Association of Research Libraries, the American Library Association, the New Jersey Library Association, library causes in Washington and in other countries, and other libraries in advisory capacities. In 1970 he was called on to preside over disciplinary hearings growing out of Princeton University campus disruptions in protest of U.S. involvement in the Vietnam War. He kept the hearings on course through angry turmoil with a clear sense of the fundamental purposes of a university.

He served the Association of Research Libraries in a variety of capacities, including a part-time appointment from 1957 to 1959 as its first Executive Secretary when it was moving toward permanent headquarters and a full-time Executive Director. In the 1960's, in a service of lasting importance to library users, he chaired the ARL Committee on Shared Cataloging, which influenced Congress to include Title II-C in the Higher Education Act of 1965. This provision enables the Library of Congress under the National Program for Acquisitions and Cataloging to assist libraries by acquiring and cataloguing promptly the world's scholarly publications. His skill in appearing as a witness before Congressional committees was useful on other occasions in fostering legislation of value to library service.

Dix carried out a wide range of assignments in ALA and its units. As Chair of the ALA Intellectual Freedom Committee during the divisive and fearful McCarthy period, he was the principal drafter of the Association's declaration on "The Freedom to Read," a statement adopted jointly by the American Book Publishers Council (now the Association of American Publishers) and subsequently endorsed by 21 other organizations. The importance he attached to a free society is stated there:

> Freedom has given the United States the elasticity to endure strain. Freedom keeps open the path of novel and creative solutions, and enables change to come by choice. Every silencing of a heresy, every enforcement of an orthodoxy, diminishes the toughness and resilience of our society and leaves it the less able to deal with stress.

His chairing of the ALA International Relations Board was the beginning of a number of international assignments: U.S. Delegate to the Conference of Asian National Commissions for Unesco, Manila, 1961; Consultant to the Ford Foundation, Baghdad, 1958; member of the U.S. Delegation to the Unesco General Conference, Paris, 1958 and 1960, serving as Vice-Chairman of the Delegation, 1960; Asian-American Assembly, Kuala Lumpur, 1963; and U.S. Department of State Government Advisory Committee on International Book and Library Programs, 1967–69.

Dix's long-time involvement in library matters reached a climax with his service as the ALA President, 1969–70, a crucial year. It was a time of national conflict between the complacency of the old ways and the new demands for meeting social obligations. To the task of preserving the Association while providing for change, he

Princeton University Library

*William Shepherd Dix*

brought his propensity to see each side of a controversy, his firmly based belief in tolerance for differing viewpoints, his concern for the individual, and his evenhanded leadership. The *Wilson Library Bulletin* summed up his contribution to the 1970 ALA Annual Conference.

> Time and again, Dr. Dix, who is said to play an outstanding leadership role at his own institution, was applauded and thanked for his patience, wit, judgment, knowledge, and almost superhuman endurance at the podium of Council, membership meetings, banquets, and in his seat at the Executive Board and on committees. Second to none of the older members in traditional library wisdom, he was also, as president, second to none of the younger dissidents in his commitment to library and association reform. Popular among all groups throughout the year, he presided over ALA in perhaps its most critical year since 1876, preaching understanding above all else.

He was a member of the American Council of Learned Societies committee to propose programs to meet the needs of American research libraries and of the Boards of Directors of the H. W. Wilson Company and of the Franklin Book Programs. He served on advisory bodies for the New Jersey State Library, Rutgers University Graduate School of Library and Information Studies, the libraries of Duke and Harvard Universities, and the Association of American University Presses. At the time of his death, he was a member of the Board of Directors of the Council on Library Resources and of the National Commission on New Technological Uses of Copyrighted Works, the latter body working for agreement among divergent interests relating to copyright.

Dix's deportment and his public addresses probably influenced his colleagues as much as his many published articles, convincing others through the force of his well-reasoned positions. Although ill with terminal cancer during the last ten months of his life (he died on February 22, 1978), he worked diligently on his retirement project of writing the history of the Princeton University Library—work that he had often put aside to meet his commitment to public groups. He was able to complete "The Princeton University Library in the Eighteenth Century," which was published as volume 40, number 1 (Autumn 1978) of *The Princeton University Library Chronicle*, and as a separate monograph by the Library. It is a worthy legacy, embodying his scholarship and his felicitous way with words.

Many honors came to him: honorary doctorates from the University of Florida and Washington College; the New Jersey Library Association's Distinguished Service Award; ALA's Melvil Dewey and Lippincott Awards and its highest honor, an Honorary Membership.

HELEN WELCH TUTTLE

# Djibouti

The Republic of Djibouti, formerly French Somaliland and subsequently the French Territory of the Afars and the Issas, became independent on June 27, 1977. It lies south of a narrow strait linking the Gulf of Aden to the Red Sea and is bordered on the southeast by Somalia and on the south, west, and northwest by Ethiopia. Pop. (1978 est.) 250,000; area 23,000 sq.km. The official language is Arabic, and French is widely spoken.

The only significant library open to the public is in the French Cultural Center, which opened in the capital of Djibouti in June 1978 with a collection of 8,000 books; in 1979 it served 2,750 readers with 15,000 books. In addition to a lending library, there is a Documentation Center with a collection of materials relating to Djibouti. Consisting primarily of periodical articles, the collection numbered over 360 items in 1979. There are small working library collections in some government ministries.

STAFF

# Dominican Republic

The Dominican Republic occupies the eastern section of Hispaniola, a Caribbean island, separated from Haiti (western section) by mountains. Pop. (1978 est.) 5,657,000; area 48,442 sq.km. The official language is Spanish.

**National Library.** In 1969 construction was authorized for a national library. The Library opened in 1971, the year in which a law required that copies of printed works and phonograph records be filed with the National Library. The Library publishes a national bibliography and provides services to the public. In 1978 it contained 311,600 volumes and 3,500 periodical titles.

**Academic Libraries.** Of the country's five university libraries, the largest and oldest is at the Universidad Autónoma de Santo Domingo, established in 1927. In 1978 it contained 160,000 volumes and 9,000 periodical titles. Its present building with space for 500 readers, opened in 1948. That year there were 1,648 students; there were 40,000 in 1978. It served as national library from 1948 to 1971 and received deposit copies of works published in the country. Under the direction of Luis Flóren Lozano, it issued a large number of bibliographies under such titles as *Dominican Bibliography, Bibliography of Dominican History,* and *Bibliography of University Professors.* There are four faculty libraries: for Economics, Agriculture and Veterinary Medicine, Engineering and Architecture, and the Humanities.

Other university libraries are at the Pedro Henríquez Ureña National University (UNPHU), containing 28,000 volumes and 1,350 periodical titles in 1978; the Technological Institute (INTEC), with 6,000 volumes and 231 periodicals; the Central University of the East (UCE), with 15,000 volumes and 100 periodicals; and the Catholic University, Mother and Teacher (UCMM), with 18,000 books in 1968 and 65,000 in 1978.

**Public Libraries.** Cultural societies founded the first public libraries in the country. The first was organized in 1860 and in 1876 came under the direction of the Amigos del País (Friends of the Nation) until 1904. Others are found at the Atheneum Amantes de la Luz (Lovers of Light) and at the Alianza Cibaeña established in Santiago in 1888. In Moca the Gabriel A. Morillo Library was founded in 1904 and another at Baní was founed in 1920; a Municipal Library at Santo Domingo was founded in 1922; and there is one at the Sociedad Renovación of Puerto Plata (1928). There is a distinction between libraries sponsored by cultural societies and public institutions in municipalities.

By 1956 there were 110 public libraries, with a total of 426,000 readers and 487,900 books loaned. By 1959, 136 libraries had served 469,900 readers, and 454,900 works had been consulted. After 1960 there was a gradual decrease that may be attributed to events such as the death of President Trujillo in 1961 and the civil war of 1965. By 1966 the number was reduced to 96 libraries with 334,000 readers and 361,150 loans.

In the 1960's and 1970's the government showed little interest in libraries. The few that were created were in private clubs; in general they have small collections of donated works, with a few subscriptions to newspapers, managed by a secretary. The largest is at the Educational Center of Bonao, financed by Falconbridge, with 10,000 volumes in 1978.

**School Libraries.** There were 27 school libraries in 1968. Foremost among them are the La Salle School

(1940) in Santo Domingo with 6,300 volumes and the Abigail Mejía School (1940) with 6,000. The library of the Loyola Polytechnic (1964) has 5,000, and the Sacred Heart School in Santiago (1960) 3,000. The majority are in private schools; in public schools, libraries are practically nonexistent.

**Special Libraries.** The majority of government offices have small libraries; two in particular may be distinguished: INDOTEC and CEDOPEX. INDOTEC (Instituto Dominicano de Tecnología Industrial), founded in 1975, specializes in industrial technology. Its information center includes a library with 2,850 volumes and 350 periodical titles (1978); an Information Unit with 4,500 documents; and a Data Bank. CEDOPEX (Centro Dominicano de Promoción de Exportaciones), specializing in commerce and exports, contains 4,800 volumes and 286 periodical titles.

In the private sector the Compañía Financiera Dominicana (Dominican Finance Company), specializing in finance, had 8,000 volumes and 186 periodical titles in 1978. One international organization has a library of note, the library of the Organización Panamericana de la Salud (OPS), specializing in public health and medicine. It held 2,000 volumes in 1978 and published the *Bibliographic Bulletin* from 1977.

**Associations.** The Dominican Association of Librarians (ASODOBI), established in 1974, extends the services of the libraries throughout the country. In 1978 it had 32 members. Its official organ is the quarterly *El Papiro* ("The Papyrus"), published since 1976. It is headquartered in the National Library.

The Association of University Libraries was established by resolution of the National Council of Institutions of Higher Learning (CONIES) in 1978. Its objectives are the creation of a system coordinating the development of the collections of the university libraries, the creation of channels of communication, and avoidance of duplication of efforts and resources.

**REFERENCES**


CEPAL, *Directorio de unidades de información para el desarollo: República Dominicana* (1978), list of libraries and information centers in areas of economic development; incomplete, but information is useful and accurate.

George Lockward, *Las bibliotecas en la República Dominicana* (1968), includes valuable statistical data.


MARISOL FLORÉN

Foto Estudio Collado

*The modern library building of the Universidad Católica Madre y Maestra in the Dominican Republic.*

## Downs, Robert Bingham

(1903– )



Robert Bingham Downs combined the careers of library administrator and library educator with outstanding leadership in professional library organizations and a remarkable publication record of books and articles. Downs was born May 25, 1903, on a farm near Lenoir, North Carolina, where he attended a one-room country school for seven years. In 1917 his family moved to Asheville, North Carolina, where he discovered the Asheville public library and started a lifelong addiction to reading. But a career in librarianship had no place in his plans then, and formal education was abandoned after one year of high school. After a variety of jobs—including construction worker, fire ranger, telephone repairman, and ranch hand in Wyoming—he returned to graduate from Trinity High School in Durham. He entered the University of North Carolina at Chapel Hill in 1923. As a student assistant in the University Library, he came under the influence of Louis Round Wilson. Receiving his A.B. in 1926, Downs enrolled in the School of Library Service at Columbia, where he received his B.S. in L.S. degree in 1927 and the M.S. in 1929. From 1927 to 1929 he was a reference assistant in the New York Public Library.

In 1929 he became Librarian of Colby College and two years later returned to the University of North Carolina to become Assistant Librarian under Louis Round Wilson. When Wilson became Dean of the Graduate Library School at the University of Chicago in 1932, Downs was made Acting Librarian and the following year was appointed University Librarian and Professor of Library Science. During the next five years he developed strong library collections, instituted a program of duplicate exchanges, and taught bibliography, history of

**Libraries in the Dominican Republic (1978)**

| Type | Number | Volumes in collections[a] | Annual expenditures (peso) | Population served[b] | Professional staff | All staff (total) |
|---|---|---|---|---|---|---|
| National | 1 | 235,000 | 189,625 | 68,469 | 4 | 77 |
| Academic[c] | 5 | 274,000 | 284,979 | 66,713 | 16 | 100 |
| Public | N.A. | N.A. | N.A. | N.A. | N.A. | N.A. |
| School | N.A. | N.A. | N.A. | N.A. | N.A. | N.A. |
| Special[c,d] | 5 | 37,150 | 255,171 | 1,188 | 6 | 22 |

[a]Books only.
[b]Readers 1977–78.
[c]Includes only those that have professional staff, an assigned budget, and a technical organization.
[d]Includes INDOTEC, CEDOPEX, Dominican Finance Company, OPS, and the Central Bank.

ALA

*Robert Bingham Downs*



books, and reference in the library school. He also began his studies in the cooperative development of library resources and, with Harvie Branscomb of Duke University, developed a plan for sharing responsibility for collecting research materials between the neighboring university libraries. His first major book, *The Resources of Southern Libraries,* was published in 1938.

The same year he was appointed Director of Libraries of New York University with the task of coordinating seven quasi-independent libraries of the University. There he centralized the technical services departments, developed a union catalogue, and reorganized the staff and services of the Washington Square Library. During this period were published his *Resources of New York City Libraries* (1942), a series of three annual surveys of "Notable Materials Added to American Libraries" in *Library Quarterly* (1940–42), and *Union Catalogs in the United States* (1942).

In 1943 he was appointed Director of Libraries and of the Library School at the University of Illinois, a dual appointment he held until his retirement 27 years later. He was designated Dean of Library Administration in 1958. At Illinois he reorganized the library staff and secured faculty rank and status for librarians, a task that earlier directors had attempted unsuccessfully. The book collection, already a notable one in many fields, grew to more than 4,000,000 volumes under his direction. Under his direction, the Library School introduced a doctoral program, a series of Windsor Lectures (honoring Director-Emeritus P. L. Windsor) to bring outstanding bookmen to the campus, the annual Allerton Park Institutes, and two serial publications, *Library Trends* (1952– ) and *Occasional Papers* (1949– ).

Downs served the University in many extralibrary activities: Chairman of the Land Grant Centennial Committee, Vice-Chairman of the University Centennial Committee, Chairman of the Senate Committee on Honorary Degrees, Chairman of the University Concert and Entertainment Board, and President of the University Chapters of Phi Beta Kappa and Phi Kappa Phi.

Downs's continuing interest in the definition and description of library resources led to the publication of his *American Library Resources: A Bibliographical Guide* in 1951, with supplementary volumes in 1962 and 1970. *Resources of Canadian Academic and Research Libraries* appeared in 1967, and after his retirement a Guggenheim Fellowship enabled him to spend a year in England to gather information for his *British Library Resources* (1973). A similar survey of Australian and New Zealand library resources was published in 1979.

Downs conducted more than 30 surveys of libraries and groups of libraries, beginning with the survey of Cornell University Libraries (with Louis R. Wilson and Maurice F. Tauber) in 1948. He was responsible for surveys of the libraries of the University of Utah (1965), the University of Georgia (1966), Purdue University (1967), and Brigham Young University (1969). He conducted state library surveys for North Carolina, Missouri, Arkansas, and Illinois and shorter reports on libraries ranging from the Library Company of Philadelphia (1940) to the libraries of the Kansas City Regional Council for Education (1964).

At the end of World War II Downs served as a consultant to libraries and library schools overseas. In 1948 he went to Japan as adviser to the U.S. Military Government on the establishment of the National Diet Library and two years later returned to help establish a library school at Keio University. In Mexico he was consultant to the National Library and the University of Mexico in 1952. He served in a similar capacity in Turkey in 1955, 1968, and 1971; in 1963 he was consultant for a new library at Kabul University, Afghanistan. He lectured at Brazilian libraries and library schools at São Paolo, Rio de Janeiro, and Belo Horizonte in 1962 and was adviser to the Interamerican Library School at Medellín, Colombia, in 1964. In 1964–65 he was consultant to the Library of the University of Puerto Rico for the establishment of its library school; in 1973 he was consultant for the University of Tunis.

Active in professional organizations throughout his career, Downs served in 1940–41 as President of the Association of College and Research Libraries and in 1952–53 as President of the American Library Association. In 1955–56 he was President of the Illinois Library Association.

In addition to his professional writing, which covers most areas of librarianship, Downs wrote various popular books. His *Books That Changed the World,* published in 1956, has been translated into 12 languages. Revised versions have appeared as *Moulders of the American Mind* (1961) and *Famous Books since 1492* (1965) and a second edition under the original title in 1978. *Famous Books, Ancient and Medieval* (1964), *Books That Changed America* (1976), *Famous American Books* (1971), and *Books That Changed the South* (1977) exemplify his interest in promoting reading.

His interest in American humor and folklore led to an early booklet on *American Humor* (1938), written with Elizabeth Downs; one on *American Humorous Folklore* (1950); one of the Windsor Lectures published in 1958 as *The Family Saga;* and a collection of stories, *The Bear Went over the Mountain* (1964). Later he wrote *Horace Mann* (1974), *Heinrich Pestalozzi* (1975), and *Henry Barnard* (1977).

Honors came to him from many quarters. The Association of American Publishers gave him the Clarence Day Award in 1963. The ALA conferred its Joseph W. Lippincott Award in 1964 and its Melvil Dewey Award in 1974. He received the Illinois Library Association's Librarian of the Year Award in 1972 and the Syracuse University Centennial Medal. He was awarded honorary degrees by Colby College, the University of North Carolina, Ohio State University, Southern Illinois University, and the University of Illinois. In 1979 he shared the first ACRL Academic Research Librarian of the Year Award with Keyes D. Metcalf.

**REFERENCE**

The Festschrift, Jerrold Orne, editor, *Research Librarianship: Essays in Honor of Robert B. Downs* (1971), contains a biography by Robert F. Delzell and a bibliography of Downs's publications.

JOE W. KRAUS

## Dunkin, Paul Shaner
(1905–1975)

As a library practitioner of merit, a philosopher of cataloguing theory and practice, a writer of pithy commentary, and a stimulating teacher, Paul Dunkin earned the recognition and respect of his fellow librarians. His ability to strip away pretense and lay bare a problem in simple, direct fashion served the profession well during the period of library growth after World War II.

Born on September 28, 1905, in Flora, Indiana, Dunkin was the son of E. W. Dunkin and Daisy Shaner Dunkin. Although he eventually traveled throughout the United States and abroad, and lived much of his life on the Atlantic Coast, Paul Dunkin remained true to his midwestern heritage, returning finally to Indiana to live after retirement from his active career.

Dunkin's undergraduate work at DePauw University in Indiana led to an A.B. degree in 1929. As a Phi Beta Kappa student, he found his greatest interests to lie in English literature and the classics. Dunkin pursued classical studies further in the completion of an M.A. in 1931 and a Ph.D. in 1937, both awarded by the University of Illinois. The relatively long interval between those two advanced degrees is explained by Dunkin's move in 1935 from Graduate Assistant in classics to Cataloguer for the University of Illinois Library. He obtained the B.S. in Library Science from the University in that year. During that period he married Gladys Hammond.

Dunkin was able to combine his classical scholarship and love of English literature with his interest in librarianship through an appointment in 1937 as Senior Cataloguer at the Folger Shakespeare Library in Washington, D.C., a position he held until 1950, when he was promoted to Chief of Technical Services. Those who recognized Paul Dunkin's continued interest in academe were perhaps not so startled as some of his other colleagues when he decided to leave the Folger Library in 1959 to assume responsibilities as Professor in the Graduate School of Library Service at Rutgers. Although the move signaled a dramatic change in focus, Dunkin's scholarly bent continued to be served as he directed master's studies and doctoral research at Rutgers. He taught during the deanship of Ralph R. Shaw, as well as during portions of the terms of Lowell Martin and Neal Harlow. Under Shaw's leadership, the Ph.D. program in library service was initiated at Rutgers, thus allowing the Dunkin "imprint" to be felt by a number of the subsequent administrators and teachers in librarianship and information services.

In addition to his teaching, Dunkin became increasingly active in the work of the library profession, especially through his responsibilities in the American Library Association. While still at the Folger Library, he had completed his first library monograph, *How to Catalog a Rare Book* (1951), and had begun his critique of the approach proposed by Seymour Lubetzky for the development of the *Anglo-American Cataloging Rules* while Lubetzky was serving as Editor of the code. Dunkin's 1956 paper, "Criticisms of Current Cataloging Practice," written for the 21st conference of the Graduate Library School of the University of Chicago, initiated a series of discussions and reflections that appeared under his name during the 1950's and 1960's.

Among the more significant of Dunkin's writings were his commentary on Lubetzky's *Code of Cataloging Rules* (1960), his "year's work" papers in *Library Resources & Technical Services* reviewing the developments in cataloguing and classification (1958–66), and his book *Cataloging U.S.A.* (ALA, 1969). Although his commentaries tended to focus on the American scene, he participated in the International Conference on Cataloguing Principles in Paris in 1961 and continued to reflect on the impact of the "Paris Principles" throughout his subsequent writings. Dunkin's style was filled with classical allusions as well as references to homely, everyday events. He was especially fond of making satirical comments about the pretensions of librarians and the preoccupations of cataloguers—a predilection that endeared him to some and caused others to react in annoyance and sometimes hostility. Despite the sharpness of his wit and the barbs ever present in his papers, Dunkin was a gentle companion and in later life gave the impression of being somewhat frail. The keen analytical mind was sometimes betrayed by the body; for example, a badly broken bone caused by a fall prevented him from serving an active term as President of the Resources and Technical Services Division of ALA.

As a result of his visibility in the field of cataloguing, Dunkin was elected and appointed to many posts in the ALA. When Esther Piercy, the founding editor of *Library Resources & Technical Services,* died in 1967, Dunkin was selected to assume her responsibilities. Meanwhile, he was also contributing the "Viewpoint" column for *Library Journal*. Not surprisingly, then, Dunkin became the recipient of the Margaret Mann Citation in 1968, awarded by the Cataloging and Classification Section of ALA. Noted as "elder statesman with a refreshingly young perspective," Dunkin was commended for his "modestly-worn erudition, grace and wit."

There is some difficulty in assessing the peculiar quality of Paul Dunkin's contributions to library service and particularly to cataloguing. He was more of an interpreter than an innovator. He tried to codify, simplify, and encourage iconoclasm among his students and colleagues. By sometimes amusing and occasionally outraging his readers, he hoped to make them reflect upon their activities and avoid taking themselves too seriously. Dunkin also rejected the "cataloguing manual" mentality, preferring to recapture the philosophical approach that he so much appreciated in the works of Charles A. Cutter. Interestingly, in *Cataloging U.S.A.* Dunkin quietly avoided mention of the plethora of cataloguing texts published in the 1940's and 1950's, perhaps in the hope that they might not even warrant a footnote in cataloguing history.

After retiring in 1971, Dunkin was designated Professor Emeritus at Rutgers. He told his friends, however, that he intended to take no further role in professional organizations and to make no postretirement speeches. His collected essays, *Tales of Melvil's Mouser; or Much Ado about Librarians,* had appeared in 1970 at the end of his teaching career. In 1973 the second edition of *How to Catalog a Rare Book* was published. Then, in 1975, his final work, *Bibliography: Tiger or Fat Cat?,* was released; Dunkin's death on August 25, 1975, preceded the official publication of that last volume.

**REFERENCES**

Doralyn J. Hickey, "Paul Shaner Dunkin, 28 September 1905–25 August 1975: An Appreciation," *Library Resources & Technical Services* (1975).

Norman D. Stevens, "The Writings of Paul S. Dunkin: A Review Article," *Library Resources & Technical Services* (1978).

DORALYN J. HICKEY

## Dziatzko, Karl Franz Otto

(1842–1903)

Karl Dziatzko was a prominent figure in the reform of Prussian librarianship that took place under the aegis of Friedrich Althoff (1839–1908), the Prussian Minister of Culture. The centralized authority of the libraries of the ten Prussian universities was such as to facilitate cooperative projects such as union catalogues, cataloguing standards, interlibrary loan networks, standard administrative procedures, and requirements for the education and certification of professional librarians. Besides doing extensive research in the history of the book, printing, and philology, Dziatzko was deeply involved in these library developments. Dziatzko was born on January 27, 1842, in Neustadt, a small town in Upper Silesia. He was educated at the Catholic Grammar School *(Gymnasium)* in Oppeln. An early enthusiasm for language and mathematics gave way to what was to become a lifelong devotion to classical philology. He entered the University of Breslau (now University of Wrocław) in 1859. After three years he moved to the University of Bonn, where he was influenced by the philologist and librarian Friedrich Ritschl (1806–76). A student in Ritschl's seminar, Dziatzko also worked in the library under Ritschl's direction. Graduating in 1863, with a dissertation on Plautus and Terence, he began his professional career as a teacher.

His early academic career was a restless one that first took him back to Oppeln and then to Lucerne. For a very brief period he was Director of the University Library at

Freiburg (Baden) and then Director of a grammar school in Karlsruhe. The decisive turning point in his career came in 1872 when he was appointed Director of the University Library in Breslau. In 1886 he was appointed Director of the Library and Professor of Library Science at the University of Göttingen.

His administrative reforms at Breslau were regarded as a model for other German universities. His rules for the revision of the catalogue at Breslau subsequently became the basis of the *Prussian Instructions* (*Preussische Instruktionen* was first published in 1899, revised in 1908, and reprinted by Harrossowitz in 1966; translated into English by Andrew D. Osborn, the University of Michigan Press, 1938). He was a key figure in the founding of the German Library Association (Verein Deutscher Bibliothekare) in 1900. His lectures and seminars on librarianship at Göttingen were the beginning of library education in Germany. He founded and edited the series *Sammlung Bibliothekswissenschaftlicher Arbeiten,* which was remarkable for the broad scope of its definition of library science. When, in 1893, by Althoff's decree, professional certification became mandatory in Prussia, Dziatzko was appointed Chairman of the examining committee.

Dziatzko's interests and reputation were international. He visited London and toured Italy to study methods of library organization. In 1900 he became a contributing editor to *The Library,* an English periodical. He died on January 13, 1903. With a singular dedication to the intellectual and scholarly dimension of librarianship that, at the same time, took into account practical matters of administration, service, and bibliographic control, Dziatzko made contributions in his life work—the perfection of librarianship and the advancement of learning—that are still a part of modern German librarianship.

**REFERENCES**

Alfred Schneider, bibliography in *Sammlung Bibliothekswissenschaftlicher Arbeiten,* 17 (1904).

Robert Langker, "The Earliest Professor of Librarianship: Karl Dziatzko of Göttingen," *The Australian Library Journal* (1960), on his role in library education.

Joseph Becker, "Karl Dziatzko," in *Der Schlesier des 17. bis 18. Jahrhunderts* (Breslau, 1928) *(Schlesische Lebensbilder,* vol. 3) on his life and times; includes references to other sources.

GORDON STEVENSON

# Eaton, John

(1829–1906)

John Eaton served as U.S. Commissioner of Education from 1870 to 1886. During his tenure he provided support for libraries through the compilation of statistics and the publication of reports and library aids, including the landmark 1876 report *Public Libraries in the United States of America.*

Eaton was born on December 5, 1829, near Sutton, New Hampshire, the oldest in a family of nine children. His early formal education was at first delayed and scanty, but he eventually earned his way through Dartmouth College, from which he received an A.B. in 1854. Between 1854 and 1859 he worked as a public school administrator, first in Cleveland, and afterward in Toledo, Ohio (1856–59), where he served as the Superintendent of public schools. In 1859 he enrolled at the Andover Seminary. When he graduated in 1861, he entered the Civil War as a chaplain with the 27th Ohio Volunteer Infantry. In 1862 General Grant placed him in charge of the many ex-slaves who were coming to the Union Army for refuge. He continued that work until the end of the war, earning the rank of Brigadier General. While in that post Eaton's educational and humanitarian ideals coalesced into a strong overall view of the central importance of public education as the key agency of social renewal that would ensure an enlightened democracy. After five postwar years of newspaper and educational work in Tennessee, President Grant appointed Eaton as the U.S. Commissioner of Education, a position in which he was able to promote his educational goals.

Eaton viewed the proper work of the Bureau of Education to be the promotion of general education through gathering and publishing educational statistics, informative reports, and other writings; presenting educational programs at public expositions; and exchanging information with other countries on the establishment of educational systems. Eaton also considered libraries to be a component of the national educational program, as essential auxiliary aids to education and culture. He had first been involved in library work in Ohio. As Superintendent of Public Instruction in Tennessee (1867–69) he insisted that each school district have a library for the aid of teachers and campaigned for each county to have a library for the general citizenry.

As Commissioner of Education he began immediately to incorporate library statistics in the annual reports of the Bureau. Between 1874 and 1876 his interest in compiling a library census led him to publish and distribute freely the special Bureau report, *Public Libraries in the United States of America: Their History, Condition and Management,* in which a variety of statistical tables were combined with a large number of general articles written by librarians to form what served for years as a fundamental handbook of library management. Eaton also correlated the issuance of the report with the initial meeting of the American Library Association in 1876, which he helped to promote.

Between 1876 and 1885 he provided annual supplements to the 1876 library statistical data and in the Bureau's 1884–85 annual report issued a fully revised library census. During this period the Bureau also published and freely distributed special circulars of information on college libraries (1880), library buildings (1881), and general library aids (1882), each written by prominent librarians. In 1884 he committed the Bureau to issuing the *A.L.A. Catalog,* a promise that kept alive the Association's interest and work on the project.

By 1885 Eaton's work had set a pattern of cooperation between the library profession and the Bureau that would continue permanently. Eaton, however, found the greatly expanded work of the Bureau to be overtaxing, and in 1886 he resigned his post. He remained active in educational concerns until his death on February 9, 1906.

**REFERENCES**

P. W. Alexander, *John Eaton, Jr.—Preacher, Soldier, and Educator,* Ph.D. dissertation, George Peabody College for Teachers (1939).

Francis L. Miksa, "The Making of the 1876 Special Report on Libraries," *Journal of Library History* (1973).

G. Smith, "John Eaton, Educator, 1829–1906," *School and Society* (1969).

M. S. Williams, "The Library Work of the Bureau of Education," *Library Journal* (1887).

FRANCIS L. MIKSA

# Ecuador

The Republic of Ecuador lies on the west coast of South America, with Colombia forming the northern frontier and with Peru on the east and south. Pop. (1978 est.) 7,814,000; area 281,334 sq.km. The official language is Spanish, but Indian languages are very common. Education is compulsory, and all public schools are free. Private schools continue to play a vital role in the education system. The illiteracy rate averages 30 percent.

The total number of libraries serving the population was estimated to be 1,752 in 1978. It should be noted,

**Libraries in Ecuador (1978)**

| Type | Number | Population served | Professional staff | All staff (total) |
|---|---|---|---|---|
| National | 1 | 7,669 | N.A. | N.A. |
| Academic | 51 | 208,097 | N.A. | N.A. |
| Public | 97 | 1,664,725 | N.A. | N.A. |
| School | 1,576 | 481,068 | N.A. | N.A. |
| Special | 27 | 38,199 | N.A. | N.A. |
| Total | 1,752 | | | |

however, that many libraries and information centers are directed by persons with little or no training in the field. The population served by all libraries in Ecuador is estimated to be 2,399,678, or about one-third of the total population of the country; almost one-half of this figure is served by only 97 municipal, or public, libraries.

The year 1968 marked a renewed effort to upgrade libraries in general, much of the momentum having been derived from the Universidad Central, which hired its first professional librarian as Director of the General Library. Decisions were made to prepare a national union catalogue, to promote the Unesco UNISIST Project, to create a NATIS (National Technical Information System), and to update the professional statutes, revise the salaries of professionals, and prepare a Professional Defense Law.

**National Library.** The Biblioteca Nacional del Ecuador, in Quito, was founded in 1792. It contains nearly 55,000 volumes, many dating from the 16th and 17th centuries. Over 7,600 students and scholars utilize that collection annually. A number of cooperative programs with the 97 municipal or public libraries have been instituted. The National Bibliography is not produced by the National Library but by the Biblioteca General of the Universidad Central and is published by that institution on a bimonthly basis and cumulated annually. Though little government support for the National Library was given over the years, there were indications that at the close of the 1970's the situation was changing; support was given by the professional community and the Asociación Ecuatoriana de Bibliotecarios (Ecuatorian Library Association).

**Academic Libraries.** There are 51 academic libraries serving over 200,000 students and faculty in Ecuatorian institutions of higher education. Perhaps the largest and most noteworthy of these is the Biblioteca General de la Universidad Central (General Library of the Central University), founded in 1826 and possessing a collection of over 170,000 volumes. Both the bimonthly *Bibliografía Ecuatoriana* and the annual *Anuario Bibliográfico Ecuatoriano* are published by the Central University General Library. Almost all academic libraries have closed stacks; most only give registered students borrowing privileges.

**Public Libraries.** Public libraries in Ecuador are called bibliotecas municipales, or municipal libraries, and many regions lack them because of limited resources and lack of trained personnel. The Biblioteca Pública Municipal de Cuenca (Cuenca Public Library) has offered numerous short courses to train personnel for public and school libraries, as has the Ecuatorian Library Association, which has sponsored 42 multileveled training programs in the capital of each province. The Biblioteca Municipal de Quito was founded in 1886 and possesses over 12,500 volumes, while the Biblioteca Municipal de Guayaquil, founded in 1862, offers a collection of more than 80,000 volumes.

Of the 97 public libraries presently serving the Ecuatorian population, the majority struggle to survive and offer minimal services that generally do not include borrowing privileges. Most are closed collections that depend heavily on donations for growth. Many public libraries must double as school libraries in the absence or inadequacy of these.

**School Libraries.** School libraries constitute over 80 percent of all libraries in Ecuador, numbering 1,576 and serving an approximate school-age population of 481,068. The majority are in private schools or offer rudimentary collections and services. Many double as public libraries, and most have irregular and insufficient hours. Generally speaking, one or several teachers with full-time class activities will be assigned to the library. The government is actively promoting improvements in the public schools, but funding continues to be a problem. The Library Association has done much to promote the concept of school libraries, and the training courses mentioned were directed toward the teachers in charge of these libraries as well.

**Special Libraries.** As in the majority of Latin American countries, special libraries and information centers are the most advanced in information management and enjoy the best funding and personnel. There are 27 special libraries in Ecuador, estimated to serve a population of 38,199. CIESPAL, the Centro Internacional de Estudios Superiores de Comunicación para América Latina (International Center of Higher Studies in Communications for Latin America) deserves special mention, having pioneered in modern information-handling techniques. CENDES, a technical information center specializing in food industry documentation, has also played a major role in the field. The Junta Nacional de Planificación (National Planning Department) has endeavored to set up a National Technical Information System, having organized the Seminario Nacional de Información Científica y Técnica (National Seminar on Scientific and Technical Information) in 1975.

**Association.** The Asociación Ecuatoriana de Bibliotecarios was founded in 1944 by Alfredo Chávez Granja, the first professional librarian in Ecuador. It has its headquarters at the Casa de Cultura Ecuatoriana (Ecuatorian Cultural Center) and has received a great deal of support from this organization. The Universidad Católica (Catholic University) has also been a staunch supporter of the AEB. After a number of periods of little activity after its inception, the AEB was revived in 1965 when four professional librarians returned from the Interamerican Library School in Colombia and initiated the publication of the *Boletín Bibliográfico Ecuatoriano*. Many courses and conferences have been offered, and the association has been very active in promoting the development of the profession in Ecuador.

MARTHA GORMAN

# Edwards, Edward
(1812–1886)



During March 1877 Melvil Dewey wrote to a lonely, unemployed, and impecunious librarian living in Oxford, inviting him to become the new *American Library Journal*'s Associate Editor for England:

> It seems eminently fitting that you to whom we have so long looked as the foremost writer and thinker in the library world should be associated with the leading librarians of the country in carrying forward this work. . . . I feel a strong personal interest in the matter because on several vital points I agree wholly with you and differ from most of our American librarians. . . . Your name on our list will vouch for your interest in our work.

Dewey's unpublished letter, now in the Edwards collection in Manchester Central Library, was addressed to Edward Edwards.

Edwards was born in Stepney, in the East End of London, in 1812. His father, Anthoney, was a bricklayer. Probably encouraged by his wife, Charlotte, a woman of some education, he unsuccessfully expanded his business activities to become "builder, chapman, and dealer" and was adjudged bankrupt in 1832. Mrs. Edwards's encouragement of her only son was more successful. She was very ambitious for him and probably taught him much herself; no record of his attendance at any school has been traced. Edwards also owed much to Thomas Binney, who became Minister of King's Weigh House Chapel in the City of London in 1829, and to Edwin Abbott, a teacher who was appointed Headmaster of Marylebone Grammar School in 1827. Edwards's education obviously continued steadily and successfully during his seven years' apprenticeship to his father, and by his early 20's he was easily able to hold his own with men of similar age who had been more formally educated.

In 1834 Edwards became a reader in the library of the British Museum, then the only large and freely available library open to the general public in London, and remained closely associated with it for the next 16 years. Following commissioned authorship on such varied subjects as coins, seals and medals, and the state, constitution, and future of New South Wales, he joined the library staff in 1839 as one of the additional cataloguers temporarily employed to prepare a new catalogue. Until 1850 his professional life was lived on three levels. He worked on the catalogue; became extremely active in the movement to establish free public libraries, publishing numerous pamphlets and articles in periodicals; and during at least the later years of the period did little or nothing to alleviate what would now be termed a serious personality clash with the head of his department in the British Museum, Antonio Panizzi. This clash was regrettable, not only because it led ultimately to Edwards's dismissal from his post but even more because both he and Panizzi were deeply concerned with making vast improvements in the Library's service to readers.

Although various proposals to establish freely available public libraries, supported wholly or in part from public funds, had been made in England earlier in the 19th century, the task of providing the authorizing legislation fell to a private Member of Parliament, William Ewart (1798–1869). Edwards acted as his information officer and was the chief witness to testify before a Select Committee of the House of Commons, chaired by Ewart, in 1849. The Committee's Reports prepared the way for the first Public Libraries Act in 1850. This Act, which, inter alia, and with numerous safeguards, empowered town councils to establish libraries and to finance them up to the limit of a local rate of one halfpenny in the pound (raised to one penny by the amending Act of 1855), was adopted most readily in large towns with substantial industrial populations. The lead was taken by Manchester, which appointed Edwards as its first Principal Librarian in 1851. He did much during the next seven years to lay sound foundations for what has become one of the greatest of British municipal library systems but, once again, did little or nothing to alleviate serious personality clashes with the members of his own governing body; Manchester dismissed him in 1858. During the remaining 30 years of his life he found salaried occupation mostly in Oxford, where he was employed, primarily as a cataloguer, in the library of Queen's College from 1870 to 1876 and in the Bodleian Library from 1877 to 1883. His permanent library reputation derives, however, not from work done in salaried posts held; Dewey put his finger on basic essentials when he referred to him as "foremost writer and thinker."

While in Manchester Edwards had also been working assiduously on *Memoirs of Libraries, Including a Handbook of Library Economy,* which was published in London by Trübner three months after his dismissal. It provides a history of libraries from the earliest evidences in Egypt and Assyria up to 1857, the second volume including an account of American libraries from the beginnings at Harvard in 1632 to the New York Public Library and the Smithsonian of 1854. Edwards's approach may also be regarded as propagandist, the libraries of the past being viewed as the predecessors of what the author regarded as the highest and most socially significant form, the municipal free public library. The second half of the second volume, "Economy of Libraries," covers book acquisition, buildings, classification and cataloguing, and "internal administration and public service," and provided librarians of the second half of the 19th century with their most comprehensive treatise. *Memoirs* can be regarded also as visionary since not only did Edwards pioneer scientific book classification in England, but he also speculated on such possibilities as national bibliographies, library associations, and even staff pension schemes.

References and discussions at the inaugural conferences at Philadelphia in 1876 and at London in 1877 make clear the continuing high reputation of *Memoirs* 20 years after first publication. By 1876, however, Edwards had supplemented it with two later works, both also published by Trübner in London: *Free Town Libraries* (1869), a mostly historical treatment in 14 chapters of which 6 cover the libraries of North America; and *Lives of the Founders of the British Museum* (1870). These two later publications may be regarded also as contributions toward the second and substantially revised edition of *Memoirs,* which the author earnestly desired but of which only a few other chapters ever found their way into print.

During the years between his dismissal from Manchester Public Library and his appointment to Queen's College, Oxford (i.e., from 1858 until 1870), Edwards had to earn his living mostly by authorship and journalism and to take advantage of whatever opportunities came his way. His publications were mostly on subjects other than librarianship. Outstanding among them was the two-volume life of *Sir Walter Ralegh* (1868), which still holds its place in the bibliography of the great Elizabethan because, as an eminent 20th-century Elizabethan scholar, A. L. Rowse, has explained: "It is admirable for its steady good judgment and is still indispensable for it contains the Letters" *(Ralegh and the Throckmortons,* [London, 1962]).

Edwards also edited a volume in the Rolls Series, *Liber Monasterii de Hyda; Comprising a Chronicle of the Affairs of England from the Settlement of the Saxons to the Reign of King Cnut; and a Chartulary of the Abbey of Hyde in Hampshire, A.D. 455–1023,* which was welcomed on its publication as a scholar's book for scholars, and was responsible for a variety of articles in the later volumes of the eighth edition of the *Encyclopaedia Britannica* on subjects as diverse as Police, Post Office, Alexis de Tocqueville, and Wool. His *Britannica* article on Libraries had been written while he was still at Manchester.

Edwards was an outstanding example of Victorian "self help." But he was always opinionated and frequently arrogant; he made enemies much too easily and often of people who, handled differently, might have befriended and helped him. He was a bad manager, of his own life, of his personal finances, and certainly of his own writing since he was seldom able to conform to limits and patterns previously agreed with his publishers. He married in 1844 Margaretta Hayward, who was nine years older than himself. Their marriage was tolerably happy for the most part, granted that Margaretta was a much more gregarious person than her husband. They had no children, and this was almost certainly a pity since Edwards, like other lonely men, seems to have had a way with children. He died in poverty in 1886, ten years after his wife, and is buried in the parish churchyard at Niton in the Isle of Wight. The Library Association maintains his grave.

**REFERENCE**

W. A. Munford, *Edward Edwards 1812–1886: Portrait of a Librarian* (London: Library Association, 1963).

W. A. MUNFORD

*John Passmore Edwards*

Library Association

## Edwards, John Passmore
(1823–1911)

John Passmore Edwards, businessman, philanthropist, and library benefactor, was born of poor parents in Cornwall, England, in 1823 and became a successful publisher of newspapers and periodicals, including a pioneer halfpenny daily, and *Mechanics Magazine,* which had itself helped to pioneer mechanics institutes, regarded in Britain as the most important and influential predecessors of public libraries. Edwards was much influenced by the transcendentalism of Channing and Emerson, became a disciple of Cobden and Bright, and supported the full program of their Manchester School. He advocated moderate liberal reform throughout his life and by the age of 60 was a rich man with much money to spend on causes appealing to him. He decided to spend largely on the welfare of the working class.

Mostly during the 1890's he presented hospitals, homes for the handicapped, museums and art galleries, a public park, schools of art and science (including a notable gift to the then new London School of Economics), and even an Oxford scholarship. But he remains best known for his public library benefactions. His library gifts were given mostly to places in his native Cornwall, where, in the later 19th century, a substantial working class population was still dependent on the declining extractive industries of tin and copper mining, and to the working class areas of east and southeast London. Towns in Cornwall benefiting included Camborne and Redruth, Falmouth, Truro, Bodmin, and Launceston; and in London, Limehouse, Poplar, Whitechapel, Southwark, West Ham, Shoreditch, and Edmonton. Edwards presented approximately 30 library buildings and also gave public and other libraries nearly 100,000 books. His British public library benefactions may be regarded as standing midway between those of local philanthropists such as Michael Bass at Derby, John Gulson at Coventry, Edmund Harris at Preston, and William Brown at Liverpool and the much greater, nationwide contribution of Andrew Carnegie.

**REFERENCES**

J. Passmore Edwards, *A Few Footprints* (1905).
T. Kelly, *A History of Public Libraries in Great Britain 1845–1975* (1977).
J. J. Macdonald, *Passmore Edwards Institutions* (1900).

W.A. MUNFORD

## Egypt (Ancient)

The principal known, written records of ancient Egypt were fixed as inscriptions, paintings, or reliefs on the walls of tombs and columns of temples; those that were portable were first entered on rolls of papyrus (or leather) but were customarily restricted to tombs and temple archive rooms. The main practices were developed in the 3d millennium B.C. under the Old Kingdom. They may account for such testimony as the sandstone stele declaration by Neferhotep (18th century B.C.) that before dispatching agents up the Nile to Thebes to begin building a temple, he consulted the ancient writings in the Atum Temple at Heliopolis (in the delta).

The use of papyrus for writing also may have begun during the Old Kingdom, but because of its fragility nothing is extant older than the 3d century B.C., and little has been determined beyond doubt. Richardson thought he had identified 21 libraries in the texts of the Book of the Dead and other sources, but Vogelsang and others, after checking the originals, concluded that Richardson had misunderstood or mistranslated key terms. There were indeed archives but no known libraries before the Ptolemaic period. (As Mogens Weitmeyer put it in *Libri* (1955–56), archival materials were stored by their nature and date; library materials were gathered into subject-related series, bore colophons including regulations of a library character, and were listed in separate catalogues.)

The three "houses of writings" and the House of the Chief of Taxation in the care of a principal courtier in the 4th and 5th dynasties (c. 2613–c. 2345 B.C.) have not been shown to be more than archives. The same holds for the celebrated 370 cuneiform tablets found at El-Amarna, mainly international correspondence of the busy 14th century B.C., in Akkadian. Verification of a sort is provided by the wall painting in the late-13th-century grave of a Ramesside high official: scribes are depicted at work in the left panel, checking and signing of documents by the chief in the center, and the wooden storage chests of the "Records Depository" occupy the right—all under the supervising eye of Thoth, god of knowledge and patron of scribes, who is represented as a baboon.

Ramses himself (II, 1304–1237 B.C.) figures in the venerable tales of the "sacred library" of "King Osymandias," renowned for its entrance inscription, "Nourishment of the Soul." Portions of the story appear to go back to the historian Diodorus Siculus (1st century B.C.), as well as later authorities like Galen, philosopher-physician of the 2d century A.D.

Diodorus' recital was studied in the mid-19th century by Lepsius, who found near the tomb of Ramses II the graves of two "librarians," father and son, which apparently encouraged him to identify the "sacred library" and "King Osymandias" with Ramses. No "sacred library" has been established beyond doubt, but the suppositions are considered reasonable because there were by that time numerous temple "libraries." The "Nourishment of the Soul" inscription, however, has never had archaeological support and is perhaps to be explained by Galen's remark that he found in the "sacred library" a medical recipe he described in terms of "nourishment."

The origins of the temple of Isis on the island of Philae, near the First Cataract, are not certain, but it is known that the building was further developed by the Ptolemies and Romans partly to attract pilgrims. A doorpost inscription referred to a bookroom designed to preserve the life-giving writings of Isis, and below the wall recesses for papyrus rolls—or for wooden jars containing them—was a life-size relief of Thoth-as-baboon with a papyrus roll.

Possibly owing something to the ideas of Imhotep, 27th-century B.C. architect-courtier, reputedly expressed in the original temple of Edfu, somewhat north of Philae, was the new Horus temple built there by the Romans as an instrument of reconciliation with the Egyptian priests. Its library is the only one in Egypt whose existence enjoys archaeological verification. The titles of 37 works were painted on a wall; their presence has been established; they are regarded as having been a sort of ready-reference collection for the staff.

SIDNEY L. JACKSON

# Egypt, Arab Republic of

The Arab Republic of Egypt in northeast Africa is bounded on the west by Libya, on the south by The Sudan, on the northeast by Israel, on the north by the Mediterranean Sea, and on the east by the Gulf of Aqaba and the Red Sea. Pop. (1978 est.) 39,636,000; area 1,002,000 sq.km. The official language is Arabic; French and English are widely spoken.

**National Library.** The National Library of Egypt (Dar el-Kutub Al-Misriyyah) was established in 1870 through the endeavors of Ali Moubarak, the Minister of Education at that time. Moubarak collected the scattered manuscripts and printed books from mosques, schools, archives, ministries, and other governmental departments. The formation of this library helped preserve what was left of Arabic books, manuscripts, and rare books from being lost or sold to foreign collectors. The library was in the palace of Khedive Isma'il until transferred to a new building in 1904. In 1960 construction on another building began. In 1971 the National Library was combined with the National Archives and the National Publishing House to form the General Egyptian Book Organization. Since 1970 the National Library has ceased to be a circulation library and has concentrated on scholarly collections, research, and preservation programs. The National Library is the legal deposit for every publication printed in Egypt. It is also responsible for compiling and publishing the *Egyptian Publications Bulletin,* which can be considered the official national bibliography of the country. Since 1955 the Library has been serving as the secretariat for the Egyptian National Committee for Bibliographic Services, which is responsible for developing plans for a national bibliographic organization.

There are about 657,105 volumes in the National Library. Of the Library's staff of about 1,000 workers, only a few have professional library science degrees.

**Academic Libraries.** Egypt has 9 national universities and about 100 technical colleges and teacher training institutes. Cairo University, which was established in 1908, is the oldest of national universities. It has an enrollment of over 100,000 students, followed by Ain Shams University, just east of the center of Cairo, which has an enrollment of 95,000. In addition to national universities there are two institutions that are not part of the national system: al-Azhar University, the world's oldest university, established in A.D. 970; and the American University in Cairo, a private institution established in 1920.

There are approximately 120 academic libraries in the country. Most of the universities have a main library to house the large library collections in the humanities and social sciences and many faculty libraries, which contain the more specialized materials in science and technology. Cairo University has a special building designed basically to be a library, and it is the sole exception of all university libraries. All the university and college libraries in Egypt suffer from a shortage of qualified librarians. The country often loses its finest librarians to institutions in other Arab countries that offer better positions and salaries. A lack of cooperation is evident among university and college libraries, as no cooperative acquisition programs exist and there is minimal interlibrary loan. Libraries at the same university do not share library resources, and no central processing exists. Students suffer from library regulations that are restrictive. Open access is very limited, with libraries usually open only during the hours when students are attending classes. Only Cairo University had introduced copy machines to serve students and faculty by the close of the 1970's.

Staffiing patterns in most academic libraries depend on the size of the institution. The library can have from 25 to 200 workers, divided into professionals, staff, library assistants, and technicians. Most libraries are inadequate for the number of students and faculty they serve.

**Public Libraries.** Although there are 159 public libraries in Egypt, only one-third of these libraries have holdings of 25,000 to 100,000 volumes and are supervised by qualified librarians. The rest are in cultural centers,

**Libraries in Egypt**

| Type | Number | Volumes in collections | Annual expenditures (pound) | Population served | Professional staff | All staff (total) |
|---|---|---|---|---|---|---|
| National | 1 | 657,105[a] | N.A. | 39,636,000 | — | 1,022 |
| Academic | 120 | 2,591,000 | N.A. | 441,000 | 432 | 805 |
| Public[b] | 159 | 1,500,000 | N.A. | 39,636,000 | N.A. | 642 |
| School | 923 | 7,749,000 | N.A. | 6,240,000 | 977 | 1,903 |
| Special | 320 | 1,605,000 | N.A. | | N.A. | 851 |
| Total | 1,522 | 14,005,000 | | | | 5,223 |

[a]Including 90,000 manuscripts and 7,105 periodical titles.
[b]This does not include 900 Mosque Libraries.

Source: Statistics were gathered by Dr. Sha'bān Khalifa, Assistant Professor, Department of Library Science and Archives, Cairo University, Egypt.

which were set up to attract young men and women who may be interested in reading or in any other social or cultural activities. These centers also usually include a theater, film projection room, music room, and a reading room with a small collection of books ranging from 500 to 3,000 volumes. At least one professional librarian is in charge of each cultural center. Public library services have been extended to farmers and the rural populace in an attempt to reduce illiteracy and to educate the villagers to the best ways of maintaining healthy communities. Other public library services do not go far beyond the very traditional services, i.e., lending books outside the library and allowing readers to read inside the building. Reader assistance is limited to showing them how to use card catalogues and how to find a book on the shelf. The libraries come under several jurisdictions, so there is no general or systematic plan for developing public libraries in the country and no way to coordinate their services.

**School Libraries.** The systematic establishment of school libraries in Egypt began in 1955, when the Ministry of Education founded the Department of School Libraries to supervise and promote school libraries all over the country. This department recommends to the Minister of Education new regulations to improve school library service; it inspects school libraries all over the country and provides standards for furniture and equipment to be used in school libraries. Until 1970 the Department of School Libraries in the Ministry of Education also operated a centralized acquisition and book-processing center that selected, purchased, and distributed books for all the school libraries in the country. Each library thereafter purchased its own books, but most of these were chosen from the selection tools prepared by the Department. Therefore, there is a kind of similarity between collections in all school libraries of the same level not only in the quality of books but also in the quantity. In many instances the collections do not correspond with the needs of pupils or teachers. School library services are very traditional. They are restricted to lending books. Collections comprise only books and a very few local newspapers and magazines. Audiovisual materials were still a novelty and microforms virtually unknown in Egyptian schools in the latter 1970's. Since 1961 the concept of school-community libraries has been introduced in Egypt, and they now provide services to the general public as well as to the students.

There are approximately 7,749,000 volumes in 923 school libraries. These libraries are serviced by a staff of 1,903, of which 977 are librarians. Each school library serves an average of 1,000 students and teachers. From 1961 more than seventy-five school libraries, 15 in Cairo alone, were open to the public.

**Special Libraries.** According to 1975 statistics, Egypt has 7 information centers and 313 special libraries: 170 in ministries and other governmental agencies, 72 in learned societies, and 71 in institutions and corporations. The special library in Egypt corresponds in collections and size with the needs of the institution it serves. The size of the collections depends entirely upon the history of the institution and the available budget. Governmental libraries contain government documents, laws, archives, and foreign materials not easily available elsewhere. In many instances services are limited to lending materials only to those who work in the institution. Information centers were established to serve researchers and scientists in government and semigovernment organizations. They are considered special libraries, although they form a superior quality of special libraries. They go beyond traditional services and provide new kinds of services that represent modern thinking in special librarianship and information services. Among the services provided by these centers, including those listed below, are indexing and abstracting, translation, bibliographic activities, and current awareness services, and some provide computerized information storage and retrieval. Information centers are recognized at the Institute of Public Administration, Iron and Steel Company, Atomic Energy Establishment, National Information and Documentation Center (NIDOC), Education Documentation and Research Center—Ministry of Education, National Planning Institute, and Ministry of National Planning. Each special library or information center varies. A library may have as few as four staff members, or it may have a staff of 100. Some libraries or centers concentrate their holdings on books, others on periodicals or documents. They may have from 3,000 to 180,000 volumes in their collections.

MOHAMMED M. AMAN;
SHA'BĀN KHALIFA

# Elmendorf, Theresa Hubbell (West)

(1855–1932)

In March 1951 the *Library Journal* selected Theresa West Elmendorf to its new Library Hall of Fame, in recognition of her long contribution to the field. In commenting on her selection, *Library Journal* took note of her exceptional knowledge of books and of her ability to interest others in reading literature. Her selection was a fitting reminder of an early library pioneer with rare ability, vision, and high ideals.

Theresa Hubbell West was born in Pardeeville, Wisconsin, on November 1, 1855; six years later her family moved to Milwaukee primarily to ensure educational opportunities for the four children. She graduated from Milwaukee's public schools and then from a school for girls in 1874. In 1877 she began her long library career as an assistant at the Young Men's Association of Milwaukee, a library that was soon to form the basis for a new municipal library. While waiting for the state legislature to pass the enabling act effecting this transfer, she kept the library open as a reading room and found time to read the 1876 report of the U.S. Bureau of Education, *Public Libraries in the United States of America.* This milestone in library literature was to form the basis of her knowledge of library theory and practice, and perhaps even the inspiration for her ideas about library service. She was appointed to the staff of the new Milwaukee Public Library and in 1880 became Deputy Librarian. Following a scandal involving the embezzlement of city funds by the Head Librarian, K. A. Linderfelt, West was appointed to the post in 1892. Her four years at the helm of Milwaukee's library were important, for it was then that a new library-museum was planned and built. She also developed her executive abilities, and the library became known as a carefully administered, patron-oriented institution.

She resigned her position in 1896 upon her marriage to Henry L. Elmendorf, then Librarian of the public library at Saint Joseph, Missouri, and a Vice-President of the American Library Association. For about a year the couple lived in London, where he managed the branch of the Library Bureau. The library profession beckoned, however, and in mid-1897 Elmendorf became the head of the newly established Buffalo Public Library, a position he held until his death nine years later. While having no official connection with the library during this time, Theresa Elmendorf acted as a silent partner and frequent adviser. She had had more experience as an administrator than he, and it seems likely she was instrumental in developing the library. At a time when public libraries traditionally closed their bookshelves to the public, Buffalo began what was called the Open Shelf Room. They also started the "Buffalo Plan," a program that included public library service to the schools of the city. Evidence of her role in the Plan is her address for the New York State

Teachers Association, which was later expanded into a booklet called *Buffalo's System of Public School and Public Library Cooperation.*

As an unpaid worker, she found time to do research, to write, and to serve in various organizations. She produced a *Descriptive Catalogue of the Gluck Collection of Manuscripts and Autographs in the Buffalo Public Library* in 1899, and in 1904 served as the Selection Editor of the ALA's *Catalogue of Books for Small Libraries.* Elmendorf as Editor was a logical choice since she was recognized as an authority on book selection. Her contributions appeared in *Library Journal* and *Public Libraries,* as well as magazines outside the profession. In 1903–04 she served as President of the New York Library Association, at which time she was also a member of the American Library Institute.

The death of her husband in 1906 forced Theresa Elmendorf to end her unpaid status, and for the next 20 years she held the position of Vice-Librarian at the Buffalo Public Library. Her new role also meant an increased participation in ALA; in 1911–12 she served as its President, the first woman to hold that position. She presided at the Ottawa conference, the second meeting held by the Association in Canada. Although she made the political mistake of suggesting a closer alliance between the two countries—at a time when Canadians were especially sensitive to such a suggestion—ruffled feelings were smoothed over, and the meetings resulted in increased cooperative library development.

It was in the area of popular bibliography that she perhaps made her greatest contribution. Her exceptional knowledge of books, and her enthusiasm in encouraging appreciation of reading in others, led her to produce a variety of reading lists and bibliographies. In 1917 *Poetry: The Complementary Life,* a selection made for Buffalo's Open Shelf Room, was published, and in 1921 a short reading list of popular books entitled *The United States* was reprinted by ALA. Her *Classroom Libraries for Public Schools,* published by the Buffalo Library in 1923, was a valuable selection aid. Even mandatory retirement in September 1926 failed to bring a halt to her efforts. In 1928 she prepared the bibliography of poems and poets for Joseph Auslander and F. E. Hill's *Winged Horse,* published by Doubleday, Doran. This was enlarged three years later into the ALA publication *Poetry and Poets: A Readers List.* Appreciation of poetry was one of her strongest characteristics, and so it was especially appropriate that this would be her last contribution to the world of books. Mrs. Elmendorf died at her home in Buffalo on September 4, 1932.

Theresa Elmendorf was a woman of unusual ability who made a major contribution to the profession and to its Association. She had high ideals and a vision of expanding library service well before its time. After her death, Mary E. Hazeltine of the University of Wisconsin Library School wrote, "Many librarians in important positions today have carried on because she awakened their appreciation of books and opened up for them insight into new realms. She was a stimulating guide and a vitalizing teacher, as well as a great librarian."

DENNIS THOMISON

# El Salvador

El Salvador, a republic in Central America, is bordered by Honduras on the north and east, the Pacific Ocean on the south, and Guatemala on the west. Pop. (1978 est.) 4,516,000; area 21,041 sq.km. The official language is Spanish.

**National Library.** The National Library of El Salvador, in the city of San Salvador, was created by presidential decree in 1870 with an initial collection of 6,000 works on theology, philosophy, law, and classical literature. A year later it was transferred to the National University and was under university administration until 1887, when it was opened to the general public. The Mobile Libraries, a division of the National Library, were founded in 1923, bringing books to amusement parks, fairs, and 226 rural communities. In 1962 the National Library became the General Directorate of Libraries and Archives and together with the holdings of the National Archives moved to the first library building constructed in El Salvador.

The National Library is the depository library under the copyright law and of documents of international organizations. The majority of books contained in the Library come from donations and exchanges with Latin American countries and with learned societies of the United States and Europe. The Library's principal departments are the Exchange Center, the International Organizations Department, Special Services for Children, and the Center for Documentation on Education. Its collection totaled 100,000 in 1974 and 110,000 in 1978. It also includes microfilm of important historical documents of El Salvador in Spanish archives.

**Academic Libraries.** The principal academic library is the Central Library of the University of El Salvador. Established in 1854, it was destroyed in 1865 and started again in 1889 with a collection of books on general

**Table 1. Libraries in El Salvador (1976)**

| Type | Number | Volumes in collections | Annual expenditures (colón) | Population served | Professional staff | All staff (total) |
|---|---|---|---|---|---|---|
| National | 1 | 124,000 | ₡40,000 | 386,600 | 1 | 30[a] |
| Academic | 13 | 190,960 | ₡645,975[b] | 53,750 | 16 | 150 |
| Public | 113 | 110,500[c] | ₡279,750 | 2,460,857 | N.A. | 193[d] |
| School | 150 | 245,000[e] | ₡260,000[e] | 855,329 | 1 | 140[f] |
| Special | 30 | 147,032 | ₡80,000[g] | 43,955 | 11 | 78[h] |
| Total | 307 | 807,492 | ₡1,025,975 | | | 591 |

[a]Twenty members of the staff have received courses in library science.
[b]Three libraries did not report their annual expenditures, and two had no library budget.
[c]Fifty-two municipal libraries did not report size of their collections or annual expenditures.
[d]Twenty-five public librarians have received courses in library science.
[e]Only 75 schools reported their number of volumes and their annual expenditures.
[f]Ten staff members have received courses in library science.
[g]Only two libraries reported their annual expenditures. They all reported not having a specific library budget but being included in the general budget of their respective institutions.
[h]Twenty-five staff members have received courses in library science.

subjects, while the University faculties founded their own libraries. The University library was the best stocked and most important library in the country, but in 1955 a fire destroyed 60 percent of its holdings, and the remains were divided among faculty collections.

In 1963 the University Rector established a Central Library and in 1966 initiated a university library system that aimed at the centralization of all library resources of the University. Because of domestic unrest, there was no centralized system in the latter 1970's, though the University authorities considered reinstituting the former library system.

The Central Library collection numbered 80,000 volumes in 1974 and 93,260 in 1978. The size of the National University Library, including the faculty collections, is 205,000 volumes, and it serves a population of 45,000 readers.

There are three other university libraries with varied collections, which include former private libraries and new bibliographic resources purchased with funds loaned by regional and international banks. The private Catholic University is well stocked and staffed.

**Public Libraries.** Until 1973 free library services were provided by the National Library and by a few municipal libraries concentrated around the capital, but their collections were small and limited. In 1973 a project called National Network of Houses of Culture was approved by the government, and 60 public libraries were founded in important cities and rural towns from 1973 to 1977. These Casas de la Cultura extend their services to surrounding communities, serving a total population of 200,000. A similar five-year plan was to establish 60 more public libraries between 1978 and 1982. This network of libraries has centralized processing and trains its own librarians.

**School Libraries.** Public and private school libraries developed rapidly in the 1960's because of educational reforms. In 1972 the Ministry of Education approved a five-year plan for public school libraries providing for 330 libraries to serve a population of 218,000 students; the number of libraries was still insufficient at the end of the 1970's. Private schools usually have good basic collections in accordance with their curricula, some surpassing 25,000 volumes. The use of audiovisual materials was introduced in the 1970's, but costs prevented the public schools from making significant use of other than book materials.

**Table 2. Archives in El Salvador (1976)**

| | |
|---|---|
| Number | 3 |
| Volume | 682 cubic meters |
| Annual expenditures | (not reported by any of the 3 archives) |
| Professional staff | 18 |
| All Staff (total) | 28 |

**Special Libraries.** Special libraries are important in the country because of the variety and richness of their holdings and because they are better funded and invariably open to the public. The oldest special library began in 1883 as the library of the National Museum. From the 1960's such libraries developed, together with their supporting organizations, in almost every bank, learned society, professional association, ministry, embassy, hospital, church, museum, industry, and commercial and business firm. The libraries of the National Coffee Company serve the many people interested in this important crop. Banks have opened their libraries to students and researchers, and the library of the Electric Company is one of the best organized.

There are many excellent collections belonging to private individuals who open their libraries part-time to university students or the general public. The Gallardo Collection in the city of Nueva San Salvador surpasses 80,000 volumes.

**Association.** The Association of Salvadoran Librarians, founded in 1947 and composed mainly of librarians without graduate training, conducts such activities as conferences, meetings, and the sporadic publication of a bulletin. The very few university-trained librarians had no separate organization in 1979.

JEANNETTE FERNANDEZ DE CRIADO

# El Sheniti, El Sayed Mahmoud
(1920–    )

El Sheniti, Egyptian library educator and administrator, participated in many important library projects and conferences around the world and contributed to significant library achievements in Egypt. He was born in Egypt on November 25, 1920. He earned a B.A. degree from Cairo University in 1940, a higher diploma in social sciences from Alexandria University in 1953, and a Ph.D. in Library Science from the University of Chicago in 1960.

El Sheniti served the Egyptian and international library profession in several capacities. He was Librarian of Alexandria University Library, 1949–51; Assistant Librarian of the Unesco Fundamental Education Center in Sirs El Layyan, Egypt, 1952–54; Director of the American University in Cairo Library, 1958–63; Unesco Documentation and Publications Expert Stationed at the Unesco Regional Center of Community Development for the Arab States in Sirs El Layyan, Egypt, 1963–68; Under Secretary of State for the Egyptian National Library and Archives, 1968–71; Senior Under Secretary of State for the Ministry of Culture and Chairman of the General Egyptian Book Organization, 1971–77; and Deputy Minister of Culture and Chairman of the GEBO, a post he held until his retirement in December 1978.

El Sheniti contributed largely to library education in Egypt as a visiting professor to the Department of Librarianship and Archives of the Faculty of Arts, Cairo University. He also worked as an expert and consultant to numerous organizations in Egypt and in other Arab countries. From 1964 to 1970 he presided over the Egyptian Library Association.

He contributed to several Unesco meetings. From 1966 to 1974 he served as a member and Chairman of the Unesco International Advisory Committee for Libraries, Documentation and Archives. He was elected President of the Unesco Intergovernmental Conference on National Planning of Documentation, Library and Archives Infrastructure, Paris, 1974; Vice-President of the International Congress on National Bibliography, Paris, 1977; and member of the International Book Committee and the International Book Year Support Committee.

El Sheniti wrote or edited numerous articles and books dealing with various aspects of library science. Noteworthy are "Book Cataloging Rules for Arabic Materials" (Cairo, 1961), "Authority List of Arabic Names" (Cairo, 1962), and "Arabic Adaptation of Dewey Decimal Classification" (Cairo, 1961).

As an administrator, El Sheniti contributed to library achievements in Egypt. Among them are centralized library activities focused around the book, i.e., public library services, national library and archives, and the state publishing industry under the umbrella of the General Egyptian Book Organization; a new modern building for the National Library and Archives; the establishment of various centers within the framework of the GEBO, such as the Arabic Book Development Center, the Bibliographic Center, the Arab Heritage Center, and the Computer and Microfilming Center.

MOHAMED M. EL HADI

# Equatorial Guinea

Equatorial Guinea is a republic in west Africa, comprising Río Muni—bordered on the north by Cameroon, on the east and south by Gabon, and on the west by the Atlantic Ocean—and the islands of Annobon and Fernando Po, which lie offshore from the mainland territory. Pop. (1978 est.) 327,000; area 28,051 sq.km. The official language is Spanish.

Equatorial Guinea, former Spanish Guinea, became independent in October 1968. The few libraries left by Spain after independence in October 1968 were somnolent, closed, or had been evacuated by 1979. No official sources documenting library services in Equatorial Guinea after 1968 were available in the following decade.

**National Library.** No National Library was established in Equatorial Guinea. Most documents published on Spanish Guinea are available in Spanish libraries. In 1979 the main Equatoguinean sources could be found in libraries in Madrid, among them the Biblioteca Nacional, Biblioteca del Instituto de Estudios Africanos, Hemeroteca Nacional, Biblioteca del Colegio Mayor Universitario Nuestra Señora de Africa, and Biblioteca de los Misioneros Claretianos; in Rome, Biblioteca del Vaticano and Biblioteca de los Misioneros Claretianos; in Geneva, Switzerland, the United Nations Library; in New York City, the United Nations Library; and at Northwestern University in Evanston, Illinois, the Melville J. Herskovits Library of African Studies.

**Academic Libraries.** In 1963 in Bata the Escuela de Magisterio (Teacher Training College) was created with a library for students' use only. In 1971 the library numbered about 3,000 volumes, covering mainly Spanish literature, books on pedagogy, and almost all publications of the Instituto de Estudios Africanos on Guinea. In 1973 the library was absorbed by the Centro de Desarrollo de la Educación, a secondary and primary school Teacher Training Center created with Unesco's assistance; in 1974 there were about 2,500 volumes. The government closed the library; it was reopened partially in 1976, but after deportation or exile of most of the students and departure of Unesco's experts, the library was not in use from 1978.

In Santa Isabel the Library of the Escuela Superior Indígena (later on called Escuela Superior Provincial) was established in 1946 for training auxiliary primary school teachers and auxiliary administrators. In 1946 it numbered 1,400 volumes, for students' use only.

Shortly before independence, the Dirección General de Enseñanza y Inspección began to organize a pedagogical library with the help of the Spanish Dirección General de Plazas y Provincias and the Instituto Pedagógico San José de Calasanz of the Scientific Investigations Council (Madrid). Its aim was to create circulation libraries for teachers and pupils in remote districts, but they did not work.

There were also some little libraries in the four Catholic seminaries, two Seminarios mayores (clerical training colleges) in Banapa and Nkuefulan, and two Seminarios menores (clerically staffed secondary schools) in Concepción and Mikomeseng.

**Public Libraries.** The Biblioteca Publica of Santa Isabel was created in 1942 by the Ministry of Education, and the institution was opened to the public in 1945. It counted 3,000 volumes at inception; the Library is in the building of the Instituto Cardenal Cisneros (presently Instituto Rey Malabo, main secondary school of the country, also created in 1942). Books were supplied by the Gobierno General de la Colonia, the Administración de Intercambios y Compras de Libros (Madrid), the Dirección General de Marrueco y Colonias (later on de Plazas y Provincias), and the Ministry of Foreign Affairs, as well as by private sources. Under the supervision of the Governor General of the Colony (later Province), the Library was directed by the Archivist of the Gobierno General. The Library administered two little circulation libraries in San Carlos (Fernando Po) and Bata (Rio Muni). In 1967 for 11,600 volumes there were 25,750 loans. There was no air conditioning in the Library, in spite of the very humid climate.

**Other Libraries.** In 1955 Father Jesús Morras founded a little private library in the Claretians Mission (Hijos del Inmaculado Corazón de Maria—missionaries established in Spanish Guinea from 1883). The library collected rare documents on archaeology, history, ethnology, and natural sciences and complete collections of various newspapers. The Library's African Museum preserved some 5,000 prehistoric stones. In response to opposition to Roman Catholicism under the Macía Nguema government, the whole library was evacuated from Fernando Po in 1974, then out of the country.

The Library of the Museo Etnográfico of Santa Isabel (about 500 volumes), managed by the Ministry of Education, was abandoned after the closing of the Ministry of Education in 1977; the Minister and other officials were assassinated.

The Dirección de Archivos, in Santa Isabel, a very understaffed service since independence, was supported by the Ministry of Education (closed in 1977). Most Equatoguinean archives have to be consulted in Spain and in other countries, principally the Archivo de las Cortes, Archivo del Consejo de Estado, Archivo de la Dirección General de Promoción del Sahara, Archivo del Ministerio de Asuntos exteriores, and Archivo Histórico nacional, all in Madrid; Archivo General de Simancas, in Valladolid; and Archivo de Indias, in Seville. Besides Spanish archives are the colonial archives of Portugal, France, England, and Germany. The Berlin archives are famous for the study of the Fang. Finally, the Vatican archives are also a rich resource. At the end of the 1970's there were no library associations.

**REFERENCES**

Sanford Berman, *Spanish Guinea: An Annotated Bibliography* (dissertation, Catholic University of America, Washington, D.C., 1961).

Max Liniger-Goumaz, *Historical Dictionary of Equatorial Guinea* (1979).

M. LINIGER-GOUMAZ

**Libraries in Equatorial Guinea (1976)**

| Type | Number | Volumes in collections | Annual expenditures (peseta) | Population served | Professional staff | All staff (total) |
|---|---|---|---|---|---|---|
| National | 0 | 0 | 0 | 0 | 0 | 0 |
| Academic | 7 | 7,000 | N.A. | 1,000 | N.A. | N.A. |
| Public | 1 | 12,000 | N.A. | 40,000 | N.A. | N.A. |
| School | 0 | 0 | 0 | 0 | 0 | 0 |
| Special | 3 | 5,000 | N.A. | 500 | N.A. | N.A. |

# Ethiopia

Ethiopia, in northeastern Africa, is bordered by Sudan on the west and north, Djibouti and the Red Sea on the east, Somalia on the southeast, and Kenya on the south. Pop. (1978 est.) 30,037,000; area 1,221,900 sq.km. The official language is Amharic.

**National Library.** Founded, together with a National Museum, by Emperor Haile Selassie in 1944, in the capital of Addis Ababa, the National Library offers loan and reference facilities to the public, acting as a central public library and as the national repository of Ethiopiana. A proclamation conferring depository privileges was enacted in 1975, a year after the Revolution.

The Library's valuable collection of several hundred Ethiopian Christian Orthodox manuscripts, some finely illuminated and dating from as early as the 14th century, also includes Ethiopian "incunabula" from the period when local printing began at the end of the 19th century. In the 1960's the Library opened branches in several provincial centers, notably Debre Zeit, Yrgalem, and Harar, stocking them with volumes from its own collection.

**Academic Libraries.** The principal resource is the library system of the University of Addis Ababa. Founded in 1961 and building on the collections of the University College of Addis Ababa established 11 years earlier, the University Library had by the mid-1970's 13 branches, including law, medical, engineering, science, agriculture, and public health. The collections were developed extensively with Ford Foundation and U.S. AID assistance. Exceeding 250,000 volumes, they include a unique library of Ethiopiana at the Institute of Ethiopian Studies, where the holdings of more than 25,000 volumes are made up of a comprehensive collection of books about Ethiopia and the Horn of Africa; some 10,000 books, mostly in Amharic, printed in the country; and a collection of more than 700 manuscripts and scrolls. The library publishes *Ethiopian Publications* (1965—), a classified list of books and periodical articles published in Ethiopia.

The University of Asmara Library was founded by Italian nuns and added collections in English after University status had been granted to the institution in 1967. It has some 60,000 volumes.

**Public Libraries.** Responsibility for these is carried by the National Library, with its inadequate funding. A number of municipal and community libraries have grown, in addition, mainly through local initiative, for example, the library at Kebri Dehar in Hararghe (1979). In 1973 a books-by-mail service was launched by the University Library, initially to provide recreational paperback reading to students on university service in the provinces, but it was later made available to the public. The service was developed after the 1974 Revolution, in cooperation with the Ethiopian Library Association, to serve students and teachers on the National Campaign for Development and Work 1974–1976, which included intensive literacy drives. Books were distributed through school or public libraries wherever these existed.

**School Libraries.** In the 1960's and 1970's the Ministry of Education attempted to improve library services in secondary schools. Courses were held to train school librarians and, with AID assistance, books were purchased and distributed.

**Special Libraries.** The most important special library in Ethiopia is that of the UN Economic Commission for Africa (1958). It has a strong collection of African government and agency documents, periodicals, and some 60,000 books on African development. Other libraries serve government agencies. The National and Commercial banks, the Institute of Public Administration, and the Police and Air Force Colleges have libraries of long standing. Among libraries sponsored by other countries are the British Council Library and the libraries of the Russian, German, French, and Italian Cultural Centers.

**Church Libraries.** For centuries thousands of churches and monasteries in Ethiopia have served as repositories of religious manuscripts used in services, teaching, and scholarship. It is estimated that some 50,000 manuscripts are housed in these churches. A project for recording them on film, initiated in 1973 by the Ethiopian Orthodox Church and Saint John's University, Collegeville, with funding from the National Endowment for the Humanities, led to microfilming more than 6,000 manuscripts in the first six years. They are kept in the Ethiopian Manuscript Microfilm Library, Addis Ababa, and the *Hill Monastic Manuscript Microfilm Library,* Collegeville (1976– ).

**Association.** The Ethiopian Library Association, founded in 1967, achieved official status as a registered society in 1969. It has been active in campaigning for better public library facilities and in training librarians.

RITA PANKHURST



# Euronet

The European on-line information network (Euronet) DIANE is conceived as a facility to enable users in any of the EEC (European Economic Community) countries to gain fast access via data terminals to scientific, technical, economic, and social information (STI) held on computer files at remote service centers. While the name *Euronet* was used originally to apply to all aspects of the project, it has presently come to be used more particularly for the specially designed data transmission network. DIANE stands for "Direct Information Access Network for Europe."

The Euronet project is the central part of two EEC action plans in STI for the periods 1975–77 and 1978–80, respectively. Responsibility for implementation rests with the Commission of the European Communities, more specifically with its Directorate General (DG) for Scientific and Technical Information and Information Management in Luxembourg. The installation and operation of the Euronet data transmission network was contracted by the Commission to the telecommunications administrations of the nine EEC member states, and a corresponding arrangement was signed in late 1975. The network was due to start commercial operations in summer 1979, with access points in all nine EEC member states. About 20 information services in Belgium, Denmark, France, the Federal Republic of Germany, Luxembourg, Netherlands, Italy, and the United Kingdom proposed to offer access via Euronet to their data bases.

A special project team within DG XIII at Luxembourg handles all STI-related aspects of the project, while the EEC telecommunications administrations set up a data network development team in Paris. A communication control center for the operations of the data network was planned for London.

The Commission and the EEC national information authorities are closely interacting within the framework of the EEC Committee for Information and Documentation on Science and Technology (CIDST). This Committee is operating on the basis of a number of subgroups, in particular the Economic and Technical Aspects Group.

The DIANE information services formed a special ad-hoc committee that voices their opinions and recommendations on all aspects of data base operations via the Euronet network. The general aim of the Euronet program is the creation of a "common market for on-line information" within the European Communities. Within the framework the project aims are directed toward new user tools for STI retrieval, central STI facilities, and STI specific sophisticated data equipment support, and furthering harmonization and promotion of all aspects of data base operation via the network. Specific priority is given, among others, to the development of a Common Command Set for retrieval purposes, installation of a data base referral facility, implementation of sophisticated "Virtual Terminals," and study of document supply problems.

Related to the Euronet DIANE project are other activities carried on by the Commission; i.e., development of information sources in special areas and of multilingual tools and the creation of a general information supply policy. The Commission publishes a bimonthly Euronet DIANE newsletter.

The Euronet DIANE project was undertaken by the Commission in contact with a large number of organizations including European user organizations and interested parties from EEC industry and research, associations of European data base operators, and of data base producers, such as ICSU-AB, CODATA, and EUSIDIC.

Mounting interest in joining Euronet was shown by non-EEC European countries; thus in 1978 Switzerland and Spain forwarded formal applications to the Commission of the European Communities for connections. The Council of Ministers of the European Community has authorized the Commission to negotiate such applications from any CEPT (Conférence Européenne des Postes et Télécommunications) countries.

H. UNGERER

ALA

*Charles Evans*

## Evans, Charles
(1850–1935)

Charles Evans, U.S. librarian and bibliographer, served a number of libraries from 1866 to 1901; from 1902 he devoted the rest of his life with single-minded dedication to his *American Bibliography,* the fundamental resource for early American imprints which secures his place in library history.

Evans was born on November 13, 1850, in Boston. After the deaths of both parents, he was placed in 1859 in the Boston Asylum and Farm School, where he received rigorous training in religion, manual labor, and academic studies. At the age of 16 Evans became an assistant at the Boston Athenaeum, the distinguished private library then under the direction of William Frederick Poole. The Athenaeum proved to be Evans's bibliographical "alma mater" and Poole his life-long mentor.

Evans was an effective library organizer and internal administrator and a leader in developing library services. But he failed to work well with supervising boards and administrators. That failure led to an uneven career as a librarian despite his achievements. He was the first Librarian of the new Indianapolis Public Library from late in 1872 until disagreements led to the end of his employment in August 1878. (He was to serve in Indianapolis again, from 1889 to 1892, but he again failed to sustain his board's support.)

Evans worked outside the library profession from 1878 to 1884. The following year he went as Assistant Librarian to the Enoch Pratt Free Library in Baltimore, but he resigned in December 1886 after difficulties with the Head Librarian. At the Newberry Library in Chicago, he worked in classification and reference from July 1892 to January 1895 and in the next year began to organize the collections of the Chicago Historical Society on a part-time assignment. Evans was Secretary and Librarian of the Society from July 1896 until the trustees dismissed him in 1901. His career as a librarian ended, but a new one was to begin.

In January 1902 Evans announced to a skeptical library community an ambitious project—a chronological, annotated record of publications printed in the U.S. from the beginning of printing in 1639 through 1820. Thereafter Evans set about achieving his objective with total commitment. By that time he had married Lena Young (1884), and they had three children (one of whom later became the golfer Chick Evans). But family and all ordinary and social obligations and pleasures were to be displaced by his relentless pursuit of his goal. He took on not only the editorial and scholarly roles that the work demanded but also all production and printing—selecting his own paper, looking for the most economical printer, and directly overseeing all the work, including handling his own order fulfillment from his home. His plan was to offer separate volumes at $15 each to an initial 300 subscribers.

He began his editorial work for each period in the Newberry and Chicago Public libraries, carefully preparing annotated slips from bibliographies and printed catalogues. Then he would visit the Library of Congress and many other libraries in the East, often discovering stacks of publications that had not been previously organized. He worked long hours to bring out his first volume (covering the years 1639–1729), published in November 1903, and did not let up in his prodigious efforts in subsequent years. With characteristic energy and devotion, he managed to issue at fairly regular intervals the next eight volumes, carrying the work through the period 1790–92 by 1915. He had about 375 subscribers at the beginning of World War I. Evans won a reputation for his bibliographical achievement and benefited from cooperation with other bibliographers and librarians who provided information. He saw his work recognized by professional peers when he was elected to membership in the American Antiquarian Society in 1910.

Increased costs and the loss of foreign subscribers during World War I interrupted his publishing program for the next decade. With the support of Theodore Wesley Koch, Northwestern University Librarian, and an ALA committee, enough sales were generated to permit continuation of the work—volume 9 (1793–94), priced now at $25, was published in 1926 and volume 10 (1795–96) in January 1929. During the Depression of the 1930's grants from the American Council of Learned Societies made possible publication of volume 11 and volume 12, covering the years 1796 and through the letter *M* of 1799. He had given up his original goal of 1820 to settle for 1800, but he did not live to complete the final volume in his revised plan. He died on February 8, 1935.

Evans attended the first meeting of the American Library Association in October 1876. He served as ALA's first Treasurer until 1878, but he was not active in the Association thereafter. ALA named him an honorary member at its Conference in 1926, and in 1934 Brown University awarded him an honorary Doctor of Letters degree.

Evans's revised plan was eventually completed in 1955 when volume 13 (*N* 1799–1800) was published by the American Antiquarian Society under the editorship of Clifford K. Shipton. The American Antiquarian Society also issued volume 14, a cumulative Index, by Roger P. Bristol, in 1959. Bristol's index to printers, publishers, and booksellers in the series appeared in 1961. After another decade of work, Bristol issued his *Supplement to Charles Evans' American Bibliography* (1970), adding 11,000 titles to Evans's original 39,000. Thus Evans's original work continues to serve as the foundation stone of American bibliographic effort.

**REFERENCE**

Edward G. Holley, *Charles Evans, American Bibliographer* (1963), includes a complete list of Evans's works and other Evans materials, pages 323–330.

EDWARD G. HOLLEY

## Evans, Evelyn
(1910– )

Evelyn Jane Alice Evans, public librarian, developed the national library service of Ghana and contributed to library service in many other developing countries. Born March 22, 1910, in Coventry, England, she served the Public Library there from 1927 to 1941. In 1931 she became an Associate of the Library Association and a Fellow in 1933. She worked in the University of Michigan Library in Ann Arbor from 1935 to 1936.

Eve Evans was British Council Librarian in the then Gold Coast from 1945 until 1949, when she was transferred to the Gold Coast Library Board. The Board became a statutory body in 1950, and she became its first Chief Librarian and later its first Director of Library Services.

In 1945 there were no significant public library services in the Gold Coast. By 1965, the time she left Ghana, there were 21 libraries and various services, including mobile units. Her philosophy was to use local resources when possible, and she early saw that she would one day have to make way for indigenous librarians. She also gave emphasis to the development of children's libraries.

In November 1961 she made a world tour to study library cooperation and national libraries. She traveled extensively in Africa and other developing areas, served as an expert on public libraries for Unesco, and advised Nigeria and Sierra Leone. In Ghana she was one of the pioneers who formed the West African Library Association in 1954, and she became its President in 1959.

In 1955 she was decorated as a member of the Most Excellent Order of the British Empire (M.B.E.) and in 1960 as Commander of the Most Excellent Order of the British Empire (C.B.E.). She was made Honorary Fellow of the Library Association in 1965.

A Unesco consultant to Liberia in 1967, she was in Ceylon from 1967 to 1970, and she drew up legislation for the Ceylon National Library Services Board.

In 1975 she was invited by the Ghana Library Board to participate in the 25th anniversary celebration of the service that she had created from scratch and which she left intact, a monument to herself, to Ghana, and to African librarianship.

ANDREW N. DEHEER

## Evans, Luther
(1902– )

Luther Evans, tenth Librarian of Congress, was Director-General of Unesco. He was born near Sayersville, Texas, on October 13, 1902. After earning a B.A. in 1924 and an M.A. in 1925 at the University of Texas, he completed a Ph.D. at Stanford in Political Science in 1927 with a dissertation on the mandate system of the League of Nations. Short-term instructorships ensued, at New York University (1927) and Dartmouth (1928–30), followed in 1930 by an appointment as Assistant Professor of Politics at Princeton, where he remained until 1935.

In October 1935 Evans was appointed Director of the Historical Records Survey in the Washington office of the Works Progress Administration. The American Imprints Inventory was perhaps their most significant project, as later edited by the Library of Congress and incorporated into the National Union Catalog. Evans remained with that office until joining the staff of the Library of Congress in 1939 as Director of the Legislative Reference Service. He was soon promoted to Chief Assistant Librarian under Archibald MacLeish and served concurrently as Director of the Reference Department. He served as Acting Head (1940–45) during MacLeish's frequent wartime absences and after his resignation in 1944. Evans succeeded MacLeish in December 1945 as the tenth Librarian of Congress, one of the rare appointments to be made from within the ranks.

Most significant of Evans's many accomplishments at the Library include the program to publish the *Cumulative Catalog of Library of Congress Printed Cards* (1947), the issuance of *Rules for Descriptive Cataloging in the Library of Congress* (1949) and *New Serial Titles* (1953), a greatly expanded readership, a 28 percent collection increase despite mounting budgetary restraints, and a democratic philosophy of management that greatly expanded the involvement of library staff in advisory groups.

In November 1945 Archibald MacLeish, then Assistant Secretary of State, invited Evans to join the United Nations delegation to the London Conference, which was ultimately responsible for the establishment of the United Nations Educational, Scientific, and Cultural Organization. In July 1953 Evans was elected third Director-General of Unesco and resigned from the Library of Congress. This move brought to a close the mounting congressional criticism of Evans's continuing extension of services to noncongressional patrons and of his heavy participation in international affairs. His UN term ended in 1958 after active involvement in such major issues as the 1956 agreement on the protection of cultural property in wartime, peaceful use of atomic energy, and the establishment of the Universal Copyright Convention. After leaving the UN, Luther Evans served as an international studies consultant at the University of Texas and directed studies for the Brookings Institution on federal department libraries and the National Education Association on educational implications of automation. He assumed directorship of the international and legal collections at Columbia University in 1962, retiring in 1971 to an ongoing professional involvement in the American Library Association, World Federalists U.S.A., United States Committee for Refugees, U.S. People for the United Nations, and the United Nations Association of the United States of America.

Library of Congress

*Luther Evans, 10th Librarian of Congress.*

**REFERENCE**

William J. Sittig, "Luther Evans: Man for a New Age," *Librarians of Congress, 1802–1974* (1977).

BETTY L. MILUM

## Extension Services

The need to make library services accessible to the public to whom they are directed has led to the development of extension services. Although the provision of library service to branch campuses of academic institutions and the pattern of linking services of special libraries within one corporation share some of the characteristics of extension services in public libraries, it is in the latter type of library that the term is most often used. Discussion of extension services in public libraries typically covers the range of such services.

**Branch Libraries.** Branch libraries serving specified geographic areas or, less commonly, specified publics such as business personnel are the major facilities of extension services. Not all libraries or library systems are large enough or serve a large enough area to require branch library service, but urban libraries and county or multicounty library systems typically are. Usually the service of branch libraries is coordinated and supported by a central library with a more comprehensive collection of materials, by a technical services unit that coordinates selection, acquisition, processing, and delivery of materials, and by such administrative services as personnel, payroll, supplies, physical maintenance, and transportation. The efficiency of the transportation service linking branch libraries to one another and to the central support services is probably the single most important contributor to the

(Top and middle) Library Association of Finland
(Bottom) Gothenberg City Library (*Göteborg, Staatsbibliothek*)

*Top and middle, one of more than 200 Finnish bookmobiles that serve the rural countryside and account for about 18 percent of public library lending.*
*Bottom, twice a year, a bookboat from the county library in Gothenberg, Sweden, visits islands off Sweden's west coast.*

quality of services provided through branch libraries.

Finding and maintaining the appropriate balance between a branch library's relationship to its community and its relationship to the rest of the library system are two of the administrative responsibilities of extension services that require clear priorities and goals, good administrative guidelines and procedures, and consistent communication. The persons who are responsible for individual branch libraries may supervise as many as 50 other employees or as few as one or two part-time workers. They must exercise judgment in deciding what they can do without referral to higher authority and must have a good sense of the relationship of their branch library to others and to the library system as a whole.

Branch library collections, personnel, and programs are distinctive in that their scope and purpose need to be carefully geared to the community that the branch library serves. Staff members must not only be sensitive to the size and composition of the community but also be informed about who its leaders are, what interests and concerns are prevalent, what organizations such as churches and schools exist in the community, and how the library's collection and programs of service can be developed to serve them all most effectively. Interest and experience on the part of library personnel can increase their competence in determining and providing appropriate services, but better understanding may be more likely when they share the same ethnic or socioeconomic background as the people with whom they work.

Services offered by branch libraries are usually comparable to those of central public libraries, differing in range and quantity more than in kind. Because branches typically serve residential areas, their services to children and young people may be more extensive than those of a central library. Among those services customarily offered to youth are storytelling, film programs, holiday observances, summer reading clubs or programs, visits to schools, class visits to libraries, orientation to the use of the library and its resources, and activities such as crafts or photography. Public programs for adults or the general public include adult education courses with emphasis on basic skills and language, film programs, art exhibits, book talks, and other activities similar to those provided for youth. While many programs may be designed to attract people to go to the library and to encourage use of its resources, that need not be the only or the prime goal of programs since the library is an educational and cultural resource, not merely a provider of materials or information. Reference service in person and by telephone, provision of materials on interlibrary loan, reading guidance, space and resources for study, and access to conference rooms and photocopying facilities are still other services that branch libraries offer to their publics.

Since branch libraries are designed to extend the library's services, their locations are of critical importance. Availability of parking, access by the public including children, the elderly, and the handicapped, and functional design and arrangement are important. Clear identification signs are essential. Locations of branch libraries may be permanent or temporary, in library-owned or rented facilities, in buildings designed or adapted for their exclusive use, or in such multiple-purpose facilities as park fieldhouses, settlement houses, schools, or community centers. Experience has shown that there are more failures than successes in library service in jointly operated facilities. Every aspect of planning, maintaining, and operating facilities cooperatively with other agencies may be somewhat more complicated than working independently because all moves should be planned and implemented cooperatively by the agencies concerned.

**Mobile Services.** The variety of mobile library service ranges from a coordinated program of bookmobile service on a regular basis through the delivery of library materials to remote areas to the use of vehicles to promote use of the library. Book drops by airplane, regular boat runs of library deliveries, and even future use of spacecraft for provision of library materials are the more extraordinary examples of this kind of library service.

In the United States provision of library materials by vehicle was an early part of public library history. Remote rural areas where population was sparse and personal transportation limited called for some kind of delivery system. A major impetus to the development of bookmobile service was the Library Services Act of 1956. Demonstrations of library service were often offered by bookmobiles, and response and use were generally enthusiastic. In the same period, the development of new housing areas and the lag in building or renting library facilities led to use of bookmobiles in shopping areas and at community centers, schools, and other locations convenient to an expanding population. Suburban and urban libraries made more use of bookmobiles to reach new publics more conveniently and to serve as testing sites for facilities to be made permanent later.

Traditional bookmobile service has emphasized the provision of books to be borrowed for home use. When stops are maintained on a regular basis over a long period of time, they have often become special service libraries bringing materials specially requested by users from a general collection maintained for the bookmobiles or from other sections of the library. The size and complexity of a bookmobile operation often require drivers and maintenance personnel, while the necessity of adapting the collection to the clientele at individual stops calls for special expertise on the part of the other library staff.

Although bookmobiles have been discontinued in many instances when new permanent public library facilities have been established, they have sometimes been adapted for new uses. In the outreach programs of the 1960's, for example, bookmobiles in housing projects often were the site of such public programs as storytelling, puppet shows, or film programs. Somtimes these were scheduled at the stop and sometimes on the mobile unit itself. The next step, development of a bookmobile with space and equipment for such programming, was a logical one.

Somewhat different in their intent but often serving the same kinds of publics are deposit collections. Rural locations of these have often been in crossroads stores or gasoline stations, but schools, union halls, factories, jury rooms, and community centers are also among the sites where these are located. In instances where public library or state library resources developed before school libraries, it was common practice to provide deposit collections to schools, either to one location or to individual classrooms. This kind of "book box" service has been considerably curtailed in recent years as school library media collections and services have improved. The missing component in providing deposit collections has been personnel, and when these collections have also become static or limited, their use and popularity have decreased. The availability of such relatively inexpensive materials as paperback books and magazines for general reading is another factor in the decline of such collections.

Mobile service to individuals whose geographic location or physical debility limits their access to libraries is also provided by some public libraries. Instances of it include the delivery of books to the homebound by volunteers or staff members on foot or in cars. The major differences between this and general bookmobile service are that this service is personalized, with deliveries usually based on requests and with no browsing opportunity available to those receiving the service.

Delivery by book truck or small mobile unit to individual cells or residential units of correctional institutions is another kind of mobile service. Senior citizens' group residences, hospitals, and long-term health care centers are other sites for which individual services are often provided in this or a similar way.

**Books by Mail.** For a number of reasons, mail or parcel delivery service to provide books to individuals may be developed as more economical than personalized delivery. Catalogues of materials available on this basis are compiled and distributed to borrowers, who make their selections and assume responsibility for returning the materials. Paperback books are often the major component of such plans, but when individuals have greater choice, including occasional selections not included in the catalogues, the benefits of the service increase, as do the costs.

In all extension services, cost and imagination are the only major limitations. The more precisely a service is targeted, such as mail deliveries to individuals, the more it is likely to be appreciated by those receiving it but also the more costly it is likely to be on the basis of number of people served or number of items provided. On the other hand, in the myriad activities and resources of a flourishing regional branch library, it is difficult to measure cost effectiveness simply because neither the public's uses and requests nor the resources of the library remain constant.

Extension services are effective and valuable when they increase the library's visibility and audience. Following the fine line between doing this and spreading finite resources too thin requires planning, judgment, evaluation, and continuous review and, when necessary, reevaluation and change of priorities and objectives.

PEGGY SULLIVAN

## Ferguson, Sir John Alexander
(1881–1969)

Sir John Alexander Ferguson, industrial court judge, bibliographer, book collector, and compiler of the *Bibliography of Australia 1784–1900,* was born in Invercargill, New Zealand, December 15, 1881. His family went to Australia when his father was appointed as minister to Saint Stephen's Church in Sydney. Attending William Street Superior Public School and later studying with a private tutor, Ferguson matriculated to the University of Sydney and earned a B.A. with First Class Honours and the University Medal in Logic and Mental Philosophy. In his law school he earned the George Wigram Allen scholarship for most distinguished arts graduate entering the school and later was awarded the Pitt Cobbet Prize for international law. Admitted to the Bar on May 27, 1905, he practiced first in equity and continued in that jurisdiction despite a developing and important practice in industrial law.

By the early 1930's J. A. Ferguson was regarded as the leading barrister in the industrial jurisdiction in New South Wales and was appointed Lecturer in Industrial Law at Sydney University. In 1936 he was elevated to the Bench of the Industrial Commission of New South Wales, and during the 17 years before his retirement he made an important contribution to the industrial affairs of his state.

Early in life Ferguson began to collect and to describe materials relating to Australia, New Zealand, and the Pacific Islands, regarding them as complementary activities. As a collector, his personal and scholarly interests found emphasis in bibliography, law, imaginative literature, social reform, military history, church affairs, the mission fields, and publishing. The influence of his father and his own lifelong association with the church led to a collecting interest in the church and missions in the Pacific areas and to the development of one of the most comprehensive collections of its vernacular publications. His *Bibliography of the New Hebrides* appeared in three parts between 1917 and 1945.

A number of other bibliographical compilations were placed aside as Ferguson devoted himself to his great compilation, the *Bibliography of Australia, 1784–1900,* the first volume of which appeared in 1941; his work on the seventh and final volume continued, despite frailty of health, into his 80th year, the checking of the proofs completed just a week or so before his death. The *Bibliography* is an important tool of the historian, the book collector, the librarian, and the dealer in rare and out-of-print books. But above all other considerations, John Ferguson saw his primary purpose, as a bibliographer and as a collector, to be the service of scholarship and research. Neither vanity nor greed led him to depart from a rational attitude to collecting by purchasing unique items at outrageous prices; his object was not to ornament his collection with priceless gems but to gather a substantial body of material of value for research.

As early as 1909 Ferguson had begun a relationship with the National Library that continued throughout his life. In 1937 he made the first transfer to the Library of part of his collection: "newspapers and periodicals illustrating the growth of all forms of political, social, economic and industrial thought in the Commonwealth." Further transfers included a large group of pamphlets in the same subject area, his "sociological pamphlets," arranged in the chronological order that he regarded as being of great importance. The continuing transfer of other subject groups left a still considerable amount of the collection in his home at his death on May 7, 1969. The Library purchased it from the Ferguson Estate and some time later, in 1975, acquired the copyright of the *Bibliography of Austrlia,* of which it published a new edition between 1975 and 1977. The Ferguson Room in the National Library is named in his honor.

Ferguson served with distinction as an office-bearer of the Royal Australian Historical Society, the Captain Cook Landing Place Trust, and from 1935 to 1965 he served as a Trustee of the Public Library of New South Wales. His old university honored him in 1955 with the degree of Doctor of Letters, and in 1961 he was knighted for services to Australian literature, bibliography, and history. Ferguson's first wife, whom he married in 1906, was Bessie Robertson, daughter of George Robertson, founder of the bookselling and publishing firm of Angus & Robertson, a factor that undoubtedly stimulated and facilitated Ferguson's interest in Australian books. The family, three sons and a daughter, had reached adulthood at the time of their mother's death in 1937, and Ferguson threw himself even more vigorously into his bibliographical and collecting activity. In 1945 he married Dorothy Johnson and in the "enlivening orbit of a growing family," a son and daughter of his second marriage, he was, in retirement from his judicial duties, to devote continuing attention to his great *Bibliography* and to his collection, which including the sections already transferred, totaled some 34,000 items at his death.

C. A. BURMESTER

# Fiji

Fiji, an independent parliamentary state, includes a group of islands in the South Pacific Ocean. It lies approximately 3,200 km. east of Australia and 5,200 km. south of Hawaii. Pop. (1978 est.) 612,000; area 18,272 sq. km. The official language is English.

**National Library.** Fiji possesses no national library, but the most significant step toward that goal was the founding of the Fiji Library Service (FLS) in 1962 as a department of the Ministry of State for Social Welfare. The FLS operates public branches in all major townships, two bookmobiles, postal loan services (1,129 correspondents), and a book box project (90 stations). Its coverage was limited to Fiji's two main islands at the end of the 1970's; and geographical obstacles were imposed by a widely spread chain of islands.

The FLS also pursues a professional staff training program for government libraries and organized an annual Fiji Certificate in Librarianship course for the training of subprofessionals. By extending its influence over technical operations and professional standards, the FLS looked toward obtaining statutory independence with its own Library Board and ultimately "national library" status. An FLS administrative headquarters was established in the capital city of Suva under a British grant. FLS hopes to incorporate the Suva City Library into its system and launch a truly inclusive national network.

**Academic Libraries.** The only university, the University of the South Pacific, established in 1967 in Suva, has the nation's largest single library, with 160,000 volumes, nine professional librarians—more professionals than in the rest of Fiji combined in 1979—and a regional clientele of 11 South Pacific nations. The University is augmented by smaller collections housed in the Pacific Theological College (25,000 volumes), Nasinu Teacher Training College (16,000), and the Fiji School of Medicine's Medical Research Library (8,000).

**Public Libraries.** Predominant libraries are the Western Regional (55,000 volumes) and Suva City (38,000). After World War II, when reading provision became more widely acknowledged as a public concern, Suva's private Carnegie Library (1909) was transformed into a public institution under city control. By 1977 the Library's single professional librarian had introduced a children's section and a bookmobile serving 25 city schools. Rural library service remains inadequate; public libraries, the FLS network, and bookshops are all confined to the towns. Books in general, and Hindi and Fijian language books in particular, are in limited supply.

**School Libraries.** Before 1940 no school libraries existed, but by the end of 1978, 20 of Fiji's nearly 800 public schools supported libraries containing from 1,000 to 7,000 volumes. Not a single trained teacher-librarian was available to run any of those libraries in mid-1979.

**Table 1. Archives in Fiji (1976)**

| | |
|---|---|
| Number | 1 government archives |
| Holdings | 4,571 cubic meters |
| Annual expenditures | F$58,000 |
| Professional staff | 2 |
| All staff | 16 |

Source: National Archives of Fiji

**Special Libraries.** British sugar interests established Fiji's first lending libraries on a subscription basis, beginning in 1882. The Ramakrishna Library of books in South Indian languages (1928) long served with Suva's Carnegie Library as the islands' major source of reading material. Special libraries number about 20, including academic and government holdings.

The 15,000-volume Indian Cultural Centre serves as a vital source of material for and about ethnic Indians, who comprise about half of Fiji's total population.

The government has maintained archives since 1954, and an official National Archives was established in 1969. An exceptional 5,000-volume local history and records li-

Caines Jannif Ltd.

*The University of the South Pacific Library in Suva, established in 1967, is Fiji's largest library.*

**Table 2. Libraries in Fiji (1976)**

| Type | Number | Volumes in collections | Annual expenditures[a] (Fiji dollar) | Population served | Professional staff | All staff (total) |
|---|---|---|---|---|---|---|
| Academic | 5[b] | 201,000 | F$75,000 | ca. 6,000 | 13 | ca. 50 |
| Public | 7 | 109,000 | F$145,000[c] | 117,000 | 5[d] | ca. 50[d] |
| School | 21[e] | 250,000[f] | N.A. | 165,500[g] | 3 | 33[h] |
| Special | 18[i] | 86,000 | [c] | N.A. | 4 | [d] |

[a]Books only.
[b]Includes university, two teacher training colleges at Nausori and Lautoka, Fiji Institute of Technology, and Corpus Christi Teachers College.
[c]Includes government expenditures on books for the Fiji Library Service, departmental libraries, and government special libraries.
[d]Public, government departmental, and special.
[e]The Fiji Library Directory (1977) listed 21 school libraries, representing the larger, more organized libraries. Statistics of schools boasting a separate room for library books (as distinct from classroom libraries) are: 132 primary schools and 59 secondary schools.
[f]Includes all texts and other books in all schools (not just in library collections, the figure for which is not known). The Fiji Library Directory gave 75,000 for the 21 schools listed.
[g]School children: primary: 132,500; secondary: 33,000.
[h]Teachers who attended library courses (subprofessional): 33; part-time teachers without training: 324.
[i]Includes specialized colleges for theology, medicine, and agriculture, in addition to government departmental and other special libraries.

brary housed in the Archives and under professional control contains rich documentary materials dating well into the 19th century. Government departments also maintain notable collections, particularly the Ministry of Education's Educational Research Centre (13,000 volumes), the Supreme Court (12,000), and the Department of Agriculture (6,000).

Growing awareness of the importance of information has led to the creation of new special libraries such as those of the Fiji Electricity Authority, the Fiji Development Bank, and the Trades Union Congress.

**Association.** The Fiji Library Association (FLA) was founded in 1972. Its membership in 1978 stood at 106 (including all 29 major libraries).

HAROLD HOLDSWORTH

# Finland

Finland, a republic in northern Europe, is bounded by Norway on the north, Sweden and the Gulf of Bothnia on the west, and the U.S.S.R. on the east. Pop. (1978 est.) 4,752,000; area 337,032 sq.km. The official languages are Finnish and Swedish.

**National Library.** The national library of Finland is the Helsinki University Library, established in 1640 in Turku as the Turku Academy Library and transferred to Helsinki in 1828 together with the Academy, which then became the Helsinki University. Its tasks include those of a national library and of a general research library. It collects all publications printed in Finland and publications written by Finns or dealing with Finland but published elsewhere, in addition to foreign literature for the study and research needs of Helsinki University. It also collects manuscripts dealing with Finnish cultural history and compiles the Finnish national bibliography and the union catalogue of Finnish research and university libraries. It receives publications on legal deposit and distributes them to other libraries. Among its resources is a special collection of Slavonic literature, started in 1820 when Finland became a grand duchy of Russia and the library received deposit copies of publications printed in that country. The library's holdings totaled 1,810,000 volumes in 1976, making it not only the oldest but also the largest library in Finland.

**Academic Libraries.** There are 22 academic libraries in Finland, a great number for a small country. Helsinki University was the only university until 1919, when Åbo Akademi, a Swedish university, was founded in Turku. Two years later a Finnish university was also founded in Turku. From their beginnings they were both remarkable, with national as well as foreign collections. In 1976 there were 1,085,240 volumes in the Turku University Library and 937,570 volumes in the Åbo Akademi Library. The first technical library in Finland was founded in 1849 in the Helsinki Technical School; it later became the Helsinki Technical University, and its library had a collection of 325,430 volumes in 1976. The Helsinki School of Economics Library was founded in 1911; it had

142,800 volumes in the late 1970's. After World War II several institutions of higher education were founded, among them the universities of Jyväskylä, Oulu, and Tampere. Only the Oulu University was actually a new institution; in Jyväskylä the Teachers' College was made into a university, and Tampere got a university when the School of Social Sciences was transferred from Helsinki and later became a university. In 1976 the Jyväskylä University Library had a collection of 699,700 volumes, the Oulu University Library 618,600 volumes, and the Tampere University Library about 398,000. These universities and other academic institutions have worked together with special libraries to provide new forms of information service, and some function as central libraries in their respective fields according to a Cabinet Statute of 1972. A special feature in the history of Finnish academic libraries was the student libraries. The student unions established libraries of their own; some of them, like the Library of the Student Body of Helsinki University, were quite remarkable. Founded in 1858, it had its own building and a collection of 200,000 volumes when in 1974 it became a part of the Helsinki University Library. The student libraries have merged with university libraries during recent years.

**Public Libraries.** The oldest public library in Finland is the library of the Regina School in Anjala, established in 1804. Its collection is now in a museum at the Central Board of Schools, where the government office for public libraries is housed. Public libraries, in the true sense of the word, came into being in the middle of the 19th century through the initiative of students and clergy. From the beginning public libraries were local municipal institutions, and state aid was not given to them until 1921, four years after the country became independent. In 1921 the State Library Bureau was set up and a group of library inspectors elected to direct library activities. The first Public Library Act was passed in 1928 and the second in 1962, giving strong support to rural municipalities and to libraries in hospitals and social institutions. The second Act also made it possible to found central regional libraries, whose main task is to serve as interlibrary lending centers, borrowing material from research and university libraries for the public libraries. Many small public libraries have been replaced by bookmobiles; thus the number of public libraries was 4,007 in 1960 and 2,903 in 1970, while the number of home loans was 15,300,000 in 1960 and 32,400,000 in 1970. Public libraries in Finland have taken on the functions of cultural centers, arranging, for example, for concerts, exhibitions, and puppet theater performances.

**School Libraries.** There is no organized system of school libraries in Finland, but by the late 1970's school libraries were included in plans for a comprehensive school system.

**Table 2. Archives in Finland (1977)**

| | |
|---|---|
| Number | 8 (the National Archives and 7 Provincial Archives) |
| Holdings | 69,067 linear meters of shelving |
| Annual expenditures | 7,399,321 Fmk (approximately $1,880,000) |
| Professional staff | 43 |
| All staff (total) | 148 |

Source: The National Archives of Finland.

**Special Libraries.** The oldest special libraries in Finland were the libraries of the scientific societies, founded in the early and middle 19th century. Most special libraries are now part of private firms and institutions. Typical of their activity are information service and documentation; documentation started in Finland in the 1940's in industrial libraries, where the first documentalists were en-

**Table 1. Libraries in Finland (1976)**

| Type | Number | Volumes in collections | Annual expenditures (markka) | Population served | Professional staff | All staff (total) |
|---|---|---|---|---|---|---|
| National | 1 | 1,810,000 | Fmk 1,204,000[a] | N.A. | 68.4[b] | 169.7[b] |
| Academic | 22 | 4,988,065 | 27,831,400[c] | 82,091[d] | 225.2[b] | 554.6[b] |
| Public | 1,890[e] | 17,228,890 | 181,387,212 | 4,693,522 | 2,300[e] | 3,500[e] |
| School | 0 | 0 | 0 | 0 | 0 | 0 |
| Special | 17[f] | 1,835,814[f] | 7,598,48 0[f] | | 85[bf] | 460.8[bf] |

Since all libraries in Finland are not included in the official statistics, the following will give only partial information. In reality the figures are higher.

[a]Staff not included.

[b]In working years.

[c]Incomplete.

[d]Contains only students and teachers. In Finland, however, the academic libraries are open to the general public.

[e]An estimated figure.

[f]The biggest libraries only. There are about 300 research and university libraries in Finland altogether.

Töölö Library

*Exterior (p. 200) and interior (above) of the Töölö branch of the Helsinki City Library, designed by Finnish architect Aarne Ervi, and opened in 1970.*

gineers. Among Finland's special libraries are such large libraries as the Parliament Library, founded in 1872 and having a collection of 411,000 volumes, and the remarkable Central Medical Library, established in 1966 and holding some 300,000 volumes. Most of the special libraries are small, however, forming a part of bigger organizations. Several of these libraries belong to an international information network and compile special bibliographies in their respective fields.

**Associations.** The Finnish Library Association dates back to 1910; it publishes a Finnish library journal, *Kirjastolehti.* The Finnish Research Library Association dates from 1929; together with the Finnish Association for Documentation it publishes the journal *Signum.* All three associations arrange meetings, seminars, courses, and national meetings of librarians are held every second year. There are other associations in the field of librarianship, book sciences, and documentation, including professional unions.

RITVA SIEVÄNEN-ALLEN

# Folger, Henry Clay
(1857–1930)

Henry Clay Folger, U.S. businessman who headed Standard Oil Company of New York, was one of the great book collectors of the late 19th and early 20th centuries. With invaluable assistance from his wife, Emily Jordan, he brought together a remarkable collection of books, manuscripts, art objects, and other materials relating to Shakespeare, his works, and his age. Folger and his wife founded the Folger Shakespeare Library in Washington, D.C., to house their collection and to make it accessible to an international community of researchers.

Henry Folger belonged to a family with distinguished American antecedents. Peter Folger, the first of the name to settle in America, emigrated from England and settled on Nantucket Island in 1635; his daughter was the mother of Benjamin Franklin. Several generations later another descendant, Charles James Folger, served President Chester Arthur as Secretary of the Treasury. Henry Folger's father was a resident of New York City who built up a prosperous wholesale millinery business and sent his son to grammar and high school in the New York area.

Henry Folger entered Amherst College in 1875. For a time his continuation at Amherst was threatened by his father's financial reverses, but timely loans from two classmates permitted Henry to complete his course of studies there, and he graduated in 1879. A career in business seemed tempting; with the help of his college roommate, Charles Pratt, whose father headed one of the affiliates of Standard Oil, Folger accepted a clerkship in the company. He also enrolled in the Columbia University Law School and two years later obtained an L.L.B. degree. A steady climb up the corporate ladder rewarded Henry Folger for his shrewd business sense and industrious dedication to the growth of the company. He became President of Standard Oil of New York and held that post until 1923, when he was made Chairman of the Board. He retired from active involvement in the company in 1928.

Despite his corporate responsibilities, Henry Folger retained a keen interest in the world of letters. The published address by Ralph Waldo Emerson on the "Tercentenary of Shakespeare's Birth," which Folger had read as an undergraduate, fired him with an enthusiastic appreciation for Shakespeare that never waned. Indeed, his marriage to Emily Clara Jordan intensified it. She was a Vassar graduate who continued to graduate school after her marriage and wrote a Master of Arts thesis on "The True Text of Shakespeare."

Their shared interest in Shakespeare led the Folgers quite early into book collecting. Starting in 1885 with a relatively cheap facsimile of the 1623 First Folio edition of Shakespeare's works, the pursuit of Shakespeareana accelerated as the Folgers' financial means to satisfy their hobby increased. Soon they were combing bookshops on both sides of the Atlantic. Rare quarto editions of Shakespeare's plays and the first folio edition of his collected works were those most sought by the Folgers, but they also looked for later editions of the plays and materials reflecting Shakespeare production down to modern times, including printed texts, promptbooks, playbills, paintings and illustrations, costumes, and memorabilia of all sorts. They wisely realized that Shakespeare could best be understood in the context of the times in which he lived; they purchased books that reveal the sources for plots and ideas contained in his plays, the works of his contemporaries in the literary world, and a wide spectrum of rare books and manuscripts depicting the society of Elizabethan and Jacobean England and, more generally, Western Europe and America in the early modern period.

The Folgers amassed a collection of some 93,000 books, 50,000 prints and engravings, and thousands of manuscripts that, for lack of space, they carefully inventoried and then stored in bank vaults and warehouses. Shortly after World War I they determined to unite their collection in a library dedicated to Shakespeare. The site they selected in Washington, D.C., was directly across from the Library of Congress, whose resources they knew would enhance the value of their own Library. The cornerstone for their Library was laid May 28, 1930. Two weeks later Henry Clay Folger succumbed to a heart attack and never saw his dream fulfilled. Mrs. Folger was present for the opening of the Library on April 23, 1932, however; she was involved closely with its operation until her death in 1936. Under the terms of Folger's will the administration of the Library was entrusted to the Trustees of his alma mater, Amherst College. Folger and his wife left the bulk of their estates to serve as endowment

Folger Shakespeare Library

*Henry Clay Folger*

to defray the operating costs of their Library. Following the lines laid out by its founders, the Folger Shakespeare Library has become an international center for the study of Shakespeare and of the Renaissance and early modern period. The Library's exhibition gallery attracts thousands of visitors each year to view items from the original Folger Collection as well as many later acquisitions. An Elizabethan theater, which is an integral part of the Library, provides thousands more with an opportunity to enjoy theatrical productions both Shakespearean and modern, concerts of Renaissance music, lectures, and conferences.

**REFERENCE**
Beety Ann Kane, *The Widening Circle—the Story of the Folger Shakespeare Library and Its Collections* (Folger Library, 1976).

PHILIP A. KNACHEL

## Food and Agriculture Organization

The Food and Agriculture Organization of the United Nations is an autonomous, specialized agency in the United Nations system. It is made up of 144 member nations who have pledged themselves to action: to raise the levels of nutrition and standards of living of their peoples; to secure improved production and distribution of all food and agricultural products; to better the condition of rural populations; and to contribute to an expanding world economy and ensure mankind's freedom from hunger and poverty.



Established in October 1945 at a conference in Québec, Canada, FAO's headquarters were in Rome from 1951; it established regional offices in Santiago, Chile; Accra, Ghana; Cairo, Egypt; and Bangkok, Thailand. There is a Liaison Office for North America in Washington, D.C., and country representatives in a number of developing nations.

The work of the organization is conducted by an international Secretariat under the leadership of a Director-General. It is governed by the biennial FAO Conference of all member countries.

FAO has a field program through which a corps of technical experts helps countries plan and execute their development programs and deal with impediments to the development of their agriculture, fisheries, and forestry. The Organization also helps developing countries to obtain financing for their development activities through arrangements with a number of lending agencies such as the World Bank. The Organization stimulates and services international consultation and negotiation in its fields of concern.

FAO is also a world source of information. It carries on a considerable publishing program through which it disseminates technical and economic information compiled from all over the world. It also operates and coordinates several international documentation systems. The International Information System for the Agricultural Sciences and Technology (AGRIS) is a current awareness system that covers literature on subjects within FAO's scope. AGRIS produces the printed monthly bibliography AGRINDEX, containing, as of January 1979, more than 350,000 records, available for consultation on magnetic tape or through direct interrogation by telephone. More than 100 countries participate in the system, which is open to all interested individual researchers and institutions.

The Current Agricultural Research Information System (CARIS) is an international information system that compiles and disseminates basic data on current research in developing countries in agriculture, forestry, fisheries, animal production, and food. It is published in directories available in English, French, and Spanish versions and also on magnetic tape. The assembled data cover 2,000 research institutions, 10,000 research specialists, and 3,300 research programs listing 20,000 research projects.

FAO also publishes a monthly analytical bulletin, the *FAO Documentation Current Bibliography,* which comes with author and subject indexes and records all the current publications and documents issued by the Organization. It is available free of charge on request.

FAO was also preparing in 1979 a Union List of serial titles regularly indexed in AGRINDEX. The List was to contain about 8,000 titles of scientific and technical journals in FAO's fields of interest and provide holding information on these journals in the 17 major agricultural libraries in the world that constitute the AGLINET (Agricultural Libraries Network) System.

*Peter Force*

Courtesy of The Newberry Library

## Force, Peter
(1790–1868)

Compiler of historical documents, bibliophile and collector, printer, editor, bibliographer, librarian, archivist, Peter Force was born near Little Falls, Essex County, New Jersey, November 26, 1790. His family moved several times before settling in New York City in 1794, where he received limited schooling. Early in his teens he became an apprentice in the printing business of William A. Davis and assumed the responsibilities of print shop foreman at about the age of 16. The New York Typographical Society elected him its President in 1812. He won a militia commission during the War of 1812 and served as marshal of printers.

Force moved to Washington, D.C., in 1815 when Davis secured a government printing contract, and they operated a lending library of over 3,000 volumes out of their printery until debts compelled them to sell the books in 1825. From 1823 to 1831 Force published a newspaper, the *National Journal,* aligned with Adams's administration. A Whig, Force participated in District of Columbia politics, sitting on the city council and winning the mayorality for two terms (1836–40). He also edited directories of government personnel, commercial statistics, and historical data intermittently from 1820 to 1836. His industriousness notwithstanding, creditors in 1830 nearly seized his property, which already included another substantial library.

Financial motives, along with a genuine veneration of America's past, inspired Force to propose in 1831 publishing for the federal government a multivolume compilation of historical documents. The idea was not original, but Force and his partner, Clerk of the House Matthew St. Clair Clarke, promised unprecedented thoroughness. Congress authorized the project in 1833. Sadly, the lucrative contract left unclear the exact scope and cost of the work, and the *American Archives,* as it became known, thus suffered repeated attacks by the frugal as well as by the politically antipathetic.

Force supervised researchers and dealers dispersed through the 13 original states and England in transcribing or purchasing pamphlets, books, newspapers, maps, government documents, and manuscripts. His preference for printed sources may reflect his lack of scholarly training. His eye for ephemeral pieces, however, preserved a number of texts from historical oblivion. Copyists received instructions on careful handling of archival materials that were exemplary for their time. Publication commenced in 1837; showing a canny sense of patriotic appeal, Force started with the fourth and fifth series (covering 1774–76) of the six (1492–1787) he scheduled to complete the work. In 1853, the Democrats having deprived the Whigs of the presidency, Secretary of State William L. Marcy refused to approve the contents of the next two volumes, and subsequent changes of administration failed to revive the *American Archives.* Truncation of the project left Force holding a huge collection of rare Americana, with obligations to match.

Even in its abbreviated form, the *American Archives* was an impressive undertaking. Major bibliographies on colonial America still cite its over 16,000 folio pages as a basic resource. Historians also continue to use Force's *Tracts and Other Papers Relating . . . to . . . the Colonies of North America* (1836–46). This four-volume work reproduced 52 pamphlets, some of which Force had already reprinted separately. Most were 17th-century London imprints, scarce even by 1836, when the *Tracts* began to appear. The set reveals Force's personal bibliophilic leanings better than the *American Archives.* "Whenever I found a little more money in my purse than I absolutely needed," he later recalled, "I printed a volume of Tracts."

Loss of income from the *American Archives* transformed Force's matchless collection into a passion he could ill afford during the last 15 years of his life. Librarian of Congress Ainsworth R. Spofford for years visited the reclusive, old man, surrounded in his Washington residence by crude tables and shelves bearing his treasures. Spofford and others yearned to relieve the owner of them; Force finally agreed for a price of $100,000. The New York Historical Society could not raise the sum, but Spofford managed with difficulty to extract the money from a wartime Congress. So the "Force Library" in 1867 became a primary foundation for future development of Americana holdings at the Library of Congress. Force died, less than a year after the collection left his home, on January 23, 1868.

Force made several noteworthy contributions to library and archival science. He created research tools that remain useful almost a century and a half later. With Spofford's good offices, he furthered the growth of the Library of Congress. Most importantly, he communicated to a young nation the vitality of his concern about collecting and preserving records of its past. His *American Archives* mark a giant step toward federal recognition of a public responsibility to assist in the dissemination of historical information. Force's publications became models that local governments and historical organizations before long emulated with happy results.

**REFERENCES**

The main body of Force's personal papers now resides in the Manuscript Division of the Library of Congress. Among the most useful published accounts are: Newman F. McGirr, compiler, *Bio-Bibliography of Peter Force 1790–1868* (1941), especially useful in locating works by Force and government document citations, Ainsworth R. Spofford, "The Life and Labors of Peter Force, Mayor of Washington," *Records of the Columbia Historical Society* (1899); and Richard W. Stephenson, "Maps from the Peter Force Collection," *Quarterly Journal of the Library of Congress* (1973), an illustrated, specialized study that includes a good general overview.

DAVID J. MARTZ, JR.

## Foskett, D(ouglas) J(ohn)
(1918– )

Library Association

*D. J. Foskett*

One of the most prominent figures in contemporary British library and information science, Douglas John Foskett was born on June 27, 1918. He had hardly begun his professional career in the Ilford Public Libraries when World War II intervened; from 1940 to 1946 he served first in the Royal Army Medical Corps and later in the Intelligence Corps.

In 1948 Foskett left Ilford to become Librarian of the Metal Box Co. Ltd., a post he held until 1957. He then became Librarian of the University of London Institute of Education until 1978, when he was promoted to the position of Director of Central Library Services of the University of London. He thus had a wide experience in public, special, and academic libraries.

His contributions to library and information science are many, varied, and important. A member of the Council of the Library Association for many years, he was Chairman (1962–63), a Vice-President (1966–73), an Honorary Fellow (1975), and President (1976). He has been a vigorous protagonist for the unity of the profession and has consistently supported the idea of a confederation among the LA, Aslib, the Institute of Information Scientists, and other related bodies. He was for some time Chairman of the LA Education Committee and influenced the forward march for librarianship in Britain in positive and beneficial ways.

Foskett also became an internationalist, having undertaken numerous missions for Unesco and the British Council and having been on lecture and observation study tours in most parts of the world. From 1968 to 1973 he was a member and rapporteur of Unesco's International Advisory Committee on Documentation, Libraries, and Archives; he also was a consultant on documentation to the International Labour Organisation. He was later a committee member of the UNISIST/Unesco and the EUDISED/Council of Europe projects. An engaging speaker, Foskett served as Visiting Professor at the Universities of Michigan, Ghana, Ibadan, and Iceland and at the Brazilian Institute of Bibliography and Documentation. He made observation tours to Czechoslovakia and the People's Republic of China.

A prolific writer on library and information topics, he wrote, among other works, *Assistance to Readers in Lending Libraries* (1952), *Information Service in Libraries* (1958), *Classification and Indexing in the Social Sciences* (1963), *Science, Humanism and Libraries* (1964), and *Reader in Comparative Librarianship* (1976). With B. I. Palmer he edited *The Sayers Memorial Volume,* a tribute to W. C. Berwick Sayers published by the LA in 1961. He contributed chapters to a number of other books and regularly contributed to professional journals.

Classification was always one of Foskett's major interests, and in 1952 he was one of the founders of the Classification Research Group in Britain. But he proved equally influential in the fields of comparative librarianship and library education and in the development of the Library Association.

K. C. HARRISON



## France

France, a republic in northwestern Europe, is bounded by the English Channel, Belgium, and Luxembourg on the north, Spain and the Mediterranean Sea on the south, the

Atlantic Ocean and the Bay of Biscay on the west, and Germany, Switzerland, and Italy on the east. Pop. (1978 est.) 53,196,000; area 544,000 sq.km. The official language is French.

**Early History: Naudé and the Bibliothèque Mazarine.** When Cardinal Mazarin, Richelieu's successor as first minister of France, arrived in Paris in 1640, he brought with him a rich personal library of 5,000 volumes, which he had collected in Rome. In 1642 he purchased the Hôtel Tubeuf on the corner of rue Neuve des Petits Champs and rue de Richelieu and decided to establish a large library on the premises. To carry out this project he chose Gabriel Naudé, who had formerly been Richelieu's Librarian.

Naudé was a scholar and book lover. Although his studies had been in medicine, his career was in books: he was, in turn, the Librarian of Cardinal Bagni, of Cardinal Barberini, and in 1642 of Cardinal Richelieu. After Richelieu's death that same year, Naudé became Mazarin's Librarian, buying large collections of books (12,000 volumes and 400 manuscripts) and compiling a catalogue. The library at the Hôtel Tubeuf was opened to the public in 1644 on every Thursday, with between 80 and 100 readers each open day. Naudé traveled far and wide in Europe buying for the collection, and Mazarin built several additions to house the 40,000 volumes handsomely bound and emblazoned with his arms.

During the Fronde (civil wars, 1648–53), however, the collection was dispersed in public sales, and Naudé died in 1653. After Mazarin's return to France that year, he rebuilt his library with the help of François Lapoterie, his new Librarian. Mazarin's library was reconstituted, and new collections, including Naudé's personal library, were bought. Mazarin, who died in 1661, left his library to the "Collège des Quatre Nations," founded according to his will for students from the four provinces conquered by France; thus began the Bibliothèque Mazarine.

**Bibliothèques Communales and the Impact of the French Revolution.** Other than the Bibliothèque Mazarine and a few collections of the 13th and 14th centuries, which were available only to scholars, there were only private libraries in France before the Revolution. The first network of public libraries was established by the Revolution. Property that had belonged to the aristocracy and to the Church, including numerous libraries, was confiscated; the libraries became the nuclei of a widespread public library system. Clerical properties were put at "the Nation's disposal" on November 2, 1789, and some months later the property of émigrés and of persons condemned by the Terror was sequestered. The total number of confiscated books was evaluated at 10,000,000 by the Abbé Grégoire in a report to the Convention dated April 11, 1794; there also were about 26,000 manuscripts (for comparison, the Royal Library contained 300,000 volumes).

In order to classify this mass of documents, an inventory had to be taken. The catalogue was actually written on playing cards. Then a Conservation Committee picked out for sale a certain number of books on theology, religion, and "ascetics." Books not put up for sale were stocked in "literary depots" in Paris and other cities, then divided among existing libraries (the Bibliothèque Nationale received 300,000 volumes) and given to "Central schools" formed in 1795 in each department. After the suppression of those schools in 1803, the books were given to the communes to create new libraries. Special libraries were also founded, including those of the Assemblée Nationale, the Cour de Cassation, the Collège de France, and the Museum d'Histoire Naturelle.

But there was a contradiction between the intentions of the authorities and their methods. The Revolutionary project was to set up libraries to serve as "a school for all citizens," but the collections confiscated from the nobility and the Church mainly consisted of works on theology, jurisprudence, and ancient literature—not what was required for popular education. Inertia prevailed, however, and the public library system that could have come into being failed to do so. Libraries were oriented toward conservation and learned studies. No acquisition policy came to balance the enormous mass of ancient documents for which the public authorities were henceforth responsible.

At the end of the Revolutionary period many large libraries in France still had not been inventoried, and they often were concerned more about ensuring the security of their collections than increasing them or opening them to the public. The librarians of these collections, so rich in history, literature, and theology, were bound to look toward the past—the paradoxical heritage of the French Revolution. This predominating influence of the past was the most striking feature of French public libraries until the 20th century; indeed, it continues to influence the whole of French librarianship.

**Bibliothèque Nationale.** The Bibliothèque Nationale is an outgrowth of the Royal Library, which dates back to the reign of Charles V (1364–80). Appreciating the manuscript treasures he inherited from his royal ancestors, he put them in the Louvre and appointed a scholar, Gilles Malet, to catalogue them. During the fluctuations of royal history, the King's Library nevertheless became dispersed, but it was enthusiastically rebuilt by Francis I, who, with the help of his ambassadors (notably in Germany, Venice, and the Middle East), bought numerous manuscripts. So, after a number of vicissitudes, the Bibliothèque Nationale, thus renamed by the Revolution, in 1721 found a permanent home on the rue de Richelieu.

*Copyright Deposit.* Legal deposit in France stems from Francis I (1494–1547), who in his Montpellier regulation of September, 28, 1537, provided that one copy of every book published in France be deposited in the Royal Library to qualify for the King's authorization. Several texts modify this ruling, the latest being a law of June 21, 1941, when two deposits were established. Each printer is required to send two copies to the municipal library in his region, and one is passed on to the Bibliothèque Nationale, and each publisher must send four copies to the Bibliothèque Nationale and two to the Ministry of the Interior.

All types of documents are subject to legal deposit rule (postcards, books, periodicals, brochures, prints, engravings, posters, music, films, records, and photographs). A decree of July 30, 1975, added audiovisual materials.

Copyright deposit statistics for 1976 are: printed books, 34,257 volumes for 25,800 titles; brochures, 10,366; official publications, 6,286; serials, 30,000 titles; maps, 6,000 sheets; engravings, 1,181; posters, 7,130; coins, 642; musical works, 2,559; records, 10,346; and microforms, 435.

*Organization.* A decree of November 19, 1977, appreciably modified the administrative structure of the Bibliothèque Nationale, taking into account the decree of July 24, 1975, which withdrew the management of French libraries from the control previously possessed by the general Administrator of the Bibliothèque Nationale.

The Bibliothèque Nationale is a public institution, which is to say by French law an institution with financial autonomy under the control of the Ministry of Universities. Its objectives are described in the decree: conservation of national production, encyclopedic documentation (mostly in the humanities), and responsibility for the Technical Cooperation Centers (the National Bibliographic Center, the National Lending Center, the National Exchange Center, and the National Center of Rare Books).

The General Administrator is assisted by a Board of

Directors, with 25 members, and a Scientific Council, which gives advice on the research program of the Bibliothèque Nationale. The Library is divided into three divisions composed of several departments: the Administrative Division, headed by the Secretary General and by a "Chargé de Mission," includes finances, personnel, publications, exhibitions, and the legal deposit; the Division of Printed Documents includes the departments of printed books, official publications, serials, and the Bibliothèque de l'Arsenal; and the division of Special Documents includes the departments of maps and charts, manuscripts, prints, coins and medals, music, performing arts, as well as the Phonotèque Nationale.

The Library's budget draws upon allocations from the Ministry of Universities and upon gifts, legacies, and the sale of publications. In 1976 it amounted to 30,523,413 French francs for collections and maintenance. The staff comprised in the late 1970's 1,150 persons, 295 of whom were professional librarians ("Conservateurs"), 248 assistant librarians, 322 stack attendants, 134 technicians (photographers, binders), and 137 administrative staff.

*Collections.* The main collections are as follows: 12,000,000 books; 300,000 manuscripts; 6,000,000 prints and engravings; 1,500,000 maps; 800,000 coins and medals; 400,000 records.

*Services.* The Bibliothèque Nationale is open for postgraduate research and served 324,434 readers in 1976 in its 884 seats. The Reference Room contains all general reference works, bibliographies, and the Bibliothèque Nationale's catalogues. Outside loans (except for exhibitions) are not permitted, but facilities for photocopies, microfilms, and other forms of reproduction are available. A Consultative Committee exists through which readers may express their desires or complaints.

In 1897 the Library launched the publication of its general catalogue of authors; the final volumes were in progress in 1978. From 1960 a new catalogue was issued that includes authors, official publications, and anonymous works. Various specialized catalogues have been published concerning manuscripts, maps, engravings, and other materials. Since 1931 the Library also has published the weekly *Bibliographie de la France* (official part), which began in 1811 and has been produced by automated production methods since 1975. The National Lending Center oversees the loans of duplicates, rare books, and manuscripts to foreign libraries.

*Central Administration in Paris.* Since Napoleon, France has always been an extremely centralized country, and the organization of the library system reflects that pattern. From 1945 to 1975 a Direction des Bibliothèques et de la Lecture Publique existed within the Ministry of National Education; all state libraries were controlled by it.

Beginning in 1975 the structure was divided and then redivided; university libraries and the Bibliothèque Nationale remained under the Ministry of Universities, which separated from the Ministry of Education, and the other public libraries came under the Ministry of Culture, where a Direction du Livre is responsible partly for municipal libraries and completely for provincial lending libraries and for the Bibliothèque Publique d'Information (BPI) at the Pompidou Center. The Service des Bibliothèques, in the central administration of the Ministry of Universities, is completely responsible for the university libraries and libraries of some public research institutes (Museum d'Histoire Naturelle, Musée de l'Homme) and partly (personnel, budget) for the Bibliothèque Nationale.

The government provides from 80 to 90 percent of the national, university, and provincial lending libraries' budgets and partly subsidizes the municipal libraries. The Service des Bibliothèques of the Ministry of Universities is responsible for personnel management, since about 90 percent of library staff is composed of civil servants.

Bibliothèque Nationale

*The main reading room of France's Bibliothèque Nationale in Paris, originally the Royal Library dating to the 14th century.*

There are corps of librarians, assistant librarians, and stack attendants, which are entered only through competitive national examinations. Membership in the corps enables staff to move from one library to another (public, university, national) without losing seniority.

Together the Direction du Livre of the Ministry of Culture and the Service des Bibliothèques of the Ministry of Universities define the library policy of France through decisions, grants, building, automation choices, and other matters.

One example of centralization is the automation of libraries. Although two university libraries (Grenoble, Nice) have created their own computerized catalogues, the main automation effort has been made at the central level by the Bureau for Library Automation, which in 1975 became the Division of Cooperation and Automation. This division, which is part of the Service des Bibliothèques, has been building a network, installing terminals linked to scientific and medical data bases, producing the national bibliography, and giving assistance to municipal libraries for their loan systems.

State control, which is total in the case of the Bibliothèque Nationale, the university libraries, and the central lending libraries, is only partial in some cases. The Ministry of Universities can appoint professional staff to libraries outside its jurisdiction (such as the Ecole Polytechnique or the Observatoire de Paris) in order to ensure library service at professional standards. It can also give grants to towns to help them build a new library. Or it may "classify" (as historical buildings are "classified") certain municipal libraries that harbor collections of great value. Professional civil servant librarians are in this case sent to the "classified" library, and grants are made to maintain the quality of the collection and guarantee the preservation of its old books and manuscripts.

Finally, the central administration directs general inspectors who visit libraries of all categories, both to check the quality of their operation and the efficiency of their staff and to advise communes on building projects and library renewals and transformations and also to assess requests for grants.

**Scientific Technical Libraries.** Besides the scientific sections of university libraries, which are entirely state supported, there are numerous scientific libraries in which state participation varies from total to none. Some scientific libraries are managed by other government departments, such as the Army. Some are entirely private. Most are called Documentation Centers and are linked to laboratories of private industry. Some, like the Institut Pasteur and Electricité de France, are mixed. Scientific technical libraries number approximately 4,000.

**Parliamentary Libraries.** The library of the Assemblée Nationale, founded in 1789, received its first lot of books from the Revolutionary "literary depots." It holds 600,000 books, 1,500 periodicals, and 1,800 manuscripts and is open to members of the Assemblée Nationale and to authorized readers. Bibliographies and reports are prepared on request on specific topics.

Use of the Senate library is reserved for its members. Like the Library of the Assemblée Nationale, it contains mostly works on law, economics, and history, though it also has a number of special collections coming from donations. It, too, goes back to the Revolution, and it possesses 500,000 books and 600 periodical titles.

**University Libraries.** These were created by a decree of 1878 that merged the libraries of the faculties and the institutes. Until 1975 universities comprised four faculties (law, humanities, medicine, and science) to which were attached specialized institutes (chemistry and mathematics among others). In 1978 there were 47 university libraries, of which 14 were interuniversity libraries serving two or more universities in one town. Taken as a whole, there are 165 sections and 13 subsections by subject in these libraries.

A typical university library contains sections in humanities, law, sciences, and medicine. A Director (a professional librarian) is in charge, aided since 1970 by a Board including faculty members, students, and library staff. The budget is paid for—up to 80 percent—by a grant from the Ministry of Universities, the remainder being made up by students' fees (15 French francs per year) and various small resources. In 1970 former large universities (30,000 students) were split into several smaller universities (6,000 students).

*Technical Organization.* Since 1962 university libraries have been divided into an active and up-to-date collection, classified according to UDC classification, on free-access shelves in the reading room, and a somewhat less active one in closed stacks and available only on loan. These libraries also are on two levels; one contains textbooks for undergraduates in the first two years of college, and one is for researchers, advanced students, and faculty members.

*Building.* France has experienced notable expansion in library construction. From 1950 to 1970 new campuses were provided with libraries, mainly one building to a section, as in Grenoble, Bordeaux, Orsay, and Orléans. In the older, established universities, such as the Sorbonne in Paris, library buildings were renovated and enlarged.

From the mid-1950's to the end of the 1970's, 120 library buildings were constructed, totaling 4,500,000 square feet (the total university library space being about 6,000,000 square feet).

*Personnel.* In 1977 total personnel in university libraries was 3,118 posts, 1,275 of which were professionals (both librarians and assistant librarians), or a ratio of one professional to 630 students.

*Collections.* Varying in quantity and quality, some collections have several million books plus incunabula and manuscripts (the Sorbonne Library, the Medical Library of the University of Paris, the Bibliothèque Sainte Geneviève, for example), whereas others are more recent (Mulhouse, Toulon). But none has the old, rich collections typical of the municipal libraries created by the Revolution. University libraries totaled 12,000,000 volumes in 1976, not counting theses and periodicals. Their annual intake of books runs roughly to 40,000.

**Municipal Libraries.** Created and operated by the communes, more than 1,000 municipal libraries exist in France. Ninety-seven percent of French cities with more than 20,000 inhabitants and 91 percent with more than 10,000 have their own libraries.

Many municipal libraries were created by a decree of January 28, 1803, that handed the old central schools libraries over to the cities. Thus was created the first national public library network. Many of these libraries, however, were not well maintained by the communes, and some were completely abandoned. Therefore, in 1839 the central government instituted tighter control over them, and in 1897 a regulation was issued proclaiming that the books and manuscripts were state property and that none could be sold or removed without government permission. The decree of 1897 introduced the concept of classification of municipal libraries: libraries were "classified" when they contained collections belonging to the state, i.e,., coming from the former "literary depots." According to a law of 1931, municipal libraries were divided into three categories, but today only two are distinguished: "classified" and "nonclassified."

Library general inspectors visit all municipal libraries, but their influence is greater on the classified since there they may advise on management and render reports to the central administration. Thus the state has real control over libraries housing state collections. The most significant difference remains in the selection of personnel. Professional librarians with a degree from the Ecole Nationale Supérieure de Bibliothécaires (ENSB) are appointed by the state to manage "classified" municipal libraries, whereas the other municipal libraries are staffed by municipal personnel.

The large, long-established libraries in major cities have set up networks of branch libraries or have started bookmobile services in order to stimulate reading among the population in their areas. Bordeaux, Toulouse, and Grenoble each have 14 branches, and Paris has 86.

New buildings have been going up at a brisk pace; municipal library floor surfaces have doubled in the last ten years. Evry, Laval, Pantin, Angers, and Metz are among the cities with new library buildings. Some towns have preferred to remodel old buildings, originally churches and monasteries, in order to obtain working libraries (Colmar, Troyes, Bayonne, Senlis). Ten new municipal libraries were opened in 1977; the municipalities themselves pay for their libraries, but they can receive grants from the state (the Direction du Livre) of about 5.7 percent toward their current budgets and 35 percent for the construction and equipment of a new library. Subsidies amounted to 600 million francs in 1977. Running expenses were 4.43 French francs per inhabitant in 1967; they rose to 11.92 francs in 1975.

The remarkable richness of the French municipal libraries was shown in a study in the late 1970's that reported they possessed: 9,158 incunabula, 69,599 16th-century books, and 221,756 18th-century books. Collections of special significance are in Dijon, Toulouse, Carpentras, and Lyons.

French municipal libraries do not possess only old books and manuscripts. From 1945 the Direction des Bibliothèques et de la lecture publique (superseded in 1975) under the direction of Julien Cain placed a new emphasis on developing reading interests among the public by creating modern collections in new buildings.

Libraries tend to form a center for cultural activities within a town. In the newer peripheral towns around Paris, for instance, the libraries are integrated with other cultural equipment and collaborate closely with organizers of plays, exhibitions, and concerts. Contemporary authors often are invited by the library to present their latest work and participate in open discussions with the public.

In Paris, municipal libraries have a special status. Having been created in 1865, well after the Revolution, they have no state collections. Despite their location at the center of the centralized state, the capital's libraries are thus not under state control. Their funds are allocated by the City of Paris—10 French francs per inhabitant in 1975. They receive visits from their own inspectors, are administered by a Library Bureau, and their professional staff is recruited through a special competitive examination.

Parisian libraries are of two kinds. The first includes research libraries such as the Historical Library of the City of Paris, in the Hôtel de Lamoignon, and devoted to the history of Paris, or the Forney Library, in the Hôtel de Sens, specializing in arts and crafts techniques, and the second standard public libraries. Since 1971 a network of lending libraries has been organized by the city around a central technical service responsible for acquisitions, catalogues, buildings, and other matters. These libraries are being created in accordance with a plan for constructing one large district library (20,000 to 22,000 square feet of floor space) in each of the Paris arrondissements and, around these, "sector" libraries (5,000 to 7,500 square feet) for each group of 35,000 inhabitants. The first large library was opened in the 18th arrondissement in 1969, with four sector libraries. They were followed by libraries in the 5th ("Buffon") and 15th ("Beaugrenelle") arrondissements. In addition the Parisian children's library, Heure Joyeuse, opened new premises seven times larger than before.

Of the 83 City of Paris libraries in 1978, 26 were district libraries. In 1953, 3,000,000 loans were made; 4,000,000 in 1976.

Of note is the Bibliothèque Publique d'Information (BPI) at the Pompidou Center in Paris, although it is not, strictly speaking, a "municipal library." The BPI depends directly on the Direction du Livre. Opened in 1977, it offers a new style of library service; anyone can enter without a card, and it provides a large collection of audiovisual materials (slides, films, tapes) with numerous readers, viewers, and recorders. More than 10,000 visitors use it daily.

**Provincial Lending Libraries.** Because smaller towns cannot support a library, the government in 1945 decided to establish "Central Lending Libraries" in each of the administrative jurisdictions known as départements (more or less the equivalent of a county). These libraries, usually set up in the departmental capital city, were intended to serve communes of fewer than 20,000 inhabitants.

There were 71 Central Lending Libraries in 1977, serving a population of 19,000,000. Each of them operates one or more bookmobiles that circulate out from a central store, distributing books at various depots in the district, which are either the local school or the town hall. The person in charge is usually a teacher or some other volunteer. Books are either left at the depot in boxes (but less and less so) or chosen by the person in charge or by local readers from the shelves of the bookmobile itself. Book deposits are also made, for example, in factories, old-age homes, and cultural centers. The bookmobile visits each town four times a year, with a stock of 3,000 books on its shelves. In 1978 there were 262 bookmobiles, with a staff of 668, giving access to 8,000,000 books. The total number of loans was 25,000,000 in 1977.

**School Libraries.** Before 1958 high school libraries existed, but only for teachers or for use in classes. From 1958 on, and mainly from 1968, "teachers' libraries" or "class libraries" were progressively brought together to form larger units (one by high school) called, since 1974, "Centre de Documentation et d'Information" (CDI). Among France's 7,150 high schools, 3,500 have a CDI. CDI's are usually managed by a teacher who, at best, received a short introductory course in library work lasting a few days. The status of a high school librarian is not officially established, and those in charge retain the status of teacher. Support comes from the regular budget under the Director of the school.

**Associations.** There are five library associations in France. The Amicale des Directeurs de Bibliothèques Universitaires (ADBU) (Society of University Library Directors), founded in 1971, consists of the Directors of all university libraries plus one section chief per library. It is thus a closed association, comprising about 100 members.

After the university reform of 1968 and the establishment of new statutes for university libraries in 1970, the Directors were aware of the need to organize in order to (1) defend university libraries vis-à-vis the public authorities, (2) study problems specific to the organization and administration of university libraries, and (3) coordinate policies and technical procedures on matters outside the

*The University of Grenoble is one of only two French university libraries to create a computerized catalogue system.*

Photopress

jurisdiction of the library service (such as photocopy prices and interlibrary loans). Membership fees are the only source of funds. The ADBU meets once a year, and this general assembly elects a board, which selects a President. The ADBU publishes no documents, but it does issue technical reports from time to time according to the needs of the profession.

The Association des Bibliothécaires Français (ABF) (Association of French Librarians), founded in 1906, is the oldest and largest association of professional librarians in France (2,500 members). Its funds come from membership fees and from modest grants. Its objectives are to defend the profession of librarian in a very broad sense; to further librarianship by studies, conferences, and reports; and to bring together all persons interested in librarianship, whatever their work, functions, categories, or opinions.

The Association is open not only to professional librarians but also to those professionally concerned with libraries, such as publishers, bookdealers, and documentalists. There are individual and institutional memberships.

The Association is organized in sections and regional groups. There are four sections by type of library—national, university, general public, and special. There are 17 regional groups.

Sections and groups elect their own councils, which choose a board (President, one or two Vice-Presidents, Secretary, and Treasurer). They also elect the national council of 30 members, which selects a board of seven to ten persons: President, four Vice-Presidents, Secretary, one or two Assistant Secretaries, and Treasurer. The council members are elected for three years.

The Association, having inadequate resources, cannot undertake extensive activities at the national level, but the regional groups are very active and are the focus for regional professional enterprises such as conferences, union catalogues, and directories of libraries. Nationally, the Association organizes colloquia, working groups, and the annual congress on a professional theme.

The Association serves as a link between state-supported and private libraries and between these and the state. It also provides a neutral forum for discussion and proposals to the government, and it develops cooperative activities. It publishes a quarterly bulletin d'information, an informal note d'information, and professional monographs (such as an elementary handbook of librarianship, a book on serials in public libraries, and another on popular scientific and technical titles).

The Association Française des Documentalistes et Bibliothécaires Spécialisés (ADBS) (French Association of Documentalists and Specialized Librarians) was founded in 1963 to bring together information and documentation professionals. In 1978 it had 1,800 members, mainly from private documentation centers. Funding comes from membership fees and grants. The Association is structured in sectorial groups (by subject: electronics, transport, and so forth) and in seven regional groups. A council elects the board, which is composed of the President, two Vice-Presidents, the Secretary General, and the Treasurer. Activities are oriented toward the improvement of information handling and transfer by means of visits, round tables, seminars, and the national congress. ADBS publishes a quarterly bulletin, *Le Documentaliste*, a monthly information sheet, and a series of monographs (Les Cahiers de l'ADBS).

The Association de l'Ecole Nationale Supérieure de Bibliothécaires (ENSB) (Association of the Ecole Nationale Supérieure de Bibliothécaires), founded in 1967, is composed, as its name indicates, of alumni of the Ecole Nationale Supérieure de Bibliothécaires in Lyons. It had about 500 members in 1979. Its funds come from membership fees and from grants from the Ministry of Universities. It is concerned with all aspects of library education, especially with maintaining the ENSB at the level of equivalent higher level educational institutions in France. It also seeks improvements in the status of civil service librarians.

The Association publishes an internal Note d'information and is a founding member of the Presses de l'ENSB, which publishes professional librarianship books. The annual general assembly elects a council of 21 members for three-year terms. One-third of the council may be renewed every year. The board is composed of eight members selected during the general assembly. The council meets at least every six months.

**Table 1. Libraries in France (1976)**

| Type | Number | Volumes in collections | Annual expenditures[a] (franc) | Population served | Professional staff | All staff (total) |
|---|---|---|---|---|---|---|
| National | 1 | 21,000,000 | Fr. 76,911,498 | N.A. | 543 | 1,150 |
| Academic | 47 | 12,000,000 | Fr. 199,700,000 | 853,934 | 1,275 | 3,055 |
| Public (BM) | 1,044 | 37,000,000 | Fr. 404,938,000 | 25,793,000 | 1,350 | 5,000 |
| School | 3,500 | 10,000,000 | Fr. 10,000,000 | 3,200,000 | 3,150 | N.A. |
| Central Lending (BCP) | 71 | 7,800,000 | Fr. 65,500,000 | 19,000,000 | 350 | 668 |
| Special | 4,000 | N.A. | N.A. | N.A. | N.A. | N.A. |

[a]Including personnel expenses.

Sources: *Bull. Bibl. France,* La Bibliothèque nationale en 1976 (1977); *Les Cahiers de la Culture et de l'Environement* (1978).

**Table 2. Archives in France (1976)**

| | |
|---|---|
| Number | c. 300 |
| Holdings | c. 200,000 cubic meters + 4,000 kilometers of microfilm |
| Annual expenditures | c. Fr. 130,000,000 |
| Professional staff | c. 800 |
| All staff (total) | c. 2,000 |

Sources: *La Gazette des Archives, Annuaire international des Archives/International Directory of Archives* (*Archivum*, 1975).

The Association des Diplômés de l'Ecole des Bibliothécaires Documentalistes (Association of Graduates of the School of Librarian Documentalists), founded in 1936, is composed of alumni of the Ecole des Bibliothécaires Documentalistes of the Catholic Institute in Paris. The annual general assembly elects a council of 12, which then elects the President. Both council and President have three-year terms. It has 500 members, whose fees constitute the main resources of the Association. It finds employment for new graduates of the School and shares with the other associations in the defense of librarianship. It publishes a half-yearly bulletin d'information.

**REFERENCES**

Maurice Caillet, "L'Inspection Générale des Bibliothèques," *Bulletin des Bibliothèques de France* (December 12, 1970; March 3, 1971).

Henri Comte, *Les Bibliothèques Publiques en France* (1977).

Georges le Rider, *La Bibliothèque Nationale en 1976,* état présent et perspectives/rapport présenté le 27 avril 1977 à Madame le Secrétaire d'Etat aux Universités par M. Georges le Rider, Administrateur Général (La Documentation française, 1977).

MARC CHAUVEINC

*Sir Frank Francis*

Library Association

## Francis, Sir Frank

(1901– )

One of the outstanding figures on the British library scene for many years, Sir Frank Francis was born October 5, 1901, in Liverpool. After graduating from Liverpool and Cambridge, he became a schoolmaster in 1925. The following year he entered the service of the British Museum, where he spent the whole of his career. In 1946 he became Secretary in succession to Arundell Esdaile, whose contributions to bibliographical scholarship he had already followed with his own. Promoted to Keeper in the Department of Printed Books in 1948, he became in 1959 Director and Principal Librarian, holding that office until his retirement in 1968. He was created Companion of the Order of the Bath (C.B.) in 1958 and knighted K.C.B. in 1960.

Francis's contributions to the library profession and to scholarship cover an unusual range and may be divided into four main categories: bibliographer and editor, teacher, administrator, and statesman.

Bibliographical and editorial work came early in his career with a regular flow of studies for the Library Association, the Bibliographical Society, and the British Museum; in 1936–53 he edited *The Library,* and in 1947–68 he jointly edited the *Journal of Documentation.* During those years he laid the foundations of his renowned course in bibliography at the School of Librarianship of University College, London (1945–59), and also for the numerous lectures he gave throughout the world.

As Keeper and Director of the British Museum, he initiated and successfully carried out a number of projects for publications based on its unique collections, culminating in the third edition of the *General Catalogue of Printed Books,* which marked an epochal advance in printing technology. He was a leading figure in the discussions that led to the founding of the *British National Bibliography* within the British Museum and lent it the full weight of his support in its early years; his authority and influence were instrumental in ensuring its success.

As a statesman of the profession, Francis set a record that is unmatched. He was President of the major associations: the Library Association, the Museums Association, Aslib, the Bibliographical Society, and the International Federation of Library Associations. He helped to set up the advisory committee on bibliography and documentation in Unesco, and as Chairman of the Trustees of the National Central Library, he guided its course until its merger with the British Museum and other libraries to form the new British Library. He was a leading member of the organizing committee for the Pahlavi National Library of Iran.

In addition he proved an enthusiastic and energetic member of many committees and working parties, and many leading British librarians have had cause to be grateful for his friendship and wise counsel. In long and controversial discussions about the nature and role of librarianship and information work, Francis constantly strove for unity among professional bodies and their members. His assertion of the value of professional qualifications was recognized by the award of the Honorary Fellowship by the Library Association, but he never neglected the value of high scholarship for all librarians. Thus, he was able in the early 1950's to give full recognition to the growing importance of information services in science and technology and played a significant role in the Committee of the Science Advisory Council.

His own interests demonstrated the same extraordinary range, testified by his membership and honorary rank in many scholarly bodies and his collection of honorary doctorates. Perhaps his major attention was given to the classics and especially to Scandinavian studies, in which he achieved international fame. Even in retirement his activity continued unabated. As Consultant to the Council on Library Resources, he became a familiar figure in the U.S., and as Master of the Clockmakers' Company, he fulfilled a role in the functions of the City of London.

D. J. FOSKETT

## Franklin, Benjamin

(1706–1790)

Benjamin Franklin stands at the beginning of the history of America's public libraries. As founder of the Library Company of Philadelphia, he initiated the first subscription library in the United States, a precursor to the modern public library.

Franklin was born January 17, 1706, in Boston, which had the largest concentration of bookshops in British America; over half of the booksellers active between 1700 and 1725 were within a quarter-mile of his birthplace. Ideally situated for one who was to be almost entirely self-educated, he received two years of formal schooling and at the age of 12 was apprenticed to his brother James, a printer. Franklin, who said of himself, "I do not remember when I could not read," began with his father's "little library consisting chiefly of Books in polemic Divinity," which he found of little use. Lending libraries were unknown, but Matthew Adams, a merchant, gave him access to his "pretty Collection of Books." Franklin went one step further, persuading fellow apprentices to borrow books from their masters' book shops, which he read and returned. His reading was eclectic, ranging from classical authors in translation through philosophy, logic, grammar, navigation, and arithmetic. *The Spectator* especially pleased him, and he used it as a model for his own writing. Franklin was vigorous in mind and body and developed a high opinion of his own ability. In 1722 there appeared in James Franklin's *The New England Courant* a series of letters signed Silence Dogood, written by Benjamin, the favorable reception of which annoyed his older brother. On two occasions when James was in trouble with the authorities, Franklin had the full responsibility for the newspaper. The already existing strain between the two grew to the point where Benjamin was eager to break his apprenticeship, which still had three years to run. In the autumn of 1723 he secretly left Boston for New York.

Unable to find work with William Bradford in New York, Franklin continued on to Philadelphia, where he was employed by Samuel Keimer, who had opened a printing shop in competition with Bradford's son Andrew. Once settled, Franklin "began now to have some acquaintances among young people of the Town, that were Lovers of Reading with whom I spent my Evenings very pleasantly." His abilities attracted the attention of Governor Keith, who promised him assistance and arranged for him to go to London to buy a press and type to open a shop of his own. Franklin arrived in England in 1724, only to find himself a victim of Keith's habit of making promises he did not keep. He found employment almost immediately with Samuel Palmer, a printer of some note, and later moved to John Watts's shop, where many noted printers had been trained. Franklin satisfied his need for books by making "an Aquaintance with one Wilcox a Bookseller. . . . Circulating Libraries were not then in Use; but we agreed that on a certain reasonable Terms . . . I might take, and return any of his Books."

When he returned to Philadelphia in 1726 at the age of 20, Benjamin Franklin had completed what amounted to his formal education, although he never stopped learning. He taught himself French, Italian, Spanish, and Latin. Opening his own printing shop in 1728, he embarked on one of the most successful business careers of any printer in pre-Revolutionary America. He started a stationer's store, made arrangements with binders, bought a lampblack house, set up as a wholesale paper merchant, and imported books. The business arrangements he entered into with printers in Newport, New Haven, New York, Charleston, and the West Indies provided a network for distributing his work. The largest part of his printing was for colonial governments; at various times he was printer to Pennsylvania, Philadelphia, Delaware, and New Jersey. Of almost equal importance were his publications on religious subjects, many of which were also subsidized. These two groups make up more than half of the output of his press between 1728 and 1748, when he went into partnership with David Hall and retired from active participation in the business. His most successful publications were the Poor Richard's almanacs and the *Pennsylvania Gazette;* the distribution of the latter was greatly helped in 1737 when Franklin became Deputy Postmaster at Philadelphia. He scarcely ever undertook the publication of a book or pamphlet on his own. His most successful such venture was the 16 editions of George Whitefield's writing and other controversial tracts occasioned by his visit to America in 1740. His best-known and handsomest piece of printing, James Logan's translation of *M. T. Cicero's Cato Major,* was a financial loss. Franklin could execute a piece of fine printing when he felt he could afford it, but in general he confined himself to sound workmanlike productions at reasonable prices. At one time he boasted of having the smallest typeface in America.

Parallel and frequently a part of his business career was Franklin's role in founding institutions and organizations for the public good. The first was the Library Company of Philadelphia. The Junto, which he had formed in 1727 for "mutual Improvement," failed in its attempt to form a small library. Soon afterward, in 1731, Franklin created the Library Company. The inspiration for it may have had its origins in Franklin's practice of borrowing books from booksellers in Boston and London, but the idea of a subscription library, owned by its members for the purpose of circulating books of general interest to those who could not afford to build their own collection, seems to belong to Benjamin Franklin. There was no counterpart in Great Britain during his stay there; the first British subscription library appeared in Scotland in 1741, the year in which Franklin printed the second *Catalogue* of the Library Company with 375 titles, and the London Library was not founded until 1785. Circulating books was not a new idea, but it had been narrowly oriented, usually around some religious interest.

The founders of the Library Company were almost all in trade, practical men who wanted useful information for self-improvement. Most of the original books were in English, and theology was held to a minimum. The Library's functions were soon expanded; it was given an air pump followed by electrical instruments, a telescope, artifacts from the Arctic, a cabinet of fossils, and other museum-like objects. On a number of occasions its rooms were used for demonstrations and lectures. The directors saw their Library as taking an active part in making practical and scientific knowledge readily and cheaply available. Until he left for England in 1757, Franklin played an active role in the Library's affairs. He was briefly acting librarian when in 1734 the Library was opened to all who would pay a rental fee. From 1746 to 1757 he was the Secretary, the principal officer. By 1776 there were at least 18 subscription libraries in America, almost all of which bore some trace of influence from the Library Company.

Although a number of other institutions with which Franklin's name is associated developed libraries, he was not closely involved. He was on the committee that selected the first books for the College of Philadelphia in 1750, but various factors, including the hostility between Provost William Smith and Franklin, meant that he had little to do with its small library. The American Philosophical Society, which he founded in 1743, did not take its present form until 1769, when Franklin was in England; until 1800 its books were all donated. After the appearance of the first volume of the Society's *Transactions* in 1771, Franklin used it to solicit gifts from the scientific writers of Europe and, even more importantly, to establish exchange arrangements with learned societies in Britain and on the Continent, to 20 of which he belonged. Likewise the Pennsylvania Hospital, founded in the early 1750's, did not decide to develop a medical library until 1762, and Franklin's only participation seems to have been an offer to seek gifts in England. His part in beginnings of the Pennsylvania State Library was more direct in that in 1752 he was the member of the Assembly who was directed, along with the Speaker, to purchase books for the newly erected library room.

With the exception of two brief periods, Benjamin Franklin spent the 28 years between 1757 and 1785 in England or France representing the interests of his country. His achievements, particularly his electrical experiments, made him a welcome addition to the literary and intellectual worlds of both countries. He continued to encourage the bookish interests of the organizations he left behind and acted as their agent in acquiring books. In London he became a close friend of England's leading printer, William Strahan, and in Paris picked up his old craft, establishing his own press in Passy. As always he bought and was given books. On his return to Philadelphia in 1785, he set about putting his library in order and designed a ladder-chair and an arm to reach books on high shelves. At his death on April 17, 1790, his library of 4,276 volumes was left to his family, who sold it at an 1803 auction that was the largest and most important to have taken place in America. Franklin's position in the history of American public libraries is well known; that some of the ideas he brought to librarianship may have predated their appearance in the mother country is not as widely recognized. Certainly the Library Company's view of itself as an active force in the educational and intellectual life of Philadelphia would seem to be one of the earliest examples of what is now taken for granted—that libraries have a responsibility that goes beyond passively providing books.

**REFERENCES**


Quotes and other material are from Franklin's *Autobiography*, edited by Leonard W. Labaree *et al.* (1964).

Austin K. Gray, *Benjamin Franklin's Library: A Short Account of the Library Company of Philadelphia* (1937), the standard history.

Margaret Barton Korty, "Benjamin Franklin and Eighteenth Century Libraries," *Transactions of the American Philosophical Society* (1965), a discursive attempt containing useful data.

Carl Van Doren, *Benjamin Franklin* (1938), the best complete biography.


THOMAS R. ADAMS

## French Cultural Center Libraries (Africa)

French Cultural Center Libraries have been organized in the capitals of the new independent countries of Africa that had been part of the French Community from 1959 to 1965. Besides the library theater facilities and a film library, the Centers offer photo workshops and sometimes other artistic facilities. They act both directly (lending books, showing films, organizing exhibitions and lectures) and indirectly (giving books to school and public libraries, training their personnel, lending films, helping theater groups).

Material used is always in French but can be of foreign origin as long as it is translated into French. When the Centers were established, it was not feasible to put either French or African trained personnel in charge of the libraries since so few were available. There has been little change in that policy; in most cases there is a French nonprofessional "librarian" and locally recruited library assistant.

Each of the 27 centers in former French colonies holds from 10,000 to 30,000 volumes, one-fourth to one-third of them children's books. Membership figures are not reliable, some Centers retaining members on the register for several years, other renewing membership cards regularly. Membership may be estimated at 2,000 to 5,000 for similar loan figures in larger Centers. Smaller ones may have fewer than 1,000 members.

Loan figures vary between 30,000 and 80,000 a year for most larger Centers except Dakar, which lends about 100,000 in most years. Smaller Centers stay just above the 10,000 mark. Figures are influenced strongly by the number of new books received in a year and to some extent by political events.

Loans to French nationals may come up to one-half or be as low as one-tenth the total for a given Center. Most of the rest of the loans are to students, either in secondary schools or in universities and technical schools. Figures on expenses are not readily available. The total book budget for the Centers (apart from gifts to schools and others) has been 400,000 to 600,000 francs since 1965, enough for 50,000 volumes in most years if good use is made of paperbacks. No breakdown per country is available. Overall budget and other resources were fairly stable for 20 years, while needs increased, particularly in former Belgian and Portuguese colonies.

**French Cultural Center Libraries**

| | Stock 1975 | Loans 1975 |
|---|---|---|
| Benin | | |
| Cotonou | 15,000 | 66,200 |
| branch | 5,000 | 30,800 |
| Burundi | | |
| Bujumbura | 9,000 | 2,000 |
| Cameroon | | |
| Yaoundé | 18,000 | 54,000 |
| Douala | 20,000 | 68,000 |
| Buea | 12,000 | N.A. |
| Central African Republic | | |
| Bangui | 11,800 | 37,800 |
| Chad | | |
| N'Djamena | 15,800 | 11,000 |
| Congo | | |
| Brazzaville | 19,000 | 30,000 |
| Pointe Noire | 16,000[a] | 11,000 |
| Djibouti[d] | | |
| Djibouti | 15,000 | 318,000 |
| Gabon | | |
| Libreville | 2,600[b] | 48,000 |
| Ivory Coast | | |
| Abidjan | 50,000[a] | |
| | 33,000[c] | 56,000 |
| Madagascar | | |
| Antananarivo | 20,000 | 75,000 |
| Mali | | |
| Bamako | 12,700 | 41,000 |
| Mauritania | | |
| Nouakchott | 26,000 | 29,000 |
| Niger | | |
| Niamey | 40,000[a] | 41,000 |
| Rwanda | | |
| Kigali | 7,800 | 2,000[c] |
| Senegal | | |
| Dakar | 30,000 | 101,000 |
| Saint Louis | 10,700 | 20,000 |
| Togo | | |
| Lomé | 23,000 | 74,600 |
| Upper Volta | | |
| Ouagadougou | 21,000 | 86,000 |
| Bobo Dioulasso | 8,000 | 20,000 |
| Zaire | | |
| Kinshasa | 13,000 | 35,000 |
| Lumumbashi | 9,400 | 20,000 |
| Bukavu | 8,500 | 8,000 |

[a]Not an actual inventory.
[b]New library; now about 15,000.
[c]Estimated.
[d]Center established 1978. Statistics from 1979.

Up to 1979 little had been done by most African governments concerned to take over the responsibility of providing non-school books to the general public. There were some indications (from Senegal, Ivory Coast, Benin) that changes may be seen in the future.

F. LALANDE ISNARD

The University of Chicago

*Herman Howe Fussler*

## Fussler, Herman Howe
(1914– )

Herman Fussler, university library administrator, scholar, and teacher, made major contributions to the improvement of library services to scholars, labored successfully to increase the general understanding of the tasks and problems of research libraries, and provides trenchant observations upon possible solutions to complex library questions. A practicing library administrator for 35 years (23 of them as Director of the University of Chicago Library), he pioneered in the development and application of new technologies and service concepts, beginning with his early contributions to library microphotography and culminating in the conception and design of the Joseph Regenstein Library of the University of Chicago (opened in 1970). The Regenstein Library is widely recognized as an attractive and efficient environment remarkably well adapted to the activity of scholarship. Fussler had also been a library educator for almost 40 years by the end of the 1970's, known as a stimulating and provocative teacher, as the possessor of a comprehensive familiarity with the literature of librarianship and with the library practitioners of his generation, and as a student and scholar distinguished for penetrating and balanced analyses of the major issues confronting the academic research library. He wrote or edited numerous significant books, articles, and reports on academic libraries, on the technologies applicable to libraries, on the ways in which the products of scholarship are disseminated, and on the management of scholarly resources. He frequently was consulted by librarians, scholars, academic administrators, and foundation officers because of his experience and perspective.

**FUSSLER, HERMAN HOWE 13**

Fussler was born in Philadelphia on May 15, 1914, the son of a physics professor. His family, after living in various parts of the country, settled in Chapel Hill, where Fussler attended the University of North Carolina. He received an A.B. degree in mathematics in 1935 and, a year later, a bachelor's degree in library science. Shortly thereafter he began studies at the Graduate Library School of the University of Chicago, where he earned the M.A. degree in 1941 and the Ph.D. in 1948.

He began his library career in 1936 at the New York Public Library as a library assistant in the Science and Technology Division. After a brief period of service there, he was invited to the University of Chicago Library to establish and direct its pioneering Department of Photographic Reproduction, with the specific mission of developing operating and technical processes, particularly in microreproduction, that would be of utility to research libraries generally. He served in that capacity from 1936 to 1946, added concurrent responsibilities as Science Librarian in the University Library from 1943 to 1947, became Assistant Director and then Associate Director of the library, 1947–48, and later in 1948 was appointed Director of the University Library, serving in that position until 1971, when he resigned to devote full time to research and teaching in the Graduate Library School of the University of Chicago. Twice during his service in the University Library his abilities were made available to other important enterprises: during 1937 he served as Head of the Demonstration of Microphotography at the Paris International Exposition, under the auspices of the Rockefeller Foundation and the American Library Association; and from 1942 to 1945 he was detached from his primary responsibilities to serve the Manhattan Project as Assistant Director of the Information Division and Librarian of the Metallurgical Laboratory.

His career in library research and in education for librarianship paralleled his career in the University Library. He became an Instructor in 1942, was promoted to Assistant Professor in 1944, and was made Professor in 1948, the year he assumed the Library directorship. For the period 1961–63 he served, in addition, as Acting Dean of the library school. His contributions to library scholarship and to the scholarly work of the University were formally acknowledged in 1974 when he was named the Martin A. Ryerson Distinguished Service Professor of Library Science. In 1977 he was Visiting Professor at Monash University in Australia.

Fussler influenced thought and action in many areas through his diligent and effective service on the boards and committees of library associations and learned societies. He served on the ALA Council from 1956 to 1959 as well as on a number of committees. He was a member of the board of the Association of Research Libraries from 1961 to 1964 and from 1970 to 1971. He was one of the initial three-man team selected to study the feasibility of a midwest storage facility for academic libraries and was active in the planning and establishment of the resulting Midwest Interlibrary Center (now the Center for Research Libraries), served on its board from 1950 to 1967, was Vice Chair of the board in 1954–55, and was Chair, 1959–60. He was a member of the Board of Regents of the National Library of Medicine (1963–67) and served on the visiting committees of various academic libraries. He was appointed by President Lyndon B. Johnson to the National Advisory Commission on Libraries in 1966.

Fussler received the Melvil Dewey Medal from ALA in 1954 and the Ralph R. Shaw Award for library literature in 1976.

Fussler served as Associate Editor for the *Journal of Documentary Reproduction* (1938 to 1942) and the *Library Quarterly* from 1949. His principal publications include *Photographic Reproduction for Libraries: A Study of Administrative Problems* (1942) and *Characteristics of the Research Literature Used by Chemists and Physicists in the United States* (1949); he edited *Library Buildings for Library Service* (1947), *The Function of the Library in the Modern College* (1954), *The Research Library in Transition* (1957); he was co-author, with Julian L. Simon, of *Patterns in the Use of Books in Large Libraries* (revised edition 1969) and editor of *Management Implications for Libraries and Library Schools* (1973) and *Research Libraries and Technology* (1973).

STANLEY MC ELDERRY

## Gabon

On the west coast of Africa, Gabon is a republic bounded on the north by Equatorial Guinea and Cameroon, on the east by The Congo, and on the west by the Atlantic Ocean. Pop. (1978 World Bank est.) 800,000; area 267,667 sq.km. The official language is French.

**National Library.** The Direction Générale des Archives, in Libreville, was begun in 1969 as the Archives and Bibliothèque Nationale. In 1972 it officially became the depository library for government-issued documents, Gabonese periodicals, and books from or about Gabon. Since 1979 it has sought to enforce the legal deposit of one copy of each title imported by the book dealers and of each dissertation prepared by Gabonese students at home and overseas. The DGABD is also interested in receiving dissertations dealing with Gabon.

The DGABD's principal departments are the Archives and the Library. Cataloguing was still under way in 1979, and there were no loan or exchange facilities planned. Owing to shortage of space, the DGABD was considering building a large center where the Archives and Library could be housed as well as a public library, a book store, a cultural center for exhibitions, lectures, shows, and museum, as well as documentation and copy centers and a cafeteria.

**Academic Libraries.** The largest academic library is the Bibliothèque Centrale of the Université Omar Bongo, established in 1972. There are about 200 periodi-

**Libraries in Gabon (1976)**

| Type | Number | Volumes in collections | Annual expenditures (CFA franc) | Population served | Professional staff | All staff (total) |
|---|---|---|---|---|---|---|
| National | 1 | N.A. | N.A. | N.A. | 1 | 16 |
| Academic | 1 | 12,000 | N.A. | N.A. | 4 | 18 |
| Public | 0 | N.A. | N.A. | N.A. | N.A. | N.A. |
| School | 4 | N.A. | N.A. | N.A. | N.A. | N.A. |
| Special | 30 | N.A. | N.A. | N.A. | N.A. | N.A. |
| Total | 36 | | | | | |

cals and 12,000 book titles. Special collections are found at the Centre Universitaire des Sciences de la Santé (Medicine Faculty), Ecole de la Magistrature (Law School), Ecole Normale Supérieure (Teachers' College), Institut Africain d'Informatique (Computer Sciences), and Institut National des Etudes Forestières (Forest Studies).

**Public Libraries.** There are no public libraries in Gabon though the library of the DGABD could function as one. The Bibliothèque Saint Exupéry, in the French Cultural Center, acts to as a public library.

**School Libraries.** Only the Lycée Léon M'Ba and the Lycée Technique Omar Bongo in Libreville and two denominational schools (in Bitam and Moanda) have small libraries.

**Special Libraries.** The principal special libraries are at the Chambre de Commerce, d'Agriculture, d'Industrie et des Mines du Gabon; the Bureau de Recherches Géologiques et Minières; the Centre Technique Forestier Tropical; the Musée des Arts et Traditions du Gabon; Radio diffusion et Télévision Gabonaise; and the Institut Pédagogique National. Both the American and French Cultural Centers maintain libraries.

**Associations.** There are very few trained Gabonese librarians and, consequently, no library association. However, DGABD staff attend international meetings, and DGABD is a member of the International Association for the Development of Libraries in Africa (AIDBA), along with the University Library; the latter is also affiliated with the Standing Conference of African University Libraries-Western Area (SCAULWA).

MARIE ELIZABETH BOUSCARLE

# Gambia, The

The Republic of The Gambia, on the Atlantic coast in West Africa, lies on a strip of land on the banks of the Gambia River; Senegal surrounds The Gambia on the north, south, and west. Pop. (1978 est.) 568,600; area 11,569 sq.km. The official language is English.

**National Library.** The National Library of The Gambia is in the capital city of Banjul. The Gambia government did not have a public or national library service of its own until April 1962, when the British Council closed its office and handed its library in Banjul to the government. The British Council, which ran a subscription library service in The Gambia from 1946, had provided the only public library in the country apart from smaller libraries in schools, government departments, mission houses, and clubs, whose materials were loaned only to their members or clients. When the book stock was transferred, it numbered 25,000 volumes, excluding phonograph records, films, and film strips, which totaled 500. On May 1, 1971, the name was changed from the British Council Library to The Gambia National Library. Before the change, Roy Flood had been sent from the British Council in London to evaluate and recommend a library service suitable for The Gambia. His recommendations for a complete reorganization of The Gambia library service were accepted.

In 1974 the British government, through the British Council and the Ministry of Overseas Development, provided 300,000 dalasis (£75,000) for the building, books, furniture, and equipment. On December 15, 1976, when the new library was opened, the collection numbered 54,620—it had doubled in the period 1962–76. Added books, manuscripts, films, recordings, and other items brought the figure to more than 60,300 by the end of 1978.

Under an act of Parliament, the National Library was made the depository library and also the Bibliographic Centre (The Gambia Library Board Act of 1976). Its six departments are the National Collection (mainly materials by and about The Gambia and the Gambians); Adult Lending; Adult Reference; Children's Lending/Reference Library; School Library Service (bulk loans to primary schools); and Mobile and Book-box services. The National Library, in summary, serves dual purposes—as a National Reference and Lending Library and also as the public library of the nation.

**Table 1. Libraries in The Gambia (1976)**

| Type | Number | Volumes in collections | Annual expenditures (dalasis) | Population served | Professional staff | All staff (total) |
|---|---|---|---|---|---|---|
| National | 1 | 54,720 | D 28,000 | 553,000[a] | 3 | 15 |
| Academic | 1 | 15,000 | 4,000 | 231 | 1 | 3 |
| Law | 2 | 20,000 | 1,000 | 500 | N.A. | 2 |
| School | 7 | 35,000 | 10,500 | 2,199 | N.A. | 7 |
| Special | 3 | 5,000 | N.A. | 1,100 | N.A. | 3 |
| Total | 14 | 129,720 | | | | 30 |

[a]Total population (1976 est.).

Sources: *Education Statistics,* 1976–77; Yundum College *Handbook* 1975–76; National Library monthly reports.

**Table 2. Archives in The Gambia (1976)**

| | |
|---|---|
| Holdings | 2,062 volumes (148,920 cu.m.) |
| Annual expenditures | D 13,000 |
| Professional staff | 1 |
| All staff (total) | 3 |

**Academic Libraries.** The only academic institution is the Teachers' Training College at Yundum, which also trains agricultural officers. Only primary school teachers are trained there. For higher education, Gambians go abroad.

An acute shortage of teachers, particularly in the provincial schools, prompted the setting up of a training center at Georgetown. Initially the training was for one year until the demand for staff in the schools sufficiently eased. The first college building was opened on March 7, 1949.

S. P. C. N'JIE

# Garfield, Eugene
(1925– )

Drexel University

*Eugene Garfield*

The library and information world has many entrepreneurs; Eugene Garfield earned a special place in that his success has a substantial intellectual component and was based upon early and deep insights regarding the structure of science literatures and the nature of scientific communication.

Eugene Garfield was born September 16, 1925, in New York City. He was raised in a Jewish-Italian family in which he, in retrospect, rejoiced, according to his warm memoir (1978) relating his experiences with his Italian stepfather to those with his intellectual mentor, Chauncey Leake. He was educated at Columbia University, earning a B.S. in 1949 in Chemistry and an M.S. in Library Service in 1954 while working at a variety of jobs to pay for his education. Self-employment, began nearly immediately after the last degree, first as a consultant to Smith, Kline and French, the pharmaceutical company, and then as the founder of a tiny company producing the predecessor to *Current Contents,* started first as a cottage industry in a converted chicken coop.

Critical years were 1960 and 1961; his small firm took on its current name, Institute for Scientific Information (ISI): He received a Ph.D. in Structural Linguistics from the University of Pennsylvania (1961). (His dissertation applied modern linguistics to the indexing of chemical information.) The most important event in 1961 was that he brought out the first citation index to a broad spectrum of science literature, genetics.

A variety of products, ideas, and special techniques and services can be identified with Garfield and his associates, but just two products, *Current Contents* and *Science Citation Index,* and their conceptualization and development, their implementation and successful management, would stand alone as major monuments to his skills, energy, and intellect. *Current Contents* capitalizes upon the researcher's urgent needs for current research information, particularly in the life sciences, and the human's enormous capability to scan text skillfully. *Science Citation Index* identified citation behavior, a means of acknowledging intellectual debt and assigning credit, as the key to a basic organizational feature of the scientific literatures, useful for retrieval, for research on the nature of science, and for science policy.

ISI marketed 25 products and employed 500 people at the end of the 1970's; Garfield continued as an active scholar, writer, and advocate.

**REFERENCES**

Eugene Garfield, *Essays of an Information Scientist* (1977), provides a basic introduction to the man and his ideas.

Eugene Garfield, *Citation Indexing* (1979), an extensive treatment of techniques.

BELVER GRIFFITH

# German Democratic Republic

The German Democratic Republic (Deutschen Demokratischen Republik, or DDR), a socialist country of central Europe, known in the West also as East Germany, was established on October 7, 1949, when Germany was partitioned into East and West Germany. It is bounded on the north by the Baltic Sea, on the east by Poland, on the south by Czechoslovakia, and on the west by the Federal Republic of Germany (West Germany). Pop. (1978 est.) 16,757,900; area 108,328 sq. km. The language is German.

**National Library.** Two libraries control the library network in the German Democratic Republic: the Deutsche Bücherei (German Library) in Leipzig and the Deutsche Staatsbibliothek (German State Library) in East Berlin.

The Deutsche Bücherei (DB), which is under the direct supervision of the Ministry for Universities and Colleges of the DDR, functions as the national library and receives for legal deposit two copies of every work published in East Germany. It was established through legal deposit regulations of 1960 and 1970. In addition, the library receives copies of translations of German publications issued outside the DDR, works in non-German languages on Germany and German-related topics, musical scores, art prints, patents, and records. Prior to 1960 the DB received, on a voluntary basis, a copy of every work published in Germany or in German-speaking countries. In the late 1970's the library's total stock exceeded 6,000,000 volumes, with an accession rate of approximately 110,000 items a year.

The Deutsche Bücherei was founded in Leipzig on October 3, 1912, by the Association of German Booksellers (Börsenverein der Deutschen Buchhändler) and served as a nonlending depository library from 1912 to 1945. During World War II little damage was done to the library's stock, although the building itself suffered some damage. The library reopened after the war on November 24, 1945, and continued to function as a national bibliographic center. It resumed publication of the national bibliography *(Deutsche Nationalbibliographie)* in August of the following year.

The German national bibliography, which began publication in 1931, provides a union catalogue of all literature published in the DDR, as well as in the Federal Republic of Germany, and of literature in foreign countries published in the German language. Since 1968 it has been issued in three series: the weekly *Neuerscheinungen des Buchhandels* (new publications in the book trade); the biweekly *Neuerscheinungen ausserhalb des Buchhandels* (new publications that cannot be acquired through the book trade); and the monthly *Dissertationen und Habilitationsschriften* (dissertations and theses). In addition to the national bibliography, the DB publishes numerous bibliographies on special subjects. These are listed in the *Bibliographie der Bibliographien,* published monthly since 1966.

The DB houses the Deutsche Buch- und Schriftmuseum (German Books and Scripts Museum). Its collection includes documents on the history of the book, on writing and paper throughout the world, and on the German Paper Museum, with an extensive collection of watermarks, comprising 213,532 original papers. The Deutsche Staatsbibliothek (German State Library) in Berlin is the central research library of the DDR. It also has legal deposit privileges and functions as an international exchange center for official and governmental publications and a central clearinghouse for national interlibrary loans, covering almost 300 libraries. Since 1971 it has been responsible for the *Zentralkatalog der DDR,* the central union catalogue of the DDR, and for union catalogues of incunabula and manuscripts. This library also stores scientific literature from all over the world. In the late 1970's its holdings included almost 5,300,000 volumes, with special collections in the Asia-Africa, Music, Maps, and Young People's Literature departments, and 40,326 periodicals; 1,800,000 volumes of the library's original collection are held by the Staatsbibliothek in West Berlin.

The Deutsche Staatsbibliothek was founded in 1661 as a court library of the Elector of Brandenburg; it is under the Ministry of Universities and Colleges. The library lends only to select users, such as students and members of industry; the DB remains primarily a reference library.

The main archives of the DDR are housed in the Zentrales Staatsarchiv, founded in 1946 in Potsdam. Its library holds approximately 135,000 volumes.

The VEB Bibliographisches Institut, founded in 1826 in Leipzig, specializes in publishing works on library science. All publications on library services in the DDR are included in the abstract journal *Informationsdienst Bibliothekswesen* (Information Service for Library Affairs), a joint publication of the DB and the Central Office for Information and Documentation in the Field of Library Science.

**Academic Libraries.** The Sächsische Landesbibliothek (Saxonian Regional Library) of Dresden, also under the Ministry for Universities and Colleges, is a major academic library of the DDR. The library dates back to 1556, when the Elector August of Saxony established a collection at Dresden Castle. Its current holdings total nearly 1,400,000 volumes and 3,000 periodicals, with 783 incunabula, 2,000 rare books, 21,300 manuscripts, 60,000 maps that relate to Saxony and adjoining areas, as well as numerous city views, musical scores, records, and tapes. It also holds the important Mayan manuscript *Codex Dresdensis*. The library maintains a catalogue of portraits and illustrations from books and periodicals and holds these portraits for 100 years. Its annual publications include *Sächsische Bibliographie; Bibliographie Bildende Kunst* and *Bibliographie Illustrierte Bücher der D.D.R.*, both on art; *Bibliographie Geschichte der Technik*, on technology; and the *Bibliographie Musik der D.D.R.*

There are seven universities in the DDR, that at Leipzig being the largest. The libraries of these universities are to some extent centralized and are all under the ministry responsible for higher education. The Universitätsbibliothek der Karl-Marx Universität, or the library of Leipzig University, was established in 1543 (the University itself was founded in 1409). Its holdings at the end of the 1970's consisted of approximately 3,050,000 books, 8,700 manuscripts, 169,000 autographs, and 2,713 incunabula.

The library of Humboldt University in Berlin, established in 1831, opened in 1833; the University was founded in 1810. There is one central library with holdings of nearly 2,000,000 volumes and more than a million dissertations and related documents. The library's numerous institutes have departmental libraries, with collections totaling approximately 1,800,000 volumes.

The library of the Technical University at Dresden was established in 1828 and holds 1,112,000 volumes, including 6,350 periodicals and 101,000 theses, as well as patents and industrial and commercial literature. There are also university libraries at Greifswald (1,869,582 volumes, including 599,302 theses, 2,104 autographs, 305 incunabula); Halle (3,511,000 volumes and 523,000 theses); Jena (2,372,340 volumes, 736,964 pamphlets, 56,867 manuscripts, 123,390 patents, 6,861 current periodicals); and Rostock (1,702,507 volumes, 4,692 manuscripts, 725 incunabula, and 4,880 journals). In the late 1970's there were 33 other academic libraries, holding a total collection of more than 31,700,000 volumes. In addition, under various ministries of the DDR, are the libraries of 233 colleges.

Tschuschke

*The German State Library in East Berlin was founded in 1661 as the court library of the Elector of Brandenberg and serves primarily as a reference library.*

**Public Libraries.** The region's first public library was established at Grossenhain in 1828. All public libraries in the DDR come under the control of the Ministry of Culture, and there is at least one public library in every community. In the late 1970's, 12,654 public libraries (Staatliche Allgemeinbibliotheken) were reported, with 31,297,365 volumes and 72,896,742 periodicals in total holdings. Library service is free to citizens of the country. One of the largest public libraries in the DDR is the Berliner Stadtbibliothek, founded in 1900 and housing almost a million volumes.

Public libraries are divided into district libraries, public research libraries, subdistrict libraries, rural central libraries, and community libraries. In 1977, 15 district libraries provided liaison between the general public libraries and the network of academic libraries. The public research libraries provide special services within the district and combine the functions of a research library with those of a cultural center. The 191 subdistrict libraries serve the population of the subdistrict capital. They also act as collection centers and provide resources and advice to other public libraries of the subdistrict. Rural central libraries, or regional libraries, service from 4 to 12 communities and function as the library center of a rural area. In late 1977 there were 407 rural central libraries and 6,418 community libraries. The smallest unit is the community library, which provides library services to villages or settlements. The collections of all public libraries include children's literature, and special children's libraries are found in all of the larger towns.

In the late 1970's there were 5,102 trade union libraries (gewerkschaftsbibliotheken), located in factories, to provide library materials to workers in industry. The National Executive of the Confederation of Free German Trade Unions is responsible for these libraries and provides the funds to maintain them. The Central Library of Trade Unions in Berlin is responsible for training the library staff. The total holdings for these libraries in 1977 were 8,302,362 volumes and 13,401,446 periodicals. Other types of public libraries include military libraries, which are available at troop locations, and libraries in homes for the elderly, prisons, and hospitals. Legislation enacted in 1978 provides for the establishment of patients' libraries, including a full-time staff, in all hospitals with more than 400 beds.

**School Libraries.** Pupils in the DDR are provided with literature related to the curriculum as well as other reading materials, according to an agreement of 1976 between the Ministry of Culture and the Ministry of Education. Education is compulsory for ten years. Frequently public libraries have service centers or branches within the schools. In the early 1970's approximately 5,300 school libraries were reported throughout the country.

**Special Libraries.** In the late 1960's approximately 12,000 special libraries in the DDR held nearly 21,700,000 volumes. About 800 of these libraries hold more than

4,000 volumes and serve about 150,000 readers. Many of these function primarily within the information/documentation system. Information and documentation centers have been established in the DDR in most areas of the humanities, social sciences, natural sciences, and technology. One such center is the Akademie der Landwirtschaftswissenschaften in Berlin, founded in 1952, whose central library holds 326,900 volumes. The Zentralinstitut für Information und Dokumentation der Deutschen Demokratischen Republik, established in 1963 in Berlin, is the coordinating body for scientific and technical information in the DDR. The institute publishes the monthly *Information/Dokumentation* and *Informatik* every two months. Library networks have been established in many fields, such as pedagogy, agriculture, medicine, and military science. Most special library networks have one central library to coordinate activities and function as collection centers.

Scientific libraries in the DDR are among the largest in the world. One of the most important is that of the Akademie der Wissenschaften der DDR (German Democratic Republic Academy of Sciences) in Berlin. The library was founded in 1700 and currently holds 290,000 volumes.

One of the oldest libraries in the DDR is that of the Thüringisches Landeshauptarchiv, founded in 1547 in Weimar and located at the Schloss (Castle) of the Duke. The library specializes in classic German literature. (Goethe was librarian there from 1797 until his death in 1832.) Branches are maintained in Gotha, Greiz, Meiningen, and Rudolstadt. Also in Weimar are the Goethe- und Schiller Archiv, which houses about 80,000 manuscripts and the works of 45 poets, and the central library of the Institute of Classic German Literature. The latter's collection consists of about 780,000 volumes on German literature, including numerous Faust studies, art, and music. The Institute issues the *Weimarer Beiträge,* a periodical on German literature, and provides information to researchers from 72 countries. There are many specialized music libraries in the DDR. The Musikbibliothek der Stadt Leipzig, founded in 1894, holds 106,534 volumes and 16,346 recordings. Its special collections include printed and handwritten music dating from the 15th century.

Leipzig is also the home of the Deutsche Zentralbücherei für Blinde (Central German Library for Blind People). Its collection includes 3,470 works on records, tapes, and cassettes, 25,140 volumes in braille, and 6,630 musical works in braille. The library also publishes books and journals for the blind and provides library materials through the mail to those with defective vision.

**Associations.** The Bibliotheksverband der Deutschen Demokratischen Republik (Library Association of the DDR) was founded in March 1964 at the Deutsche Staatsbibliothek in Berlin, where delegates from 110 libraries gathered to establish a body that would promote cooperation among all types of libraries, including academic, public, and trade union libraries. The association is seated permanently in Berlin. Membership is open only to institutions. In 1977 there were 1,507 members, consisting of libraries, scientific institutions, and documentation and information centers. In that same year the association published 11 titles relating to librarianship. Its official journal is the *Informationsblatt des Bibliotheksverbandes,* which is issued six times a year. The association is affiliated with IFLA and publishes German translations of IFLA conference papers. It also sponsors conferences, seminars, and workshops on relevant topics and works toward the establishment of library networks by subjects and regions.

STAFF

# Germany, Federal Republic of

The Federal Republic of Germany, in central Europe, is bordered by Denmark and the Baltic Sea on the north, the German Democratic Republic and Czechoslovakia on the east, Austria on the south and southwest, Switzerland on the southwest, France, Luxembourg, Belgium, and the Netherlands on the west, and the North Sea on the northwest. Pop. (1978 est.) 61,352,700; area 248,629 sq.km. The official language is German.

The foundation of contemporary librarianship in Germany dates back to the Reformation, but the development of modern librarianship in Germany—as well as in other large European nations—began in the early 19th century, a result of attempts during the Romantic period to maintain the ecclesiastical libraries that were abandoned because of political events. Rare book collections, particularly from monasteries, were generally transferred to libraries of princes, and in turn became part of national and state libraries—the central research libraries of the individual states of the German Empire—in the course of the 19th century. Meanwhile, university libraries gained greater prominence after the reform of German universities during the first decades of the century. The University of Göttingen—already in possession of an efficient library during the 17th and 18th centuries—was a model for new university libraries in already established and newly founded universities. National, state, and university libraries assumed the guiding functions in library work in Germany.

During most of the 19th century a university library was run by a professor of a certain discipline, but later it was headed by a library professional, as library science came into being. However, the "professor-librarian," as represented by Friedrich Ritschl (classical philology), Karl Richard Lepsius (Egyptology), and Adolf Harnach (theology), still existed into the 20th century.

In addition to research libraries, public libraries, originally financed by private contributions, were established in the 19th century. Later the Anglo-American model influenced German public library development with the "Bücherhalle" ("bookhall"). During the second decade of the 20th century, the Bücherhalle's emphasis on instruction was replaced by an emphasis on the education of its readers, exemplified by Walter Hofmann and Erwin Ackerknecht. Only after World War II did German libraries again turn toward the Anglo-American public library tradition.

World War II marked a significant turning point in the Germany library system. In the course of the ravages of war, many libraries were destroyed. The largest German library, the Preussische Staatsbibliothek in Berlin (Prussian State Library), was divided among both German states after the German partition. The reconstruction of research libraries after 1945 was based on the traditional patterns of library administration as described in the *Handbuch der Bibliothekswissenschaft (Handbook of Library Science),* by Fritz Milkau and Georg Ley (1931–42), which guided research libraries for almost 40 years.

German university libraries at the end of the 19th century felt restricted due to the better financed libraries of the university faculties and seminars which the director of the university library could not influence. Also the number of personnel in research libraries was generally insufficient up to the middle of the 1960s. Central services, like cataloguing by a national library, did not exist in Germany, so that libraries with only a small number of employees had to handle a considerable amount of work. The reestablishment of German sciences after both of the World Wars created a strong demand for foreign literature. In order to assure that the required literature for research would be available in the Federal Republic of Germany, the Deutsche Forschungsgemeinschaft (German Research Society) founded a system of special collections in the German research libraries whereby approximately 40 libraries collect newly published foreign literature relevant for scientific research in their specific field of science. Since 1949 this literature has been available to all users through an interlending system among German libraries.

In the early 1960's a trend toward new universities brought about changes in research libraries. These changes included the opening of the stacks to the public and the consolidation of the central university library with the faculty libraries, along with the participation of professors in the book selection done by special consultants and the introduction of electronic data processing. Data processing also led to the establishment of regional library centers in the 1970's, which provide data processing services for the libraries of individual regions.

After the war the public libraries became oriented to the Anglo-American library system. In a very short period the public library replaced the German "Volksbücherei" ("people's library"), first in the large cities and somewhat later in smaller cities and towns. The closed-stack library was replaced by open stacks, and comprehensive information services were developed. Efficient library centers with large collections were founded, and the collections of the "Volksbüchereien," which had been restricted mainly to belles lettres, was significantly enlarged with other types of materials.

**National Libraries.** A comprehensive single national library has never existed in Germany; however, beginning in 1912 the Deutsche Bücherei ("German Library") in Leipzig collected all German publications and published a national bibliography. After the partition of Germany into two states, a new library for these tasks, the Deutsche Bibliothek, was founded in 1948 for the Federal Republic. It became a federal state institution on March 31, 1969. One of its tasks is the comprehensive collection and bibliographical registration of German literature—not only publications of the Federal Republic but also the German language publications of the German Democratic Republic, Austria, Switzerland, and Luxembourg, as well as of the non-German-speaking countries all over the world.

Besides collection and bibliographical registration the Deutsche Bibliothek handles central services for all libraries. It maintains the German office of the International Serials Data System, a CIP-Service for central cataloguing of new German publications, and operates the on-line data bank Biblio-Data for bibliographical searching which contains all German titles since 1972.

**State Libraries.** There are two large state libraries, the Bayerische Staatsbibliothek ("Bavarian State Library") in Munich and the Staatsbibliothek Preussischer Kulturbesitz ("Prussian State Library") in Berlin, which handle certain central services for the Federal Republic. The Staatsbibliothek Preussischer Kulturbesitz is mutually financed by the federal government and all German federal states, while the Bayerische Staatsbibliothek is a library of the state of Bavaria. These two libraries handle the supply of ancient and foreign literature and they are the largest German libraries. Along with the Deutsche Bibliothek they carry out community functions for all German libraries. The ISBN-agency is affiliated with the Staatsbibliothek Preussischer Kulturbesitz, which library established the serials data bank for the German libraries. The Bayerische Staatsbibliothek takes care of the German communications format for electronically stored title entries.

*Central Special Libraries.* Since 1959 there exist four central special libraries—for medical sciences in Cologne, technology in Hannover (TIB), worldwide economics in Kiel, and agricultural sciences in Bonn.

*Other State Libraries.* There are state libraries in the individual German states (Staats- und Landesbibliotheken), which supply materials within a certain federal state or a region. Some of these libraries additionally serve as university libraries, such as the Staats- und Universitätsbibliothek Hamburg ("State and University Library Hamburg") and the university libraries in Münster and Bonn. All of these libraries have the right of legal deposit for their respective regions and in most cases publish a regional bibliography.

*Computer Centers.* In order to meet the data processing needs of libraries, special data processing centers were established in some federal states, e.g., in North-Rhine Westphalia (University Library Center) and in Berlin, where the Deutsche Bibliotheksinstitut ("German Library Institute") performs these tasks. In other federal states such centers are under construction. In 1978 the Federal Minister for Research and Technology instituted a plan for uniform equipment in a projected seven centers. These centers will operate an on-line data base for the libraries of their respective region, will make their services available to all libraries, and will be responsible for centralized planning for the region's libraries.

**City Libraries.** The city research libraries in Germany have a very old tradition, traceable to the late Middle Ages in many cases. However, the largest and most important ones received new responsibilities in the 20th century because of their integration into universities; e.g., in Cologne, Frankfurt, Hamburg, Bremen, and Düsseldorf. The trend toward public libraries after World War II also affected city research libraries, and in many cases they were consolidated with public libraries to create new and efficient library systems; e.g., in Hannover, Essen, München, and Wuppertal.

**Academic Libraries.** University libraries have a dominant role in German librarianship; next to the public libraries of the large cities, they have the greatest number of readers. The expansion of universities in the Federal Republic from 1960 had a considerable influence on number and structure of university libraries. The number of universities and technical institutes in 1964 totaled 25. By 1979 the number had doubled. In addition, a completely new type of university, the Fachhochschule ("professional university"), specializing in more practical education, was created. There are approximately 50 of these institutions in the Federal Republic, so the number of academic libraries has increased to about 100 during the last 15 years.

The structure of university libraries has also changed. The library system of the old universities was characterized by a central university library and a number of independent faculty and seminar libraries (quite often several hundred in one university). Recent developments now favor a university library that simultaneously manages individual faculty libraries; this type is referred to as a "single-line" university library.

**Public Libraries.** This type of library developed to quite an extent after World War II. Today all cities have big libraries with many branches that house a comprehensive literature selection for the public. Since the beginning of the 20th century, the special literature demands in smaller towns and provinces have been covered by state library branches (Staatliche Büchereistellen); these branches have advising functions and keep bookstocks that are available for smaller libraries for completing their collections.

**Special Libraries.** The Federal Republic of Germany has a great number of special libraries, many with quite comprehensive holdings. The approximately 1,500 special libraries range in size from several thousand to several hundred thousand volumes. The parliamentary and public agency libraries do have a special status, the largest being the Bibliothek des Deutschen Bundestages ("Library of the House of Parliament").

Larger industrial enterprises and business associations also maintain significant libraries, available to all readers in the republic. Both of the established churches (Roman Catholic and Protestant) also maintain library systems that include public and research libraries.

Since 1962 the government has developed a documentation and information system, financed mutually by the federal government and the federal states. Under the

**Libraries in the Federal Republic of Germany (1978)**

| Type | | Volumes in collections | Annual expenditures (mark) | All staff (total) |
|---|---|---|---|---|
| National | 3 | 10,900,000 | DM 9,600,000 | 1,245 |
| Academic | 56 | 48,200,000 | DM 80,000,000 | 5,519 |
| State Libraries | 22 | 9,800,000 | DM 8,700,000 | 984 |
| Public | 8,685[a] | 51,500,000 | DM 66,800,000 | 5,434 |

Sources: Verein deutscher Bibliothekare, *Betriebsstatistik 1978. Information Deutsches Bibliotheksinstitut Berlin* (1979).
[a]The total number of public libraries is 13,588. Statistical data, however, are available only from those included here.

Government Program for Advancement of Information and Documentation (I & D Program), a central institution for research and development was established, the Gesellschaft für Information und Dokumentation (Institute for Information and Documentation) in Frankfurt. An additional 16 centers are planned for special fields, with four now operating. These documentation centers work with their area libraries to supply needed materials.

**Associations.** *Deutsche Bibliothekskonferenz* (German Library Conference). The large library associations of the Federal Republic of Germany are united in the German Library Conference, which is the official partner of the federal government and the federal states regarding all library affairs. The President is one of the chairmen of the member associations and changes in a one-year rotation.

*Deutscher Bibliotheksverband* (German Library Association). This association comprises libraries and their financing institutions. Until the foundation of the German Library Institute in 1978 this association was responsible for all library development and research in the Federal Republic.

Up to now the library foreign office (Bibliothekarische Auslandsstelle) has been part of this association. This office is responsible for international contacts, particularly for invitations to foreign librarians to visit German libraries and for trips by German librarians to foreign countries.

*Verein Deutscher Bibliothekare* and *Verein der Diplombibliothekare an Wissenschaftlichen Bibliotheken* (Association of German Librarians and Association of Certified Librarians in Research Libraries). Librarians in research libraries are members of these two associations. The Verein Deutscher Bibliothekare has been particularly responsible for the official work of research libraries for more than 50 years. The new German cataloguing rules (RAK) and new library loan rules are examples of these initiatives. This association also organizes meetings of the Deutsche Bibliothekartag (German Librarian's Forum). Since some official work has been assumed by the Deutsches Bibliotheksinstitut, these associations' work has been somewhat more restricted to professional tasks. These associations publish the *Zeitschrift für Bibliothekswesen und Bibliographie*.

*Verein der Bibliothekare an Öffentlichen Bibliotheken* (Association of Librarians in Public Libraries). This association is a personnel-oriented organization for librarians of public libraries. It deals mainly with professional matters and publishes *Buch und Bibliothek* (Book and Library).

*Arbeitsgemeinschaft der Spezialbibliotheken* (Working Forum of Special Libraries). The Working Forum of Special Libraries represents a loose union of all special libraries in the Federal Republic. They hold a congress every two years that deals with problems of special libraries.

**National Planning.** Germany's system of federal states and local governments precludes a single statute or administration governing libraries, and regulations concerning them are issued by individual states or local jurisdictions. For example, each federal state has its own legal deposit statute. There are, however, several organizations which coordinate library-related activities.

Matters of concern on the federal level are addressed by the Federal Government-Federal State Commission for Educational Planning and Advanced Research, which is among the organizations responsible for libraries financed by the federal government and states. This commission is also responsible for the German Library Institute in Berlin (founded 1978), which is devoted to library research. The Deutsche Forschungsgemeinschaft (German Research Society) has supported the work of research libraries. Among the federal states, a committee within the Permanent Conference of Ministeries of Culture and Education considers the problems and needs of public libraries. In 1973, the several library and information-related organizations, supported by the Federal Ministery for Education and Science, developed a plan for library development in the Federal Republic, which contains standards for all types of libraries.

GÜNTER PFLUG

*Conrad Gesner*

The Newberry Library

## Gesner, Conrad

(1516–1565)

Conrad Gesner, Swiss humanist scholar, discovered in bibliography an appropriate expression for his profound intellectual adventurousness. Born into a large Zurich family on March 16, 1516, he was assigned to live with two family friends, both of whom encouraged his studies. One was Johann Jacob Amman, who taught him Latin and was a friend of Erasmus. The Battle of Kappel in 1531, which took the life of Zwingli, also claimed Gesner's father, and Conrad returned home to support his mother. In 1533 he traveled to Bourges on a fellowship but returned home the next year following the strong French reaction to Protestantism. He married in 1535, at the age of 19. His first published book, a Greek-Latin dictionary (1537), coincided with his appointment as Professor of Greek at the newly founded university in Lausanne. Four years later he left for a chair in physics and natural history at the Collegium Carolinum in Zurich, where he resided until his death. Honors were bestowed on him by nearby royalty; scholars went to visit him and contributed to his vast correspondence. He died on December 13, 1565, during one of the frequent plagues of Zurich.

Gesner produced 72 "books" that were published in his lifetime and left 18 more unfinished. Alongside the *Bibliotheca universalis,* his best-known work is the *Historia animalium,* four volumes of which appeared 1551–58 and a fifth posthumously in 1587. His work in botany began with an edition of Valerius Cordus of 1561 and was not completed in print until the *Opera botanica* of 1751–71. In both zoology and botany, his work was mostly that of a collector and organizer; he remains the leading modern scholar up to the time of Linnaeus. In philology, his several dictionaries take second place to the *Mithridates* of 1555, in which parallels in 130 languages are presented and the Romany language is discussed for the first time. His medical studies were collected in the *Epistolarum medicinalium* of 1577, while his culinary insights are seen in his 1563 edition of Willich's cookbook, *Ars magirica.* He also worked and published extensively in geology and mineralogy; his studies of fossils were probably the result of his love for mountain climbing, the reports that he did the latter for exercise and amusement notwithstanding.

Gesner's *Bibliotheca universalis* was issued in four folio volumes by a friend, the Zurich publisher Christopher Froschauer. The first volume (1545) is the author catalogue. Next come the *pandects,* a classified subject-index to the first volume, with 21 subdivisions of the world of knowledge. The second volume (1548) contains 19 subjects; theology alone comprises the third volume (1549); while the material on medicine was never published. The fourth volume (1555) is an appendix with additional titles. Gesner's colleagues soon discovered the importance of this work. Two abridgments quickly appeared (1551, 1555); supplements were issued as early as 1555; and expanded new editions were assembled by his pupils Josias Simler (1574) and Johann Jacob Frisius (1583). Gesner's entries include not only author and title information but also frequent imprints, chapter and section headings or other contents descriptions, and occasional critical observations. Not only does Gesner cite the published editions he knew about but also he frequently gives credit to authors for their unpublished or unfinished works, even for works that were known to have been projected. It is hardly correct to see Gesner as the "father of bibliography," since Tritheim, Erasmus, Nevizzano, Leland, and Champier all did important work before him, but the dimensions of Gesner's achievement are many times more vast. The logical planning that was called for, no doubt, was conspicuous in first inspiring his monumental efforts.

**REFERENCES**

Among the few substantial essays in English, see

J. Christian Bay, "Conrad Gesner (1516–1565), the Father of Bibliography: An Appreciation," *Papers of the Bibliographical Society of America* (1916).

D. W. KRUMMEL

# Ghana

Ghana, known before independence in 1957 as the Gold Coast, is a republic of West Africa on the coast of the Gulf of Guinea and is bounded by Upper Volta on the northwest and north, the Ivory Coast on the west, Togo on the east, and the Atlantic Ocean on the south. Pop. (1978 est.) 10,775,000; area 238,533 sq. km. The official language is English.

**National Library.** Even though Ghana has been in the forefront of library development in black Africa, the idea of a national library was not given the importance that the institution deserved. The result is that a national library as an institution with statutorily defined functions does not exist in the country. In 1961 the Padmore Research Library was founded by the Ghana Library Board in memory of the West Indian Pan-Africanist, George Padmore, to support research on African Affairs. It was envisaged that the Library should form the nucleus of the country's national library. Thus from its birth the Research Library on African Affairs, the name given to it in 1966 after the overthrow of the first Republic of Ghana, has been performing those functions usually performed by national libraries throughout the world; that is, the collection, preservation, and dissemination of the nation's intellectual output.

The Research Library on African Affairs is in the capital city of Accra and is administered by the Ghana Library Board. A building extension designed to increase the capacity of the library from 20,000 to 50,000 volumes was completed. Services include compilation of the *Ghana National Bibliography,* which lists all the publications issued in Ghana within the periods covered. It acquires everything written or published in or about Ghana. This includes materials not normally mentioned in the press and other media. Staff are sent to all parts of the country to fulfill this responsibility. The Library, in its capacity as the national bibliographic center for Ghana, is the national agency for the administration of the ISBN system.

The Research Library cooperates actively with other Africana libraries in Ghana in order to pool library resources. Union lists of certain types of library material are kept so that each library is aware of their existence. Africana libraries that enter into this cooperative endeavor are the Institute of African Studies Library, Legon; the Africana Library of the Balme Library, University of Ghana, Legon; and the Africana Library of the University of Cape Coast.

The Library has an active program for the collection and preservation of oral tradition. This covers not only oral literature but also history, music, and dance, on film, tapes, and records.

**Academic Libraries.** The genesis of academic librarianship in Ghana can be traced to the foundation of Achimota College in 1948. The library of the College originally started as a Teachers' Training College Library, but it developed as the basis of a university library. Its facilities extended to other institutions of comparable nature throughout Ghana. In 1951 the Achimota Training College moved with its library to Kumase to become a department of the Kumase College of Technology, now the University of Science and Technology. From Kumase College of Technology the Achimota stock continued to circulate to form the basis for the libraries of the University College of Cape Coast, now University of Cape Coast, the School of Administration of the University of Ghana, and the Teachers' Training College at Winneba. There are three well-developed academic libraries serving the needs of the country's three universities—namely, the Balme Library of the University of Ghana, Legon; the University of Science and Technology Library, Kumase; and the University of Cape Coast Library, Cape Coast.

One feature that all the academic libraries have in common is that their policies are supervised and directed by committees of the universities' Academic Boards. The chairman is invariably the Vice-Chancellor of the university. The libraries are allocated a portion of the funds provided periodically by the central government.

The Balme Library, the main library of the University of Ghana, is the largest academic/research library in Ghana. It grew up with the foundation of the University College of the Gold Coast in 1948. When the library moved into its permanent building at Legon in 1959, the collection totaled 119,000 volumes. The new building was designed to accommodate 350 readers and 250,000 books. But with the adoption of the Report of the Com-

**Ghana Library Association** 502
**Ghana Library Board** 195, 220–221
***Ghana National Bibliography*** 388
**Ghana, University of, Balme Library**
*illus.* 220

Jean E. Lowrie

*The Balme Library of the University of Ghana, Legon, Accra, is the largest academic library in Ghana.*

mission on University Education by the government of Ghana in 1961, it became obvious that the building needed extensions to accommodate its new facilities, its increasing library resources, and its staff. That is, the Balme Library had to change its complexion when the University College became a full-fledged University of Ghana. In response to this new situation, an Africana Library was established to support the work of the Institute of African Studies and, with the annual student intake increased, a Students' Reference Library was created to meet the increased demand for basic textbooks. Between 1961 and 1965 the Balme Library expanded rapidly in staff, materials acquired, and services provided. The bookstock increased to over 200,000 volumes. The collection comprises 297,957 volumes and 5,192 periodical subscriptions (1977).

The Balme Library maintains a Union Catalogue of its departmental libraries: the Law Library and the libraries of the Faculty of Agriculture, the departments of Physics, Chemistry, Zoology, Biochemistry, and Nutrition and Food Science. Other library facilities at the University had not been integrated in the Balme Library Catalogue by the end of the 1970's. If all library resources on the University campus were integrated, the total bookstock would be over 400,000 volumes.

Since 1963 the Balme Library has been a repository for United Nations documents, especially material produced by the parent body, UN, Unesco, FAO, and Economic Commission for Africa (ECA). Publications of all other agencies of the UN are kept in the main library.

The University of Science and Technology succeeded the Kumasi College of Technology, which was established in 1951 and was opened officially in January 1952 with some 200 Teacher Training students transferred from Achimota to form the nucleus of the new College. The Library was started with the collection of books that formed the library of the Teacher Training College at Achimota.

The Library of the University of Cape Coast started as a college library when the University College of Cape Coast was established in 1962 with the primary purpose of producing "graduate teachers in Arts and Science subjects for the Secondary Schools, Teacher-Training Colleges, Polytechnics and Technical Institutes in the country." The library began with some 650 volumes transferred from Kumase. When the college achieved university status in 1971, the stock stood at 65,000 excluding unbound volumes of periodicals. The stock now stands at more than 100,000. More than 1,000 serial and periodical titles are received through subscription and donations.

The University's development plan at the end of the 1970's envisaged a student population of 5,000 and a central library, incorporating both the Arts and Science libraries, which would contain 350,000 volumes with a seating capacity for 1,200 readers. Work on the new library had started by 1979.

**Public Libraries.** Ghana was the first black African country to create a nationwide public library system. In 1928 Bishop Aglionby, the Anglican Bishop of Accra, mooted the idea of providing a library service for the "growing literate" in the cities. He donated an initial amount of £1,000 and persuaded the then British Colonial Government to support the public library movement in principle.

The coming of the British Council to Ghana in 1943 marked an important phase in library development in the country. The Council started at the onset to develop a countrywide service. It thus initiated an articulated pattern to be later adopted by the Ghana Library Board when it was established in 1950. The Council made available to the Board the services of its librarian, Evelyn J. A. Evans, who developed upon this foundation a service that reflected in every detail her experience in the British County Library System, and the Council's entire bookstock was transferred to the Board.

This background and experience facilitated the establishment of the Ghana Library Board with authority to "establish, manage and maintain" libraries in Ghana. The history and development of the Board is the history of public librarianship in the country. Since January 1950, when the ordinance establishing the Gold Coast Library Board came into force, the Board has been closely identified with the growth and development of this type of library.

With the 27,000 books inherited from the British Council in 1950, the Board set out to establish temporary libraries in the regional capitals and to lay the foundation for the building of permanent regional and branch libraries throughout the country. Thus between 1951 and 1955, branches with children's facilities were opened at Cape Coast and Kumasi (1950), at Sekondi (1952), at Ho (1955), and at Koforidua and Tamale (1955). By 1955 the volume of books had risen from 27,000 to 120,000 and in 1960 the bookstock stood at 266,666.

The aim of the Board is first to provide general reading material for the literate population not enrolled in any formal education program. The second aim is to acquire materials that will satisfy the information needs of the literate public. Textbooks similar to those used in schools are provided in fairly large numbers. The Board had more than doubled its bookstock by 1975 to bring the total stock to almost 600,000 volumes.

The Board maintains a Children's Library Service. Beginning with only three children's libraries in Accra in 1950, the Board established 30 children's branch libraries throughout the country. Wherever the Board opened a branch library for adults, it also opened one for children.

Rural people comprise 60 percent of the population, and many are illiterate. The 1970 population census showed that about two-thirds of the adult population is illiterate. The Board was not able to include service to the illiterate majority in its operations because of limits of finance, unsuitability of the books to satisfy local needs, transportation, and the high demand for textbooks.

The rural library service dates back to 1945, when the British Council provided a postal service to its country members—that is, subscribers of the British Council Library living in the rural areas. By 1959 this system had developed into the mobile library service with the provision of book boxes—stout wooden boxes specially designed to stand all kinds of travel and rough treatment. The Book Box Service, as it came to be called, was open to anyone who lived in a place where a library had not been established. For an annual fee, a box of 50 books of the reader's own choice was sent to a subscriber, and one could subscribe to as many boxes as one could afford. This service attracted many schools, community and social centers, mines and other enterprises, hospitals, and individuals.

**School Libraries.** School and college libraries also come under the authority of the Ghana Library Board. In 1968–69 the Board in association with the Ministry of Education and the British Council appointed a committee to "probe the . . . position of school and college libraries and identify the problems that have to be solved." (College in this context refers to the Teacher's Training College and the Polytechnic.)

The committee reported in 1970 and identified the problems facing the school and college libraries as unsuitable accommodations, poor furniture, the total absence of racks for periodicals, and a dependence on the interest and enthusiasm of the Headmaster or Principal. The greatest defect was the lack of proper organization. Practices varied widely, and there was no consistency of library procedure. A total bookstock of 350,000 volumes was found to be in the 245 such institutions in the country.

Following these revelations, the committee recommended that the Ghana Library Board be asked to run the libraries in these schools and colleges and that additional grants be made available for the acquisition of books and services. Thus it was that the School and College Department of the Board was established in 1972. This department is responsible for the order, supply, and cataloguing of books to schools. It also arranges regular visits to advise and offer professional guidance and assistance in the use of the library and prepares booklists and conducts seminars for teacher/librarians and library clerks in the 245 schools and colleges in the country. Two publications, *Manual for School Libraries in Ghana* and *A Suggested List of Books for Secondary Schools and Training Colleges in Ghana,* were issued by the Department.

**Special Libraries.** In industrialized countries like the United Kingdom and the United States of America, special libraries are found in industries, but in developing countries like Ghana such libraries support scientific and social research in various institutions or are built around special collections. In a study carried out by the Central Reference and Research Library of the Council for Scientific and Industrial Research, 71 such libraries were identified. Even though not all the 71 libraries recorded in the directory may be said to be supporting some research activity, their collections serve the special purposes of the institutions they serve.

The most important group of special libraries serves the research institutions of the Council for Scientific and Industrial Research (CSIR). The Council's Central Reference and Research Library, founded in 1964, coordinates and supplements collections and services of the Council's institute libraries. Such libraries with the dates on which they were founded are the Animal Research Library (1964), the Institute of Aquatic Biology Library (1965), the Building and Road Research Institute Library (1951), the Cocoa Research Institute Library (1937), the Food Research Institute Library (1963), the Forest Products Research Institue Library (1960), the Crops Research Institute Library (1950), the Soils Research Institute Library (1945), the Industrial Research Institute Library (1967), and the Water Resources Research Unit Library (1968).

Among the other special libraries may be mentioned the Ministry of Agriculture Library, which was established in 1926.

The Ghana Institute of Management and Public Administration Library was founded in 1961 to serve the special needs of the Institute, a postgraduate professional training and research institution. The scope of the Library, whose stock totals over 50,000 books and monographs, covers management, public administration and finance, law, economic and development planning, local government, and international relations.

The University of Ghana Medical School Library was founded in 1964. The stock grew from 2,000 volumes in 1964 to over 20,000 in 1976, including resources of the Ministry of Health and the National Institute of Health and Medical Research.

The Volta River Authority (1964) Library supports the activities of the Authority mainly in the field of water resources, hydroelectric power generation and distribution, dams, inland water transportation and irrigation, and to a lesser extent economics, law, agriculture, resettlement schemes, and other subjects.

All the banks in the country have libraries attached to their financial operations. They include the Bank of Ghana library, the Ghana Commercial Bank library, and the Capital Investment Bank library. The Economic Library of the Central Bureau of Statistics (1948) has played a useful role by providing services to government statisticians and planners with its stock of 35,000 volumes. A number of departments and corporations run small special collections, but these have not been developed to any great extent.

**REFERENCES**

L. Agyei-Gyane, Compiler, *Directory of Special and Research Libraries in Ghana* (Accra: CSIR, 1977).

Evelyn J. A. Evans, *A Tropical Library Service: The Story of Ghana's Libraries* (London, 1964), an authoritative work on public library development by the first Director of the Ghana Library Board.

Ghana Library Board, *The Ghana Library Board Silver Jubilee Brochure 1950–1975* (Accra, 1975), covers 25 years of the Board's history and analyzes the place of the Board in the public library system in Ghana.

John Harris, *Patterns of Library Growth in English-speaking West Africa* (University of Ghana, 1970), gives useful statistics on libraries in Ghana and other West African countries.

H. DUA-AGYEMANG

## Gjelsness, Rudolph H.
(1894–1968)

Rudolph H. Gjelsness, library educator, consultant, and scholar, was the first recipient (1954) of the Beta Phi Mu award for distinguished service to education for librarianship. He was born in Reynolds, North Dakota, on October 18, 1894. Following his graduation from the University of North Dakota in 1916, Gjelsness became a high school principal in Adams, North Dakota, but resigned a year later to join the American Expeditionary Force. His interest in librarianship had its origin following the Armistice in 1918 when he was detached from the Army to serve as Reference Librarian with the AEF in Beaune, France. Returning to the United States in 1919, Gjelsness enrolled in the University of Illinois's library school and received the B.L.S. degree in 1920. His first professional library position was as Order Librarian

ALA
*Rudolph H. Gjelsness*

for the University of Oregon; in 1922 he became Senior Bibliographer at the University of California. A fellowship from the American Scandinavian Foundation in 1924 permitted him to spend a year in Norway, the home of his ancestors.

Gjelsness's first contribution to library literature appeared in the July 1925 issue of *Public Libraries* and was entitled "A Librarian's Year in Norway." Writing from Norway, he closed the article with, "When I return, I shall be interested in a position where I could develop or organize something." That opportunity came quickly with his appointment by William Warner Bishop as Assistant Librarian and Chief Classifier for the University of Michigan. In the summer of 1927 Gjelsness was given his first opportunity to contribute to library education, teaching a course in national and regional bibliography in Michigan's new library school.

From 1929 to 1932 Gjelsness was Chief of the Preparation Division of the New York Public Library and a Lecturer in library science at Columbia University. From 1932 to 1937 he was Head Librarian at the University of Arizona. In 1937 he consented to return to Michigan as Professor of Library Science with the tacit understanding that in due course he would succeed Bishop as head of the Library School. This appointment came in 1940 and continued until his retirement in 1964. During the 24 years that Gjelsness chaired the Department of Library Science, the University conferred 2,269 degrees in Library Science, including 47 doctorates.

Active in association work, Gjelsness chaired the ALA Committee on Cataloging and Classification from 1930 to 1933, and from 1935 to 1941 he headed the Catalog Code Revision Committee. He was Editor-in-Chief of the *A.L.A. Catalog Rules: Author and Title Entries* (1941). He was Treasurer of ALA from 1941 to 1947 and was President of the Association of American Library Schools in 1948–49.

Strongly committed to international librarianship, Gjelsness co-directed a summer school at Bogotá, Colombia, in 1942 and spent a year away from Michigan (1943–44) as Director of the Benjamin Franklin Library in Mexico City. A sabbatical year (1962–63) was spent as Library Consultant to the President of the University of Baghdad in Iraq.

Following his retirement in 1964, Gjelsness returned to the University of Arizona Library to head its Special Collections Division. After a summer teaching assignment at Michigan in 1968, he went to the University of Puerto Rico to assist in the founding of the Graduate School of Librarianship. He was killed by an automobile in a hit-and-run accident on his second day in Rio Piedras, August 16, 1968.

Luther College and the University of North Dakota awarded him honorary degrees, and in 1966 a Festschrift was published in his honor by the University of Virginia, *Books in America's Past*. His articles and books, which number in excess of 80, pertain largely to issues in library education, international and comparative librarianship, cataloguing and classification, the history of books and printing, and Norwegian literature. He translated a number of Norwegian short stories and novels into English.

RUSSELL E. BIDLACK

## Gleason, Eliza Atkins
(1909–     )

Eliza Atkins Gleason, librarian and educator, was the first Dean of the School of Library Service, Atlanta University, and the architect of a library education program that trained more than 90 percent of all black librarians in the United States. She was born in Winston Salem, North Carolina, on December 15, 1909, to Simon Green and Oleona (Pegram) Atkins. Her father was the founder and first President of Slater State College, now Winston Salem State University, and her mother was a teacher.

After graduating from Fisk University in 1930 as a member of Phi Beta Kappa, Eliza Gleason received the Bachelor of Science degree from the Library School of the University of Illinois in 1931. In 1936 she received the Master of Arts in Library Science from the University of California at Berkeley. She studied at the University of Chicago Graduate Library School and in 1940 became the first black person to receive the Ph.D. in Library Science. She was married to Maurice F. Gleason, a physician, in 1937.

The Dean of the School of Library Service, Atlanta University (1940–46), which opened in 1941, Gleason was aware that the success of the program, even in a period of segregation and rampant discrimination against black persons, depended on a philosophy that was responsive to current human needs but at the same time capable of being remodeled and reshaped when necessary. She wrote, "these objectives are enunciated with the full recognition that no institution can long remain an active force unless it is sensitive to contemporary life, which implies a willingness to accept change. A program of this kind, therefore, predisposes that the objectives of the School of Library Service of Atlanta University are not static but that they may be altered according to the best judgment of the school in what seems to it to be the present and long-term needs of library service with special reference to the Negro" *(Library Quarterly,* July 1942).

Gleason's professional career has been distinguished, wide, varied, and productive. From 1931 to 1932 she was Librarian of the Louisville Municipal College. In 1932 she accepted the position of Head of the Reference Department and Assistant Professor at Fisk and served there until 1936. From 1936 to 1937 she was Director of Libraries at Talladega College, where she became aware of the lack of public library service to black people in the South and began to open the college library resources to black citizens in the surrounding communities. Her interest in access to public libraries for black Americans is reflected in her landmark dissertation, *The Southern Negro and the Public Library* (1941).

In 1953 Gleason became Head of the Reference Department of the Wilson Junior College Library in Chicago. From 1953 to 1954 she was Associate Professor and Head of the Reference Department of the Chicago Teachers College Library. In 1954 she returned to library education as Associate Professor of Library Science, Illinois Teachers College, Chicago, serving until 1963. From 1964 to 1967 she was Assistant Librarian at John Crerar Library in Chicago. She served as Professor of Library Science, Illinois Institute of Technology, from 1967 to 1970. In 1970 she became Assistant Chief Librarian in charge of the regional centers, Chicago Public Library.

Writing in *Illinois Libraries* (April 1972) about the establishment of the Chicago Public Library's regional library centers, Gleason manifests her continuing interests in students and education:

> In planning for Regional Center service, what potential users did the Chicago Public Library have in mind? It had in mind "students"—students of all kinds. Can one imagine a greater boon for the high school teen-agers who are in honors or accelerated courses, or for junior college students whose programs are terminal, or for junior and senior college students whose own college libraries may be inadequate or on the wrong side of town when they have time to study? And finally, there is that vast hoard of "students" who are not enrolled in formal courses but who wish to pursue a subject in depth.

In the 1974–75 academic year she again returned to library education and served as Professor of Library Science at Northern Illinois University.

Active in professional associations, Gleason was the First Afro-American to serve on the ALA Council; she was a member from 1942 to 1946. In 1964 Fisk bestowed upon her its Alumni Award for outstanding accomplishments.

In addition to her book on *The Southern Negro and the Public Library: A Study of the Government and Administration of Public Library Service to Negroes in the South* (1941), she wrote *A History of the Fisk University Library* (1936) and a large number of journal articles.

A woman of great energy and resourcefulness, Gleason led an active community life. She was elected and appointed to many positions of leadership. In 1978, for example, she was appointed to the Chicago Public Library Board. While most people are in or considering retirement as they begin their 70th year, she demonstrated her vitality by beginning a new career for the benefit of humankind—in the fall of 1978 she was appointed Executive Director of the Chicago Black United Fund.

E. J. JOSEY

## Greece (Ancient)

Libraries of public character are attributed by ancient writers to certain 6th-century tyrants of Greek cities, notably Polycrates of Samos and Peisistratus of Athens. Much more is known of the latter than of the former, but we lack the original documents that might have described Peisistratus' supposed library of papyrus rolls of contemporary poetry and drama. Leading scholars believe that any progress in library organization that may have been made under Peisistratus can be determined only by checking the practices of the later libraries of the Ionian cities, which were so important in Greek commerce and culture. Of note during the 5th century were such private libraries as those of the celebrated playwright Euripides, who collected works of poets, dramatists, and philosophers. His passion for books was ridiculed publicly by his rival, Aristophanes. Some writers argue that at least the theater public of that day was conscious of the book, but nothing certain is known about these libraries.

By contrast, when one considers philosophical schools, some encouraging deductions become possible. Socrates is understood to have worked exclusively through oral discourse. His pupil Plato likewise believed that the written word was a burden on free discussion and creative thinking, although it seems probable from the testimony of his writings that much material referred to by him and his students was being checked in a book collection of some sort even though none is mentioned. Besides, Plato's own prose is indebted to some of the very poets he banned from his ideal society, and at least one of his (and Isocrates') students established a library.

Furthermore, if one relies on a modern translation (McKeon edition), Aristotle, speaking briefly of writers on husbandry and household economy in *The Politics,* explains that he did not go into detail because "any one who cares for such matters may refer to their writings." This seems to imply the presence of one or more libraries accessible to the student, or of stores selling such works at prices within student means, but this is not certain. The sole established fact is that Aristotle's personal library was not a part of his Lyceum in either a physical or legal sense.

In the later case of Zeno, the founder of Stoicism, the personal library may have been perceived as an integral part of teaching. In any case, Antogonos Gonatas, who seized power in Macedonia in 276 B.C., tried to attract the septuagenarian Zeno to court and offered him slaves to copy books; but, reportedly, he felt physically unable to leave Athens.

The question of libraries arises also in connection with a number of other educational institutions of pre-Alexandrian Greece. Medical teaching was established by Hippocrates and his associates early in the 4th century, and the early 3rd century witnessed the intellectual enrichment of the gymnasium curriculum. Both enterprises may have had "book" collections among their resources, but there is no evidence as yet.

Most vexing are the uncertainties regarding the books owned by Aristotle, thanks to his prominence and the gaps and contradictions in the record. That he left them (d. 323 B.C.) to disciple Theophrastus is accepted by scholars on the basis of ancient writers' testimony; it is also known that Theophrastus (d. 288 B.C.) bequeathed his collection (including the Aristotle legacy) to his pupil Neleus. Though these facts promote little argument, one must be cautious, since Aristotle's will says nothing of either his school or books, while his legal status as a "metic" prevented him from owning real property in Athens. Did Neleus take the books (which ones?) to his hometown, Skepsis, less than 50 miles north of Pergamum? Were they hidden in a cellar to conceal them from energetic agents seeking books for Pergamum? Did they deteriorate from neglect until found and bought by a rich young Athenian, Apellicon, or were they actually stolen by him right in Athens or were they in the meantime purchased by representatives of Ptolemy II Philadelphus (reigned 285–247 B.C.) for the great library in Alexandria? It seems fairly clear that when Sulla conquered Athens in 86 B.C., he took to Rome what came to be labeled "Aristotle's library," which was confiscated from the late Apellicon's property; that some blundering efforts were made to restore the documents and the texts they contained; and that sometime in the middle of the 1st century B.C. they were properly edited by the scholarly Andronicus of Rhodes, usually referred to as the 11th Director of the Lyceum. Finally, it is clear—and distressingly important—that a danger of misinterpretation awaits every step, thanks to the dual meaning of *biblia*: when did the author refer to the writings of Aristotle or Theophrastus and when to their entire libraries?

SIDNEY JACKSON

## Greece

Greece, a republic on the southern Balkan Peninsula, is bounded by Albania on the northwest, Yugoslavia and Bulgaria on the north, and Turkey on the northeast and extends into the Mediterranean Sea; it lies between the Ionian Sea on the West and the Aegean Sea on the east, occupying most of the islands in the Aegean. Pop. (1977 est.) 9,284,000; area 131,990 sq.km. The official language is Greek.

**National Library.** The National Library of Greece was begun in 1829 on the island Aegina, first capital of the modern Greek state, and it was transferred to Athens in 1834. The National Library is one of the four copyright libraries of Greece. Principal collections are the manuscript section, Greek literature, geography, history, and rare books. The collection totals 1,500,000 items, 4,500 manuscripts, 130 incunabula, and 2,500 rare books. It also includes historical archives, such as documents pertaining to the War of Independence in 1821 and the archives of the Philhellenic committee of London, family records, and other materials.

**Library of Parliament.** At Old Palace, Athens, the Library of Parliament, founded in 1845, provides research and lending services mainly to the members of the Parliament. The collection totals 1,200,000 volumes in Greek and in other languages and special collections on political, social, and economic sciences and history. It maintains complete files of Greek and foreign periodicals and newspapers.

An Annex, Benaki Library, housed in the old Parliament House in Athens, has a collection of 45,000 books,

Arthur Plotnik

*The National Library of Greece, established in 1829 in Aegina, was moved to Athens in 1834.*

mainly literature, history, and modern Greek literature. It includes the Psychari Library donated by E. Benaki and the private collections of political leaders of Greece.

**Academic and Special Libraries.** Libraries of special interest include Gennadious Library, Athens (c. 60,000 items; modern Greece: history, travel, literature; printed catalogue); the Library of the Archaeological Society (65,000 volumes; archaeology and history of ancient Greece); the American British, French, German, Italian, and other archaeological school libraries, which have excellent collections; and the National Research Foundation Library (2,000 titles of scientific periodicals, no books).

Democritos, the Atomic Research Library, Eugenides Foundation Library, and Benaki Phytopathological Research Institute are the main special libraries of the Athens area. Another of special interest is the Library of the Academy of Athens.

University libraries were still at early stages of development at the close of the 1970's. Much remained to be done. The largest is the Library of Salonica University.

**Public Libraries.** The idea of the modern public library was not developed in Greece until after World War II. Thereafter a number of public libraries were established in the provinces, introducing lending and children's sections.

**Library Association.** In the 1970's the Greek Library Association made strong efforts toward improving Greek libraries and librarianship in the country. Efforts were concentrated on legislation and education of librarians through seminars, congresses, and the establishment of two library school courses: a YWCA one-year course (1962—77) and a state-school three-year library program (1977).

K. THANOPOULOU

Records of the National Archives

*Wayne Clayton Grover*

## Grover, Wayne Clayton

(1906–1970)

Wayne Clayton Grover, Archivist of the U.S., was born in Garland, Utah, September 16, 1906, to George F. and Mary Clayton Grover. Graduated from the University of Utah in 1930, he received the M.A. and Ph.D. degrees from the American University in 1937 and 1946, respectively. In 1935 he married the daughter of United States Senator Elbert Thomas (Democrat, Utah), Esther.

Grover worked as a journalist and as a congressional aide between 1930 and 1935. He joined the staff of the National Archives in 1935, during its first year. One of the first persons to receive training as an archivist, he was given a variety of assignments at the Archives. He served as a Records Consultant in 1941–42 with the Office of Strategic Services. In 1943 Grover was commissioned a Captain in the Army, and he became Chief of its records management branch in the Adjutant General's Office. As such he was the War Department's principal staff officer for its pioneering records management program, and he inaugurated the Army's system of records centers. Although he was discharged a Lieutenant Colonel in 1946, he remained in his job as a civilian. He was decorated with the Legion of Merit for his work.

In 1947 the National Archives was confronted with a reduction in staff, a great preservation backlog, and the need to bring the records glut of the federal government under control. The Archivist of the United States, Solon J. Buck, decided to make use of Grover's demonstrated ability by naming him his deputy as Assistant Archivist. Grover was responsible for mending his agency's relations with Congress and getting the Archives to work more efficiently within its slender resources. When Buck resigned as Archivist in 1948, he recommended that Grover be his successor. President Truman nominated Grover, and the Senate confirmed his appointment in June.

During his first year as Archivist, Grover managed to improve his agency's funding and to reduce the backlog of material needing preservation. Nevertheless, the long-range outlook for proper support of the National Archives's programs was poor. Grover was able to get the Hoover Commission on the Organization of the Executive Branch of the Government to champion the establishment of a comprehensive federal records management program. Only that, he believed, would lead to efficiency, economy, and effectiveness in the use of federal records and would assure a smooth flow of records of enduring value to the Archives. The Hoover Commission, however, recommended that the National Archives lose its status as an independent federal agency and that a new bureau deal with records management. In 1949 Congress did place Grover's agency, as the National Archives and Records Service (NARS), under the General Services Administration (GSA), but Congress also clearly intended that NARS become the government's records management service and provided increased funding for that purpose.

Grover became the architect of the many-faceted organization that the National Archives and Records Service became, partly because of his vision and partly because of the opportunities offered him by incorporation into GSA. Previously, his agency had been chiefly concerned with archives, although it also operated the Franklin D. Roosevelt Library and the Federal Register Division and was involved in promoting records management. Grover's first important step was to gain enactment of the comprehensive Federal Records Act of 1950, which officially made NARS into the government's records management agency. This enhanced the likelihood of preserving federal archives for research use, as well as the improved management of records by government agencies. It was most important for the information sciences and for research that Grover won his fight to have records dealt with during their life span on the basis of archival as well as managerial principles.

Grover was responsible for more than the enduring—though occasionally rocky—marriage of archivists and records managers. He upgraded NARS's display program, the centerpieces of which were the Declaration of Independence and the Constitution, which he procured from the Library of Congress in 1952. He inaugurated a facsimile program and expanded his agency's outstanding micropublications and film preservation operations. In 1950 he resuscitated the National Historical Publications Commission, the work of which has enriched the nation's documentary publications. Under Grover's sponsorship the Federal Register Division in 1957 began a valuable new series, the *Public Papers of the Presidents of the United States*. It was Grover who guided the systematization of the acquisition and administration of the papers of recent Presidents and their associates in the Presidential Libraries Act of 1955. Moreover, under his supervision NARS made considerable inroads on its problems of preservation and description. His agency grew from 341 employees when he became Archivist to 1,716 by the time of his retirement in 1965.

Grover did not deal easily with the General Services Administration. Although it provided NARS with increased resources, GSA, with its management orientation, increasingly was criticized for posing a threat to archival professionalism. Grover used the occasion of his retirement to argue for his agency's return to independent status. Although his campaign was unsuccessful, it resulted in better funding for NARS and expansion of its programs. The issue continued to be raised by archivists and historians. Grover remained active in other ways after his retirement, including advising President Johnson on the development of his Presidential Library.

In recognition of Grover's services, Brown and Bucknell universities and Belmont Abbey College bestowed honorary degrees upon him. He received the GSA's Distinguished Service Award in 1959 and one of the National Civil Service League's Career Service Awards in 1961. During his career, Grover was President of the Society of American Archivists, Vice-President of the International Council on Archives, and a member of the United States Commission for Unesco. He was the author of articles in a wide array of professional publications. Yet his real monument was the remarkably broad-based institution that NARS became during his tenure as Archivist of the United States. Grover died in Silver Spring, Maryland, June 8, 1970.

**REFERENCE**

Donald R. McCoy, *The National Archives: America's Ministry of Documents, 1934–1968* (1978).

DONALD R. McCOY

## Guatemala

Guatemala, a republic in northern Central America, is bordered by Mexico on the west and north, Belize on the northeast, the Caribbean Sea on the east, Honduras and El Salvador on the southeast, and the Pacific Ocean on the south and southwest. Pop. (1978 est.) 6,620,500; area 108,889 sq.km. The official language is Spanish.

**National and Public Libraries.** The National Library of Guatemala was founded in 1879 in Guatemala City. A dependent of the Ministry of Public Education, it preserves the national bibliographic heritage and also functions as a public library, the largest in the country in 1979. It occasionally produces and publishes works of national significance. Service is provided to over 125,000 readers annually and includes a special service for children. The total collection of volumes in the national library is 350,000, including that of the periodicals library, which operates independently within the same building.

Ninety-three small public libraries exist throughout the republic. Of these 93 libraries, 64 in different areas of the country fall under the direction of the National Library, while the remaining 29 are under the direction of the Bank of Guatemala, which is their sponsor. Their total collection is 74,000 volumes. Service is provided to approximately 232,500 readers annually throughout the republic.

**Academic Libraries.** The Central Library of the Universidad de San Carlos, the autonomous state university, is the largest academic library in the country. It was established at the new university city in 1966; however, as the faculties that had continued to function in other areas of the capital moved to the new site, their respective libraries were also incorporated into the Central Library, beginning in 1974. The collection comprises 150,000 volumes and 447 journals. Service was provided to 155,000 readers in 1978.

The library of the Universidad Rafael Landivar (1963) has 20,000 volumes and 60 journals and served 30,000 readers in 1978. The library of the Universidad Francisco Marroquín (1972) has 9,788 volumes serving 37,500 readers in 1978. The library of the Universidad José Cecilio del Valle provided service to 37,500 readers in 1978. Founded in 1966, it holds 16,555 volumes and 373 journals. The library of the Universidad Mariano Gálvez (1966) contains 5,000 volumes, serving 5,000 readers in 1978. All five of these libraries are in Guatemala City.

**School Libraries.** In some educational establishments, especially at the secondary level and in state schools, there are small libraries. However, the largest collection does not exceed 3,000 volumes, and they lack professional personnel. The use of these libraries is restricted to faculty and students. No law exists whereby these institutions are required to maintain libraries.

**Special Libraries.** The most important special libraries are in the capital. The Library of the Bank of Guatemala, founded in 1946, serves interests in banking, currency, and economics. Its collection totals 31,000 volumes and 320 journals. In 1978 it provided service to 60,000 readers, including the Bank's officials and the general public. In keeping with the cultural program of the Bank of Guatemala, its library established 29 public libraries throughout the country, of which 9 (district) are in the capital. The Library of the Instituto de Nutrición de Centroamérica y Panamá (INCAP), founded in 1949, specializes in nutrition and allied sciences. Its basic functions are research, teaching, and providing technical assistance to the area countries, and it also serves the general public. Its collection numbers 33,798 volumes and 864

**Libraries in Guatemala (1978)**

| Type | Number | Volumes in collections | Annual expenditures (quetzal) | Population served | Professional staff | All staff (total) |
|---|---|---|---|---|---|---|
| National | 1 | 350,000 | N.A. | 700,504 | 4 | 32 |
| Academic | 5 | 201,343 | N.A. | 43,277 | 15 | 82 |
| Public | 93 | 74,000 | N.A. | 6,810,535 | N.A. | 93 |
| School | N.A. | N.A. | N.A. | N.A. | N.A. | N.A. |
| Special | 3 | 84,798 | Q 32,000[a] | 600[a] | 10 | 31 |

Source: Questionnaire.
[a]Includes only INCAP library (see text).

journals. During 1978 it served 33,330 readers. In 1976, 45 percent of its collection was destroyed by fire resulting from the earthquake of February 1976, but this material has since been replaced.

The Library and Documentation Center of the Instituto Centroamericano de Investigación y Tecnología Industrial (ICAITI), founded in 1956, serves industry and business; it also functions as the regional coordinator of the OAS Program of Information and Technical Assistance for Business in Central America and the Caribbean. It conducts training in documentation services. Its collection totals 20,000 volumes, and 300 journals. In 1978 service was provided to approximately 10,000 readers. Other institutions that contribute to the economic development of Guatemala, and whose holdings include important collections of journals and documents, are the Instituto Técnico de Capacitación y Productividad (INTECAP), Guatexpro Centro Nacional de Promoción de las Exportaciones (GUATEXPRO), and the Secretaría Permanente del Tratado General de Integración Económica Centroamericana (SIECA).

GUILLERMO PALMA R.



## Guinea

Guinea, a republic of West Africa, on the Atlantic Ocean, is bounded by Guinea-Bissau on the northwest, Senegal and Mali on the north and northeast, Ivory Coast on the east, and Liberia and Sierra Leone on the south. Pop. (1978 est.) 4,762,000; area 245,857 sq.km. The official language is French.

**National Library.** When Guinea obtained independence from France in October 1958, it had no professional librarians. The only library open to the general public, and the largest library in the former French territory, was the research library of the Institut Français d'Afrique Noire (IFAN) in the capital city of Conakry. It was strongest in history and natural sciences, and it served as the nucleus of the new National Library. The stock had reached 11,000 books and 300 periodicals when it was moved to another building in 1967. In early 1959 staff were recruited, and during the 1960's short training courses were introduced.

**Academic Library.** The nation's first school at the university level, the Institut Polytechnique, appointed its first professional librarian in 1965; at that time the collection numbered 20,000 volumes.

**Public Libraries.** Efforts were made to expand public library service beyond the capital of Conakry through the Partie Démocratique de Guinée (PDG), which is responsible for certain quasi-government functions. It began its program with about 600 volumes per lot (30 lots), mostly donated by friendly governments.

Little current information on library service was available at the end of the 1970's; evidence from what was known was that there had been no radical change over the decade.

F. LALANDE ISNARD

## Guinea-Bissau

Guinea-Bissau, an independent republic of West Africa, is bounded by Senegal on the north, Guinea on the east and south, and the Atlantic Ocean on the west. Pop. (1978 est.) 949,400; area 36,125 sq.km. The official language is Portuguese. Before Guinea-Bissau, a former overseas province of Portugal (Portuguese Guinea), gained its independence in 1975, the Museum and Public Library of Bissau was the only significant library. Its restricted schedule of hours and out-of-date collections limited use. The Center of Scientific Investigation, under the Ministry of Culture, was founded after independence; it received the collections previously held by the Museum and Public Library. It was being reorganized at the end of the 1970's.

Three secondary and eight primary schools operated libraries in the capital of Bissau.

Two special libraries that operated in the late 1970's were the Library of Legal Sciences, planned to become part of a new university, and the library of the Statistics Service, under the Ministry of State for Planning. The most important library activities center in Bissau.

MARIA MANUELA CRUZEIRO

## Guyana

Guyana, a republic on the Atlantic coast, is bounded by Venezuela, Brazil, and Suriname, in South America. Pop. (1978 est.) 845,000; area 214,970 sq.km. The official language is English.

**National and Public Libraries.** The National Library of Guyana in Georgetown had its origin in the Public Free Library service, which was established in 1909. In 1950 an act of the Legislative Council empowered the Library authority to extend the library service beyond Georgetown, initiating the rapid development of a countrywide service; the Law Revision Act of 1972 empowered the National Library to perform the dual functions of both a national and a public library. The law also designated the National Library a legal deposit library, which entitles it to one copy of every local imprint, and it published the Guyanese National Bibliography from 1972.

The National Library provides service through the operation of several units. The Adult Reference and Lending Departments, a Juvenile Department, and one branch library together serve Georgetown. Two branch libraries outside Georgetown, a Rural Services Department comprising 17 Rural Library Centers, and two bookmobiles jointly provide service to the rest of the country. Additional public library services are provided by the John F. Kennedy Library, with collections devoted exclusively to U.S. books.

The resources of the National Library total an estimated 184,956 items, including manuscripts and phonograph records and a valuable special collection of research material on Guyana. It is also a depository for Unesco publications.

**Table 1. Archives in Guyana (1976)**

| | |
|---|---|
| Number | 1 |
| Holdings | 4,000 linear feet |
| Annual expenditures | G$35,000 |
| Professional staff | 4 |
| All staff (total) | 11 |

Source: *National Archives of Guyana.*

**Academic Libraries.** The University of Guyana Library, established in 1963, is the only academic library in the country. It supports the teaching and research programs of the University with a total collection of some 150,000 items, including manuscripts and nonprint materials. The Library is a partial depository for the publications of the United Nations and its several agencies and in 1972 was designated a legal deposit library for Guyanese imprints. Of special importance is the Library's Caribbean Research Collection, an extensive collection of material on Guyana and the Caribbean that is considered, because of its many unique holdings, to be perhaps the world's largest collection of material on Guyana. The University Library operates an international gifts and exchange program and is the local center for international lending activities related to the British Library Lending Division. Other international loan activities are also undertaken.

**Table 2. Libraries in Guyana (1976)**

| Type | Number | Volumes in collections | Annual expenditures (dollar) | Population served | Professional staff | All staff (total) |
|---|---|---|---|---|---|---|
| National | 1 | 184,956 | G$450,472 | 175,000 | 5 | 66 |
| Academic | 1 | 150,000 | G$685,000 | 3,000 | 13 | 65 |
| Public | 1 | 7,654 | N.A. | 1,900 | 1 | 4 |
| School | 18[a] | N.A. | N.A. | N.A. | N.A. | N.A. |
| Special | 24 | 115,000 | N.A. | 9,178 | 7 | 49 |

[a]Excludes primary schools.

Sources: *Guide to Library Services in Guyana; Annual Reports.*

**School Libraries.** Except for the organized libraries in the 12 largest secondary schools in the country, school libraries were still largely in their formative years in the late 1970's, particularly in the primary level of the education system. There are six libraries in postsecondary colleges such as colleges of education, most of which are small collections of books and audiovisual materials.

**Special Libraries.** The Medical Science Library and the Library of the Department of Mines and Surveys are perhaps the largest and best organized special libraries in the country; although primarily committed to serving the organizations to which they are attached, these libraries do provide a limited service to the wider community. Most other special libraries are small units attached to government departments. Most of these are as yet small collections, a few of which were in the process of being developed by 1979. The Library of the Caribbean Community Secretariat (CARICOM) supports the needs of officers concerned with development in the Caribbean at the regional level. Limited service is also given to researchers and students from the Guyanese community.

YVONNE STEPHENSON

# Haines, Helen

(1872–1951)

Helen Elizabeth Haines, teacher, reviewer, and advocate of intellectual freedom, influenced generations of students of librarianship through her book *Living with Books: The Art of Book Selection* (1935, 1950). A native of New York City, Haines was born on February 9, 1872. Privately educated, she held only one degree, an honorary M.A. conferred by the University of Southern California in 1945.

After undertaking free-lance work as an indexer and writing *The History of New Mexico from the Spanish Conquest to the Present Time, 1530–1890* (New Mexico Historical Publishing Company, 1891), Haines was employed by R. R. Bowker, publisher of library indexes and journals, in 1892 on the recommendation of Mary Wright Plummer, library educator and family friend. She held a number of editorial positions before she was appointed Managing Editor of *Library Journal* in 1896, a position she held until ill health forced her resignation in 1908.

The *Proceedings* of the American Library Association were published annually in *Library Journal,* and Haines became the Association's recorder. She served on the Council and the Executive Board; in 1906 she was elected Second Vice-President.

In Pasadena, California, where Haines moved in search of health, she began a career as book reviewer and activist in library affairs. A book review column, "The Library Table," was begun in the *Pasadena News* in 1910 and continued for 40 years. Her reviews appeared in other newspapers and periodicals, including the *New York Herald Tribune,* the *Nation,* and the *Saturday Review of Literature,* and she gave series of book talks for the Pasadena, Long Beach, and Los Angeles public libraries. Her articles on library legislation, book selection, and other topics appeared in state and national library journals.

Haines's advocacy of high literary standards in the selection of materials for libraries was brought to the attention of library educators, and in 1914 she began to teach book selection and the history of books and libraries at the training class of the Los Angeles Public Library. When the class became a library school and, in 1932, part of the University of Southern California, Haines became a full-time faculty member. She lectured to book selection classes at the University of California at Berkeley and prepared and conducted correspondence courses in book selection for the American Correspondence School of Librarianship and the Columbia University Home Study Department. She taught at Columbia University during summer sessions.

Columbia University Press gave Haines a grant that enabled her to write *Living with Books: The Art of Book Selection* (1935), which, published by Columbia, became a standard text in library schools and a reference tool in libraries. Appreciative of contemporary as well as traditional literature, comprehensive, liberal in outlook, and delightfully readable, it became the book-oriented librarian's bible. *What's in a Novel,* also published by Columbia Press (1942), an analysis and appreciation limited to contemporary literature, largely of the more or less popular mainstream, did not serve as broad a purpose.

By 1950, when a new edition of *Living with Books* was published, again by the Columbia University Press, the climate had changed. Haines, then 78 years old, again exhibited an open, liberal attitude toward the books of the period, including those on politics, religion, and science. It was inevitable that she should be accused of a pro-Soviet bias, and not surprising that many librarians should timidly reject the book. Long a defender of intellectual freedom, and one of the founders of the Committee on Intellectual Freedom of the California Library Association in 1940, Haines had foreseen and warned against censorship from within libraries.

Recognized as an outstanding library educator, a brilliant speaker and author, and a principal force in encouraging in librarians a love of books and high critical standards, Haines was given the Joseph W. Lippincott Award for outstanding achievement in librarianship by ALA in 1951. Her eloquent speech of acceptance measured the power of the book in the past and foretold its continuing influence in the future. Helen Haines died in Altadena, California, on August 26, 1951.

**REFERENCES**

Helen E. Haines, "Living with Books," *Library Journal* (1951).

Everett T. Moore, "Innocent Librarians," *ALA Bulletin* (1961), describes attack on Haines as "a propagandist for the Stalinist way of life" by Oliver Carlson in *The Freeman,* (1952, and the point-by-point answer given by Elinor S. Earle in *ALA Bulletin* (1952).

Everett T. Moore, "The Intellectual Freedom Saga in California," *California Librarian* (1974), an account of Haines's activities and leadership in intellectual freedom.

RUTH WARNCKE

# Haiti

Haiti, a republic in the Caribbean Sea, occupies the western third of the island of Hispaniola and is bounded by the Dominican Republic on the east and the Atlantic Ocean on the north. Pop. (1979 est.) 6,000,000; area 27,700 sq.km. The official language is French, spoken by 20 percent of the population; the national language is Creole.

**National Library.** The Bibliothèque Nationale was created in 1940. Under the direction of Max Bissainthe (1942–57), the Library's Haitian collections grew from 280 titles in 1942 to more than 6,000 in 1957. Bissainthe was also responsible for the compilation of the Haitian retrospective bibliography *(Dictionnaire de Bibliographie Haitienne* (1951). The National Library suffered great losses during the 1960's, and its Haitian collection was reduced to 860 titles and its total holdings to 7,000 volumes. The Library had no acquisitions budget in the 1970's, and it does not receive depository copies of Haitian imprints.

**Academic Libraries.** Haiti's 16 schools of higher education, 9 of which form the official Université d'Etat d'Haiti, are served by 11 libraries with a total collection of about 55,000 volumes. The libraries of the Faculties of Agriculture (38,000 volumes approximately) and of Medicine (10,000 volumes) are the most notable. They have well-organized collections and qualified personnel. The Faculty of Medicine, with a separate lending collection of 2,287 volumes, was the only academic library with an acquisitions budget in 1979. All libraries limit student access to the stacks and permit only in-house consultation of books and magazines.

**Public Libraries.** The French Institute (Institut Français d'Haiti) maintains the only modern public library in the country. Financially supported by the French government, it has a collection of over 34,000 items arranged on open stacks and available on loan. It has a children' section—the only such facility in the country—and a sizable, ever expanding collection of Haitiana. The head, a professional librarian, from 1974 compiled the national bibliography published in *Conjonction,* the scholarly review of the French Institute.

There are other small public libraries in Port-au-Prince and the largest provincial towns. As a rule, they reach only a small fraction of their potential users, an estimated 10 to 20 percent of the population who can read.

**School Libraries.** Of the country's nearly 3,000 elementary and secondary schools, which serve approximately 570,000 children, an estimated 25 percent have what can be better described as deposits of old books rather than as libraries. Two private schools in the town of Cap-Haitien—Collège Regina Assumpta and Collège Notre-Dame—are exceptions: their libraries house almost 40,000 volumes on open shelves, and collections are heavily utilized.

**Table 2. Archives in Haiti (1976)**

| | |
|---|---|
| Number | 18 |
| Holdings | 964.3 cubic meters |
| Professional staff | 4 |
| All staff (total) | 250 |

Source: Bruno Delmas, *Haiti: Etat des systèmes d'information des pouvoirs publics et propositions de réorganisation et développement (Unesco, 1979).*

**Special Libraries.** The library of the Institution Saint Louis de Gonzague, associated with a Catholic school, specializes in the history and culture of Haiti and is the country's principal research library. It has over 20,000 monographs, serials, and other documents. The fast-growing library of the Ministry of Planning (Ministère du Plan) specializes in Haitian government documents and technical reports.

**REFERENCE**

Wilfrid Bertrand and Daniéla Devesin, "Bibliothèques haitiennes aujourd'hui," *Conjonction* (1975), a complete survey of Haiti's libraries, including a brief history and statistical data.

LYGIA MARIA F. C. BALLANTYNE

# Hamer, Philip May
(1891–1971)

Historian and teacher of history, librarian and archivist, Philip Hamer was born in Marion, South Carolina, November 10, 1891. He received a B.A. from Wofford College in Spartanburg, South Carolina, M.A. at Trinity College (now Duke University), and Ph.D. in History

**Table 1. Libraries in Haiti (1976)**

| Type | Number | Volumes in collections | Annual expenditures (gourdes) | Population served | Professional staff | All staff (total) |
|---|---|---|---|---|---|---|
| National | 1 | approximately 7,000 | G 250,000[a] | 100,000 est. | N.A. | 16 |
| Academic | 11 | approximately 55,000 | G 35,000[b] | 4,500 | 13 | 40 |
| Public | 13 | approximately 70,438 | G 57,000[c] | 1,000,000 est. | 2 | 44 |
| School | 7 | approximately 49,400 | N.A. | 570,000 | N.A. | 22 |
| Special | 13 | approximately 64,000 | N.A. | 10,000 est. | 2 | 36 |
| Total | 45 | approximately 245,838 | | | | 158 |

[a] Salaries and operating expenses only.
[b] Represents acquisitions budget of the School of Medicine.
[c] Represents acquisitions budget of French Institute library.

Sources: Wilfrid Bertrand and Daniéla Devesin, "Bibliothèques haitiennes aujourd'hui," *Conjonction* (1975), supplemented by data collected through interviews. Estimates of population served are based on data contained in H. Wiesler, *La Scolarisation en Haiti* (Port-au-Prince, 1978).

Philip May Hamer

Records of the National Archives

(1918) at the University of Pennsylvania. After a year as Professor of History at the University of Chattanooga, he went to the University of Tennessee at Knoxville, where he served as Associate Professor of History, 1920–26, Professor of History, 1926–35, and Chairman of the Graduate School, 1930–34.

Hamer was popular as a teacher, but he also loved research and writing history, and he published many articles on East Tennessee, the Revolution, Indian relations, the southwestern frontier, and a four-volume history of Tennesee (1933). He helped organize the East Tennessee Historical Society, of which he was President, 1926–28. Later, he was a founder of the Southern Historical Association, Editor of its *Journal of Southern History,* and in 1938 its President. His presidential address, delivered at New Orleans, "The Records of Southern History," was published in volume 5 of the Association's *Journal.*

Hamer joined the staff of the newly established National Archives in 1935 as a deputy examiner of records and was assigned to survey the records of the Interior Department, which had in its file rooms, basements, and attics much that intrigued him. But not only records in the District of Columbia were of interest to him. On January 1, 1936, he became the National Director of the Survey of Federal Records outside the District of Columbia, a project supported by Works Progress Administration funds. Hamer accepted this responsibility without special compensation, depending on the $3,500 a year he was receiving as Deputy Examiner. He prepared *The Manual of the Survey of Federal Archives,* a mimeographed pamphlet of 29 numbered leaves, which was sent to appointed regional directors, members of advisory committees, and some of the key workers.

When the Survey of Federal Records was legally terminated on June 30, 1937, most of the records of the federal government in the 48 states had been surveyed and reported, but the work of compiling and making available the information thus secured remained unfinished. Responsibility for such activity was transferred to the Historical Records Survey, of which Luther H. Evans was National Director, and members of the staff of the Survey of Federal Records both in the field and in Washington were also transferred. Hamer was appointed, again without pay, as Associate National Director. The intended *Inventory of Federal Records* in the states got out of hand because records of the federal agencies were stored in 58,840 rooms in 24,536 buildings and in volume amounted to 5,080,694 linear feet. By the end of 1940, 333 volumes with a total of 36,168 pages had been published in mimeograph form and distributed to libraries throughout the country. Hamer's interesting reports on the problems of the Survey of Federal Records from 1936 to 1940 may be found as appendices in the second to sixth Annual Reports of the Archivist of the United States. He also gave a number of speeches, one of them to the newly organized Society of American Archivists.

In April 1936 he was appointed Chief of the Division of the Library in the National Archives. It was expected that the Library would consist of some 50,000 or 60,000 volumes—mainly American history and biography—printed government documents, and many pamphlets and journals. Many older copies of printed documents could be secured from federal agencies that no longer needed them. His achievement—a good, working library—is still evident, for next to the Library of Congress the National Archives Library is the best and most convenient repository of American history in the District of Columbia.

In 1938 Hamer was appointed Chief of the Reference Division, into which the Library Division had been merged, a position he held until 1944. During those years his staff members not only took care of the Library but ran the central search room, requesting records from the custodial divisions for historians wishing to examine federal records.

From 1944 to 1951 Hamer was Director of Records Control. The change in title indicated that Hamer and his staff members, while still handling reference work, had become increasingly concerned with the preparation of guides, inventories, and other finding aids, and had taken over much of the work of the Classification and Cataloguing Divisions, which had been abolished in 1939 and 1941. The first adequate *Guide to the Records in the National Archives* (684 pages), published by the Government Printing Office in 1948, was "prepared under the immediate direction and editorial supervision of Philip M. Hamer," according to the Archivist's foreword. Hamer was also responsible for planning and directing a special guide in two volumes to *Federal Records of World War II* (1950).

Hamer had also been serving as Secretary of a National Historical Publications Commission, 1946–51, established as part of the Act of 1934 creating the National Archives. Not much had been done before 1946 because of the demands of World War II, but Hamer, who had always been interested in making documentary sources more available, felt it was time to get that program going. He had the support of Solon J. Buck, the Archivist, who by law chaired the Commission. President Truman, upon being presented with volume one of Julian Boyd's *The Papers of Thomas Jefferson,* asked the Commission to canvass scholars and plan a similar program for publishing the papers of other American leaders. The Federal Records Act of 1950 gave the Commission additional authority, and in 1951 Hamer was made Executive Director, a full-time assignment that he held until his retirement in 1961. In 1954 he transmitted to the President the Commission's *A National Program for the Publication of Historical Documents* (106 pages), which he had prepared after discussions with history teachers, historical societies, and others interested in the publication of source documents. The Commission also proposed the preparation of a guide to the archival and manuscript collections of the nation, which Hamer and his staff planned, prepared, and published in 1961. It describes the holdings of more than 1,000 archival agencies, historical societies, and libraries in the United States and is still a basic tool of the scholarly historian.

The Commission labeled as priority projects the publication of the papers of Benjamin Franklin, John and John Quincy Adams, Alexander Hamilton, and James

Madison. Hamer helped to get all of them started, along with a project for the "Documentary History of the Ratification of the Constitution and First Ten Amendments." He worked with certain scholars and universities to start additional projects for John C. Calhoun, Henry Clay, John Jay, Andrew Johnson, John Marshall, James K. Polk, and Woodrow Wilson, among others.

In October 1960 Hamer was elected the 16th President of the Society of American Archivists, and in 1961 he gave the presidential address at the annual meeting in Kansas City. His subject was "Authentic Documents Tending to Elucidate Our History" (published in *The American Archivist,* volume 25).

Hamer wanted to see published the papers of Henry Laurens, who had represented South Carolina in the Continental Congress and served two years, 1777–78, as its President. Hamer felt that he had been one of the forgotten Revolutionary leaders. Upon Hamer's retirement from the Commission on November 30, 1961, he continued to work on the project in the National Archives building, where the papers of the Continental Congress were preserved. He chose as his Associate Editor Professor George C. Rogers, Jr., of the University of South Carolina, another repository for many papers. Much collecting and editing had been done, and two volumes were published by the University of South Carolina Press, before Hamer died on April 10, 1971. A third volume, upon which he had worked, was published in 1972; others followed.

OLIVER W. HOLMES

# Handicapped, Services to

Most special library service for handicapped individuals is concerned with those who cannot read ordinary print because of visual or physical limitations. The reading needs of these persons are met by providing books in special forms—braille, large print, or recorded. A few libraries also supply special devices to enhance limited vision and provide electronic reading machines.

Special library service for blind readers is well established after more than one hundred years of experience; however, the special reading needs of other sensory-impaired persons—primarily the deaf—have not been seriously considered until recently. Although deafness is generally recognized as a serious disability, it is not usually recognized as a handicap to reading. Probably for this reason, special library service for deaf persons has played no significant role in the public library service of the U.S.; the few available special library collections are in schools and institutions. They consist mostly of captioned movie films, slides, filmstrips, sign-language instructional materials, and storybooks for children.

Other handicapped persons—the mentally retarded, emotionally disturbed, the learning disabled—could benefit from the use of reading materials and special library service. Among the present limited number of such special materials are high-interest, low-vocabulary publications. Special editions of Boy Scout merit badge manuals for learning-disabled Scouts, for example, are popular and have been helpful. These collections are small and are most frequently found in institutions and organizations with a special interest in serving this group of handicapped individuals rather than in public libraries.

Thorough and independent studies are lacking, but it appears that by the late 1970's deaf and other groups of handicapped individuals did not have access to adequate library service. The needs of these persons and the feasibility of providing them with special materials through a nationally coordinated special library service parallel to the services provided to blind and physically handicapped individuals was being studied.

THE BLIND AND PHYSICALLY HANDICAPPED

Federally sponsored national library service in the U.S. for blind and physically handicapped individuals originated with the Pratt-Smoot Act of March 3, 1931, which enabled the Library of Congress to establish a collection of embossed books for circulation to legally blind adult residents of the U.S. and American citizens living abroad. It also authorized the Librarian of Congress to arrange for other libraries to serve as local or regional centers for circulation of such books; 13 were designated after consultation with the American Library Association and the American Foundation for the Blind. The free mailing privileges granted in 1903 for mailing braille books were extended to those circulating from the Library of Congress collection.

The Adult Blind Book Project began on July 1, 1931, with priority on selection of titles to be embossed. A 1933 amendment provided for books on records. Talking-book service was launched in October 1934; by 1935, 100 copies of 27 titles—including the Bible, Shakespearean plays and sonnets, historical documents, and fiction—were available for circulation through 24 cooperating libraries. Further legislation in 1952 deleted the word *adult* from the basic law, paving the way for service to blind children. In 1962 music services were added, and in 1966 severely physically handicapped individuals were included as recipients of special services.

**The NLS.** As of 1978 the National Library Service for the Blind and Physically Handicapped (NLS) of the Library of Congress distributed special reading materials for blind and physically handicapped individuals through a cooperating network of 56 regional and 101 subregional libraries. In public, city, and state libraries and in a few instances in private institutions, these libraries provide library service to eligible persons in their service areas. As

Hennepin County Library

*Hennepin County Library, Minnesota, provides extensive services to the homebound and handicapped people.*

of fiscal year 1977, the Library collection included more than 5,387,000 volumes and containers; of these, 13,291,000 were circulated to 570,810 individuals.

**Selection.** Reading tastes of blind and physically handicapped individuals are generally indistinguishable from those of the public at large, and NLS selects materials accordingly. The generosity of copyright owners in granting permission to reproduce materials allows NLS to select from the same wide choice of materials available to the general public. Books are selected after consultation with advisory committees composed of librarians and other specialists and must be reviewed in national book-trade publications, library periodicals, and leading newspapers or must appear on best-seller lists of national circulation or be recommended by readers. Selection is not made until a copy of the print book has been examined.

A braille book contains the entire text of a print book, while a talking book is the recording of the complete text of a print book read aloud by a person professionally trained for reading. The high cost of producing braille and talking books in sufficient quantity generally limits the number of titles to those meeting the widest reader preference, to assure the best use of available funds. An average talking book of seven records cost $5,500 to $6,600 in the late 1970's for an edition of 1,100 copies; an average novel recorded on cassette tape cost about $6,050 in an edition of 1,100 copies; press-braille books averaged four volumes per title and cost about $4,300 for an edition of 70 copies. Braille and talking books are produced for NLS by organizations concerned primarily with handicapped individuals. Four principal presses produce books and magazines in press-braille under contract with the Library.

**Materials and Services.** NLS provides regional libraries with a basic collection of recorded books and books in braille, which are supplemented by single copies of local volunteer-produced books in braille or on cassette tapes. Single copy titles are generally available on interlibrary loan.

*Music Collections.* The NLS Music Services Program, established in 1962, is the major national source for music scores, textbooks, and instructional materials in formats usable by blind and other disabled persons. These materials are provided to readers directly rather than through the network of cooperating libraries, and the collection includes audio demonstrations of actual playing styles and techniques; music theory, appreciation, and history; and beginning, intermediate, and advanced instruction for piano, organ, and guitar.

The *Musical Mainstream,* which contains reprints from print music periodicals, original articles, announcements, and lists of recent acquisitions, is a bimonthly NLS magazine produced in recorded, braille, and large-print editions. A braille edition of *Music Article Guide*—a quarterly annotated index of significant, signed feature articles from American music periodicals—is also distributed; on request, articles in the index are recorded and provided for patrons.

*Children's Books.* The juvenile collection serves preschoolers through young teenagers. Each year the Newbery and Caldecott Award books are produced. Recommendations of the Children's Advisory Committee are considered in selecting children's books for production in braille or recorded form. Book selection for handicapped children presents special problems. The text of a book must stand on its own, independent of illustrations, diagrams, or graphs. Although verbal explanations of some illustrative material are possible, children's books that depend largely on illustration may be unsuitable for transcription or recording. A notable development is the production of print books with transparent page overlays of braille transcriptions. Thus, a blind parent and a sighted child or a blind child and a sighted parent can read together.

Library of Congress

*Daniel J. Boorstin, 12th Librarian of Congress, narrating his book* An American Primer *in a studio of the National Library Service for the Blind and Physically Handicapped. When completed, the book was made available in 1,500 copies for approximately 600,000 users of the LC program.*

*Periodicals.* Magazines constitute a large proportion of material available in recorded format. More than 50 popular titles, recorded on flexible discs, are mailed directly by producers to the readers. Other magazines in braille, large print, and recorded form are available to readers by subscription from nonprofit organizations. The number of magazines in special form is, nevertheless, very small compared with print magazine availability.

Before specific new magazine titles are selected for the national program, most are tested through the *Talking Book Magazine of the Month* and the *Braille Magazine of the Quarter.* Production of braille and recorded editions of the *New York Times Large Type Weekly* is a cooperative venture of the Library and the *New York Times* and provides for a national-circulation newspaper to blind and physically handicapped readers. *Talking Book Topics* and *Braille Book Review,* available in special forms for handicapped readers, are bimonthly magazines published by NLS containing announcements of new books, articles, and newsnotes.

*Cataloguing.* Since 1955, when braille and talking books were first catalogued centrally and cards printed and distributed to the regional libraries, NLS has advanced to a computer-produced microfiche catalogue, *Reading Material for the Blind and Physically Handicapped,* first distributed to network libraries earlier in 1977. This system was designed to include listings of all available loan materials. Revisions can be processed, and complete new editions are produced quarterly at a fraction of the cost of print material.

*Interlibrary Loan.* If a request for braille or recorded material from a reader cannot be filled by the regional library, it may be serviced through a multistate center or the NLS Resources Coordination Unit. Cooperating network libraries produce significant amounts of single-copy recorded and braille materials. Interlibrary lending of these materials is aided by the use of the computerized catalogue.

*Education.* To serve handicapped persons and others interested in their welfare, the NLS program maintains a national reference and referral service on all aspects of blindness and other physical handicaps. A public education effort is made to reach unserved handicapped persons. NLS sponsors programs for locating and reaching potential users and participates in programs and exhibits at conferences, sponsors magazine articles, issues mass mailing of publications, and conducts other outreach activities.

*Standards.* To promote high standards in library service for blind and physically handicapped individuals, NLS sponsors biennial conferences for network librarians. NLS staff members serve as area consultants and visit each of the regional and subregional libraries periodically to ensure smooth functioning of the program, resolve service problems, and provide leadership in introduction of innovative practices.

Revision of standards for service is in progress by the American Library Association with funds provided by the Library of Congress. The revised standards cover four major areas: (1) administration, including organization, budget, volunteers, and reports; (2) resource development, including network responsibilities, selection, bibliographic control, and duplication of recorded and braille material; (3) service to users, including circulation and reader advisory service; and (4) public education and information.

**Research and Development.** These have long played important roles in improving service for handicapped readers, including the development of the long-playing record in 1934 and more recently the four-track cassette and reduced recording speeds.

A number of innovative ideas for reading machines are being studied, with the objective of developing a machine capable of scanning printed material and providing an interpretation of it in a form understandable to blind and physically handicapped readers. Such a method would permit independent reading of ordinary printed material and would be a valuable addition to present reading techniques. Examples include the Kurzweil Reading Machine, a computer-assisted device that scans a print page with an optical character recognition system. It breaks down the characters into basic print elements, translates them into basic sound elements, and puts them together into synthesized speech.

Cassette equipment that accepts, stores, and displays braille on a tactile board has been developed by several manufacturers; such electronic equipment is compact, portable, and enables the user to read braille on an electronic tactile display rather than on paper. The Saltus Reader is designed for use by visually impaired persons or by physically handicapped individuals who lack sufficient manual dexterity to handle printed books or magazines. The reading machine is a metal box that holds either a book printed in large type on a reel of paper or individual pages encased in pockets of a continuous roll of plastic. A motor advances or rewinds the paper one page at a time or at a continuous rate. Telebook, developed by Mitre Corporation under contract with the Library, is another new concept being tested for talking-book service. Readers dial a central telephone number and request that specific talking books or magazines be played over FM radios via cable television lines.

**Volunteers and Associations.** For almost a century volunteers have performed indispensable services for handicapped readers. More than a score of philanthropic and nonprofit organizations continue to augment the national program in valuable ways. Volunteers transcribe hand-produced braille books in single copies or very small editions to meet special needs. They supplement talking-book collections by recording on standard magnetic tape many of the small but growing lists of specialized and scholarly titles. The Telephone Pioneers of America is a volunteer organization of senior telephone industry employees who spend many hours repairing and restoring talking-book machines. NLS cooperates with related associations and libraries to further mutual goals. Close liaison and cooperative projects are carried on with Recording for the Blind, Inc., the National Braille Association, Hadley School for the Blind, and others active in producing or circulating reading materials. In addition, professional associations directly related to service to blind persons include the American Association of Workers for the Blind, the Association for Education of the Visually Handicapped, and professional library organizations.

**Other Countries.** The principle that special services should be provided for handicapped persons unable to use public libraries was conceived in the United States in 1868 when the Boston Public Library established a department with embossed books. A similar project began in 1882 in the United Kingdom when the Lending Library for the Blind was founded as a charitable venture; in 1916 its name was changed to the National Library for the Blind, and it now provides large-print books for partially sighted readers as well as braille and Moon type. In 1934 the Royal National Institute for the Blind (RNIB) set up the British Talking Book Service for the Blind. As elsewhere, however, circulation of braille in Europe decreased considerably during the first decade of talking books. In Britain three agencies provide talking books. Books recorded on cassettes are available to any adult who registers either as blind or unable to read ordinary print. Playback machines can be rented for a modest fee, but local authorities or voluntary agencies often pay these charges.

The largest producers of braille in the United Kingdom are RNIB, the National Library for the Blind, and the Scottish Braille Press. RNIB's publications include children's books; works on the law, medicine, and philosophy; the twin journals *Monthly Announcements* in braille and *New Beacon* in print; and its most successful publication, the braille *Radio Times*. RNIB also operates a library of braille books for blind students in evening and university classes. The Scottish Braille Press issues more than 40 magazines.

In the Scandinavian countries, where development of public libraries and care of blind individuals is often parallel, an entirely different pattern of organization exists in the supply of books for blind readers. In Denmark the state is entirely responsible for such activities; in the three other countries this service is run by state-supported associations. Braille and talking books in Denmark are distributed directly to blind readers—usually by mail from the National Library for the Blind. Branches of public libraries that are located in hospitals have an interlibrary loan relationship with the National Library for the Blind. Larger hospital libraries have deposits of books from the National Library, and hospital administrations purchase tape players for patient use.

In contrast, Swedish and Norwegian activities are the responsibility of associations of blind individuals. The talking-book library in Oslo, Norway, provides a national service, and there are three braille libraries located in Bergen, Trondheim, and Oslo. The librarian in charge of the library also coordinates and controls braille services. Absence of a strong central braille collection reflects a historical situation in that each braille library was founded independently as a charitable center. The central Swedish library for blind individuals is at the Association of the Blind in Stockholm. It has library departments for braille and talking books and departments for literature, adult education, and university studies. Apart from libraries at schools for blind persons, the Association of the Blind runs the only braille library in Sweden.

As in the majority of European countries, Sweden's library for blind readers was originally created on a philanthropic initiative. A state grant for library activities was made for the first time as recently as 1953. Sweden is in a special position because public libraries participate actively in the distribution of talking books; several now follow the example of the Malmö library in 1955 and record talking books, most usually for literature of local or regional interest or books largely in dialect. Otherwise, talking-book production is concentrated in the Bibliotekstjanst (the Library Bureau) in Lund, which sells to local libraries.

The Nederlandsche Blindenbibliotheek (Dutch Library for the Blind) has been lending braille books since 1895. When talking books on open-reel tapes were introduced in 1958, the number of readers increased rapidly; most talking books are now recorded on cassettes. There are four libraries in the Netherlands that circulate braille and talking books. Two agencies produce and distribute taped periodicals, and a coordinating center for student literature is located in Amsterdam. All four libraries have their own sound-recording facilities for production of talking books. All libraries have a full range of conventional braille-printing equipment, and the Nederlandsche Blindenbibliotheek has up-to-date machines that produce braille books via punched tapes.

West Germany's library service to the blind is decentralized. The Marburger Studienanstalt has extensive braille and tape resources and specializes in foreign language and formal education materials. Libraries in Hamburg, Stuttgart, Muenster, and Essen supply both braille and talking books, while services at Karlsruhe, Cologne, Hanover, and Bonn circulate braille only, and those at Berlin, Saarbruecken, and Munich provide talking books only. All talking-book services—except that at Essen, which is part of the city library system—belong to a coordinating organization and operate as a unified system. Each serves its own region and holds the same basic stock.

The Arbeitsgemeinschaft Deutscher Blindenhoerbuechereien coordinates production and distribution through seven member talking-book libraries. Despite the absence of an up-to-date union catalogue, libraries often advise readers where to obtain specific braille titles. The reader may apply directly, or the library may obtain the book for the patron. Of the seven talking-book libraries belonging to this organization, five have their own production facilities, and the titles they produce are available to the others.

Library of Congress

*An early user listens to recorded books, circulated by the Adult Blind Book Project. The project began in 1931 at the Library of Congress.*

Perkins School for the Blind, Watertown, Mass.

*A student at the Perkins School for the Blind operates a Kurzweil Reading Machine. The computer-assisted device scans a print page automatically and synthesizes speech.*

The Japan Braille Library was established in 1940 with a collection of 700 braille books. A recorded book system was launched in 1958; now the library produces both press-braille and single-copy transcribed braille books. Recorded books are read by professional announcers and radio personalities. Braille and recorded books can be mailed anywhere in the country to blind persons registered with the library. Since 1965 the library has also maintained a department to distribute inexpensive for-sale items such as a radio for listening to sound without a television set, tape recorders, braille typewriters, and watches.

The advanced design of the Tokyo Metropolitan Central Library (Tokyo Toritsu Chuo Toshokan) to accommodate handicapped visitors is noteworthy. Entranceways are negotiated easily by persons in wheelchairs; closed-circuit television sets magnify print for partially sighted readers; and soundproof rooms are available for volunteers to read to blind individuals.

The Republican Central Library for the Blind in Moscow supervises the decentralized network of library services in the Soviet Union. Regional centers provide libraries for blind readers. In some cases these are departments of public libraries. The libraries use bookmobiles for blind residents of remote areas.

Each state library is regarded as autonomous. The Central Library does not control the system formally but offers assistance to libraries on questions of method and administration. It helps state libraries maintain contact with one another through seminars, workshops, and reports. It also channels book requests from the state libraries to publishing organizations.

During a period of rapid expansion of services between 1956 and 1962, most regional or provincial libraries with divisions for blind readers handed over their collections to special state libraries. These facilities increased from 26 to 54 during the same time; however, they have retained diversified service patterns based on cooperative relationships with factories, workshops, and other agencies, as well as direct distribution by mail and personal deliveries to readers' homes by truck. In those republics where state libraries are not yet operational, smaller libraries of associations for blind individuals attempt the work as possible.

In 1963 the All-Russian Society for the Blind set up a studio to record talking books for distribution to regional libraries. Talking books are recorded by schools and factories through local radio installations during working hours and lunch periods if production conditions permit. A blind person may use earphones to listen to talking books in the reading room or attend a group reading of the more popular works. More and more blind persons are acquiring tape recorders—sold to members of the Society of the Blind on favorable terms—and are beginning to take talking books home to read. Talking and braille books are sent free through the mail.

**International Cooperation.** As a result of a proposal by NLS Director Frank Kurt Cylke, a formal Working Group was established by the Hospital Library Section of the International Federation of Library Associations (IFLA) at its 1977 meeting in Brussels, Belgium, to consider library services for blind and physically handicapped readers since many countries are seeking closer contact with the United States on this topic. At the 1978 IFLA meeting in Czechoslovakia, the Working Group addressed these issues: (1) library services for handicapped persons should be as similar as possible to those provided nonhandicapped persons; (2) library services for handicapped individuals belong in a library, not a social welfare setting; (3) copyright; (4) bibliographic control; (5) postal and customs regulations; (6) format; (7) research and development.

THE DEAF

Available figures indicate that there are more than 13,000,000 persons in the United States with some hearing impairment. About 2,000,000 persons suffer from deafness, the most extreme form of hearing impairment; among these about 400,000 (2 of every 1,000) lost their hearing before reaching the age of 19 or were never able to hear. That U.S. public libraries are doing very little to fill these needs may be attributable to the general impression that deafness imposes no handicap in reading and, thus, there is no need for special library service.

The consequences of impaired hearing are variable according to the age at which hearing loss is sustained and the degree of that loss. Hearing loss at an early age has a profound effect on development of language skills—including learning to read. A child born deaf will not acquire language or speech through the normal mechanism of auditory feedback and reinforcement. That child will struggle through life with the inconsistencies of the English language and the intricacies of reading printed matter. In old age the consequences of impaired hearing for those who have been deaf since their youth entail persistence and, possibly, intensification of the difficulties experienced earlier in life. Books may be of little interest as the language problems that accompany deafness occurring at an early age may have kept the individual from developing the skills necessary to enjoy and profit from reading. Yet all deaf persons, including the aged deaf, have need for information to enhance the quality of life and to keep the mind active and interested in the surrounding world.

Some public libraries have sponsored programs for deaf readers. These programs, based on librarians' observations of local interests, feature heavily illustrated materials, popular novels that have been made into movies, and simply written materials dealing with skills for coping with modern life. Nonprint materials—films, slides, and filmstrips, particularly those with captions and subtitles—seem to be more popular among these patrons.

This scattered population, however, does not have equal access to the few special programs sponsored by libraries with aggressive outreach programs and policies. Further, there are no independent data to show what kind of materials and service would be of greatest benefit. A nationwide survey of the reading tastes and library service needs of the deaf population is needed. Benefits from special library service to individuals who became deaf after reaching maturity should be identified, and the feasibility of establishing a coordinated national library service for deaf individuals should be studied.

THE MENTALLY RETARDED

Traditionally, public libraries have not attempted to serve mentally retarded individuals. Because they may not read, have a limited vocabulary, and may not be able to talk, they have never been included in the library's public. Recent changes in public attitudes, improved and enlightened care, training, and psychological assessment have led to greater efforts to bring these persons into community life. These efforts include attempts to bring them the benefits of library service.

The Independent Living Program, an experimental library program for retarded adults conducted with the John E. Runnells Hospital, Berkeley Heights, New Jersey, was designed to train retarded adults to successfully handle routine household duties and normal everyday activities. Since traditional print materials were not appropriate, the program relied heavily on audiovisual materials. Twice monthly library visits were planned. Those people with slight reading skills were given adult library cards; they borrowed from filmstrips, tapes, records, paintings, sculpture, and, in a few instances, children's books and magazines. Through these means, a heretofore unreachable public of the nonreading, institutionalized patrons was in fact reached.

This experiment has implications for other communities. While the mentally retarded comprise only about 3 percent of the total population, the total number of these persons is significant. Certainly the public library should play an important role to help mentally retarded persons develop to the highest potential. There is need for a national reference service on mental retardation to organize and coordinate information. Coordinated bibliographic efforts would help the public and professionals by bringing together approaches to problems and materials from different disciplines.

**REFERENCES**

Rhea Joyce Rubin, *Bibliotherapy Sourcebook* (1978).

Donald E. Schauder and Malcolm D. Cram, *Libraries for the Blind—An International Study of Policies and Practices* (1977).

Maryalls G. Strom, *Library Services to the Blind and Physically Handicapped* (1977).

Frank Kurt Cylke, ed., *Library Services for the Blind and Physically Handicapped—An International Approach* (1979).

Keith C. Wright, *Library and Information Services for Handicapped Individuals* (1979).

FRANK KURT CYLKE;
ALFRED D. HAGLE

## Hanson, J(ames) C(hristian) M(einich)

(1864–1943)

J. C. M. Hanson's was perhaps the greatest individual influence on the bibliographical organization of libraries in the United States during the first half of the century. Hanson was born March 13, 1864, at Sørheim, his father's farm, in the district of Nord-Aurdal in the Valdres Valley of Norway. The sixth of eight children of Gunnerius

(Gunnar) and Eleanore Adamine Röberg Hansen, he was christened Jens Christian Meinich Hansen. His boyhood friends in Iowa called him Jim, which he, to his later regret, formalized as James. The change in the spelling of his surname was inconsistent. By 1897 he had adopted "J. C. M. Hanson" as his signature, although he sometimes reverted to "Jens" or "J. C. M. Hansen" in his writings for the Norwegian-American press.

Because Hanson's father was a government official, *lensmand* for the district of Nord-Aurdal, the family would not ordinarily have been among those emigrating to the United States, but Hanson's mother's half-brother, Hans Röberg, had settled in Decorah, Iowa. He offered an education to one of the boys in the family, and in the summer of 1873 Hanson, who was then only nine, left Norway in the company of the Reverend Ove J. Hjort for the trip to Iowa. Because of his age he could not enroll in the preparatory department of Luther College until the following year. In 1882, at the age of 18, he received a B.A.

Hanson had no definite career plans and was persuaded by the Reverend Ulrich V. Koren, a member of the college Board of Trustees, that Concordia Seminary in Saint Louis was the proper goal for a Luther graduate. Hanson stayed at Concordia for only two years. He felt no real call to the ministry, and the lack of adequate financial support would have made the third and final year exceedingly difficult even had he wished to remain. Instead he accepted a position in the fall of 1884 as Principal of Our Saviour's Church school in the Norwegian community in Chicago, *Klokker* (Deacon) for the church, and Superintendent of its Sunday School. He supplemented his income by teaching English to adult Scandinavians in the Montefiore Evening School and by pitching for several commercial baseball teams. After saving enough money for a year's graduate study, he enrolled at Cornell University in 1888.

In his second year at Cornell, Hanson was awarded the President White Fellowship in history and political science. His research required extensive use of the library, which was at the time undergoing reclassification. He became acquainted with the Acting Librarian, George William Harris, whose influence, according to Hanson, led him to decide on librarianship as his life's work. Accordingly, in September 1890 Hanson joined William Frederick Poole's prestigious training ground at the Newberry Library in Chicago. Among the many benefits gained there, the formation of his lifelong friendship with Charles Martel was not the least.

In 1893 Hanson was appointed Head Cataloguer at the University of Wisconsin. His experience in the planning and implementation of complete reclassification and recataloguing was to prove invaluable to him later at the Library of Congress.

Hanson was appointed Superintendent of the Catalogue Department at the Library of Congress in August 1897 by the newly appointed Librarian of Congress, John Russell Young. In beginning the new catalogue during Young's brief administration, Hanson laid the groundwork for the success of cooperative, later centralized, cataloguing by his carefully considered modifications of Charles A. Cutter's *Rules for a Printed Dictionary Catalogue* to conform to the best practice of the time and thereby "facilitate" the use by other libraries of the Library of Congress cataloguing. The resulting entries, printed for the copyright books in the subdivision *Books proper* of the *Catalogue* of the Register of Copyrights, were welcomed enthusiastically in a *Library Journal* editorial.

The Montreal conference of the American Library Association in 1900 heralded an era of cooperation in cataloguing. The ALA Publishing Board established an Advisory Committee on *Cataloging* Rules with Hanson as Chairman. (The name of the committee, which became a special committee of the ALA in 1906, varies; the predominant form was Catalog Rules Committee.) The reconciliation of the numerous divergent views on the many disputed points of cataloguing was credited by William Warner Bishop to Hanson's "thoroughness and patience." His wholehearted commitment to cooperation in cataloguing, which is dependent on agreement on rules, was a major factor in his successful leadership.

This achievement was crowned by the further cooperation with the Library Association's Catalogue Rules Committee in the mutual acceptance, with only eight differences, of *Catalog Rules: Author and Title Entries,* commonly known as the Anglo-American code of 1908. The official ALA motion thanking the Catalog Rules Committee noted that thanks were due "especially" to Hanson, who "has done more to bring the English and American committees into harmony, and has borne the burden of the final editing of the Code." The catalogue cards produced at the Library of Congress under his direction were generally acclaimed for their excellence. Their quality and the general acceptance of the cataloguing rules were major factors in the success of the Library of Congress card distribution service. The card distribution service, in turn, led to an unprecedented national standardization in cataloguing practice.

Hanson's influence on subject cataloguing in the United States was equally powerful and long lasting. Cutter's "dictionary" principle was radically modified for the new catalogue. Because of the anticipated size of the catalogue, Hanson thought the dispersion of related headings would be too great. Subject topics were therefore subordinated extensively, and independent headings were deliberately inverted to group the headings together. Although some of the principles underlying the system have been modified over the years, the *Library of Congress Subject Headings* remains virtually the standard list of subject headings in use in the United States today.

Within two months of his arrival at the Library of Congress, Hanson was able to bring Charles Martel from the Newberry Library as one of his two chief assistants. Hanson always accorded to Martel the credit for the Library of Congress Classification, but he himself had a major role in its beginnings, primarily in its conception and notation. Hanson, too, carried the responsibility for convincing both Young and Young's successor, Herbert Putnam, of the need for a new classification scheme.

In 1910 Hanson moved to the University of Chicago as Associate Director of the library. This was his third library reorganization, and he became one of the leading voices for cooperative cataloguing to supplement centralized cataloguing as the most efficient and economical means of bibliographical organization. He was appointed to the faculty of the newly established Graduate Library School of the University of Chicago in 1928.

That same year Hanson led the team of cataloguing experts sent by the Carnegie Endowment for International Peace to assist in the reorganization of the Vatican Library. The Vatican Library's *Norme per il catalogo degli stampati,* which reflected the influence of the Anglo-American code of 1908, was another step toward international agreement in cataloguing. Even after his retirement in 1934, Hanson continued to work for international cooperation in cataloguing as the only route for the future. In furtherance of this cause he compiled his monumental work, *A Comparative Study of Cataloging Rules Based on the Anglo-American Code of 1908; with Comments on the Rules and on the Prospects for a Further Extension of International Agreement and Co-operation* (1939).

Hanson was the author of numerous articles on technical library matters, book reviews, and frequent contributions to the Norwegian-American press. "Corporate Authorship versus Title Entry" (*Library Quarterly,* 1935) is perhaps his most frequently cited article, but his earlier paper on "Rules for Corporate Entry" (*Library Journal,* 1905) is especially valuable for its analysis of the problems.

Hanson's scholarship and the integrity of his character inspired respect; his kindliness, modesty, and generous spirit evoked the affection of his colleagues, staff, and students. His feeling for Luther College was strong. He was appointed to its Board of Trustees in 1920; in 1931 it bestowed on him the honorary LL.D. degree. In 1928 he was appointed Knight and Commander of the Order of Saint Olav by the Crown of Norway. Hanson died at Green Bay, Wisconsin, on November 8, 1943.

**REFERENCES**

The Hanson Festschrift issue of the *Library Quarterly* (1934) includes a chronological bibliography of Hanson's publications. The bibliography, with a continuation to May 1943, is also in Hanson's autobiography, *What Became of Jens?,* edited by Oivind M. Hovde (Luther College Press, 1974).

The largest collection of Hanson's papers is in the University of Chicago Libraries; a smaller collection of personal papers is in the Luther College Library, Decorah, Iowa. The manuscript materials relating to Hanson's work at the Library of Congress are in the Library of Congress Archives. These sources, as well as secondary sources, are documented in Edith Scott, "J. C. M. Hanson and His Contribution to Twentieth-Century Cataloging" (Ph.D. dissertation, University of Chicago, 1970).

EDITH SCOTT



## Hasse, Adelaide Rosalie

(1868–1953)

Indexer, writer, and bibliographer, Adelaide Hasse was born in Milwaukee, Wisconsin, on September 13, 1868, and raised in an environment shaped by individuals who challenged both her mind and her ability to do unusual things in an unusual way. Her father, Dr. Hermann Edward Hasse, was a well-known physician, surgeon, and botanist who, with other members of a distinguished family, created a noteworthy learning environment for his five children. There is no evidence that Adelaide attended any private schools or attained a college education, but from childhood she was educated to think, to examine, to challenge the obvious and the easy. As a result, she developed analytical skills and a critical acumen that played an important role in her library career.

When her family moved to the West Coast, Adelaide Hasse began her library career in 1889 under the leadership of a woman of unique characteristics, Tessa L. Kelso of the Los Angeles Public Library. At that time, there was no school of library science other than the prototype Dewey enterprise in New York; those who came to the field learned by example and by doing. Several decades later Hasse recalled Kelso's tremendous impact on her life as one "which gave point and direction to my natural bent." At the Los Angeles Public Library, Kelso asked her young apprentice to organize the library's collection of U.S. government publications. Since there were few guidelines or procedures, Hasse applied her own logical approach, devised a classification scheme, and began a checklist of items. The success of her methods, especially in a field where so little was known, quickly came to the attention of persons in key positions in Washington, D.C. Because of the requirements of the Printing Act of January 12, 1895, an office had been organized that, among other responsibilities, was to prepare and print an index to government publications. As a result of her pioneer work in Los Angeles, Adelaide Hasse was invited to serve in Washington as the first Librarian of the Office of the Superintendent of Documents.

Hasse arrived in the capital in May 1895; the following year the first of her major bibliographies was published by the Government Printing Office. *The List of Publications of the U.S. Department of Agriculture* initiated a life as an indexer and bibliographer that was not concluded until Hasse, in her 80's, came out of retirement to help edit a microfilm publication of records of the United States. During the nearly 60 years in which she served in a variety of library and bibliographic positions, Adelaide Hasse produced dozens of articles for the library and popular press as well as compiling a series of checklists and bibliographies that are unparalleled in their value and coverage. Among the titles are two remarkable indexes that were still key resources in the 1970's. The first, published in 13 volumes from 1907 to 1922, is the *Index of Economic Material in Documents of the States of the United States.* Financed by the Carnegie Institution of Washington, it was, as R. R. Bowker noted in 1920, "a life work for any less persistent and industrious person." The second set, a three-volume *Index to United States Documents Relating to Foreign Affairs, 1828–1861,* was also funded by the Carnegie Institution and was published from 1914 to 1921.

Adelaide Hasse's arrival in Washington in 1895 occasioned a burst of activity typical of her dedication and enthusiasm for her work. The duties of her position called for the collection of existing documents from all the government departments and then for them to be organized and housed. She uncovered an amazing amount of material; in six weeks nearly 300,000 documents had been retrieved and roughly inventoried. Hasse's story of this experience, along with an autobiographical commentary on many aspects of her professional career, is described in a privately published pamphlet, written in 1919, entitled *The Compensations of Librarianship.*

Although Adelaide Hasse remained in Washington for only two years, 1895–97, her efforts there are especially recognized because she developed a classification for government documents. The scheme was expanded in the *Checklist of United-States Public Documents, 1789–1909,* and served as the structural basis for the *Monthly Catalog.* Her organization of the Library of the Superintendent of Documents so impressed John Shaw Billings, Director of the New York Public Library, that she was offered a position "to build up what Dr. Billings wished to be a great document collection."

Hasse's career in New York is divided into two distinct phases: (1) the period from 1897 until Billings's death in 1913 when she was able to develop a model public documents collection; and (2) the final six years during which, in her own eyes at least, her accomplishments and her position were destroyed. In both instances, the particular natures of her employers apparently were key factors.

John Shaw Billings was an outstanding librarian, even in an era of unusual library leaders; his vision and his administrative skills were instrumental in establishing the New York Public Library. In fact, only a man of his scholarship and achievements could have impressed Adelaide Hasse, who brought a special aptitude of her own to the library profession. Billings recognized her brilliance and dealt with her acerbic personality in such a way as to encourage and enhance her contributions. During the years of his administration, she was instrumental in building a collection of documents from an unorganized base of 10,000 items to nearly 300,000 catalogued volumes. Hasse's reputation as an expert on government publications was also evident in the contributions she made to the American Library Association; she served first as a member and later as Chair of the Committee on Public Documents, and she spoke and wrote often on the collection and administration of government publications. As life member number 779 of the ALA, she regularly participated in conferences, was a member of the Committee on Library Schools, and was elected to Council from 1908 through 1913.

In addition to her capable development of the documents collection, Hasse was also involved in serving the assorted publics of the Library. Her ability to retrieve specialized information from the vast resources of the government was extended to other data bases as well. Since her perception of direct service to the business world predated many of her colleagues, Public Documents and then the Economics Division of the Library emerged as major service centers. It was during this productive period, the first decade of the 20th century, that she also began a massive index of economic material and was able to uncover, during a trip to Europe, a copy of the "lost" *Bradford Journal,* which she later edited for publication.

Billings's death in 1913 marked the beginning of the end for much of Hasse's work in the New York Public Library, although six years elapsed before the Board of Trustees terminated her employment. The new director, E. H. Anderson, was not of the same mind and pursuits as his predecessor. Several personal and professional factors were involved, but before many months had passed, Hasse and Anderson were stubbornly set in a pattern of action and reaction that, given Anderson's power as Director, could end only in Hasse's removal. She made it clear that she considered Anderson incompetent and destructive of her work of 16 years; he, in turn, rallied the staff and the Board, charged her with insubordination, and asked for her resignation. Hasse refused and was fired in the fall of 1918.

The emotional character of the library conflict and the nature of the accusations leveled against Hasse, some of which involved rumors of pro-German sympathies in a traumatic war climate, might have debilitated a lesser personality. Hasse, however, was neither incapacitated nor silenced. In 1919 she used her own financial resources to publish *The Compensations of Librarianship,* a statement of professional interests, an accusatory and spirited explanation of the situation leading to her firing, and a credo of continuing dedication to library work. Moreover, she was able to provide positive evidence that the U.S. government perceived no treacherous tendencies, since she left New York in 1918, a few weeks after her termination, to work for the Department of State. For the next 30 years, until she retired in 1941, Hasse was employed in a series of responsible positions in Washington including the War Labor Policies Board (1918–19), the War Industries Board (1919–21), the office of the Assistant Secretary of War (1921), the Brookings Institution (1923–32), the Works Progress Administration (1934–39), and the Temporary National Economics Committee (1939–41). After she retired, she continued to live in Washington until her death on July 29, 1953, at the age of 84.

In reviewing Adelaide Hasse's long life, it is important to emphasize the amount of her publication, which includes nearly 24 monographs and some 50 articles. She was an incisive and perceptive commentator on numerous facets of library service as well as a compiler of excellent checklists and bibliographies, many of which identified difficult-to-locate government publications. Hasse was an early advocate of library service for special groups and, in Washington during the 1920's, helped to organize the local chapter of the Special Libraries Association, served as its first President, and edited the association journal, *Special Libraries.* She applied her expertise and organizational skill concerning government resources in her employment as a lecturer at George Washington University from 1933 to 1937 and, near the end of her career, at Catholic University.

Although the precise motivation and expectations of Adelaide R. Hasse cannot be interpreted precisely, it is well established that she had a confidence in the role of libraries and librarians that inspired a personal commitment that never waivered. Writing in *The New Republic* in January 1918, at a period in her life that for her was verging on the catastrophic, her question to the library profession was "Why Not?" Hasse felt keenly the failure of the profession to function as a "public service organization." Yet, beneath the critical question there existed a sense of that which might be. She asked then, and throughout her career, regardless of consequences, "What is there so very incongruous about taking just one more step and by so doing galvanizing the present inert mass into a pulsating service plant?" Her life was an example of that one more step.

LAUREL A. GROTZINGER

## Hewins, Caroline Maria
(1846–1926)

Caroline Maria Hewins was a pioneer in children's library work and, for 50 years, Librarian of the Hartford Public Library.

She was born October 10, 1846, in Roxbury, Massachusetts. Her paternal forebears had come from England to Sharon, Massachusetts, in 1656. Her father was a well-to-do Boston haberdasher. In her infancy the family moved to Jamaica Plain, and when she was seven to West Roxbury, where they occupied a five-acre estate, ample for their nine children of whom she was the oldest.

ALA

*Caroline Maria Hewins*

A precocious, bookish child, Hewins was reading by the age of four and later enjoyed reading and telling stories to her younger sisters and brother. These experiences, which inculcated a life-long love of children's books, were described in her memoir, *A Mid-Century Child and Her Books* (1926). Education at home and at private schools was followed by Eliot High School in Jamaica Plain and then the Girls' High and Normal School of Boston, which prepared her for teaching.

While at Normal School Hewins was much impressed with the Boston Athenaeum, where she was required to do some research. Upon graduation she arranged to work at that library in 1866–67 under the guidance of its famous Librarian, William Frederick Poole. For a number of years thereafter she taught in private schools in the Boston area and took courses at Boston University.

In 1875, learning that the Young Men's Institute of Hartford, Connecticut, needed a librarian, she applied and was accepted. The Institute, a subscription library, served a membership of about 600 with a collection of some 20,000 volumes. Though few children used the library, Hewins sought by means of extensive discarding of objectionable books and purchase of desirable titles to improve the children's collection and raise reading standards. Without neglecting her other duties she became a pioneering specialist in work with children. An innovative administrator, she instituted many programs that later became standard practice in youth libraries, including clubs, book talks, storytelling, nature walks, a doll collection, and dramatics. She used the children's own book reviews as guides to book selection.

Membership in the library was opened to the schools; reading lists were provided for teachers; and eventually classroom libraries were sent out, making the Hartford Library a leader in the movement for cooperation between public and school libraries. A concern for disadvantaged youth led her to live for 12 years at the North Street Settlement House, where she founded a drama club and a branch library. On her frequent trips abroad Hewins wrote letters to her young patrons that were often published in the *Hartford Courant* and later were published as a book, *A Traveller's Letters to Boys and Girls* (1923). Despite her prominence in the growing field of children's libraries, it was not until 1904 that she was able to persuade the trustees to establish a separate children's room, followed in 1907 by the appointment of a full-time children's librarian.

Caroline Hewins was nationally recognized as an authority on the selection of books for children. When the Institute was absorbed by the older Hartford Library Association in 1878, she started the quarterly *Bulletin of the Hartford Library Association,* primarily to list new acquisitions and including perhaps the first selected lists of children's books. These led in 1882 to the publication by Frederick Leypoldt of *Publishers' Weekly* of her *Books for the Young: A Guide for Parents and Children* (reprinted 1884) and later by the American Library Association of her *Books for Boys and Girls: A Selected List* (1897, rev. 1904, 1915). In these lists and elsewhere she expressed her philosophy of book selection for children. Her emphasis was heavily on the classics; modern books had to meet her exacting standards, and "series" books were rejected. She deplored an apparent tendency to denigrate the bookish child.

Although Hewins is remembered as a children's librarian, she also capably ran a growing city library. The Hartford Library Association became a free library in 1892 and the following year adopted the name of Hartford Public Library. By 1925, the last year of her administration, it had a collection of 150,000 volumes in the main library, branches, and deposit stations.

A founder in 1891 of the Connecticut Library Association, she served as President in 1912–13 and was also prominent in the Hartford Librarians' Club. In 1893 she was largely responsible for establishing the Connecticut Public Library Committee, a forerunner of the state library commission, for which she served as volunteer Executive Secretary and "library visitor" for many years. The Educational Association, later the Parent Teachers Association, occupied her organizational abilities in 1897. She lectured at library schools and educational workshops and taught children's literature to Hartford teachers and librarians.

Caroline Hewins probably joined the American Library Association at its 3rd Conference in Boston in 1879. Recorded as the first woman to speak from the floor of an ALA Conference, she subsequently read many papers at those meetings. She was a Councilor from 1885 to 1888 and again from 1893 to 1902 and Vice-President in 1891. In 1897 she was one of two women in the American delegation who read papers at the 2nd International Conference of Librarians in London; she spoke on children's books as seen by children themselves. A meeting of children's librarians that she called at the Montreal Conference of ALA in 1900 resulted ultimately in the establishment of its Children's Section. Hewins published extensively in library and educational periodicals, with well over half of her writings on children's library work.

In 1911 Trinity College of Hartford awarded her an honorary Master's degree, the first woman to be so honored by this men's college. On February 15, 1926, at a celebration of her 50 years of service, the Hartford Librarians' Club gave her funds to establish the Caroline M. Hewins Scholarship Fund for Children's Librarians. During the same year, though retired, she remained active at the Library until she died in Hartford on November 4 after a brief illness.

Cheerful, energetic, intelligent, and capable, she had been one of the most eloquent supporters of the public library movement, particularly as it contributed toward a fuller life for children, and an exemplar of the increasing role of women in the professions. Her collection of children's books is now in the Connecticut Historical Society. The Caroline M. Hewins Lectureship, an annual presentation at New England Library Association meetings, was established by Frederick G. Melcher in 1946. When ALA celebrated its 75th anniversary, Hewins was one of 40 persons named to the "Library Hall of Fame."

**REFERENCES**

Jennie D. Lindquist, "Caroline Maria Hewins," in *Notable American Women, 1607–1950* (1971).

Mary E. Root, "Caroline Maria Hewins," in *Pioneering Leaders in Librarianship,* edited by Emily M. Danton (ALA, 1953).

BUDD L. GAMBEE

*Edward Gailon Holley*

ALA

## Holley, Edward Gailon
(1927– )

Edward Holley contributed to the library profession as a scholar, university library administrator, library school dean, and as President of the American Library Association.

He was born on November 26, 1927, in Pulaski (Giles County), Tennessee. His close contact with libraries began when he started working at the local public library on Sunday afternoons during high school. It continued at David Lipscomb College, where he worked as a library Assistant. Indeed, Holley became de facto Librarian during his senior year, when there was no regular librarian. After his graduation in 1949 (B.A. in English, magna cum laude) Holley was persuaded by the Dean to stay on as Librarian. He also attended George Peabody College, where he earned a Master's in Library Science and English in 1951.

Holley then went on to the University of Illinois at Urbana-Champaign to a professional position at the Photo Reproduction Library and to begin work on a library science doctorate. From 1953 to 1956 he was called into active service from the U.S. Naval Reserve. Upon his return he served as a Graduate Assistant in the University of Illinois Library Science Library, 1956–57, and as Librarian of the Education, Philosophy, and Psychology Library from 1957 to 1962.

He was awarded the Ph.D. in Library Science at Illinois in 1961; his dissertation, *Charles Evans: American Bibliographer*, was published by the University of Illinois Press in 1963 and won the Scarecrow Press Award for Library Literature the same year.

From 1962 through 1971 Holley served as Director of Libraries at the University of Houston. During his tenure 126,000 sq.ft. were added to the existing 93,000 sq.ft. of library space, and the collection grew from 300,000 to 665,000 volumes with more than double the number of periodical subscriptions.

In January 1972 Holley was appointed Dean and Professor at the School of Library Science of the University of North Carolina, where he strengthened the faculty with many outstanding appointments and inaugurated a doctoral program.

His numerous activities included Chairperson of the U.S. Office of Education's Advisory Council on College Library Resources (1969–71); Editor for the Association of College and Research Libraries Publications in Librarianship Series (1969–72); President of the Texas Library Association (1971); Chairperson of the ALA Publishing Board (1972–73); and President of ALA during 1975–76.

Holley became a member of Beta Phi Mu and in 1971 received a Council on Library Resources Fellowship, during which he made a study of urban university libraries in the United States. Among his works are *Raking the Historical Coals: The ALA Scrapbook of 1876* (1967), *Resources of Texas Libraries* (with Donald Hendricks, 1968), and many articles on academic libraries, copyright issues, and other topics. He contributed "ALA at 100" to *The ALA Yearbook* (1976).

A distinguished library historian, he was a major contributor to, and member of the Advisory Board for, the *Dictionary of American Library Biography* (1978).

Early in 1978 Holley spent two weeks in Japan at the invitation of the Japanese Ministry of Education, visiting university libraries and giving public lectures, and was a visiting scholar at the University of Hawaii Graduate School of Library Studies for one week.

GEORGE S. BOBINSKI

# Honduras

Honduras, a republic in Central America, is bounded by the Caribbean Sea on the north, Nicaragua on the south and east, El Salvador on the south and west, and Guatemala on the west. Pop. (1978 est.) 3,438,388; area 112,088 sq.km. The official language is Spanish.

**National Library.** As of 1972 there were an estimated 225 library collections in Honduras. Most of the major libraries in the country are government libraries. The largest is the Biblioteca Nacional de Honduras in the capital city, Tegucigalpa. Founded in 1880, it had holdings of 100,000 volumes by the early 1970's. It shares with other libraries the legal deposit of three copies of each book published in Honduras, but enforcement of the law is not rigorous. From 1961 the National Library published an *Anuario Bibliográfico Hondureño.*

**Special Libraries.** The government also maintains several special libraries each with a collection of a few thousand volumes, emphasizing archaeology, art, law, administration, and the humanities.

**Academic Libraries.** In higher education, the library of the Universidad Nacional Autónoma de Honduras has shown significant progress. The library has grown from 25,000 volumes for over 3,000 students early in the 1970's to 98,000 volumes for 13,000 students in 1978. It has subscriptions to 348 periodicals. Its staff performs centralized cataloguing and other services for the University's two branch campus libraries as well as for the National Medical Library and its branch library, which are part of the University.

**Public Libraries.** In the early 1970's there were 32 public libraries with a total holding of 50,000 volumes. Some of these may in fact be primary school libraries.

**School Libraries.** In the area of primary school libraries, Honduras showed its greatest initiative. In 1967 the government of Honduras, in cooperation with Unesco, began the School Library Pilot Project. Under the direction of a librarian, the program was designed, among other things, to teach students the use of various kinds of library materials and to provide communities with public library facilities where none existed. The project was planned to have two stages. The first, from 1968 to 1972, was under the direction of Unesco, which provided extensive technical assistance. It was hoped that by 1972 there would be 396 primary school libraries serving a school population of 218,869. Schools were divided into four categories, depending on the size of the schools' enrollment in conformity with Honduras Fundamental Law on Public Education. Twenty-three libraries were opened before 1970. The second stage, beginning in 1973, was directed by the Ministry of Education. As previously agreed upon, Unesco ended its participation in the project at the close of the first stage. Progress after 1973 was slow.

**Association.** Honduras has a Librarians' Association, which has stressed better methods of organization for public libraries.

Cooperation with librarians from other countries has centered mainly in the Primary School Pilot Project. Honduras was working in the 1970's with Costa Rica on a similar program and would like to extend the project to other countries in Central America. Librarians from the National University have participated in the Consejo Superior Universitario Centroamericano, a group made up of other national universities in Central America and designed to promote cooperation among them.

Overall, libraries in Honduras, where the illiteracy rate exceeds 50 percent, the system for publishing and distributing books is antiquated, and the political climate has often stifled unapproved ideas, have been few, small, and poorly financed. They also lack professional staff. There has been little coordination among libraries, and librarians have not been well organized. Beginning in the late 1960's, however, especially through the Primary School Pilot Project and the National University, these trends began to be reversed.

DANIEL W. BARTHELL

**Holmes, Oliver Wendell,** U.S. jurist **315**

**home library movement,** alternative to public library service to children in Japan **132**

**Hong Kong Library Association 240**

# Hong Kong

Hong Kong, a British colony off the southern coast of China, comprises Hong Kong Island and islets nearby; Kowloon Peninsula; and the mainland areas of the New Territories. Pop. (1978 est.) 4,566,900; area 1,046 sq.km. The official language is English.

More than 300 libraries serve Hong Kong. *Library Services in Hong Kong,* a directory compiled by Lai-bing Kan and published in 1975, recorded 88 libraries open to the general public and children, 45 government department and British Armed Forces libraries, 119 school libraries, 21 postsecondary and university libraries, 36 special libraries, and 8 club and society and private libraries.

Hong Kong Polytechnic

*The multilevel Hong Kong Polytechnic Library's collection totaled 100,000 volumes in 1978.*

**National Library.** Since Hong Kong has no national library or national bibliographical center, the Urban Council Libraries serve part of the functions of a national library. Under the Hong Kong Books Registration Ordinance, publishers and printers submit five copies of every title published and printed locally to the Urban Council Libraries. Based on those deposits, *A Catalogue of Books Printed in Hong Kong* is issued quarterly.

**Academic Libraries.** The major academic libraries include the two universities, the University of Hong Kong and the Chinese University of Hong Kong, Hong Kong Polytechnic, Baptist College, and Lingnan College. The University of Hong Kong Library was established soon after the university opened its doors to students in 1912 and had approximately 600,000 volumes in mid-1978. The Chinese University of Hong Kong maintains a library system: a University Library and three branch libraries at the colleges. The entire collection amounted to more than 600,000 volumes in mid-1978. Approximately 54 percent of the stock are in Oriental languages, principally Chinese. The Hong Kong Polytechnic Library had more than 130,000 volumes in 1978.

**Public Libraries.** The libraries of the Urban Council, Urban Services Department, Social and Community Centres of the Social Welfare Department, Adult Education and Recreation Centres of the Education Department, the Caritas Centres, and the Boys' and Girls' Clubs Association serve the general public in the urban and rural areas. The City Hall Library, opened in March 1962, is the headquarters of the Urban Council Libraries. The whole network of Urban Council Libraries comprises 16 libraries (including two mobile libraries) with a total of 907,300 volumes in March 1978.

**School Libraries.** With few exceptions, most of the secondary and primary schools in Hong Kong have inadequate library facilities, managed by teachers and clerical staff. The *Library Services* directory (1975) recorded statistics supplied by 119 schools serving approximately 122,500 students. The libraries surveyed provided an average of seven volumes per secondary student and seven volumes per primary student. In September 1974 Hong Kong had more than 1,300,000 students enrolled; the total student population could be served better by their schools. The Department of Education of the Hong Kong government planned in the late 1970's to develop the school libraries as resource centers under the direction of teacher librarians.

**Special Libraries.** Many government department libraries are specialized and serve primarily the staff of their own departments. The Hong Kong Productivity Centre, Hong Kong Trade Development Council, Federation of Hong Kong Industries, Hong Kong Management Association, and Hong Kong Tourist Association, among others, maintain libraries and information services to serve the commerce and industry sectors. The Union Research Institute specializes in materials relating to Communist China. Besides these, there are several medical libraries in hospitals and other special libraries in some business firms and factories.

**Archives.** The Public Records House has the largest collection of official documents. From 1972 that office collected the old documents and records from more than 20 government departments, some dating back to 1844.

**Hong Kong Library Association.** Established in 1958, the Association had a membership of 247 in 1978, including five categories: personal, student, corresponding, institutional, and honorary. The Association publishes a *Journal* and a *Newsletter*.

**REFERENCE**

L. B. Kan, *Library Services in Hong Kong* (Hong Kong Library Association and the Chinese University of Hong Kong, 1975).

LAI-BING KAN

# Hungary

Hungary, a people's republic in central Europe, is bounded by Czechoslovakia on the north, Romania and a section of the U.S.S.R. on the east, Yugoslavia on the south, and Austria on the west. Pop. (1978 est.) 10,670,800; area 93,032 sq.km. The official language is Magyar.

The Library Law of 1976 and subsequent decrees of the Council of Ministers (1976) and the Ministry of Culture (1978) fundamentally reorganized library services in the Hungarian People's Republic. Thirteen major categories of library systems, regional library networks, switching centers, coordination centers, and specialized fundamental collections now exist, while 120 major libraries operate as national switching centers for information and as cooperation centers in their particular subject fields. Each of the 16,000 libraries in Hungary is an active member of at least one network or system. The Hungarian Ministry of Culture implements and administers the Library Law, assisted by the National Library Council and the National Széchényi Library.

**National Library.** The National Széchényi Library (1802) in Budapest, with a collection of over 5,500,000 volumes, is Hungary's largest library. It is the coordination center for all public library systems and regional networks. As the national library, it (1) collects all materials printed in Hungary as well as foreign publications that relate to the republic, (2) conducts the international exchange of publications, (3) acts as depository library, (4) serves as the clearinghouse for national and international interlibrary loans, (5) compiles and publishes current and retrospective national bibliographies, (6) performs R & D tasks, (7) maintains a central registry of incunabula and other rare library items, (8) provides assistance with the conservation and protection of library materials, and (9) assists in the training and continuing education of librarians through its Center of Library Science and Methodology (1959).

The Library directly supervises three special libraries of national significance: the Bajza József Library in Gyöngyös (1475), the Antal Reguly Science Library in Zirc (1720), and the Helicon Library in Keszthely (1745).

**Academic Libraries.** Libraries of higher educational institutions include eight systems: four in science (Budapest, Debrecen, Pécs, Szeged), three in technology (Budapest, Miskolc, Veszprém), and one in economics (Budapest). The main library forms the core of each system, which usually consists of institutional, clinical, and branch libraries. All academic libraries are active in regional library networks, and many serve as national switching centers. Holdings of these libraries range from 500,000 to 2,500,000 units.

The largest system serves the Lóránd Eötvös University (1561) in Budapest. The main library has over 1,500,000 units, while the total system boasts about 2,500,000, particularly strong in the humanities.

**Public Libraries.** There are three types of public library systems in Hungary: council, trade union, and armed forces. Each public library is part of a local system and contributes to the activities and services of one of the five regional networks. Library needs of nationalities are served by 11 collections in the South Slavic, German, Romanian, and Slovak languages. While the National Széchényi Library coordinates the work of most public library systems and networks, the Gorkii State Library (Budapest) coordinates the collections for nationalities. The 10,494 public libraries of Hungary (1977) contain over 35,000,000 units (32,900 library items per 10,000 persons).

The Ervin Szabó Municipal Library (1904) in Budapest, with over 100 branches and extensions and total holdings of close to 2,000,000 volumes, is the leading public library system in the country.

**Table 1. Libraries in Hungary (1976)**

| Type | Number | Volumes in collections | Annual expenditures (forints) | Population served | Professional staff | All staff (total) |
|---|---|---|---|---|---|---|
| National | 1 | 5,368,734 | Ft 5,601,019 | 10,572,094 | 165 | 533 |
| Academic[a] | 495 | 12,271,968 | Ft 75,362,468 | 119,690 | 463 | 1,515 |
| Public | 9,770[b] | 34,112,362 | Ft 90,937,560 | 10,572,094 | 1,962 | 10,166 |
| School[c] | 4,901 | 14,176,723 | Ft 36,381,964 | 1,453,113 | N.A. | N.A. |
| Special[a] | 1,337xf | 26,259,554 | Ft 190,767,873 | N.A. | 801 | 3,652 |
| Total | 16,504 | 92,189,341 | Ft 399,050,884 | | | |

[a]As of December 31, 1974.
[b]Out of the 9,770 public libraries, 5,064 are maintained by councils and 4,706 by trade unions. These figures include central as well as branch libraries.
[c]As of September 1, 1976.

Sources: *Statistical Yearbook, 1975; Statistical Information of the Ministry of Culture: Scientific and Special Libraries* (1974); *Statistical Information of the Ministry of Culture: Public Libraries* (1976); personal correspondence with the Information Department, Center for Library Science and Methodology, National Széchényi Library, Budapest (Vera Gerő, Head); 1977 data concerning the number of public libraries and their holdings are published in the statistical yearbook of the COMECON [Sovet Ekonomicheskoi Vzaimopomoshchi, Sekretariat, *Statisticheskii ezhegodnik stran chlenov Soveta Ekonomicheskoi Vzaimopomoshchi—1978* (Moskva: Statistika, 1978)].

**School Libraries.** Special library systems unite the over 4,000 (1976) elementary, high school, and educational research libraries in Hungary. Holdings of these systems total about 14,000,000 (1976). The libraries of local pedagogical continuing educational institutes serve as centers for the school library systems. The work of the metropolitan and county school systems is coordinated by the National Pedagogical Library and Museum (1877 and 1958), which is the national switching center for information in the educational field.

**Table 2. Archives in Hungary (1976)**

| | |
|---|---|
| Number | 70 |
| Holdings | 173,534 linear meters |
| Annual expenditures | FY 52,303[a] |
| Professional staff | 388[b] |
| All staff (total) | 549[b] |

[a]Excluding special state archives and church archives.
[b]Excluding church archives.

Source: The Information Department, Center for Library Science and Methodology, National Széchényi Library, Budapest (Vera Gerő, Head).

**Special and Research Libraries.** Over 1,300 special and research libraries and information centers exist in Hungary, with total holdings of about 26,000,000. They belong to several nationwide special and research library systems (e.g., the Academy of Sciences library system and information systems of medicine, metallurgy, transportation, archives, statistics, labor, and agriculture). Member libraries participate in the activities of their respective regional networks. The National Central Technical Library and Documentation Center (1883), the Information Center of the Ministry of Agriculture and Food (1946), and the National Medical Library and Documentation Center (1960) coordinate the work of various special and research library systems.

**Association.** Headquartered at the National Medical Library in Budapest, the Hungarian Library Association has over 1,500 regular members. The activities of the Association are directed by its President and Secretary. It receives the financial support of the Ministry of Culture and acts as the intermediary between the government and the Hungarian library community. The Magyar Könyvtárosok Egyesülete holds regular conferences.

IVAN L. KALDOR

## Hutchins, Margaret
(1884–1961)

Margaret Hutchins made significant contributions to librarianship through outstanding practice, teaching, and a seminal monograph, *Introduction to Reference Work.* Born September 21, 1884, she graduated from Smith College in 1906 with a Bachelor of Arts degree. After receiving a Bachelor of Library Science from the University of Illinois, she became a Reference Librarian there and lecturer in the library school. Together with Alice S. Johnson, who held similar positions in the library and library school at Illinois, and Margaret S. Williams, an instructor in the New York State Library School, Hutchins wrote a text published by H. W. Wilson in 1922 as *Guide to the Use of Libraries: A Manual for College and University Students;* a revised edition was published by Wilson in 1925.

Hutchins left Illinois in 1927 to become a reference specialist in the Queens Borough Public Library, New York. In 1931 she joined the staff of the School of Library Service at Columbia University, where she taught for many years, retiring as an Associate Professor in 1952. While at Columbia, Hutchins wrote the monograph that is her major contribution to librarianship—*Introduction to Reference Work* (1943). Dedicated to Francis Simpson, a teacher at Illinois, and Isadore Gilbert Mudge, a teacher at Columbia and Head of the Reference Department at its library, the book expressed its aim—"to describe and interpret reference work as the reference librarian sees it for the information of administrators of libraries and other librarians and library school students."

The Hutchins monograph bears some resemblance to James Wyer's *Reference Work* (1928) in that it describes the process of reference work rather than the contents of individual reference books. Wyer's work, however, had been based on a literature survey and visits to some 50 libraries; Hutchins did not repeat such an investigation. Instead she relied on her "thirty-five years' devotion to the subject, two thirds of which were spent in actual prac-

**hybreda,** Renaissance script for vernacular texts **476**

tice of reference work" to support "an attempt to interpret the essence of reference work in its universal aspects." The 28 chapters of the work are organized into seven sections: the Scope of Reference Work as a Branch of Library Service, Reference Questions, Selection of Reference Material, Organization of Reference Materials, Organization and Administration of Reference Service, the Less Common Functions of a Reference Librarian (including Advising Readers, Teaching the Use of Books and Libraries, Reporting Literature Searches, Work in Connection with Interlibrary Loan, Participating in Public Relations), and In Conclusion (Evaluating and Reporting Reference Work).

Recent developments in library service, ranging from the availability of data bases for on-line searching to the establishment of Information and Referral services in public libraries, make Hutchins's *Introduction to Reference Work* seem very old-fashioned, but her comments on the reference interview are noticeably modern. Indeed, she was first to use the phrase "reference interview," and her chapter on that subject anticipates much that is currently discussed in articles and dissertations on the communication skills needed by reference librarians.

Hutchins died at the age of 76 at Bayshore, Long Island, on January 4, 1961.

MARY JO LYNCH

# Iceland

Iceland, a republic, is an island in the North Atlantic Ocean near the Arctic Circle. Pop. (1978 est.) 222,500; area 103,000 sq.km. The official language is Icelandic.

**National Library.** Landsbókasafn Íslands was founded in 1818, instigated by members of the Icelandic Literary Society in Copenhagen. Donations were immediately solicited in Denmark, but it was not until 1825 that space was provided in the cathedral loft in Reykjavík. Through gifts, purchases, and a comprehensive exchange program, the Library grew. It moved first to the Althing (Parliament) building and then to its own home in 1909.

Since 1886 the National Library has received deposit copies of all works published in Iceland. Later they are distributed to libraries in each of the four regions in Iceland, the University Library, and to the University of Copenhagen in Denmark and the University of Manitoba in Canada, with which Icelanders have special cultural ties.

The Library's holdings include an extensive collection of manuscripts and printed books, which in 1974 numbered about 319,000 (or about 1.5 volumes per capita). Since the founding of the University Library in 1940 and Iceland's independence in 1944, the National Library has been responsible for acquiring materials in the humanities, while the University Library oversees collections of scientific books. In 1970 the Althing passed a resolution authorizing the building of a joint library and the eventual merging of the two collections. Among the National Library's activities are the publication in Icelandic of "The Icelandic National Bibliography" since 1974, union lists of foreign language materials acquired anywhere within the country, and a catalogue card distribution service.

**Academic Libraries.** Háskólabókasafn, the University of Iceland Library, is the principal academic library in the nation, although there are libraries in some other specialized institutions. In Reykjavík, it held more than 170,000 volumes in 1975. Its collections include materials to support the full range of general curricula and numerous research programs in Icelandic Studies, vulcanology, and fisheries. On campus, the Stofnun Árna Magnussonar (Icelandic Manuscript Institute) is the principal repository of the nation's extensive literary heritage, which includes manuscripts of the sagas from as early as the 12th century.

**Public Libraries.** Because of Iceland's long-standing tradition of reading, the literacy rate is virtually 100 percent. Public libraries are found in all population centers, and bookmobiles provide service to many outlying settlements. Per capita circulation in 1974 was approximately eight items from public libraries alone. Services are provided to hospitals, asylums, and other institutions and, typically Icelandic, collections of materials ("bookboxes") are regularly prepared for ships in the country's fishing fleets. The state pays a small sum of money to Icelandic authors whose works have been acquired by libraries, to compensate for royalties not gained from direct sales; writers of Icelandic-language works have a small potential market (probably no more than 150,000 buyers). The public library system is similar to that found in other Nordic countries and is quite progressive in most respects.

**School Libraries.** In 1974 libraries were mandated for all schools by a law of the Icelandic Parliament; by 1984 all schools were to have a library. In Reykjavík, by early 1976, more than half of the schools had libraries, many of them modern facilities similar to media centers in the U.S. A centralized service center in Reykjavík handles acquisitions, cataloguing, and other processes. In some of the smaller towns, school and public library functions are provided by the same institution.

**Special Libraries.** Several small special libraries support research centers (such as the National Energy Authority and the Marine Research Institute) and the specialized training schools (e.g., those in marine engineering and the health-related professions). An extensive collection of materials is held by the Nordic House, a cultural center supported by the Nordic countries. The U.S. International Communication Agency also maintains a modern library.

**Associations.** People working in Icelandic libraries become members of Bókavardafélag Íslands (The Association of Icelandic Librarians), founded in 1960. It has approximately 120 members. Félag Bókasafnsfraedinga (Association of Professional Librarians), established in 1973, has approximately 40 members with university-level training, frequently in the United States, Britain, or

Kenneth C. Harrison

*The National Library of Iceland originated in 1818 and moved to this building in Reykjavík in 1909.*

**Libraries in Iceland (1974)**

| Type | Number | Volumes in collections | Annual expenditures (krona) | Population served | Professional staff | All staff (total) |
|---|---|---|---|---|---|---|
| National | 1 | 319,000 | 24,482,000 I.kr. | 215,000 | 5 | 7 |
| Academic | 2 | 91,000[a] | 16,000 I.kr.[a] | N.A. | 6½ | 8½ |
| Public | 251 | 1,033,000 | 117,506,000 I.kr. | 215,000 | 7 | 168 |
| School | N.A. | N.A. | N.A. | N.A. | N.A. | N.A. |
| Special | 20 | N.A. | N.A. | N.A. | N.A. | N.A. |

[a]Obvious errors in source, but more accurate data not available.

Sources of information: *Unesco Statistical Yearbook, 1977* (Paris: *Unesco*, 1978), pp. 731–78.

one of the Scandinavian countries. The University of Iceland provides professional training in combination with another study area in a three-year program. Graduation from it is regarded as necessary for admission to the professional library ranks.

CHARLES WILLIAM CONAWAY

# Indexing and Abstracting

This article covers the processes of indexing and abstracting and includes sections on the following: indexing (types of indexing systems, standards, thesauri), abstracting (definitions, use, types of abstracts, writing abstracts, and standards), use of computers in abstracting and indexing, and major organizations in the field. Theories of classification are not covered here (see Classification).

INDEXING

**Definition.** Indexing has been defined as "the process of analyzing the information content of recorded knowledge and expressing this information content in the language of the indexing system." John Rothman has defined an index as "a systematic guide to items contained in or concepts derived from a collection." He further describes the operations in the process of indexing as:

> (1) scanning the collection, (2) analyzing its content, this content analysis being based on predetermined criteria of use of the collection and the index, (3) tagging discrete items in the collection with appropriate identifiers, and (4) adding to each identifier the precise location within the collection where the item occurs, so that it may be retrieved. Additional functions, which may but need not be performed by the same indexer, are: (1) cumulating the resulting entries into a cohesive, consistent whole, (2) establishing rules for the selection of identifiers, (3) establishing a pattern of interrelationship of identifiers (through cross references, tracings, and scope notes), (4) establishing the format of the locator, and (5) determining the physical form in which the completed index is to be published or otherwise made available for use. Note that the process of indexing does not include the actual production (for example, printing) of the completed index; and that the term is never applied to using an index.

**Traditional Controlled Vocabulary Systems.** Traditionally, indexing has involved a deductive method of organization. Knowledge is divided into broad subject categories or disciplines, each category is subdivided, and each subcategory is further subdivided. The organizational scheme is based on subject disciplines, and the scheme is hierarchical. In such systems, classification numbers are usually assigned to categories and subdivisions with allowances for the addition of new subcategories. The Dewey Decimal Classification and the Library of Congress Classification systems are examples of this type of indexing system. These systems were originally developed to organize collections of books on shelves in libraries and to permit browsing in shelf areas arranged by classification number. A list of the hierarchical subject headings used provides an index to the classification numbers.

As each document is added to a collection, the indexer makes a decision about the subject content of the document by asking himself what the document is about. Subject headings and corresponding classification numbers are selected from the lists. This type of indexing is sometimes referred to as indexing by assignment, because subject headings are assigned to the document. The vocabulary in this type of system is controlled, and subject terms are linked together, or bound, to represent a discipline or subcategory of a discipline (e.g., 20th-Century French Literature). The indexer selects subject headings that best describe the document and that, it is hoped, will be ones later used by people who try to retrieve the document. Usually three or four subject headings are selected, and often only one classification number is selected because that number determines where the document will be placed on the shelves.

**Natural Language Systems.** After World War II there was a definite shift from the exclusive use of traditional indexing systems with controlled vocabulary to systems using uncontrolled vocabulary in the form of natural language. This shift was precipitated by the large in-

Wayne State University Library

*The* New York Times Index, *which includes brief synopses of articles, shown in use in the reference room's index area at G. Flint Purdy Library, Wayne State University, Detroit, Michigan.*

crease in the number of technical reports issued during the war and by the need to identify quickly those reports and journal articles, rather than books, that contained current information in science and technology. A principal figure in the movement toward natural language systems was Mortimer Taube, who developed the idea of UNITERMS in the United States.

Taube recognized that only a portion of the documents added to a collection are ever used, and he argued that time and effort should not be put into providing costly subject analysis of all documents at the input stage, when they are added to a collection, but rather into retrieving effectively all relevant documents from a collection at the output stage, in response to a specific request.

Taube's idea represented a change to the use of the natural language in which the documents are written. The choice of subject terms was based on the author's words rather than the indexer's. Thus, the indexer no longer asked what the document was about but instead extracted terms from the document itself. This type of indexing is frequently referred to as "indexing by extraction" because words are extracted from the document, rather than being assigned by an indexer.

This new type of indexing put the responsibility for joining or coordinating terms on the user of the collection (or an intermediary), and the distinction arose between precoordinate and postcoordinate indexing systems. Traditional systems had precoordinated the terms by joining them into subject headings, while natural language systems kept each term separate, requiring coordination of terms during searching. Because of problems with synonyms and the need to bind together some terms that always appeared together (such as New Jersey), the system was modified to permit some precoordination of terms.

**Types of Indexes.** Traditional controlled vocabulary indexing systems use subject headings consisting of words joined together. Examples of this type of indexing are subject headings used for classifying books in library catalogues, back-of-the-book indexes, and the periodical indexes, such as those published by the H. W. Wilson Company, which use hierarchical subject headings. Several types of indexing systems have been developed to use the natural language of documents, many of which were designed specifically for technical report collections and for indexing journal articles. These include concept coordination and rotated and permuted indexing systems.

"Concept coordination" refers to indexing systems that list document numbers grouped under the key word that was assigned to each document. As each new document is received, the natural language key words are extracted from it, and the number for the document is listed on the card or part of the file for that key word. To find documents on subjects A and B, the cards or sections of the file for A and B are examined, and the lists of document numbers are compared to see which document numbers appear in both places. The former Cross Index published by *Biological Abstracts* and manual concept coordination cards are two examples of this type of index.

Rotated indexes are most frequently seen as Key Word in Context (KWIC) or Key Word Out of Context (KWOC) indexes, produced by rotating each significant word in the title of a document so that it appears alphabetically in the index. The advantages of this type of index are that it is very inexpensive to produce because no intellectual effort is needed and that it can be produced very quickly. The major disadvantage is that there is no control over the vocabulary, and synonyms appear in different places and—because many titles are not very meaningful or complete—a subject approach only through the words that appear in the title may be insufficient. The Institute for Scientific Information's *Permuterm Subject Index* is a classic permuted index in that each significant word in a title is linked with each "co-term," which is every other significant word in the title. Rotated indexes do not necessarily link the words in the title with each other.

**Faceted Classification Schemes.** A different type of indexing scheme was developed in 1933 to allow for more flexible coordination of subject approaches to documents. In his Colon Classification, S. R. Ranganathan proposed that documents be analyzed by generic concepts, which he called facets. Rather than organizing knowledge by subject disciplines, the scheme organizes knowledge according to five facets: Personality, Matter, Energy, Space, and Time (PMEST). Each document is described according to these facets, and numbers corresponding to each of the facets are assigned. The numbers are then joined together with a system of punctuation marks into a chain.

**PRECIS.** The PREserved Context Indexing System (PRECIS) is a multiple entry system that was developed to replace chain indexing in the *British National Bibliography*. The order of elements assigned is designed to preserve the meaning in every entry through the use of relational operators with concept strings. Indexers identify concept strings (e.g., curriculum, secondary schools, Canada) and determine the order in which the elements should appear. The elements are then shunted into the lead by computer, and each significant element appears alphabetically in the index, followed by a string of the other related elements in the designated order. See and see also references are used to refer to preferred and related terms. PRECIS is not dependent on any specific classification scheme, and it is used for many types of documents, including books, periodical articles, and dissertations. Its use for multilingual indexing is being investigated.

**Thesaurus Development.** A thesaurus is a postcoordinate listing of terms showing relationships among terms, specifically the generic relationship of broader and narrower terms and other relationships of synonyms and related terms. A classic thesaurus uses natural language key words, and it lists the key words to show the relationships among the terms. The precise definition of broader and narrower terms is a necessary trait of a true thesaurus. This generic relationship must always be true for it to be established as broader-narrower relationship in a thesaurus. Although a list of subject headings may look like a thesaurus (and sometimes is even called a thesaurus), it differs from a true thesaurus in that it uses precoordinate subject headings that are derived deductively by dividing a subject area into subdivisions, and it is not based on natural language key words.

A useful and comprehensive set of guidelines for thesauri exists as the American National Standards Institute Standard (Z39.19–1974), *Guidelines for Thesaurus Structure, Construction and Use.* This standard presents rules and conventions for the structure, construction, and maintenance of a thesaurus of terms and also serves as an aid in using existing thesauri. Maintenance is costly and time-consuming but is an essential part of thesaurus development.

**Standards for Indexing.** There is no single standard for indexing, primarily because there are so many different types of indexes and indexing systems. The ANSI standard on *Basic Criteria for Indexes* (Z39.4–1968 [R1974]) was under revision at the end of the 1970's. Unesco issued a series of Indexing Principles (included in the NFAIS Indexing kit), but these are general guidelines developed to be independent of any specific system. The 1979 revision of the ANSI standard was expected to be the most useful American standard or guideline for indexing.

ABSTRACTING

In order to sift through the large quantity of literature on any topic to identify those documents of interest, a searcher often relies on abstracts to provide summaries of the literature. Abstracts are usually consulted to determine the need for reading the complete document and are not intended to serve as a surrogate for the document. An abstract is a summary of a larger work. As Ben H. Weil and his colleagues have noted, there is a constant thread throughout many definitions of *abstract* and its synonyms of "'fewer words, yet retaining the sense'; 'condensation and omission of more or less of detail, but retaining the general sense of the original'; and 'a brief or curtailed statement of the *contents* of a topic or a work' and a *part* which represents typically a large and intricate whole' " [author's emphasis].

**Use of Abstracts.** There are numerous uses of abstracts, including the nine enumerated by Charles L. Bernier: (1) translation into languages other than that in which the original document was written; (2) facilitating selection of documents; (3) a substitute for the original document—a point of disagreement between Bernier and most abstracting and indexing services); (4) time-saving; (5) more convenient and less expensive organization of documents into related groups than can be done with the original documents; (6) retrospective searching; (7) more accurate selection of literature to be read or translated than through titles alone or titles plus annotations; (8) facilitating indexing by concentrating the indexable subjects to speed indexing and by eliminating the language problem; and (9) facilitating the preparation, acquisition, and searching of documents through ease of physically organizing (e.g., copying, cutting and pasting) abstracts. Additional uses include current awareness services and a memory-aiding device to remind a researcher of which articles he has read without having to scan the entire article again.

**Types of Abstracts.** These are generally defined by purposes, although Borko and Bernier also categorize them by whom they were written and by form. The three most common types are informative (or informational or comprehensive), indicative (or descriptive), and an annotation. These have been defined by Weil et al. as follows:

> The "informative," "informational," or "comprehensive" abstract, one that is still complete enough in its distillation "to communicate knowledge." This type of abstract contains the significant findings, arguments, and applications; states the scope; and usually at least indicates such other important aspects of the document as methods and equipment used.
>
> The "indicative" or "descriptive" abstract usually restricted to descriptive statements about the contents of the document.
>
> The "annotation," in which a few words or a sentence are added to a title by way of further description, explanation, or even critical comment. Annotations are usually indicative, it is difficult to make them informative.

Two additional types of abstracts defined in terms of purpose are the "title-only" abstract and the "slanted abstract." These are defined as follows:

> The "title-only" abstract, where the title of a document is used without amplification to describe the document's contents. Titles usually state subjects, not findings, so are usually indicative rather than informative.
>
> The "slanted" abstract, in which the information or description reported is oriented to a specific "discipline" or to an industrial or governmental field or "mission." In such abstracts, emphasis may sometimes be placed on methods, equipment, or findings that were only incidental to the author's major purpose; the latter may even be omitted or minimized.

**Writing Abstracts.** Weil et al. provide a clear and succinct discussion of technical abstracting. The authors identify four purposes of abstracts and suggest that informative abstracts may well be the most desirable type of abstract because they transmit salient facts from the document rather than simply indicating that certain information exists in it.

The authors provide a list of rules and a description of techniques for writing abstracts. In summary, the first sentence of an abstract should be a topical sentence containing the most important findings, conclusions, and recommendations of the document, and it may serve as a one-sentence abstract of the abstract. If properly prepared, it will contain most of the terms needed for indexing. Brevity is essential, and stock phrases should be avoided. Direct statements in the active voice are preferred to indirect statements in the passive voice.

**Standards for Abstracts.** The most comprehensive official standard for abstracts is the ANSI Z39 standard, which was approved in 1970 (ANSI Z39.14–1971) and revised in 1978. The abstract of the 1970 version summarizes the recommendations as follows:

> Prepare an abstract for every formal item in journals and proceedings, and for each separately published report, pamphlet, thesis, monograph, and patent. Place the abstract as early as possible in the document. Make the abstract as informative as the document will permit, so that readers may decide whether they need to read the entire document. State the purpose, methods, results, and conclusions presented in the document, either in that order or with initial emphasis on findings.
>
> Make each abstract self-contained but concise; retain the basic information and tone of the original document. Keep abstracts of most papers to fewer than 250 words (preferably on one page), and abstracts of short communications to fewer than 100 words. Write most abstracts in a single paragraph. Normally employ complete, connected sentences; active verbs; and the third person. Employ standard nomenclature, or define unfamiliar terms, abbreviations, and symbols the first time they occur in the abstract.
>
> When authors' abstracts are employed in secondary services, precede or follow each abstract with the complete bibliographic citation of the document described. Include pertinent information about the document itself (type, number of citations, etc.) if this is necessary to complete the message of the abstract.

**Computers.** Computers have been used since the 1950's to produce indexes of all types, although much less work has been done in using computers to abstract. Several studies indicate that computers are being used to prepare extracts, rather than true abstracts, which range in quality from fairly good to disappointing, primarily because of problems related to the complexity of the language itself and the need for human intervention to interpret and edit the abstracts. Research is still under way to prepare acceptable abstracts using computers.

Several types of indexes have been produced by computer, including the KWIC, KWOC, and citation indexes mentioned above. Also, many abstracting and indexing services use computers as an aid to human indexers and to detect spelling errors and perform routine functions. In most cases humans still perform the majority of indexing.

With the ability to make the complete abstract, title, and indexing terms available for computer searching, indexing entered a new era. The computer can provide an "index" to every word, author's name, word in a journal title, etc., which is input into the computer. Questions are arising concerning whether expensive indexing is really necessary with this new ability. Problems of synonyms, variations in spelling of the same word, and

Texas State Library

*Computer-assisted indexing of Confederate pension records, much used by genealogical researchers, provides easier record access.*



multiple-language data bases are taking on new dimensions. Research is currently under way to determine what the effect of on-line searching will be on the indexing of data bases. It is likely that new theories on indexing, and perhaps new techniques for indexing, will become available in the near future.

**Major Organizations.** Several organizations are involved to some extent in the fields of indexing and abstracting, including the large professional associations, such as the American Library Association and the American Society for Information Science. Most prominent among those organizations devoted to the field are the American Society of Indexers (ASI) with its British counterpart, the Society of Indexers, and the National Federation of Abstracting and Indexing Services (NFAIS). ASI is a national nonprofit organization for indexers and those employing indexers, with members throughout the United States and Canada and a total membership in 1979 of approximately 350. ASI is concerned with all forms of indexing, both manual and computerized. Its activities include meetings, workshops on free-lance indexing, publications, and an award in cooperation with the H. W. Wilson Company for excellence in indexing. Among its publications is the *Register of Indexers,* an annual self-selected listing of individuals available to do indexing. The Society of Indexers is a similar organization in Great Britain. The two societies are formally affiliated and share in publishing a journal, *The Indexer.*

The National Federation of Abstracting and Indexing Services is an umbrella organization of approximately 40 abstracting and indexing services in the not-for-profit and government sectors. Founded in 1958, it concentrates its activities in the areas of educational seminars, an annual technical conference, publications including the "Indexing in Perspective" education kit, a bimonthly newsletter, active participation in standards work, and research. From 1968 the Federation presented a series of seminars on indexing in the U.S., Canada, and the U.K. Under Unesco sponsorship, the Federation presented an indexing seminar for representatives from 15 countries, including 11 developing countries, in Warsaw, Poland, in 1976. NFAIS is frequently called upon to represent the abstracting and indexing community in national projects such as the Network Advisory Committee of the Library of Congress and the CONversion of SERials (CONSER) project. The Federation is also active in international activities, such as the Unesco General Information Programme's U.S. National Committee and the International Organization for Standardization.

**REFERENCES**

Harold Borko and Charles L. Bernier, *Abstracting Concepts and Methods* (1975).
———. *Indexing Concepts and Methods* (1978).
Everett H. Brenner et al., *NFAIS/Unesco Indexing in Perspective Education Kit* (1979).
Ben H. Weil, I. Zarember, and H. Owen, "Technical Abstracting Fundamentals," *Journal of Chemical Documentation* (1963).

TONI CARBO BEARMAN

# India

India, a federal republic in southern Asia, lies on a peninsula that juts out into the Indian Ocean; the Arabian Sea is on the west and the Bay of Bengal on the east. India is bordered on the north and from east to west by Burma, Bangladesh, China, Bhutan, Nepal, and Pakistan. Pop. (1977 est.) 625,810,000; area 3,287,782 sq.km. The official languages are Hindi and English.

**National Library.** The National Library of India was established as the Imperial Library in 1903 in Calcutta, then the country's capital, by an act of the government passed in 1902. It was given its present name by the Imperial Library (Change of Name) Act passed by India's Constituent Assembly in 1948, when it moved to its 30-acre campus at Belvedere in southwest Calcutta. The Compulsory Deposit of Books and Periodicals Act of 1954, amended in 1956, made it a depository library; the other two are the Connemara Library, Madras, and the Central Library, Bombay.

When the Imperial Library was founded by Lord Curzon, then Viceroy and Governor-General of India, it took over the holdings of the Calcutta Public Library (established in 1836) and the Imperial Secretariat Library (1891). Consequently it had then—as it has now—some features of both a public and a departmental library. Any Indian citizen who is at least 18 years of age can obtain a reading room ticket and a borrower's ticket free of charge. Only books in print are issued on loan against deposit of money. Central and state government officials are permitted to borrow books without deposit. The Library has an interlibrary loan service covering libraries in India and abroad.

The National Library's collection totaled 1,476,752 volumes in 1974 and 1,607,528 books in 1978. It has about 60,000 Indian and foreign official documents, including the publications of the UN and other international bodies and 72,000 maps. Among its rare items are about 2,000 books in European languages published between the 15th and 18th centuries and another 3,000 rare titles published in India. It receives annually about 20,000 books and 18,000 periodicals in English and Indian languages under the Delivery of Books Act and purchases about 9,000 books a year. It subscribes to about 800 foreign periodicals. The Library's reading rooms have 500 seats for its average 1,000 daily readers.

The Library staff is about 800, more than 200 of whom are professional librarians holding degrees or diplomas in library science. It falls under the Union Ministry of Education and Culture, which set up an Advisory Committee for three years to advise the union government about its structure, function, and governance. The National Library of India Act of 1976, which grants the Library statutory autonomy, had yet to come into force by mid-1979.

The Indian National Bibliography begun in 1956 is compiled and published by the Central Reference Library, which is in the National Library campus and is headed by its Librarian.

**Academic Libraries.** India's 105 universities, 10 institutions deemed to be universities by the University Grants Commission, and another 10 learned bodies of national importance contain academic libraries. The country's 3,227 colleges of arts, science, and commerce, 108 engineering colleges, 200 medical colleges, 543 teacher training colleges, and 2,569 intermediate colleges have libraries, some of which are more than 100 years old. The most important academic libraries in the country are those of Calcutta, Bombay, and Madras universities, all founded in 1857. An older academic library is that of Presidency College, Calcutta, founded as Hindu College in 1817. Some missionary colleges, such as the Scottish Church College, Calcutta, predates the three important universities by more than a quarter of a century.

**Public Libraries.** Public libraries in India are as old as the introduction of the New Learning in the country in the early decades of the 19th century. It is, however, from the country's attainment of independence in 1947 that notable efforts have been made to establish a network of such libraries in the cities, towns, and villages within the country's 22 states and 9 union territories. The Unesco figure for public libraries in India in 1956, given as 24,026, is misleading because it includes libraries of all descriptions to which the public have any access. Central and state governments have a policy of establishing public libraries that are supported by public funds and open to the public free of charge. Four of the 22 states of the country had passed library acts by 1979, and many more planned to do so. In 1972 the central government established the Raja Rammohun Library Foundation in Calcutta to help build a national library system. In 1977–78 the Foundation gave assistance to 26 state central libraries, 397 district libraries, and 3,000 libraries in semi-urban and rural areas. The national library system was expected in 1979 to keep pace with the government's attempt to reduce the illiteracy rate, which was 70 percent of the population.

**School Libraries.** India's 84,213 high schools all have libraries, the oldest with particularly rich collections. A scheme calling for two years of preuniversity education after high school required a large number of schools to enlarge their collections to include books for the use of students who though still in high school are actually pursuing collegiate courses. Another problem for India's school libraries is that they must provide textbooks for students in fairly large numbers.

**Special Libraries.** *The Directory of Special and Research Libraries,* published by the Indian Association of Special Libraries and Information Centres in 1962, lists 173 special libraries, the majority of which are supported by the government. Among these are libraries of the central government institutions: the Geological Survey of India, Calcutta (established in 1851), Botanical Survey of India, Howrah (1890), Archaeological Survey of India, New Delhi (1902), Zoological Survey of India, Calcutta (1916), and Anthropological Survey of India, Calcutta (1946). National laboratories, such as the National Physical Laboratory, and other national institutes for scientific research, such as the Bhaba Atomic Research Centre, Bombay, have large collections of books and journals in their respective areas of research. Other important special libraries of the country include the Medical Library and the Law Library in New Delhi. The Asiatic Society, Calcutta (1784) has a large collection of books and manuscripts relating to Indian literature, history, and philosophy.

In 1979 India's national government and state governments were working toward establishing a national library system from a plan offered in the report of the Advisory Committee for Libraries, which was appointed by the Union Ministry of Education in 1959. In the 20 years following, leading librarians and educators seriously reflected on the question of a sound national library system. Their ideas and plans are reflected in the Indian Library Association's work, which celebrated its 25th anniversary in 1979. A national library policy was expected to emerge when all 31 states and union territories have their library acts and when an instrument of cooperation among all libraries becomes necessary for the sharing and economy of library resources. That instrument may be embodied in a central government policy resolution or act.

**REFERENCES**

B. S. Kesavan, *India's National Library* (1961).
Subodh Kumar Mookerjee, *Development of Libraries and Library Science in India* (1969).
Jibananda Saha, *Special Libraries and Information Services in India and in the U.S.A.* (1969).

R. K. DAS GUPTA

# Indonesia

Indonesia is the fifth most populous nation in the world, with 141,000,000 people spread unevenly over 13,667 islands covering an area of 1,904,569 sq.km. The most densely populated is Java, an island of 137,187 sq.km., with 88,000,000, inhabitants. The official language is Bahasa Indonesian. Telecommunication facilities are not well developed. Obtaining information through library services is not a rooted tradition.

**Proposed National Library.** A national library was still lacking as was a legislated national library service in the late 1970's, but plans for a national library were under way. Preparations for its development were entrusted to the Centre for Library Development, Department of Education and Culture. Meanwhile, library services were performed under loose agreements between libraries joining a national network program.

Centers that act as national focal points were set up in the fields of science and technology, biology and agriculture, health and medicine, and social sciences. As national focal points in their respective fields, the centers have among others the responsibility to develop a national collection and to improve national services. Resource sharing among libraries is receiving considerable attention in development to offer accessibility of literature information to all levels of users. Besides government support, library development has also received bilateral and unilateral aid from various sources, including Unesco, USIS, US-AID, the Asia Foundation, British Council, and Colombo Plan. Usually aid from these sources is in the form of experts or grants for overseas study and training.

**Academic Libraries.** Most of the colleges and universities in Indonesia, and thus also their libraries, are comparatively young, especially those outside Java. Only the Faculty of Medicine, University of Indonesia, in Jakarta and the Institute of Technology in Bandung existed long before Indonesia grained its independence in 1945.

Most libraries in Indonesia are government owned. Several private ones belong to the Islamic institutes, Theological Seminaries, and also Teachers' Training Colleges.

More centralized university library services remained to be developed, as many universities still maintained departmental libraries in the late 1970's. An integrated university library system was being managed by the Directorate of Higher Education, Department of Education and Culture, but development was hampered principally by the limited supply of qualified senior librarians.

**Public Libraries.** Public libraries, also mostly government owned, are usually managed by the local government and the Department of Education and Culture. In fact, libraries are essentially reading rooms open for pastime reading. They had not reached a state of service adequate for public use for most reference purposes.

At the end of the decade of the 1970's, the reading hunger of the newly literate was partly met by neighborhood libraries—small collections, usually privately owned, serving the inhabitants of a small community.

**Special Libraries.** Special libraries, many of which are attached to research institutes, are better off than other types of libraries.

**Table 1. Libraries in Indonesia (1976)**

| Type | Number | Volumes in collections | Annual expenditures (rupiahs) | Population served | Professional staff | All staff (total) |
|---|---|---|---|---|---|---|
| National | N.A. | N.A. | N.A. | N.A. | N.A. | N.A. |
| Academic | N.A. | 448,913 | 185,238,000[a] | 206,102 | 22 | 220 |
| Public | 265 | 914,000 | 143,432,500[a] | N.A. | N.A. | 472 |
| School | 2,800 | 2,800,000 | 24,925,000[a] | N.A. | N.A. | 1,785 |
| Special | 92 | 1,354,639 | 557,304,188[a] | N.A. | 215 | 592 |

[a]Not including salaries and building.
Sources: Directorate of Higher Education; Center for Library Development; National Scientific Documentation Center.

The four library centers with national functions cited previously grew from special libraries. Several of the established ones are growing to become specialized centers in their field of interest. In the Indonesia library development, the special libraries could be considered as promoters of new approaches in library and information services.

**Table 2. Archives in Indonesia (1976)**

| | |
|---|---|
| Total number | 1 |
| Holdings | 15 linear km. |
| Annual expenditures | Rp. 220,000,000 |
| Professional staff | 10 |
| All staff (total) | 120 |

Source: National Archives.

**School Libraries.** There are 83,500 primary schools and 12,755 secondary schools in Indonesia (1977 census); most provide insufficient libraries to support class assignments. Free access to the collections is still very reluctantly accepted by school heads because of limited budgets the schools receive for collection building. Facilities for training of teacher librarians were offered by the Teacher Training Colleges in the 1970's.

**Associations.** The Indonesian Library Association, founded in 1954, was the only library association existing in the country. Throughout its history it has undergone several times changes of names and coverage of activities. At one time it was also an association for archivists.

Later, between 1969 and 1973, people working in special libraries felt they needed their own association and thus formed the Indonesian Special Library Association.

Although the small group flourished well, many believed that the small number of professionals in the associations was not considered advantageous to the development of the profession. A new combined association was started in 1974. Many constraints exist in making the association strong, of which the most obvious ones are the lack of strong personnel with driving power and the lack of funds for operation.

A national agency, in charge of publishing *Bibliografi Nasional Indonesia* ("Indonesian National Bibliography"), is in the Office of Bibliography and Deposit created in 1953. This office has also published many other bibliographies and checklists for reference purposes. The compilation of a true national bibliography was hampered in the late 1970's by the absence of a depository act.

"Yayasan Idayu," privately owned, is also active in bibliographic work and publishes *Berita Bibliografi Idayu.* This private institute has an outstanding collection of Indonesia publications published since 1945.

**REFERENCE**

Philip Ward, *Indonesia: Development of a National Library Service* (1975).

LUWARSIH PRINGGOADISURJO

# Information Science Education

Librarianship has repeatedly been faced with a "crisis of identity." Are libraries simple "storehouses," or are they "centers for information"? Which do librarians regard as important, the "medium" or the "message"? These are not idle questions, nor are the answers obvious. They were explicit in the arguments that reverberated loudly at the hearings of the Royal Commission on the Library of the British Museum in 1847–49 concerning the relative importance of the author-title catalogue and the subject catalogue. At that time the answer was clear: the role of the library was to preserve the records of the past and to assure that they were available for the needs of the future; although both catalogues were needed, the author-title catalogue was the more urgent in order to tell whether the library held a particular book. The results of that decision have set the tone for libraries ever since.

But the ever increasing demand for "information" has forced librarianship into a reexamination of that answer made over 100 years ago. Clearly, the historical role of the library as preserver of the records of the past is still an important one. "Information" does not exist in abstract form but only as data recorded in some record, and, therefore, even for those whose interest is only in the information, the record in which it is recorded must be preserved and made available. But should libraries continue to regard this as their *primary* function?

Whatever the answer may be, it will have a profound effect on the nature of libraries and their relationship to their users. It is therefore imperative that library education help the student to understand the nature of "information," the processes by which it is generated, the extent to which those processes can be provided by libraries, and the extent to which they have been formalized and can be provided by computers.

Of course, this has been well recognized, and information science is becoming an integral part of library education, an increasingly important part of the librarian's professional and operational responsibility, and a part of the theoretical foundations of librarianship. What, then, is "information science"? The purpose of this article is to define it, with emphasis on its relevance to library education.

**Definitions.** First, it is essential that one establishes some definition so as to have a common basis for communication in this article.

*Information.* It is clear that *information* has had a variety of meanings. Some people identify it with transmission over communication lines and will measure it by the statistical properties of signals; some have identified information with recorded facts; others, with the content of text; still others, with the experience stored in the human mind. Information science deals with information, and we must have a suitable definition, even if it is at the most elementary level. The following is the operational definition of *information* that will be used in this article:

> *Information* is a property of data resulting from or produced by a process that produced the data. The process may be simply *data transmission* (in which case the definition and measure used in communication theory are applicable); it may be *data selection*; it may be *data organization*; it may be *data analysis*.

It is important to note that given this definition, information is dependent on the processes that produce it. Although some of its properties may be subject to investigation independent of the means of performing those processes, the important and interesting ones cannot be. That means that "information" can best be studied in the context of specific "information systems."

*Information Systems.* If one considers any complex phenomenon, one may be concerned with a variety of things about it—its physical structure, its cybernetic response to environment, its chemical and metabolic balance, or its information processing. Thus a person can be viewed as a complex of bones and muscles, capable of performing mechanical tasks; as a chemical factory processing ingested food, water, and air and converting it to metabolic energy; or as a thinking human being, taking in sensory data, making decisions, and controlling its physical and chemical structure. A library can be viewed as a physical structure, with physical records and a mechanical flow of materials; as an administrative organization, with the assignment of people to a variety of tasks; or as an information-processing system taking in data and providing it out again in response to requests.

If the aspects of interest in a system are the ones that we identify as information processing, the system then becomes an information system. Hence,

> An *information system* is that set of aspects of a general system (a natural phenomenon, a physical construct, or a logical construct) that are identified as information producing.
>
> This leads to a very natural definition of Information science:
>
> *information science* is the study of information-producing processes in any information system in which they may occur.

This means that while information science may in principle be concerned with pure analysis of processes, it depends upon the methodologies of specific disciplines. For example, RNA and DNA can be studied for the information processes that they embody and, as such, are information systems of vital interest to information science. But it would be impossible to study, in any real sense, the means by which they transmit, select, and even analyze "data" (represented by various configurations of amino acids) without the use of microbiology. It is therefore more appropriate to talk in terms of "information science in genetics" or "information science in social theory" or "information science in documentation" than to talk of "information science" in isolation from specific systems.

**Information Systems.** What then are the "systems" with which information science is concerned?

*The Computer.* The computer has been an especially important context for information science, for very clear reasons. The raison d'etre for the computer is its data processing capabilities. Furthermore, those capabilities are very well defined and can be measured in very precise ways; the computer is therefore a relatively predictable system to study.

*Computer-Based Information Systems.* Because the computer has been used in an increasing variety of applications, the resulting computer-based information systems have become a fruitful spawning ground for information science activities. They embody information-producing processes considerably more complex than those of the computer itself. The result has been the growth of "systems work" or "application work"—the body of techniques by which an organization is studied and by which alternative systems for information processing are designed and evaluated. Since the primary focus of systems work is on the information processes in these areas of application of computers, it has been natural to identify information science with systems work on computer applications, although, again, to do so unnecessarily limits the scope of the field.

*Libraries and Information Centers.* Libraries and information centers, as institutions, exist for the information functions they serve. Furthermore, the information processes they use—cataloguing and indexing, for example—are relatively well formalized. As a result they provide ideal subjects for study by information science, and there has been a corresponding interest on the part of libraries and information centers in utilizing the insights that information science could provide. Indeed, the extent of interest on both sides has been so great that some have identified information science with library science, but it seems clear that to do so unnecessarily restricts the scope of information science.

*Social Systems and Biological Systems.* That a social system or biological system can be regarded as an "information system" may seem somewhat unnatural. But it is clear that each performs processes upon what we regard as data (symbolic representations). For example, an elected official can be treated as a symbol of his constituency; there are clearly defined mechanisms for selection of such symbols, and these constitute "information generating processes." Similarly, the "genetic code" is made up simply of arrays of amino acids, but these can be regarded as data (symbolic representations). Economics is concerned with processes upon symbols of capital; psychology, with processes upon symbols of response; and so on.

**Information Science Education.** Programs for education in information science have been defined in such a variety of ways that it is almost impossible to extract a common curriculum from them. The following lists a few of the existing kinds of programs:

(1) Some have identified information science with computer science. They include coursework in the methodologies of engineering (for study of the computer hardware) and of mathematics and logic (for study of the software).

(2) Some have identified information science with the use of computers in libraries; such schools will imply that they have an "information science curriculum" if they added one or two courses on "data processing in the library."

(3) Some have identified information science with "science information" and usually regard it as synonymous with "documentation." Such schools will add courses on "Indexing and Abstracting," "the Management of Information Centers," and "Mechanized Information Retrieval" as their curriculum in information science.

(4) Some have identified information science with the design of information systems in various fields of interest. Usually they will call their curricula "Information Systems" curricula and include courses on system design and the application of computers.

(5) Some regard information science as a discipline in its own right that, although applicable in many fields, has its own problems of research interest and its own "discipline." Such schools will include both theoretical courses

(usually drawn from the formal disciplines of mathematics, logic, and perhaps linguistics) and applied courses (from fields like psychology, engineering, or microbiology).

*Historical Development.* The development of these various kinds of curricula is a relatively recent phenomenon. In fact, the earliest identifiable recognition of the field in librarianship (not in name, but in fact) was at Western Reserve University, under the guidance of Dean Jesse Shera. In the middle 1950's James W. Perry and Allen Kent founded the Center for Documentation and Communication Research as an adjunct of that library school.

In the subsequent five to ten years, a number of short courses, workshops, conferences, and other forms of instruction were launched at a number of other universities—at UCLA, American University, Drexel, University of Washington, and Georgia Institute of Technology. However, all of these were, like that at Western Reserve, essentially outside the structure of formal academic curricula.

In viewing these ad hoc educational programs, it is important to recognize that the several types of context outlined above were thoroughly intermixed. In fact, one of the predominant concerns was with development of computer-based information systems in support of science and technology in the post-Sputnik era. The result was continuing confusion between "science information," "computer science," "information systems design," and "information science." Even with that confusion, however, the steadily increasing number of such programs provided clear evidence of a real need for formal instruction. In 1961 and 1962 two conferences were held at Georgia Institute of Technology at which, for the first time, the various aspects of the field were more or less clearly delimited and the goals for formal curricula defined.

Almost immediately various schools initiated formal programs in information science. The ones started at Georgia Institute of Technology (Vladimir Slamecka), Ohio State (Marshall Yovits), and Lehigh University (Robert Taylor and Don Hillman) were all outside of librarianship as such, but they have retained a close association to librarianship. The ones at the University of Chicago (Don Swanson), Case Western Reserve (Perry, Kent, and Alan Goldwyn), UCLA (Robert Hayes and Harold Borko), Pittsburgh (Allen Kent), and other universities, however, were established as integral parts of library schools. From 1964 to 1967 these programs became well established in their respective schools. A series of conferences were held during that period at which representatives of the several programs met to exchange

**Various Course Emphases**

| Representative Courses | Theory Oriented | Computer Oriented | Systems Oriented | Operations Oriented | Usage Oriented |
|---|---|---|---|---|---|
| *Core Courses* | | | | | |
| Introduction to Information Science | C | C | C | C | C |
| Information System Design | C | C | C | C | C |
| Seminar in Information Science | C | C | C | C | C |
| *Formal Disciplines* | | | | | |
| Calculus | Prereq. | Prereq. | Prereq. | — | — |
| Programming | Prereq. | Prereq. | 1 | 2 | — |
| Symbolic Logic | 1 | 1 | 3 | — | — |
| Recursive Functions | 1 | 1 | 3 | — | — |
| Linguistics | 1 | 2 | 2 | — | — |
| *Applied Disciplines* | | | | | |
| Statistics | 3 | 3 | 1 | — | 3 |
| Operations Research | 3 | 3 | 1 | 2 | — |
| Psychology | 2 | 3 | — | — | 1 |
| Information Theory | 1 | 1 | 3 | — | — |
| Systems Analysis | — | 3 | 1 | 2 | 3 |
| Methods of Social Res. | — | — | 2 | — | 1 |
| *Computer-Oriented Courses* | | | | | |
| Computer Hardware | 3 | 1 | 2 | 3 | — |
| Compiler Construction | 3 | 1 | — | — | — |
| Data Base Management | 3 | 1 | 1 | 2 | — |
| Info. Retrieval Sys. | 1 | 1 | 1 | 1 | — |
| Management Info. Sys. | — | 3 | 2 | — | 2 |
| *Management-Oriented Courses* | | | | | |
| Managerial Accounting | — | — | 1 | 3 | — |
| Organization Theory | 3 | — | 2 | — | 2 |
| Info. Center Mgt. | — | — | 1 | 1 | 3 |
| *Service-Oriented Courses* | | | | | |
| Sources of Info. | — | — | 2 | 1 | 3 |
| Catal., Class., Index., Abst. | 2 | 2 | 2 | 1 | 3 |
| Documentation | — | — | 2 | 1 | 2 |
| Computer Ref. Serv. | — | 2 | 2 | 1 | 1 |

C — Core, required of all students
Prereq. — Prerequisite for specialty
1 — Required for specialty
2 — Recommended for specialty
3 — Elective for specialty

views and experiences—at Chicago and Western Reserve in 1964; Warrenton, Virginia, in 1965; and London in 1967. Various syllabi and reports on curriculum development were informally distributed. In the years since then virtually every library school in the country has added courses focused on one or another of the kinds of subject matter identified with information science.

*Structure of Curricula*. These varied curricula with specific focus on information science can best be summarized in the framework shown in the table. As it shows, an information science curriculum consists of courses designed to provide the student with the intellectual orientation and technical tools necessary for successful professional work and research in this field. The student must understand the problems in *utilization* of recorded information, the methods in *operation* of information systems, the techniques in their technical implementation, and their underlying theoretical structures. The curriculum should provide a common core of technical knowledge, integrated by a framework of the total field; it should provide directions of specialization within the field; and it should bring the student to the point of successful independent work. The direction for specialization will normally be in one of four aspects—the information *specialist*, concerned with utilization; the *manager* of an information system, concerned with operational techniques; the system *designer*, concerned with technical problems in implementation; and the *information scientist*, as such, concerned with the theoretical foundations of the whole field. Any particular curriculum will tend to emphasize one or another component, reflecting the orientation of the faculty and school. To some extent, however, each of the components should be explicitly recognized if the curriculum is properly to be characterized as an "information science" curriculum.

*Course Requirements*. The student's program should comprise an integrated course of study in the theoretical and practical foundations of information handling. They should provide an interdisciplinary program with emphasis on research and basic principles of information science. Within this general scope, there are five areas of coursework: (1) system design and integration, (2) organization of information records, (3) management of information activities, (4) use of equipment, and (5) theory and research. Each student should complete a common core of courses providing knowledge in each of these areas, together with coursework integrating them into a coherent whole so as to be able to understand how all of the parts fit together. The student should also complete required, recommended, and elective courses, as identified in the table, specializing in one or another of the component areas. Finally, the student should engage in active research in the chosen area of specialization, completing a dissertation or thesis. Such a program for study should require at least two years for a Master's-level degree.

Because of the interdisciplinary nature of information problems, the course work of the curriculum is likely to be drawn from a number of departments and schools. Thus, for an information science program associated with a library school, one might find the following:

(1) The core courses of the information science curriculum (Introduction to Information Science, Information System Design, and Seminar in Information Science), those that integrate the diverse tools into a single focus, can properly be provided by the library school, since librarianship is a profession completely concerned with the handling of information as such.

(2) Courses providing the students with knowledge of the technical tools of system design—statistics, operations research, optimization techniques, and the like—are likely to be taken in the departments of Mathematics, Engineering, or Business Administration.

(3) Courses providing knowledge of the technical tools of information service—bibliography, cataloguing and classification, indexing and abstracting, and reference—would almost certainly be taken in the library school.

(4) Courses acquainting the students with the tools of management would normally be taken in Business Administration (managerial accounting, for example), but the library school may well cover them in courses on library administration and the management of special types of libraries.

(5) Courses focusing on the computer may be taken in a number of schools or departments, but some specialized courses in this area may be offered by the library school: Data Base Systems, Information-Retrieval Systems, Management Information Systems, and Library Data Processing.

Research occupies a central role in an information science program, providing the means for the students to develop and explore a research problem in the design of modern information systems. It also provides an instructive experience in preparing a proposal for a definite project, scheduling the work that needs to be done, and carrying out the work itself. Consequently, the student is better able to evaluate his own capacity and that of others to execute projects.

*Information Science in Library Education*. A library school, however, is likely to treat information science as a component of an MLS degree program rather than as a degree objective in itself. As a result, the library school is likely to emphasize the "operations oriented" component, as shown in the table, with at best minimal attention to the other components. The core courses—Introduction to Information Science, Information System Design, and a seminar in information science—will bear a much greater burden. Consequently, they will tend to be more superficial and less technical than they would be in an information science curriculum as such.

One crucial problem faced by a library school in including an information science component in its program is whether and how to integrate it with the traditional components of the MLS curriculum. If not properly handled the information science courses can become an isolated enclave, bearing little relationship to the remainder of the MLS curriculum. Fortunately, progress in computerization of library technical processes and services now makes it not only feasible but essential to include coverage of this aspect as part of the traditional courses in cataloguing and reference. That part of an information science orientation, at least, can easily be integrated into an MLS program. The more theoretical and technical course work, however, is difficult to encompass within the framework of an MLS program. As a result, coverage tends to be superficial.

**Standards.** As of 1979, there were no established standards for education in information science, although the American Society for Information Science (ASIS) has frequently considered developing some.

**Accreditation.** As of 1979, there was no recognized accrediting body for information science. However, the American Library Association explicitly recognized information science, in its 1972 *Standards for Accreditation,* as an essential component of MLS programs.

(See also Librarianship, Philosophy of, by Jesse H. Shera.)

**REFERENCES**

Don R. Swanson, editor, *The Intellectual Foundations of Library Education* (The 28th Annual Conference of the Graduate Library School, July 6–8, 1964).

A. J. Goldwyn and Alan M. Rees, editors, *The Education of Science Information Personnel—1964* (1965).

Laurence B. Heilprin and others, editors, *Education for Information Science* (1965).

ROBERT M. HAYES

## Institutionalized, Services to the

In the last several years, institution libraries have reached an unprecedented level in the development of library service programs and in the delivery of service to the user. In the U.S., the Library Services and Construction Act admendments of 1966, which provide federal funds for institution libraries, gave that service a strong impetus. In addition, the social climate provided a sympathetic environment for the growth of institutional library service. The involvement of libraries in social programs made service to institutions feasible.

State library agencies are leaders in the development and promotion of institutional library service. Each state has a person at the state level responsible for library service to the institutionalized, usually as an institutional consultant. Consultants assist in the establishment, development, and improvement of library service in institutions. A discussion group, the Institutional Library Services, in the Association of Specialized and Cooperative Library Agencies of the American Library Association, acts as a clearinghouse for an exchange among state level personnel of information that is of special concern to institutional consultants.

Many statewide studies have been funded to explore the need for institutional library service and to set up statewide plans. Studies to evaluate present performance or to develop long-range planning programs have been funded. States that have sponsored these studies and reports include Florida, Illinois, North Dakota, Ohio, and Washington. Specialized studies of single institutions, of a type of institution, and of pilot programs have resulted in published reports. These publications have increased the information available on which to base decisions in the present and future development of institution libraries.

Studies have shown and experience has proved that the library needs of the institutionalized are as divergent and as varied as the backgrounds of the individuals themselves. Library service to the institutionalized has always been directed toward the individual and continues to be. Because there are many who do not fully realize the positive gains to the institutionalized from library service, librarians are taking the initiative in introducing and providing institution library service to individuals. These services have been funded initially, to a great extent, by the Library Services and Construction Act, Title IV, Part A, State Institutional Library Services, later combined into Title I, Library Services. Other funding at the federal level that has stimulated the program has come from the Law Enforcement Assistance Administration, the Elementary and Secondary Education Act, Social Security, and the Comprehensive Employment and Training Act (CETA). Funding also has been provided by federal revenue sharing and state and local funds as well as from private organizations and foundations. Federal funds have supported training institutes and fellowships through the Higher Education Act, Title II-B, providing preparation for institution library service. Federal legislation and regulations that have had a positive effect on institution library service include the Education of All Handicapped Children Act and the regulations pursuant to section 504 of the Rehabilitation Act of 1973.

*Below, bringing library materials to the hospitalized, and to the incarcerated (p. 253), in Sweden.*

Stockholms Staatsbibliothek

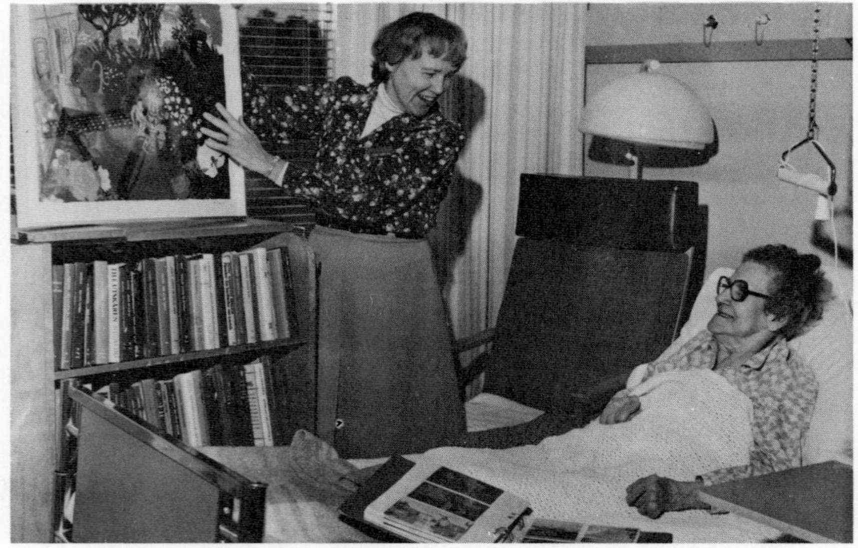

Standards for library service also have considered library service to the institutionalized directly or indirectly. *Standards for Library Functions at the State Level* (ALA, 1963) recommended an official relationship between state libraries and institutional libraries for the purpose of establishing library service to the institutionalized. The 1970 revision of these standards describes the state library agency's role as that of supplementing the institution libraries with resources and services, providing advisory and consultative services, coordinating the statewide program of library service to the institutionalized, and assisting in in-service training programs. Other standards relating to library service in institutions include *Standards for Library Service in Health Care Institutions* (ALA, 1970) and the *Minimum Standards for Public Library Systems* (ALA, 1966). Standards for library service that have been developed or are in the development or revision process in the late 1970's include service to adult and juvenile offenders, the mentally retarded, the developmentally disabled, the deaf, the blind and visually handicapped, and the hospital patient. State standards also have been developed for library service relating to the institutionalized. The implementation of all standards is gradual and uneven but is being accomplished. Another positive element in the development of library service to the institutionalized is the National Commission on Libraries and Information Science's expression of concern for the institutionalized user.

It is difficult to determine the number of institution libraries in existence in the United States. In 1970 the national census reported that 2,160,280 persons were living in institutions. This means that for every 100 persons counted in the 1970 census, 1 was in an institution. Institution libraries have existed almost since the beginning of the institutions themselves. Librarians, however, seldom have been the decision makers. The decisions usually have been made by the administration of the institution. In some instances, they were made by personnel in the education program. With the new surge of improved institution library service, a library coordinator position has been established in some states for all institutions or for a group of institutions. The number of qualified library staff members has been increasing. Librarians are now in decision-making roles as well as in service positions.

Many patterns of library service exist in institutions. Included are : (1) all library service provided by the institution, (2) all library service provided by outside libraries, (3) primary library service provided by the institution with supplementary service provided by outside libraries, and (4) primary library service provided by the institution with supplementary and additional primary service by outside libraries. The outside libraries include all types with state libraries and public libraries as the chief providers of service.

The services and materials available to the institutionalized differ in type, number, and quality. Materials are available in all suitable formats. Bookmobile service is provided. When this service is not feasible or when supplementary service is needed, rotating collections or deposit collections are placed in the institutions. The libraries sponsor reading-aloud activities, bibliotherapy sessions, creative writing groups, storytelling, and field trips. Books-by-mail service has also been utilized to serve the institutionalized user. Telephone reference is a service found in some institution libraries as is request delivery service. Other services provided include group discussions on subjects in library materials, organized library-use courses, reader-interest profiles, and bibliographies for the staff and for the residents. Information booklets telling where the released residents can find services, including library services, in their home communities are available. Extension services are often provided within an institution for those who cannot go to the library. These services are implemented in the form of book carts, deposit collections, or auxiliary libraries. Audiovisual production services are part of the library program in some institutions.

As a result of all of these efforts, many elements of improved library services have been developed in institutions. These include the following: (1) In-service training plans are in use. Formal training for library service, while improved in availability and quality, is not widely accessible. Library training programs do, in some instances, offer courses leading to a Master's degree, but continuing-education programs are more available to assist in the training of librarians for service to the institutionalized. In-service training supplements formal training and provides paraprofessional and clerical training.

(2) Interlibrary loan services are widely used. There is an increasing knowledge of materials in libraries outside the institution. The interrelationship between the public libraries and the institutional libraries is of special importance. The public library is of continuing importance because residents are released to the communities.

(3) Materials and services are provided for both staff and resident library programs. A library service to the staff is made available to enable the staff to keep up to date with institutional care. For the residents, the library service is provided to meet the recreational, educational, vocational, and therapeutic needs. In some instances a resident/staff library serves all people in an institution.

(4) Overall planning has been developed for institution libraries at the state level. In some institutions the overall planning is assisted by a staff advisory committee; a resident library committee assists in material selection, library management, public relations both within and without the institution, program planning, interlibrary loan processing, and with orientation planning and implementation. An outside advisory committee of interested citizens assists in relating the institutional library service to the community as well as helping to develop an institutional library program.

(5) Cooperative programs between the institution libraries, public libraries, school libraries, and academic libraries have been developed. Each year the number of states with statewide arrangements for institution and outside library cooperation grows. Some individuals must remain in an institution all their lives. The institution library, along with other libraries, assists in the development of a sense of worth in the individual and creates interest in the world outside the institution. In some states the degree of cooperation varies from one area of the state to another.

(6) Legal materials are increasingly available to the institutionalized, especially in correctional institutions. While the number and types of materials are not yet adequate, a strong beginning has been made.

An unevenness exists in the United States in the services provided in specific library programs in different types of institutions. Even with the remarkable advances in library service to the institutionalized, few institution libraries can meet adequately the needs of the individual. Overall there exists a lack of resources, programs, space, and staff. While there are outstanding examples of exemplary programs of library service in institution libraries,

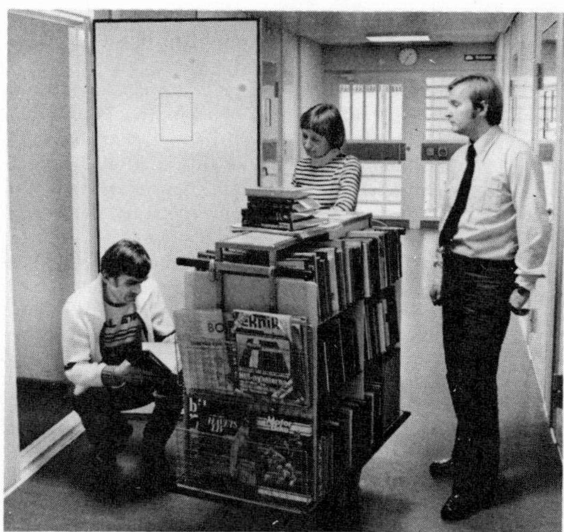

they are few in number. Institution library service is expensive to establish and to maintain at any effective level. Problems that exist in institution libraries include outdated book collections or collections unsuited to the service, lack of qualified staff, inadequate physical facilities, and underfinancing. Because priorities have not always been high for institution libraries, library service needs have been inadequately met.

Programs of library service are operating in some institutions which will stand the test of both the satisfaction of the user and fiscal accountability. A concept of service underlies institution library service—an assumption that services available in communities, including library service, are available in institutions—the institutionalized have a right to access to books and other informational materials. The result of this concept of service is visible through an increasingly effective provision of quality library service in institution libraries comparable to those services available to the public and made available to the institutionalized on an individual basis.

**REFERENCES**

Harris C. McClasky, issue editor, "Institution Libraries," *Library Trends* (1978); the needs of the library users in institutions are discussed as well as the response of the libraries to the needs.

Jane Pool, issue editor, "Library Services to Correctional Facilities," *Library Trends* (1977); the current state of correctional library service is examined. Included are the history, environment, standards, training and research, and alternate service patterns in different types of facilities and in several countries.

Eleanor Phinney, editor, *The Librarian and the Patient* (ALA, 1977), is a comprehensive discussion of the principles of librarianship related to the needs of the individual patient. The objectives of the total service program of an institution library are examined.

PHYLLIS I. DALTON

# International Association of Agricultural Librarians and Documentalists

The International Association of Agricultural Librarians and Documentalists (IAALD) was founded in 1955 to promote, internationally and nationally, agricultural library science and documentation as well as the professional interests of agricultural librarians and documentalists. The term *agriculture* is interpreted in its widest sense and includes forestry, agricultural engineering, veterinary science, fisheries, food and nutrition, and agricultural and food industries.

There were approximately 520 members from some 60 countries at the end of the 1970's. Membership is open to agricultural librarians and documentalists as individuals, corporate bodies (national and multinational associations of agricultural librarians and documentalists), and institutions (libraries, documentation centers, research and educational institutions, and official bodies).

In pursuing its objectives, IAALD encourages collaboration between agricultural libraries and documentation centers in various countries, particularly through the loan and exchange of literature and other documents. This has been formalized by the establishment of AGLINET, a cooperative document supply system supported by the major agricultural libraries of the world. The Association assists in the coordination of activities and projects dealing with agricultural bibliographies and abstracting services. It cooperates with international, regional, and national organizations in the field of agricultural information. In particular, IAALD supported and took part in the development of the FAO-sponsored international agricultural information system, AGRIS.

The organs of the Association are the General Assembly, the Executive Committee, and the Secretariat. The General Assembly of all members meets every five years and lays down general policy, amends the Constitution, appoints officers and members of the Executive Committee, and establishes membership fees. The Executive Committee consists of a President, two Vice-Presidents, a Secretary/Treasurer, at least six but not more than ten members, and a representative from each recognized national or multinational association of agricultural librarians and documentalists. The Executive Committee calls the General Assembly and directs the Association between meetings of the General Assembly. The Secretariat handles the current affairs of the Association under the direction of the Secretary/Treasurer.

IAALD holds a World Congress every five years. The 1980 Congress was scheduled for Manila, Philippines, on the theme of "Agricultural Information to Hasten Development." Regional Congresses are held at other times. The Association from 1956 published a *Quarterly Bulletin,* free to members. In addition to the *Proceedings of the World Congresses,* it published *World Directory of Agricultural Libraries and Documentation Centres* (1960), *Current Agricultural Serials* (2 volumes, 1965 and 1967), and *Primer for Agricultural Libraries* (1967, revised 1979).

IAALD is affiliated with IFLA (International Federation of Library Associations and Institutions) and to FID (International Federation for Documentation) as an international member. It has close contact with regional and national associations in its field, who are represented on its Executive Committee. D. E. GRAY

# International Association of Law Libraries

The International Association of Law Libraries (IALL), established in 1959, is a professional organization of lawyers, legal information specialists, bibliographers, and law librarians. The IALL Constitution describes the goals and objectives as follows:

> The purposes of the Association are to promote on a cooperative, non-profit and fraternal basis the work of individuals, libraries, and other institutions and agencies concerned with the acquisition and bibliographic processing of legal materials collected on a multinational basis, and to facilitate the research and other uses of such materials on a world-wide basis.

IALL members represent 54 countries on 5 continents. The membership is composed of individuals and institutions specifically interested in the transmission of law-related information throughout the world and international cooperation on the level of official and private documentation. For that purpose, IALL is affiliated with other international organizations such as the International Federation of Library Associations and the Federation for International Documentation. IALL is also developing close working relationships with such specialized organizations as the Association of Parliamentary Libraries and the Association of International Libraries.

The main purpose of IALL is to emphasize the pooling and dissemination of legal and documentary sources and publications among its members as well as other lawyers, law librarians, and legal bibliographers. This purpose is advanced through a vigorous and active publication program and regular institutes and meetings of the membership.

For several years prior to the June 1959 meeting in New York when the IALL was born, a small group of legal information specialists—William R. Roalfe, then Law Librarian and Professor of Law at Northwestern University, William B. Stern, Foreign Law Librarian at Los Angeles County Law Library, and Kurt Schwerin, Assistant Librarian and Associate Professor of Law at Northwestern University—carefully and laboriously laid the ground-work for the IALL. Their work was the result of constant frustrations involved in source work on foreign and international law. Having experienced the raised standards, higher efficiency, and improved status brought about in the U.S. by the American Association of Law Libraries, they felt similar results could be achieved on an international level. Roalfe was elected the first President of the Association when it was established in 1959.

The IALL Board of Directors is comprised of representatives from throughout the world. IALL Headquarters migrates with the President of the Association. IALL committees include IALL regional advisory councils and a committee to establish an International Bureau of Law Library Appointments and Career Opportunities under the direction of Betty Taylor of the University of Florida Law Library.

A formal program of institutes was inaugurated by IALL in 1964. These institutes address a wide range of legal research, bibliography, and documentation subjects. The following were held or planned by the late 1970's:

- 1975: Workshop on selected problems of the European Communities in Bergisch-Gladbach, Federal Republic of Germany. Round table discussion on the law library profession, held in conjunction with the International Federation of Library Associations General Conference in Oslo, Sweden.
- 1976: Round table conference on the significance of legal literature and documentation in developing countries in Lausanne, Switzerland.
- 1977: IALL course on the legal literature of socialist countries in Budapest, Hungary. Round table discussion of law library development in conjunction with IFLA meeting at Brussels, Belgium.
- 1978: Workshop on the Japanese law and legal literature in Tokyo, Japan.
- 1979: Meeting on Latin-American legal literature in Quito, Ecuador (spring).

Results of the IALL meetings are published in the *International Journal of Law Libraries.*

IALL regularly publishes a journal, a newsletter, and a directory. *The International Journal of Law Libraries* (vol. 1, 1974– ) appears three times annually. It contains articles on problems and concerns of law librarianship, current surveys of legal literature, bibliographies, and book reviews. The IALL Newsletter appears at least six times a year. It contains brief review notes of recent publications and bibliographical news of interest to law librarians. The IALL also publishes a *Directory* of its personal and institutional members, the only updated listing of specialists in international legal information throughout the world.

IGOR I. KAVASS

## International Association of Metropolitan Cities Libraries

INTAMEL was founded in 1968. Membership is open to all public libraries in cities (or countries) of more than 400,000 inhabitants. INTAMEL promotes the exchange of professional experience among its members and helps to ensure the development of standards for libraries in metropolitan areas all over the world.

In summer 1966 the public library of Prague invited a number of librarians from various European countries to help in finding a common basis for closer international contact between the library systems in large cities. Geoffrey Chandler (Liverpool) proposed that a general foundation meeting be held in his city in 1968. Chandler himself was chosen President, for the next three years, with K. C. Harrison (Westminster) serving as Treasurer. More than 100 members entered the organization during the following months, including libraries from the developing countries. INTAMEL pointed its activities in two main directions: efforts were made to give practical help to urban libraries in industrial areas, while at the same time INTAMEL tried to provide assistance to the developing countries.

The annual meeting of 1969 took place in Gothenburg, Sweden. Tokyo was chosen as meetingplace for the 1970 conference in order to give librarians working in East Asia a chance to participate. At the annual meeting in Baltimore (U.S.) in 1971, Harry Campbell (Toronto) was elected President. He succeeded in getting financial aid to ensure the participation of a great number of librarians from developing countries at the annual meetings in Rome (1972), as well as in New Delhi (1973), where a special seminar for those members was held subsequent to the conference. At the 1974 conference in Hamburg and Hannover (Federal Republic of Germany) a new President and a new Treasurer were elected: Keith Doms (Philadelphia) and Kenneth Duchac (Brooklyn). They led the INTAMEL delegation in Lagos (Nigeria) in 1975. Paris (1976) and Rotterdam (1977) were the next conference sites. From 1977 Jürgen Eyssen (Hannover) was President, with Friedrich Andrae (Hamburg) as Treasurer.

INTAMEL had some 130 members in 35 countries in all continents in 1979. Particular efforts are made to include the big cities in Communist countries, only three of which (East Berlin, Prague, and Zagreb) had become members by the late 1970's. The General Assembly, in the course of the annual meetings, is the main governing body of the organization. The President is elected for a term of three years. The honorary Treasurer serves at the same time as the Head of the Secretariat and is located in the country where the President resides.

INTAMEL initiated many programs. General statistics of the member libraries are brought up-to-date year by year. Other efforts have been made in book exchange and the recommendation of significant books or materials that may be helpful for reference work in other countries. A questionnaire gathered information on special collections held by the member libraries. Staff exchanges have been arranged as well. The general statistics and INTAMEL news are distributed to the members in order to enhance closer connection among them.

In 1978 INTAMEL was granted Round Table status within IFLA

JÜRGEN EYSSEN

## International Association of Music Libraries

The International Association of Music Libraries (IAML) [Association Internationale des Bibliothèques Musicales (AIBM); Internationale Vereinigung der Musik Bibliotheken (IVMB)] was formed shortly after World War II to promote worldwide cooperation in all aspects of music librarianship, bibliography, and documentation, such as cataloguing, interlibrary loan, training, and the creation of new tools for research. Among its early members were many distinguished scholars and music librarians. Annual meetings, one-third of which is an international congress, have been held in cities from Montreal to Jerusalem and Århus to Lisbon.

The membership as of 1978 was approximately 1,700 individuals—music librarians, scholars, bibliographers, archivists, and documentalists from 37 countries. Each country is represented through its own national association on the IAML Council, its governing body. IAML is organized into Professional Branches and Working Committees, each also represented on the Council and each reflecting its primary concerns and areas of activity. The Professional Branches include Broadcasting Libraries, Public Music Libraries, Music Research Libraries, Libraries in Academies, Conservatories and Music Colleges, Record Libraries, and Music Information Centres. The three Working Committees are Bibliographical Research, Cataloguing, and Education and Training. Each committee has its own goals and projects and at the same time interacts with others to refine ideas and enhance productivity.

IAML has played a central role in the implementation and publication of the "three R's" of international musicology: *Répertoire international des sources musicales* (RISM); *Répertoire international de littérature musicale* (RILM); and *Répertoire international d'iconographie musicale* (RIdIM).

RISM, founded in 1952, is concerned with the gathering and publication of bibliographies of all sources in music and music literature to 1800—from the writings of the Hebrew and Greek theorists, through vast repertories of monophonic and polyphonic music and the writings about music through the centuries, to the extant printed editions and manuscripts of Dittersdorf, Boccherini, and Michael Haydn, among others.

RILM, founded in 1966, deals with current music literature. It sponsors *RILM Abstracts* (1967– ), published quarterly in New York, which contains citations to and abstracts of the current music literature from many countries and in many languages, accompanied by a detailed computer-generated index. RILM is producing a series of annotated bibliographies entitled *RILM Retrospectives,* including *Thematic Catalogues in Music, French Dissertations in Music,* and *Congress Reports in Music.*

RIdIM, established in 1971, is concerned with the accumulation, classification, cataloguing, interpretation, and reproduction of visual materials relating to music, the training of iconologists, and the publication of checklists, bibliographies, iconographies, and scholarly studies. The Research Center for Musical Iconography, founded in 1972 at the City University of New York, serves as the international RIdIM center for the collection and classification of iconographical materials.

Reports on the progress of the "three R's," as well as reports of IAML congresses, conferences, and meetings, and other IAML news, reviews, and communications, are published in *Fontes Artis Musicae,* the association's quarterly journal, founded in 1954 under the editorship of Vladimir Fédorov and currently edited by Rita Benton. Other IAML or IAML-assisted publications include: *Documenta Musicologica; Catalogus Musicus; Terminorum Musicae Index Septum Linguis Redactus; The Guide for Dating*

*Early Published Music;* the *Directories of Music Research Libraries* (RISM, Series C); the *RIdIM Newsletter;* the *RILM International Thesaurus;* the professional cataloguing manuals; and various national newsletters.

IAML cooperates with the International Musicological Society (IMS) on the RISM, RILM, AND RIdIM projects and with the International Council of Museums on the RIdIM project. In addition, it actively participates in projects with the International Federation of Library Associations (IFLA) and the Unesco-sponsored International Music Council (IMC). IAML became a member of IFLA in 1976 and is represented on several of IFLA's Standing Committees and its Music Round Table. Under the sponsorship of the IMC, IAML is taking the lead in collaboration with the IMS, the International Society for Music Education, and the Music Information Centres Commission in the implementation of a new international documentation project entitled *World Inventory of Sources of Music Information* (WISMI). In addition, IAML has spawned a sister organization, the International Association of Sound Archives (IASA), and has served as a model for an international association of art libraries.

In response to a changing world and as a reflection of advances in current communications, IAML is working with or experimenting with computers, information retrieval, automated photocomposition of words and music, and revolutionary methods of text and sound storage to organize and maintain vast collections of books, scores, and discs, as well as archives, documentation centers, and bibliographical projects. Future goals and projects of IAML include a Unesco-supported plan to assist third world countries in the establishment and expansion of their music libraries and documentation centers, and a reexamination of the functions and goals of IAML in relation both to the profession and the public it serves; this will probably result in an expansion to represent more accurately the myriad activities of IAML members, as well as a change of name to something like International Association of Music Libraries, Archives, and Documentation Centers.

**REFERENCE**

Barry S. Brook, "Fontes at Twenty-five—IAML at Thirty," *Fontes Artis Musicae* (1978). Discusses history of IAML. Article is in English, French, and German.

BARRY S. BROOK

**INTERNATIONAL ASSOCIATION OF SCHOOL LIBRARIANSHIP 509**

## International Association of School Librarianship

The International Association of School Librarianship (IASL) was founded in 1971 in Kingston, Jamaica, during the Annual Conference of the World Confederation of Organizations of the Teaching Professions (WCOTP). There were 512 members and 14 association members in 1978. Members include librarians, media specialists, educators, publishers, and interested lay persons.

During the early 1960's those school librarians and educators interested in school library service who attended WCOTP meetings discussed the need for an international forum for people who had this concern. In 1967 the American Library Association's International Relations Committee gave the AASL a small grant that made it possible to bring together a group of 30 educators and librarians at the Vancouver WCOTP meeting. Those present decided to establish a committee and charged it with the following directives: (1) to plan a program on school library service for the 1968 meeting in Dublin; (2) to conduct a survey on the status of school library programs in WCOTP member countries; (3) to move toward a formal committee status within WCOTP. An international steering committee representing the United Kingdom, Kenya, Paraguay, Malaysia, Australia, and the United States was formed. The group in Dublin voted to ask WCOTP to create an ad hoc committee for school library development.

Meetings were held in Abidjan, Ivory Coast, in 1969 and in Sydney, Australia, in 1970. It was during the meeting in Sydney that the concept of an independent organization was approved in principle. A charter was drawn up, IASL was incorporated in the state of Illinois, and the Association was inaugurated in 1971 in Kingston, Jamaica. The new officers were installed by the Secretary General of WCOTP, John Thompson. Those first leaders were President, Jean E. Lowrie, U.S.; Vice President, Margot Nilson, Sweden; Treasurer, Phyllis Hochstettler, U.S.; Directors represented Jamaica, Canada, England, Australia, Nigeria, and Singapore. The objectives of the Association are (1) to encourage the development of school libraries and library programs throughout all countries; (2) to promote the professional preparation of school libraries; (3) to bring about close collaboration between school libraries in all countries, including the loan and exchange of literature; (4) to encourage the development of school library materials; (5) to initiate and coordinate activities, conferences, and other projects in the field of school librarianship.

A newsletter was established immediately under the editorship of M. Bernice Wiese, Baltimore, Maryland, and it was published on a quarterly basis thereafter. The *Newsletter* is a perquisite of membership. A Memorial Fund honoring Miss Wiese, who died in 1977, will support the publication of special monographs highlighting unusual activities in school librarianship at the international level. In addition to the *Newsletter,* IASL has published the Proceedings of its annual conferences since London (1972); *Persons to Contact for Visiting School Libraries/Media Centers,* 2d edition, revised and enlarged in 1977; *Directory of National School Library Associations* (1978); and a biennial membership directory.

IASL is also responsible for the Unesco Cooperation Action Program 554, "Books for School Libraries in Developing Countries"—Africa, Asia and the South Pacific, Central and South America. Approximately $20,000 worth of book coupons were distributed over a four-year period. Through its research committee IASL has cooperated with the School Library Standing Committee of the International Federation of Library Associations, of which it is a member, in the Unesco-supported effort to write international guidelines for school library/media centers. It is cooperating with the Organization of American States, Library Division, to survey the status of school library programs in Latin America. IASL is also working informally with the International Reading Association and the International Board for Books for Young People. It has maintained its affiliation with WCOTP and follows the geographic pattern of that organization in holding its annual meeting in a different quarter of the globe each year.

A sample of the program themes over the years gives an indication of the emphases IASL has promoted: school libraries and cultural involvement; crucial issues in school library development and professional education; school library: its role and function; and educational changes and implications for library service.

In 1978 a Secretariat was established to promote continuity of programming for the association. Officers in 1978 represented Jamaica, Denmark, U.S., Canada, Colombia, Philippines, Australia, and Nigeria. Future plans include the development of regional chapters, a move aimed toward strengthening cooperative efforts and material support for program expansion, and the development of a portfolio on evaluation techniques and formats.

JEAN LOWRIE

International Association of Sound Archives 256

## International Association of Technological University Libraries

The International Association of Technological University Libraries (IATUL) was founded in Düsseldorf in May 1955 as an international forum for the exchange of ideas relevant to librarianship in technological universities around the world. In September 1955 it was recognized as a subsection of the International Library Associations division of IFLA.

Membership is open to the libraries of technical universities and to other higher educational institutions. IATUL statutes stipulate that ordinary membership can be accorded to the library of any technological university that grants doctorates. In the late 1970's there were slightly more than 100 member libraries, primarily from North and South America, Asia, Australia, New Zealand, and Europe. In addition, representatives from 21 countries had been given observer status.

The Association is governed by a Board consisting of a President, Secretary, Treasurer, First and Second Vice-Presidents, and three committee members elected by member libraries; the Board meets three or four times each year. IATUL established temporary headquarters at the library of the University of Technology at Loughborough in England.

The primary goal, the exchange of information among university technological libraries, is accomplished mainly through publication and written communication, although international conferences are held every three years. Seven such conferences had been held by 1979; future conferences were scheduled to be held every two years. Important areas of interest have related to any activities concerned with scientific information, the use of information resources in science and technology, library organizations and buildings, and the use of data processing in libraries and information systems.

The official publication is the *IATUL Proceedings*, 1966– , issued on an irregular basis but approximately annually from 1975. The *Proceedings* contain articles (usually in English or German), reviews of published research, and digests of lectures, as well as news of the association and bibliographic information.

**REFERENCES**

D. Schmidmaier, "The History of the International Association of Technological University Libraries (IATUL)," *IATUL Proceedings* (1976), pp. 42–45.

STAFF

## International Atomic Energy Agency

The International Atomic Energy Agency (IAEA) was established on July 29, 1957, with headquarters in Vienna, Austria. Its main objectives are to "seek to accelerate and enlarge the contribution of atomic energy to peace, health and prosperity throughout the world" and to "ensure so far as it is able, that assistance provided by it or at its request or under its supervision or control is not used in such a way as to further any military purposes."

The IAEA is an intergovernmental organization directed by a Board of Governors composed of representatives from 34 member states and a General Conference of the entire membership of 110 states. It has its own program and its own budget ($75,000,000 in 1979) financed by contributions from member states. Although autonomous, the IAEA is a member of the United Nations system and reports on its work to the General Assembly and other United Nations organs. Its staff of about 1,500 persons is headed by the Director General, who is responsible for the administration and implementation of the Agency's program. Five Deputy Directors General head the departments of Administration, Research and Isotopes, Safeguards, Technical Assistance and Publications, and Technical Operations.

The IAEA establishes safety standards for all types of nuclear activity, prepares feasibility and market studies, operates three laboratories, and, in more than 70 countries, applies safeguards to nuclear materials to ensure that they are used only for their intended peaceful purposes. The Agency advises governments on atomic energy programs and on the physical protection of nuclear materials. It awards fellowships for advanced study, arranges equipment loans, finances small research contracts or programs, and acts as an intermediary in arranging the supply of nuclear materials.

In the field of nuclear information the IAEA acts as both collector and disseminator. Each year it organizes 10 to 15 large international conferences and symposia and about 100 smaller meetings and publishes many of their proceedings. The Agency also publishes two journals, *Nuclear Fusion* and *Atomic Energy Review*.

In order to foster the exchange of information, the IAEA established in 1970 the International Nuclear Information System (INIS). INIS provides a comprehensive abstracting and indexing service for the world's literature on the peaceful uses of atomic energy. Contributed by 60 participating countries and 13 international organizations, the information is disseminated bimonthly both on magnetic tape and as an abstract journal, *INIS Atomindex*. Each year some 70,000 new references are added to the INIS files, which by 1978 contained 400,000 references. The INIS Clearinghouse supplies microfiche copies of documents that are not commercially available. In 1978 INIS established an experimental facility giving organizations in some countries direct on-line access to the INIS files stored on the IAEA computer. INIS conducts an extensive training program for staff of information centers in member states.

Through its nuclear data program, the Agency serves as an international data center and coordinates the worldwide compilation, analysis, evaluation, exchange, and dissemination of nuclear and atomic data in cooperation with more than 15 centers. A comprehensive annual reference index on neutron data, *CINDA*, and numerous reports and handbooks of bibliographic and numerical data are published. The *IAEA Bulletin* (bimonthly) contains articles on current activities of the Agency and its member states; the *INIS Newsletter* (quarterly) reports new developments in INIS.

**REFERENCE**

*INIS Today: An Introduction to the International Nuclear Information System* (1978).

HANS W. GROENEWEGEN

## International Board on Books for Young People

The International Board on Books for Young People (IBBY) is the only international organization related to professional work in all disciplines concerned with the creation, promotion, study, and reading of children's literature.

Founded in Zurich in 1953 by Jella Lepman, then Director of the International Youth Library, it grew in membership from a few Western European sections to some 40 national sections, which are spread throughout the world. The American Section combines the membership of children's librarians in the American Library Association and publishers of children's books belonging to the Children's Book Council. The latter's headquarters organization serves as secretariat for the American Section and its affiliated Friends of IBBY, whose membership includes authors, illustrators, and educators as well as publishers and librarians. Its semiannual *Newsletter,* with some 20 pages of fresh articles, lists, and news, is edited by John Donovan, Executive Director of the Council.

IBBY's aims, summarized by Leena Maissen (international secretariat, Basel, Switzerland), include (1) bringing together those persons who are concerned about good books for young people; (2) promoting the availability of such books and access to them by encouraging their production to fit worldwide needs, associating them with communications media, such as radio, television, the press, films, and recordings, and encouraging the growth of libraries for the young; (3) encouraging translations and assisting in the making available of books of international quality; (4) initiating, encouraging, or advancing research in children's literature and its illustration and organizing the publication on an international scale based on the results of such research; and (5) advising international or national individuals, groups, institutions, or organizations, with information on books for the young and on the training of librarians, teachers, editors, writers, or illustrators.

Work by the sections at national levels forms an impressive basis for international activities. The national sections present national awards, compile lists of best books of the year, organize exhibits, book weeks, seminars, and conferences, and celebrate IBBY's International Children's Book Day on April 2 (Hans Christian Andersen's birthday). For this day, national sections serve in turn as sponsors, supplying an author's message and an artist's poster to be made available internationally.

Of first significance on the international level are IBBY's biennial Hans Christian Andersen Medals, one for an author, presented first in 1956, and another for an illustrator, introduced in 1966. An honors list, presenting books from a recent two-year period, has three categories of titles named by the sections and automatically listed without jury action: for text, illustration, and, beginning with 1978, translation.

*Bookbird,* the only international periodical on children's literature, is IBBY's journal, issued three times a year from the Austrian Section's offices in Vienna. It includes articles, national lists of outstanding books, reviews of professional works, and news of national and international conferences and prizes.

The biennial congress moves from country to country. In Athens, 1976, the theme was "Folklore and Poetry." The Würzburg Congress of 1978 focused on "Aspects of Modern Realistic Stories for Children and Young People." Conference papers have appeared in *Bookbird* and in bound *Proceedings.* For 1978 an international bibliography was published, *Modern Realistic Stories for Children and Young People* (Arbeitskreis für Jugendliteratur, IBBY Section of the Federal Republic of Germany), and a catalogue of the "best books" submitted by member countries for exhibition.

IBBY has a permanent representative to UNICEF in New York and is a member of the International Book Committee with commitment to the International Year of the Child. It has submitted to UNICEF and Unesco a policy statement: "Priorities in Children's Books and Related Materials for Intellectual Development of Children." It has also issued a statement, "Children's Books for a Better World," for the International Year of the Child 1979.

VIRGINIA HAVILAND

## International Council of Scientific Unions

In 1931 the final Assembly of the International Research Council (IRC) became the first Assembly of the International Council of Scientific Unions (ICSU). The IRC had been founded in 1919 as an outgrowth of the earlier International Association of Academies, which had its first meeting in 1899. ICSU has two types of members, the International Scientific Unions, of which there are 18; and the National Members, Academies of Science, Science Research Councils, among others, of which there are 68. There are also 14 Scientific Associates and 4 National Associates.

The principal objectives of the Council are (1) to encourage international scientific activity for the benefit of humankind; (2) to facilitate and coordinate the activities of the International Scientific Unions; (3) to stimulate, design, and coordinate international interdisciplinary scientific research projects; and (4) to facilitate the coordination of the international scientific activities of its National Members.

In addition to the International Scientific Unions, each of which has its own objectives and structure, ICSU functions through a series of ten Scientific and Special Committees, five Inter-Union Commissions, two Permanent Services, and other groups. These are concerned with interdisciplinary and inter-Union activities, such as the International Geophysical Year, launched by ICSU in 1957, and the International Biological Programme (1964–74), the results from which are being published in a series of 30 volumes.

The ICSU meets every two years in General Assembly with representatives of the National and Scientific Union Members and of all the subsidiary bodies. The General Committee—composed of 18 representatives from the Scientific Unions, 12 from the National Members, and the Officers—meets every year. The Secretariat of ICSU is at the Hôtel de Noailles, Paris, made available by the French Ministry of Education. Secretariats of six other ICSU bodies, including those of the Committee on Data for Science and Technology (CODATA) and of the ICSU Abstracting Board (ICSU-AB), are also housed there. The other Secretariats, of the unions, committees, commissions, and others, are spread throughout the world.

ICSU has a Policy Group on Scientific Information that provides advice to the officers. It organizes annually a meeting which brings together the principal bodies in ICSU concerned with information—the Committee on Data for Science and Technology (CODATA), ICSU Abstracting Board (ICSU-AB), Federation of Astronomical and Geophysical Services, World Data Centres Panel (WDC), several of the Scientific Associates, and a number of other such organizations to discuss future projects, ensure cooperation, and try to avoid unnecessary duplication.

ICSU has relationships with several United Nations agencies. The feasibility study for Unesco's World Scientific and Technical Information System (UNISIST) followed a decision of the 1966 ICSU General Assembly and developed into a joint study with Unesco after the Unesco 1966 General Conference. ICSU currently has a joint program with the World Meteorological Organization, the Global Atmospheric Research Programme.

ICSU publishes a *Year Book* that provides information about the various members of the ICSU family and the addresses of the officers of these bodies. The *ICSU Bulletin* provides information about ongoing activities in ICSU. The ICSU AB publishes occasionally a *Survey of the Activities of ICSU, Scientific Unions, Special and Scientific Committees* and *Commissions of ICSU in the Field of Scientific Information.* In 1979 it was in the process of publishing the *International Serials Catalogue* (ISC) together with an index/concordance. The catalogue includes more than 30,000 serial titles covered by one or more of the Abstracting and Indexing Service Members of ICSU AB.

F. W. G. BAKER

# International Council on Archives

The International Council on Archives (ICA) was founded in May 1948 at a meeting convened by Unesco to establish a worldwide organization of the archival profession. A provisional constitution was adopted, and the first International Congress on Archives met in Paris (1950) to establish the ICA formally.

ICA was created to improve the worldwide standards of archival administration and practice and to advance archival theory. The Council aids professional relations between archival institutions and organizations in order to stimulate the interchange of ideas and information, to solve archival problems, to ensure the physical preservation of mankind's archival heritage, and to support archival development and training in all countries.

The concerns and issues of the international archival community, as expressed in ICA publications and meetings, include the intellectual control of records, preservation, microreproduction, greater access to archives, and technological advances in the creation, control, and preservation of archives. The programs of the Council emanating from these goals are implemented by the ICA congresses, committees, regional branches, and the Executive Secretary.

The membership of ICA is composed of public archival authorities on international, national, and subnational levels (category A members); professional associations (category B); state, local, and private institutions (category C); individuals (category D); and honorary members (category E).

In August 1978 there were 731 members of ICA, including 112 countries represented by their national archival authorities. One hundred seventy-one archivists from 36 countries and 7 international organizations are individual members. In the early history of the Council the membership centered in Western Europe, with Eastern European countries joining ICA later; in recent years the membership growth has come from the third world countries as national archival institutions were established there.

Seven regional branches of ICA in the third world work to develop archival institutions and staff as integral parts of the information systems in those countries. The regional branches are Asociación Latinoamericana de Archivos (ALA), Arab Regional Branch (ARBICA), Caribbean Regional Branch (CARBICA), East and Central African Regional Branch (ECARBICA), Southeast Asian Regional Branch (SARBICA), South and West Asian Regional Branch (SWARBICA), and West African Regional Branch (WARBICA). These branch organizations sponsor conferences, seminars, and publications to make known the need for sound archival programs, to preserve the national heritages of the member countries, and to educate archivists, librarians, government officials, and the general public.

The governing bodies of the ICA are the General Assembly, the Executive Committee, and the Bureau of the Council. The General Assembly meets once every four years during the International Congresses on Archives to conduct the business activities of the Council, elect officers, and act on resolutions and recommendations concerning the professional interests of the worldwide archival community.

The Executive Committee is vested with the governing powers for the years between General Assembly meetings. It is composed of the ICA officers, 12 elected members, and a number of ex officio members. The Bureau, a smaller governing body made up of the ICA officers, meets as often as necessary between the annual sessions of the Executive Committee to expedite the business of the Council and to advise the Secretariat of ICA. The Executive Secretary is in Paris and coordinates the programs of the Council and maintains liaison with Unesco and other international organizations.

The ICA committee structure includes committees on Publications, on Archival Development, on Professional Training and Education, on Automation, on Conservation and Restoration, on Microfilm, on Sigillography, on Business Archives, on Literature and Art Archives, the Coordinating Committee for the Guide to the Sources of the History of Nations, and the ICA/International Records Management Federation Joint Committee on Records Management. Sections, which are organized around professional interests, include the Section of Archival Associations and the Section of Archivists of International Organizations. The committees and sections issue newsletters and hold annual meetings on topics of specific interest to their members.

The International Congresses on Archives are the quadrennial meetings of ICA; subjects selected by the Executive Committee and the national organizing committee are discussed. Reports, prepared by specialists on the basis of original research and international inquiries, are presented at the plenary sessions and are followed by discussions and interventions. Meetings were held in Moscow in 1972 and in Washington, D.C., in 1976. The plenary sessions at the Washington Congress included the following topics: records management, the technological revolution in archival and records administration, greater access and use of archives, and the worldwide growth of the archival community. The 1980 Congress was scheduled to be held in London.

In 1954 the President of ICA, Charles Braibant (France), decided to convene an annual meeting of the leaders of the profession (directors of national archival institutions and presidents of national archival associations). These meetings, called the International Round Table Conferences on Archives, are held each year when an international congress is not held to study one or two major problems of archival administration. The 1978 Round Table Conference was held in Nairobi, Kenya, and discussed "Standards of the Archival Profession and Institutions." The 1979 Conference was in Guadeloupe.

The International Council on Archives has associate and consultative relations with Unesco as a Category A international nongovernmental organization cooperating with Unesco. The Council receives a subvention and grants from Unesco for research and publications. Cooperation between ICA and the General Information Programme of Unesco centers around international projects, missions, and meetings and is an ongoing process aimed at assisting the archival institutions in developing countries. ICA also has close links with the International Federation of Library Associations and the International Federation for Documentation, the representatives of the other two professional sections of the Unesco General Information Programme.

The Council publishes a number of journals and volumes for the international community of archivists. *Archivum* is an annual journal devoted to special topics. *International Journal of Archives* was to begin publication in 1980 as a semiannual professional journal to serve the needs of the world archival community through the exchange of information and ideas on archival theory and management. The *ICA Bulletin* is a semiannual newsletter of ICA programs and meetings. The Council, with the assistance of Unesco, also publishes studies and handbooks for developing countries on such topics as microfilming, archival buildings, access policies, professional training, and restoration techniques. ICA and Unesco have also cooperated in publishing a series of archival guides entitled *Guide to the Sources for the History of Nations*. By 1979 two series were complete: nine volumes for Latin America (1974) and eight volumes relating to Africa south of the Sahara (1977). Other series were being prepared for North Africa, Asia, and Oceania. They are intended to encourage and facilitate research in the histories of the developing countries, particularly when many sources for those histories are in Europe and North America.

The International Archival Development Fund is the ICA instrument for financially supporting third world archival institutions. The Fund, established in 1974, assists the world's developing countries in building effective modern national archival structures and services. Administered by the ICA Treasurer, Executive Secretary, and Committee on Archival Development, the Fund seeks monies from international organizations, private foundations, and other sources for projects, missions, and meetings; most of the funds are used for training and national archival planning in the developing countries.

**REFERENCES**

*International Council on Archives Directory 1979* (1979).

Oliver W. Holmes, "Toward an International Archives Program and Council, 1945–1950," *American Archivist* (July 1976).

Morris Rieger, "The International Council on Archives: Its First Quarter Century," ibid.

JAMES B. RHOADS



# International Federation for Documentation (FID)

The Fédération Internationale de Documentation (FID), an international, not-for-profit, nongovernmental organization, was founded in September 1895 as the Institut International de Bibliographie (IIB). The IIB was one of the resulting resolutions of the Conférence Internationale de Bibliographie, which was assembled by Paul Otlet and Henri LaFontaine, the two persons regarded as the founders of FID. The objectives of this Conference, held under the endorsement of the Belgian government, were to establish the Institut, to create a Répertoire bibliographique universel (RBU) classified according to the Dewey Decimal Classification, and to form a Bibliographic Union between governments.

The members of IIB could be individuals, institutions, or associations, and there was no limit placed upon the size of the membership. This pattern of membership remained until after World War I. Today FID is composed of national members, only one being accepted from each country, and international members, being international organizations active in the field of documentation. Apart from national and international members FID accepts associates, a type of interim membership, and institutional and personal affiliates. The membership in 1979 was 72 national members and 2 international members. In addition there were about 300 affiliates from some 68 countries, 11 of these not represented by a national member.

When the IIB was founded, its essential functions were "to provide encouragement for the study of classification in general and to promote a uniform and international system of classification in particular." The purpose of FID has broadened in the ensuing years, and the original objectives of the IIB are now only a part of the Federation's purpose. Today the aim and nature of FID, as summarized in the preamble of its Statutes, is "to promote, through international cooperation, research in and development of documentation, which includes inter alia the organization, storage, retrieval, dissemination and evaluation of information, however recorded, in the fields of science, technology, social sciences, arts and humanities.

"The nature of the Federation has been and should continue to be principally that of a federation of national members. This means that the principal responsibility in the government of the Federation remains in the hands of bodies representative of various countries, whereas it is agreed that individuals participate as specialists in the work of the Federation."

FID realizes that with limited resources it cannot handle the whole range of problems of documentation and information that call for study and action within this broad aim. It is therefore prescribed in the framework of its present program structure that priority fields and activities be defined that FID handles most effectively, taking into account information programs of related intergovernmental and nongovernmental organizations, such as Unesco and IFLA, among others.

The two major interests of the founders of the IIB were the development of the Decimal Classification and the Universal Bibliographic Repertory (RBU). The two were not developed independently, and the former resulted in the subsequent development of the Universal Decimal Classification (UDC). The first complete edition of the UDC was published in French in 1905 as IIB publication 63 and bore the title *Manuel du répertoire bibliographique universel*.

Because of World War I the IIB remained stagnant for a number of years, but 1924 marked a turning point with the Institut being reorganized and becoming a federation with five national members: Belgium, France, Germany, the Netherlands, and Switzerland. Up to the time of the War the IIB had remained an international organization made up of individual and organizational members. This reorganization of the Institut changed its emphasis, and the RBU became only one of its tasks. At the same time, the UDC was recognized as having achieved an enhanced importance in the affairs of the IIB. The Classification Committee, which was formed in 1921, became in 1924 the official body through which the IIB exercised its control over the UDC. The Dutch national member, Nederlands Instituut voor Documentatie en Registratuur (NIDER), assumed the Secretariat for the Committee, and Frits Donker Duyvis, who was to later serve as FID Secretary General for many years, was appointed Secretary.

In 1931 the IIB became the Institut International de Documentation (IID), a name that continued until the present name was adopted in 1938. This 1931 name change, to incorporate the word *documentation,* signaled a clear separation from the word *bibliography* (work on the RBU had long since ceased) and an emphasis on practical aspects.

For almost 30 years the FID Secretariat was housed in Brussels with the Office International de Bibliographie, a semigovernmental Belgian organization. After 1924 the Netherlands and Belgium shared the Secretariat until 1938, when it was completely taken over by The Hague, and F. Donker Duyvis became the sole Secretary General—a position he had shared with the founders from 1924 to 1938.

After World War II FID had added only three new national members to the first five of 1924. With the increased interest in documentation in the postwar years, membership gradually increased, and by 1958 there were 28 national members, including seven outside Europe, making FID truly a world organization.

It was also during this time that the first committees other than the Classification Committee and its subcommittees were established. Ten FID committees presently help to carry out the FID professional program. They are FID/CCC, Central Classification Committee, along with its 30 subcommittees for revising the UDC; FID/CR Classification Research; FID/DT Terminology of Information and Documentation; FID/ET Education and Training; FID/II Information for Industry; FID/LD Linguistics in Documentation; FID/PD Patent Information and Documentation; FID/RI Research on the Theoretical

Basis of Information; FID/SD Social Sciences Documentation; and FID/BSO Broad System of Ordering.

FID has established two regional commissions, FID/CLA Latin American Commission (1960) and FID/CAO Asia and Oceania (1968). The two commissions, in turn, have several of their own committees that assist in carrying out regional programs: in Latin America CLA/UDC Universal Decimal Classification, CLA/CCN National Union Catalogues, CLA/ET Education and Training, and CLA/II Information for Industry; in Asia CAO/AG Agricultural Information and Documentation and CAO/II Information for Secondary Industry.

The highest authority of the FID is the General Assembly, which meets biennially and is composed of representatives of national and international members. The FID Council meets twice yearly to carry out the decisions of the General Assembly and tasks assigned it by the *FID Statutes.* The Council is composed of the President, three Vice-Presidents, the Treasurer, 14 Councillors (including the Presidents of regional commissions), and ex officio the Secretary General. Between meetings of the Council the Executive Committee, made up of the officers and the Secretary General, may meet if there is a need. The daily operation of the Federation is handled through its Secretariat in The Hague and through the secretariats of the regional commissions.

FID cooperates with the programs of several other international organizations: the Unesco General Information Programme (PGI), the International Federation of Library Associations and Institutions (IFLA), International Council on Archives (ICA), and International Organization for Standardization (ISO).

In addition to an active monograph publications program FID publishes the monthly *FID News Bulletin,* the quarterly *International Forum on Information and Documentation* (in Russian and English), *R&D Projects in Documentation and Librarianship* (bimonthly), and the *Extensions and Corrections to the UDC* (annual). The *Bulletin* includes two special quarterly supplements: the "Document Reproduction Survey" and the "Newsletter on Education and Training Programmes for Specialized Information Personnel."

The biennial *FID Directory,* replacing the former *Yearbook,* provides information on membership, committees, and historical information on the Federation.

**REFERENCES**

W. Boyd Rayward, *The Universe of Information: The Work of Paul Otlet for Documentation and International Organization* (1975).

*The ALA Yearbook* and the *FID Annual Report* provide summaries of the activities of each year.

*FID Publications: An 80 Year Bibliography 1895–1975* and the current list of *FID Publications* provide a bibliographical survey of many publications.

KENNETH R. BROWN

# International Federation of Library Associations and Institutions (IFLA)

**History.** The 50th anniversary Conference of the American Library Association in Atlantic City and Philadelphia in 1926 marked the beginning of the concept of an international library organization. Three months earlier at the International Congress of Librarians and Booklovers in Prague, the spiritual father of IFLA, Gabriel Henriot, had already voiced an appeal for a standing international library committee. The idea materialized in Edinburgh on September 30, 1927, during the celebration of the 50th anniversary of the Library Association (U.K.), when representatives of library associations from 15 countries signed a resolution that can be regarded as the founding of IFLA. Isak Collijn, the Swedish National Librarian, was elected first President. The most skillful negotiator was Carl H. Milam, Secretary of ALA, who agreed to draft the statutes. The first IFLA Constitution was approved in Rome in 1929 during the first World Congress of Librarianship and Bibliography, which took place under IFLA auspices.

IFLA

*IFLA commemorative stamp, issued on the occasion of its 50th anniversary, Brussels, 1977.*

The new organization was predominantly an association of library associations, aiming at the organization of regular world conferences. Originally, IFLA was a meeting point for leading librarians from Europe and America and continued as such for a long time. In the early years notable personalities—genuine representatives of their profession—defined IFLA's profile. It became a kind of "conference family," where personal friendships led to close cooperation in such areas as international loan and exchange, bibliographical standardization, and library education.

At the only prewar IFLA session outside Europe (Chicago, 1933), the second IFLA President, William Warner Bishop, acted as host. During five years as President, he guided IFLA through the first years of economic crisis as membership reached 41 associations from 31 countries, including several library associations from outside Europe and the U.S. (China, India, Japan, Mexico, Philippines). IFLA could not yet boast of true universal international membership, however. That was not to be achieved for 40 years.

Marcel Godet, Director of the Swiss National Library at Berne, was IFLA's third President from 1936 to 1947. Through Godet and Secretary Breycha-Vauthier, IFLA took part in the Advisory Committee on Literature for Prisoners-of-War and Internees, which distributed significant numbers of books to various camps. (Breycha-Vauthier also worked at the League of Nations Library at Geneva during the war.)

IFLA's first postwar session at Oslo in 1947, funded by a grant from the Rockefeller Foundation, was attended by 52 delegates from 18 countries. One important result of this conference was a formal agreement between Unesco (IFLA has Consultative Status A with Unesco) and IFLA concerning future cooperation. In 1948 they organized an International Summer School on Public Library Practice in Manchester, attended by 50 librarians from 21 countries who from that time worked to better public librarianship (the first standards for public libraries were a result of this cooperation). Another Oslo resolution of lasting significance was the recommendation to accept an international format for catalogue cards.

In the postwar period IFLA developed slowly, perhaps too slowly, because its structure and lack of funds hampered effectiveness. Its profile was still defined by individuals who gave their time and expertise to IFLA during meetings but turned their attention between meetings to their national duties. Since 1951 a series of proposals for reorganization was launched, based on a fundamental criticism about the lack of constructive programs, but they were too vague to lead to concrete results. By 1958 IFLA had grown to 64 member associations from 42 countries. The organization was basically similar to its prewar antecedent until the International Conference on Cataloguing Principles (Paris, 1961), for which the Council on Library Resources allotted a grant of $20,000, generated major activity for IFLA in the cataloguing field.

In 1962 IFLA's first permanent central secretariat was established by a Unesco grant; Anthony Thompson became the first full-time IFLA Secretary General. During this time IFLA began to exhibit real strength in the realm of programming; in 1963 the Federation published *Libraries in the World,* a long-term program for IFLA, which distinguished itself by an imaginative and realistic view on IFLA's possible future development. Gradually the importance of sections for types of libraries and committees for types of library activity increased, enabling IFLA to react adequately to urgent library problems. IFLA's firmness of purpose became exemplary and resulted in steady growth. When Thompson resigned in 1970, the Federation had 250 members in 52 countries.

In 1971 an energetic President, Herman Liebaers, National Librarian of Belgium, brought the Secretariat to The Hague. As President he managed to interest several funding bodies in the work of IFLA. He launched the UBC (Universal Bibliographic Control) program and brought the librarians of the third world into IFLA. With support from the Council on Library Resources, a small, effective secretariat was strengthened at The Hague, and a permanent office for UBC was set up in London. A regional office at Kuala Lumpur in Malaysia was founded with assistance from the Canadian International Development Agency, and a program for the various world regions was developed.

When Liebaers left IFLA and the library profession in 1974, IFLA had grown into a beehive of activity and could claim virtually universal international membership with 600 members in 100 countries. Liebaers had the vision and drive necessary to adapt IFLA to the demands of modern society. He also had the foresight to use the services of a Program Development Group, a core of experts who paved the way for some major IFLA projects (Universal Bibliographic Control, Universal Availability of Publications, public library development) but who also had a keen eye for smaller, but nevertheless valuable, projects. The *IFLA Medium-Term Programme 1976–1980* is the result of this group's work.

**Organization and Structure.** After years of sometimes heated discussions, a new structure for IFLA was approved by the Council in Lausanne in 1976. The new Statutes define the purpose as follows:

> to promote international understanding, cooperation, discussion, research and development in all fields of library activity, including bibliography, information services and the education of personnel, and to provide a body through which librarianship can be represented in matters of international interest.

*Membership.* The name of the organization was expanded to include *institutions* (libraries, library schools, bibliographic institutes). It became the International Federation of Library Associations and Institutions (IFLA). Since 1976 IFLA has had two main categories of members, Association and Institutional. Both have voting rights in all matters and meetings. However, in Council meetings Association Members have more votes than Institutional Members, at least 51 percent, with 5–20 votes for the joint Association Members in any one country. A relatively new category is the Personal Affiliate, with no voting rights. There is also the opportunity for Consultative Status for related international organizations. Among those with Consultative Status are FID (International Federation for Documentation), ICA (International Council on Archives), ICAE (International Council on Adult Education), ISO (International Organization for Standardization), IPA (International Publishers Association), and ISDS (International Serials Data System). Other international organizations, mainly concerned with librarianship, tend to join IFLA as International Association Members with voting rights; for example, IAML (International Association of Music Libraries), IATUL (International Association of Technological University Libraries), COMLA (Commonwealth Library Association), LIBER (Ligue des Bibliothèques Européennes de Recherche), and ACURIL (Association of Caribbean University, and Institutional Research Libraries). INTAMEL (International Association of Metropolitan Cities Libraries) functions as a Round Table in IFLA.

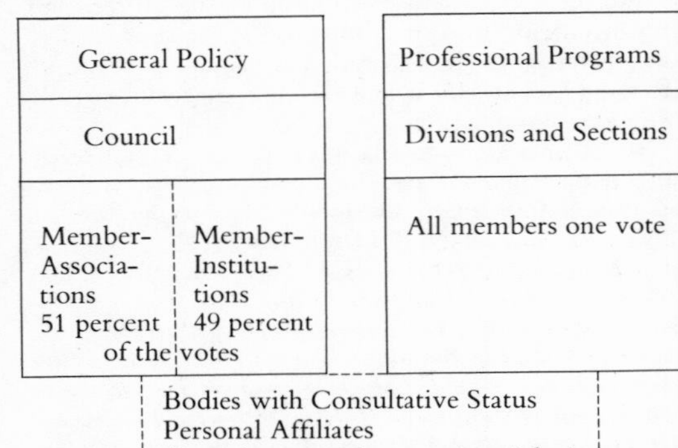


*Steering Bodies.* The main steering bodies are the Executive and Professional Boards; the first has full powers of administration and management, and the latter is concerned with the coordination and planning of professional activities. The Executive Board consists of an elected President and seven elected members, with the Chairperson of the Professional Board an ex-officio member. The Professional Board is composed of the Chairpersons of the eight Divisions.

In May 1979 the Executive Board decided to establish a Programme Management Committee for the coordination of IFLA's Professional Focal Points. It was to direct and coordinate the IFLA programs for Universal Availability of Publications (UAP), Universal Bibliographic Control (UBC) and International MARC. This organizational structure became effective on September 1, 1979.

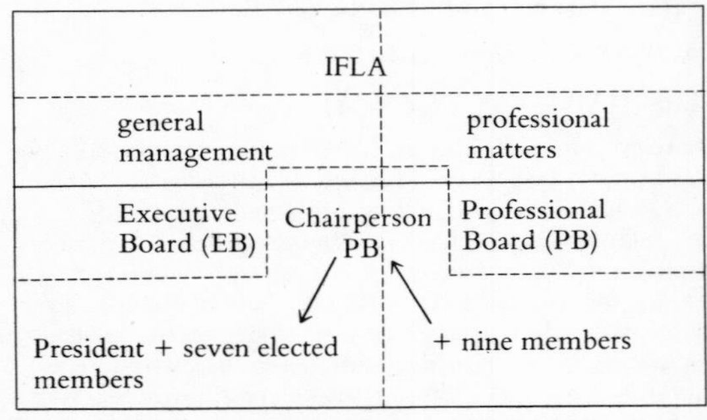


*Subunits.* In the new IFLA the Sections can be considered the core of the organization; they are grouped to-

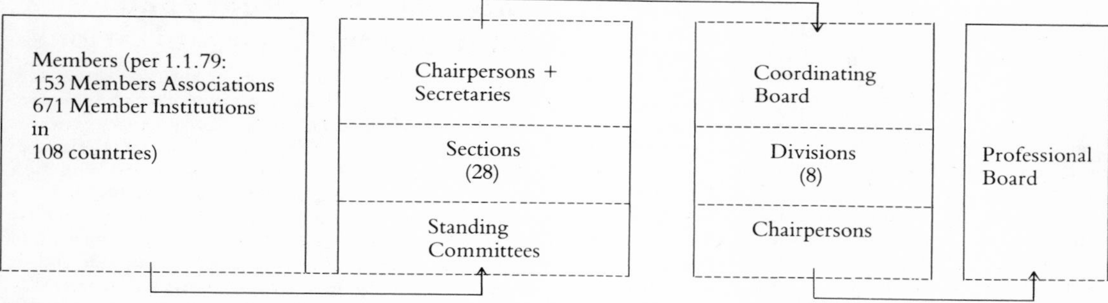


gether in Divisions for coordination purposes. Members and affiliates register for the Sections of their choice and can nominate and elect persons for membership on Standing Committees, the core groups of experts that develop the program of the Section and ensure its execution. The Chairpersons and Secretaries of the Sections form the Coordinating Board of the Division to which they belong. The Chairpersons of the Divisional Coordinating Boards automatically form the Professional Board.

In the professional field IFLA has two other, less formal, means for the performance of professional tasks: Round Tables and Working Groups.

*Headquarters.* The Association is headquartered in the Netherlands Congress Building, The Hague, Netherlands. The staff consists of the Secretary General, the Coordinator of Professional Activities, and three administrative staff members. They are responsible for daily management of the organization, liaison with related organizations, coordination of professional groups and units within IFLA, maintaining secretariats of Executive and Professional Boards, and issuing periodical publications.

*International Office for UBC.* At the British Library Reference Division, the International Office for UBC is staffed by the Director, one program assistant, one bibliographical assistant, and two administrative assistants. The office initiates, monitors, and promotes international/regional projects in the context of Universal Bibliographic Control; stimulates national systems of UBC; serves working groups in the field; promotes bibliographical standardization; and issues publications on aspects of UBC.

*Office for International Lending.* The British Library Lending Division, Boston Spa, is the host for the Office for International Lending, staffed by the Director and one assistant. It serves as a clearinghouse for difficult loan requests, promotes standardization of loan methods, and compiles statistics on international lending. The bureau is gradually developing into the focal point for IFLA's program for Universal Availability of Publications (UAP).

*Regional Bureaus.* Two regional bureaus were operating in 1979 at Kuala Lumpur, Malaysia, and Dakar, Senegal. Consultations with FID to plan a joint bureau in Latin America and with ICAE to found a joint bureau in Nairobi were also under way. The tasks of such bureaus are the promotion and coordination of regional programs and of national projects that can serve as models for other countries.

**Programs.** The IFLA *Medium-Term Programme 1976–80* describes a variety of activities, based on two approaches. Library operation can be looked at from two points of view, one treating all operations as elements in the functioning of an integrated whole—the library; the other viewing each operation as a separate activity with its own techniques. These approaches have been expressed in IFLA by the growth of two kinds of groups, one consisting of librarians responsible for a particular type of library and another consisting of librarians concerned with the techniques appropriate to a particular operation that is common to various types of libraries. The 28 Sections of IFLA, with the additional Round Tables and Working Groups, all have their own programs, ranging from sophisticated university management studies to professional training of school librarians, from the establishment of regional brăille centers in the third world to the availability of official publications, and from improvement of the status of librarians to the development of public library work. There are, however, two major programs that cut across the Sections and on which IFLA concentrates most of its resources and efforts: UBC and UAP.

*UBC.* Under the title UBC, IFLA launched in 1974 as a major policy objective the promotion of a worldwide system for the control and exchange of bibliographic information. The purpose of the system is to make universally and promptly available, in a form that is internationally acceptable, basic bibliographic data on all publications issued in all countries. The concept of UBC presupposes the creation of a network made up of component national parts, each of which covers a wide range of publishing and library activities, all integrated at the international level to form the total system. The UBC program was adopted by Unesco and has received support from the Council on Library Resources and from national libraries all over the world.

*ISBD.* The achievement that may appeal most to the imagination of librarians is the successful series of International Standard Bibliographic Descriptions (ISBD), published by the UBC Office, adopted by the majority of national bibliographies, and used by cataloguers all over the world. IFLA has accepted responsibility for the maintenance and monitoring of the ISBD's. The UBC office was also responsible for the working documents for the important Unesco/IFLA International Congress on National Bibliographies held at Paris in September 1977. The impact of this conference is reflected especially in the agreements reached on the standardized production of national bibliographies.

*UAP.* The full benefits of UBC can be realized only through universal availability of the recorded literature. As with UBC, the guiding principle of UAP is that of national contributions to an international system—each country should be responsible for supplying its own native publications by loan or photocopy on request to other countries. The program encompasses such topics as interlibrary lending systems, exchange of publications, legal deposit, copyright, and cooperative acquisition schemes.

The Unesco General Conference in November 1978 decided to include UAP in the Unesco program for the coming years and to aim at an Intergovernmental Conference on UAP in 1981. IFLA was to be involved in the preparation of this Conference and the provision of working documents. The first projects that IFLA planned in this field with the assistance of Unesco are a comparative study of alternative national systems of ensuring availability and the collection of statistics on international lending, to identify trends and problems areas.

*Libraries in Developing Countries.* A third major IFLA

objective is the development of library work in the third world. With assistance from the Canadian International Development Agency (CIDA), IFLA has managed to strengthen considerably the participation of librarians and libraries from Asia, Africa, Latin America, and the Caribbean in IFLA's work. The World Wide Seminar in Seoul, June 1976, was the first major IFLA conference ever held in a developing country. The IFLA General Conference for 1980 was scheduled for Manila. CIDA funds were also utilized for studies on the cataloguing of African authors' names and on the status of librarians, as well as for preparation of a compendium for courses in library science for South Asian use and for the organization of a training seminar for school librarians in Central America. Projects under way are manifold and cover such varied topics as the compilation of uniform headings for Indonesian computer bodies; a comparative survey of library and subprofessional needs in Gambia, Sierra Leone, and Liberia; and the provision of library services to the rural areas of Ghana.

Unesco sponsors every second year a "presession seminar" for librarians from developing countries, held prior to the IFLA General Conference. Other projects focusing on special needs in the regions are developed by specialized IFLA groups, such as the Working Group of Libraries for the Blind and the Section on Library Buildings.

**Conferences and Meetings.** Although emphasis has gradually been moved from the annual meetings to continuing projects, the importance of regular personal contact must not be underestimated. IFLA holds General Professional Conferences with some 130 meetings during the conference each year. Every second year (in odd years) such conferences are combined with a Council meeting, where the IFLA business affairs (elections, budget, rules) are dealt with. Planned sites are: Manila, 1980; Leipzig, 1981; Montreal, 1982; and Munich, 1983.

Within the new structure, Divisions and Sections are also encouraged to hold separate meetings, preferably in the regions. In 1979 the first meetings of that kind were the World Conference of Special Librarians, with the participation of the IFLA Division of Special Libraries (Honolulu), and a meeting of the IFLA Round Table of National Centres for Library Services (Jerusalem).

**Publications.** Periodical publications of the Association are the quarterly *IFLA Journal and International Cataloguing; IFLA Annual* and *IFLA Directory* are issued yearly.

IFLA Publications is a monograph series, published by K. G. Saur (Munich, London). Numbers 12 and 13, which appeared in 1978, were *Library Service to Children: An International Survey,* edited by Colin Ray, and *Letters for the International Exchange of Publications: A Guide to Their Composition in English, French, German, Russian, Spanish,* by Alex Allardyce.

Another monographic series, UBC Publications, is published by the IFLA International Office for UBC and includes the *International Standard Bibliographic Descriptions* (general, monographic publications, serials, nonbook materials, cartographic materials) and several publications on uniform headings, cataloguing, machine-readable cataloguing, serials, and standardization.

**REFERENCES**

*IFLA's First Fifty Years: Achievement and Challenge in International Librarianship,* edited by W. R. H. Koops and J. Wieder (1977), contains eight chapters on the history of IFLA as well as views on IFLA's future.

*IFLA and Contemporary Library Problems,* special issue of *IFLA Journal* (1977), contains articles on IFLA's role in various fields of library work.

MARGREET WIJNSTROOM

## International Library and Bibliographical Organizations

International library or bibliographic organizations now fulfill a wide range of functions. Among these functions are: (1) the lending or exchange of documentary materials; (2) the regulation of international commerce related to these materials (postal and tariff regulations, copyright agreements, publishing and distributing rights, and censorship); (3) the generation, standardization, exchange, or publication of bibliographic data in various formats for books and nonbook publications and of indexing and abstracting data for journal articles and related materials; (4) the creation, maintenance, and operation of international information systems of various kinds; (5) the provision of moral, technical, and financial assistance to developing countries to help them improve their use of existing documentary materials and information systems; and (6) the publication of reports, manuals, directories, monographs, and proceedings—a technical and general support literature about operations, systems, and procedures that represents the deliberations of expert bodies of personnel about problems of international interest.

**Early History.** Perhaps the first organizations to take on an international cast were the German book fairs of the 16th century, which drew buyers and sellers of books from all over Europe and England. The famous *Messkatologe,* begun in 1564 by Georg Willer, listed what was available and contained entries for books outside the German states, though, naturally enough, books published within them predominated. Various series of these catalogues were published until the late 19th century, though entries for non-German material began to decline in the 17th century. In 1617 John Bill began to publish an English edition of these catalogues; he soon began to add English titles (the catalogues already contained some), and from 1622 to 1626 these additions took the form of regular, separately titled supplements.

In the last half of the 17th century, the rise and increasingly rapid proliferation of journal literature added complexity to a bibliographic problem that, with the diffusion of printing and the widespread adoption of the vernacular, had already become serious. Nevertheless, until the latter part of the 19th century, the problem was dealt with first only by individuals and then by formal groups acting at a national level. While much individual and later corporate effort was expended on the development of national bibliographic control, where the works created reached beyond national bounds, most of them tended to seek universality of scope. Among the enormous number of works of this kind, one of the first and greatest was Gesner's *Bibliotheca Universalis* (1545). Derived from the Frankfurt *Messkataloge* were Georg Draud's *Bibliotheca Classica. . . , Bibliotheca Exotica. . . ,* and *Bibliotheca Librorum Germanicorum Classica* (1611–12, revised 1625). At the end of the 17th century, Raffaele Savanorola finished his *Orbis Litteraris.* Occupying some 40 folio volumes, it was never published and disappeared some time in the 19th century. Francesco Marucelli's *Mare Magnum. . . ,* a catalogue intended to list everything known to have been written, was compiled at about the same time; it, too, was never published but survives in 111 volumes copied sometime after 1751 from the now lost manuscript.

The idea of universal bibliographic control, of which the works mentioned above are imperfect manifestations, exercised a potent fascination on bibliographers from the 17th through the 19th centuries. In 1631 Petrus Blanchot published his *Idea Bibliotheca Universalis,* a proposal for a universal subject index. In the 1840's and 1850's the idea sprang up more vigorously than ever, though apparently independently, in France, the United States, and England in association with attempts to compile and publish library catalogues. Danjou in France, Charles Coffin Jewett in the United States, Charles Wentworth Dilke, Andrea Crestadoro, and later Sir Henry Cole in England, all had different schemes, to say nothing of the fin de siècle schemes of Bonnage in France and Vander Haeghen in Belgium.

**The 19th Century.** A major scheme for the control of scientific literature in the 19th century was the Royal Society's *Catalogue of Scientific Papers.* Universal in scope, this catalogue was almost self-consciously national in execution, though foreign academies and learned societies were consulted for recommendations as to journals to be indexed. It was published in four series between 1867 and 1925 with a supplementary volume for the period 1800–83.

A little known, more limited attempt at scientific bibliography that seems to have had some success internationally was initiated in 1889 by the Société mathématique de France, which sponsored a Congrès international de bibliographie des sciences mathématiques in Paris. The *Répertoire bibliographique des Sciences mathématiques* came into being in 1893 and had two forms: a simple retrospective bibliography published in Paris from 1893 to 1912 on cards and the *Revue semestrielle des publications mathématiques,* a current bibliography with abstracts, which appeared under the auspices of the Société mathématique d'Amsterdam. This bibliography continued in the latter form until 1934, when it merged with the *Jahrbuch über die Fortschritte der Mathematik,* which ceased publication in 1942. Both the *Revue* and the *Jahrbuch* used the classification, revised from time to time, of the *Répertoire bibliographique des Sciences mathématiques*.

Such ventures are evidence of a growing, but incomplete, internationalism in bibliography. Two other 19th-century forms of bibliographical or bibliothecal internationalism should be mentioned: the first may be described as regulatory and involved governments; the second was essentially consultative and collegial. In 1817 a limited scheme was implemented for the exchange of dissertations between German universities, the Akademischer Tauscheverein; by the early 1880's 50 European universities and academies had become involved in this venture. In the 1840's and 1850's Alexandre Vattemare, a famous ventriloquist and quick-change artist who desired to stimulate the exchange of publications between governments, set up an Agence centrale des échanges internationaux in Paris to coordinate this work. He was eventually able, if only briefly, to interest many governments in his ideas, including 18 state legislatures and the Congress of the United States. The major development in this area, however, was an international intergovernmental conference, which culminated a number of earlier conferences, at Brussels in 1882. Here were signed two official conventions governing the international exchange of documents: *Convention A* dealt with the exchange of government publications generally; *Convention B* dealt with parliamentary gazettes, journals, and annuals. While these conventions were never widely adopted, they remained in force and under scrutiny into the middle of the 20th century.

International copyright had been a subject of debate for much of the early part of the 19th century, and various bilateral agreements were concluded between European states and England in an attempt to protect the rights of authors internationally. As early as 1858 a major international congress in Brussels deliberated on the subject, and the movement then begun quickly gathered force leading to an official convention signed in Berne in 1886. A permanent bureau directed by Henri Morel and sponsored by the Swiss government was set up in 1888 to act as the headquarters for what has since become generally known as the Berne Copyright Union.

As the 19th century progressed and as literature proliferated and libraries grew, librarians and bibliographers began locally, nationally, and internationally to seek mutual stimulation and enlightenment through formal association. In 1868 a Société bibliographique was created in Paris and in 1878 held the first of three international, decennial conferences that "in a series of reports would trace the scientific and literary movement of the ten-year period in order to provide ample materials and accurate information to all students." These gatherings, though strongly French, attracted some few participants from Italy, Belgium, England, Luxembourg, and elsewhere. Similar conferences were the International Conference of Librarians in London in 1877, which was enlivened by a large contingent of American librarians, and the 20th-anniversary conference of the Library Association of the United Kingdom, which had been founded at the 1877 conference. Other international conferences were held, for example, on the occasion of the international exhibitions of Paris in 1900, San Francisco in 1904, and Brussels in 1910, but no permanent organization was created either to perpetuate the conferences themselves or to allow them to undertake some corporate activity of international value. Curiously the 1900 conference had resolved that it should reconvene every five years (it did not), and the 1910 "Congrès de Bruxelles" was organized by an avowedly "Permanent Commission for the International Congresses of Archivists and Librarians," of which no more was heard.

**Before World War I.** For bibliographical organization, the year 1895 is a watershed. In that year the International Institute of Bibliography was created in Brussels by Paul Otlet and Henri LaFontaine. The Concilium Bibliographicum was in the process of being set up in Zurich by Herbert Haviland Field, and the consultations with foreign academies and learned societies undertaken by the Royal Society, prior to calling an international conference to explore the creation of an *International Catalogue of Scientific Literature,* were well advanced.

The International Conference on Bibliography, held in Brussels in 1895, created the International Institute of Bibliography (IIB), and the Belgian government undertook to support a headquarters organization for it, the International Office of Bibliography (OIB). The aim of the new organization was to create a universal bibliography or catalogue (Répertoire Bibliographique Universel) that would be organized both by author and, by means of a radical expansion of the Dewey Decimal Classification and a sophisticated development of the mechanics of the classification's notation, by subject.

The Concilium Bibliographicum had a limited goal: to compile centrally and to distribute on cards or as supplements to major journals or reviews the current bibliography of zoology and related subjects. Agreements between the Concilium and the International Institute of Bibliography were made even as both organizations completed their initial arrangements. The latter adopted the three-by-five-inch card as the basis for its work (it had originally proposed to use a card of a quite different size), promoted its use as an international standard, and confided to Field and his colleagues the development of the UDC in the areas of the Concilium's interest. In its turn, the Concilium undertook to develop the UDC, to use it on its bibliographical notices, and to send copies of its cards and other bibliographical publications to Brussels. As well as being published in card form, the zoological portion of the Concilium's work appeared as a supplement to the *Zoologischer Anzeiger,* the physiological portion as part of the *Zentralblatt für Physiologie,* and the protozoological portion in the *Archiv für Protistenkunde.* Support for the Concilium was provided by Field himself and by local sources (the Swiss Confederation and the city and canton of Zurich principally), by international sponsors (the International Congress of Zoology and the

French Zoological Society), and from revenues generated from the sale of its bibliographical services.

The first International Conference on a Catalogue of Scientific Literature was held in London in 1896, and others followed in 1898 and 1900. Sponsored by the Royal Society, these conferences led to the creation of a complex organization to govern and produce the catalogue. It was governed by an International Convention that met in 1905, 1910, and 1922 and was administered by an International Council that met regularly at more frequent intervals. A Central Bureau, supervised by the Director of the Catalogue, Henry Forster Morley, prepared the work for publication; regional bureaus in participating countries, such as the Smithsonian Institution in the U.S., transcribed onto slips of a standard size and weight references to their national scientific literature. Detailed specifications as to form of entry, content, punctuation, and abbreviation were followed in producing these slips. The first issue of the *International Catalogue of Scientific Literature,* divided into 17 different subject areas, appeared in 22 volumes in 1901. Annual issues appeared in 1914, when World War I produced the Catalogue's quietus.

**Between the Two World Wars.** The end of World War I marks a major turning point in the development of international bibliographic organization and control. A sustained period of development was abruptly terminated during the war, and the return of peace provided an opportunity for conscious choice as to whether the effort and expense of resuming prewar bibliographical ventures were worthwhile. These ventures, overlapping each other to different degrees, had involved the creation of a formal mechanism to procure the international cooperation of scholars, the centralization of publishing and consultative activities in ambiguously supported, nationally based headquarters, and the provision of conventional enumerative bibliography. After the war it seemed that new organizations for the cooperation of scholars were necessary and that conventional bibliography of the kind provided before the war was no longer enough.

The *International Catalogue of Scientific Literature* was not resumed at all after the war. Though the work of the Concilium Bibliographicum was continued for a time, and a special grant from the Rockefeller Foundation assisted Concilium's flagging finances, it too fell rapidly into a decline from which it did not recover. Despite the German occupation of Brussels during the war, the facilities and collections of the International Institute of Bibliography were unharmed, and for a short time it seemed as if the Institute's postwar future was secure. Nevertheless, the Belgian government began to withdraw its support from the vast, overextended complex of organizations (Galais Mondial or Mundaneum) of which the IIB was part, and in 1924 the IIB's members decided to reorganize the Institute, stressing its dependence from the failing center in Brussels, the importance to it of national members, and the need to revise the UDC, now long out of print and out of date. The reorganizations begun in 1924 were continued under the presidencies of Allan Pollard, an Englishman (1927–30), and J. Alingh Prins, a Dutchman (1931–37). Emphasis was placed on decentralization of activity and federalism of organization. Annual congresses began in 1927, and in 1931 the Institute changed its name to International Institute of Documentation (and changed it again in 1937 to International Federation for Documentation, FID). Its work was limited to the continuous revision and translation into various languages of the UDC (the second full edition was issued in 1932), the publication of the journal *Documentatio Universalis* (1930–32) and its successor *IID Communicationes* (later *FID Communicationes*), and to the annual congresses. Bibliography, especially the preparation of a centralized universal bibliography of doubtful utility, technically inadequate and poorly supported, was subordinated first to the elaboration of a classification that, at least theoretically, could be used to bring a form of standardized access to any bibliography or catalogue anywhere, and then later, as the 1930's progressed, to the study of documentary reproduction, especially by microphotography, the techniques and uses of which the Institute had been exploring since 1906.

*The League of Nations.* The most important institution for the world of learning after the war took an organizational form different from any that had preceded it. Though at first not conerned with this area, the League of Nations in 1922 created an International Committee on Intellectual Cooperation and appointed to it 12 eminent scholars from a variety of disciplines and countries. Receiving inadequate financial support from the League from the start, the Committee was given permission in 1924 to appeal directly to governments for assistance. The French government offered to set up in Paris and in part fund what would be an executive arm and headquarters organization for the Committee, the International Institute of Intellectual Cooperation, frequently referred to as the Paris Institute. The whole was called the League Organisation of Intellectual Cooperation.

Among a wide range of tasks addressed by the International Committee on Intellectual Cooperation were the organization of relief for intellectual workers in central and eastern Europe, improvement in the international exchange of publications, improvement in international copyright, and the coordination of bibliography. Indeed, one of the first subcommittees set up by the Committee was for bibliography.

Over a period the League Organisation of Intellectual Cooperation arranged consultations through the Subcommittee on Bibliography, and later its Committee of Library Experts, on how the bibliography of a diverse group of subjects might be improved; it proposed major modifications in the treaties governing the protection of intellectual property and the international exchange of publications; it held conferences, conducted surveys, and issued a great many publications. Some of these were directories, some bibliographies, and some, like the *Index Bibliographicas* and the *Index Translationem,* were continued after World War II by Unesco.

Because of lack of resources and the conception of its role as primarily investigative and advisory, it was a matter of policy that the League Organisation of Intellectual Cooperation did not attempt to carry out major projects of work. Rather, it sought to identify those that were of international importance and, whenever possible, sometimes by the provision of subsidies, to encourage other existing organizations to undertake them. From the start it had sought a viable relationship with the International Institute of Bibliography. But despite the signing of an agreement between the two bodies in 1924, the relationship between them, already delicate because of the personalities involved, gradually deteriorated to such a degree that to some outside observers, such as Ernest Cushing Richardson from the United States, the settlement of the differences between the organizations was the crucial test of the League's ability to bring about successful international cooperation in intellectual matters.

*IFLA.* League cooperation with the International Federation of Library Associations (IFLA) was more successful than with the International Institute of Bibliography, partly because there could be no clash of vested interests or organizational philosophy between the two. From its inception in 1927, IFLA was deeply influenced by the League Organisation and by a long-held but unfulfilled hope in the Paris Institute of setting up as part of its Section on Scientific Relations an International Library Advisory Service. In 1926 a proposal to create a permanent professional library organization, one function of which would be to work with the Paris Institute, had been made at the International Conference of Librarians and Booklovers in Prague. In 1927 at the annual meeting of the Library Association (of the United Kingdom), an International Library and Bibliographical Committee was formally created. This became the International Federation of Library Associations in 1929, and in that year the first World Congress of Librarianship and Bibliography was held. According to the statutes of the new association, its excecutive committee was to be called the International Library Committee, which would meet annually, while the association as a whole was to assemble at least once every five years. IFLA cooperated closely with the League Organisation in the publication of several directories and guides. The *Acts* of the International Library Committee and the *Proceedings* of the 1929 Rome-Venice conference and the 1935 Madrid-Barcelona conference provide evidence of the evolution from the limited, occasional prewar library conferences of a permanent international library community, characterized by continuous if fragile links between members, sustained formal communication, and some corporate activity.

The League Organisation of Intellectual Cooperation also worked closely with the International Federation of National Standardizing Associations (ISA). The latter body was formed in 1926, and in 1938 a technical committee, ISA-46, was devoted to studying standardization in documentation. This technical committee was a direct forerunner of the present ISO TC 46.

General cooperation between the League Organisation and the International Research Council was a goal pursued by both over a period of years, though its achievement was hindered in part because of the relatively long intervals between the meetings of the Council. A committee appointed by the Council in 1925 recommended in 1928 that a joint Council/League commission should be set up. In 1937 a formal agreement was reached for consultation and cooperation between the Council and the Paris Institute, which had, in any case, already referred matters to the Council for advice (including some matters of bibliography).

Thus, essentially by 1930 a pattern of international bibliographic and library organization had emerged, the outlines of which can still be discerned beneath the increasing international complexity and activity characteristic of the period after World War II. At the center in the 1930's was the permanent international intergovernmental organization of the time, the League of Nations as represented by its International Committee on Intellectual Cooperation and the technical agency it directed, the International Institute of Intellectual Cooperation in Paris. Its work took a number of forms. First was the publication, often as the result of international surveys, of guides, directories, and bibliographies. Next was the summoning of meetings of experts to consider issues of importance. Finally was the attempt to stimulate and coordinate the work of international nongovernmental organizations active in major areas of League interest: here lie the negotiations, successful and complete to varying degrees, between the League and IFLA, FID, ISA, and the International Council of Scientific Unions.

**After World War II.** As World War II drew to its close, there was no question that a new organization dealing with matters of education, culture, and science should be created as part of the United Nations family of organizations then being planned. Moreover, there was no doubt that part of the work of the new organization, which was to be called Unesco, should be concerned with libraries and bibliography. A rather grandiose plan, put forward by Theodore Besterman for an International Library and Bibliographic Clearing House within the Unesco secretariat, was soon abandoned as unrealistic. Unesco's program for libraries, bibliography, documentation, archives, and related subjects has grown over the years in strength, scope, and complexity. Its early conferences on science abstracting (1949) and the improvement of bibliographical services throughout the world (1950) culminated in the UNISIST (World Scientific and Technical Information) program adopted by an intergovernmental conference in 1971 and its NATIS (National Information Systems) program adopted by an intergovernmental conference in 1974. These and related programs were brought together in the General Information Programme (PGI), an intersectoral program attached to the Office of the Directorate in order to facilitate coordination and development of work and to reduce duplication of effort and organizational conflict.

Unesco, like the League Organisation of Intellectual Cooperation, continued to rely on the help of other organizations. IFLA has been able to bring about considerable international agreement in the standardization of cataloguing practices throughout the world, and its Universal Bibliographical Control Program (UBC), administered through a specially funded International Office for UBC, has attracted much international support, while its other programs, especially the Universal Availability of Publications (UAP), are developing considerable impetus. FID, while continuing to support the UDC, has collaborated closely with Unesco in developing and maintaining the ISORID program (International Information System on Research and Development in Documentation) and in devising the Broad System of Ordering (BSO) within the framework of UNISIST. Like IFLA it continues to hold a range of general or special meetings, issues publications, and acts jointly with other organizations in supporting workshops, conferences, seminars, and so on. The International Council of Scientific Unions created an Abstracting Board (ICSU-AB), which first met in 1955, and this has become an important international forum for the major abstracting and indexing services in the world.

The advent of the computer as a major tool in information processing and the development of machine-readable bibliographic data bases to some degree underlie aspects of UNISIST's program of systems interconnection. They have also led to the development of a number of international information systems, such as INIS (the International Nuclear Information System of the International Nuclear Energy Agency) and AGRIS (Agriculture Information System of the Food and Agriculture Organization). A number of other systems were under development as the 1980's began. Such systems are similar to the *International Catalogue of Scientific Literature;* their differences, however, are crucial. The subject and scope of the present systems are specific, and the systems constitute relatively minor parts of the work of major, broadly based intergovernmental organizations. Another contemporary development predicated on the computer revolution is the emergence of regional networks for the exploitation of bibliographic data bases, such as Euronet/Diane, which was scheduled to become operational in late 1979.

International library and bibliographic organization in the last quarter of the 20th century is complex. It involves a great many nongovernmental associations—some with fairly general and some with quite specific goals. It involves a number of intergovernmental organizations, some maintaining international systems, some such as Unesco or ISO responsible for development, coordination, and support of the work of other organizations. There are regional organizations and global ones. There are international agreements of various degrees of formality, ranging from intergovernmental conventions on copyright, exchange of documents, and the international flow of educational and cultural materials to expressions of approval of vaguely formulated programs of international desiderata. There are internationally drawn-up and maintained procedures and tools that are under constant scrutiny, development, and revision and that are accepted nationally with varying degrees of completeness. While much remains to be done, an established organizational basis and a widespread international awareness suggest that continuous achievement in the future is inevitable.

**REFERENCES**

Edward Carter, "The Birth of Unesco's Library Programmes," in *Med Boken Som Bakgrunn; Festkrift Til Harold L. Treterås* (1964).

S. Steven Falk, "The International Committee on Intellectual Cooperation: Its Work for Bibliography" (unpublished M. A. thesis, University of Chicago Graduate Library School, 1977).

Katherine Oliver Murra, "Some Attempts to Organize Bibliography Internationally," in Jesse Shera and Margaret Egan, editors, *Bibliographic Organization* (1951).

W. Boyd Rayward, *The Universe of Information: The Work of Paul Otlet for Documentation and International Organisation* (1975).

W. BOYD RAYWARD

## International Organization for Standardization

The International Organization for Standardization was created in 1946 following a meeting in London of the International Federation of the National Standardizing Associations. Delegates from 25 countries cooperated to create the new international organization, whose purpose would be to "facilitate the international co-ordination and unification of industrial standards." ISO comprised in 1979 the national standards institutes of 84 countries, of which 65 were member bodies and 19 correspondent members. Correspondent members are normally organizations in developing countries that do not yet have their own national standards bodies; most are governmental institutions, and they normally become full members after a few years. They do not take part in technical work.

The scope of ISO extends to both technical and nontechnical standards and is not limited to any particular branch, although it does not deal with the electrotechnical field, which is covered by the International Electrotechnical Commission. The object of the organization is to promote the development of world standards with a goal of facilitating the international exchange of goods and developing cooperation in intellectual, scientific, technological, and economic areas.

The technical work of ISO is accomplished through technical committees; the creation and scope of the committees are determined by the ISO Council. Within the determined scope the individual committee decides its own program and creates subcommittees and working groups. One hundred fifty-seven technical committees existed by the end of 1978, with 590 attendant subcommittees and 1,193 working groups. Each technical committee and subcommittee has a secretariat assigned to an ISO member body. A new item may be introduced into an ISO working program through a proposal usually made by a member body but that may be made by some other international organization. If an item is accepted, a new technical committee may be created, or it will be referred to the appropriate existing committee. Any member body that is interested in a subject for which a committee has been authorized has the right to be represented on that committee; representatives are designated either as observers or as participating members, who have the right to vote and to participate in meetings and one of whom acts as the committee's secretariat.

**ISO/TC 46.** Standardization in the field of information, documentation, librarianship, and related information handling, including information systems and interchange networks as applied to documentation, is the subject of ISO Technical Committee 46 (ISO/TC 46). The Committee had its origins in 1938, when the German Technical Committee of librarianship within the Deutscher Normenausschuss proposed that ISA-46 be set up and took over its secretariat. The secretariat was later held by NOBIN (Nederlands Orgaan voor de Bevordering fan de Informatieverzorging) and was reallocated in 1966 to DNA (since 1975, DIN, Deutsches Institute für Normung). Twenty-eight participating members and 15 observing members, who are nominees of the respective national standards institutions, carry out the standardization work. Eight other ISO technical committees and 37 international organizations also participate.

ISO publishes numerous documents and periodicals, including *ISO Catalogue,* an annual list of ISO standards that is updated quarterly, and *ISO Technical Programme,* a semiannual list of all draft ISO standards. *ISO Bibliographies* list all standards and draft standards in a given field. An overall view of ISO activities can be obtained in the *ISO Annual Review,* while the *ISO Bulletin* supplies monthly news. Information on technical committees is available in published Directives for the technical work of ISO. ISO also began to publish a series of handbooks containing selected ISO standards in particular fields.

ISO has granted liaison status to approximately 340 international organizations with ISO technical committees and subcommittees. Further details can be found in ISO's publication *Liaisons.*

JOHANNA EGGERT

## Iran

Iran, a republic in western Asia, is bounded by the Caspian Sea and the U.S.S.R. on the north, Pakistan and Afghanistan on the east, the Persian Gulf and Gulf of Oman on the south, and Turkey and Iraq on the west. Pop. (1977 est.) 35,686,000; area 1,648,000 sq.km. The official language is Farsi (Persian).

Although the history of 2,500 years of Iran's contributions to civilization, knowledge, and scholarship refers to outstanding libraries with rich collections, the modern concept of library services was introduced there only 25 years ago. The first library school was established in Tehran University as recently as 1966; hence there is a shortage of professionally qualified librarians, a factor that affects the slow development of modern library services in Iran.

**National Library.** "Ketabkhaneh Melli" of Iran was established in 1935; it holds approximately 100,000 volumes in a wide variety of subjects; and it has an outstanding manuscripts collection. It receives one copy of each publication produced in the country, and it publishes the *National Bibliography of Iran.* Services to other libraries and participation in national library development, which are normally considered as national library functions, are in part performed by other organizations such as the Tehran Book Processing Center and the Iranian Documentation Center, both established in 1968 by the Ministry of Science and Higher Education.

**Academic Libraries.** The first Western-style university was founded in Tehran in 1934. By 1975 there were 10 universities and 132 colleges and technical institutes in Iran, and the number increased during the late 1970's. Except for newer and smaller universities, Iranian universities have no centralized library system; each faculty (school) within each university has its own independent library. In recent years, Tehran, Tabriz, and Esfahan universities have created central libraries that operate independently.

The Tehran University library holds approximately 500,000 volumes serving 18,000 students and 2,000 instructional staff. The collections of other major university libraries range from 6,000 to 12,000 volumes each serving 4,000 to 6,000 students. The teaching methods generally employed in older universities, which principally require memorization of the professors' lecture notes, do not encourage the use of the library. Library services include limited reference and bibliographical services, photocopying service, and interlibrary loan. Open access is replacing the old closed access system.

**Public Libraries.** According to the Library Act of 1965, which authorized the establishment of public libraries in Iran, each municipality is to allocate 1.5 percent of its revenue to public library services. Since 1965 over 300 public libraries have been established. Most of their users are high school students, and book collections range from fewer than 500 to more than 6,000 volumes. A 1975 survey of 97 public libraries revealed that 58 libraries have fewer than 2,000 volumes each. Tehran, with a population of 4,500,000, is served by a main public library and 16 branches serving over 40,000 registered borrowers.

**School and Children's Libraries.** Through the Institute for the Intellectual Development of Children and Young Adults, founded in 1965, the most modern and advanced library services in Iran are provided for children. There is a network of some 80 children's libraries in Tehran and other cities, with approximately 350,000 registered users. The Institute operates 4 bookmobiles serving over 420,000 children in schools, hospitals, orphanages, and day-care centers.

According to the School Building Act, one room or a section of a room in each school must be allocated for a library, and a certain amount of the budget must be set aside for books. In reality, however, only a very limited number of schools, mostly in Tehran, offer only minimal library service.

**Special Libraries.** The establishment of special libraries, documentation centers, or information centers is a recent development in Iran. Notable examples are the Central Bank Library with more than 35,000 volumes and 6,000 bound serials; the Razi Institute Library, which holds over 6,000 books in biology and pathology and subscribes to more than 100 scientific journals; the Oil Consortium libraries in Tehran and Ahvaz; the Iranian National Oil Company Information Center, with its collections on petroleum engineering; and the Informatics Center of Plan and Budget Organization, which deals with data on all aspects of national development.

**Library Association.** The Iranian Library Association was founded in October 1966 "to promote the adoption of more effective systems of library service and to encourage the development of librarianship as a profession." Its membership is open "to those who are, or have been, employed in library service or who have been enrolled in or graduated from a library school." In 1975 the Association had 949 members.

**REFERENCES**

"Iran," *Herald of Library Science* (1975).
"Iranian Library Association," *IFLA Annual* (1976).
P. B. Mangla, "Libraries in Higher Education in Iran," *International Library Review* (1976).
J. Haider Jalaloddin, "Scientific Research and Information Facilities in Iran," *Special Libraries* (1976).

FARIDEH TEHRANI
NASSER SHARIFY

# Iraq

Iraq, a republic in southwest Asia, is surrounded by Turkey on the north, Iran on the east, Syria and Jordan on the west, Kuwait and Saudi Arabia on the south and southwest, and the Persian Gulf on the southeast. Pop. (1977 census) 12,171,500; area 437,522 sq.km. The official language is Arabic.

**National Library.** The National Library, founded in the capital city of Baghdad in 1920, is under the direction of the Ministry of Information. The Library has also functioned as a public library for some time. The National Library and the Central Library of the University of Baghdad are both depositories of all Iraqi publications according to laws of 1963 and 1970. The National Library maintains a legal deposit center that holds more than 51,000 volumes, while the Central Library of the University of Baghdad acts as exchange and national bibliographic center. The book production in Iraq in 1975 was 638 titles, according to the Arab League Educational, Cultural and Scientific Organization.

The University of Baghdad Central Library has issued the National Bibliography, a semiannual publication, since 1963; issues a catalogue of the Library holdings in Arabic and other languages; and has issued the Bibliographical List of Government Publications since 1969. The National Library has issued the Depository Bulletin monthly since 1971.

**Academic Libraries.** The first academic libraries in Iraq were established in the 1930's, almost at the same time as college study was begun there. Those colleges were incorporated in the University of Baghdad in 1958. The University established its Central Library in 1960 and moved it to a central building in 1965. The Central Library and the 22 independent college libraries possess around 750,000 volumes. The central library has about 220,000 volumes of books, 10,000 maps, and 1,500 Arabic manuscripts on microfilm. It acquires annually about 10,000 volumes and subscribes to 2,000 periodicals.

The Al-Hikma University Central Library was established in Baghdad in 1956 and transferred to a modern building in 1962. The Library has an up-to-date collection of about 50,000 volumes on the subjects taught in its three main departments: English, physics, and business. The Al-Mustansiriyah University Library, founded in Baghdad in 1963, was housed in a new building in 1966. The University of Mosul Central Library, founded in 1965, has a collection of about 190,000 volumes and subscribes to 1,700 periodicals. The University of Basrah Central Library was founded in 1964. The other noteworthy academic libraries are those of the University of Sulaimaniyah (founded in 1969), the Academy of Fine Arts (1967), and Usul-al-Din (Islamic Studies) College.

**Public Libraries.** The Iraqi local government municipalities offer public library services as one of their responsibilities. Public libraries in the major cities of Iraq number 25; noteworthy are the Child Library, founded in 1964, and the Public Library in Mosul, the oldest in the chain of the public libraries, founded in 1930.

**School Libraries.** School libraries are not well developed. The large secondary, vocational, and technical schools maintain sizable libraries administered mainly by nonprofessional personnel.

**Special Libraries.** More than 45 special libraries have been established in Iraq to serve the officials and researchers in the government departments, research centers, banks, and companies. The Library of the Iraqi National Museum in Baghdad, founded in 1934, is the largest of these, containing about 100,000 volumes and 12,000 manuscripts. Others of note are in the Ministries of Education, Information, Health, Agriculture, Justice, Planning, and Transport and at the Foundation of Scientific Research.

The Iraqi Scientific Documentation Center was established in Baghdad in 1972. Attached to the Foundation of Scientific Research, the Center coordinates the libraries of the institutes and centers belonging to the Foundation—such as the Date Palm Research Center, Building Research Center, Biological Research Center, Agriculture Research Center, Petroleum Research Center, Natural Resources Center, and Institute of Applied Research. The

Scientific Documentation Center assists in organizing these libraries and unifies technical processing, abstracting, and bibliographical services. The Center offers its services to persons engaged in scientific research and development, including those working in universities, research centers, government establishments, and industries, as well as experts and consultants of the United Nations Development Programme (UNDP) projects.

The Department of Documentation and Industrial Information of the General Organization for Engineering Industries, established in 1971, offers industrial information services to Iraqi industries. The Documentation Center of the Iraqi National Petroleum Company, founded in 1965, takes care of petroleum data processing in the country. The Department of Documentation and Studies, established by the Ministry of Education in 1967, offers educational documentation services to educators, researchers, planners, teachers, and students of education in Iraq.

**Associations.** There is an Iraqi Library Association, but its professional activities are limited. The Arab Regional Branch of the International Council on Archives (ARBICA), founded in Baghdad in 1973, organizes meetings, publishes a professional bulletin, and collects professional archival materials.

MOHAMED M. EL HADI

# Ireland, Republic of

Up until 1922 the entire island of Ireland, separated from Great Britain by Saint George's Channel, the Irish Sea, and the North Channel, was a de jure part of the United Kingdom of Great Britain and Ireland. Following a rebellion (1916) and a War of Independence, self-government for the 26 counties having predominantly nationalist populations was achieved; the six northeastern counties, which had unionist majorities, remained part of the United Kingdom. The information that follows refers to the twenty-six counties in the state now known as the Republic of Ireland. Pop. (1977 est.) 3,199,000; area 70,283 sq.km. Official languages: Irish, English.

Marsh's Library

*Archbishop Marsh's Library, founded in Dublin in 1702, was the first public library in Ireland. A magnificent example of a scholar's library, it contains collections of some of the earliest English printers, Cicero's "Letters to His Friends" (1472), 17th-century music manuscripts, and mementos of Jonathan Swift.*

**National Library.** The National Library of Ireland is in the capital, Dublin. It is a State Library and dates from 1887, when the then Government acquired the library of the Royal Dublin Society to form its nucleus. This society—which still flourishes—was in the 19th century a center of intellectual and cultural interest. The original library has been expanded and updated on a continuing basis and today is the major reference resource for material relating to Ireland. Its collection includes manuscripts, maps, pamphlets, tracts, and unique holdings on microfilm of Irish manuscripts, the originals of which are in many places throughout the world. Its staff are continually active in bibliographical fields, and a former Director, Richard Hayes, published a monumental work, *Manuscript Sources of Irish History*. The library does not lend, but it provides an extensive photocopy service. Its Educational Division has the task of making people aware of the resources available.

**Academic Libraries.** The most important academic libraries in Ireland are those of the two university foundations—Dublin University (Trinity College) and the National University of Ireland, which has four constituent Colleges: Dublin, Cork, Galway, and Maynooth. Of these by far the most important is that of Trinity College Dublin, which was established by Royal Charter (Elizabeth I) in 1592. Since 1801 it has been a legal deposit library and, though now outside the United Kingdom, retains the right to receive a copy of any book published in that country. It is a modern university library with vast collections appropriate to the various schools within the foundation. But besides the material needed for the work of the University, Trinity Library houses a priceless collection of ancient Irish manuscripts, chief of which is the *Book of Kells*. This transcription of the four Gospels executed by Irish monks is accounted by many experts to be the finest illuminated manuscript in the world. The Library is rich in other manuscripts and incunabula and attracts scholars and visitors in great numbers. Trinity does not lend to individuals but cooperates in interlibrary lending schemes.

The libraries in the constituent Colleges of the National University of Ireland at Dublin, Cork, and Galway are of more recent origin and, in general, are geared to the courses taught at the Colleges. The library in Dublin, however, is the most extensive. It contains much archival and manuscript material including unpublished papers of Irish historical and political notables. The Dublin library also houses an extensive collection of books and periodicals on librarianship; the College has the only School of Library and Information Studies in the republic. The College of the National University at Maynooth (County Kildare) was formerly reserved as a seminary for aspirants to the Roman Catholic priesthood. It now admits lay students, and its library has a heavy concentration of works on philosophy and theology.

In addition to these older established libraries, newer academic foundations such as the National Institute for Higher Education and five Regional Technical Colleges are in the process of building appropriate libraries. Specialist academic libraries are fairly numerous in Dublin and include Chester Beatty Library (Oriental Arts), Kings Inns (Law), Royal Irish Academy (Science, Humanities, particularly relating to Ireland-Irish manuscripts).

**Public Libraries.** Public libraries have been established in Ireland since 1855. There are 22 library authorities whose areas comprise entire counties, two whose areas comprise adjacent counties amalgamated for library purposes, and two small areas within counties that retain separate library identities: Bray (County Wicklow) and Dun Laoghaire (County Dublin). The four largest cities, Dublin, Cork, Limerick, and Waterford, are each independent library authorities. The highest concentration of service is in the capital, Dublin, staffed at IFLA-recommended levels and directed by professionally qualified librarians. In the rest of the country the Chief Librarian and top aides are professional librarians. It is estimated that over 90 percent of the entire population of Ireland is within reach of public library service, but actual use varies according to concentrations of population and the quality of the service between 50 percent and 20 percent. The central government retains an overview of library services through the Department of the Environment, which is advised by a statutory body—the Library Council (Public Libraries Act 1947). The Council recommends levels of assistance and grants, approves the siting and extent of new projects, and also advises local authorities on library matters.

**School Libraries.** School library provision is, in general, part of the public library service. The state gives special financial aid to local authorities on a per capita basis for the National Primary Schools but does not give library subvention for schools at higher levels. There are, therefore, no reliable statistics of library provision in these. School library stocks are geared toward class and project work and do not cater to recreational reading, which is regarded as being the province of the children's departments of the public libraries.

**Special Libraries.** There were no up-to-date statistics about the number of special libraries in Ireland at the end of the 1970's, but most larger organizations are believed to have some sort of book or information provision. In particular, the following may be cited: the Oireachtas (Parliament); the government departments of Agriculture, Education, Labour, Foreign Affairs; the Electricity Supply Board; Institute of Public Administration; Irish Tourist Board; and Irish Export Board. A list of 74 special libraries appeared in *An Leabharlann,* the journal of the Library Association in Ireland, in the issue for September 1967.

**Associations.** The Library Association of Ireland (Cumann Leabharlann na h-Eireann) was founded in 1928 and has a membership of some 300; its founding members included James Barry and Christina Keogh. In addition to conducting seminars, conferences, and other programs, the Association publishes *An Leabharlann: The Irish Library*.

The Irish Association for Documentation and Information Services (IADIS), headquartered at the National Library, was founded in 1967 to support special library and information work. It published the *Union List of Current Periodicals in Irish Libraries* (1975) and sponsors the *Irish Publishing Record,* a bibliography of Irish imprints with a directory of Irish publishers. School librarians may participate in the Irish Association of School Librarians (Cumann Leabharlannaithe Scoile, CLS), founded in 1962. Its official journal is the *C.L.S. Bulletin,* and it conducts summer courses in school librarianship. The Irish Society for Archives is an organization for the country's archivists.

ROBERT J. CASEY

# Islamic Libraries

(7th to 17th centuries)

Islam evolved early in the 7th century A.D. from an Arabic civilization that was basically nomadic but one with a scripture *(ahl al-kitāb).* This predisposed the victorious Arabs to enrich their literary heritage with that of their Persian and Byzantine neighbors soon after they conquered them. The Qur'ān (Koran), the Arabic revelation, encourages learning and knowledge. Although the word *knowledge* as used in the Qur'ān has a religious connotation, later such sayings as "Seek ye knowledge from the cradle to the grave," "The search for knowledge is incumbent on every Muslim," "Seek ye knowledge even into China," and the like were broader and became commonplace. Since religion was the focal point in the Islamic state, it is in regard to the Qur'ān that the first library transaction can be observed—the deposit of a copy of this work with Ḥafṣah, one of Prophet Muḥammad's widows.

The private library was the preponderant type of library in early Islam. Private libraries were owned mainly by scholars interested in those branches of knowledge that developed from the study of the Qur'ān and the traditions of the Prophet, such as grammar, theology, law, and history. Eventually the collections of these libraries found their way into the mosques that had developed adjunct libraries rather early in their efforts to supplement religious instruction. The most famous mosque library is that of al-Azhar in Cairo, which was founded in the 9th century but gained university status in the 18th. It should also be noted that since in many instances the private libraries were accessible to other scholars and sometimes even to the general public, there was a gradual transition from the private library to the later public libraries.

During the Umayyad Caliphate (661–750) scholarly interests extended to the natural sciences. This interest particularly in mathematics, astronomy, and medicine, came to the fore during the Abbaside Caliphate (750–1258), when under al-Ma'mūn (813–33) a House of

Bibliothèque Nationale

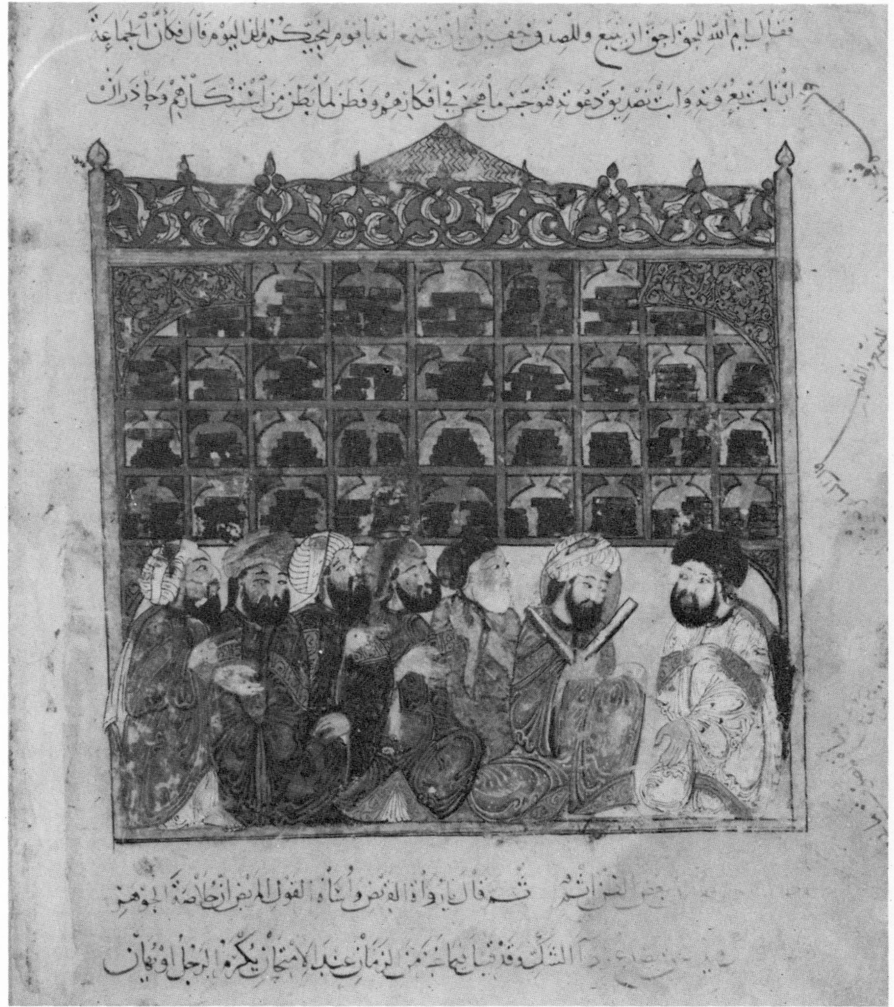

*Interior of an Islamic library from an illuminated manuscript of al-Hariri in the Bibliothèque Nationale in Paris.*

Wisdom *(Dār al-Ḥikmah)* was established in Baghdad that was open to all. It was this academy that contributed extensively to the understanding of Greek philosophy and science. Under its head and chief translator, Ḥunayn ibn Isḥāq, Greek manuscripts were acquired and translated into Arabic, often through the Syriac medium. Greek works that were lost in the original were frequently preserved only through these translations.

A similar institution was founded in Cairo during the Fāṭimid rule (909–1171). After the dissolution of this library at the end of the Fāṭimid reign, much of the collection was acquired by the Secretary of Saladin, Qāḍī al-Fāḍil, and was named al-Fāḍilīyah after him.

The third most important library of the Middle Ages in Islam was the court library of the Umayyad rulers of Cordova, Spain (750–1031). Although apparently less accessible to the public, its holdings were extensive.

These three libraries cannot be considered national libraries in the strict sense of the word, but they were the most outstanding central institutions in these countries and were—if indirectly—financed by public revenues. Unfortunately, these libraries were often short-lived because frequent political upheavals destroyed the libraries and their collections.

During the Seljuks (1037–1300) the colleges *(madrasah)* came into prominence and with them the college library. The wazir Niẓām al-Mulk, who during a period of 20 years was the virtual ruler of the realm, built numerous colleges throughout the empire; the best-known one was in Baghdad and named al-Niẓāmīyah. Al-Ghazzālī, the famous philosopher, was one of the outstanding teachers there. At that time the monastic library also came into existence in conjunction with the rise of the derwish orders; its significance was minimal, however, compared with that of the European monastic library.

The Ottoman Turks (1299–1923) made Constantinople their capital, and consequently the principal library activity followed to that city. G. Toderini, visiting the city in the early 18th century, reports on 13 major libraries, many of them open to the public, and gives an insight into their holdings.

While the strength of the Islamic library collections was first measured in camel loads, numbers do exist for later periods; these, however, cannot always be taken at face value. Volume numbers up to half a million for major libraries during the Middle Ages are probably not exaggerated, as most of these libraries had full-time manuscript copyists *(nāsikh)* on their staffs. Other members of the library staff were the Superintendent *(ṣāḥib),* one or more Custodians *(khāzin),* and Assistants *(farrāsh).* The scribes often belonged to the local guild and as such sometimes wielded considerable power; fearing for their jobs, they successfully opposed the introduction of printing into Constantinople until the beginning of the 18th century.

The arrangement of books usually was by subject, stored in compartments that could be locked. Since the books were stored on their sides, a practice that contributed to the deterioration of the outer covers and the title and colophon pages, the titles were written on labels attached to the spine and were written on the foreedge to facilitate identification. When catalogues existed, they usually were in book form. The lack of proper ventilation and the presence of vermin contributed to the damage of the manuscripts. The mosque libraries, not usually being equipped to forestall or repair deterioration, suffered most in this respect, while the caliphal libraries were financially best suited to house the collections in air-conditioned premises and to repair them when damage occurred. Unfortunately it was the latter library that bore the brunt of the attacks by the human enemy—the thieves, sectarians, and Mongol invaders.

**REFERENCES**

O. Pinto, "The Libraries of the Arabs during the Time of the Abbasides," *Islamic Culture* (1929).

*Index Islamicus* provides references under "Libraries."

MIROSLAV KREK

# Israel

Israel, a republic in the Middle East, is bordered by Lebanon on the north, Syria on the northeast, Jordan on the east, Egypt on the southwest, and the Mediterranean Sea on the west. Pop. (1978 est.) 3,695,600; area (excluding occupied territory from the June 1967 war) 20,700 sq.km. The official languages are Hebrew and Arabic.

**National Library.** The Jewish National and University Library (JNUL) in Jerusalem serves a dual purpose as the National Library of Israel and of the Jewish people throughout the world and as the Library of the Hebrew University. The Library was begun in 1884 as a small collection that merged with a library of the B'nai B'rith Lodge in Jerusalem in 1890. The World Zionist Organization assumed responsibility for it in 1920 and named it "the Jewish National Library." In 1925 it was incorporated into the Hebrew University. Since its foundation, private donors and organizations throughout the world have been collecting and sending books and archives to JNUL, and every effort was made to find and add to its collection material salvaged from Jewish communities annihilated by the Nazis in Europe during World War II. Priority is given to acquiring Hebrew and Jewish manuscrips, incunabula, and rare books. It collects Israeli publications by means of the Legal Deposit Law acted upon by the Knesset, or parliament, even before statehood. The JNUL collects material about Israel, Palestine, Jews, or Judaism, material that is written in Hebrew script or Jewish language, and all that is written in specific areas by Jews, regardless of country of publication. Thus, a rapid, although somewhat random, growth resulted, from a few thousand volumes at its foundation to 424,338 volumes in 1948 and over 2,000,000 volumes by 1977. Its collection of Judaica and related subjects is one of the finest in the world. There is also one of the largest and best organized collections on Arabic and Islamic subjects in the Middle East.

JNUL is composed of the main library and about 70 departmental libraries that serve the Hebrew University. It publishes *Kiryat Sefer,* an annotated bibliography of books published in Israel; books about Jews, Judaism, and Israel published all over the world; and an *Index of Articles on Jewish Studies.*

**Academic Libraries.** The libraries in Israel's seven universities are developing slowly but steadily in spite of severe budgetary restraints. By the mid-1970's the size of the collections in the academic libraries (excluding JNUL) ranged between 200,000 and 700,000 items. Absence of formal acquisitions policies contributed to gaps in the collections, and this problem is aggravated by a fragmentation of the collection and services among a central and departmental libraries, all of which compete for the limited funds and manpower.

All academic libraries follow the JNUL's tradition of also providing public library services to the community at large. Moreover, academic libraries fulfill national roles as well; for example, the Technion extends information services to the country's scientific and research institutions and to industrial companies, and the Haifa University Library prepares one of Israel's main bibliographic tools, the computer-based annual *Index to Hebrew Periodicals,* and other computer-based bibliographic materials.

In the late 1960's the government, which provides some 70 percent of the academic institutions' budget, initiated measures toward the introducton of interlibrary cooperation in order to achieve more efficient academic library services. The committee established to this end, Israel Standing Committee of National and University Libraries (SCONUL), has already succeeded in carrying out such projects as the establishment of interlibrary lending, the regular updating and publication of the *Israel Union List of Serials,* and the provision of a central cataloguing agency using MARC tapes (MARCIS). Through cooperation with the National Grants Committee, SCONUL has been tackling other problems.

**Public Libraries.** The Israeli public library has its roots in age-old traditions. Jews have always attributed great importance to reading and learning, which were considered lifelong occupations of every man. In every Jewish community from the Middle Ages on, there was a Beit Midrash, or House of Learning, which can be considered a prototypical public library, inasmuch as it served as the cultural and social center of the community and fulfilled roles characteristic of the modern public library. There was also a tradition of assigning a public role even to private collections.

The traditional attitudes toward books and reading persist in modern Israel, where there is a significantly high percentage of readers. Although Israelis were slow to recognize the importance of libraries as providers of information and as culturation or acculturation agencies, this trend changed in the 1960's when the Library Section of the Ministry of Education and Culture began taking measures for the active development of libraries. Local authorities were encouraged to establish libraries, especially in new rural settlements and development towns.

The Library Law of 1975, although slowly implemented because of financial difficulties, provided for the establishment and further development of public libraries. The law decrees that it is the local authorities' duty to establish and maintain libraries; these libraries are to extend services free of charge, including reference and circulation. Out of 779 settlements, 556 had library services in the late 1970's, but only 42 library systems with 169 branches were under the supervision of the Ministry of Education. Their number was expected to grow when financially possible.

There is much interaction between academic and public libraries; for example, the public libraries of the southern region are aided by the library of the Ben Gurion University, and the same role is fulfilled by the Haifa University Library in the north. In addition to providing direct service to citizens, the academic libraries "adopt" the public libraries of their region and advise them in the organization of their collections, provide bibliographic services, and donate books to them.

The Center for Public Libraries, founded in 1965, is another agent for the aid of public libraries, providing such centralized services as central cataloguing, centralized book acquisition, and book processing for libraries. The Center also publishes bibliographies, reference books, and a periodical devoted to librarianship, *Yad la-Kore.*

**Kibbutz Libraries.** The kibbutz (collective settlement) population has access to the highest proportion of library books per capita in Israel—84,000 people (3.4 percent of the entire population) have at their disposal 1,883,000 volumes. Some 37 percent of kibbutz residents are active readers. Until the late 1960's books were scattered throughout the settlements in small, often disorganized collections, but since then serious attempts have been made to apply some method to kibbutz libraries.

**Arab Libraries.** In towns of mixed Jewish and Arab

David Harris

*The Jewish National and University Library in Jerusalem serves as the national library of Israel and as the library of the Hebrew University. Its collection of Judaica is one of the largest in existence and its Arabic and Islamic holdings are extensive.*

**Table 1. Libraries in Israel (1977)**

| Type | Number | Volumes in collections | Annual expenditures (pound) | Population served | All staff (total) |
|---|---|---|---|---|---|
| National | 1 | 1,200,000 | I£27,000,000 | N.A. | 196 positions |
| Academic | 7 | 4,200,000 | approximately I£300,000,000 | 62,000 | 910 |
| Public | 757 | 5,570,000 | approximately I£55,000,000 | 2,798,400 | 1,063 |
| School | approximately 500 | N.A. | N.A. | approximately 150,000 | N.A. |
| Special | approximately 400 | N.A. | N.A. | N.A. | N.A. |

Sources: a survey of University and National Library; a survey of Unit for Public Libraries at the Ministry of Education and Culture.

**Table 2. Archives in Israel (1977)**

| | |
|---|---|
| Number | 26 |
| Holdings | 30,000 cubic meters (90 kilometers of shelves) |
| Annual expenditures | I£25,000,000 in 1978–79 |
| Professional staff | 95 |

Source: Director of the National Archives.

population, the public libraries serve both Jewish and Arab readers, and Arab students and teachers make use of the Arabic collections at the university libraries. However, the general public in purely Arab settlements have little access to libraries. Recently, the government has begun to encourage Arab local authorities to establish libraries.

**School Libraries.** In most Israeli schools there is some kind of a book collection, usually numbering a few hundred to a few thousand, and children are taught to use books as information sources. Until recently collections were kept in classrooms in closed cabinets for circulation only, and no attempt was made to teach library use. From the 1970's there was increasing awareness that the lack of school libraries affects educational performance and that public libraries can only in part replace them. Efforts are being made toward the organization of libraries in schools and integration of library use instruction into general education.

**Special Libraries.** Israel has some 400 special libraries linked to research institutions, hospitals, professional associations, government agencies, and industrial plants. A few libraries provide selective dissemination of information (SDI) services and provide aid in editing scientific papers.

The Center for Scientific and Technological Information (CSTI) was established in 1961 by the National Council for Research and Development to organize the provision of scientific information in Israel.

**Other Libraries.** *Parliamentary Library.* The parliamentary library has a relatively small collection for the use of members of the Knesset. It also receives deposit copies of Israeli publications, but unlike JNUL it does not serve as a depository library; the books are distributed among other libraries.

*Religious Libraries.* Many libraries and book collections of religious nature are used by the orthodox segments of the population. The Jewish religious libraries are in synagogues, orthodox Jewish educational institutions, local religious councils, and rabbinical courts. There are also a number of private collections.

Christian religious libraries can be found in monasteries and missions and near churches. Although some serve the general public, many are limited to the use of researchers.

Muslim religious libraries have been founded and promoted mostly by the Muslim Religious Endowment (WAQF), although there are many private collections as well, and there are also libraries in mosques.

*Foreign Libraries.* Foreign libraries of a secular nature are sponsored either by foreign governments or by nongovernmental public bodies in their respective countries. Their collections fulfill a public library function to Israel's new immigrants.

**Associations.** The Israel Library Association (ILA) is the professional organization for Israeli library personnel and archivists. The number of its members grew from 150 at its foundation in 1952 to about 2,000 in 1977. The Israel Society of Special Libraries and Information Center (ISLIC) was founded in 1966 to extend professional aid to special librarians and establish foreign and local contacts in the field of special librarianship. It publishes the *ISLIC Bulletin,* which deals with problems of special libraries.

**REFERENCES**


Shmuel Sever, "Some Aspects of Public Library Development in Israel," *Library Quarterly* (1968), trends in modern Israeli librarianship based on cultural traditions.

———, "The Arab Library in Israel," *Library Quarterly* (1979).

Curt D. Wormann, "Education for Librarianship Abroad: Israel," *Library Trends* (1963), an overview of Israeli library and library education by the single most influential professional leader during the first generation after Israel's independence.


SHMUEL SEVER

# Italy

Italy, a republic in southern Europe, comprises the Apennine Peninsula, Sicily, Sardinia, and various other islands. Italy juts out south into the Mediterranean Sea and is bordered on the north and west by France and Switzerland and on the north and east by Austria and Yugoslavia. Pop. (1978 est.) 56,600,400; area 301,262 sq.km. The official language is Italian.

**National Libraries.** There are eight national libraries in Italy. The National Central Libraries in Rome and Florence are the most prominent, and both receive materials under the deposit laws of 1886 and subsequent modifications. The National Central Library in Rome, officially known as the Biblioteca Nazionale Centrale Vittorio Emanuele II, opened its new building in 1975. The Library collaborates with its sister Central Library in Florence to produce bibliographies of Italian and foreign materials. Their most important bibliography is the *Bibliografia Nazionale Italiana* (BNI), primarily produced by the staff in Florence using computer methods. The *Catalogo dei Periodici 1958–67* is part of the BNI. The Central Library in Rome also produces catalogue cards, still little used by libraries in Italy owing to the retention of local classification and cataloguing procedures. The National Central Library in Rome holds over 2,000,000 books and pamphlets, 2,000 incunabula, and 6,000 manuscripts.

The National Central Library of Florence opened to the public in 1747 with 30,000 volumes and 3,000 manuscripts. It contains nearly 4,000,000 books and pamphlets, 25,000 manuscripts, and about 4,000 incunabula. As does its counterpart in Rome, this library serves the general public and acts, in fact, as the major public library in Florence.

The other six national libraries in Milan, Venice, Turin, Naples, Bari, and Palermo are also open to the public. These six libraries serve as depositories for materials printed in their respective regions.

**Academic Libraries.** Academic libraries have undergone great stress because of enormous increases in student enrollments, which grew from 245,000 in 1960 to nearly 1,000,000 in 1978. Libraries in higher education reflect the fragmentation and specialization of university organizational structure. Faculties of literature, law, and medicine, among others, are quite autonomous and are subdivided into special aspects of their respective disciplines. Libraries are generally designed to serve these separate faculties and their subdivisions. Probably the largest single library is at the University of Florence, the Biblioteca di Letture e Filosofia, with over 1,300,000 books and pamphlets. There are more than 40 other institutes and similar libraries at the University. Its Central Medical Library has over 75,000 volumes in addition to 350–400 volumes in each of the 14 other special medical libraries. This characteristic pattern of specialization results in about 100 faculty and institute libraries at the University of Palermo, while the University of Rome has about 120 libraries with holdings exceeding 1,100,000 volumes. Several major university libraries are governed by the national Ministero per i Beni Culturali e Ambientali.

There are many restrictions on lending in Italy, especially in academic and special libraries, resulting in great reliance on use of materials in the library. Moreover, as many academic libraries have limited staff members, the hours of access to the collections are limited, frequently only 20 hours a week.

The European University Institute Library at San Domenico di Fiesole, Florence, employs a fully integrated automated system. It cooperates with the National Library, the Tuscan Region, and the University Library in a shared, computer-based cataloguing system. This program began in 1979.

**Public Libraries.** According to Unesco's *Statistical Yearbook 1976,* about 57 percent of Italy's 56,000,000 people are served by public libraries. Correspondence, interviews, and annual reports, however, suggest that this figure is high and that 37 percent is a more realistic estimate. The national government has jurisdiction over 44 libraries, all of them called *biblioteche pubbliche statali,* or state public libraries. These 44 libraries are of various types—national, academic, and special. All are open to the public. They do not, however, include public libraries as the term is widely used, that is, libraries governed by local authorities and devoted to serving people of all levels of education with a wide variety of interests. Public libraries of this sort are known as popular or communal (municipal) libraries in Italy.

In recent years many plans and programs have been drawn up to develop library systems. One such plan would create library systems within provinces (which include many communes or municipalities). The other major approach conceives systems developed by the 20 regions of Italy, each of which includes many provinces. By the late 1970's, drafting of regional library laws was in progress, the major obstacles being lack of funds and lack of consensus on organizational strategy.

The most prominent provincial system is in Bologna. The Bologna Provincial Consortium includes 23 libraries and 21 reading rooms *(sale di lettura),* serving about half of the 850,000 people in this province. The Consortium's libraries function as cultural resource centers; in addition to providing traditional services, such as lending books and providing reading and reference rooms, libraries are centers for musical concerts, art exhibits, and programs of lectures, discussions, and demonstrations about a wide range of issues—historical and contemporary. This broad definition of library activities is shared widely in Italy, but few public libraries are able to put the ideal into practice.

The Consortium's budget in 1978 was 459,000,000 lire, 65 percent of it from the regional government. Libraries in this system hold 181,000 volumes and 430 current periodical titles. Although the budget was nearly double that of 1974, it barely managed to maintain the earlier level of service, since the number of libraries and reading rooms had nearly doubled in that four-year period. Further, as with all libraries, increase in the cost of books was great: average book costs rose from 3,500 lire in 1974 to 6,000 in 1977.

The city of Bologna is not a part of the Consortium. Its holdings should be considered in addition to those of the Consortium. The city has a central library and 16 branch libraries for 550,000 people. They have 120,000 volumes and 218 current periodicals with a 1978 budget of 90,000,000 lire.

Vera Fotografia

*The Vatican Library in Rome dates from the 13th century and is open to the public, but collections are restricted to use by qualified scholars.*

Because it is probably the best developed municipal library, the public library of Milan merits special attention. It effectively serves 42 percent of the total population of 1,708,000. The 1977 budget of 2,123,000,000 lire supported a large central library and 33 branches. The city system has 1,747,000 volumes, including 215,000 in school libraries. The public library administers the school libraries in the city. Its 1977 loans exceeded 1,400,000 in addition to use of 2,777,000 books, records, and other materials in the libraries. There were nearly 600 exhibitions, concerts, and other activities—all managed by a staff of 300, of which 57 are full-time librarians.

Although planning for regional library systems is longstanding, no region had formed a true system or network by the 1970's. Tuscany was developing one in the mid-1970's, but it retrenched its service to cover only six provinces—Florence, Massa-Carrara, Leghorn, Arezzo, Pistoia, and Empoli. Its objectives still constitute a model for regional systems. These include a collective regional catalogue, a special library for science and technology, bibliographic information services for the region's libraries, regional microfilm archives, guardianship of library and archival holdings, a restoration laboratory, and professional training.

*Five Regions.* Following is a description of public li-

**Libraries in Italy (1972)**

| Type | Number | Volumes in collections | Population served[a] | All staff (total |
|---|---|---|---|---|
| National[b] | 8 | 11,293,000 | 45,574 | 863 |
| Academic | 3,060 | 55,114,000 | 1,148,105 | N.A. |
| Public | 8,686 | 16,979,000 | 2,944,163 | N.A. |
| School | 12,042 | 22,495,000 | 3,360,510 | N.A. |
| Special | 3,876 | 51,047,000 | N.A. | N.A. |
| Total | 27,672 | 156,928,000 | | |

[a]Registered borrowers.
[b]1974 data. Staff includes 148 with diplomas and 183 trained on the job.

Source: Unesco, *Statistical Yearbook,* 1976.

Theodore F. Welch

*The National Central Library, Rome, occupied this new building in 1975. One of eight Italian national libraries, it is officially named the Biblioteca Nazionale Centrale Vittorio Emanuele II.*

**"It's Fun to Read,"** N.Y.C. television series **70**

**IVMB:** *see* article International Association of Music Libraries

braries in 5 of the 20 regions (data for the others are not available):

Piedmont (1978): budget 3,370,000,000 lire; 576 communities, 3,500,000 served; holdings 3,500,000 volumes, 8,000 periodicals; participates in interlibrary loan; no central cataloguing.

Lombardy (1978) (see also Milan Public Library, above): budget 11,500,000,000 lire; 1,188 of 1,546 communities have libraries serving about 10 percent of the 8,500,000 inhabitants; holdings 5,600,000 volumes and 12,300 current periodicals in public libraries (1975), about 14,500,000 more volumes in university and school libraries; interlibrary loan facilities; cataloguing center in trial state (1979).

Friuli-Venezia-Giulia: budget 300,000,000 lire; 219 libraries in 4 provinces with 1,250,000 population; holdings 2,500,000 volumes; has interlibrary loan, no central cataloguing.

Abruzzo (1978): budget not reported; 128 communities, 850,000 of 1,200,000 people served; holdings 1,500,000 volumes, 1,500 periodicals; three district systems share collections and catalogue books for 77 libraries in their districts.

East Sicily (1977) (provinces of Catania, Messina, Rugosa, Siracusa, comprising about 50 percent of Sicily's population): budget 253,000,000 lire, including value of gift volumes; 106 of 195 communities served (2,300,000 total population in the 195 communities); holdings 1,500,000 volumes, 2,510 periodicals; little interlibrary loan, plan for centralized cataloguing (1979).

School libraries frequently are under the jurisdiction of local public libraries as exemplified by Milan. School libraries generally have meager resources and, like libraries of other types in Italy, are often understaffed.

**Special Libraries.** The thousands of special libraries in Italy serve an enormous range of needs for contemporary materials, including all of the sciences, art, and professions. Many of these are affiliated with universities and are known as institute libraries. The most important special libraries—in number and kind—are primarily devoted to serving scholars in the humanities, history, literature, and philology. Their collections are particularly strong in the Middle Ages and the Renaissance. The national government controls some of the most prominent of the world famous libraries, such as the Biblioteca Medicea Laurentiana and the Casanatense.

Few libraries in Italy enjoy the benefits of computerization of any of their operations. An exception is a special library, the Institute of Legal Documentation in Florence, which provides computerized bibliographic services based on about 1,000 Italian law journals to lawyers, law students, and legislators.

**Vatican City.** The Biblioteca Apostolica Vaticana is a distinguished library with roots in the 13th century, but its modern origin more correctly dates from the 15th century. It has grown from a few hundred volumes to holdings of 700,000 printed works, 62,000 manuscripts, and tens of thousands of maps, prints, and other items. Major exhibition rooms are open to the public, but use of the collections is restricted to qualified scholars.

**Association.** Established in 1930, the Associazione Italiana Biblioteche (Italian Library Association) has 1,300 members participating in activities covering the spectrum of interest in librarianship. Working groups and conferences on education, legislation, automation, and networks have produced reports testifying to the intense interest in solving the many problems of Italian libraries.

**REFERENCES**

Ray L. Carpenter, "Contrasting Developments in Italian Libraries," *International Library Review* (1976), is an analysis of selected Italian libraries and librarianship as of 1974.

*La Pubblica Lettura in Toscana: Indagine Preliminare sulle Strutture Bibliotecarie degli Enti Locali al 1972* (Dipartimento Istruzione e Cultura, 1974), a highly detailed report on reading and libraries in Tuscany, unique in its comprehensiveness and its usefulness as a basis for library planning.

Rose Segre, "University Libraries in Italy: The Crisis Persists," *College and Research Libraries* (1974), is a concise report on the current status of academic libraries.

RAY L. CARPENTER

# Ivory Coast

Ivory Coast, a republic in West Africa, is bordered by the Gulf of Guinea on the south, Liberia on the southwest, Guinea on the northwest, Mali and Upper Volta on the north, and Ghana on the east. Pop. (1978 est.) 7,205,000; area 322,463 sq.km. The official language is French.

**National Libraries.** The Bibliothèque Nationale in Abidjan, the capital of Ivory Coast, was founded in 1968 with the merger of the holdings of the former territorial library and those of the Institut Français d'Afrique Noir in Abidjan. The building, dedicated in January 1974, includes conference and lecture rooms, reading rooms, a film library and screening rooms, a popular circulating collection, and a noncirculating research collection. In 1965 the holdings of the former territorial library numbered 6,000 volumes, increasing to 10,000 volumes and 650 current serials by 1974, and by 1977 to 21,000 volumes and 750 serials. Supplementing the Bibliothèque Nationale collection are the individual libraries maintained by the Assemblée Nationale and many of the cabinet ministries.

**Academic Libraries.** The principal academic library is the Bibliothèque Universitaire, on the main campus of the national university in an Abidjan suburb. The library is open only to students, faculty, and researchers affiliated with the university; however, students of other specialized colleges as well as individuals demonstrating a bona fide need may use the library after paying a nominal fee. The library has 61,000 volumes and 1,625 serials and can arrange international library loans with the stipulation that borrowers pay shipping costs.

Some university research institutes maintain their own specialized libraries. The library in the Institut d'Ethno-sociologie contains 4,200 volumes (300 in English) and 40 serials specializing in sociology, ethnography, and economic development. The holdings of the Institut de Linguistique Appliqué number 200 volumes and 28 serials pertaining to applied linguistics, African linguistics, and oral traditions. Additional libraries at the Ecole

**Table 1. Libraries in Ivory Coast (1976)**

| Type | Number | Volumes in collection | Annual expenditures (franc) | Population served | Professional staff | All staff (total) |
|---|---|---|---|---|---|---|
| National | 1 | 63,320[a] | CFA 1,500,000 | 921,000[b] | 16[b] | 43[b] |
| Academic | 11 | 91,790 | CFA 500,000[c] | N.A. | 16[d] | 36[d] |
| Public | 3 | 77,000 | CFA 2,000,000[e] | 1,094,000 | N.A. | 7[f] |
| Special | 24 | 65,093[g] | CFA 2,920,000[h] | N.A. | 14[i] | 32[j] |
| School | 89 | 60,000 | N.A. | N.A. | N.A. | N.A. |

[a]Includes holdings of the national library and the Assemblée Nationale's library.
[b]For the Bibliothèque Nationale.
[c]Total for one library.
[d]Total for four libraries.
[e]Budget of the Bibliothèque Centrale.
[f]For the Bibliothèque Centrale.
[g]Total represents holdings for 20 of the 24 libraries.
[h]Total for four libraries.
[i]Figures for six libraries.
[j]Figures for nine libraries.

Nationale Superieure de Travaux Publiques (3,000 volumes), the Ecole Nationale Superieure Agronomique, and the Ecole de Stastitique (1,300 volumes) also provide for specialized academic needs. The library of the Ecole Nationale d'Administration, serving both students and members of the national government, contains over 10,000 volumes and 100 serials as well as 500 documents and studies on Ivory Coast.

**Table 2. Archives in Ivory Coast (1976)**

| | |
|---|---|
| Number | 2 |
| Holdings | 1,500 linear meters |
| Professional staff | 15 |
| All staff (total) | 19 |

**Public Libraries.** In 1952 the colonial government established a municipal library in Abidjan. By 1963 it contained over 5,000 volumes. The library was reorganized in 1969 and by the end of the 1970's had over 50,000 volumes. In 1964, as part of a Unesco pilot project, the government installed a public library in one of the busiest markets in the Abidjan area. From a collection of 3,500 volumes in 1964 the holdings of the Bibliothèque Centrale de Lecture Publique grew to 19,000 volumes and 70 periodicals in 1976. The only other public library is the 8,000-volume collection of the Centre Culturel Jacques Aqua in Bouaké, the second largest city.

**Special Libraries.** The holdings of larger special libraries reflect the importance of agriculture for the development of Ivory Coast. The two technical libraries of the Office de la Recherche Scientifique et Technique Outremer (ORSTOM) and those of the Institut de Recherche Agronomique Tropicale et Cultures Vivrières (IRAT) at Bouaké, the Institut Français du Café, du Cacao, et Autres Plantes Stimulantes, and the Centre Technique Forestier Tropicale de la Côte d'Ivoire contain important works on plant and soil sciences, geology, ecology, and tropical agriculture. There is also an important geology library in the Societé pour le Developpement Minier de la Côte d'Ivoire. Other research institutes maintain smaller libraries having for the most part fewer than 500 volumes. The library of the Institut Africain pour le Developpement Economique et Sociale, however, includes over 30,000 volumes and 250 serials focusing on the social sciences and economic development. Also concentrating on economic development is the collection of the Bureau National d'Etudes Techniques du Developpement (BNETD), with 2,000 volumes and 60 serials. Finally, the French, German, and American cultural centers in Abidjan maintain libraries on the history and culture of their respective countries.

**School Libraries.** With the stated objectives of helping students with classwork, stimulating thought, and encouraging reading for pleasure, the government set up libraries in all secondary schools, though most of the libraries have fewer than 1,000 volumes. In 1973 there were 60,000 volumes divided unequally among the 89 secondary school libraries, with the lion's share going to the more prestigious, though not always larger, urban schools.

ROBERT E. HANDLOFF

# Jamaica

Jamaica, a parliamentary state, lies in the Caribbean Sea south of Cuba. Pop. (1978 est.) 2,115,000; area, 10,991 sq. km. The official language is English.

**National Library.** The National Library of Jamaica began with the enactment of the Institute of Jamaica Act (1978) and is a department of the Institute, founded in 1879. The West India Reference Library, established by the Institute in 1894, forms the nucleus of the collection of this national institution. In 1976 the collection included 29,000 books and pamphlets, 1,900 manuscripts, and other items totaling 280,000. It has been used extensively by scholars for historical research on Jamaica and the other West Indian islands.

**Academic Libraries.** The University of the West Indies, Mona, Kingston, has the primary academic library in Jamaica. It functions as a regional library, as it serves a regional institution. The main collection in 1977 totaled



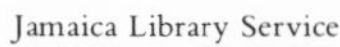
Jamaica Library Service

*The main building of the National Library of Jamaica, Kingston, opened in 1978 as part of the Institute of Jamaica, established in 1879.*

284,842, with 90,000 manuscripts, microforms, maps, and other items. The library is a depository for the printed publications of the United Nations.

The Medical and Science Libraries, with collections of 78,429 and 161,806, respectively (1977), are its two branches. There are also four independent libraries at the Mona Campus—the Institute of Social and Economic Research (1948), the Documentation Centre of the School of Education (1967), the Norman Manley Law Library (1963), and the Department of Library Studies (1963). The Library of the College of Arts, Science, and Technology, with a collection of 25,000 items, is the largest of the other academic libraries, which include the United Theological College, the School of Agriculture, and eight teacher training colleges.

**Public Libraries.** The Jamaica Library Service, established by an act of Parliament in 1949, provides a free public library service and is responsible for the operations of the Schools Library Service. The Service is organized from a coordinating headquarters in the capital city of Kingston with a network of service points consisting of 13 main libraries in each capital town, 135 branch libraries (94 of which are part-time), 50 book centers, and 238 bookmobile stops. Special services are provided to hospitals and correctional institutions, and a postal service is also provided in rural areas. In 1976, 2,478,871 books were circulated to 526,009 users. The stock includes 1,098,000 volumes, periodicals, pamphlets, filmstrips, slides, and records. Special collections include West Indian literature, horticulture, the theater, and foreign languages (French, Spanish, and German). Educational and cultural programs are conducted by all libraries.

The two Junior Centres of the Institute of Jamaica, Kingston, serve young people between the ages of 8 and 12. Their collections number over 25,000, and they provide a wide range of educational and cultural activities.

**School Libraries.** The Schools Library Service is administered by the Jamaica Library Service on behalf of the Ministry of Education. The Service for Primary Schools began in 1952 and was extended to the Junior Secondary Schools in 1969.

Five bookmobiles, with a stock of 2,000 books each operating from five regional centers, visit each primary and comprehensive school at least three times a year. At each visit teachers may select 200–1,000 books, depending on the school's enrollment and accommodation. The stock in 1976 totaled 551,928 and served an enrollment of 334,651 pupils.

The 80 Secondary School Libraries (formerly Junior Secondary Schools), unlike primary schools, all have organized library rooms. The total bookstock of these libraries was 136,310. There are also well-established libraries in many of the traditional high schools.

**Special Libraries.** In recent years much interest has been shown by business, industrial, and professional organizations in the provision of libraries. The largest of these is the Alcan Technical Information Centre attached to Alcan, one of the Bauxite Companies.

Many important libraries are attached to government ministries and agencies. These include those of Education and Agriculture, the Supreme Court, the Bureau of Standards, and the Scientific Research Council.

**Associations.** The Jamaica Library Association (1950) and the Commonwealth Library Association (1972) are headquartered in Kingston, and both maintain professional collections. LEILA THOMAS

## Jameson, J. Franklin
(1859–1937)

John Franklin Jameson—historian, teacher, editor, manuscript librarian, and administrator—was born September 19, 1859, in Somerville, Massachusetts, the son of John Jameson, a schoolmaster and lawyer, and his wife, Mariette Thompson Jameson. Jameson's intellectual promise and habits of hard work were evident in early boyhood. He was graduated from the Roxbury Latin School and, in 1879, as valedictorian from Amherst College. While in college he set course on becoming a historian. Unable to finance graduate study in Germany, he taught high school for a year before going to the newly established Johns Hopkins University. His Ph.D. in 1882 was the first history doctorate awarded there.

Present at the beginnings of the historical profession in the United States, and later of the archival profession, Jameson had the rare opportunity to found and shape important institutions. He was one of the founders in 1884 of the American Historical Association and in 1895 of the *American Historical Review,* which he edited with great distinction until 1928 (except for 1901–05).

For the two decades after taking his doctorate, Jameson held history professorships at Hopkins (1882–88), Brown University (1888–1901), and the University of Chicago (1901–05). But it was not as a teacher that Jameson made his mark.

On leaving Chicago, Jameson became the second Director of the Bureau of Historical Research of the recently (1902) founded Carnegie Institution of Washington. As an adviser to Carnegie's first President, Daniel Coit Gilman, Jameson had helped formulate Carnegie's historical programs, which centered on identifying, evaluating, and publishing guides to the archives of the federal government and of bodies of archival material abroad with bearing on American history. This work eventually made clear the abysmal state of the federal government's archival practices and the pressing need for an archives building and an appropriate agency to administer the whole enterprise. Jameson politicked actively for a quarter-century for an archival establishment and was rewarded for his efforts by the construction of the National Archives building in 1934.

In 1927 Jameson became the first incumbent of a chair of American history at the Library of Congress as well as Chief of the Manuscript Division. He actively enlarged the division's role in fostering scholarship by expanding its program of photocopying records from foreign institutions (made possible by the guides he had published at Carnegie) and by acquiring many important new collections. Jameson was responsible for the policy formulation of the Division but also supervised closely all the routine work of his staff.

Although Jameson's bibliography is lengthy, most entries were edited pieces, reports, or reviews; this remarkable historical statesman was far more intent on administering great projects than in producing large-scale interpretive works himself. Still, two of his books, *The History of Historical Writing in America* (1891) and *The American Revolution Considered as a Social Movement* (1926), were of considerable influence in their day and for some years after.

Jameson died September 28, 1937, while still occupying his posts at LC.

**REFERENCES**

Elizabeth Donnan and Leo F. Stock, editors, *An Historian's World: Selections from the Correspondence of John Franklin Jameson* (American Philosophical Society, 1956). Includes biographical sketch.

Ruth Anna Fisher and William Lloyd Fox, editors, *J. Franklin Jameson: A Tribute* (1965), memoirs by 14 contributors.

The major collection of Jameson's papers is in the Manuscript Division of the Library of Congress.

JOHN B. HENCH

# Japan

A constitutional monarchy of eastern Asia, Japan comprises an archipelago including the four main islands of Hokkaido, Honshu, Kyushu, and Shikoku. Pop. (1978 est.) 114,689,500; area 377,582 sq.km. The official language is Japanese.

**National Library.** The National Diet Library (NDL)—Kokuritsu Kokkai Toshokan—in the national capital, Tokyo, was formed under law in 1948 by combining the libraries of the upper and lower houses of the two-chamber legislature with the collections of the former Imperial Library. Serving first the informational needs of the national legislators, it also serves the nation as a whole in a variety of ways through its one department and six divisions, based on the U.S. Library of Congress model. The Research and Legislative Reference Department, and Administrative, Acquisitions and Serial Publications Processing, Circulation, Reference and Bibliography, and Interlibrary Services divisions maintain close association with the 33 NDL branch libraries of the government ministries and agencies. The law provides that all Japanese publications are to be deposited at NDL. This forms the basis of the national bibliography and other catalogue records used by libraries in Japan and abroad.

The National Diet Library's main collection exceeded 3,600,000 in 1977, and nearly 6,700,000 volumes are maintained when the collections of all the branches are included. The budget was approximately $16,000,000, nearly three times the amount spent in 1970. In 1977 the total acquisitions exceeded 217,000 volumes. NDL seats over 1,200 readers and was staffed by 845 full-time employees in the late 1970's.

The Library was moved to its permanent quarters adjacent to the National Diet in 1961. Constructed in two stages, the building was completed in 1968 and contains 73,674 sq.m. of floor space. Total stack capacity is 4,500,000 volumes. Pneumatic tubes deliver call slips from the main hall to the closed stacks, from which requests for in-house consultation of the collections are sent by vertical conveyors back to the main reading hall. Over 11,000 legislative reference inquiries are handled annually, and book circulation to the Diet exceeds 20,000 titles a year. About 150,000 reference inquiries were received from the general public during the period April 1977 to March 1978, and 9,550 volumes were loaned to domestic libraries during the same period. Two hundred thirty-five institutions receive NDL printed catalogue cards. Of the 5,100,000 cards prepared, 4,100,000 were distributed during the 1977–78 fiscal year. During that period 3,230,000 photocopies were made of original texts, and 239,000 hard copies were made from microforms. NDL has exchange relations with 636 organizations in 101 countries, including 35 international organizations.

Principal publications number 37, 9 of which are compiled by computer, and include the computer-generated Japanese National Bibliography, in both annual and weekly editions, accessions lists, directory of Japanese scientific periodicals, directory of special collections in Japanese libraries, and a large number of specialized catalogues, bibliographies, and abstracting services. Western books are processed by using LC MARC tapes. There is a central processing unit, and as of the late 1970's the staff had developed a number of subsystems that will lead ultimately to the "Japan MARC" for monographs with multicharacter data processing capacity. Some 2,006 *Kanji* (Chinese characters) as well as *Kana* (Japanese phonetic characters), Western alphanumerics, and other significant symbols and marks are available on keyboard. Most *Kanji,* composed of one or more component parts called "radicals," fall into one of 40 geometrical patterns. With the addition of 139 pure radicals, it is possible to construct *Kanji* that are not listed in the 2,006 keyboard *Kanji.* In addition to *Kanji* display terminals, a system developed by Nippon Electric Company is used for processing and typesetting of up to 5,717 different characters and symbols.

Theodore F. Welch

*The earliest library in Japan is thought to be the Yumedono (Hall of Dreams), established on the grounds of the Horyuji Temple near Nara in A.D. 702.*

**Academic Libraries.** As of 1977 there were 1,234 libraries housed in national, public (local), and private institutions of higher education, including junior colleges, over half of which are privately sponsored. The largest academic library in Japan is the University of Tokyo, part of the national academic system, with its general library and independent 29 faculty and institute libraries. Founded in 1877, the general library contained 768,000 volumes in 1977, of which 298,000 were in Western languages. More than 300 junior colleges support libraries. Important private university libraries include Tenri Central Library, with its superlative rare book collections; Keio University, Japan's largest private institution of higher education; and International Christian University, long held as a model of Western academic librarianship in Japan.

Academic libraries are not governed by legislation as are public and school libraries, and hence their structures and functions vary widely. Competition on campuses for book funds makes a strong centralized library system rare in Japanese academia. Faculties and research institutes enjoy an independent status and often have their own library budgets, staffs, and reading rooms. Few libraries are headed by a trained librarian. The post is usually awarded to a senior professor, often just before his retirement. There is a strict ranking order among national libraries, beginning with the University of Tokyo, followed by Kyoto University and five others, which form an elitist core of seven. Some 81 in total, national university libraries form their independent association and rarely deal with the private university libraries or local university library associations.

**Public Libraries.** The Library Law of April 1950 provides the basis for the establishment and activities of the 1,133 libraries (as of 1977) operated at the local level. Of this number, all but 32 are financed by public funds.

There are 388 bookmobile units operated by these libraries, primarily in cities. Within the 47 prefectures, including Okinawa, were 75 libraries. In 1977, 74 percent of all Japanese cities maintained libraries, while only 10 percent of towns and villages provided municipal library service. Qualified staff throughout public libraries averages 47 percent and serve some 113,226,000 constituents with 135,640,000 volumes at a ratio of 45 per 100 residents in prefectures and 74 volumes per 100 in cities. At the city-town-village level, an average of 4.7 percent of the residents were registered library borrowers in 1977.

The roots of modern public libraries can be clearly traced to the activities of national leaders who observed libraries in Western countries during Japan's dramatic attempt in the early 1870's to emulate foreign ways, institutions, and technologies. Beginning with the Shojakukan in 1872, libraries for public use were built quickly throughout the country until well into the 1920's. The basis for their existence, however, was markedly different in Japan from that in the West, where they had enjoyed centuries of developmental growth in response to a community-based need for sharing informational resources among an enlightened citizenry. By Western standards, public libraries have never fully developed or been utilized by the Japanese.

In addition to the factor of national administration, rather than popular demand, which led to the creation and development of modern public libraries, deeper traditions relating to book ownership have hindered library development. Premodern libraries were generally private, limited in use to a fixed clientele, and widely regarded as treasure houses of literary, religious, or family archives. The tendency toward book ownership by individuals who have little regard for or reliance upon institutional holdings still exists today.

**School Libraries.** The School Library Law of 1953 demanded that all schools in Japan establish libraries, and this requirement had nearly been universally achieved by the late 1970's. Fewer than 5 percent of the more than 30,000 schools had libraries in 1970. Although precise roles, activities, and collections are delineated by law, secondary schools have more adequate libraries than have elementary and middle schools. Public funding generally lags significantly behind private contributors for school library facilities. The law provides for the position of teacher-librarian, whose credentials indicate qualifications as both teacher and librarian. Schools have been reluctant to hire, and pay for, such highly qualified staff and have created a lesser post of school librarian in an attempt to economize.

Children's libraries exist also as elements within public libraries or as separate independent operations usually fostered by individuals in the community. While school libraries reflect the rigid curriculum of the institutions they serve, children's libraries, especially for preschoolers, offer free reading and a less controlled environment. The Japanese school system, with its emphasis on preparation for college entrance from the primary grades on, does not encourage extracurricular reading among students, who must learn lessons and memorize texts with an aim toward successful passing of examinations. School libraries and their staffs reflect this concentration in the restricted nature of their collections and services.

**Special Libraries.** Special libraries for literature, medicine, industry, economic development, and other purposes abound and numbered in excess of 2,000 by the late 1970's. The Japan Information Centre of Science and Technology (JICST), attached to the office of the Prime Minister in Tokyo, collects information from worldwide sources and functions as a major resource in the industrial and trade-centered Japanese economy. The Nomura Research Institute of Technology and Economics in Kamakura and the Mitsubishi Research Institute in Tokyo are two of the country's largest private research centers.

Aside from JICST, which abstracts about 2,000 journals dealing with science and technology, there were no commercially available data bases of Japanese-generated information of relevance to special libraries in 1978, with the exception of medical special libraries; a sophisticated cooperational information-sharing system is tied in with the U.S. MEDLARS program. Depending on the institution and area of research performed, reliance on Western source materials varies from 30 percent to 70 percent in all research undertaken. Informal methods of person-to-person contacts, meetings of professional societies, and sharing of limited editions of research reports comprise the mainstream of information flow among special librarians and researchers.

**Other Libraries and Collections.** The earliest library formed in Japan is believed to be the Yumedono ("hall of dreams") established in A.D. 702 by Prince Shōtoku on the grounds of the Hōryūji Temple near Nara. Many special collections and libraries of interest have since come into being. Untei, built by Isonokami no Yakatsugu (729–81), was a private collection that was made available to anyone wishing to read the primarily Chinese

**Table 1. Libraries in Japan (1976)**

| Type | Number | Volumes in collections | Annual expenditures (yen) | Population served | Professional staff | All staff (total) |
|---|---|---|---|---|---|---|
| National[a] | 34 | 6,596,021 | 5,034,359 | 111,937,000 | 1,135 | 1,224[b] |
| Academic[c] | 1,170 | 91,092,000 | 54,441,940,000 | 5,417,709 | 9,232 | 7,495[b] |
| Public[d] | 1,083 | 48,630,000 | 81,935,700,000 | 111,937,000 | 3,621 | 7,639 |
| School | 40,523 | 202,700,000 | 17,160,000,000 | 19,830,103 | 9,000 | 10,600 |
| Special | 2,006 | Books: 29,445,808 Periodicals: 491,546 titles | 27,041,728,000 | Admin/Engr.: 5,650,000 Researcher & Assts.: 28,593 | N.A. | 9,860 |
| Total | 44,816 | 378,955,375 | 180,584,402,359 | 254,800,405 | | 36,818 |

[a]Includes only National Diet Library and its branches in the government ministries, agencies, etc.
[b]Figures shown are totals for permanent and temporary staff; distinctions between professional and nonprofessional are not generally made in Japan.
[c]Shown are totals on national, public (local), and private university libraries, including 365 junior college libraries.
[d]Includes prefectural and municipal libraries.

classics and scriptures it contained. Although there are few who could take advantage of its openness, it is often referred to as Japan's first public library.

In addition to the private libraries of wealthy citizens, great warriors in later years came also to own reknowned collections. Two such collections are the Kanazawa Bunko and the Ashikaga Gakkō Bunko, both believed to date from the 13th century. Collections from these two "warrior libraries" *(buke bunko)* are still extant. The great shogun Ieyasu Tokugawa (1542–1616) maintained a variety of collections that have survived to the present, with the Shizuoka (Aoi) Bunko, Hōsa Bunko, and Nanki Bunko being among the most prominent. A summary of noteworthy historical collections is not complete without mention of the Seikadō Bunko, formed by two generations of the Iwasaki family of Mitsubishi fame. Likewise, the Sonkeikaku Bunko of the Maeda Clan contained treasures typical of the premodern library: Chinese classics, printed scriptures, old manuscripts, household records, Heian and Kamakura period books and works of art, as well as valued handicrafts of the Edo period.

Surviving to date in the Imperial system is the Zushoryō, first begun by edict to create an "imperial department of books," which today is known as the Shoryōbu on the palace grounds in Tokyo. The Jingū Bunko, Ise, is the main repository for the written heritage of the Shinto religion. Important modern collections are contained in the Nihon Kindai Bungakukan (Museum of Modern Japanese Literature), privately sponsored and maintained since 1967 in Tokyo. A counterpart government center for premodern literature exists in the form of the Kokubungaku Kenkyū Shiryōkan (National Institute of Japanese Literature), established in 1972 in Tokyo. The national archives, formed in 1971 to collect all post-1868 archival materials in one location, absorbed the collections and functions of the Naikaku Bunko (Cabinet Library).

**Table 2. Archives in Japan (1976)**

| | |
|---|---|
| Total number | 1 since 1971 |
| Holdings | 520,000 items |
| Annual expenditures | 64,485,000 yen |
| Professional staff | 47 |
| All staff | 53[a] |

[a]Figures shown are totals for permanent and temporary staff; distinctions between professional and nonprofessional are not generally made in Japan.

**Associations.** The Japan Library Association (JLA), formed in 1892, is the largest of all associations in membership (approximately 5,000 individuals and 1,000 institutions by the end of the 1970's) and represents the full spectrum of libraries by type. From 1906 JLA sponsored an all-Japan Conference and from 1907 published *Toshokan zasshi,* which carries the English subtitle *The Library Journal.* The articles are invariably written in Japanese. Of major concern to this monthly bulletin are study opportunities for members, foreign and local news, and articles of general appeal. Another major library association that survived World War II is the Japan Institution for Library Science, which traces its ancestry back to the very active and scholarly League of Young Librarians. *Toshokan-kai (Library World)* is published by the Institution bimonthly and generally carries articles of scholarly research in themes related to domestic librarianship.

The Special Libraries Association (JSLA) dates from March 1952. The National Diet Library and its many branches and government agencies serve as the backbone for the organization, and the headquarters has continuously been placed inside NDL. JSLA is divided into seven

Theodore F. Welch

*Central catalogue hall of the Tenri University Library, Tenri, Japan.*

district councils geographically distributed throughout the country, guided by a central council in Tokyo. District councils collect for their constituent members central government documents as well as local documents and related research material. JSLA publishes irregularly a bulletin that serves as a news and coordinating device among council members. *The Directory of Special Libraries* was published in its third edition in 1976. The Japan Medical Library Association (JMLA) loosely traces its origins back to 1927, when only three institutions formed an earlier effort. A half century later a league of over 50 medical libraries, composed only of institutional members, represents the membership. Several dental school libraries are included in the membership. The Association's headquarters is at Tokyo University Medical Library. Interlibrary cooperation effected by the JMLA is an outstanding example of sharing in Japan, and the most successful documentation activity in the country occurred under its sponsorship.

**REFERENCES**


Theodore F. Welch, *Toshokan: Libraries in Japanese Society,* (ALA, 1976), is the principal and most comprehensive resource, covering in detailed descriptions libraries of all types, the legal bases for libraries, and bibliographical sources in English and Japanese. See also by Welch articles in *Encyclopedia of Japan* (in preparation): 28 articles on specific libraries and important collections.

Louise Watanabe Tung, "Library Development in Japan," *The Library Quarterly* (1956), provides excellent coverage of premodern Japanese Library development.

George Chandler, "Japan," *Libraries in the East* (1971), is a noninterpretive outline of libraries by type.


THEODORE F. WELCH

## Jast, Louis Stanley
(1868–1944)



Louis Stanley Jast was one of the great pioneers in the development of the British public library service. He was an inventive practicing librarian, an engaging writer on librarianship, and the best speaker in the profession in his day.

Jast was born at Halifax, Yorkshire, August 20, 1868. He was the son of an exiled Polish army officer, and

Library Association

*Louis Stanley Jast*



his family name, which he changed in 1895, was Jastrzebski. Jast began his library career in 1887 at the Halifax public library, where he was thoroughly grounded in all the pettifogging routines that were then the very essence of public librarianship. Not until he became his own master was Jast able to exercise his latent talents.

In 1892 Jast became Librarian of the small town of Peterborough. Soon afterward he discovered the Decimal Classification, which in later years he listed among the books that had most influenced his life. Under its spell he waged his first campaign, for the wider use of close classification in public libraries. This gained him the friendship of James Duff Brown, pioneer of open access in British public libraries. Jast joined forces with Brown not only on the platform in propagating the elements of "the new librarianship" but also in the pages of the *Library World,* the independent monthly journal that Brown had founded and also edited.

In 1898 Jast became Librarian of Croydon, a rapidly growing commuter town on the fringe of Greater London. There, with the backing of a sympathetic committee and a hard-working staff, Jast created a truly dynamic library service. Under his direction the Croydon libraries became a workshop for new ideas. Among the many novelties were the card catalogue, the reference information service, the library bulletin, lectures, reading circles, exhibitions of books and pictures, and liaison with the local schools.

Running the Croydon libraries was not enough to absorb Jast's boundless energy. From 1905 to 1915 he served as Honorary Secretary of the Library Association (LA). No one was better qualified for the post, but not even Jast's sparkle and enthusiasm could bring the LA prosperity. Its membership and resources remained obstinately small. The two major events during Jast's term of office were the inauguration in 1910 of a register of qualified librarians and the framing and publication, in collaboration with the American Library Association, of the well-known *Cataloguing Rules: Author and Title Entries* (1908).

In 1915 Jast became Deputy Librarian of Manchester and in 1920 Chief Librarian. His main preoccupation as Chief was the planning of the new central library, which was long overdue. Jast's contention that one could have a useful library "with books and brains and any sort of protection against the weather" was broadly true, but for him it was rather a sour truth. The new building he planned and longed for was not opened until July 1934, by which time he had been retired for two and a half years. Throughout his service at Manchester the central library was housed in "temporary" huts.

Apart from its circular shape, due to the nature of the site, and its great circular reading room—modeled on the reading room of the British Museum, which Jast greatly admired—the most interesting feature of the new Manchester Central Library was the book stack. This formed the core of the building, and the public rooms were grouped around it and above it. Jast called it "an integrated stack" and was very proud of it.

Jast had given much time to studying the design of large libraries in Britain and America. His mature thoughts on the subject, first presented in a lecture in December 1926, were published in pamphlet form as *The Planning of a Great Library* (1927). Jast enunciated four principles of library planning: (1) a properly designed library should not be a building containing books but books in an appropriate setting; (2) there are limits to the value of subject departmentalization; therefore, the stock should be kept as intact as possible; (3) the book stack should be "the central nerve ganglion of the whole building"; and (4) in the collaboration between librarian and architect, the premier role should be assigned to the librarian.

With regard to the second principle, Ernest A. Savage, a zealous advocate of subject departments and busy at that time forming as many as he could in his awkward Victorian central library at Edinburgh, said that in planning the new Manchester library Jast had "raised the standard of specialization without exposing it to too strong a wind." Jast, however, had played a significant part in the development of subject specialization in Britain; at Croydon he had given some attention to the collection of local materials and had made the central library the base for an elaborate photographic survey of the county. During World War I he had made nationally a strong plea for the creation of special public library services for businessmen. In 1917 he organized a commercial library at Manchester and in 1922 followed it with a technical library.

Jast's final practical contribution to librarianship was the mobile library. In 1931 he converted a former single-decker bus (he called it a "bibliobus") to provide a library service for Manchester's new housing projects.

Jast's interest in librarianship continued throughout his retirement, when his particular interests were library cooperation, professional education, and the need for a centralized cataloguing bureau. He died on December 25, 1944.

Jast was a successful librarian who also had ambitions to become a successful author. His poetry and plays are of little merit, but he was an agreeable belletrist, and his professional writings were often spiced with genial witticisms.

Although Jast is undoubtedly an important figure in British library history, his achievements are not as fully appreciated as they should be. This is partly because the only biography of him is too slight to do him full justice and partly because he wrote no major work on librarianship and most of his essays and speeches remain uncollected.

**REFERENCES**

There is a short biography of Jast: W. G. Fry and W. A. Munford, *Louis Stanley Jast: A Biographical Sketch* (1966).

There are numerous obituary appreciations in the *Library World* (1945) and several in the *Library Association Record* (1945). Collectively they provide an excellent likeness of a librarian who was highly esteemed.

There is a vivid account of Jast's work at Croydon in Ernest A. Savage, *A Librarian's Memories* (1952).

The best account of the library Jast planned at Manchester is the one by his successor as City Librarian, Charles Nowell, "Manchester Central Library," *Library Association Record* (1934).

JAMES G. OLLÉ

# Jenkinson, Sir Hilary

(1882–1961)

(Charles) Hilary Jenkinson was founder and leader of the British archive profession.

He was born in London November 2, 1882, the son of William Wilberforce Jenkinson, and was educated at Dulwich College and at Pembroke College, Cambridge, being a Scholar of both. At Cambridge he was placed in the First Class of the Classical Tripos. In 1905 he sat the entrance examination for the Home Civil Service and was placed in the Public Record Office. For Jenkinson this was a vital moment of decision, whether or not to apply for transfer to another department offering more evident prospects of advancement. For reasons that he never disclosed Jenkinson elected to remain at the Public Record Office, and the national archives gained their greatest archivist.

During his earlier years in the Office, Jenkinson

worked mainly on medieval records (in particular those of the Exchequer of Receipt), reducing their chaos to order and developing, from study of their vicissitudes, the principles that he was later to expound for the administration of both ancient and modern records. From 1916 to 1920 he served as an Artillery Officer and on the General Staff, then returned to the direction and reorganization of the Literary Search Room (the "Round Room") that he had undertaken in 1912 and was to continue until 1929.

In 1922 he took charge of Repairs and Binding and, relinquishing the Round Room in 1929, took charge of the Repository. In these closely related fields his most important work as an Assistant Keeper was done. Under his direction the physical care of records—not only the skilled repair of damage and decay but also their prevention through proper conditions of storage—was developed to a craft and a science, and the two departments became a center of study, experiment, and teaching.

In 1938 Jenkinson was appointed Secretary of the Public Record Office, and as its principal administrator he devised and directed the wartime program of ARP (air-raid precautions), of dispersal of records and staff to improvised repositories in the country, and of their return after 1945. In 1947 he became head of the Office as Deputy Keeper; though postwar shortages frustrated many of his plans, he was able, by establishing the "intermediate repository" at Hayes, to lay the foundations for the Records Administration Division, the Office's most significant postwar development.

Though his official career was distinguished, it was Jenkinson's extracurricular activities that gave him his unique standing and reputation. From 1911 until 1935, and again in 1938 and 1949, he was Maitland Lecturer at Cambridge. From 1920 he was Lecturer, and from 1925 to 1947 Reader, in Diplomatic and English Archives in the University of London. During the same period he published, as Charles Johnson's collaborator, *English Court Hand* (1915) and independently *Palaeography and Court Hand* (also in 1915) and *The Later Court Hands in England* (1927). These lectures and writings established Jenkinson as a leading authority on palaeography and diplomatic, and as the exponent of a new theme, already latent in his notable work for the Surrey Record Society, that the study of administrative history is the key to all work on records.

The establishment in 1932 of the British Records Association carried Jenkinson's influence and reputation into wider fields. Jenkinson was a founder of the Association and, as its joint Honorary Secretary for 15 years and thereafter as Chairman of its Records Preservation Section, he personally drafted most of the Association's influential *Reports* and *Memoranda* and led the campaigns that *inter alia* established the *National Register of Archives* and, ultimately, a nationwide network of local record offices, besides saving countless archives from destruction.

All Jenkinson's extraofficial activities that related to archives (and few did not) were undertaken with the same boundless energy and conviction. Jenkinson was the original and most persistent advocate of the postgraduate diploma in Archive Studies at University College, London. Halfway between the official and the personal, and as important as either, was Jenkinson's appointment in 1943 as Archives Adviser to the War Office, in which capacity he planned and in part directed the rescue and preservation of archives in the war zones of Italy and Germany. In Italy the operation was successful, while in Germany a much more extensive program was less so; but in both countries his work served as the basis of postwar reconstruction and greatly augmented Jenkinson's international reputation.

Jenkinson was a prolific writer for print, though few of his publications were in book form. The monograph upon which his fame securely rests is the *Manual of Archive Administration,* first published in 1922. This treatise, the first and the latest to be based upon English experience and practice, became at once the authoritative guide to all British archivists. Revised, reissued, and supplemented but still not superseded, the *Manual* remains required reading for archivists everywhere. Nor is it any disservice to Jenkinson's memory to recall that Charles Johnson's *The Care of Documents* preceded the *Manual* by three years and that C. G. Crump's magisterial article "Record" in the *Encyclopaedia Britannica* was published in 1911. These men, with M. S. Giuseppi, were the young Jenkinson's mentors. Jenkinson was the youngest of the brilliant group who deduced and defined the principles of archival administration in England. He made it his task to examine these principles, to expound them with his own prophetic fervor, and to apply them in practice with a master's hand. No less he was the first of his English colleagues to perceive the relevance to native theory and practice of the manual of Müller, Feith, and Fruin, then accessible only in a French translation.

Jenkinson was a man abounding in energy, of mind and of body, most eloquent in all his causes and equally fertile of expedient. His Protean personality was not seen by all his contemporaries in the same guise; to an opponent Jenkinson could appear obstinate, unreasonable, devious. To those who enlisted under his banner Jenkinson was their most courageous, resourceful, and inspiring leader—able to evoke deep and lasting affection. In the years since his death old differences have been laid to rest, and his stature has steadily grown, as the founder and leader of the British archive profession.

Jenkinson was made a Commander of the Order of the British Empire (CBE) in 1943 and was knighted as Sir Hilary in 1947. He was an Honorary Fellow of University College, London, and received the honorary degree of LL.D. from the University of Aberdeen, to whose library he left the greater part of his books. He was President of the Society of Archivists, of the Surrey Archaeological Society, of the Surrey Record Society, and of the Jewish Historical Society. He was a Vice-President of the British Records Association and an Honorary Member of the Society of American Archivists. From 1947 until his death he was a Commissioner of the Royal Commission on Historical Manuscripts. He died at Arun House, Horsham, Sussex, on March 15, 1961.

**REFERENCES**

A bibliography of Jenkinson's writings (1909–56) by Roger Ellis and William Kellaway is printed in *Studies Presented to Sir Hilary Jenkinson,* edited by J. Conway Davies (1957), which includes also an important *Memoir* (unsigned, by H. C. Johnson, later Keeper of Public Records). Further "Recollections of Sir Hilary Jenkinson," by Roger Ellis, are printed in *Journal of the Society of Archivists* (1971). Jenkinson's own small archive of personal papers is accessible at the Public Record Office.

ROGER ELLIS



# Jewett, Charles Coffin
(1816–1868)

Trustees of the Boston Public Library
*Charles Coffin Jewett*

Charles Coffin Jewett's contributions to American librarianship are most durable. His career spanned the earliest days of the transition from the medieval to the modern in librarianship in America. Through his ingenuity and diligence, and his service in great institutions of national prominence in America, he was one of the founders of American librarianship. He was a logical thinker and was articulate in presenting his views. His perspicacity led to major innovations in librarianship that were proved of value in practice in three of the nation's leading libraries at their earliest period of modern growth. He helped crystallize the profession, and although he did not live to see the creation of the American Library Association in 1876, his support of the librarians' conference of 1853 was a catalyst for the permanent union.

Jewett was born in Lebanon, Maine, on August 12, 1816, one of several children of Paul Jewett, a New England minister. One of Jewett's brothers, John, achieved fame as the publisher of *Uncle Tom's Cabin*. Little is recorded about Jewett's early life, but following family influence and the normal route to education and employment, Jewett set out to gain a college education and to join the ministry. He entered Dartmouth College in 1831 but quickly transferred to Brown University, his father's alma mater, from which he graduated in 1835. He served briefly as preceptor at Uxbridge Academy in Massachusetts. In fall 1837 he entered Andover Seminary.

Jewett early evinced an interest in books and bibliography. As a student at Brown he and a classmate, William Lawton Brown, arranged, classified, and catalogued a collection of books belonging to one of the student societies. At Andover he assisted Oliver Alden Taylor, the Librarian, in the preparation and publication of the *Catalogue of the Library of the Theological Seminary*; as a result he was appointed Acting Librarian of the Seminary. Upon his graduation he became the Principal of Day's Academy in Wrentham, Massachusetts, but a few months later, in 1841, left to become Librarian at Brown.

Jewett was Brown's first full-time Librarian. Prior to his appointment it had been usual for a professor to hold that post. Brown's library program, however, had been expanded by its President, Francis Wayland. With an endowment of $25,000 for books and a new building, which the library shared with the University's chapel, the library program was too demanding to be managed as a part-time activity.

Jewett's first major task was to prepare and publish a new catalogue. It followed the plan of the Andover catalogue, being divided into two parts: (1) an author listing and (2) an alphabetical and classified subject index with cross references. It took two years to complete and was widely acclaimed for its arrangement and careful preparation.

The catalogue done, Jewett turned his attention to building the library collection. He traveled extensively in Europe, buying books and pamphlets and collections not only for the University but also for a few scholarly friends who entrusted him with funds to use at his discretion. Jewett was judicious and prescient in his selections, and the Brown University Library became one of the leading academic research libraries of its time.

Perhaps as important as book buying was Jewett's effort to learn more about bibliography. He spent time in England with Anthony Panizzi, Keeper of Printed Books in the British Museum. It is evident from his letters that Jewett formed important opinions about national libraries, bibliography, and all of the then-modern aspects of library science in this part of his trip.

Jewett returned to Brown in 1845. His book-buying feat placed him in the ranks of the leading scholar-bibliographers of his day. He joined the faculty at Brown and became a very popular professor of modern languages and literature.

All during Jewett's formative years as a librarian, events were transpiring in Washington, D.C., that would lead inevitably to his move to national prominence there. From 1835 to 1846 Congress had been arguing over the manner in which it could achieve the goal of the will of an English scientist, James Smithson, to operate an institution to "increase and diffuse knowledge among men." The opinion in Congress was strongly divided into two camps, one proposing the creation of a national library and the other the establishment of a scientific research and study agency. This division of opinion was transferred to the Regents of the agency, to be known as the Smithsonian Institution, when it was finally created in 1846.

The proponents of science seemed to prevail, and the Regents' choice for its Secretary and first chief operating officer of the Institution was Joseph Henry, a professor at Princeton University and then America's leading scientist. Several of the U.S. senators who were strong proponents of a national library, and who had been active in obtaining the legislation to establish the Smithsonian, served on its first Board of Regents. They kept the issue of the future of the Institution alive by promoting the appointment of an assistant secretary qualified to be the Institution's Librarian. As one of the best known and most energetic of American librarians, Jewett was the Regents' choice, and he entered their service in 1847.

The Regents were persuaded that they had full authority to spend the Institution's funds as they thought appropriate and never authorized the maximum budget for the library as allowed by congressional action. They devoted most of the funds in the early days to the construction of the first Smithsonian building, much to the dismay of both Henry and Jewett. With his usual devotion, Jewett managed to complete a list of the publications of the learned societies of the world; he established gift and exchange relationships with most of them, and by 1855, regardless of inner turmoil, the Smithsonian had thus acquired probably the finest library collection of these publications in the country.

Most of Jewett's attention, however, was focused on a novel and colossal plan for a national, centralized library catalogue production facility. In Jewett's time libraries generally printed their catalogues. Jewett devised a plan whereby the libraries could produce their catalogues from stereotype plates made and kept at the Smithsonian. Cataloguing copy would be provided by libraries, but duplicate cataloguing could be avoided by sharing the plates. The Smithsonian proposed to do the collating of entries and the printing of the catalogues.

An obvious requirement for the success of such a venture was a set of standard cataloguing rules. Here Jewett's acquaintance with Panizzi emerged, for Jewett's rules were based on Panizzi's own cataloguing rules. Along the way, in order to know his market, Jewett prepared the first major inventory of public libraries in the United States. The Smithsonian published his *Notices of Public Libraries,* prepared from descriptions provided by the libraries themselves, as an appendix to the 1851 *Annual Report* of the Regents of the Smithsonian.

Jewett described his cataloguing plan to the librarians of the United States at the 1853 librarians' conference, which he chaired. He noted that his plan could be carried out only by an agency at the national level, and that it could not be successful without the endorsement and cooperation of other libraries. The conference unanimously adopted resolutions acknowledging the need expressed by Jewett and supporting his national cataloguing plan.

His plan came to naught, however. The materials from which the stereotype plates were made warped and hence could not be made into a suitable printing surface. Of greater consequence, however, was the unwillingness of the Secretary of the Smithsonian to commit the Institution and its resources to the effort required to sustain a national library operation. In the end, with Jewett's departure from the Smithsonian, the chief advocate for a national library was without the national platform required for operating such an important national program. Still, every element of shared cataloguing and of national distribution of cataloguing copy from Washington, D.C., as it was finally put into place by the Library of Congress nearly 50 years later, was laid out in Jewett's plan.

The relationship between Jewett and Henry was never easy. Jewett assumed that he had been employed by the Regents as their direct assistant to head an independent library department. He refused to help Henry with any general duties and carried on a campaign among friends to overrule Henry's intent to make the Institution the national home for scientific research and publication. By 1854 Henry could no longer tolerate Jewett's actions, and with the Regents' approval he dismissed Jewett (January 1855).

Jewett remained prominent in American librarianship even after leaving the Smithsonian. He was employed at the Boston Public Library, first as a cataloguer, then as an acquisitions librarian, and finally as the Library's first Superintendent from 1858 until his death ten years later. At the Boston Public Library Jewett applied himself with his characteristic conscience, devoting his ingenuity to the problems of his library. As usual, his solutions to several key problems served as models for innovations in other libraries. Among other things he replaced the circulation record book with separate slips for each book circulated, thus introducing flexibility and management control of collections into what was formerly a cumbersome function. Under Jewett's direction the Library grew to over 150,000 volumes, second in size only to the Library of Congress. Jewett died on January 9, 1868.

**REFERENCES**

Joseph A. Borome, *Charles Coffin Jewett* (ALA, 1951).
Michael H. Harris, *The Age of Jewett: Charles Coffin Jewett and American Librarianship, 1841–1868* (1975).
Geoffrey Hellman, *The Smithsonian: Octopus on the Mall* (1967).

RUSSELL SHANK

# Joeckel, Carleton Bruns

(1886–1960)

As a librarian, Carleton Joeckel was a unique blend of practitioner and theoretician. In his research he never lost touch with the realities of his profession. As a teacher, he was distinguished by his ability not only to impart knowledge but also to maintain fruitful contact with his students. Carleton Bruns Joeckel bequeathed a twofold legacy to the library profession: his published works, which stand as a monument to his productive scholarship, and a generation of librarians imbued with his philosophy of free public library service for everyone.

Joeckel was born in Lake Mills, Wisconsin, January 2, 1886, and attended the University of Wisconsin, obtaining his A.B. degree in 1908. Having chosen librarianship as a career, Joeckel entered the New York State Library School in 1908 and completed the B.L.S. degree in 1910. His library career began in 1910 as secretary to the Librarian of the Saint Louis Public Library. In 1911 he moved to Berkeley, California, where he was Assistant Reference Librarian and Superintendent of Circulation of the University of California until 1914. Writing in 1936, Sidney B. Mitchell, Founder-Director of the University of California School of Librarianship, remembered young Joeckel as leaving "a permanent impression of a quick, alert body and mind, of a habit of not talking unnecessarily and of intolerance of vague, dreamy ideas and of shams of any kind." So favorable was Joeckel's impression on the Head of the University Extension Division (who was also Chairman of the Board of the Berkeley Public Library) that in 1914 he was offered the post of Librarian. Except for a two-year leave of absence (1917–19) for service in the Army in the United States and overseas, Joeckel remained Librarian until 1927.

According to Mitchell, during Joeckel's tenure,

> he put his library on the map, built up a professional staff, made it easy for his younger untrained college graduates to go to library school, encouraged ambitious members to try out their ideas, made it evident that a humanized as well as an efficient service was to be expected by his public, extended the service by new branches, built branch buildings and secured the passage of a building fund for a main library building (since erected), even though a bond issue for new school buildings was defeated.

It was during his years as Director of the Berkeley Public Library that Joeckel's interest in the training of librarians developed. Destined to become deeply committed to library education, Joeckel in his first experience in teaching was a lecturer in public library administration in the unit that was to become the School of Librarianship of the University of California.

Joeckel's career took a new direction when in 1927 he left California for full-time teaching at the University of Michigan. Joining the faculty of the Department of Library Science as Associate Professor, he was promoted to Professor in 1930. He strengthened the teaching faculty, chiefly in the areas of library administration and book selection. His contract with the University included the opportunity to pursue advanced study in political science, which culminated with a Master's degree in 1928.

On receiving an ALA fellowship, Joeckel took a year's leave of absence for advanced study at the University of Chicago Graduate Library School (1933–34). After obtaining his doctorate in 1934, he resumed his teaching post at the University of Michigan for another year. In 1935 he joined the faculty of the University of Chicago Graduate Library School, where he remained the next ten years.

During his Chicago years Joeckel's career flourished. The University of Chicago was the only institution in the country offering a doctoral program in librarianship at that time, and Joeckel's dissertation, *The Government of the American Public Library* (1935), was the first comprehensive study of the public library and governmental relations. This trail-blazing treatise won for Joeckel the confidence and respect of the professional library community. It laid to rest the skepticism of some practitioners who maintained that librarianship was not a sufficiently comprehensive field in which to pursue doctoral study. A perceptive observer of the American library scene and a supporter of the Ph.D. program in librarianship, Wilhelm Munthe, Director of the University of Oslo Library, asserted, "This treatise alone is sufficient documentary evidence in justifying the existence of the [Graduate Library] school," since it "placed American library research on a higher plane."

Joeckel quickly became immersed in the spirit of research and publication that pervaded the University. Beginning in 1937 Joeckel, in collaboration with faculty colleague Leon Carnovsky, undertook a survey of the Chicago Public Library and documented the findings and recommendations in *A Metropolitan Library in Action* (1940). Their report was hailed as "a source book on the methodology of public library research" because it provided a framework for an objective approach to the study of problems in public libraries of all sizes. In 1938 Joeckel's report *Library Service,* prepared for President Franklin D. Roosevelt's Advisory Committee on Education, was released by the U.S. Government Printing Office.

Joeckel's expertise in the theory and practice of librarianship brought him in 1940 an invitation from the newly appointed Librarian of Congress, Archibald MacLeish, to serve as Chairman of the Librarian's Committee, whose charge was to make a comprehensive survey of the processing departments of the Library of Congress. MacLeish characterized the confidential report submitted by the Committee that Joeckel chaired as "one of the most important documents in the history of the Library." He used the recommendations of the Committee as the framework for a complete reorganization of the processing operations.

Of the many facets of librarianship to which Joeckel gave his attention there was none that he believed in more

ALA

*Carleton Bruns Joeckel*

firmly or advocated more ardently than the concept of larger units of library service. As early as 1929 he had introduced this concept, an audacious one at that time, at the annual meeting of the Michigan Library Association. Three years later he put this perspective into sharp focus in a provocative address given before the ALA Council and published in the ALA *Bulletin* (1933):

> The typical public library unit is still so small and weak as to be seriously lacking in administrative efficiency, and the area it serves is unnecessarily circumscribed. . . . [The librarian] has been so absorbed in the library problems of his own town or city that he has overlooked the fascinating possibilities of expansion of the units of library service. . . . Sweeping changes in the complicated structure of local government are being recommended on all sides. The public library must adapt itself to them.

Throughout his career, Joeckel was actively involved in professional organizations. Recognition of his charismatic leadership came early in his career, as evidenced by the offices he held. He served as President of the California Library Association (1919–20) and of the Michigan Library Association (1930–31). He was a member of the Illinois Library Association's Executive Board (1935–45) and of the American Library Institute (1937–45). Joeckel joined the American Library Association in 1910, the year in which he graduated from the New York State Library School. Although he was to participate in many committee activities during the next 40 years, probably the most constructive was those of the Federal Relations Committee and of the Post-War Planning Committee, of which he was Chairman.

Joeckel was a staunch champion of federal aid to libraries. His conviction that all citizens in a democratic society are entitled to have free access to adequate library resources and services permeated his thinking and writing. Joeckel advocated a nationwide program of library service to be funded jointly by the federal, state, and local governments. "Without federal aid," Joeckel wrote with characteristic forthrightness, "the establishment of a national minimum standard of library service is quite simply and literally impossible."



Joeckel played a major role in the establishment in 1937 of the Library Services Division in the Office of Education, the first federal agency established with the specific responsibility for fostering a national program of library development. He was the motivating force behind the passage of the Library Services Act in 1956.

As Chairman of the Post-War Planning Committee, Joeckel was the chief architect of the *ALA Post-War Standards for Public Libraries* (ALA, 1943) and (with Amy Winslow) the author of *A National Plan for Public Library Service* (ALA, 1948), prepared for the Committee on Post-War Planning.

Some of Joeckel's most significant writing appeared as papers in the proceedings of library institutes: "Realities of Regionalism" in *Library Trends* (papers presented before the GLS Institute, 1938); "Library Extension Today" in *Library Extension; Problems and Solutions* (papers presented before the GLS Institute, 1946); "Service Outlets as the Reader Sees Them" in *Reaching Readers: Techniques of Extending Library Services* (papers presented at the Library Institute sponsored by the University of California School of Librarianship and the ALA Library Extension Division, 1947). A noteworthy article entitled "National Leadership from Washington," written in collaboration with Willard O. Mishoff, appeared in *The Library of Tomorrow* (ALA, 1939). Joeckel's editorial accomplishments were also impressive. They include: *Current Issues in Library Administration* (papers presented before the GLS Institute, 1938), *Library Extension, Reaching Readers, Post-War Standards for Public Libraries,* and his contributions to *The Library Quarterly* as Associate Editor from 1936 to 1945 and as Advisory Editor from 1946 to 1959.

Through his extensive writings and other professional activities, Joeckel made a notable impact on the American library scene in the 1930's and 1940's, but it was through his teaching and his influence on his students that he contributed most significantly to the library profession. From his initial venture into teaching at the University of California in the 1920's to his return to the Berkeley campus in the mid-1940's, Joeckel's concern was focused largely on his students. His intellectual vigor and personal integrity earned their respect; his appealing and vibrant personality won their affection. A demanding professor, Joeckel expected his students to measure up to his standards. His seminars were stimulating experiences, challenging his students to critical thinking. Joeckel was major professor to many doctoral candidates who went out in all directions from Chicago to assume positions of high professional responsibility.

With the retirement of Louis Round Wilson in 1942, Joeckel was appointed Dean of the Graduate Library School, and Leon Carnovsky, a faculty colleague, was appointed Assistant Dean. In spite of war-born personnel shortages, Joeckel maintained the School's traditional strength in advanced seminars, research, and publishing. During his deanship he sponsored three summer institutes: The Library in the Community (1943); Library Extension: Problems and Solutions (1944); and Personnel Administration in Libraries (1945).

To carry out his plan of devoting some of his later years to research and writing, Joeckel resigned from his administrative post at GLS in 1945 and returned to Berkeley. Still vigorous in health, he resumed academic pursuits at the University of California by joining the faculty as Professor of Librarianship. Four years later ill health forced him to take a leave of absence, and one year later, in 1950, he retired for a second time.

Recognition of Carleton Joeckel's professional accomplishments came in the form of various honors. The American Library Association conferred upon him the first James Terry White Award for his notable professional writing (in 1938) and the Joseph W. Lippincott Award for his distinguished service to the profession (in 1958). Honorary life membership in the Association was conferred upon him in 1954.

Joeckel died April 15, 1960, in Oakland, California.

MARY LUELLA POWERS

## Jones, Virginia Lacy
(1912– )

Virginia Lacy Jones, library educator and leader, received the 1973 Melvil Dewey Award and the 1977 Joseph W. Lippincott Award, both bestowed by the American Library Association for distinguished services to the profession. Each award may be viewed as a fitting tribute to a distinguished career. From the time she entered the profession, her personal commitment, desire to excel, and ability seemed to destine an important role in the future development of library services. She became the second Afro-American to receive the Ph.D. in Library Science.

Jones was born on June 25, 1912, in Cincinnati, Ohio. The daughter of Edward and Ellen Louise (Parker) Lacy, she moved with her family to Clarksburg, West Virginia, where she attended public school. Her junior and senior high school years were spent in Saint Louis, Missouri, in order to facilitate her entry into Stowe Teachers College, but instead she entered Hampton Institute (Virginia). She received a Bachelor of Science in Library Science there in 1933 and later the Bachelor of Science in Education.

Her professional experience was begun at Louisville Municipal College, the Negro branch of the University of Louisville. There she met Rufus E. Clement, President of the College, who had a significant influence on her career. In 1937 she received the first of two fellowships from the General Education Board, allowing her to complete a Master in Library Science degree at the University of Illinois in 1938 and a Doctorate at the University of Chicago in 1945.

When Clement moved to Atlanta University as President in 1938, he offered her a position as cataloguer. She became a part of Clement's plan for a library school to replace the recently closed Hampton Institute Library School. Moving to Atlanta in 1939, she was involved in the planning that led to the opening of the library school in 1941. She served on the faculty until 1945, when she was appointed Dean.

She was supervisor of the Prairie View Regional Summer Training Center for librarians, one of four sponsored by the General Education Board from 1936 to 1939. While working at Louisville Municipal College, she, along with Ann Rucker, spearheaded the establishment of the Library Section of the Kentucky Negro Education Association. Following her move to Atlanta, she worked in concert with Mollie Huston Lee of Raleigh, North Carolina, and Charlemae Rollins of Chicago to raise publishers' awareness of negative images of blacks in children's books. She also assisted in the establishment of a Field Service Program, sponsored by the Carnegie Corporation of New York, which brought consultant services to libraries serving Negroes in several southeastern states.

Additional professional activities have included four terms as a member of the ALA Council and one term as a member of the Executive Board, Association of American Library Schools (Secretary-Treasurer, 1948–54, Board of Directors, 1960–64, President, 1967), Beta Phi Mu, and many other associations and projects. Activities outside the library profession include work for the National Endowment for the Humanities, the Southern Association of Colleges and Schools, Atlanta Area Teacher Education Service, Atlanta Sister City Project, Delta Sigma Theta Sorority, and Atlanta University Women's Club.

A. P. MARSHALL

# Jordan

Jordan, a constitutional monarchy in southwest Asia, is surrounded by Syria on the north, Iraq on the east, Saudi Arabia on the east, southeast, and south, the Gulf of Aqaba on the south, and Israel on the west. Pop. (1978 est.) 2,971,000; area (including Israeli-occupied territory from the 1967 war) 95,396 sq.km. The official language is Arabic.

**National Library.** Jordan does not have a national library or a depository law, but there are some regulations concerning the delivery of copies of all new publications to the Department of Publications at the Ministry of Information. This is in compliance with the Publications Law and not with legal deposit regulations. Also, the Publications Services at the Ministry of Education receives a copy of almost all publications issued in the country. Registration of the nationally produced publications in an annual list has been performed by the Jordan Library Association since 1969. The *Bulletin of Arab Publications* (1977), issued annually by the Arab League Educational, Cultural and Scientific Organization, listed 104 Arabic titles as the Jordanian book production in 1975.

**Academic Libraries.** The principal academic library is the Jordanian University Library, established in 1962. Its general collection numbers about 150,000 volumes and over 1,700 periodicals. The University Library is a depository for all publications issued by the United Nations, Food and Agriculture Organization, and the World Health Organization. Monthly accession lists have been issued by the University Library since 1969.

Theodore F. Welch

*American Cultural Center Library, Amman, Jordan.*

**Public Libraries.** The country possesses eight municipal public libraries in the major principal towns. Noteworthy among them is the one in the capital city of Amman, founded in 1960. The book collections total about 50,000 volumes in Arabic and English and some 260 periodicals. It houses two separate sections for children and the blind. The second major public library in Jordan is in the city of Irbid; it was founded in 1957 and possesses about 12,000 volumes.

**School Libraries.** The Library Section at the Ministry of Education serves school libraries in the country. Only the major secondary schools possess libraries with modest book collections. They do not have standardized procedures, furniture, and equipment. School libraries are mostly managed by personnel without professional qualifications.

**Special Libraries.** About 26 special libraries were founded in the 1960's and 1970's, mainly in Amman. They serve the wide interests of researchers, scholars, and government officials in the country. Noteworthy are those of the Royal Scientific Society (founded in 1970), the Institute of Public Administration (1968), the Center of Building Materials (1973), the Industrial Development Bank (1969), the Jordanian Central Bank (1964), the Chambers of Commerce (1962), the National Planning Council (1965), the Ministry of National Economics (1967), the Authority of National Resources (1966), the Ministry of Industry and Commerce (1966), the Ministry of Finance (1973), and the Jordanian Petroleum Refinery Company (1962).

A National Documentation Centre was established under the responsibility of the Ministry of Culture and Youth in Amman according to the legislation of October 1975. Also, the Ministry of Education established the Educational Documentation and Publication Centre to serve educators, researchers, students, administrators, and foreign organizations. Both documentation centers offer local consultation, loan, SDI, translation, preparation of bibliographies, and inquiry services through traditional nonconventional methods.

**Association.** The Jordan Library Association (JLA) was founded in 1963. Considered the most active professional library association in the Arab world, it collects documents, publishes bibliographies and directories, and organizes training programs and seminars. JLA disseminates professional information through a quarterly library journal *(Rissalat Al-Maktaba),* issued from 1965. The Association published a directory of libraries in Jordan and an adaptation of the *Anglo-American Cataloging Rules* in

1970. The *Palestinian-Jordanian Bibliography* is compiled by the JLA and has been published annually as one issue of its journal since 1970. The *Bibliography* is considered the national bibliography of Jordan.

MOHAMED M. EL HADI

# Kenya

Kenya, an independent republic in eastern Africa, is bounded by Sudan and Ethiopia on the north, Somalia on the east, Tanzania on the south, and Uganda on the west. Pop. (1977 est.) 14,337,000; area 590,367 sq.km. The official languages are Swahili and English.

Kenya has no national library in the conventional meaning of the term. The Kenya National Library Service runs a nationwide public library service with a headquarters in Nairobi. Most scholarly researchers use the University of Nairobi Library Service. Both of the libraries are legal deposits for Kenyan publications.

**Academic Libraries.** The major academic library is the University of Nairobi Library Service, comprising the main university library and eight sublibraries in the various campuses of the university. The main library covers the fields of commerce, social sciences, humanities, and engineering, while libraries in other campuses serve the sciences, medicine, agriculture, and veterinary medicine. The total bookstock in 1978 was about 260,000 volumes and 3,500 current periodical titles.

Kenyatta University College is a separate but constituent college of the University of Nairobi, housing the Faculty of Education. The bookstock of its library in 1978 was approximately 80,000 volumes, with 1,300 periodical titles.

There are in addition academic libraries of various sizes in the main postsecondary training institutions such as Egerton College (agriculture), Kenya Institute of Administration, Kenya Polytechnic, Kenya Science Teachers College, Kenya Technical Teachers College, and the Mombasa Polytechnic.

Africana Publishing Corp.

The McMillan Memorial Library, Nairobi, founded in 1931, is the main library of the Nairobi City Library Services.

**Public Libraries.** The public library services are provided through the Kenya National Library Services Board Act, which empowers a government-appointed board to equip and operate libraries in the country. In 1978 the Service was operating eight libraries in the country, including the headquarters library in Nairobi, with plans to start two new libraries each year until there is one in each of Kenya's 50 districts and municipalities. The bookstock of the entire Service in 1978 was about 170,000 volumes, of which 60,000 are in the headquarters library.

The Nairobi City Council operates a separate City Library Service with a main library and two branches. The City Library Service had a bookstock of 150,000 volumes in 1977. Other libraries open to the public are operated by foreign missions, notably the American Library in Nairobi; the British Council Libraries in Kisumu, Mombasa, and Nairobi; and the French, German, and Indian Information/Cultural Centres in Nairobi. Their stocks range from 7,000 to 16,000 volumes.

**School Libraries.** There is no organized national school library service. Of the nearly 1,400 secondary schools in 1977, only about 420 were maintained or assisted with government grants. The older and larger libraries have 6,000 to 10,000 volumes, and many of the others have small classroom collections. The large majority of the rest are Harambee (self-help) Schools, and most of them have no libraries at all. Practically none of the 8,500 primary schools have libraries, although some maintain small class collections.

All primary teacher training institutions have libraries, although their sizes differ greatly, from 2,000 volumes in the smallest to 18,000 in the largest. The Kenya Institute of Education Library assists in arranging short courses for staff running libraries in schools and teacher training colleges.

**Special Libraries.** The *Directory of Libraries in Kenya* (1977) lists 55 special libraries, mainly in ministries and departments of government, research organization, and training institutions of various kinds. The largest, and one of the oldest, is the Ministry of Agriculture Library with over 70,000 volumes and 800 periodicals. Other notable special libraries are those in the following organizations: Central Bureau of Statistics, 26,000 volumes; High Court Library, 60,000; Kenya Agricultural Research Institute, 40,000; Mines and Geology Department, 26,000; National Archives, 25,000; National Public Health Laboratories, 20,000; and Veterinary Research Laboratories, 42,000.

International organizations with offices in and around Nairobi have established libraries, including the United Nations Environment Programme (UNEP), the International Laboratory for Research on Animal Disease (ILRAD), and the International Centre of Insect Physiology and Ecology (ICIPE). First established in the 1970's, their libraries are still modest in size, but they have grown rapidly and their holdings are of great importance.

**Association.** The East African Library Association was formed in 1956, with most members located in Nairobi. In 1962 it began publishing the *East African Library Association Bulletin,* and in 1964 branches were formed in Uganda and Tanzania. At a 1972 conference it was decided that the East African Library Association should be disbanded and that each country should organize its own national association. Thus, the Kenya Library Association was founded in 1973.

**Libraries in Kenya (1978)**

| Type | Number | Volumes in collections | Annual Expenditures (shilling) | Population served | Professional staff | All Staff (total) |
|---|---|---|---|---|---|---|
| Academic | 8 | 450,000 | shs.10,000,000 | 10,000 | 40 | 200 |
| Public | 18 | 380,000 | N.A. | 1,000,000 | 25 | 130 |
| School | N.A. | N.A. | N.A. | N.A. | N.A. | N.A. |
| Special | 55 | 700,000 | N.A. | N.A. | 20 | 150 |

Sources: Directory of Libraries in Kenya; various Annual Reports.

Membership is open to individuals and institutions connected with the administration and management of libraries or interested in the Association's aims and objectives. It publishes a journal entitled *Maktaba* (the Kiswahili word for "libraries") and had 210 members in 1978.

**REFERENCE**

Anna-Britta Wallenius, *Libraries in East Africa* (1971).

JOHN NDEGWA

# Keppel, Frederick Paul

(1875–1943)

Frederick Paul Keppel, foundation administrator, was a leading figure in the growth of American libraries. He was born July 2, 1875, in Staten Island, New York, and spent most of his early years in Yonkers, New York, where he attended the public schools. His parents, Frederick and Frances Keppel, were Irish immigrants. Upon completing high school, he worked for two years in his father's print-selling shop and then entered Columbia University, graduating with an outstanding academic record in 1898. He obtained a position with Harper and Brothers in the same year but thought himself unsuited for the publishing field.

In 1900 he took a position as Assistant Secretary at Columbia University, rapidly advancing to Secretary of the University in 1902 and then to the deanship of Columbia College in 1910. Wanting to serve his country in World War I but too old at 42 to volunteer for military service, Keppel went to Washington as a confidential clerk in the War Department. His administrative talents and ability to deal with people tactfully were quickly noticed by his superiors, and within a year he was made Third Assistant Secretary of War. After the war he held administrative posts with the American Red Cross (1919–20), in Paris with the International Chamber of Commerce (1920–22) and for a brief period was Secretary of the Plan of New York. In December 1922 he was elected President of Carnegie Corporation of New York but did not actually assume his duties until October 1923.

Keppel was the fourth President of Carnegie Corporation of New York, an educational philanthropy whose name is closely associated with the early growth of libraries in the United States and abroad and with the nurturing and development of the library profession.

His earlier positions had given Keppel the understanding and skills to shape the foundation's policy, philosophy, and programs for the 18 years he was President, 1923–41. Because the Carnegie staff was quite small, he made extensive use of outside advisers and expertise. He was frank, but warm and courteous, concise, a persuasive speaker, and he hated bores. He rarely put off decisions. His grantmaking was sometimes criticized for ranging too widely and not demonstrating any particular strategy, but he saw his role as being the administrator of a public trust, which made it encumbent upon him to dispense allocations in a variety of subject areas and projects and to do so fairly and representatively.

Libraries, particularly public libraries, he saw as among the major facilities for lifelong learning. Although he did not initiate the Corporation's relationship with the American Library Association, Keppel depended heavily on the ALA to identify needs and to develop programs that would enhance librarianship and service to the public. Andrew Carnegie had started that relationship and actually gave the Association its original endowment grant of $100,000 in 1902. During Keppel's tenure $86,000,000 was given away; of that amount, approximately $30,000,000 went for library projects, and over $3,000,000 of that went directly to the ALA for its activities. Included in this sum were additional endowment grants of $2,000,000 (paid 1926–33). This kind of support for the Association and for a diverse group of library projects was part of the Corporation's long view regarding libraries.

*Frederick Paul Keppel*

Carnegie Corporation of New York

Three commissioned evaluative reports, two by well-known and respected scholars Alvin S. Johnson and Charles C. Williamson and one by Carnegie staff member William S. Learned, contributed immeasurably to the Corporation's ultimate decision to revise its giving policy with respect to libraries. Johnson's 1919 report carried the recommendation that the Corporation cease providing assistance to communities for the construction of library buildings and that funds instead be made available for upgrading the training of librarians and for improving services. Williamson examined the training of librarians and concluded that what was needed was university training instead of that provided by public libraries, and that a library school should be established that would offer graduate-level courses. Learned specifically recommended that the ALA expand its services to librarians and that the foundation finance demonstration projects that would represent innovations in library service, particularly to rural communities. Accordingly, the Corporation provided the funds to set up the first graduate school of library science at the University of Chicago in 1926, with an endowment grant of $1,000,000. It made grants for training for librarianship, for book purchases to colleges and universities, for various kinds of experimental service projects, and for the development of other library schools. The ALA, assisted by Keppel, worked closely with the colleges and other organizations to implement many of these other programs and to strengthen the Association itself.

After retiring from the Corporation in 1941, Keppel became a member of the War Relief Control Board in Washington and still later a member of the Board of Appeals on Visa Cases at the Department of State. He remained as an educational consultant to the foundation.

Throughout his life Keppel gave innumerable speeches and lectures and wrote many books. His published works include *Columbia* (1914), *The Undergraduate and His College* (1917), *Education for Adults and Other Essays* (1926), *The Foundation* (1930), *The Arts in American Life,* with R. L. Duffus (1933), and *Philanthropy and Learning* (1936). He received honorary degrees from a number of distinguished colleges and universities including Harvard, Columbia, Michigan, Pittsburgh, and Toronto.

Keppel died September 8, 1943.

**REFERENCE**

Florence Anderson, *Carnegie Corporation Library Program, 1911–1961* (1963).

GLORIA PRIMM BROWN

## Kesavan, B. S.

(1909– )

Bellary Shamanna Kesavan, Indian library educator and administrator, was Librarian of the National Library, Calcutta, 1947–62, and first Director of the Indian National Documentation Centre (INSDOC), New Delhi, 1963–69. He was born on May 10, 1909, in Mylapore, Madras, India. He was educated in Mysore and London, where he took an M.A. in English Literature at the University of London and earned a Diploma in Librarianship at the School of Librarianship and Archives, University College, London. He also had advanced training in Sanskrit and German.

Kesavan taught English at Mysore University (1929–44) and was Assistant Secretary of the Council of Scientific and Industrial Research in New Delhi, 1944–46. He served as educational adviser to the Ministry of Education in New Delhi from 1946 to 1947. Kesavan provided outstanding leadership to the Indian library and information community for more than two decades. The two national institutions he headed, the National Library in Calcutta and INSDOC of the Council of Scientific and Industrial Research (CSIR), provide evidence of his skill for building and organization. From 1947 to 1962 the National Library was developed from a mere storehouse of books to an active organization with national stature and international recognition. Apart from the tremendous growth of the document collection through purchase, gift, exchange, and deposit and the generation of new services for users, the retrospective bibliographical projects of the National Library for different subjects such as Indian anthropology, Indian botany, and Indian literature were significant contributions. Another important bibliographic project that was planned and brought out under the editorship of Kesavan for the Sahitya Akademi was the selective retrospective bibliography of books published from 1901 to 1953 on humanities in all the principal languages of India including English. Another achievement was the launching, in 1956, of the *Indian National Bibliography of Current Indian Publications,* a landmark in India's bibliographic history. Kesavan's other major contribution was the development of the Indian National Scientific Documentation Centre (INSDOC), which was established with technical support from Unesco. In 1963 he became the first Director of INSDOC, which was until then under the administrative control of the National Physical Laboratory. Kesavan went about his new task with imagination and creativeness. The initiation of the National Science Library, the vigorous effort for the compilation of the *National Union Catalogue* of scientific serials to integrate and consolidate national resources and to create a computerized data base, starting of an advanced training course in documentation and reprography, the publication of *Indian Science Abstracts,* development of programs to introduce computer-based information services, providing improved facilities for printing and reprographic services, building up translation potential, and setting up of the INSDOC Regional Centre at Bangalore were some of the major contributions during his tenure from 1963 to 1969.

He also gave leadership, direction, and advice to the development of library documentation and information services in Council of Scientific and Industrial Research Laboratories and many research and development institutions, universities, and public sector undertakings. In effect he sowed seedlings for a national information system for science and technology.

Kesavan's international activities were also distinguished. He was the Vice-President of the International Federation of Documentation from 1964 to 1966, a member of the International Advisory Committee on Bibliography, Documentation, and Terminology of Unesco, and a member of the Expert Committee for Organizing the Library and Documentation in Unesco. He directed the Unesco Regional Seminar on the Development of National Libraries in Asia and the Pacific Area at Manila in February 1964.

Among his publications are a book on the national library (1961) and a small monograph on *Documentation in India* (1969), an abridged version of which was published in *Library Trends* (1969).

After retirement from his official career in 1969, Kesavan served international organizations like the United Nations Development Programme and the World Health Organization. He continued to work thereafter with enthusiasm for the cause of libraries and librarianship.

T. N. RAJAN

*Frederick Gridley Kilgour*

Arthur Plotnik

## Kilgour, Frederick Gridley

(1914– )

Frederick G. Kilgour, library administrator, lecturer, writer, and editor, is best known as head of OCLC—the national shared cataloguing system that pointed to a new era in librarianship. He was born January 6, 1914, in

Springfield, Massachusetts, and he entered Harvard College in 1931. He received his baccalaureate degree four years later. In his senior year at Harvard he was appointed Circulation Assistant in the Widener Library, where he remained for seven years, eventually becoming Chief of the division. During the latter summers of this period he attended the School of Library Service at Columbia University.

Called to war duty in 1942, Kilgour moved to Washington, D.C., where except for overseas service he remained for almost six years. Until 1945 he served in the Office of Strategic Services, as Executive Secretary of the Interdepartmental Committee for the Acquisition of Foreign Publications, attaining the naval rank of lieutenant (j.g.) and earning the Legion of Merit. For the following three years he was Deputy Director of the Office of Intelligence Collection and Dissemination in the U.S. Department of State.

In 1948 Kilgour returned to academic life as Librarian of the Yale University School of Medicine, a position he held until 1965. During these years he wrote and lectured extensively in both librarianship and the history of science and technology, and became active in the Medical Library Association (Secretary-Treasurer, 1950–52), the American Library Association, and other professional organizations. In 1961 he was a prime mover in one of the major early library automation efforts, the Columbia-Harvard-Yale Medical Libraries Computerization Project. As Yale's first Associate University Librarian for Research and Development between 1965 and 1967, he oversaw that library's entry into automation studies and processes.

In 1967 Kilgour was called to what appeared to many at the time to be a most unprepossessing assignment but that later proved to be a development of great significance to American librarianship, the directorship of the Ohio College Library Center (OCLC). Technically a creature of the Ohio College Association, OCLC had actually been conceptualized two years earlier by Kilgour and Ralph Parker as consultants to the OCA, and he now found himself brought west to implement his own recommendations. Building from his successes and failures in automation at Yale, Kilgour was soon able to deliver batch-processed catalogue cards to his Ohio college library clients. By 1971 OCLC's shared cataloguing system was available on-line in the state of Ohio, and within two years after that it could be used elsewhere through other academic library consortia, first in the East, then the South, then the West. In 1978 it was reorganized as a national service. These developments did not come about without criticism, of both OCLC and Kilgour, but they led nonetheless to dramatic changes in academic and other library operations.

Kilgour participated actively in library professional affairs, serving as the founding Editor of the *Journal of Library Automation,* and as author, lecturer, and international consultant. In 1974 he received the Margaret Mann Citation and in 1978 the Melvil Dewey Award from the ALA for his distinguished service to the profession. His wife, Eleanor Margaret Beach, worked with him on many projects.

**REFERENCE**

David L. Weisbrod, "Margaret Mann Citation, 1974: Frederick G. Kilgour," *Library Resources & Technical Services* (1974).

DAVID KASER

## Korea, Democratic People's Republic of

North Korea, or the Democratic People's Republic of Korea, occupies the northern half of the Korean Peninsula in eastern Asia. It is bounded on the north by China and the Soviet Union, on the south by South Korea, on the east by the Sea of Japan, and on the west by the Yellow Sea. Pop. (1978 est.) 17,078,000; area 121,200 sq.km. The official language is Korean.

The State Central Library in Pyongyang functions as a national library. Little information was available in the West on library holdings. In the 1970's there were provincial libraries at North Hamgyong, South Hamgyong, North Pyongan, South Hwanghae, North Hwanghae, Kangwon, Chagang, South Pyongan, and Ryanggang. In addition, there were city libraries in Kaesong and Chongjin and two scientific libraries: the Pyongyang Scientific Library and the Library of the Academy of Sciences in Pyongsong.

The Academy of Sciences Publishing House, founded in 1953, publishes works on science, chemistry, geology, metallurgy, physics, biology, history, mathematics, meteorology, education, and economics. The Academy of Social Sciences and the Academy of Medical Sciences, both in Pyongyang, publish works in their respective fields.

There is one university in North Korea; the Kim Il Sung University in Pyongyang, founded in 1946, has faculties in history, philosophy, political economics, law, philology, foreign literature, geography, geology, physics, mathematics, chemistry, and biology. The Kim Chaek Polytechnic Institute and the Pyongyang Medical Institute are also in Pyongyang. In the late 1970's there were 82 institutions of higher and professional education in all of the main towns. These included colleges of engineering, agriculture, fisheries, and teacher training. In addition, there were also 57 factory (engineering) colleges. Statistical and other information was not available on library service in these institutions.

The Library Association of the Democratic People's Republic of Korea was established in 1953. The Association is affiliated with IFLA; its headquarters are in the Central Library at Pyongyang.

STAFF

## Korea, Republic of

The Republic of Korea, or South Korea, in southeast Asia, is bounded by the Sea of Japan on the east and by the Yellow Sea on the west and by North Korea. Pop. (1978 est.) 36,628,000; area 98,799 sq.km. The official language is Korean.

**National Libraries.** The Central National Library was started in 1923 and was reorganized after the Japanese left Korea in 1945. Administratively it is under the Ministry of Education and serves the country by acquisition and preservation of the national literature, bibliographic services, and exchange services between domestic and overseas libraries. It has 600,200 volumes, including 180,000 rare books, Chinese and Korean classics. Major publications are *The Monthly Bulletin* and *The Korean National Bibliography*.

The National Assembly Library was established in 1951 to serve members and committees of the Assembly and provides information and materials for legislative reference and research work. It serves government officials, as well as the public, with bibliographical services, research, and technical services. The Library has 470,356 volumes, including 9,838 rare books. Two of its major publications are *The National Assembly Library Review* (monthly) and *The Index to Korean Periodicals* (quarterly). Both libraries became depository libraries under the Library Law of 1963. The services rendered by the two libraries overlap in many ways, and a movement was under way in the late 1970's to unify the two libraries into a single, strong national library.

**Academic Libraries.** Academic libraries increased in number and were physically extended after World War

The Central National Library

*The Republic of Korea's Central National Library, Seoul.*

II as part of the promotion of higher education systems. Academic libraries include university and college libraries as well as junior and teachers' college libraries supported either by the government or private institutions. According to the *Statistics on Libraries in Korea 1977,* academic libraries serve 5,983,000 users with 7,766,200 volumes.

Most academic libraries suffered during the Korean War, 1950–52. They subsequently were active in building up the collections and reader services, however, and those who had not already built were involved in new library building plans in the late 1970's. Seoul National University Library, the largest academic library, has a modern building centrally located on a new campus supported by the government. The Kujang Kak, the Royal Library Collection of classic literature, is preserved in a specially designed section of that library.

Other major university libraries are at Yonsei, Korea, and Ewha universities. They are supported by private institutions and provide more special services that reflect their longer histories.

**Public Libraries.** Public libraries were introduced to Korea only in the beginning of the 20th century. Because they were introduced by the Japanese during an occupation, the image of the public library suffered. A few prospered, but public libraries were not generally popular or well supported until the enactment of the Library Law in 1963. Still small in number, public libraries came to perform a real function in encouraging intellectual interests and filling recreational needs. Local and city governments are financially responsible for encouraging the development of public libraries under the overall supervision of the Ministry of Education. There were 114 public libraries in Korea according to *Library Statistics, 1977*. The number was still far too small compared with the population they have to serve. Accordingly a five-year plan for public libraries, released by the Ministry of Education, proposed a plan to be effective by 1983 to set up one or more libraries in 92 communities that have no public libraries. The Ministry also disclosed plans to increase the number of professional librarians and allocated a budget of 17,500,000,000 *won* ($35,000,000) for that purpose.

**School Libraries.** After the Korean War, the most notable increase in library numbers was seen in school libraries. Though many see school libraries as indispensable in modern education, the lack of understanding among school administrators and the shortage of teacher librarians hampered growth and presented problems of maintaining school libraries as instructional media centers in the late 1970's. There were about 4,000 school libraries in Korea with 11,500,000 volumes to serve 31,000,000 students. School libraries outnumbered all other libraries in Korea, but their facilities and services required improvement if they were to meet student needs.

**Special Libraries.** Special libraries are among the growing forces in Korean librarianship. A new demand for information on sciences, technology, and business administration increased. This growing interest among scholars, administrators, and businessmen has helped them to recognize the importance of library service in their organizations. It caused the fast development of special libraries in research institutes, business firms, mass media systems, and both governmental and nongovernmental organizations.

Due to better understanding by administrators and better financial support, special libraries have grown fast. Staffed by trained librarians, they not only are more adequately financed than others but enjoy better interlibrary

**Libraries in the Republic of Korea (South) (1976)**

| Type | Number | Volumes in collections | Annual expenditures (*won*) | Population served | Professional staff | All staff (total) |
|---|---|---|---|---|---|---|
| National | 2 | 1,070,537 | 959,828,000 | 645,253 | 96 | 373 |
| Academic | 156 | 7,766,161 | 2,039,813,000 | 5,983,000 | 584 | 1,388 |
| Public | 114 | 1,174,252 | 1,061,731,000 | 7,419,263 | 189 | 867[a] |
| School | 4,024 | 11,500,247 | 923,925,094 | 31,066,068 | 1,785[a] | 4,024[a] |
| Special | 121 | 1,763,247 | 1,938,681,000 | 448,263 | 164 | 611 |
| Total | 4,417 | 23,274,444 | 6,923,978,094 | 45,561,847 | 2,818 | 7,263 |

[a]Estimated number.

Sources of information: Korea, Ministry of Education, *Statistical Yearbook of Education, 1976* (Seoul, Korea, 1977); Korean Library Association, *Statistics on Libraries in Korea, 1977* (Seoul: KLA, 1977).

cooperation. The best example is the Science Park Complex composed of KIST (Korea Institute of Science and Technology), KDI (Korea Development Institute), ADD (Agency for Defense Development), KAIS (Korea Advanced Institute for Science), and KORSTIC (Korean Scientific and Technological Information Center) located within the Seoul Research and Development Project, which undertakes joint cooperative acquisition, technical processing, and service.

**Associations.** Established in 1945, the first library association was called the Chosun Library Association. In 1955 it was reorganized as the Korean Library Association, known as KLA. The objectives of the Association are to promote library development and cooperation among individual and institutional membership and to promote international library cooperation. The Association holds an annual conference, and the Board of Directors meets regularly during the other months. A Technical Advisory Committee with eight subcommittees meets as necessary. The KLA office consists of the President, a Vice-President, and the Executive Secretary and his staff.

The Association has regional associations, and divisions are by types of libraries. Statistics for 1977 showed KLA membership as 507 individual members and 511 institutional members. The Association sponsors activities such as an annual National Library Convention, Book Week, and Library Week as well as workshops and a materials distribution center service to the member libraries. KLA publishes the *KLA Monthly Bulletin,* a *Library Science Series,* revisions of the *Korean Decimal Classification System* and *Cataloging Code, Statistics on Libraries in Korea,* and many other tools.

The Korean Library Science Society was started in 1970 by the members of library science school faculties and individuals interested in advanced studies in the field of library science. The Society promotes Korean librarianship by seminars, lectures, and an annual publication, *Tosogwanhak* ("Studies in Library Science").

The Korean Bibliographical Society was organized in 1968 by librarians and scholars interested in bibliographical service. It also sponsors seminars and lectures, and publishes a journal, *Sujihak* ("Bibliographical Studies").

The Korean Micro-Library Association was inaugurated in 1960. It is a grass-roots effort to reach individuals at the village and farm level. Each "library" of approximately 60 titles is self-contained in a wooden bookcase that holds upwards of 300 volumes. The original 60 titles are selected in accord with the recipient villagers' needs and interests; for example, agriculture, stock-raising, gardening, fishing, or homemaking. Each recipient is responsible for adding new volumes. The Village Reading Club runs the library, and books are lent free of charge. The Association, first operated under the auspices of the Ministry of Education, is sponsored by the Ministry of Home Affairs, which had provided a total of 35 libraries as of 1978. It publishes *Monthly Micro-Library.*

A study for a National Library Plan was in process at the end of 1978 and had received funding from one of the major business groups in Korea.


**REFERENCES**

David Kaser and others, *Library Development in Eight Asian Countries* (1969).

Pongsoon Lee, "The Korean Libraries: From Their Origin to the Present," *Proceedings of IFLA Worldwide Seminar* (1976).

Ke Hong Park, "Libraries and Librarianship in the Republic of Korea," *Proceedings of IFLA Worldwide Seminar* (1976).


PONGSOON LEE

## Krupskaya (Ulianova), Nadezhda Konstantinovna
(1869–1939)

Printed courtesy of *Soviet Life*

*Nadezhda Krupskaya*

Nadezhda Krupskaya, the wife of Lenin, was prominent in Communist Party and Soviet state activities, one of the founders of the Soviet educational system, and a pioneer in the development of Soviet libraries. She was born February 26, 1869, in St. Petersburg (now Leningrad). She graduated from secondary school in 1887, and in 1890, while a student of the Woman's College in Saint Petersburg, she became a member of a Marxist circle. In 1891–96 she taught at a Sunday evening school for workers and propagated revolutionary ideas.

She met V. I. Lenin in 1894, and soon they were married. With him she took part in the organization of the Revolution in Russia. In August 1896 Krupskaya was arrested and joined Lenin in his exile in the village of Shushenskoye and later in Ufa. At that time she wrote her first work, *The Woman-Worker.* During 1901–05, together with Lenin, she lived in Germany, Great Britain, and Switzerland and was active in the revolutionary movement and the publishing of the Marxist newspapers *Iskra* and *Vperyod.* On her return to Russia in November 1905 she worked as the Secretary of the Central Committee of the Bolshevik Party. From the end of 1907 until April 1917 she again lived in exile with Lenin, continuing her revolutionary activities.

At the same time, she became interested in the study of popular education in Russia and in western European countries and in 1915–16 became a member of the Pestalozzi pedagogical society in Switzerland and the Berne and Fribourg pedagogical museums. In that period she also wrote one of her major works, *People's Education and Democracy,* which dealt with the development of popular education in the U.S., a problem that she had examined in a number of her earlier works.

After the establishment of the Soviet government in Russia in November 1917, Krupskaya became one of the leaders of the Commissariat of People's Education (from 1929 serving as Deputy of the People's Commissar), where she took an active part in the preparation of the first legislative acts on people's education and became the chief organizer of cultural and educational work in the country. She taught at the Academy of Communist Education and was the founder of a number of voluntary societies, including "Away with Illiteracy" and "Children's Friend," and chaired the Society of Teachers-Marxists. She was a member of ruling bodies of the Communist Party and the Soviet government.

Krupskaya played a prominent role in activities directed toward the elimination of illiteracy, the organization of the Soviet school system, and the establishment of cultural foundations for a new society. She appreciably contributed to the elaboration of the most important problems of Marxist education: the definition of the objectives of Communist education, preschool and primary education, the connection between the school and public life, professional and technical training, the content of curricula, and the education of the different nationalities of the Soviet Union. She was editor of a number of journals, including *Public Education, People's Teacher, Extra-Scholastic Education,* and *School for Adults.* Her literary production totals over 5,000 items, among which are a number of reminiscences of Lenin, representing significant primary sources for his biography.

She devoted much time to librarianship, to which she accorded an integral role in education and the development of public life. She had expert knowledge of bibliography in Russia, was acquainted with many western European libraries, and displayed a keen interest in U.S. libraries. She took part in the preparation of major legislative acts on libraries, including the decree "On the Centralization of Librarianship in the RSFSR" (1920) and the resolution of the Central Executive Committee, "On Librarianship in the USSR" (1934). The most significant meetings and conferences in the field were held under her guidance, and she gave speeches on book distribution, problems of library science, and bibliography. Such journals as *The Red Librarian, In Aid of Self-Education, Book Bulletin, What One Should Read,* and others were founded on her initiative. She wrote hundreds of articles on librarianship, publishing, bibliography, lifelong education, and self-education.

The scope of her activities can be classifed along three major lines. First, she was an ardent propagandist of the ideas of Lenin, who regarded the establishment of libraries as an inseparable part of the Socialist state policy in the field of culture, and considered the establishment of an integrated system of different types of libraries, evenly distributed throughout the country and provided with all facilities required, as a necessity. Krupskaya's many speeches and articles, which were imbued with these ideas, and especially a widely known work, *What Lenin Wrote and Said about Libraries* (1929), helped to enhance the prestige of libraries in Soviet society.

Second, during the first two decades of Soviet power, Krupskaya headed the organization of a library system and the popularization of libraries and their use by wide sections of the public. She showed great concern for all aspects of librarianship, including the publication of needed materials and the most effective methods for their distribution according to the needs of different social and cultural groups. Krupskaya devoted much time to the development of children's literature and the organization of school and children's libraries. She encouraged the establishment of libraries in both cities and villages, supported the organization of reference and information services, encouraged the use of interlibrary loan, and supported the participation of all libraries in the country's economical, social, and cultural development. As early as 1918 Krupskaya initiated the opening of a number of library schools. She argued that raising the standards of librarianship was possible only if qualified personnel with sound training were available. She paid significant attention to the development of bibliography, especially to the compilation of recommendatory bibliographical lists and indexes, and to the evaluation of books and the definition of their relevance for each category of reader. She considered it important to teach broad sections of the population how to use libraries, choose books, and educate themselves.

Third, the work of Krupskaya in elaborating fundamental principles of library science deserves attention. The first library research institutions, such as the Research Institute of Library Science and Recommendatory Bibliography, were established on her initiative, as were the formulation of training programs in librarianship and bibliography for secondary schools and universities. She stressed the need for constant attention to the reading needs of the broad masses and for constant improvement of forms and methods for book publishing; the need for a purposeful policy in selecting book collections and servicing readers—a policy that would be in keeping with the objectives of building a new society; the need for combining the dissemination of professional and technical knowledge in library activities with efforts at developing a harmonious personality; the need for understanding the cultural heritage of all the peoples of the world and for promoting humane qualities that would serve higher human ideals.

Krupskaya's writings are widely published and studied, and many books and articles have been written about her. Many libraries and educational and other institutions were named after her. An annual Krupskaya medal is awarded to the best teachers and librarians in the Soviet Union. Krupskaya died in Moscow on February 27, 1939.

**REFERENCES**

The collected writings of Krupskaya are *Pedagogicheskie sochineniya* ("Pedagogical Works," in Russian) 11 volumes (Moscow, 1957–63); *O Bibliotechnom Dele* ("On Librarianship") (Moscow, 1957, 1st ed.; 1976, 2nd ed.); *Reminiscences of Lenin;* translated by Bernard Isaacs (Moscow, 1959); *Memories of Lenin;* translated by E. Verney, 2 volumes (London, 1930–32); *Memories of Lenin* (London, 1942).

A bibliography of her works and literature about her is *Nadezhda Konstantinovna Krupskaya: Bibliografia Trudov i Literatury o Zhizni i Deiatelnosti* ("Bibliography of Works and Literature about Life and Activities"), 2 volumes (Moscow, 1969–73).

S. Simsova, *Lenin, Krupskaya and Libraries* (1968).

GEORGIJ FONOTOV

# Kuwait

Kuwait, an independent constitutional monarchy, lies on the northwest coast of the Persian Gulf and the northeast coast of the Arabian Peninsula. Kuwait is bordered by Iraq on the north and northwest and by Saudi Arabia on the south and southwest. Pop. (1978 est.) 1,198,500; area 16,918 sq.km. The official language is Arabic.

**National Library.** The National Library of Kuwait, the National Heritage Center, is closely affiliated with and supervised by Kuwait University Libraries Department. The Center was established in 1971 on a recommendation from the Kuwaiti Cabinet. Five copies of all printed publications issued in Kuwait must be deposited in the Center according to the legal deposit law of March 1972; only 63 books were reported by the Arab League to have been published in Kuwait in 1975. The functions of the Center are gathering and making available all printed and nonprint materials concerning and issued in Kuwait, the Gulf States, and the Arabian Peninsula, as well as issuing national and specialized bibliographies. The library holdings of the Center total about 10,000 volumes.

**Academic Libraries.** The principal academic library in Kuwait is that of the Kuwait University, which was inaugurated in 1966. Its growing library system comprises the Central Library, six college libraries, a separate library for periodicals, and the National Heritage Center. The book collections in all libraries of Kuwait University total about 250,000 volumes. Acquisitions, cataloguing, classification, compiling bibliographies, audiovisual services, reference, and other functions are performed centrally by the Department of Libraries, which administers all libraries of the University.

The Kuwait University Libraries Department has issued *Selected Bibliography on Kuwait and Arabian Gulf,* two volumes for foreign and Arabic sources (1969–70), which is considered the nucleus of the national bibliography; *A List of Books and Publications Received by the Kuwait University,* a computer printout since 1973; *Selected Bibliography on Arab Civilization* in 1970; and other specialized bibliographies. The Kuwait Institute of Scientific Research has issued two editions of a union list of periodicals in the libraries of the Gulf States.

**Public Libraries.** Public library services in Kuwait came into existence with the establishment of the Central Public Library in 1936. The public library system consists of the Central Public Library and 18 branch libraries mostly in the suburban shopping centers of the city of Kuwait. The public library system is administered by the Public Libraries Department of the Ministry of Education. All operations, such as acquisitions and technical processing, are done centrally by the Central Public Library. New books and catalogue cards are distributed regularly to each branch library. Periodicals are acquired and processed separately. The book collections of the public library system total about 180,000 volumes.

**School Libraries.** The School Libraries Department of the Ministry of Education, established in 1954, is responsible for establishing and developing school libraries, providing them with library materials and personnel, and operating a book processing center for book distribution. The administration of individual school libraries is a responsibility assigned to each school principal. There are 270 school libraries serving elementary, intermediate, secondary, vocational, and technical schools.

**Special Libraries.** Government departments, research centers, banks, and other enterprises possess special libraries with sizable collections. Noteworthy among these libraries are those of the Ministry of Education, Ministry of Foreign Affairs, Ministry of Endowments, the Kuwait Institute of Scientific Research, the Arab Planning Institute, the Planning Board, the Kuwait Fund for the Arab Economic Development, the Central Bank of Kuwait, and the Kuwait National Petroleum Company. The Documentation and Information Section of the Kuwait Institute of Scientific Research performs a leading role in scientific documentation, particularly with regard to computerized bibliographies and specialized professional training.

MOHAMED M. EL HADI

# Lancaster, F(rederick) Wilfrid

(1933– )

F. Wilfrid Lancaster, library educator, became a major influence in the fields of information systems and the evaluation of library services. Born September 4, 1933, in Durham, England, Lancaster studied at Newcastle-upon-Tyne School of Librarianship (1950–54) and became Fellow of the Library Association of Great Britain (by thesis) in 1969. Lancaster began his professional career in 1953 as Senior Assistant, Newcastle-upon-Tyne Public Libraries. His subsequent positions include Senior Librarian for Science and Technology, Akron Public Library; Resident Consultant and Head, Systems Evaluation Group, Herner and Company, Washington, D.C.; Information Systems Specialist, National Library of Medicine; and Director of Information Retrieval Services, Westat Research, Inc. From 1970 Lancaster served on the faculty of the University of Illinois, Graduate School of Library Science, with the rank of Professor from 1972.

Lancaster's contributions have been made through writing, teaching, and consulting. Major publications include *Towards a Paperless Information Society* (1978), *The Measurement and Evaluation of Library Services* (1977), *Information Retrieval On-line* (1973), *Vocabulary Control for Information Retrieval* (1972), *Information Retrieval Systems: Characteristics, Testing and Evaluation* (1968), and *Evaluation of the MEDLARS Demand Search Service* (1968). In addition, Lancaster edited 5 books and wrote more than 70 articles and technical reports by the late 1970's. His publications were recognized by the American Society for Information Science with best book awards in 1970 and 1975 and a best paper award in 1969. In 1978 Lancaster received the Ralph Shaw Award for the outstanding contribution to the literature of library science for *The Measurement and Evaluation of Library Services.* His consulting includes work for the Central Intelligence Agency, Center for Applied Linguistics, National Library of Medicine, and the National Library of Australia. He completed a set of guidelines on the evaluation of information systems and services for Unesco and the Food and Agriculture Organization.

Lancaster's work deals principally with the underlying intellectual problems and conceptual frameworks of information retrieval systems, rather than technical aspects of computing and systems design. His major contributions have been in the areas of vocabulary control, interaction between system and user, evaluation of systems effectiveness, and, in his later work, the implications of advanced information systems for the future of libraries in society. Lancaster's strongest impact was on the development of criteria and procedures for the evaluation of systems performance, mainly through the extension, refinement, and application of concepts pioneered by the Cranfield studies. His *Evaluation of the MEDLARS Demand Search Service* (1968) represents a landmark investigation, not particularly for its influence on the later development of the MEDLARS system, but as a demonstration of the application of refined methods for testing, analyzing, and evaluating the performance of an operational information retrieval system.

The more general significance of Lancaster's work results from his ability to combine a rigorous and thorough approach with a clarity of expression that renders advanced concepts of information retrieval accessible to the student and the practicing librarian without oversimplification. Lancaster's work, therefore, might be viewed as an attempt to bridge several important divisions in the information professions. His early work on vocabulary control and systems evaluation provides a connection between practice and theory for the technically oriented designer of information systems. His recent work, particularly the *Measurement and Evaluation of Library Services* (1977), serves to narrow the gap between the library profession at large and the growing body of research relevant to measurement and evaluation. Lancaster's most significant contribution to the literature of library and information science, assessed at a point still relatively early in his career, may well be his stimulation of interest in the possibility that theory and research may have some practical utility in the field.

JOE A. HEWITT

# Laos

Laos, proclaimed a people's democratic republic in December 1975, is bounded by China on the north, Vietnam on the northeast and east, and Cambodia on the south. Pop. (1978 est.) 3,546,000; area 236,800 sq.km. The official language is Lao.

**National Library.** The National Library of Laos in Vientiane includes the National Museum and National Archives. On the grounds of the School of Fine Arts, it is under the direction of the Ministry of Education. The extent of the National Library's holdings and the degree of continuity in its operations allowed by the Communist government in the late 1970's are uncertain, but the government allowed this and similar institutions (including Buddhist institutions) to function. Prior to the change of government in 1975, the National Library received aid from the French and U.S. governments, private foundations, and Western scholars. The Rockefeller Foundation presented 9,000 volumes, mainly in French, on a wide range of subjects. Other contributions were made by the Asia Foundation and by the U.S. Library of Congress. In 1974 the Director of the National Library, Prachit Soulisak, told a representative of the U.S. Library of Congress that he had compiled a list of 84,000 titles available in Lao at various temples and libraries throughout the country; he said the list gave the locations of each item, but the list had not been published by the mid-1970's.

The Lao Library Association was closely associated with the National Library and was physically housed in a building behind the Library. Prior to 1974 the Association published a considerable number of monographs. Also associated with the National Library was the Siaw Savath Society, which was organized to publish theses of Lao students who studied abroad.

The National Library of Laos published *Lao National Bibliography,* 3 volumes (1968–72); *Bibliographie de Laos,* Institute Française d'Extreme Orient, with a supplement covering the years 1962–70, was compiled by the Director of the Lao National Library.

**Academic Libraries.** Before 1975 the Buddhist Institute in Vientiane was one of the most important centers of scholarship in Laos. It maintained a substantial collection of works, many in Pali and Sanskrit, for the use of its students and foreign scholars. The Institute apparently remained open, but the extent of its activities was unknown in the West.

Sisavangvong University, in Vientiane, is the only university in Laos. Library facilities of its faculties of medicine, law, and education were mainly provided by Western governments and foundations and are not extensive for research purposes. The law faculty published a law journal as of 1974.

**Public Libraries.** Apart from the National Library, which had 850 registered borrowers at the end of the 1960's, there are not believed to be any public lending libraries, in the Western sense, in Laos. The library of at least one major temple, the Wat That in Luang Prabang, performed some of the functions of a public library, however. In 1971 it reportedly had a 5,000-volume collection, with many contemporary works in Lao and Thai, and it circulated about 100 books a month to residents of Luang Prabang. Most temples have a teaching function, and many serve as community centers; some of the larger ones have collections of manuscripts in Pali and Sanskrit.

Prior to the Communist takeover in 1975, a number of foreign governments (the United States, France, and Britain) operated libraries and reading rooms in Vientiane and other major towns. These were often heavily patronized. With U.S. economic assistance, a program of providing modest library facilities in rural areas also enjoyed some success.

**School Libraries.** The French *lycées* and the normal and technical schools in Laos each had relatively modest library facilities (mainly provided through foreign-aid programs) that were reserved usually for the use of their own students and faculties.

**Special Libraries.** The Directorate of Archaeology in the Ministry of Culture had a collection of manuscripts; in 1974 it reportedly planned to incorporate these into the National Library's collection. The U.S. Agency for International Development also maintained collections of documents on foreign assistance to Laos. (AID was expelled from Laos in 1973.)

PETER A. POOLE



## Lara, Juana Manrique de (1899– )

Juana Manrique de Lara, Mexican librarian, introduced modern librarianship to Mexico through teaching, writing, and official duties as Inspector General of Libraries. Born in the village of El Cubo, Guanajato, in Mexico, on March 12, 1899, she studied first in her native state and later in Puebla. A marked vocation toward teaching led her to graduate from the Normal School of Puebla. Inclined as well toward books, she enrolled in the first National School of Archivists and Librarians in Mexico City, studying there during the years of the Revolution, 1916–17.

She continued her studies in the United States to prepare as a professional librarian, one of the first Mexican women to do so. De Lara graduated from the School of the New York Public Library in 1924. Returning to Mexico, she dedicated herself to teaching library science. She taught at the early Library School of the Secretariat of Education and at the National School of Archivists and Librarians. The courses were many and the years were long, and her enthusiasm was contagious. For her pupils she published a number of valuable books such as the *Manual of the Mexican Librarian,* which she modestly described as advice for persons in charge of libraries, and which went through several editions. Other best-sellers for Mexican librarians, so lacking in tools, were her *Elementary Notions concerning the Organization and Administration of a Small Library, Elements of the Organization and Administration of School Libraries,* and *Guide to Headings of Material for Dictionary Catalogues;* another work supplied a need in Mexican literature, *School Libraries and Children's Literature*—lists of books for children in primary grades and youth in secondary schools; a valuable work written in collaboration with another distinguished librarian, Guadalupe Monroy Baigen, was *Pseudonyms, Anagrams and Initials of Mexican Authors.* She wrote numerous articles in specialized magazines of the U.S., Mexico, and countries of Central America.

She was for many years Inspector General of Libraries, Director of Libraries of the Secretariat of Education, and other specialized branches, in all of which she left her impress of positive activity totally dedicated to the culture of her country.

ERNESTO DE LA TORRE VILLAR

## Law Libraries

PURPOSES AND OBJECTIVES

The dynamic growth of law library collections in the 20th century has been reflected in the changing role of the law librarian from a mere custodian of law books to an information specialist, organizing, managing, supervising, and coordinating legal research activities of the bench and bar, academia, and other institutions concerned with law.

Law in the books has always been a formidable challenge to lawyers seeking legal authority. There was a time, around the turn of the 17th century, when the English lawyer had to contend with only 5,000 reported cases. Today the American lawyer can consult millions of judicial opinions, increasing at the annual rate of approximately 50,000 published American appellate opinions alone. There is also a mass of federal and state legislation supplemented annually by hundreds of huge volumes of codes aggregating about 500,000 pages by themselves. Then there are the tens of thousands of pages of legal periodicals, government documents, administrative law and regulations, foreign law, and international law as well as topical looseleaf services.

In the years since World War II, this challenge has been heightened by the increasing relevance of economic, sociological, and scientific data in legal research so that the mere process of identifying, locating, and referring to these materials confounds not only the practicing lawyer but the legal scholar as well. It is not for naught that the late Chief Justice Arthur T. Vanderbilt of New Jersey noted in this context, "The first thing about our legal system that strikes a European or Latin American lawyer is its sheer bulk."

Law libraries have always been practitioner oriented. Lawyers generally seek legal authority in court decisions and statutes relevant to the solution of factual problems in a specific jurisdiction. These primary repositories of the law can easily be arranged chronologically on open shelves by jurisdiction or state. Hence, there was little need for the practitioner to depend on a law librarian either to arrange or organize these materials for use or to assist in locating relevant authority. We find, for example, that in England in 1646, as a result of an inquiry into the loss of books in the library of Gray's Inn, the chapel clerk was appointed Library-Keeper, with an extra annual salary of £5. In 19th-century America the tital of "Librarian" was given often to the custodian of the building where the law library was located, or to its janitor. Obviously such a position did not require any special education or knowledge.

The tremendous growth of law book collections in the 20th century, however, the "information explosion," and the increasing demand for interdisciplinary materials in legal research have changed the concept that a law library is merely a collection of books in which legal authority can be found, and that can easily be arranged on shelves, alphabetically by author, or jurisdictionally under date or title. Today, as a result, law librarians function more as information specialists, coordinating the research activities of their institutions. They are more than reference assistants and bibliographers; they organize law libraries and their collections of legal materials for efficient and economic use. They suggest sources of information the lawyer can use and, even more significantly, law librarians are trained to locate such sources when they are initially unknown to them.

In actual research, law librarians can find legal citations or references, suggest sources of information, verify and translate citations, interpret abbreviations, assemble materials for specific projects, prepare bibliographies, and explain the use of legal materials in the library. Law librarians, moreover, must possess judgment and legal background to anticipate the research needs of lawyers and resourcefulness to analyze legal materials and recognize their relevance to a particular subject or problem.

Law books are highly technical tools that are difficult to use properly on occasion. Law librarians can skillfully use indexes, conversion tables, tables of cases, citations, and other technical finding tools. They provide significant assistance to legal researchers because of their thorough familiarity with legal and nonlegal bibliographies, as well as of many important nonlegal sources. They know where to find the answers to questions involving business, medicine, history, the social sciences, economics, and the applied sciences. Often the law librarian is the "silent partner" in the research activities of lawyers, judges, and scholars.

This changing role of law librarianship has been reflected in rising demands on the educational and professional qualifications held not only by head law librarians but by the rank-and-file staff members as well. Standards established by the American Bar Association and the Association of American Law Schools for law school librarians have been generally accepted as basic requirements for professional status.

With some exceptions, law school librarians are the most highly qualified in the field. As of December 1978 about 241 law school librarians, 402 private law firm librarians, 240 county and bar librarians, 130 government law librarians, 121 court librarians, 88 state law librarians, and 100 company law librarians were members of the American Association of Law Libraries.

Characteristically, other law librarians seek to obtain the same qualifications as law school librarians possess, to meet the test of professional acceptance. The professional careers of many law librarians suggest this trend in that they have moved from private law firm libraries, bar libraries, and the other types of law libraries to law school libraries and vice-versa. It would appear that there is a commonly accepted core of professional and educational achievement prerequisite to success in law librarianship.

The American Bar Association standards for law librarians are part of its *Standards for the Approval of Law Schools* (1977). Its Standard 605 provides that "the law library [of an ABA accredited law school] shall be administered by a full-time law librarian whose principal activities are the development and maintenance of the library and the furnishing of library assistance to faculty and students, and may include teaching courses in the law school." Substandard 605 (c) provides that "the law librarian should have a degree in law or library science and shall have a sound knowledge of library administration and of the particular problems of a law library."

Law schools accredited by the Association of American Law Schools have set the most demanding professional standards, and AALS accreditation contributes significantly to a law school's standing. AALS Executive

The University of Chicago Law School

*The University of Chicago Law School Library, designed by Eero Saarinen. Five floors of stacks and reading space rise above a first-floor lounge.*

Committee Regulation 8.3(a) provides that "the librarian should have both legal and library education and . . . should have met the certification requirements of the American Association of Law Libraries."

The American Association of Law Libraries was founded in 1906 "to promote librarianship, to develop and increase the usefulness of law libraries, to cultivate the service of law librarianship and to foster a spirit of cooperation among the members of the profession." It had 14 regional chapters at the end of the 1970's and a number of Special Interest Sections. It publishes the *Law Library Journal, The Index to Foreign Legal Periodicals, The Directory of Law Librarians,* a *Biographical Directory of Law Librarians, AALL Publication Series, Current Publications in Legal and Related Fields,* and *AALL Newsletter* and a *Recruitment Checklist.* The AALL had over 2,800 active members in 1979.

The certification program of the AALL is a "formal recognition that a person has attained a standard of competence in law librarianship recognized by the AALL." It is voluntary and is granted to those persons who qualify as following:

1. A graduate degree in library science from a school accredited by the American Library Association and a degree in law from an American Bar Association-approved law school or admission to the Bar of a state plus two years of professional library experience
2. A degree in law from an ABA-approved law school or admission to the Bar of a state plus four years of professional library experience
3. A library science graduate degree from an American Library Association-approved school plus six years of professional library experience or eight years of experience and a graduate degree in library science from an accredited library school
4. Twenty years of responsible professional law library experience and outstanding contribution to the profession [This is the "no degree" requirement.]

The great interest in law librarianship has encouraged library schools to offer courses in the field. Among them are library schools at Columbia University, the University of Washington, the University of Illinois, Western Reserve, Drexel, Pratt, the University of California at Berkeley, Rosary College, the University of North Carolina, and the University of Maryland. The American Association of Law Libraries sponsors educational programs that are given credit for accreditation purposes.

An analysis of the 1977 *Biographical Directory of the American Association of Law Libraries,* by the staff of the American Bar Association, showed that of the 1,221 entries in the Directory, 322 had obtained the LLB degree or its equivalent JD and 22 the Master of Law degree; 516 had a professional library science degree. Many of the younger persons entering the profession of law librarianship today have both the law degree and the library science degree.

There are many types of law libraries that employ law librarians:

*Bar Association Libraries* serve practicing lawyers and are keyed to the research demands of litigation and client counseling. Among them are some of the leading law collections in the country, such as that of the Association of the Bar of the City of New York.

*Company Libraries* are maintained by legal departments of business enterprises. Here legal and related materials on the type of industry represented are collected—e.g., insurance, transportation, communications, international business transactions. Some of the larger collections of this type are held by the Prudential Insurance Company in Newark, the Library of the American Telephone and Telegraph Company in New York, and the General Motors Corporation in Detroit.

*County Law Libraries* are supported with public funds wholly or in part. They serve the courts, public officials, and the bar. Among this group is found the Los Angeles County Law Library, the largest practitioners' collection in the country. The states with the most county law libraries are California, Ohio, Pennsylvania, Florida, Massachusetts, Maine, Michigan, Arizona, and Washington. Thirteen states had no county law libraries in 1979.

*Court Libraries.* There are more than 100 formally organized court libraries employing professional law librarians. Many more small court libraries are not in charge of professional librarians but are maintained by clerks or secretaries. The largest number of court libraries, including those of the federal courts, are concentrated in New York state.

*Government Libraries* comprise those of state and local governments as well as federal departmental and agency law libraries. Most of the federal law libraries are in Washington, D.C. Probably the largest law library in the world is that of the Library of Congress, with about 1,400,000 volumes. Its divisions (American, British, European, Far Eastern, Hispanic, Near Eastern, and North African) suggest the comprehensiveness of its collection. Among other important U.S. government libraries are the U.S. Supreme Court Library, the Department of Justice, the Treasury, and the Federal Trade Commission.

*Law Office Libraries.* Law office collections range from a small number of volumes to approximately 55,000. Besides the usual law books, they may contain records and briefs of cases before various courts, memoranda, and forms of all types. The largest number of law office libraries are in New York, California, and Illinois.

*Law School Libraries.* These employ more law librarians than any other types of law libraries. Depending upon their location, resources, teaching, and research programs, law school libraries are used by law students and faculty exclusively, and when publicly funded, they are often used by the bench and bar of the area. The 1977 statistical survey of law school libraries and librarians indicates that of 162 law school libraries, 32 contain over 200,000 volumes. Harvard Law School has over 1,000,000 books in its library collection and Columbia, Michigan, Yale, and New York University, over 500,000 volumes.

*State Law Libraries.* Service may be provided either by independent libraries or by divisions of other state agencies. Some of them provide legislative reference services and exchanges of state legal materials, case reports, and statutes. Their primary function is to serve the state officials in all three departments of state government. Their collections range in size from 30,000 volumes to over 1,000,000 with 15 having more than 100,000 volumes. The more important state law libraries can be found in Massachusetts, Minnesota, New York, Rhode Island, New Jersey, and Wisconsin. Of course, the Law Library of Congress can be included here as well.

In essence, a law library is one of the "special libraries." A law librarian is basically a specialist in legal bibliography. In law schools, law librarians often teach a course in legal bibliography or subject courses in the law school. Professionally, law librarians also write and edit law texts and assist in the revision of statutes and the preparation of indexes. The law librarian is often called upon to act as a consultant to the Bar and other law libraries. As experts in legal bibliography, law librarians write book reviews, participate in workshops and institutes, and contribute to the professional growth of law librarianship.

JULIUS J. MARKE

SERVICES TO USERS

The effective law library was long known as a happy combination of books and people. Today the functional legal information center is a harmonious union of people, materials, and technology. This subtle change in nomenclature is important because it implies modern service to a demanding clientele.

The raison d'être for a legal information center is service to what are probably the most influential and powerful forces in society—the executive, legislative, and judicial branches of government and the advocates of the legal profession. The role of the legal information center is vital because the missions of its users are essential in the civil and criminal matters inherent in society. Without law there would be no order; without well-organized, readily accessible legal information, the President and governors, the legislators, the judges, the lawyers, and the public who must contend with law and regulation would be severely impeded in their activities.

The traditional law library selects and acquires legal materials for the use of its audience, catalogues and classifies these materials so that many individuals may benefit from their content, and answers questions on a variety of legal and other subjects. These functions constitute the traditional role, but in an age of a rapid evolution in information they are not enough to satisfy legal professional needs properly.

**Current Context.** More people live on our planet today than the sum of all the people who ever lived before in recorded history. People must have information to survive in our world, and as the population increases it becomes necessary to find better ways of distributing needed information. Information is being produced faster by more people than in the past. In law this condition is reflected both in additional court decisions, because there are more people litigating, and in increased legislation, because society has become more complicated in human relationships and in scientific development. The number of specialized subjects is also increasing rapidly. For example, law must regulate space exploration, satellite communications, environmental pollution, toxic chemicals—areas for which there was little if any law a generation ago.

No longer does the word *information* apply only to things that are printed; rather, it also includes such other materials as film, slides, videotape, videodiscs, and computer tapes and discs. The library must become a media center that will allow its patrons communication with sources of information in perhaps many different locations. Information science is concerned with discovering better ways to get the right information quickly to the person who needs it and with finding information efficiently at a later time, once it is stored in libraries and other centers of information.

The legal information system the law library profession envisions for the U.S. will deliver information to judges and lawyers, faculty and students, and the general public. To satisfy this objective it must meet three basic requirements: first, it should be able to tell a user where to find information; second, it should be able to deliver this information; and third, it must respond within the time limits the user imposes.

The law library information operation will therefore be concerned with the way people create information, index or label it, store it, find it, analyze it, send and receive it, and use it. In carrying out this mission there are at least three basic tools for law library personnel: first, computers, because they can process information in the form of words as effectively as they compute numbers; second, telecommunications, because this technology is capable of distributing word and picture information at great speeds to widely dispersed places; finally, micrographics, because microform technology allows large quantities of information to be condensed into a small space.

With the financial support of the Association of American Law Schools and the American Association of Law Libraries, leading law libraries are working together to build a legal information network that will link the information, books, and audiovisual materials of many law libraries and legal information centers into one significant system. Using telecommunications it will then be possible to make the information resources of the whole network available to any single user in the country.

Law librarians seek to further their leadership in the application of advanced modern technology to law by utilizing electronic retrieval systems such as LEXIS and WESTLAW for reports of court decisions, statutes, and administrative law and by providing for the automation of library and bibliographic processes through RLIN and OCLC. The data base systems developed by Lockheed, Systems Development Corporation, and others should provide access to subjects related to law, such as energy and the environment. Leading law firms already utilize computers and will increasingly expect new lawyers to be knowledgeable in their operation. The law library is thus the true laboratory of the law where its patrons must experiment and learn to use the new tools of the profession.

**Staff.** Effective service requires a professionally qualified staff. The legal profession has been slow in grasping the advantages provided to law libraries by library school graduates. Because there are no effective or enforceable standards for personnel in many county, court, and law firm libraries, such libraries are typically quite poorly organized and maintained. With the advent of certification and accreditation procedures developed by professional associations, this situation may be expected to improve. Professional librarians are now typically the employees of choice in law firm, government, and bar association libraries. In academic libraries the personnel may be lawyer-librarians with some training in information science.

The smaller a law library collection is the more important it is that the person in charge of the library have professional training, because with a limited collection available the librarian will need knowledge of sources of information off-premises. The law firm in the late 1970's was backing into the 20th century by discovering the value of professional librarians as information finders and organizers on both the legal and factual sides of legal causes.

**Services.** Well-designed and equipped physical facilities are critical to providing law library services and access to materials. Upon entering a library the patron should see a directory upon which all service elements are mapped. Next, by various architectural techniques, the patron should notice first an information outlet where he or she may inquire about a particular problem and be directed to the proper department. Typically, provision will be made for access to the collections through card catalogues, micrographic devices, or computer terminals,

Library of Congress Law Library

*The reference materials used in LC's Law Library are of particular importance to legal researchers.*

and additional standard bibliographic services and indexes will be provided. Copying and typing facilities are standard. Enclosed course reserve materials areas in law school libraries, reference rooms, audiovisual and computer instructional facilities, discussion rooms, rare- or restricted-book areas, and lounges are other features often included in modern libraries. Reference services will vary among law libraries according to the institutions they serve. Law school libraries may provide more traditional academic library reference services, while in law firm libraries the staff play an integral role in research.

Access to law libraries and their materials similarly varies according to institutional setting. By national policy, the courts of last resort in each jurisdiction and accredited law school libraries with government depository status are urged to make their federal documents collections available to the general public. County law libraries are typically open to the public, while bar association and court libraries are often restricted to use by judges and attorneys. Special regulations may govern the use of law libraries in colleges and universities where space may be a factor in providing acceptable service to law students and faculty who will receive top priority. Firm law libraries are normally restricted to use by members of the firm. Relatively few public libraries maintain extensive collections of legal materials, and as library support in many communities is curtailed, this condition may be expected to continue. At the same time, however, there is a growing interest in providing access to legal materials to public library patrons.

Library personnel are not permitted to give legal advice, though they may point out standard reference sources. Legal materials may baffle the layman who has not been instructed in their use, so educational materials may be made readily available for self-instructional purposes. There is a body of literature that shows the difficulty in refraining from giving legal advice while providing access to complex legal tools.

Interlibrary loans of legal materials may be restricted to secondary materials inasmuch as primary materials—statutes and cases—are essentially reference works in sets. The procedure for interlibrary loan would be the same as in general libraries, subject to the aforementioned restrictions.

DAN HENKE

COLLECTIONS

Law library collections reflect the characteristics of the clientele they are designed to serve. While core collections in sole practitioners' libraries will have contents similar to those of the larger law libraries, the expanded collections will vary in accordance with the information expectations of the users. Even within the different types of legal communities served, vast differences may be observed in the collections assembled for use. For example, one law school may teach the rudiments of the law practice and require a library primarily of the practitioners' tools, while another may emphasize research and writing requiring extensive resources for faculty and student investigation. Law firm and corporate libraries collect books in the areas of their lawyers' specialities and outside the core collection may concentrate on highly specialized titles in limited fields of practice within the firm or corporate environment. Bar associations, courts, and governmental libraries acquire resources consistent with the interests of the constituencies that they serve. The Law Library of Congress, for instance, acquires materials on a worldwide basis because of the demands for research materials and reports from Congress.

**Materials.** Law library collections differ from other types of special library collections in that serials comprise the largest proportion of the content, often to the extent of two-thirds of the collection. This is due to the nature of the law itself. The state legislatures produce volumes of laws, known as session laws, which when codified become "codes" or "statutes" and when reproduced by commercial vendors along with cases and notes are given titles of "annotated codes" or "annotated statutes." Courts concurrently expound their opinions in "decisions" that are published as "reports" and are later consolidated into "annotated reports," digests, encyclopedias and eventually incorporated into "annotated codes" or "statutes"; thus, the magnitude of these serial publishing programs becomes evident when 50 states and the federal system are multiplied by the number of courts and volumes that each court publishes in one year.

Even the smallest library must maintain the current laws and court opinions in its state and federal law and opinions when applicable. Beyond the primary law books, indexing tools are an essential part of legal research. As the scope of legal research activity increases, the library must parallel or exceed that activity by providing the information resources to support the demand. Growing libraries may expand toward resources of the region in which they are located—the states around them or significant states with similar legal controversies—while the larger libraries will collect nationwide and selectively in the international fields. Ultimately, the largest libraries will amass worldwide collections.

Libraries that support extensive writing projects must invest in research tools beyond the basics in laws and court reports. Law firms that have a large appellate practice, corporate legal research units, law schools that emphasize research and writing and maintain student publications, bar associations, and courts and government agencies engaged in brief writing require secondary sources of the law to assist with formulating research products and framing the final outcome of the query searched. Libraries will acquire some or all of these, depending upon their research requirements. Publications such as law reviews and legal periodicals, encyclopedias, dictionaries, and treatises fill this kind of need. Many professional associations publish a legal journal, and nearly every law school publishes a law review, edited by its students, with articles by leading practitioners, judges, faculty, and some student works. The *American Bar Association Journal* and the *Harvard Law Review* are but two of the approximately 400 legal periodicals indexed in the *Index to Legal Periodicals*.

Two national encyclopedias, the *American Jurisprudence 2nd* and *Corpus Juris Secundum,* purport to cover the basic American law principles, documented with cases that have enunciated these principles. Additionally, state encyclopedias cover local law. A number of law dictionaries define legal terms citing to court opinions, among them *Black's Law Dictionary* and *Ballentine's Law Dictionary*. Other legal information is published in books that exhaustively treat a legal subject with supporting documentation, referred to as treatises; often their authors are authorities in their fields, and their works are frequently cited by name as the outstanding exposition on the law in a particular area, such as *Prosser on Torts*. *Shepard's Citations* has long served the legal profession by leading legal searchers through a maze of cases and statutes citing to a case or law being searched. In the natural sciences this method of research through citation is used in *Science Citation Index*.

The passage of Public Law 95-261 in 1978 afforded law school libraries the opportunity of becoming depository libraries for U.S. government publications, and many have done so. Dramatic increases in information services, collection content, and volume count will result from this effort to secure additional resources for law libraries and will enhance the libraries' abilities to serve their patrons more effectively.

**Notable Collections.** Accumulation of law book collections has been an ongoing activity for many years. The first law library established in the U.S. was the Law Library Company of Philadelphia, formed in 1802 by a group of lawyers. Three years later the first law library book catalogue for this library listed 249 volumes. The Boston Social Law Library opened in 1804. Two state libraries that have excellent law collections were also established in this period, Pennsylvania in 1816 and New York in 1818. The Harvard Law School, founded in 1817, established a library with the nucleus from the college library, gifts, and some purchases; by 1826 the library had 1,752 volumes. One of the better known American bar associations is the Association of the Bar of the City of New York, which was incorporated in 1869 and within two years had acquired 6,000 volumes. From these beginnings law libraries have increased astronomically both in quality and quantity of collections as well as in numbers of libraries. The Boston Social Law Library contains more than 177,000 volumes, the State Library of Pennsylvania Law Library over 121,000 volumes, and the New York State Law Library over 240,000 volumes. Ranking among the largest law libraries in the U.S. are the Association of the Bar of the City of New York Law Library at more than 397,000 volumes and the Los Angeles County Law Library with more than 618,000 volumes. The largest law library is the Law Library of Congress at about 1,400,000 volumes and at least 1,600,000 when volumes in the Library of Congress are combined with the law collection.

The most spectacular growth in law library collections has occurred in law school libraries. From its humble beginnings in 1817, the Harvard Law School Library collection has consistently ranked the largest among law schools over the years, numbering 1,336,000 volumes in 1978. A span of some 600,000 volumes separates Harvard from those following in size: Columbia 651,000; Yale 590,000; New York University 523,000; and those in the 400,000-volume range—University of California at Berkeley, the University of Texas at Austin, and the University of Minnesota.

Some early common law collections were known to exist in England, but most law school libraries were not independent of parent universities. The Bodleian Library at Oxford enjoys a long history, but its law collection was incorporated into the main collection even though in 1878 a concession was made to shelve the law collection separately from the remainder of the collection. A new building completed in 1964 first housed a separate Bodleian Law Library with 192,000 volumes, the largest law library in the British Commonwealth today. Another law library in London enjoys a worldwide reputation for excellence. Assembling a law book collection under a cooperative acquisitions policy with four colleges of the University of London, the Institute for Advanced Legal Studies possesses an extensive common-law collection in addition to holdings in the law of Western European countries; in 1977 the collection numbered 130,000 volumes.

One of the most outstanding library systems with a world reputation is in West Germany. The five Max Planck Institutes, in different cities, are devoted to legal studies on foreign and international law, dealing with criminal, public, and private law, patents, copyrights, and unfair competition as well as legal history. Their combined libraries with more than 402,000 volumes form a unique law collection.

Other libraries of excellence throughout the world that deserve mention are: York University Law Library (Toronto) at 174,000 volumes (1977), the largest law school library in Canada; the Law Courts Library of Sydney, Australia, with 130,000 volumes; the University of Singapore Law Library with 68,000 volumes (1977); the University of Tokyo, Faculty of Law Library at 347,000 volumes (1977), and the Japanese Ministry of Justice Library with 213,000 volumes (1977); and the combined libraries of the Institute of Legal Studies and the Law School Library at the University of Lagos, Nigeria, for the best law collection in Africa.

**Collection Development.** Budgets and space are probably the two most significant delimiters to growth in law libraries. Ideally, a library should have every law title that its clientele could possibly desire at the time the need arises, but few, if any, libraries can operate in this kind of environment. Therefore, some kind of judgment must be made in the selection of types of legal information to be furnished. In those libraries where each aquisition must be justified, a library committee of attorneys may make the selections for the library. In other libraries the librarian may have more freedom in selection of materials for the collection. In some governmental libraries a central purchasing agency must approve the acquisitions. In law school libraries, where nearly all of the librarians have both professional degrees, the selection of materials for the collection remains largely the librarians' prerogative.

Guidelines for the contents of law school libraries are provided by the Association of American Law Schools and the American Bar Association. Designated types of books are required for the normal teaching function of accredited law schools. Sufficient flexibility is permitted so that the law school libraries may acquire the basic required library tools and in addition purchase related materials to meet the specific interests of the faculty at each school.

As a further aid to book selection the Association of American Law Schools sponsored the publication in 1967 of a series of 48 pamphlets of *Law Books Recommended for Libraries* in subject areas from Admiralty to Water Law and Foreign and International Law. Supplements for each were issued beginning in 1974. Books are ranked in A, B, C order for priority in ordering. The "A" ranked books are recommended for purchase in all law school libraries. Medium libraries should possess the "B" ranked books, and the only the largest law school libraries would be expected to own the "C" type books, which are primarily official government publications and materials in foreign languages. A survey conducted by the American Association of Law Libraries Special Networks Committee concluded that these rankings are largely valid, in accordance with the holdings of libraries in the various categories that checked their collections against the list.

Supreme Court of the U.S.

*Main reading room in the U.S. Supreme Court Library.*

A standard publication comparable to *Books in Print* is published for law libraries, *Law Books in Print.* Begun in 1957 and continuing in bound editions and paper supplements, the title remains as the primary authority for determining availability of current editions and prices of books still in the market place. Other bibliographies cover book selection, and publishers and dealers of course provide advertisements, brochures, a sales slip service, and catalogues for examination. Emphasis in law book buying is generally on the most current publications; interest in retrospective collections depends upon the availability of funds beyond those required for the current collection. A survey conducted in a general university library indicated that the majority of their book buying consisted of titles more than one year on the market, whereas the vast majority of the law book buying was prepublication or current-year publications. Thus, law libraries are constantly under pressure to stay current with new publications.

Sizable law book collections, while an asset for study and research, can become a liability where space is concerned. A general rule of thumb in the academic world points out that collections tend to double in ten years. Many law school libraries, having felt this pinch already, are housed in new buildings, moving into new buildings, or planning new ones. Some housed in relatively new buildings are already searching for additional space. Restrictions in funding, particularly from public sources, and the space crunch combine to challenge the resourcefulness of librarians in coping with demands for access to more information and at the same time finding places to store it.

Despite mixed user reactions, some law librarians are purchasing large quantities of microform with the intent of providing information in an easily storable format; in 1978 the University of Virginia and the University of Florida law school libraries ranked first and second in number of equivalent volumes held in microform: 95,000 and 75,000 volumes, respectively. The entire set of state session laws from territorial days to the present are available in microfiche. State court reports can be purchased in film or fiche. Congressional documents have been produced in microfiche, eliminating the storage and clerical chores involved in checking in separate pamphlets. Many other titles can be acquired from commercial sources to fill in sets that are impossible to obtain now in complete form except in rare instances when a used set comes on the market. Microform solves the problem of completeness, physical damage to books, and care and maintenance of aging collections. The pros and cons about forms of media apply equally as well to the law collection as to the general libraries, and they are adequately covered elsewhere in the library literature.

**Resource Sharing.** Libraries are looking toward resource sharing as budgets and space are increasingly limited. No longer can any library hope to be completely self-sufficient. Interlibrary lending and borrowing have been traditional among law libraries as they have been in the general library field, although they may not be as formalized. In metropolitan areas, law libraries have been cooperating in sharing resources for many years. As more law firms hire professional librarians and information managers, this activity is likely to grow. Smaller libraries will tend to lean on the larger libraries for information support in the more esoteric sources and infrequently used titles. This tendency has been evident for years, and larger libraries tend to suffer or to feel that they do, in meeting the constant demands of the smaller libraries to the detriment of their own library patrons. Consequently, many larger libraries are now imposing fees for lending materials and have thereby effectively cut off a rich source of information for less fortunate library patrons.

Two on-line cataloguing systems were formed originally to provide shared cataloguing data so that librarians over the country would not be cataloguing the same title and taking the time needlessly to handle each and every book. These systems, OCLC and RLIN, are developing rapidly, and as their data bases increase, so does their value for other purposes. OCLC experimented with an interlibrary loan function on-line to assist in the borrowing and lending of library materials. A number of law school libraries participate in OCLC, so an interlibrary loan function may become very valuable for law libraries. Even if a library does not participate in the on-line loan system, it is possible to determine what other libraries possess law titles and to write or telephone for a book loan.

As budgets become more limited and acquisitions agreements become more prevalent, the on-line systems will be even more valuable in determining if a title has been purchased by another library within the geographical area, or within the same size agency or institution, or if at all in the country. Cooperative acquisitions arrangements are more realistic with a tool like on-line cataloguing that is within the means of most law libraries.

**Audiovisual Materials.** In addition to law books and information in the microform format, many new libraries are now expanding resources to include audio cassettes, video cassettes, films, etc. Condyne and the State Bar of California are two large producers and distributors of audio tapes on current topics of the law. Many libraries provide these for patrons to acquire knowledge of supplemental areas of the law or in continuing legal education to update legal studies. This format has even become popular with those who have cassette players in their automobiles, so they can learn and drive simultaneously.

Videotapes have become a very popular medium for self-instruction in trial tactics and other practical subjects. Videotaping for self-criticism has become an acceptable teaching method in law schools as well as in continuing legal education seminars for lawyers, faculty, and judges. Although collecting video equipment and software requires a sizable investment of funds and employment of skilled personnel, the results are often worthwhile. Many law schools are now providing audiovisual services, either as a library function or through a separate department created for this purpose. A number of companies are producing legal tapes, including the American Trial Lawyers Association, the National Practice Institute, the Hastings College of Trial Advocacy, and the American Bar Association.

**Data Bases.** A natural movement from television to computerized research and instruction is inevitable. Computerized legal information is relatively new as compared with systems operating with general, scientific, and medical data bases. A latecomer in the field, computer-assisted research and instruction are making rapid strides and gaining in popularity and momentum. In contrast to systems available to other libraries, the legal data bases are searchable in full text, thus providing greater research capability and in-depth accessibility to information. The two operating systems are LEXIS and WESTLAW, which are predominately case data bases. LEXIS, a product of Mead Data Central, first went on-line in 1969 for Ohio. Subsequently, as use increased and its reputation grew, other states were added to the system. By 1979, 19 state data bases were searchable, with 5 more added in that year along with a substantial federal case, statutory, and administrative law data base. WESTLAW is a by-product of book production from the West Publishing Company, the largest law book publishers in the world. WESTLAW, first offered in 1975, contains cases from all states back to 1967 and with retrospective cases in selected states.

Both systems are available at commercial rates and special academic rates. Various preferences for use prevail—some users learn how to use the systems individually, while others depend upon library staff or specially designated professionals to frame the queries and search the data bases. In law schools, learning how to use the systems is heavily emphasized, whereas in law firms, courts, and other legal units, only one or two persons may become skilled in computerized searching. Approximately one-third of the law schools in the country have taken advantage of the special rates. It is too early yet to observe the impact of this training upon the legal community; however, it is safe to predict that law students who have consistently been successful in computerized legal research will no doubt influence the acquisition of these systems.

AUTOCITE, a Lawyer's Cooperative Publishing Company system that displays a case history, can be leased at communication and computer connect time costs through LEXIS. Data bases in other subjects with applicability to law can also be added to the law library's computer capabilities. Law libraries at the close of the 1970's were looking forward to the creation of a legal periodicals index data base on-line.

As of 1979 no automated system could be searched in lieu of traditional manual research because of the inadequacy of content of available data bases. But as information accessibility increases in automated form, expertise in searching improves, equipment costs decline, and more customers are added to systems, adequate data bases will develop for current, and eventually for all, research.

Computer-assisted instruction for law programs is only slowly gaining in popularity in law libraries. Law programs, primarily in courses for trial practice, are available in both the EDUCOM and PLATO systems, but as yet few law schools or libraries have acquired the systems as a part of their curriculum or as a library service.

BETTY TAYLOR

ADMINISTRATION, GOVERNANCE, AND FINANCE

There have been changes, sometimes dramatic and frequently subtle, in how law libraries function and why, in the 1960's and '70's. The causes are many. In large part the changes developed from greater dependence on law libraries, brought on by greater involvement of law and government in life itself as society becomes more complex. There has been a wider demand for law library service, stimulated by such diverse movements and trends as consumerism, equal rights, and interdisciplinary awareness. Other contributors to change include the technology explosion, the increasing availability of nonbook media, and inflation. Such factors have led to changes in varying degrees among the different types of law libraries and have resulted in alterations yet to be perceived in the nature of law librarianship.

Some preliminary information on the different types of law libraries is necessary for the discussion that follows. Generalizations and distinctions can then be made regarding how and why such entities function and how they are supported.

Law school libraries, with a few exceptions, are a part of a law school that in turn is part of a university. Authority for their existence can derive from institutional fiat, from a mandate of the university's governing board, or in the case of some tax-supported institutions, from legislative enactment. Funding can come from tuition, endowment, grants, legislative appropriation, or any combination of these sources.

The label "governmental law libraries" describes an array of law libraries serving the different levels of government. On the federal level there are very large law libraries, including the Law Library of the Library of Congress and the Department of Justice Library. Other law libraries serve agencies and other units in such specialized areas as the military, civil service, civil rights, agriculture, energy, taxation, labor relations, and a host of others. The states, their administrative agencies, and the county and municipal units have analogs of these federal governmental law libraries. Most states have a "state law library," meaning that library that has the primary responsibility of meeting the law information needs of state government. The actual title, mission, and governance of this entity, which is clearly recognized by law librarians, varies widely from state to state.

The federal and state court systems frequently have law libraries serving a particular court or group of courts. These are commonly referred to as supreme court libraries, court of appeals libraries, or some other term describing the type or types of courts served.

There are hundreds of county law libraries throughout the United States, which exist primarily to assure that litigants and their attorneys have access to law books, although other persons may also use these resources. County law libraries range greatly in size. The Los Angeles County Law Library in California and the Cook County Law Library in Chicago, Illinois, are among the largest law libraries anywhere; both have comprehensive library collections and large staffs. Other county law libraries have only a few thousand volumes and are staffed part time by a clerk attached primarily to another unit. County law libraries will normally derive their authority from state statutes, and their funding may come from appropriations from the state or county or from a portion of the fees charged to litigants for filing required papers relating to their business with the court.

Law firm libraries have been growing in numbers and size, and the employment of professional librarians in them has been increasing. Funding comes from the firms' revenues. Corporate law libraries are quite similar to law firm libraries. They serve the attorneys in the law department of a corporation. These libraries can be found among the larger manufacturers, banks, insurance companies, and public utilities.

Finally, there is a miscellaneous category of law libraries that does not fit into any of the above groupings, although resemblances may be close in some instances. Included here are bar association law libraries, such as the American Bar Foundation Cromwell Library of the American Bar Association and the Association of the Bar of the City of New York Library. Some learned societies and other organizations devoted to law, including the American Judicature Society and the American Society of International Law, maintain law libraries. These libraries are usually funded from members' dues and sometimes additionally by grants from charitable and other foundations.

**Governance.** The majority of head law school librarians answer to the dean of the law school. Less typically, the law library will be a part of the campus library system, but, even in this case, logic and tradition will compel a very close relationship between the law school and library. The head librarian, in most cases, will also be a member of the faculty. Law school librarians will unabashedly refer to the library as "the laboratory of the law school."

The problem of autonomy (whether the law library is part of the law school) versus centralization (whether the law library is a branch of the general library) is of great concern to academic law libraries. Two of the main issues raised in this concern are the subjection of the law library budget to the approval of the law school dean, rather than to the university librarian, and a complete in-house library, including staffing, book ordering, and processing.

The majority of county libraries are governed by a board of trustees, or board of directors or library committee, usually with a judge, county administrator, county commissioner, or other county official as a member. The head librarian is selected by that governing body but then exercises control over management of personnel below that position.

A similar situation exists in the law firm library. Usually there is a library committee, with one or two partners in the firm designated as "library partner," and it is to them that the head law librarian must report or seek approval. The law firm administrator and law librarian must also work closely together. In line with the trend toward compartmentalization and specialization in legal practice, firms are employing more professional law librarians to maintain their libraries, and this, at times, can cause tensions between a new professional who wants to run his or her own shop and the administrator, partner, or legal secretary who used to have control.

Government agency libraries (including court libraries) serve their respective clienteles in much the same manner as law firm libraries. Overall governance will be handled more or less formally by a library committee, a single attorney or judge, or the judges or staff of attorneys acting as a committee of the whole. The majority of state law libraries are administratively placed under the judicial branch (viz. the state supreme court). The others come under a variety of organizational arrangements, including being under the state library, the department of education, the legislature, the attorney general, or as independent agencies.

The library committee, whether advisory or governing, is found within all types of law libraries. The nature of the library committee's activities is determined by its function rather than by the size and type of law library, although size has an indirect relationship to the amount of authority exercised by the head law librarian. The library committee best serves the librarian by advising on matters of general policy, the development of library resources, and means of integrating the library program with the other functions of the law firm, school, agency, or other institution. On the one hand, the library is an agency whose functions and services are varied and affect many; on the other hand, it is a tight, complex agency whose inner workings are largely unknown to those it serves except for certain obvious lending and reference functions performed at the circulation desk. The law library thus needs information from the governing committee about new policies, new courses and new instructors in the academic law library setting, and new firm members and areas of practice in the law firm setting, because almost inevitably such matters have a direct bearing on the needs of the library and the services it should be able to provide. The library committee should be advisory to the librarian.

**Finance.** Law school libraries are funded through tax revenues in the case of public institutions and through tuition income in the case of private universities. In both instances, such funds can be supplemented through endowments, gifts, grants, and library use fees. County law libraries may obtain funding through earmarked portions of filing fees required of litigants or by appropriation or allocation of funds by the governmental unit of which the library is a part. Portions of bar membership dues and income from photocopy machines, investments, and book sales are also sources of funds. Law firm and corporate law libraries are allocated funds by the governing members of the law firm, frequently through the office manager or legal administrator. Other private law libraries, such as a membership library or a bar association library, derive their budgetary funds through membership fees and dues. It is possible for the law librarian to supplement regular funds through creative measures such as forming a Friends of the Law Library group from a nucleus of users, or from alumni in the law school library setting.

Other ways of supplementing the library budget are through charging fees for reference work and research, for interlibrary loan requests, and for photocopying. Almost universally, however, fees are charged only to recover costs of services to secondary patrons and not as a means of raising extra revenue.

Some law libraries have initiated publication programs to supplement funding, and others exchange or sell surplus books to other libraries or to book publishers.

**Administration.** The administration of the law library involves planning, policymaking, budget management, and personnel management.

*Goals and Policy.* Each type of law library necessarily plans its policies around the clientele it serves. Law librarians tend to identify closely with their clientele, namely practicing lawyers, judges, government lawyers, law school teachers, and law students. Many have law degrees or some law training, and all have an interest in the subject matter and profession of law. This fosters close and sympathetic communication between librarian and patron in setting library goals and policy. The academic or university law school librarian must, of course, accommodate the needs of students and faculty. But other problems, such as the relationship with the general library and outside use of the law library by other law patrons, must be considered. A continuing problem for the larger law school libraries in metropolitan areas is the heavy use they get from practicing attorneys and from students in smaller law schools. Even the largest of law firm libraries cannot afford to keep all of the law books that might be needed (e.g., all the legal periodicals, outside state materials, and government documents). The government library (federal, state, municipal, county, court) must serve the needs of the local courts and practitioners and yet deal with problems generated by outside use of the facilities by the public. It is only in the law firm or corporate law library that the clientele is strictly defined; yet even there, sharing of resources is an important factor, and a thriving interlibrary loan activity takes place both ways among law firms and other institutions and individuals.

*Organizational Structure.* Administration of the law library involves departmentalizing the activities of the library to carry out its objectives. The determination of departmental groupings is based largely on the size of the library. In the small law library—for example in a law firm or government agency—there is little need for departmentalization. All functions are performed by one person or a small number of personnel. However, since almost all law libraries are relatively small, versatility and flexibility are highly valued among law librarians. In the larger library, delegation and departmentalization are essential, nevertheless. The organizational structure parallels that of similarly sized general libraries.

The traditional functional organization provides separate departments for cataloguing, circulation, and reference; not infrequently the last two areas are combined into a single department. In this bifurcated functional organization all library activities are considered as either readers services or technical processes.

Because of the integrating tendencies of automation, law libraries, like other libraries, are witnessing the dissolution of the old compartments of ordering, serials, binding, cataloguing, and final book processing. These units are tending to blend into one rather homogeneous technical processing section. In public services, there has always been a tendency to treat public services as a single activity, without the usual subdivision of circulation, reference, interlibrary loan, and so on. There are several reasons for this. For one thing, circulation tends to be a less distinct activity in law libraries. Few, if any, books circulate outside the premises. Where there is any charging out, it will be to offices, carrels, or other locations on the premises. Due dates, recalls, overdues, and fines, for example, are generally not significant. Charged materials are usually quickly retrievable and therefore regarded as information location problems like any other problem a reference librarian deals with.

*Personnel Administration.* No administrative duty of the librarian is more important than effective selection of staff. Time spent on all other areas of administration will not be as effective without a competent staff to work toward goals and carry out policies and programs. In working with relatively small staffs conducting essentially a personalized service, the quality of each member is critical. It is important in the law library to find staff with law-related experience beyond generalized library experience or at least to place newcomers to this subject field in a position where they can learn about law materials and special needs of law library users.

The effectiveness of the library requires a well-qualified and numerically adequate staff. The typical library staff consists of librarians and nonprofessional assistants, augmented with student or part-time help. Often, the head law librarian possesses both a law degree and a library science degree, and in many of the larger law libraries other librarians may possess both of these degrees. There are few such positions in the private law firm, although there is a trend in that direction.

Professionalism is a current issue in librarianship, and paraprofessionals are in the middle of the controversy. Proposed solutions include certification standards promulgated by such groups as ALA, AALL, and ACRL and minimum requirements for professional librarian positions. Most objections to the use of paraprofessionals in the library system are centered on the argument that expanded employment of paraprofessionals will displace professionals. However, many library tasks can be performed with efficiency by paraprofessionals.

The head law librarian is usually selected by the library's governing body or library committee, which then delegates the authority of selection of lower-level library positions to the head librarian. It is common for the librarian to nominate the professional and clerical staff, and it may be required that the latter be selected from a municipal or state civil service eligible list in certain public institutions. The governing body of the library frequently passes on the librarian's nominations of professional staff members, but such authority may be delegated to the head librarian, along with authority to hire clerical staff members.

In well-established organizations the practice of permitting the librarian to make all recommendations of personnel, supporting such nominations with full data and references, has been demonstrated as effective procedure. Universal to recruitment and selection is the job description, which usually includes title, salary, and minimum qualifications and lists basic responsibilities for that position. Job descriptions are used also to organize job hierarchies within the law library and set up salary classifications. Flexibility is important in establishing minimum qualifications to allow for consideration of on-the-job training or related coursework in lieu of a job requirement. Recruitment also involves considerations of affirmative action requirements and whether the administrator must select from civil service roster or other institutional eligibility lists.

Staff size in relation to the physical size of the library will vary according to the function that the law library serves. For example, a very small law firm library may have more than one staff member because of the attorney reliance on the librarian as a source of information and research. In the larger academic library, staff size in proportion to library size may be much smaller, because of a relatively greater reliance on the collection itself, rather than the personnel.

Administration of the law library involves allowing for interaction between individual personnel and the greater organization of the library. Participatory management is the style and philosophy frequently encountered in law libraries.

*Budget.* The budget of a law library affects nearly every major consideration in its administration, including collection development, book selection, staff size, physical plant, equipment, attendance at professional meetings, and even use of telephones. It is customary in some law libraries to classify the budget by object or type of material, thus establishing separate categories of expenditure for treatises, periodicals, continuations, supplies, equipment, and such other items that local practice may identify. Most law libraries utilize such line-type budgets, while others, especially law firm libraries, may prepare lump-sum budgets, or categorize by department or area of law rather than type of material.

Many law school libraries use comparative statistics to justify budget expenditures. The results of a statistical survey of law school libraries and librarians are published annually in the May issue of the *Law Library Journal* to monitor law library expenditures.

In some of the smallest law firm libraries, budgets are not yet a fixture of the law librarian's position. However, they are of growing concern as the firm realizes the impact of expenditures of its library and the need to keep track of and control over that investment.

The overwhelming budgeting concern among all library administrators is decreasing financial support, coupled with inflation. One or both of these factors are affecting all types of law libraries. A number of alternatives are being considered and tried in law libraries. Microform offers economies in initial cost and shelving space, and law libraries in particular are attracted to this medium because so much of their material is available in microform. But lawyers, who are used to finding their information in large, premium quality texts with all of the bibliographic and typographical conveniences, often resist this format.

The economies, if any, and other impact of automation (aside from information retrieval) have been late in coming to law libraries, probably because as relatively small economic units they often cannot afford the high capital costs. Law library administrators have had to look toward linking up with larger units or networks or to the purchase of commercially packaged systems.

One result of more stringent budgets has been a lowering of expectations among law library administrators.

York University

*York University in Toronto provides comfortable study areas among the stacks in the Osgoode Hall Law School Library.*

The enthusiastic buying of materials in the allied social and technical sciences during the 1960's has lessened considerably. Few libraries now attempt to be "complete" in any of the broad areas. Even the largest, best supported libraries find it difficult to cover an area such as all foreign law. All of this, of course, is not unique to law libraries but reflective of current conditions in all areas of librarianship and in society in general.

**REFERENCES**

Ronni F. Begleiter, "The Private Law Librarian—A Complete Library Professional," *Law Library Journal* (February 1978).

Ann M. Carter, "Budgeting in Private Law Firm Libraries," *Law Library Journal* (February 1978).

Joseph Myron Jacobstein, "Law Library Administration," *Library Trends* (January 1963).

MORTIMER SCHWARTZ

MEASUREMENT AND EVALUATION

The problem of measurement and evaluation of libraries has puzzled law librarians and those responsible for the administration and funding of law libraries during most of this century. Standards were adopted early by both the American Bar Association (ABA) and the American Association of Law Schools (AALS). Members of the American Association of Law Libraries (AALL) participated actively in the preparation of these standards, which were and still are largely quantitative and applicable only to law school libraries. Little had been done until the late 1970's to develop standards for court, government, bar association, or law firm libraries. The available standards have been useful especially when tied to an enforcement process, as in the accreditation of law schools; whether voluntary standards, without supporting enforcement, can be effective remains to be tested. At best, the development of standards and their application have been slow and painful.

Similarly, statistical information has been available for the law school libraries for many years but for other types of libraries only recently. Statistical information for law libraries is useful for comparison and serves as a basis for future planning by library administrators and the profession as a whole. Librarians are able to evaluate their libraries on a quantitative basis or at least compare their libraries with others, but in doing so, problems have arisen.

The far more difficult question, whether *qualitative* measurement and evaluation is possible, remains the subject of much argument. Because of this difficulty, library standards have tended more to be guidelines based on practices in existing institutions than to be standards in a qualitative sense. Statistical information provides a basis of comparison and in that way reinforces those standards, but many have urged the development of qualitative standards by which law libraries could be measured in accordance with recognized standards of excellence as to size, structure, clientele, resources, services, and staff. If libraries could be graded in relation to each institution's potential, each library would have a guide for the improvement of its collection and of its services. The argument for qualitative standards has continued steadily but without resolution.

Perhaps because of the lack of qualitative standards, quantitative comparisons are made and have become qualitative by application. Thus "big becomes better" even though it is clear that volume count alone reveals little about the quality of a collection or a library's adequacy for its mission. Volume count—absent accurate physical counting based on agreed practices and with uniform conversion of microforms and other nonbook resources to equivalent volumes—stands, at most, as a questionable basis for comparison, be it quantitative or qualitative. The AALL Committee on Bibliographic Standards prepared recommended definitions and guidelines for nonprint and nonbook library resources that, if adopted and followed, will relieve the problem but unfortunately not resolve it.

**Law School Libraries.** The Association of American Law Schools, organized in 1900, promulgated the first statement of minimum requirements for law libraries. Member schools were required to own, or have convenient access to, a library containing the reports of the state in which the school was located and of the United States. These requirements have been amended and refined as legal education has changed and the role of law libraries and law librarians in that educational process has developed. The By-laws and Executive Committee Regulations of the Association (1978) now recommend a minimum collection of 60,000 volumes, a full-time librarian who is a full, participating member of the faculty, and, for a library of 60,000 volumes or more, three professional assistants.

In 1921 the American Bar Association adopted formal standards to be used in the approval of law schools. These first standards required only that an approved law school provide an adequate library for the students. The *Standards for the Approval of Law Schools* (1977) require now that a law school maintain and administer a library adequate for its program. No minimum volume count or minimum number of professional staff is specified, although a list of required titles is included.

The United States Commissioner of Education, in the Department of Health, Education, and Welfare, has recognized the American Bar Association as the national accrediting agency for legal education. The Council on Postsecondary Accreditation similarly has recognized the American Bar Association's program of accreditation. Law schools are inspected as part of the provisional accreditation process and after full approval are reinspected once every seven years.

Although there are differences in the ABA Standards and the AALS requirements for membership, both associations are concerned with the same basic operations. In recent years ABA and AALS have conducted joint inspections of member schools. Law librarians were included as members of the site inspection teams during the 1970's, and an ABA manual, "Suggestions for Law Library Inspectors," appeared in 1976. It contains a checklist that has proved useful in the evaluation of the library.

Statistics on law school libraries are available in the annual *Review of Legal Education in the United States,* published by the American Bar Association, while a more detailed statistical survey is published annually in the May issue of the *Law Library Journal.* Such data are extremely helpful in comparing collections, growth rates, budgets, staff, etc., and in providing useful information on hours, seating capacity, etc. Unfortunately, the utility of this information is restricted by the lack of uniformity in reporting practices.

These statistics were used by Charles Kelso in the AALS "Study of Part-Time Legal Education" (1972) and later in "Adding Up the Law Schools" published in *Learning and the Law* in 1975. Peter Swords and Frank K. Walwer, in *The Costs and Resources of Legal Education* (1974), also used these data in measuring law school resources. In the Kelso study, six factors are indexed: number of students, student/volume ratio, student/faculty ratio, number of faculty, faculty/volume ratio, and volumes in library. As these are "added up" it must be noted that three of the six originate in volume count. In the Swords and Walwer study, three factors are used: median Law School Admissions Test score, median faculty salary, and number of volumes in the library. Obviously it is critical that the total volume count reported be as accurate as possible if it is to be used in this way.

**Nonacademic Law Libraries.** The first general study of law libraries outside the law schools appeared in 1953 as part of the Survey of the Legal Profession sponsored by the American Bar Association, published as *The Libraries of the Legal Profession* by William Roalfe, then Law Librarian and Professor of Law at Northwestern University. The focus of this study was on all types of law libraries serving the legal profession except those in the law schools, which were studied elsewhere. Roalfe concluded that much more information was needed about the libraries serving the legal profession, their collections, their staffs, and their funding. He emphasized the need for better libraries located throughout the nation and available to all segments of the legal profession. The availability of these libraries to the general public was not studied, and little or no attention was given to this matter for another quarter century.

Standards for nonlaw school libraries have been available only in the late 1970's. The State, Court, and County Law Libraries Special Interest Section of AALL has prepared *Standards for Supreme Court Law Libraries* (adopted 1977 and revised 1978), *Federal Court Libraries* (adopted 1978), and *County Law Libraries* (adopted 1978). Their effectiveness, without an enforcement procedure, remains to be tested. Whether similar standards can, or will, be developed for other types of nonacademic libraries remains a challenge to the profession.

A report entitled "Improving the Federal Court Library System" was prepared in 1978 for the Federal Judicial Center on the libraries of the federal courts. The study, which focused on management, budget and procurement, personnel, use and facilities, and the need for future planning, was submitted to the Judicial Conference of the United States for consideration.

Statistical information on nonacademic law libraries has become increasingly available. A survey of law firm libraries and librarians first appeared in 1974, and an annual survey of law libraries serving a local bar has appeared since 1976. Both surveys seek to provide the kind of basic information on collection, income, expenditures, staffing, and salaries previously available only for law school libraries and have proved useful for comparative purposes. Unfortunately, the same problems encountered in the use of such data discussed above apply here.

**Professional Qualifications.** The argument over the professional qualifications for law librarians began early. Many have felt, and some still feel, that the administration of the law library is a fairly simple matter that can be learned in a short period of time and that does not require professional education. Those who argued for professionally qualified librarians generally favored law training, with only a few preferring the library degree. It was not until after World War II that librarians with degrees in both law and library science appeared in any number. Today, most head librarians in the law schools have both degrees, and in fact the AALS membership regulations state that the head librarian should have both degrees and meet the Association's certification requirements.

The focus of attention has now shifted to the educational requirements for supporting professional staff and to the need for continuing education for librarians at all levels of the profession. The American Association of Law Libraries has concerned itself with both the education and continuing education of its members. The programs at annual meetings have sought to provide educational opportunities for the membership. In 1964 the Association began a series of Rotating Institutes in response to the increasing demand for education, and two series were completed before the Association discontinued them. Most head librarians, and an increasing number of supporting professional staff, enter the profession with library degrees. Librarians with advanced degrees in related areas, especially computer science, are also part of the profession today. AALL's Education Committee has presented a variety of programs to meet needs for continuing education.

The AALL has operated, since 1961, an active program for the certification of law librarians. The Association grants certification to applicants with various combinations of education and experience: (a) law degree, library degree plus two years of professional experience; (b) law degree and four years of professional library experience; (c) library degree plus six years of professional library experience; (d) 20 years of responsible professional law library experience and outstanding contributions to the profession (no degree requirement). From 1961, when the certification program began, through the 1978 annual meeting, 704 persons were certified, including charter certifications.

The debate continues. How much education can and should be expected of one entering the profession? Does "certified law librarian" mean "professional law librarian," and if so should the certification of persons without professional education in law or in library science be continued? Will continuing education be required to maintain certification? Obviously the application of educational requirements and standards is far from certain or uniform, and the pattern for the future remains to be designed.

BETTY LEBUS

## LAW LIBRARY COOPERATION

Cooperation among law libraries occurs in various ways. There are the traditional interlibrary loan procedures, which do not differ from those of other types of libraries. Most law libraries, especially those of university law schools, will lend materials to other libraries and will borrow when needed, using standard American Library Association interlibrary forms. Perhaps the only distinguishing feature is that more materials in a law library are of a reference nature and do not circulate under any circumstances. Increasingly, however, law libraries are providing photocopies in lieu of lending of the item itself.

But law libraries do participate in other forms of cooperation. At universities, although nearly all law school libraries are administered as part of the law school rather than as a branch of the university library, the acquisition of library materials is frequently coordinated. This occurs because of the commonality of interest among law professors and historians, political scientists, sociologists, economists, and criminologists. Moreover, agreement is frequently reached on the most effective place to house certain government documents, such as reports of administrative agencies, and other interdisciplinary materials. Sometimes the university as a whole will be better served to have some of these materials shelved in the law library with other sets shelved elsewhere on campus.

Cooperation may also occur on an interlibrary basis. In large cities law firm libraries in the same or nearby buildings will agree that one will buy an expensive set and the other another. Larger law libraries in the same metropolitan area will frequently assume responsibility to share the acquisition of foreign law. One library may assume responsibility, for example, for legal materials of Latin America, while one or more will collect European legal materials.

While there has been much discussion of a national coordinated scheme of cooperation among law libraries, in practice cooperation has been limited to local areas with informal agreements among the cooperating libraries. While much has been accomplished by such arrangements, the lack of an organized and planned program has had its effect. Cooperative schemes organized with the best of intentions have faltered with change of personnel, either at the level of the law librarian or at a higher administrative position.

Several factors, however, now point to an increased and more organized effort toward cooperation among law libraries. These factors are inflation, an ever expanding growth in the subjects of law, and the development of computer-based library networks. The extent of the growth of the law in recent years is perhaps not generally realized, even by lawyers. Society seems to feel that any new societal problem can be solved only by passing new legislation.

Some subject areas of the law developed in the 1960's and '70's include computer law, energy law, environmental law, fair employment practices, nuclear regulation, and pollution control, to name only a few. All of these are primarily examples of domestic law; many other examples from international and comparative law could also be cited. This growth in the law by itself has had a significant impact on the acquisitions policies of law libraries. With the added impact of inflation, the pressure for cooperation indeed becomes urgent. A *Library Journal* survey of price indexes reveals that between 1970 and 1979 the price index for legal periodicals has increased by 140 percent and for legal series by 160 percent.

Law libraries, therefore, perhaps even more than some other types of libraries, now have the impetus to enter into cooperative agreements. As national and regional networks became operational, law libraries were quick to participate. Law school libraries frequently joined with their university libraries, although usually arranging to keep their records separately identifiable. In a few instances a law school library has joined a network different from that of its university library when it appeared the network would better meet its needs. Law libraries not connected with universities have also joined networks, either through joining a regional network or directly with a national one. However, while law libraries have taken advantage of the developing modern technology, the effect has been to diversify the cataloguing data of the various law libraries, impeding the further development of shared acquisitions and cataloguing programs among law libraries. Some of the larger law libraries, such as the University of Texas, Cornell, and the University of Florida, are in the OCLC system, while many of the larger research law libraries, such as the Los Angeles County Law Library, University of California at Berkeley and Davis, Stanford, the University of Michigan, and Columbia are in the Research Library Information Network (RLIN) of the Research Libraries Group (RLG). Others are in yet a different network.

**A Law Library Network.** Among law librarians,

however, there is a felt need for a common data base for legal materials. Larger law libraries do about 50 percent original cataloguing, and records on most of this important material are not available to those law libraries not in the same network or not in any network. To remedy this situation, a number of law librarians met in the latter part of 1975 and recommended the creation of a national law library network. The concept of a network based on a subject, rather than on geography, is rather new and raised many different types of problems. In order to measure the feasibility of a law network, the American Association of Law Libraries, in cooperation with the Association of American Law Schools, engaged a consultant, Brett Butler, to advise on the matter. His 1978 report, *Toward a Law Network: Survey and Evaluation,* indicated that such a subject network is indeed feasible. The report recommends that the AALL sponsor the development of a law information network (LAWNET). This network, among other things, would assume the responsibility for the development of law libraries standard subject headings, standards for the format of bibliographic records, standards for the content of a law data base, and other necessary standards. The report further recommends that LAWNET should proceed to build a composite data base by merging selected machine-readable files gathered from those law libraries currently inputting their records into a network. Once the data base is created, and procedures have been developed for maintaining and updating it, LAWNET should arrange to have such a service available on-line and also available for distribution to smaller law libraries on microfiche. It further recommended the development of a "LAWNET Location Guide," which would provide listings by title and control number for all monographs and serials in the LAWNET data base along with location code. The AALL was exploring at the end of the 1970's ways of implementing the recommendations for the creation of LAWNET

This development has tremendous possibilities not only for law libraries but for other types of libraries. First, it may become a prototype for the feasibility of creating a national network by subject that may be of interest to other types of special libraries such as music, art, or engineering. Second, it will provide for an intelligent basis for shared acquisitions and cataloguing; for example, one large law library might assume all the responsibility for the original cataloguing of German materials, another for French, and still another for Italian. Under such a system all other law libraries would not have to do any original cataloguing for legal materials from those geographic areas.

Similarly, as the system grows, law libraries can start to develop coordinated acquisitions programs to ensure that all necessary legal research materials are available without unnecessary duplication. Attention will also be given to document delivery.

The significance of this program to other types of libraries should be self-evident. The need for legal materials in nonlaw libraries is growing. Large public libraries have to supply information to their patrons who may be interested in such diverse subjects as the control of the environment or of nuclear energy or even, for example, to provide information to irate citizens who want to know their rights when their reservations are not honored by an airline. Similarly, more and more undergraduate programs are emphasizing courses in which access to legal materials is necessary. Yet, with declining budgets these libraries are finding it more and more difficult to maintain an adequate legal collection. The development of LAWNET as proposed by the American Association of Law Libraries will make legal materials available, not only to other law libraries, but to other libraries in need of legal materials.

In summary, the fact that law libraries have not had a national law library, such as the National Library of Medicine, or the National Library of Agriculture, has hindered the development of cooperation among law libraries. Considerable cooperation has developed in the past, and now under the leadership of the American Association of Law Libraries concerted efforts are being made for the coordination of cooperation on a national level. As this develops, and as law libraries increase their participation in other national plans for better bibliographic control, not only law libraries will benefit but all libraries will be able to better meet the growing demand of the public for legal information.

J. MYRON JACOBSTEIN

LAWS AND LEGISLATION

Any attempt to describe briefly the legislative foundation for U.S. law libraries is perilous indeed. There are several aspects to this hazard. First, the definition of what a law library is is subject to a criticism of being arbitrary; that criticism may be rebutted if the library is denominated a law library by its senior authority or governing rules. However, when the collection is an integral component of a larger administrative unit, or, although physically distinct, the collection is referred to as the "state library," "legislative library," or "department library," the definition of law library must be based on the nature of its collection, its services, and its primary clientele and is necessarily subjective. Second, many law libraries cannot trace their birth to specific legislation. Rather, in many if not most instances libraries have evolved from informal office collections to major resources as an adjunct to the mission of the senior agency without initial statutory approbation. Third, the sovereign independence of 50 state legislatures as well as that of the federal government results in a variety of approaches in the formulation of law library statutes that discourage their classification and the development of broad generalizations about them. Notwithstanding these inherent limitations, the following article attempts to give an initial description of the patterns of law libraries as affected by law and legislation.

**Federal Legislation.** In 1832 direct statutory action was responsible for the creation of the paramount federal law library, the Law Library of Congress. It was established as one of the two administrative units of the Library of Congress, and it was the intention of the lawmakers to form a convenient collection of law books for the use of the Supreme Court, which at that time was also located in the Capitol. As activities of the Library of Congress and the Supreme Court evolved, however, particularly when the Supreme Court was given its own building in 1935, the specific purpose of that early statute seemed to be lost. In 1977, however, under a reorganization plan proposed by the Librarian of Congress whereby the law library would have lost its status as one of the coequal departments of the Library of Congress as articulated in 1832, becoming instead one of several subject departments, the 150-year-old law was recalled as the keystone of a vigorous defense of the status quo. Focusing on the language of the early statute, supporters of the Law Library of Congress as a coequal administrative unit, including members of the legal profession in legal education and the practicing bar, as well as the law library community, argued strongly in official communications and in hearings before the Joint Committee on the Library of Congress that the special status should be maintained. Faced with these strong representations, the Library of Congress withdrew its immediate plan to reorganize insofar as the Law Library was concerned and indicated that it would subject the matter to further study and subsequent review. The Law Library of Congress continues to stand as a distinct unit within the Library of Congress. Through its specialized organization along worldwide regional lines, the Law Library serves its primary clientele, the members of Congress. Additionally, it serves as one of the nation's capital resources in the collection of legal materials on a global scale.

Also within the Library of Congress there was created by statute in 1946 a separate department for the analysis, appraisal, and evaluation of legislative proposals. Originally called the Legislative Reference Service, it changed its name in 1970 to the Congressional Research Service. Since this unit does not manage large book collections, it is not exactly a library; and as its interest ranges much more widely across the subject spectrum than merely the law in a narrow sense, it is not exactly a law library. Yet, because it does directly serve the legislative branch and, further, because the Service's enabling act specifically authorizes the appointment of American public law specialists, it can be asserted that a law library was created. This institution serving the federal legislature exemplifies a type of legislative law library that is frequently found in state government.

Two other most significant congressional libraries, those of the House of Representatives and the Senate, although again not specifically law libraries, have a substantial legal content and are representative of libraries that began somewhat informally. The House and Senate were no doubt collecting books, documents, and other material for their own use from the earliest days, but in the spring of 1792, both bodies passed simple resolutions that specifically charged the Secretary of the Senate and the Clerk of the House to procure or purchase library materials for their respective use. Subsequent legislative history provides ample evidence of legislative recognition of the existence of these libraries. Appropriations, debates about library space, and statutory provisions for appointment of librarians and administrative control all contribute to understanding the legislative support that has encouraged the development of two libraries, each in access of 200,000 volumes.

The Library of the Supreme Court similarly evolved over a period of time without benefit of specific statutory creation. The legal collection created in 1832 for the use of the Justices ultimately developed into the Law Library of Congress. When the Court occupied the Supreme Court Building in 1935, it satisfied its law book needs by gift, with duplicates from the Library of Congress, with a small collection that had served the Court's Conference Room while it was in the Capitol, and by purchase with supplemental appropriations. The Supreme Court Building, constructed with space for a major library, is indicative of initial legislative approval and support for the nation's largest library exclusively devoted to the judicial function.

The libraries of the several courts of appeals and district courts also developed both informally and by statute. When books were necessary to carry out the legal work of the judiciary, they were acquired as a function of regular court procurement. In 1948, however, possibly in reaction to the growth of these libraries and the need for appropriate supervision, statutory authority was granted to each court of appeals to appoint a librarian and necessary library assistants. In a companion statute, the appointment of a Marshal for the Court of Customs and Patent Appeals was authorized, which statute charged that officer with the buying of books and supplies and supervision of the library. In 1954 the Tax Court was specifically authorized to make purchases of those library reference books and materials necessary to execute its functions.

Although no specific statutory authority seems to exist for the law libraries of the several executive departments, they have no doubt come into being either, as in the Departments of Commerce and Interior, by virtue of the authority establishing the general library of those departments or, as in the Departments of Energy and Justice, as concomitant resources to the departments' meeting their larger statutory mission. Thus the combination of explicit statutory authority to establish libraries and the implicit authority to collect library books as part of required resources provided the framework for the law libraries of the federal government to grow and prosper since their early beginnings. In the District of Columbia alone there are now 56 United States government libraries listed in the geographical directory of the American Association of Law Libraries.

Law libraries nationally have of course been affected by those laws that have an impact on libraries generally. Some law libraries have benefitted from federal grants applicable to library building projects through the Library Services and Construction Act. Others have received some federal support for collection development. Law libraries feel the pressures of increased postage costs and regulatory limitations on the meaning of the special "library rate." But in each of these instances the law library reacts to the legislation as a library and not in any particular way because it is a law library, and thus these laws have not had any unique meaning for law libraries. One law, however, that does deserve special mention is the Depository Library Act. Although this law has been of immeasurable benefit to the general library community, and it did for many years permit state libraries and the highest state appellate court libraries to become depositories for U.S. government publications, the 1978 amendment allowing all approved law school libraries to request depository status was of substantial importance. Additionally, even though a number of law school libraries had, over time, become depositories in their own right under the historical provision of the Act, most law school libraries, including several major research centers, had never been able to take advantage of depository benefits. This extension of the Act resulted in a great flurry of interest in documents by law librarians in the months that followed. While other laws may have been more significant in the development of the library of a particular institution, the depository law is in some measure the federal legislation that has had the single greatest impact on law libraries nationally.

**State Legislation.** The laws that resulted in the formation of law libraries in the several states generally follow the pattern outlined for the federal government. In general, librarians tend to classify these law libraries under three major heads: state law libraries, supreme court libraries, and county law libraries. Since state and supreme court libraries so frequently overlap in their functions and governance, joint treatment of them is appropriate.

*State and Supreme Court Libraries.* The respondents to a 1974 survey of state and supreme court law libraries indicated a wide disparity of organizational structures. Two libraries indicated they were units of legislative or administrative departments. Two other libraries were units of the state Attorney General's office. Two libraries were units of the legislative council, while four libraries were part of a larger, more comprehensive state library. In four instances the judicial branch shared a law library with a department of education, while there were six examples of the judicial and executive branches of government sharing the same law library. Finally, 29 law libraries were units of the judicial branch exclusively. Statutory review supports the responses from the librarians themselves. The statutes of 37 states specifically establish either a state law library, a law department of a state library, or a law library for the supreme court. Twenty-one states, including 18 of these 37, have established a legislative reference service that is also, in some instances, a department of the state library or the state law library. With this variety of organizations, some resulting from statutes that are based upon the earliest state administrative relationships and others on evolutionary development, it is difficult indeed to generalize about state law libraries. Most state statutes do, however, attempt to authorize law library service for the judicial branch. By placing superintending control in the hands of the state supreme court or a committee upon which one or more members of the supreme court sit, there is at least the opportunity that the court will receive appropriate service. The method of financing the state and court libraries is uneven, resulting in some libraries that are extremely strong, while others are of more modest circumstances. One library receives at least part of its financing from the sale of its court reports, another from a $15 tax on newly admitted lawyers, a third from a fund composed of court fees, and a fourth from the proceeds of a state land grant. In most instances the laws are silent as to the specific services that the library is required to render, although several do specifically require that the library be open to the public. Several libraries by statute and others, imitating the U.S. Supreme Court, by court rule prohibit the circulation of books from the court building. In one state the librarian is guilty of a misdemeanor if an unauthorized person borrows a book from the library! Another anomalous piece of legislation is the state statute that limits the appointment of a librarian to "any woman over 21 years of age." William B. Roalfe noted in his 1953 study, *The Libraries of the Legal Profession,* that "the service provided by state court libraries sometimes leave a great deal to be desired and most of them operate on a level well below that maintained by the best examples." A quarter of a century later the statutory base of the state and court libraries had not changed substantially.

County law libraries are authorized by 35 states and consequently represent, at least potentially, a major resource for providing legal materials. Once again the minds of legislators have conceived a plethora of methods to fund county law libraries. Seventeen states use a system of filing fees and fines to support law libraries, while an additional 14 states have fixed appropriations. Five states use a combination of filing fees and appropriations, while the balance rely for funds on other miscellaneous fees.

There seems to be no particular advantage to the major types of funding in achieving a substantial level of library support. California, for example, uses the fee system; Ohio uses fines; New York relies on appropriations. In each of these states strong county law libraries have resulted, although Ohio with 44 county law libraries and California with 58 seem to provide a more extensive county law library system. In fact, the existence of substantial populations and the volume of litigation probably have a greater impact on law library development than the particular statutory method devised to support law library service. It is evident, however, that a financial support mechanism that is tied directly to litigation, such as filing fees or fines, will tend to provide a level of support that will automatically move upward as the demands increase. A survey of county law libraries in California indicates that a filing fee funding system (limited to a maximum of $7 but with recommendations from the Council of County Law Libraries that it be increased to $12) has resulted in an array of law libraries roughly proportional to the general and lawyer populations in their respective counties. Los Angeles County, with 7,000,000 people and 17,000 lawyers, has a great research law library of over 575,000 volumes. San Francisco County, with 700,000 population and nearly 5,000 lawyers, has almost a quarter of a million law books. Calaveras County, on the other hand, with about one lawyer for each 1,000 of its 13,000 inhabitants, has a library of just under 5,000 books. Legislative developments in most states have not matched, and probably, because of more limited means, cannot be expected to match, the resources of the County Law Library in Los Angeles, but the challenge of more generous funding for county law libraries in more populous counties in other jurisdictions still awaits the legislative ingenuity of many of the states.

**REFERENCES**

Rachel Hecht, "Survey of Federal Court Libraries," *Law Library Journal* (1974).

Jacquelyn Jurkins, "Development of the County Law Library," *Law Library Journal* (1969).

Alex Ladenson, editor, *American Library Laws,* 4th ed. (1973) and supplements.

Bethany J. Ochal, "County Law Libraries," *Law Library Journal* (1974).

ROGER F. JACOBS

## Lebanon

Lebanon is a republic of the Middle East on the eastern shore of the Mediterranean Sea. Pop (1978 est.) 3,152,000; area 10,230 sq.km. The official language is Arabic.

**National Library.** The Lebanese National Library (which is also a public library but without borrowing privileges) was placed under the Ministry of National Education in 1922 and started with the personal collection of Viscount Philippe de Tarazi at the National Museum. In 1937 it moved to its present location—the Parliament building. Although the copyright deposit law of November 1941 and its amendment in 1959 exist, the Library could never enforce it. The Library's aims and objectives were never defined, and it never had a qualified librarian. No recent inventory had been taken, and its collection of 100,000 volumes and 2,000 rare manuscripts was partially burned and partially looted during the Lebanese civil war of the mid-1970's.

**Academic Libraries.** The American University of Beirut (AUB), "the Jafet Complex" comprising four libraries, is the richest in funds and qualified staff. Beirut Arab University is academically affiliated to the University of Alexandria, Egypt. Its four libraries holding a collection mainly in Arabic place it as best among Arabic Lebanese libraries.

At Lebanese University the six Faculties and two Institutes (a total of 8) were split into 16 after and because of the Lebanese civil war. Thus it had at the end of the 1970's 16 libraries plus the 3 libraries of the *Mohafazat* (Prefectorate) of Bekaa, North and South, totaling 19. A fact worth mentioning is the opening of a four-year program leading to the first B.A. in Library Science at the Faculty of Information and Documentation (First Branch).

At Beirut University College Stoltzfus Library is noted for its well-organized collection and its Documentation Center of the Institute for Women Studies in the Arab World, its Children's Library, which serves as a multimedia learning center for education students as well as being the only Children's public Library in Lebanon, and its first successful two-year program leading to the degree of Associate in Applied Science in Library Science (sophomore level). Haigazian College Library possesses a good collection on Armenology. At Saint Joseph University seven libraries possess a good collection mainly in French. The University of the Holy Spirit at Kaslik Library was developing at a fast rate.

**Public Libraries.** A law obliging each municipality to have a public library exists, but the libraries are small and lack financial support.

**School Libraries.** There are approximately 50 schools in Lebanon with libraries that are like storerooms for the use of the teaching staff only. The library at the International College rates best among them.

**Special Libraries.** Special libraries are increasing at a rapid rate primarily in the private sector. The statistical table includes a selection. A decree of January 1978 estab-

**Libraries in Lebanon (1978)**

| Type | Number | Volumes in collections | Annual expenditures (pound) | Population served | Professional staff | All staff (total) |
|---|---|---|---|---|---|---|
| National | 1 | 100,000 | £L10,000 | N.A. | N.A. | 24 |
| Academic | 37 | c. 922,150 | c. £L3,292,000 | c. 53,000 | 15 | c. 139 |
| Public | N.A. | N.A. | N.A. | N.A. | N.A. | N.A. |
| School | N.A. | N.A. | N.A. | N.A. | N.A. | N.A. |
| Special | 13 | 177,000 | c. £L918,500 | c. 22,400 | c. 4 | 48 |

Sources: Direct interviews; Aida Na'man, *al-Tajheez al-ilmi wa al-taknology li Kita' al-maktabat wa al-tawthig* (Scientific and Technological Preparation for the Library Sector and Documentation), Beirut: Lebanese Library Association (1973).

lished an Institute of National Archives centered in Beirut. This institute is administratively and financially independent. No statistics on archives in Lebanon were available from public sources.

**Lebanese Library Association.** Founded in 1960, the LLA is a member of IFLA. It has no government-allocated budget or its own premises. It approved the Library Science program taught at the Faculty of Information and Documentation of Lebanese University.

AIDA KASSANTINI HAFEZ

*Gottfried Wilhelm Leibniz*

Library of Congress

## Leibniz, Gottfried Wilhelm

(1646–1716)

German philosopher, mathematician, scientist, jurist, historian, linguist, and librarian, Leibniz contributed extensively in many disciplines; this article concentrates on his contributions to librarianship and information science.

Leibniz was born in Leipzig on July 1, 1646, into a pious Lutheran family; his father was a professor and his mother the daughter of a professor at the University of Leipzig. A precocious boy, Leibniz learned to read early and widely; he taught himself Latin in the library of his father, who died when Gottfried was only six years old. From 1653 to 1661 he attended the local Nicolaischule, where among other subjects he acquired a knowledge of Greek and was impressed by the study of Aristotelian logic.

When he was nearly 15 he entered the University of Leipzig. He obtained a broad general education but concentrated on the study of philosophy and law. In 1662 he earned a Bachelor's degree, in 1664 a Master's degree of the Philosophical Faculty. A year later he obtained a Bachelor of Laws degree. Then he began to work on his doctoral dissertation, *Dissertatio de arte combinatoria (Dissertation on the Art of Combination),* which he published in 1666. His dissertation was influenced by the combinatorial logic of the Spanish mystic Raymond Lully. In this work he formulated a model that is a theoretical forerunner of modern computer logic; he saw his art of combination and permutation as a logical calculus and a logic of discovery that could lead to significant new insights. But when he wanted to obtain his Doctor of Laws degree during the same year, a majority of his faculty refused it because they felt that he was still too young. Disappointed, he left his native city and moved to Altdorf, a university town close to Nürnberg, where at age 21 he earned a Doctor of Laws degree with distinction for his dissertation *On Perplexing Cases.* But he refused to accept a teaching position at the University of Altdorf.

In Nürnberg Leibniz met the retired statesman Johann Christian von Boineburg (1622–72), who had been formerly the most prominent minister of Johann Philipp von Schönborn (1605–73), the ruling Archbishop and Elector of Mainz. With Boineburg's recommendation, Leibniz obtained a position of legal counselor at this court and was assigned the task of revising and improving the German legal code. Von Boineburg owned a sizable private library and invited Leibniz to become his part-time librarian. Between 1668 and 1673 Leibniz had a classed catalogue prepared for this collection. The catalogue was rediscovered after World War II and consisted of four volumes with 9,840 main entries. Its major divisions corresponded to those that the German bibliographer and clergyman Georg Draud had used for his *Bibliotheca classica,* which had first appeared in 1611. A second edition was published in 1625, and both editions were available in Boineburg's collection. The 15 main classes were further subdivided by many alphabetically arranged subject headings, several of which were sometimes used for the same work. But the death of Boineburg brought the work to a halt; the catalogue is incomplete, and the syndetic devices are sparse. A general alphabetic author index has not been found.

In 1672 Leibniz was sent on a diplomatic mission to Paris, where he decided to stay for almost four years. In this vibrant metropolis he devoted himself to intensive studies and became acquainted with a number of the most renowned scientists. He also got to know the prominent librarians of the City, among them N. Clément, who introduced him to the rapidly growing Bibliothèque du Roi and its policies. His studies in Paris and visits to London in 1673 and 1676 broadened his intellectual horizons and established many scientific contacts for life. In 1673 he was elected a Member of the Royal Society.

**Major Contributions to the Profession.** The need for a regular income forced him to accept a position as

Counselor and Librarian at the court of Duke Johann Friedrich of Brunswick-Lüneburg, who owned in 1676 a private library of some 3,310 volumes, among them 158 manuscripts. Later Leibniz was also appointed Historiographer at the court, and he held these positions until his death in 1716. Unfortunately, the intellectual Johann Friedrich died in 1679, and his successor, Ernst August, did not appreciate libraries as much as his cosmopolitan brother. Leibniz was able to provide Ernst August with valuable historical and genealogical information that helped him to become Elector of Hanover in 1692. Nor did library support improve under his son Georg Ludwig, who succeeded his father in 1698 and became King George I of Great Britain in 1714.

In addition to his library duties at the Hanoverian Court, Leibniz was in 1690 appointed Librarian of the valuable Ducal Library at Wolfenbüttel, which was owned by another line of the Guelph dynasty. This library had been founded by the learned Duke August the Younger and held in 1661 some 28,000 volumes of printed works, including 2,000 incunabula, and about 2,000 manuscripts. Duke August had been his own librarian and prepared a classed catalogue using 20 classes derived from Konrad Gesner's *Pandectae*. But here again the succeeding dukes did not share Duke August's enthusiasm for the library and provided little financial support for its upkeep and extension.

In Hanover and Wolfenbüttel Leibniz worked hard to extend and improve the collections through purchases of current works and advantageous auctions. The Hanoverian collection grew very rapidly and served the princes and the court. At Wolfenbüttel he ordered the production of an alphabetical author catalogue, which was completed before 1700, and he was successful in having the first separate German baroque library building contructed. It was a rectangular library topped by a cupola and a dome light. Increased shelving space was provided by means of galleries and shelving that surrounded the supporting pillars. Against Leibniz's wishes it was built as a wooden structure, and no furnace was allowed in the building to provide heat in the winter.

More important than his actual achievements were Leibniz's novel ideas, which he spread in letters, memoranda, and petitions. As a leading scholar in several disciplines, he was fully aware of the importance of libraries for the advancement of knowledge. He advocated a universal library that should contain the original ideas of mankind that have been recorded. Such a library was not to be measured by the number, rarity, or fancy bindings of its volumes but by the balance, accuracy, and up-to-dateness of the information contained in them. The main task of the librarian was to collect works with up-to-date information, organize them efficiently, and make them readily available for use. For speedy access good catalogues would be needed; while he himself favored classed catalogues, he also stressed the need for alphabetical author and subject catalogues. He personally designed two classification schemes for libraries.

Throughout his life he was most concerned with the research needs of scientists and scholars. In order to avoid needless duplication of efforts and to make results of research speedily available, he planned and promoted the construction of abstracting and indexing tools. The abstracted information was to be indexed and integrated into a demonstrative encyclopedia that was to be organized with the help of a detailed and complex universal classificatory language, his *characteristica universalis*. For this purpose he stressed the need for division of labor and sought the help of scientific societies. He himself was the founder and first President of an academy of sciences in Berlin and the moving spirit behind the founding of the academies in Vienna and Saint Petersburg. When he died on November 14, 1716, in Hanover, he had accomplished great tasks but was keenly aware of the tremendous work that still remained to be done.

**REFERENCES**

Leibniz, *Sämtliche Schriften und Briefe* (1923– ).

Kurt Müller, *Leibniz-Bibliographie: Die Literatur über Leibniz* (1967).

Lindsay Mary Newman, *Leibniz (1646–1716) and the German Library Scene* (1966).

Hans Georg Schulte-Albert, "Gottfried Wilhelm Leibniz and Library Classification," *Journal of Library History* (1971).

Hans Georg Schulte-Albert, "Leibniz's Plans for a World Encyclopaedia System," unpublished Ph.D. dissertation, Case Western Reserve University (1972).

HANS GEORG SCHULTE-ALBERT

## Leland, Waldo Gifford

(1879–1966)

Waldo Gifford Leland, historian, archival advocate, and administrator, was a key figure in the creation of the National Archives. He was born in Newton, Massachusetts, on July 17, 1879, to Luther Erving and Ella M. Gifford Leland. He was graduated from Brown University in 1900 with a B.A. degree and membership in Phi Beta Kappa. Coming from a family of schoolteachers, Leland aimed at a career as a college professor, which to him "seemed likely to be less confining, more lucrative and to have more prestige than at the level of the schools." He leaned toward the social sciences, particularly sociology. Although he had studied little history at Brown, only part of a course taught by the great J. Franklin Jameson, he was persuaded by Jameson to do some graduate work in history before plunging into sociology. He went to Harvard for his advanced work, taking an M.A. in 1901 and beginning work on a Ph.D., and never did make the plunge into sociology.

Leland never completed his doctorate in history either, for in 1903 one of his professors, Albert Bushnell Hart, convinced him to go to Washington for six months to assist Claude H. Van Tyne in compiling a report for the recently (1902) established Carnegie Institution of Washington on the condition of the archives of the federal government. His decision to accept the post started him on a lifetime of work of the highest importance in the world of scholarship, history, and archives but kept him from becoming the teacher he had set out to be.

The survey of the government's archives took the collaborators to basements and attics, warehouses and car barns, doorways and corridors all over Washington—wherever neglectful or ignorant civil servants had placed federal records when they ceased to be current. File clerks and high officials, with few exceptions, welcomed them and were cooperative. The condition of the precious records they found varied considerably, but many were in advanced stages of deterioration. The immediate result of the research by Van Tyne and Leland was the publication in 1904 of the *Guide to the Archives of the Government of the United States in Washington,* which appeared in a revised and enlarged edition three years later. This assessment of the state of the federal archives had, in the long run, a profound influence on the course of archival development in the government.

After finishing the description of the archives, Leland stayed on with the Carnegie Institution's Department of Historical Research, of which his old Brown history professor, Jameson, had become Director in 1905. One of the major projects Jameson directed was the compilation of a series of guides to source material for the study of American history in foreign archives and libraries. Leland's assignment was Paris, and he directed Carnegie's work there from 1907 to 1914 and again from 1922 to 1927. The published result was the two-volume *Guide to Materials for American History in the Libraries and Archives of Paris* (1932–43). In addition to being colleagues at the Carnegie Institution, Jameson and Leland were also close associates in the American Historical Association, Leland being the Association's Secretary (1909–20) and Jameson the Managing Editor of its journal, the *American Historical Review*.

Leland's work at the Carnegie Institution placed him center stage in the archival world, then just beginning the process of professionalization. In 1909 he spoke on "American Archival Problems" at the first American conference of archivists. Three years later he published in the *American Historical Review*, at Jameson's request, an article entitled "The National Archives: A Programme," which recited the litany of the government's neglect of and indifference to its own official records and set forth a bold plan of action to remedy the dismal situation. This article served as a public manifesto to accompany Jameson's backstage politicking for a national archives establishment. The creation of the National Archives in 1934 justified the quarter-century effort by Jameson, Leland, and others, though Leland modestly claimed no part of the credit for himself.

Many considered Leland the "dean of American archivists," but Leland confessed he was "somewhat embarrassed to find myself described as an archivist, a title to which I have no claim. I have never had charge of records, public or private." At most, he thought, he was an "archivist by association." Still, his colleagues in the new archival profession bestowed great honors on him. He served in 1940 as second President of the Society of American Archivists (founded in 1936, of which he was a charter member), was made an Honorary Member in 1949, and a Fellow in 1958. His portrait was painted and hung in the National Archives building in Washington.

Throughout his long career, Leland maintained an active interest in the affairs and problems of libraries, especially the Library of Congress. When he first went to Washington in 1903 to be interviewed for the job with the Carnegie Institution, the site of the appointment was the Library of Congress building. His first meal in the capital city was at the famous Round Table presided over by the Librarian of Congress, Herbert Putnam. Leland noted years later, "I was impressed to the point of being awed." Putnam was one of the two most influential men in Leland's professional life, the other being Jameson. Putnam in fact asked Leland on the day after Jameson's funeral in 1937 to succeed Jameson as Chief of the LC Manuscript Division and as occupant of the library's chair of American history. Leland refused Putnam's invitation, which "was one of the hardest things I have ever had to do." Nevertheless, Leland served LC in a number of advisory capacities and sat on numerous committees, including the planning committee that, following World War II, examined the question of the future role of LC.

On leaving the Carnegie Institution in 1927, Leland became the Secretary, or chief administrative officer, of the American Council of Learned Societies (ACLS). The ACLS had been founded in 1919 to provide United States representation in the newly established International Union of Academies, and Leland had been present as Secretary at the organizational meeting of ACLS. He remained the chief executive, his title being changed in 1939 to Director, until 1946. One of the major achievements of his administration was the sponsorship of the *Dictionary of American Biography*.

Much of Leland's work was in the sphere of national and international cooperation in the humanities. This global concern led him also to take a role as a U.S. delegate in the establishment of Unesco at the end of World War II, and he served as the U.S. representative to the third Unesco General Conference in Beirut in 1948.

Leland died in Washington on October 19, 1966.

**REFERENCES**

The major collection of Leland's papers is in the Manuscript Division, Library of Congress. He wrote a brief memoir, "Some Recollections of an Itinerant Historian," *Proceedings of the American Antiquarian Society* (1951).

JOHN B. HENCH

## Lesotho

Lesotho, formerly Basutoland, a British protectorate from 1868, became independent in 1966. Surrounded entirely by South Africa, the country, which is a monarchy, varies in altitude from 5,000 to 11,000 feet; the climate is dry and rigorous with temperatures ranging from 93° F (34° C) to 3° F (−16° C) and rainfall averaging about 29 inches per annum. The area is 30,355 sq.km. Lesotho is a purely African country, the few European residents being government officials, traders, missionaries, and artisans. The estimated population (1979) is about 1,200,000, the largest town being the capital, Maseru, with a population around 20,000. The languages are English and Sesotho (official).

**National Library.** Work on the Lesotho National Library Service began in May 1976, and the Library opened its doors to the public in July 1978.

**Public Library Service.** A public library service is offered to residents of Maseru, and a free postal loan service is operated for persons outside Maseru. Books are also lent to some 85 secondary schools throughout the kingdom. Services provided include adult and children's lending and reference libraries, magazine and newspaper reading room, and a special collection of material on and about Lesotho. Premises for branch libraries were acquired in Mafeteng and Leribe (old capital), and the five-year development plan includes library coverage in the remaining seats of district administration, viz., Mohale's Hoek, Teyateyaneng, Quthing, Mokhotlong, Butha Buthe, Qacha's Nek, and Thaba Tseka. Initial funding for the library of £247,500 was provided by the British Council through the Ministry of Overseas Development. The bookstock comprised a total of 29,000 in 1979.

**Academic and Other Libraries.** Other libraries in Lesotho include that of the National University of Lesotho in Roma, which has 118,000 books and periodicals, and the library of the National Teachers Training College in Maseru (15,000 volumes). Smaller collections exist in government departments, educational and vocational training establishments such as the Lesotho Agricultural College and Lesotho Institute of Public Administration, and foreign agencies such as the British Council and United States Information Service.

**Association.** A professional body, the Lesotho Library Association, was formed in 1979.

VINCENT FORSHAW

## Liberia

Liberia, a republic in western Africa, is bordered by Sierra Leone on the northwest, Guinea on the north, Ivory Coast on the east, and the Atlantic Ocean on the south and west. Pop. (1978 est.) 1,716,900; area 97,790 sq.km. The official language is English.

**National Library.** In 1978 legislation was passed by the National Legislature creating a Center for National Documents and Records, which merged the Public Library System and Bureau of Archives. Liberia does not have a national library, but the public library system and the academic libraries are providing national leadership in library development.

**Academic Libraries.** The University of Liberia Libraries, established in 1862 in Monrovia, is a national institution operated by the government. Cuttington Uni-

**Libraries in Liberia (1978)**

| Type | Number | Volumes in collections | Annual expenditures (dollar) | Population served[a] | Professional staff | All staff (total) |
|---|---|---|---|---|---|---|
| Academic | 2 | 190,000 | N.A. | N.A. | 10 | 69 |
| Public | 9 | 47,400 | N.A. | 11,712 | N.A. | N.A. |
| School | 103 | 160,176 | N.A. | 35,680 | N.A. | N.A. |

[a]Registered readers.

Sources: Director of Libraries, University of Liberia; University Librarian, Cuttington University College; and Director of Public Libraries, Republic of Liberia.

versity College Library, in Suakoko, Bong County (1888), is a private institution operated by the Protestant Episcopal Church of Liberia.

The University of Liberia Library System maintains four professional reading rooms for law, medicine, agriculture/forestry, and engineering. It holds a collection of Africana and serves as depository center for the United Nations, Unesco, and other international organizations. Cuttington University College maintains a central library.

**Public Libraries.** Liberia's first Public Library System was organized in 1826 by the American Colonization Society, but little progress was made until 1937, when the National Legislature passed the act that gave birth to the public library movement. In the early 1950's a national library committee was formed and charged with planning the System. In 1958 the first professionally trained public librarian was employed. The System's headquarters, in Monrovia, operates and coordinates a number of branch library reading rooms in counties and territories.

**School Libraries.** By modern library standards and structure, Liberia's school library program has yet to be organized. Many schools suffer from an acute lack of funding. School librarians are not professionally trained. Few schools can afford trained library personnel, nor do they have adequate funds to build collections.

**Special Libraries.** Certain attempts by a few ministries and agencies of the government and private organizations are being made to organize special library services, but growth is relatively slow. Those services that exist are unstructured owing to lack of trained library personnel and funding.

The Liberian Institute of Public Administration Library (1975) does provide source materials for instructors to prepare their lectures and provides collateral readings for trainees and public civil servants. It has two professionally trained librarians and a number of semiprofessionals. Its collection totals approximately 4,000 volumes and contains about 600 government documents. The Library subscribes to some 70 specialized journals.

**Association.** The Liberian Library Association (LLA), organized in 1977, attempts to improve and develop library services and librarianship throughout the country. Its membership includes practicing as well as professionally trained librarians.

**REFERENCE**

C. Wesley Armstrong, *Role of Information Resources in National Development: A Descriptive Study and Analysis of Library Resources in West Africa* (Ph.D. dissertation, Graduate School of Library and Information Sciences, University of Pittsburgh, 1971).

C. WESLEY ARMSTRONG

# Librarianship, Philosophy of

**The Retrospective View.** "The Best Books for the Most People at the Least Cost" can hardly be called a philosophy of librarianship, but for many years it was, either implicitly or explicitly, all that the profession had. Terms were never defined nor cultural or social relationships examined. It was a creed rather than a philosophy, a dedication to a faith. Indeed, Oliver Garceau speaks at some length about the "library faith" in *The Public Library and the Political Process* (1949):

> Out of [the library's] past has come what we may call *the library faith*. It is a fundamental belief, so generally accepted as to be often left unsaid, in the virtue of the printed word, the reading of which is good in itself, and upon the preservation of which many basic values in our civilization rest. When culture is in question, the knowledge of books, the amount of reading, and the possession of a library—all become measures of value, not only of the individual, but also of the community.

Seen in the light of this *faith*, it may not be surprising that the present writer and his contemporaries in library school often observed that had all of us been born a generation earlier, we would likely have been ministers of the Gospel.

Pierce Butler remarked, in *The Reference Function of the Library* (1943), that librarians generally have been indifferent to a philosophical rationale for their profession:

> Some librarians dislike and distrust theory. They recognize clearly that the world needs efficient library service far more than it needs theoretical opinions. They fear, not without cause, that our quest for a professional philosophy may involve a neglect of practical values. Other librarians . . . are certain that the field of librarianship is amenable to rational analysis and that this analysis will reveal basic laws and principles. . . . They believe that a sound theory of librarianship can be developed without any sacrifice of practical efficiency. Moreover, they believe that such a sound theory must be established before librarians can become even reasonably competent in certain practical areas of their activity.

There are good historic reasons for the librarians' ambivalence, not to say indifference and neglect, concerning the philosophical raison d'etre of the library as a social organism. Over the millennia libraries created, by their very existence, their own rationale, their own philosophical justification. From the time of the ancient Sumerians and Egyptians libraries have been created because they are needed. Custody of the record of the culture was necessary for the transmission of that culture from generation to generation and beyond the reach of individual human memory—for training the priesthood, for commercial and other transactions for which preservation was necessary, and for carrying on affairs of state. As the medieval universities arose, libraries were necessary because the book-centered educational system required them. The early librarians were scholars who not only gave the books in their custody the needed protective care but also worked with the texts themselves. It was the innovation of the modern public library that created the philosophical need, not only for its justification but also for its guidance as an institution.

The modern public library is rooted in those small, voluntary associations of people who banded together in England and Colonial America to acquire the books they needed in their work and for their general stimulation but could not procure in sufficient quantity for themselves. Their collections were very similar to the personal library of the gentleman scholar. These social libraries, as they were called, spread along the east coast of Colonial America and were carried into the interior as it was opened by the pioneer settlers. Some, such as the Boston Athenaeum and the Redwood Library of Newport, Rhode Island, were sufficiently strong to survive periods of severe economic stringencies, but most of them fell by the wayside as their most enthusiastic supporters either died or moved away. By the beginning of the 19th century it was apparent that voluntary support was inadequate for the book requirements of the new nation, and readers turned to suport from municipal funds. Thus the public library was born and with it the need for a pragmatic justification to elicit public support. It was the *public* library, then, as a new generic institutional form that was part of the public sector (of local government specifically), that created a demand for its justification. Edward Everett and George Ticknor found themselves in sharp disagreement about the kind of book collection the new Boston Public Library should have when they set themselves the task of writing the institution's first official report. Oliver Wendell Holmes asked, "What is a library but a nest to hatch scholars?" and Horace Mann saw the public library as "the crowning glory of our public schools." All of the early advocates of legislation in support of public libraries stressed that the institution was essential to an enlightened electorate, without which a democracy could not survive.

After the Civil War and the restabilization of the federal government, public libraries spread throughout the country, and though few of them could be called opulent, many were enriched from, if not actually created by, Andrew Carnegie's generosity. That these libraries were desirable was readily acknowledged even by those who did not use them. They played important roles in the lives of many American young people, especially in the acculturation of the immigrants who at the turn of the 20th century were flocking to U.S. shores in increasing numbers. Not until the advent of the Great Depression in the 1930's did librarians suddenly awaken to the realization, and its implications, that they really were a part of the public sector, that they were created by society, and that what affected the social fabric of which they were a part also had serious implications for them. It was a rude awakening, but even then not many librarians struggling against economic misfortune thought it necessary to ask themselves, "What is our function in society, and why are we here?" Librarians, by temperament and training, have always been a pragmatic breed not much given to philosophical speculation.

As a result, librarians and their libraries in recent decades have assumed a wide variety of activities in the hope that by their very diversity they will attract increased public support: adult education, service to the aged, aid to the disadvantaged, programs for the physically handicapped, and many other social functions wholly admirable in themselves. But librarians failed to ask whether the library is really the best agency to be involved with such public services. Even in the sharply defined world of bibliography librarians have not been able to resolve the argument over the *quality* or *demand* theories of collection building. Over the centuries the library has been an elitist institution; can it, or should it, shed its heritage and strive to be as many things to as many people as possible? Questions like this are very stubborn, and no philosophical guides have evolved. The librarians talk glibly of library science, and indeed strive to endow it with scientific principles, but neglect the fact that librarianship has emerged from a humanistic tradition.

**Definition and Purpose.** An assembly of books is not a library, nor is a library only a place where books are kept; a library in the sense one is concerned with here is an organization, a system designed to preserve and facilitate the use of graphic records. It is a social instrument created to form a link in the communication system that is essential to any society or culture. Without communication there can be no society, and without some form of graphic record and a means for the preservation of that record there can be no enduring culture. The library may from time to time assume certain marginal functions, but its basic purpose remains generically the same—a link in the communication chain that is concerned with the custody of recorded knowledge. Its fundamental concern is with the communication of knowledge, ideas, thought, but because those intangibles are embodied in physical objects—books and other graphic records—it is easy to mistake the physical object rather than its intellectual content as the reality. A book qua book is nothing more than a physical representation of what the author thought he said, and its utility varies directly with what the reader brings to it in understanding.

The modern library, in the Western world at least, is an integrated system of three interrelated and interdependent parts held together by an administrative authority, the purpose of which is to keep the triad in harmonious balance (proportion) and to see that aims and objectives are adequately realized. The three parts, which may also be known as functions or operations, are: acquisition, organization, and interpretation or service.

*Acquisition* requires that the librarian should know what materials are to be procured to meet adequately the legitimate needs of the patron, or anticipated patron, and how these materials are to be acquired. Bibliography in the larger sense is the keystone of acquisition, for it is from bibliography that one learns about the materials to be acquired.

*Organization* involves putting the materials, or the representation of those materials, together—in catalogues or other ordered files—in such a way as to make them available when needed. Organization also necessitates the analysis of the materials by subject or any other aspect that is believed to be useful to the patron. Order is essential, because it is only through order, relationship, that the human mind can comprehend the intellectual or other aspects of the graphic record. Man cannot "think chaos"; order is heaven's first law, and nowhere is it more essential than in the organization of a library.

*Interpretation,* or service, is the rationale for the library; it is the goal for which the above two exist. Accumulating books and arranging them, no matter how expertly done, has little value if the system is not used. "Books are for use; every book its reader; and every reader his book" were the first three of S. R. Ranganathan's Five Laws of Library Science (see further his biography). The fact that these are not really laws but precepts does not destroy their validity; they are the rationale of the library, no matter what kind, size, or type it happens to be.

Administration (management) is necessary because there must be an operational focus, an authority to make decisions and impose standards. Administration is unproductive in that it does not "create" anything; it builds no collections, leaves behind it no taxonomic structures or analyses of the library's materials, and provides no direct apparent and tangible service to the user. Moreover, it should be held to a minimum. That administration is best that administers least, but this is not to say that administration is unimportant. At its best administration can achieve acceptible results under the most severe restrictions; at its worst it can leave the best library system in ruins. As libraries grow in size and complexity, the role of administration becomes increasingly important.

The library may also be viewed as operating in three spheres: the mechanistic, the one of maximum content, and the one of maximum context.

*Mechanistic Sphere.* This sphere encompasses all the physical operations involved in the total library process. Here are included all the "tools" the librarian uses in the performance of library tasks, including software and hardware, to borrow the terminology of the computer engineer. Such tools may be designed for either the librarian or the patron, or both.

*Maximum Content.* The sphere of maximum content includes the totality of the library's intellectual resources. The term maximum is used, not to suggest that the collections of the library should be as big as possible, but instead to suggest that the resources should be aligned to user needs to the greatest degree possible, given the library's available economic support. The term content also includes the resources of other libraries through various forms of interlibrary cooperation.

*Maximum context* refers to the social and intellectual environment in which the library operates. The library's first responsibility is to its own culture, but this mandate does not exclude consideration of other cultures and other social goals. How far the library can or should go in stimulating alterations in its culture (that is, in the social context) is a philosophical question that has not yet been answered, if indeed it can be. A serious problem for the librarian is created when the goals of society itself are unclear or when the society is in a state of flux.

**Society, Culture, and the Communication System.** A society, as understood by the anthropologist, is composed of people working together to achieve common ends and to satisfy common needs. Culture is that body of knowledge, understandings, and beliefs held in common by a society. The culture is interpreted, nurtured, and enforced by institutions. Institutions are those large, powerful bodies in the society, such as those associated with family, religion, law, and education, that through their agencies, e.g., the church, courts, and schools, implement their power. Institutions set standards of conduct, grant rewards for adherence to the culture, and exact penalties for violations. Institutions in general dominate the society, and one departs from their dicta at one's peril. Libraries, then, are molded by the culture and kept in line by such institutions as the church, state, courts, and education. Libraries are generally thought of as an agency of the institution of education, and rightly so, but they are also subjects of the state, law, and even religion. Thus the social context, as defined above, is a complex interacting system that works in many ways its wonders to perform.

The culture is the totality of knowledge and beliefs of a society, maintained by a trinity: physical equipment, scholarship (in the broad sense of that which is known or believed), and social organization. The physical equipment is composed of tools of any kind, from stone axes to the most sophisticated computer or other mechanical or electronic mechanism. The scholarship is the totality of the products of thought, and the social organization is the system by which the whole is held together. Language is essential to a culture, and, indeed, many anthropologists consider language the essence of culture, without which culture cannot exist. Language, either spoken, written, or kinesic, is a system of symbolic representations commonly understood and accepted by those in the culture. It is basic to the communication system in a culture, and the library is part of that system.

Because the library is an important agent in the communication system in society, how a society, or culture, acquires, absorbs, and disseminates knowledge must find accommodation in the librarian's professional philosophy. Douglas Waples was long convinced of the importance to librarianship of the study of the social effects of reading, and though he did not find the answers he sought, he at least opened the problem through his probing and did much to reveal its importance to the philosophy of the library profession. Information science, on the other hand, seems to be concerning itself primarily with the effectiveness of the communication channels in society and has not as yet addressed itself to the origins and growth of knowledge and the impact of that knowledge on its coeval culture. Moreover, information scientists seem to be aligning themselves with the natural sciences, which deal with physical phenomena, things, whereas the library and librarians deal with ideas and knowledge and their communication; hence librarianship is much closer to the humanities than to the "hard" sciences.

Thus there emerges a need for a new discipline, or science, of communication. This will emphatically not be a reworking of the old area of mass communication with which we have become, it must be admitted, rather tediously familiar. We are concerned here with a body of knowledge about knowledge itself. How knowledge has developed and been augmented has long been a subject of study, but how knowledge is coordinated, integrated, and put to work is yet an almost unrecognized field of investigation. We have, from the most ancient times, our systems of logic and our formulations of systematic scientific method. We know with some exactitude how knowledge of this kind is accumulated and transmitted from one generation to another. Philosophers have speculated for generations about the nature of knowledge, its sources and methods, and the limits of its validity. But the study of epistemology has always revolved about the intellectual processes of the *individual*. Psychologists carried the philosophers' speculations into the laboratory and made some progress in examining the mental abilities and behavior, again, of the individual. But neither epistemologists nor psychologists have developed an orderly and comprehensive body of knowledge concerning intellectual differentiation and the integration of knowledge within a complex *social* structure. The sociologists, though they have directed their attention toward the behavior of people in groups, have paid scant heed to the *intellectual forces* shaping social structures.

The new discipline that we here envisage, and which for want of a better name we have called "social epistemology," will provide a framework for the effective investigation of the whole complex problem of the intellectual processes of society—a study by which society as a whole seeks to achieve a perceptive or understanding relation to the total environment. It will lift the study of intellectual life from that of the individual to an inquiry into the means by which a society, nation, or culture achieves an understanding relationship with the totality of the environment, and its focus will be upon the production, flow, integration, and consumption of all forms of communication throughout the entire social pattern. From such a discipline should emerge a new body of knowledge about, and a new synthesis of the interaction between, knowledge and social activity.

But though social epistemology will have its own corpus of theoretical knowledge, it will be a very practical discipline, too.

Because of the emerging science of information, librarianship is, for the first time in its long history, compelled to formulate, self-consciously, its role in society, to examine critically its intellectual foundations, and to view itself holistically—as an integrated system that serves man, both as an individual and as a member of society, throughout life. Despite the obvious relationship of librarianship to its coeval culture, the library has been recognized as a sociological entity only within the last half century. The rise of the public library in the United States coincided with important new developments in sociological theory, and the beginnings of a search for status encouraged all lines of inquiry that might help to establish the librarian's claim to being professional.

Public librarians are improving their skills in working effectively with other educational and social agencies in their service areas, and they are being called upon to participate in large-scale community programs for nonreaders, the functionally illiterate, the undereducated, and the culturally deprived. In recent decades, especially within the past few years, the public library has broadened and strengthened its role in the thinking and decision making of the community. In no way do these auxiliary functions diminish the library's independence, initiative, or social prestige. Programs for the professional education of the librarian have reflected changes in educational philosophy as well as in the theory of librarianship.

**Personal Knowledge.** Though the library is the creature of society, it does not reach the individual as do the mass media. Each must seek the library and its resources out for himself, and it is through the individual that the library achieves its social goals. Therefore, for the library, "the proper study of mankind is man."

It is important to librarians that they be supported as much as possible by an understanding of those psychological and other mental processes through which the individual receives and assimilates knowledge, that they know as much as can be known, given our present limitations, of the cognitive process. For the librarian the basic questions are: What is knowledge, how do we learn, and how does the assimilation of knowledge by whatever means influence behavior? What reading, in the generic sense, does to people was long ago addressed by Waples, but we are still ignorant of the influence that knowledge exerts on our behavior. Yet the problem of the nature of personal knowledge still eludes us. We are still unable to define a book other than to say that it deals in symbolic representations of what the originator intended to say.

Because most of our communication is carried out through symbolic representations—either written, oral, or through gestures and other forms of physical representations—the problem of communication, linguistics, and symbolization lies at the very heart of what the librarian is trying to do.

Thus librarians should remember that their primary concern is with ideas rather than physical objects. But because physical objects often embody or represent conceptualizations, the one is easily mistaken for the other. Librarianship touches all subject fields and is dependent on all of them for its intellectual and professional substance.

The philosophy of librarianship, as it is evolved, must encompass all forms of human activity, both physical and mental, not only because the library's shelves hold the record of the human adventure but also because those holdings represent and can respond to the needs of all human life.

All philosophy begins in an appreciation of our own ignorance—in asking ourselves the fundamental questions. "We have all the answers," Archibald MacLeish once told his staff when he was Librarian of Congress; "it is the questions we do not know."


**REFERENCES**

Pierce Butler, *An Introduction to Library Science* (1933).

Conrad H. Rawski, editor, *Toward a Theory of Librarianship* (1973).

Jesse H. Shera, *The Foundations of Education for Librarianship* (1972).

*Knowing Books and Men* (1976).


JESSE H. SHERA

## Library and Information Science Research

*Webster's New Collegiate Dictionary* defines *library science* as "the study or the principles and practices of library care and administration" and defines *librarian* (librarianship) as "a specialist in the care or management of a library." *Information science* is defined as "the collection, classification, storage, retrieval, and dissemination of recorded knowledge treated both as a pure and as an applied science." This definition of information science is what many of us have been taught is the role of a library. All of these definitions seem to us inadequate: a combination of them is much more appropriate.

Pierce Butler states in *An Introduction To Library Science* (1933), "the basic elements of librarianship consist in the accumulation of knowledge by society and its continuous transmission to the living generation so far as these processes are performed through the instrumentality of graphic [sensible] records." This definition is sufficient to encompass not only traditional views of library and information science but systems, information, and communication theory as well. It imposes no restriction on medium of recording or mode of transmission of knowledge, if the word *graphic* is changed to *sensible*.

The purpose of research in the library and information science field is to try to find the best methods of acquiring, organizing, storing, accessing, retrieving, and disseminating information (or data). In a more general sense, library and information science research is the study of the human communication process.

The term *research* may itself be defined as "careful or diligent search" or as "studious inquiry or examination." By combining this definition of research with Butler's definition of library and information science given initially, we clearly develop a sense of the scope of library and information science research.

**Goal of Library and Information Science Research.** Alan MacGregor reports a common aim for this research is "to contribute in some way to the improvement (optimization, if you will) of communication so that the user receives, at his moment of need, the relevant and pertinent facts or opinions with the shortest delay consistent with acceptable cost (acceptable both to user and to the system). . . . Research in our field concerns itself with the transfer of information rather than increment to knowledge." This aim is very much in line with the Five Laws of Library Science of Ranganthan, covered in his biography in this *Encyclopedia.* Lewis Stieg, in his article in *Library Trends* (Winter 1978), provides a good review of works on the theory and purpose of librarianship.

A simple model of the research process in library and information science is shown in the accompanying Figure. This model is an adaptation of the general communication model reported by Claude Shannon and Warren Weaver in their *Mathematical Theory of Communication* (1964). The inputs from library science and information science may be viewed as forming a single input source so that the inappropriateness of the distinction between them can be emphasized. In the model, Feedback indicates that we can (and should) learn from previous research findings, although this frequently does not occur.

**Subject Areas for Research.** The true scope of library and information science is as yet unclear since the discipline is really in its emergent stage. Nevertheless, indications of the scope of library science may be given by enumerating the subject areas that have been addressed thus far. The following is a brief, representative, but certainly not an exhaustive, list of subject areas; the list is derived from the index in Charles H. Davis's compilation, *Doctoral Dissertations in Library Science* (1976):

Academic and research libraries
Acquisition and book selection
Alphanumeric coding
Bibliography
Book storage
Cataloguing and classification
Dewey Decimal classification
Evaluation of library science
History of books and printing
Information analysis centers

A companion work, *Computer Science, a Dissertation Bibliography* (1977) yields an equally diverse sample of subjects.

To obtain a clear picture of related dissertation topics, one would need to study not only *Dissertation Abstracts* but *American Doctoral Dissertations* and then to add lists from individual universities that do not take part in these services. There is also *Master Abstracts* for the M.L.S. works. Other publications that report on thesis and dissertation research, such as *Library Quarterly, Library Research,* and *Journal of Librarianship,* provide insight into current research activity in the field. Research outside the library school is reported in publications of ERIC and NTIS.

**Research Methodology.** Sound research is based chiefly upon the scientific method, which provides a framework within which hypothesis testing and inferential thought may be carried out in a disciplined manner. *Webster's New Collegiate* defines *scientific method* as "principles and procedures for the systematic pursuit of knowledge involving the recognition and formulation of a problem, the collection of data through observation and experiment, and the formulation and testing of hypotheses." Much of what has been called research in library and information science, however, has not been conducted using the scientific method, and often there is doubt about what has been learned.

Within the framework of the scientific method, many specific methodologies may be used in conducting library and information science research. Examples of these methodologies, most of which are shared with many other subject areas, include: operations research; mathematical; analytical; historical; survey; experimental; modeling and simulation; and statistical methods. Because librarianship has not had a scientific orientation, a good deal has been published regarding research methods. For example, the July 1964 issue of *Library Trends* contains the proceedings of a 1963 conference on research methods sponsored by the University of Illinois Graduate School of Library Science. A second conference, also sponsored by the University of Illinois, was reported in *Research Methods in Librarianship; Measurement and Evaluation* (1968).

The use of operations research methods was the subject of the 1971 University of Chicago annual conference, the proceedings of which were published in the January 1972 issue of *The Library Quarterly*. The use of this research methodology can best be followed through the programs and publications of the Operations Research Society of America and the Institute of Management Science, and examples of its application in library settings have appeared in the library literature in such works as Churchman's *Introduction to Operations Research* (1957), Wagner's *Principles of Operations Research* (1975), and Brophy's *Reader in Operations Research for Libraries* (1976). Bibliometrics, which involves the application of mathematical methods to library and information science problems, has been the subject of several publications, including articles by Ferrante and Moll in *Collection Management* (Fall 1978) and by Narin and Moll in the *Annual Review of Information Science and Technology* (1977). Exemplifying the use of analytical methods is the research on paper and card stock, binding materials, and so on. The Council on Library Resources, Inc. and other agencies have supported a good deal of work on the preservation and restoration of library materials, research that also employs analytical methods. The historical, or historiographical, method has been used extensively in library and information science research. David Kaser reports that historical methods formed primary use in 11–12 percent of the research reported in library science dissertations between 1971 and 1976 and observes that the benefit of historical research is that it provides "a new awareness of the difference between transient and perpetual issues."

Survey methodology also has been used frequently. It permits the researcher to collect data necessary for testing hypotheses from widely dispersed sources or to obtain answers to specific research questions. Survey methodology involves the construction and testing of returns; great care is required in questionnaire construction to ensure that the precise desired data are obtained and that they enable the researcher to determine the validity of responses, the bias of responses, and the nature of the sample (represented by responses) as compared with the nature of the population surveyed. A particular type of survey method, called the Delphi Technique, has grown in popularity in assessing future events and trends. It draws on specialists' judgments reinforced under certain controls to reach reliable consensus.

**Funding Sources.** The Office of Libraries and Learning Resources (OLLR) within the Office of Education, U.S. Department of Health, Education and Welfare, provides major federal support for U.S. libraries. However, only a small part of OLLR funds ($1,000,000 for FY 1978, under the Library Services and Construction Act) was available for library and information science research.

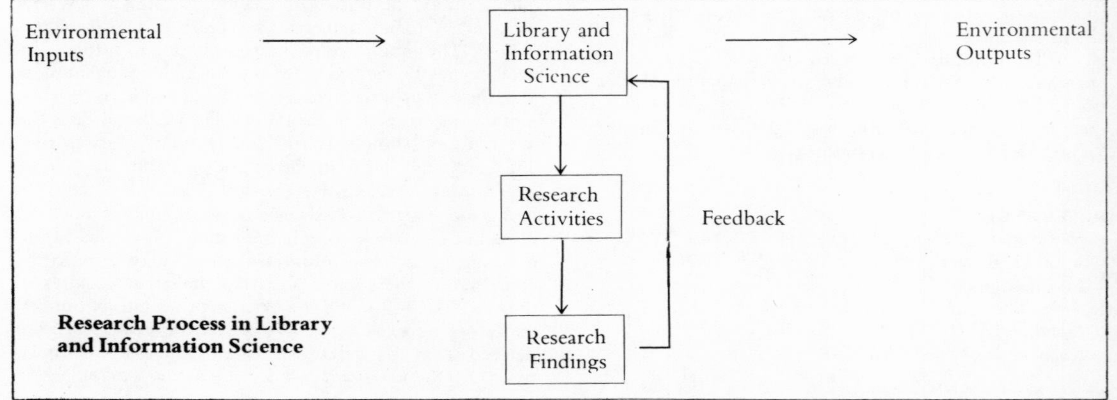


**Research Process in Library and Information Science**

The Library Research and Demonstration Program's abstracts and directory provide complete and regular accounting and overview of the research conducted under this program. The National Science Foundation (NSF), through its Information Science and Technology programs, provides a good deal more support (some $4,600,000 in FY 1977) for library and information science research. The National Library of Medicine (NLM) also funded approximately $1,000,000 a year in library and information science research under the Medical Library Assistance Act of 1965. Summaries of funding by OE, NSF, and NLM are provided annually in *The ALA Yearbook* in the article "Research."

The Council on Library Resources, Inc., is the major private agency in the U.S. that funds research in library and information science. The nature and scope of CLR's involvement in research may be traced in its newsletter and annual reports.

In Great Britain, the Office of Scientific and Technical Information (OSTI) has funded research in library and information fields, including some research of the Classification Research Group. Government agencies concerned with scientific and technical information, documentation, education, or other fields similarly support research in other countries as well, either by funding individual research projects or by supporting governmental or private research projects, institutions, and documentation centers.

International organizations, such as Unesco, the International Atomic Energy Agency, IFLA, and many others, are actively involved in conducting or supporting research through publications, conferences, and seminars and the development of information systems. Unesco has been particularly prominent internationally in conducting statistical and other research and in supporting the projects of other international organizations and national associations.

There is a fairly well-defined cyclic nature of funded research, and it usually requires many talents and skills (rarely possessed by a single person) to successfully complete the cycle. The cycle is described in the accompanying Table.

In reality, there is no such thing as an unfunded project, so the funded research cycle applies to all research projects.

**Future.** The need for more research in library and information science and a much greater adherence to scientific method in the research conducted in turn suggest that graduate library and information science programs should emphasize research in (rather than the practice of) library and information science. The attempt to understand all facets of library and information science demands an understanding of the research methods, both old and new, through which understanding of the field may be gained. Because of the complex nature of library and information science, Howard L. Resnikoff of the National Science Foundation underscored, in particular, the need for new research methods and approaches. Resnikoff says,

> The information system does not scale; it is unique, too large to be copied for purposes of tests and too important for our economy, for our civilization, to be ignored. Thus the establishment of an intensive program of analysis, of research into the nature of information and of the information systems on which we depend, stands forth as an intelligent, a desirable, and indeed necessary commitment on behalf of the people of any nation. (*Information Management,* February 1979).

The purpose of research in library and information science is to find the best methods of acquiring, organizing, storing, accessing, retrieving, and disseminating information (or data). We do not yet have a wide understanding and use of basic research methodologies, and changes in our educational programs and processes are called for if we are to correct this situation. Changes in academic programs also will foster the discovery of new methods of research into the human communication process. After all, library and information science is a social metaphor.

**REFERENCES**

Earl R. Babbie, *Survey Research Methods* (1973).

David Kaser, "Advances in American Library History," *Advances in Librarianship* (1978).

Harold Linstone and Murray Turoff, *The Delphi Method: Techniques and Applications* (1975).

Alan MacGregor, "Some Trends in Research and Development in Documentation," *Journal of Documentation* (1978).

**Cycle of Funded Research**

| *Step of cycle* | *Description of step* | *Talent or skill needed* |
|---|---|---|
| Idea | An idea susceptible to scrutiny through the scientific method. | Good ideas. |
| Methodology | Workable methodologic for conducting the research. | Knowledge and experience to properly structure a research project so as to obtain meaningful results. |
| Proposal | A written document describing the ideas, methods, and resources needed for carrying out the project; the expected results and benefits to be obtained. | Writing talents and organization skills. |
| Funding | Commitment of resources in support of the idea. | Person or group with the capital resources. |
| Management | Organizing, directing, controlling project resources, applying methodology to "prove" the idea. | Staff who can "orchestrate" complex ventures. |
| Analysis | Examination of collected data to derive useful conclusions. | Keen analytical abilities. |
| Report | A document similar to a proposal but reporting findings, not conjectures. | Good writing abilities. |
| Dissemination | Dissemination of research results through publication and presentation. | Knowledge of the audience and good writing and other communication skills. |
| Idea | An idea prompted (perhaps) by the results of the previous research project. | Ability to draw good ideas from the work of others. |

Howard L. Resnikoff, "The Need for Research in Information Science," *Information Management* (1979). For articles on various methods, see Allen Kent and Harold Lancour (editors), *Encyclopedia of Library and Information Science* (1968– ).

NEAL K. KASKE;
JAMES E. RUSH



# Library Education, Comparative

Despite the long history of libraries themselves, "library schools are, apart from the early stirrings in the United States, largely a twentieth century phenomenon." To this comment by Gerald Bramley might be added J. Periam Danton's observation that outside the United States and Europe this phenomenon has been most evident in the years after World War II. In looking at these comparatively recent developments in different parts of the world, certain themes recur—the role of the professional association whose influence may extend beyond national boundaries; the changing patterns of higher education affecting the establishment and location of schools in some countries; the increase in the number of faculty needed to staff these schools; concerns with meeting the needs of different levels of library education, from technician through to doctoral programs with continuing education also assuming increasing importance; plus the many established international links affecting the curriculum and concerns for equivalency of qualifications.

The two most influential associations in library education have been the American Library Association (ALA) and the Library Association of the United Kingdom (LA). Each has stood for a different approach. ALA has accredited the program of study by which individuals have been recognized as professionally qualified librarians. The LA has granted its recognition to those individuals who have met its requirements. The picture is not quite as clean cut as might appear at first glance. There are other factors at work, such as, in North America, the Medical Library Association (MLA), which grants its certification to those individuals who meet its requirements. In the U.K. it is now possible to obtain an educational qualification in librarianship outside the LA's examination structure. However, the Association retains control of the Register of Chartered Librarians (those individuals it officially recognizes by designation as either an Associate or a Fellow of the Library Association, A.L.A., or F.L.A.). If employers continue to seek those with the professional qualification, in addition to whatever educational qualification a person has, this will maintain the LA's power in this area.

ALA's long involvement with library education may be seen as beginning formally in 1924 with the establishment of its Board of Education for Librarianship, later replaced by the Committee on Accreditation (COA). COA's concern is with the first professional degree, commonly referred to simply as the M.L.S. (The actual title of the Masters degree awarded varies from institution to institution, as do the titles of the schools themselves, to the confusion of many outsiders.) The mechanics of COA's control over the M.L.S., exercised on behalf of ALA, is considered in ACCREDITATION, as is the extension of ALA's influence to another country, Canada; by arrangement with the Canadian Library Association, COA grants recognition to first professional degree programs offered by seven Canadian universities. Although there have been periodic suggestions that Canada develop its own internal system of recognition or accreditation, it would seem that at the present time the delegation of power of entry to the profession in Canada to ALA meets the wishes of the majority of librarians in Canada.

**International Cooperation.** This is an interesting example of international cooperation in library education, but it is not unique. For example, schools developed in countries where British influence has lingered have, in some instances, retained the practice of employing external examiners. These persons serve as assessors for the examinations conducted by the schools themselves. Nigeria and the West Indies are two examples where schools there still follow this practice, with American, British, and Canadian external examiners employed in recent years, together with librarians from within the countries themselves.

An international library school was talked about as early as 1904, by Guido Biagi writing in *Library Journal*. The most recent discussion has taken place in IFLA and FID, but there has been no really concrete progress. Unesco has been suggested as a sponsoring agency, but the location of the proposed school, language of instruction, curriculum, recruitment of faculty, all present problems that so far have been and may continue to be insurmountable. On a more modest scale, perhaps the most successful example of international cooperation in recent years has been the International Graduate Summer School (IGSS) held annually at the College of Librarianship Wales (CLW). CLW is a residential college devoted exclusively to librarianship, located in Aberystwyth, which is also the home of the National Library of Wales. The faculty of the Summer School changes from year to year, although there is some degree of continuity. The majority are drawn from North American schools and CLW itself, with a few from other European countries and further afield. To increase its appeal to students from North America, the IGSS is cosponsored with the Graduate School of Library and Information Science of the University of Pittsburgh, whose former Dean, Harold Lancour, served as Codirector in its early years. Pittsburgh issues transcripts for courses completed, thus facilitating transfer of credit to M.L.S. programs in the United States and Canada. The international flavor of the School has been further enhanced by students from other overseas countries, often specially funded by the British Council.

Different examples of international cooperation in formal education for librarianship can be found in the establishment of regional schools serving more than one country. Regional schools would seem to have much to commend them, especially in those areas where resources are limited. They permit the bringing together of faculty and institutional support to meet the needs of a student body drawn in the main, although not exclusively, from the host region. The language of instruction may also be a unifying factor, as is the case of the Inter-American Library School, Medellín, Colombia, established in 1956 for Spanish-speaking countries, or the University of Dakar's School for Librarians, Archivists, and Documentalists, founded in 1963 to meet the needs of French-speaking countries in Africa. It has had strong support from the French government and Unesco; its founding Director came from France.

Other regional schools are those in Uganda and the West Indies. The East African School of Librarianship, established in 1963 at Makerere University College, Kampala, Uganda (later Makerere University), aims to train librarians from Kenya, Tanzania, and Uganda. It has had support from Unesco, various foundations, and Scandinavia, which provided its first Director, Knud Larsen. The difficult political situation in Uganda in the 1970's was not conducive to its development. The West Indies school began in 1971 at the Mona campus, Kingston, Jamaica, to serve Jamaica, Trinidad and Tobago, Barbados, Grenada, Guyana, and the British Associated States and Colonies in the Caribbean. Its first two Directors, Dorothy Collins from the United States and Frank Hogg from Britain, were supported by Unesco, as have been other staff appointments. Additional support has come from Canada through governmental agencies and with the cooperation of the library schools at Western Ontario and Dalhousie, which have made available faculty members to teach at the West Indies school.

Many schools in North America have established links with schools in different parts of the world. ALA's International Library Education Committee has tried to establish a record of these arrangements, but the informal and short-lived nature of many of these enterprises has hindered the compilation of a central register. The paucity of records makes accurate comparisons impossible, but the impression remains that faculty members from British library schools are more active in visiting for varying periods overseas schools than are their North American counterparts. The strong supporting role of the British Council has influenced this state of affairs.

**The Library Association.** The Library Association's own direct influence on library education has been more international in scope in many ways than that of the ALA. The most obvious and immediate impact of the LA's educational program has been within the United Kingdom itself, but its ramifications have been much wider. The history of library education in the U.K. has been well covered in the literature. In 1885 the LA began its system of administering an examination system to assist in determining who would be regarded as professionally qualified librarians. This system did not require attendance at a library school, and until the end of World War II preparation for these examinations was by attendance at part-time classes for those fortunate to live in metropolitan centers, at short summer school courses, or by home study or correspondence courses. It was essentially a nongraduate profession. (The small school at London University was the solitary exception offering a full-time program essentially for those holding a baccalaureate degree.) The LA did permit overseas candidates to sit for its examinations, so a small but influential number of librarians did obtain a professional qualification from the United Kingdom when, as for instance in Australia, there was no domestic system of library education.

Full-time library schools became the feature of post-World War II education in the U.K. Initially these schools, located in technical colleges rather than universities, prepared their students for the centrally administered examinations of the LA. In 1980 the picture is very different. The schools are generally now located in universities or polytechnics and offer a bewildering array of first degrees with librarianship as a "major" or "minor," postgraduate diplomas (i.e., a one-academic-year program open to those with an academic first degree), Masters degrees (generally a research degree earned by thesis), and doctoral degrees. This conversion from an essentially nongraduate profession to one offering this wide range of options has caused much debate within British librarianship, as the pages of the *Library Association Record* in recent years bear ample testimony. The LA Council has been well aware of the implications of this change for its members, particularly those whose education took place pre-1964, after which degree programs became more common. The LA's Working Party on the Future of Professional Qualifications reported in September 1977 a proposed plan to reorganize the Association's system of qualifications, adding a new category, Licentiate (L.L.A.), as a first step before the associateship or fellowship. It was also proposed that those who began their studies after 1981 would have to be graduates. The 1978 Annual General Meeting of the Association, while accepting the Working Party report, rejected the idea of an all-graduate profession. However, this action may well become irrelevant, as the two-year program for the LA's examination seems destined to wither away. Recent incoming students have consistently opted for degree programs so that now only two schools still offer what was once the standard two-year course for nongraduates in preparation for the LA's examinations. Meanwhile, the LA continues to arrange overseas centers at which candidates may sit for its examinations, although it has given notice that overseas examinations will be withdrawn at the end of 1980. (It has to be remembered that 10 percent of the LA's membership is overseas.)

This influence of the LA, whereby overseas candidates sat for its examinations, was understandable when there was no alternative method of qualification within the country itself. In countries such as Ghana and Nigeria, the first full-time library schools prepared their students for the examinations of the LA in Britain but soon changed to offer their own degree programs. In Australia when the Library Association of Australia (LAA) became established as an examining body, the pattern of Britain was followed. The students prepared themselves for LAA's centrally administered examinations, first at part-time courses and later at full-time schools. The Association has now decided to become an all-graduate profession with the LAA moving toward an accrediting role akin to that of ALA. Somewhat as in the United Kingdom, these new full-time schools in Australia are located in both universities and other institutions of tertiary education. In New Zealand the decision was taken to move to university-based education for professional librarians; in 1980 the Victoria University of Wellington offered programs for graduates, and the Wellington Teachers' College a Certificate of Library Studies. They replaced the former graduate and nongraduate programs of the New Zealand Library School, which was linked with the National Library.

**Issues.** The creation of full-time schools in various countries in the post-World War II years has created the need for faculty members to staff them. As in library systems themselves in countries developing their services, staff have often been recruited from outside the country itself, a practice continuing today. An interesting approach to international cooperation in library education has been the program at the Department of Library and Information Studies at the Loughborough University of Technology in the United Kingdom. This began in 1974 to educate "teachers from institutions concerned with library education in the non-industrialized countries in order to expand and help to improve the quality of library education in those countries." Despite all this cross-fertilization there seems to be one major area of library education that has so far defied definition, and that is an acceptable system of equivalency and reciprocity of qualifications. ALA's Committee on this subject wrestled with the problem for some years before voting itself out of existence as unable to provide a working definition. It has left in place a series of Country Resource Panels, now administered by the International Library Education Committee of ALA, which give opinions on the level of non-North American qualifications. The Canadian Library Association committee on equivalency of qualifications also dissolved itself, unable to draft an acceptable working definition. The Commonwealth Library Association (COMLA) took upon itself as one of its first objectives the drawing up a system of equivalencies. IFLA's Section on Library Schools and Other Training Aspects has established a Working Group to review "equivalence and reciprocity between national professional qualifications." This group circulated a questionnaire and planned to make its report in 1980. Another area in which IFLA has been involved is in developing guidelines for a model curriculum with which it has associated a proposal in a related field—"Guidelines for Curriculum Development in Information Studies"—prepared for Unesco. These were considered at the 1979 IFLA Congress in Copenhagen.

What still remains at issue is how many librarians are needed and at what level. While the distinction between the technician and professional librarian is generally understood, there are still differences of opinion over how much education is needed, especially for the latter category. If a simple quantitative approach is taken, then the number of years of high school and tertiary education can be determined. How many years should be devoted to academic subjects and how many to professional studies, i.e., library science? The Canadian two-academic-year (or four-term) program for the first professional degree may become the norm for North America. Whether it does or not, the place of advanced degrees between the M.L.S. and Ph.D. is still unclear. From the European viewpoint the impact of equivalency and reciprocity of qualifications between member nations of the European community will be of concern especially in two areas—the level of qualifications and the amount of practical experience built into the professional qualification. Despite the many efforts of the Continuing Library Education Network and Exchange (CLENE) and the work of ALA and other professional associations in the U.S., there does not yet appear to be any clear consensus of what continuing education is needed for the library profession. The CLA, the LA, and the LAA—in countries with now well-established programs for professional library education—are all working toward clarifying their roles in continuing education. Similarly there does not yet appear to be any certainty of whether or not the schools are recruiting and producing the right people in the right numbers. Finding some of the answers to these questions will be the real challenge for the remainder of the 20th century.

**REFERENCES**

Amadou Bousso, "University of Dakar, School for Librarians, Archivists and Documentalists," *Unesco Bulletin for Libraries* (1973).

Russell Bowden, "Improving Library Education in the Developing Countries: A Unesco and Loughborough University Experiment," *Unesco Bulletin for Libraries* (1976).

Gerald Bramley, *World Trends in Library Education* (1975).

J. Periam Danton, "The Diffusion of Library Education since World War II," *Library and Information Science* (1971).

*Development of Public Libraries in Africa: The Ibadan Seminar,* Unesco Public Manuals, no. 6 (1954), an example of the many international conferences and short courses devoted to library education held in many different parts of the world. Some, like this one, have been important in influencing later developments.

Library Association, "Working Party on the Future of Professional Qualifications: Recommendations and Implementation," *Library Association Record* (1977, 1979).

NORMAN HORROCKS

## Library Education, Curriculum

For the past several decades, library education as reflected through curriculum content and structure has changed at a very sluggish pace and only in small increments or with minor variations; however, fundamental and more rapid curriculum revision has been characteristic of the 1970's. Several factors are playing roles in precipitating curriculum change:

(1) The revision, adopted in 1972, by the American Library Association of the *Standards for Accreditation* of library education programs leading to the first professional, i.e., M.L.S., degree. The previous standards had been in effect since 1952. The new standards, which encourage flexibility, are more guidelines than standards; each school, therefore, has great latitude in curriculum development, and most curricula are reflections of the predominant philosophy of librarianship at the institution that offers the program.

(2) Due in large part to fellowships available for doctoral study in librarianship through the Higher Education Act of 1965, there has been a notable influx into library schools of library educators holding the doctoral degree. While these library educators agree that M.L.S. education is, most importantly, professional education, they bring to education for librarianship concerns and experience that encompass more than the day-to-day operational concerns of library institutions.

(3) Increasingly, undergraduate, library technical assistant, joint-degree, sixth-year certificate, and Ph.D. programs are important components of library education programs. In the institutions where these programs exist, they have effects upon the curriculum available to M.L.S. students.

(4) The crosscurrents generated by the far-reaching, extensive technological, societal, and bibliographical developments of the 1960's and 1970's have been embraced, or at least accepted, by the majority of library educators. One indicator of the acceptance of the great changes affecting the library environment is the trend toward changing library school names to include the more encompassing term "information." Schools of library science are now being renamed to "schools of library and information science" or similar names.

In order to accommodate these and many other factors, curriculum content and structural change have become highly characteristic of contemporary library education programs. Some M.L.S. programs contain rearranged and augmented required curriculum components, while a number of these and some others have extended the number of credit hours required for the M.L.S. degree. The modal number of graduate level academic credits required to complete the degree remains 36 semester hours or its equivalent in quarter hours, but requirements vary from as few as 30 to more than 60 semester hours. Because most library educators and many practitioners agree that the basic knowledge now required for librarianship has expanded and, to a lesser degree, concur that librarians should develop a certain, although undetermined, level of competence in an area of specialization prior to receiving the M.L.S. degree, it is understandable that there appears to be a trend toward lengthening the number of credit hours required for the first professional degree. This trend is probably the key harbinger of fundamental curriculum change taking place in library education today.

**Fundamentals in Library Education.** The ALA's Committee on Accreditation (COA) gives the following as the basic content areas that all M.L.S. programs must cover: (1) an understanding of the role of the library as an educational and information agency; (2) an understanding of the theories of collecting, building, and organizing library materials for use; (3) a knowledge of information sources and an ability to assist the user of library materials in locating and interpreting desired items; and (4) knowledge of the principles of administration and organization to provide information services. Translated into curriculum structure in M.L.S. programs, these four content areas constitute what has come to be known as the "core." It is significant that three of the four content areas refer to library specifically, while the fourth speaks only of information services; the COA itself seems to suggest that there is more to library education than training for work in library institutions.

Because curriculum revision, especially at the level of the core, is so characteristic of today's library schools, it is difficult to describe a typical core curriculum, especially in number of credit hours that may be required of all students; however, most typically the core, often the only required curriculum component, ranges from 6 to 12 semester hours. These hours remain largely devoted to the traditional content areas of librarianship that came into acceptance in the 1940's and 1950's; i.e., courses including a combination of reference, materials selection, cataloguing and classification, and administration. It is the limitation of this largely skill- and principle-based library, institution-focused, and separated curriculum that has come under serious scrutiny in the 1970's. Integration and expansion of core content appears to be the present direction, even though there is no national agreement as to the basis for an *integrated* core in librarianship; still, a significant number of schools are creating and implementing such curricular structures.

The first attempt at offering an integrated core curriculum was undertaken in the 1960's through the leadership of Jesse Shera at Case Western Reserve University. Since then, many schools have introduced and revised variations of an integrated core. Some include a required foundations of librarianship course, coupled with a small number of separate, largely skill-based courses. Another approach is a totally integrated core, usually consisting of 9 to 12 credit hours that may be taken either in a block or in a sequence of a primary 6 hours followed by 3 to 6 additional hours. These integrated core curricula subsume substantial parts of the traditional core of reference, cataloguing, materials selection and administration and add significant components dealing with foundations, communications, the research process, media, and most notably information science. The emphasis of the integrated core is on the view that there are elements common to all types of library and information services that include both theoretical and philosophical, as well as skill fundamentals. The central institutional focus remains the library, but other institutional and independent work roles are included.

In those schools with the longest experience with integrated core curricula, notably Drexel University and the universities of North and South Carolina, the integrated core approach has had influence on the entire curriculum, especially in reducing redundancy and providing individual faculty with a shared knowledge of what is included in the common knowledge base of those students who have completed the core.

An abbreviated, generalized outline for a hypothetical integrated core curriculum is as follows:

I. Libraries and Society
 A. Communications
  Information—its meaning, interpretation, dissemination
 B. Library role in the communication process
  User needs; comparison with other information agencies; library and information science as a profession
 C. Social role of information institutions
  Meeting the needs of clients
 D. Political context of information institutions
  Library in its institutional setting, its administrative structure, means of support, legal base
 E. Freedom of information, intellectual freedom, and copyright
 F. Forms of communication media
  Film, audio tape, other media
II. Library Services and Materials
 A. Information institutions as service systems
 B. Mechanization of library services
  Computer usage; computer language and programming
 C. Collection development
  Types of materials; types of collections; types of libraries and users; technique and principles of selection and acquisition; selection tools
 D. Collection access
  Bibliographic descriptions; subject analysis and description; physical access

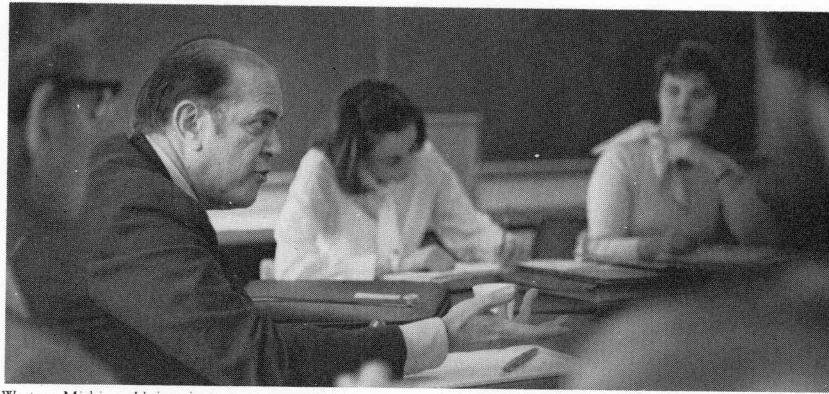
Western Michigan University

*Alphonse Trezza, Executive Director of NCLIS, addresses students as a Visiting Scholar at the School of Librarianship, Western Michigan University, 1976.*

 E. Information seeking
  Reference services; materials and automated services; reference interview
III. Research (as a means of studying concerns in library and information science)
 Problem identification, research techniques, design, data collection and treatment. Communication of research results.
IV. Management
 A. Planning, organizing, staffing, directing, controlling
 B. Systems analysis
 C. Effectiveness measurement
 D. Interlibrary cooperation and organization

Returning to the traditional core of reference—cataloguing and classification, administration, and selection—it can be easily seen that the integrated core does indeed subsume these elements, but important elements emphasizing conceptual and methodological concerns are added. Especially noteworthy are: (1) the comparison of libraries and librarians with other institutions and professions and occupations that provide information services; (2) identification of information user needs and behaviors and the role of the librarian in identifying and responding to them; (3) introduction of technology and information science to all who will become professional librarians; (4) recognition of knowledge of the content and process of research as essential to all library professionals; and (5) acknowledgment of the increasing responsibility of all professional librarians in the management of library operations.

The emphasis on the core of librarianship in library education curricula, especially the inclusion in the core of the concerns of and contributions from information science, indicates the strong desire of library educators to keep the traditional generalist curriculum and to head off a possible bifurcation of the discipline into librarianship *and* information science. This task of unification, however, may well be beyond the capacity of most programs

Missouri State Library.

*Edward P. Miller, Dean of the Library School at the University of Missouri, Columbia, consults with three graduate students who are studying information science under fellowships awarded by the U.S. Office of Education.*

of library education as they are presently structured. The possibility of the American Society for Information Science's (ASIS) taking on a role in the accreditation of library education programs could contribute to the melding of library and information science education into a single discipline and profession, although it could force divisions and might (emphasizing might) lead to a slow and agonizing demise of traditional library education.

The curriculum of librarianship, which through the 1960's had been relentlessly oriented to the institutional structure of the library, continues to emphasize specialization in the profession by the type of library institution in which the professional might expect to work. But there were indications by the end of the 1970's that this emphasis was declining and that specialization in the field would focus increasingly upon type of client served (e.g., student, researcher, recreational user) or information function pursued (e.g., indexer/abstracter, collection developer, information interpreter, information manager), without regard to the institutional setting of the professional. The development of integrated core curricula is one of the key indicators of this shift.

**Specialist Areas.** So long as the vast majority of M.L.S. degree holders continue to find employment in library institutions, and so long as these institutions require only that their beginning professionals possess the degree without much regard to the courses taken to obtain that degree, true educational specialization will be concentrated in on-the-job experience and post-M.L.S. programs. Only one school accredited by the ALA claims to have a specialist or single-purpose, as opposed to generalist curriculum; that program is in school/media librarianship. Regardless of the many reasons given for continued reliance on the generalist curriculum, a growing number of library educators and practitioners concur that specialist preparation is needed. They agree that the 36-hour M.L.S. curriculum is insufficient for educating specialists unless a school chooses to educate a single type of librarian with all courses, after the core curriculum, focused largely upon a single subject area, functional area, or type of library. Even then 36 hours may be too limited. Some library educators and employers believe that more library education programs should choose to declare a specialty or perhaps small groups of specialty curricula. For example, a school might state that it is single purpose in the education of public librarians including perhaps tracks for urban and rural public librarians. This type of specialist school might have in its curriculum, in addition to the 12-hour core, such course offerings as the following distribution:

*Required of all students:*
Political Environment of the Public Library (3)
Economics of Public Service (3)
Systems of Libraries (3)
Administration of Public Libraries (3)

| *Rural Tract* | *Urban Tract* |
|---|---|
| Rural Sociology (3) | The City (3) |
| Regional Planning (3) | Urban Planning (3) |
| Rural Libraries (3) | Metropolitan and Suburban Libraries (3) |
| Rural Economics (3) | Urban Economics (3) |
| Resources for Small Public Libraries (3) | Resources for Large Public Libraries (3) |
| Rural Library Research (3) | Urban Library Research (3) |

This type of specialist program offered totally within the library school could also be developed for academic librarianship including tracks for university, college, and community college librarians. Since the COA has approved of the single-purpose program as appropriate for school/media librarianship, there seems to be little compelling argument that it would not be appropriate for other types of librarianship.

Another type of single-purpose curriculum that could be developed within the offerings of a single-purpose school might be the reference specialist. As in the past, many generalist librarians still decide to concentrate in reference service without regard to type of library in which they might find employment. These students take courses in reference, totaling at least 15 semester hours. The 15 minimum hours would probably include:

Introduction to Reference Service (3)
Resources for the Humanities (3)
Resources for the Social Sciences (3)
Resources for Science and Technology (3)
Government Publications (3)

In today's complex information environment, a single-purpose curriculum of some depth for a reference specialist might well include:

Introduction to Reference (3)
Resources for the Humanities (3)
Resources for the Behavioral Sciences (3)
Resources for the Social Sciences (3)
Resources for the Sciences (3)
Resources for Technology (3)
U.S. Government Publications (3)
Government Publications (Exclusive of U.S.) (3)
Serial Publications (3)
Nonprint Media (3)
On-line Bibliographic Resources and Services (3)
Information User Studies (3)
Administration of Reference Services (3)

This hypothetical curriculum represents a total of 39 semester hours of which only 3, Introduction to Reference, might be concentrated in the core. Additional single subject resource courses could well be included, boosting the number of credits to well over 40. In fact, a school that chooses to be a reference specialist school could reasonably develop tracks for social science specialists, humanities specialists, and others.

Another route to specialist preparation is through cooperation with other academic departments. While the specialization program by type of library could be pursued in this manner, for example, having those pursuing academic librarianship taking courses in schools of education and public administration, this path to specialization is especially appropriate for educating subject specialists. Prospective art librarians might profitably take a variety of courses in art history and fine arts as well as special courses in the library school. While many students might choose a joint master's degree program, it would be possible to gain appropriate preparation for a specialty with fewer hours than those needed for a joint degree, provided, of course, that the specialist program is well designed.

One area of specialization in the M.L.S. curriculum that has been called for especially by library practitioners is a management specialization. It is unclear whether practitioners are calling for an actual specialization or for an extension of the M.L.S. curriculum for *all* librarians in the area of management. There is considerable evidence, based upon research studies, continuing education needs assessments and programs held at professional meetings, that professional librarians are increasingly being utilized in management and various supervisory positions. Traditionally, library schools have offered only the core course in general library administration and then planned for additional administrative knowledge to be gained through students' taking type-of-library courses. A number of library schools, responding to the need to provide additional administrative knowledge, have introduced advanced general administration courses. Many schools offer courses in such analytical skills as systems analysis. Courses in the administration of specific library functions such as technical services and public services are also offered at some schools, and many courses dealing with library networking or cooperative systems emphasize administrative aspects. The most prevalent means for providing concentration in administrative aspects of librarianship is through cooperation with other academic departments. M.L.S. students may be encouraged to take courses such as personnel management or organizational behavior in schools of business or public administration.

Only the largest library schools in number of faculty can hope to provide more than one or two programs of library specialization to their students, although many schools are able to offer individual specialized courses such as law, map, music, or archival librarianship. The individual specialized course does not amount to specialization. These courses are typical in most traditional library education curricula because they are offered based on the expertise available from a particular full-time or adjunct faculty member.

The future development of specialization programs within the 36-hour M.L.S. degree is problematic. It is especially difficult for publicly supported library schools to abandon the generalist library education program, as they are expected to educate and train librarians for all types of libraries within their states. Further, the development of specialized library education programs would best be accomplished through a national plan for library education. Although a number of writers have called for such a national plan, none is on the horizon. Again, it appears that the most likely changes to occur in the education of librarians are that (1) curriculum content will be shifted to emphasize development of competence in the technologically oriented aspects of the information environment, and (2) the number of credit hours required for the first professional degree will increase.

Library education curricula have entered into a period of scrutiny and change, and curricular change will continue to be the most characteristic element of library education in the 1980's. The inclusion of flexible course structures, such as Issues in Librarianship or Resources in Special Literatures, which will allow library educators to respond rapidly to changes in library and information science, will become essential elements in the curriculum.

**Association of American Library Schools.** The Association of American Library Schools (AALS), founded in 1915, has as its mission promoting excellence in education for library and information science as a means of increasing the effectiveness of library and information services. The goals of the Association are: (1) To provide a forum for the active interchange of ideas and information among library educators and to promote research related to teaching and to library and information science; (2) to formulate and promulgate positions on matters of mutual interest to library education; and (3) to cooperate with other organizations on matters of mutual interest.

Membership in the Association is open to both institutions and personal members. Institutional memberships are granted upon request to any school with a program accredited by the American Library Association, Associate Institutional memberships may be granted to other schools that offer graduate degrees in librarianship or cognate fields. Personal members must be full-time educators or librarians employed full-time in accredited programs; any person outside these categories may be an Associate Personal member.

The curriculum of library education programs is of vital concern to the membership of AALS. Because this membership is principally made up of faculty of accredited library schools and schools that plan to seek accreditation, the emphasis on curriculum is greatest at the M.L.S. level. The 1977 annual meeting of AALS was devoted to the core curriculum, and the Association supports both a general Curriculum Interest Group and several interest groups that emphasize specific curricular components such as adult services, on-line bibliographic services, library history, and research methodology. With the discontinuance of the Library Education Division within the ALA, AALS will undoubtedly find itself cooperating more fully with ALA in library education matters. Indeed, the membership of ALA Council's Standing Committee on Library Education (SCOLE) is largely composed of members of AALS. Of chief concern to both SCOLE and AALS is the continued development and availability to potential information professionals of excellent programs of library education. Perhaps AALS and SCOLE will join together to develop a national plan for library education, at least at the M.L.S. level, that will aid in the assurance that tomorrow's information professionals will have access to educational programs of quality that contain both core and specialist components.

**REFERENCES**

Martha Boaz, "The Future of Library and Information Science Education," *Journal of Education for Librarianship* (1978).

Herbert Goldhor, editor, *Education for Librarianship: The Design of the Curriculum of Library Schools* (1971).

Gerald Jahoda, "Education for Information Science," *Annual Review of Information Science and Technology* (1973).

Kathryn A. Oller, editor, "Education for Librarianship: A New Approach to the Core," *Drexel Library Quarterly* (1974).

Jesse Shera, *The Foundations of Education for Librarianship* (1972).

JANE ROBBINS CARTER

## Library Education, History

The history of U.S. library education parallels the history of the country's library development, particularly in the period after 1876. Prior to that institutionalization of librarianship, represented by the founding of the American Library Association, the publication of the *American Library Journal,* and the ascendancy of Melvil Dewey and his colleagues, librarians were trained in a variety of informal and individual ways. Some learned library practice by "personal confrontation" and by reading and consultation with senior colleagues. Others found brief observation periods in similar libraries a useful training experience. For the fortunate few, apprenticeships could sometimes be arranged as a short but formal program of training in library techniques.

*A class in Bibliography at Pennsylvania State University, c. 1894.*

A summer library school session at the University of Iowa, c. 1930.

University of Iowa Archives

By 1876 some prominent librarians were concerned enough about the provision of a formal training program to call for the establishment of "schools of bibliographical and bibliothecal training" in order to produce persons who could "guide the formation of and assume management within the fast increasing libraries of our country." This call for an established educational program resulted in an 1883 proposal presented to the young ALA by Melvil Dewey. Dewey described his School of Library Economy, to be established as a central training agency for instruction and practice in library work.

Dewey was able to see his proposed school become reality in 1887 when Columbia University agreed to an experimental four-month program of lectures, library visits, directed readings, and work experiences for a class of library staff people. The Columbia program lasted two years until Dewey's disagreement with the University trustees over the admission of women to a Columbia education. In 1889 Dewey took the school to the New York State Library at Albany, where he began to plan and execute the kind of library education program that has been a model ever since. He developed a two-year course combining classroom instruction with practical fieldwork or apprenticeship experiences.

Several of Dewey's students went on to establish library schools in other cities and states—notably at Drexel in Philadelphia, Pratt Institute in Brooklyn, and the Armour Institute in Chicago. By 1900 these four schools had been formally reviewed by an ALA committee chaired by John Cotton Dana, and in 1907 library school faculty members met together at an ALA conference. A Round Table of Library School Instructors was formed in 1911 and then broke away from ALA in 1915 to become the Association of American Library Schools (AALS).

That same year the Carnegie Corporation, in its distribution of Andrew Carnegie's fortune, began investigating library training and education. Its commission to Charles Williamson to prepare a critical report on library schools and training was part of a broader program that also included funding for training programs at the public libraries in New York, Pittsburgh, and Atlanta.

In the years after World War I the ALA once again took a leadership position in the planning efforts for a standardized library training experience. Williamson's report, *Training for Library Service,* was published in 1923; in 1924 the ALA established the Board of Education for Librarianship (BEL). Williamson described 14 schools in his report, criticizing them for curricular inadequacies and poor financial and faculty arrangements. The BEL then took on the tasks of supervising these schools, of developing standards, and of commissioning institutes and textbooks. Its *Minimum Standards for Library Schools* were adopted in 1925 and provided guidelines for library training programs on both the undergraduate and graduate levels.

The first advanced graduate program, including a program leading to a doctoral degree, was established in 1926 at the University of Chicago. This noteworthy program, staffed by a faculty trained in the traditional disciplines and heavily devoted to research, provided an excellent leadership model for library education and was the first landmark institution to appear in the 40 years that had elapsed since Dewey and his School of Library Economy. A number of other schools were founded in the decade after Chicago's Graduate Library School, including the first Canadian school, which opened at McGill University in 1929.

The 1930's and the Great Depression saw a slowing in the expansionist phase begun by the establishment of the BEL and the GLS, but those library schools that were firmly established in major U.S. universities survived both depression and the world war that followed.

In the academic boom times after World War II the need to reexamine the revised accreditation standards put forth by the BEL in 1933 was obvious. The Board was joined in its deliberations on revision by the AALS and by the ALA's Library Education Division, which had been established in 1946. The new *Standards for Accreditation* and a *Statement of Interpretation* appeared in 1951 and 1952, respectively. By 1957 all U.S. library schools had been reviewed, and most of those offering graduate training leading to the terminal Master's degree were accredited.

Another 1956 ALA action affected library education. The BEL was eliminated and its functions absorbed by two ALA organizations. The Library Education Division was to serve as the umbrella unit to promote library education in the profession, while a new unit, the Committee on Accreditation, was separately established as the body charged with both accreditation of the first professional degree and the maintenance of the *Standards* themselves.

The turbulent 1960's saw an enormous growth in library education programs, supported partially by an influx of federal aid from the Office of Education and caused in part by the rapid expansion in library buildings and services also funded by the government in the late 1950's and 1960's. A number of graduate library schools added doctoral programs and research institutes; others added continuing education and sixth-year certificate programs. Federal funding was also made available for scholarship aid, and an emphasis was placed on the recruitment of persons into library education in order to meet the perceived need for both practitioners and library educators.

The ALA also responded to the enlarging sphere of interest in library education and service by establishing the Office for Library Education in 1966. That office was involved with the twin issues of library education and the human resources necessary for library service. Its formal paper on *Library Education and Manpower* (later revised and published as *Library Education and Personnel Utilization*) prepared under the direction of Lester Asheim, was published in 1966 and recognized the need for a variety of persons and levels of library training, including the paraprofessional or library technician.

Curricular changes also occurred during the 1960's as library education attempted to respond to changing social institutions and cultural expectations, as well as to technological and behavioral developments. Student needs to seek specializations and subject skills also added pressure for curricular change.

By the 1970's, however, the flood of federal funding was ended. Library schools began to tighten and change curricular and faculty emphases away from vast research studies and innovations and back toward the traditional terminal Master's degree program and continuing education programs. The ALA Office for Library Education was restructured in 1971 as the Office for Library Personnel Resources. Its mandate was far broader and included library personnel and staffing issues as well as training and library education.

The *Standards for Accreditation* were revised by the Committee on Accreditation in 1971 (published 1972), and all U.S. and Canadian schools were reexamined for accreditation of their first professional degree programs. Periodic reaccreditation was mandated, and a formal pattern for the new accreditation process was established. The tightening economic and political mood of the U.S. was reflected in the spare and cautious atmosphere prevailing in library education as it entered the decade of the 1980's.

The history of the British experience with library education differs in one vital way. Until recently certification of librarians, rather than accreditation of degree programs, forms the basis for professional recognition in the British Isles and in those nations whose educational and professional programs have been influenced by the British pattern. The librarian seeking professional recognition in the British system had to take the examination set by the Library Association. For many years the candidates obtained their basic professional knowledge through a program of practical apprenticeship, personal reading, in some cases by correspondence courses, or by some course work at part-time centers, in what was essentially the American 19th-century mode. Only after World War II were full-time colleges of librarianship established, such as those at Aberystwyth and Loughborough, initially to prepare candidates for sitting the Library Association examinations. (The one pre-war exception was at the school at London University.) The acceptance of these formal educational programs for librarians forms the basis for a basic shift in British library education proposed in a Library Association (U.K.) Working Party Report in 1977.

**REFERENCES**

Gerald Bramley, *A History of Library Education* (1969).

Charles Churchwell, *The Shaping of American Library Education* (ALA, 1975).

Donald G. Davis, Jr., "Education for Librarianship," *Library Trends* (1976).

Edward G. Holley, "Librarians, 1876–1976," *Library Trends* (1976)

Jesse Shera, *The Foundations of Education for Librarianship* (1972).

ELLEN GAY DETLEFSEN

## Library Education, Specialization in

The definition and role of specialization in library education have undergone several changes that reflect the history of library schools and libraries in the United States in general. In the 19th century curricula were entirely devoted to library functions; gradually courses by type of library were added, and today the large majority of library schools offer courses on special subjects and services. Function-oriented courses have remained as foundation or core curriculum throughout this development.

The first program in "library economy," established by Melvil Dewey at Columbia in 1887, covered the major practical processes of daily library operations. Technical/clerical procedures were taught together with a minimum of the intellectual content of bibliographic organization.

All library schools in the 19th and early 20th centuries taught the four basic components of library operations: cataloguing and classification, reference (combining both bibliographic documentation and services), book selection, and administration. Courses on the history of books and libraries, or the library in society, constituted the framework for this "quadrivium," as Jesse Shera has referred to the early core curriculum.

At the turn of the century the need for preparation for specific library services, to public or academic libraries for example, was recognized. Gradually courses by type of library were added to the original curriculum, and these were considered specializations. While several efforts to improve the quality of library education (the Williamson Report of 1923 and others) were made over the next decades, the major changes concerning the subject content of library curricula occurred in the 1960's and 1970's. Responding to technological developments, to the intensification of research, and to the expansion of social services, library schools developed specializations by subject and by services.

In 1951, six years after World War II, the American Library Association had already acknowledged, in its first official standards for graduate library education, that the study of specialized service in general or special libraries could occupy a place in the basic program that was to include principles and practices common to the various types of libraries and library services. As the demand for specialization increased and the core courses had to incorporate more complex concepts and operations, as well as introductions to the contemporary information environment, the extension of the traditional one-year curriculum had to be considered. Two approaches were taken in the 1960's: (1) a two-year Master's program, offered now in Canada and in a few schools in the U.S., and (2) advanced certification programs in subject or professional areas. The first formal post-Master's specialist course was introduced at the Columbia University Library School in 1961, and by 1975 Gerald Bramley could note that 20 schools offered a sixth-year specialist course.

In 1967 the report of an ALA committee to consider a national plan for library education had stated that "the significance of specialization in various fields of librarianship should be considered and its place in the overall pattern [of library education] determined." In 1970 ALA had accepted the Library Education and Manpower policy statement, prepared by its Office for Library Education. Part 30 of this document relates to specialization, noting that library schools should make knowledge in other fields available to students, either through the appointment of staff members from other disciplines or through permitting students to cross departmental, divisional, and institutional lines in reasoned programs in related fields. Thus after a slow start the development intensified and was acknowledged and supported by ALA. In all discussions and recommendations, the need for proper balance between the core and the specialized courses was stressed, together with the concern for the quality of the subject courses.

In the *Carnegie Commission Report on Higher Education of 1972* E. H. Schein and D. W. Kommers stressed the need for more flexibility in the professional school curriculum, "more transdisciplinary curricula that integrate several disciplines into new professions that will be more responsive to the new social problems of today's and tomorrow's society." In the same year ALA upgraded the 1951 standards, demanding explicit objectives for specific educational programs. Three years later, in 1975, a task force of the Association of American Library Schools recommended that programs should provide opportunities for students to develop a specialty in a particular subject discipline or library function. In 1977, 55 out of 59 accredited library schools in the United States integrated specializations into their curricula, evidence of the social sensitivity of American library education.

**Types of Specializations.** In October 1977 a survey of specializations was conducted at the request of the Association of American Library Schools. Short questionnaires and a request for current bulletins were sent to the 59 accredited programs of library and information science. The bulletins from all schools were received, and the three schools that had not answered the questionnaire were contacted by telephone.

The following courses were considered as specializations in this survey:

1. Courses designed for specific information needs outside the immediate library/information/communication professions; e.g., art, law, music.
2. Fields within the broader library/information/communication professions for which no formal graduate programs exist; e.g., archives, publishing.
3. Courses related to current social concerns, for which formal programs are emerging, and where—interestingly—teaching, research, and library information service programs develop in many instances in close exchange; e.g., gerontology and new urban service programs.

Not included as specialties were

1. Courses on special librarianship (offered at several schools) because they are considered "type of library" courses, like those dealing with public or school librarianship. They may include, but do not focus on, discrete subjects or professions.
2. Media courses (film, TV, and so forth) since most nonbook media constitute integral parts of library resources and services and are included in basic library courses.
3. Management, systems analysis, and computer courses because they too constitute part of the contemporary librarian's basic education.
4. Joint Ph.D. programs between schools; e.g., the School of Information and Library Studies at the State University of New York at Buffalo offers a Ph.D. in cooperation with the Department of Higher Education. The final degree is a Ph.D. in Higher Education with a specialization in academic librarianship.

According to the survey the following subject specialties were offered in 1977:

| *specialties* | *schools* |
|---|---|
| Medicine* | 36 |
| Law | 31 |
| Archives | 23 |
| Rare books | 22 |
| Music | 11 |
| Art | 10 |
| Publishing | 7 |
| Area programs** | 5 |
| Ethnic studies | 5 |

* This topic includes Health Services and Pharmacology.
**This topic includes Latin American, Southeast Asian, and African area bibliography courses.

Other specialties that were taught by fewer than five schools were:

| | |
|---|---|
| Social issues: | Drug information<br>Gerontology<br>Disadvantaged/Handicapped<br>Prison services<br>Urban programs |
| Subjects: | Geography/Maps<br>Performing arts<br>Theology |

Several schools indicated that they were in the process of developing specialty courses and joint professional programs, especially in the areas of archives, medicine, and urban studies. Programs in cooperation with academic disciplines like history of English were also increasing; thus, unless current trends are changing drastically, specialization will increase in the foreseeable future. This development is also encouraged by former students' responses, which are predominantly positive in respect to the effect of special courses on both their credentials and their job satisfaction.

Some schools offered one course in a specific subject area, while others offered whole sequences. With special seminars, independent study, and fieldwork credits, the exact number of course offerings may be slightly higher than the results indicated. It was clear, however, that the majority of schools offered at least one course in some specialty: 20 schools offered courses in four or more subject areas; 35, one to three; while 4 schools indicated no special subject course offerings.

Approximately 30 programs offered joint courses with other departments that were described under a variety of headings in their bulletins as "Special Programs," as "Double Master's," or as "Interdisciplinary Programs." In some school bulletins the special courses were listed with the general description of the Master's and Ph.D. programs, while others listed them separately. Case Western Reserve, for example, in its 1978 school bulletin enumerated the following library services sequence: Public Library Program, Academic Library Program, School Library Program, Health Sciences Librarianship and Health Sciences Information, Law Librarianship, Children's Library Program, Music Librarianship, Special Libraries, Services to Disadvantaged, Archives Management and Administration, Drug Information Program. In addition, students can enter joint programs with the School of Management and others.

Special courses are offered primarily on the Master's level. They fall into the following pattern:

Courses offered in the school by a regular faculty member;
Courses offered in the school by an adjunct lecturer, often a practitioner;
Courses offered in cooperation with the respective subject department—this pattern applies to both Master's and Ph.D. programs;

***Library General Information Survey*** **511**
**library hand,** legible handwriting for library records **142**

Courses offered in any other department, to be taken as an elective or as part of a special program;
Courses offered through a variety of special seminars.

Some schools give credit for nonacademic workshops at governmental agencies (archives, social agencies).

**Impetus for Specialist Programs.** The current proliferation of these courses is a direct reflection of the state of our civilization. Today the special information needs of most professions have become complex to an extent that general reference and referral services are not able to meet adequately.

The implementation of the specialized courses can be traced to several direct causes. In some cases professional organizations, either by suggesting standards or by approaching schools with requests, were responsible for the initiation of programs. At Syracuse University, for example, the university archivist on returning from the 1964 annual meeting of the Society of American Archivists sent a memorandum to the library school stating, "It was unanimously acknowledged that there is an acute shortage of trained archivists in this country," and that "the consensus was, that library schools initiate archival training programs. Many felt that the library school should limit itself to offering an introductory or general course in archives and manuscripts, which would be part of the normal training program for librarians. In this way, the librarian would at least be familiar with the principles and techniques used in processing archives and manuscript collections."

In other instances courses were initiated even prior to the founding of a professional organization and before specific needs were formulated publicly. This was the case not only in new fields of endeavor, such as environmental or area studies, but also in conventional disciplines like the fine arts, where library school courses were offered before the Art Libraries Society of North America (ARLIS/NA) was founded in 1973. With the unprecedented increase in museum activities, art research, and new visual media, the need for organized resources emerged almost overnight, and some schools responded as soon as they recognized this phenomenon.

Some professional organizations, in addition to initiating courses, now also monitor their quality. The Music Library Association, for example, developed guidelines for courses in this field, and the Medical Library Association opted for certification examinations for individual librarians, rather than for the accreditation of library school programs. This process is, however, much debated, and various means for the quality control of special programs are currently under review. Special courses have also been initiated through direct requests from communities or through grants available from foundations and government.

The decision to offer a special program is usually influenced by one or several of the following factors:

*The University*. Strong departments, special programs, campus facilities, especially the library system and museum, are essential in any consideration of alternative specialties.

*The Community*. In larger communities other academic institutions and governmental and private agencies often provide ideal partners for cooperative programs, including fieldwork. In cities like Chicago, New York, or Washington, D.C., library schools have unique opportunities, and course titles like "Federal Library Administration" or "Federal Library Resources" appear.

*Interest of Faculty Members and Deans*. This is, naturally, a stong factor in the decision to implement new courses, and the professional competence and motivation of those in charge are essential to the quality of the program.

The currently offered specialties introduce students to the information requirements of new fields and at the same time strengthen their professional background for work at existing institutions, especially research libraries. In a large university any subject bibliographer must meet more than the M.S.L.S. requirements of the past; an advanced degree in the specific field is usually required. Thus the subject specialty courses in library schools are not added to develop an amateur chemist or lawyer through one course (a criticism that is sometimes ventured against subject-oriented courses in library schools). Rather, they are designed to introduce students with a subject background to the current state of bibliographic organization and services in their field. There is little doubt that most students who enter a library school with advanced degrees in a subject field need, in addition to their familiarity with the substantive content, an introduction to the resources (e.g., book and nonbook media, data bases) and bibliographic organization (concepts and methodology) of their own specialty.

The efforts to upgrade the library profession and the paucity of beginning teaching positions are an unpredicted coincidence. Thus many students graduating with Master's and Ph.D. degrees in various subjects in the humanities and the social sciences, and without job prospects in conventional teaching positions, may greatly enhance their chances for employment with an additional Master's degree in Library and Information Science. History graduates, for example, with a degree in librarianship and an archives specialization, will have a variety of options. They will also gradually provide historical societies, historical museums, and archives with qualified staff members who, in addition to being historians, have a professional background in the organization and administration of collections and programs.

Naturally the general library/information science program can gain immensely from the admission of students with subject graduate degrees and from the addition of special courses. With the expansion of both, the library's mission and its services, many of the alternative specialties have become as important for general librarianship as they are for special libraries and for the new information professions mentioned earlier.

**Implementing Programs.** In the development of specializations in library school curricula the following considerations are essential:

1. Can the course, courses, or new units be integrated into the school's curriculum without constituting patchwork and/or without negatively affecting the school's program?
2. Can the new courses meet desirable standards; i.e., what are the faculty qualifications and resources?
3. Does the market justify the initiation of the specialty, even if interest and resources are ideal?
4. Should schools emphasize double Master's programs rather than the addition of single courses, or should both be done?
5. Should the schools individually, or ALA, and/or the Association of American Library Schools monitor regional patterns and try to promote a reasonable distribution of special courses throughout different parts of the country?
6. What are the general librarianship/information science courses required by students who want to specialize but may later change to another area of librarianship?

As all schools wrestle with these issues, and as these discussions bring library educators and professional organizations into closer exchange, the warning of Jesse Shera and others should be heeded: a loss of quality of library school programs might result from the proliferation of specialization. If specialized courses are merely a reaction to superficial trends, they can indeed weaken the profession just as too much standardization and regulation would do serious harm. Where the previous considerations are taken seriously, the thoughtful integration of specializations can only add to the experience of students whether their interest is in systems design, in bibliographic organization, or in any other area of librarianship.

All specializations can be seen as components that together constitute librarianship in its broad generic sense. Just as the generic book is more than a physical entity, libraries were already described by E. C. Richardson in 1914 as organized information systems whether of natural or man-made origins; the process of coding and carrying codes from place to place and from period to period constituted for him the character of the library. In a similar vein, Unesco looks at libraries in a broad context, together with museums and archives, as agencies that are involved in the organization and dissemination of information and that must consider their mission together.

The inclusion of subject and service specialties in the education of library/information specialists adds, aside from conceptual and practical implications, an intellectual dimension that has been largely neglected in the past. The majority of librarians without adequate subject knowledge have not been able to transmit information together with the perception of meaning in this information. With subject graduate degrees, and with subject and service courses added to the library/information curriculum, this essential dimension is added.

The question is not whether to accept or reject the integration of courses in law or medical librarianship but how to progress most effectively in the implementation of specializations. Wherever this process is already successful, it takes place in the spirit of dynamic complementarity between theory and practice, between professional responsibilities and the needs of society.

**REFERENCES**

Gerald Bramley, *World Trends in Library Education* (1975).

Charles D. Churchwell, *The Shaping of American Library Education* (ALA, 1975).

Antje Bultmann Lemke, "Alternative Specialties in Library Education," *Journal of Education for Librarianship* (1978).

Jesse H. Shera, *The Foundations of Education for Librarianship* (1972).

ANTJE BULTMANN LEMKE

# Libya

Libya, a socialist republic in northern Africa, is bordered by the Mediterranean Sea on the north, Egypt on the east, Sudan on the southeast, Chad and Niger on the south, and Tunisia and Algeria on the west. Pop. (1977 est.) 3,014,100; area 1,749,000 sq.km. The official language is Arabic.

**National Library.** From 1955 the university library acted as a national library for the country. In January 1979 construction of the National Library building in Benghazi was completed. Thereafter it worked separately under the supervision of the Information and Culture Bureau. It is well furnished and has modern library equipment. The Library's collection consists of books, manuscripts, films, periodicals, and other items.

In 1970 a division for national bibliography was established under the supervision of the Cultural Department. That office was able to publish the first volume in 1971; it contains books and periodicals from 1866 to 1971. Five more publications had been published by 1977.

**Academic Libraries.** The Central Library of Garyounis University, Benghazi, was founded in 1955. The four main departments are acquisitions, classification, periodicals, and registration. The Library uses the Dewey Decimal Classification System for non-Arabic books, and there is an amended system that is used for Arabic books collection. Cataloguing for both Arabic and non-Arabic books is done according to Anglo-American Cataloguing Rules and LC Subject Headings. The total number of the subscriptions of various periodicals is about 1,500. An audiovisual department plays an active role, making available films, slides, videotapes, and listening and recording tapes. Also, videotapes, cassettes, and microfilms are produced by that department. The Library moved into a new building on January 1, 1974; the monumental building houses 1,000,000 volumes and 3,000 seats. Besides the Central Library, Garyounis University has seven branch libraries of the faculties.

At El-Fateh University the first library was established in 1957 when the Faculty of Science was opened. A temporary Central Library was set up later in the building of the Faculty of Science, but mainly library services were still being carried by each faculty library at the end of the 1970's. In 1975 a decision was made to build a new building for the Central Library. There are seven faculties, each with well-equipped and furnished libraries.

There are five higher institutes for technical education in different parts of the country. Founded between 1972 and 1977, the institutes have their own libraries, which provide needed periodicals, books, films, and other materials to the teaching staff and to students. The institutes cooperate to cover any shortage that may occur.

**Public Libraries.** Public library service started in Libya near the end of 1950 on a limited scale. These libraries were under the Ministry of Education. In mid-1960 the Ministry of Information and Culture introduced a new service at the "Peoples' Cultural Centers." The main role of the centers was "to guide the public in the light of governmental policy."

Both public libraries and the cultural centers came under the administration of the Secretary of Information and Culture. These are regularly provided with new books, magazines, newspapers, and governmental publications. They numbered 154 in the whole country at the end of the 1970's. All the technical service work is centralized.

**School Libraries.** From 1960 considerable effort was made to establish libraries in secondary, preparatory, and vocational schools. By the end of 1978 almost all of them had small libraries. Services of these libraries improved very slowly because of lack of trained personnel, proper facilities, and sufficient collections of printed and nonprint materials of high quality. There remained the need to pay full attention to the development of school library services.

**Special Libraries.** These libraries have become indispensable for the main governmental departments and other organizations. Special libraries up to 1970 numbered only 8 in the whole country; that number had increased rapidly up to 21 by the end of 1978. Each library maintains material relating to its special activities.

**Other Libraries.** Libraries were established by religious and social groups to serve the country when there were no public libraries. The collections of these libraries are mixed and cover all subjects, but mostly in manuscripts and old printed books. They have a limited membership and offer no good facilities or services. The trend is for them to be combined into public libraries.

AHMED M. GALLAL

# Liebaers, Herman

## (1919– )

Herman Liebaers, Librarian, 1943–54, on the staff of the Royal Library of Belgium and Director, 1956–73, and Grand Marshal of the Court of Belgium from 1974, led in strengthening IFLA and international librarianship. Born at Tienen, Belgium, on February 1, 1919, Herman Liebaers was educated in Brussels and at the University of

Ghent, but like so many young Europeans of his generation he was caught up in World War II and the consequent occupation of Belgium. Thus he spent most of 1943 in German captivity. On return to Brussels he came into librarianship and into his eminent career at the Royal Library by mere chance when that Library needed a staff member with academic training in Germanic language and literature but who was, obviously, not pro-German. During his early career in the Royal Library, where his first task was to translate the existing French subject catalogue into Dutch, he not only achieved his library certification in 1944 but also continued his scholarly studies, receiving his Ph.D. from the University of Ghent in 1955. His study of the 19th-century Dutch poet Hélène Swarth, together with her correspondence, was subsequently published by the Royal Flemish Academy of Language and Literature.

Another significant element in his early career came by way of a five-month visit to the United States during 1950–51, when he was a consultant at the Library of Congress and visited many U.S. libraries, museums, and art galleries. During the next few years he conducted summer courses in Flemish art for foreign art historians under a program sponsored by the Belgian-American Educational Foundation.

In 1954 Liebaers left the Royal Library (permanently, he thought at the time), spent half a year as Librarian of the European Council for Nuclear Research (CERN), and then returned to the United States until 1956 as a Fellow and Associate Secretary of the Belgian-American Educational Foundation. He returned to the Royal Library in 1956 as Director, a position he held until 1973.

Under his forceful directorship the Belgian Royal Library in many ways set high standards for the other ancient national libraries of Western Europe. The impressive new building, which was dedicated in 1959, not only functions efficiently but is also an appropriate component of the national cultural center of Brussels. In establishing an effective modern scientific and technical documentation service, Liebaers dispatched the Chief of the new facility to Kansas City to spend a term under the tutelage of Joseph Shipman at the Linda Hall Library. On quite another front the Library's rich Burgundian heritage of rare books, manuscripts, coins, and prints was extended and brought into public view and scholarly use through an impressive and handsome series of exhibitions and catalogues. Under his direction legal deposit was established for the Library, and the national bibliography was modernized.

In 1973 Liebaers returned to the United States on a leave of absence as Consultant to the Council on Library Resources with the intention, at least in the minds of his friends, of producing an analysis of American research libraries—sort of an update of Wilhelm Munthe's *American Librarianship from a European Angle* (ALA, 1939). But before the year was out, his career took a decided change when King Baudouin appointed him Grand Marshal of the Court of Belgium. Thus he left the Royal Library and moved, metaphorically at least, across the way to the Royal Palace. In 1974 he also resigned as President of the International Federation of Library Associations. The new royal appointment, with its high state responsibility for advising the Court, recognized Liebaers's crucial role in Belgian cultural and intellectual life, his extensive international experience, and his notable diplomatic talents. When asked what the function of a Grand Marshal might be, Liebaers himself suggested that the inquirer should "look up a medieval manuscript or incunabulum."

But Liebaers's library career reached far beyond Belgium and the United States, through the agency of the International Federation of Library Associations and Institutions (IFLA), to which he gave increasing attention in the years following 1956. He was Chairman of its National and University Libraries Section from 1959 to 1964, joined the IFLA Executive Board in 1963, was elected a Vice-President in 1964, became First Vice-President in 1967, and then in 1969 was elected President succeeding Sir Frank Francis for the term 1969–72, as well as for a second term beginning in 1972 but ending prematurely with his resignation in 1974. At that point he was elected Honorary President of IFLA.

But beyond this mere chronology is a major and successful career devoted to strengthening IFLA and moving it into the modern world and thereby energizing international librarianship. During his presidency IFLA was enabled to establish a permanent Secretariat in The Hague, to solidify its fiscal position, with generous support from the Council on Library Resources, and thereby to mount a succession of aggressive projects, notably the Universal Bibliographic Control program and more recently that for Universal Availability of Publications.

Sir Frank Francis had grasped the international significance of the American Shared Cataloging Program which led to the National Program for Acquisitions and Cataloging Program (NPAC), but it was under Liebaers's leadership that this was crystallized into the powerful UBC program. Similarly, Liebaers sensed the symbolic importance of Unesco's International Book Year Project of 1972 and saw to it that IFLA was the prime mover in the worldwide success of the Unesco project. For that service the Association of the German Book Trade awarded him its Interprofessional Award at the Frankfurt Book Fair in 1973. During his IFLA tenure Liebaers traveled extensively, particularly in the third world, taking the message of books and libraries wherever he went. In these years third world membership in IFLA expanded rapidly, and IFLA entered into an active regionalization program in order to take the IFLA program into all corners of the world.

For these and other efforts Herman Liebaers was widely honored: In 1956 he was named a Laureate of the Royal Flemish Academy of Language and Literature and in 1970 a Professor of Librarianship and Bibliography in the Free University of Brussels; the University of Liverpool awarded him an honorary doctorate in 1971, and in 1973 the Library Association of the United Kingdom named him an Honorary Vice-President; he became an Honorary Member of the Special Libraries Association in 1974 and of the American Library Association at its centennial meeting in 1976.

**REFERENCES**

A bibliography of Herman Liebaers, by Robert Gabriel, appeared in the Belgian journal *Mens en Taak* (1975). A volume of Liebaers's own reminiscences was announced by Nijhoff in 1979.

ROBERT VOSPER



# Ligue des Bibliothèques Européennes de Recherche (LIBER)

The idea of LIBER first took shape in a bar in Frankfurt am Main in August 1968 when, at the instigation of the Swiss Library Association, the acting President and Secretary, K. W. Humphreys and K. Garside, of IFLA's Section on National and University Libraries called an informal discussion. A Steering Committee, set up under the chairmanship of J. P. Clavel, decided on the proposed structure, type of membership, and draft statutes. A questionnaire to some 300 libraries elicited a 45 percent affirmative response to the proposal to establish the Ligue. The Council of Europe invited representatives from Western European countries to a meeting in Strasbourg in March 1971, at which the Ligue was legally constituted.

Large research libraries were then offered membership; about 150 joined. Membership applications now must be approved by the Executive Committee. The present membership of 180 libraries are in Austria (3), Belgium (8), Denmark (5), Finland (1), France (33), Germany (39), Iceland (1), Italy (17), Luxembourg (1), Malta (1), Monaco (1), Netherlands (10), Norway (4), Portugal (1), Spain (5), Sweden (5), Switzerland (8), United Kingdom (36), and Vatican (1). While most members are university libraries, there are also some national libraries in the organization.

The aim of LIBER is to find through cooperation practical ways of improving the services the member libraries provide by holding conferences and meetings of experts, collaborating with other bodies, making surveys and studies, and issuing publications. Since its inception LIBER has organized meetings on a number of subjects—shared cataloguing; library buildings; exchange of staff; library management; the publication, exchange, and bibliographic control of theses; collection building; interlibrary loans; the administration of manuscript and rare-book collections and map collections.

The activities of LIBER are directed by an Executive Committee elected for three years (renewable once) by members at the Annual General Meeting. The Board elects its President, Secretary, and Treasurer. (The Secretariat may be within the President's library or elsewhere.) LIBER has Working Parties on Acquisitions from the Third World, Exchange of Staff, and Library Management. As of 1978 it was in the process of setting up Groups, initially for map librarians and for manuscript and rare-book librarians. There are plans to develop Group organization and to set up more Working Parties, and such issues as professional education in Europe, information networks, user education, and the publication of statistics on prices for materials will figure in LIBER's programs.

From the beginning LIBER decided to publish a *Bulletin* twice a year; in addition, two supplements appeared covering the University Library Buildings Conference and the Meeting of Experts on Shared Cataloguing. A *LIBER Newssheet* began regular publication in autumn 1978.

One of LIBER's major problems is that it is entirely dependent on members' subscriptions. The cost of publication takes most of its income, so expenses for meetings must normally be met by members' own institutions. Initially the Council of Europe gave some valuable financial support to LIBER, but a change of policy in the Council resulted in LIBER's ceasing to be so closely associated with the Council's library program.

LIBER is a member of IFLA and has a close relation with it, and particularly with some of its Sections. A continuing question is that of extending membership to libraries in Eastern Europe.

**REFERENCE**

K. W. Humphreys, "Ligue des Bibliothèques Européennes de Recherche (LIBER)," *The Bowker Annual of Library and Book Trade Information* (1978).

K. W. HUMPHREYS

## Lippincott, J(oshua) B(allinger)

(1813—1886)



J. B. Lippincott's business life as a printer, binder, publisher, bookseller, and distributor was conducted in such a way that his publishing peers referred to him as "the Napoleon of the book trade." His business philosophy is reflected in the motto of his old-line house, *Droit et Avant* ("Right and forward," or roughly, "Be sure you are right and then go ahead").

An only child, Lippincott was born in Juliustown, Burlington County, New Jersey, on March 18, 1813. Little is known of his childhood years. He had a common school education and began working at the age of 13. From all accounts, his nonbusiness life was private. Little is recorded concerning it, other than noting that the business, banking, and educational community of Philadelphia benefited from his leadership as a member of the boards of directors of the Philadelphia and Reading Railroad, the Farmers' and Mechanics' Bank of Philadelphia, the Philadelphia Saving Fund Society, the Pennsylvania Company for Insurance on Lives and Granting Annuities, and the Board of Trustees of the University of Pennsylvania.

Lippincott began his book-oriented career in 1827 as a clerk in a Philadelphia store owned by a bookseller named Clarke. Creditors subsequently closed on Clarke, and in 1832 Lippincott was designated as the store's manager. He paid close attention to the business and to his personal finances and by 1836 had saved sufficient funds from his earnings to purchase the business, thus launching J. B. Lippincott and Company.

Lippincott was energetic and increasingly successful. He was fast making his mark as a substantial publisher of bibles, prayer books, and general literature. Lippincott gave special attention to the manufacturing aspects of the book, and his interest in elegant bindings made his books popular with booksellers. He also retailed books and did contract printing.

In 1850 he made the major decision to purchase the entire stock of books and stationery of Grigg and Elliott, Philadelphia—at that time the country's largest wholesalers in the field. Although many in the trade considered it an unwise purchase, Lippincott meant it to help him become the foremost publisher in Philadelphia. It was this transaction that more than any other occasioned people to call him "the Napoleon of the book trade."

An early business practice followed by Lippincott was to take in his assistants as partners, thus the imprint Lippincott, Grambo, and Company in the first part of the 1850's. During the period 1855–85 publications bore "J. B. Lippincott & Company."

Lippincott's early catalogue was distinguished by its comprehensiveness. Its notable works ranged from bibles, religious books, and tracts to major reference titles. In 1855 the first edition of *Lippincott's Pronouncing Gazetteer of the World* was published; subsequent editions continued in print for almost a century. In 1858 the firm began publishing Webster's *Blue-Back Speller*. Other successes under Lippincott's direction were *Allibone's Dictionary of Authors* (beginning with the second volume in 1870), a number of excellent editions of the *Unabridged Dictionary* by Webster, which the firm gave up in 1876 when it began publication of *Worcester's Dictionary,* and *Lippincott's Pronouncing Dictionary of Biography and Mythology*.

Lippincott was a publisher of periodicals as well, which he began in 1857 with the *Medico-Chirurgical Review,* edited by Samuel D. Gross. Other periodicals included *The Medical Times* and *Annals of Surgery*. In 1868, under the editorship of Lloyd Smith, Librarian of the Library Company of Philadelphia, Lippincott launched *Lippincott's Magazine*. In the years immediately following the Civil War, Lippincott expanded into the medical field publishing textbooks and handbooks. Early examples of his success were Da Costa's three-volume *Medical Diagnosis, Principles and Practice of Surgery* by Agnew, and the *Photographic Atlas of Diseases of the Skin* by Fox. A widely used handbook is *The Dispensatory of the United States of America;* with the 27th edition in 1973 it remains the oldest continuously published reference work under private ownership in the world. He is also credited with the publication of *A Handbook of Nursing* (1878), the first nursing textbook in the United States.

Another of Lippincott's noteworthy contributions was the massive Chembers' *Cyclopaedia of English Literature*. He was the first American publisher of this title, and this nine-volume facsimile edition, illustrated with wood engravings and original maps, was important in establishing Lippincott's business with publishers on the Continent and in Great Britain.

While Lippincott was especially strong in books of reference and medicine, he also issued a sizable list of general books. Included were standard and deluxe editions of the works of Bulwer-Lytton, Scott, Thackeray, and Dickens, as well as Foster's three-volume biography of Charles Dickens. In 1871, under the editorship of Horace H. Furness, Lippincott published *Romeo and Juliet,* the first volume in its outstanding *Variorum Edition of Shakespeare*.

Important government-sponsored works were executed by him, most notably Henry Schoolcraft's *History of the Indian Tribes,* published in six folio volumes and costing nearly $100,000. Lippincott's business acumen was displayed in his securing the copyright and plates for the 15 volumes of Prescott's historical works from the Boston firm of Phillips, Sampson and Company, and from Prescott's heirs.

Some of the important works published by Lippincott were the romances of Miss de la Ramé, better known by her nom de plume, Quida; an edition of Scott's Waverley Novels; *The Life of John Quincy Adams,* edited by his son Charles Francis Adams; and Bigelow's life of Benjamin Franklin. Other noteworthy publications were *The Writings of Albert Gallatin* and an accompanying title, *Life of Gallatin,* by Henry Adams. During Lippincott's time the idea of a series of books on a common, nonfiction theme was being developed. In 1869 Lippincott produced the "Reason Why Series."

The panic of 1873 was devastating to a number of publishers and booksellers and resulted in demands for a national trade association that would regulate the retail price of books based on the cost of production. A national convention was held July 21–23, 1874, at the summer resort of Put-in-Bay on Lake Erie, and J. B. Lippincott was represented at this first American Book Trade Association (ABTA) convention at which the historic "20 percent rule" was made. The rule provided that publishers and booksellers would agree not to sell at a discount greater than 20 percent on miscellaneous books and schoolbooks to libraries, large book buyers outside the trade, professional people and teachers, or of more than 10 percent on medical books.

Although the Lippincott firm was in attendance at Put-in-Bay, it opposed the rule, fearing that so sudden and drastic a marketing decision would adversely affect its trade. Lippincott's position subsequently moderated in objection to being called "the only holdout in the industry." Its condition for signing was that all books must be sold at the published retail price, except for a maximum discount of 20 percent to libraries, school teachers, and buyers outside the trade who purchased more than $100 net at any one time. This proposal caused much argument over a number of months, but at the second ABTA convention in July 1875 it was announced that Lippincott had finally signed the agreement. By this time Lippincott shared the distinction with Appleton of owning one of the two largest bookstores in the United States.

In order to supply his vast empire, Lippincott developed an outstanding physical plant, moving to various locations in Philadelphia. In 1861 the firm erected a magnificent new marble building on Market Street, between Seventh and Eighth streets. Subsequent additions were built until it was the largest book publishing, distributing, and manufacturing office in the world.

In December 1879 Lippincott discussed his business with *Publishers' Weekly:*

Twenty-nine presses are kept constantly running to meet the demands of our business. The average number of books printed by them is 2,000. Our business extends from the Atlantic to the Pacific, from Newfoundland to Texas. From 25,000 to 30,000 boxes of books are annually shipped to our various customers, and about 100,000 express packages. A manuscript is brought into the establishment and comes out a bound volume. The entire book is manufactured under this roof. Here it is printed, bound, published, sold, and distributed.

In 1884 Lippincott's health began to fail. Realizing this, he reorganized the firm in February 1885. It was incorporated with a capital of $1,000,000, and he personally held 9,970 of the 10,000 shares of stock. The new name of the firm was J. B. Lippincott Company; he was the president and owner and the first publisher to incorporate in the United States.

On January 5, 1886, Joshua Ballinger Lippincott died at his home in Philadelphia.

**REFERENCES**

Stuart Freeman, *Centennial Reflections: J. B. Lippincott Company in the 1870's* (1976).

J. B. Lippincott Company, *The Author and His Audience; With a Chronology of Major Events in the Publishing History of J. B. Lippincott Company* (1967).

Charles A. Madison, *Book Publishing in America* (1966).

John Tebbel, *A History of Book Publishing in the United States,* 2 volumes (1972, 1975).

RICHARD FITZSIMMONS

# Li Ta-chao
(1888–1927)

Li Ta-chao, a founder of the Chinese Communist Party, honored as China's first revolutionary martyr, is considered the father of modern Chinese librarianship. Born on October 6, 1888, in the village of Ta-hei-t'o, Hopei Province, Li was raised in an upper middle class environment. Between 1907 amd 1913 he studied at the Peiyang College of Law and Political Science in Tientsin, concentrating on political economy and foreign languages. Upon graduation Li furthered his schooling at Waseda University in Tokyo. Returning from Japan in 1916, he began several years of political activism in Peking and Shanghai. The two greatest concerns of the young Chinese intellectuals in the early 20th century were the encroachment of foreign interests, on one hand, and the inevitable transition of a nation from the Middle Kingdom to a modern, industrialized state on the other. A leading voice of the intelligentsia was *Hsin Ch'ing-nien* ("New Youth"), for which Li wrote extensively and became a member of the editorial board in 1918. Soon after his appointment Li was asked to assume the position of Head Librarian at Peking University.

Li's career as Librarian of one of China's leading universities was to have a tremendous impact on modern history. During his tenure, from 1918 to the mid-1920's, he utilized to its fullest measure the library's potential as a center for political activism. By directing the traditional functions of a university library (i.e., the systematic acquisition and distribution of materials, utilization of space for private study and small discussions) toward the promulgation of the philosophies of Marxism, Li Ta-chao organized enough support to begin China's journey toward revolution.

Li's office was the center of much research and study. He collected and translated a major corpus of Marxist and Leninist works and made them available to students and faculty. His Marxist Research Society attracted many individuals to his office, which became known as the *hung-*

Courtesy of The Harvard University Press

*Li Ta-chao*

*lou* or the "Red Chamber." Among his early followers was a young library assistant named Mao Tse-tung, who worked with Li and attended many sessions in the Red Chamber. Years later Mao would credit Li with his initial introduction to Marxism and the beginning of his own political development.

In 1919 a series of events known as the May Fourth Movement would focus on the far-reaching importance of Li's work. For several weeks intensive riots and demonstrations prevailed in several major cities as the Chinese voiced their opposition to foreign presence on their native soil. Li and the Peking University Library served a unique role during this politically volatile time, directing the earliest activities of the Marxist leaders of modern China.

Li Ta-chao's career, although vitally important, was brief. By the mid-1920's Li and other faculty members had been forced to leave the University, as the government was becoming increasingly hostile to Communists. Eventually Li was arrested in Peking and, on April 28, 1927, was executed.

The political activism of Chinese libraries in the decades following the founding of the People's Republic was strongly influenced by the work of Li Ta-chao. It has been written that if Chinese librarians study political and cultural materials, work diligently to improve their knowledge, and actively impart this information to the people, the profession will approach Li's ideal of the library after the Marxist revolution. The example of the Red Chamber, according to this view, places a responsibility upon Chinese librarians that is unique in the history of the profession.

**REFERENCES**

Nearly all writing on Li Ta-chao's career in librarianship is in Chinese and untranslated as of the end of the 1970's. Two works that address this subject and draw from the original materials are

Maurice Meisner, *Li Ta-chao and the Origins of Chinese Marxism* (1967), the most comprehensive evaluation of Li Ta-chao in a western language, with extensive translations and historical background to Li's library years.

Diane M. Nelson and Robert B. Nelson, "The Red Chamber: Li Ta-chao and the Sources of Radicalism in Modern Chinese Librarianship," *Journal of Library History, Philosophy and Comparative Librarianship* (Spring 1979), which, in addition to tracing Li's development as political activist and librarian, presents translations of later Chinese writings concerning the impact of Li Ta-chao's career on modern practices in the People's Republic.

DIANE M. NELSON;
ROBERT B. NELSON

## Locke, George Herbert

(1870–1937)

George Locke, educator and librarian, was one of two Canadians elected President of the American Library Association. He directed the fortunes of the Toronto Public Library (TPL) for nearly 30 years (1908–37), during which it expanded from a small system with a staff of 26 to a major institution boasting a large central building, 16 branches, and a staff of 232.

Locke was born in Beamsville, Ontario, March 29, 1870. Educated at Victoria College, University of Toronto, he received the B.A. and M.A. degrees in Classics. He then did graduate study and teaching in educational theory, first at Chicago, later at Harvard. From 1899 to 1903 he was Associate Professor at Chicago, then was appointed Dean of the College of Education. He was Editor of the *School Review* (1900–06), a prestigious journal of American secondary education. After a year in Boston as an Assistant Editor with the publishing firm of Ginn & Co., Locke returned to Canada as Dean of the School of Education at McGill University, Montreal. From McGill he was invited to TPL in 1908.

Locke brought neither formal training nor prior library experience to his new position, but he had a personal concept of the public library as a social institution. Probably developed from his work in education, Locke's concept of the library contained two major components: the library should bring the pleasures of literature to the general public for recreation, and it should play a major role in continuing adult education. For him, librarianship was as educational in character as the teaching profession, although it offered no specific formal instruction and served a more varied clientele.

He used his term as ALA President (1926–27) to reiterate his conviction that the public library was an intellectual public utility that would help preserve and inspire the democratic state. Its resources, properly interpreted by librarians, would allow citizens to prepare for intelligent service to society and to become informed about workings of the democratic process. His years on the ALA Executive Board produced definite views concerning the most desirable role for the Association. Librarians served a social institution, and Locke felt their professional association needed strong personal leadership. Since the membership exceeded 10,000 by the mid-1920's, Locke urged alternating full membership meetings with regional meetings every second year. He also urged a two-year term for the ALA presidency to prevent erosion of power by the permanent general staff.

Furthering an active professional life, Locke produced a substantial body of publications, for both educational and library journals, and works for the general public. He wrote two works of popular Canadian history and a study of English history for the ALA's "Reading with a Purpose" series. He was a member of the American Association for the Advancement of Science, the Dominion Education Association, and several Canadian and American library associations. For his services to the community the University of Toronto awarded him an LL.D. in 1927. He died on January 28, 1937, and was mourned in three countries—Canada, the U.S., and the United Kingdom—and most of all by the city of Toronto.

MARGARET ANDERSON

## Lubetzky, Seymour

(1898– )

Seymour Lubetzky, the greatest theoretician of descriptive cataloguing in the 20th century, was born around 1898 in Zelwa, a town then part of Russia, later of Poland, and now in the U.S.S.R. He went to Los Angeles, California, in 1927, where he became a student at the University of California (now UCLA). Graduating in 1931, he moved to Berkeley, attended the University of California at Berkeley, and earned a Certificate in Librarianship from the School of Librarianship on that campus.

In 1936 Lubetzky went to work at the UCLA Library, eventually becoming a cataloguer. While there he wrote a number of articles questioning the then-current library practice with respect to capitalization, the use of unnecessary title added entries, and the division of library catalogues. These articles displayed the talent that caused the Library of Congress to hire him to look into current cataloguing practices in 1943.

From 1942 to 1943 Lubetzky worked in a shipyard in the San Francisco Bay area so that he might contribute to the war effort in a tangible fashion. By creating a uniform set of parts descriptions, he was able to reorganize the shipyard's stock and thereby save many thousands of dollars.

Lubetzky's first assignment at the Library of Congress in 1943 was temporary only but later led to his being appointed Chief of the LC Catalog Maintenance Division, where he was responsible for the planning for the publication of the ongoing *National Union Catalog* (the closest equivalent to an American national bibliography). Finally, he became Specialist in Bibliographic and Cataloging Policy. It was in this last position that he made his most important theoretical contributions.

Lubetzky's first major endeavor at LC was the simplification of the rules for description. His studies led to the 1949 publication of *Rules for Descriptive Cataloging in the Library of Congress (Adopted by the American Library Association).* He turned his attention next to the rules for entry found in the *A.L.A. Cataloging Rules for Author and Title Entries, Second edition* (1949). His analysis and critique of those rules is found in his *Cataloging Rules and Principles,* published by LC in 1953. *Cataloging Rules and Principles,* one of the classics of library literature, questions previous practice with respect to the form of heading for both personal and corporate authors as well as the very structure of previous cataloguing codes. In addition, it provides the outline for a future code.

As a result of the favorable reaction to *Cataloging Rules and Principles,* Lubetzky was appointed editor for a revised cataloguing code. The revision contemplated by Lubetzky is found in two major drafts—*Code of Cataloging Rules: Bibliographic Entry and Description* was issued in 1958; *Code of Cataloging Rules: Author and Title Entry* was issued in 1960, with its appendant *Additions, Revisions and Changes* appearing in 1961. These drafts are characterized by the clear statement of the objectives of cataloguing and the rigorous pursuit of those objectives in the form of rules addressed to bibliographic conditions instead of the unsystematic case-by-case approach found in previous cataloguing codes.

Lubetzky was unable to finish work on the revised code because of the press of duties connected with his appointment as Professor at the new School of Library Service at UCLA in 1961 as well as unwillingness to compromise on important points in the new code. Some of Lubetzky's major findings, however, were incorporated in the "Statement of Principles" formulated at the International Conference on Cataloguing Principles (ICCP) held in Paris in 1961. Although the 1967 *Anglo-American Cataloging Rules* (AACR) was based on the ICCP principles, rather than the Lubetzky drafts, Lubetzky's influence is nevertheless apparent in AACR.

Probably the most definitive statement of Lubetzky's views is to be found in his 1969 report, *Principles of Cataloging; Final Report, Phase I: Descriptive Cataloging.* Among other major points, Lubetzky insists that a catalogue must deal with works, not books, as the fundamental objects to be catalogued, that main entry is a useful device for identifying works and bringing together the various editions of a work, that corporate bodies are authors of their publications. These, and other conclusions of Lubetzky, have permanent value even though they may have passed out of fashion in the second edition of AACR.

Lubetzky was awarded the ALA Margaret Mann Citation in 1955, a Doctor of Laws degree by UCLA in 1969, and the ALA Melvil Dewey Award in 1977. The citation for the Dewey Award states that Lubetzky's achievements assure recognition of his "position as the greatest influence on cataloging theory since Cutter."

MICHAEL CARPENTER

## Luhn, Hans Peter
(1896–1964)

Hans Peter Luhn was one of the early information scientists. He came to information science by way of engineering. His interest was in the use of machines to aid in the retrieval and dissemination of information and the use of devices for the preparation of indexes and abstracts. Luhn's name will always be associated with Key Word in Context (KWIC) indexes and Selective Dissemination of Information (SDI), but beyond these two methods he pioneered in the use of mechanical—and later electronic—devices for the processing of textual material.

Hans Peter Luhn, known to his friends as Pete, was born in Barmen, Germany, on July 1, 1896. He completed secondary school (gymnasium) in Germany and then went to Sankt Gallen, Switzerland, to learn the printing business. His father was a well-known printer in Germany, and it was expected that Luhn would join the business. At this early age, Luhn already showed an inventive mind and took great interest in technical matters, physics, and statistics.

His stay in Sankt Gallen was interrupted by World War I, in which he served in the German Army as a communications officer in France, Turkey, Romania, and Bulgaria. After the war Luhn continued his studies in Switzerland but also found time to invent a double-entry bookkeeping machine to record both debits and credits on ledger cards. In connection with that work he first became acquainted with Hollerith machines, the punched card equipment then coming increasingly into use.

In the early 1920's Luhn switched to the textile field, first as a free-lance designer and then as an agent for a German textile firm, which he represented in 1924 in the United States with the hope of establishing textile plants there. Because of financial problems the mission failed, and Luhn was forced to look for a job. After working in a bank, he again joined the textile business as Assistant to the President of a company in Pennsylvania. It offered him the opportunity to show his inventiveness, and from 1927 to 1930 he was able to obtain ten patents. One of these, the Lunometer, a device used to count threads in fabrics, is still marketed.

In 1933 Luhn established himself as an engineering consultant. The number and type of patents granted him during this period demonstrate the scope of interests and the inventiveness of the man: foldable raincoat, game table, recipe guide, apparatus to determine thickness of thread, and many others.

The recipe guide was Luhn's first invention related to information retrieval. Marketed as the Cocktail Oracle, it enables a user of this "optical coincidence" system to determine quickly which cocktails he could prepare with the ingredients available on his shelf.

Luhn's interest in documentation, now called information retrieval, began in the late 1940's when he was asked by IBM to find a solution to the problem of searching chemical compounds that could be represented in coded form. Luhn's solution was to record the codes on punched cards, and he developed a machine (which became known as the Luhn Scanner) to search files of these specially encoded cards. Luhn soon recognized the limited capacity of the punched card and of the equipment used to process it if one tried to apply it to searching files of textual information or index terms, for example. His inventiveness was demonstrated over and over again as he came up with new schemes, such as "Super-imposed Coding" and "Row by Row Searching" to overcome the limitations of the available equipment.

With the beginning of the computer age in the early 1950's Luhn was able to find solutions to the problems he encountered in the storage and retrieval of information by using computer software, rather than having to invent machines to overcome the limitations of conventional punched-card equipment. He saw the great potential offered by computers to solve the problems created by the rapidly growing volume of scientific and technical literature. He wanted to understand these problems in depth

Library Association

*Lionel R. McColvin*



and so participated in many meetings and conferences of librarians and documentalists.

One of the highlights of Luhn's career was his participation in the 1958 International Conference on Scientific Information in Washington, D.C. At that conference he discussed and demonstrated a method of automatically preparing abstracts of documents. Actual conference papers, the texts of which were available on Monotype tape as a by-product of publishing them in the conference proceedings, were abstracted automatically by a computer using a program developed by him.

In 1958 Luhn wrote a paper entitled "A Business Intelligence System" in which he proposed an automatic method to provide current awareness services to scientists and engineers faced with the ever growing volume of literature. Luhn's techniques assumed the availability of text in machine-readable form and would consist of automatic abstracting and matching of these abstracts against interest profiles of users, which he called action points. The result of a match would be a notice containing the abstract and relevant bibliographic information sent to a subscriber. Such systems of disseminating information on a selective basis are in use, known as SDI systems.

Another professional triumph for Luhn was the adoption by the American Chemical Society in 1960 of the Key Word in Context (KWIC) method of indexing and the publication of *Chemical Titles* by this method. Luhn had been advocating the use of computers for the preparation of permuted indexes to cut the costs and delays inherent in the conventional indexing methods.

Luhn died August 19, 1964. Throughout his career, but especially as an information scientist, Hans Peter Luhn always searched for the simple solution.

**REFERENCE**

A bibliography of Luhn's papers related to information science has been published in Claire K. Schultz, editor, *H. P. Luhn: Pioneer of Information Science, Selected Works* (1968).

STEPHEN E. FURTH

## MacAlister, John Young Walker
(1856–1925)

John Young Walker MacAlister, the best known British medical librarian of his day, was born in Scotland in 1856. He had served an appropriate double apprenticeship prior to his appointment as Librarian and Secretary of the Royal Medical and Chirurgical Society in London in 1887. His early medical training at Edinburgh having been abandoned because of illness, he had instead obtained library posts in Liverpool and Leeds. From 1887 until his retirement he built up his employing society into the great Royal Society of Medicine, an achievement appropriately recognized by his Sovereign, who conferred a knighthood on him in 1919. But in 1887 he was appointed Honorary Secretary of the Library Association (LA), and it was in this capacity, and in that of Proprietor and Editor of its official organ, *The Library,* from its inception in 1889 until its supersession by *The Library Association Record* in 1899, that he is best remembered.

MacAlister was immensely influential as a leader of others, and he drove the infant Library Association at a pace comparable to Melvil Dewey's during the early years of the American Library Association. He provided the LA with offices and a meeting place in his employing society's headquarters in Hanover Square, West London, and stimulated its members, and particularly its younger members, with ambitious ideas and untiring encouragement, both in person and through the pages of *The Library.* He was a prominent clubman at a time when the London clubs were at the height of their power and importance and persuaded his extensive and influential acquaintances to do all possible to help and support the LA. "Mac," as he was always known to his contemporaries, was almost too ambitious for the LA, since its very small membership and limited financial resources proved discouragingly restrictive. But the recollections of such prominent librarians as James Duff Brown, L. Stanley Jast, and Ernest Savage leave a later generation in no doubt as to his standing with them.

MacAlister was largely instrumental in gaining for the Library Association its Royal Charter of incorporation in 1898 but took a lesser part in its activities after his resignation from the Honorary Secretaryship in the same year. His interest and active participation in professional affairs were renewed during the years of World War I when serving as LA President from 1915 until 1919. He died in 1925.

W. A. MUNFORD

## McColvin, Lionel R.
(1896–1976)

Lionel R. McColvin was the outstanding public librarian of his generation in Britain. From the mid-1930's until his retirement in 1961 he dominated the public library scene, not just in his own country but internationally as well. Born in Newcastle upon Tyne on November 30, 1896, McColvin was the son of an artist. His first library post was at Croydon, where he worked as Reference Librarian under W. C. Berwick Sayers. Early professional advancement resulted in his becoming Deputy Librarian of Wigan Public Libraries in 1921, and in 1924 he was appointed Chief Librarian of Ipswich. He earned both these appointments before his 28th birthday, an early age to become a Chief Librarian in Britain. After seven years at Ipswich he became Chief Librarian of Hampstead, a northern suburb of London, and remained there until 1938, when he was appointed City Librarian of Westminster, one of the most important posts in British public librarianship.

Westminster was to be McColvin's final position; indeed it would have been difficult if not impossible for him to have advanced further. He was due to retire at the end of 1961, but in December 1960 he suffered a series of strokes that left him with loss of memory. He remained City Librarian of Westminster until his official retirement date on November 30, 1961, but was on sick leave for most of that year. He lived on until January 16, 1976, and was able to enjoy his retirement, apart from his amnesia.

McColvin was active in the Library Association all his life. He was elected to the LA Council in 1925 at the early age of 29, and it would not be far from the truth to say that he dedicated his life to the Association. He was Honorary Secretary from 1934 to 1951, a title that no longer exists but that was akin to being Prime Minister of the Association. It was during these years that McColvin struck up a rapport with Percy Welsford, the full-time, paid Secretary of LA, a working relationship that was to be extremely fruitful for British librarianship.

The LA Council soon recognized that it possessed an outstanding person in McColvin, and in 1936 he was sent to the U.S. to study library administration on behalf of the Association. At that time most public library systems in Britain had been in existence for 50 or more years, and many could be described only as Augean stables more than ready for a cleanup. To draw attention to this state of affairs, the LA sent a number of senior librarians, including McColvin, on tours of Britain with the object of investigating libraries and making recommendations for improvements.

World War II put an end to thoughts of radical improvements in libraries. McColvin, who had served in the British Army during the latter part of World War I, was too old to be called for active service in the second conflict, but he could still look after LA affairs, and he remained in close touch with Percy Welsford. During the darkest days of the war, the LA asked McColvin to undertake a one-man survey of public libraries in Britain, and to its credit the Westminster City Council agreed to release their City Librarian for that assignment.

The result of McColvin's tours, undertaken in bombed wartime Britain, often in conditions fraught with discomfort and danger, was the publication in 1942 of his report *The Public Library System of Great Britain.* It soon became known as the McColvin Report and was immediately debated at great length both inside and outside the profession.

McColvin's investigations had convinced him that there were too many public library authorities in Britain and that the majority of these were too small to function efficiently, being without the financial resources necessary for effective service. His answer was to redraw the local government map of the country, creating fewer but larger authorities, and in this respect he was years ahead of his time. It was not until 1965 that there was a reorganization of local government in London, with similar moves in England, Wales, and Scotland in 1974 and 1975. The result of these changes was a reduction in the number of public library authorities from over 500, as there were in McColvin's day, to 170. In this way, McColvin's dream came true nearly 40 years after his report. Furthermore, the new local government boundaries bore some striking resemblances to McColvin's suggestions in 1942.

After World War II McColvin became a great library traveler, performing missions for Unesco, the British Council, and other agencies. He visited Australia, New Zealand, the Middle East, the U.S., Germany, Turkey, Scandinavia, and elsewhere. With Bengt Hjelmqvist he founded the Anglo-Scandinavian Public Library Conferences, held triennially from 1958. He attended IFLA General Council meetings and in 1953 was elected Chairman of its Public Libraries Section. Alone and unaided, he drafted standards for public library service, which were printed in *Libri* in 1958; these formed the basis for the IFLA *Standards for Public Libraries,* which were published in 1973.

Meanwhile, back in Britain, he still continued to serve on the LA Council, on the Executive Committee of the National Central Library, and on the British Council Advisory Panel on Libraries. A great advocate of the principle of free access to public libraries, he successfully campaigned against library charges as a member of the Roberts Committee. He was elected President of the LA in 1952 and became an Honorary Fellow in 1961.

McColvin wrote 20 books, the first being *Music in Public Libraries* in 1924. This was followed by works on book selection, assistance to readers, children's libraries, and other topics. Among his best works were *Music Libraries* (with Harold Reeves, 1937–38), *The Personal Library* (1953), and *The Chance to Read* (1956). In addition to his books he was a prolific contributor to conferences and to professional journals. In 1971 the LA published a Festschrift for McColvin entitled *Libraries for the People,* edited by his former Deputy at Westminster, R. F. Vollans, and including contributions from a formidable array of international librarians such as Louis Shores, Helle Kannila, Bengt Hjelmqvist, E. Allerslev Jensen, and Anders Andreassen. It was a tribute that McColvin richly deserved.

**REFERENCE**

Robert L. Collison, "Lionel Roy McColvin: A Bibliography of His Writings," in *Libraries for the People: International Studies in Librarianship in Honour of Lionel R. McColvin* (1968).

K. C. HARRISON

## MacLeish, Archibald
(1892– )

Library of Congress

*Archibald MacLeish, poet, statesman, and 9th Librarian of Congress.*

Writer and poet Archibald MacLeish was the first well-known figure from outside the library profession to be nominated and confirmed as Librarian of Congress. The controversy surrounding his nomination, especially the bitter opposition of the American Library Association, has obscured his achievements from 1939 to 1944 as Librarian of Congress and his unique role as an eloquent spokesman on behalf of libraries and librarianship. MacLeish's chief administrative accomplishments were a thorough reorganization, development of the first explicit statements of the institution's objectives (the "Canons of Selection" and a statement of reference and research objectives), and a concern for procedures and morale that brought the administration and the staff of the Library of Congress into accord for the first time in many years. Furthermore, he permanently enlarged the role of the Library of Congress as a repository of the American intellectual and cultural tradition. His contribution to the profession centered on his frequently expressed belief that librarians must play an active role in American life, particularly in educating the American public to the value of the democratic experience.

Archibald MacLeish entered public life for the first time at the age of 47 when, on July 10, 1939, the local postmaster in Conway, Massachusetts, administered his oath of office as Librarian of Congress. MacLeish already was a man of several successful careers. Born in Glencoe, Illinois, on May 7, 1892, he attended Hotchkiss preparatory school in Connecticut before entering Yale in 1911. A star athlete at Yale, he also was elected to Phi Beta Kappa. After entering Harvard Law School, he served in the U.S. Army in France during World War I, then returned to Harvard, where he was an Editor of the *Harvard Law Review* before graduating in 1919. Law practice with a prominent Boston firm was forsaken in 1923 for Paris, where he established close ties with the American writers living on the Left Bank and published several collections of verse. He returned to the United States in 1929, joining Henry Luce's new *Fortune* magazine, for which he wrote articles on political and cultural subjects for the next nine years. During that period he continued to write verse and drama, the subjects reflecting his liberal social and political views. Such opinions consolidated MacLeish's intellectual sympathy with the New Deal and contributed to his departure from the Luce organization. They also paved the road to his nomination as Librarian of Congress.

From the start President Franklin D. Roosevelt looked outside the profession for a successor to Librarian of Congress Herbert Putnam. In choosing MacLeish, Roosevelt followed the advice of his friend Felix Frankfurter, the Supreme Court Justice, who informed the President that "only a scholarly man of letters can make a great national library a general place of habitation for scholars." The nomination was announced at a press conference on June 6, 1939, at which Roosevelt proclaimed that the job of Librarian of Congress required not a professional librarian but "a gentleman and a scholar."

The American Library Association was shocked. Not only had Roosevelt ignored its own candidate for the job, the ALA Executive Secretary, Carl H. Milam, but the President also had ignored all offers of ALA assistance. Even worse, in the ALA view, his nominee had no library experience. At its annual meeting in San Francisco on June 18, the ALA adopted a resolution opposing the nomination because "the Congress and the American people should have as a Librarian . . . one who is not only a gentleman and a scholar but who is also the ablest Library administrator available." The ALA testified unsuccessfully against the nomination in the Senate hearings. On June 29, 1939, by a vote of 63 to 8, the Senate confirmed the President's choice, and Archibald MacLeish became the ninth Librarian of Congress.

When the new Librarian officially began work on October 2, the Library had a book collection of approximately 6,000,000 volumes, a staff of about 1,100, and, in fiscal year 1939, a direct appropriation of approximately $3,000,000.

The new Librarian immediately tackled the most pressing internal problems left behind by Putnam. Studies were undertaken of the Library's cataloguing, acquisitions, personnel, and budget policies. The results were distressing, and MacLeish and his senior staff asked for a substantial increase in the Library's budget request to remedy the many problems. The request was for $4,200,000 and included 287 additional positions. The Appropriation Committee approved 130 of the new positions and encouraged the new Librarian to continue his "industrious and intelligent" beginning. In response to the Appropriation Committee's report and to carry on the investigations already begun, MacLeish appointed on April 10, 1940, a special Librarian's Committee to analyze the operations of the Library—especially its processing activities. The report of that Committee, headed by Carleton B. Joeckel of the University of Chicago Graduate Library School, served as a catalyst for MacLeish's reorganization—a functional restructuring that served as the basis of the Library's administrative structure for the next three decades.

While the administrative reorganization probably was MacLeish's single most significant achievement, it was only one of his accomplishments. He also enhanced the Library's reputation as a major cultural institution, not only because of his own prominence as a poet but also by inaugurating the first series of poetry readings. He brought many prominent writers and poets to the Library, including war refugees Aléxis Saint-Léger Léger and Thomas Mann and U.S. poet Allen Tate, who served both as Poetry Consultant and as the first Editor of the newly established *Quarterly Journal of Current Acquisitions*. Relationships between the Library and scholarly and literary communities were improved through a new program of resident fellowships for young scholars and the formation of the Fellows of the Library of Congress, a group of prominent writers and poets.

MacLeish, a wartime librarian, quickly became a leading American spokesman for the cause of democracy. Speaking before the ALA on May 31, 1940, he asserted that librarians "must become active and not passive agents of the democratic process." The organization that had so bitterly opposed his nomination a year earlier applauded vigorously, and relations between the Library of Congress and ALA were on the mend. At the annual conference of the Association in June 1942, ALA President Charles H. Brown introduced MacLeish as "a man of whom we librarians are very proud," and the Librarian received a thunderous ovation before delivering his address, "Toward an Intellectual Offensive."

MacLeish and Luther H. Evans, his Chief Assistant Librarian, inaugurated a staff *Information Bulletin* and created a staff advisory committee. In April 1942 MacLeish announced the formation of the Librarian's Council, composed of distinguished librarians, scholars, and book collectors who would make recommendations about collection development and reference service. Weekly meetings with department directors were started, and in 1943 the Library administration began holding informal monthly meetings with the professional staff.

During the war MacLeish helped Roosevelt in many ways. Those activities meant that he served only part-time as Librarian of Congress, which makes the many achievements of his administration especially remarkable. In October 1941 the President directed him to assume, in addition to his duties as Librarian, supervision of the government's newly established Office of Facts and Figures. The appointment was controversial, both because of the publications produced by the new office and because the Librarian's additional duties often kept him away from the Library. In June 1942 the Office of Facts and Figures was combined with other agencies to form the Office of War Information, which MacLeish served part-time as an Assistant Director. The Librarian also drafted speeches for the President and represented the government at various meetings, as in March 1944 when he went to London as a delegate to the Conference of Allied Ministers of Education, a forerunner of the United Nations. MacLeish apparently expressed a wish to leave the Library of Congress as early as the summer of 1943, but he stayed in office until December 19, 1944, when he resigned to become an Assistant Secretary of State, in charge of public and cultural relations.

Archibald MacLeish's relatively brief administration was one of the most fruitful in the history of the Library of Congress. The accomplishments were not his alone; in fact, as he was the first to acknowledge, his colleagues Luther H. Evans, Verner Clapp, and David C. Mearns played major roles. The style, tone, and motivation, however, came directly from the Librarian. He provided the Library of Congress and the library profession with inspiration and a badly needed sense of perspective. His succinct statement of the purpose of the Library in the first issue of the *Quarterly Journal of Current Acquisitions* (1943), for example, stands today as both a summary and a challenge: "The first duty of the Library of Congress is to serve the Congress and the officers and agencies of government. Its second duty is to serve the world of scholarship and letters. Through both it endeavors to serve the American people to whom it belongs and for whom it exists."

**REFERENCES**

Nancy L. Benco, "Archibald MacLeish: The Poet as Librarian," *Quarterly Journal of the Library of Congress* (1976).

Edward J. Mullaly, *Archibald MacLeish: A Checklist* (1973), contains lists of works by and about MacLeish.

Dennis Thomison, "F. D. R., the ALA, and Mr. MacLeish: The Selection of the Librarian of Congress, 1939," *Library Quarterly* (1972).

JOHN Y. COLE

# Madagascar

Madagascar, a republic on the island of Madagascar and others in the Indian Ocean, lies off the southeastern African coast. Pop. (1978 est.) 8,776,000; area, 587,041 sq.km. The official languages are Malagasy and French.

**National Library.** The National Library, instituted in 1961 following the country's independence, inherited the collection of 80,000 volumes from the former Library of the General Government created in Antananarivo in 1920. The Library received its works thanks to a legal trust while acting as a public library for the capital as well as a documentation center for research.

From 1961 to 1973 the National Library, while fulfilling its former roles, served as the national center for the promotion of books and reading and libraries. The extension of these activities led to the creation of the National Library Service in 1973. The Library Service consists of a division for the promotion of books and reading whose main role is promoting the art of writing, the rights of authors, publishing, and the pleasure of reading, and in collaboration with the Malagasy Book Office publishes the national bibliography. The National Library is the other element; it has a collection of 150,000 printed books, manuscripts, periodicals, photos, and maps. It continues to receive legal trust moneys; it assures the conservation of national patrimony; and it plays an important role as a public and research library because of its extensive collection on Madagascar. A new building devoted to the whole of this service was under way in 1979.

**University Library.** The University of Madagascar in Antananarivo has a library that specializes in different disciplines in the University. It was created in 1960 and has a collection of 100,000 works. Following decentralization of the University, five regional centers were attached to it, the oldest being the Toliara Center.

**Public Libraries.** A program to promote public libraries in the Fivondronanas (subregional constituencies grouping several former communes) was launched in 1978 and was to proceed gradually over several years. It consists of stimulating the former municipal libraries and former information centers and creating new libraries. The Library Service ensures the technical training of personnel.

**School Libraries.** About ten were actively working with a well-defined staff in 1979, essentially supported by funds from school cooperatives or private funds. About 40 were still in the beginning stages with a limited number of books.

**Special Libraries.** The Malagasy Academy Library in Antananarivo, created in 1905, is a specialized library in language, literature, art, social and political sciences, and fundamental and applied sciences. It has a collection of 30,000 works and receives 50 periodicals. It also exchanges materials with other library systems. The National Research Center Library offers studies, reports, and results of research concerning Madagascar. The Malagasy Book Office in Antananarivo was created in 1971 to publish and diffuse works tending to develop the pleasure of reading, to promote a book policy on a national scale, and to serve as a center of information concerning questions touching on the domain of books and as a resource for writers.

**Association.** The Association of Archivists, Librarians, Documentalists and Museologists was formed in September 1976.

JULIETTE RATSIMANDRAVA

## Malawi

Malawi, a republic in central southeastern Africa, is bordered by Tanzania on the north, Mozambique on the east and south, and Zambia on the west. Pop. (1977 prelim. census) 5,571,576; area 118,577 sq.km. Official languages are English and Chichewa.

**National Library.** In the absence of a national library, the National Archives established a reference library section in 1958. It is the only legal deposit library in the country, holds the most comprehensive Malawiana collection, and is responsible for the publication of the *Malawi National Bibliography* (1965– ). Over 30,000 items are held by the library.

**Academic and School Libraries.** The University of Malawi has the country's only academic library, with three constituent libraries at the Polytechnic, Bunda College of Agriculture, and Chancellor College, where the main library is situated. Established in 1965, the library had some 152,000 volumes in 1974, growing to over 179,000 in 1978. Special collections in the main library include Malawiana in printed works or microfilmed documents. Though mainly for use by university staff and students, resources of the libraries are made available for reference to the public, and borrowing privileges are obtained on payment of a small deposit.

Libraries also exist in teacher training colleges, technical schools, secondary schools, and some primary schools. Bookstocks range from 2,000 to 6,000, consisting mainly of textbooks and general reading material.

The National Library Service of Malawi

*Headquarters of the Malawi National Library Service in Lilongwe, established by an act of Parliament in 1967.*

**Public Libraries.** A 1967 act of Parliament established the National Library Service Board with power to promote, establish, equip, manage, maintain, and develop libraries in Malawi. A library service was started in 1968 in Blantyre, and further developments include the establishment of a headquarters in Lilongwe, regional libraries in Mzuzu and Blantyre, and branches in Limbe and Lilongwe. In addition to these service points, there is a countrywide postal loans service, as well as library centers in various types of schools, units of land development projects, district community centers, rehabilitation centers, and Young Pioneer bases. This service helps supplement the meager library resources that often exist in most institutions; 132 were being served in 1979. The National Library Service has over 106,000 volumes. Registered borrowers number 25,000, and many more use the Service through the library centers. It issues over 250,000 books from its service points annually.

Small library units exist in district community centers and in church centers, and it is in these units that the National Library Service chiefly operates. In some cases books lent by the Service are the only reliable stock for the library. Other libraries open to the public are the British Council Libraries in Blantyre, Zomba, and Lilongwe, American cultural centers in Blantyre and Lilongwe, and the French Cultural Center in Blantyre. The British Council operates postal as well as book-box services, in addition to the normal book lending and reference facilities from service points, along with an audiovisual service.

**Special Libraries.** A number of special libraries are found in government ministries, departments, research institutions, and statutory bodies. There is a wide variation in their size and organization. The Central Library of the Ministry of Agriculture and Natural Resources is Malawi's most notable special library.

**Association.** The Malawi Library Association, founded in June 1976, organizes lectures and meetings and training courses for Library Assistants and publishes the *MALA Bulletin*. Librarians, archivists, and others working in information services participate in this association.

RODRICK S. MABOMBA

## Malaysia

Malaysia, an independent federation of 13 states in Southeast Asia, comprises two distinct land areas—West Malaysia on the Malay Peninsula and East Malaysia on the island of Borneo. The two areas are separated by the South China Sea. Pop. (1977 est.) 12,600,000; area 329,736 sq.km. The official language in the constitutional monarchy is Bahasa Malaysia.

Library development in Malaysia has been relatively recent, much of it taking place in the 1970's with the establishment of the National Library, as well as several university, special, and public libraries.

National Library of Malaysia

*The Universiti Perttanian Malaysia Library was founded in 1971.*

**National Library.** The National Library of Malaysia was established under the National Library Act, 1972. In January 1977 the National Library, hitherto linked administratively to the National Archives, was established as a separate department under the purview of the Ministry of Housing and Local Government. The Library provides mainly reference, bibliographic, lending, and training facilities. It has a collection of over 110,000 volumes, receives materials under legal deposit, and publishes the *Bibliografi Negara Malaysia* (Malaysian National Bibliography) and the *Indeks Majallah Malaysia* (Malaysian Periodicals Index). The National Library is also actively involved in promoting the development of public library services within the country and in coordinating the utilization of the nation's library resources.

**Academic Libraries.** Academic libraries comprise the libraries within the country's five universities, in the Colleges of Further Education, and in the Teacher Training Colleges. University libraries include those at the University of Malaya (1959), the Universiti Sains Malaysia (1969), the Universiti Kebangsaan Malaysia (1970), the Universiti Pertanian Malaysia (1971), and the Universiti Teknoloji Malaysia (1972). The University of Malaya library had a collection (1979) of 607,000 volumes; the Universiti Kebangsaan Malaysia, 165,000; the Universiti Sains Malaysia, 150,000; the Universiti Pertanian Malaysia, 70,000; and Universiti Teknoloji Malaysia, 48,000. These libraries are well developed and are among the major resources of published information in the country. They provide mainly lending, reference, and reprographic facilities.

Libraries at Colleges of Further Education include the Mara Institute of Technology, the Tunku Abdul Rahman College, and the Ungku Omar Polytechnic. Apart from the collection of 109,000 volumes at the Mara Institute of Technology, the collections at the other institutions mentioned are relatively small.

The Teacher Training College libraries generally are small, and only a few—such as the Malayan Teachers College in Penang, the Specialist Teachers Training Institute in Kuala Lumpur, and the Gaya Teachers Training College in Sabah—have collections approximating 20,000 volumes.

**Public Libraries.** Public library services are provided by individual states, while the National Library provides services within the Federal Territory of Kuala Lumpur. Ten states have established State Public Library Corporations based on state laws. In Johore, Sabah, and Sarawak, however, public library services are provided by state and local government authorities without the support of legislation. Public library collections generally are small, with services at an embryonic state as of 1978. They tend to be confined to the state capital cities; several states, however, including Selangor, Kedah, Sabah, and Sarawak, maintain a network of branch libraries as well as a mobile library service.

**School Libraries.** School libraries fall within the purview of the Ministry of Education. There are over 6,000 schools in Malaysia, many with their own libraries. Most individual collections are under 2,000 volumes, although there are several schools with collections of over 15,000. The Ministry of Education is giving greater attention to the further development of school libraries and in 1978 was collaborating with the Malaysian Library Association to prepare a blueprint for school library development in Malaysia.

**Table 2. Archives in Malaysia (1976)**

| | |
|---|---|
| Number | 5 |
| Holdings (in cubic meters) | 36,191 linear feet (Headquarters only, Branches N.A.) |
| Annual expenditures | M $1,218,685 |
| Professional staff | 15 |
| All staff | 137 |

Source: *Anggaran Perbelanjaan Arkib Dan Perpustakaan Negara Malaysia 1977.* (Estimates of Expenditure, National Archives, and Library)

**Special Libraries.** There are a number of special libraries, the oldest of which are found in research bodies. These include the Institute for Medical Research, the Rubber Research Institute, and the Forest Research Institute. Newer libraries are in the Malaysian Agricultural Research and Development Institute, the Tun Ismail Atomic Research Centre, and the Standards and Industrial Research Institute of Malaysia. Government ministries and departments such as the ministries of Agriculture, Commerce, Defense, Foreign Affairs, the Prime Minister's Department, the Economic Planning Unit, to name just a few, have also established special libraries.

Collections vary; most special libraries consist of less than 2,000 volumes, although some are relatively sizable. There are 18,000 in Bank Negara (Central Bank) Malaysia, 65,000 in the Dewan Bahasa dan Pustaka, 65,000 in the Ministry of Agriculture, 69,000 in the Economic Planning Unit, and over 91,000 in the Rubber Research Institute.

**Professional Association.** The Malaysian Library

**Table 1. Libraries in Malaysia (1976)**

| Type | Number | Volumes in collections | Annual expenditures (Malaysian dollar) | Population served | Professional staff | All staff (total) |
|---|---|---|---|---|---|---|
| National | 1 | 93,576 | M $1,415,225 | 800,000 | 26 | 90 |
| Academic | 32 | 1,492,249 | 7,322,505 | 40,000 | 163 | 862 |
| Public | 24 | 820,444 | N.A. | N.A. | 30 | 299 |
| School | N.A. | N.A. | N.A. | N.A. | N.A. | N.A. |
| Special | 116 | 830,268 | N.A. | N.A. | 59 | 411 |

Source: *Directory of Libraries in Malaysia,* Kuala Lumpur (1978).

Association is the only professional library association in Malaysia, concerned mainly with the establishment and development of libraries.

**REFERENCES**

Lim Huck Tee, *Libraries in West Malaysia and Singapore: A Short History* (Kuala Lumpur: University of Malaya Library (1970).

Donald Earlian Kingsley Wijasuriya, *The Barefoot Librarian,* library developments in Southeast Asia with special reference to Malaysia by D. E. K. Wijasuriya, Lim Huck Tee, and Radha Nadarajah (1975).

D. E. K. WIJASURIYA

# Mali

Mali, a republic in West Africa, the former French Sudan, is bounded by Algeria on the north, Mauritania, Senegal, and Guinea on the west, Ivory Coast on the south, and Upper Volta and Niger on the east. Pop. (1977 est.) 6,468,200; area 1,240,142 sq.km. The official language is French, though more than 15 languages are spoken.

**National Library.** The National Library, which provides traditional library services (cataloguing, acquisitions, circulation, bibliography, and publication), is in Bamako, the capital of Mali. It became the National Library in 1960 as a branch of the Institute for Scientific Research of Mali and in 1962 as a branch of the Institute for the Humanities of Mali. By 1966 it had its own quarters, distinct from those of the National Archives and of the Research Department. In 1973 it became an autonomous unit, although it remained the headquarters for the researchers of the Institute for the Humanities of Mali. In 1976 it was integrated into a network of documentation within the Division for the Arts and Letters, later the Division for the Cultural Inheritance of the National Department for Arts and Culture, Ministry for Youth, Sports, Arts, and Culture.

Its first collections were African-oriented, geared toward the former FOA (French Occidental Africa, Afrique Occidentale Française) and the former French Sudan. The collections were mainly books and periodicals in history, ethnography, and sociology and occasionally in the natural sciences.

The National Library is in charge of the copyrighting and of the loan program with other countries; it houses a bindery and the main public library, and it is also the headquarters for the Librarians, Archivists, and Library Researchers Association of Mali (AMBAD, Association malienne des bibliothécaires, archivistes, et documentalistes).

The National Library owns about 5,000 books, mostly in French, fewer in English and in national languages (especially the Bamanan). The relatively old collection was projected to be increased rapidly and be more diversified. The National Library, as all other libraries in Mali, suffers from a lack of qualified staff and from the absence of an interloan program with other libraries in Mali and in other countries.

Within the Ministry for Youth, Sports, Arts, and Culture of the National Department of Arts and Culture, Division of Cultural Inheritance, is a branch for libraries and documentation centers, in charge of promoting a policy for reading (the founding of libraries, the training of librarians, and the management of the national library). This branch carries out inspection, replacing a former unit concerned with inspection of archives, museums, and libraries, part of the Ministry of National Education.

**Academic Libraries.** In 1962 a system of professional schools (hautes écoles supérieures) was chosen over the traditional university set-up. The main libraries are often libraries specializing in the fields covered by the schools of which they are part. Examples are the library of the Ecole Normale Supérieure (training school for high school teachers), founded in 1962; the library of the Ecole Nationale d'Administration (training qualified staff for government, legal practice, and finances); the library of the Institut Polytechnique Rural of Katibougou (training agricultural engineers, water and forestry specialists, and veterinarians), heir to the Agricultural Technical College of Katibougou; the library of the Ecole Nationale de Médicine (training doctors, pharmacists, and dentists), founded in 1970; and the library of the Ecole National d'Ingénieurs (training engineers in every specialty), heir to the School of Public Works for French Occidental Africa. None of them owned more than 3,000 works at the end of the 1970's.

**Libraries in Mali**

| Type of Library | Number |
|---|---|
| National Library | 1 |
| Library, university level | 6 |
| School libraries | 30 |
| Public libraries | 32 |
| Special libraries | 6 |
| Total | 75 |

Note: These are approximate figures owing to absence of data. They do not take into account family libraries. The number of public libraries is uncertain.

**Public Libraries.** Before 1960 several public libraries existed in the main towns of the districts, municipalities, military camps, and some central jails; the most important one was in Bamako. They failed because of lack of staff. They were replaced by foreign documentation centers, all in Bamako, the most important being the French documentation center, the Soviet documentation center, and the American documentation center, plus a private center, the Center Djoliba.

In 1976 a campaign for public reading was launched; it aimed for the opening of 44 public libraries within five years at the district *(cercle)* level; 21 were open by 1979. Every public library starts with a collection of 300 books, going up to 500 the second year and up to 1,000 toward the end of the third year. Such public libraries own a variety of works of general interest and black African ones; they include also a shelf for young children.

**School Libraries.** All 25 high schools of Mali own a library, as do some other important schools. These libraries collect mainly textbooks. None owns over 1,000 works.

**Special Libraries.** Libraries exist in important government departments; examples are the library of the Nigerian Office (Office du Niger) in Ségou and the library of the Institute for Rural Economics in Bamako (Institut d'économie rurale).

The Ahmed Baba Center for Documentation and Historical Research in Tombouctou was founded in 1973; the role of the regional center is to collect, to keep, and to make use of the Arabic manuscripts of every origin and in every discipline. Arabic manuscripts often are in national languages (Peul and Songhoi mainly) written in the Arabic alphabet.

Private family libraries include mainly Arabic manuscripts. They are located in Tombouctou, Gao, Djenné San, Ségou, Macina, Nioro, Banamba, Dia, and Bandiagara, among other places.

Oral traditions are the main source of information for Mali, where over 15 languages are spoken; some of these use the *tifinar,* the Arabic alphabet, and more and more often the Roman alphabet. Two centers are in charge of collecting and keeping oral traditions: the Institute for the Humanities (Institut des Sciences Humaines) of Mali in Bamako and the National Broadcasting Corporation of Mali in Bamako (Radiodiffusion Nationale du Mali).

**Association.** The Librarians, Archivists, and Library Researchers Association of Mali (AMBAD) was founded in March 1978. Headquarters are in Bamako.

ALPHA OUMAR KONARE

## Malta

Malta, a parliamentary state, comprises the islands of Malta, Gozo, and Comino. Lying in the Mediterranean Sea, Malta is southwest of Sicily and northeast of Tunisia. Pop. (1978 est.) 326,000; area 316 sq.km. The official languages are Maltese and English.

**National Library.** The Knights of Malta established a library in 1555 that was fused with the Biblioteca Publica on its creation in 1776. In 1797 the library of the Hospital of the Order of Saint John was also added, and in 1812 the collection was transferred to Valletta, Malta's capital city. Between 1920 and 1950 the Biblioteca's Melitensia was developed, legal deposit was established, and the British Government renamed the library Royal Malta Library (RML). In 1964 the Malta Garrison Library closed down and gave most of its 50,000 books to the RML. The Library became the National Library in 1977 and is now the national depository for United Nations and Council of Europe publications, which are housed in the European Documentation Centre (set up in 1974, when the National Library transferred its lending functions to the Public Lending Library). The strengths of the NL's over 346,000 volumes are its Melitensia, Maltese newspapers and periodicals, and fine printing, bindings, and manuscripts. The NL is essentially a national and public reference library and offers no special services to members of Parliament.

**Academic Libraries.** The largest academic libraries are those of the New University of Malta (NUM), before 1978 known as the Malta College of Arts, Science and Technology, or MCAST, and of the Old University of Malta (OUM), before 1974 known as the Royal University of Malta, or RUM, both at Msida. The MCAST library dates from the early 1960's, and in 1975 the library of the men's College of Education was integrated with it. The total stock is 35,600 volumes. OUM originated in 1952, but its main library dates back to 1830. In 1959 a new library building was inaugurated, but by 1967 it had to be moved again to its present modern building. It holds a checklist of all periodicals concerning Malta. The library primarily serves undergraduate studies. Total stock is 165,000.

**Public Libraries.** The Public Lending Library (PLL) near Valletta dates to 1974, but its origins lie in the Biblioteca of 1776. Gozo, a sister island of Malta, had its first public library in 1839. It became state owned in 1853 and is a legal deposit library of 100,000 books, including records of local administration between 1560 and 1814 and rare books. The PLL has the largest collection of children's books in Malta and offers facilities to the blind. It takes overall responsibility for 47 district libraries (established in the 1920's), housed in primary schools. There are plans to revive these libraries and have them serve as town or village libraries in the evenings and as school libraries during the day.

**School Libraries.** All the 38 state secondary schools were equipped by the end of the 1970's with reference collections and similar efforts to improve the 95 state primary schools were begun. A special collection of filmstrips, slides, books, and other items for use in school projects and a reference section on libraries are available at the PLL, which also supplies bulk loans of fiction to schools and issues a regular information leaflet. School libraries are run on a part-time basis by teachers, most of whom have some rudimentary training in librarianship. The 5 main state school libraries were founded in the late 1950's and early 1960's and individually hold about 6,000 books. No recent survey of libraries in the 71 private schools is available, but about 6 of them have good libraries, one of which houses a 5,000-volume children's library. The Seminary, a secondary school for those training for the priesthood, has the largest of these school libraries, with a stock of 9,000 books.

**Special Libraries.** Religious libraries date from around 1533, according to the earliest known reference to a collection of such books. Forty years later the Franciscan Friars Minor founded a library. The Capuchins, Jesuits, and Dominicans established libraries in 1588, 1592, and 1600, respectively, while the Society of Saint Paul (SSP) set up theirs in 1910. Starting in the mid-1960's, a revival led to the introduction of Universal Decimal Classification in the Biblioteca San Agathae of the SSP (10,000 volumes) and the Capuchins' library (23,000). The Franciscans' library became the "Provincial Library," and the Jesuits founded the John XXIII Memorial Library, with 6,500 books on contemporary theology.

There are two corporate libraries: the Central Bank of Malta Library (3,500 volumes), set up in 1968 as a reference library, and the Chamber of Commerce Library, for members and government officials. The range of smaller special libraries includes the Archaeology Library, the Teachers' Institute Library, the Marine Biology Laboratory Library, the library of the Malta Federation of

**Libraries in Malta (1978)**

| Type | Number | Volumes in collections | Annual expenditures (pound) | Population served[e] | Professional staff[e] | All staff (total)[e] |
|---|---|---|---|---|---|---|
| National | 1 | 346,600[a] | £M 45,000 | 326,000 | 2 | 31 |
| Academic | 3 | 200,600 | £M 80,000 | 3,200 | 6 | 25 |
| Public | 2 | 100,000 | £M 70,700 | 326,000 | 1 | 26 |
| School[b] | 42 | 45,000 | £M 3,000 | 16,000 | 0 | 42[c] |
| Special[e] | 20 | 70,000[d] | £M 2,000 | N.A. | 5 | 15 |

[a]Includes archival collections of approximately 7,000 manuscripts, which is administered and used as part of the Library's holdings.
[b]Private schools excluded. No information available.
[c]Indicates full-time teachers acting as part-time librarians.
[d]Excludes the newspaper collection.
[e]Approximate figures.

Sources: *Annual Reports* of Public Lending Library (unpublished) and of the Old University Library. Some information supplied privately by the librarians of the Public Lending Library, the old and new universities, and the National Library.

Professional Bodies (MFPB), the Social Action Movement Library, libraries of several cultural institutes, the *Times of Malta* newspaper library, a parish library, and a private circulating library.

**Associations.** The Library Association (Valletta), a member of IFLA since its creation in 1969, is the main professional association and has a small library in the Old University. The Professional Librarians of Malta Association was founded as a member of MFPB.

**REFERENCES**
P. T. Biggs, "Malta: The Library Scene and Its Setting," *International Library Review* (1973).
"Problems of Librarianship in Malta," *Focus* (1973).

NORBERT BONNICI

*Fujio Mamiya*

Theodore F. Welch

## Mamiya, Fujio

(1890–1970)

Fujio Mamiya made contributions to the Japanese library world that have much in common with some of Melvil Dewey's contributions to the American library world, and he has been called the Dewey of Japan.

Born on July 26, 1890, in Tokyo, Mamiya finished his higher primary school in 1902, and he joined, as an apprentice, the Book Division of Maruzen Co., Ltd., the oldest and largest import trader of foreign books and stationery in Japan. Although his formal school education was short, he felt strongly the importance of reading as a method of self-education, and he was devoted to improvement of Japanese libraries in his later years.

In the days he worked for Maruzen, he came to the attention of a businessman in the typewriter trade. With his aid Mamiya made a trip to the U.S., a long-cherished desire. In 1915 he attended training classes of typewriter corporations in New York. He returned to Japan in 1916 and worked in the Kurosawa typewriter shop for five years.

In 1921 he retired from the Kurosawa shop and commenced the Mamiya shop in Osaka, producing and selling library supplies. His shop developed successfully. In 1927 the League of Young Librarians, a research group for libraries, was organized under his leadership. The Japan Library Association had existed long before the League started, but the League emphasized "the standardization of norms and forms." From 1928 *Toshokan Kenkyu* ("Library Study") was published quarterly as a bulletin of the League and as the only research journal for libraries in Japan. It was forced to cease in 1943 by increasingly severe war limitations.

He made efforts to promote international standard size cards through his library supply business. In addition, he established at his office the Mamiya Library, consisting of about 3,000 volumes of foreign books on library science. Unfortunately, the Library was destroyed in fire with the Mamiya shop during an air raid in May 1945. In 1950 he founded the Japan Library Bureau in Tokyo. The Japanese government recognized his long distinguished service for the Japanese library world with formal awards in 1961 and 1966. Another interest of his was the movement to promote romanization of the Japanese alphabet, to which he devoted efforts all his life. Mamiya died at the age of 80 on October 24, 1970.

TOSHIO IWASARU

## Mann, Margaret

(1873–1960)

A brilliant and imaginative teacher, Margaret Mann revolutionized instruction in cataloguing. In an obituary, the *Australian Library Journal* described her as "one of the most outstanding librarians of the twentieth century."

She was born April 9, 1873, in Cedar Rapids, Iowa. After graduating from Chicago's Englewood High School in 1893, she entered the new Department of Library Economy at Armour Institute, Chicago, under the direction of Katharine Sharp. Armour was one of four library schools founded between 1887 and 1893 and the first in the Middle West. Entering students were at least 20 years of age and had to have a high school education; the entrance examination stressed a knowledge of authors and their works (in French, German, Latin, Greek, and English), some background in history, and a familiarity with current events. Students put in 40 hours a week during their year's study and were awarded certificates if successful. In addition to attending classes, they worked for various members of the library staff and gave some hours each week to the Institute.

Mann was one of 12 applicants (22 tried) to pass Armour's entrance examination. She finished the first-year course with superior grades and was employed as a cataloguer for the Institute's new 10,000-volume library. At the same time, she began a second year of study in the Armour library school, and by 1896 she was teaching cataloguing at Armour and summer courses at the University of Wisconsin.

In September 1897 Armour moved to the University of Illinois (as the University of Illinois State Library School) with Katharine Sharp as Director of the School and Librarian of the University. Mann became an instructor; her course in the cataloguing and reference use of public documents was the first of its kind to be offered anywhere. She organized and supervised the Catalog Department in the university library and in 1900 was named Assistant Librarian.

In 1903 Mann became Head of the Cataloging Department at the Carnegie Library of Pittsburgh, where she prepared for publication the Library's classified catalogue, a monument of its kind and a valued reference tool for many years. During her years in Pittsburgh, Mann taught cataloguing regularly in the Library's training school; offered courses at Western Reserve and in Riverside, California; lectured; wrote; and began serving the American Library Association. She had become ALA member number 1,527 in 1896, when Katharine Sharp was a member of Council. In 1909–10 she was Chairman

School of Library Science, University of Michigan
*Margaret Mann*

of ALA's Catalog Section; during 1910–13 she was a member of the Committee on Catalog Rules for Small Libraries; and she was elected to Council for the first of three five-year terms beginning in 1912. In 1914 she was appointed by the Executive Board to a Special Committee to Study Cost and Methods of Cataloging, in 1917 to the Decimal Classification Advisory Committee (for one year), and also in 1917 to the Catalog Rules Committee, where she served—except for one three-year lapse—until 1932. Her *List of Subject Headings for a Juvenile Catalog* was published by ALA in 1916.

In 1919 Harrison Craver, under whose directorship Mann had worked in Pittsburgh, employed her again in New York at the United Engineering Societies Library. From the separate catalogues and collections that had merged to form the Library, Mann created one collection arranged by a relatively brief Dewey number and a classified catalogue arranged by the Brussels (Universal Decimal) classification. During these years she was instrumental in organizing a system of regional cataloguing groups that became ALA's Council of Regional Groups. She was active on the Committee on Library Training from 1920 to 1924, was appointed to the Executive Board of ALA to fill a vacancy during 1921–22, and served on the Fiftieth Anniversary Committee in 1923–24.

In 1923 the ALA set up a library school in Paris, which was an outgrowth of reconstruction work with war-damaged libraries in France carried on by the American Committee for Devastated France. Sarah C. N. Bogle, Director of the Ecole des Bibliothècaires and Mann's friend from the Pittsburgh days, asked Mann to teach in the Paris Library School in 1924. The School's international student body was taught in French and took courses for eight months, followed by a six-week summer course. Subjects were not taught in discrete parts, as in most American schools at the time, but in large groups. Mann's cataloguing course, for example, included work with the ALA and French cataloguing codes; Dewey Decimal, Brunet, Cutter, Library of Congress, and Universal Decimal classifications; shelflisting; and the making of dictionary and classified catalogues.

By the time Mann returned to the U.S. in 1926, William Warner Bishop had formed a new library school at the University of Michigan, Ann Arbor. They had met at Armour, where he was an instructor. Years later they served together on ALA Council and on the Catalog Rules Committee, where Bishop found Mann an ally against the proponents of constant change in the code. In 1923, when he left the chairmanship of the Committee (then called the Committee on Cataloging), she was appointed in his place.

Bishop's concern to find capable instructors for the school led him to Mann. By 1926 she was internationally recognized both as cataloguer and as teacher of cataloguing. Reporting to Michigan's President of Mann's qualifications, Bishop wrote: "Without exception every one in the country says that Miss Margaret Mann, now teaching cataloguing and classification . . . in Paris, . . . is the best teacher of these subjects to be found anywhere. In this opinion I heartily concur. There are certain obstacles to her appointment . . . chief of which is the fact that she has had no college work whatever. . . . Personally, I think the University of Michigan is big enough to employ the best teachers irrespective of their academic preparation. Miss Mann is distinctly one of the exceptions which prove the rule. . . . Despite her lack of academic study, she is one of the best-read people I have ever met in my life." Later she was offered one of three full-time positions in the new school.

Inasmuch as Mann's fame rests chiefly on her excellence as a teacher of cataloguing, her views on the subject and methods of communicating it are worthy of attention. The organization of her Paris course does not seem unusual today until it is contrasted with other styles of teaching cataloguing. The three schools that followed Dewey's at Albany—Pratt, Drexel, and Armour—were connected with circulating public libraries. While they could not offer students the resources of a large academic library, they could offer actual practice in library routines. Following the first plan of Dewey's school, they emphasized technique almost to the exclusion of principle. The Pratt Institute *Circular* for 1922–23 lists separate courses in classification (44 hours), cataloguing (120 hours), and subject headings (15 hours); these were taught by two different people. There was also a course in what was called library economy, described as covering "the minor records of a library, as accessioning and shelf listing, also order work, book numbering, the filing of cards, binding and rebinding, charging systems, care of supplies, and many of the routine . . . processes." The University of Illinois Library School *Circular* for 1924–25 shows courses in classification and subject headings (which included book numbers and shelflisting) and cataloguing (including the making of dictionary and classified catalogues and the ordering of Library of Congress cards). Summer courses offered at the University of Michigan prior to the opening of the library school covered not only cataloguing and classification but such topics as accessioning, card alphabeting, and the physical preparation of books for the shelves.

In contrast to this fragmented approach, with emphasis on activities she felt were largely clerical in nature, Mann insisted that cataloguers needed to develop critical judgment and executive ability; "emphasis on technical details," she wrote, "will never make a good cataloger." She saw the library catalogue as a service instrument for library staff and users and attempted to teach every facet of the subject in its relation to the needs of users. Her style was quite unlike that of other cataloguing teachers, one of whom is described thus: "He read to the students from the cataloguing rules of Charles Cutter, adding his own interpretations, and drawing upon the examples of other cataloguing codes where appropriate."

In 1926 the Board of Education for Librarianship asked Mann to write the cataloguing volume in a series of seven basic textbooks sponsored by ALA and funded by the Carnegie Corporation. *Introduction to Cataloging and the Classification of Books* was published in mimeograph form by ALA in 1928 and in bound form in 1930; a second edition came out in 1943. Regarded as a classic in its own time, it won an influence that still continues.

Mann's book followed the organization of her course. She felt cataloguing training should begin with a study of books, since students would have some familiarity with them while they lacked techniques of librarianship. Next, subject approach was discussed, and students learned classification and the use of subject headings. This was followed by cataloguing and then by topics related to the administration of a catalogue department. Although Mann believed in laboratory practice for students, she felt card sets should be made by typists. Apparently, she was one of the first library school instructors to use audiovisuals as an aid to the teaching of cataloguing when she used a reflectoscope to display title pages on a screen.

When William Warner Bishop was immersed in problems of cataloguing the Vatican Library in the late 1920's, Mann served as an adviser on cataloguing and trained several cataloguers sent to Michigan from the Vatican. She surveyed cataloguing and classification conditions at the library of Teachers College, Columbia University; this survey led to a revision of its catalogue. The ALA Executive Board in 1931 appointed her to a committee to study the possibilities for cooperative cataloguing among research libraries; the project begun as a result of this work was funded by the General Education Board. In 1932 she shared in a Carnegie Corporation grant and spent her sabbatical year studying library education in Europe.

Mann retired from teaching in 1938 when she was 65, although she continued to be active on ALA's Catalog Code Revision Committee until 1942. In 1945 she moved to Chula Vista, California, where she died on August 22, 1960.

CONSTANCE RINEHART

# Martel, Charles
(1860–1945)

Charles Martel, the chief architect of the Library of Congress classification, was born March 5, 1860, in Zürich, Switzerland. James Bennett Childs has stated that Martel's name was originally Karl David Hanke and that he was the son of Franz and Maria Gertrud Strässle Hanke. Franz Hanke was a publisher and antiquarian bookseller, and Martel credited his education to his association with the bookstore, but he also completed the Gymnasium course in 1876 and attended the University of Zürich during 1876–77. In 1876 Martel spent five months visiting the United States. He returned to the U.S. in either late 1879 or early 1880 and became a citizen in 1887 under the name of Charles Martel. From 1880 to 1892 he taught in schools in Missouri and Nebraska and was employed in a law office in Council Bluffs, Iowa.

Martel had served as a volunteer in various libraries, and he chose librarianship as a full-time career in February 1892 when he joined the staff of the Newberry Library in Chicago. Eight months later Librarian William Frederick Poole recommended an increase in salary "because of his very great ability and enthusiasm." Poole's further evaluation in a report in October 1892 would be confirmed by others: "a quiet, scholarly man, indefatigable, and working in season and out of season." Martel was involved in both cataloguing and classification and was in charge of the Department of Arts and Letters (1893–96) and of early printed books and manuscripts (1896–97).

While at the Newberry, Martel formed a lifelong friendship with his colleague J. C. M. Hanson. Within two months after Hanson's arrival to head the bibliographical reorganization of the Library of Congress consequent to its move from the Capitol, Librarian John Russell Young appointed Charles Martel as Assistant in the Catalogue Department, one of the two top-salaried positions, effective December 1, 1897. When Martel joined Hanson, the Library of Congress acquired "a team which has never been equaled anywhere," according to William Warner Bishop (*Library Quarterly,* January 1948).

Martel's analysis of the existing classification, his first assignment, was submitted to Young by the end of the month. Although it included an outline of a new scheme, it was the notation, not the scheme itself, that was emphasized. He described the new scheme merely as an eclectic one "combining the best features of those in use in other reference libraries." Moreover, the arrangement for class Z (Bibliography and Library Science) had been "modified so as to disturb as little as possible the existing order" of the collection. These emphases may have been made in deference to the Assistant Librarian, Ainsworth Rand Spofford, an articulate foe of close classification.

Hanson always rejected any credit for the classification, as he reminded Herbert Putnam:

> Aside from some preliminary planning of the notation, I am afraid that my claims to association in the construction of the Library of Congress classification are very slight. Soon after 1898 I was forced to give almost all my time to the cataloguing, leaving the details of the classification very largely to Mr. Martel (March 25, 1915; University of Chicago Library Archives).

Work on the reclassification began in January 1898 but was suspended when, after Young's death in January 1899, Herbert Putnam was appointed to succeed him. The project was not resumed until January 18, 1901, when the reclassification of United States history into classes E and F, prepared by Martel in 1898–1900, was undertaken with an enlarged staff. A number of subject specialists worked with Martel in developing the other schedules.

In 1901, beginning with classes D (Universal and Old World History) and Q (Science), and in subsequent classes, a second letter for the major subdivisions was introduced to permit "the beginning of operations simultaneously at various points in the system" (Report of the Librarian of Congress . . . June 30, 1902). In 1911 Martel introduced another notational modification in subdivisions needing provision for many names, by incorporating the initial letter in the number for the subdivision and assigning the Cutter author number from the second letter in the name.

The pressure to complete and publish the classification schedules was so great that a detailed description of the philosophical basis of the system could not be written for publication until 1911. Martel first wrote it as part of a larger paper, "Classification: A Brief Conspectus of Present Day Practice," read at a meeting of the New Zealand Library Association in April 1911. The part on the Library of Congress scheme was sent for reading at the Pasadena meeting of the American Library Association in May of the same year.

Martel also made a major contribution in descriptive cataloguing. For 28 years after he was appointed Chief of the Catalog Division in October 1912 (to succeed Charles H. Hastings, who had served during the interregnum following Hanson's resignation in October 1910), Martel guided Library of Congress cataloguing on a level generally accepted as authoritative. When he reached the statutory retirement age of 70 in 1930, he filled the specially created position of Consultant in Cataloguing, Classification and Bibliography. On June 30, 1932, President Herbert Hoover, on Putnam's recommendation, exempted Martel from the provisions of the Retirement Act by Executive Order, citing Martel's "irreplaceable knowledge of the collections of the Library of Congress and his rich bibliographical and technical experience."

In 1928 William Warner Bishop asked Martel to head a commission of cataloguers to assist in the reorganization of the Vatican Library, a project supported by the Carnegie Endowment for International Peace. Martel at first refused, but he reconsidered when Hanson, who was next approached, refused to go without him. The cataloguing rules they worked out with the Monsignors Tisserant and Mercati constituted the original draft of the Vatican Library's *Norme per il catalogo degli stampati*, a major step in international library cooperation. Martel also assisted in the translation into Italian of the needed parts of the Library of Congress Classification. Martel retired on May 1, 1945, and died two weeks later, on May 15.

**REFERENCES**


James Bennett Childs, who investigated Martel's early life as part of a planned biography, included his sources in his biography of Martel in volume 17 (1976), *Encyclopedia of Library and Information Science,* and the *Dictionary of American Biography* (3rd Supplement). In addition, he wrote an article (edited for publication by John Y. Cole) for the *Dictionary of American Library Biography* (1978).

Leo E. LaMontagne, *American Library Classification with Special Reference to the Library of Congress* (1961), pp. 234–51.

Edith Scott, "J. C. M. Hanson and His Contribution to Twentieth-Century Cataloging" (Ph.D. dissertation,

University of Chicago, 1970), pp. 177–227, documents manuscript sources.

Harriet Wheeler Pierson, "Charles Martel," *Catalogers' and Classifiers' Yearbook* no. 9 (ALA, 1941); frontispiece is a portrait of Martel, the original of which hangs in the Descriptive Cataloging Division of the Library of Congress.

EDITH SCOTT

# Martin, Allie Beth

(1914–1976)

Tulsa City–County Library

*Allie Beth Martin*

Allie Beth Martin was an outstanding educator, a skillful politician, a talented writer, a respected leader, and a dedicated librarian. She was born in the small town of Annieville, Arkansas, on June 28, 1914, to Carleton Gayle Dent and Ethel (McCaleb) Dent. She attended public schools in Seattle, Washington, and Batesville, Arkansas. While attending Batesville's high school Martin lived with her grandfather, who had a primary influence on her life and the course it would later take. It has been said that she decided as a child that she wanted to become a librarian.

Following her graduation from high school in 1932, Martin enrolled at Arkansas College in Batesville, where she majored in foreign languages and English while working part-time in the college library. She graduated in 1935 with a B.A. and became the first Librarian of the Batesville Public Library. A year later she moved to Little Rock, where she was in charge of the junior college library. The following year she joined the Arkansas Library Commission as Assistant to the Executive Secretary. She married Ralph F. Martin, a journalist, on October 6, 1937, and later resigned from the Commission. In 1939 she received a B.S. in Library Science from George Peabody College for teachers in Nashville, Tennessee. She moved with her husband to Arkansas, when he entered medical school and she served as Director of the Mississippi County Library in Osceola, Arkansas, and later, from 1942 to 1947, returned again to the staff of the Arkansas Library Commission. In 1945 she was elected President of the Arkansas Library Association, and she served as Editor of the *Arkansas Libraries* until 1947. During her husband's internship and residency in New York, she attended Columbia University School of Library Science and received her Master's degree in 1949.

In 1949 the Martins moved to Tulsa, Oklahoma, where Dr. Martin practiced medicine until his death in 1968, and she joined the Tulsa Public Library and spent her first year serving in various departments. In 1950 she worked as a children's librarian, following that with the position of extension librarian, in which she served until 1961. Martin edited the *Oklahoma Librarian* from 1953 to 1954 and was elected President of the Oklahoma Library Association in 1955. She was later honored by OLA with the Distinguished Service Award.

The condition of the Tulsa Public Library in the late 1950's was typical of many libraries of that time. The Central Library, built with Carnegie funds in 1916, was overcrowded and in a state of disrepair, as were the four branch libraries. Allie Beth Martin became actively involved in convincing the community of the need for new and improved library facilities. A first bond issue failed, only to be overwhelmingly approved when presented the second time on November 14, 1961. The bond issue included $3,800,000 for construction of a new Central Library and building and renovation of 20 branch libraries and an annually recurring levy for the operation of the Tulsa City-County Library System. In 1963 Allie Beth was named Director of the library system she was instrumental in creating. The Library, under her leadership for 13 years, became well known throughout the United States for its innovative and forward-looking programs.

Martin served as President of the Southwestern Library Association (1969–70) and led the regional association into an active leadership role in continuing education and cooperative projects.

A member of the American Library Association from 1935, she served in many capacities: on the executive boards of the Public Libraries and Children's Services Divisions, and as Chairperson of the ALA Membership Committee. *Strategy for Public Library Change: Proposed Public Library Goals* was published by ALA in 1972. She was elected to the ALA Council for the term 1972–76 and to the Executive Board in 1973. In 1974 she became President-elect and was inaugurated President in July 1975 at the San Francisco conference. Three months later she underwent surgery for cancer. She continued with her work as President and as Library Director until her death on April 11, 1976.

Martin received many awards and honors during her lifetime and following her death; a regional library of the Tulsa System was named for her, as was a national library award and a lecture series.

PAT WOODRUM

# Maunsell, Andrew

(d.1595)

Andrew Maunsell, a member of the London Drapers' Company, is remembered today almost entirely for his bibliographical work. Though not a member of the Stationers' Company, as early as 1578 he obtained a license to publish *The State of Swearinge and Swearers,* and thereafter until 1595 was active as a bookseller and publisher, particularly of theological works. At that time there was no general printed catalogue of English works, with the partial exception of the *Scriptorum illustrium majoris Britanniae . . . catalogus* of John Bāle (Wesel, 1548; another edition Basel, 1557–59). In the *Catalogue of English Printed Books,* which occupied Maunsell in the last years of his life, he attempted the preparation of a true national bibliography, and in a form that presented many advances in bibliographical technique.

In *The First Part of the Catalogue of English printed Bookes: which concerneth such matters of Divinitie, as have bin either written in our owne Tongue, or translated out of anie other language,* published by Maunsell from his shop in Lothbury in 1595, he explained his purpose and method in the prefatory address to the Master of the Stationers' Company. He justified his work on the ground that it was as necessary for the bookseller to have such a catalogue "as the Apothecarie his *Dispensatorium,* or the Schoolemaster his *Dictionarie.*" In distinction to Bale and other earlier compilers, he pointed out that he was including only printed works and only works that he had personally examined, and he had arranged his entries so that books on the same subject were grouped together. Another advance was that alphabetical arrangement was by surnames, not forenames; anonymous works were listed by title and by subject. He took care to record translators, printers and publishers, date of publication, and format. Deliberate exclusions were noted: "The auncient Popish Books that have been Printed heere, I have also inserted among the rest, but the Bookes written by the fugitive Papistes, as also those that are written against the present government, I doe not thinke meete for me to meddle withall."

*The First Part* (which was arranged on the dictionary principle, with author, title, and subject entries in a single alphabet) was followed later in the same year by *The Seconde Part,* which listed works on "the Sciences Mathematicall, as Arithmetick, Geometrie, Astronomie, Astrologie, Musick, the Arte of Warre, and Navigation: And also, of Phisick and Surgerie" arranged on the same general principles. A third part was promised in the preface to this volume. It was to deal with "Humanitie," which

Maunsell defined as "Gramer, Logick, Rethoricke, Lawe, Historie, Poetrie, Policie, &c. which will for the most parte concerne matters of Delight and Pleasure." However, since it was difficult to collect information, and "so tedious to digest into any good methode," Maunsell had thought it wise to publish the first two parts to test public reaction before completing his work. We must be grateful that he did so: though public reaction was favorable, Maunsell's death late in 1595 was to prevent the completion of his labors. As compiler of the first effective national bibliography on scientific principles, Maunsell is a figure of considerable importance. His *Catalogue* was reprinted in 1962 as part of the Gregg/Archive Press series of English Bibliographical Sources.

RODERICK CAVE

## Mauritania, Islamic Republic of

Mauritania, a republic in West Africa, is bounded by Western (Spanish) Sahara on the northwest, Algeria on the north, Mali on the east and southeast, Senegal on the southwest, and the Atlantic Ocean on the west. Pop. (1977 est.) 1,420,000; area 1,030,700 sq.km. The official languages are Arabic and French.

**National Library.** The national library system in the Islamic Republic of Mauritania was instituted by a law of July 10, 1962, which foresaw, in particular, the establishment of an integrated system comprised of (1) a national conservation library of all the nationally printed documents and the essentials of the written civilization; (2) public and school libraries; and (3) study libraries for the use of universities, institutes, laboratories, and others.

The National Library of Mauritania in Nouakchott, the capital, was created on January 27, 1965, by a decree put into application by the law of 1962. It comprises a conservation library, a documentation center on Mauritania, and a study and research library. To fulfill the three functions vested in it, the National Library is responsible for (1) receiving and conserving all publications subject to the formalities of the legal trust instituted by a law of June 27, 1963; (2) acquiring, through purchasing, exchanges, or gifts, all the works existing abroad concerning Mauritania; and (3) constituting a universal research collection. Realizing the weakness of resources in the country, the National Library of Mauritania has been led to serving also the roles of school libraries and public reading programs.

The National Library is responsible, further, for the establishment and application of policies concerning the development of libraries and documentation throughout the entire country. The administration of the legal trust is one of its functions, and it is responsible for setting up the national library in the country; the collection of that institution totaled 20,000 volumes and 175 periodicals in 1975 and 25,000 volumes and 225 periodicals in August 1979. The manuscript department, which had 3,500 works in 1975, was attached in 1979 to the Mauritanian Institute of Scientific Research, which had nearly 2,500 others.

**Academic Libraries.** At the close of the 1970's there was no university in the Republic of Mauritania, but many schools of higher learning with the status of university institutes existed. Each one of those schools had its own library. They included a School of Education created in September 1970, which had a library with nearly 10,000 volumes; a national School of Administration created in 1966 with a library of approximately 12,000 volumes; and a School of Elementary Education Training, created in 1965, which had a library of more than 8,000 volumes.

**Public Libraries.** Apart from the department of public reading of the National Library, there were no other state public libraries as of 1979. The public libraries in existence were those of the cultural centers of several accredited embassies in Mauritania, including France, Libya, Egypt, the U.S.S.R., and Syria, among others. A governmental project foresaw the eventual establishment of a cultural center housing a library and public reading room in each regional capital.

**School Libraries.** There is a library in each secondary school for the use of its teachers and students, but they were in embryonic stages in the latter 1970's, since not one of the collections exceeded 1,500 works.

**Special Libraries.** Several special libraries or documentation centers are within the jurisdiction of various departments of different government ministries or semiprivate organizations. Among examples are the documentation service of the National Society of Mine Imports (SNIM), which has a collection of books and documents close to 13,000 titles; the documentation service of the National Society of Rural Development (SONADER); the documentation service of the Administration of Studies and Programming of the Ministry in Charge of Special Projects; the documentation division of the Administration of Mines and Geology; the documentation project of the Ministry of Rural Development; the documentation service of the National Pedagogical Institute; and the Mauritanian Institute of Scientific Research Library.

**Associations.** The Mauritanian section of the International Association for the Development of Libraries and Archives (AIDBA) in Africa formerly existed in the country. In May 1979 a new association was created. Continuing the work of the AIDBA, and named the Mauritanian Association of Librarians, Archivists, and Documentalists (AMBAD), it established headquarters in Nouakchott; a Directory Committee of 17 members included the Director of the National Library who served as President.

OUMAR DIOUWARA

## Mauritius

Mauritius, a parliamentary state, lies east of the island of Madagascar in the Indian Ocean. It includes the island of Mauritius and the dependencies of Agalega, Cargados Carajos Shoals, and Rodrigues. Pop. (1978 est.) 920,000; area 2,040 sq. km. The official language is English.

**National Library.** The Mauritius Institute Public Library and Museum is considered to be the national library of the island and is in the capital of Port-Louis. The library has a Natural History Museum attached to it, and together they form the Mauritius Institute. The library started in 1902 with a collection of about 7,000 books donated by the eminent lawyer Sir Virgil Naz. The library is state owned and has the right of legal deposit. It now has a bookstock of about 52,000 volumes, lending and reference general sections, a particularly strong Mauritiana collection, and a research section on the natural sciences. The Mauritius Institute is also the depository library for Unesco publications.

**Academic Libraries.** The University of Mauritius, a developmental university started in 1968, has three schools: Agriculture and Sugar Technology, Industrial Technology, and Administration, all with about 1,000 students, both full- and part-time. The library contains about 50,000 volumes. About 400 periodicals are acquired, and 350 are received on an exchange basis. The library of the Institute of Education started operations in 1975, though courses for the training of secondary school teachers started in 1977. The library now consists of 5,000 volumes and 60 periodicals and caters to a student population of 585 and a staff of 76. Courses in the Mahatma Gandhi Institute's School of Mauritian, African, and Oriental Studies had not started by early 1979, but its library was already operating with a bookstock of 5,000, mainly donations from the Indian and French governments. The Mauritius College of Education, formerly called the

**Mauritius Association of Booksellers 348**
**Mauritius Library Association 348**

**Table 1. Libraries in Mauritius (1976)**

| Type | Number | Volumes in collections | Annual expenditures (rupee) | Population served | Professional staff | All staff (total) |
|---|---|---|---|---|---|---|
| National | 1 | 50,000 | Mau.Rs. 50,000 | 450,000 | 2 | 8 |
| Academic | 4 | 60,000 | N.A. | 14,000 | 8 | 26 |
| Public | 6 | 142,500 | Mau.Rs. 228,000 | 300,000 | 3 | 43 |
| School | 140 | N.A. | N.A. | N.A. | 5 | N.A. |
| Special | 1 | 16,800 | N.A. | N.A. | 1 | 4 |

Teachers Training College, is concerned with the training of primary school teachers. Its library has a bookstock of 20,000 volumes.

**Public Libraries.** Public library service is provided mainly in the urban areas. In Port-Louis it is provided by the Mauritius Institute and the Port-Louis city library. The latter, established in 1851, is the largest municipal library, with a bookstock of over 40,000 volumes. There are four other municipal libraries in the district of Plaines Wilhems, namely, the library of the municipalities of Beau-Bassin–Rose-Hill, Quatre-Bornes, Vacoas-Phoenix, and Curepipe.

The rural areas are not so well provided with public library service. A library has been opened in Mapou, in the north of the island, by the Pamplemousses-Riviere du Rempart District Council, with a bookstock of about 5,000 volumes; it is a rare example of public library service in the rural areas.

**Table 2. Archives in Mauritius (1976)**

| | |
|---|---|
| Number | 1 |
| Annual expenditures | Mau.Rs. 2,500 (for books only) |
| Professional staff | 1 |
| All staff (total) | 6 |

Source: Ministry of Education and Cultural Affairs.

**School Libraries.** Among the 250 government primary schools, about half have libraries, which began mainly through the efforts of parent-teacher associations. A book box service is in operation in the schools that have no libraries. The 6 government secondary schools and the 13 secondary schools run by religious bodies have fairly good libraries, but among the 130 private secondary schools few have good libraries.

A Library Organizer, attached to the Ministry of Education and Cultural Affairs, is responsible for the government primary and secondary school libraries and for providing professional advice to the private school libraries. The Library Organizer also advises the Ministry generally on all library matters.

**Special Libraries.** The Mauritius Sugar Industry Research Institute, at Reduit, promotes, by means of research, the technical progress and efficiency of the sugar industry in Mauritius. Its library has 17,500 volumes; holdings of serial publications total 659, of which a large number are received on an exchange basis. The Legislative Council library limits its services to the members of the legislative Assembly. The Supreme Court library, which has a good collection of law books and law reports, is limited to the members of the legal profession.

There are libraries in some government departments, notably the Ministry of Agriculture, the Ministry of Economic Planning and Development, and the Ministry of Health. There are some libraries in foreign missions, the most important of which are the British Council library, situated in Rose-Hill, Le Centre d'Enseignement et de Documentation (the library of the French embassy) in Port-Louis, and the library of the Indian High Commission, also in Port-Louis.

**Libraries for Children.** Apart from the library services for children in schools, each of the five municipal libraries has a children's section. There is also a junior library in Rose-Hill, run by the Ministry of Education and Cultural Affairs. The Bibliothèque Saint Joseph, which caters to children, is a Catholic Church enterprise that started in about 1968. In five parishes there is a children's library in a room on the church precincts, open in the afternoon and run on a purely voluntary basis. A small fee is charged for the loan of books. These libraries are very popular with children, and the number of book loans is very high.

**Association.** The Mauritius Library Association, founded in 1974, numbers about 50 members of the library profession, including 15 librarians who have had their training in countries such as the United Kingdom, France, Canada, India, Jamaica, and Australia. Though booksellers have an association of their own, some members of the Mauritius Association of Booksellers are also members of the Mauritius Library Association.

S. JEAN-FRANÇOIS

# Medical Libraries

PURPOSES

Medical (health sciences) libraries form a distinct group, although they fall within the general heading of special libraries. The main purposes of medical libraries are in three areas, teaching (education), research, and patient care. Some libraries will be involved in all three areas, others in only one or two.

The scope of teaching that medical libraries are required to support increased enormously in the 1970's. With the greater emphasis on public health and the recognition of the impact of the environment on health, the main subjects that now fall within the scope of a medical library include almost every discipline except some of the pure sciences and the arts. With an increased emphasis on the patient and his recovery and rehabilitation, through bibliotherapy, music therapy, and art therapy, even materials in the arts may be collected. As the requirements for continuing education of medical professionals in all health service areas have increased, the demands on the library for support services and materials for such programs have also risen.

The libraries that deal with research similarly serve a wide and varied user population depending on their parent body. Libraries in commercial institutions such as pharmaceutical corporations may have a very narrowly defined role that ties very closely to the research programs of the institution, whereas the library supporting research in a university setting will find that the research topics it supports are very broad and are usually heavily interdisciplinary.

Libraries that are primarily concerned with patient care are to be found in hospitals and such related institu-

McGill University

*The McIntyre Medical Sciences Building houses McGill University's Medical Library in Montreal, Canada.*

tions as chronic care centers, and it has been traditional to think of patient libraries as relating more closely to the public library. With increasing emphasis and awareness of the problems of patient education and patient rights and responsibilities, however, the patient care library has a much wider role and one that is increasing in importance. Moreover, many hospitals find that it is more economical to combine the patient care library with the library services that are provided for the professional staff. The standards of the Joint Commission on the Accreditation of Hospitals have recently been strengthened for hospital libraries and now call for a minimum of professional consultative services on a regular basis if the hospital is not able to employ a full- or part-time professional librarian. The standards also require that the librarian be graduated from a school that has been accredited by the American Library Association and have certification from the Medical Library Association or provide documented equivalent training and/or experience.

Medical librarians are largely alone among professional library groups in the development of certification and recertification programs by their major professional body, the Medical Library Association. The Certification Code, which went into effect on January 1, 1978, calls for recertification of librarians at five-year intervals by completion of a specified number of hours of continuing education programs or by examination. The Medical Library Association, which is the second-oldest U.S. national library association, has developed an extensive continuing education program to serve the needs of its more than 5,000 members, and this program was begun as early as 1964 in its present form. The programs are held annually at the Association's meeting and given regionally, either in conjunction with its regional groups or in cooperation with local library groups. The first international presentation of its courses took place in September 1979 in Helsinki as part of the first regional meeting (for North Europe) of the IFLA Section of Biological and Medical Sciences Libraries.

Medical libraries vary greatly in size and run the gamut from the largest, the National Library of Medicine, located on the campus of the National Institutes of Health in Bethesda, Maryland, to very small working collections in hospitals. The National Library of Medicine plays an important role in setting national and international standards for cataloguing and has a major influence on U.S. libraries in such areas as catalogue organization and the provision of cataloguing information (now available in an on-line form through the services of OCLC, Inc.). It is, of course, not necessarily the size of the collection that guarantees its ability to serve the information needs of its user population effectively but rather the degree to which that collection reflects the scope of the interests of the library's community of users. Attempts have been made to codify the purposes and operation and management of medical school libraries. Medical school libraries also provide a wealth of statistical information about their operations to permit comparative studies and to assist other institutions in keeping pace with general trends in the field. These statistics are published annually.

Medical libraries play a major role in the information transfer process in biomedicine. They form part of a highly structured network of medical libraries that provide basic library services to all health professionals and that are, in the United States, organized on a regional basis. The regionalization and cooperative interaction among medical libraries take the form of improved and speeded document delivery services, coordinated collection development, and the education of the staff of medical libraries.

Library automation began in medical libraries at the beginning of the 1960's, and medical libraries now use automated services very heavily. The world's first on-line bibliographic information-retrieval system in biomedicine began operation in 1968 (after three years of planning and development) under the aegis of the State University of New York. This was followed shortly by the MEDLINE services of the National Library of Medicine, and there are currently a number of sources, both commercial and noncommercial, for searching the world's biomedical and scientific bibliographic information on-line. These services are used extensively in medical libraries throughout the world.

Medical libraries are characterized by their highly developed sense of service, in common with many other special libraries, and do more for their users than has been considered common or proper in many libraries. The tradition that a researcher must perform all of his own library research personally has passed; the time element and the volume of work to be done have changed the perception of what a library may or can do for a user, just as the medical profession has accepted the presence and services of the nurse practitioner and midwife. Medical libraries engage in extensive outreach programs to try to make the task of the health professional in getting and using information as easy as possible. In recent years the highly personalized services of clinical medical librarians have become increasingly common. For those institutions that can afford the expense of the service, the results are gratifying, and health professionals have responded enthusiastically.

On the international scene, the reorganization of the International Federation of Library Associations and Institutions has resulted in the formation of a Section of Biological and Medical Sciences Libraries within the Division of Special Libraries. Besides providing substantive programs at the annual IFLA meetings, the work of the Section aims toward improving reference tools in biomedicine by the compilation of a list of on-line data bases in biomedicine and eventually a world list of biological and medical sciences libraries.

As will be seen from the following sections that provide much more detail about the programs and activities of medical libraries, they have been in the vanguard of progress in the library profession in a number of areas such as automation, research in library management, and provision of services. There is every expectation that such progress will continue. IRWIN H. PIZER

*Pan American Health Organization's Regional Library of Medicine, in São Paolo, Brazil.*

COLLECTIONS

The terms *medical libraries* and *health sciences libraries* have been used rather loosely to define medical center libraries, hospital libraries, and medical school libraries. Although there are general statements concerning collection development that can be attributed to all types of medical libraries, there are differences in policies and methods of collection that depend upon the size and type of the library.

The purpose of any library is service to its community; an essential factor in carrying out this function is adequate resources. Although no library can acquire all the material requested by its users, it should contain at least the primary titles needed to fulfill its mission. H. G. Weiskotten in his *Medical Education in the United States* (1940) stated: "Perhaps no department is more vital to the educational and research programs of the medical school than its library. Indeed, if a medical school is to be appraised by a single criterion, the library might well serve." Although he specifically mentions medical schools, the quote can be applied to all types of medical libraries and their parent institutions. Yet it is very often the library that is poorly financed and/or is the first to have its budget cut in times of budget constraints. The librarian must be in touch with the institution's purpose, philosophy, and activities; without this current knowledge the library cannot meet the changing needs of its users. With the increase in volume of published literature and the escalating prices of materials, it is imperative that the librarian use wisely the dollars allotted to the library.

**Acquisitions Policy.** The preparation of an acquisitions policy is important as a guide in the selection process. The policy should include the definition of any areas in which the library will collect at different levels of sophistication, i.e., graduate versus undergraduate for allied health personnel, or at different levels of support, i.e., exhaustive, comprehensive, educational, working collection. (Exhaustive Collection = collect everything published in a given subject(s) area. Comprehensive = collect all material in a given subject(s) area to support research. Educational = collect material needed to support education function of the institution. Working collection = minimal collection in a subject(s) area—one or two texts, a few primary journals, a reference tool.)

In many libraries the chief librarian does the major part of selection. In other cases the acquisitions librarian does the selection, as well as carrying out the actual procedures involved in acquiring the material. In larger libraries subject bibliographers do the selection, or it is part of the reference librarians' function, or a combination of one or more of the above. Although user input should be encouraged, the librarian should be responsible for the selection of materials. The librarian must prove to the library's users that s/he has the expertise to select materials needed (within budgetary constraints) to support the function of the institution that the library serves.

Weeding of the collection must be considered as an integral part of an acquisitions policy. Not only is weeding necessary because of space limitations in most libraries but out-of-date and little-used materials on shelves tend to diminish the usefulness of the collection.

**Materials.** In any type of medical library the majority of the collection will be journal literature—about two-thirds serials and one-third books. It thus follows that the bulk of the library's acquisitions budget will be used for serials. There are several aids that can be used in selecting serial titles. For the small medical library and/or hospital library there are such tools as Alfred N. Brandon and Dorothy R. Hill, "Selected List of Books and Journals for the Small Medical Library," *Bulletin of the Medical Library Association* (1979), and the list of journals indexed in the *Abridged Index Medicus,* a list of 100 common journals that the National Library of Medicine expects most medical libraries to own. Each library's individual needs must be considered in the selection process. Other aids directed toward hospital, medical school, or other health science libraries will be used. These include the American Hospital Association's *Administrator's Collection* (1978) or Fred Roper et al., *Introduction to Reference Sources in the Health Sciences* (1979).

Larger medical libraries must go beyond these, and for the health sciences library serving medicine, dentistry, nursing, and other allied health fields, the task of selection becomes much more complex. Use of indexing tools, publishers' catalogues, or approval plans may be part of collection development activity.

Although the smaller medical library will have a few reference aids, the larger medical library must have all the major indexing and abstracting tools in the fields served by them. Computer literature searching is a fact of life today, and even the small hospital library has access to MEDLARS by having its own terminal or shared access with other hospital libraries. The larger libraries have access to numerous data bases in addition to those of the National Library of Medicine. *Psychological Abstracts, BIOSIS Previews, Chemical Abstracts, Excerpta Medica,* and *Management Contents* are just a few data bases available and of interest to medical libraries. Use of this service leads to demands upon the library to acquire the items retrieved in the literature search. While interlibrary loan comes into play here, the librarian will be aware of what titles are being requested most frequently, to identify those that should be added to the collection.

The various professional associations issue publications that can be of great value to the hospital library, particularly those of the American Hospital Association, the American Medical Association, and the National League for Nursing. The U.S. Department of Health, Education and Welfare (HEW) issues a tremendous amount of material in the health care field, as do state and local government agencies. The *Monthly Catalog of Government Publications* is a tool that can be used for selection of government documents, and many government publications are free to libraries.

Every medical library will contain some historical, archival, and/or rare book collection. Very often the library becomes the depository for the archives of the institution, although recently institutions have realized the importance of maintaining archives properly and have employed an archivist to collect, maintain, and house the archives. In the hospital setting the archivist's position is usually separate from the library, while in the university-affiliated health sciences library the archivist may be a member of the library staff. The archives can be a separate section in the library or part of the special collections area. The historical rare book collection of the small medical library will be minimal and probably will have been acquired by gift. The size of the historical and/or rare book collections in larger health sciences libraries can vary depending upon the interest of its users in this area, budget for purchase of this type of material, and gifts acquired by the library; many health sciences libraries have substantial collections of rare materials. Many health sciences libraries have established Friends of the Library groups, which often contribute single titles, collections, or funds to purchase rare books.

The acquisition of nonprint material by health sciences libraries increased tremendously in the 1970's, an increase evident in both hospital library and the larger health sciences library. In some institutions the audiovisual section is not an integral part of the library but part of a division of medical education or attached to an AV production unit within the institution, although the collecting, housing, and servicing of AV materials are appropriate functions for the library. Audiovisual materials include a variety of formats—films, slides, videotapes, filmstrips, models, and other forms in use in health care applications. Various bibliographic tools are available for selection. AV-Line, from the National Library of Medicine, lists audiovisual titles with full cataloguing information; all materials listed on AV-Line have been previewed and rated by selected previewers, and the rating for each title is provided. The National Medical Audiovisual Center in Bethesda and the National Audiovisual Center in Washington, D.C., issue catalogues of AV material that can be used for selection. There are also some commercial catalogues available, and some medical schools that have developed large AV collections issue catalogues of their holdings, such as Southern Illinois University, University of Connecticut, and Indiana University.

**Cooperation.** Although cooperative activities among medical libraries are discussed elsewhere, it should be noted here that cooperation in collection development is vital in view of the growth in the volume of published literature, increased costs, and reduced or stable budgets. The Regional Medical Library (RML) Network concept of the National Library of Medicine has encouraged the development of consortia among hospital libraries so that hospital libraries could develop their collections and share resources. The library literature is filled with references to various networks being formed by university libraries in order to share resources and cataloguing. Cooperative acquisition of periodicals is somewhat easier to achieve than cooperative acquisitions of monographs, with union lists of serials particularly helpful in deciding whether or not to acquire a given title. In some instances libraries divide acquiring material by subject or language. By cooperating in this manner libraries are free to purchase what they want but Library A can eliminate certain titles or languages, knowing that Library B will get them and share those titles, and vice-versa. Thus, more resources are available within a given region. The latest development in serials is the possibility of the establishment of a National Periodicals Center, whose purposes as stated in the draft legislation proposal of July 1979 are:

1. To provide reliable and timely document delivery from a comprehensive collection of periodical literature
2. To complement and augment local, state, regional, and other periodical resources

National Library of Medicine

*The National Library of Medicine. At left is the Library's Lister Hill National Center for Biomedical Communications.*

Wayne State University

*The Shiffman Medical Library serves Detroit's Wayne State University.*

3. To contribute to the preservation of periodical materials

The NPC will include all subject areas except clinical medicine. Medical librarians are concerned about this and have raised questions, particularly about how the NPC will relate to the RML network and how nonmedical libraries will obtain medical materials. Also of concern are such issues as copyright and charges for loans.

Selection of quality titles requires time and a knowledge of appropriate literature. As financial resources for building collections diminish, more emphasis is being placed on analysis and evaluation of the library's collection. Use studies are being utilized to determine which titles are the most heavily used. The library's collection, large or small, must be made known to the users of the library so that the collection can be fully utilized. Acquisitions lists, newsletters, and library lectures are some methods of informing the user about the library and its collection.

Owsei Temkin in his address at the opening of the Medical College of Ohio library said,

> For a library is not only a gathering point for students, professors, practicing physicians, and others interested

in medicine. It is also the point where past, present, and future meet. The library makes available knowledge accumulated up to the present day, knowledge that we assimilate with an eye to things to be done in practice or in research, be it today, tomorrow, or at some distant time. Thus, a medical library is a monument to the Hippocratic aphorism: "Life is short, the art is long." It is a monument to the short lives of those whose deeds and thoughts have passed into the stream of the medical art that flows on endlessly.

CECILE E. KRAMER

LAWS AND LEGISLATION

**International Scene.** The international awareness generated by copyright revision and the trend toward development of national networking information systems has heightened the legislative consciousness of medical librarians throughout the world. Traditionally, library legislation made a positive impact on medical libraries by engendering public support for health information services. However, in the mid-1970's medical librarians began to feel the negative effect of copyright revision because it threatened the freedom with which library services have usually been rendered. Recently the question over legality of public access to data bases has cast another gloomy shadow on the prospect of developing national networking systems.

Legislative interest in medical librarianship already exists in the United States and is growing rapidly in other countries. In 1977 the Medical Library Association (MLA) moved toward steady rather than spasmodic involvement in legislative affairs by expanding the role of its Legislation Committee. In 1979 the 45th International Federation of Library Associations and Institutions (IFLA) Council and Conference, which met in Copenhagen, chose the theme, "Library Legislation and Management." The intent of the IFLA program was to share information on legislative issues affecting numerous library associations. Obviously, the concerns for legislative solutions to problems of disseminating information throughout the world extend beyond the discipline of medical librarianship. However, the IFLA papers raised issues that need more specific exploration in the literature and further discussion in future international meetings.

Stimulated by both national concern and Unesco, a number of countries have been establishing national networking systems for information services. In the networking systems health and biomedicine are usually handled as an individual section. The principles for establishment of these systems usually emanate from executive decree or legislative authority. This subject still remains as unexplored territory in the literature, and therefore, developing a cohesive description is beyond the limits of this presentation. However, it can be noted that in a 1975 National Science Foundation report entitled "Scientific and Technical Information Services in Eight Latin American Countries," Scott Adams outlined the work of various technical assistance agencies, such as Unesco's Division for Scientific and Technological Information and Documentation (UNISIST), Department of Libraries, Documentation and Archives (DBA), the Pan American Health Organization (PAHO), and others that have achieved considerable progress in enhancing the legal and political environmental aspects of information transfer. While the approach of the eight individual countries that he cites varies slightly, the ultimate purposes are to develop national linkages between scientific and technical information in a realistic manner and to implement multilateral agreements for regional cooperation.

The PAHO attempt to create regional services at the Biblioteca Regional de Medicina (BIREME) in São Paulo, Brazil, has been reasonably effective. The U.S. National Library of Medicine served as a technical consultant to assist Argentina, Peru, Chile, Columbia, Uruguay, and Venezuela to establish a regional medical library to serve as backup resource to the member states. Services include interlibrary loans, exchange of journals, training of librarians, and access to MEDLINE computer bibliographic searches. With the demonstrated success of BIREME and assistance from the World Health Organization (WHO), other regional approaches are being attempted.

In a paper presented at the 1979 IFLA meeting, Estelle Brodman reported the importance for joint action of biomedical librarians through organizations such as IFLA, Unesco, ESCAP (Economic Social Commission for Asia and the Pacific), WHO, and MLA. In further discussion Brodman added that the major concern of developing countries is to feed and clothe the population; therefore, creating strong libraries naturally has lower priority. For this reason regional approaches and cooperative programs seem the most economic and efficient solution to information transfer. The trend toward creation of regional medical library groups is growing rapidly. However, legislative efforts have been generally haphazard in the international arena, and this has resulted in inconsistent support by individual countries and organizations

**The United States.** *The National Library of Medicine.* In a tripartite governmental structure such as that of the United States, authority is given by the legislature to develop national programs through congressional enactment of legislation that is signed into law by the President. The system works efficiently in the United States because once laws are passed, Congress often appropriates funds to conduct the programs. This legislative basis has been the mechanism for developing national information and library services in the health sciences, and it has been the primary means of modernizing medical library services throughout the nation. Generally, Congress has consistently supported health and library legislation that has enabled the National Library of Medicine (NLM) to develop networking and cooperative programs at a steady pace that can serve as a model to other countries.

The basis for support of a national library of medicine in the U.S. dates back to 1836 with the collection in the Surgeon General's Office. In 1922 that library became the Army Medical Library, and in 1952 it was changed to the Armed Forces Medical Library. As a result of legislation sponsored by Senators Lister Hill and John F. Kennedy in 1956, the Armed Forces Library became the National Library of Medicine. It was then authorized as the nation's major collector and distributor of health sciences information. Since that time various pieces of legislation have expanded the authority of the NLM. After Congress authorized funds to build the library on the campus of the National Institutes of Health in Bethesda, Maryland, it enacted the Medical Library Assistance Act of 1965 (MLAA) authorizing the NLM to develop a grant program to provide aid to the nation's medical libraries. In 1968 the National Medical Audiovisual Center and the Lister Hill National Center for Biomedical Communications were established by statute as part of the NLM.

Funds appropriated by Congress have supported the NLM's bibliographic contributions in print and nonprint format. Most notable have been the preparation of *Index Medicus,* the comprehensive bibliography of medical literature, and development of MEDLARS (Medical Literature Analysis and Retrieval System), the computer bibliographic service from which the major data bases of NLM have been created. Another on-line bibliographic retrieval service named TOXLINE is a result of the Toxicology Information Program established at NLM in 1967. Recently NLM created the Toxicology Data Bank, which stores and retrieves information about toxic substances.

The basis for the regional approach to networking and cooperation was authorized by the MLAA in 1965.

This legislation set into motion a series of programs that strengthened the nation's medical libraries and enabled essential coordination and cooperation.

*The Medical Library Assistance Act.* Several reports and conferences conducted in the mid-1960's substantiated the fact that American medical libraries needed to be improved so they could keep pace with increased information demands of health professionals. Passage of a vital piece of legislation in October, 1965, known as the Medical Library Assistance Act, Public Law 89–291 (MLAA), responded to this need by authorizing the NLM to administer an extramural program to upgrade medical libraries and to organize regional and local relationships by encouraging sharing of skills and resources. This legislation became the basis for more clearly defined roles and responsibilities between the medical library community and the NLM.

The underlying philosophy of this legislative program was reflected in future extensions of the MLAA with only minor amendments. To fulfill the changing needs of health professionals, the MLAA was periodically revised, consolidated, and extended. Overall, however, the Act's flexibility has allowed the administering agency to make modifications and to implement new programs without changing the legislative language. (See Table 1).

Considered noncontroversial legislation, the MLAA has traditionally enjoyed strong congressional support. Extensions have been easily obtained, but full funding or even adequate appropriation levels to fulfill the expectation of the Act are yet to be achieved. Although a good beginning was made toward achieving the tenets of the Act, limited funds have prevented more substantial accomplishments. During the past few years moratoria and terminations of essential library programs were a result of low funding levels. In addition, inflation multiplied the effect of inadequate funding.

In administering the MLAA programs, the NLM monitors the changing needs of health professionals and the medical library community to assure that they are fulfilled. Although Table 2 indicates little fluctuation during a 14-year span, in reality some subtle programmatic changes have occurred. For example, training support shifted from medical librarians to computer specialists in medicine, and a recently developed research program for computers in medicine with specially earmarked funds has been launched. Thus, new precedents are constantly being established that can potentially change the manner in which the Act is administered.

The active programs authorized through the MLAA that most directly affect medical librarianship are the Regional Medical Library, Resource Improvement, Training, and Research Grants programs.

*The Regional Medical Library Program* (RML) is noted for its mainstay support of document delivery to health professionals. Through existing libraries the NLM developed a network with hierarchical interconnections that made cooperative service and resource sharing viable. A system for interlibrary lending and exchanges was established in 11 regions. (See Table 3.)

*The Resource Improvement Grants Program.* Another vital component of the MLAA, this program was originally conceived as a means of supplementing library support. Grants were awarded on a formula basis according to budget size and number of patrons served. In 1970 the program was split into Resource Improvement and Resource Project Grants. The Improvement grants were designed to assist small hospital libraries. Of the great variety of activities funded through the Resource Project Grants, probably the most innovative aspect was consortium development for sharing of resources.

*The Training Program* has undergone a series of evolutionary steps designed to improve the skills of health professionals involved in transfer of information. In 1965 this program concentrated on sponsoring medical library trainees at the undergraduate and graduate levels. In the 1970's additional training programs were supported in response to manpower needs for biomedical information personnel to assist ongoing scientific research. Eventually the medical library trainee program was phased out and replaced by training for health professionals in computer sciences and technology. In 1978 a small trial program was established to support medical library management interns.

*The Research, Development, and Demonstration Program* supports projects that improve storage and retrieval of biomedical information, communication of biomedical research, effectiveness of biomedical teaching, and communications of health care. Largely through this program, support is given to advance the current state of the art of information sciences related to health. As a result of two conferences conducted in 1974 and 1975, future research goals have been emphasizing the need for health practitioners to retrieve actual information rather than references to documents.

*The Research Support for Computers in Medicine Program* was recommended in January 1978 by a task force on review of the NLM's research grant program. This new program was designed to foster the growth and advance of computer sciences in the health field and to promote research in an environment conducive to interdisciplinary collaboration.

**The Copyright Act of 1976.** Public Law 94–553, signed on October 19, 1976, by President Gerald R. Ford and in force as of January 1, 1978, represents one of the most recent controversial pieces of legislation to affect medical libraries. Although the antiquated copyright law of 1909 was in need of revision, the ambiguities and inconsistencies of the new law created so many possibilities for varying interpretations by librarians, publishers, and producers of print and nonprint materials that guidelines representing different points of view were prepared by associations of each special-interest group. The MLA responded to the needs of its membership by appointing a subcommittee to draft a copyright brochure entitled *The Copyright Law and the Health Sciences Librarian.* The brochure was prepared to assist medical librarians in applying the revised copyright law to their individual settings.

In addition, the MLA presented its position to Congress and worked with the Council of National Library Associations' (CNLA) Committee on Copyright Law Practice and Implementation to present testimony to the National Commission on New Technological Uses of

**Table 1. Renewals of the Medical Library Assistance Act**

| Years Implemented | Title of Acts | Dates Signed |
|---|---|---|
| 1966 | Medical Library Assistance Act of 1965, P.L. 89–291 | October 22, 1965 |
| 1971 | Medical Library Assistance Extension Act of 1970, P.L. 92–212 | March 13, 1970 |
| 1974 | Health Programs Extension Act of 1973, P.L. 93–45 | June 18, 1973 |
| 1975 | Heath Services Research, Health Statistics and Medical Libraries Act of 1974, P.L. 93–353 | July 23, 1974 |
| 1977 | Biomedical Research Extension Act of 1977, P.L. 95–83 | August 1, 1977 |
| 1978 | Biomedical Research Extension Amendments of 1978, Title II of the Community Mental Health Centers Extension Act of 1978, P.L. 95–622 | November 9, 1978 |

**Table 2. Amounts Awarded by Program under the MLAA for FY 1966–79 (dollars in thousands)**

| | 1966 | 1967 | 1968 | 1969 | 1970 | 1971 | 1972 | 1973 | 1974 | 1975 | 1976 | 1977 | 1978 | 1979[1] |
|---|---|---|---|---|---|---|---|---|---|---|---|---|---|---|
| Construction | $ 0 | $ 0 | $10,000 | $1,250 | $ 0 | $ 0 | $ 0 | $ 0 | $ 0 | $ 0 | $ 0 | $ 0 | $ 0 | $ 0 |
| Training[2] | 432 | 812 | 922 | 1,310 | 983 | 1,000 | 1,234 | 720 | 720 | 891 | 1,389 | 1,208 | 1,360 | 1,472 |
| Special scientific projects | 34 | 33 | 54 | 85 | 5 | 5 | 100 | 76 | 95 | 153 | 72 | 109 | 248 | 215 |
| Research | 741 | 1,357 | 1,473 | 1,321 | 990 | 590 | 640 | 665 | 900 | 1,292 | 1,353 | 1,180 | 1,110 | 1,592 |
| Publications | 745 | 588 | 582 | 300 | 267 | 280 | 311 | 389 | 340 | 614 | 617 | 738 | 1,050 | 764 |
| Resource grants | 24 | 3,328 | 3,548 | 2,800 | 2,105 | 2,231 | 2,505 | 2,298 | 2,211 | 1,469 | 726 | 1,773 | 2,078 | 2,008 |
| Regional medical libraries | 0 | 105 | 680 | 2,088 | 1,807 | 1,886 | 2,047 | 2,501 | 3,104 | 2,194 | 3,351 | 3,086 | 3,018 | 2,849 |
| Total | $1,976 | $6,223 | $17,259 | $9,154 | $6,157 | $5,992 | $6,837 | $6,649 | $7,370 | $6,613 | $7,508 | $8,094 | $8,864 | $8,900 |

[1]Rounded figures.

[2]Support in the later years reflects an effort to promote the integration of computer technology into all phases of clincial medicine.

Copyrighted Works (CONTU). MLA agreed to abide by the existing law until the review scheduled for five years from the law's taking effect.

Because document delivery services in the health sciences are largely handled through photocopied articles, the current regulations may have an adverse effect on health libraries, their constituents, and those who subscribe to health publications. If the cooperative arrangements built by the RML network are cut through restrictions imposed by the Copyright Law, the existing transfer of biomedical information will be directly impeded. This could result in increased subscriptions and operating costs for health sciences libraries.

**Other National Health Legislation.** It has become more and more apparent to American medical librarians that other pieces of health legislation can restrict or support their ability to provide information services. A selected number of acts are cited here because of their direct impact. The National Health Planning and Resource Development Act (Public Law 93–641) created Health Systems Agencies (HSA) to plan for the nation's health care system. This legislation opened the possibility for a close alliance between HSA's and RML services to sponsor innovative library programs and to prevent unnecessary duplication. Medical librarians have played a role in providing HSA staff with information related to data gathering and research. Renewal legislation was anticipated in the fall of 1979.

The National Consumer Health Information and Health Promotion Act (Public Law 94–317), administered through the Bureau of Health Education, Center for Disease Control (CDC), authorized a program to support development of patient/consumer education materials. Although Title XVII applies to the information services, it remains unfunded, and in 1979 the CDC began negotiating contracts to develop resources in patient education.

The Comprehensive Health Manpower Training Act of 1971 (Public Law 92–157) authorized establishment of Area Health Education Centers. The program was designed to decentralize education and training programs for health professionals and to improve their distribution in underserved areas. Medical librarians have played a key role in providing information services to satellite facilities of university programs and developing a communication network to link university resources to the community.

Hospital Cost Containment bills were unsuccessfully introduced in the 95th Congress. Despite raised expectations of the White House, President Carter was unable to acquire passage of an act before Congress adjourned in 1978. Hospital librarians believe cost containment is already exercised to the ultimate through resource-sharing programs. Therefore, any further attempts to reduce library operating budgets would detrimentally affect services.

Recently the Department of Health, Education, and Welfare took another approach to adhering cost containment by issuing new regulations implementing Section 223 of Public Law 92-603 (Amendment to the Social Security Act, Title XVIII), redefining criteria for Medicare reimbursements. The criteria established based on bed size and geographic location impose hardships on tertiary-care teaching hospitals that may ultimately affect library budgets.

**General Legislation Affecting Medical Librarians.** The concern of medical librarians with respect to general legislation that impacts on libraries also reflects the interests and needs of health care consumers and health professionals. Three important acts are outlined briefly.

The White House Conference on Libraries and Information Services, held November 15–19, 1979, and authorized as part of Public Law 93-568, is one of the major pieces of legislation focusing on national library issues. Medical librarians served on advisory, planning, and preconference committees at the state and national level. Important resolutions recommending national information networks and national library programs were endorsed by the conferees in 1979.

The Postal Amendments of 1976 (Public Law 94-421) made it possible for publishers and distributors to mail materials to libraries at the fourth-class rate. However, an oversight made no provision for materials to be returned at the same rate. Passage of the Postal Service Reform Act of 1979 (H.R. 79) proposing extensions of book rate and fourth-class library rate for materials mailed from libraries can rectify the past problem, and this is important to the cooperative MLA Exchange program.

The Public Printing Reorganization Act of 1979 proposes a revision of Title 44 of the *U.S. Code* to reorganize the structure and operations of the Government Printing Office. The three major concerns of medical librarians are: (1) the replacement of the Joint Committee on Printing by a presidentially appointed seven-voting-member Board of Directors, (2) any potential transfer of control of health-related audiovisuals away from the National Medical Audiovisual Center, (3) any transfer away from NLM of administrative control of its data bases. Measures that could restrict access to health information are an anathema to the medical library profession.

The famous Williams and Wilkins suit of 1968 alleging copyright infringement by the NLM and NIH stimulated greater legislative awareness among medical librarians that was enhanced during preparation of the Copyright Act of 1976. Its impact was felt throughout the world. Since then, medical librarians have recognized the need to maintain vigilance over impending legislation, to sponsor supportive library legislation, and to be knowledgeable about health legislation that impacts on the mission of providing health information.

**Table 3. Eleven Regional Medical Libraries and States**

| Region | States | Operational |
|---|---|---|
| 1—New England<br>New England Regional Medical Library<br>The Francis A. Countway Library of Medicine<br>Boston, Massachusetts | Connecticut<br>Maine<br>Massachusetts<br>New Hampshire<br>Rhode Island<br>Vermont | Oct. 1967 |
| 2—New York<br>New York and New Jersey Regional Medical Library<br>New York Academy of Medicine<br>New York, New York | New Jersey<br>New York | Feb. 1970 |
| 3—Mid-Eastern<br>Mid-Eastern Regional Medical Library<br>College of Physicians of Philadelphia<br>Philadelphia, Pennsylvania | Delaware<br>Pennsylvania | July 1968 |
| 4—Mid-Atlantic<br>Mid-Atlantic Regional Medical Library<br>National Library of Medicine<br>Bethesda, Maryland | Maryland<br>North Carolina<br>Virginia<br>Washington, D.C.<br>West Virginia | N/A |
| 5—East Central<br>Kentucky-Ohio-Michigan Regional Medical Library<br>Wayne State University<br>Detroit, Michigan | Kentucky<br>Michigan<br>Ohio | April 1969 |
| 6—Southeastern<br>Southeastern Regional Medical Library<br>A. W. Calhoun Medical Library<br>Woodruff Research Building<br>Emory University<br>Atlanta, Georgia | Alabama<br>Florida<br>Georgia<br>Mississippi<br>Puerto Rico<br>South Carolina<br>Tennessee | Jan. 1970 |
| 7—Midwest<br>Midwest Regional Medical Library<br>The John Crerar Library<br>Chicago, Illinois<br>(University of Illinois at the Medical Center—1/80) | Illinois<br>Indiana<br>Iowa<br>Minnesota<br>North Dakota<br>Wisconsin | Nov. 1968—Dec. 1979 |
| 8—Midcontinental<br>Mid-Continental Regional Medical Library<br>University of Nebraska Medical Center<br>Omaha, Nebraska | Colorado<br>Kansas<br>Missouri<br>Nebraska<br>South Dakota<br>Utah<br>Wyoming | July 1970 |
| 9—South Central<br>South Central Regional Medical Library<br>University of Texas<br>Health Science Center at Dallas<br>Dallas, Texas | Arkansas<br>Louisiana<br>New Mexico<br>Oklahoma<br>Texas | Feb. 1970 |
| 10—Pacific Northwest<br>Pacific Northwest Regional Health Sciences Library<br>University of Washington<br>Seattle, Washington | Alaska<br>Idaho<br>Montana<br>Oregon<br>Washington | Oct. 1968 |
| 11—Pacific Southwest<br>Pacific Southwest Regional Medical Library, Center for Health Science<br>University of California<br>Los Angeles, California | Arizona<br>California<br>Hawaii<br>Nevada | Sept. 1969 |

## REFERENCES

Scott Adams, *Scientific and Technical Information Services in Eight Latin American Countries: Developments Technical Assistance Opportunities for Cooperation,* National Science Foundation, NTIS #PB253 202 (1975), provides comprehensive background on establishment of national information systems in eight Latin American countries.

Estelle Brodman, "Biomedical Library Management and Legislation in Developing Countries in Southeast Asia," paper presented at IFLA Congress 1979, Copenhagen, Denmark, makes numerous recommendations to IFLA on joint actions to aid biomedical libraries in developing countries.

Arthur J. Broering, "Medical Library Resource Grants: The Past and the Future," *Bulletin of the Medical Library Association* (1971), reviews progress of the resource grants funded through the MLAA in 1970.

Martin M. Cummings and Mary E. Corning, "The Medical Library Assistance Act: An analysis of the NLM Extramural Programs 1965–1970," *Bulletin of the Medical Library Association* (1971); detailed description of the administration and implementation of the MLAA.

Department of Health, Education, and Welfare, Public Health Service, National Institutes of Health, *Communication in the Service of American Health . . . A Bicentennial Report from the National Library of Medicine,* DHEW Publication No. (NIH) 76256 (1976); excellent historical background that includes establishment of the Extramural Programs and the international impact of NLM.

"Renewal of the Medical Library Assistance Act," *Bulletin of the Medical Library Association* (1978), outlines the recommendations of the MLA Legislation Committee for extension of the MLAA in 1978.

NAOMI C. BROERING

## SERVICES

The contemporary health science library offers its users a myriad of innovative services that are designed to meet the information needs of the health professional engaged in patient care, biomedical and related research, and education. It has placed special emphasis upon computerized information retrieval, extension and outreach programs, document delivery, library instruction, and audiovisual services. The contemporary health science library also is responsive to societal needs and has expanded the scope and breadth of user services to accommodate the information needs of the sophisticated health consumer who emerged in the late 1970's. An overview of the development and implementation of public services in the health science library provides a foundation for reviewing the dynamic array of services that are available to library users today.

Prior to the 1920's medical librarians were employed primarily to acquire, organize and maintain collections of medical literature. Only the physician who provided economic support to the library was entitled to use the collection. In these libraries, then commonly referred to as "doctors' libraries," it was the physician who independently accessed and interpreted the medical literature. As the size of medical library collections reached the point when the typical user encountered difficulty in exploiting the available resources, the physician found it necessary to rely upon the librarian for assistance, and user services programs evolved.

During the 1920's medical librarians, employed by private medical society libraries and in the libraries of the sizable academic institutions, provided substantial reference services to users. Noteworthy was the exceptional situation at the American College of Surgeons in Philadelphia, which in 1926 had ten employees to handle reference services for 6,000 members.

Document delivery also received early attention. In the 1920's the American Medical Association (AMA), the American Dental Association (ADA), and other society libraries distributed "package libraries" to members. The package library consisted of selected reprints relevant to the member's information query. (The ADA's Bureau of Library Services continues to maintain this popular service on a worldwide basis to members.) In 1928 the New York Academy of Medicine began operation of a delivery

Los Angeles County Public Library

*Consumer Health Information Program and Services (CHIPS), of the Los Angeles County Public Library and the Harbor-UCLA Medical Center, uses bilingual volunteers to answer or refer health questions from the community.*

service for its members who resided in the New York metropolitan area. Thus, the Academy took the library to the membership. As librarians gained familiarity with user needs, they began to investigate the resources of other medical libraries to supplement local holdings and subsequently laid the foundation for interlibrary resource sharing.

During the years following World War II, monumental progress was achieved in biomedical research and technology. New branches of medicine were born, particularly in program areas that received heavy government funding (e.g., aerospace medicine, nuclear medicine, etc.). A direct result of these developments was the generation of recorded information with an unprecedented momentum. The medical library exerted every possible resource to backup the health scientist's research efforts; this was the era of unlimited reference service. Nevertheless, the medical library community realized that in order to cope effectively with the rampant growth of biomedical literature and to render comprehensive user services to a clientele with expanding interests and needs, mechanized methods for information storage and retrieval were mandated.

**On-Line Services.** Health professionals were the first group of library users to realize, on a large-scale basis, the benefits of computerized information storage and retrieval systems. In response to the call for improved bibliographic retrieval systems in the late 1950's, the National Library of Medicine (NLM) in Bethesda, Maryland, developed and mounted MEDLARS (*MED*ical *L*iterature *A*nalysis and *R*etrival *S*ystem). From 1964, when MEDLARS became operational, until 1971, when MEDLINE (*MED*LARS on-*LINE*) became available, health professionals' requests were processed against the data base in batch mode. Since 1971 the number of MEDLINE terminal locations has increased dramatically. Much of this growth has been in the hospital setting. From a total of 120 institutional users of MEDLINE in mid-1973, the user population grew to 1,003 domestic users and 189 foreign terminal locations in August 1979. Health science libraries that serve academic institutions and major research facilities also commonly use other data bases, in the social, physical, and behavioral sciences.

The capability of searching the health science literature by computer has enabled the library to expand the scope of reference and interlibrary loan services. The primary application of on-line systems remains the production of bibliographies, tailored to the user's specific information request. However, on-line systems have also revolutionized current awareness services; user profiles can be stored in the search system that automatically generates periodic updates (usually monthly). These printouts furnish the user with current citations well in advance of their appearance in the printed indexes. Many of the data bases accessed by the health science library contain abstracts of articles. These abstracts, which frequently assist the health professional in deciding if the complete article should be consulted, are particularly popular with residents who are preparing for patient rounds. Both health science librarians and library users have come to view automated search services as a tool that supplements, but does not replace, manual reference services.

**Reference and Outreach Services.** Users of health science libraries find that reference services have been designed to furnish timely, accurate, and relevant responses to their queries. Medical librarians have formal training in health science bibliography. They communicate fluently using concise medical terminology and display a solid knowledge of biomedical concepts and processes when interpreting and analyzing the library's information resources. Like other types of special libraries, the health science library performs in-depth reference services for the user. Frequently the librarian assumes the major responsibility for locating, evaluating, and summarizing the literature. Typically, library staff members verify citations, compile bibliographies, provide Selective Dissemination of Information (SDI) services, make referrals for translations, and respond to reference questions at all levels, simple to complex. The primary users of the health science library have come to expect the provision of these basic services. No review of these services will be furnished here. Instead, an overview of several newer user services, which incorporate the basic reference activities, will be given.

Today's health science librarians assume an active role in the information transfer process. Perhaps no one program illustrates this philosophy better than the Clinical Medical Librarian (CML) program, wherein the librarian, as a member of the health care delivery team, interacts directly with health professionals in the patient care setting. The CML makes patient rounds with the medical staff and assesses their information needs as they arise. Upon returning to the library, the CML searches the health science literature using manual or automated retrieval systems, evaluates articles for relevancy of content, and forwards photocopies of the selected articles to the health professionals. While the medical staff may request that the CML research a specific topic, questions are often anticipated, and the CML provides information before it is requested. User evaluations of the Clinical Medical Librarian programs reveal that interns and residents particularly find value and merit in having the information specialist readily available to assist in determining information needs and providing immediate solutions.

Another user service that supplements educational efforts and relates directly to the provision of better patient care is Literature Attached to Charts (LATCH). At the medical staff's request (usually submitted by telephone), the health science librarian selects and locates current literature on some aspect of a patient's illness. Photocopies of the articles are then sent to the hospital, where they become part of a patient's chart. This program allows any individual reviewing the patient's case, whether as a primary physician or as a consultant, to have immediate access to pertinent background information.

A third example of taking library services to the health community is the Circuit Rider Librarian program. This librarian travels from one library to another in order to provide reference support to the personnel in health care institutions that are unable to support a full- or even part-time professional librarian. In addition, Circuit Riders provide health professionals with access to the regional interlibrary loan network and collect and process materials for the individual library's collection. Circuit

Riders, usually based in large academic health science libraries, also serve as liaisons between the remote user and the library sponsoring the program. Thus, they can rely on comprehensive health science collections to resolve complex user questions.

The contemporary health science library has expanded its service population to include professional laypersons (lawyers, environmentalists, etc.) and the general public. The consumer health education movement, brought about by increased emphasis on "informed consent" and patient rights, has activated a strong plea from the general public for access to health-related information. The health science librarian possesses the expertise to disseminate biomedical information, and the provision of user services to the public appears to be a logical extension of existing activities.

Two successful projects serve as prototypes for establishing viable reference and referral services for the public. The Community Health Information Network (CHIN) is a cooperative program between Mount Auburn Hospital in Cambridge, Massachusetts, and six area public library systems. The joining of collections and the sharing of personnel resources facilitate the dissemination of information at the appropriate level of sophistication. The individual with more sophisticated health information needs may obtain reference services directly from the hospital library. A project coordinator, stationed at the hospital library, assists in identifying accurate health information materials for the non-health professional. The second program, CHIPS (Consumer Health Information Program and Services/Salud y Bienestar), is a bilingual consumer health information and referral service. Working together, the Los Angeles County Carson Regional Library and the Los Angeles County Harbor General Hospital Regional Medical Library make services available to a population of over 2,000,000 people of multiethnic backgrounds. Activities include the selection and purchase of health education materials, the establishment of a joint interlibrary loan program that benefits the users of both libraries, the maintenance of a clearinghouse for brochures, display materials, posters, etc., and the operation of a TEL-MED system. This latter service permits the public to listen to tapes on health-related topics over the telephone. Components of both projects have been replicated by health science libraries nationwide.

Hospitalized patients also need health information in order to make sound judgments related to their personal care and course of treatment. Many health science libraries offer patient education services; print and audiovisual materials are provided that teach the patient and the family about pathological conditions and self care. The U.S. Veterans Administration Hospital libraries conduct one of the most extensive patient-education programs in existence.

**Document Delivery Services.** A large majority of the users of the health science library judge the library services principally upon the accessibility of materials and the success of document delivery services. Failure to obtain required documents can seriously impede the progress of research projects, patient care, and educational activities. Most circulation services in the health science library closely resemble those employed by other types of libraries. However, the exceptional component of document delivery services to the user of the health science library is the extensive provision of interlibrary loan (ILL) services.

The bibliographies produced from on-line data bases have stimulated users to request an all-time high volume of items through interlibrary loan. Users have come to expect that if the library supplies the citation, it should also be responsible for supplying the document cited. Fortunately, the advent of automated information retrieval was accompanied by the formalization of the interlibrary loan network for health science libraries in the United States. The Medical Library Assistance Act of 1965 authorized the Regional Medical Library Program, which divided the country into 11 regions. The National Library of Medicine serves as the Regional Medical Library (RML) in the mid-Atlantic area, and ten large biomedical libraries have been given this responsibility in the remaining geographical areas. The RML program has encouraged local resource sharing through prescribed referral channels. NLM serves as a national backup resource for those requests that cannot be filled at the regional level. Thus, this program ensures that the library user's ILL request will be routed and filled in an orderly and expeditious fashion.

Wayne State University

*A reference interview is the starting point for the complex research conducted in medical libraries.*

In addition to the RML network, health science librarians may tap many other sources and networks. Medium-sized and smaller health science libraries report that consortia participation has improved their ability to fill user requests. Many librarians willingly forward user requests to national medical libraries in foreign countries when the material is not available domestically. An important international resource is the British Library Lending Division, Boston Spa, which exchanges photoduplications for prepurchased coupons, thus eliminating the necessity of paying for single documents in foreign currency. When rapid and guaranteed delivery is crucial in supplying a user with a journal article, some librarians rely on commercial services such as the Institute for Scientific Information's OATS (Original Article Tear Sheets) program.

Health science libraries use a variety of methods to expedite document delivery requests. Union lists in print, microfiche, and on-line formats provide necessary holdings and location information. Libraries that process a high number of ILL's transmit requests via TWX (Tele-Typewriter Exchange Network) machines or through the facilities of OCLC, Inc. The 60 member libraries of The Medical Library Center of New York (MLCNY) forward requests and documents to each other via a daily delivery service. An MLCNY request that is submitted and accepted by telephone is processed so quickly that the material can be in the hands of the user the next day. Recently, health science libraries have begun to experiment with telefacsimile equipment as a mode of transmitting hard copy instantly over long geographic distances.

The combination of networking and telecommunications has enabled the health science library to achieve a high success rate in filling document delivery requests. Health science libraries have been pioneers in network development, and acknowledgments from the health care community reinforce continued efforts toward advancement of document delivery services.

**Instructional Services.** An analysis of user services offered by medical school libraries in 1968 indicated that instructional services were generally poorly developed. Since the initiation of public services in the health science library, instruction to users on a one-to-one basis has been commonplace. However, programs that have been developed since 1968 show that the library can and does provide effective instruction to health science students in the areas of research methodology and literature evaluation, especially when it is integrated within the school's curriculum. Health science librarians also are invited to deliver guest lectures in the classroom in order to prepare students for an upcoming research assignment. Course content may include the detailed analysis of biomedical reference materials, application of computerized data bases, use of a controlled thesaurus, methodology for conducting a review of the literature, format of a bibliography, or writing of an abstract. Courses aimed at developing library skills of research assistants or other ancillary personnel, often the heaviest library users, also have proved to be worthwhile endeavors.

**Audiovisual Services.** As audiovisual resources assumed an increasingly important role in the education and the continuing education of the health professional, health science libraries concurrently strengthened the scope of audiovisual services offered. During the 1950's and the 1960's, medical librarians debated the merits of incorporating multimedia services into the library operation versus housing media in an autonomous learning resources center. In the 1970's the medical librarian came to view audiovisual and other nonprint media as viable resources for providing curricular support in the education of health professionals. Multimedia services are now provided by most health science libraries, large and small.

Typically, the library user can expect comprehensive multimedia reference service including assistance with arrangements for previewing sessions, compilation of bibliographies, and selection of materials. Undergraduate and graduate students, who constitute a primary media user group, find that audiovisuals are particularly effective in demonstrating techniques such as changing a catheter or performing periodontal surgery. Many libraries also provide users with access to computer-assisted instruction programs. The University of Illinois PLATO system enables the student to select from numerous preclinical and clinical programmed sessions and to interact with the program to measure comprehension, to sharpen decision-making skills, or even to editorialize on recent biomedical journal articles. This and other systems using discs, slides, and audiotapes appear to be the way of the future.

Libraries have recently begun to house diagnostic skill centers. Users work with models or other devices that simulate visual, tactile, and/or auditory manifestations of pathological conditions. Mannequins with slides projected behind the eyes teach ophthalmologic diagnosis. The "Gynne" model is used to familiarize students with the basic gynecologic examination, and Recording Resusi Ann, a life-sized model, has become an important tool in teaching cardiopulmonary resuscitation techniques. These and other materials accommodate many user needs as well as, if not better than, print resources.

With the current requirements for recertification of health professionals, AV media represent a viable alternative to traditional instruction. By having available audiovisual programs such as the Network for Continuing Medical Education, a videotape series, health professionals can earn CE credit in the local library without having to travel to professional meetings.

Thus, the state of the art of user services in the health science library has advanced rapidly during the 20th century. Technological, professional, political, and economic factors have influenced and will continue to influence the development of these services.

**REFERENCES**


Estelle Brodman, "Medical Libraries around the World," *Bulletin of the Medical Library Association* (1971).

———, "Users of Health Science Libraries," *Library Trends* (1974.)

Louise Darling, "Changes in Information Delivery since 1960 in Health Science Libraries," *Library Trends* (1974).

M. C. Langer, "User and User Services in Health Science Libraries, 1945–1965," *Library Trends* (1974).

G. Werner, "Users of On-Line Bibliographic Retrieval Services in Health Science Libraries in the United States and Canada," *Bulletin of the Medical Library Association* (1979).


WILLIAM D. WALKER

ADMINISTRATION

**Governance.** Primary medical libraries, or health sciences libraries as many now prefer to call them, have principal roles in education, commercial organizations, clinical or health research organizations, health-related professional organizations, and in government agencies. There governance is a function of their organizational role.

Hospital libraries make up the largest group of medical libraries. They have functional roles in education, in the clinical organization (the hospital), and in government agencies (such as the Veterans Administration Hospitals). The hospital's organization chart will usually show the hospital librarian reporting to the hospital administration on matters of budget, personnel, and daily operation. A library committee, made up of the hospital administrator and members from the medical and nursing staff, is usually functional for such roles as library policy determination, library effectiveness review, continuing development of the library, and an advisory role regarding book and journal selection.

Cami L. Loucks, Trinity Lutheran Hospital, Kansas City, Missouri

*The computer terminal is the vital link between the medical library and access to the vast medical literature.*

Libraries for health-related professional organizations are some of the oldest medical libraries in the United States. The principal role of these medical society or academy libraries is in the continuing education of the practicing physician. The library operates within the governance structure of the medical society, and the librarian will normally report to the society board or a designated member of that board.

Perhaps the largest employer of professional medical librarians is the medical school library. Since the medical school library will normally be a part of a university system, it will normally fall under one of two governance structures: (1) as an integral part of the university library system; or (2) as a library independent of the university library system but under the governance of the medical or health sciences school.

Few medical school libraries exist as independent entities while at the same time serving medical or other health sciences schools. Of some 138 medical libraries in the United States and Canada, perhaps 10 percent are independent entities, while over 60 percent are under the governance of the medical school. The remaining 30 percent or so fall under the university library system.

When under the governance of the university library system, the medical school library director would report to the university librarian or some other administrator in the university library system. In the second case, under the governance of the medical school, the medical school library director would report to the administration, normally the dean, of the medical school or, particularly where the library also supports other health sciences programs, to a vice-president or similar administrative officer in charge of health science affairs. Neither situation is necessarily better for the medical school library. When reporting is through the university librarian, several of the library's functions are also normally found to emanate from the university library, particularly its technical processing functions. There may be no difficulty with this in a particular situation, but as a general rule the emphasis on currency in the medical library is much more pronounced than it is in the general university library, and the built-in delays through double processing can frustrate the serious medical librarian's service programs. This, along with other reasons in support of the library governance being directly under the medical school, is reported in a survey by Virginia Parker as follows:

(1) The library is responsible to, and is the responsibility of, the school it serves, which generates *better support* for the library on the part of the medical school administration.

(2) Medical school affiliation makes possible the *recruitment of personnel* to meet the special needs of a medical library. Those on the professional staff view themselves more as health professionals than as university librarians.

(3) A library that is independent of the university library system orders, catalogues, and processes its own books in a way that serves its own users, and there is no time lag. It is *free to set policies* regarding circulation, interlibrary loan, and other services tailored to medical school needs.

(4) Being a recognized department of the medical school *improves communications with the users*.

(5) Members of *medical school faculties* are accustomed to experimentation with new methods and equipment and are, therefore, *sympathetic with a library administration that is creative*.

The governance structure for the medical school library, then, while it may differ from library to library, establishes its policymaking structure. The functions and goals of the medical school library's advisory structure, on the other hand, are often much less understood. When the medical librarian reports to the university librarian, an advisory committee made up of members from the health sciences community can be a valuable asset. A library committee in such circumstances can assist the medical librarian in obtaining not only fiscal support but also support for policies, personnel, and processing. An advisory committee's role under the other structure can be much less well defined, however. When the medical school library director reports to the health sciences administration, even such a committee's advisory functions, in the realities of faculties' priorities, will demand innovation from the library director. When the medical school library has a direct channel to the health sciences administration, a library advisory committee will assume a policymaking role, particularly with setting external library policies (circulation and other public services policies), while in others the committee will act merely as a sounding board to assist the director in policy determinations for the library. While an advisory committee can potentially play a significant role in assisting to achieve goals, a policymaking committee where there is competent library staff (and this is true in the hospital library as well) is potentially a liability, for the medical librarian must continue to assume responsibility for *all* of the library's policies the committee notwithstanding.

Cami L. Loucks

*At St. Luke's Hospital in Kansas City, the Medical Library supports medical education programs as well as patient health care.*

**Finance.** Medical library directors are as concerned as the executive officers of other organizations about applying current management techniques to their budgeting processes. While the incremental line-item budget is common in the medical library, a combination of budgeting techniques is perhaps more often used. Program budgeting, zero-based budgeting, and incremental budgeting are rarely found in their pure form. Since budgets, along with statistical data on library activities, are still most commonly used in libraries as control devices—that is, the primary focus is on "how much," rather than on "what," "why," or "how"—the use of a budget in a medical library as a tool for translating management plans into financial terms is still in its infancy. When applied in consideration of the consequences of eliminating programs, and of letting all programs compete for the library's limited resources, zero-based budgeting is a move toward answering the more meaningful organizational performance questions and should therefore become a much more prevalent budget tool in the future.

The medical library's budget is prepared by the library director, along with others on the library staff, and is submitted for approval to the person to whom the director reports. A budget request will normally include personnel, acquisitions (including processing), maintenance and operations (supplies, printing, etc.), communications, travel, automation, and equipment. In the medical school library, the three main parts of the library budget—personnel, acquisitions, and other expenses—normally fall, in the better libraries, close to a 60:30:10 percent ratio, which can be used as a guideline for standard budgeting in those libraries but not as a substitute for a planned budget. In actuality, however, these ratios in most medical school libraries seem to be moving toward a heavier acquisitions budget percentage, bringing it closer to 40 percent of the total, with personnel slipping closer to 50 percent. This reflects the tremendous inflationary pressures in book and particularly journal prices (the latter accounting for about 70 percent to 80 percent of the medical library's acquisitions budget), while salaries, on the other hand, continue to remain not only behind the inflation rate but also too often behind other comparable professional salaries.

In the hospital library, the major source of financial support is from the hospital's operating budget. Other sources of funding may include medical staff dues or contributions, grant funds, and Medicare. Medical society libraries must rely for the most part on annual dues assessed to their memberships.

**Management.** Both medical school libraries and hospital libraries tend to see their mission or purpose solely as one to further the mission of the larger institution of which they are a part. The medical school library's mission is usually stated in terms of its contributions to the teaching, research, and service goals of the health science institution. The AMA-MLA Guidelines for Medical School Libraries state that the purpose of the medical library is to serve its community. The hospital library's purpose is usually stated in terms of the three major functions of the hospital: patient care, education, and research, with the major commitment being patient care. Medical society libraries from their founding have played a significant role in the continuing education of the practicing physician, and even though there are yet some significant society libraries in the United States, this function is being taken over more and more by hospitals and medical school libraries.

While there can be little argument with these mission statements, which have been fairly universally adopted, some medical libraries are beginning to see their mission to their user community in less reactive, more assertive terms. To contribute in various and detailed ways to the teaching, research, and service goals of the larger institution to serve the library's user community in general is clearly what the medical library does indeed do, but this says nothing about what it considers the desired results of these activities to be. With more and more medical libraries adopting current management techniques, including marketing, strategic planning, budgeting techniques, and Management by Objectives (all are taught as continuing education courses through the Medical Library Association's CE program), the ultimate goal of the medical library is being scrutinized more carefully now than ever before. Performance measurement is a concept the medical librarian is beginning to work with. With the publication of the *Annual Statistics of Medical School Libraries in the United States and Canada* in 1978, comparative statistical information for medical school libraries has become readily available, and similar comparative data are being considered for hospital libraries. A next step for medical libraries will be to develop management information systems toward determining their performance effectiveness. Before the medical library will be able to truly assess its performance, it first must define in clear and meaningful terms its organizational direction.

Since the large majority of hospital libraries are small and staffed by one librarian, their internal structure is relatively simple. The librarian must function in the several roles that are quite distinct in larger libraries, from acquisitions and cataloguing to reference services and management. The medical school library or the larger medical society library, on the other hand, will have an internal organizational structure differing little from that of a general academic library. The separation into departments—cataloguing, acquisitions, serials, reference, interlibrary loan, circulation, audiovisual—is fairly standard. Some names are changed—audiovisual departments become learning resource centers or media centers; reference departments may be called information services departments—and some departments are combined, such as acquisitions and serials. In addition, there may be some distinction given to the collection development functions in the larger medical libraries. Further differing details in organizational structure will depend upon the particular library and the management style in operation in it. Some medical libraries are large and complex enough to need an associate director along with directors in charge of the technical and public services divisions, but the two divisional directors alone are more commonly found. Some library directors do not adopt the divisional structure at all but prefer to operate under a flat structure, with each department head reporting directly to the library director.

With the average (mean and median) number of librarians in 1978 in a medical school library at eight to nine, there is little more than one librarian for each of the major functions; covering about 53 to 57 reference desk hours each week requires the help of most of these librarians. A pattern whereby the librarian functions as generalist, and perhaps an over-activitied generalist, is still predominant. When the cataloguing librarian is not cataloguing, she or he is handling reference desk duties and perhaps even conducting data base searches. It is the feeling of some medical librarians that the generalist approach not only dilutes the quality of the service the library is capable of giving, but has built into it an inability of the library to respond to anything but the most common, and too often the most superficial, needs of the medical library's community. Librarians are almost inherently activity prone; they conceive their ultimate purpose to be of service to their community, by definition a reactive role. All too frequently what gets left out in this picture are the innovative services, which are the basic ingredients of an assertive and forward-looking library service.

**REFERENCES**

Gertrude L. Annan and Jacqueline W. Felter, editors, *Handbook of Medical Library Practice,* 3rd ed. (1970).

Lois Ann Colaianni and Phyllis Mirsky, *Manual for Librarians in Small Hospitals* (1978).

Virginia Parker, "The Relationship of Medical School Libraries to University Library Systems," *Bulletin of the Medical Library Association* (1977).

RICHARD A. LYDERS

MEASUREMENT AND EVALUATION

Measurement and evaluation have long been an integral part of the health science library scene. The picture has been a fragmented one for an assortment of reasons, not the least of which is the great variety of agencies that harbor health-related libraries. These libraries not only span the customary library divisions of special and academic but also within these categories may represent the interests of host institutions that are private or public, for profit or nonprofit, small or large, or any size in between.

Individual libraries, especially those in academic settings, are sometimes challenged further by the strikingly disparate and sometimes diametrically opposed needs of several classes of users. The classical conflict between the needs of faculty and students is well known to all academic libraries. Further, the research use of materials by basic scientists can be quite dissimilar in nature from its use by those engaged in the day-to-day delivery of health care.

The factors that tie libraries in the field into a cohesive whole include not only the subject matter of the information and materials they handle but a surprising similarity in the goals they seek to achieve. The second of these helps to provide a rationale for the strong interest in measures of *effectiveness* as a tool for evaluation. While the many differences between libraries in the field might make other common measures difficult to devise and use, shared or interlocking goals make measurement of effectiveness a satisfactory approach for health science libraries.

Over a period of years, health science libraries have used a series of complementary and overlapping mechanisms in an effort to evaluate their collections, services, and other relevant library qualities. The pattern that has emerged has been similar in many ways to that followed in other fields of librarianship, beginning with the search for acceptable standards against which to measure adequacy, followed by the collection and analysis of statistics to allow for comparisons among libraries, and culminating in the development and application of tools designed to assess effectiveness of library operations in meeting the needs of library users. While all of these approaches continue to be used today as circumstances require, the emphasis given to each has shifted.

**Standards.** The variety of standards for health-related libraries reflects the rich variety of library types within the field. In 1972 Helen Yast, then Director of Library Services at the American Hospital Association (AHA), reviewed in *Library Trends* the genesis of standards for library service in health care institutions. This study indicated the large number of organizations with an interest in the subject ranging from the American Library Association to the Association of American Medical Colleges. In consequence, a large number of standards have been produced over the years.

The Joint Commission on the Accreditation of Hospitals (JCAH) first made mention of libraries in their 1953 hospital standards. Always stated in the most general of terms, these guidelines only recently, with the assistance of the Medical Library Association (MLA), have become sufficiently specific to be meaningful to hospital administrators and helpful to hospital librarians.

During that period when a great many libraries were significantly out of line with what was generally considered adequate, it was expedient to provide reasonable numerical standards for the purpose of bringing these libraries up to a specified minimum level. For hospital libraries in some geographic areas, this continues to be true today. However, once the greater number of libraries addressed reach this level, this type of standard loses its effectiveness as a change agent and tends instead to preserve the status quo. When a certain degree of leveling off has been reached within a field, numerical standards become obsolete as evaluative tools.

A more recent development along these lines, intended to assist in the area of collection development, is lists of books or journals appropriate for libraries of various sizes and types. The most notable of these are the regularly revised Brandon list of books and journals for the small medical library, which appears in the *Bulletin of the Medical Library Association,* and the Sterns and Ratcliff "core lists." (A bibliography of 19 such lists published between 1967 and 1977 for health science libraries appeared in the July 1978 *Bulletin of the Medical Library Association.*) Small and medium-sized hospital libraries find these lists useful for evaluating and updating collections.

While it is difficult to write and apply standards for hospital libraries, the issue of complex variables is no less a problem for health science libraries in academic settings. These range from smaller libraries such as those serving schools of nursing or pharmacy alone to large multidisciplinary libraries serving several schools, clinics, hospitals, and research centers. The needs of these libraries are addressed, at least in theory, by the standards written for university libraries as well as by the now outdated guidelines sponsored by the Association of American Medical Colleges (AAMC) in 1965 and prepared under a National Library of Medicine contract by a distinguished panel of medical librarians. The newly formed Association of Academic Health Science Library Directors is now in the process of examining the AAMC's various efforts to assist medical school libraries in order to determine how they can be brought up to date.

As tools for evaluation, many standards leave much to be desired, though they may serve other useful purposes. According to F. Wilfrid Lancaster, "For evaluation purposes, standards should be precise, quantifiable and measurable." The trend today appears to be for standards to state their requirements in terms of generalized goals. This may make standards appropriate starting points for evaluation, rather than tools for the evaluative process itself.

**Statistics and the State of the Art.** Additional influences that forced a search for alternatives to standards for evaluating health science libraries included the accelerated pace of medical research including interdisciplinary research, the resulting growth of the overall body of knowledge concerning medical, premedical, and related subjects, and the concomitant growth in the literature that reflected this knowledge, the growing interest and influence of the National Library of Medicine (NLM), and the impact of the Medical Library Assistance Act.

During this time of rapid change in the 1960's, the collection of comparative statistics assumed a new importance. While individual libraries had collected a variety of statistics as by-products of library operations for inclusion in various internal and management reports, major efforts were made in the early and mid-1960's to collect these nationwide in order to define the general state of hospital and academic medical libraries. The Medical Library Association and others conducted several major surveys reported between 1963 and 1967. The major effect of these national surveys was to make visible the uneven profile of health-related libraries in the United States. The information provided by the studies supported the recommendations of the President's Commission on Heart Disease, Cancer, and Stroke concerning medical libraries, and to the extent that these efforts resulted in the Medical Library Assistance Act they were successful. However, much of what was collected appeared to be redundant to other items in the surveys; the data collected were of questionable reliability and of minimal value in exploring effectiveness.

The currently published *Annual Statistics of Medical School Libraries in the United States and Canada,* now compiled by the Houston Academy of Medicine, Texas Medical Center Library, is a somewhat more carefully constructed review and is in a continuing state of refinement to ensure reliable and consistent reporting. Another significant source of statistics about medical school libraries is the series of statistical compilations in the form of directories and profiles developed by Susan Crawford, Director of the library of the American Medical Association (AMA) under contract to the NLM.

**Evaluation for Effectiveness.** In contrast to both the standards and comparative statistics approaches were those studies that focused on the effectiveness of the libraries' collections and services in meeting the needs of users. These began by analyzing the effectiveness of individual libraries' internal abilities to meet needs, advanced to measure their capability of providing needed materials regardless of source, and later attempted to measure the success of national systems and networks in meeting users' needs.

Frederick G. Kilgour's studies at Yale's Medical Library in the early 1960's, for instance, studied items circulated to determine the characteristics of library materials most in demand by users. His discovery that a very small percentage of journal titles accounted for a large percentage of the total journal circulation supported earlier findings made by others in studies of general library collections. Kilgour later combined efforts with T. P. Fleming of Columbia to identify that core of biomedical journals that would satisfy 79 percent of all items circulated by the two libraries. A 1966 investigation by L. M. Raisig and others used interviews with researchers returning monographs to determine how users had identified needed materials, the use to which borrowers had put the library materials, and how useful the material had been. The age of the material circulated was also determined and, as in the case of the journal studies, the results supported earlier observations that most materials circulated are of recent origin. Similar studies were conducted by other researchers. Reviews based on citation analysis had been popular as early as the mid-1940's and were also used throughout the 1960's and since, in efforts to evaluate collections of libraries, individual scientists, and hospital core collections among others.

One of the most intensive efforts in the area of measurement of satisfaction from the viewpoint of the user was that made by the Institute for the Advancement of Medical Communications (IAMC) for the National Library of Medicine. The intended end product of this work was not the evaluation of libraries but the development of tools whereby evaluative studies could be done. This group, led by R. H. Orr, developed methods for collecting objective data suitable for planning and guiding local, regional, and national programs. Beginning its work in 1966, the IAMC focused on the following five goals:

> (1) to develop a method of measuring quantitatively a library's capability for providing the documents its users may need; (2) to develop a standard procedure for making an "inventory" of all the services a library offers its individual users; (3) to develop a method for identifying, enumerating, and characterizing the user population that constitutes a library's primary responsibility; (4) to assess the responsibility of measuring quantitatively a library's capabilities for providing certain types of "reference service"; and (5) to evaluate alternative methods for measuring utilization of the library's services.

These efforts were concentrated on academic libraries serving biomedical populations. The studies also focused on assessing effectiveness in terms of how well the users were served rather than in terms of how the library went about its business.

The user orientation of these later studies influenced, or at least forecasted, a persistent trend. Many recent evaluations of both traditional and innovative library services now measure success in terms of user satisfaction rather than in numbers of units of service provided. Though R. Tagliacozzo rightly warns of the pitfalls of oversimplified interpretations of user satisfaction studies, the trend toward measuring library effectiveness in terms of meeting user needs rather than meeting some arbitrary standards is a firmly established one in health science libraries.

**REFERENCES**

F. Wilfrid Lancaster, *The Measurement and Evaluation of Library Services* (1977).

R. H. Orr et al., "Development of Methodologic Tools for Planning and Managing Library Services," "II. Measuring a Library's Capability for Providing Documents," "III. Standardized Inventories of Library Services," *Bulletin of the Medical Library Association* (1968).

Irwin H. Pizer and A. M. Cain, "Objective Tests of Library Performance," *Special Libraries* (1968).

L. M. Raisig et al., "How Biomedical Investigators Use Library Books," *Bulletin of the Medical Library Association* (1966).

R. Tagliacozzo, "Estimating the Satisfaction of Information Users," *Bulletin of the Medical Library Association* (1977).

VIRGINIA H. HOLTZ

LIBRARY COOPERATION

Like public and research libraries, specialized health science libraries have been forced to recognize that the doctrine of self-sufficiency could no longer exist. Because of escalating costs and rapid accrual of information, a shift in philosophy was necessary to reassess adequately the need to expand services while continuing to consider the quality of materials and their distribution. As the health science community became more aware of its growing need for more of the world's expanding biomedical information, the resource requirements of any library to meet these needs became more challenging. Librarians could no longer be territorially possessive of their collections in even the largest of libraries, nor was it possible for any library to have on-site access to all materials requisite for their primary clientele. On the other hand, the reality of paring their collections and entering into cooperative arrangements was discouraging to librarians. Desperation measures of drastic reduction of subscriptions were common before a rational examination of the total acquisition policies of the field of librarians could take place. The planning for cooperative activity and incorporation of smaller units eventually forced innovative solutions.

**Medical Library Assistance Act.** Historically, the responsibility for the emergence of a network concept in U.S. medical libraries must be credited to the National Library of Medicine (NLM) under the Medical Library Assistance Act (MLAA). In 1965 the President's Commission on Heart Disease, Cancer and Stroke studied the medical librarianship of the U.S. and found it wanting. Poor facilities, lack of resources and services, and staff inadequately educated to the advancing technology were among their findings. Under the MLAA of 1965, NLM met the challenge and began to develop the nationwide Biomedical Communication Network (BCN). The MLAA played a key role in supporting the development of this network potentially enabling the NLM to fill biomedical information needs of over 5,000,000 health care personnel. Potentially affected were approximately 8,000 health institutions, including over 7,000 community hospitals, over 550 colleges, universities, and professional schools in the health sciences, and approximately 470 medical research society, health care, and industrial organizations.

Beyond the over 1,400 grants awarded under the MLAA for research, resources, training, construction, and publications, the Regional Medical Library network was established to provide programs to meet the information needs of the health care professionals and research community. Within the Regional Medical Library Program (RMLP), grants were awarded to meet the changing information needs. Developing consortia was viewed as necessary to meet the goal of self-sufficiency for hospital libraries, the least tended area of medical librarianship until the early 1970's. Grants were made available to support this emerging development in 1976.

Initially, under the RMLP the country was segmented into 11 Regions, each with a Regional Medical Library (RML). On a decentralized basis, each RML was responsible for promoting document delivery. Selected primary libraries with major medical collections in each state of any Region were designated as Resource Libraries. Interlibrary loan requests among Resource Libraries, and from other health science libraries to Resource Libraries, for document delivery were reimbursed by NLM. This interlibrary document delivery activity impacted on lending patterns and collection development among Resource Libraries. In the mid-1970's NLM, satisfied that the steps toward filling the goal of document delivery by Resource Libraries were established, shifted its concern toward the limited resources or absence of health science libraries at the grass roots. Focusing on this large segment of the U.S. where health care information needs were not being met, NLM began to fill the void through the Biomedical Communication Network.

**Structure.** In the health science cooperative arena, the three recognized configurations are in operation: the BCN hierarchy, the consortium distribution, and the MEDLARS network as a star. (They follow the three traditional patterns for network structure: the *star network,* whereby one network member holds all resources with all members utilizing these resources; the *hierarchical network,* wherein network members share resources, with the majority of needs satisfied before requesting service to the next greater resource center and remaining unfilled requests referred to the "library of last resort"; and the *distributed network,* in which network members hold different resources that are shared among members.)

Consortium development, as an example of a cooperative subregional network, was one solution to NLM's direction that Regional Medical Libraries develop libraries at the sub-Resource Library level of the BCN hierarchical structure. The success of this development can be attested by the Midwest Health Science Library Network's 37 consortia with 553 members. For document delivery, requests are initially tendered to other consortium members within a distributed network configuration. If the request is not filled, it is sent to a Resource Library, which fills the request from its collection or refers it to another Resource Library. If the request cannot be filled at this level, it is referred to the "library of last resort," the National Library of Medicine. The NLM in turn has agreements with the British Library Lending Division. Through the BCN the 25-bed hospital's library manager truly has access to the same resources as a large medical school or research organization.

Area Health Education Center (AHEC) libraries are participants in two configurations: as distributed in their AHEC to AHEC cooperation, and as part of a star structure in their relationship with their local medical school library in supporting the clinical experience for students, interns, and residents. Departmental libraries of large medical schools work most often in a star configuration.

The MEDLARS/MEDLINE computerized on-line bibliographic network within the BCN can be described as a star configuration with all terminals connected to the NLM data bases through use of two major communication networks, TYMNET and TELENET. With more than 1,000,000 literature searches performed in 1978 by 945 institutions using the network, the necessity for sharing costs of system operations requires mandatory economies.

**Governance.** Medical library networks use a variety of governing structures. Within the BCN at the Regional Medical Library level, there is usually a policy-setting body as well as an advisory group in place. In varying degrees they include representatives of all levels of libraries, i.e., basic units, Resource Libraries, Regional Medical Library, as well as sub-units of the Region, and nonlibra-

**Network Structure**

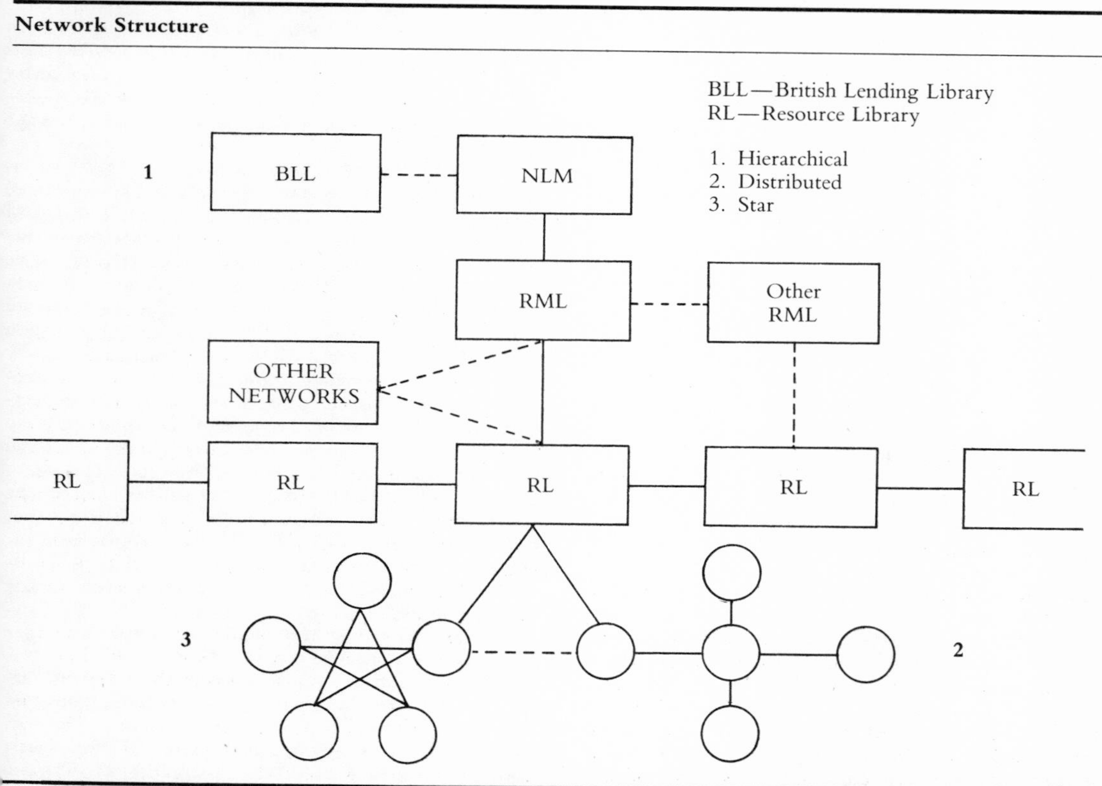

rians, e.g., university faculty, medical professionals. (The Regional Medical Library is the library of last resort in a Region, contracting library for the NLM to administer the contractual funds for developing activities including cooperative programs within the Region. Resource Libraries are libraries with large health science collections subcontracted to the Regional Medical Library primarily for document delivery. Most Resource Libraries have assumed other resource and leadership responsibilities within their respective states. Basic units are health science libraries within the Region that are not Regional Medical Libraries or Resource Libraries.)

At the consortium level a coordinator or chairperson and secretary may discharge the organizational management of the group on an elected or rotating basis. Consortia may have formal governance with contractual agreements, Bylaws, and an institutional administrative advisory council or may be organized informally. In a majority of cooperative arrangements, monies are not involved; interlibrary loans which may require exchange of funds are generally handled with a periodic statement or balance of payment on an individual institution-to-institution basis.

**Function.** As an example of a wide-ranging, discipline-based, single-type form of library cooperation, health science libraries are certainly one of the most advanced in the country. Within the single-type cooperative concept there is relative homogeneity of the network components; however, no two participants are identical, in either organizational structure or needs. The 25-bed hospital obviously has different information requirements from those of the medical school or pharmaceutical research division.

At the outset of interlibrary cooperation, document delivery was the single function and principal reason for forming, and motivation for joining, cooperative networks; however, with recognition of the potential that cooperation holds, many cooperative ventures have developed into multitype function networks.

The University of Pittsburgh survey of networks, cited by J. G. Williams in *The Structure and Governance of Library Networks,* produced a multifaceted list of 21 functions in which library networks are involved:

1. interlibrary loan
2. reference
3. delivery
4. acquisitions
5. union lists
6. continuing education
7. bibliographic access
8. photocopying
9. circulation
10. communications
11. publications
12. cataloguing
13. processing
14. storage
15. literature searching
16. collections development
17. abstracting/indexing
18. referral
19. consulting
20. accounting and management
21. microfilming

Each of these functions has been used by health science library networks.

The Medical Library Center of New York with its 59 members is an example of a uniquely designed multifunction network. It was established for the purpose of cooperative acquisitions and storage of medical library materials. Further cooperation has led to creation of the Union Catalog of Medical Periodicals (UCMP), one of the major computerized union lists of serials, and the Union Catalog of Medical Monographs and Multimedia (UCOM). OCLC, Inc., is yet another example of a multifunction network currently including cooperative cataloguing, interlibrary loan transmission, and serial records components.

**Funding.** Funding for cooperative activities comes in a variety of ways. The following channels are the most significant:

1. *National Library of Medicine:* Under the MLAA ever larger portions of the NLM budget have been devoted to the Regional Medical Library Program—approximately $105,000 in 1967 and $3,000,000 in 1978.

2. *Regional Medical Library:* RML programs are carried out under contract between NLM and the ten other Regions (NLM is the RML for Region IV). RML's and Resource Libraries contribute substantial staff time and effort over and above contract funds. Many activities are carried out voluntarily by hundreds of librarians through Regional Committees and projects.

3. *Consortia:* In the main, consortia are not grant funded. Activity costs are absorbed by individual institutions, e.g., printing of union lists. The exceptions are the NLM Resource Improvement Grants for consortium development and Resource Project Grants for large-scale consortium projects. Fees for service may be applied to nonmembers requesting service. Dues, per-bed fees, and entry fees are other means of sharing costs of consortium activities.

**International Cooperation.** Mention should be made of international health science library cooperation and its impact on country-to-country relationships, intracountry relationships, and the use of cooperation and exchange by varied means.

*International Congresses.* The first Congress of the International Congress on Medical Librarianship in 1953 enabled the 300 attendees from 37 countries to share experiences and ideas on education, classification, history of medicine, and international health science library cooperation. The second Congress in 1963, with 900 attendees from 58 countries, discussed health science library education, documentation, information dissemination, and MEDLARS. The third Congress in 1969 centered on health science library computer applications and network and national regional planning, while the fourth Congress in 1980 will focus on medical librarianship for developing countries.

*Medical Library Association (MLA).* The Medical Library Association in the U.S. has provided strong links for health science library cooperation, as the international congresses have offered opportunities for librarians to exchange information in one-to-one contact with colleagues from other countries. MLA's Committee on International and National Cooperation administered an international fellowship program with $94,000 from the Rockefeller Foundation. Forty-three Fellows from 29 countries spent time in the U.S. on a work-study-travel program. In 1974 the Committee initiated a library-to-library project and now matches 40 pairs of libraries from 28 countries. Cooperative activities in reference referral, distribution of basic lists and directories, and translation services are encouraged. The MLA Exchange program has been historically active in cooperative activity. The Exchange, together with Unesco, distributed duplicate materials to libraries in countries ravaged by World War II. In 1979 there were 84 overseas and 67 Canadian institutional members of the Exchange.

*National Library of Medicine.* During John Shaw Billings's administration of the Surgeon-General's Library, international exchange was initiated in 1881. Presently it has 810 exchange partners in 87 countries throughout the world. In response to request for service from developing countries NLM has provided interlibrary and audiovisual loans, as well as MEDLINE, distribution of *Current*

*Catalog, Index Medicus,* and *Abridged Index Medicus.* Under the Special Foreign Currency Program (PL 480) originating in the Agricultural Trade and Assistance Act of 1954, NLM has received funds to translate biomedical literature, develop bibliographic tools, and prepare critical reviews. International MEDLARS bilateral agreements to share the bibliographic data base have been negotiated with 143 non-U.S. MEDLARS Centers in 11 countries.

NLM, in sharing its resources and expertise, has stimulated many cooperative biomedical communication activities. Mutual benefits have accrued from these collaborative efforts to work toward the common goal of dissemination of biomedical information.

The impact of the Lister Hill National Center for Biomedical Communication's efforts to marry the minicomputers and the videodisc console is exciting indeed. The Center's capability for satellite communication will continue to affect the future of health science library cooperation. Materials will be available to single libraries as well as networks in electronic form, e.g., videodiscs and other technologies of the future. The prospects of reduced costs of electronic document delivery loom on the horizon.

In addition to biomedical information networks in countries such as Great Britain, Japan, and Canada, there is an emergence of similar networks in Czechoslovakia, Hungary, and Germany. The World Health Organization (WHO), Pan American Health Organization (PAHO), and Unesco have also provided bases for coordination of cooperative usage of health science library resources on a world spectrum.

**Other Cooperative Activities.** Health science library networks are moving in the direction of internetwork cooperation with non-health science library networks. Again, NLM has been in the forefront as a lead mover in initiating discussions. Through the Regional Medical Library Program, the TALON (Texas, Arkansas, Louisiana, Oklahoma, New Mexico) and Midwest regions have held meetings with state library directors, heads of library agencies, and other networks to discuss ways in which non-health science and health science libraries can work together to furnish maximum information to their respective clientele.

Consortia are making progress toward interconsortium sharing at the local level in each state. Interstate cooperation at the consortium level is already being experimented with.

The professional library organizations—the Medical Library Association, the Special Libraries Association, and the American Library Association—are working in concert to resolve problems involved with cataloguing rules, the closing of the Library of Congress card catalogue, and the establishment of National Periodical Center, which will affect the entire library community.

Health science librarians today are far better qualified at the entry level, in view of highly specialized training in medical librarianship and their practicum experience. Building on this increased level of professional development, perhaps the greatest impact on the success of any network has come from the contributions of individual personnel involved in network planning, management, and activities.

**REFERENCES**

Mary E. Corning, "National Library of Medicine: International Cooperation for Biomedical Communications," *Bulletin of the Medical Library Association* (1975).

Beth A. Hamilton and William B. Ernst, Jr., *Multitype Library Cooperation* (1977).

Donald D. Hendricks, "The Regional Medical Library Program," *Library Trends* (1975).

Allen Kent and Thomas J. Galvin, editors, *The Structure and Governance of Library Networks* (1979).

RUBY S. MAY

# Melcher, Daniel

(1912– )

Daniel Melcher, publishing executive, contributed to library service as an innovator in developing professional publications, reference services, and methods for improving book production and distribution.

Melcher was born July 10, 1912, at Newton Center, Massachusetts, the son of Marguerite Fellows Melcher and Frederic Gershom Melcher (later President of R. R. Bowker Company). Daniel Melcher was graduated from Harvard College (A.B.) in 1934. In 1934 and 1935 Melcher was a publicity assistant at the London publishing house of George Allen and Unwin and an assistant and student of publishing methods at other houses in London and Leipzig, Germany. From 1936 to 1942 he worked in a variety of sales promotion and management capacities at Henry Holt and Company, Oxford University Press, Alliance Book Corporation, and Viking Press, all in New York City. During World War II he worked in Washington with the U.S. Treasury Department's War Finance Division, first as publishing consultant and then as National Director of its education section. In 1946 he was Director of the National Committee on Atomic Information, also in Washington.

When he joined the R. R. Bowker Company, New York, in 1947, Melcher was appointed Publisher of the firm's *Library Journal.* He quickly began developing the 70-year-old magazine into a major publication dealing with every aspect of the library profession, and in 1954 he founded, as an adjunct, *Junior Libraries* (*School Library Journal,* beginning 1961).

At the same time, Melcher had been working on the idea of a series of current in-print directories of American books. He devised the procedures by which the directories could be edited and produced, and in 1948 the firm launched the annual *Books in Print,* with author and title indexes. There followed, also under Melcher's vigorous direction, *Paperbound Books in Print* (1956), *Subject Guide to Books in Print* (1957), *Forthcoming Books* (advance listings), and *American Book Publishing Record* (catalogue listings, current and cumulative, in Dewey cataloguing sequence, 1961).

Meanwhile, Melcher was writing articles on library questions for *LJ* and on book distribution and book manufacturing for *Publishers' Weekly.* He contributed to the automated "belt press" concept of book manufacturing. His concern for distribution made him a major force in the mid-1960's in establishing the International Standard Book Numbering System.

Melcher became a Director and General Manager of Bowker in 1956; Vice-President, 1959; and President, 1963–68. After Bowker acquired Jaques Cattell Press, biographical directory publisher, Melcher was its Board Chairman, 1961–67. He took part in the Bowker stockholders' decision to sell the firm to the Xerox Corporation January 1, 1968, and was then Bowker Chairman under Xerox but resigned early in 1969.

He was Board Chairman of Gale Research Corporation, 1971–73, and thereafter an independent consultant. He was a member of the ALA Council, 1972–74, and from 1969 a board member of Institutes for Achievement of Human Potentials, with a special interest in the ways by which very young children can learn to read.

With Nancy Larrick, Melcher wrote a basic guide, *Printing and Promotion Handbook* (1949, 1956, 1967), and, with Margaret Saul Melcher, *Melcher on Acquisitions* (ALA, 1971).

He married, in 1937, Peggy Zimmerman, later a children's librarian; they had one son, Frederic G. Melcher II. After her death (1967), he married Margaret Saul, who had been editor of *School Library Journal.*

CHANDLER B. GRANNIS

ALA

Frederic Gershom Melcher



## Melcher, Frederic Gershom
(1879–1963)

Frederic Gershom Melcher, editor, publisher, bookseller, and book collector, became one of the most influential and respected figures in the world of books not only in the United States but throughout the world during his 45 years with the R. R. Bowker Company. Rarely has a single person had such familiarity with all the aspects of bookmaking, bookselling, and book acquisition. Melcher's devotion to books began early when as a child he read in the public libraries of Newton, Massachusetts; later (in 1947) he honored a pioneer children's librarian, Caroline M. Hewins, by establishing a lectureship on New England children's literature and naming it for her.

Born on April 12, 1879, in Malden, Massachusetts, the son of Edwin Forrest Melcher and Alice Jane Bartlett, he grew up in Newton Center and graduated from high school in 1895. He took the "Institute course," to prepare for the Massachusetts Institute of Technology, but the illness of his father and the difficult times following the depression of 1893 (combined with his own disinclination to become, as he put it, "a chemist or a civil engineer") made it necessary for him to seek a job instead.

Through the influence of his maternal grandfather, he obtained a position in the mailroom at Lauriat's famous bookstore in Boston. He remained there 18 years and handled its large library business for a time, built up its children's department, and eventually became one of its most successful salesmen. His discernment in judging and recommending current books earned him a reputation that began to spread beyond the Boston area; Arnold Bennett, for example, credited him with initiating the demand that led to the American success of *The Old Wives' Tale* in 1908.

His activity in professional organizations fostered his growing reputation: he was President in 1912 of the Boston Booksellers' League and delivered some rousing remarks at both the 1911 and 1912 American Booksellers Association conventions. One member of the audience, W. K. Stewart, soon after asked him to be Manager of his Indianapolis store, and in March 1913 Melcher and his family (he married Marguerite Fellows on June 2, 1910) moved to Indianapolis.

The store served as the heart of Indiana's thriving literary activity. Melcher not only met Riley, Tarkington, Ade, Nicholson, Hubbard, and other writers and artists but also discussed book design and fine printing with Edwin Grabhorn, who set up his Studio Press in Indianapolis in 1915. During these years Melcher was becoming active in local and state library associations and speaking before library groups as well as writing for *Publishers' Weekly* and addressing the 1918 ABA convention. He was therefore widely known, and his knowledge of the book trade was thorough, when in 1918 an editorship of *Publishers' Weekly* became available. He joined the Bowker Company, publisher of the journal, in May 1918 as Vice-President and was associated with *Publishers' Weekly* for the next 40 years, first as Managing Editor and then, after Bowker's death in 1933, as Co-editor with Mildred C. Smith.

His intense interest in all aspects of the book and his belief in the interdependence of all parts of the book world were reflected in his handling of *PW*. One of his first actions was to institute a column on bookmaking and book design; another was to devote certain issues each year to children's books. He kept abreast of new developments and maintained personal contact with hundreds of people in the field through extensive travel, both in the United States and abroad, serving as a delegate to the International Publishers' Congresses and, following World War II, making trips to Europe and Japan for the State Department and the War Department. His editorials over the years amount to a compendium of informed and sensible commentary on all that was taking place.

In 1934 he succeeded R. R. Bowker as President of the company; under his direction the Bowker lists, while continuing to offer basic book trade tools for libraries and booksellers, increased their attention to bibliophilic books and works of scholarly bibliography. Bowker became the American publisher of Michael Sadleir's "Bibliographia" series, issued a series of state imprint bibliographies for the Bibliographical Society of America, and published John Carter's great *Taste and Technique in Book-Collecting* (1948—dedicated to Melcher in its 1970 printing), as well as important books on collecting by Mary Benjamin, Jacob Blanck, Howard Peckham, and Colton Storm, and *American Book-Prices Current*. The distinction of this list underlies the comment made by John Carter, one of Melcher's many English friends in the trade, in his 50th-anniversary address to the Bibliographical Society of America, when he singled out three firms, Bowker in New York and Constable and Hart-Davis in London, as having been particularly hospitable to bibliography.

In these years Melcher continued to be tireless in his professional service for such groups as the American Booksellers Association (Secretary, 1918–20), National Association of Book Publishers (Executive Secretary, 1920–24), New York Booksellers' League (President, 1924–25), American Institute of Graphic Arts (President, 1927–28), and New York Library Association (President, 1935–36) and in his work in connection with the Copyright Committee, the NRA code, the Council on Books in Wartime, and the American Civil Liberties Union, among others. As of 1959 Melcher, approaching his 80th birthday, gave up his long editorship and presidency and became Chairman of the Board; he remained active, however, and attended the International Publishers' Congress in Spain in 1962, the year before he died, on March 9, 1963, in Montclair, New Jersey.

Melcher's influence, through *PW* and the Bowker Company and through his wide acquaintance, was pervasive during the second quarter of the 20th century. But his influence has been and will continue to be felt in another way—through his generosity in establishing awards and disposing of his own collections. Children's books were always one of his special interests: besides being a founder in 1919 of Children's Book Week, he set up in 1922 an annual award for excellence in children's books, the Newbery Medal, and in 1937 added to it the Caldecott Medal for children's book illustration. He commissioned and donated these medals, but with characteristic modesty he did not wish his name attached to them. As the most prestigious awards in their field, however, they will remain one of his best memorials. Among the other awards indicative of his temperament and aims are one he established in 1940 for the Indiana library most active in promoting regional history or literature and another that he set up in 1943 for creative publishing (named after Mathew Carey and Isaiah Thomas). His name will also be remembered for his collecting, and he often expressed his delight in the feel of a well-made book. The many friends who had the pleasure of examining his books at his house in Montclair, New Jersey, would be glad to know that much of the collection can still be consulted in libraries: his private press books are in the university libraries at Princeton and Syracuse; his Vachel Lindsay collection is in the Lilly Library at Indiana University; and his extensive collection of books about books is handsomely housed and effectively maintained (and kept up to date) in the library named for him at the R. R. Bowker Company.

A bestower of awards, he sought none for himself, but they inevitably came to him as the premier ambassador of the book world. In 1945 he was given the medal of the American Institute of Graphic Arts (he had been President of the AIGA in 1927 and helped organize its Book Clinic in 1931) and in 1950 a plaque from the Children's Library Association; in 1955 at the Newbery-Caldecott dinner he was informed that a Melcher Scholarship had been established in the field of library service for children; in 1958 he was awarded an Honorary Litt.D. from Rutgers and the following year one from Syracuse; and in 1962 the Regina Medal was presented to him by the Catholic Library Association for his work with children's literature. Contributors to the book published in connection with the May 1945 dinner commemorating his first 50 years in the book trade were in agreement about the position he occupied; B. W. Huebsch, for instance, called him the leader "by tacit consent," and Marion E. Dodd labeled him the "number one liaison man to all the branches of the book world." The London *Bookseller* in 1954 referred to him as "the dean of the *corps diplomatique* of the American book-trade," and after his death it pronounced him "without doubt the greatest all-round bookman the English-speaking world has produced." His broad knowledge, his engaging personality and sense of humor, his infectious enthusiasm for books, his encouragement of newcomers in the field, his skill in bringing together people of diverse interests, and his vigorous championship of professional and humanitarian causes all have combined to make him a legendary figure.

**REFERENCES**

*Frederic G. Melcher: Friendly Reminiscences of a Half Century among Books and Bookmen,* edited by Mildred C. Smith (1945). In addition to the editor's introduction, a preface by Christopher Morley, and a memoir of his early years by Melcher, this volume contains pieces by Charles E. Goodspeed, D. Laurance Chambers, Harry Hansen, Harry L. Gage, Harry M. Lydenberg, B. W. Huebsch, Bertha E. Mahony Miller, and Marion E. Dodd. (The entry in *Current Biography 1945* is based largely on this book.)

Helen Adams Masten, editor, "Frederic G. Melcher Memorial Issue," *Top of the News* (1964). In addition to an assessment by the editor and two autobiographical essays by Melcher, this issue contains articles by Storer B. Lunt, Irene Smith Green, Ruth Gagliardo, Mildred C. Smith, Anne J. Richter, Leonore St. John Power Mendelson, and Ruth Hill Viguers.

Irene Smith, *A History of the Newbery and Caldecott Medals* (1957), contains information drawn from Melcher's correspondence files.

G. THOMAS TANSELLE

## Metcalf, Keyes Dewitt

(1889–  )

Keyes Dewitt Metcalf achieved international recognition for his contributions as a library administrator at the New York Public Library, as Director of the University Libraries at Harvard during a period of vigorous growth, and as consultant to the library world at large. He became a leader of the profession who won the admiration of generations of librarians.

Metcalf was born April 13, 1889, in Elyria, Ohio, the son of a railroad engineer. One of 17 children, he went to work while still in high school as a page in the nearby Oberlin College Library, where his brother-in-law, Azariah Root, was Librarian. As a student at Oberlin between 1907 and 1911, he continued his work in the Library as well as playing on the college football and track teams. After graduation he served for a time as Root's Executive Assistant.

Metcalf enrolled in 1911 in the first class of the New York Public Library School, earning its certificate in 1913 and its diploma in 1915. While a student there he worked in the main reading room of the then new and still palatial building at Fifth Avenue and 42nd Street, beginning a relationship with that institution that was to extend over the next quarter-century. He served successively as its Chief of Stacks, Chief of the Order Division, Executive Assistant, and finally—from 1928 to 1937—was in charge of the entire massive operation as Chief of the Reference Department.

Metcalf's accomplishments at the NYPL alone would have been enough to assure him illustrious recognition in the annals of American librarianship. Together with its Director, Harry M. Lydenberg, he furnished a substantial measure of leadership to the library profession through his increasing involvement in the work of the American Library Association. Also during this period he married the former Martha Gerrish, and they became parents of a daughter, Margaret, and a son, William. Widowed in 1938, he later married Elinor Gregory.

Metcalf began the second portion of his tripartite career when President James B. Conant of Harvard persuaded him in 1937 to go to Cambridge, Massachusetts, as Librarian of Harvard College and Director of University Libraries. The first person ever to fill that post who was not himself a Harvard graduate, and the first trained Librarian, Metcalf instituted many significant changes in library operations between that time and his retirement 18 years later.

Faced early in his incumbency by a worsening space situation in the Widener Library, then only two decades old, Metcalf soon conceived a multifaceted library plant development program calculated to accommodate Harvard's extensive collections for almost a half-century. The program included construction of a special building for rare books and manuscripts, completed as the Houghton Library in 1942; a remote facility for joint storage of seldom-used materials, completed in the same year as the New England Deposit Library; a library for undergraduates, the Lamont Library, opened in 1949; and a structure for additional stacks and services beneath the southeast corner of the Harvard Yard, added as the Pusey Library in 1977. This network of libraries, all interconnected above and below grade with Widener, created in effect a library campus within the University campus. Another integral part of Metcalf's plan for meeting the University's library spatial requirements was a calculated move toward intentional but controlled physical decentralization of libraries. All of these developments were implemented during and after Metcalf's administration in accord with the concepts described in his annual report for the year 1939–40.

Metcalf's program for housing the collections was only one of many major accomplishments that took place during his tenure. Among other things, he altered markedly the character of Harvard's library staff by bringing in large numbers of men and women trained in library schools, a change that brought the library system closer to the mainstream of American librarianship and gave it a more professional, cosmopolitan cast. His concern for the collections themselves manifested itself in the remarkable accessions of rare materials, the vast increase in general holdings (from 4,000,000 to 6,000,000 volumes), and the establishment of a strong library book selection program. He also elicited important modifications in the way in which the University administered and funded its library affairs, in keeping with the needs of contemporary scholarship.

As head of the world's largest university library during this period of vigorous library growth, Metcalf thus experienced first—and frequently solved—many of the problems of sheer size that would later plague other institutions. Other libraries found it always to their benefit, when faced by a problem resulting from size, to look first at how Harvard had responded to it. In this way Metcalf

ALA

*Keyes Dewitt Metcalf*

and his associates, whom he was particularly adept at selecting and developing, came deservedly to be viewed as a principal fountainhead of creativity and innovation in the field of research librarianship.

In 1955 Harvard University conferred emeritus status upon Keyes Metcalf, but this meant only that he could then embark full-time upon a third career—one already well established—as adviser and consultant-extraordinary to the library world at large. Especially active in the field of building planning, this work took him in the next quarter-century to all of the continents on the globe, save Antarctica, and involved him in a phenomenal 600 assignments. In 1965 he produced his landmark work, *Planning Academic and Research Library Buildings,* which brought the impress of his expertise to bear upon hundreds of additional buildings.

Metcalf remained professionally active throughout his long career. He served on innumerable boards and committees of ALA and was President, 1942–43. The historian of the Association of Research Libraries, of which Metcalf was for five years Executive Secretary, rates him that Association's all-time most influential participant. He was a founding member and President of the American Documentation Institute, later the American Society for Information Science. He was Adjunct Professor of Library Service at Rutgers from 1955 to 1958, and his bibliography of published writings extends to more than 180 items. These accomplishments have brought him many prestigious awards and recognitions, including 13 honorary doctor's degrees and the unique 50th Anniversary Medal of Achievement from the New York Public Library in 1971.

Great industry, boundless energy, and enviable endurance have pervaded his work at every point. He also became well known for his unexampled humanity, his patience, his humility, and his gentleness. A gregarious but slightly shy man, quick to smile and easy to know, Keyes Metcalf continued in the tenth decade of his life to fulfill a felicitous father-image for generations of American librarians.

**REFERENCES**

Keyes D. Metcalf, "Six Influential Academic and Research Librarians," *College and Research Libraries* (1976).

Edwin E. Williams, "The Metcalf Administration, 1937–1955 and Keyes D. Metcalf, a Bibliography of Published Writings," *Harvard Library Bulletin* (1969).

DAVID KASER

## Metcalfe, John Wallace
(1901– )

John Wallace Metcalfe, Australian library leader and educator, won an international reputation for his contributions to the history and theory of cataloguing and classification. He was born in Blackburn, Lancashire, England, on May 16, 1901. When he was six, the family moved to New Zealand, then moved again three years later to Adelaide, South Australia. When Metcalfe was 11, they moved yet again to Sydney, New South Wales (NSW). There Metcalfe would remain for the rest of his professional life, destined to play an important role in the intellectual life of the city and state.

Metcalfe attended a state school in Marrickville, a Sydney suburb, and took his first library position at the age of 16 as an Assistant in the Fisher Library of the University of Sydney. He graduated from the University with First Class Honours in History in 1923 and on December 1 of that year was appointed an Assistant in the Public Library of New South Wales, the oldest and then probably the largest and most influential reference and research library in the Australian Commonwealth. Nine years later he had risen to the position of Deputy Principal Librarian. In 1942 he was appointed Principal Librarian, a position he was to hold until 1959, when he became Librarian of the University of New South Wales.

During his years in the Public Library of New South Wales, Metcalfe was active in creating and supporting the Free Library Movement. Established in 1935 as an organization for laypeople, the Free Library Movement had as a major aim the creation of free public libraries in municipalities and shires throughout the country, supported partly by local taxes and partly by state subsidy. It was founded by Geoffrey Remington and others after the results of the Munn-Pitt survey of Australian libraries were published. Metcalfe's involvement was also intensified by his experience in 1934–35 of studying libraries in Great Britain, Europe, and the United States on a grant from the Carnegie Corporation. Largely as a result of the activity of the Free Library Movement, the NSW Minister for Education set up in 1937 a Library Advisory Committee with Metcalfe as member and Secretary. He was responsible for much of the Committee's report and for the attached draft bill that became the basis for the Library Act of 1939. Owing to the war, the provisions of the Act were not fully implemented until 1944, and in that year Metcalfe, as Principal Librarian of the Public Library of NSW, became ex officio Executive Member of the Library Board of NSW. Created under the act, the Board was to encourage and oversee the development of public libraries throughout the state and to recommend the disbursement of state subsidies to them.

In 1935 Metcalfe became the first Australian to be admitted by examination as a Fellow of the Library Association (FLA) of the United Kingdom. His interest in the education of librarians, the systematic provision of which was also an aim of the Free Library Movement, led him to set up training classes in the Public Library of NSW in 1937 or 1938. The library school thus created continued for many years and enabled Metcalfe and his associates to put their stamp on a whole generation of Australian librarians. His *General Introduction to Library Practice,* part of which was prepared in collaboration with others, formed the basis for instruction in the library school and went through three editions (1940, 1943, and 1955) with various formats and supplements.

In 1937 Metcalfe organized the Australian Institute of Librarians, which became the Library Association of Australia in 1949 and which was granted a Royal Charter in 1963. Until recently a major function of the Association was that of a professional examining body for librarians, and Metcalfe served as Chairman of its Board of Examiners from 1943 to 1958. He was General Secretary of the Association from 1937 to 1938 and again from 1950 to 1953, President from 1946 to 1948, and again President from 1957 to 1959. He was the first Editor of the Association's journal, *The Australian Library Journal,* and wrote most if not all of the unsigned copy for many of the early issues.

After 35 years of service with the state government in the Public Library of NSW, Metcalfe resigned in 1959 to become the first Librarian of the University of NSW, a position he accepted partly because of the opportunity it gave him of creating a post-graduate school of Librarianship in the University. The School was opened in 1960 and initiated a new pattern of education for librarians in Australia.

Metcalfe wrote widely on a variety of professional subjects. His major books are *Information Indexing and Subject Cataloging: Alphabetical, Classified, Coordinate, Mechanical* (1957), *Subject Classifying and Indexing of Libraries and Literature* (1959), *Alphabetical Subject Indication of Information* (Rutgers Series on Systems for the Intellectual Organisation of Information, vol. 3, 1965), and *Information Retrieval, British and American, 1876–1976* (1976). He also wrote voluminously on many educational, cultural, and community matters in Australian local and national journals and newspapers, the latter of which, in his heyday in the Public Library of NSW, consulted him frequently for or reported his forceful, pithy, sometimes controversial views.

In 1947 Metcalfe was appointed to the Australian delegation to the Unesco General Conference in Mexico City, and upon its conclusion, at the invitation of the Carnegie Corporation and the British Council, was once again able to visit libraries in the United States and Great Britain. In October 1956 he was seconded for nine months as a consultant to Fisher Library at the University of Sydney. Metcalfe retired from the University of NSW and from professional life in 1968.

**REFERENCE**

W. Boyd Raymond, editor. *The Variety of Librarianship: Essays in Honour of John Wallace Metcalfe* (1976), contains a full bibliography of Metcalfe's writing together with a list of published items about him in the *Australian Library Journal.*

W. BOYD RAYWARD

# Mexico

The Federal Republic of Mexico, the northernmost country of Middle America, is bounded by the United States, the Gulf of Mexico, Belize, and Guatemala and, on the west, by the Pacific Ocean. Pop. (1978 est.) 66,944,000; area 1,972,550 sq.km. The official language is Spanish.

In Mexico, as in most other countries, there are public libraries, school libraries, academic libraries, and special libraries. Their different stages of development are due mostly to the lack of planning at a national level; the absence of library systems; the scarce amount of human, bibliographic, and economic resources; and the past indifference of local authorities.

The outlook for libraries has improved, mostly because some institutions, such as UNAM (Universidad Nacional Autónomo de Mexico, National Autonomous University of Mexico), CONACYT (Consejo Nacional de Ciencia y Tecnología), and Secretaría de Educación Pública (Ministry of Education), among others, were giving libraries attention and support in the late 1970's and finally came to realize what libraries have always been in the country—a need.

Of approximately 13,840,000 volumes in the country, 58 percent are found in the Federal District; distribution of books and libraries is uneven.

**National Library** The Biblioteca Nacional de México (National Library of Mexico) and the Hemeroteca Nacional de México (National Library of Periodicals of Mexico) are part of and are coordinated by the Instituto de Investigaciones Bibliográficas (Bibliographical Research Institute) of UNAM.

The Biblioteca Nacional de México was founded by presidential decree in 1867 in Mexico City, the capital. It is a depository library for all material published in Mexico and offers information and research services to all kinds of users. The general collection has 1,500,000 volumes, with a strong emphasis on the humanities. The old and rare book collection comprises approximately 41,750 books and 45,000 manuscripts. It is rich in historical material and offers a vast amount of primary source material on Mexico. The bibliography section has some 7,000 volumes of bibliographies from all over the world.

The Library publishes the *Anuario Bibliográfico* (Bibliographic Annual), which covers all material published in Mexico from 1958 to 1963. As of 1967 the bibliographic production of Mexico is covered in the periodical publication *Bibliografía Mexicana*.

Theodore F. Welch

*Decorated with mosaics by Diego Rivera, the Universidad Nacional Autónoma de México, is one of the world's most striking library buildings.*

The Hemeroteca Nacional is for periodical publications what the Biblioteca Nacional is for books. The collection of newspapers and journals is an important resource, especially notable for Mexico City newspapers, some of which date from the 18th century. The materials are available for internal use or through interlibrary loan. Other services available include reference, research, photocopying, and microfilming.

For many years the files of newspapers and periodicals were part of the Biblioteca Nacional. As the collection grew it became necessary to relocate them; in 1944 the Hemeroteca Nacional was established.

A project to house both libraries under the same roof was begun in the late 1970's.

**Academic Libraries.** Even though many university libraries still lack the collections, facilities, and professional staff necessary to offer adequate library service, it is within this group that libraries have had the major impulse to develop during the 1970's. Collections have grown and improved considerably as institutions have realized the importance of the library in the university and have allowed larger budgets for acquisitions and for better-paid professional librarians. (A high percentage of professional librarians work in university libraries.) The Escuela Nacional de Agricultura (National School of Agriculture), Instituto Tecnológico y de Estudios Superiores de Monterrey (Technological Institute of Monterrey), El Colegio de México, Universidad Iberoamericana, and Universidad Metropolitana are among those that designed and built new library buildings in the late 1960's and the 1970's.

**Metropolitan Free Libraries Association** (London) **410**

**Metropolitan Toronto Library** (Canada) **113**
*illus.* **111, 114**

**Mexican Association of Librarians** **370**

**Michigan Library Consortium,** U.S. regional network **480**

**Michigan, University of, Department of Library Science** **90**

**Libraries in Mexico (1976)**

| Type | Number | Volumes in collections | Annual expenditures (peso) | Population served | Professional staff | All staff (total) |
|---|---|---|---|---|---|---|
| National | 1 | 1,810,000 | N.A. | N.A. | N.A. | 300 |
| Academic | 450 | 4,306,955 | N.A. | N.A. | N.A. | 2,233 |
| Public | 579 | 2,906,319 | N.A. | N.A. | N.A. | 1,327 |
| School | 472 | 1,842,342 | N.A. | N.A. | N.A. | 1,092 |
| Special | 333 | 2,971,347 | N.A. | N.A. | N.A. | 1,156 |
| Total | 1,835 | 13,836,963 | | | | 6,108 |

**Public Libraries.** Scattered over the country, following no plan nor belonging to any system as such, public libraries throughout Mexico remained neglected, functioned inadequately, and faced many serious problems as of 1978. Early that year the Secretaría de Educación Pública (Ministry of Education) created the Dirección General de Publicaciones y Bibliotecas, which started a program to promote public libraries including centralizing acquisitions and technical processes; supplying libraries with new and useful books and other materials; organizing a variety of workshops, courses, and seminars for their staff; offering technical assistance; organizing public services in general; and remodeling old library buildings and building new ones.

Among public libraries offering the most notable collections are the Biblioteca de México, Biblioteca del Congreso de la Unión, and Biblioteca Pública del Estado de Jalisco.

**School Libraries.** There is no school library system; as with public libraries, this sector has long been neglected. Though it is generally understood that where there are schools there must be libraries and while the need for them is recognized and accepted, most schools both at the elementary and secondary level do not have them. Only 10 percent of all primary and 50 percent of all high schools in the Federal District have libraries, and only a few of them are adequate. Private schools, by contrast, are required by the Secretaría de Educación Pública to have libraries, providing a few good ones.

**Special Libraries.** There are some 300 special libraries and information centers in Mexico, most of them in Mexico City. These libraries employ, together with academic libraries, the largest number of library professionals and information specialists of the country.

Most special libraries possess the necessary economic and bibliographic resources to function properly. Some of the best libraries in Mexico are those specialized libraries and information centers that grew in the 1970's in response to the needs of developing technology and industry. Among the most significant collections are the ones at the libraries of Banco de México, Banco Nacional de México, Nacional Financiera, Instituto Nacional de Antropología e Historia, and Instituto Nacional de Energía Nuclear, but there are many good, smaller, and even more specialized libraries that serve an important and highly specialized group of users.

**National Associations.** AMBAC, the Asociación Mexicana de Bibliotecarios (Mexican Association of Librarians), was founded in 1954. It had 455 members in 1978. Two of its main objectives are the professional improvement of its members and the promotion of libraries, library service, and librarianship throughout the country. It has several committees, among them the Publishing Committee, which publishes a quarterly newsletter, *Noticiero de la AMBAC,* and a directory of Mexican librarians; the Committee for the Promotion of Libraries; the Bibliographic Committee; and the Committee for Meetings, Conferences, and Congresses, which organizes a yearly Congress and other periodic meetings.

AMBAC has several regional associations; and as affiliate ABIESI, Asociación de Bibliotecarios de Instituciones de Enseñanza Superior e Investigación (Association of Librarians of Higher Learning and Research Institutions), founded in 1957 by a group of academic librarians. It has 60 institutional members and 120 personal members. It has set the standards for interlibrary loan in the country, organizes specialized courses and seminars of general interest for the library profession, and publishes two irregular series: *Cuadernos* and *Archivos.*

**REFERENCES**

Paul Bixler, *The Mexican Library* (1969).
Rosa María Fernandez de Zamora, *Apuntes para la historia de las bibliotecas universitarias de México* (ABIESI, 1975).
Estela Morales Campos, "Las bibliotecas universitarias en México," *Bibliotecas y Archivos* 7 (1976).
Carl M. White, *Mexico's Library and Information Services: A Study of Present Conditions and Needs* (1969).
Mexico Secretaria de Educacion Publica, *Directorio de bibliotecas de la República Mexiana,* edited by Cecilia Culebra y Vives, 2 vol. (1979).

CARMEN E. DE GARCÍA MORENO

# Micrographics

Micrographics is that field of information management concerned with the creation and utilization of microimages, images too small to be discerned by the unaided eye. Most microimages are representations of textual and graphic information and are produced by the highly precise photographic techniques of microphotography. Microimages are recorded on both transparent and opaque media, which collectively are called microforms. Transparent microforms are called microfilm, and opaque microforms are referred to as micro-opaques.

The earliest experiments in microphotography were carried out in the mid-1800's, and some microfilm copies of rare and valuable materials were exchanged between research libraries in the early part of this century. It was not until the 1930's, however, when specialized microfilm cameras were built by Eastman Kodak, that micropublishing became a reality. During the 1960's when American higher education was expanding rapidly, many academic libraries augmented their basic collections with microform editions of otherwise unavailable works essential to undergraduate instruction and graduate research. The information compaction offered by microforms has proved attractive to libraries, especially industrial, technical, and other special libraries, many of which operate within severe space constraints. Microphotography has likewise served as an effective and relatively economical means of preserving the information content of deteriorating printed materials, especially newspapers. Recently a new type of micrographic technology, *computer output microfilming* (COM), has been widely applied to the management of libraries and to their bibliographic records.

**Types of Microforms.** Based on their physical forms, microforms are of two types: roll and flat. Roll microforms are available in several widths, only two of which—16-mm and 35-mm—are commonly found in libraries. By historic precedence, 35-mm microfilm is the de facto standard for roll microforms in academic and research libraries. This film width permits the use of relatively low reductions that result in more legible microimages from newspapers, deteriorating manuscripts, and other difficult-to-copy materials. Even though most serials, monographs, typewritten reports, and other recently published materials can be legibly recorded on 16-mm microfilm, many academic libraries have a considerable investment in 35-mm microfilm and associated display equipment. For these libraries, the acquisition of 16-mm microfilm would introduce the added complications and extra costs of a mixed-media system. On the other hand, critics of the 35-mm format point to the limited selection of newer, more convenient display equipment as a major deterrent to user acceptance of that medium. Because 16-mm microfilm is widely used in business applications, a number of up-to-date display devices are available. Consequently, many industrial libraries prefer the 16-mm width for roll film applications. Cartridges and cassettes can be used to facilitate handling of 16-mm roll microfilm, with a resulting favorable effect on user acceptance.

Two thousand letter-size pages can be recorded on a 100-foot roll of 16-mm microfilm at a 24-to-1 reduction ratio. Flat microforms, on the other hand, are designed for applications where the recording of smaller numbers of related images is desired. Because they are often used to group a number of related images and thereby segregate them from unrelated images, flat microforms are referred to as *unitized* microforms. The dominant flat microform is the *microfiche* (often abbreviated to *fiche*), a rectangular sheet of microfilm bearing microimages in a grid of rows and columns. While microfiche are made in a variety of sizes, the national and international standard size is 105 by 148 mm. Information capacity varies from 60 to over 400 images, depending primarily on the reduction ratio used. In the United States microfiche became popular in the mid-1960's as a means for disseminating technical reports by government agencies. In conjunction with the increasing use of COM over the last decade, a number of relatively low-cost, high-quality microfiche readers have been developed, resulting in intensified interest in microfiche as an alternative to roll microfilm even in applications where unitization is not a primary consideration. A variant form of microfiche, called *ultrafiche*, employs proprietary technology to achieve extremely high reductions and thereby increase fiche capacity to upward of 3,000 images. Ultrafiche have, in the main, been used for micropublishing "package libraries" and for compacting and unitizing parts catalogues.

Other flat microforms resemble microfiche but have somewhat different application characteristics. A *microfilm jacket* is a unitized, transparent carrier for strips of roll microfilm. Since the individual strips of film are replaceable, jackets have been used to miniaturize vertical files and other document collections that require updating. Microprint, a proprietary product of Readex Microprint Corporation, is a unique flat microform that consists of miniaturized page images printed on both sides of an opaque cardstock. Other micro-opaques, notably those sold under the trade names Microcard and Microlex, are no longer in production, although many research libraries retain large files of them. A group of hybrid microforms—aperture cards, card jackets, and jacket cards—combine transparent microimages with opaque cardstock (for eye-readable and card-punch information) in a single

Texas State Library

*Microfilm publications, like this edition of the 1850 U.S. Census, decrease storage space and make materials more widely available.*

medium. They are used widely in business and industry but have seen little application in libraries.

**Production of Microforms.** The oldest method of producing microforms, source document microphotography, involves microfilming physical document pages. Several types of cameras are used for this purpose. Rotary cameras, which employ a high-speed document transport mechanism and film the documents "on the fly," have proven popular in banking and other businesses. The limited resolution capabilities of rotary cameras make them impractical for books and other library materials, although they can be used to microfilm library business records. Quite a number of libraries have used rotary cameras to make security copies of their card catalogues. However, some authorities question the utility of these copies. Planetary cameras, which microfilm stationary documents positioned on a flat surface, typically offer the high resolution required for research materials and are preferred in library applications requiring 16-mm or 35-mm microfilm. A special type of planetary camera, the step-and-repeat camera, is designed to create microfiche.

The silver halide process remains the dominant technology in source document microfilming. It offers excellent resolution and is the only microphotographic process that, properly applied, can assure long-term image stability. Because it requires wet chemical processing in a darkroom, it is time-consuming and inconvenient. As a result, several manufacturers have developed source document cameras employing alternative recording technologies. The 3M 1050 Step-and-Repeat Camera, for example, records microimages on dry silver microfilm that is exposed to light and developed by heat alone. The A. B. Dick/Scott System 200 Record Processor employs a variant of the electrostatic process used in office copiers to produce microimages on a transparent sheet of film. The resulting microfiche can later be reinserted in the camera for the addition of new images. By 1979, the Bell and Howell Company had introduced a similar "updatable" microfiche system, and another system had been announced by the 3M Company. For the duplication of existing microforms, many users prefer diazo or vesicular microfilms. Although unsuited to use in cameras, these duplicating films are less expensive and more convenient to work with than silver halide duplicating film.

The need to record rapidly the voluminous results of computer processing has led to the development of COM, a technology by which computer-processed data are converted directly to human-readable information on microfilm without the creation of intervening paper documents. In the most prevalent COM recording technique, the output of a computer is displayed as a page of human-readable characters on the face of a cathode ray tube and automatically photographed onto silver halide microfilm by a built-in camera. Several newer COM recorders employ laser beams to "write" directly onto microfilm. These recorders utilize dry silver film that, conveniently, is developed by heat as a part of the same continuous process. Regardless of recording method, the speed, quality, and versatility of COM recorders compares very favorably with those of high-speed computer printers, and COM usually has a significant cost advantage when multiple copies are needed.

The current intense library interest in COM has been stimulated by the success of OCLC and other MARC-derivative services that have enabled libraries to create conveniently machine-readable files of their holdings. An increasing number of public, academic, and special libraries have replaced card and book catalogues with COM counterparts on microfiche or 16-mm microfilm. COM has proved especially attractive as an economical medium for the publication of the union catalogues of library systems. A number of vendors of acquisitions and cataloguing services have developed programs to create COM catalogues from library-supplied OCLC tapes or other machine-readable MARC or non-MARC records. Two vendors have developed motorized 16-mm microfilm readers specifically for the display of COM catalogues. Library COM applications are not, however, limited to catalogues but include patron files, circulation records, serials listings, and other computer-generated reports.

**Micropublishing.** While early library microform programs emphasized the filming of research materials by the library itself, most libraries now purchase micropublications from micropublishers, broadly defined as producers of information in multiple-copy microform for sale to the public (including libraries). The library market is now served by both institutional and commercial micropublishers. The former group includes the Library of Congress, the National Archives, the Government Printing Office, other libraries, historical societies, and various cultural and government agencies. Their micropublishing programs are typically based on their own holdings and, in many cases, developed as a by-product of preservation microfilming or interlibrary loan activities. The ranks of commercial micropublishers include conventional book publishers, microfilm service bureaus, very small companies, and divisions of large corporations; the content and number of their offerings are equally varied. Some have extensive lists of titles; others offer only a few.

Micropublications can be divided into three groups: original, simultaneous, and retrospective. Original micropublications contain information published for the first time in any form. The microfilming of doctoral dissertations by University Microfilms in 1938 was probably the earliest instance of original micropublishing. Other original micropublication programs include the publication of technical reports on microfiche by ERIC and NTIS, scholarly monographs on highly specialized subjects published by university presses, a relatively small number of limited circulation serials, and certain MARC-derivative bibliographies such as *MARCFICHE* and *Books in English*.

Simultaneous micropublications, those issued at the same time as their paper edition counterparts, have experienced only limited acceptance, apparently because the cost differential between the two formats—paper and microforms—is usually too small to overcome the resistance many persons have to the latter. The simultaneously micropublished versions of some technical journals, however, appeal to foreign subscribers to whom they can be air-mailed at reasonable cost.

Retrospective micropublishing (or micro-republishing, as it is also called) is the republication in microform of material previously published in paper form. It is a form of reprinting and represents the dominant type of micropublishing to the library market. The earliest retrospective micropublishing programs dealt with a particular type of publication, such as serials, newspapers, or out-of-print books. While these programs remain important, more recent micropublishing projects are based on themes or established bibliographies. These collections can be viewed as anthologies, some on a grand scale; the largest of them contain tens of thousands of individual titles on roll film, fiche, or both.

The growth of micropublishing has given rise to the need for improved bibliographic control of micropublications, and recent years have seen important developments in this area. At the national and international levels, a number of trade bibliographies and related publications are designed to enable libraries to identify and understand the offerings of various micropublishers. These publications include: *Microform Review,* a leading selection aid for micropublications; the *Guide to Microforms in Print;* its companion *Subject Guide to Microforms in Print;* and the *Micropublishers Trade List Annual,* a collection of micropublishers' catalogues on microfiche accompanied by a

General Libraries, University of Texas at Austin

*Newspapers, preserved and stored on microfilm, are available for research at the University of Texas at Austin.*

hard copy index. In addition to these bibliographies, four Library of Congress printed catalogues facilitate the identification and location of microforms made from various research materials. The *National Register of Microform Masters* is a main-entry catalogue of master microforms created by both commercial and institutional micropublishers and reported on a voluntary basis. Microform masters of newspapers are reported in *Newspapers in Microform: United States, 1948–72* and *Newspapers in Microform: Foreign Countries, 1948–72.* Locations of microform masters and use copies of archives and manuscripts are reported in the *National Union Catalog of Manuscript Collections.* Locations of microform copies of monographs available for use by library patrons are reported in the *National Union Catalog.*

These improvements in national bibliographic control in the U.S. have been accompanied by similar local improvements. Recognizing the difficulties inherent in identifying and locating individual items in micropublished sets containing thousands or tens of thousands of titles, a number of major micropublishers have developed special bibliographic tools to support their offerings. These tools may take the form of catalogue card sets, book-form indexes, or both.

**Display Equipment.** The acceptance of microforms by library users has since the beginning suffered from the inadequacies of reading machines and other display devices. While there remains much room for further development, the quality of microform readers has improved significantly. These improvements are especially notable in newer microfiche readers, most of which are of modular design and incorporate high-quality optics, straightforward operating controls, and easily interchanged lenses. Libraries can select from a number of satisfactory models at prices under $300. In addition, several roll microfilm readers have been developed specifically for library applications. Notable features of these readers include screens large enough to display an entire newspaper page and simplified operation with instructions imprinted on the reader itself. Prices for these readers, however, exceed $1,000. The development of roll film readers for library COM applications has already been mentioned.

Libraries whose users require paper enlargements of microimages can select from a number of reader/printers. Prices for this equipment remain relatively high: $1,500 to $3,000 for a microfiche reader/printer; $2,500 to $5,000 for a roll microfilm reader/printer. Xerox and the Bruning Micrographics Division of AM International sell high-speed enlarger/printers that are designed to make single or multiple plain paper copies of microfiche images. The prices of these devices are high.

**Future Trends.** The micrographics industry is moving toward a closer identification with data processing and automated office technologies, as the increasing popularity of COM indicates. Other trends include the development of updatable microfiche systems suitable for use in paperless office environments, the emerging integration of microforms with word processing and electronic mail systems, and the growing number of hybrid systems that combine micrographic storage of document images with computer-based manipulation of index data. These developments have significant potential for the improvement of information storage and dissemination in libraries. Their application, however, is not significantly widespread to permit accurate assessment of their likely impact.

**REFERENCES**

Pamela Darling, "Microforms in Libraries: Preservation and Storage," *Microform Review* (1976).

William Saffady, *Computer Output Microfilm: Its Library Application* (ALA, 1978).

———, *Micrographics* (1978).

WILLIAM SAFFADY;
CARL M. SPAULDING

Courtesy of The Newberry Library

*The Cloisters, Gloucester, western England, showing carrels.*

## Middle Ages, Libraries in the

The period from the extinction of the Roman Empire in the West in 476 to the discovery of America in 1492 and the rise of European nation-states is on the whole one of the darkest in the history of culture, books, and libraries. But a tenuous connection survived between the great libraries of the ancient world and the beginning of libraries as they are understood today. This great extent of time was far from being uniform and can be subdivided into four periods that showed different characteristics of library development. The first period, up to the end of the 6th century, witnessed the final collapse of the ancient classical heritage. The second period, up to the 9th century, saw its replacement by the Christian institution of monasticism as the refuge of a tradition of letters. The third period commenced with the slow growth of medieval cultural institutions after the devastations of the last phase of the barbarian invasions—the raids of the Vikings, the Saracens, and the Hungarians in the 9th and 10th centuries—which gravely impaired social institutions and destroyed many monasteries and their libraries. It closed with the rise of the universities in an age of increased clerical literacy in the service of church and state. The final period of the Middle Ages showed a rapid increase in the production of books in manuscript and, at the end, in printed form, as well as rapidly growing literacy among the middle-class laity, the beginning of the new learning of the Renaissance, and the physical development of libraries in the older institutions.

Dom David Knowles, in his *Religious Orders in England* (1955), gives a relevant definition: "A library is to our thinking a large and comprehensive collection of books, gathered together according to a carefully prepared scheme to serve determined purposes, and housed from the beginning in a building designed to accommodate both the books and those who wish to consult or study them." If we are to understand the history of libraries as instruments of scholarly work or preservers of the intellectual heritage at this early period, it is necessary to put together all scraps of information that survive relating to the provision of books. Evidence is provided by literary and historical references and archaeology, as well as by catalogues of medieval collections and by the books themselves that have survived the devastation caused by negligent or intentional destruction. With the caveat that literacy—even literacy in Latin—is not learning, and that learning does not predicate the existence of libraries, the thread can then be traced. There is a single constant throughout the library history of the Middle Ages: the universality of the manuscript in codex format, written on folded leaves of vellum and bound between stout wooden boards, the physical form common to the earliest liturgical manuscripts and some incunabula printed after the age of paper had begun. Provision for storage and use of the codex explains the origin of library architecture.

The format of classical pagan literature had been the papyrus roll, whose physical survival necessitated repeated copying. Neglect and damp, even more than deliberate or accidental destruction by Christians and barbarians, had probably reduced the stock of Roman literature before the beginning of the medieval period, although the tradition of collecting the classics survived among wealthy Romans and provincials in Italy and Gaul into the 6th century. Nevertheless, one of the most vital cultural services of Christian institutions was the preservation of pagan literary works throughout the Middle Ages by copying them in permanent form. Christian hostility to pagan writings had been tempered even before the institution of the Christian Roman Empire by Constantine in the 4th century, through the habit of regarding them as in some sense precursors of Christian revelation, and later they were viewed as sources for grammatical teaching. The Christian Boethius (480–524), the last Roman philosopher, furnished a link between the pagan and Christian traditions, since he studied in the library of his father-in-law, Symmachus, heir of the last great pagan family of Rome. His *De consolatione philosophiae* describes the glazed book presses ornamented with ivory in his own library. Boethius's career as minister to the conquering Gothic king Theodoric is paralleled by that of a more significant figure in the history of libraries, Cassiodorus (502–597).

**Monastery Libraries.** After his retirement from the court of Ravenna and the siege of Rome in 546, Cassiodorus founded the monastery of Vivarium in southern Italy, where he established a *scriptorium* and a library. His *Institutiones* was to serve as a bibliographical guide for future monastic collections and included a detailed account of the making of books. He describes the arrangement of the library, contained in nine *armaria* or book presses, the majority of which held theological works and the remainder liberal arts and sciences. The *Etymologiae* of a Spanish bishop, Saint Isidore (c. 560–636), was even more influential in the organization of knowledge in the Middle Ages. This encyclopedia cites over 150 pagan and Christian writers and contains chapters on libraries, librarians, and their duties. His poem *Versus titulis bibliothecae* indicates that his private library occupied 14 to 16 presses containing from 400 to 500 volumes.

Saint Benedict (c. 480–547?) provided the key to the development of the monastic orders. His *Regula,* on which all later monastic rules were based, secured the place of writing and literacy in the Latin language. Chapter 48 mentions the word *bibliotheca,* though it is uncertain whether it means a room or a collection of books; more significant was the ample provision of time for reading sacred writings and the insistence on manual labor, later to be interpreted as including the work of the *scriptorium.* In the 500 years after Benedict, the copying of books inspired by his Rule—and consequently the survival of learning—was confined almost exclusively to monastic institutions. The root of the Benedictine tradition did not come from the schools of Christian learning in the later Roman Empire but rather from the Eastern monasticism that developed in Egypt. Originally communities of ascetic and usually illiterate hermits, Coptic monasteries, by the time of Saint Pachomius in the 4th century, had codified the place of cloistral reading of the Scriptures, the Fathers, and works of devotion. Archaeological evidence of their use of books can be traced through as late as the 13th century.

The most significant advance of Christianity in the Middle Ages was the tide of conversion that flowed from Rome to England and from the British Isles back to the pagan German lands. Its leaders, devoted to monasticism, regarded books as the life blood of Christianity, and the monasteries they founded developed a vital library tradition of incalculable importance in preserving and transmitting European culture. The missionaries and monasteries can be placed in a family tree that reached to and from the north of England and returned to Italy. Pope Gregory the Great dispatched Saint Augustine to the Kentish kingdom in 597. Saint Augustine, the Easterner Theodore of Tarsus, his successor as Archbishop, and Hadrian, an African monk who had been Abbot of a south Italian monastery, brought books from Rome to Canterbury. The cathedral monastery of Christ Church and the abbey of Saints Peter and Paul, later Saint Augustine's, both established libraries that existed until their destruction in the 16th century. The Northumbrian Benedict Biscop, pupil and successor of Hadrian as Abbot of Saint Peter's, journeyed to Rome several times collecting books and founded the twin monasteries of Wearmouth (674) and Jarrow (681).

Saint Ceolfrid, Abbot of both monasteries, also traveled to Rome, where he probably acquired the *Codex Grandior* that may have belonged to Cassiodorus. The *Codex Amiatinus,* written under his direction for presentation to the Pope, copied its frontispiece, a unique pictorial record of an early library book press. It was at Jarrow that the Venerable Bede (673–735) composed his many scriptural, historical, and scientific works, which evidence the richness of the book collection available to him. His pupil Egbert, Archbishop of York from 732 to 766, founded a cathedral school and library, and this collection served as a source of copies made for monasteries of the Frankish Empire.

Christianity came to Northern England not only from Rome but also from the Celtic church of Ireland. Little can be conjectured about the book collections of Irish monasteries, but Saint Columbanus (543–615) brought books to the monasteries founded by him in his missionary journeys to the Continent. Luxeuil in Burgundy (founded 590) and Bobbio in northern Italy (f. 612) developed great *scriptoria* and libraries, as did the houses founded by his disciples—Saint Gall, in Switzerland (f. 614), and Saint Riquier, in northern France (f. 625–645). A 9th-century plan of Saint Gall indicates a bookroom connected with a *scriptorium,* and in the abbey remains one of the most magnificent of monastic libraries. The library at Bobbio transmitted some of the most ancient books of the Western world to modern times.

The Englishman Boniface, the apostle of Germany (680–755), founded bishoprics and monasteries in the pagan areas east of the Frankish kingdom. When he was martyred by the Frisians, books were in his baggage. The sees of Mainz, Wurzburg, and Salzburg became centers of religious and political influence with schools and libraries. Boniface's monastery of Fulda (f. 744) was to be the most powerful in Germany, housing a *scriptorium* famous for illuminated manuscripts and a great library, of which an 8th-century catalogue survives. Charlemagne, the first of the Frankish emperors, called Alcuin of York to be master of his palace school, and Alcuin became his trusted minister. As the Abbot of Tours, he sent for books from England to add to the library. Alcuin revived Frankish monasticism under his royal patronage. Monasteries such as

Fleury (7th century) and Corbie (f. 657) created collections of manuscripts that were to be matched by those in German lands, such as Reichenau (f. 724), Lorsch (f. 763), and Corvey (f. 822). Classics copied in the Carolingian minuscule hand were to transmit their clear calligraphy to the scholars of the Renaissance. The letters of Lupus, Abbot of Ferrieres (842–860), an indefatigable collector of both classical and Christian titles, document the bibliographical cooperation between monasteries in the period before the devastation inflicted by the Northmen eliminated learning in most of the British Isles and gravely affected it on the Continent.

The period from the 10th to the 12th centuries witnessed first a slow and then a rapid recovery that brought about a rebirth of monastic institutions and their libraries. In England the efforts of Saint Dunstan (924–988) were succeeded by those of Lanfranc (1005–1089), teacher, Prior of Bec in Normandy, and Archbishop of Canterbury. His influential recension of the Benedictine Rule made specific references to the lending and reading of books. Norman prelates rebuilt English abbeys and renewed their collections. After the Saracen sack of Monte Cassino, Abbott Desiderius in the 11th century raised its library and *scriptorium* to its highest level. The greatest age of monasticism was ushered in by the foundation of the new orders of reformed Benedictinism, the "Black Monks" of Cluny (f. 910) and the "White Monks" of Citeaux (f. 1098); both evolved international systems of daughter houses that spread over Europe. The primary concern of their monastic life was not learning but a communal spiritual life in isolation from the world. The Cluniacs placed emphasis on liturgical worship, and the early Cistercians restricted on principle the collecting and reading of books to devotional requirements. The copying of manuscripts was religious work prescribed by the Rule, rather than a method of building up holdings, but along with their great building and economic activities, libraries were created. The first catalogue of Cluny itself in the 13th century enumerates nearly 600 works, and by this time most of the important houses of Black Monks also had sizable collections. Cistercian foundations, such as Fountains in England and Fossa Nuova in Italy, made careful architectural provision for protecting their books, and these developed over the centuries.

The fundamental unit of monastic book storage remained the classical *armarium,* a large wooden cupboard with shelves on which the bindings were laid flat. Sometimes it was recessed into stonework, which has survived. It was usually in the east walk of the cloister between the chapter house (where books were distributed on an annual basis during Lent for the monks' private reading) and the side door of the church. The usual location for study and writing was under the windows of the south walk of the cloister, which in the later Middle Ages was frequently glazed and fitted with wooden carrels. When space became inadequate, storage rooms were built adjoining the chapter house. The book regulations of other orders, such as the Carthusians (f. 1084) and the Premonstratensians (f. 1120), were generally similar to those of the Benedictines. The Carthusians, who lived in detached cells, were allowed the loan of two books at a time. Supervision of books and readers was allotted to the precentor, the official primarily responsible for the maintenance of church services, which included the care of the liturgical books used in the choir. By the end of the 12th century, the provision of libraries in large and small monastic houses was so close to universal practice that an epigram was coined: "A cloister without books is like a castle without an armory."

Episcopal establishments were frequently centers of learning throughout the Middle Ages, and the teaching of famous scholars encouraged the accumulation of books. This was particularly true in cities of northern Italy. A catalogue of the library of Cremona was made shortly after the death of Bishop Liutprand (902–972), diplomat and classicist, and other early records refer to collections at Novara, Vercelli, Monza, and Ivrea. At Verona the Capitular Library can claim lineal descent back to the 5th century, when manuscripts were written that survive to the present. North of the Alps, Archbishop Hincmar of Reims (805–822) and Gerbert, a teacher in the cathedral school there who became Pope Sylvester II (999–1003), acquired notable collections. The latter's pupil Fulbert created a library at Chartres; Beauvais and Rouen also possessed rich libraries. The see of Bamberg (f. 1007) maintained a famous school and inherited the library of the Emperor Henry II in 1024. Prior to the rise of the universities, the educational influence of the cathedral schools and their libraries had outstripped that of the monasteries. Thus when Peter Lombard, the authority on canon law, died in 1160, he bequeathed his books to the cathedral of Notre-Dame in Paris.

**University Libraries.** Before the end of the 12th century, the University of Paris, which had its roots in the cathedral school, had become the center of the scholastic philosophy that generated a new professional literature for the clergy and largely outmoded older medieval writings. The need for books for thousands of students became pressing. The primary response of university authorities was to regulate the book trade by controlling the *stationarii* who supplied the textbooks. The many professional scribes, principally laymen, copied an *exemplar,* writing by the *pecia* for fixed prices. Public library facilities were a secondary growth. The many student hostels in Paris and the daughter university of Oxford were for the most part too small and poor to assume such a function. The growth of larger residences for masters and students, such as the Sorbonne (f. 1257), with substantial buildings and a regulated community life made the formation of libraries possible. The Sorbonne library was organized and catalogued in 1289, and library rules exist from 1321. The collection, as was customary in monastic as well as academic institutions, was divided into two parts: books constantly referred to were chained in the great library, those available for loan or rarely used being secured in a separate room. By 1338 over 300 volumes were in the first location and over 1,000 in the second. At Oxford and Cambridge during the 14th and 15th centuries, the smaller halls were gradually squeezed out by endowed colleges, which erected library facilities of a pattern that has survived to the present day. Libraries common to the university as a whole were of less importance and were founded at a relatively late date. Oxford's collection, bequeathed by Thomas de Cobham in 1327, was housed in a room above the University Church. At Cambridge a university library did not exist until the first half of the 15th century.

The new mendicant orders of friars quickly assumed a dominant role in the universities. The Dominicans (f. 1215) produced famous teachers of philosophy and were soon followed by the Franciscans (f. 1210). Their convents established working collections of books, largely academic and pastoral in content. Dominican instructions of the 1250's include precise library regulations, as do Franciscan constitutions of 1260. The catalogue of the Franciscan mother-house at Assisi in 1381 describes a large collection carefully classified, labeled, and shelved. Substantial libraries were established by the friars in other urban centers. In England the Augustinian collection in York numbered over 600 works in 1372, and in 1429 Sir Richard Whittington built the Greyfriars' convent in London with a substantial library.

**Other Libraries.** Throughout the Middle Ages the popes of Rome must always have required books and archives, but the history of the papal library is fragmented and puzzling. Earlier collections of books and archives probably suffered destruction during the repeated sacking of the city—by the Vandals in 455, the Saracens in 846, and the Normans in 1084. The exile of the papacy to Avignon during the 14th and 15th centuries dispersed the library described in the earliest surviving catalogue of 1295, but records of the existence of libraries go back as far as Pope Damasus (366–84). Archaeological excavation has revealed remains of the building used as a library by Pope Agapetus (535–36), an associate of Cassiodorus. Gregory the Great (590–604) complained of an inadequate library, though the collection may have increased when Pope Zacharias (741–52) transferred it to the Lateran. The title of librarian existed from the time of Hadrian I (722–95), and names are known for librarians of the 11th century.

The separation between Western and Eastern forms of Christianity was a consequence of the division of the Roman Empire. The Eastern or Byzantine Empire, Greek in language and Orthodox in religion, maintained in isolation from the West a continuity of both cultural tradition and imperial authority. Evidence of Eastern libraries exists intermittently over the whole period. Many emperors, from Theodosius II at the end of the 5th century through the Nicaean rulers after the Latin conquest, maintained libraries that may have afforded a degree of public access. A traveler's reference of 1437 gives a glimpse of stone benches and tables used in consulting the palace collection. The contents can be presumed to have included, besides law and theology, works of Greek literature and science. Byzantine encyclopedic works and digests refer to classical works now lost. Higher educational institutions, both theological and secular, such as the academy established by Theodosius II (408–50) and those founded by the Emperors Leo the Philosopher in the 9th century and Constantine Monomachus in the 10th, must have had extensive book collections. The Patriarchate maintained schools and libraries. Monastic collections, such as those at the Lavra on Mount Athos and Saint Catherine's on Mount Sinai, were widely distributed, though usually small. About 825 Saint Theodore, Abbot of Studium, regulated his monks' reading and copying. A Greek monastery that can be singled out because its library still survives in situ and largely intact is one founded by the monk Christodoulos in 1088 on Saint John's island of Patmos in the Aegean. The looting of Constantinople by the Latins in 1204 began the flow of Greek manuscripts to Italy, and the pace accelerated until the final conquest of the city by the Turks in 1453. The acquisitions of Western travelers were supplemented by books brought by emigré Greeks, such as Cardinal Bessarion, who bequeathed his library to the Republic of Venice in 1472. Italian libraries became the home of Greek literature and philosophy, which transformed the culture of the Renaissance and superseded the medieval tradition of learning.

The last two centuries of the Middle Ages witnessed greatly increased production of books and a corresponding growth in accommodation for them among collegiate and monastic institutions. The latter declined drastically in intellectual influence but maintained economic power that enabled them to erect buildings to house, not the products of their own *scriptoria,* but rather scholastic works coming to them by gift or bequest, often from their members who had attended university. At Oxford, the great abbeys of Gloucester and Durham maintained their own halls of residence. The latter was bequeathed but apparently did not receive the rich collection of Richard de Bury (1287–1345), royal civil servant and Bishop of Durham. His *Philobiblon* gives valuable insight as to the state of contemporary learning and libraries. At Canterbury, Archbishop Henry Chichele erected a library building in the early 15th century, and other English cathedral foundations did likewise, a development that was matched in France, as at Rouen. An exceptional 15th-century monastic collection was formed by John Tritheim (1462–1516), Abbot of Sponheim, who acquired 2,000 volumes, many of them printed. Incunabula from other south German monasteries have reached many modern collections, a large proportion of them having found their way into the Bavarian State Library as the result of confiscation during the Napoleonic period.

Oxford colleges had relatively small collections up to the beginning of the 14th century. Later foundations, such as New College (f. 1379), All Souls (f. 1437), and Magdalen (f. 1458), all included libraries in their building plans. These long, narrow rooms had equidistant windows on both sides between which were set lecterns, with the volumes resting on the sloping tops, either at standing height or at sitting height with benches placed between, under the windows. As the books were customarily chained, the length of the desks and the narrow shelf below limited the number of books. This system became universal in larger libraries throughout western Europe. It is exemplified in the library built by the University of Oxford over the Divinity School between 1444 and 1487 and named in honor of its benefactor, Duke Humphrey of Gloucester.

The universities had trained many clerics who possessed private libraries—Chaucer's Clerk of Oxenford, with his 20 books, must have been typical of many thousands. But country gentlemen and lawyers, too, began in the 14th and 15th centuries to acquire considerable collections, evidence of which is found in wills, inventories, and records of gifts. Like other valuables, these were habitually stored in the stout wooden chests universally used throughout the period. Culturally, the laymen's holdings were significant because of the high proportion of books in vernacular languages, only occasionally present in institutional libraries. An outstanding German private collection was formed by the physicians Hermann (1410–85) and Hartmann (1440–1514) Schedel, burghers of the wealthy free city of Nuremberg, most of which survives in the Bavarian State Library. A number of German cities established public libraries for their citizens during the 15th century, Brunswick being the earliest in 1413.

The greatest lay libraries were in the hands of royalty, and these were to become predecessors of the national collections of the future, although bequest, sale, or plunder destroyed their continuity. Kings and emperors throughout the Middle Ages had occasionally been patrons of learning. Charlemagne installed two libraries in his capital of Aachen—as recorded by his biographer Einhard, himself a book collector—and his example was followed by his son, Louis the Pious (814–40), and his grandson, Charles the Bald (840–77). Regrettably, there is no trace of the books of the brilliant Emperor Frederick II, which must have reflected his contacts with the Greek and Muslim cultures of southern Italy and Sicily. In the later Middle Ages kings became less peripatetic, and residence in fixed centers of government made the establishment of royal libraries feasible. Foremost among these were the collections of the French royal house, a good part of whose holdings were literary and historical works written in or translated into French. John II (1350–64) bequeathed his taste for books to both branches of his descendants—the Kings of France and the Dukes of Burgundy. His eldest son, Charles V (1364–70), installed a library of three floors in the Louvre with a resident librarian. His third son, John, Duke of Berry (1340–1416), was a munificent patron of scribes and illuminators. His fourth son, Philip the Bold (1363–1404), commenced the collection of the Dukes of Burgundy, augmented by his successors. Partially dispersed after the Netherlands passed under Habsburg rule, the remainder became the nucleus of the Belgian Royal Library.

Two English princes of the House of Lancaster

Courtesy of The Newberry Library

*Medieval scribe at work.*

amassed book collections. John, Duke of Bedford and Regent of France (1389–1435), in 1424 bought the library formed by Charles V. Humphrey, Duke of Gloucester (1391–1447), an early patron of humanist learning north of the Alps, gave hundreds of volumes to the University of Oxford, and after his death King Henry VI gave some of the remainder of his library to King's College in Cambridge, although only a few of his books survived the Reformation. A unique royal library was formed by Matthias Corvinus, King of Hungary (1440–90), allied by marriage with the royal house of Naples, also great collectors. His magnificent Renaissance manuscripts were looted by the Turks after the capture of Buda in 1526, and all but a tiny proportion perished through neglect.

The libraries established by the princes of Italy were of the greatest cultural significance because their collections reflected the new learning of the Renaissance. City tyrants cooperated with the passionate enthusiasm of humanist scholars in the discovery and copying of manuscripts of the Latin and Greek classical writers and in preserving them in libraries. Princely families, such as the Este of Ferrara and Modena, the Gonzaga of Mantua, and the Visconti and Sforza of Milan, formed sumptuous collections that had a propaganda value in reflecting the liberality and culture of the ruling house. Typical were the manuscripts of Federigo da Montefeltro, Lord of Urbino (1444–82), commissioned from the Florentine dealer Vespasiano da Bisticci. The earliest of the great Humanists, the poet Petrarch (1304–74), possessed a substantial library that he intended to, but never did, bequeath to form a public library in Venice.

The leading center of Renaissance learning was Florence. At the beginning of the 15th century two friaries maintained libraries accessible to the citizens, the Carmelites and the Augustinians of San Spirito, to which Petrarch's disciple Boccaccio (1313–75) bequeathed his books. The first citizen and de facto ruler of Florence, Cosimo de Medici, founded the Dominican house of San Marco, and in 1444 built a library in it designed for public use. He arranged for his donations to be supplemented by the bequest of the many classical manuscripts of the scholar and bibliophile Niccolo Niccoli (1363–1437). His fellow Humanist, Poggio Bracciolini (1380–1459), traveled in southern Germany and France from 1415 to 1417, buying, borrowing, or stealing manuscripts of classic authors from the most ancient monastic libraries. The private library of the Medici, greatly increased by Lorenzo the Magnificent (1449–92), did not find a permanent home in San Marco, but most of it—after a sojourn in Rome in the early part of the 16th century with the Medici popes, Leo X and Clement VII—returned to Florence to be incorporated in the Biblioteca Medicea-Laurentiana. It is worth noting that the library's fittings, designed by Michelangelo before 1571, are a final example of the medieval lectern system. The example of San Marco was copied by Malatesta Novella, Lord of Cesena, in a library he had built in the Franciscan convent in 1447, which survives with the original collection, desks and benches intact. The most magnificent Renaissance library housed the papal collection, recreated by the Humanist Pope Nicholas V (1447–55) and enlarged by Sixtus IV (1471–84), who installed the Humanist Bartolomeo Platina as Librarian in 1475 and provided appropriate quarters and fittings. Though these were replaced by the present building in the 16th century, the continuity of the collection extends to the Vatican Library of today.

The libraries of Italy were to have a happier destiny than the medieval libraries north of the Alps. As the latter were representatives of an outmoded philosophy of learning and a hostile religion, the era of the Reformation was to witness their neglect and frequently their total elimination. In England hundreds of monasteries were destroyed with the loss of almost all their books between 1536 and 1540—Durham Cathedral alone retaining an appreciable percentage—and from 1549 to 1551 the university collections were purged. In France and Germany, many libraries suffered similar dispersal and loss in the popular tumults and wars of the 16th and 17th centuries. The social and political upheavals of the French revolutionary era were hardly less destructive. While contemporaries rarely cared, posterity was to mourn the irreplaceable loss of a thousand years of cultural achievement.

**REFERENCES**

Anthony R. A. Hobson, *Great Libraries* (1970).
Raymond Irwin, *The Heritage of the English Library* (1964).
Burnett Hillman Streeter, *The Chained Library* (1970).
James Westfall Thompson, *The Medieval Library* (1957).
Francis Wormald and Cyril E. Wright, editors, *The English Library before 1700* (1958).
*Medieval Scribes, Manuscripts and Libraries: Essays Presented to N. R. Ker* (1978).

JOHN R. T. ETTLINGER

## Milam, Carl Hastings
(1884–1963)

Carl Hastings Milam held the principal executive position, first as Secretary and later as Executive Secretary, of the American Library Association from 1920 to 1948. He was born in Harper County, Kansas, on October 22, 1884. Although a native of Kansas and resident of Illinois during most of his adult years, Milam considered himself an Oklahoman, having lived there from 1893 to 1907. He attended the University of Oklahoma, where, as a student who had to earn part of his living, he worked as one of two student assistants to Milton Ferguson, then the only professional librarian on the staff of the University Library. Through Ferguson's influence he decided on a career in librarianship and entered the New York State Li-

ALA

*Carl Hastings Milam*

brary School after his graduation from Oklahoma in 1907. After completing his studies, he worked as a cataloguer at Purdue University (1908–09).

When Chalmers Hadley resigned in September 1909 as Secretary and organizer of the Indiana Public Library Commission to become Secretary and Executive Officer of the ALA, Carl Milam followed him at the Commission, thus providing in his formative years as a librarian both academic and public library experience. That position prepared him for his later work with ALA, of which he had become a member while student assistant at the University of Oklahoma Library. As Secretary at a time when many public libraries were being organized and needed Commission assistance, he provided advice both in his travels throughout the state and from headquarters in Indianapolis. He prepared reports and forms, spoke to various groups on behalf of libraries, developed programs for continuing education of librarians, and initiated the founding of the first state organization of public library trustees.

After four years with the Commission, Carl Milam resigned late in 1913 to accept the post of Librarian of the Public Library of Birmingham, Alabama, the largest in the state. In 1917 he took leave to work with the Library War Service in Washington, D.C., but returned to Birmingham several times during his leave, finally resigning in 1919.

Milam was one of several assistants to Herbert Putnam, Director of the Library War Service, financed initially by the Carnegie Corporation of New York and by contributions to ALA of $50,000 from libraries and individuals. When Putnam went overseas after the Armistice in 1918, Milam became Acting Director and succeeded Putnam as Director in 1919. Armistice did not lessen the work of the Library War Service either in the U.S. or in the camps overseas; delays in demobilization and the return of servicemen from overseas increased the workload because servicemen needed morale-maintaining activities, opportunities, and information that the wartime libraries could provide. During the months it took to close the libraries, decisions about disposition of buildings and books had to be made. Before and after Armistice Milam worked long hours and showed his administrative abilities in recruiting, selecting, and assigning personnel, planning, policymaking, and public relations. He negotiated skillfully with army officers, government officials, nongovernmental agencies, and other representatives concerned with library service to armed service personnel in the U.S. and abroad.

Work with the Library War Service led Milam directly into ALA's Enlarged Program, of which he was named Director in 1919 and was thus at the same time Director of both the Library War Service, which was terminating its activities, and the Enlarged Program, which was just beginning. At the March 1920 meeting of the ALA Executive Board, the Board considered, among other matters, the resignation of George B. Utley as Secretary and a report by Milam as Director of both the Library War Service and the Enlarged Program. In his report Milam suggested the feasibility of consolidating the two programs in Chicago. The Board abolished the Enlarged Program directorship, merged the responsibilities of that program with those of the Secretary of ALA, and offered the new post to Milam, who became the 12th Secretary but only the 4th paid, full-time executive officer of the Association.

It is difficult for anyone who was not involved closely with Carl Milam during a considerable period of his career to appreciate his abilities as a librarian and administrator. His tenure spanned the 28 years from the end of World War I to the end of World War II and covered the period of rapid growth and change within both the Association and the profession of librarianship. Membership swelled from 4,464 in 1920 when Milam took office to 18,283 when he resigned in 1948 to accept the librarianship of the United Nations Library in New York. He served under 29 Presidents of ALA and was involved in many major reorganizations of the Association—beginning in 1923, through the first three Activities Committees, and through part of the changes that resulted from the investigations and reports of the Fourth Activities Committee.

Milam had to organize a growing, diverse, and increasingly specialized staff to match the growth and diversification of ALA interests and activities. His energies were also directed toward the substantive matters that concerned the Association: improved library services; welfare, salaries, and annuities for librarians; technical bibliographical improvements; publishing; education for librarianship; international relations; better statistical measurements of effectiveness of libraries; federal aid for libraries; and a host of other concerns. In pursuit of the Association's interests, Milam developed strong working relationships with many foundations, including the Carnegie Corporation of New York, Carnegie Endowment for International Peace, Laura Spelman Rockefeller Memorial, Julius Rosenwald Foundation, General Education Board, and the Rockefeller Foundation, as well as with federal agencies and congressional representatives. These relationships bore fruit in support for a wide range of large and small projects, including such major ones as endowment funds for ALA, federal aid for libraries, aid for foreign libraries affected by World War II, establishment of U.S. libraries abroad, and experimentation with microfilm and cooperative cataloguing. Milam also maintained a rapport with other national associations, including the Adult Education Association, the Special Libraries Association, and the Canadian Library Council and its successor, the Canadian Library Association.

Milam capped his career by becoming Librarian of the United Nations Library in 1948 and was responsible for its development from its early beginnings at Hunter College and Lake Success to its move to new quarters at the present UN headquarters in New York City. Milam's program for the Library emphasized the provision of aggressive service to the UN Secretariat. While there would be a relatively small working library and a dependence placed on the rich library resources of the New York City area, a goal was set for completeness in collections of documents and publications of the UN and its many specialized agencies. He believed that a legislative reference type of service should be developed for the UN Secretariat and staff primarily but that it might also serve other agencies, the communications media, international governmental agencies, and affiliated nongovernmental organizations, as well as educational institutions, scholars, and writers.

At the expiration of his UN contract on May 1, 1950, Milam and his wife, Nell Robinson, whom he had married in 1910, returned to their farm near Barrington, Illinois. He grew irises and Christmas trees and engaged in some professional work after returning to Barrington, but the care of his wife, who died in 1956 of a progressively debilitating disease, came to require his constant attention.

In late 1961 he returned to New York for the dedication of the new UN Library building on the invitation of UN Secretary-General Dag Hammarskjöld. During a two-day symposium held after the dedication ceremonies, Milam was praised for his contributions to the organization, functioning, and continuing direction of the UN Library, then renamed the Dag Hammarskjöld Library.

Carl Milam died on August 26, 1963, just after he had sold the Barrington farm and was preparing to move to Jamaica, Iowa, to be near one of his two daughters, Mary Milam Seidler, and her family. The Carl H. Milam

Memorial Lecture was established by the ALA in 1971. The first lecturer was Herman Liebaers, then Director of the Royal Library in Brussels and President of the International Federation of Library Associations.

**REFERENCES**

Doris Cruger Dale, editor, *Carl H. Milam and the United Nations Library* (1976).

Peggy Sullivan, *Carl H. Milam and the American Library Association* (1976). MARION A. MILCZEWSKI

## Moore, Anne Carroll

(1871–1961)

Anne Carroll Moore, children's librarian, author, editor, and critic, formed the Children's Department of the New York Public Library, made many contributions to a new profession, and had significant influence on the creation and publishing of children's literature.

Anne Carroll Moore was born on July 12, 1871, in Limerick, Maine. She was christened Annie, but years later, at the suggestion of her editor, she changed Annie to Anne in order to avoid confusion with Annie E. Moore, who was engaged in a related field of work. In *Roads to Childhood* (1920) she wrote about her parents, her seven older brothers, and especially the influence her father had on her childhood and youth. In her home her lawyer-father read aloud, there were vigorous family discussions, she had her own books, and there seemed to always be a family celebration. When she was ten years old, she was sent to Limerick Academy; "No doubt it was the Academy that gave Anne early control of a lucid style in speaking and writing that was to make her a distinctive critic and essayist in her day," according to her biographer, Frances Clarke Sayers. Anne Carroll Moore entered Bradford Academy in 1889, completed her courses in two years, and graduated in 1891. She returned to Limerick to read law with her father, but the death of both parents brought that plan to an end. Four years later, in 1895, she entered Pratt Institute in Brooklyn, New York, for library training. At the end of this period she was asked by Mary Wright Plummer, Director of the Pratt Institute Free Library, to become Librarian of the Children's Room—"the first in the country to be included in an architect's plan, and the first to make the circulation of books subordinate to familiar acquaintance with books and pictures in a free library" (*Horn Book,* January–February 1942). Her years there were marked by bringing together children, books, and pictures. Moore was not content to know the children who came to the library; she went where they were—to the schools, settlement houses, streets. She established the Children's Library as a focal part of the community. When the room was closed to circulation, she read aloud to the children. This aroused an interest in storytelling and, though she never attempted to tell a story herself, she recognized its value in introducing children to stories. She was convinced of it when she heard Marie Shedlock, the great English storyteller, tell Andersen's stories.

It was from this meeting that storytelling came to the New York Public Library when Anne was asked to form a children's department there. She reported to work on September 1, 1906. Her first responsibility was to bring together under her leadership all those who in any way had been assigned to work with children while at the same time she visited the 36 branches in Manhattan, the Bronx, and Staten Island. She began immediately to train those working with children. Her lectures consisted of such subjects as open shelves, reading aloud, book selection, and administration—all pioneering in children's work. Five years later, May 23, 1911, the main library at 5th Avenue and 42nd Street was opened, and within it was a Central Children's Room. Over the years this room was to become nationally and internationally known for its collections, staff, programs, and influence on authors and illustrators. Meanwhile, Anne Carroll Moore was also guiding the growth of work in the branches so that upon her retirement she had one of the strongest children's departments in the United States.

The New York Public Library

*Anne Carroll Moore*

Her contributions to the profession were many. In 1900 she was chosen as President of the first Round Table organization of librarians actually in charge of children's work at the American Library Association's Annual Conference in Montreal, and in 1901, at the invitation of the American Library Association, the Round Table became a section of ALA and Anne Carroll Moore was its first Chairman. She had been active since her first ALA Conference in 1896. In the fall of 1918 Franklin K. Mathiews of the Boy Scouts of America and Frederic Melcher, editor of *Publishers' Weekly,* went to the office of Anne Carroll Moore to discuss a plan to encourage authors of children's books and to interest others in the children's book world. Children's Book Week, later known as Book Week, was devised in order to celebrate books and reading. There followed the Caldecott and Newbery medals, which Frederic Melcher established under American Library Association auspices. It was in 1918 that Ben W. Huebsch, a prominent publisher, asked Moore to prepare and deliver a series of lectures to a group of distinguished book people—heads of publishing firms, editors, booksellers, writers, artists—on the subject of children's books. It was in 1918 that Macmillan Publishers announced the first separate department for the publishing of children's books under Louise Seaman Bechtel, a close associate of Moore. In the years to follow, Anne Carroll Moore worked closely with children's editors and their authors and illustrators. She exposed her staff, through meetings and branch library visits, to many of the great literary figures of the day. Her staff and exhibits in Central Children's Room represented many nations, and she had enduring friendships with such book people as Beatrix Potter, Leslie Brooke, Walter de la Mare, Padraic Column, and Ruth Sawyer Durand.

In 1918 *The Bookman,* the chief American literary journal of its day, asked Moore to contribute articles and reviews of children's books at regular intervals. There had been frequent but sporadic reviewing of children's books by distinguished writers and illustrators, but, up to that time, there had been a lack of sustained criticism of children's books. She did so from 1918 to 1926. From 1924 to 1930 Moore edited a weekly page of criticism of children's books in *Books* of the *New York Herald Tribune.* Its logo was "The Three Owls," and subsequent books by her carried that title. In 1936 she offered "The Three Owls Notebook" as well as her editorial advice to the *Horn Book.* Her page was last published in 1960, but she continued as one of the Associate Editors. She also contributed lists and articles to journals and publications too numerous to name here. It would be difficult to measure the stimulating effect of such criticism upon the writing, illustrating, and publishing of children's books.

Moore retired from the New York Public Library on October 1, 1941. She died on January 20, 1961. "One person more than any other gave shape and content to the new profession, to the greatest degree and in the fullest measure: Anne Carroll Moore, of Brooklyn's Pratt Institute and the New York Public Library. To be sure, confluence of period and place set the stage for her achievement, but the color and character of her accomplishment derived from the quality of her imagination; her courage and stubborn determination; her shrewd, New England practicality; her logical, analytical mind, which, like a pyrotechnical display, could turn and light up the sky with its rocketing commitment to joy" (Frances Clarke Sayers).

Books by Anne Carroll Moore include *Nicholas: A Manhattan Christmas Story,* with drawings by Jay Van Everen (1924); *Nicholas and the Golden Goose,* with drawings by Van Everen (1932); and Introduction to *The Art of Beatrix Potter,* with an appreciation by Anne Carroll Moore (1954).

Books edited by her are *Roads to Childhood* (1920); *New Roads to Childhood* (1923); *Cross Roads to Childhood* (1926); and *My Roads to Childhood: Views and Reviews of Children's Books* (1939). Others include *The Three Owls: A Book about Children's Books* (1925); *The Three Owls, Second Book* (1928); *The Three Owls, Third Book* (1931); *Knickerbocker's History of New York,* by Washington Irving, illustrated by James Daugherty (1928); and *The Bold Dragoon and Other Ghostly Tales,* by Washington Irving, illustrated by Daugherty (1930). "Children's Books Suggested as Holiday Gifts," published by the New York Public Library as an annual list, was edited by Anne Carroll Moore from 1918 to 1941. She issued other lists and wrote numerous articles. She received honorary degrees (Pratt, 1955; University of Maine, 1940), the Regina Medal of the Catholic Library Association (1960), and other honors, including the first Constance Lindsay Skinner Gold Medal from the Women's National Book Association (1940).

**REFERENCE**

Frances Clarke Sayers, *Anne Carroll Moore* (1972), a biography.

AUGUSTA BAKER

# Moraes, Rubens Borba de

(1899– )

Rubens Borba de Moraes as General Director of the National Library was responsible for significant innovations and development in Brazilian libraries. He was born in Araraquara, in the state of São Paulo, on January 23, 1899. He studied at the Collège de l'Université de Geneva, Switzerland, where he received the degree of *licencié es lettres* in 1919. His first work was written in French and published in Switzerland. When he returned to São Paulo, Moraes associated himself with a group of avant-garde writers and artists. He participated in the celebrated Week of Modern Art in 1922 and collaborated in journals of the Brazilian Modernist movement. He was one of the founders of the futurist periodical *Klaxon* (1922–23). In 1932 he participated in the constitutionalist revolution against the federal government.

In 1934, with a fellowship from the Rockefeller Foundation, he studied library organization and operation in the United States. Returning to São Paulo in 1935, he was appointed Director of the Municipal Public Library, and in 1936 he established the first university course in library science, with a U.S. orientation. In 1938 he founded the São Paulo Librarians Association. He reorganized São Paulo's public library in a modern building, planned and built under his guidance, and directed its opening in 1942. A year later he published *O problema das bibliotecas brasileiras* (1943), a comparative essay on European, American, and Brazilian libraries in which there appeared the concept of the library network as a solution to the problems of Brazilian libraries.

From 1945 to 1947 he was the General Director of the National Library in Rio de Janeiro. He introduced the dictionary catalogue, the Dewey Decimal Classification, free access by readers to reference collections, and a more liberal philosophy in relations with the public. During this same period, he was Professor of Bibliography and Reference in the National Library course.

In 1947 he was invited by the United Nations to direct the UN Information Service in Paris, where he remained until 1951. During this time he published the *Manual bibliográfico de estudos brasileiros* (1949), which he edited with William Berrien. This collective work was the first critical survey of Brazilian studies in the fields of humanities and social sciences and contained contributions by Brazilian and foreign experts. He then became the Director of the UN Library in New York City, a position he held until 1959. From 1963 to 1970 he was a professor at the University of Brasilia, teaching the history of books and libraries and Brazilian bibliography. During his teaching career he published *Bibliografia brasileira do periodo colonial* (1969), a critical bibliography of Brazilian works published before 1808. In 1971 the University awarded him the title of Professor Emeritus. In 1975 he was elected Honorary President of the 8th Brazilian Congress of Librarianship and Documentation, held in Brasília.

Moraes' other major publications include the *Bibliographia brasiliana* (1958–59; 2nd edition revised, 1979), a bibliographical essay written in English on rare books about Brazil, and *O bibliofilo aprendiz* (1965), an introductory guide for those who wish to collect rare books, ancient or modern. In addition to his important contributions to Brazilian librarianship and bibliography, Moraes translated, introduced, and edited a number of works by foreign authors about Brazil and São Paulo in two serials, the *Biblioteca Historica Brasileira* and the *Biblioteca Historica Paulista.* His *Livros e bibliotecas no Brasil colonial* (1979) covers libraries, book printing, and commerce in colonial Brazil.

EDSON NERY DA FONSECA

# Morgan, J. Pierpont

(1837–1913)

The collector's role assumed by J. P. Morgan evolved from several fortuitous circumstances—a well-to-do father, an international education, and a time of economic expansion. In Morgan's time, big U.S. corporations were in need of capital funds; the House of Morgan arranged capital for the railroad, steel, banking, and insurance companies. Morgan was an aristocrat who dominated every situation with his powerful personality.

Morgan's first acquisition was typical for a 14-year-old—a presidential signature, that of President Fillmore. The collection grew slowly during Morgan's first 45 years. Upon the death of his father, Junius Spencer Morgan (1890), and the formation of the firm of J. P. Morgan & Company in 1895, Morgan began to buy on a grand scale.

Junius Morgan had been a collector and owned a George Washington letter as well as the original manuscript of Sir Walter Scott's *Guy Mannering.* Pierpont Morgan's interest was probably stimulated by his father's possessions. That interest was further enhanced by the efforts of his nephew, another Junius Morgan, who was an ardent collector of books, prints, and manuscripts. Over the next several decades, the collection grew apace, with group and individual purchases, each adhering to the principle of selectivity first established.

Examples of the acquisitions include a Gutenberg Bible on vellum, the 1459 Mainz Psalter, the four Shakespeare Folios, and the original autograph manuscripts of Keats's *Endymion* and Dickens's *A Christmas Carol.* Collections purchased en bloc included a fine run of Aldine imprints in hand-tooled leather bindings. Several collections of illuminated manuscripts were acquired, including the Duke of Hamilton's famous "Golden Gospels" and a select group of 270 Rembrandt etchings. By 1905 Morgan had purchased some 700 incunabula, among them 40 from the press of William Caxton. Besides the printed works and manuscripts, the Morgan collections include outstanding early written records such as seals, tablets, and papyri. The collections are unusual in that a high percentage of the holdings are unique copies.

In 1906 Morgan had a library building constructed adjacent to his New York home at 36th and Madison in New York City. Designed by the noted architectural firm of McKim, Mead, and White, it is styled as a Renaissance palazzo. With a grandiose interior that has been carefully preserved, the J. Pierpont Morgan Library has become a noted structural landmark. The original building was expanded with a large annex in 1928, and two additions were later made, in 1962 and 1977.

After the books and manuscripts were moved into the new building, Morgan seemed more determined to increase the scale and depth of his collection. Joining him in this effort was a talented librarian, Belle DaCosta Greene, who became a model as a private collector's librarian. She served 43 years in the post, guiding the growth of the library during the time of the transition from a private collection to an invaluable research resource.

The Library sponsors many publications and exhibits and supports an active research program; its vast resources are available at the Library to scholars. The success of the Morgan Library probably far exceeded the founder's vision of its usefulness.

**REFERENCES**

*An Introduction to the Pierpont Morgan Library* (The Morgan Library, 1974).

Francis Henry Taylor, *Pierpont Morgan as Collector and Patron, 1837–1913* (1957).

DONALD D. HENDRICKS

## Morocco

Independent from March 3, 1956, after 44 years as French protectorate in the majority of its territory an Spanish in the northern area and the Saharian provinces Morocco, a constitutional monarchy of northwest Africa is bounded by the Mediterranean on the north and the Atlantic Ocean on the west, Algeria on the east, and the Western Sahara on the southwest. It lies north of the Sahara and faces Europe across the Strait of Gilbraltar. Pop. (1977 est.) 18,359,000; area 458,730 sq.km. (does not include purported division of Western [Spanish] Sahara between Morocco and Mauritania). The official language is Arabic. [STAFF]

**National Library System.** Founded in 1921 in Rabat, the General Library and Archives of Morocco (BGA) played an important part in the country's national library system. Originally conceived as a library of special studies on the Maghreb and Muslim west, it first was made up of collections from the Moroccan Institute of Higher Studies. The buildings were constructed and inaugurated in 1924. The acquisition of private libraries and of 1,500 manuscripts, stamps, and ancient maps has built up the initial collection. At the same time, a collection of general culture has been developing, that of the human sciences and public reading material, which has answered the needs of public users, European for the most part.

In 1926 it was established by decree as a public institution, and the decree foresaw as well the establishment of a place for the administrative archives more than ten years old. A decree of January 27, 1931, on Moroccan public libraries authorized it to subsidize them and gave it the right to inspect those libraries. However, the creation of a library division in the Ministry of Cultural Affairs, after independence, eliminated that role, and only 6 percent of them were still annexed in 1979: Rabat-Chellah, Sale, Kenitra, Meknes, El Hajeb, and Ifrane.

The BGA collection at the close of the 1970's totaled 234,943 works, 4,500 periodicals, a quarter of which were in Arabic (the majority of these documents are in French), 10,762 Arab manuscripts, and 1,480 microforms. These collections answer the needs of specialized researchers of ancient and modern Morocco and Islamic Spain as well as those of the students of the School of Arts and Sciences.

Founded in 1939 by the Spanish authorities, the Tetouan General Library played in the northern area a comparable role to that of the BGA before the independence and reunification of Morocco. Its specialized collection on the area, mostly in Spanish and Arabic, totals 60,000 volumes, 2,220 periodicals, and 1,500 manuscripts, and in its archives are some 20,000 historic documents, 60,000 administrative documents, and 35,000 photographs. Attached to the Library Division of the Ministry of Cultural Affairs, it supervises the public libraries in Asilah, Larache, Ksar el Kebir, and Tangier.

The National Documentation Center (CND), created in Rabat in 1968, was charged by a decree of 1972 with documentation about economic and social development of Morocco, especially government publications, and its publication, organization, retrieval, and distribution among other responsibilities, including representation of Morocco in international congresses.

The CND had indexed and recorded on tape by 1979 approximately 80,000 references to documents produced by the different organs of the government, the documents themselves being preserved on microfilm.

The Library of the CND was conceived to meet needs for special interests in the information sciences (2,900 works and 157 periodicals).

**Academic Libraries.** The famous Kairouyyin University in Fez, one of the first in the world, was founded in 1400. It is now attached to the State Ministry in Charge of Cultural Affairs. At the Hassan II University in Casablanca are about 20,000 works in the Law School (1973 estimate). Works at the University totaled 197,600 in 15 libraries. (Those figures exclude the Universities of Marrakesh and Oujda, created comparatively recently, and the higher schools dependent on the technical ministries, considered to be specialized schools.)

**Public Libraries.** Sixty-five libraries have been opened to the public in 28 cities in the kingdom, for an urban population of 6,781,200 inhabitants (1977 statistics), of whom 46 percent are estimated to be literate.

Only ten of them date prior to the independence of Morocco; the first three were opened in Casablanca in 1918, in Fez in 1920, and in Marrakesh in 1923, then two in Tetouan in 1937 and 1939. The first American library was opened in Casablanca in 1941 with the arrival of the Allies during World War II. Public library service is offered by the Ministry of Cultural Affairs (18 libraries; 100,000 works); municipalities (13; 263,000); other ministries (4; 2,500); the foreign cultural centers (23; 257,500); and cultural associations (7; 51,000). The total was 65 libraries and 674,000 works at the close of the 1970's.

The documentary collections of the public libraries dependent on the government are almost all in Arabic, and those of the libraries of the cultural centers are mainly composed of works in the language associated with the center (French, English, Spanish, German, and Russian). There are 2,138 manuscripts in Arabic in three of the libraries dependent on the State Ministry in Charge of Cultural Affairs. Two French cultural centers organized a reading section for children in Rabat and Fez.

**School Libraries.** A survey in Rabat indicated that 80 percent of the secondary schools have a library; the majority of the collections were estimated at 1,300 works as an average, made up chiefly of school books. The lending of a small number of books for pleasure reading found there has never been free.

In the primary schools initiatives were undertaken, by the school directors or teachers, to build a small collection of works with the financial aid of the parents or of the school cooperative, or with modest contributions from the students.

**Special Libraries.** One hundred and nine specialized libraries were recorded in 1973, 31 of which were private and 78 governmental (7 belonging to the upper schools and 8 to the Institute of Research); 74.3 percent were concentrated in Rabat and Casablanca, and 80 percent of their documentary collection (195,000 works) was found in Rabat. The oldest is a private library, founded in 1917 by the Association of Public Works and Buildings, followed in 1920 by the creation of the library of the Bureau of Research and Mine Investments by French authorities. Three-fourths of the special libraries have been created since independence; major subject areas are agriculture, mines and industry, education, Islam, and sociology.

The Royal Library contains a collection of historic archives and Arab manuscripts and the Libraries of Zaouias a collection of Arab manuscripts belonging to religious brotherhoods.

**Professional Association.** An association for information specialists was created in July 1973.

G. HARIKI

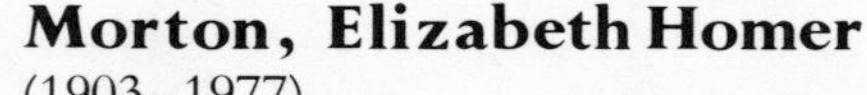

## Morton, Elizabeth Homer
(1903–1977)

Canadian Library Association

*Elizabeth Homer Morton*

Elizabeth Homer Morton was the founding Executive Director of the Canadian Library Association. She was the best known Canadian librarian of her generation and perhaps the most esteemed, as much for her qualities of heart and mind as for her formal achievements. Born on February 3, 1903, in Tunapuna, Trinidad, of Canadian parentage, she was privately educated until 1919. She did her high school studies in Saint John, New Brunswick, and then took an arts degree (1926) at Dalhousie University in Halifax, Nova Scotia.

Brief service as a teacher in Cape Breton, Nova Scotia, convinced Morton of Canada's urgent need for better library service, and she decided to become a librarian. She took the librarian's course given by the Ontario Department of Education and then worked in the Cataloguing Department of the Toronto Public Library. Returning to New Brunswick, she was employed as a teacher and school librarian and then as Secretary of the New Brunswick Library Commission. In 1931 she rejoined the staff of the Toronto Public Library, this time as a member of the Reference Department, where she remained until 1944. From 1936 to 1943 she also served as Secretary of the Ontario Library Association.

The decisive step in Morton's career came in 1944 when she left the security of library employment to become the full-time Secretary of the Canadian Library Council, a struggling organization whose main purpose was to pave the way for the formation of a national library association. When the Canadian Library Association/Association Canadienne des Bibliothèques was actually established in 1946 (in good part because of her efforts), it was wholly logical that Morton be selected as its initial Executive Director. She held that position until her retirement in 1968.

In the fledgling years of the CLA/ACB, Morton was in effect the one-person team on whom the continued existence of the Association depended. The Association had large ambitions, a small membership, and a precarious funding, and it had to accommodate itself to a taxing diversity of regional, cultural, and professional interests. Aided by a very small staff, Elizabeth Morton served as initiator, organizer, lobbyist, counselor, convener, and editor. Her most visible accomplishments were the establishment and continued supervision of the *Canadian Periodical Index* (the first major index of Canadian periodicals), the *Canadian Newspaper Microfilm Project,* and the Association's two journals, *Canadian Library Association Bulletin* (now *Canadian Library Journal*) and *Feliciter.* She also edited the *C.L.A. Occasional Papers* series.

Less visible but perhaps even more important was the influence that Elizabeth Morton wielded behind the scenes. Her excellent contacts in governmental and educational circles did much to muster support for the formation of Canada's National Library (1950). Her advice was sought in many library appointments and policy decisions. She was, unobtrusively, the originator as well as the executor of major developments within the Canadian Library Association itself.

To mark her retirement from the CLA in 1968, the Association published an impressive book of essays on Canadian librarianship. She was made a member of the Order of Canada in 1968 and was awarded honorary doctorates by the University of Alberta (1969) and Sir George Williams University (1970).

After leaving the CLA, Morton continued to be active for a decade. She took a Master's degree from the Graduate Library School of the University of Chicago (1969), operated her own consulting firm, assisted in the National Library's survey of resources, and acted as library consultant for Unesco in Trinidad. She lectured at various library schools and worked on several books.

Elizabeth Morton died in Ottawa on July 6, 1977.

SAMUEL ROTHSTEIN;
MARION GILROY

## Mozambique

Mozambique, an independent republic on the southeast coast of Africa, is bordered on the west by Malawi, Zambia, Rhodesia, and South Africa, on the east by the Indian Ocean, on the north by Tanzania, and on the south by Swaziland and South Africa. Pop. (1977 est.) 9,899,000; area 799,380 sq.km. The official language is Portuguese; Bantu languages are widely spoken.

The National Library of Mozambique, founded in Maputo in 1961, houses about 110,000 volumes. Mozambique does not issue a national bibliography of its own, but bibliographical references to publications about or of Mozambique are listed in the *Boletim de la Bibliografia Portuguesa.* The journal *Documentario trimestral,* issued in Mozambique from 1935, lists publications deposited, under copyright law, during the previous four-month period. Archival materials are kept at the Arquivo Histórico de Moçambique, Maputo, founded in 1934. In the late 1970's the collection consisted of 7,468 volumes. There is one university in Mozambique, the Universidade Eduardo Mondlane (formerly the Universidade de Lourenço Marques), founded in Maputo in 1962. The language of instruction is Portuguese. There are approximately 80,000 volumes in the general and departmental libraries of the university, plus 8,600 periodicals. Educational facilities in Mozambique are not highly developed. Although there were almost 600,000 students in primary schools in the early 1970's, the attrition rate beyond the second and third years is high. Most primary students are in special African schools. The Roman Catholic missions operate more than half of the primary schools. Neither public nor school library systems had been established in the 1970's. There is a city library in Maputo, the Biblioteca Municipal, which holds approximately 8,000 volumes.

The Mozambique Institute of Scientific Research, founded in Maputo in 1955, houses a library and documentation center, the Biblioteca e Centro de Documentação e Informação, established in 1977 under the Ministry of Education. The library's collection consists of approximately 2,000 scientific volumes; in the late 1970's it was in the process of reorganization. The Institute publishes works on ecology, the natural sciences, earth sciences, and the social sciences, particularly on Mozambique history. There are two other notable libraries in Maputo. The Direcção dos Serviços de Geologia e Minas, founded in 1930, specializes in mining research and geological studies. The collection consists of nearly 16,000 books. Research findings are published in the society's *Boletím.*

The Instituto de Algodão de Moçambique (Cotton Research Institute), founded in 1962, houses 2,500 volumes and 210 journals. There was no organized library association in Mozambique in the 1970's.

STAFF

## Mudge, Isadore Gilbert

(1875–1957)

Isadore Gilbert Mudge was America's foremost reference librarian and for many years the author of the standard *Guide to Reference Books.* Born in Brooklyn, New York, on March 14, 1875, Mudge was the daughter of well-educated parents. Her father, Alfred Eugene Mudge, was a respected Brooklyn lawyer and the stepson of Charles Kendall Adams, who served as President of Cornell University and the University of Wisconsin and was instrumental in building important libraries at each institution. Mudge's mother, Mary Ten Brook, was the daughter of Andrew Ten Brook, a noted historian and at one time the Librarian at the University of Michigan.

Mudge was named in the memory of her aunt, the name Isadore having come originally from a popular romance. Nothing is known about her early years. In 1889 she enrolled in the Adelphi Academy in Brooklyn; graduating at the top of her class in Spring 1893, Mudge entered "Grandfather's university" the following fall, though by then Charles Kimball Adams had moved from Ithaca to Madison.

At Cornell, Mudge excelled in her studies and was elected to Phi Beta Kappa in her junior year. She majored in history and took classes with some of the most distinguished professors in the country, including Moses Coit Tyler and George Lincoln Burr. Of the two, Burr was the more influential. She enrolled in every course he offered and later revealed that it was the training she received from him that started her on her career as a reference librarian.

In September 1898, 15 months after her 1897 graduation from Cornell, she enrolled in the New York State Library School at Albany, the famous school established by Melvil Dewey at the time he became State Librarian. She excelled at the Library School, completing the two-year program in 1900 and receiving the B.L.S. degree with distinction.

Mudge seems to have made a favorable impression on Dewey during her residence in Albany. Although there is no evidence of a close friendship between the two, Dewey—at the peak of his career—does appear to have recommended Mudge for her first two library positions. The first of these was at the University of Illinois, where Dewey's close friend and former star pupil, Katharine Lucinda Sharp, was not only the Director of the new library but also had established an important library school in Urbana that was already beginning to compete with Dewey's own school. Mudge arrived on the Urbana campus in 1900 and was put in charge of the Reference Department and made Assistant Professor in the library school. She stayed for three years, working hard to develop the reference collection and provide services for researchers. She also met Minnie Earl Sears of the Cataloging Department, a woman who would be her companion and collaborator for several decades.

In 1903 Mudge resigned her position at Illinois to accept the directorship of the Bryn Mawr College library. Dewey recommended her for this job as well, just as he had trained and recommended the previous two Directors of that library. Accompanied by Sears, who would become Head of the Cataloguing Department there, Mudge took charge of an entire library for the only time in her life. It was a responsibility she may not have enjoyed; nothing is known about the work she did there, and she was always reticent about the details of her Bryn Mawr experience. In 1907 she took a one-year leave of absence from the position but did not return when the year was over.

After seven years of library work, Mudge went to Europe accompanied by Minnie Earl Sears. They traveled and worked on their *Thackeray Dictionary* (1910). After their return to the United States there followed a number of projects and part-time appointments: Mudge taught in the library school at Simmons College in Boston in 1910 and 1911, reviewed reference books for *Library Journal,* and assisted William D. Johnston in compiling *Special Collections in Libraries in the United States* (1912). Johnston was the Director of the Columbia University library, and her association with him on this project led to her eventual appointment in 1911 at Columbia, where she spent the rest of her professional career.

The year before that appointment, however, Mudge began another association that would also occupy the rest of her career and would make her the best-known librarian of her generation. At the 1910 conference of the American Library Association, Mudge was asked to take over the editorship of Alice Bertha Kroeger's *Guide to the Study and Use of Reference Books.* Kroeger had brought out editions of this work in 1902 and 1908 before she died in 1909. Mudge began her editorial work by preparing a two-year supplement to the 1908 edition. Under Mudge's editorship, the *Guide* became the standard book of librarianship, and Mudge was to see it through four editions.

While preparing that first supplement, she was appointed to the Columbia University library by Johnston. Her first position as Gifts and Exchange Librarian (February 6, 1911) was followed a few months later by the appointment as Reference Librarian, and she remained in that position for the next 30 years. Mudge said that she had "set her mind on wanting Columbia from the days that I was at Cornell." By the time she arrived on the Morningside Heights campus, Columbia had already established itself as a university of the highest quality. Under the direction of President Nicholas Murray Butler, its graduate faculties were producing more Ph.D.'s than any other university in the country. But the library at Columbia was woefully inadequate to support so much advanced scholarship.

Mudge began at once to develop the reference collection and quickly won the support of Butler himself. He discovered her resourcefulness in satisfying his own bibliographical needs, and with his help Mudge was able to build the finest reference collection in existence. Moreover, she provided thorough and expert guidance to that collection for students and faculty alike. The reference service she had begun at Columbia was unique at that time. It took several years for these services to gain recognition in the library, but gradually more and more scholars realized how helpful her knowledge could be in their research. In fact, it became clear with the passing years that her methods contributed significantly to the research and instruction at Columbia.

Throughout her years at Columbia, Mudge had the ongoing project of preparing editions and supplements to her *Guide to Reference Books,* a work that has had a distinguished history. Mudge's first edition (but the third edition since 1902) appeared in 1917, and it became the most frequently used reference book in every research library; it greatly enhanced every reference library by providing a guide to all kinds of reference books in many languages. Other editions of the *Guide* appeared in 1923, 1929, and 1936, and the tradition established by Mudge at Columbia was continued by her successors Constance Winchell and Eugene Sheehy. Under Mudge's editorship, the *Guide* became so well known that, as her biographer John Waddell pointed out, " 'Mudge' became not merely a woman's name, but a noun, an adjective, and a verb upon the lips of librarians and students in the entire English-speaking world."

ALA

*Isadore Gilbert Mudge*

During the 1920's and 1930's Mudge was the undisputed authority on reference books, and the Columbia reference department served as a model for reference departments at other institutions. Mudge-trained librarians were constantly being sought to fill newly created reference positions throughout the country. Some neophyte librarians studied with Mudge at Simmons College, where she continued to teach from time to time, and at the New York Public Library's Library School, where she also occasionally offered courses. Others studied with Mudge at Columbia after a merger in 1926 of the Albany Library School and the New York Public Library School formed the School of Library Service at Columbia. Mudge became Associate Professor there and from 1927 on regularly taught Bibliography and Bibliographical Methods, a course that made lasting impressions on the many students, who in turn spread Mudge's methods far and wide.

With Minnie Sears's death in 1933, Mudge's life began to slow down. The 1936 edition of the *Guide* was the last one she edited, and it was extremely difficult for her to complete. She had never honored deadlines, and as she grew older her habits became impossible for her publisher. Finally, it was decided by the ALA that a new editor should be sought to prepare the next edition of the *Guide.* Constance Winchell became the new editor, and Mudge retired from the Reference Department in 1941, continuing her teaching just one year longer. She moved to the Westchester home that she and Minnie Sears had purchased years before. She died on May 16, 1957, at the age of 82.

**REFERENCES**

The only full study of Mudge is John Neal Waddell, "The Career of Isadore G. Mudge: A Chapter in the History of Reference Librarianship" (unpublished Ph.D. dissertation, Columbia University, 1973).
Laurel L. Grotzinger, "Women Who 'Spoke for Themselves,' " *College and Research Libraries* (1978).

PAUL COHEN

Arthur Plotnik

*Lawrence Quincy Mumford, 11th Librarian of Congress.*

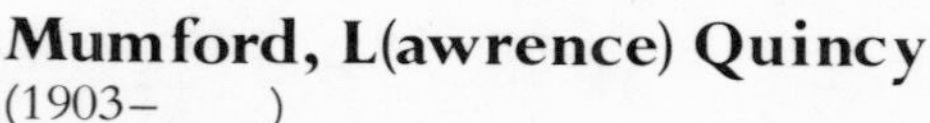

## Mumford, L(awrence) Quincy (1903–    )

Lawrence Quincy Mumford, 11th Librarian of Congress, directed LC during a period of great growth, from 1954 to 1974. He was born on a farm in Ayden, North Carolina, on December 11, 1903. Mumford received his A.B. from Duke University in 1925 and the M.A. from Duke in 1928. His library career began when he was a student assistant in the Duke University Library; in 1926 he became Head of its circulation department, and in 1928 the Acting Chief of Reference and Circulation. While at Columbia University (1928–29), where he earned a graduate degree in library science, Mumford was an assistant in the library.

In 1929 he joined the staff of the New York Public Library as a reference assistant. There he served as General Assistant in charge of the Director's Office (1932–35), Executive Assistant and Chief of the Preparation Division (1936–43), and Executive Assistant and Coordinator of the General Service Divisions (1943–45). In 1940, at the request of the then Librarian of Congress, Archibald MacLeish, Mumford was granted a leave of absence to organize the Processing Department of the Library of Congress and to serve a year as its Director. In 1945 he was appointed Assistant Director of the Cleveland Public Library and in 1950 became its Director, a position he held until his appointment as Librarian of Congress in 1954 by President Dwight D. Eisenhower. He was the first Librarian to have a professional degree in librarianship. In an editorial headed "Librarians' Librarian" the *Washington Post* on April 28, 1954, wrote,

Lawrence Quincy Mumford, newly nominated by the President to be Librarian of Congress, seems ideally qualified for that great office by attributes of mind and experience. A professional librarian for the past 25 years, he is the president-elect of the American Library Association and was one of the candidates recommended to the President by the association. He served a term in the Library of Congress some years ago and is now the director of the Cleveland Public Library. This is manifestly a merit selection by the President and deserves the warmest public approbation.

The Library of Congress made remarkable progress during Mumford's 20 years as Librarian (1954–74). Congressional appropriations increased from about $10 million to almost $100 million. In 1958 the Library was authorized to use U.S.-owned foreign currencies under the Agricultural Trade Development and Assistance Act, to acquire books for itself and other U.S. libraries, and to establish acquisition offices in foreign countries such as Egypt, India, Indonesia, Israel, and Pakistan. In 1965 the Higher Education Act authorized the establishment of the National Program for Acquisitions and Cataloging (NPAC), which greatly expanded the Library's foreign procurement program and inaugurated a system to speed up the acquisition, cataloguing, and dissemination of cataloguing data for "all library materials currently published throughout the world which are of value to scholarship." Under this program the Library established additional overseas offices in Austria, Brazil, France, Germany, Great Britain, Japan, Kenya, Norway, Poland, Spain, and Yugoslavia. This improved service to the nation's libraries resulted in great savings in cataloguing costs nationally and improved access to research materials.

As a result of studies of space requirements for the Library, which began during Mumford's administration, Congress in 1965 authorized the construction of the Library's third major building, the James Madison Memorial Building. It was to double available space and was scheduled for occupancy by 1979.

The application of automation to the Library's processes and services began and made substantial progress during Quincy Mumford's service. Following the publication in 1964 of a feasibility study, published as *Automation and the Library of Congress,* the Information Systems Office was established. In 1965 the Machine Readable Cataloging (MARC) project began, which became the basis for the revolution in the rapid distribution of cataloguing information utilizing computers and communication technology.

Other notable advances at LC under Mumford include the organization of the papers of the Presidents; the beginning publication of the *National Union Catalog of Manuscript Collections* and the *National Register of Microform Masters;* the establishment with the cooperation of the Bureau of the Budget of the Federal Library Committee; the tremendous expansion of the National Books for the Blind program to include the physically handicapped; the establishment of a separate Preservation Office and expansion of preservation research and services including motion picture preservation in cooperation with the American Film Institute; the beginning of the *Pre-1956 National Union Catalog* project, scheduled to exceed 600 volumes; the huge expansion of the Congressional Research Service under the Legislative Reorganization Act; and the establishment of the Cataloging-in-Publication program in cooperation with publishers.

Another way of measuring the significant growth in resources and services of LC under Quincy Mumford is to cite the growth of collections, from about 33,000,000 items in 1954 to almost 74,000,000 in 1974, and the more than 50 percent increase in staff to a total of more than 4,500 in 1974.

Mumford served as President of the Ohio Library Association, 1947–48, and of the American Library Association, 1954–55. He also was President of the Manuscript Society (1968–70), a member of the Lincoln Sesquicentennial Commission (1958–60), and he was on the President's Committee on Libraries (1966–68), named to review the recommendations of the temporary National Advisory Commission on Libraries. During his service as Librarian of Congress, he was a member of the Board of Advisors of the Dumbarton Oaks Research Library and Collection, the Sponsors Committee of the *Papers of Woodrow Wilson,* the U.S. National Book Committee, the National Trust for Historic Preservation, and a number of other advisory boards. He received several honorary degrees.

JOHN G. LORENZ

## Munn, Ralph

(1894–1975)

Ralph Munn was a library administrator and educator, consultant, author, and leader in professional organizations. He was born in Aurora, Illinois, on September 19, 1894, grew up in Colorado, and attended the University of Denver, where he earned an A.B. degree in 1916 and an LL.B. degree in 1917. After service with the U.S. Army in France from April 1917 to July 1919, he attended the New York State Library School at Albany, from which he received the B.L.S. degree in 1921. He was married to Anne Shepard, also a librarian, on June 6, 1922.

His first professional position was in the Seattle Public Library, where he served as Reference Librarian, 1921–25, and Assistant Librarian, 1925–26. He then became Librarian of the Flint (Michigan) Public Library, 1926–28. From 1928 to 1964 he served as Director of the Carnegie Library of Pittsburgh. He served also as Director, and later Dean, of the Carnegie Library School of Carnegie Institute of Technology, 1928 to 1962, when the school was transferred to the University of Pittsburgh.

Throughout his long and distinguished career, Ralph Munn was actively involved in international interests and concerns as a professional librarian and citizen. In 1934, commissioned by the Carnegie Corporation, he surveyed the libraries of Australia and New Zealand and made recommendations for their development and for the selection of librarians to study library practice in the United States. As a result, he became known as the "father of the modern library movement in Australia and New Zealand."

Nine years later, in 1943, he was retained by the City Planning Commission of New York City to survey library needs and select sites for new branch libraries in New York's five boroughs.

In 1947 he undertook a good-will tour of libraries of Central and South America for the United States Department of State and as a representative of the American Library Association. While on that mission, he spoke in Lima, Peru, on the occasion of a presentation of 10,000 American books given to the Peru National Library, which had been rebuilt following a fire. For his work in behalf of the reconstruction of the Library, the Peruvian government awarded him the degree of Knight of the Order "El Sol del Peru." In 1950 he served as Chairman of the U.S. delegation to a Unesco Library Seminar in Malmo, Sweden, to determine the needs of public libraries throughout the world.

Throughout his career Ralph Munn never deviated from his conviction that the public library's primary role was educational, informational, and cultural. This conviction brought into clear focus the issue of demand versus quality. In 1938 he implemented a revised book selection policy that sharply defined and limited the purchase of light, recreational fiction and effectively eliminated the acquisition of books that he categorized as "shopping bag fiction." As a result, the Carnegie Library of Pittsburgh gained remarkable status as a distinguished local institution, widely recognized for the quality of its collections and services.

Under his administration Carnegie Library expanded its services significantly. He frequently appeared before governmental bodies to seek necessary funds for library facilities, collections, and services. Ralph Munn sought to make libraries more responsive to the needs of young people who, he once said, "are required to read books I never heard of until I got to college."

Through his leadership, unified library services were established in Pittsburgh with the merger of the Carnegie Free Library of Allegheny and Carnegie Library of Pittsburgh in 1956. Also in 1956 Carnegie Library contracted with the County Commissioners of Allegheny County to give service to county residents. Free borrowing privileges were extended, and bookmobile services were operated in those parts of the county unserved by local libraries. In his judgment, achievement of the difficult merger with the Carnegie Library of Allegheny and implementation of contractual services with the county were the most significant innovations of his administration. Previously he had established the Downtown Branch and Business Branch, and in 1958 he published his *Plan for the Federation of Libraries in Allegheny County*.

Ralph Munn was persistent in his efforts to improve public library service throughout Pennsylvania. In 1930–31 and in 1958 he served on the Governor's Commission on Public Library Development. His participation in the work of the 1958 Commission contributed to the formation of a state library system under which Pennsylvania was divided into 29 districts, with Carnegie Library of Pittsburgh as the headquarters for all of Allegheny County and parts of Butler and Westmoreland counties. As a result of its outstanding science and technology collections, the Carnegie Library became designated the resource in that field for the entire state. In 1959 he was the first recipient of the Distinguished Service Award given by the Pennsylvania Library Association for outstanding service by a Pennsylvania librarian to the library development in the state.

His longtime associate, Elizabeth Nesbitt, observed that as Dean of the Carnegie Library School, Ralph Munn "insisted upon maintenance of standards in admission and performance of students, and upon honesty and fairness to employer and employee in placement of students." In 1936 the Carnegie Corporation published his *Conditions and Trends in Training for Librarianship*.

Ralph Munn was constant in his advocacy of cooperation among libraries. Cost and space factors, community needs, and the interdependence of libraries caused him to assume leadership in 1942 in coordinating the acquisition of costly research materials by the University of Pittsburgh, Carnegie Institute of Technology, and Carnegie Library. The results of this early work provided a foundation that led to the formation of the Pittsburgh Regional Library Center nearly 25 years later.

Always conscious of cost effectiveness in his management of Carnegie Library, he sought to keep overhead costs as low as possible in order to make available maximum funding for collection development and informational services. He introduced laborsaving devices and employed management techniques and principles of financial administration that were sensible and effective. He was one of a small cluster of progressive library administrators who established a public relations office in the mid-1940's.

Ralph Munn was respected universally for his professional as well as personal integrity. His unusually well-balanced judgment was combined with an unerring sense of timing that contributed greatly to his effectiveness as an administrator, planner, and strategist. His lifelong interest in young people inspired him in his work and en-

ALA

*Ralph Munn*

riched his personal life. Through his international activities, and long before the Fulbright Program was implemented, he welcomed many young librarians from abroad, including Australia, the Netherlands, and Scandinavia. They were added to the staff of the Carnegie Library, where they received the same salaries, benefits, and opportunities as their American colleagues. He took great interest in their professional development and provided many opportunities to participate in staff activities and community cultural events.

Whether writing or speaking, he had an extraordinary gift for clarity and grace. He was a keen observer, responsive, and always interested in others. His commanding and courtly presence was temporized by inner warmth and a fine sense of humor. Ralph Munn was forthright, perceptive, considerate, and kind. He possessed the qualities of a master teacher who willingly shared his insights and experience with many younger librarians.

He felt strongly that able women were too often denied equal opportunity to advance in a profession where women predominated. His concern was deepened in the years following World War II, when men were actively recruited into library schools. This prompted him to write an article on this subject, published in 1949, which included the following statement:

> Throughout the predictable future [librarianship] is sure to be mainly a women's occupation. It should therefore be kept attractive to the ablest of women.
>
> We must have men for many positions, to be sure. But let us make certain they they are men who give every promise of raising the standard and the prestige of the profession as a whole, and not those who are merely seeking a shabby security in positions to which able women should advance (*Library Journal,* November 1949).

A much respected leader in the American library movement throughout his long and distinguished career, he maintained active membership in professional organizations. He was the president of the American Library Association, 1939–40, and of the Pennsylvania Library Association, 1930–31. He was an effective public speaker and made key addresses on many auspicious occasions, including the dedicatory address for the new American Library Association's Headquarters building during the Association's 1963 Conference in Chicago.

Ralph Munn was honored by the University of Pittsburgh, which conferred upon him the honorary degree of Doctor of Letters in 1940. In 1960 Waynesburg College in Pennsylvania bestowed upon him the honorary degree of Doctor of Laws.

As a private citizen he was intensely interested in community affairs. He was a member of the board of the Foreign Policy Association of Pittsburgh and Chairman of the United Services Organization Council during both World War II and the Korean War. He was also a member of the H. C. Frick Educational Commission, the Health and Welfare Federation of Allegheny County, and the Pittsburgh Rotary Club. A local precedent was set when he invited two women from his staff to assist him in the presentation of a program to the Rotary Club in the early 1940's.

Upon his retirement, effective October 1, 1964, he was appointed Director Emeritus by the Board of Trustees of the Carnegie Library of Pittsburgh. Shortly thereafter a fund was established to support the Ralph Munn Lecture Series, subsequently a program for precollege students of the Greater Pittsburgh area.

Following his death in Pittsburgh, January 2, 1975, the American Library Association adopted a resolution expressing its sense of loss and appreciation for his contributions to the library profession. The resolution characterized Ralph Munn as exemplifying "the highest ideals of the library profession in his activities as Association official, library administrator and educator, author, consultant and citizen."

KEITH DOMS

# Namibia

Namibia, formerly South West Africa, is bounded on the west by the Atlantic Ocean, on the north by the Kunene and Okavango rivers separating it from Angola, on the south by the Orange River separating it from South Africa, and on the east by Botswana and South Africa. The Caprivi Strip, a narrow strip of land of nearly 300 miles, extends Namibia eastward to the borders of Zambia. Pop. (1977 est.) 905,200; area 824,268 sq.km. Afrikaans, German, and English are the primary languages spoken. In addition, dialects of the Khoisan and Bantu language families are spoken.

**National Library.** The Administration Library, in the capital city of Windhoek, to some extent serves as the national library of Namibia. It was begun in 1926 with a nucleus of books originally the property of the German administration and was known until 1957 as the Library of the Legislative Assembly. Administratively, it forms part of the South West Africa Library Service, instituted by ordinance in 1968 as a subsection of the Department of Education. In 1951 all S.W.A. publications were required by law to be deposited here. The Library also serves as a research and special library for the legislature (the Legislative Assembly and currently the National Assembly) and administration. Reference, loan, and interlibrary loan facilities are available both to government officials and to the general public, of all races, notably the numerous correspondence students of the University of South Africa, Pretoria. The Library is a depository for United Nations publications. It also houses an Africana collection, specializing in Namibiana, which includes both legal deposit and purchased material.

The book stock in 1979 was approximately 32,000 volumes, excluding an undetermined number of periodicals, newspapers, and official publications. A small percentage of the collection is decentralized in departmental libraries throughout the administration. A retrospective Namibian national bibliography, which includes approximately 1,500 entries on books, reports, and articles dealing with Namibia, was published in 1977: *Namibische Nationalbibliographie (NNB), 1971–1975.*

**Academic Libraries.** Namibia has no university. Students seeking a university education usually went to South Africa or elsewhere to study. The Government Archives (or Staatsarchiv), founded in Windhoek in 1939, is probably the main academic library in Namibia. Supervised by the Department of Education, the institution contains a collection of 2,939 books, official and private documents dating from the period of German rule, 2,668 maps, 5,115 photographs, and a Namibiana collection. There are three other libraries of academic importance. The State Museum Library in Windhoek has a collection of 3,000 books, special collections in Namibiana, archaeology, mammalogy, and ethnology. It also publishes *Cimbebasia,* 1962– , which reports the results of original research in the social sciences and natural history. The Museum Library in Swakopmund, founded in 1951, has a collection of 1,000 volumes and a special collection of Namibian newspapers covering the period 1898–1938. The South West Africa Scientific Society Library, established in Windhoek in 1925, has a collection of 8,400 books and publishes a *Newsletter,* an *Ornithological Newsletter,* and a *Botanic Newsletter.* The library of the Windhoek College of Education opened in May 1979.

**Public Libraries.** Local ordinances make provision for library facilities to the general public (whites only at the end of 1979) through the Library Service for South West Africa. Books and services are provided free of charge. In 1979 12 public libraries, mainly in the larger towns, were affiliated with the Library Service. Eventually the Service will be extended to outlying areas by means of depots and traveling libraries.

A Book Distribution Service is available by mail to individuals who cannot make use of existing library facilities. Four subscription libraries exist, and there is a public library at the nonwhite township of Katatura, which is run by the Municipality of Windhoek. All these libraries together have a book stock of approximately 150,000 and serve about 20 percent of the total population of Namibia.

The largest public library in Namibia is the Windhoek Public Library, which has a collection of 52,000 volumes, with special collections in Modern Dutch and Modern French literatures. The Library is a member of the South African interlibrary lending system.

**School Libraries.** The appointment of an Organiser of School Library Services in early 1966 represented the first step toward the development of school libraries. In 1968 all books in stock in the School Library Division of Library Services for South West Africa were catalogued. A completely centralized system was developed, whereby the School Library Division was in charge of the selection, purchasing, classification, and cataloguing of books for school libraries. School Library Services are under the direct control of the Chief Inspector of Education. The libraries of Black and Coloured schools, according to the population categories defined there, came under control of the Department of Education and Training and the Department of Coloured Relations of the Republic of South Africa and not the administration of South West Africa.

In the 1970's three distinct school systems existed: one for whites, one for Coloureds, and a third for blacks, the black system being divided into further subgroupings to enable instruction to be given in the students' mother tongues. Education was compulsory only for white students up to the age of 16 and was not compulsory for black students, the majority of whom entered the labor market after only a few years of schooling. Constitutional developments during 1979, including the representation of all ethnic groups at central government level for the first time, have led to proposals for an improved educational system in the territory.

**Special Libraries.** Three libraries of special interest in Namibia are the Supreme Court library, the Water Affairs library, and the Weather Office library. The first is used for research on legal problems and is not open to the public. Use of the second is restricted to the staff of the Department of Water Affairs for research on water-related issues. The Weather Office Library specializes in meteorology. One other important special library is that of the Society for Scientific Development, which holds 4,500 volumes, including an Africana collection of 2,000 volumes. The library of the Agricultural Technical Services is for the use of that department.

There was no formal library association in 1979.

PATRICIA B. PIETERSE
S. H. VAN DEN BERG

# National Bibliographies

The following list of 100 current national bibliographies was compiled from the catalogues and collections, and with assistance from the staff, of the Library of Congress. While it is as exhaustive as possible, no claim for completeness can be put forward. Some national bibliographies that are said to exist could not be traced in any of the library catalogues or holdings lists that were examined.

For this article, it was decided, rather arbitrarily, to regard as "current" any national bibliography known to be active during the 1970's, even if its coverage lagged considerably behind the imprint date. Some of the bibliographies included on this basis may have suspended or ceased publication recently because of revolutionary changes in various parts of the world (e.g., Ethiopia, Iran). To keep entries relatively short, each country has been limited to one title, with the exception of Czechoslovakia, which issues separate bibliographies for its two major languages. In cases where the national bibliography is issued in various parts covering different types of publications, only the part dealing with trade books is listed. With few exceptions, details about frequency, cumulations, title changes, subseries, and bibliographies that antedate the establishment of the current national bibliography have been omitted. Additional information of this kind can be found in the published sources listed under *References*. In the absence of a bona fide national bibliography, an entry is provided for the next best available source produced by local agencies (such as individual booksellers, book trade organizations, university or public libraries, or learned societies). It should be noted that some of these substitutes, especially in the case of the smaller territories, include writings published elsewhere about the area in addition to items published locally. The current title and imprint are given in the vernacular, and, in most cases, a starting date is given. Titles in non-Roman alphabets have been transliterated. If the issuing agency does not appear as corporate author, as publisher, or in an "at head of title" note, it is supplied in a drop note.

ALBANIA

*Bibliografia kombëtare e Republikës Popullore të Shqipërisë: Libri shqip. Bibliographie nationale de la R.P.A.: les livres albanais.* 1958+ Tiranë, Botim i Bibliotekës Kombëtare.

ALGERIA

Algiers (City). al-Maktabah al-Watanıyah. *Bibliographie de l'Algérie.* 1.+ année; 1. oct. 1963+ Alger, Bibliothèque nationale.

Added title page: *al-Bībliyūghrāfyā al-Jazā'irīyah.*

ARGENTINA

*Bibliografía argentina de artes y letras.* 1 + enero/marzo 1959+ Buenos Aires, Fondo Nacional de las Artes.

AUSTRALIA

*Australian National Bibliography.* Jan. 1961+ Canberra, National Library of Australia.

AUSTRIA

*Oesterreichische Bibliographie; Verzeichnis der österreichischen Neuerscheinungen.* Bearb. von der Österreichischen Nationalbibliothek. 1945+ Wien, Hauptverband des österreichischen Buchhandels, 1946+

BANGLADESH

Bangladesh. Directorate of Archives and Libraries. *Bāṃlādeśa jātīya granthapañjī. Bangladesh National Bibliography.* 1+ 1972+ Ḍhākā, Bāṃlādeśa Ārakāibhs o Granthāgāra Paridaptara, Śikshā, Saṃskṛti, o Krīṛā Mantranālaẏa, Gaṇaprajātantrī Bāṃlādeśa Sarakāra.

BARBADOS

*The National Bibliography of Barbados.* Jan./Mar. 1975+ Bridgetown, Public Library.

BELGIUM

*Bibliographie de Belgique. Belgische bibliografie.* 1.+ année; jan. 1875+ Bruxelles, Bibliothèque royale Albert Ier.

BENIN

*Bibliographie du Bénin.* 1.+ année; 1976/77+ Porto-Novo, Bibliothèque nationale, 1978+

BOLIVIA

*Bibliografía boliviana.* 1962+ Cochabamba, Los Amigos del Libro, 1963+

BOTSWANA

*The National Bibliography of Botswana.* v. 1+ 1969+ [Gaberones] Botswana National Library Service.

BRAZIL

*Bibliografia brasileira mensal.* nov. 1967+ [Rio de Janeiro] Instituto Nacional do Livro.

BULGARIA

*Bŭlgarski knigopis.* 1897+ Sofiia, Narodna biblioteka "Kiril i Metodiĭ."

BURUNDI

*Bibliographie courante.* In *Revue universitaire du Burundi.* v. 1+ 1. trimestre 1972+ [Bujumbura] Université officielle de Bujumbura.

Compiled by Pol P. Gossiaux. Lists books, articles, and periodicals relating to Burundi.

CANADA

*Canadiana.* Jan. 15, 1951+ Ottawa.

Compiled and edited by the Cataloguing Branch, National Library of Canada.

CHILE

Santiago de Chile. Biblioteca Nacional. *Anuario de la prensa chilena.* 1877/85+ Santiago de Chile, 1887+

Retrospective volume covering 1877/85 was published in 1952.

CHINA, PEOPLE'S REPUBLIC OF

*Ch'üan kuo hsin shu mu. Quan-guo xinshumu. National Bibliography.* 1950+ Pei-ching, Wen hua pu, Ch'u pan shih-yeh kuan li chü, Pan-pen t'u shu kuan, 1951+

CHINA, REPUBLIC OF (TAIWAN)

*Chung-hua min-kuo ch'u pan t'u shu mu lu.* 1970+ T'ai-pei, Kuo li chung yang t'u shu kuan.

Supersedes *The Monthly List of Chinese Books* (1960–69).

COLOMBIA

*Anuario bibliográfico colombiano "Rubén Pérez Ortiz."* 1951+ Bogotá.

At head of title: Instituto Caro y Cuervo. Departamento de Bibliografía.

COSTA RICA

*Anuario bibliográfico costarricense.* 1956+ San Jose, Impr. Nacional, 1958+

At head of title: Asociación Costarricense de Bibliotecarios. Comité Nacional de Bibliografía "Adolfo Blen."

CUBA

*Bibliografía cubana.* 1917/20+ La Habana, Consejo Nacional de Cultura.

At head of title: Biblioteca Nacional José Martí.

CZECHOSLOVAKIA

*České knihy.* 1951+ V Praze.

Compiled by Národní knihovna.

Supersedes *Bibliografický katalog,* pt. A, *Knihy české* (1933–50).

*Slovenská národná bibliografia. Séria A: knihy.* roč. 21+ 1970+ Martin, Matica slovenská.

Continues *Slovenské knihy* (1951–69) which superseded *Bibliografický katalog,* pt. B, *Knihy slovenské* (1946–50).

DENMARK

*Dansk bogfortegnelse. The Danish National Bibliography. Books.* 1841/58+ Udarb. af Bibliotekscentralen. Ballerup, Bibliotekscentralens Forlag, 1861+

ECUADOR

*Anuario bibliográfico ecuatoriano.* 1975+ Quito, Universidad Central del Ecuador, Biblioteca General.

Published as the sixth issue each year of *Bibliografía ecuatoriana.*

EGYPT

*al-Nashrah al-Miṣrīyah lil-maṭbūʻāt.* al-Sanah 1.+ 1956+ [al-Qāhirah] Dār al-Kutub wa-al-Wathā'iq al-Qawmīyah.

Added title page: *Egyptian Publications Bulletin.*

EL SALVADOR

*Guión literario.* año 1+ enero 1956+ San Salvador, Dirección General de Publicaciones del Ministerio de Educación.

ETHIOPIA

*Ethiopian Publications.* 1963/64+ Addis Ababa, Haile Sellassie I University, Institute of Ethiopian Studies, 1965+

FINLAND

*Suomen kirjallisuus. Finlands litteratur. The Finnish National Bibliography.* 1544/1877+ [Helsinki] Helsingin Yliopiston Kirjasto, 1878+

FRANCE

*Bibliographie de la France.* 1.+ année; nov. 1811+ Paris, Cercle de la Librairie.

GERMAN, DEMOCRATIC REPUBLIC

*Deutsche Nationalbibliographie und Bibliographie des im Ausland erschienenen deutschspraghigen Schrifttums.* Bearb. und hrsg. von der Deutschen Bücherei. *Reihe A: Neuerscheinungen des Buchhandels.* 3. Jan. 1931+ Leipzig, VEB Verlag für Buch- und Bibliothekswesen.

GERMANY, FEDERAL REPUBLIC OF

*Deutsche Bibliographie. Wöchentliches Verzeichnis. Amtsblatt der Deutschen Bibliothek.* A: *Erscheinungen des Verlagsbuchhandels.* 1. März 1947+ Frankfurt am Main, Buchhändler-Vereinigung.

GHANA

*Ghana National Bibliography.* 1965+ Accra, Ghana Library Board, 1968+

GREECE

*Hellēnikē vivliographia.* 1971+ Athēnai, Vivliographikē Hetaireia tēs Hellados, 1975+

Added title page: *Greek National Bibliography.*

GUYANA

*Guyanese National Bibliography.* Jan./Mar. 1973+ Georgetown, National Library.

HUNGARY

*Magyar nemzeti bibliográfia: könyvek bibliográfiája.* 32. évf.+ aug. 15, 1977+ Budapest, Országos Széchényi Könyvtár.

Continues *Magyar nemzeti bibliográfia,* which began publication jan./márc. 1946.

ICELAND

*Íslensk bókaskrá. The Icelandic National Bibliography.* 1974+ Réykjavík, Landsbókasafn Íslands, 1975+

A continuation of "Islenzk rit," which appeared in *Árbók Landsbókasafns Íslands,* 1945–75, and *Bókaskrá Bóksalaféélags Íslands,* 1937–73.

INDIA

*Indian National Bibliography.* v. 1+ Jan./Mar. 1958+ [Calcutta] Central Reference Library.

INDONESIA

Indonesia. Kantor Bibliografi Nasional. *Bibliografi nasional Indonesia.* 1963+ [Djakarta] Kantor Bibliografi Nasional, Departemen Pendidikan Dasar dan Kebudajaan.

IRAN

Teheran. Kitābkhānah-i Millī. *Kitābshināsī-i millī* 1+ [1963]+ Tihrān.

Added title page: *National Bibliography, Iranian Publications.*

IRAQ

Bagdad. Jāmiʻat Baghdād. al-Maktabah al-Markazīyah. *al-Nashrah al-ʻIrāqīyah lil-maṭbūʻāt.* 17 Tammūz/Kānūn al-Awwal, 1963+ Baghdad.

IRELAND

*Irish Publishing Record.* 1967+ [Dublin] School of Librarianship, University College Dublin.

ISRAEL

*Kiryat sefer, rive'on le-bibliografyah shel bet ha-sefarim*

*ha-le'umi veha-'universita'i bi-Yerushalayim.* shanah 1+ [Jerusalem, 1924]+
Added title page: *Kiryat Sefer, Bibliographical Quarterly of the Jewish National and University Library, Jerusalem.*

ITALY
*Bibliografia nazionale italiana.* anno 1+ genn. 1958+ Firenze, Biblioteca nazionale centrale.

IVORY COAST
*Bibliographie de la Côte d'Ivoire.* 1969+ [Abidjan] Bibliothèque nationale [1970]+

JAMAICA
Institute of Jamaica, Kingston. West India Reference Library. *Jamaican National Bibliography.* 1964+ Kingston, 1965+
*Jamaican National Bibliography, 1964–1970 Cumulation* (322 p.), compiled by Rosalie I. Williams and covering accessions for the period 1960–70, was published by the West India Reference Library in 1973. Further quinquennial cumulations are planned.

JAPAN
*Zen Nihon shuppanbutsu sōmokuroku.* [1948]+ [Tōkyō] Kokuritsu Kokkai Toshokan.

JORDAN
*al-Bibliyūghrāfīyā al-Filastīnīyah al-Urdunīyah.* 1969+ In *Risālat al-maktabah,* al-Sanah 5.+ Ādhār 1970+
Compiled by Maḥmūd al-Akhras. Title varies. Appears annually in the March issue.
The compiler has published in book form, under the same title, cumulations for 1900–70 (['Amman] Jam'īyat al-Maktabāt al-Urdunīyah, 1972. 265 p.) and for 1971–75 (1976. 353 p.).

KOREA, REPUBLIC OF
*Taehan Min'guk ch'ulp'anmul ch'ongmongnok.* 1945/62+ [Seoul] Kungnip Chungang Tosŏgwan
Added title page: *Korean National Bibliography.*

LAOS
*Bannanukrom haeng chat, National Bibliography of Laos.* 1968+ Vientiane, Ho Samut Haeng Chat.

LIBYA
*al-Bibliyūghrāfiyah al-'Arabīyah al-Lībīyah.* 1866/71+ Ṭarābulus, Wizārat al-I'lām wa-al-Thaqāfah, Idārat al-Marākiz al-Thaqāfiyah al-Qawmīyah.
First three volumes are entitled *al-Bibliyūghrāfiyah al-Waṭanīyah al-Lībīyah.*
Added title page, 1972+: *The Arab Bibliography of Libya.*

LIECHTENSTEIN
*Liechtensteinische Bibliographie.* 1.+ Jahrg.; 1974+ Vaduz, Liechtensteinische Landesbibliothek.

LUXEMBURG
*Bibliographie luxembourgeoise.* [1.]+ année; 1944/45+ Luxembourg, P. Linden.
At head of title: Bibliothèque nationale, Luxembourg.

MADAGASCAR
*Bibliographie annuelle de Madagascar,* 1964+ Tananarive, Bibliothèque universitaire et Bibliothèque nationale.

MALAWI
National Archives of Malawi. *Malaŵi National Bibliography; List of Publications Deposited in the Library of the National Archives.* 1965+ Zomba.

MALAYSIA
*Bibliografi negara Malaysia. Malaysian National Bibliography.* 1967+ Kuala Lumpur, Perkhidmatan Perpustakaan Negara, Arkib Negara Malaysia.

MAURITANIA
Nouakchott. Bibliothèque nationale. *Liste mensuelle des nouvelles acquisitions.* juil. 1973+ Nouakchott.
Publication had been suspended, but efforts were being made as of 1979 to resume issuance or begin a new periodical.

MAURITIUS
Mauritius. Archives Dept. *Memorandum of Books Printed in Mauritius and Registered in the Archives Office.* 1893+ Port Louis.

MEXICO
*Bibliografía mexicana.* enero/feb. 1967+ [México] Biblioteca Nacional de México, Instituto de Investigaciones Bibliograficas.
At head of title: Universidad Nacional Autónoma de México.

MONGOLIA
*Bibliografiâ mongol'skikh knig izdannykh v MNR.* 1945+ Ulan Bator, Gosudarstvennaiâ publichnaiâ biblioteka MNR.

MOROCCO
*Bibliographie nationale marocaine,* 1962+ Rabat, Bibliothèque générale et archives du Maroc.

THE NETHERLANDS
*Brinkman's cumulatieve catalogus van boeken.* 1.+ jaarg.; 1846+ Alphen aan den Rijn, A. W. Sijthoff.

NEW ZEALAND
*New Zealand National Bibliography.* Feb. 1967+ Wellington, Alexander Turnbull Library.
Supersedes in part the *Index to New Zealand Periodicals, and Current National Bibliography* (1950–65).

NIGERIA
*National Bibliography of Nigeria.* 1973+ Lagos, National Library of Nigeria.
Continues *Nigerian Publications: Current National Bibliography* (1950–72).

NORWAY
*Norsk bokfortegnelse. The Norwegian National Bibliography.* 1814/47+ Oslo, Norsk Bokhandlerforening, 1848+

PAKISTAN
*The Pakistan National Bibliography.* 1962+ Karachi, Govt. of Pakistan, Directorate of Archives & Libraries, National Bibliographical Unit.

PAPUA NEW GUINEA
*New Guinea Bibliography.* no. 1+ Nov. 1967+ Boroko, Papua, University of Papua New Guinea Library.

PERU
*Anuario bibliográfico peruano.* 1943+ Lima [Biblioteca Nacional, Instituto Nacional de Cultura] 1945+
Current coverage is now being provided by *Bibliografía nacional: libros, artículos de revistas y periódicos,* no. 1+ enero 1978+ (Lima, Biblioteca Nacional).

PHILIPPINES
*Philippine National Bibliography.* Jan./Feb. 1974+ Manila, National Library of the Philippines.
Preceded by *Philippine Bibliography* (1963/64–70/72), issued 1965–73 by the University of the Philippines Library in Quezon City.

POLAND
*Przewodnik bibliograficzny; urzędowy wykaz druków wydawnych w Rzeczypospolitej Polskiej.* [rocz. 1]+ 1944/45+ Warszawa, Biblioteka narodowa.
Supersedes *Urzędowy wykaz druków* (1928–39) and its predecessor, *Przewodnik bibliograficzny* (1878–1933).

PORTUGAL
Lisbon. Biblioteca Nacional. *Boletim de bibliografia portuguesa.* v. 1+ ano de 1935+ Lisboa, 1937+

PUERTO RICO
*Anuario bibliográfico puertorriqueño; índice alfabético de libros, folletos, revistas y periódicos publicados en Puerto Rico.* 1948+ San Juan, Estado Libre Asociado de Puerto Rico, Departamento de Instrucción Pública, 1950+

ROMANIA
Bucharest. Biblioteca Centrală de Stat. *Bibliografia Repub-*

*licii Socialiste România: cărţi, albume, hărţi.* 1952+ [Bucureşti]

SENEGAL
*Bibliographie du Sénégal.* no 40+ 1972+ [Dakar, Archives du Sénégal]
Continues *Bulletin bibliographique des Archives du Sénégal* (1963–71).

SEYCHELLES
*Bibliographical Notes.* In Seychelles Society. *Journal.* no. 2+ Oct. 1952+ Victoria, Mahé.
Compiled by J. F. G. Lionnet. Lists "papers on the natural history and related subjects of the Seychelles and neighbouring archipelagoes."

SIERRA LEONE
Sierra Leone. Library Board. *Sierra Leone Publications.* 1962/63+ Freetown, 1964+

SINGAPORE
*Singapore National Bibliography.* 1967+ Singapore, National Library.

SOUTH AFRICA
*South African National Bibliography. Suid-Afrikaanse nasionale bibliografie.* 1959+ Pretoria, State Library [1960]+
Continues *Publications Received in Terms of Copyright Act no. 9 of 1916,* issued by the State Library, Apr. 1933–58.

SPAIN
*Bibliografía española.* 1958+ Madrid, Ministerio de Educación Nacional, Dirección General de Archivos y Bibliotecas.

SRI LANKA
*Srī Laṅkā jātika grantha nāmāvaliya. Ilaṅkait tēciya Nūṟpaṭṭiyal. Sri Lanka National Bibliography.* v. 1+ Jan. 1963+ Koḷamba, Śrī Laṅkā Jātika Pustakāla Sēvā Maṇḍalaya.

SWAZILAND
*Swaziland National Bibliography.* 1973/76+ Kwaluseni, University of Botswana and Swaziland.

SWEDEN
*Svensk bokförteckning. The Swedish National Bibliography.* jan. 1953+ Redigerad av Bibliografiska Institutet vid Kungl. Biblioteket i Stockholm. Stockholm, Svensk bokhandel.

SWITZERLAND
*Das Schweizer Buch. Le livre suisse Il libro svizzero.* Hrsg. von der Schweizerischen Landebibliothek. 1.+ Jahrg.; Jan./Feb. 1901+ Zürich, Schweizerischer Buchhändler- und Verleger Verband.

SYRIA
*al-Nashrah al-maktabīyah bi-al-kutub al-ṣādirah fi al-Jumhūrīyah al-'Arabīyah al-Sūrīyah.* 1970+ [Dimashq] al-Jumhūrīyah al-'Arabīyah al-Sūrīyah, Wizārat al-Thaqāfah wa-al-Irshād al-Qawmī, Mudīrīyat al-Marākiz al-Thaqāfīyah al-'Arabīyah wa-al-Maktabāt.

TANZANIA
*Printed in Tanzania.* 1969+ Dar es Salaam, Tanganyika Library Service, 1970+

THAILAND
*Bannānukrom hāeng chāt.* [1962/67]+ Krung Thēp, Hō Samut Hāeng Chāt, Krom Sinlapākon, Krasūang Su'ksāthikān [1977]+

TRINIDAD AND TOBAGO
*Trinidad and Tobago National Bibliography.* v. 1+ Jan./June 1975+ [Port of Spain] Central Library of Trinidad and Tobago.

TUNISIA
*Bibliographie nationale de la Tunisie.* 1.+ année; 1. semestre 1969+ Tunis, Bibliothèque nationale, 1970+
Added title page: *al-Bibliyūghrāfiyā al-qawmīyah al-Tūnisīyah.*
Retrospective coverage is provided by *Bibliographie nationale; publications non-officielles, 1956–1968,* compiled by the Bibliothèque nationale (Dār al Kutab al-Qawmīyah) and published in Tunis by Service documentaire (1974. 167, 165 leaves).

TURKEY
*Türkiye bibliyografyası.* 1934+ Ankara, Türk Tarih Kurumu Basımevı.

UGANDA
*Uganda Bibliography.* In *Library Bulletin and Accessions List.* no. 55+ Jan./Feb. 1965+ [Kampala] Makerere University College [Library]

UNION OF SOVIET SOCIALIST REPUBLICS
*Knizhnaīa letopis', organ gosudarstvennoĭ bibliografii SSSR.* g. 1+14 īūlīa 1907+ Moskva, Izd-vo "Kniga."
Issued by Vsesoīuznaīa knizhnaīa palata.

UNITED KINGDOM
*British National Bibliography.* 1950+ London, British Library, Bibliographic Services Division.

UNITED STATES
*Cumulative Book Index.* 1898/99+ New York, H. W. Wilson Co.

URUGUAY
*Anuario bibliográfico uruguayo.* 1946–49; 1968+ Montevideo. Biblioteca Nacional, 1947–51; 1969+
*Bibliografía uruguaya,* which began publication in 1962, is still being issued by the Biblioteca del Poder Legislativo, but its coverage is about five years behind.

VENEZUELA
*Bibliografía venezolana.* año 1+ enero/marzo 1970+ Caracas, Centro Bibliográfico Venezolano.
In 1977 the Centro Bibliográfico Venezolano of the Biblioteca Nacional resumed publication of the *Anuario bibliográfico venezolano* with the issuance of a volume covering the years 1967–68 (386 p.). There were plans to continue the *Anuario* on a current basis and to produce retrospective volumes to cover the 1955–66 gap.

VIETNAM
*Thư'mục quốc gia Việt Nam.* Hà-Nội.
At head of title: Cộng Hòa Xã Hội Chủ Nghĩa Việt Nam, Thư' Viện Quốc Gia.
Publications of South Vietnam were formerly covered by *Thư' tịch quốc-gia Việt-nam; National Bibliography of Vietnam,* issued in Saigon beginning June 1968 by Nha Văn-Hkô và Thư'-Viện Quốc-Gia, Bộ Van-Hóa Giáo-Dục và Thanh-Niên.

YUGOSLAVIA
*Bibliografija Jugoslavije; knjige, brošure i muzikalije. The Bibliography of Yugoslavia; Books, Pamphlets and Music.* god 1+ 1950+ Beograd.

ZAIRE
*Bibliographie nationale.* no. 5+ 1974+ Kinshasa/Gombe, Direction des Arts et Culture, République du Zaïre.
Continues *Bibliographie nationale retrospective des publications zaïroises ou relatives à la République du Zaïre, acquises par la Bibliothèque nationale.*

ZAMBIA
*The National Bibliography of Zambia.* 1970/71+ Lusaka, National Archives of Zambia.

ZIMBABWE RHODESIA
*Rhodesia National Bibliography.* 1967+ Salisbury, National Archives, 1968+
Continues *List of Publications Deposited in the Library of the National Archives* (1961–66).

**REFERENCES**

Marcelle Beaudiquez, ***Bibliographical Services throughout the World, 1970–74.*** (1977).

*Commonwealth National Bibliographies, An Annotated Directory* (1977).
Ligue des Bibliothèques Européennes de Recherche, *Acquisitions from the Third World; Papers of the Ligue des Bibliothèques Européennes de Recherche Seminar 17–19 September 1973,* edited by D. A. Clarke (1975).
Eugene P. Sheehy, "Bibliography: National and Trade," in his *Guide to Reference Books,* 9th ed. (ALA, 1976).
*Synoptic Tables Concerning the Current National Bibliographies,* compiled by Gerhard Pomassl and a working group of the Deutsche Bücherei (1975).
Irene Zimmerman, *Current National Bibliographies of Latin America, A State of the Art Study* (Center for Latin American Studies, University of Florida, 1971).

RUTH S. FREITAG

## National Libraries

DEFINITIONS AND PURPOSES

There were 100 national libraries in the world at the end of the 1970's (see accompanying table). These are either officially titled as the national library of the country or are so characterized by their governments and their scholarly communities. But the matter of definition—what a national library really is—remains a problem. While the national library is accepted as being a unique form of institution, and while the national library is generally perceived as being dissimilar from public, academic, or special libraries, for nearly a century the profession has been unable to agree on a single, accepted definition.

In the first half of the 20th century, library scholars tried to define the institution in terms of universals: what are the characteristics of single national libraries that are common to all national libraries? Numerous essays pursuing this approach were published before it was abandoned with the reluctant discovery that the diversity among elements was too great —scarcely a single characteristic could be described as appearing in *most* national libraries, much less *all.*

The search then shifted to broad, general descriptions rather than precise, limiting particularizations. Herman Liebaers suggested in a 1958 Unesco study:

> The main characteristic of a national library is without doubt the leading place it occupies compared with other libraries in the country. This position is due to the extent and encyclopaedic character of its collections, the variety of material held and the diversity of specialized departments and services. It thus has a general and a national responsibility: within the profession, in all cases; outside it, more often than not.

The participants in the conference for which this study was prepared rejected it in the course of the meeting, on the grounds that "there were too many exceptions" to make it useful as a working description.

Scholars then tried to define the concept in terms of fundamental functions, and K. W. Humphreys' conclusion, prepared for a study of "The Role of the National Library" , met general acceptance for a time. Humphreys identified the fundamental functions of a national library as being: the possession of an outstanding and central collection of the nation's literature; the acquisition, in connection with this, of all current published material by means of a legal deposit; the extensive coverage of foreign literature for the nation's scholars; the publication of the national bibliography; and the establishment of a national bibliographic center which, as a rule, entails the publication of catalogues.

As time progressed, the Humphreys definition failed to satisfy the national librarians so that, in 1973, an IFLA colloquium on the subject tried to focus on the essential *tasks and obligations* required of national libraries. The participants sought to determine what a national library *does* rather than what it *is.* The sponsors identified the following that they believed to be typical:

- Collecting and preserving the nation's literature
- Collecting foreign literature for research and teaching
- Caring for special forms of records such as maps, music, pictures, films, etc.
- Maintaining a collection of manuscripts and rare books bearing on the nation's heritage
- Preparing appropriate bibliographic information
- Indexing the national literature and publishing a national bibliography
- Distributing catalogue cards
- Keeping a "national central catalogue"
- Controlling the nation's lending services
- Participating in the international exchange of publications
- Providing advisory service to other libraries
- Training the nation's librarians
- Coordinating acquisition policy, documentation projects, and automation at the national level
- Fostering international cooperation at the "supra-regional" level.

But this attempt failed to survive the conference. By the close of the meeting for which it was designed, almost every element on the list had been rejected by enough of the participating national librarians to make it inappropriate to be called a "common characteristic." Yet there was still a need for an official definition (if only to decide on who should be invited to national conferences), so the Unesco meeting noted above finally concluded that the only definition common to all was, "The national library of a country is the one responsible for collecting and conserving the whole of that country's book production for the benefit of future generations."

This description held shakily until it was finally rejected by a substantial proportion of the national librarians of the developing countries. They maintained that the quoted task was not the obligation of the national libraries

Arthur Plotnik

*Reading room in the National Library of Greece.*

but properly belonged to the state and local *universities,* and thus the hoped-for definition reached the point that Arundell Esdaille, Secretary of the British Museum, had anticipated in 1934: "Uniformity is not to be expected; the political and social traditions of one country will produce a quite different type of library service from those in another."

**Three Types.** Clearly the concept of the national library has meaning within the library profession and is a useful, distinctive term. Yet, why is it so hard to define? It seems to become workable from a taxonomic point of view if the 100 national libraries are divided into three admittedly disparate types. The majority of these provide unique services; most are recognized as holding a position of primacy among the libraries of their nation—and all share the increasing problems that face "national libraries" at the present time.

*First Generation.* National libraries can be grouped into three fairly clear-cut modes; the first might be called First Generation. These are the traditional, the classic national libraries that initially come to mind when the term is used in Western librarianship. Approximately 20 in number, all were founded in or before 1800 and are in the traditional mode of the Library of Congress, the British Museum, and the Bibliothèque Nationale. They were originally established as an ornament of nationalism, and their collections began either with acquisition of royal holdings (as in France, Austria, and Denmark) or with the acquisition of large private libraries (as with the Library of Congress's Thomas Jefferson volumes or the British Museum's Sir Hans Sloane). Once established, they grew inexorably under forced deposit arrangements, which were in turn tied to the copyright or to permission-to-publish by the nation's book trade.

Thanks to the deposit procedures, these collections grew comprehensively. There was little selection; production of a work within the national borders gave the material standing as a part of the record of the national heritage. The vast breadth of the collections soon led to new obligations to the scholarly communities who used them. The logical first step was the development of bibliographic controls to make the holdings useful. This in turn stimulated national bibliographies, special bibliographies, union catalogues, national bibliographic standards, and finally professional training for the nation's librarians.

The very size of these founding libraries generated a reciprocal standing in their nation's cultural life. They demonstrated the nation's interest in and support of intellectual activities, and they were thus soon housed in magnificent buildings built at public expense. Private treasures were given to them, enhancing their collections and the prestige of the donors. Having brought all recorded knowledge into a single place, they became the most efficient centers for research within their countries: one-stop, million-book "encyclopedias" to explore, analyze, and then use for more writing—which would in turn be housed, catalogued, and explored. The quantity of use neither matched the size of the collections nor approached the use rate that fell on the university or municipal libraries of the time, but the quality of use reflected the highest levels of scholarship and attracted the most creative minds of the contemporary societies.

*National Library, Singapore.*

National Library, Singapore

ALA

*Reading room beneath the dome of the Bibliothèque Nationale, France.*

Such national libraries excelled in superlatives. The Viennese had more papyri, the Danish more Icelandic sagas, the Irish more illuminated vellum—and the Reading Room of the British Museum exceeded Saint Peter's in the breadth of its dome. They were elitist; in many of the European versions, the user had to be introduced in writing by others who had been granted access. Students were resisted everywhere, and service was frequently designed to dissuade any researcher who had any but the highest motivation to use the collections; the turnaround time between book request and book delivery almost always exceeded 24 hours and frequently involved many days. They nevertheless became the center of librarianship in each of their countries and inexorably became a major element in preserving the national memory and fostering research and scholarship. Their acceptance and tradition generated the Second Generation of national libraries.

*Second Generation.* This group of national libraries appeared after the Napoleonic Period and came to an end with World War II; it totals approximately 50. While they may well have begun in the image of the original 20, they developed into quite different institutions along the way. Those in Latin America began as literary and historical collections, usually housed in splendid buildings, but frequent changes of government brought about inadequate funding and constant variation in staffing. Their large, centrally situated buildings became involved in wars and revolutions, for which they were commandeered for purposes other than the accumulation and preservation of books; their collections were frequently dispersed and forced to begin anew. Thus when many of the Latin

American national libraries arrived in the 20th century, they were old in history but new in collections and services.

Many of the Second Generation institutions began as adjuncts to the national governments and were established to support parliaments. Thus Canada, Australia, and New Zealand focused first on materials to aid the legislature and from that locus expanded to science and the humanities.

Finally, the founding of another group (e.g., Switzerland, Greece, Israel) coincided with the development of educational and community libraries, and the national libraries therefore found themselves in competition with other institutions for funding and attention. These libraries, again, began as hopeful duplicates of the original 20, but straitened circumstances forced them to specialize in services that only a central, national collection could provide, and let many of the peripheral tasks be shifted to local universities and public libraries. Central bibliographic services were common (although the book trades in many of the countries still provided the national bibliography), and most of these libraries accumulated the history and accomplishments of the nation, but the great collections rarely materialized.

The result of major wars, frequent changes of government, and dramatic shifts of national purpose was, for most of these libraries, a selective series of targets and objectives. Instead of being all things to scholarship and the national memory, each took certain tasks as their primary purposes and built on them. Their collections vary widely in size, from Bolivia's 26,000 volumes to the U.S.S.R.'s Lenin Library at 27,000,000. Housing ranges from the National Library of Tunisia, in an old Turkish barracks that was originally used as a jail, to the splendor of the National Library of Canada.

Toward the end of the period, a new technique was developed to solve problems of use, storage, and support: the division of the national library into separate elements located in varying parts of the nation. In the British system, the National Library of Wales was established in 1909 and the National Library of Scotland in 1925. In Italy the national library was divided among fully developed institutions in Florence, Naples, Rome, Venice, Palermo, and Turin, and in Yugoslavia the national library appears in Belgrade, Zagreb, Ljubljana, Sarajevo, Skopje, and Cetinje.

*Third Generation.* Begun at the close of World War II, the Third Generation comprises approximately two dozen libraries, and they are radically different from the first in their objectives. While the older states started with inherited collections and grew larger around their books, the new states picture their national libraries as integrated systems, fully developed, usually headquartered in the national capital but reaching as a network out toward the provincial and local libraries. The national library usually runs a library school, loans books, and maintains the national bibliography. Frequently they were created to meet the need for a central point for the deposit of international documents (of the United Nations, World Health Organization, Unesco, and other organizations) and for a central point for international exchange and receipt of foreign book grants.

Several began as essentially government libraries (Nigeria's, and even the National Diet Library of Japan) that then received broader responsibilities and ultimately became the center of major networks of acquisition and use.

Many of the new countries called on library specialists from the developed countries to study their needs so their systems could grow according to professional plans. Western specialists, frequently expecting to duplicate the systems of the industrial nations, soon revised their thinking and universally turned to much more integrated systems. Hans Panofsky suggested a symbolic approach

National Library of Switzerland

*Students use a reading room of the National Library of Switzerland.*

would be a single building with a door labeled National Library "at one entrance, Public Library at another, University Library at a third, and perhaps Government Archives on a fourth side." Uganda, Ethiopia, Sri Lanka, and Sudan concluded that the traditional research collection of a national library more properly belonged to the universities and that the national library should be the center of a national public library network as well as supporting government activities at the national, state, and local level. Reference, research, and the record of the national experience belonged to the educational system. (This division of labor is hardly restricted to Africa and Asia; Iceland, Norway, Czechoslovakia, and Israel followed the same pattern.) A national library that forms the center of a Ministry of Education public library configuration is found in Panama, Guatemala, and Ghana. In Libya, Tunisia, and Malaysia the national library became the central warehouse for book loan and distribution, and Colombia and El Salvador opened branches of the national library in municipal centers throughout their countries.

## SERVICES TO USERS

While it is obvious that, given this wide variety of institutions, one can find an example of almost every library service somewhere among the national libraries, there are certain trends that can be identified as either being common to a large number of the institutions or suggesting the way of the future.

**Access.** Which books are acquired and kept varies widely, but what is done with them can be safely generalized. Only in the Third Generation national libraries are loan programs common. In the more traditional institutions, books must be used either within the building or through interlibrary loan to other libraries. In Latin America use only on the premises is almost universal. Many of the major European institutions limit the user himself; while the British Library has liberalized its own rules, the traditional rules for the British Museum are typical on the Continent:

> Permission to use the reading rooms is given, not in the rooms or the departments themselves, but in the Director's office. Applicants must be 21 years of age . . . ; they must give evidence of a definite study, and of se-

rious need for the Museum Library, and not (as is common) a mere fancy to read there rather than in a local public or special library; they must be recommended by some person in a responsible position; and they must not be reading for an examination.

Access to the Irish National Library is limited to "bona fide researchers and to graduate students."

The developing countries tend to be more liberal. The National Library of Liberia serves all members of the public over 16 years old. Ethiopia's National Library is open to all "and there is no charge for reading on premises." Two books may be borrowed at a time and kept for a month.

Hours of access vary widely. In Latin America, most national libraries are open from 9:00 to noon and then reopen from 7:00 to 10:00 in the evening. Guatemala points with pride to its 8:00 to noon, 3:00 to 9:00 service.

In Europe, book delivery to the central reading rooms is commonly on a 24-hour turnaround; a book requested at a certain time one day will be made available at approximately the same time the next. Several of these libraries permit patrons to write in advance, so the library will have a book waiting for the visitor, providing the patron has been previously approved and sufficient lead time is provided. The literature suggests that this response time is not seriously challenged by researchers in the humanities but is the source of increasing resentment by users in the scientific and technological fields. This factor, plus the increased need for specialized attendants for technological materials, accounts for a general increase of special reading rooms in many national libraries. Indeed, many national libraries are even splitting off their medical, agricultural, scientific, and governmental departments into separate institutions using different techniques of retrieval and offering different time scales of service. Examples are Canada, India, Great Britain, and the United States.

**Bibliographical Services.** While reader service varies markedly among the national libraries, bibliographical services are uniformly triumphant, effective, and ever expanding. Some form of deposit arrangement appears in the majority of the institutions (80 of the 100 in 1979 were primary depositories of their national publishing), and one of their earliest obligations was thus the preparation of printed cards, printed catalogues, and the ultimate preparation of the national bibliography. The latter service is the one most frequently agreed upon by the national libraries; 61 of the 100 produce a national bibliography. National bibliographies appear in either author or subject arrangements (rarely both); of the 61 identified, the subject order is the more common.

In the developed countries the national bibliography frequently indexes periodicals and newspapers as well as monographs, but this is not typical in the developing nations. In the past the traditional national libraries commonly prepared special bibliographies for their scholarly patrons and prepared printed catalogues for other libraries. Both of these services diminished in the 1960's and 1970's. Hopes for the computerization of the indexing were common in the 1970's, but one national library after another has had to delay or abandon this technique as either being too expensive, given their present budgets, or to await more reliable systems and equipment to support their plans.

Union catalogues are a common service of national libraries regardless of age. All European national libraries maintain union catalogues, but many are comparatively recent. The Dutch Union Catalogue at The Hague began in 1921, the Swiss at Berne in 1927, Yugoslavia's in 1956, Spain's in 1942, and the British Union Catalogue in 1931. When the national library produces a national bibliography, the national union catalogue in most cases contains only "foreign" (those in other than the national) languages; the Bibliothèque Nationale's union catalogue of foreign works began in 1921 in Paris. In Germany, the union catalogues are both prepared and housed in the various provinces and therefore are in multiple parts that together add up to a single whole.

Throughout Europe the catalogues are simply location tools; few supply interlibrary loan service as well. In the developing countries, on the other hand, the union catalogues are an essential part of the interlibrary loan network and solve other problems at the same time. The National Library in Taiwan, for example, maintains four union catalogues: one of Chinese rare books, one of Chinese documents, one of Chinese serials, and one of "nonrare stitch-bound books." The union catalogue department issues Chinese catalogues for the nation's libraries and establishes the national cataloguing rules.

Photoduplication services are common among the national libraries. They are used both as an adjunct of preservation and as a substitute for loan. Older materials rarely circulate anywhere, but programs to preserve deteriorating bookstocks are still rare. The Central State Library of Romania provides a Center for "book pathology and restoration," and Taiwan's National Library is converting all its rare Chinese books to microform and distributing them to the public and university libraries. But difficulties with preservation appear everywhere. Costs are high, qualified staff are scarce, and few user groups support the search for funds.

COLLECTIONS

In no area are the national libraries' disparities more apparent than in their collections. In the classic model of a national library, the characteristics of size (enormous size, as a rule) and preoccupation with the receipt and preservation of the intellectual activities of the nation were the primary distinctions that set them apart from other libraries. They were the one national institution responsible for preserving the national memory. They were comprehensive in the extreme. But the newcomers concentrate on current, working collections, frequently linked with provincial libraries by lively interlibrary loan networks and in some cases boxes of books delivered and picked up by trucks on daily or weekly schedules. Their thrust is

National Free Library of Rhodesia

*Reading area of the National Free Library of Rhodesia, Bulawayo.*

immediate use; eternal preservation is the least of their worries.

Some of the sharpest ironies and most difficult dilemmas fall in this area. Peru, for example, is torn between the need to act as the nation's archive of volumes (the one place where a copy of everything needed by its scholars can be found) while the demands made on its collections are so great—indeed, the use so insatiable—that its Librarian despairs over the mutilation of the collection while watching volumes wear out from use or disappear from a dozen causes with frightening speed. The European national libraries are torn between supporting intricate interlibrary loan networks with their provincial and municipal libraries while at the same time recognizing that, as a rule, they can secure a copy by airmail more quickly from other national libraries outside their own borders than rely on the domestic sources they are dedicated to fostering. Similarly, the temptation is great for these mature libraries to divide the various intellectual specializations among universities and professional associations and let these pursue, organize, and service the works in each's area of expertise—which all too quickly eliminates the national library's raison d'être.

Some of the chief ironies surrounding the national libraries come from the requirements of legal deposit, which has come to be not a boon but a millstone. The obligations of cataloguing, housing, and preserving the totality of a national print production are overwhelming. Simply because a work is published by a countryman does not guarantee its usefulness to the nation, but individual librarians are reluctant to be the agent who interrupts a tradition of comprehensive collecting carried on with vigor for centuries. The National Library of Austria represents the problem in a curiously difficult form, but its dilemma affects every national library of the West. The Austrian library was begun in the mid-14th century and has had legal deposit for over 400 years. It served an empire of 50,000,000 people with many differing national traditions until 1918, when the nation was divided and thereby reduced to a population of 7,000,000. The library, however, is still trying to collect all significant material produced that relates to the "lost" ethnic groups—not from a political context but simply to keep the early holdings of centuries in continuing use. Since these holdings are so extensive, the ethnic scholars still come from all over central Europe to use them, and the present generation is reluctant to destroy the continuity of the collection.

ADMINISTRATION AND FINANCE

National libraries differ administratively from other forms of libraries in at least two ways. Most other libraries have a specific, often limited clientele or audience, as in a university community, a municipality, or a professional elite. On the other hand, the national library tends to serve as a link to the entire spectrum of the nation's literate population. It thus demands more complicated relationships outside its walls than do most libraries. It requires ties to the academic community as users, the industrial community as patrons, the government community as employer, the publishing community as producer, and so on—and the greater the number of links, the greater the support for the national library. According to David Mearns, "It seems to be a rule of life that where national libraries prosper, their activities are identifiable with and allied to the interests of many and diverse groups." The breadth of this diversity provides many advantages: national libraries tend to enjoy greater policy independence than most libraries, and they have a momentum (almost glacier-like) that protects them from attack, major elimination of funds, and certainly of interruption or extinction.

Size, on the other hand, embodies serious costs for

National Library of Austria

*National Library of Austria displays selections from the treasures held in its collection.*

the national library. Its collections grow faster than any other collection in the nation since of all the nation's libraries it alone is collecting comprehensively. Similarly, since it attempts to preserve the nation's heritage, it can rarely weed and discard materials, and thus it grows ever larger. This, in turn, has an impact on building, which again is an especially difficult issue for national libraries. Their traditional location at the center of government, which in turn is usually in the center of the nation's largest city, makes expansion doubly difficult. Most national libraries have tried to solve the problems by displacing certain components of their service to satellite, suburban locations, but in doing so they have threatened the traditional advantage of the great, central ("one-stop") research collection, where the user can explore regardless of format or subject. While the U.S., Britain, France, Spain, Italy, the U.S.S.R., The Netherlands, and others have cleared central space and built new buildings to keep the central collection strong, they have at the same time moved serials, documents, motion pictures, music, newspapers, processing, or interlibrary loan units to the periphery. Ireland, Mexico, and Denmark at the end of the 1970's were displacing collections to adjacent universities; the U.S., Canada, Britain, and Australia cut out major parts of their collections to establish separate libraries for medicine, agriculture, science, or government. Yugoslavia, Italy, and Germany were dividing their collections by region or national origins, while Latin American libraries were dividing by age—the recent materials in the center city, older at the periphery. But all dispersion is at the expense of comparative research.

**Organization.** Within the walls of the national library there is likely to be greater diversity of administrative units than in any other form of library institution. With a collection covering the entire span of the nation's creative skills, most national libraries have many small, highly specialized reading rooms, units, divisions, and departments. This division along with the library's vast size, makes it easier for the administrator to break up tasks into specializations (and thus the worker can better fit his skills, interest, and training to the particular job), but it shatters the general sense of purpose. The worker has more trouble remembering why he is doing his task and how it relates to others. While such specialization was originally thought to speed up flow-through, it may well have passed the point of profit and is now becoming counterproductive in the great institutions. Each step must redo some of the preceding, reread some pages, recheck certain previous steps. In the Library of Congress this fragmentation has reached such a point that English-language materials may be touched by 65 different pairs of hands between mail room and shelf, and foreign materials as many as 50. Similarly, the staff quickly divides into the "recorders" and the "users"—processing and reference—and it becomes increasingly easy to forget the linkage.

A corollary to the complexity of the organizational structure of the national library is its differing types of personnel. The staff is likely to be divided almost equally between librarians and technical specialists. The skills of acquisition (dealing with publishers, booksellers, and importers) and cataloguing (creating the national bibliography, preparing catalogues, and loading the bibliographic data banks) require professional librarians. Service to highly specialized audiences, such as social scientists, medical scientists, energy scientists, linguists, and specialists in international affairs, requires specialized training to anticipate the needs of the users and "speak their language" in serving them quickly and accurately.

While in the past the most highly trained practitioners of all these bibliographic and research arts were drawn to the great national libraries, this is no longer the case on any continent. The specialists are being pulled toward the great universities, the research laboratories of the industrial complex, the library schools, and the government agencies "where the action is." Thus the professional literature reports in every language the failure of the national libraries to compete for the outstanding scholars in their traditional fields.

It is obviously hopeless to try to present a "typical" organizational scheme of the 100 national libraries, but a small sample might be useful.

*Example: Denmark.* The Royal library of Copenhagen has experienced a series of reorganizations and is presently tightly departmentalized into 16 sharply defined units, 10 departments organized by format and 6 by service. It has a Danish Department with its own catalogues and staff (relatively unchanged since the early 1700's and caring for a complete collection of everything printed in Denmark since the 15th century) but also two "Foreign Departments"—one concentrating on the acquisition of books (selected by a staff of 40 full-time subject specialists) and a parallel department of foreign serials. The departments of Manuscripts, Maps and Prints, Oriental Manuscripts, Judaica, Music, Rare Books, and National Bibliography are traditional.

But the Department for Public Relations is less so in European national libraries. It conducts a publicity program through radio, television, and the scientific press, carries on an intensive traveling exhibition program, and conducts courses for students on how to use the national library. Its primary purpose is to widen the circle of library users. The Department of Service to the Institute and Other Libraries is also unusual, representing a close and continuing relationship with the National universities, the Royal Academy of Music, the Scandinavian Institute for Asian Studies, and other institutions. The departments of Descriptive Cataloguing, Classification, Readers' Service, and Technical Services (primarily binding and photoduplication) are also traditional.

*Brazil.* The National Library of Brazil is divided into five sections: Acquisition and Processing, General Reference, Special Reference, Divulgation (publications, cultural promotions, and exchanges), and Conservation; and three services: copyright, reprography, and administration.

*DDR.* The Deutsche Staatsbibliothek in East Berlin has departments of Acquisition, Cataloguing, and Lending, a Reference Bureau, and departments of Manuscripts, Oriental Books, Incunabula, Music, Cartography, Children's Literature, and Reprography.

*Switzerland.* This national library is organized around six departments: Acquisition, Catalogues, Periodicals, Circulation, Special Collections, and the Swiss Union Catalogue. The Director's Office contains an administrative unit of personnel and accountancy and a technical services unit of reproduction and bookbinding—all four elements within the Director's immediate supervision.

**Finance.** There seems little unique about national libraries' budgetary needs per se. Their requirements parallel those for any large, central library. Most require adequate acquisition money readily at hand so they can secure small production or regional material quickly before it is lost, but many are spared the cost of intranational purchasing since their materials come free through deposit arrangements.

Most national libraries are treated as separate entities by their parent governments, and the libraries strive to keep this independence intact, thus avoiding direct competition with other agencies within a ministry or department. Most receive their funds through annual budgets, and most are favorably treated. Although few get as much funding as they want, even fewer are cut back from previous levels unless the entire national budget is reduced.

*National Library of Wales, Aberystwyth.*

Joel Lee

LIBRARY COOPERATION

In a world of increasing international interdependency, it might be assumed that the great national libraries would be at the forefront of international library cooperation. While there has been much discussion in this area, the anticipated results have been limited. Some national librarians believe that this is less a failure in implementation than a recognition that what international cooperation was genuinely needed has already been accomplished; hoped-for additions are really linked to secondary needs, which are pushed ever further back by lack of space, resources, and the absence of demands by user elites. Very real achievements have involved a number of areas.

The first area of international cooperation to be explored historically was that of documents exchange. This activity was initiated between the major national libraries as early as 1840, when the United States Congress passed a special bill to establish "a system of international exchange of public documents." These protocols grew steadily, so that by the 1950's well over 100 were operating. The national gazettes, legislative debates, and state papers were universally exchanged, and the documents of cabinet-level ministries and departments followed spottily thereafter. The majority of the programs were developed as formal diplomatic exchanges negotiated as treaties or international agreements—not as professional library dialogues.

Programs of acquisition exchange were started to repair the damage of World War II, and many of these continued into the 1960's and 1970's after the initial purpose had been satisfied. In the United States the Library of Congress's National Program for Acquisition and Cataloging was broadly active; the members of the French Union continued to support each other even after independence (with much help from the French government itself); and the traditional members of the British Commonwealth used the empire avenues to expand cooperative ventures.

Bibliographic programs expanded, notable among them the Library of Congress MARC program with its computerized data base and automated union catalogues. Cooperative cataloguing built machine-readable data bases, and "MARC tapes" were first exchanged with Canada and then increasingly sent to other nations. IFLA programs for the cooperative formulation of cataloguing principles were developed.

Interlibrary loan would appear to be an obvious area of cooperative potential, but this has started very slowly and shown little expansion. The original logic suggested that as national libraries are usually the primary custodians of foreign books in a country, and as national libraries are usually the source of last resort for advanced research, they are the obvious libraries to exchange materials with other national libraries dealing with institutional peers. It has not so developed. Experience has shown that from 60 to 80 percent of all interlibrary loans involve books published in the past five years; thus serious researchers tend to buy foreign books rather than rely on their national libraries to borrow them for them. While the remaining 20 to 40 percent frequently do come through international exchange from abroad, the numbers have never been as large as the potential would have suggested.

Graciela Sánchez Cerro

*National Library of Peru*

The majority of successful programs in international cooperation can be traced to the following organizations working in the field: Unesco, the International Federation of Library Associations (IFLA), the International Federation for Documentation (FID), the International Council on Archives, and the Inter-Parliamentary Union.

LAWS AND LEGISLATION

National libraries differ legally from traditional libraries in two major respects: their relation to the sovereign gov-

*Special collections of the National Library of Poland, Warsaw, are housed in the historic Palace of the Republic.*

National Library of Poland

ernment and their role in the copyright or deposit system of the nation.

**Authority.** Other libraries are governed by a college board, a local government, or a corporation, but national libraries are usually the creation of the national government and thus may be either directly responsible to the ruling body or a part of the government's cabinet ministries. They appear in three modes. Some are independent agencies with independent authority; some have legally fixed responsibilities with "firm primacy" within larger governmental units; and some function with traditional momentum and continue without written rule but exercise authority by common consent.

The guiding charters usually spell out four elements: who appoints the chief librarian, where the money is to come from, to whom the librarian reports, and what the obligations of the institution are. Any of these elements can be missing—indeed, some national libraries can find little law relating to their institutions in any of their codes, and they find this so useful they are actively reluctant to change it.

The Swiss National Library is under the Department of the Interior. The Austrian National Library is run by the Ministry of Science and Research. The Library of El Salvador is an agency of the Ministry of Culture; the Italian National Library is under the Ministry of Fine Arts; and the National Library of Venezuela is a department of the National Institute of Culture and Fine Arts. The Royal Library of The Netherlands falls under the Department of Education and takes some pride in its lack of charter or statutes, although its internal regulations date back to 1884. This relationship to the Ministry of Education also appears in the Stockholm Royal Library, the National Library of Ireland, and the Tunisian National Library. The Jewish National and University Library has no link to the government of Israel at all and is financed by private contributions and university funds as an independent agency.

**Deposit Laws.** The first nation to use a deposit law to fill its national library with free, automatically forwarded books is thought to be Austria, in 1575. Sweden in 1661. Denmark in 1697, and Spain in 1716 followed this precedent, and by the time the Library of Congress embraced the idea in 1846 it was long established. Of the 100 national libraries cited in this article, 80 are at least one of the deposit points for the product of the national publishing industry (see table). Multiple deposit of free volumes is common; Great Britain, for example, deposits one copy of all new books with the British Museum, the Bodleian Library at Oxford, the University Library at Cambridge, Trinity College in Dublin, and the National Libraries of Scotland and Wales.

In some nations it is the printer, not the publisher, who must make the deposit, thus denying the national library books printed abroad—a practice that is increasingly common with color work even in the developed countries. In the United States much material from universities, museums, and scholarly societies is deliberately published without copyright to encourage scholarly use and thus is not sent to the Library of Congress for inclusion in either its collections or its published catalogues. Most copyright and deposit laws were written in the days of books, maps, and newspapers, but they have been amended repeatedly to cover photographs, films, recordings, and now the multiple forms of electronic capture and storage. While such laws have the advantage of acquiring comprehensive collections with little cost or search effort, the disadvantages of increasing problems of space, proper preservation, and complexities of storage and retrieval are eroding the profitable trade-off.

PROBLEMS AND TRENDS

What is the future of national libraries? Once again, the future seems to vary sharply among the three types of national libraries. The initial 20, the great institutions of the 17th and 18th centuries, are the most stressed. They are having difficulty adjusting their traditional role of encyclopedic accumulation and total preservation to a society that seems to be focusing on precise data, instantly produced. Their two primary sponsors—the scholarly and the governmental communities—seem to have changed their informational needs and turned to different ways of satisfying them.

On the university campuses of the nations, wide-ranging, interdisciplinary research has been replaced by precise, narrowly defined searches for specific, specialized pieces of fact. The great, comprehensive collections of the initial 20 libraries have proved to be difficult to shift to the kind of quickly accessible materials, served by specially trained personnel, providing the kinds of rapidly changing bibliographic needs that are demanded by this specialized clientele.

The national libraries that supported their governmental communities found another inherent conflict. Governments needed immediate data, ephemeral, constantly changing, totally disposable, but perpetually responsive. The national libraries had developed grand skills of acquisition, careful bibliographic control, highly professional preservation and storage techniques—for materials long since discarded by their governmental users. The latter, like their scientific counterparts, have been attracted to the splitting off of their informational support facilities and thus are further weakening the central institution.

The great libraries have two powerful advantages, however—because of their size and the professional skills of their staffs, they may well be in the best possible position to take advantage of the computer. If the world of automation goes to vast, centralized storage, the already encyclopedic collections of the national libraries provide the potential for exploiting automation's ability to store and manipulate great quantities of data with blinding speed.

A corollary to their comprehensive nature is the national libraries' preeminence in "foreign" (nonnational, outside-the-borders) acquisition. No institution in any nation has proved to be as efficient at accumulating research materials from around the world as the national libraries. Unfortunately, this stimulates yet another conflict that makes finding the proper role for the national libraries so difficult. Since the great libraries have the greatest concentration of stored data in their countries, they might be expected to support a major amount of the use of this material. But they are universally ill-equipped to sustain such demands and thus have had to build a wall of "last resort" around their collections—further alienating their audiences and lowering their visibility even to specialists who would be the most appropriate users of their holdings.

The Second Generation libraries, on the other hand, appear to be remarkably at peace with their roles. Having fitted their aspirations to reality along the way, they have been accepted by their nations and seem to be living comfortably with the responsibilities assigned them. The Second Generation libraries have proved to be especially adept in generating popular interest and pride in their nation's culture and traditions. They have cared for their national intellectual patrimony with skill and are now frequently the leading source of national programs relating to the national history and customs. They seem to be a major source of pride for their communities and are enthusiastically a part of their nation's cultural scene.

The Third Generation seems to be in an even healthier state. While their future seems to be "all before them," they have been recognized by their governments as a major partner in the building of the new nations and are deeply involved in the professionalization of the government cadres. They frequently are the central institution in adult education and literacy programs and are often the primary link between distant communities and provincial centers of population. Their potential impact in their nations seems to grow steadily, and their popular support is equally heartening.

Indeed, in no area of international librarianship is the national library the object of severe criticism. In this day of fashionable challenge to all public roles, librarians may take heart that the national library is firmly accepted; the only discussion is how it can be most effectively used.

**National Libraries (1979)**

| Country | Name of library | Place | Date founded | Number of volumes | Legal depository? | Produces national bibliography? |
|---|---|---|---|---|---|---|
| Albania | National Library | Tirana | 1922 | 450,000 | Yes | Yes |
| Algeria | Bibliothèque Nationale | Algiers | 1963 | 650,000 | Yes | Yes |
| Angola | Biblioteca Nacional de Angola | Luanda | ? | 25,000 | No | No |
| Argentina | Biblioteca Nacional | Buenos Aires | 1810 | 682,794 | Yes | No |
| Australia | National Library of Australia | Canberra | 1902 | 1,625,000 | Yes | Yes |
| Austria | Österrichische Nationalbibliothek | Vienna | 1526 | 2,237,000 | Yes | Yes |
| Bangladesh | National Library | Dacca | 1971 | 10,000 | Yes | No |
| Belgium | Bibliothèque Royale Albert I | Brussels | 1837 | 3,000,000 | Yes | Yes |
| Benin | Bibliothèque Nationale | Porto Novo | ? | 7,500 | No | Yes |
| Bolivia | Biblioteca y Archivo Nacional de Bolivia | Sucre | 1836 | 26,000 | Yes | No |
| Botswana | Botswana National Library Service | Gaborone | 1968 | 130,000 | Yes | Yes |
| Brazil | Biblioteca Nacional | Rio de Janeiro | 1810 | 1,800,000 | Yes | Yes |
| Bulgaria | Kiril i Metodi Narodna Biblioteka (Cyril and Methodius National Library) | Sofia | 1878 | 1,307,993 | Yes | Yes |
| Burma | National Library | Rangoon | 1952 | 49,123 | Yes | Yes |
| Cambodia | Archives et Bibliothèque Nationales | Phnom Penh | 1923 | 31,000 | Yes | ? |
| Canada | National Library | Ottawa | 1953 | 500,000 | Yes | Yes |
| Chile | Biblioteca Nacional de Chile | Santiago | 1813 | 1,200,000 | Yes | Yes |
| China | National Library | Peking | 1912 | 4,400,000 | No | No |
| China (Taiwan) | National Central Library | Taipei | 1928 | 500,000 | Yes | Yes |
| Colombia | Biblioteca Nacional | Bogota | 1777 | 400,000 | No | No |
| Congo | Bibliothèque Nationale Populaire | Brazzaville | ? | ? | No | No |
| Costa Rica | Biblioteca Nacional | San José | 1888 | 175,000 | Yes | No |
| Cuba | Biblioteca Nacional "José Marti" | Havana | 1901 | 531,329 | Yes | Yes |
| Czechoslovakia | Stâtni Knihovna České socialistické republiky (State Library of the Czech Socialist Republic) | Prague | 1958 | 4,600,000 | Yes | Yes |
| Denmark | Det Kongelige Bibliotek (The Royal Library) | Copenhagen | 1657 | 2,100,000 | Yes | No |
| Dominican Republic | Biblioteca Nacional | Santo Domingo | 1971 | 153,955 | Yes | No |
| Ecuador | Biblioteca Nacional | Quito | 1792 | 55,000 | Yes | No |
| Egypt | Dar el-Kutub (Egyptian National Library) | Cairo | 1870 | 1,500,000 | Yes | Yes |
| El Salvador | Biblioteca Nacional | San Salvador | 1870 | 95,000 | Yes | No |
| Ethiopia | Ethiopian National Library | Addis Ababa | 1944 | 100,000 | No | No |

**National Libraries (1979)—Continued**

| Country | Name of library | Place | Date founded | Number of volumes | Legal depository? | Produces national bibliography? |
|---|---|---|---|---|---|---|
| France | Bibliothèque Nationale | Paris | 1480 | 7,000,000 | Yes | Yes |
| German Democratic Republic | Deutsche Staatsbibliothek | East Berlin | 1661 | 5,298,515 | Yes | No |
| | Deutsche Bücherei | Leipzig | 1912 | 6,400,869 | Yes | Yes |
| Germany, Federal Republic of | Deutsche Bibliothek | Frankfurt | 1946 | 2,036,671 | Yes | Yes |
| | Staatsbibliothek Preussischer Kulturbesitz | West Berlin | 1661 | 2,730,000 | No | No |
| | Bayerische Staatsbibliothek | Munich | 1558 | 4,000,000 | No | No |
| Ghana | Central Reference and Research Library | Accra | 1964 | 6,500 | Yes | No |
| Greece | National Library | Athens | 1828 | 1,000,000 | Yes | No |
| Guatemala | Biblioteca Nacional | Guatemala City | 1879 | 352,000 | Yes | No |
| Guinea | Bibliothèque Nationale | Conakry | 1960 | 10,000 | Yes | No |
| Guyana | National Library | Georgetown | 1909 | 151,879 | Yes | Yes |
| Haiti | Bibliothèque Nationale | Port-au-Prince | 1940 | 19,000 | No | No |
| Honduras | Biblioteca Nacional | Tegucigalpa | 1880 | 55,000 | Yes | No |
| Hungary | Országos Széchényi Könyvtár (National Széchényi Library) | Budapest | 1802 | 2,035,110 | Yes | Yes |
| Iceland | Landsbókasafn Islands (National Library of Iceland) | Reykjavík | 1818 | 320,000 | Yes | Yes |
| India | National Library | Calcutta | 1902 | 1,579,845 | Yes | No |
| Iran | National Library | Teheran | 1935 | 100,000 | Yes | Yes |
| Iraq | National Library | Baghdad | 1963 | 51,000 | Yes | Yes |
| Ireland | National Library | Dublin | 1877 | 500,000 | Yes | No |
| Israel | Jewish National and University Library | Jerusalem | 1892 | 2,000,000 | Yes | Yes |
| Italy | Bibloteca Nazionale Centrale | Florence | 1747 | 4,000,000 | Yes | Yes |
| | Bibloteca Nazionale "Vittorio Emanuele III" | Naples | 1804 | 1,531,936 | No | No |
| | Bibloteca Nazionale Centrale Vittorio Emanuele II | Rome | 1876 | 2,500,000 | Yes | No |
| | Bibloteca Nazionale | Palermo | 1782 | 440,534 | No | No |
| | Bibloteca Nazionale Marciana | Venice | 1468 | 1,210,000 | No | No |
| | Bibloteca Nazionale | Sagarriga-Visconti-Volpi | 1865 | 250,000 | No | No |
| | Bibloteca Nazionale Universitaria | Turin | 1723 | 850,000 | No | No |
| Ivory Coast | Bibliothèque Nationale | Abidjan | 1971 | 22,000 | Yes | Yes |
| Japan | National Diet Library | Tokyo | 1948 | 6,726,031 | Yes | Yes |
| Korea, North | State Central Library | Pyongyang | ? | 1,500,000 | Yes | Yes |
| Korea, South | National Central Library | Seoul | 1925 | 438,318 | Yes | Yes |
| Laos | Bibliothèque Nationale | Vientiane | ? | ? | Yes | Yes |
| Lebanon | Bibliothèque Nationale | Beirut | 1921 | 100,000 | Yes | No |
| Libya | National Library | Benghazi | 1966 | ? | No | Yes |
| Luxembourg | Bibliothèque Nationale | Luxembourg | 1798 | 540,000 | Yes | Yes |
| Madagascar | Bibliothèque Nationale | Antananarivo | 1961 | 150,000 | Yes | Yes |
| Malaysia | National Library | Kuala Lumpur | 1971 | 43,500 | Yes | Yes |
| Mali | Bibliothèque Nationale | Bamako | 1913 | 6,000 | ? | ? |
| Malta | National Library | Valleta | 1555 | ? | Yes | No |
| Mauritania | Bibliothèque Nationale | Nouakchott | 1965 | 10,000 | Yes | Yes |
| Mexico | Biblioteca Nacional | Mexico City | 1833 | 1,000,000 | Yes | Yes |
| Morocco | Bibliothèque Générale et Archives | Rabat | 1920 | 230,000 | Yes | Yes |
| Mozambique | Biblioteca Nacional | Maputo | 1961 | 110,000 | No | No |
| Nepal | National Library | Katmandu | ? | ? | No | No |

**National Libraries (1979)—Continued**

| Country | Name of library | Place | Date founded | Number of volumes | Legal depository? | Produces national bibliography? |
|---|---|---|---|---|---|---|
| Netherlands | Koninklijke Bibliotheek (Royal Library) | The Hague | 1798 | 1,000,000 | No | No |
| New Zealand | National Library | Wellington | 1966 | 419,000 | Yes | Yes |
| Nicaragua | Biblioteca Nacional | Managua | 1882 | 70,000 | ? | ? |
| Nigeria | National Library | Lagos | 1962 | 100,000 | Yes | Yes |
| Pakistan | National Library | Islamabad | ? | 10,000 | Yes | No |
| Panama | Biblioteca Nacional | Panama City | 1892 | 200,000 | No | No |
| Paraguay | Biblioteca y Archivo Nacionales | Asuncion | 1869 | 44,000 | No | No |
| Peru | Biblioteca Nacional | Lima | 1821 | 661,232 | Yes | Yes |
| Philippines | National Library | Manila | ? | 360,637 | Yes | Yes |
| Poland | Biblioteca Narodwa | Warsaw | 1928 | 3,160,245 | Yes | Yes |
| Portugal | Biblioteca Nacional | Lisbon | 1796 | 1,000,000 | Yes | Yes |
| Romania | Biblioteca Centrală de Stat (Central State Library) | Bucharest | 1955 | 7,001,494 | Yes | Yes |
| Saudi Arabia | National Library | Riyadh | 1968 | 16,000 | No | ? |
| Sierra Leone | National Library | Freetown | 1961 | 398,000 | Yes | ? |
| Singapore | National Library | Singapore | 1884 | 971,717 | Yes | Yes |
| South Africa | South African Library | Cape Town | 1818 | 520,000 | Yes | No |
| | State Library | Pretoria | 1887 | 700,000 | Yes | Yes |
| Spain | Biblioteca Nacional | Madrid | 1712 | 3,000,000 | Yes | No |
| Sri Lanka | Ceylon National Library Services Board | Colombo | 1970 | ? | No | Yes |
| Sweden | Kungl. Biblioteket (Royal Library) | Stockholm | Early 17th century | 2,000,000 | Yes | Yes |
| Switzerland | Bibliothèque Nationale Suisse-Schweizerische Landesbibliothek | Berne | 1895 | 1,500,000 | Yes | Yes |
| Syria | Al-Maktabah al Zahiriah (Zahiriah National Library) | Damascus | 1880 | 77,000 | Yes | Yes |
| | Al-Maktabah al-Wataniah (Wataniah National Library) | Aleppo | 1924 | ? | no | No |
| Tanzania | National Central Library | Dar es Salaam | 1964 | 1,000,000 | Yes | Yes |
| Thailand | National Library | Bangkok | 1905 | 820,910 | Yes | Yes |
| Togo | Bibliothèque Nationale | Lomé | ? | 7,000 | No | Yes |
| Tunisia | Bibliothèque Nationale | Tunis | 1885 | 500,000 | Yes | Yes |
| Turkey | Milli Kütüphane (National Library) | Ankara | 1948 | 596,697 | Yes | Yes |
| Union of Soviet Socialist Republics | V. I. Lenin State Library | Moscow | 1862 | 28,216,000 | No | No |
| United Kingdom | British Library | London | 1753 | 17,080,000 | Yes | Yes |
| United States | Library of Congress | Washington, D.C. | 1800 | 18,240,295 | Yes | No |
| Uruguay | Biblioteca Nacional | Montevideo | 1816 | 500,000 | Yes | No |
| Venezuela | Biblioteca Nacional | Caracas | 1833 | 400,000 | Yes | Yes |
| Yugoslavia | Narodna biblioteka Socijalističke Republike Srbije | Belgrade | 1832 | 729,172 | Yes | No |
| | Nacionaina i sveučilišna biblioteka (National and university library) | Zagreb | 17th century | 1,069,471 | Yes | No |
| | Narodna i univerzitetska knjiznica (National and university library) | Ljubljana | 1774 | 1,150,000 | Yes | No |

**National Libraries (1979)—Continued**

| Country | Name of library | Place | Date founded | Number of volumes | Legal depository? | Produces national bibliography? |
|---|---|---|---|---|---|---|
| | Narodna i univerzitetska biblioteka Bosne i Hercegovine (National and university library of Bosnia and Herzegovina) | Sarajevo | 1945 | 670,000 | Yes | No |
| | Narodna i univerzitetska biblioteka "Kliment Ohridski" (National and university Library Kliment Ohridski) | Skopje | 1944 | 1,100,000 | Yes | No |
| | Centraina narodna biblioteka S R Crne Gore (Central National Library of the Socialist Republic of Montenegro) | Cetinje | 1946 | 370,000 | Yes | No |
| Zäire | National Library | Kinshasa | ? | ? | Yes | Yes |
| Zambia | National Archives | Lusaka | 1947 | 11,500 | Yes | Yes |
| Zimbabwe Rhodesia | National Free Library | Bulawayo | 1943 | 50,000 | ? | No |

**REFERENCES**

Marcelle Beudiquez, *Bibliographical Services throughout the World, 1970–74* (1977).

Arundell Esdaile, *National Libraries of the World,* 2nd ed. (1957).

*International Librarianship: Surveys of Recent Developments in Developing Countries and in Advanced Librarianship, Submitted to the 1971 IFLA Pre-session Seminar for Developing Countries Sponsored by Unesco* (1972).

Miles M. Jackson, ed., *Comparative and International Librarianship: Essays on Themes and Problems* (1970).

David C. Mearns, "Current Trends in National Libraries," *Library Trends* (1955).

Symposium on National Libraries in Europe, Vienna, 1958, *National Libraries: Their Problems and Prospects* (1960).

CHARLES A. GOODRUM

# Naudé, Gabriel

(1600–1653)

Gabriel Naudé was one of the first men to attain distinction as a professional librarian. This he achieved partly through his labors in assembling and organizing the library of Cardinal Mazarin but mainly for his celebrated treatise on library economy, *Advis pour dresser une bibliothèque (Advice on Establishing a Library)*. Strangely, the *Advis* was published when Naudé was quite young and his library experience fairly small. It was first published in Paris (1627) and dedicated to Naudé's first employer, Henri de Mesme, *President a Mortier* in the Parliament of Paris.

Naudé was born in Paris on February 2, 1600. For several years he studied medicine, but apparently he never practiced. Having become Librarian to de Mesme, he remained one—serving a succession of illustrious bibliophiles, including, for a short period, Cardinal Richelieu, and also Queen Christina of Sweden. But his most important appointment and most ambitious assignment was as Librarian to Cardinal Mazarin, for whom he assembled a magnificent and unusually large library of 40,000 volumes, which he collected himself from all over Europe. Mazarin fell from power in 1652, and his library was ruthlessly dispersed; some years later it was reconstituted, but Naudé did not live to see it, having died at Abbeville July 29, 1653.

The Mazarine Library reflected exactly Naudé's own enlightened views on how the library of a wealthy private collector should be organized and administered, views that he had already expressed with boldness and clarity in his *Advis*. Naudé believed that such a library should include books valuable for their content, rather than their rarity or beauty; that they should be housed with due attention to natural lighting and freedom from dampness and household noises; and that they should be arranged by subject and made freely accessible to deserving scholars with few books of their own. These were the particular characteristics of the Mazarine Library, which was dedicated *a tous ceux qui y vouloient aller estudier* ("to all those who wish to go there to study").

Although the *Advis* was reprinted, and translated into Latin and English—the English edition, London (1661), was a translation by scholar diarist John Evelyn—its circulation was small. All the same, it is probable that it was of some influence in library development. It is generally agreed that it influenced the library career of Gottfried Leibniz.

To be ahead of one's time may be a disadvantage, as well as a distinction. Naudé belonged, in spirit, to the modern world of freely accessible public libraries and was, within the limitations of his day, an ideal librarian.

**REFERENCES**

The best modern editions of Naudé's pioneer treatise are, in French, *Advis pour dresser une bibliothèque*

(Leipzig, 1963), and in English, *Advice on Establishing a Library* (1950).

Jack A. Clarke, *Gabriel Naudé 1600–1653* (1970), a full biography that is readable and scholarly.

JAMES G. OLLÉ

## Near East, Ancient

The principal Babylonian sites where written records have been found are Uruk (now Warka) and Ur (now El-Mukajjar) in southern Babylonia; Shuruppak (now Farah), almost in the middle of the area; and present-day Jamdat Nasr (ancient name unknown), north of Babylon. Oldest, heralding the new role of writing, are the tablets of the so-called Uruk-Jamdat Nasr period (3100–2700 B.C.), whose messages are clear to us about very little so far. Somewhat later are those of Ur level III, 400 tablets and many more fragments of varied content. Nikolaus Schneider studied the economic items among them, concluding (1940) that the tablets had been distributed among clay containers by subject and date and that the clay containers had tags indicating their respective contents. It is hypothesized that literary and religious texts may have been handled likewise and that the edifice in which the tablets were found had housed a school associated with the nearby temple. The temple area proper yielded religious and astronomical texts; they are ascribed to the 3rd millennium B.C., but exact dates have not been fixed.

A little later than Ur, in turn, are the Early Dynasty II and III (mid-3rd millennium) tablets recovered at Farah (ancient Shuruppak), some 40 miles southeast of Nippur. The numbered series among them contain lists of commodities, quantities, and persons in connection with either temple accounts or school exercises; included are lexicons and incantation texts. There are also unnumbered lists of things like writing signs, for study, and tablets bearing early examples of known Sumerian literature and lexical texts. Neither the temple nor the school tablets demonstrate the existence of a library, but they do testify to preservation of older written materials and to the development of at least rudimentary organizational devices.

Furthermore, the temple records raise the distinction between archives and libraries. Probably most widely accepted are the criteria of Mogens Weitmeyer (1955–56) that archival materials were stored by their nature and date; library materials were gathered into subject-related series, bore colophons including regulations of a library character, and were listed in separate catalogues.

Nearer the close of the 3rd millennium, it appears, are the thousands of tablets surviving from Lagash (present-day Tello), numerous enough for the site to be called "Tablet Hill" since de Sarzec found it in 1894. They are organized in individual rooms, which had plastered walls, containers along the walls, and surfaces on which to place tablets (for reading?). Of particular interest is the evidence that each room had tablets in only one corner, perhaps leaving space for additions. Access to any one of the rooms was provided only through a hole in the ceiling, which brings to mind storerooms or even graves rather than library facilities.

**Second Millennium.** Surviving from Ur and Nippur, particularly, and other sites are numerous tablets documenting the culture of the age of Hammurabi (18th century B.C.). The subjects were from the past: legends of ancient Sumerian gods, kings, and heroes like Gilgamesh. The literary forms similarly derived from long practice, polished in a scholastic style. The script was cuneiform and mainly in Sumerian, but use of vernaculars was beginning, notably the Akkadian used by the Babylonians, into which Sumerian writings were increasingly being translated. Sumerian remained, like Latin in a later day, preferred for learning and literature. Serving religion were Sumerian myths, hymns, and psalms praising gods

Courtesy of The Newberry Library

*The principal written Babylonian records, clay tablets like those depicted here, tell us very little about Babylonian libraries.*

and kings; incantations and prayers of the private sort; and, most important, divination—primarily haruspicy or prediction from entrails. Equally prominent were mathematics texts. The significance of scribes, moreover, is evident from writings about their education both serious and humorous.

Revealed as a commercial center that flourished early in the 2nd millennium, until crushed by Hammurabi about 1750 B.C., was Mari, on the Euphrates. Presently on the Syrian-Iraqi border, it is still important to the nomads. Its ancient remains cover more than 100 acres. The palace is believed to have occupied more than 6 acres, and more than 260 chambers, courtyards, and corridors have been identified. Scholars are satisfied that the building was both the king's residence and an administrative center with workshops and archives. The surviving 20,000 tablets bear mainly diplomatic and household economic records of three unconnected periods of Assyrian rule, and it is considered definite that they were shelved in separate groups.

At ancient Alalakh, a few miles northeast of Antioch, were found tablets in a western dialect of Akkadian constituting an archive of a state of consequence for perhaps 75 years soon after the fall of Mari. It seems to have benefited from trade between the sea and Aleppo, some 50 miles east of Alalakh, and the timber of the Amanus mountains north of the town. Most of the extant tablets are administrative, a few lexicographical and literary, throwing much light on Hurrian activities; but, as at Mari, nothing of a library nature has been established to date.

The world of tablets in cuneiform apparently included also, by the 16th century B.C., archives at the Hittite capitals in Anatolia. The extant data revealing bilingual dictionaries—documents like the Hittite and Akkadian testament of Hattusili I and facilities much like those at Lagash—are interpreted by some to indicate a temple or state library. The degree to which the organized resources included known Hittite historical writings and supernatural or anecdotal literature is not established. Yet there are historical-critical evidences that Assyrian, biblical, and Greco-Roman historiography were influenced by the novel separation from mythology of the "Ten-Year Annals" of a 14th-century Hittite ruler, Mursili. The apparatus for such influence seems likely to have included "book" collections.

The expansion of the Hittite Empire and growing complexity of Near Eastern commercial and diplomatic activity signaled by the Amarna letters are among the events reflected in the 14th- and 13th-century tablets excavated at Ras Shamra, a Syrian coastal town about seven miles north of Latakia. Their contents encompass administrative, economic, ritual, and literary themes, often in more than one language and supported by bilingual word lists. They were found in buildings, both public and private, of ancient Ugarit, not just in the center but at various locations. The Ba-al temple is held to have had a library, not just archives. The nearby house of the chief priest possessed mythological and religious texts not only in the official North Canaanite dialect but also in Hurrian, the language of an important minority; also on hand were vocabularies and other items suggesting that the establishment performed also the functions of a seminary for training temple scribes. Not far from the palace were spacious homes of high officials, at least one of whom owned a library; the variety of its contents is perhaps implied by a surviving lexicographical tablet with equivalents linking Ugaritic and Hurrian with Sumerian and Babylonian. Conspicuous in the artisans' quarter was an imposing stone edifice that had housed a library of texts in Babylonian cuneiform, some astrological and some literary, perhaps used for teaching.

Fairly well documented is the 14th-century activity in Assyria-Babylonia of the "Middle Kassite" period. The Babylonian heritage of religious hero-poems, wisdom literature, theology, philology, prognostication, medicine, and astronomy was collected, edited, translated, and arranged by learned Babylonian scribes in series of numbered tablets. From the traditions of the Kassite rulers came additional cults and cult literature, magic, and demonology. It seems likely that library collections played an important part in that work, which anticipates the later achievements at Alexandria.

In any case, "omens" (predictions), hymns, prayers, and lexicographical texts from the mid-13th-century reign of Shalmaneser I of Assyria became part of a collection expanded by the conquests of Tukulti-Ninurta, the great Assyrian king of the late 13th century. According to a Sumerian-Akkadian epic, indeed, the latter carried off the tablets that distinguished the libraries of Babylonia. Involved were the usual omens, prayers, and incantations, as well as medical texts. Some of them appear to have turned up among the remains of the library established at the Assur temple early in the 11th century by Tiglath-Pileser during his days as Crown Prince.

**Assurbanipal's Library.** For the most impressive legacy, testifying beyond serious challenge to a library, one jumps five centuries to Assurbanipal, "King of the World, King of Assyria" (668–*c.* 631). In 1850 Austen Henry Layard crowned several years' labor at Nineveh sites near Mosul, in far northern Iraq, by identifying "Chambers of Records." In 1854 Hormudz Rassam found an important portion of a library in a nearby structure. The subsequent half-century of excavations added more enlightenment. Some 20,000 tablets and fragments, preserved in the British Museum, owed their enlightening condition to the destruction of Nineveh in 612 by the Medes, so thorough that the sites had lain virtually undisturbed for more than 2,400 years. It is clear from the huge assemblage of Assyro-Babylonian and Sumerian writings and his own correspondence that Assurbanipal built his library partly by welcoming copies from any possible source. Those sources may include the temples, whose plundering by his soldiers is noted in the records of his reign.

The library included the main works of Akkadian literature. More particularly, Leo Oppenheim inventoried the tablets as follows: more than 300, each of which bears from 80 to 200 individual omen texts; 200 with lists of cuneiform signs and combinations, including Sumerian-Akkadian dictionaries; more than 100 Sumerian incantations with interlinear Akkadian translations; 100-plus with proverbs, cycles of conjuration, among others; 200 miscellaneous, including reference works for court diviners and magicians and handbooks for education, research, and the training of scribes; and some 35 or 40 with epic literature. King Assurbanipal himself could read, and it may be assumed that, as elsewhere in the ancient Orient, writings could be used by priests, officials, and merchants, but that was probably all.

Assurbanipal's concerns presumably explain in part the directions that led to stocking his library with exceptional tablets. By comparison with many other Assyro-Babylonian survivals they consist of notably finer and better baked clay than the usual, and the script achieved marked elegance and clarity by means of physically tight inscribing. The correcting and editing was of matching quality.

How the tablets were stored is not known, not from any direct evidence at the library, at any rate. Layard reported in 1853 that he had found two small rooms whose floors were piled a foot or more high with broken clay tablets and cylinders, most of which had probably fallen there from a higher room, and adjoining chambers with similar but slighter remains. Nothing further can be inferred from Rassam's narrative; we hear that additional fragments of the same tablets or belonging to the same series have been found scattered in various places, but thanks to the inexperience and carelessness of excavators or local handlers and arrangers we do not know from which of the two palaces involved any given fragment came. It can hardly be doubted that there were once a definite order and supervision, but we have neither knowledge of them nor any basis for reconstructing them.

Extraordinary care led to the discovery of subscripts on the tablets. Besides the ownership stamp, "Palace of Assurbanipal, King of the World, King of Assyria," precise data were furnished, the equivalent of book or manuscript description. It is now agreed that they were not created by Assurbanipal or his staff but borrowed from available models. These practices had been known at the state (?) library of the Hittites at Boghazköi, and it is no longer doubted that the seeds were planted in oldest Babylon.

That Assurbanipal was collecting systematically is plain from the tablet and series indexes, indexes that furnish at the beginning of each tablet in a series the number of lines on each tablet, and series indexes that bring together the titles of various series whose contents are related. The extant collections do not include index tablets of a bibliographical character or catalogues.

For indicators there were plain, oddly shaped little clay markers, which bear nothing but a series title, perhaps to facilitate finding the series, and which lay on the pile of series items or on the reed or clay receptacles that contained them. Such a receptacle was called *girginakku,* a designation that seems to have carried over to the whole library—like *biblio-theke;* at least the chief was called *rab girginakku,* or supervisor thereof. It may be that the scion of an old scholarly family, whose tablet collection Assurbanipal apparently acquired, was the actual organizer and first director of the royal library.

**REFERENCE**

Ernst Posner, *Archives in the Ancient World* (1973).

SIDNEY L. JACKSON

# Nepal

Nepal, a constitutional monarchy, is bounded by Indian states on the east, south, and west and by China on the north. Pop. (1977 est.) 13,136,000; area 140,798 sq.km. The official language is Nepali.

**National Library.** The Nepal National Library in Patan near Katmandu was established in 1955 when the government of Nepal consolidated the collection of a royal priest with the bound volumes from the Bir Library, a collection begun in the 14th century by a Malla king. The library has 70,000 books and pamphlets in South Asian languages on history, culture, and religion. It has published lists of its holdings in Nepali.

**Academic Libraries.** The principal academic library is the Tribhuvan University Central Library in Kirtipur near Katmandu. The University was chartered in 1959, and in 1962 the Library was given its core collection of 12,000 books from the Lal Durbar Central Library, an American aid project started in 1959. Under the leadership of the Librarian, Shanti Mishra, the general collection of the Library grew to 68,000 volumes in 1973 and 76,000 volumes in 1976, and it has been a United Nations depository since 1964. There is a special collection of 3,000 volumes on Nepal, all Tribhuvan University theses, and also many books in Nepali, Newari, Hindi, and Sanskrit. It has manuscript, map, and microfilm collections. There is a public reference section, and the Library grants memberships to the academic community for library use. It is in a pagoda-style building constructed under the auspices of the Colombo Plan.

The Documentation Center of the former Centre for Economic Development and Administration is also in the University Library. This collection of 5,000 items on economic development in Nepal was started in 1971, and it includes government documents, foreign assistance agency reports, and foreign dissertations on Nepal.

Tri Chandra College, established in 1918 in Katmandu, had 7,000 volumes in 1959 and almost 18,000 volumes in the mid-1970's. The books are kept in locked cases. Other schools and colleges in Nepal have inadequate libraries.

**Public and Foreign Libraries.** There were no public libraries in the late 1970's, but citizens' groups in Katmandu and other towns established small, private reading rooms to compensate in part for that lack of library service. In addition, the circulating libraries of the British Council and the U.S. International Communications Agency perform some functions of public libraries in Katmandu since they loan a variety of books to readers at no cost. China, India, and the U.S.S.R. also support reading rooms that are well used. The U.S. Agency for International Development maintains a small collection of reports on development in Nepal, as does the Swiss Association for Technical Assistance.

Tribhuvan University Library

*Tribhuvan University Library in Kirtipur, Nepal's principal academic library, is the country's only library existing in a separate building of it own.*

**Special Libraries.** The government's Department of Archaeology administers the National Archives and the Kaiser Library in Katmandu. The National Archives of Nepal preserves the historical and religious documents from the former Bir Library. This collection contains about 30,000 manuscripts in most South Asian languages and in Chinese and Tibetan. It has about 1,200 palm leaf manuscripts, 1,000 historical letters, ancient scripts, and government documents dating back to 1920. The manuscripts were being microfilmed in the late 1970's by the German Oriental Society. The Kaiser Library was founded by Field Marshal Kaiser S. J. B. Rana, who began collecting books on all subjects around 1909; the Library was given to the government in 1968. It has 30,000 volumes, including many rare books on Nepal and South Asia, along with old maps and photographs from the Rana era (1846–1951).

Other government special collections include the Geological Survey Department (geological reports and maps), the Mining Department (mineral surveys), the Nepal Industrial Development Corporation (industrial feasibility studies), the Nepal Rastra Bank (reports of international banks), Radio Nepal (tapes of folk music), and the Royal Drug Research Laboratory (publications on the flora of Nepal).

The Madan Memorial Trust Library, started in 1955, is a private collection that concentrates on Nepali language and literature. It holds 8,000 volumes and has photographs, manuscripts, and tape recordings of Nepalese writers and scholars. It also has documents and political handbills from the post-Rana period (after 1951).

**REFERENCES**

E. W. Erickson, "Libraries in Nepal," *Wilson Library Bulletin* (1961); an American adviser describes the library scene in Katmandu, 1958–59.

S. Mishra, "Library Movement in Nepal," *Unesco Bulletin for Libraries* (1974); summarizes the history of libraries in Nepal.

GARLAND L. STANDROD

**Libraries in Nepal (1976)**

| Type | Number | Volumes in collections | Annual expenditures (Nepalese rupee) | Population served | Professional staff | All staff (total) |
|---|---|---|---|---|---|---|
| National | 1 | 70,000 | N.A. | N.A. | N.A. | N.A. |
| Academic | 2 | 94,000 | N.A. | N.A. | N.A. | N.A. |
| Public | N.A. | N.A. | N.A. | N.A. | N.A. | N.A. |
| School | N.A. | N.A. | N.A. | N.A. | N.A. | N.A. |
| Special | 16 | 64,000 | N.A. | N.A. | N.A. | N.A. |

Sources: B. M. Gyawali and G. L. Standrod, compilers, *Information Resources on Nepal* (Kirtipur: Documentation Centre, Centre for Economic Development and Administration, 1973); and N. Mishra and S. Mishra, "Nepal, Libraries in," in *Encyclopedia of Library and Information Science* (1976).

# Netherlands

The Kingdom of the Netherlands lies on the North Sea, bounded by Belgium on the south and the Federal Republic of Germany on the east. Pop. (1978 est.) 13,897,900; area 41,160 sq.km. Much of the country is below sea level. The official language is Dutch.

**National Library.** The Koninklijke Bibliotheek (Royal Library) in The Hague functions as the national library of the Netherlands. It was founded in the French revolutionary era in 1798 and grew rapidly during the next few decades. Its collections in the late 1970's numbered about 1,100,000 printed works (including the largest collection of Dutch incunabula and books printed in the early 16th century), 1,500 medieval manuscripts, 120,000 letters, and 4,500 other manuscripts. It houses the largest chess collection in Europe, the Bibliotheca Van der Linde-Niemeijeriana. In the later 19th century it was decided to restrict the Library's collecting activities to the humanities and the social sciences. Although a legal deposit system for books and periodicals had not been accepted by Parliament by 1979, a voluntary deposit scheme was started in 1975; publishers send copies of their works free of charge up to a certain price limit. The Library's national services include the maintenance of an International Exchange Bureau for books and the Dutch Union Catalogues for books and periodicals. The latter was converted from a card catalogue into a series of computer-based printed volumes. The Library is headquarters of a consortium of research libraries guiding a national Project on Integrated Cataloging Automation (PICA), operative from 1979. PICA was planned to be a central cataloguing institution for participating libraries and for the automation of the Library's own accessions department. By virtue of office, the Librarian is Director of the Museum Meermanno-Westreenianum (Museum of the Book) and of the Dutch Literary Museum.

**Academic Libraries.** Twelve libraries in the Netherlands are directly connected with universities or technical colleges. The oldest is the University Library of Leiden, founded shortly after the establishment of the University in 1575. In the next century or so it incorporated the private collections of scholars such as Vossius, Scaliger, and Perizonius. It has about 7,000 medieval manuscripts as well as an outstanding collection of Oriental manuscripts.

The largest university library is probably that of the Municipal University of Amsterdam. Begun as a city library in 1578, it holds more than 2,000,000 volumes and houses one of the world's most important collections of judaica, the Bibliotheca Rosenthaliana.

Other university libraries are connected with the universities of Utrecht and Groningen, the Free (Calvinist) University of Amsterdam, and the Catholic University in Nijmegen. Apart from the main holdings of these libraries a great number of books are in university institutes, especially where the university has become very much decentralized (as in Utrecht).

Delft Technical University has the most important collection of technical works and also maintains a Union Catalogue for such literature. Wageningen Agricultural University is (with some 400,000 volumes) the main center for books on agricultural and related subjects.

**Public Libraries.** Popular reading libraries were common in Holland from an early date, although a public library system was fully developed only in the 20th century. With the increase in numbers, the denominational rift in Dutch society also split the public library world: apart from the general public libraries both Protestants and Catholics started public library systems of their own. All received government subsidies and held the same ideal of educating the people by making them read. They all gave priority to books for study and did not attract the large groups of people who wanted to read for recreation. But whereas the general libraries did not wish to select their books by other standards than inherent quality, Protestant and Catholic leaders felt that an "indiscriminate" supply of books would disturb their particular flocks. During the 1960's this segregation relaxed and disappeared, uniting public libraries in the Nederlands Bibliotheek en Lektuur Centrum [NBLC; Dutch Center for (Public) Libraries and Literature]. Popular works were acquired in large quantities, branch libraries multiplied, and the reading public came to the libraries in previously unknown numbers. A moderate annual fee is required, except for those under 18. The Public Library Act of 1975 ruled that the central government was to pay all costs of staff and 20 percent of all other expenditure, the remaining 80 percent to be supplied by the provincial and local authorities.

Until comparatively recently the research libraries were able to cope with the demand for study books, but the enormous increase in the numbers of students, both at the universities and at training colleges, required some extension of the library system. Interlibrary lending solved some of the problems, but in addition 12 libraries were designated as regional supporting libraries (including several larger public libraries as well as provincial and municipal libraries). Additional government grants enabled them to buy bibliographical tools and to equip reading rooms.

**School Libraries.** Most secondary schools maintain libraries of their own, and the same is true of vocational training colleges for social workers, primary school teachers, and such. They are usually of little import on the national library scene and employ very few professional librarians.

**Special Libraries.** Although enormously varying in scope and number of volumes, many special libraries are actively engaged in documentation and information retrieval work of a kind only hesitatingly entering the academic libraries; thus the Economic Information Service

**Table 1. Libraries in the Netherlands (1976)**

| Type | Number | Volumes in collections | Annual expenditures (florins) | Professional staff | All staff (total) |
|---|---|---|---|---|---|
| National | 1 | 1,100,000 | Dfl. 1,595,000 (for books) | N.A. | 184 |
| Academic | 12 | N.A. | N.A. | N.A. | N.A. |
| Public | 414 | N.A. | Dfl. 48,073,196 (for books) | N.A. | N.A. |
| School | approx. 4,500 | N.A. | N.A. | N.A. | N.A. |
| Special | N.A. | N.A. | N.A. | N.A. | N.A. |

Source of information: Koninklijke Bibliotheek and NBLC (see text).

(of the Ministry of Economic Affairs) serves industry at large through its 85,000 books, 2,500 periodicals, and 1,500,000 microfiches but also through the data base Informecon. The library of the Royal Dutch Academy of Sciences in Amsterdam has extensive holdings of periodicals in medicine and the natural sciences; the 2,000 periodicals used for the Excerpta Medica abstracts are kept there. An institution of a different type well worth mentioning is the International Institute for Social History in Amsterdam with its widely known collections on socialism and the labor movement.

A number of research libraries that cannot be classed under other headings deserve brief treatment. Most of the country's larger libraries are in the former province of Holland, which traditionally carried most weight in national affairs. Several provinces have libraries of regional importance, especially those of Friesland and Zeeland. These are 19th-century foundations. The oldest municipal library is found in Deventer, in the province of Overysel: this Athenaeum Library dates from the 1560's and is a flourishing research library.

**Table 2. Archives in the Netherlands (1976)**

| | |
|---|---|
| Total number | 81 (General State Archives + 11 State Archives in the Provinces + 69 Municipal and Regional Archives) |

**Associations.** From 1922 to 1975 Dutch university librarians and a number of public and special librarians met in the Rijkscommissie van Advies inzake het Bibliotheekwezen (State Advisory Committee on Library Affairs). In 1975 this task was assumed by the Bibliotheekraad (Library Council). It was felt that the old Advisory Committee was mainly concerned with research libraries, and that a new forum should be created. The new Library Council's work is regulated by law; it is organized in two departments, one for research and special libraries, the other for public libraries. The Council includes nonlibrarians as members.

Librarians in general had their professional organization, the Nederlandse Vereniging van Bibliothecarissen (NVB; Dutch Association of Librarians). Public librarians came to feel that their interests demanded an organization exclusively their own; from 1975, therefore, the NVB comprised librarians working in research and special libraries, while public librarians were organized under the NBLC, cited previously. To provide the necessary unity the Federatie van Organisaties op het gebied van het Bibliotheek-, Informatie-en Documentatiebestel was created in the same year, 1975 (FOBID; Federation of Organizations in the Field of Library, Information, and Documentation Services).

**REFERENCE**

*Libraries and Documentation Centres in the Netherlands* (NBLC, 1978).

H. VAN DER HOEVEN

## Netherlands Antilles

The Netherlands Antilles, a group of six islands within the Leeward Islands in the Caribbean, consists of Curaçao, Aruba, Bonaire, Saint Eustatius, Saba, and the southern part of Saint Martin. Pop. (1977 est.) 245,000; area 993 sq.km. The official language is Dutch.

The Willemstad Public Library *(Openbare Bibliotheek)*, established in Curaçao in 1922, functions as a national library for the Netherlands Antilles. There are two branch libraries, plus a bookmobile that serves suburbs. Although there is no legal deposit law, this library tries to purchase all works printed in, or about, the six islands of the Netherlands Antilles. Its collection of Caribbeana consists of approximately 6,000 volumes. These are the only noncirculating volumes in the 110,000-volume accumulation. Holdings are mainly in Dutch, although the Library has some works in English and in Spanish. There are only a few titles in Papiamento, the patois spoken by most people in the Netherlands Antilles.

The Public Library of Aruba opened in 1944 in Oranjestad and houses approximately 120,000 books. Holdings are in Dutch, English, Spanish, French, and Papiamento. Another branch in the suburb of Saint Nicholas has been in operation for many years. The Caribbeana collection is a noteworthy feature of the Oranjestad main library. Most of the collection circulates, although a deposit is required for some of the older works. Only the rarest items must be used on the premises.

Adults must pay a membership fee to join these public libraries; membership is free to children.

The Central Historical Archives (Centraal Historisch Archief), founded in Willemstad in 1969, contains all archival publications of the Netherlands Antilles, concentrating on government documents. The library is in close contact with the National Library in The Hague and is making copies of all documents there that relate to the Netherlands Antilles. Only government officials may borrow materials, but the collection is accessible to students and others during restricted hours. The library collects periodicals related to archival matters, publishes two newsletters describing old and new acquisitions, and restores and laminates Caribbeana documents.

Arthur Plotnik

*Caribbean libraries range widely in scope. Nevis, above, has a small local collection; Curaçao has a national library for the Netherland Antilles.*

The University of Aruba, founded in 1970, comprises colleges of liberal arts and sciences, business administration, languages, preprofession sciences, and education. In the late 1970's the library housed more than 3,000 volumes.

The Institute of Higher Studies of the Netherlands Antilles was to become the University of the Netherlands Antilles by the end of 1979. The library was opened in 1970 and houses approximately 80,000 volumes, mainly books on law, economics, business administration, and sociology. Students are allowed to borrow books, the number of titles dependent on their class standing. The library subscribes to approximately 100 periodicals and has an active interlibrary loan operation. In addition, the library maintains a union catalogue of all library holdings within the Netherlands Antilles.

There are some special libraries in the Netherlands Antilles. The Oranjestad Sportburo was established in Aruba in 1978 as an outgrowth of a new government bureau in charge of coordinating physical activities in the schools. This circulating library has about 600 books on sports-related topics, half in English and the other half in Dutch.

The main public libraries at Oranjestad and Willemstad both have special collections on music, including musical scores and works related to music, particularly that of the Netherlands Antilles.

The Stichting Wetenschappelijke Bibliotheek (Scientific Library Foundation), founded in 1950 in Willemstad, has an extensive music collection in addition to works on the pure and applied sciences. Holdings include musical scores, printed music, and books on music of the Netherlands Antilles, with a special collection of music by Curaçao composers. Publications of the foundation include a union catalogue of all nonfiction books in the Netherlands Antilles, plus *Curaçao Folklore, Curaçao Music,* and *Nansi Stories.*

Other special libraries connected to research institutes in Curaçao include those of the Caraibisch Marien-Biologisch Instituut, with more than 3,000 volumes, and the Meteorologische Dienst van de Nederlandse Antillen (Meteorological Service of the Netherlands Antilles).

The Association di Biblioteka i Archivo di Korsow (ABAK—Association of Libraries and Archives) was established in 1972 and is affiliated with IFLA. The association is housed in temporary headquarters in Willemstad, Curaçao. There is no official publication.

BARBARA FOSTER

# New Zealand

New Zealand, a parliamentary state, lies in the South Pacific Ocean; the Tasman Sea separates the country from Australia. New Zealand comprises North and South islands and Chatham and Stewart, among other islands. Pop. (1978 est.) 3,151,400; area 269,057 sq.km. The official language is English.

**National Library.** The National Library was established by act of Parliament in 1965 and came into being in 1966 by a merging of the existing National Library Service, the Alexander Turnbull Library, and the General Assembly Library. The National Librarian is an officer of the Crown, responsible to the Minister of Education. A statutory Board of Trustees exists to advise the Minister on the state and development of the National Library and to promote the development of library services in New Zealand. The Library is financed by an annual appropriation by Parliament.

The Library provides the normal national bibliographical and interlibrary loan services and manages the national collections. Its Extension Services Division provides book loans, information services, and technical assistance to public libraries in towns with populations under 75,000 and to elementary and secondary schools.

The Alexander Turnbull Library, an institution for scholarly research, was founded in 1918 as the result of a bequest; its collection reflects the interests of its donor—the Pacific, New Zealand history and literature, English literature (particularly the mid-17th century and the work of John Milton)—with additional strengths in early printed books and the development of the art of printing. The General Assembly Library, established in 1858 as the library of Parliament, was for a time a library of historical research because of the strength of its holdings, but in recent years by transfer of stock and by internal reorganization it has reverted to its primary role as a parliamentary reference library.

**Academic Libraries.** There are six autonomous universities at Auckland, Hamilton, Palmerston North, Wellington, Christchurch, and Dunedin, and an agricultural college at Lincoln. The libraries of the universities are financed through their parent bodies by government grants. The resources and services of the libraries were generally in a poor state until the early 1960's, when a number of advances were made following the recommendations of a Government Committee of Inquiry on Universities (the Parry Report). All libraries are now housed in new buildings; grants for purchases of books and serials have been increased; and salaries and conditions of employment for professional staff have become competitive with those in other sectors. At the time of the Parry inquiry the holdings of all the university libraries were some 818,000 volumes; by 1974 there were over 2,743,000 volumes.

The collections of all these libraries are generally adequate for undergraduate studies, but the growth of postgraduate studies within New Zealand—a matter of official policy—has not been matched by the development of specialized book collections in the university libraries. A recent survey of university libraries (McEldowney, 1973) addressed itself to this question.

There are 8 colleges for training elementary and secondary school teachers and 17 technical institutes that provide tuition for apprentices and other technical students. These institutions are financed by the central government and controlled by autonomous boards. The financial grants for library purposes are determined according to Department of Education formulas, but standards are well below the best that obtain in other comparable countries. The New Zealand Library Association has published standards for these institutions but has not gained direct official recognition of them.

**Public Libraries.** Public library service, other than that supplied to isolated settlements and rural communities, is exclusively the responsibility of local government—boroughs or counties. Finance for the service is derived from a land tax. The period of most rapid development of public libraries, 1945 onward, coincided with or was a consequence of the abandonment of the subscription and rental library systems. In 1938 there were 104 libraries operated by local bodies; by 1959 there were 164; and by 1974, 268.

All libraries in cities and most of those in boroughs provide free lending and reference services to their residents, but special services in light fiction, sound recordings, and art reproductions are normally operated on a rental basis. There is a strong emphasis on lending, but increasing attention is being given to information and reference work and to services that are directed at particular groups.

Efforts to promote the reorganization of service into larger units by way of pilot schemes or cooperative ventures by local bodies saw little success, and it was clear at the end of the 1970's that the reorganization would have to await the reorganization of local government in gen-

**Table 1. Libraries in New Zealand (1976)**

| Type | Number | Volumes in collections | Annual expenditures (dollar) | Population served | Professional staff | All staff (total) |
|---|---|---|---|---|---|---|
| National | 1 | 4,244,721 | NZ$2,918,990 | 3,150,000 | 157 | 380 |
| Academic | 34 | 2,743,341 | NZ$7,695,618 | 115,916 | 220 | 819 |
| Public | 268 | 4,783,748 | NZ$6,229,633 | 2,429,333 | 275 | 1,786 |
| School | 1,067 | 5,458,722 | NZ$1,452,257 | 545,658 | 70 | 4,755[a] |
| Special | 174 | 2,551,802 | NZ$2,263,828 | 182,348 | 136 | 525 |
| Total | 1,544 | 19,782,334 | NZ$20,560,326 | | 858 | 8,265 |

[a]Includes adult voluntary workers.

eral, a policy of both of the major parties in central government.

**School Libraries.** Formal education at the elementary and secondary stages is the responsibility of central government, financed by annual appropriations through Parliament and the Department of Education. There are no formal links between school libraries and public libraries, and the National Library's School Library Service has only limited powers to operate within the schools.

The state of school libraries is generally poor. The concept of libraries as resource centers has not been established; there are no standards for staffing or book purchasing, funding is inadequate, and libraries are not directed by professional librarians. The Minister of Education set up a working party in 1977 which developed a set of recommendations that, if effected, would remedy the deficiencies in the school library system.

**Table 2. Archives in New Zealand (1976)**

| | |
|---|---|
| Number | 1 |
| Holdings | 474,830 linear meters |
| Annual expenditures | $321,395 |
| Professional staff | 11 |
| All staff | 35 |

Source: Wilfred Smith, *Archives in New Zealand: A Report* (Wellington: Archives and Records Association, 1978).

**Special Libraries.** In numbers this has been the fastest-growing sector in the library field since World War II. In 1959 there were 98 special libraries recorded in the *Census of Libraries;* by 1974 the number was 174, and the development continues. The strength of this group was such that a Special Libraries Section was formed within the New Zealand Library Association in 1971.

These libraries exist in order to meet the information needs of their parent bodies, but some of them—by virtue of the extent of their resources—are functioning as national collections in their subject fields, as with the libraries of the Ministry of Works and Development, the Department of Agriculture and Fisheries, the Department of Scientific and Industrial Research, and the Department of Health.

**Association.** The New Zealand Library Association was constituted in 1935 as the successor to the Libraries Association of New Zealand, founded in 1910. The new association, by admitting personal members, became a wider forum for discussion and cultivation of library matters. It became a powerful force in the development of library service, initiating or stimulating a wide range of activities—bibliographical projects, library training, the introduction of free library service, promotion of the National Library, interlibrary loan, publication of standards, promotion of regional library service, and sponsorship of surveys. The Association publishes the monthly newsletter *Library Life* and the quarterly journal *New Zealand Libraries.* BRIAN K. MCKEON

## Nicaragua

Nicaragua, a republic and the largest country of Central America, lies between the Pacific Ocean on the west and the Caribbean Sea on the east; it is bounded by Honduras on the north and Costa Rica on the south. Pop. (1977 est.) 2,312,000; area 128,875 sq.km. The official language is Spanish.

**National Library.** The National Library of Nicaragua was founded in 1882. At its inception it occupied the National Palace; it later transferred to its own building in the western sector of Managua, the capital of the republic. After the earthquake of 1972 it was transferred again to the National Cultural Center in the northeastern section of the capital. The National Library originally contained approximately 5,000 volumes; by the close of the 1970's it held 36,000, of which 20 percent consisted of Nicaraguan bibliography. The remainder were works of reference, textbooks, and other items, including works for leisure reading. The library was named after Rubén Darío (1867–1916), the great Hispanic-American poet who in his earlier years was employed in it as Assistant Librarian. In the beginning the Rubén Darío National Library functioned with a staff of three employees; it had a staff of 24 by 1979. Although none was a graduate librarian, a number had taken special training courses. This library in the late 1970's was undergoing a period of reorganization, with an expectation that by the early 1980's it would fulfill the objectives of a truly national library. It attended in the meantime to the immediate needs of the student body of Managua.

**Academic Libraries.** Academic libraries were assigned to the following institutions of higher education: Autonomous National University of Nicaragua, Central American University, National Educational Center, Polytechnic University, Autonomous Private University, and the National School of Agriculture and Cattle Breeding. The libraries have a total of 105,226 volumes.

The principal academic libraries, in stock, organization, and function, are those of the National University in Managua and León, the Central American University, and the National Educational Center in Managua.

**Public Libraries.** From 1968 efforts were made to augment the quality and quantity of public libraries, and up to December 1978 ten were in existence in the departments of Managua, Chinandega, Estelí, León, Jinotega, Matagalpa, Granada, and Carazo.

The public libraries in the cities of Jinotepe, Jinotega, and Chinandega, established by Rotarians, are preeminent. Others are the product of the joint efforts of municipalities, the Ministry of Education, and some citizens aware of the importance of libraries in the development of nations. All of them are within urban zones and are used largely by students at lower, intermediate, and higher levels of learning.

**Special Libraries.** At the end of the 1970's there were six special libraries, all in the capital at Managua: in

**Libraries in Nicaragua (1978)**

| Type | Number | Volumes in collections | Annual expenditures (córdoba) | Population served | Professional staff | All staff (total) |
|---|---|---|---|---|---|---|
| National | 1 | 36,000 | ₡ 360,000 | 4,500 | N.A. | 18 |
| Academic | 7 | 105,226 | ₡3,129,400 | 32,583 | 10 | 169 |
| Public | 10 | 20,985 | ₡ 98,783 | 3,490 | N.A. | 10 |
| School | 168 | 109,500 | ₡ 184,800 | 233,850 | N.A. | 168 |
| Special | 6 | 71,518 | ₡1,896,532 | 1,588 | 3 | 21 |
| Total | 192 | 343,229 | ₡5,669,515 | | | 286 |

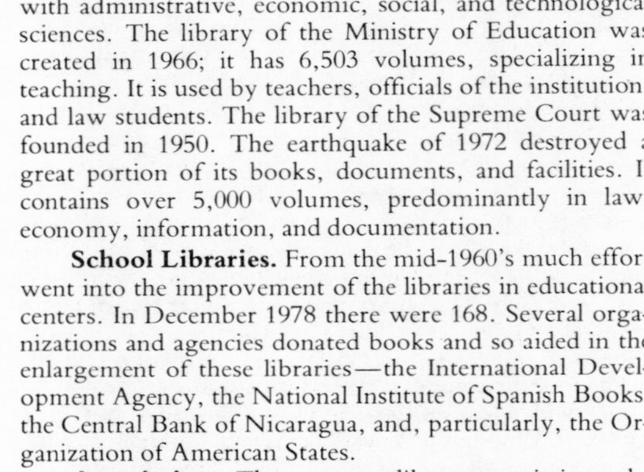

the Central American Institute of Business Administration, the Central Bank, the Supreme Court, the Ministry of Education, the National Bank, and the Bank of America. The library at the Central American Institute was established in 1968 with fewer than 500 volumes; by 1979 it stocked 18,679 works and 345 periodicals and films and other audiovisual items. The library at the Central Bank, founded in 1961, was damaged in the earthquake of 1972 but thereafter largely recovered. It contains 35,901 books and 702 periodical titles; 80 percent of the contents deal with administrative, economic, social, and technological sciences. The library of the Ministry of Education was created in 1966; it has 6,503 volumes, specializing in teaching. It is used by teachers, officials of the institution, and law students. The library of the Supreme Court was founded in 1950. The earthquake of 1972 destroyed a great portion of its books, documents, and facilities. It contains over 5,000 volumes, predominantly in law, economy, information, and documentation.

**School Libraries.** From the mid-1960's much effort went into the improvement of the libraries in educational centers. In December 1978 there were 168. Several organizations and agencies donated books and so aided in the enlargement of these libraries—the International Development Agency, the National Institute of Spanish Books, the Central Bank of Nicaragua, and, particularly, the Organization of American States.

**Associations.** There are two library associations: the Special University Libraries and the Nicaraguan Association of Librarians. The former was created in 1969, comprising 20 libraries. The Association of Librarians was established in 1965. Both associations endeavor to motivate librarians to improve service to the public within their limited financial means by offering lectures and courses, expositions, professional meetings, and workshops.

Progress in library service was seen mostly from July 1975 with the benefit of advice of the OAS. New interest was shown in improving the quality of the libraries, seriously damaged by the quake of 1972, and in facilities offered to the users.

LUISA CARDENAS PEREZ

## Nicholson, Edward Williams Byron

(1849–1912)

Library Association

*Edward Williams Byron Nicholson*

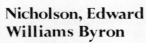

Edward Williams Byron Nicholson, founder of the Library Association and Librarian of the Bodleian Library, was born on March 16, 1849, and educated at Tonbridge School, Kent, publishing a catalogue of the school library in 1866. At Oxford he studied classics but spent much time writing for undergraduate journals. He graduated B.A. in 1871 and M.A. in 1874. His involvement in Oxford Union debates revealed an excitable character, while his duties as Librarian of the Union introduced him to the practical problems of librarianship.

By accepting the post of Superintendent and Librarian of the London Institution in 1873, Nicholson hoped to gain a foothold in literary circles. He completely reorganized this moribund proprietary institution; the reference library of 60,000 volumes was recatalogued and classified according to a decimal scheme, while the circulating library was increased, issues rising sixfold in five years. A letter from Nicholson to *The Times* in 1875 produced a flood of new members (and income). Popular guest lecturers were secured; in February 1876, 700 people heard John Ruskin, while 200 had to be turned away.

The 1876 Philadelphia Conference of Librarians, resulting in the organization of the American Library Association, impelled Nicholson—aged 27 and completely unknown—to invite British librarians to support a similar venture, with the aim of establishing a Library Association of the United Kingdom. The International Conference of Librarians, held at the London Institution on October 2–5, 1877, and attended by 216, was a great success, particularly because of the American librarians present.

Nicholson and Henry R. Tedder were the main forces behind the Metropolitan Free Libraries Association, whose aim was promoting public libraries in London. Several violent public meetings discouraged them from continuing direct action, and Nicholson and Tedder instead drafted a public libraries bill to make the provision of libraries easier. This bill was introduced, with the support of the LA Council, in Parliament in 1881 but unsuccessfully. The LA was necessarily run by London-based nonpublic librarians, though resented by provincial public librarians who drafted a rival bill, which also failed. These events and the growing belief that the LA was too indolent to encourage new developments in librarianship made Nicholson resign from its Council in 1881. He was never suited to work with people of opposing views.

Nicholson's election as Bodley's Librarian in 1882—which forced him to abandon his literary plans—was unexpected, since he lacked scholarship and experience. Although the Curators wanted an energetic person capable of undertaking a large-scale reorganization, the arrival of an outsider was ill received, especially by Sublibrarians Adolf Neubauer and Falconer Madan. However hard Nicholson worked at improving the Bodleian, he worked even harder at arguing against their continual opposition.

Nicholson found the Bodleian in a depressing state: "Always undermanned as it had been, always undermoneyed, and almost always underroomed, its organization, fairly advanced at some points, was in most respects absolutely rudimentary or non-existent." (Bodleian Curators papers, untitled fly-sheet by Nicholson, February 8, 1899). For years the annual income never exceeded £9,000, with expenditure only a little less. Nicholson complained about the Bodleian's poverty to the London *Daily News* in 1894 and at the Bodleian Tercentenary in 1902. His public appeals were vindicated when, from 1907, the Library was aided by Lord Brassey's Oxford University Endowment Fund.

The Bodleian's stock increased from approximately 500,000 to 1,000,000 items under Nicholson, mainly because of rigid enforcement of the legal deposit privilege (he even claimed Valentine cards and tram tickets). He was more parsimonious about purchasing books and manuscripts. Nicholson's weakness was in trying to be a perfectionist; he spent large sums on unnecessary binding and catalogued all acquisitions in detail. Notable accessions included the Saint Margaret's Gospel Book, bought for £6, and a First Folio Shakespeare, acquired after Nicholson raised a public subscription, despite opposition from Library Curators.

Nicholson's most obvious achievements were the underground bookstore—the first constructed on such a scale—and the conversion of the Picture Gallery into the Upper Reading Room, amid tremendous dissension. Nicholson published a cataloguing code in 1883 and devised an elaborate classification scheme. The latter provided the basis for producing "the greatest subject-index the world has ever seen," according to Nicholson (memorandum to the Curators, February 13, 1909), but lack of money and staff thwarted Nicholson's hopes. Much to Nicholson's mortification, his deputy, F. Madan, was authorized in 1890 to commence the abbreviated *Summary Catalogue of Western Manuscripts*. The Bodleian's Oriental catalogues show Nicholson's desire for detailed cataloguing.

Nicholson formed a "Select Library" of open-access reference books, exhibited manuscripts, established a photographic department, and published facsimiles. Yet he encountered opposition over minor matters, such as extending opening hours or the seating and heating arrangements. He employed boys for routine duties and undergraduates for cataloguing. Despite ingrained prejudice, he appointed a female assistant librarian. Duties were recorded in the *Staff-Kalendar*, the first published library manual of its kind.

Nicholson's tenure was marred by perpetual animosity between himself and Madan, who thought that the Library's scholarly calm had been replaced by continual disorganization. The Curators tried to "fetter" Nicholson, as he was fond of saying, but he would not be muzzled. In 1898 he threatened to take them to law if they persisted in persecuting him. Nicholson suffered his first nervous breakdown in 1901 and became increasingly incapable of administration, though he would not admit it. He died on March 17, 1912.

**REFERENCES**


Henry R. Tedder, "E. W. B. Nicholson . . . In Memoriam," *Library Association Record* (March 1914); personal reminiscences by Nicholson's closest Library Association colleague.

Strickland Gibson, "E. W. B. Nicholson (1849–1912): Some Impressions," *Library Association Record* (May 1949); account, by a former colleague, of Nicholson's work at the Bodleian.

Sir Edmund Craster, *History of the Bodleian Library, 1845–1945* (1952), pp. 152–245; detailed account of Nicholson's Bodleian work.

K. A. Manley, "Edward Williams Byron Nicholson," *Encyclopedia of Library and Information Science*, volume 19 (1976), includes bibliography of Nicholson's major writings, though he published little on librarianship.

K. A. Manley, "E. W. B. Nicholson and the London Institution," *Journal of Librarianship* (January 1973).


K. A. MANLEY

## Niger

Niger, a republic of north central Africa, is bordered on the east by Chad, on the west by Upper Volta and Mali, on the northeast by Libya, on the northwest by Algeria, and on the south by Nigeria and Benin. Pop. (1978 est.) 4,986,000; area 1,186,408 sq.km. The official language is French, but Sudanic dialects are widely spoken.

Niger does not have a national library, and there are few libraries in the country. The Ministère du Plan, founded in February 1976 in Niamey, took over the functions of the Centre de documentation, which was under the Commissariat général au développement. Its primary function is to gather and conserve documents on Niger, as well as the documents of other countries. Its holdings include almost 23,000 volumes, mainly periodicals and documents. Strongest subjects in the collection are economics, statistics, technical reports of ministries and public and private organizations, and social affairs. The Centre publishes bibliographies and catalogues. The Centre does not function as a national library.

The Archives Nationales in Niamey, founded in 1913, houses a collection of documents through the 19th century but in the late 1970's was in process of reorganization.

The Institut de recherches en sciences humaines (IRSH), founded as the Centre IFAN de Niamey in 1944 and later in 1964 as the Centre nigérien de recherches en sciences humaines (CNRSH), was integrated with the Université de Niamey in 1973. The Institut has a limited scholarly library of about 6,500 volumes. Approximately 60 percent of the collection is in French, and the remainder is in English, Arabic, and African languages. The Institut issues on an irregular basis, approximately three times a year, the *Études nigériennes*.

Niger does not have a national bibliography, nor was there evidence of significant bibliographic activity at the end of the 1970's. There is no legal deposit in Niger.

There is no public library system.

The educational system in this country was not adequately developed. The Ministry of National Education is responsible for primary schools, secondary schools, and teacher training colleges. Literacy programs were ongoing in the 1970's and were conducted in the major African languages of the country.

There is one university, the Université de Niamey, which was founded in 1971 and attained university status in 1973. Its library is that of the IRSH, cited previously. In addition, it houses approximately 3,300 volumes in the sciences and 500 volumes in medicine.

The École nationale d'administration du Niger was founded in Niamey in 1963 to train civil servants and other officials. Its library consists currently of approximately 14,000 volumes, 100 current periodicals, and 70 maps.

Two notable special libraries are those of the Centre régional de recherche et de documentation pour la tradition orale, founded in 1968 in Niamey in cooperation with Unesco, with a collection of approximately 5,000 tape recordings of songs, tales, fables, and other records in the major African languages spoken in Niger; and that of the Commission du fleuve Niger (Niger River Commission), founded in 1971 in Niamey. Its documentation center provides abstracting services in agricultural production, stock farming, fish breeding, pedology and geology, and hydrology.

There was no formally organized library association in Niger at the close of the 1970's.

STAFF

## Nigeria

Nigeria, a republic and federation of 12 states in western Africa, is bordered by Niger on the north, Chad and Cameroon on the east, the Gulf of Guinea on the south, and Benin on the west. Pop. (1977 est.) 78,660,000; area 923,800 sq.km. The official language is English.

**National Library.** The National Library of Nigeria, established under the National Library Act of 1964, contained holdings of approximately 160,000 items at the end

United Nations

*Students at the library at the Federal Advanced Teacher's College in Lagos.*

of 1977. Microfilms of Nigerian newspaper files and of other materials unavailable in any other form are among the special materials contained in its collection.

Designated as the nation's official depository and main bibliographic service center, the Library is also responsible for preparing the National Union Catalogues and for collecting library statistics. Of equal importance are the research services it provides to the general public, officials of the federal and state governments, Nigerian diplomatic missions, and various statutory corporations. The Library supports intellectual efforts in all activities directed toward national progress and development through its coordination of Nigeria's resource sharing program. It manages the country's interlibrary loan system and provides leadership in the library component of the NATIS program while representing the country in the General Information Programme of Unesco.

**Academic Libraries.** A variety of academic libraries are found in Nigeria's 13 universities, 14 polytechnical institutes, and numerous special colleges of education, science, and technology. The oldest of these libraries is at the University of Ibadan, established along with the University in 1948. It maintains a notable collection of Africana and in conjunction with the Department of Library Studies has organized the Abadina Media Resource Centre to provide information services to the various schools on the campus.

In 1977 aggregate holdings among all academic libraries amounted to over a million items. A survey of academic library collections was under way in 1979, with the goal of better utilizing and developing the strengths of individual libraries, particularly in professional disciplines such as law, medicine, and architecture.

**Table 2. Archives in Nigeria (1976)**

| | |
|---|---|
| Number | 4 |
| Holdings | N.A. |
| Annual expenditures | N.A. |
| Professional staff | 139 |
| All staff (total) | N.A. |

Source: Prototype survey on library resources.

**Public Libraries.** State and local governments presently administer public libraries. After the first Eastern Regional Library Act of 1955, six states promulgated comprehensive library service laws, and all 19 states operated library services in some form by the end of the 1970's. Under a local government reform program initiated in 1977, many states moved to consolidate the nearly 300 local libraries of varying size and quality that remained outside the state library systems.

The state services embrace a wide spectrum of activities, ranging from service delivery to the general public at established points to mobile libraries, book box deposit service to schools and other institutions, and boat delivery service along rivers in certain areas. Some state services serve government departments, prisons, and hospitals.

Public library services still reach only a small percentage of the literate population, which is in itself still small relative to the entire population. Readers are mostly young people of school age, generally not beyond the age of 25. Library facilities are primarily in urban areas, where a large portion of the literate population reside.

**School Libraries.** Inaugurated in the 1960's, school library service is still in the process of development, although several promising programs have been initiated. The state of Lagos inherited the Unesco school library service pilot project established for Nigeria in 1965. Although the project's influence is restricted to Lagos State, it generated considerable library development, mostly in high schools. In addition, the project operates an information resource center and provides continuing education to teachers.

The states of Anambra and Imo have organized school library associations that stimulate the development of individual school libraries. The state of Bendel's library directs the development of school library services, and to this end it has established a Book Depot to ensure a steady supply of materials to the state's schools.

**Special Libraries.** Numerous government departments, private companies, and other organizations main-

**Table 1. Libraries in Nigeria (1976)**

| Type | Number | Volumes in collections | Annual expenditures (pound) | Population served | Professional staff | All staff (total) |
|---|---|---|---|---|---|---|
| National | 1 | 158,000 | ₦ 1,940,000 | N.A. | 35 | 570 |
| Academic | 44 | 1,168,030 | ₦ 5,294,354 | 132,626 | 369 | 1,527 |
| Public | 56 | 890,917 | ₦ 2,442,292 | 579,310 | 26 | 91 |
| School | N.A. | N.A. | N.A. | N.A. | N.A. | N.A. |
| Special | 60 | 644,450 | ₦ 755,812 | N.A. | 72 | 593 |

***Nihon Shoshi no Shoshi,***
"Bibliography of Japanese Bibliographies" **34**

tain special collections. The most significant holdings are those of the Central Bank of Nigeria, the Nigerian Institute of International Affairs, the West African Examinations Council, the Geological Survey located in Kaduna, the Federal Department of Agriculture at Ibadan, the Institute of Management Technology in Enugu, the Federal Institute of Industrial Research at Oshodi, and the Centre for Management Development in Lagos.

**Association.** The Nigerian Library Association, founded in 1962, grew out of the earlier West African Library Association, established during the British colonial period. The NLA is governed by a Council and operates state chapters known as divisions. Interest groups form special sections within the NLA, while the Council organizes committees on subjects of interest approved by the membership. The official organ of the Association is the quarterly journal *Nigerian Libraries*.

SIMEON B. AJE

# North Atlantic Treaty Organization

The North Atlantic Treaty Organization (NATO) was founded in 1949 to serve needs of the Western European Community for mutual defense of national boundaries. The organization represents an alliance of 15 nations—Iceland, Great Britain, the United States, the Federal Republic of Germany, Italy, Greece, France, Denmark, Canada, Belgium, Luxembourg, Netherlands, Norway, Portugal, and Turkey.

Of particular interest is the purpose and function of the NATO Science Committee, established in December 1957 as a result of the report submitted by the Committee on Non-Military Cooperation, formed in May 1956 to advise the North Atlantic Council on ways to improve and extend cooperation in nonmilitary fields and to develop greater unity within the Atlantic Community.

The Science Committee is the key body in the organization directed at promoting research in all fields of science. One of its primary functions is to ensure proper dissemination of scientific and technical knowledge to all segments of the world community and particularly to developing countries. The Science Committee, headed by the Assistant Secretary General for Scientific and Environmental Affairs, receives its financial support from the NATO budget, which is contributed by the member nations of the alliance. The program consists of four major elements: (1) the Science Fellowship Program, (2) Special Science Program, (3) Research Grants, and (4) Advanced Institutes Program.

**Technical Programs.** *Science Fellowship Program.* This was the first program established by the Science Committee and was aimed at aiding postgraduate and postdoctoral students in the pure and applied sciences to study at institutions outside of their own country. In 1973 an additional aspect of the program was established to support lectures by senior scientists on advanced topics that have not been published previously. The program also supports visits by scientists.

*Special Science Program.* This program is organized around a number of panels, guided by internationally eminent experts in the respective areas. Support is provided for conferences, symposia, and other activities.

The Air Sea Interaction Panel studies the exchange of energy in the ocean and the atmosphere and the subsequent effect on weather, climate, and marine life. The Marine Sciences Panel concerns itself with pollution, marine organic balance, and marine biology in general. The Human Factors Panel studies issues relating to man-machine interaction, including a number of psychological/-physiological processes. The Systems Sciences Panel promotes the application of systems theory to prevailing institutional problems and issues. The Eco-Sciences Panel stimulates and supports conferences on the status of the environment and its preservation. The Materials Science Panel studies issues regarding scarce material resources and the application of these resources to essential needs. It explores the development of new resources.

*The Research Grants Program.* This program provides "seed money" to promote exploratory research in experimental, theoretical frontiers, with emphasis on basic rather than applied research. The small grants provide for travel and living expenses of researchers, for expenses in the management of the research, among others.

*The Advanced Study Institutes Program.* Established in 1958, the program is headed by the Director of the Scientific Affairs Division. Its primary purpose is the dissemination of advanced knowledge and the formation of contacts among scientists from different countries. This program does not support conferences but, rather, institutes that are high-level teaching activities aimed at updating the knowledge of scientists in specific areas. Proposals for institutes are considered by an advisory panel of distinguished scientists who convene semiannually to evaluate and approve the programs proposed. In 1972 the Division approved an Institute in Information Science, which was held in Seven Springs, Pennsylvania. In 1973 an Institute in Information Science was held in Aberystwyth, Wales, and in 1978 another was held in Crete. Fundamentally these institutes reflect the Division's interest in promoting interdisciplinary programs. The Division encourages the publication of all the proceedings of the institutes, and a library of approximately 800 volumes contains such proceedings.

**REFERENCES**

*Two Decades of Achievement in International Scientific and Technological Cooperation, NATO Science Programmes: Report of the Scientific Affairs Division* (1978).

M. N. Ozdas, "Twenty Years of Scientific Cooperation," *NATO Review* (1978).

ANTHONY DEBONS

# Norton, Margaret Cross
(1891– )

Margaret Norton, Illinois State Archivist, during a career of more than 35 years, played a leading role in redirecting an emerging archival profession toward public service, entitled to public support, and important for public administration, at a time when many saw care of public records as an adjunct to the primary concerns of the historical profession. Born in Rockford, Illinois, to Samuel and Jennie Adams Norton, on July 7, 1891, Margaret Norton attended Rockford College and the University of Chicago, where she received a Ph.B. in History in 1913, followed by an M.A. in History in 1914. She then enrolled in the New York State Library School at Albany; after her graduation in 1915, she became a Cataloguer at the Vassar College Library. Norton became a Cataloguer in the Department of History and Archives of the Indiana State Library in 1918, although she spent the early part of 1919 and the 1919–20 academic year working on a Ph.D. in History at the University of Chicago. Late in 1920 she became Cataloguer for the State Historical Society of Missouri, a position she held until April 1922.

At that time few states had archival programs, although Alabama, Mississippi, North Carolina, Delaware, and South Carolina had established state agencies with archival responsibilities. Several quasipublic state historical societies, including Minnesota and Wisconsin, served as repositories for archival materials; and some state libraries, including Pennsylvania, Virginia, and Texas, had begun to acquire and store permanently valuable public records of their states. In Illinois the Secretary of State had long been legal custodian of the state's records; a Division of Archives and Index was established in his office in 1873, but it became concerned principally with current matters and did not develop along archival lines. In 1921 the legislature created three divisions in the Illinois State Library; on April 1, 1922, Margaret Cross Norton became Archivist of Illinois when she was designated Head of the Archives Division.

Using storage space in the state library stacks in the Centennial Building, Norton began to bring together the state's valuable records. Searching through steam tunnels, under the Capitol steps, and in attics, she acquired much of the material. During that period she contributed two volumes of *Illinois Census Returns,* published in 1934 and 1935 as volumes 14 and 16 of the *Collections of the Illinois State Historical Library*.

Norton first attended a meeting of the Public Archives Commission of the American Historical Association in 1923. Established in 1899, the Commission had as its goal the establishment of a national archives to facilitate the research of historians. Seven years later she became a member of the Commission, continuing until it was replaced by the Society of American Archivists (SAA) in 1936. A charter member of the SAA, she served as its first Vice-President, and in 1937 she became a Council member. She was elected fourth President of SAA, serving from 1943 to 1945, and in 1946 she began a two-year term as Editor of *American Archivist*.

At the same time, she became active in the National Association of State Libraries; she served as Secretary-Treasurer for five years beginning in 1933. She had served earlier as Chairman of an Archives Committee with members Charles B. Galbreath (Ohio) and George S. Godard (Connecticut). That Committee soon became inactive, and in 1935 an Archives and Libraries Committee was created with Norton first as a member and then as Chairman for 1942. Thus, for a period of more than ten years, she was one of the links between the National Association of State Libraries and the ALA on the one hand and the Public Archives Commission of the American Historical Association and the Society of American Archivists on the other.

Of even greater significance, however, was Margaret Norton's warning, as early as 1930, against allowing historians to preempt the field of archival care and preservation. She pointed out that public records were the product of governmental activity and were primarily designed to serve governmental needs. Speaking before the National Association of State Librarians in 1930, she asserted that the proper care of archives was an administrative concern of state government and not merely an adjunct to the historical field. "The archivist," she maintained, "should be a public official whose first interest is business efficiency, and only secondarily should he be interested in history. If the public records are cared for in a way that preserves their proper provenance, the historian not only of today but also of tomorrow will be as well served as the public official."

Seven years later she repeated the principle of the value of archives for administrative purposes: "An archives department is the governmental agency charged with the duty of planning and supervising the preservation of all those records of the business transactions of its government required by law or other legal implication to be preserved indefinitely."

The 1930's were doubly important to Margaret Norton's professional career. First, the state arsenal adjacent to the Capitol grounds in Springfield burned in 1934; responding to the outcry of patriotic and veterans organizations, the 1935 General Assembly appropriated money for a state archives building, and additional funds were obtained from the Public Works Administration. The building was dedicated during the Second Annual Meeting of the SAA in 1938. In the same year, the reorganization of the Illinois State Library began; it was completed in 1939 with the revision of the State Library Act. As a result of the reorganization, *Illinois Libraries,* formerly a publication of the Library Extension Division, became the official publication of the state library, and Margaret Norton became a regular contributor. The section initially entitled "The Archives of Illinois" and, after March 1942, "Illinois Archival Information" comprised what Ernst Posner called "the first American manual of archives administration." Articles were appearing elsewhere, but Norton's writings in *Illinois Libraries* specifically addressed the problems of the state archivist. Although devoted to the principles and philosophy of archival administration, they were based to a large extent on her own practical experience. She wrote at a time when the only discussions of archival practice originated in European experience, and her articles made *Illinois Libraries* essential reading for archivists. Norton also published articles in the *American Archivist* and in publications of the National Association of State Libraries and ALA.

After 1947 Margaret Norton wrote infrequently for *Illinois Libraries*. Her last article appeared in October 1956, when she discussed the relationship between the archivist and the records manager—a discussion that raised certain questions that are still debated.

Margaret Cross Norton retired as Illinois State Archivist on April 15, 1957. Her career spanned more than 35 years, the climax of which was a successful statewide records management survey. Norton continued to live in Springfield.

**REFERENCE**

Thornton W. Mitchell, editor, *Norton on Archives: The Writings of Margaret Cross Norton on Archival & Records Management* (1975).

THORNTON W. MITCHELL

# Norway

Norway, a constitutional monarchy in northern Europe, lies in the western section of the Scandinavian Peninsula. It is surrounded by Sweden on the east, Finland and the U.S.S.R. on the extreme northeast, the Atlantic Ocean and the North Sea on the west, and the Arctic Ocean on the north. Pop. (1978) est.) 4,077,000; area 323,886 sq.km. The official language is Norwegian.

**National Library.** In Norway the tasks of a national library are dealt with by the Royal University Library in Oslo (Universitetsbiblioteket i Oslo). It has had the right to legal deposits throughout its existence (from 1812) with the exception of the years between 1839 and 1882. The act of legal deposits of 1882 was revised in 1939.

The national collections contain, besides books and serials proper, music and maps and material (e.g., manuscripts and pictures) connected with the country's outstanding personalities.

The Norwegian national bibliography *(Norsk bokfortegnelse)* is published by the Royal University Library in Oslo and is also available on microfiche.

**Academic Libraries.** Academic libraries comprise those attached to the universities, those belonging to state colleges, and libraries serving the regional colleges. The four university libraries in Oslo, Bergen, Trondheim, and Tromsø each count a number of branch libraries administered centrally but detached to the respective faculties and institutes.

The Royal University Library in Oslo dates back to 1812, when the first Norwegian university was established, but the Library only became fully operational several years later. Donations in the 1820's resulted in a collection of about 60,000 volumes, which gradually was built up to reach 4,000,000 by the end of 1978.

**Table 1. Libraries in Norway (1976)**

| Type | Number | Volumes in collections | Annual expenditures (krone) | Population served | Professional staff | All staff (total) |
|---|---|---|---|---|---|---|
| National / Academic | 95 | 6,451,002 | Kr. 21,932,650[a] | N.A. | 381 | 590 |
| Public | 1,385 | 11,253,567 | Kr. 159,102,396 | N.A. | 574 | N.A. |
| School | 3,661 | 4,807,196 | Kr. 10,775,122[a] | 592,906 | N.A. | N.A. |
| Special | 216 | 3,436,451 | Kr. 12,000,000[a] | N.A. | 232 | 490 |
| Total | 5,357 | 25,948,216 | | | | |

[a]For books, periodicals, binding.

Sources: Statistical yearbook 1977; Bok og Bibliotek (1978).

The Library has from its very beginnings served wider interests than those of the Oslo University teaching staff and students, being the largest of its kind in the country. The Library concentrates 60 percent of all research literature in the country. While not officially designated as a clearinghouse, the Library mediates a large part of international loans. Efforts at separating the national tasks from the university requirements, dictated, as they were, by the sheer volume of literature, resulted in placing the relevant recent literature in faculty libraries at the university campus. The last to move to new premises was the medical library, in June 1978. But the central functions (budget, staff, catalogue) are still in the hands of the university via the university library, which receives occasional state grants to be able to fulfill its national tasks.

The Tromsø University library is the youngest and consequently the smallest of the four university libraries, while the Trondheim University library operates with two departments, one for humanities, the other for science and technology—a distinction due to historical development. The university library in Bergen is based on the Bergen Museúm, founded in 1825, while the University was established in 1948. Though large parts of the holdings in university libraries necessarily duplicate each other, efforts at coordinating acquisition of periodicals have led to interesting results.

Other academic libraries attached to colleges cover the fields of commerce, agriculture, veterinary medicine, physical education and sports, architecture, and theology. Regional colleges, of which there are ten in the country, represent a venture in decentralizing education. Their libraries had to be built up from scratch in most cases but have received increased attention, reflected in better budgets. The fields of subjects that the libraries cover are somewhat different from traditional university subjects; this in due time should give rise to specialized collections.

**Table 2. Archives in Norway (1976)**

| | |
|---|---|
| Number | 9 |
| Holdings | 6,000 cubic meters |
| Annual expenditures | 12,900,000 |
| Professional staff | 65 |
| All staff | 110 |

Note: The Archive of the Labour Movement is not included.

Source: The Director of the National Archives of Norway.

**Public Libraries.** Through library legislation public libraries have been compulsory in every municipality since 1947. There are in all 1,385 public library units. Because of the geographical structure and the population pattern, it is nevertheless in practice difficult to reach every inhabitant. Through bookmobiles and a bookboat along the coast, outreach service is provided. Under the Library Act of 1971, municipalities are obliged to give financial support to the libraries. In addition, libraries get state grants, varying according to the financial situation in the municipalities.

**County Libraries.** To supplement and support public and school libraries there are 20 county libraries in Norway. They get financial support from the county, according to the Library Act, and the county municipality is entitled to government grants, provided the library works in accordance with the regulations given by the state. A subject distribution plan is in operation between the county libraries.

**School Libraries.** Such libraries are compulsory in every elementary school, and there are over 3,600 school libraries in Norway. A certain amount per pupil for books must be granted from the municipality, which again is entitled to government grants. The amount is given according to the same percentage scale as that for public libraries.

**Special Libraries.** These belong to both state and private institutions and range in magnitude, with a few exceptions, from about 5,000 to 50,000 volumes. The best known among the exceptions are the Library of the Parliament (Stortingsbiblioteket), the Nobel Library, and the library of the Central Bureau of Statistics, while some of the smaller ones either endeavor to cover a modern subject in depth, as does the library of the Atomic Institute, or follow up a line of traditional interest, such as the library of the Whaling Museum. All are primarily oriented to serve their principal institutions, but their collections are also accessible to others through interlibrary loans.

**Other Libraries.** The National Office for Research and Special Libraries (Riksbibliotektjenesten) was estab-

*The Vestre Toten Public Library, Raufoss. Municipalities in Norway are required by law to give financial support to libraries.*

Vestre Toten Public Library

Daniel Bernstein, Waltham, MA
*Felicia Adetowun Ogunsheye*

lished in 1969 and charged with coordinating the functions of academic as well as special libraries. It is headed by the National Librarian and had a staff of 14 in 1978.

The State Directorate for Public and School Libraries (Statens Bibliotektilsyn) main tasks are (1) to supervise and control and render advice to public and school libraries in accordance with the Library Act; (2) to assist and advise the Ministry in matters concerning public and school libraries; (3) to work for further development and strengthening of the libraries' activities on the whole spectrum of cultural work.

The Norwegian Library Bureau (A/L Biblioteksentralen) was inaugurated as a cooperative society on February 4, 1952. The state, the local authorities, and the Norwegian Library Association are the part owners of the concern. It is a service institution for public and school libraries of Norway, enjoined with the tasks of providing books, library material and equipment, and bibliographical aids.

**Associations.** The Norwegian Library Association (Norsk bibliotekforening), founded in 1913, has the following sections: Special and Research Librarians (and Libraries); Public Librarians; Part-Time Librarians; and Public and School Libraries. It had 2,500 individual members and 700 institutional members (1978).

The Association of Norwegian Research Librarians (Norske Forskningsbibliotekarers Forening), founded in 1948, had 680 members. The Municipal Library Workers' Union (Kommunale Bibliotekarbeideres Forening), founded in 1957, had 510 members.

The Norwegian Library Union (Norsk Biblioteklag), founded in 1946, had 465 members, and the Norwegian Part-Time Librarians' Union (Norske Deltidsbibliotekarers Yrkeslag), founded in 1963, 650.

ELSE GRANHEIM

## Ogunsheye, Felicia Adetowun
(1926– )

Felicia Adetowun Ogunsheye, educator and author, became the first Nigerian head of a library school. She was born on December 5, 1926, in Nigeria, attended elementary school in various parts of the country, and took her secondary school education in Queen's College, Lagos, from 1939 to 1945. She proceeded to the Higher College, Lagos, where she obtained a Teaching Diploma in 1949. She attended Newham College, Cambridge, where she was graduated with a B.A. with honors in Geography in 1952, followed by an M.A. at the same university in 1956.

Felicia Ogunsheye, who married Ayo Ogunsheye, an economist and at one time a faculty member of the University of Ibadan, started her working life as a teacher, first in high schools for girls and later in the Nigerian College of Science and Technology, 1956–57. She joined the University of Ibadan Library as Assistant Librarian in charge of maps in 1958, and she took charge of the African and Map Collection in 1960.

At Simmons College, Boston, Massachusettes, she earned a Master's degree in Library Science in 1962. She returned to her post, finding time to lecture in a new Institute of Librarianship. In 1963 she became a full-time lecturer and was named Senior Lecturer. Ogunsheye was appointed Acting Director in 1970. When the Institute was redesignated the Department of Library Studies, she became the first Head, rising in rank to Professor in 1973. From 1977 she served as Dean of the Faculty of Education of the University. In the field of bibliography, her studies and publications are extensive. She initiated the Abadina Media Research Project, a pilot library set up on the campus of Ibadan University for the children of Abadina, a satellite village created for the low-income, nonacademic staff of the University, providing direct library services and facilities for the children and offering research facilities. The center is headquarters of the Nigerian School Library Association, of which Ogunsheye became President.

A member of the Council of the Nigerian Library Association, she was Vice-President, Acting President, and President in succession in the years 1966 to 1971, which included the Nigerian Civil War years of 1967 to 1970.

She served on many committees, panels, and boards, including the National Library Board of Nigeria, and from 1971 participated regularly in the activities of IFLA, serving on some of the Standing Advisory Committees.

A tireless organizer, she played a key role in making the Department of Library Studies of the University of Ibadan an active center of the pursuit of knowledge in librarianship. She also became President of the Association of African Library Schools. She was first Secretary of the Nigerian Council of Women Societies and West African Council of Women Societies. She served as President of the Women's Improvement Society and the Nigerian Society of University Women. Simmons College awarded her an honorary doctoral degree, and she received the International Alumni Award (1979).

S. B. AJE

## Oman

Oman, an independent sultanate, lies on the southeast coast of the Arabian Peninsula. It is surrounded by the Gulf of Oman on the north, the United Arab Emirates on the northwest, Yemen (Aden) on the southwest, Saudi Arabia on the west, and the Arabian Sea on the east and south. A small, northern section of Oman is separated from the main area by the United Arab Emirates. Pop. (1978 est.) 843,000; area 213,380 sq.km. The official language is Arabic.

The sultanate of Oman does not possess a national library. The Directorate of the Omani Heritage of the Ministry of Information and Tourism, established in Muscat in 1973, collects manuscripts, books, documents, and other library materials relating to the Oman's historical past. Book production in the sultanate is negligible. Legal deposit and national bibliography had not been instituted as of the late 1970's.

The country has not instituted a higher education system. There were no universities and colleges as of 1979. The government sends the Omani high school graduates abroad, especially to other Arab countries, for university education. Similarly, a system for public library services cannot be found in the sultanate, although the library of the Directorate of Omani Heritage offers some public library services. The large mosques in the sultanate preserve sizable collections on Islamic studies but are not organized according to library schemes.

School libraries cannot be traced in the country. The secondary school attendance totaled 200 students in 1975–76. Records on special libraries in the country were not available as of 1979.

MOHAMED M. EL HADI

## Organization of American States

The Organization of American States (OAS), composed of 25 member states of Latin America, the Caribbean, and the United States, has its General Secretariat in Washington, D.C. It is the formal outgrowth of the Pan American Union as the central operational organ of the "Inter-American System," resulting from the first International Conference of American States in 1890. The principal purposes of the Organization enunciated in its 1948 Charter are the maintenance of peace and security and the attainment of mutual understanding among the American peoples. In pursuit of this second objective, the OAS has carried out activities related to bibliographic control, copyright legislation and legal deposit, international exchange of publications, free circulation of books among member states, and, more recently, the development of national and regional systems for library and information services and their organization and staffing.

Historically, the activities and projects in support of improved library and information services and systems have been shared principally by the Columbus Memorial Library, the Library and Archives Development Program of the Regional Programs of Cultural and Educational Development, and the scientific and technological information projects of the Regional Program of Scientific and Technological Development. The 1969 meeting of the Inter-American Council for Education, Science and Culture (CIECC) charged the Library Development Program (LDP) with executing a new project on school and university libraries as a part of the OAS educational program as well as a new archives program. A proposal to integrate the information services and activities of the entire Secretariat, mandated by CIECC, and for the development of an inter-American network for transmitting automated bibliographic information had been approved in principle by the end of the 1970's and was under study for implementation.

The objectives of the Library Development Program include collaboration with member states to improve access to information through developing the institutions, mechanisms, and media of communication of knowledge and information, to formulate national information policies, and to integrate the services of archives, libraries, and documentation centers. The LDP is also concerned with improving training and advanced studies for library and archival school professors, for the personnel of archives, libraries, and documentation centers, for staff of publishers and producers of audiovisual information media, and for technicians in restoring and preserving documents. It is further concerned with converting the traditional library into learning resource centers for formal, informal, and continuing education.

Direct services for national and multinational projects requested by member states are given principally through technical assistance by experts under contract with the OAS. OAS provides assistance in advisory services and training, for scholarships and fellowships and travel grants for training programs, and for the organization of technical meetings. LDP training programs consist of fellowships for postgraduate study by Latin American librarians in graduate schools of the United States and Puerto Rico, with preference given to teachers of library and information sciences and those charged with developing national library and information systems, and scholarships for the shorter-term courses in multinational projects. Travel grants are given for short-term courses and in-service training programs in Europe in archives management, book production and distribution, and public library services.

Special attention is given to strengthening regional and national library schools capable of serving as regional and multinational centers, including those in Colombia, Costa Rica, and Jamaica, and to the development of schools of library and information science at the graduate level in Brazil and Mexico, as well as the elevation of the undergraduate program of the Inter-American Library School (EIBM) of the University of Antioquia, in Medellín, Colombia, to the graduate level.

Other multinational and inter-American centers of the LDP are: (1) Centro Interamericano de Formación de Archiveros at the University of Córdoba in Argentina; (2) CENTRO/MIDCA, Centro Taller para Restauración y Microfilmación de Documentos para Centro América y el Caribe in Santo Domingo, Dominican Republic; beginning in 1978 (3) Centro Interamericano para la Normalización de las Técnicas Bibliotecarias, University of Costa Rica in San Jose; (4) Centro Interamericano para la Transferencia de Información Bibliográfica Automatizada in the National Council for Science and Technology (CONACYT) in Mexico City, with responsibility for continuing the production of the MARC manuals in Spanish initiated by the OAS in 1978, for aiding the National Library in automating its national bibliography in the MARC format, and designing the MARCAL project and testing it for Latin America; and (5) the Proyecto Interamericano de Literatura in the Gentro de Capacitación "El Macaro," in the state of Aragua, Venezuela.

The OAS/LDP provides planning and advisory and supervisory services for various multinational projects financed by outside funds: (1) the Spanish translation of the Dewey Decimal Classification; (2) Project LEER for selecting books for the Spanish-speaking population of the United States and conducting regional training institutes; and (3) the Seminars on the Acquisition of Latin American Library Materials (SALALM), for which the OAS served as Executive Secretariat for 18 years.

Continuing projects of a regional and national nature directly related to multinational projects were being carried out in the late 1970's: (1) a new Centro Catalográfico Centroamericano at the University of Costa Rica Library, to be absorbed into the multinational project on standardization, with connecting national cataloguing centers in Nicaragua and Panama; (2) centralized and cooperative cataloguing projects in Chile, Colombia, Costa Rica, Mexico, and Paraguay, which tend toward automation, and the creation of national or regional data bases, with possible on-line access to OCLC: (3) national school library systems in Costa Rica, Colombia, Chile, and Bolivia; (4) a learning resources center at the Salvadorean normal school; (5) educational documentation centers in Chile and Peru; and (6) a pilot project in Trujillo, Peru, for national university library system planning, including providing technical information to industry.

The role of public libraries for mass communication was being advanced through OAS projects in Venezuela with the Banco del Libro and through the Casas de la Cultura in Colombia and El Salvador. In El Salvador a new project also began to produce easy-to-read materials in Spanish for new adult literates.

In archives development, assistance was given to Peru, Colombia, Costa Rica, Barbados, and Trinidad for the improvement of their national archives and for developing national archival systems, to Panama and Colombia for the restoration of documents, to Jamaica for records management, and to Paraguay for university archives. Technical meetings have been held on library acquisitions, standards for library schools, and international cooperation for library and information services, on the development of national public library systems and services, on materials in Spanish for public and school libraries, planning for the archives development program and for the training programs of the LDP, on the integration of information services of archives, libraries, and documentation centers, on book selection, centralized cataloguing, and automation, on scientific documentation and national systems of scientific and technical information, on educational documentation, on planning for a bilingual learning resources center and children's book center, on information services of large university library systems, planning centralized cataloguing services, the development of the MARCAL format and its approval for Latin American libraries, on subject headings in Spanish, on library automation, and on the coordination of OAS projects in centralized cataloguing and standardization, the bilingual authority control system, and library automation with MARCAL.

In addition to the bibliographic publications of the Columbus Memorial Library, the Library and Archives Development Program has issued *Inter-American Library Relations* in English and Spanish, as well as a series of *Manuales del Bibliotecario, Estudios Bibliotecarios, Reuniones Bibliotecológicas,* and *Cuadernos Bibliotecológicos*. Responsibility for producing many classes of publications shifted to the centers and projects in the field, which by the close of the 1970's were issuing journals and newsletters, technical manuals, bibliographies, conference reports, and other publications.

In the planning and development of an inter-American network for the transmission of automated bibliographic information, much remains to be done in support of standardization, information management, and coordination of efforts of many organizations and institutions into a common program; substantial financial support for such a cooperative effort remained necessary if the information needs of Latin America and the Caribbean were to be met in the future.

**REFERENCES**

Various articles and reports by Marietta Daniels Shepard, such as "Analysis of the Library Situation in Latin America," *Cuadernos Bibliotecologicos,* no. 53 (1970), and, in the same series, no. 55, ". . . To Gain Access to Knowledge" (1971).

"An Inter-American Network for the Transmission of Bibliographic Information: Plans and Progress," IFLA/Unesco Pre-Session Seminar for Librarians from Developing Countries (Antwerp, 1977).

MARIETTA DANIELS SHEPARD

## Otlet, Paul-Marie-Ghislain

(1868–1944)

It is largely due to Paul-Marie-Ghislain Otlet, Belgian lawyer, bibliographer, and internationalist, in a lifelong collaboration with Henri LaFontaine, that there exist the International Federation for Documentation (FID), the Union of International Associations (UIA), and a major bibliographical tool still in widespread international use, the Universal Decimal Classification (UDC). He also initiated in Europe the formal study of documentation, a term he popularized and gave its specialized contemporary meaning. His work and that of friends and followers had considerable influence in the United States, especially in the founding of the American Documentation Institute, now the American Society for Information Science.

He was born August 23, 1868, and his family was wealthy and of some social importance; as he grew up he was surrounded by notable figures in the literary, artistic, and intellectual circles of Brussels. His education was at first private and then in the hands of the Jesuits until he transferred in 1866 from the Université de Louvain to the Université Libre de Bruxelles, where he earned a law degree in 1890. He then married his cousin Fernande Gloner and joined an old family friend, Emile Picard, as a *stagiaire* (trainee) at the Palais de Justice.

W. Boyd Rayward
*Paul-Marie-Ghislain Otlet*

But the law was of no vital interest to him, and he longed for some inspirational work of social and intellectual value. In 1891 he was to find both in the recently formed Société des Etudes Sociales et Politiques. At this time he began his collaboration with Henri LaFontaine, a former *stagiaire* of Picard's, now an international jurist of some reputation, and 15 years Otlet's senior. LaFontaine had directed a section for bibliography in the Society, and the disciplines of bibliography seemed to fire Otlet's imagination. In a seminal paper, *Un Peu de Bibliographie* (1892), he addressed the question: "How can the social sciences be given the positive and documentary character of the natural sciences?" Some of the answers, he believed, could be found in new forms of bibliography practiced on an international scale.

In 1893 the two friends expanded their work and became codirectors of what they now called the International Institute of Sociological Bibliography. Otlet's discovery of Melvil Dewey's Decimal Classification in 1895 led them to seek yet further expansion. Under the sponsorship of the Belgian government and with financial support from Ernest Solvay, industrialist and social theorist, they convened the first International Conference on Bibliography to discuss the problems involved in this expansion. The conference resolved that a catalogue truly universal in scope should be attempted, that an International Institute of Bibliography (IIB) should be formed to further the work, that the Decimal Classification should be adopted en bloc as the basis for the subject arrangement of the catalogue, and that a documentary union of governments should be created to support it. The Belgian government provided a headquarters for the Institute, and an International Office of Bibliography (OIB) was established by Royal Decree, September 17, 1895 (an official documentary union was never achieved, though the idea was raised again in 1908, 1910, and 1919).

The Universal Bibliographic Repertory (RBU) grew rapidly. By 1903 its various parts together contained over 6,000,000 notices; the number in the 1930's was variously estimated as between 12,000,000 and 15,000,000. An on-demand search service was instituted, and the service gradually expanded in the number and variety of consultations made of it. The Office began bibliographical publications of its own, directed others, and persuaded numerous bibliographical publishers to adapt their publications to meet minimum requirements for easy incorporation of entries into the RBU (thus becoming what were called "contributions" to the "Bibliographia Universalis").

The classification was to provide subject access to the RBU and was developed as the repertory grew. For Otlet and LaFontaine the Decimal Classification and the three-by-five-inch card, with its promise of indefinite intercalation, constituted a modern technology that for the first time in history made possible the creation of an up-to-date universal subject catalogue of infinite extensibility and correctability. On the one hand, they interested a cadre of prominent European scholars and scientists in developing the tables of the classification; on the other, Otlet gradually elaborated those technical features that were to make it distinctive and the first "faceted" classification. These features were a series of common subdivisions and methods for extending or elaborating classification numbers using combinatorial symbols of a prescribed function and order. The sophistication of the system was to enable it to express what Otlet called "all the nuances of ideologico-bibliographical analysis" of documents. The first full edition of the classification with a detailed discussion of principles, rules, and practices appeared in 1905 as *Manuel du répertoire bibliographique universel*.

The process of expansion and revision in Belgium of the American edition of the classification was conducted in close consultation with Melvil Dewey and his assistants in the United States in Otlet's rather one-sided hope that concordance between the two versions might be maintained. As the years passed, however, divergencies inevitably increased: the purposes of the two classifications and the philosophies guiding their elaboration were too different for much mutual understanding or accommodation to be achieved.

The first decade of the 20th century brought many developments in the IIB's work. The Institute held conferences in 1897, 1900, 1908, and 1910. In 1905 a Universal Iconographic Repertory, a "documentary repertory of pictorial material," was begun, arranged by UDC and intended to provide an illustrative supplement to the RBU. In 1907 came an Encyclopedic Repertory of Dossiers, in which brochures, pamphlets, and periodical and newspaper articles were assembled; its purpose was to give the RBU a substantive component, to constitute a kind of encyclopedia for which the RBU could theoretically act as a table of contents, its essential function for knowledge as a whole in Otlet's view. Also in 1907 a Collective Library of Learned Associations was opened, bringing together the libraries of a variety of national and international associations and societies, the number of which grew rapidly with the years, their collections as a whole providing a kind of documentary backup for the RBU.

Paralleling Otlet and LaFontaine's widening concern with the international organization of knowledge was their increasing interest in the problems of international organizations themselves, for, as Otlet observed, "The proper organization of documentation considered in the widest sense of the term is today one of the foremost functions to have devolved on international associations." In 1906 the two friends founded a Central Office of International Associations and mounted first a survey of those having headquarters in Belgium and then, in collaboration with Cyril Van Overbergh and the Belgian Sociological Society, a survey of international organizations more generally. In 1909 they coedited with Alfred Fried the *Annuaire de la Vie Internationale*; this directory, begun by Fried in 1904, was enormously expanded and was prefaced by a long, comprehensive analysis by Otlet of the structure, government, and functions of international organizations. They published a subsequent edition of the directory independently of Fried in 1910–11. Above all, in 1910 they organized the first World Congress of International Associations, a highly successful affair at which the Union of International Associations (UIA) was founded and for which the Central Office henceforth acted as headquarters.

A number of the associations taking part in the Congress in 1910 supported Otlet's proposal that the left wing of the Palais du Cinquantenaire should become an international museum. The government approved, and Otlet conceived of the huge building as a preliminary location for a Palais Mondial, a vast center of internationalism. In this were to be conjoined the bibliographic services of the IIB, the international library, the international museum, secretarial and publishing services for the associations, and ultimately an international university. Here, Otlet hoped, they would be developed as an integral whole with the support of governments and associations. The organization, rationalization, and propaganda for the Palais Mondial became the major preoccupations of the rest of Otlet's life. A second, even larger World Congress of International Associations was held in 1913, and plans for a third in San Francisco in 1915 were also begun. The museum had grown vigorously in the interim, and some attempt to consolidate the collections and services originating with the RBU in 1895 in the Palais Mondial was made before the outbreak of World War I put an end to such efforts.

During these prewar years Otlet had grown in importance internationally and in Belgian official and intellectual circles. The course of his personal life, however, had not been smooth. He had had two sons, Marcel and Jean, the latter killed in the war, but his marriage eventually failed, and in 1908 he and Fernande were divorced. In the early years of the new century, after a series of crises, the Otlet family fortune was almost wholly lost, and Otlet was to be plagued by legal and family problems associated with its dissolution. He married in 1912 a wealthy Dutchwoman, Cato Van Nederhasselt, whose income helped support him and his institutes for the rest of his life.

During the war he lived mostly in Paris and was an active member of the European movement for a League of Nations (Société des Nations). An integral part of the international order Otlet hoped to see established after the war was the creation by the League of an organization for intellectual relations with the Palais Mondial at its center. Otlet and LaFontaine had some influence on the League's eventual creation of an International Committee on Intellectual Cooperation.

After the war the primary task confronting the two friends was to resume their work in Brussels. They found that their institutes and collections had been unharmed by the occupation government and carefully maintained by a small, devoted staff. In 1920 they held the first of what were called Quinzaines Internationales, or International Fortnights (others were held in 1921, 1922, and 1924), during which meetings of the IIB, the UIA, and other international associations were held. Otlet now called for the creation of an International University and sought for it the patronage of the League of Nations. The League, however, impoverished, politically insecure, and only recently established in Geneva, was prepared to offer no more than sympathy and encouragement for the new enterprise.

Otlet and LaFontaine's various undertakings, now increasingly identified with Otlet, at first seemed successfully recovered after the war, and they had been completed by the foundation in 1920 of what was rather extravagantly named an International University. They fell fairly soon, however, on difficult times. Otlet could not interest the League in offering them any concrete support; its Committee on Intellectual Cooperation, created in 1922, soon went in directions that he regarded as inimical to the Palais Mondial and all it stood for. Efforts to collaborate with the Committee and with its executive arm, the International Institute for Intellectual Cooperation in Paris, failed and led to bitterness on Otlet's part and suspicion of him on that of League officials. The support of the Belgian government became increasingly uncertain until, in 1924, for a short period it actually resumed occupancy of the Palais Mondial for a trade fair.

It became clear that something needed to be done for the IIB lest it be lost and buried in the Palais Mondial. Assisted by LaFontaine, the Institute gradually began to assume an independent existence. New personalities began to move it in new directions, even changing its name in 1932 to the International Institute of Documentation. Otlet disliked and resisted all of the changes that this essentially new generation of supporters effected. He restored the Palais Mondial, which he now began to call the "Mundaneum," as best he could after the dislocations of 1924, and continued to seek support for it. His opposition to the trends in the Institute toward decentralization and federalism was silenced in 1934 when the Belgian government once more closed the Palais Mondial, this time effectively for good. The UIA's last meeting was held in 1924, though Otlet continued to issue publications in its name, and the Germans tried to use it for their purposes during the occupation of Brussels in World War II.

In all of these interwar years of struggle and disappointment, Otlet continued to act as one of the Secretaries-General of the IIB along with LaFontaine and eventually Frits Donker Duyvis. While it was open, he regularly lectured at the Palais Mondial. He worked rather ineffectively and controversially on the revision of the UDC, the completed second edition of which finally appeared in 1932. He gave courses in librarianship and documentation in Brussels and wrote ceaselessly on the broad international questions that interested him. As grand old men of European documentation, he and LaFontaine were much feted at the World Congress of Universal Documentation held in Paris in 1937 jointly with the International Institute for Intellectual Cooperation. Here the IIB's name was again changed, to the International Federation for Documentation. Otlet, however, continued to speak of it as part of that vast intellectual edifice, the Mundaneum, to the elaboration of which so much of his life had been devoted, and in protest against the changes that had occurred in the IIB he cut it out of his will.

A lifetime of research and writing culminated in the publication in 1934 of *Traité de la Documentation* and in 1935 of *Monde: Essai d'Universalisme.* These are large, slightly absurd encyclopedic works from which little insight seems possible for they contain no theories and offer no arguments, positions, or proof. Earlier writings, however, remain landmarks in the formal study of documentation and internationalism and have been too much neglected.

Otlet died on December 10, 1944, preceded by LaFontaine by a year. After World War II both the FID and the UIA were resurrected. The former still issues the UDC in a variety of translations and editions though allowing it no exclusively central place in its work; the latter has taken up the *Yearbook of International Organizations* as a major task and has made of it an indispensable reference tool.

**REFERENCES**

Otlet's MS diary and the archives of the IIB are preserved in the Mundaneum in Brussels.

Samuel Bradford, "Fifty Years of Documentation," in his *Documentation* (1948).

F. Donker Duyvis, "International Federation for Documentation," *Journal of Documentary Reproduction* (1940).

A full-length study of Otlet is W. Boyd Rayward, *The Universe of Information: The Work of Paul Otlet for Documentation and International Organisation,* FID Publication 520 (1976), which contains a comprehensive but occasionally inaccurate bibliography of Otlet's writings. A translation of a selection of these and an improved bibliography by Rayward is in preparation.

W. BOYD RAYWARD

# Pakistan

Pakistan, a federal republic in southern Asia, is bordered by Afghanistan and the U.S.S.R. on the north, China on the northeast, India on the east and southeast, and Arabian Sea on the south, and Iran on the west. Pop. (1977 est.) 74,540,000; area 796,095 sq.km. The official languages are Urdu and English.

**National Library.** There was no national library in Pakistan in 1979. The *Fifth Five-Year Plan (1978–83)* includes provisions for a national library in the capital city of Islamabad. The National Library of Pakistan would house a collection of 600,000 volumes. Designed as a research and reference library, it would promote public library service in the capital area (Rawalpindi-Islamabad) even though public education and libraries are responsibilities of local and provincial government.

The former national library in Karachi (founded 1950) changed its name in 1954 to Liaquat Memorial Library and was more of a community library with 55,000 volumes in 1967 when the decision to house the national library in Islamabad was taken. It is still a depository library for Pakistani publications under the Copyright Ordinance of 1967 and houses the National Bibliographical Unit, which publishes *The Pakistan National Bibliography* (1962– ) at annual, but irregular, intervals. The Unit along with another, the Acquisition Branch, established in 1976, will later move to Islamabad. The International Book Exchange Centre (1958), housed with the Central Secretariat Library in Karachi, will also move to Islamabad.

**Academic Libraries.** University libraries, 15 in all, are the most advanced group. They hold collections of 1,608,458 volumes (1978) and serve a student population of 34,470 (1976–77), contrasted with 1,066,288 volumes and 19,091 students in 1973. The 50.8 percent increase in bookstock is still short of student growth (80.6 percent).

Notable university library bookstocks are at Punjab (founded in 1908, 283,000 volumes), Karachi (1952, 174,394), and Sind (1947, 123,308). The Punjab University Library in Lahore has a rich collection of manuscripts (18,256) in Arabic, Persian, Urdu, Sanskrit, and Gurmukhi. It published three-volume catalogues in Persian, Urdu, and Arabic (1942–48) and two volumes in Sanskrit (1932–41). Its special collections also have historic and scholarly significance. A catalogue of its Sherwani collection was publishhed in three volumes (1968–73).

The Dr. Mahmud Husain Library, as the Karachi University Library is called, is notable both in size and content. It publishes a number of catalogues; they include those of collections on Quaid-i-Azam Mohammad Ali Jinnah, the founder of Pakistan (1976), and Allama Iqbal, the national poet (1977), whose birth centenary years were celebrated in 1976 and 1977, respectively. The Freedom Movement Archives, housed in the Library, contain rare materials on the All-India Muslim League, the political party that founded Pakistan.

Of 508 college libraries, 229 libraries held a collection of 1,913,492 in 1974. The collections vary from 2,000 in Riaz Girls College, Karachi (nationalized 1972), to 60,000 in Dayal Singh College, Lahore (founded 1910).

**Public Libraries.** The *Education Policy* (1972–80) proposed a system of 50,000 public libraries to eradicate illiteracy, but modern public libraries have yet to emerge. The *Fifth Five-Year Plan (1978–83)* proposes to establish community-oriented libraries in 1,000 villages.

Nevertheless, 242 libraries are called public libraries, and 78 had 972,566 volumes in 1974. Some of these are the oldest libraries in the country. The Punjab Public Library in Lahore (founded 1884) holds the country's second-largest collection (210,900). It holds 1,200 manuscripts in Arabic, Gurmukhi, Persian, and Urdu and published catalogues of Arabic and Persian manuscripts in 1957, 1963, and 1966. Its special collection, *Baitul Qur'ān,* holds microfilms and translations of Qur'ānic literature and tape recordings of recitations of the *Qur'ān.* Dayal Singh Public Library in Lahore (1908) published a catalogue of its Arabic and Persian manuscripts in 1974. It held 104,800 volumes in 1978.

Among the libraries run by provincial governments, the Central Library, Bahawalpur in Punjab (1948), with a collection of 75,000 (1978) and Divisional Public Library, Khairpur in Sind (1955), with a collection of 21,500 (1974) also operate mobile libraries.

At the municipal level, the public library system under the authority of the Karachi Metropolitan Corporation comprises 1 central library, 13 branch libraries, 1 reference library, and 3 reading rooms. It provides free lending service and is the first of its kind in the country. The central library (Frere Hall Library—now Karachi Metropolitan Public Library) opened in 1851 and holds a collection of 35,888 volumes. Other libraries in the system opened in the 1950's.

**School Libraries.** Primary schools do not normally maintain libraries. The limited number of secondary schools have libraries, but they are the most neglected in Pakistan. Of 413 secondary schools in Karachi, with 118,377 students (1978), only 72 have libraries, with collections totaling 479,763. Only four are served by a librarian. Individual collections vary from 2,000 to 15,740 volumes. The situation in other parts of the country is generally the same. The bookstock in Lahore, for example, varies from 200 to 30,000 volumes. The *Fifth Five-Year Plan (1978–83)* proposed to establish small libraries in primary schools and train teachers in the maintenance and use of small libraries in primary and lower secondary schools.

**Special Libraries.** These fare better in funding. From 40 in 1947, numbers grew to 242 in 1974. The collection in 178 such libraries in that year totaled 1,368,026.

A centralized documentation center was established in Karachi in 1957 under a Unesco subsidy. Called Pakistan Scientific and Technical Documentation Centre (PANSDOC) until 1974, it relocated to Islamabad with a new name—Pakistan Scientific and Technological Information Centre (PASTIC). Working under the Pakistan National Science Foundation, the Centre is redesigning its structure and services as a decentralized network. In its new role, PASTIC was to become PakSTI-network and coordinate the country's resources in social and economic sciences. As an experiment, a computer-based union catalogue (NASLIST) of 250 books was prepared in 1978.

PASTIC, however, remained unchanged at the end of the 1970's; it had yet to develop into a full-fledged system. It publishes *Pakistan Science Abstracts* (1961– ) and has a library of 6,000 volumes. It is a member of the Commonwealth Translation Index Scheme and participates in the National Technical Information Service of the U.S. Department of Commerce. Pakistan is interlinked with INIS and AGRIS through its special libraries.

**Table 2. Archives in Pakistan (1976)**

| | |
|---|---|
| Number | 3 |
| Holdings | N.A. (317,400 pieces) |
| Annual expenditures | 1,381,824 |
| Professional staff | 23 |
| All staff (total) | 119 |

Sources: Archival centers.

**Other Libraries.** Rental libraries, popularly known as *anna* libraries, exist in sizable numbers in large cities. In Karachi alone, in 1970, 214 such libraries held 412,379 volumes; in 1964 they numbered 104 and held 223,945 volumes. Hatim Alavi Memorial Library, Karachi (founded 1977), is the country's only library for the blind and is run by a social welfare organization.

**Associations.** Among the first local library associations were the Punjab Library Association (1948) and Karachi Library Association (1949). The former still exists, although it was suspended for a few years in the early 1950's. The Pakistan Bibliographical Working Group

University of Karachi

*The Dr. Mohamed Husain Library, University of Karachi, houses the Freedom Movement Archives of Pakistan's founding political party, the All-India Muslim League.*

(1950), founded as a result of the Unesco-Library of Congress world survey of bibliographical activities, still survives after many slack years. The Group has a number of publications. The *Pakistan National Bibliography (1947–61)* is the most important; two fascicules of the *Bibliography*, covering General Works, Philosophy, Religion, Social Sciences, and Languages, were published by the National Book Centre (now Council) of Pakistan (1972, 1973).

The Pakistan Library Association (1957) organizes annual conferences and publishes proceedings. It also publishes an irregular *Newsletter*. The Association, among other activities, fostered the idea of free public library service, invigorated the activities of local associations by holding joint sessions, fought for the grant of teachers' salary and status to the librarians, and surveyed the reading habits in Pakistan (1972). Its headquarters are rotated every two years to one of the five capital cities in the following order: Karachi, Lahore, Islamabad-Rawalpindi, Peshawar, and Quetta.

In 1960 a civic group, Society for the Promotion and Improvement of Libraries (SPIL), was formed. It held a number of seminars, conferences, and workshops during 1961–74 and published their proceedings.

ANIS KHURSHID

**Table 1. Libraries in Pakistan (1976; see notes)**

| Type | Number | Volumes in collections | Annual expenditures (rupee) | Population served | Professional staff | All staff (total) |
|---|---|---|---|---|---|---|
| National | 1[a] | 10,000 | 1,940,000 | 72,368,000[b] | 10 | 29 |
| Academic | 523[c] | 3,521,950[d] | 13,796,061[e] | 296,576[f] | 169[g] | 620[h] |
| Public | 240[i] | 972,566[j] | 1,748,113[k] | 5,380,000[l] | 36[m] | 103[n] |
| School | 72[p] | 479,763 | 99,000[q] | 266,381[r] | 5[s] | 11[s] |
| Special | 242[t] | 1,368,026[u] | N.A. | N.A. | N.A. | N.A. |

[a]On ad hoc basis (see text)
[b]Estimates (1976)
[c]In 1978
[d]Of 15 universities and 229 colleges only
[e]Only for universities; in colleges, book budget varies from 2,000 to 16,000
[f]In 1974 (colleges) and 1976–78 (universities)
[g]Figures for colleges N.A.; generally from 1 to 2 in each college
[h]Figures for colleges N.A.; generally between 2 and 11 in each college
[i]In 1974
[j]For 78 libraries
[k]For Karachi system; others vary from 449,880 to 240,000/less
[l]Literate population (1960)
[m]For Karachi system; others vary from 3 to 10
[n]For Karachi system; others vary from 26 to 40
[o]Secondary only
[p]In 1978 (Karachi only)
[q]For 4 libraries
[r]In 413 schools
[s]For 4 libraries
[t]In 1974
[u]Of 178 libraries

Source: Library Survey by Department of Library Science, University of Karachi, 1974.

University of Panama

*The Simón Bolívar Inter-American Library, formerly the Central Library established in 1935, opened on the campus of the University of Panama in 1978.*

## Panama

Panama, a republic of Central America, is bounded by the Caribbean Sea on the north, the Pacific Ocean on the south, Colombia in South America on the east, and Costa Rica on the west. (The Canal Zone bisects the Isthmus of Panama.) Pop. (1978 est.) 1,825,000; area 76,650 sq.km.

**National Library.** A decree of January 31, 1942, authorized the establishment of the National Library of Panama. With initial holdings of 10,000 volumes originally at the Colón Library, which had been donated by the Municipal Council of the Ministry of Education, it was founded on July 11, 1942. The Colón Library of the Municipality of Panama, dated from October 12, 1892, was discontinued in 1941 by disposition of the District Council. The National Library serves as a repository of the nation's bibliographic production, including all of the literature relating to the history of Panama. Its newspaper section contains the most complete collection of the dailies of the country. The collection totals 100,000 volumes.

**Academic Libraries.** Academic libraries are under the aegis of the country's two universities—the University of Panama (the national university) and the Santa María La Antigua University, a private institution. The University of Panama has two libraries—the Central Library and the Simón Bolívar Inter-American Library, the latter with two sections on medicine and law. Three others are independent of the Central Library—the Library of Dentistry, another at the Institute of Criminology, and a third at the Central American Institute of Administration and Supervision of Education.

Simón Bolívar Inter-American Library (Central Library), the name from 1978, was established immediately after the establishment of the University of Panama in October 1935. The Library was reorganized in 1941 under the direction of Gastón Lyton. In 1951 it was transferred to La Colina, now part of University City. In 1978 it was moved again to new facilities on the campus. The new buildings were named Simón Bolívar Inter-American Library and given responsibility for the acquisition and organization of material from the Libraries of Medicine, Law, and five Regional University Centers at Colon, Penome, Chitre, Santiago, and Chiriqui. The collection totals 258,000 volumes, 850 periodicals, and 21,000 graduate theses. The Library of the Central-American Institute of Administration and Supervision of Education (ICASE) was established May 11, 1970. The collection consists of 5,000 volumes and 100 periodicals.

The Library of the University of Santa María La Antigua was established at the beginning of the University on April 27, 1965. The collection consists of 50,000 volumes, including imported magazines, 135 periodical titles, and 270 graduate theses. It publishes an annual, *Boletín Informativo,* and bibliographies of existing material.

**Public Municipal Libraries.** Supported by the municipalities of each district, the name derives from the sustaining organizations and not from their primary purpose or services. There were 11 in Panama City in 1979. All offer mostly material for primary school students. The Mayor's Department of Education is in charge of the libraries of the Municipality of Panama.

**School Libraries.** These serve primary and middle-grade students in their own schools or groups of schools. In Panama City are libraries of the José Dolores Moscote Institute, founded in 1959 (more than 10,000 volumes), and the Octavio Méndez Pereira Library, part of the Isabel Herrera Obaldía Professional School in Paitilla (more than 10,000 books). A Unesco pilot project was organized with the cooperation and technical advice of the National Library and the Association of Librarians of Panama. It serves the following schools: Republic of Cuba, Republic of the Argentine, Republic of Peru, and the Chorrillo Community. The libraries of the University of Panama and the Ministry of Education by the late 1970's were well advanced in their projects, sponsored by the Organization of American States, to improve library services in the 1980's.

**Special Libraries.** The Library of the Department of Census and Statistics of the Comptroller General of the Republic was founded in 1914. It serves the public interested in the statistics of Panama as well as other countries and is equipped to reproduce documents. Its collection in 1978 totaled 48,000 books.

The Medical Library of the Social Security General Hospital, established March 31, 1969, contains medical information available to medical personnel working in the social security hospitals, in the city, and in the interior. Its collection consists of 600 books.

The Bio-Medical Library of the Commemorative Gorgas Laboratory is in the City of Panama. The Institute maintains an office in Washington. Its collection embraces more than 10,000 volumes, besides 504 periodical titles. The contents consist of books and reviews covering preventive tropical medicine and certain facets of biology, a result of investigations conducted in the laboratory. It

**Libraries in Panama (1976)**

| Type | Number | Volumes in collections | Annual expenditures (balboa) | Population served | Professional staff | All staff (total) |
|---|---|---|---|---|---|---|
| National | 1 | 100,000 | N.A. | N.A. | 0 | 66 |
| Academic | 8 | 388,000 | 218,660 | N.A. | 22 | 87 |
| Public | N.A. | N.A. | N.A. | N.A. | N.A. | N.A. |
| School | N.A. | N.A. | N.A. | N.A. | N.A. | N.A. |
| Special | 6 | 109,600 | N.A. | N.A. | 7 | 22 |

[a]Includes Central Library, University of Panama, and Library of Santa Maria La Antigua University.

Sources: Personal interviews with library heads.

serves the requirements of its scientific personnel and collaborators and the scientific community of the area, in particular of the medical doctors of Saint Thomas and Children's Hospitals. It receives photocopies of articles of the U.S. National Library of Medicine and exhaustive bibliographies prepared under the MEDLARS and GRACE systems.

Gorgas Hospital Medical Library, founded in 1918, is of interest to clinical medicine, with 25,000 books and periodicals.

The Smithsonian Tropical Research Institute, established in 1925 and supported by the U.S. government, is located in the area of the Canal. It has a fairly complete collection of 16,000 volumes. It serves all persons in Panama and the Canal Zone without regard to nationality. It is much used by patrons from the University of Panama.

The Amador Washington Library of the International Communication Agency (ICA) was created in 1952. In 1964 a fire destroyed its physical plant and its collection, and in that year it was recreated with the same staff and new books under its present name. It has a collection of 10,000 volumes and 17,000 microforms. It offers all readers service concerning books published in the U.S.

**Association.** The Panamanian Association of Librarians was established on March 6, 1951. A law approved by the National Assembly in 1956 regulated the profession of librarian and established the National Service throughout the country. Librarians created a guild. The Association participated in national and international activities contributing to the organization and improvement of the libraries in Panama. The Association publishes an annual bulletin. It has also published a bibliography of literature by Panamanian women, 1970–74. At the end of the 1970's it addressed issues concerning the recognition of librarians' professional stature within the sanction of law; the law of 1956 was considered to have failed to achieve its goals.

VICTOR U. MENDIETA ORTIZ

## Panizzi, Sir Anthony
(1797–1879)

Sir Anthony Panizzi (Antonio before knighthood) is one of the greatest figures in library history. Posthumously, Panizzi's reputation has grown ever more lustrous. To Arundell Esdaile he was the most creative force in the history of the British Museum; to Albert Predeek he was "the greatest lawgiver the library world has known"; to Edward Miller, his biographer, he was "a librarian of librarians, perhaps the greatest we have yet seen."

He was born September 16, 1797, at Brescello, a small town in the Duchy of Modena in northern Italy. After studying at the University of Parma, he practiced law for a while at Brescello. Unfortunately, the Duchy was then under Austrian domination and vitually a police state; when it became known that Panizzi was a member of a secret society working against the government, he was obliged to flee the country. For a short time he lived in Switzerland, but in 1823, like a number of his compatriots, he found refuge in England.

For several years Panizzi eked out a living as a teacher of Italian at Liverpool. In 1828 he was appointed first Professor of Italian Language and Literature at the new University of London, but since students were few and the remuneration small, the appointment turned out to be a barren honor. In 1831 he joined the staff of the British Museum.

Although the British Museum had been founded by an act of Parliament in 1753, in 1831 it was still a random miscellany of museum specimens, books, and manuscripts, in the care of scholarly but unenterprising officials who enjoyed a peaceful but pensionless service. The Museum's income was slender, and it lacked a vital sense of purpose. The Department of Printed Books, which Panizzi joined as an extra assistant, was among the least regarded of the departments, even though it embraced several former private collections of considerable importance. Among them were the Old Royal Library and the King's Library. It was the gift in 1823 of the latter, the magnificent private library of George III, that forced the BM's Trustees to provide a new building, on which work had just begun when Panizzi joined the staff.

Although his knowledge of libraries was then slight, by dint of travel- and correspondence he had become very well informed by 1836, when he was called upon to give evidence to the Parliamentary Select Committee on the condition and management of the Museum.

In 1837 Panizzi was appointed Keeper of the Department of Printed Books. In this capacity he not only did most of the things for which he is best remembered but had to endure the strongest attacks from his enemies, both within the Museum and outside it. In 1856 Panizzi was appointed Principal Librarian (i.e., Chief Officer) of the BM, but owing to ill health he had to resign in 1866. He died in London, April 8, 1879.

Although Panizzi was not lacking in friends, he had to suffer virulent criticism and hatred throughout most of his career at the BM, partly because he was regarded as a foreign upstart and partly because he refused to budge an inch when he believed he was right—as he usually was.

Some librarians are remembered for the work they did for their own libraries; others are remembered for their contribution to librarianship at large. Panizzi belongs squarely to the former group. In the 1980's the great circular Reading Room of the British Museum, which to many people was Panizzi's finest achievement, will be vacated when the British Library, of which the former BM Library is now part, takes over its elaborate new headquarters at Somers Town, near London's Saint Pancras Station. No longer, then, will one be able to say, in a literal sense, *Si monumentum requiris circumspice* ("If you seek a monument, look around"). But this was never an altogether satisfactory verdict on Panizzi's achievement, which may be more profitably considered under five headings: bookstock, building, staff, service, and cataloguing.

**Bookstock.** The vast increase in the bookstock of the BM Library since the 1850's has been due mainly to the action taken by Panizzi, as Keeper of the Department of Printed Books, to enforce the law of legal deposit, under which the Museum was entitled to receive one copy of every new British publication. In recent years it has several times been suggested that deposit at the British Library should be selective to prevent the acquisition of "rubbish." Panizzi, however, was unwilling to speculate on the probable needs of scholars of the future; he insisted on receiving everything. On the other hand, he recognized the disadvantage to scholars of having a national library with a stock based almost entirely on deposited publications and random donations. By securing regular and generous book funds and using them largely to acquire European and American publications, he gave the stock of the BM Library proper dimensions.

**Building.** Panizzi's reputation as a library planner rests securely on his successful advocacy (the conception was not entirely his own) of a great circular reading room with extensive surrounding stacks, both fabricated of cast iron, at that time little used in building construction. The addition of these desirable amenities meant the sacrifice of the Museum's inner quadrangle, but the result was accommodation for readers and books without parallel in any other library in the world.

**Staff.** Panizzi's particular solution to the staffing

British Museum

*Sir Anthony Panizzi*

problems of the BM was to secure for its personnel civil service conditions of employment, including security of tenure. The benefits to the Library were very clear toward the end of the century, when there were several outstanding men in its service who were quite willing to make their work at the BM a lifelong career.

**Cataloguing.** A remarkably large part of the history of the BM Library during the Panizzi period is concerned with the complicated story of Panizzi's troubles with the catalogue. When Panizzi joined the BM staff, the main catalogue was urgently in need of revision; the task of preparing a new one was still in hand when Panizzi became Keeper. One way and another the problems that this catalogue generated bothered Panizzi almost continuously for the next 13 years. The main difficulty was that the Trustees and Panizzi could not agree as to what kind of catalogue should be provided, but close behind it was the petty interference of the Trustees with the day-to-day work of the cataloguers.

When he was but an assistant librarian, Panizzi had made up his mind as to what was desirable and feasible: an alphabetical name catalogue in manuscript form, compiled throughout by the application of a new, comprehensive code of cataloguing rules. In the end this is what was achieved, but only after long, bitter, and widely publicized wrangling.

The first step was to convince the Trustees that an alphabetical catalogue was preferable to a classed one; the second was to get them to approve a new catalogue code, the famous *91 Catalogue Rules,* which Panizzi drew up with the help of his colleagues. The most difficult step was the third. Panizzi realized that printing the alphabetical catalogue would be inadvisable until the entire stock had been catalogued. This proposition the Trustees would not accept, even after Panizzi had demonstrated the folly of premature printing by actually having one specimen volume printed. Panizzi won in the end, but under the worst possible conditions. The Royal Commission, which was appointed in 1847 ostensibly to "examine the constitution and government of the British Museum," was, in effect, an ill-advised attempt to impeach Panizzi for incompetence and insubordination. Unable to prove his inefficiency on any other count, Panizzi's accusers turned to his long-standing quarrel with the Trustees over the catalogue. In their final report (1850) the Commissioners accepted all Panizzi's arguments and agreed that his refusal to print the catalogue was justified. The eventual benefits of this fortunate end to a disagreeable episode were the compilation of an incomparable reading room catalogue and following it, at the end of the century, the publication of the world-famous BM *Catalogue of Printed Books.*

**Service.** The standard of service built up by Panizzi was, for its day, very high. One aspect of it, by itself, indicates the kind of man Panizzi was—his refusal to favor some readers more than others. His statement to the Select Committee in 1836 on this matter is his most familiar pronouncement:

> I want a poor student to have the same means of indulging his learned curiosity, of following his rational pursuits, of consulting the same authorities, of fathoming the most intricate enquiry, as the richest man in the kingdom, as far as books go, and I contend that Government is bound to give him the most liberal and unlimited assistance in this respect.

Rather less familiar is Panizzi's observation to the Royal Commission, in 1849: "I never felt the skin of any reader and they are all treated alike."

One of Panizzi's arch enemies outside the BM was author Thomas Carlyle. One of the reasons Carlyle played a major role in founding the London Library in 1841 was his failure to obtain from Panizzi special privileges as a reader at the BM. This quarrel had the beneficial effect of enriching the metropolis with one of the finest learned subscription libraries in the world.

**Evaluation.** Panizzi could not have done all that he did alone. Although he was a hard taskmaster (one member of his staff described him as "a thorough-going tyrant"), he inspired in most of his lieutenants loyalty and willing cooperation. Prominent among those who helped him in all his endeavors was Thomas Watts, his right-hand man; outstanding among those who hindered him was Sir Frederic Madden, the brilliant but querulous Keeper of the Department of Manuscripts. The story of Panizzi's ceaseless arguments with Madden and the Museum's Trustees would make a volume in itself. It is a part of Panizzi's life that cannot be ignored, since the progress he made in spite of it is all the more remarkable. Furthermore, the existence of this powerful opposition led Panizzi to explain and defend his actions as he might never have done otherwise. Although he published a fair amount on language and literature, he published hardly anything on librarianship.

It is now generally understood that the British national library should be the apex of the British library system, which is precisely what the new British Library is. But in Panizzi's day there was no national public library network; there were not even many academic libraries. Edward Edwards, who worked with Panizzi for a while, visualized a nationwide public library service and helped to prepare the way for it. Panizzi was not a protagonist in the public library movement, but this was not to his discredit; the BM's affairs absorbed him utterly.

Panizzi's name is more familiar than the names of most librarians of the past; that may be due, in some measure, to his friendship with many of the leading political figures of his day and a role he played in the struggle for the unification of Italy. Nevertheless, it is undeniable that his work for the British Museum Library was of seminal importance. He took over several valuable but static collections and left behind him a large, coherent, working library, so organized and so sustained that its continuance as a great national library was scarcely in doubt.

**REFERENCES**

The best full-length biography of Panizzi, which makes good use of Panizzi's official papers, is *Prince of Librarians: The Life and Times of Antonio Panizzi of the British Museum* by Edward Miller (1967). Arundell Esdaile, *The British Museum Library: A Short History and Survey* (1946), provides a concise but authoritative description of conditions at the BM before and after the Panizzi regime. It also shrewdly assesses Panizzi's reforms.

Because Panizzi himself published little on the BM Library and his work for it, the evidence he gave to the Select Committee and the Royal Commission, which was published verbatim in their respective reports, is particularly useful. Complete facsimiles of both reports were published by the Irish University Press in their British Parliamentary Papers series, *Report from the Select Committee on the Condition, Management and Affairs of the British Museum, 1836* (1968) and *Report of the Commissioners on the Constitution and Government of the British Museum, 1850* (1969).

See also the excellent symposium on Panizzi in *British Library Journal* (1979).

JAMES G. OLLÉ

# Papua New Guinea

Papua New Guinea, an independent parliamentary state in the western South Pacific, includes the eastern section of New Guinea and various islands. The country is north of Australia and separated from it by the Torres Strait. Pop. (1977 est.) 2,908,000; area 462,840 sq.km. The official language is English.

**National Library Service.** The National Library Service (NLS), in the capital of Port Moresby, was established in 1975; by 1978 it had absorbed the Public Library Service, National Film Library, School Libraries Service, and National Archives. Under the Copyright Act of 1978 and the Statutory Deposit Act of 1979, it is one of three depository libraries. In 1978 it occupied the new National Library building, Australia's independence gift to the nation. Research and loan services are provided to national government officials and to the general public; films are loaned to government, educational, and cultural organizations throughout the country. The NLS also oversees library services to the Parliament and government departments. A central processing service is available to school and public libraries.

The NLS had no stock of its own in 1976, but by 1978 it had 40,000 volumes and approximately 6,000 films in the National Library building and 20,000 volumes in its Ela Beach Library.

**Academic Libraries.** Papua New Guinea has two universities, the University of Papua New Guinea (UPNG) and the Papua New Guinea University of Technology (PNGUT). By the end of 1977 the UPNG Main Library, established in 1965, held 184,000 volumes and the Medical Library and the Goroka Teachers College Branch Library 20,000 volumes each. The PNGUT Library, established in 1968, had a collection of 50,000 volumes by the end of 1977.

The UPNG Main Library maintains an extensive New Guinea Collection, and the PNGUT Library operates a comprehensive audiovisual service. Both are depository libraries.

**Public Libraries.** The Commonwealth National Library (of Australia) established the Public Library Service of the Territory of Papua and the Mandated Territory of New Guinea in 1936. In 1962 there were 9 public libraries with a total stock of 57,000 volumes. By 1976 there were 190,000 volumes in 24 libraries, one in each of the urban centers, which together serve 20 percent of the population. The national literacy rate in English was estimated at 14 percent in 1971, and it may be assumed that public library stocks are used mainly by nonindigenous persons. Experiments were conducted between 1949 and 1964 with the establishment of 260 village libraries, but they proved unsuccessful. Many libraries have only part-time staff, and most collections are small and outdated. The Headquarters Library at Ela Beach provided a central selection and processing service, but devolution of national government powers in 1978 removed responsibility for library services to each of the 19 provincial governments.

Information Office, PNGUT

*The Matheson Library, Papua New Guinea University of Technology, was remodeled in 1977 and accommodates 500 seated patrons. Local artists created the mural and sculpture.*

**Table 2. Archives in Papua New Guinea (1976)**

| | |
|---|---|
| Number | 1 |
| Holdings | 90,000 linear feet |
| Annual expenditure | K48,000 |
| Professional staff | 1 |
| All staff (total) | 13 |

Source: Office of National Librarian.

**School Libraries.** The establishment of the School Libraries Office in 1966 facilitated book box schemes, library subsidies, and professional advisory services, and in the mid-1970's a central processing service was introduced. Most of the 620,000 school children in the mid-1970's had no library services. Those libraries available are predominantly in the high schools and technical schools, but only in rare instances do they have trained staff or substantial collections, as responsibility for funding rests with individual schools.

**Special Libraries.** The Parliament, Department of Justice, Office of Forests, and the Bougainville Copper Company, in the North Solomons Province, are among the major special libraries. The Library of the Prime Minister's Department has an extensive collection of rare historical documents, and the Research Library of the Department of Education provides a postal loan service to teachers throughout the country.

The Papua New Guinea Institute of Public Administration, established as the Administrative College in 1961, has special collections in government, New Guineana,

**Table 1. Libraries in Papua New Guinea (1976)**

| Type | Number | Volumes in collections | Annual expenditure (kina) | Population served | Professional staff | All staff (total) |
|---|---|---|---|---|---|---|
| National[a] | N.A. | N.A. | N.A. | N.A. | N.A. | N.A. |
| Academic | 3[b] | 314,000 | K314,000 | 3,600[c] | 30 | 138 |
| Public | 24 | 186,330 | N.A. | 2,800,000[d] | 1 | 50 |
| School | 98 | 401,858[e] | K100,000[e] | 700,000[e] | — | 133 |
| Special | 20 | 140,248 | K300,000[3] | N.A. | 4[e] | 60 |

[a]The National Library existed only on paper until 1978.
[b]Includes PNG Institute of Public Administration (IPA).
[c]Excludes IPA, as most courses are for a few weeks or months only.
[d]Total estimated national population.
[e]Estimatic ns based on incomplete figures.

Sources: M. Obi, *Directory of Libraries,* and L. Baker, *Development of University Libraries in PNG.*

and library science. In 1977 its collection totaled some 50,000 volumes.

**Associations.** The Papua New Guinea Branch of the Library Association of Australia, established in 1967, was the forerunner to the Papua New Guinea Library Association (PNGLA), formed in 1974. Current activities include an annual conference and publication of a quarterly journal, *Toktok Bilong Haus Buk.* A School Libraries Association of Papua New Guinea was formed in 1970, but it had lapsed by 1976.

**REFERENCES**

Kwami Avafia, "Library Development in Papua New Guinea," *Libri* (1975), surveys all types of libraries and contains some statistics, based on 1973 survey.

Leigh Baker, *Development of University Libraries in Papua New Guinea,* Master of Philosophy thesis, PNGUT (1978), includes survey of libraries and librarianship, plus detailed treatment of university libraries; utilizes 1977 data gathered specially.

Harold Holdsworth, *The Development of Library Services in Papua New Guinea* (1976), report on a consultancy visit in September 1975; includes brief report on libraries visited, extensive survey of current situation, and forecasts and recommendations for the future.

LEIGH R. BAKER

# Paraguay

Paraguay, a republic of South America, is bounded by Bolivia on the northwest and north, Brazil on the east, and Argentina on the southeast, south, and west. Pop. (1978 est.) 2,888,000; area 406,752 sq.km. The official language is Spanish.

**National Library.** The National Library, in the capital of Asunción, was founded in 1869 under the name of Municipal Library. The Director General of Archives, Libraries, and Museums of the Nation traces the founding of the National Library to the Paraguayan humanist Juan Silvano Godoy, who set up his own library on March 25, 1909. This library was later acquired by the state.

The holdings of the National Library have been developed over a period of time, primarily through the incorporation of such important libraries as the Biblioteca Americana of Juan Silvano Godoy and the personal library of Enrique Solano López, son of Marshal Francisco Solano López. Similarly, the National Library received books donated by the Institute of External Dissemination and the embassies of Chile, West Germany, and Israel.

The valuable collection of the National Library contains about 40,000 volumes and is divided into the following sections: national authors, national periodicals—from all eras of Paraguayan printing; international authors—materials from many continents.

The collection of the National Library did not grow as it should have during the 1970's because of a precarious economic situation that did not enable it to maintain its collection up to date. Copyright law does not require the deposit of all works published by Paraguayan writers. Moreover, deficiencies in the organization of materials make bibliographic and reference services difficult. Nevertheless, many of the materials of the National Library are unique and are used by historians, researchers, and students.

**Academic Libraries.** Paraguay has two well-defined systems of academic libraries, one belonging to the National University of Asunción (UNA), the other to the Catholic University Our Lady of Asunción. The UNA operates a system consisting of a Central Library and 16 other libraries of the University's faculties, schools, and institutes. Beginning with the years 1977–78, the Organization of American States sponsored a multinational project devoted to improving university library services

*Library of the National Institute for Technology and Standards in Asunción.*

through the establishment of a union catalogue. Seventeen university libraries had cooperated in this system of information by 1979; the union catalogue itself is in the Central Library of the UNA. The collections of the various libraries that comprise the UNA system totaled 48,300 volumes in 1976; by 1978 the total had climbed to 76,000 volumes. One notable donation to the Central Library was the collection of former President Félix Paiva (1937–39), consisting of 660 volumes in the fields of political science, law, and general culture.

The Pope Paul VI Central Library of the Catholic University was created in 1962 and presently contains approximately 20,000 books, as well as 12 titles of official publications and 56 other journal titles. During the 1970's the collection was considerably enriched through the acquisition of a number of personal libraries, such as the Tupí-Guaraní Collection (1971) and the 500-volume collection of Paraguayan works of Diego Amarilla (1972). Other collections include the *Gaceta Oficial* from 1869 to 1975 (continually updated), that of Monseñor Secundino Núñez consisting of 3,8000 volumes (1974), and the 2,000-volume collection of Juan Santiago Dávalos (1976).

In addition to possessing the best single collection in Paraguay, the Central Library of the Catholic University has the best continuing working budget. The Catholic University also operates a number of faculties in Asunción and has extended its services to many areas of the country, providing university-level courses in the cities of Encarnación, Concepción, Coronel Oviedo, Pedro Juan Caballero, Presidente Stroessner, and Villarica. A library of 2,000 volumes and a large reading room supports the teaching program in Villarica.

**Public Libraries.** Exact information on the public libraries of Asunción is difficult to find, but from all evidences the first public library was the Municipal Library of 1869, which later became the National Library. The present municipal library became a public library in 1932 at the suggestion of Sra. Sirvillán G. de Guanes, and in 1943 it grew by 343 volumes through a donation from the Argentine Commission on Intellectual Cooperation. The Library was officially organized in 1962 and maintains a collection of 6,000 volumes. The most valuable section of the Municipal Library is its collection of out-of-print books.

In addition to the Municipal Library, the city of Asunción has five other libraries, which belong to different foreign embassies: those of Argentina, Brazil, the

**Table 1. Libraries in Paraguay (1978)**

| Type | Number | Volumes in Collections | Annual expenditures (guaraní) | Population served | Professional staff | All staff (total) |
|---|---|---|---|---|---|---|
| National | 1 | 40,000 | Gs. 8,630,400[a] | 2,800,000 | — | 10 |
| Academic | 19 | 98,000 | Gs. 16,704,000 | 24,150 | 14 | 51 |
| Public | 15 | 46,850 | Gs. 8,268,000 | 734,400 | 3 | 32 |
| School | 47 | 156,300 | Gs. 20,958,000 | 44,000 | 13 | 91 |
| Special | 17 | 42,170 | Gs. 28,568,000[b] | 4,500 | 11 | 64 |
| Total | 98 | 383,320 | Gs. 83,128,400 | 3,607,050 | 41 | 248 |

[a]Included annual expenditures of the Library, archive, and musseo.
[b]ITAIPU includes annual expenditures of the library and archive.

Sources: Interviews and visiting libraries.

**Table 2. Archives in Paraguay (1978)**

| | |
|---|---|
| Number | 12 |
| Holdings | 1,964 cubic meters |
| Annual expenditures | N.A. |
| Professional staff | 2 |
| All staff (total) | 105 |

Sources: Interviews and visiting archives.

United States, Spain, and Mexico. With a total of some 23,360 volumes, these libraries provide information services to their members.

Nine other small municipal libraries are known to exist in the interior of the country, with a combined total of 17,500 volumes. These libraries are organized and run by the small cities that they serve. Although they rarely have reliable annual budgets, the information services that they are able to provide indicate some interest in their support on the part of the municipalities they serve.

**School Libraries.** Paraguay enjoys quite a few school libraries, owing, in part, to the 1976 law promulgated by the Ministry of Education and Culture. This law establishes a series of standards for school libraries in the country, including the regulation that the library should have at least three books per student in the school. In addition, the "Renovated Curriculum" concept calls for greater emphasis on school libraries.

Quality varies among the existing school libraries. A study by the School of Librarianship of the UNA found 47 organized school libraries, 7 of which have sufficient budgets and are administered by professional librarians. The information services of these libraries are much superior to those of the other 40, which are lacking in technical and administrative development and in professional personnel.

**Special Libraries.** The majority of the special libraries oriented toward research were created during the 1960's; those organized during the 1970's were more oriented toward the government, that is, centralized public organisms such as the Ministry of State and other governmental units. Because they are so recent and, indeed, are still in the early stages of development, special libraries in Paraguay scarcely have a history of their own. Presently, many of them evidence interest in documentation services and often publish information bulletins and bibliographies relating to their institutions.

One of the most important special libraries is that of the Documentation Center of ITAIPU (the binational Paraguay-Brazil enterprise constructing the world's largest hydroelectric dam on the Paraná River), which issues three monthly publications, including a scientific journal index.

The Library and Archives of the Documentation Center of ITAIPU had an excellent budget of 10,980,000 guarani ($90,036) in 1978 and is well equipped with modern machines and well staffed by competent professionals. It offers efficient information service to researchers from the company as well as to other persons in the community. A branch of the library operates in the city Presidente Stroessner, on the Paraná River about 350 kilometers from Asunción.

The library of the National Institute for Technology and Standards (INTN), one of the best of its kind, provides services to researchers, teachers, and university students. It concentrates on storage and selective dissemination of information in the areas of foodstuffs, wood, textiles, leather goods, and construction materials. It receives a wide variety of periodical publications on standards and technology from many countries. Among its publications is *Boletin de Informacion Tecnica Industrial,* which contains numerous annotated bibliographies.

**Library Associations.** Two library associations operate in Paraguay: the Association of Librarians of Paraguay (ABIPAR) and the Association of University Librarians of Paraguay (ABUP). The former was founded on May 17, 1962, by a group of five Paraguayan librarians and had 62 members by the end of the 1970's, including librarians, booksellers, writers, and friends of libraries. The latter dates back only to July 20, 1974, when it was founded by 17 librarians. Its membership, totaling 51, consists of graduates of the School of Librarianship of the UNA, united for the purpose of elevating the status of the library profession in Paraguay.

YOSHIKO MORIYA DE FREUNDORFER (translated by Edwin S. Gleaves)

# Penna, Carlos Victor
(1911– )

Carlos Victor Penna, library author, educator, and administrator, worked for library advancement in Latin America as a Unesco specialist and contributed concepts of library and information service planning that led to the Unesco NATIS program. He was born in Bahia Blanca, Buenos Aires Province, Argentina, on October 1, 1911. He attended school in Cayupán and Maza, small towns in the provinces of Buenos Aires and Pampa, and in 1927 he began studies at the Escuela de Mecánica de la Armada, which he left in 1931, unwilling to adapt to the military regimen required there. In 1933 he began work at the Library of the Estado Mayor de la Marina as a page in charge of stack maintenance. When he was promoted to the position of Cataloguer, he applied modern cataloguing techniques for the first time in Argentina, having translated and experimented with some of the Vatican "Rules for the Cataloguing of Book Materials" and the Universal Decimal System. He later organized the centralized cataloguing of the books of more than 100 libraries in Marina—the first cooperative venture of this nature practiced in Latin America. Penna also pioneered in the introduction of microphotographic techniques applied to the organization of the Central Catalogue of the University of Buenos Aires, which he directed in 1943 after returning from library studies at Columbia University in New York City in 1941. Penna also organized the Library School of the Social Museum of Argentina and introduced modern information management methods into the curriculum. The School had a great impact not only in Argentina but on a continental scale, and the text materials written by the faculty have been utilized by library schools all over Latin America.

In 1945 Penna began traveling in a way that later enabled him to fully participate in information work on an international level. First he visited La Paz, Bolivia, together with Augusto Raúl Cortázar, to reorganize the Mariscal Santa Cruz Library. In 1947 he participated in the Assembly of American Librarians. In 1950 he traveled to Cuba to teach courses at the Library School of the Friends Society of Cuba and also made several visits to Uruguay to assist A. Gropp in the development of the Library School that the North American had organized in Montevideo. In 1951 Penna became a Unesco specialist, first assigned to the Western Hemisphere Regional Center in Havana, Cuba. From Havana, as a specialist in the area of library development, Penna worked hard for the betterment of libraries all over Latin America. In 1964 he was transferred to the main offices of Unesco, from which he retired in 1971 as Director of the Division for the Development of Documentation, Libraries and Archives.

Upon leaving Unesco, Penna made his home in Palma de Mallorca, Spain, serving as an expert of the Iberoamerican Education Office. In 1974 he moved again, this time to the United States, where he taught subjects such as library and information services planning at Pratt Institute and acted in an advisory capacity with the Coordinating Commission of the National System of Library and Information Services of Venezuela.

Penna published more than 120 journal articles and professional papers. Among his many books and projects are *Catalogación y clasificación de libros* (1st ed., 1949; 2nd ed., 1964); direction of the translation of *Sears List of Subject Headings for Small Libraries* (1949); *Manual de Bibliotecología* ("Manual of Librarianship"), in collaboration with other authors (1968); direction of the Kapelusz Editorial Series, together with E. J. Sabor, *Bibliotecología: planeamiento de servicios bibliotecarios* ("Librarianship: The Planning of Library Services"; 1968), also published in English, French, Japanese, Arabic, and Turkish; *Planeamiento de servicios bibliotecarios y de documentación* (*Planning Library and Documentation Services;* 2nd ed., by Sewell and Liebaers, 1970), also published in English and French; and *Servicios de Bibliotecas e Información: nueva concepción Latinoamericana* ("Library and Information Services: A New Latin American Concept"; 1972).

EMMA LINARES

## Peru

Peru, a republic in western South America, is bordered by Ecuador and Colombia on the north. Brazil on the east, Bolivia on the east and south, Chile on the south, and the Pacific Ocean on the west. Pop. (1978 est.) 4,376,100; area 1,285,215 sq.km. The official languages are Spanish and Quechua.

**National Library.** The Biblioteca Nacional, or National Library of Peru, was founded in 1821 by José de San Martín. Although it was partially destroyed by fire in 1943, it was possible to reopen it in 1947, and copies of the first publications printed in Peru and the Americas are still among its most prized possessions. It contains over 661,200 monographs, 171,300 manuscripts, 11,643 maps, 7,512 musical scores, 7,564 photographs, and 1,585,600 issues of periodical publications and newspapers and thus offers an impressive collection to the student and scholar alike, especially in that pertaining to Peruvian history, literature, and law.

The National Library was once called the Biblioteca Pública, or public library. However, although open to the general public, no borrowing privileges are permitted by law of the republic. It publishes the *Anuario Bibliográfico Peruano* ("Annual Bibliography of Peru"), as well as the *Boletín de la Biblioteca Nacional* ("National Library Bulletin"), the *Gaceta Bibliotecaria del Perú* ("Peruvian Librarian's Gazette"), and other publications.

The Archivo General de la Nación, founded in 1861, and the Biblioteca del Instituto Nacional both complement the National Library's activities, the latter having participated closely in the identification and classification of Peruvian publications.

**Academic Libraries.** Academic libraries in Peru exist in almost every institution of higher learning, these numbering at least 200. They are generally closed collections offering access only through the card catalogue and limiting borrowing privileges to registered students. Required text materials are usually available in multiple copies and constitute the most heavily used portion of these collections.

The Biblioteca Central of the Universidad Nacional Mayor de San Marcos (San Marcos National Higher University Central Library) was founded in Lima during the 16th century and possesses over 450,000 volumes. It was originally the owner of a large portion of the colonial collection, presently housed in the National Library.

The Biblioteca Central de la Pontificia Universidad Nacional Católica del Perú (National Peruvian Pontifical Catholic University, Central Library), although founded as recently as 1917, possesses an ample collection of over 130,000 volumes, many of a recent, technical nature.

The Biblioteca de la Universidad Nacional de San Augustín in Arequipa deserves special mention as an example of the decentralization trend taking place in many Latin American academic libraries. The central library coordinates 12 specialized libraries that possess a total of 97,800 volumes above and beyond the basic collection of 33,250 monographs, 1,200 pamphlets, and over 530 periodical publications.

In many cases academic libraries function more as study halls than as information centers, as students and professors alike have only comparatively recently begun to utilize modern research methods and tools. Libraries slowly are becoming equipped to handle these new demands on their collections, services, and personnel.

**Public Libraries.** Public libraries in Peru are generally referred to as bibliotecas públicas municipales, or municipal public libraries. There were an estimated 500 such libraries in Peru in the latter 1970's. The majority possess small collections of donated materials and are directed by persons with little or no training in modern library methods.

Several exceptions to this broad generalization exist, principally in the major urban centers. The Lima Municipal Library, founded in 1935, has a collection of about 16,000 volumes, relatively small owing to the role played by the National Library also located in Lima and the consequent recent founding of the Lima Public.

The Arequipa Public Municipal Library was, on the other hand, founded earlier than the Lima Public and contains over 28,000 volumes. The Casa de la Cultura (Cultural Institute) of Peru is housed in that library, giving an indication of the humanistic nature of the collection.

Surprisingly, the largest public library in Peru is in Callao. The Biblioteca Pública Municipal Piloto (Callao

Municipal Pilot Public Library) was founded as recently as 1936 and reorganized in 1957. It offers a broad collection of over 48,500 volumes to the general public.

Public libraries in Peru are generally not lending libraries, as is true in the majority of Latin American public libraries. Public library services have often been merged with the functions of the National Library, and only recently have these two different types of service begun to be separate in practice. Public libraries in Peru receive technical assistance from the Oficina Nacional de Bibliotecas Populares Municipales, located in the National Library.

**School Libraries.** The majority of existing school libraries in Peru are found in private and very large public primary and secondary schools mainly in the several major cities. Most of these are directed by untrained personnel, in many cases teachers with full class schedules. These factors generally lead to less than adequate collections and services and even affect access to the library, given usually irregular and insufficient working hours.

The OAS sponsored the Programa de Bibliotecas Escolares, or School Library Program, in conjunction with the Peruvian Ministry of Education, for several years during the early 1970's and was still active in this area in the latter 1970's. One of the several tangible results of this program was the creation of two scholarships for school librarians and two for professors of librarianship to study on a postgraduate level outside the country. The first two scholarships were designed to provide immediate leadership in the field, and the latter were intended to create a long-range multiplying effect toward the future development of the field.

Audiovisual aids are generally underutilized or unavailable and many times are not considered the responsibility of the school library. The Dewey Decimal System is generally used for classification purposes, but a number of school libraries are uncatalogued and unclassified because of the lack of trained personnel.

**Special Libraries.** The *Directorio de Bibliotecas Especializadas del Peru* ("Directory of Peruvian Special Libraries") was published by ABIISE, Agrupación de Bibliotecas para la Integración de la Información socioeconómica (Consortia of Libraries for the Integration of Socioeconomic Information) in 1972, serving as an update of the Peruvian Library Association's 1969 *Guia de Bibliotecas Especializadas.* The Directory lists 100 special libraries out of a total of 130 identified during the survey period. The libraries included may be broken down equally into three types, one-third each being in the social sciences, the applied and basic sciences, and the humanities, or geared to the broad concerns of a particular institution. A cross section of the above categories, also equaling about one-third of the total, were directly related to government offices, such as ministries.

A number of special libraries in Peru deserve special mention: INTINTEC—Instituto de Investigación Tecnológica Industrial y de Normas Tecnicas (Industrial Technology and Standards Research Institute) has a fine hard technology information and documentation center, while ESAP—Escuela Superior de Administración Pública (School of Public Administration) and ESAN—Escuela de Administración de Negocios para Graduados (Graduate School of Business Management) both have specialized in the area of soft technology. Socioeconomic information sources are by far the most developed and coordinated in Peru, thanks to the efforts of ABIISE.

Some significant collections of manuscripts and valuable historical materials are found in convents and monasteries. A number of these are open to the public.

**Associations.** The two major professional associations are the APB, Asociación Peruana de Bibliotecarios (Peruvian Library Association), and ABIISE. Both have played a vital role in the development of libraries and librarianship in Peru.

A trade group of sorts, called the Asociación de Empleados de la Biblioteca Nacional, exists for the employees of the National Library, and the Cámara Peruana del Libro (Peruvian Book Council) has worked closely with the Library Association in a number of areas and has made important donations to various libraries.

MARTHA GORMAN

## Petherick, Edward Augustus
(1847–1917)

Edward Augustus Petherick, bookseller, publisher, bibliographer, and book collector, provided a collection that formed the basis of what is now the National Library's large and important body of materials relating to Australia, New Zealand, and the Pacific Islands. He was born on March 6, 1847, at Burnham, Somerset, England, the eldest of nine surviving children of Peter John Petherick, stationer-librarian, and his wife, Ann, née Press. The family sailed from Bristol to Melbourne, Australia, arriving in March 1853 with, among other things, 400 books to sell. Edward, able to read from the age of five, attended Alfred Brunton's Public School in Melbourne part-time while working for his father. It was not long before he became employed in the bookselling and stationery firm of George Robertson, who was impressed by Edward's precocious knowledge of books and enthusiastic application to his duties. After ten years' experience with the firm, Petherick was chosen in 1870 to reorganize the London office, which he quickly transformed and continued to manage until Robertson restired in 1887. That year Petherick set up his own business in London. His Colonial Booksellers' Agency at 33 Paternoster Row had a capital of $800 and was backed by a number of publishers and assisted by Australian banks supporting distributing branches in Sydney, Melbourne, and Adelaide. At this time he began publishing, issuing quarterly the *Colonial Book Circular and Bibliographical Record,* later changing its title to *The Torch,* and in 1889 launched his *Collection of Favourite and Approved Authors.*

As early as 1865 Petherick had collected titles for a catalogue or bibliography of Australiana but put it aside when he went to England in 1870. In 1878 he made a fresh start with it, commenting, "The business of the London department being well organised, I took up the work again; but finding I could do little without the books, I began to collect them—as they came within my grasp, and the savings of a limited salary." In 1882 he won public recognition as a bibliographer by publishing the *Catalogue of the York Gate Geographical and Colonial Library.* Its success prompted William Silver, the owner, to enlarge his collection with help from Petherick, whom he commissioned to prepare a second edition, subtitled *An Index to the Literature of Geography, Maritime and Inland Discovery, Commerce and Colonisation;* it was published by John Murray in 1886. When Silver died in 1905, Petherick arranged the sale of the York Gate Library to the South Australian Branch of the Royal Geographical Society of Australasia. With tireless industry, inexhaustible energy, and bachelor freedom, he became involved with many learned societies and corporate activities—from the Royal Geographical, Hakluyt, and Linnean Societies to the Royal Colonial Institute and the Library Association—becoming a life member of all. He wrote numerous reviews, letters, and articles, many of which remain unpublished.

Petherick's publishing venture continued until 1894, when the Australian bank crisis and his own lack of financial reserves forced him into bankruptcy with debts of about $50,000. His book stocks were sold to E. W. Cole, a Melbourne bookseller, and his *Collection of Favourite and Approved Authors* was taken over by the London publishers George Bell & Sons. On March 1, 1892, in Dorset, Petherick had married a widow, Mary Agatha Skeats, née

Annear, and it was mainly with her help that he met his financial difficulties and succeeded in saving his own collection of Australiana. Broken by business failure, he became a cataloguer with the antiquarian booksellers Francis Edwards & Co. and between 1895 and 1908 produced a series of outstanding catalogues of Australasian material. As means permitted, he continued collecting and devoted great effort to completing his *Bibliography of Australia and Polynesia;* he prepared a printed prospectus of it in 1898 but was unable to arrange publication.

As his collection grew, Petherick became anxious that it should pass to the Australian people and, even before the federation of the Australian States in 1901, he approached two premiers with an offer to present his collection to "Federated Australia," but no action resulted. Nor did anything result when he wrote to Prime Minister Barton in March 1901, his approach at that time being premature. In 1908, however, he and his wife took the collection to Australia and soon negotiated with the Federal Parliament. Its Library Committee on May 27, 1909, recommended acquisition of the collection "in consideration of an annuity of $500 a year, Mr. Petherick to render during the currency of the annuity such services in the Commonwealth Library as the Committee may from time to time prescribe." The collection consisted of some 10,000 volumes, 232 boxes of pamphlets, and some manuscripts, maps, and pictures. It was accompanied by the sheets of the still unpublished *Bibliography* of about 100,000 entries.

Petherick tended his collection from 1909 to 1917, distressed by the casual recognition that Australians made of his overseas achievements and the small encouragement they gave him to develop his collection further, compensated only by a belated appointment as C.M.G. in 1916. Predeceased by his wife on May 10, 1915, Petherick died in Melbourne on September 17, 1917. He is commemorated today in the Petherick Reading Room of the National Library of Australia.

**REFERENCE**

The papers and correspondence of E. A. Petherick are held in the National Library of Australia, Canberra.

C. A. BURMESTER

*The Asian Development Bank Library in Manila houses an extensive book and pamphlet collection on finance and economics.*

Theodore F. Welch

# Philippines

A republic of the western Pacific Ocean, about 500 miles (800 km.) from southeastern Asia, comprises an archipelago of about 7,100 islands. Pop. (1977) 45,028,000; area 300,780 sq.km. Official languages are Pilipino and English.

**National Library.** The National Library of the Philippines, in the capital city of Manila, traces its origin to the American Circulating Library, a subscription library established in Manila in 1900 to serve the information and recreational needs of American soldiers, which was donated to the Philippine government in 1901. It has led a checkered life, with several changes in name, functions, and administrative organization. The name National Library was used from 1964, and thereafter it performed the functions of a national library, a public library, a copyright office, a registrar for priests and ministers desiring authorization to solemnize marriages, and a historical museum. It likewise served as legal depository of all books and other materials published and printed in the Philippines from January 1976, when a Presidential Decree on Legal and Cultural Deposit was promulgated. The various functions are discharged through nine major divisions: Acquisitions Division, Bibliography Division (responsible for the compilation of a current Philippine National Bibliography), Catalog Division, Extension Division (exercises supervision over all provincial, city, municipal, district, and barrio libraries, and deposit stations in the Philippines), Filipiniana and Asia Division (houses over 20 special collections), Public Documents Division (serves as depository of local and foreign government documents), Publication Division, Reference Division, and Administrative Division (under which the Copyright Office and Legal Deposit Section are).

In 1964 the National Library had accessioned only 280,999 books, but as of the end of 1977 the collection had reached a total of 1,044,092 volumes. Its serials collection consisted of 7,474 titles, while its microform collection numbered 2,434 pieces/reels.

The *Philippine National Bibliography* (1974– ) is issued by the National Library bimonthly, with annual cumulations. It follows a classified arrangement, with an author-title-series index and a subject index. Preceding this, the University of the Philippines Library issued the *Philippine Bibliography,* 1963/64–1970/72 (5 vol.), an author listing of Filipiniana materials by type: nongovernment publications, government publications, and theses and dissertations. A milestone in Philippine national bibliographic activities was the publication in 1974 of *Philippine Retrospective National Bibliography: 1523–1699,* compiled by Gabriel A. Bernardo with the assistance of Natividad P. Verzosa and edited by John N. Schumacher. This is a chronological list of 760 foreign and Philippine imprints for the period.

**Academic Libraries.** While each of the 689 institutions of tertiary education in the Philippines (645 private and 44 state-supported) have library facilities as required by Bureau of Higher Education regulations, very few have adequate book resources, sufficient library personnel, and adequate financial support. Most of the libraries are small.

An in-depth study of the resources of private higher education conducted by the Fund for Assistance to Private Education in 1976 showed that 331 of the 645 private colleges and universities had a combined total book collection of 4,771,081 volumes, 224,083 serial titles, and 44,393 pieces of nonprint materials. The biggest book holdings were reported by the University of Santo Tomas (oldest university, found in Manila) with 232,159 volumes, followed by Saint Louis University (Baguio City) with 167,127 volumes. Other universities with relatively large library collections are the University of San Carlos (Cebu City), 162,604 volumes; University of the East (Manila), 146,841 volumes; Far Eastern University (Manila), 126,994 volumes; Ateneo de Manila University (Quezon City), 123,600 volumes; and Silliman University (Dumaguete City), 101,549 volumes.

The University of the Philippines Library System is the biggest of the state-supported academic libraries, with a total book collection of 823,384 volumes, 19,249 serial titles, and 30,951 pieces of nonprint materials as of December 31, 1977. On the other hand, libraries in 13 colleges and 7 universities that are state-supported reported a total book collection of 324,658 volumes and 1,725 serial titles in 1973.

**Table 2. Archives in the Philippines (1976)**

| | |
|---|---|
| Number | 17 |
| Holdings | 2,590,825 cubic meters[a] |
| Annual expenditures[a] | N.A. |
| Professional staff | 25 |
| All staff (total) | 68 |

[a]Only for 13 of the archives.

Sources: The institutions themselves.

**Public Libraries.** Public library services in the country are inadequate, and they do not reach all the people. As of September 1978 there were only 457 public libraries in the Philippines: 34 provincial, 31 city, 282 municipal, 58 barrio, 31 district, and 21 deposit station libraries, very many fewer than the number required to provide library services to both urban and rural populations. Depending almost entirely on the financial support of the local governments although their establishment, organization, and supervision are the responsibility of the Extension Division of the National Library, the libraries vary greatly in the size of their collections and staff as well as the services they offer. The majority of them, however, have inadequate resources. The combined total resources of the 457 libraries are 1,104,757 volumes of books, 36,979 government publications, 605 newspapers, and 70 periodicals.

Bookmobiles were introduced in Quezon Province, Nueva Ecija, and Cebu, with the financial support of the National Library.

**School Libraries.** Public school libraries, along with public libraries, remain neglected although it has been a requirement for a long time that all schools, public and private, must have libraries. Most are one-room libraries with inadequate resources, for there has been no regular financial support from the government. They have to depend on gifts, donations, and voluntary contributions from individuals and institutions to build their collections. On the other hand, libraries in private schools such as Ateneo de Manila, De la Salle, and Xavier School, which have a regular source of income (library fees), have good and up-to-date collections including audiovisual materials and provide effective services to their clientele.

**Special Libraries.** The number and types of special libraries grew in the 1970's, reflective of the economic growth and development of the country and the national priorities. The largest number of special libraries in the Philippines are government agency libraries, with 95 out of 229 libraries noted in a 1975 listing of this type. Some of the oldest special libraries, the Supreme Court and Weather Bureau libraries, for example, and likewise some of the youngest special libraries, for example, the Bureau of National and Foreign Information and the National Computer Center libraries, fall into this category. The second largest group of libraries consists of libraries of the private sector—of business corporations and industrial firms, law and accounting firms, etc. Business-finance is the subject coverage of the largest number of libraries, while science and technology are the subjects covered by the second largest number of libraries.

More than 70 percent of the special libraries have fewer than 5,000 books in their collections. Only three libraries have more than 30,000 volumes each: the Law Library of the University of the Philippines, the Supreme Court Library, and the International Rice Research Institute Library and Documentation Center, which maintains the largest collection on rice and publishes the *International Bibliography of Rice Research.* The Asian Development Bank Library in Manila has rich book and pamphlet collections on finance and economics, while the Scientific Library and Documentation Division, National Science Development Board, is the premier scientific library in the country. The latter offers a manual SDI service to 500 selected users in the country. Other special libraries such as the Philippine Council for Agriculture and Resources Research Library and the Human Resources Division Library of San Miguel Corporation offer current awareness services to their clientele.

**Associations.** The Philippine Library Association is the national library organization and serves as the voice of the profession. Established in 1923, it represents 24 library organizations of different subject and geographic orientations. The awakening of national consciousness on the need to establish public libraries all over the Philippines and the recognition of the library profession may be attributed largely to the efforts of the Association. It pub-



**Table 1. Libraries in the Philippines (1976)**

| Type | Number | Volumes in collections | Annual expenditures (peso) | Population served | Professional staff | All staff (total) |
|---|---|---|---|---|---|---|
| National | 1 | 126,701 | P4,081,971 | 2,703,018 | 114 | 249 |
| Academic | 689 | 5,878,855[a] | N.A. | 911,579[b] | 664[a] | 1,378[a] |
| Public | 439 | 830,481 | P 827,229 | 3,384,910 | 20 | 792 |
| School | | N.A.[c] | N.A.[c] | | | |
| Special | 229[d] | 986,621[d] | N.A. | N.A. | 457[d] | 1,121[d] |

[a]Data for only 352 libraries.
[b]Number of students only.
[c]No statistics, more or less complete, are available from the Ministry of Education and Culture.
[d]Data for 1975.

Sources: The National Library of the Philippines; the Fund for Assistance to Private Education-Private Higher Education Sectoral Area Study on Library Resources; the University of the Philippines Library; the *Directory of Libraries in the Philippines;* the "Directory of Special Library Resources and Research Facilities," *ASLP Bulletin* (1974).

lishes the quarterly *Bulletin of the Philippine Library Association* and the *PLA Newsletter.*

**REFERENCE**

Concordia Sánchez, *The Libraries of the Philippines* (1973).

URSULA G. PICACHE

## Platina, Bartolomeo
(1421–1481)

Italian librarian and Humanist, Bartolomeo Platina was born into the Sacchi family in 1421 at Piadena (thus "Platina") near Mantua and died at Rome on September 21, 1481. In his earlier years he was a tutor for the children of Marquis Ludovico Gonźaga at Mantua. From 1457 to 1461 he studied Greek at Florence, and the following year he became Secretary to Cardinal Francesco Gonzaga in Rome. Two years later Platina was one of the Humanist scholars employed by the papacy to draft social letters and documents in an elegant calligraphic hand, on a staff that generally consisted of 70 "abbreviators." When Pope Paul (1464–71), dissatisfied with their work, abolished the office, the 70 picketed the papal residence for 20 days in formal protest. As organizer and leader, Platina further offended the Pope by insisting upon arbitration and drew a three-month prison sentence when he threatened to appeal before kings and princes for a public hearing of the abbreviators' problems.

Shortly after his release, Platina and other dismissed scholars formed a study group to read Latin writers, as opposed to the Greek. The Pope, however, favored the study of early Christian writers, or at least such classics as did not breathe an air of immorality and paganism, and claimed that the writings of Juvenal, Ovid, Plautus, and Terence could only corrupt children. For his contrary opinions Platina and other scholars were arrested, and he was sentenced to a year in prison.

The Vatican library at Rome was in many ways the most important of Renaissance libraries. Fifteenth-century popes were not only spiritual leaders of the world but secular rulers of territorial states. Other princes in Italy encouraged and developed manuscript and book collections; some popes also felt it a civic duty to become library patrons.

In 1474 Platina published the first part of his *Lives of the Popes,* a readable book that achieved wide circulation, and the following year Pope Sixtus IV appointed him Vatican Librarian. Pope Nicholas V (d. 1453) had initiated the idea of a library, but it was Platina's administrative genius that made the plan feasible, causing the Pope to create an annual library budget to support book purchases, regular salaries for the librarian, two assistants, and three copyists, and the operation of a book bindery.

It was the Pope's aspiration to create in Rome the foremost library anywhere. Platina was authorized to plan a library building to hold writings collected by earlier popes and to accommodate future acquisitions. He was given a free hand in construction and in the selection of artists and craftsmen. The library, occupying the ground floor of the papal palace, consisted of four halls for books and readers: one for Latin writings; another for Greek works; a third, the *Secreta,* was set aside for valuable manuscripts; and papal archives and registers were assigned to the fourth, the *Pontificia.* Renowned painters, such as the Ghirlandaio brothers and A. Romano, decorated walls and ceilings with paintings, while the talents of Melozzo da Forli resulted in the famous fresco "Pope Sixtus IV Appoints Platina as Vatican Librarian." Special efforts were made to accommodate patrons, including portable heating devices for their convenience during chilly Italian winters. The originality of posted regulations in Latin requesting silence and order prompted one patron in 1513 to make a copy: "When in the Library let no one speak vociferously with another nor be troublesome; and when he is going from place to place, let him not climb the steps and scrape them with his feet. Let him close the books and replace them in their proper places. Everyone may read whatever he wishes wherever he wishes. Whosoever acts otherwise will be ejected in dishonor and will henceforth be denied entrance to this place."

Three copyists *(scriptores)* were hired to reproduce Latin, Greek, and Hebrew manuscripts, and Platina also had regular funds to dispatch book agents to European countries in what a contemporary writer, Vespasiano, viewed as a new epoch in the manuscript book trade. Platina's success in developing the holdings may be measured by noting the library's growth. When he assumed his duties in 1475, his inventory listed 2,527 volumes. The materials were divided between Latin and Greek volumes, with none in the Italian vernacular. Though there was increasing emphasis on theology and philosophy, one-fourth of the holdings were ancient classics. Six years later in a report prepared eight days before Platina's death, the number had increased to 3,499, an annual increase of 162 volumes. The library's only rival was the 3,000-volume collection of Matthew Corvinus of Hungary.

**REFERENCE**

J. W. Clark, "On the Vatican Library of Sixtus IV," *Cambridge Antiquarian Society Proceedings and Communications* (1899).

REDMOND A. BURKE

*Mary Wright Plummer*

ALA

## Plummer, Mary Wright
(1856–1916)

Mary Wright Plummer, library educator and leader, attempted throughout her professional life to communicate her enthusiasm for broadly based liberal education and cultural experience and for practical professional training. She was born on March 8, 1856, at Richmond, Indiana, to Jonathan W. and Hannah A. (Ballard) Plummer, who valued their Quaker heritage and passed it on to their children. Attending the Friends Academy in Richmond until she was 17, she moved about 1873 with her family to Chicago, where her father was employed as a wholesale druggist. Except for attending Wellesley College, 1881–82, she spent her early adulthood with her family—teaching, writing poetry, and generally educating herself, including mastery of several modern languages.

In January 1887 she enrolled in the first class of Melvil Dewey's new library school at Columbia College, where she first made her mark. At the September 1887 conference of the American Library Association she reported on the school to curious members in a talk that was later published in *Library Journal* as "The Columbia College School of Library Economy from a Student's Standpoint." Upon completing the program at Columbia she worked as cataloguer at the Saint Louis Public Library for two years.

In the fall of 1890 she went to Pratt Institute Free Library in Brooklyn as both a librarian and an instructor for the training class. Following a year's tour of European libraries she became head of both operations in 1895—a demanding joint position she filled until 1904, when at her request she concentrated on directing the developing library school. In 1911 she became the first Principal of the new library school of the New York Public Library, where she served until her death in 1916.

Active in state and local library organizations, she was enthusiastic about the early planning that led to the establishment of the Association of American Library Schools in 1915. She had previously chaired the ALA's Committee on Library Training (1903–10). Elected the Association's second woman President for 1915–16, she did not live much beyond the end of her term; she became ill, and her presidential address of June 26, 1916, had to be read to the Asbury Park, New Jersey, Conference in her absence. She died September 21, 1916, in Dixon, Illinois.

At both Pratt and the New York Public Library she attempted to help the schools respond to the contemporary and unique needs of students and institutions, rather than to the uniform patterns of the emerging university schools. This resulted in flexible admission requirements and a greater emphasis on practice work. All the while, she hoped that the esteem in which scholarly librarianship was held in Europe could be approached in her homeland. Concerned about the status of women in librarianship, she was nevertheless patient in temperament and preferred to work for change slowly by encouraging individual achievements in the conventional manner.

During her Pratt years a book of poetry and several children's titles appeared. Her *Hints to Small Libraries,* originally published in 1894, appeared in its fourth edition in 1911. She contributed to *Library Journal, Pratt Institute Monthly,* and the *ALA Bulletin,* as well as the "Training for Librarianship" chapter to the ALA *Manual of Library Economy* (1913). Her 1909 talk before the New York State Library Association appeared in the *Sewanee Review* (1910) as "The Seven Joys of Reading" and has been reprinted several times. Her 1916 presidential address to the ALA, "The Public Library and the Pursuit of Truth," appeared in *Library Journal* and in the conference proceedings.

DONALD G. DAVIS, JR.

# Poland

Poland, a socialist republic in eastern Europe, borders the Baltic Sea on the north, East Germany on the west, Czechoslovakia on the south, and the Soviet Union on the east. Pop. (1978 est.) 35,000,000; area 312,677 sq.km. The official language is Polish. The earliest mention of libraries in Poland is of cathedral and monastic libraries at the beginning of the 11th century. The oldest cathedral library, in existence since A.D. 1000, is in Gniezno. The next most important event was the establishment of the library at the University of Cracow when it was founded in 1364. The art of printing came to Cracow in 1473–74; the first printed book in Polish vernacular was published in 1513.

Beginning in the 16th century, many of the Polish kings and nobles founded their own libraries. Small fragments of these private collections have survived wars and confiscations and can be found in the rare collections of today's Polish libraries. The first city libraries were founded in 1535 (Poznan) and 1596 (Gdansk).

**National Library.** Early in the 18th century the Zaluski brothers founded a library that they donated to the nation in 1747, making Poland the first country to possess a true national library. In 1780 a legal deposit law was enacted, and by 1790 the library had become one of the largest in Europe, with approximately 400,000 volumes. The history of this national library reflects the history of libraries in Poland as affected by wars, confiscation, and wanton destruction. After the partition of Poland by its big neighbors, the library was confiscated in 1794 and carried away to Saint Petersburg by order of Empress Catherine II. After World War I, when Poland regained independence, a new National Library was established in 1928. That library sustained great losses (80 percent of the collection) during World War II through deliberate destruction and looting by Nazi occupants—including 2,200 incunabula and 50,000 volumes of pre-1800 Polish books.

National Library of Poland

*The National Library of Poland, Warsaw, comprises a number of buildings. The historic Palace of the Republic houses special collections of the National Library, which traces its origins to 1747.*

The Biblioteka Narodowa is in Warsaw. It is scattered among a number of buildings, but by the end of the 1970's a new building had been planned for construction. The collections totaled 3,000,000 volumes with strengths in the social sciences and humanities. The Library collects all Polish publications in any form, as well as foreign Polonica. As the central library of the state, the National Library also performs the following functions: compiling statistics on publishing and library activities; coordinating activities of all Polish libraries; standardizing library procedures and technology; compiling the national bibliographies, as well as other bibliographic tools; conducting research on reading habits and the spread of knowledge about books; advising on the appropriate reading materials; and printing and distributing library catalogue cards.

**Academic Libraries.** There are some 90 academic libraries in Poland (including main libraries and branches) with about 33,000,000 volumes. The Jagiellonian Library at the University of Cracow (founded in 1634) is preeminent among them, with a bookstock of 2,000,000 volumes, exceptionally strong manuscript collections, and the largest collection of incunabula in Poland. All Polish works published before 1800 are collected. The University Library in Warsaw (founded in 1817), with over 1,800,000 volumes, is the next most important of the academic libraries.

**Public Libraries.** In 1976 there were approximately 9,100 public libraries (including branches) with collections of over 77,000,000 volumes. During 1976 some 7,200,000 readers (of a total population of 33,000,000) made use of public libraries; 142,000,000 volumes were circulated. All public libraries in Poland are part of a national network—in every administrative unit and rural district there is a library belonging to this network. Among the large public libraries are those in Warsaw, Szczecin, Torun, Lodz, Cracow, Poznan, and Bydgoszcz.

**Trade-Union Libraries.** Some 6,000 trade-union libraries hold collections of over 17,000,000 volumes,

**Libraries in Poland (1976)**

| Type | Number | Volumes in collections | Annual expenditures (zloty) | Population served | Professional staff | All staff (total) |
|---|---|---|---|---|---|---|
| National | 1 | 3,000,000 | N.A. | 33,000,000 | N.A. | N.A. |
| Academic | 90 | 33,000,000 | N.A. | N.A. | N.A. | N.A. |
| Public | 9,100 | 77,000,000 | N.A. | N.A. | N.A. | N.A. |
| School | 25,000 | 100,000,000 | N.A. | N.A. | N.A. | N.A. |
| Special | 8,000 | N.A. | N.A. | N.A. | N.A. | N.A. |
| Trade-Union | 6,000 | 17,000,000 | N.A. | N.A. | N.A. | N.A. |
| Total | 48,191 | | | | | |

mostly fiction. This network of trade-union libraries supplements the network of public libraries.

**School Libraries.** In Poland school libraries are found in all primary, secondary, and vocational schools—about 25,000 libraries in total. Their joint bookstocks amount to over 100,000,000 volumes.

**Special Libraries.** There are about 8,000 scientific or vocational libraries and centers of scientific, technical, and economic information. They include the Main Medical Library of Warsaw, the Central Agricultural Library, the Main Communication Library, the Library of the Main School of Planning and Statistics in Warsaw, the Central Statistical Library, the Central Military Library, and the Seym (Parliament) Library.

There is a National Center for Scientific, Technical, and Economic Information. In 1974, on the recommendation of the Minister of Science, Higher Schools, and Technology, a national system of scientific, technical, and organizational information (SINTO) was established.

**Association.** The Polish Library Association, founded in 1917, had over 13,000 members in the late 1970's. It publishes works on the theory and practice of librarianship and on bibliography and two journals, *The Library Review* (from 1927) and *The Librarian* (from 1929). It has been a member of IFLA since its beginning in 1929.

**REFERENCES**

A. Freibish, "Polish Libraries: Their Structure, Organization and Aims," *International Library Review* (1977).

Richard Lewanski, *Guide to Polish Libraries and Archives* (1974).

R. C. Usherwood, "Rising from Ruin: Impressions of Polish Libraries," *Wilson Library Bulletin* (1976).

GEORGE S. BOBINSKI



## Pollard, Alfred William

(1859–1944)

Alfred William Pollard, librarian and bibliographer of early printed books, produced with G. R. Redgrave the *Short-Title Catalogue* for the period 1475–1640. He was born in London on August 14, 1859, and was educated at an excellent London school. Taught by John Wesley Hales, he studied English literature, notably Chaucer and Shakespeare, whose texts he later reexamined and edited. His admission to the University of Oxford was a natural progression; he entered Saint John's College in 1877 with an open scholarship and earned a B.A. Honours degree in Classical Studies and Philosophy.

Pollard proved to be a brilliant addition to the staff of the Printed Books Department of the British Museum Library when he went to work there in 1883. He married a graduate of Cambridge University in 1887, who, with her own intellectual interests, constantly inspired and stimulated his work. They had two sons and a daughter; both sons were killed in World War I, a double tragedy for which Pollard's solace was intensive scholarship and bibliographical research. He became Keeper of Printed Books in the British Museum in 1919 and in the same year was appointed honorary Professor of Bibliography at the University of London. He retired from the Museum in 1924 but remained mentally active and productive until 1935, when he suffered some brain damage after an accident.

He was associated with a bibliographical journal, *The Library,* for nearly 46 years and was officially recognized as co-editor in 1899. In the London Bibliographical Society, founded in 1892, Pollard was appointed Secretary in 1893, and under his guidance it became a prestigious organization. Eventually, *The Library* became the official publication of the London Bibliographical Society.

The high quality of Pollard's work was recognized by various institutions. In 1907 he became a Fellow of King's College, London, and in 1921 received the honorary degree of Doctor of Letters from the University of Durham. He was made a Fellow of the British Academy in 1922, and that year he was invested as a Companion of the Order of the Bath by King George V. He was also known and admired by scholars and librarians in the United States and collaborated, by mail, with the scholar Henrietta Bartlett in the compilation of a *Census of Shakespeare's Plays in Quarto* (1916). During his only visit to the U.S. he catalogued the rich library of an eccentric bibliophile, General Rush C. Hawkins, in Providence, Rhode Island. In 1921 he was elected an Honorary Foreign Corresponding Member of the Bibliographical Society of America.

All his awards cannot be listed but even those named here prove that he had a great reputation as a bibliographer. His work, however, must be assessed in historical perspective and his aims analyzed in the light of his performance. Most of his early research into 15th-century printing was done in collaboration with Robert Proctor, who joined the British Museum Library's staff in 1893. Both were keenly interested in "fifteeners," as they were sometimes known, or "incunabula"—books produced during printing's infancy in the second half of the 15th-century. Proctor and Pollard cooperated in an ideal partnership. Proctor possessed the meticulous assiduity and patient precision necessary for the measurement and identification of typefaces, and Pollard concentrated on early book illustration.

In his obituary of Proctor, Pollard condones his partner's obsession with "fifteeners" but also, characteristically, sees the other side of the picture. Of Proctor's work at Oxford with J. G. Milne in the library of Corpus Christi he said, "I gather that the responsible librarian was a little alarmed at the enthusiasm with which the fragments of printers' or binders' waste were extracted from the old bindings, and despite the extraordinarily interesting finds which have been made in book-covers, there is much to be said on the librarian's side." Proctor had, according to Pollard, an enormous ability to labor and concentrate on bibliographical detail, but he was not an innovator. He "had one of the brains which require some outside influence to kindle them into activity."

Pollard regarded himself as a journalistic bibliographer while recognizing the importance of the work undertaken by men of the caliber of Proctor. When the latter died suddenly in 1903, Pollard reluctantly but dutifully took on the burden of compiling a full-scale catalogue of the early printed books in the British Museum Library. Curiously, but not unnaturally, the section concerning the incunabula of the United Kingdom has not yet been completed. Pollard's ambivalent attitude toward bibliographical tasks of this nature preserved a sense of balance in the undertaking. In the words of his colleague at the Museum, Victor Scholderer, Pollard's "precision with which he kept the wood in focus could prove uncommonly disconcerting to a disciple bemused with the multitude of trees."

Although Pollard was bored by the tedious processes involved in the recognition of typefaces, he saw their importance in the training of beginners in the cataloguing of early printed books. His sense of humor was such that he could not take minutiae too seriously, and combined with this was an awareness of humanity. It is significant that his presidential address to the Edinburgh Bibliographical Society in 1923 was entitled *The Human Factor in Bibliography*.

It was in a lighthearted vein at a meeting of the London Bibliographical Society in January 1918 that he made the proposal for the publication of the work that became his chief contribution to bibliography: *A Short-Title Catalogue of Books Printed in England, Scotland, and Ireland and of English Books Printed Abroad, 1475–1640,* produced in collaboration with G. R. Redgrave. The vast compilation of over 26,000 items took about nine years to prepare. Pollard received the assistance of numerous bibliographers, but in the last resort he was the editor and did much of the work himself. He believed that in the extensive bibliographical field, speed and production were more important than detail. The "S.T.C.," as it is now known, was not intended as a final product. Pollard makes this clear in his preface:

> One object of this preface is to warn all users of this book that from the mixed character of its sources, it is a dangerous work for any one to handle lazily, that is, without verification. The main workers on it on the average are septuagenarians.

Pollard's view of bibliography's function was succinctly expressed as the enumeration of books and the provision of a basis for textual criticism. Because he had an open mind, he did not expect his judgments and conclusions to be regarded as final and irrevocable, but he did expect other scholars to be stimulated by his work to undertake further investigations. All bibliographers are indebted to him for his scientific approach to an occupation formerly regarded as a bibliophilic hobby.

**REFERENCES**

G. Murphy, *A Select Bibliography of the Writings of A. W. Pollard* (1938), includes notes and an autobiographical essay, "My First Fifty Years."

J. Dover Wilson, *Alfred William Pollard, 1859–1944* (1948).

MARGARET WRIGHT

# Poole, William Frederick

(1821–1894)

ALA

*William Frederick Poole*

William Frederick Poole was Librarian of the Boston Athenaeum, of the Chicago Public Library, and of the Newberry Library. He was one of the outstanding librarians of the 19th century. He was born in Salem, Massachusetts, on December 24, 1821, the son of working-class parents. Young Poole was compelled to abandon his studies at 12 and seek employment in a variety of occupations. Through his mother's encouragement, at the age of 17 he was able to enroll in the Leicester Academy while at the same time undertaking to teach in the local schools. In 1842 he entered Yale University but after one year was obliged again to suspend his education for financial reasons. He turned to teaching a second time and three years later resumed his college career at Yale, from which he graduated in 1849 with election to Phi Beta Kappa.

To supplement his income, during his junior year at Yale he became the Assistant Librarian of the Society of Brothers in Unity, a student literary and debating organization. The society provided its members with a collection of books and periodicals to help them find material for their debates and other forensic exercises. Although the library maintained a catalogue of the book collection, there was no similar key to the contents of periodicals. In his strong desire to assist the students, Poole fell upon the idea of compiling an index to the periodical collection. He therefore promptly undertook the task of preparing an index of some 200 volumes of magazines in manuscript form. Since there was only one copy of the index, Poole soon realized that it would need to be published. Through the efforts of Henry Stevens, who was a former Librarian of the Society, he was able to convince G. P. Putnam to publish it. As a result of this work he received considerable recognition both at home and abroad. The first edition of the index was quickly sold out, and Poole began to compile a second edition, which was issued in 1853.



In the interim, although he indicated some leanings toward the legal profession, Poole became determined to pursue librarianship as a life career. In 1851 he received a temporary appointment as Assistant Librarian of the Boston Athenaeum and shortly thereafter became the Librarian of the Mercantile Library Association of Boston, one of the leading social libraries in the country. Poole threw himself into his new responsibilities with vigor. He managed the moving of the library to new quarters, enlarged the book collection, and published a printed catalogue of its holdings. In issuing the catalogue, he introduced an innovation in that the author, title, and subject entries were listed in a single alphabetical sequence, thus resulting in a precedent that became a standard practice for many libraries to follow, popularly referred to as the dictionary catalogue. During his tenure at the Mercantile Library he attended the first library conference, which was held in New York in 1853. Poole was treated as one of the important delegates at the conference. An advance copy of the second edition of his periodical index was on display at the meeting, and a resolution approving it was adopted by the members present.

In 1856 Poole was offered the position of Librarian of the Boston Athenaeum. The Athenaeum was one of the prestigious libraries of the country, and this appointment offered Poole considerable visibility. He remained there for 13 years, and during this period he was responsible for a number of important improvements in the physical quarters of the Library as well as in its services. He expanded the book collection and devised a classification scheme that was pragmatic in nature. Poole did not advocate strict subject classification, nor did he believe that it was possible. The professional staff was also enlarged and trained under his direction. Several of his assistants, among whom were Caroline M. Hewins, William I. Fletcher, and Charles Evans, were later to become nationally prominent librarians. In his leisure moments Poole was engaged in working on his periodical index and in writing, particularly in the field of early New England history. He published a new edition of Edward Johnson's *Wonder-Working Providence of Sion's Saviour in New England* together with a lengthy scholarly introduction that afforded him recognition as a historian. From 1858 to 1870, he served as a member of the Visiting Committee for the Harvard Library.

Serving the reading and research needs of the intellectual elite of Boston, who were members of the Athenaeum, was doubtless an enriching experience for Poole. Nevertheless in 1869 Poole felt the need for greater professional opportunities, and therefore he tendered his resignation to the proprietors of the Athenaeum. For the next few years he served as a consultant and adviser to a number of libraries throughout the country. In some instances his services were limited to the selection of books; in other cases it involved a complete reorganization of the library, as in the case of the Naval Academy library in Annapolis and the Cincinnati Public Library. His work in Cincinnati led to a full-time appointment as Librarian in 1871. In a short period of time he transformed a feeble institution into a strong and vibrant organization second only to the Boston Public Library. Under Poole, the Cincinnati Public Library opened its reading room on Sundays, increased the circulation of books significantly, and organized a special room for fine arts and decoration to serve commercial designers. This may well be the first subject department to have been established in a public library.

His tenure in Cincinnati, however, was brief, for in January 1874 he became Librarian of the newly established Chicago Public Library. Even before he accepted the position in Chicago, he had advised library leaders in Peoria on the drafting of legislation relating to the legal structure of public libraries for Illinois. Poole was familiar with Ohio and Indiana library legislation, which placed public libraries under the jurisdiction of public school boards of education. He found this governing authority unsatisfactory, and he proposed the concept of a library board appointed by the mayor of a municipality that would be free from excessive political interference. The Illinois Public Library Act of 1872, under which the Chicago Public Library was established, bore the fruits of Poole's advice.

Poole's first task upon assuming his duties was to organize a book collection and to provide suitable quarters for the Library. There was a gift of some 8,000 volumes received from the people of Great Britain following the Chicago fire of 1871, but they were largely reference and scholarly works. What was needed was a large collection of books for circulating purposes to meet the reading needs of the average user. Poole with the assistance of his staff promptly undertook the acquisition, cataloguing, and classification of the initial collection. Since Poole was essentially a pragmatist rather than a purist or a perfectionist on issues relating to cataloguing and classification, the work proceeded with dispatch. Poole designed a classification scheme that was based on utility rather than theory. It was divided into 20 major subjects or classes. Each class was assigned a letter of the alphabet. His book notation system consisted of a single letter followed by a serial number. Books in each class were numbered serially beginning with one and running continuously as books were added. Provision was made for subclasses by reserving in advance blocks of numbers for each subclass. With his characteristic flare for producing results, Poole managed to have an ample collection of circulating books ready for use within four months after he took office.

Since a printed catalogue was not possible, Poole decided on a device that he called a "finding list." This printed publication contained a sampling of the collection, with the titles arranged by subject and with the call number included. For a time there was a small charge made for a finding list. In later years the lists were published by a commercial firm that carried some advertising, and the lists were distributed free. Poole was a firm believer that the public library was an important educational institution, and he strove to make its influence felt in the community. In 1884 he expanded library service to the outlying areas of the city through a system called "station delivery." Neighborhood stores whose proprietors agreed to accept orders for library books were designated as stations. Orders were picked up by library messengers each day and the books delivered as promptly as the service would permit. The storekeepers were paid a small fee for the service they performed. Under Poole's strong leadership, the Chicago Public Library became the largest circulating library in the United States.

At this period in his professional career, Poole was undoubtedly one of the outstanding librarians of the day, if not the most eminent, second only to Justin Winsor. In 1876 he served on the organizing committee to form the American Library Association at a meeting that was held in Philadelphia. At that historic conference he was elected Vice-President of the newly established association, and served in that capacity for eight years, to be followed by two terms as President. A cooperative proposal, suggested by Poole, for the preparation of his index to periodicals was adopted at the 1876 meeting. Under his plan, librarians from both the United States and England would participate in the indexing project, to be coordinated by Poole and William I. Fletcher. This project came to a successful conclusion with the publication of the third edition of *Poole's Index to Periodical Literature* in 1882, receiving wide applause. During America's centennial year Poole was also invited to contribute an article to the U.S. Bureau of Education Report on *Public Libraries in the United States of America*. His paper was entitled "The Organization and Management of Public Libraries" and can be described as a distillation of the principles and practices of library administration at that time. In 1877 he attended the International Conference of Librarians held in London and served as Vice-President for the meeting.

In 1887 Poole resigned from the Chicago Public Library to become the first Librarian of the Newberry Library, which came into being under a munificent bequest of Walter L. Newberry, an early business giant of Chicago. The Newberry was to be a reference library, and Poole at what would be retirement age for many accepted a new challenge. Poole's contribution to this institution lay in the development of its rich collection and in his architectural plan for the building. Although this was his first opportunity to plan a completely new building, he had become a specialist in library architecture. Poole was an innovator in the field since he believed that a library building should be functional rather than monumental. Instead of the traditional large hall with a high vaulted ceiling, Poole advocated a number of large rooms, each 50 feet in width, which could accommodate a number of subject departments to be administered by subject specialists. With the use of steel beams, which were coming into general use as a result of the new Chicago school of architecture, such a building was possible. Despite the opposition of the architect, Henry Ives Cobb, the Board adopted Poole's plan. To assist him in the operation of the Library, Poole recruited an impressive array of assistants who laid the professional groundwork for the future development of the famous Library.

Poole was a dynamic person and found time to pursue the writing of history in addition to his full-time responsibilities as a librarian. He delved into two major areas involving colonial New England and the early West.

His writings were based on deep research into original sources and exhibited the highest degree of scholarship. For his historical studies he was elected President of the American Historical Association in 1888. Poole was also very active in the literary life of Chicago. He was a founding member of the Chicago Literary Club, and his historical bent furnished him with material for a number of papers that he delivered at meetings of this organization.

Poole died on March 1, 1894, leaving a legacy of professional accomplishments and attainments that would be difficult to match.

**REFERENCES**

*Annual Reports of the Board of Directors of the Chicago Public Library* (1874–86).
William Landrum Williamson, *William Frederick Poole and the Modern Library Movement* (1963).

ALEX LADENSON

Jorge Alves

*Formerly the Royal Public Library of the Court created in 1796, the National Library in Lisbon moved to a new building in 1979.*

# Portugal

Portugal, a republic on the western Iberian Peninsula, lies on the Atlantic Ocean, and is bounded by Spain on the north and east. Pop. (1978 est.) 9,832,800; area 91,632 sq. km. The official language is Portuguese.

**National Library.** Created in 1796 by Queen Mary I, the National Library of Lisbon was designated as the Royal Public Library of the Court. The first collection was that of the Real Mesa Censória, now extinct. Until 1969 the Library was in the ancient Convent of Saint Francisco in the city. It was transferred in 1969 to a new building built expressly for the Library.

The Library holds approximately 2,000,000 volumes, together with printed works, codified manuscripts, incunabula, collections of miscellaneous manuscripts, stamps, maps, geographic charts, and periodicals. It also has a valuable collection of medallions, coins, and other ancient items. Of special significance is its music section.

**Academic Libraries.** The most important university library is in Coimbra; it is the General Library of the University and was created in the 16th century. Its original installation, situated in a magnificent edifice on the patio of the University, is characteristic of the baroque style, typical of all the surrounding region. The Library moved to a new building expressly built for it in the university zone of the city. This Library's growth and evolution give it the characteristics more properly of a national library rather than those of a university library. Its collections consist of approximately 1,000,000 volumes, including publications, incunabula, and manuscripts, some very rare and of great value.

**School Libraries.** Secondary schools have libraries, some of them signally important for the antiquity and richness of their collections; an example is the one of the secondary school of Passos Manuel, in Lisbon, which inherited the library of the Convent of Jesus.

**Public Libraries.** Public libraries of special interest are in Porto, Evora, and Lisbon. The one in Porto, the most important, was instituted in 1833, and its first bibliographic collections were the books of convents abandoned in the face of approaching troops during the political wars of the period. It possesses actually approximately 800,000 volumes and has a valuable collection of incunabula together with a notable collection of manuscripts. It was made a Municipal Library in 1896.

**Special Libraries.** Of significance are the Scientific Academic Library of Lisbon, the Portuguese Academy of History, and the libraries of the National Academy of Belas Artes and those of the Geographic Society. Other special libraries notable for the richness of their collections include those associated with the following institutions: Calouste Gulbenkian Foundation (art history); National Institute of Statistics (statistics); Camara Pestana Institute (biology and toxicology); Center of Philological Studies (linguistics); National Laboratory of Civil Engineering (civil engineering); and Laboratory of Nuclear Physics and Engineering (nuclear energy). Two others are the Ajuda Library in Lisbon and the library of the Mafra Convent.

**Association.** The Portuguese Association of Librarians, Archivists and Documentalists serves the professionals within these specialties. It was instituted in 1973 with the legal recognition of its statutes.

MARIA MANUELA CRUZEIRO

**Libraries in Portugal (1976)**

| Type | Number | Volumes in collections | Annual expenditures | Population served | Professional staff | All staff (total) |
|---|---|---|---|---|---|---|
| National | 3 | 3,137,611 | N.A. | N.A. | N.A. | N.A. |
| Academic | 5 | N.A. | N.A. | N.A. | N.A. | N.A. |
| Public | 117 | 5,893,139 | N.A. | N.A. | N.A. | N.A. |
| School | 756 | 1,768,716 | N.A. | N.A. | N.A. | N.A. |
| Special | 179 | 2,255,949 | N.A. | N.A. | N.A. | N.A. |
| Total | 1,062 | | | | | |

Source: *Estatísticas da Educação* (Instituto Nacional de Estatística, 1977).

# Posner, Ernst

(1892–    )

Ernst Posner, often affectionately referred to as the Dean of American Archivists, has been a major influence on the development of archival education and administration in the United States. Many archivists practicing today were students of Posner's and the approach to archival education he initiated after he emigrated to the U.S. from Germany. But his career as an archivist did not begin in the

U.S.; he achieved success as an archivist in Germany before he arrived with his wife, Katherina, in America in July 1939.

Ernst Posner was born on August 9, 1892, the youngest of three children, into a cultivated, liberal German family. His father was a doctor of philosophy as well as an M.D. who practiced and taught as a urologist at the University of Berlin while he was coeditor of a journal of urology. His Uncle Max, a historian recognized for his contributions to 18th-century intellectual history, was also an archivist. All family members wrote, enjoyed music and literature, and spoke and read several languages. It was in this intellectual and challenging atmosphere that Posner grew to manhood.

He attended the University of Berlin, where he graduated in 1910. After two years of required military service in 1911 and 1912, he left the Army as a reserve noncommissioned officer to reenter the university for graduate study in auxiliary historical sciences and in comparative administration. World War I interrupted his studies, and he returned to the German Army to serve from 1914 to 1918, when he was mustered out as a reserve lieutenant and awarded the Iron Cross, First Class. He resumed his studies again, and in 1920 he received two degrees, one for the teaching licentiate and one for the doctorate. He was now prepared to become either a teacher or an archivist. While he eventually became both, initially he chose to pursue his career as an archivist.

In November 1920 Ernst Posner became a professional archivist at the Prussian Geheime Staatsarchiv. From the beginning he was highly regarded. Soon he became the administrative assistant to the director in charge of building and personnel. He discharged this responsibility so ably that in 1930, as a 37-year-old archivist and scholar, he was among those mentioned for the position of Director.

Posner also found time to write and edit. Between 1922 and 1934 he published four papers and reports and contributed to a comprehensive bibliography of German history. He also wrote annual review articles about new literature on the history of Prussia. From 1922 until 1938 he served on behalf of the Prussian Academy of Sciences as the editor of Volumes 11 through 15 of the *Acta Borussica,* continuing the documentary publication dealing with the internal history of Prussia during the 18th century. It was during this period that Posner became a teacher, serving from 1930 until 1935 as a faculty member of the Institute for Archival Science and Advanced Historical Studies connected with the Geheime Staatsarchiv. January 30, 1933, the date on which Adolf Hitler came to power, was the beginning of the end of Posner's archival career in Germany. As a Jew he was gradually made to resign all of his archival, editing, and teaching positions. During the Krystallnacht pogrom in November 1938 Posner was arrested and spent six weeks in Sachsenhausen concentration camp. His archival career in Germany was over.

With the help of several American historians, among them Eugene Anderson, Waldo Leland, Merle Curti, and Solon J. Buck, Posner and his wife made their way to the United States. They settled in Washington, D.C., where Ernst Posner joined with Solon J. Buck at the American University to teach one of the first courses offered in the U.S. on the history and administration of archives. In 1942, when Buck succeeded R. D. W. Connor as Archivist of the United States, Posner was made solely responsible for teaching the course. Over the next several years he designed and added other courses to develop a major archival education curriculum. By 1957 American University could boast a certificate and degree program in archival administration and records management. The curriculum Posner developed became a model for archival education programs that were to be created in other institutions throughout the United States.

Posner's summers were busy, too. In 1934 the summer Institutes on Archives Administration, which Posner directed for 16 years, were initiated. They were designed as introductory or continuing education courses primarily for prospective archivists or for those who had on-the-job archival experience but no formal schooling in archival administration. In 1950 Posner started a summer Institute on Genealogical Research; 1954 was the start of Institutes in Records Management. With the cooperation of Colonial Williamsburg and the National Park Service, Posner presented summer Institutes on the Interpretation of Historic Sites during 1949 and 1950.

From 1939 until 1945 Posner served as a part-time member of the American University faculty, first as a Lecturer and after 1940 as an Adjunct Professor. In 1945 he became Professor of History and Archives Administration and was made Dean of the Graduate Division. Two years later he became Director of the School of Social Sciences and Public Affairs and in 1955 was appointed Dean of the Graduate School. He took time off in 1957 when he was awarded a Guggenheim Fellowship and Fulbright research grant to work on his history of archival development in the ancient world. After he returned from his leave in Rome, he resumed his chairmanship of the history department, which he retained until he retired from academic life in 1961.

While pursuing his career as academician, Posner also had time to participate in other professional activities. For many he was uniquely qualified by virtue of his German background and experience. In 1943 and 1944 he served, consecutively, two bodies concerned with the protection of cultural treasure in countries torn by World War II. The first was the Dinsmore Committee of the American Council of Learned Societies; the second, an official body, the American Commission for the Protection and Salvage of Artistic and Historic Monuments in Europe (the Roberts Commission). For the first time he wrote a number of reports on archival establishments in Europe and Asia. He also prepared manuals on German and Italian record practices for the U.S. War Department.

A member of the Society of American Archivists from 1939 and an honorary member from 1965, Posner served the organization long and ably. He was a member of its Council, 1947–51; Vice-President, 1953–54; and President, 1955–56. He was Chairman of several of its important committees as well as a member of the editorial board of its scholarly journal, *The American Archivist.* He often represented the Society in international archival meetings. From 1958 he served intermittently as lecturer on American archival administration and practices at the Germany Archives School at Marburg.

Posner is remembered for his writings as well. In the U.S. one of his most famous works, researched and written on behalf of the Society of American Archivists between 1961 and 1964 and supported by a grant to the Society from the Council on Library Resources, was *American State Archives,* published by the University of Chicago Press in 1964. This signal work was an examination and evaluation of archival agencies throughout the United States and Puerto Rico. *Archives and the Public Interest: Selected Essays by Ernst Posner,* edited by Ken Munden, was published by the Public Affairs Press, Washington, D.C., in 1967. Posner's major work *Archives in the Ancient World* (1972), a study of the development of archives from the Tigris-Euphrates civilization to the division of the Roman Empire into eastern and western halves, appeared to acclaim in 1972.

Posner received wide recognition for his accomplishments. In 1958 he became a Fellow of the Society of American Archivists. The American Association for State and Local History honored him in 1963 by presenting him with its first Award of Distinction. The Society of American Archivists gave Posner a Certificate of Appreciation in 1964, and in 1965 *American State Archives* was awarded the Waldo Gifford Leland Prize. For *Archives in the Ancient World* he won his second Waldo Gifford Leland Prize in 1973. Posner settled in Europe, where he continued his researches in archival history.

MARY LYNN McCREE

## Power, Effie Louise
(1873–1969)

Effie Louise Power, pioneer children's librarian, educator, and author, directly influenced the development of services to children in three major cities, Cleveland, Saint Louis, and Pittsburgh. She was born February 12, 1873, near Conneautville, Pennsylvania. When she was 13, her family moved to Cleveland, where she graduated from Central High School. William Howard Brett, a neighbor of the Power family, invited her to take the Cleveland Public Library's entrance examination and thus brought to library service a protégée who caught his inspirational spark. Throughout her career, Power kindled it in others.

Power began her library work as an apprentice in autumn 1895, then left for about three months to be school librarian at her former high school. Returning to the Public Library, she took charge of the "Junior Alcove" under Brett's supervision. His plans for a children's room materialized in 1898, and Power became the first children's librarian in the Cleveland system, a post she filled until 1902. One of her first contributions was to change the handling of nonfiction books for children. Such books had been kept out of the children's alcove on the theory that children read nonfiction only under coercion from adults. Each day Power went through the library gathering up biography, history, and nature books suited to children and arranged them on the counters in the children's alcove. Each day the books disappeared, and so did the assumption that children would check out only fiction.

Service to children profited when in late 1901 the Cleveland Library moved to new but temporary quarters that provided a large and pleasant basement room for the children's department. For the first time, Power and her two assistants had sufficient space to bring the children together for storytelling. The following year, having established the children's room on firm principles and practices, Power decided to add to her practical experience a more formal foundation of knowledge and technique. Brett noted in his annual report for 1902 that she was spending the school year studying work for children in the training program for children's librarians at the Carnegie Library in Pittsburgh. She received her diploma in 1904.

Power returned to Cleveland after a year's study only to direct her talents in new directions. Brett had long advocated that the Cleveland City Normal School introduce a course in children's literature and the use of books. At the last moment, the candidate selected to teach the course refused the invitation, and Power was given a leave of absence to fill the position. She taught at City Normal School from 1903 to 1908. During summer 1906, she earned a teaching certificate at Columbia University. Although accounts differ, some claiming she did not return to the Cleveland Public Library until 1920, certain information indicates that she returned to the Library in 1908 and stayed for a year as the children's librarian.

Power became first assistant in the children's department of the Carnegie Library of Pittsburgh in 1909 and also taught in the library school there. In March 1911 she was appointed Supervisor of Children's Work in the Saint Louis Public Library. Less than a year later, when the Library was moved to a new building, she demonstrated her belief in preparing the young to take civic pride in their library. After the general public had inspected the new building, she held a special opening; 1,000 children were taken in groups on tours of inspection and heard short talks by members of all departments.

Power stated her principles in *How the Children of a Great City Get Their Books,* first published as part of the annual report of the Saint Louis Public Library for 1913–14. Her standards for book selection were high. After being approved by the librarians, a book had to win the approval of the children before it was duplicated to any great extent. Stating the library's responsibility for books placed on open shelves, and recognizing the dependence of parents and librarians in smaller libraries on the lists put out by the Saint Louis Library, Power expressed her conviction that children's librarians must know not only "a good book but the best book for each particular need."

About this time, Power's leadership took on a national character. A member of the American Library Association since 1906, she chaired the Children's Section in 1912–13 and again in 1929–30 and served on Council (1914–19). She joined the National Education Association in 1896, serving as President of the Library Department in 1916–17 and chairing the Committee on Elementary School Libraries (1914–18).

Power returned to Pittsburgh in 1914 as Supervisor of the Carnegie Library's schools division and later as Head of the Children's Department (1917–20). During her years in Pittsburgh, she worked for the introduction of libraries in the city's high schools and for courses in the use of books and libraries in the Teachers' Training School.

In 1920 she again returned to the Cleveland Public Library as director of work with children. She also taught at Western Reserve University, as Instructor until 1925 and as Assistant Professor (1925–29), and continued her practice begun in 1918 of teaching in library schools throughout the country. One of her contributions in these teaching stints was to help develop cooperative programs between the public library and the schools.

The American Library Association asked her to write a textbook on library work with children; this first authoritative text on the subject, *Library Service for Children* (1930), was widely used in the United States. Her revision of the work was published by ALA in 1943 under the title *Work with Children in Public Libraries.* In addition, she wrote numerous professional articles that reveal both a sense of history and a sense of humor and was the coauthor, author, or compiler of several other works. In 1928 she collaborated with a Cleveland teacher, Florence Everson, in writing a collection of stories about pioneer life, *Early Days in Ohio.* In an attempt to bring to storytellers the best of world literature she compiled four collections of stories for children: *Bag o' Tales* (1934), *Blue Caravan Tales* (1935), *Stories to Shorten the Road* (1936), and *From Umar's Pack* (1937). After her retirement, she wrote another book for children, *Osceola Buddy, a Florida Farm Mule* (1941).

Allegheny College awarded Power an honorary Master's degree in 1934. Three years later when she retired from the Cleveland Public Library, Columbia University offered her a position as Instructor in the School of Library Service; she taught there until 1939. Retiring to Pompano Beach, Florida, she succeeded in inspiring the citizens to raise funds for a new library to replace one destroyed by a hurricane 20 years earlier.

Power seems in retrospect to have been the ideal librarian. In addition to her work as an influential practitioner, she, as an educator and author of professional books and articles, indirectly influenced the libraries in which her students and readers worked. She always held to essentials. Children's work would develop in direct proportion to the support given by knowledgeable administrators to well-trained and dedicated children's librarians determined to maintain the highest standards in services and collections. Throughout her long and varied career, she demonstrated a willingness to leave a comfortable position in order to meet the challenge of a new situation. Never could it be said of Effie Louise Power that she stopped growing professionally. She died on October 8, 1969.

MARY E. KINGSBURY

# Prasad, Sri Nandan

(1921– )

S. N. Prasad, archivist and Director of the National Archives of India, was born on September 18, 1921, in Varanasi, Uttar Pradesh. Prasad obtained from Allahabad University M.A. (History, 1944) and D.Phil. (1948) degrees and entered the field of archives in 1949 as Senior Research Officer, Historical Section, in the Indian Ministry of Defence; he was later its Director (1964–69). He administered and utilized confidential military records of the government of India in those capacities.

In 1969 he was selected to head the National Archives of India as its Director. During the decade of his stewardship (1969–79) he was chiefly responsible for setting up an Institute of Archival Training and new record centers at Jaipur and Pondicherry. He also contributed to the framing and implementation of archival policy by the government of India for better records management, acceleration in acquiring documentary materials in India and from abroad, better conservation, greater facilities for users by way of reference aids, publication development, easier access, and improved techniques of reproduction. As Secretary of the Indian Historical Records Commission he provided effective leadership to Indian archivists. The expansion of the National Archives reflected his able guidance.

He joined the International Council on Archives, first as a member of its Executive Committee (1969–76), later as the only Asian member of the Committee on Archival Development (1972–76) and Vice-President (1976–80). He acted as a rapporteur at the Moscow Congress of ICA (1972) and presented a comprehensive report on "Technical Assistance: Viewpoint of Developing Countries." He represented India, the third world, and the International Council on Archives at numerous meetings and provided expertise to Unesco as well. He took the lead in setting up the South and West Asian Regional Branch of the ICA (SWARBICA) in 1976.

Noted as a military historian, Prasad wrote *Expansion of Armed Forces and Defence Organization* (1956), *Reconquest of Burma* (1958), *Paramountcy under Dalhousie* (1964), and *Survey of Work Done on the Military History of India* (1976). Articles in professional journals cover a wide range of subjects.

N. H. KULKARNEE

# Priolkar, Anant Kākbā

(1895–1973)

Bibliophile and Marathi scholar, A. K. Priolkar was born in 1895 at Priol (Goa, India). For the collection and preservation of old manuscripts and incunabula, i.e., Marathi books printed prior to the year 1867 when an Act of Registration of Books was passed, he not only created a consciousness but also developed his own concept of an ideal library for the Marathi language. In a book entitled *Marathi Granthānche Adarsha Sangrahālaya* (1967), he maintained that besides all the available printed books in Marathi, such a library should procure (a) all the works translated into Marathi with their originals; (b) works of Marathi authors translated into other languages; (c) the first editions of Marathi books that have gone out of print; (d) microfilm copies of Marathi books that are not available in Indian libraries; and (e) the manuscripts and correspondence of important Marathi authors.

Educated at Dhārwār and Sāngali, he obtained a B.A. at Bombay University in 1923 in Marathi language and literature. He served as a secondary teacher for a couple of years and then as a clerk for two decades in the Bombay Municipality.

In spite of his clerical position, Priolkar had a craving for literary pursuits. He composed poems under the pseudonym "Arunodaya," edited and reviewed old Marathi works, and wrote learned treatises on linguistic subjects and skits and articles of topical interest.

He made his first debut as a research scholar and pioneering textual critic by bringing out an authentic critical edition of Raghunath Pandit's *Damayanti-Svayamvar* in 1935. In 1948 he became Reader and then in 1950 Director of the Marathi Postgraduate and Research Institute, Bombay. As the head of the Institute he guided Ph.D. students in Marathi and edited its prestigious quarterly, *Marathi Samshodhan Patrika,* for 12 years, bringing to light many a rare work in Marathi and its dialects. He was chiefly responsible for bringing to light Marathi and Konkani books by foreign missionaries settled in Goa in the 16th and 17th centuries. He also prepared a critically reconstructed edition of Muktesvar's *Adiparva* in four volumes (1951–59). His biographical writings on 19th-century figures indicate his interest in the history of Bombay in that century.

His English work, *The Printing Press in India* (with an essay on Konkani printing by J. H. Da Kunha Rivara), is a scholarly and succinct account of the beginnings of printing and publishing in the various Indian languages. Priolkar always strived for authenticity, and his writings show a rare objectivity, diligence, and scrupulous accuracy. He was elected the President of the All Marathi Literary Conference at Kārwār in 1951. His best-known works include critical editions on *Raghunāth Panditavirachita Damayanti Svayamvar* (1935) and *Mukteshvarkrit Mahābhārat Adiparva,* vol. 1 to 4 (1951–59); biographies of *Dādobā Pāndurang* (1947) and *Bhāu Dāji* (1971); and in English a treatise on *The Goa Inquisition* (1961).

**REFERENCE**

*Prof. A. K. Priolkar Smriti-Granth* (Bombay, 1974).

S. G. MALSHE

# Public Libraries

PURPOSES AND OBJECTIVES

Since the mid-1960's the objectives of public libraries and library systems in many parts of the world have been the subject of regular review, and they have been examined and reexamined by users and librarians alike to determine if they respond adequately to the needs of each community. This concern can be found in countries with well-established library systems, as well as in those with very few public libraries. That such an activity should be carried on in various parts of the globe is not surprising. The tide of social change that has swept through a wide variety of countries has been a powerful force, producing movements for more access by citizens to education and learning. So also has been the effect of technological advances in the production and distribution of the printed word. The need for books, information, and all types of published materials has been growing constantly.

The public library has traditionally been in the forefront of the institutions that have responded to such a demand. In the 1980's it is not a question of "Should the public library respond?" that is asked but rather, "How can it best contribute to social change and economic development, and how can it meet the needs of a wider circle of users?" Public libraries today represent a focal point for the aspirations of many citizens, as well as for governments and public agencies.

Each decade has seen considerable changes in the goals and objectives of local, regional, and national public library systems. What has been considered as the objective of a public library system by one generation is normally revised and altered in light of the changing conditions faced by the next generation. The results achieved by public library services must also be considered at the same time as the goals and objectives of that service. If the library accomplishes little, then it can expect little support from the citizens.

This situation is not new. For over 200 years the public library has been undergoing revision and reassessment and has developed new goals and objectives in order to meet the needs of a constantly changing pattern of demands. Such an evolutionary process has often meant the disappearance of a particular form of library service and the appearance of new services and new forms of organization. The library has been the initiator of activities later taken over by other institutions, and it has left these in their care and gone on to develop fresh approaches. The mercantile, special, technical, and business collection, the community reference information service, the continuing education course for adults, and the local history collection often had their beginnings in the public library. Along with the evolution of these and other services, there has been a constant transformation of the library's stock of materials.

Public library collections pass through many phases, from being the private possession of a few persons to being owned by a group or private association and eventually becoming the public possession of an entire nation. Public libraries' materials have alternatively found themselves hoarded and divided, fought over and bartered, suppressed and exhibited. Those in charge of the public library and its collections have had to take into account the policies set through changing social conditions in the libraries' communities. The public library will continue in this manner as long as it attempts to perform a public function. In this it is unlike its progenator, the private library, which has often been able to maintain a fixed policy for decades.

It is not known how many public library systems exist today, and no single list of their goals and objectives can be prepared. The Union of Soviet Socialist Republics has over 350,000 libraries in a network for the use of the public. In the U.S. there are over 8,300 separate community public library systems, with an unknown number of separate branches and parts. Czechoslovakia claims 45,000 separate libraries that serve the public, and Canada reports statistics on 739 public library systems organized to meet the needs of 23,000,000 people. With such wide differences in services, and with very large differences in financial support, there can be no general statement of public library purposes and goals that applies universally.

The Unesco Public Library Manifesto, first issued in 1949 and revised in 1972 by the International Federation of Library Associations and Institutions (IFLA) on the occasion of the International Book Year, is a broad charter of public library goals. It does not cover the full variety of purposes and activities to which the public library can lend itself, but it does lay down certain basic requirements that must be met. Any statement of public library purpose that incorporates these requirements can be said to be unique for those who prepare it; yet it is unlikely that it will apply directly to other societies and to other library contexts without review and alteration.

The statements contained in this article are based on what a number of people in various countries have seen to be the scope and function of today's public library. The article deals mostly with the patterns of public library service common to North America and, in part, to several European nations. It should also be pointed out that this article does not give an extensive historical appraisal of the public library, which can be found in other sources. The article is based mostly on a review of public library events of the decade 1968–78 as seen in Europe and North America. The purposes and objectives of the public library are accordingly described in relation to three basic concerns: (1) the needs of people who use the libraries; (2) the need to ensure that the library is located in a suitable place; (3) the need to provide for effective means of operating it and developing its services.

Bulawayo and District Publicity Association

*Mzilikazi Memorial Library, Bulawayo, Zimbabwe Rhodesia.*

**Public Library Manifesto** (Unesco) **441, 445**

**Needs of Library Users.** The following statements, chosen from the United Kingdom, the United States, and Canadian declarations of purposes, highlight the views of public library leaders in these countries with regard to services to users.

The Public Library Research Group of the London and Home Counties Branch of the Library Association of the United Kingdom set out in 1971, under headings of education, information, culture, and leisure, the following objectives for public library services in that country:

| | |
|---|---|
| EDUCATION: | To foster and provide means for self-development of the individual/group at whatever stage of education, closing the gap between the individual and recorded knowledge. |
| INFORMATION: | To bring to the individual/group accurate information quickly and in depth, particularly on topics of current concern. |
| CULTURE: | To be one of the principal centres of cultural life and promote a keener participation, enjoyment and appreciation of all the arts. |
| LEISURE: | To play a part in encouraging the positive use of leisure and providing material for change and relaxation. |

The following subobjectives were listed for those responsible for organizing public libraries:

> To promote the use of public libraries as education agencies for the individual; to promote the creation of specialized resources; to promote the use of public libraries as information centres; to promote the use of public libraries as referral points to specialized sources of information; to promote and encourage the use of public libraries as centres where individuals can take part in the arts in a positive way; to encourage the public librarian to assume the role of initiator and organizer of cultural events; to encourage the public librarian to liaise with local societies and cultural organizations, fostering the creative use of leisure in the field of the

Josephine Riss Fang

*Shanghai Library, the largest public library in the People's Republic of China (above and p. 443).*

arts; to promote and encourage the use of public libraries as "special library" agency for local associations and cultural organizations; to promote and encourage the use of public libraries as cultural information centres; to promote the provision of general leisure material for the individual; and to promote the provision of leisure and amenity services to special groups in the community.

In 1977 the American Library Association's Public Library Association, having conducted a review over a number of years of the standards set out a decade earlier, issued in its "Mission Statement for Public Libraries" the following statement of public library objectives:

> Society needs an agency to operate as it were, in the eye of the revolutionary storm, to keep the radical new thrust in some continuity with the past. Society needs an agency to preserve and make widely accessible the record of human experience—to stimulate thoughtful people everywhere to discern positive insights and values from the past, and to assimilate them into the new order. The mass media—the press, T.V., radio, etc. —of their nature tend to concentrate exclusively on the current scene.
>
> Because change now moves so rapidly, the majority of individuals and institutions today suffer future-shock—a sense of alienation from the world and from themselves, a sense of powerlessness in coping with, let alone controlling, the direction of life.
>
> Therefore, society needs an agency to identify relationships in the fast-flowing river of change, to maintain the record of new ideas, technologies, values, so that individuals and institutions will be able to perceive and then control the direction of change as it relates to each person's particular life experience.

The Canadian Library Association's Council adopted the following statement on intellectual freedom at its Annual Conference in June 1974:

> Every person in Canada has the fundamental right, as embodied in the nation's Bill of Rights, to have access to all expressions of knowledge, creativity and intellectual activity, and to express his thoughts publicly. This right to intellectual freedom is essential to the health and development of Canadian society.
>
> Libraries have a basic responsibility for the development and maintenance of intellectual freedom.
>
> It is the responsibility of libraries to guarantee and facilitate access to all expressions of knowledge and intellectual activity including those which some elements of society may consider to be unconventional, unpopular or unacceptable. To this end, libraries shall acquire and make available the widest variety of materials.
>
> It is the responsibility of libraries to guarantee the right of free expression by making available all the library's public facilities and services to all individuals and groups who need them.
>
> Libraries should resist all efforts to limit the exercise of these responsibilities while recognizing the right of criticism by individuals and groups.
>
> Both employees and employers in libraries have a duty, in addition to their institutional responsibilities, to uphold these principles.

Many countries in all parts of the world have similar declarations adopted by the library profession, the governing body for library development, or the national associations of librarians. It is one of the main requirements of any active library development group that it update and review on a regular basis both the statement of the purposes of public libraries and the ways in which these purposes are being carried out.

**The Location of the Public Library.** It is not often appreciated that the location of a public library is a key factor in determining how it will be used. For this reason, unless the library adopts as a goal that of being easily available, it will seldom reach its objective of full use by all citizens.

A basic factor in success or failure is the decision on specific location and type of service to be provided. This lesson has been well learned through experience in most of the countries that have understood the value of access to knowledge for all citizens. A related criterion is that location must be considered with respect to the other educational and cultural services of a community or nation. This includes both location in a physical setting and the relation of the library service to the planning and financing of a balanced range of social, educational, and cultural opportunities for citizens. Where there is coordination of all libraries in a country, the greatest use will result.

Examples of unified systems of public libraries can be found in most socialist countries and range from Cuba to the Ukraine. In Czechoslovakia the number and levels of libraries that made up the unified library system in 1975 were the following:

**Table 1**

| | Number | Holdings (volumes) (million) | Circulation (million) | Readers (thousand) |
|---|---|---|---|---|
| Public Libraries | 13,056 | 14.7 | 72.6 | 2,224 |
| Research Libraries | 17 | 20.7 | 5.8 | 210 |
| University Libraries | 83 | 11.5 | 4.4 | 216 |
| Scientific Institute Libraries | 125 | 3.6 | 0.8 | 52 |
| School, Agricultural, Health, Administrative, and Other Libraries | 8,904 | 12.3 | 10.5 | 816 |
| Trade Union Libraries | 27,807 | 60.2 | 26.9 | 2,482 |
| Total | 44,992 | 150.0 | 121.0 | 6,000 |

Such a broad array of libraries within the country meant that they were used annually by 52 percent of the citizens as a whole and 70 percent of the city population.

A recent study in Canada of public library use indicated that in those provinces where there was adequate provision of library buildings and library outlets there was high use, while those areas that were deficient in library outlets had low use. It was also shown that use decreased with the distance that persons had to travel to reach the public library. In Canada in 1978 the national average percentages for public library users as proportions of the adult population were 25 percent active users and 18 percent low users. The provinces with the highest percentage of active users were British Columbia and Ontario. The province of Quebec showed the lowest use, with 14 percent active users and 12 percent low users.

Those countries that are able to ensure that the locations for libraries, whether in schools or in community centers, will be readily available to adults and children reap the greatest benefit from their investment in providing books and other library materials.

**Provisions for Operation and Development.** The objective of a trained and qualified staff is basic to achieving success in the public library. The range and quality of resources that must be provided, the need to have up-to-date materials, and the need to select materials appropriate for users' needs have made qualified staff a prime necessity. This is why most countries provide at least 60 percent of the public library budget to secure a qualified staff and why there are increasing numbers of both professional full-time and part-time staff employed in most countries.

The situation with respect to qualified staff varies greatly among libraries throughout the world. While there are some variations between European and North American public library staff provision, there is a far greater disparity between the number of staff in Asian, African, and Latin American public libraries compared with European and North American libraries. The following figures from the mid-1970's indicate how far many countries have to go in order to secure an adequate number of trained people to meet their public library needs.

The proper staffing for public libraries is a crucial matter for all countries, and part of the basic goals and objectives of a library must include targets for achieving the effective use of human resources in organizing and operating public library services.

Emphasis in considering goals has been placed on meeting user needs, providing adequate facilities, and employing qualified staff. Additional objectives also prevail, set by different countries in the light of their cultural and national priorities. On a worldwide basis these objectives have been summed up in the General Information Programme (PGI) of Unesco, established in 1974 and imple-

**Table 2**

| Country | Year | Number of Employees (Public and National Libraries Combined) | | Full-Time Public and National Library Staff per 100,000 Population |
|---|---|---|---|---|
| | | Full-Time | Part-Time | |
| *Africa* | | | | |
| Ghana[1] | 1971 | 288 | 33 | 3.3 |
| Kenya[1] | 1971 | 45 | — | .3 |
| Nigeria | 1971 | 503 | — | .7 |
| Uganda[1] | 1974 | 80 | — | .7 |
| *Latin America and the Caribbean* | | | | |
| Jamaica | 1976 | 944 | 31 | .4 |
| Cuba | 1971 | 506 | — | .05 |
| Mexico | 1975 | 1,017 | — | .02 |
| *Asia* | | | | |
| Iraq | 1974 | 271 | — | 2.5 |
| Malaysia | 1974 | 211 | 17 | 2 |
| Philippines | 1974 | 1,257 | — | 3 |
| Sri Lanka[1] | 1974 | 547 | 33 | 4 |
| Thailand | 1974 | 369 | 91 | 1 |
| *North America and Europe* | | | | |
| U.S. | 1974 | 33,153 | — | 16 |
| Canada[1] | 1973 | 5,501 | 1,070 | 25 |
| Ukrainian S.S.R. | 1974 | 34,602 | — | 81 |
| Poland | 1974 | 12,392 | 32 | 37 |
| Netherlands | 1974 | 2,716 | 3,518 | 20 |
| Denmark | 1974 | 4,448 | 108 | 89 |
| Yugoslavia | 1974 | 4,086 | 362 | 19 |

[1]Public library only.

Source: Unesco, *Statistical Yearbook* (1976).

Library Association

*Story hour in the Children's Room of the Dudley Public Library, England.*

mented by a Unesco Intergovernmental Council through Unesco's worldwide program. Through the PGI there is the possibility for examining the role of the public library on a worldwide basis and for supplementing individual national efforts by cooperative action with other countries.

Within such a broad framework the task of providing access to education and cultural resources can be carried out at either the local, regional, national, or international level. Such cooperative measures are essential in order to provide for an equitable distribution of the printed and published materials of the world to all those who need them.

H. C. CAMPBELL

SERVICES TO USERS

The specific services that any particular public library offers may constitute a relatively short list, but the range of possibilities is extremely broad. This is a natural corollary of two basic characteristics of the public library: it has a broad charge, subject to multiple interpretations, and it serves, potentially at least, everyone.

In general, all statements of purpose of a public library say something to the effect that a public library supplies materials and services to a community in order to support that community's educational, informational, cultural, and recreational needs. The public library, by definition, is open to everyone who lives within a particular geographic area. For a specific locality it is possible to be fairly definite about the demographic, occupational, or socioeconomic characteristics of public library users and potential users but, in general, the possibilities are limitless.

To all residents of an area, and to all on an equal basis, the public library offers library services—a phrase that once meant a circulating collection of books but that today embraces many different things ranging from story hours for children to data base searches for business. This section surveys the services offered by contemporary public libraries in the United States. Where possible and appropriate, comments will be made about practices in other countries.

**Types and Range of Services.** Statistics have been available for many years describing the number of public libraries in the United States, their holdings, budget, and personnel. Counts of items circulated have also been recorded, but the range of different items available and the characteristics of persons borrowing from public libraries are not known on a national scale. In addition, no national data exist that describe the number of other services (i.e., besides circulation) available from public libraries and the use of these services. Statistics on public library services in other countries are similarly scarce. The Unesco *Statistical Yearbook* records holdings, budget, and personnel for public libraries in each nation but says nothing about services.

In 1978 the U.S. National Center for Education Statistics (NCES) convened a panel of experts to consider whether it would be feasible to gather and analyze meaningful data on public library users and public library services in the U.S. The panel concluded that a number of different studies should be conducted; its report, *Approaches to the Study of Public Library Services and Users* (1979), presents a rationale and a description of the recommended studies. One is an inventory of library services to be taken by asking a national sample of librarians to respond to an exhaustive list of possibilities. The panel considered lists of services used in several earlier studies and prepared a draft instrument that might be used.

**Table 3. Informational, Educational, Recreational, and Cultural Services Offered by the Public Library**

*Educational**
- Book Reviews/Book Talks
- Concerts (Live or Recorded)
- Craft Demonstrations
- Cultural Exhibits
- Field Trips
- Film Showings
- Formal Courses
- Lectures
- Literacy Tutorials
- Reading Improvement Classes
- Story Hours
- Training of Volunteers
- Workshops on Program Planning

*Informational*
- Advice on Use of Materials
- Answers to Complex Questions
- Answers to Simple Questions
- Bibliographies on Specific Subjects
- Community Calendar
- Current Awareness Services (SDI)
- Data Base Searches
- Information on Program Resources
- Referrals to Community Sources for Information
- Translations

*Recreational**
- Concerts (Live or Recorded)
- Craft Demonstrations
- Cultural Exhibits
- Field Trips
- Film Showings
- Story Hours

*Cultural**
- Book Reviews/Book Talks
- Concerts (Live or Recorded)
- Cultural Exhibits
- Film Showings
- Lectures

*A number of services may be considered either educational or recreational or cultural depending on the perspective of the participant or the content of the event.

Because the panel believed that making a collection of materials available for use is the most basic library service, the draft instrument begins with a section listing over 40 types of material and asking the responding librarian to indicate if a particular type is:

(1) available through the local library system
(2) available through a cooperative arrangement or federated system
(3) not available in my library system but available to anyone in the community through some other agency
(4) not available in my community

The second choice here recognizes that cooperative arrangements of various kinds supplement the collection and services of a local library. The third choice recognizes that the public library is one of a number of agencies providing print and audiovisual materials and related services to a community. Both of these factors are taken into account when planning a public library collection and service program.

From one perspective, everything a library does is a service, but it is also possible to think of services as those activities that library staff perform in direct response to client requests or in anticipation of client interest. Services in this second sense are given in Table 3, which is an adaptation of a list in the NCES panel's draft instrument. In the draft survey the respondent is asked to indicate for each service one of the four choices given for materials in the previous paragraph.

In most cases these services are available to all persons in the library service area. Frequently, however, public library staff will tailor some of these services to the needs of persons sharing specified characteristics in common, thereby developing a special program for such groups as the blind and/or physically disabled persons, business people, children, deaf persons, ethnic group(s), government officials, homebound persons, illiterate persons, institutionalized persons, senior citizens, and young adults.

One of the controversial issues currently facing the public library community in the United States is the question of whether a public library may, should, or must charge fees for expensive services such as data base searches. On the one side are those who assert that it is unethical for the public library to provide special services to those who can pay; on the other are those who insist that unless the public library charges for technological or labor-intensive services, it will not be able to offer them at all, and other agencies will develop to fill the need.

Although the 1972 Unesco Public Library Manifesto states that a public library "should be maintained wholly from public funds, and no direct charge should be made to anyone for its services," fees are frequently charged in European libraries. While such a practice has not been common in the United States, it has been suggested that public libraries in the United States will have to abandon their "information should be free in the public interest" ethic in view of the rapidly changing technological and economic forces affecting information distribution today.

**Public Library Programs.** Much less controversial, but still a matter of debate for public libraries in the United States, is the extent to which public libraries should sponsor such special events as lectures, cultural exhibits, concerts, and field trips. Story hours and other events for children are usually accepted, but events for adults often raise questions. Those opposed claim that these events are the legitimate domain of other agencies in the community and should not distract staff time and energy from the services "proper" to a library. Those in favor put forth one of two arguments: (1) that these events are good public relations for the library and bring into the library people who might otherwise not come in; or (2) that these events are extensions of material on library shelves and provide needed enrichment to the life of a community. This second argument is more in keeping with the 1975 joint report of the Library Advisory Councils of England and Wales on *Public Libraries and Cultural Activities*. It is also congruent with the Unesco Public Library Manifesto, which states that

> The public library is a natural cultural centre for the community, bringing together as it does people of similar interests. Space and equipment are therefore necessary for exhibitions, discussions, lectures, musical performances and films, both for adults and children.

In the United States the National Endowment for the Humanities adopted this view of the public library and supported numerous public library programs involving the humanities. But contradictory evidence comes from such documents as a long-range plan for the Baltimore County Public Library (1977), which provided that if the budget were to be cut, programming for adults would be dropped since response to it was meager.

The educational role of the public library is a more traditional one, though the present movement toward "nontraditional" education in the United States has encouraged libraries to develop innovative ways to respond to their public's interest in "lifelong learning" or "continuing education." At the other end of the educational spectrum are library programs to assist people who lack literacy skills. Public library interest in such programs has increased substantially during recent years.

**Public Library Facilities and Services.** In addition to these highly visible services, public library staff are regularly involved in providing a service that is often taken for granted—orientation to the library and its holdings. The orientation may provide one or more of the following to groups or individuals: an explanation of the library's catalogue; an explanation of reference sources; an explanation of machines and equipment; maps, brochures, etc., explaining the library; tours of the library.

Another "hidden" service of the public library is the provision of space and equipment for activities related to library materials and services. A public library may provide: an auditorium/lecture room; a conference/meeting room; a facility for producing audio or visual material; a film-viewing room; photocopying equipment; space for individual reading, listening, or viewing; typewriters; calculators. The importance of appropriate physical facilities was stressed in the Unesco document, which states that

> The public library building should be centrally situated, accessible to the physically handicapped, and open at times convenient to the user. The building and its furnishings should be attractive, informal and welcoming, and direct access by readers to the shelves is essential.

A very different perspective on the library as a place comes from C. Walter Stone, who observed in a 1967 *Library Trends* article that it was important to think of the

Bibliothèque Nationale, Paris

*The circulation desk is a hub of activity in the Municipal Library, Montreuil, France.*

*The Kyoto Prefectural Library, which follows a policy of limited circulation, is noted for strong local history collections.*

Theodore F. Welch

library not as a place but as "a far-flung network composed of units of various sizes and types, each of which may perform similar as well as different functions, but all of which will be linked together electromechanically." Through this linking people everywhere will have access to the information and knowledge they need regardless of the form it takes or its actual location.

Public libraries have not yet reached the technological level Stone sketched. Most, however, offer services far beyond those available in a particular building. Bookmobile services have been commonplace for many years in both rural and urban areas. In some countries mobile units may take the form of horse-drawn wagons or even boats. Public library units in systems routinely offer intrasystem loans to their users, and most public libraries will also go outside the system to request interlibrary loans. Many libraries send material to users by mail, and telephone reference service is available from all but the smallest libraries. A number of public libraries have begun to offer reference service and programming via cable television.

No one public library offers all of the services just discussed, and no one library user takes advantage of them all. Taken as a whole, however, the varied services described here constitute a rich resource for the people. Services offered by public libraries will probably change considerably in the next 10 or 20 years owing to technological, economic, and political forces currently influencing both public services and the information community.

**REFERENCES**

Arthur D. Little, Inc., *Into the Information Age* (ALA, 1978), includes challenging suggestions for the future of public library service.

Lowell Martin, "Demographic Trends and Social Structure," *Library Trends* (1978), a perceptive analysis with suggestions for changes in services of public libraries.

Margaret Monroe, "A Conceptual Framework for the Public Library as a Community Learning Center for Independent Study," *Library Quarterly* (1976), a challenging view of the library's role in a learning society.

W. Boyd Rayward, editor, "The Public Library: Circumstances and Prospects," *Library Quarterly* (1978), the proceedings of a University of Chicago Graduate Library School conference. See especially articles by Thomas Childers, Mary Jo Lynch, Mary K. Chelton, and Mae Benne.

John S. Robotham and Lydia LaFleur, *Library Programs: How to Select, Plan and Produce Them* (1976).

MARY JO LYNCH

COLLECTIONS AND MATERIALS

Collections in public libraries in the U.S. range in size from the New York Public's 9,000,000 or more volumes to Elk Township, Michigan's 900 volumes. They range in form from books, periodicals, reports, and clippings through recordings, films, and microforms to data bases on magnetic tape. They range in content from the most scholarly to those in basic English for the functionally illiterate. They range in focus from materials for preschool children to materials for the aged. They include special materials for the handicapped, such as talking books or Braille titles. They are as diverse as public libraries themselves, but always collections are at the heart of all public library service.

Collections are the concrete expressions of the public library's mission. In the words of the *Guidelines for Public Library Service* endorsed by the ALA's Public Library Association (1979):

> Materials should be selected to support the cultural, informational, educational and rehabilitative functions of the library. Relative emphases within these four objectives should be determined by analysis of individual community need and by the availability of resources in all types of libraries within the community.
>
> Materials should be selected to meet the needs of as wide a variety of target groups as live within the community, including the literate, the illiterate, the educated, the uneducated, children, adults, aged people, majority and minority cultures.

These imperatives only reemphasize the position on collections expressed by the ALA's *Minimum Standards for Public Library Systems* (1966):

> The public library as an institution exists to provide materials which communicate experience and ideas from one person to another. The function is to assemble, organize, preserve, and make easily and freely available to all people the printed and nonprinted material that will assist them to:
>
> Educate themselves continually
> Keep pace with progress in all fields of knowledge
> Become better members of home and community
> Discharge political and social obligations
> Be more capable in their daily occupations
> Develop their creative and spiritual capacities
> Appreciate and enjoy the works of art and literature
> Use leisure time to promote personal and social well-being
> Contribute to the growth of knowledge.

Although the centrality of materials to the library's mission seems philosophically obvious, its importance is not always reflected in budget allocations. In a study made by the American Library Association of 56 public library budgets, 1974–76, it was documented that materials accounted for only 9–11 percent of total expenditures. The skyrocketing costs of library materials, both print and nonprint, and the escalating range of materials available make this statistic even more ominous.

**Selection of Library Materials.** Theories of materials selection vary among public libraries from the "demand" position of the Baltimore (Maryland) County Public Library ("BCPL is committed to collecting, not a broad array of materials that librarians feel users should read or use, but those materials which most users do read or use") to the "should" position of many public libraries who base selection on principles of quality, authenticity, and social value. On this continuum most public libraries attempt to find a middle ground.

All public librarians agree however—in theory, if not in practice—that selection of materials should be made within the context of a written policy that articulates the objectives of the individual library or library system. The ALA Standards describe this policy statement as follows:

> This statement should be approved and supported by the governing body. It sets forth the purposes, levels of quality, and community needs to be reflected in acquiring materials. It describes the scope and emphasis and defines the limits of the collection; it affirms the institution's position on supplying resources on controversial subjects; and records the policies which govern withdrawals.

The materials selection policy is perceived by the library profession to be a guideline for the day-to-day selection and maintenance of the collections, a bulwark against attacks on intellectual freedom by community groups and individuals, and a statement to the library's public about what it can expect. However, as Ann Bender of the Brooklyn Public Library admitted during an ALA Preconference Institute on Collection Development held in June 1977,

> In most public library situations, particularly in branches, the library must be so responsive to the immediate needs of its public, needs which are often fast changing, that collection development statements may become obsolete as soon as they are written.

The ALA Standards enunciate the board principles that should underlie materials selection policy, such as:

> Materials acquired should meet high standards of quality in content, expression, and form.
>
> Within Standards of purpose and quality, collections should be built to meet the needs and interests of people.
>
> Library collections should contain opposing views on controversial topics.

As Bender wryly comments, however:

> The preparation of a collection development policy involves more than the mere writing down of general principles. It involves:
>
> 1. Knowing the community and its needs, actual and projected.
> 2. Careful analysis of the existing collection and determining its strengths and weaknesses.
> 3. Establishing a weeding policy.
> 4. An estimate of possible or likely fluctuations in the materials budget.
> 5. Considering the rates of inflation in books and materials prices.
> 6. Considering which items may be deemed part of a core collection, which must be replaced continually, and how much to set aside for new materials.
> 7. Considering what and how much to purchase in nonprint forms and what the relationship of such materials will be to the existing collection.
> 8. Considering factors of space, rate of deterioration of materials, optimum size of the collection and its elements, loss rates, etc.
> 9. Knowing what other library resources are available in the community either through other agencies in the same public system or in private, academic, and nonacademic libraries in the same community and assessing the degree to which cooperation in collection development is possible.

Diechmanske Public Library, Oslo

*Listening facilities, as well as circulating collections, are among the services that Norwegian public libraries provide.*

**Materials Other than Print.** Most libraries agree that public library collections should include more than print materials, although it must be acknowledged that the vast bulk of the human record is still in print and that extensive nonprint collections are probably the exception rather than the rule especially among smaller public libraries.

The ALA Standards proposed that:

> To provide a reservoir of knowledge and aesthetic enjoyment which supplies inquiring minds, library materials [should] include a variety of forms:

| | |
|---|---|
| Books | Films, slides, filmstrips |
| Periodicals | Music scores |
| Pamphlets | Maps |
| Newspapers | Recordings |
| Pictures | Various forms of microreproduction |

The later Guidelines are even more explicit and extensive in their concept of library resources:

> Library resources should include multiple forms—print, non-print, audio, visual, magnetic tape, etc.
>
> Human information resources in the community, as well as recorded experience should be considered part of the library's material. Community resource files, including information on organizations and agencies, their officers, activities, services, speakers, etc. should be maintained in all public libraries. Hardware to make use of microforms, audio and visual tapes, and slides, films and filmstrips, videocassettes, etc. should be available for community use.

Canadian Library Association

*Winnipeg Public Library*

The Audiovisual Committee of the Public Library Association published in 1975 *Guidelines for Audiovisual Materials and Services for Large Public Libraries* and *Recommendations for Audiovisual Materials and Services for Small and Medium Sized Public Libraries.* These are quantitative guidelines, proposed within the context of the following assumptions, stated in the former document:

1. Librarians are concerned with the products of imagination, intellect, and spirit.
2. All formalized communication formats are of interest to librarians.
3. Audiovisual materials and services should have equal weight, concern, familiarity, and support of library administrations and staff as those of printed materials. Integration of planning and programs, regardless of subject, format, or age level served, is required for the library to continue as a relevant agency.

These guidelines recommend that all public libraries, regardless of size,

> offer a variety of audiovisual resources [whether from their own collections or through a regional system], a minimum of 10–15 percent of the library's resources budget for audiovisual resources, and that once an audiovisual department is established and operative, 10–15 percent of its materials budget be allocated for repair and replacements. Variables affecting basic staff and materials requirements recognized by the guidelines are:
>
> a. population served
> b. area of service in square miles
> c. number of 16mm titles
> d. hours open per week
> e. accessibility
> f. range of media

Although these guidelines would meet with little or no disagreement in principle from public libraries, the degree to which the specific, quantitative recommendations are being met is uncertain. In 1979 the Brooklyn Public Library was allocating 5 percent of its materials budget to audiovisual materials. The comment made by Lowell Martin in 1969 when he surveyed the Chicago Public Library in *Library Response to Urban Change* is probably still relevant today:

> One of the shortcomings of public libraries is a concept of resources limited to the book or at most to the book and the magazine rather than to the full range of communication media.

Increasingly, however, as Kathleen Molz has pointed out, public libraries are confronting the realities of a public who no longer depend upon print as the primary medium for news and information, who no longer have the leisure and education necessary for serious reading, and who indeed may not have mastered even basic reading skills needed for day-to-day coping. In this environment nonprint materials are certain to become increasingly emphasized in public library collections.

**Intellectual Freedom and Public Library Materials.** Problems relating to the preservation of intellectual freedom and guaranteeing the right to read are central to collection development in the public library. At first glance it would seem that the basic policies of materials selection are clear as enunciated in the Library Bill of Rights, first adopted by the ALA Council in 1948 and last amended in 1967:

> The Council of the American Library Association reaffirms its belief in the following basic policies.
>
> 1. As a responsibility of library service, books and other library materials selected should be chosen for values of interest, information and enlightenment of all the people of the community. In no case should library materials be excluded because of the race or nationality or the social, political or religious views of the authors.
> 2. Libraries should provide books and other materials presenting all points of view concerning the problems and issues of our times; no library materials should be proscribed or removed from libraries because of partisan or doctrinal disapproval.
> 3. Censorship should be challenged by libraries in the maintenance of their responsibility to provide information and enlightenment.
> 4. Libraries should cooperate with all persons and groups concerned with resisting abridgment of free expression and free access to ideas.
> 5. The rights of an individual to the use of a library should not be denied or abridged because of his age, race, religion, national orgins or social or political views.

Despite the apparent clarity of the Library Bill of Rights, it has become necessary over the years to define its application in library practice by a series of "interpretations," also adopted by the ALA Council at the recommendation of ALA's Intellectual Freedom Committee. A summary of these interpretations follows.

The statement on *Free Access to Libraries for Minors,* approved in 1972, affirms that *only* the parent may restrict *only his or her* child from access to library materials, and that the librarian is not in loco parentis. The statement opposes library procedures, such as restricted reading rooms for adults only, closed collections for adults only, and interlibrary loans for adults only that limit access of minors to library materials. The statement affirms the *right* of children to *all* library materials rather than to only a part of a library's collection and sources.

The *Statement on Labeling,* first adopted in 1951 and amended in 1970, opposes the techniques of labeling as "a 'censor tool,' a means of predisposing readers against library materials." Librarians, the statement declares, are neither advocates of the ideas found in their library collections nor infallible about what should be considered suspicious.

*Expurgation of Library Materials,* adopted in 1973, defines *expurgation* as "deletion, excission, alteration, or obliteration" of any portion of any document or literary work (or film). Such expurgation is declared a violation of the Library Bill of Rights because it imposes a restriction on the rights of library users to the full ideas the work was intended to express.

*Reevaluating Library Collections,* adopted in 1973, while endorsing the "continuous review of library collections to remove physically deteriorated or obsolete materials," warns against the abuse of this procedure as a kind of "silent censorship" of those materials considered too controversial or disapproved of by segments of the community.

The reevaluation warning followed by two years a *Resolution on Challenged Materials,* adopted by ALA in 1971, which declared that

> as a matter of firm principle no challenged library material should be removed from any library under any legal or extra-legal pressure, save after an independent determination by a judicial officer in a court of competent jurisdiction and only after an adversary hearing, in accordance with well-established principles of law.

*Restricted Access to Library Material,* adopted in 1973, opposes such library practices as closed shelves, locked cases, and "adults only" collections. While the statement recognizes that these limitations differ from direct censorship activities such as refusal to purchase or subsequent withdrawal of controversial publications, they do constitute a form of "subtle" censorship and should be avoided.

Recognizing that maintaining principles of the Library Bill of Rights can be complicated, if not hazardous, the ALA, as early as 1962, adopted the statement *How Libraries Can Resist Censorship.* This statement recommends that public libraries as a matter of standard operating procedures:

1. Maintain a definite materials selection policy. It should be in written form and approved by the appropriate regents or other governing authority. It should apply to all library materials equally.
2. Maintain a clearly defined method for handling complaints. Basic requirements should be that the complaint be filed in writing and the complainant be properly identified before his request is considered. Action should be deferred until full consideration by appropriate administrative authority.
3. Maintain lines of communication with civic, religious, educational, and political bodies of the community. Participation in local civic organizations and in community affairs is desirable. Because the library and the school are key centers of the community, the librarian should be known publicly as a community leader.
4. Maintain a vigorous public relations program on behalf of intellectual freedom. Newspapers, radio, and television should be informed of policies governing materials selection and use, and of any special activities pertaining to intellectual freedom.

The public library profession recognizes its responsibilities: (1) to meet the general library and information needs of all users, actual and potential, young and old, educated and undereducated, handicapped or well; (2) to consider materials selection within the context of total available resources in a community, since no one library can provide access to the whole human record; (3) to defend the free flow of ideas against all censorship by means of a responsible, defensible selection policy; and (4) to provide materials in whatever form is appropriate to the ideas expressed and to the users to whom the ideas are disseminated.

San Diego Public Library

*One of the many public library buildings funded by Andrew Carnegie is in San Diego.*

**REFERENCES**

Lester Asheim, "Not Censorship but Selection," *Wilson Library Bulletin* (September 1953), a classic in its lucid consideration of the selector's role.

Ann Bender, "Allocation of Funds in Support of Collection Development in Public Libraries," *Library Resources & Technical Services* (1979).

Mary Duncan Carter, Wallace Bonk, and Rosemary Magrill, *Building Library Collections* (1974), discusses the value of selection policies in all types of libraries.

Leroy Merritt, *Book Selection and Intellectual Freedom* (1970), a basic text on the theory and practice of book selection.

R. Kathleen Molz, "The Changing Capacities of Print and the Varying Utilities of Libraries," in *The Metropolitan Library,* edited by Ralph Conant and R. Kathleen Molz (1972), a thoughtful exploration of the nonprint revolution.

GENEVIEVE M. CASEY

FINANCE AND ADMINISTRATION

The public library in the United States has since its beginnings shown that it is adaptable to the changing social environment because it sprang from democratic idealism and not from autocratic condescension. As a voluntary institution with no mandate in law, it flourishes on the goodwill of the citizen but for the same reason often lacks the scholarly aspirations of academic libraries. The quality of a public library's performance in the U.S. is necessarily related to the wealth of its constituents and to their attitudes toward books. In these circumstances financial support and library excellence vary greatly across the nation. Annual tax support in 1979 ranges from less than $1 per capita in the poorest jurisdictions to well over $20 in others.

**Finance.** The key distinguishing feature of the public library in the United States is its local governance. In the absence of federally imposed standards, state and local standards set the performance levels, but even so, most state library boards lack legal authority to impose penalties and are resigned to an advisory role, leaving the local library to succeed or fail as it will. Of the 50 states only Hawaii has made the public library a function of state government. Elsewhere the library is a creation of county, city, town, or village as permitted by state law. The diversity thus spawned by this decentralization is representative of the American preference for local decision making for human service. Reliance on local autonomy leads to an occasional jewel like the Boston Public Library, but more often local poverty nurtures inadequate libraries and in some sparsely populated areas none at all.

Houston Public Library

*The Houston Public Library's modern downtown building uses granite on exterior and interior walls (above and p. 451). A concrete concourse beneath the library plaza connects the building to the old Central Library.*

Local pride, however, may succeed in overcoming poverty to help local leaders form strong libraries. Some declining cities of the northeastern section of the nation still boast superior institutions and support them well from a shrinking tax base in preference to other public services; Cleveland, Ohio, is a case in point.

The fiscal mainstay of the local public library has long been the property tax, while taxes other than those on real property are tapped in some states. (These exceptions will not be discussed here, since in general about 90 percent of library tax support originates in real estate, the remainder in grants from state or federal sources.) For most cities the property tax began to lose its reliability in the mid-1960's as taxpayers offered resistance to the mounting cost of local government. The changing climate manifested itself dramatically in California, where in 1978 a statewide referendum placed a ceiling on property tax rates. The stricture in the flow of tax revenues, whether it occurred slowly or suddenly, fostered a growing sense of pessimism about the future of the public library. Anecdotes of individual library service reductions due to budgetary stringency were numerous in the mid-1970's, and they occurred in all regions of the nation, prompting some library scholars to gloomy prophecies of library collapse. Fiscal starvation was not the only blow dealt to public libraries in the 1960's and 1970's, since social disintegration in urban areas and the as-yet-unassessed influence of television also depressed library use, shaking the complacency, if not the confidence, of librarians. These seismic shifts in the political, social, and economic environments of the library did not occur without library response. In 1970 a group of trustees of U.S. city libraries formed the Urban Libraries Council both to publicize and to combat the declining fortunes of libraries. Later in the decade a group known as the National Citizens Emergency Committee to Save Our Public Libraries assumed a similar role.

Not all the developments in the world of public libraries were negative; certain contrary trends gave hope that fiscal defeats were isolated phenomena. Over a 15-year span beginning in the mid-1960's, the Chicago Public Library tripled its budget and by the end of the 1970's had won approval of a plan to build a new main library in the downtown area. In other regions of the nation, state legislatures moved to appropriate additional money to compensate for the deficiencies in local budgets. Minnesota and New York both substantially raised the level of state aid in their 1978 legislative sessions. These back eddies in the general downward flow of public library fortunes suggest that by the late 1970's the limits had been reached in effective operation of decentralized library systems and that henceforth if the public library in the United States is to thrive, it will come to depend more upon state and federal intervention than it has historically been willing to do. Any significant change in the budgetary mixture of libraries will inevitably bring with it a redistribution of power over them, it may be assumed. State and federal money will be followed by compulsory adherence to regulations from above, in the view of many observers, and, despite warm ideological arguments in favor of the virtues of local management, those views are not likely to prevail. The same tide that carried the victory for regionalized school systems during the period immediately following World War II was beginning to tug at the foundations of the local public library in the 1970's; how fast and how far movements toward centralized administration of public libraries will go is still conjectural. Thoughtful students of library government see an eventual partnership in the financing of libraries—a partnership that would assign about 20 percent of the support to the federal government, 30 percent to the states, and the remaining half to local government. The suggested proportions may vary from observer to observer, but the consensus for a fiscal partnership is already in place.

**Administration.** One striking feature of public libraries in the United States is their historical dependence on lay boards of governors, commonly designated as trustees, even though such boards frequently have only nominal or advisory authority. Library boards symbolize the democratic character of the library, and they exemplify the original motive of founders: to keep the library at some distance from politics. The public library is analogous to the public school with respect to its governance, for both sprang from the same generous social impulse and both developed complementary missions to educate the masses. Local lay control may be somewhat anachronistic in a management-oriented society where the professional overrides the proprietor, as it were; yet the library board provides stability and continuity by slowing the rate of library adaptation to cooperative enterprises and computerized bibliographic control. Some boards had their origins in the private libraries that were the antecedents of contemporary public libraries, and it is not unusual today to find self-perpetuating boards with memberships largely confined to local elites. More commonly boards are appointed by publicly elected officers; a few are elected by popular vote at the polls. Boards may possess taxing and budgetary authority, but just as often their control over money is nominal.

Important as they are, the governance and financing of libraries have not been all-absorbing matters for library managers in the most recent decades. There have been other preoccupations, some of them felt by all institutions, most particularly those affiliated with education. The overriding development in the library community has been the search for means to collaborate among institutions. The quest for larger and more complex combinations has been spurred both by economic necessity and by a desire to enlarge the influence and effectiveness of the library. If local control had the virtue of guaranteeing autonomy, it also threatened small libraries with impotence in a complex environment requiring machines and speedy communications. The thrust toward collaboration was fueled by the desire to equalize service by tapping the resources of the large, powerful library for the benefit of the citizen who did not have direct access to it. Coincidentally, the advantages of cost cutting through diminution of redundant operations became evident. Among the cooperative efforts most frequently advocated (and practiced) in recent years are shared cataloguing, interlibrary loan, reference referral, cooperative book buying, union lists of serials, reciprocal borrowing privileges across jurisdictional boundaries, and automated circulation-control systems.

The internal organization of public libraries is a matter of some interest, and in larger libraries with multiple buildings and services the organizational strategies call for careful planning. Aside from the housekeeping services of supplies and maintenance, public library activity falls into four major components: book selection, cataloguing, book circulation, and reference work. Variations on these basic themes are universally observable, but the four elements are the generic ingredients for all libraries. In small libraries the activities may be carried on by one librarian, while in larger libraries the activities are subdivided and allocated among many librarians.

*Urban Libraries.* The large urban library or the regional library system in a populous suburban area is more complex than the basic model would suggest. Many ancillary activities may flourish in the large library. Program specialists, publicists, readers' advisers, coordinators of work with young children or adolescents—all are representative of what may be found in a major institution. The urban library is normally characterized by an ample—sometimes monumental—building housing a major book collection located at the center of the commercial area of the city, accompanied by a spread of smaller, domestically oriented branches designed to serve residents in their neighborhoods. These outlying units are ordinarily further augmented by mobile services and outreach efforts within hospitals, for example, or in the homes of immobilized residents. Some big-city libraries have also assumed the more complex task of maintaining service for blind and physically handicapped readers. A typical urban library is likely to invest 50 percent of its annual budget in its downtown location; in the very largest cities the public library may, in the range and complexity of its collections, achieve the stature of a strong university library. The chief characteristic that distinguishes the city library from an equally complex suburban library system is the central building itself. By many standard measures, suburban systems perform extremely well in meeting citizen reading demands. The core city main library, however, remains a unique institution. A few of the finest research libraries in the United States are public: New York, Boston, Philadelphia, Cleveland. In many cities the public library is still the provider of library service with public schools, although in the 20 years after 1955, as schools tended to create and manage their own library systems, the public library withdrew.

The uniqueness of the city main library inadvertently established city-suburban rivalry for tax dollars. The flight of the middle class to the suburbs caused city libraries to serve the same people who, after leaving the taxing area, continued to patronize the library but no longer supported it. The stress caused by this demographic pattern is not unique to library services, but it poses extremely serious problems for library boards and directors trying to maintain high standards of service primarily for nonresidents. The imbalance between the tax support and library patronage has been rectified constructively in some jurisdictions through contracts designed to divert suburban tax revenues into the city. Mergers have also been a useful response. Despite these examples of success, many cities have not been able to resolve the problem. Evidences of interest in a totally different solution are beginning to appear—the designation of central city libraries as state resources, thereby giving the state government a stake in the maintenance of a city's intellectual treasures. In Michigan, for example, the state totally underwrites the cost of operating the main library of Detroit.

Public libraries, like most human institutions, develop personalities that transcend cultural and national barriers. Significant similarities from city to city or nation to nation are useful in identifying the basic imperatives that distinguish public libraries. Because the main, or central, library of a city system differs both in size and service sophistication from a branch library, the organizational structure will tacitly recognize the distinction. Typically a large public library divides its public service administration into two units, one for main library and one for all the other services. The intricacy of the web of working relationships thereafter will be determined by the relative size of the library and the city it serves. This model has become universal and is to be found in all those nations that boast public libraries.

Long before the central library became too heavy a burden for cities to carry, New York by historical accident created a dual library system: a popular service system of branches, and a main research center. By creating, in effect, two separate libraries, the world-famous center on Fifth Avenue, privately funded, and the branch system, publicly funded, actually anticipated a course of action now being imitated. In 1976 Toronto, starting from altogether different premises, divided its main library from its branch system and created a new board representing the entire district to control the main and now independent unit. The branch system continues as before under its separate board. New York City and Toronto may not be typical, but one way or another library leaders are emphasizing the distinction between main and branch libraries. A new pattern may be emerging, and it is possible that Toronto's example will be imitated.

*Services.* Since its inception during the years immediately preceding the Civil War, the public library in the United States has exhibited certain pragmatic qualities: it has shown a willingness to tinker and experiment, to seek for practical improvements in service. The public library movement is tireless in its quest for new service objectives. Service to the blind today is being augmented by use of radio broadcasts. Efforts to ease communications with deaf people through teletype are now being employed. Specialized programs to combat illiteracy are strongly advocated. Whether these techniques will survive is less important than the fact that they indicate a continuing vitality in the library world. On the larger scene, it is to be noted that migrations of populations

National Library of Poland

*Mosaics and billboard-high signs identify the municipal library of Zielona Góra, Poland.*

across the globe have provided new targets of library opportunity. In English-speaking countries that heretofore were insistent on linguistic assimilation by immigrants, the tendency now is to accept polyglot populations. In the United States the second and growing language is Spanish; community book collections are being shaped to reflect the new demographic makeup. In Canada the interaction of French and English is important, but in Toronto, where at least 39 languages were spoken by its citizens, one branch library featured books in 23 of those languages. Melbourne in Australia has learned to acquire books in Turkish, Greek, and Balkan languages for some of its branch libraries, a task made difficult by the enormous distance from the supply source. The Netherlands comes to grips with linguistic diversity brought in by those who migrated from the Dutch East Indies after World War II. The Soviet Union faces staggering language problems with its 91 nationalities. It attempts to deal with them through bilingual publications provided through its libraries—with Russian on one page and the national language on the facing page.

*Management Concerns.* Automation is increasingly prevalent in the public library, and both the complexity and the high costs of computers have begun to accentuate the differences between large and small libraries. Before World War II it was reasonable to perceive a large library as differing only in scale from the smaller institution. Today the larger library performs activities, gives services, or possesses equipment not to be found at all in small independent units. Technology has increased dependence upon larger systems by small libraries, thereby fostering creative responses through the shared programs referred to earlier. Out of necessity the collaborative efforts among libraries have proliferated so that now large libraries find themselves tied into many intricate and specialized service networks.

The potential economies implicit in shared resources are increasingly attractive to library administrations hard pressed for money. Because the operating costs of large libraries tend to rise irrespective of the amount of public service rendered, the acquisition, storage, and maintenance of complex collections are not easily managed. Library administrators substitute sharing for endless growth. Many large American libraries have probably reached their practical physical growth limits and will cease to be self-sufficient. Compression of information into computers or into microforms is one substitute for costly storage space. A library of 1,000,000 volumes, expanding at the annual rate of 5 percent, would have to add 6,000 linear feet of shelving annually and would double its inventory in about 14 years if it took no action to inhibit exponential growth. Because society is less and less willing to pay for large warehouses of little-used materials stored in buildings where the economic value of the property is highest—namely the heart of the business district of the city—library administrators face difficult choices.

Collaboration among libraries may have had its origin in technology, but it is also hurried along by the world of expanding information. Libraries have also looked to common pools of stored books as a way to relieve the discomfort of growth, but more often than not book depositories have been of greater interest to academic libraries. One notable exception is the active participation of the Boston Public Library in the New England Deposit Library. Another technique of public libraries within a geographical cluster has been the assignment of major acquisition responsibilities in subject fields among its various members, at the same time increasing accessibility to those scattered collections by interlibrary loan. A national periodical center is under consideration as one more effort to inhibit collection growth. Electronic transmission of information stored in print is only beginning to be developed, but it gives promise of further relief.

Guidelines have been developed within the American Library Association, as well as in state associations, to measure the performance of individual libraries. These guidelines address such matters as size of buildings and collections, rate of additions to or withdrawals from collections, the ratio of branch libraries to population, the optimum distance between units, the ratio of employees to population, the ratio of professionals to clerks, desirable levels of budget, the kinds and duration of education of librarians—to identify only some of the matters of interest.

The quality of the intellectual and professional capabilities of staff members has been a constant concern of library administrators. The training of staff was seen as an inescapable responsibility for public libraries as early as the 19th century. By the turn of the century major city libraries had established intramural training schools for librarianship before there was a ready supply in the academic market of graduates. Many library schools had their origins in public libraries, and over the years public library administrators have been the champions of high-quality academic preparation for librarianship. In the 1960's and early 1970's, when professionals appeared to be in short supply, library administrators advocated cultivation of paraprofessionals trained by community colleges. As a result of these efforts curricula were established to produce staff with skills at a level midway between clerical and professional.

While the many forces at work in society operate to disturb the serenity of a library administrator, those same forces are equally disturbing to the employees of libraries. Shrinking budgets have provoked inevitable disputes about remedies, and to the degree that remedies have not been agreed upon, employee dissatisfaction has risen. The growth of unions in the professional ranks has been rapid. Laws permitting bargaining between public agencies and employees have sanctioned the movement. The historical justification for unionism—pay and working conditions—has recently been augmented by rising pressure for employees to have a role in managerial decisions. Today's library administrator is likely to be less autocratic and, indeed, to possess less authority, than the administrators of the period before World War II. Increasingly administration has come to demand as much of diplomatic art as of technical skill. Library professionalism is less deeply associated than formerly with the humanistic disciplines. As the need for technical knowledge has increased, the library profession has opened its ranks to include newer specialties: in computers, in data banks, in microforms, in measurement and evaluation. The bookish scholar is no longer the dominant personality in library administration. Managerial training is gradually displacing literary or bibliophilic scholarship as the primary qualification for library directors. The internal environment of the large city library is a rich tapestry of contrasting interests that go to make up the whole. The range of a library's programming and the demand for many specialists within the staff create a cosmopolitan environment of unusual complexity.

As previously noted, suburban libraries in the United States are not charged with the responsibility for maintaining massive research collections in large, monumental buildings. They perform more efficiently and at lower cost in circulating books, their chief activity. Because they also deal with clienteles of higher income and broader education than are normally to be found in cities, the suburban libraries appear as more ably managed than city libraries, intensifying political conflict for limited library tax dollars. While the social need is greater in the city than in the suburbs, the flow of money is away from the cities, thereby defeating the democratic ideal of equalization of opportunity.

It is generally true to say that important local or regional information is to be found in the public library, and most public libraries take their local history seriously. It was almost a spontaneous thing for public libraries to become a haven for documents relating to local history. Even in communities with independent academic libraries or historical societies, the public library is likely to have acquired resources not obtainable elsewhere. In the absence of competing institutions, the public library often is the sole possessor of local historical information. Libraries occasionally are called upon to play a role with respect to public archives, but archival responsibility is assigned in accordance with local initiatives, traditions, or legal structures.

The library board, which is so important a feature of the American public library, is often absent elsewhere in the world. In Europe the library is either a function of the educational system or a department of local government under the city council or its equivalent. Library boards are, however, to be found in Canada. The decentralized Australian system has strong state libraries in all the chief cities of the nation. In New South Wales, for example, the public library of Sydney is independent of the state library, but in Western Australia the state library manages all the public libraries and indeed carries on all the book selection for the state's local libraries.

Soviet libraries, while numerous, are seeking to develop some autonomy under the organized supervision of the central directorate in Moscow. Book selection is governed by rigid selection, and even local budgets are set by the Ministry of Culture. In support of efforts to advance socialist thinking, the state subsidizes the publishing of children's literature, making attractive books readily available in large quantities at low prices.

*The Future.* The last two decades of the 20th century will put heavy pressure on library managers. The destabilizing forces of revolution and energy depletion that are agitating all institutions pose a particularly unsettling challenge to libraries. As reading declines, as illiteracy spreads, as video-telecommunications make inroads on the library's traditional clientele, how will the profession respond? Problems appear now where all was thought to be safe and secure. In the United States children's use of public libraries, once the staple of public library services, has been halved since the mid-1950's; in most cities children's circulation is now only about one-third of the total. Americans are using their libraries more heavily as information sources rather than as reading centers, a phenomenon also reported elsewhere in the world.

Libraries now have the capability of answering reference questions by means of access to remote data banks in preference to using printed sources. While faster, the service is more expensive, and it can drive up the cost of reference service to unacceptable levels. This phenomenon is bringing into question the validity of the "free" public library. Increasingly the "free" library is being challenged by economists and politicians, many of whom advocate placing the cost burden on the beneficiary of the service rather than on the tax rolls. Such political opinions generate strong resistance among traditionalists who hold to egalitarian standards. This battleground will be fought over in the decades ahead, and in the dust of conflict the library director will require diplomatic arts to maintain a stable and safe institution. Whatever the outcome in this conflict, or any of the others, one point is indisputable: the tempo of change is speeding up, and the pressures on the managers are growing. Yet library administrators who delay decisions while awaiting a clearer view of the field will not serve their institutions well. A flexible posture is required, a willingness to move with emerging forces and still retain inviolate the fundamental principles of librarianship. It is not an easy period in public librarianship, but it may yet be the most fertile in ideas.

New York Public Library

*The Research Libraries of the New York Public Library, on Fifth Avenue. New York Public is one of the largest and most notable libraries in the world.*

**REFERENCES**

Roberta Bowler, editor, *Local Public Library Administration* (1964).

Edward N. Howard, *Local Power and the Community Library* (ALA, 1978).

Ann E. Prentice, *Public Library Finance* (ALA, 1977).

Dorothy Sinclair, *Administration of the Small Public Library,* 2nd ed. (ALA, 1979).

Joseph L. Wheeler and Herbert Goldhor, *Practical Administration of Public Libraries* (1962).

ERVIN J. GAINES

MEASUREMENT AND EVALUATION

As public library systems throughout the world become more sophisticated, more time is spent on measuring and evaluating their performance. In the 1960's and early 1970's there was a tendency to centralize work within each country and to rely on ever more detailed quantitative measures. There is some evidence to show that in the 1980's the emphasis will be on decentralization and on qualitative rather than quantitative measures.

**Standards.** The tendency toward qualitative measures is particularly noticeable with the development of new public library standards. Traditionally standards have been compiled centrally by a professional association

Jacksonville Public Library System

*From the Circulation Desk of the Haydon Burns Library, Jacksonville, Florida, readers enter the Browsing Collection and New Books Area.*

or a government department. They were expressed in numerical terms and related to inputs—that is, to the number of staff, number of books, and number and size of service points. Furthermore, they were compiled with the implicit assumption that what was appropriate in one part of the country was generally appropriate elsewhere.

The newer forms of standards tend to reject this assumption and accordingly are framed in rather different ways. Modern standards start from the proposition that public library systems should themselves calculate what is appropriate in their particular circumstances. There is much more emphasis on providing a framework or methodology, which can then be used to calculate the number and proportion of inputs required for a given output, or level of service. The end results of this approach are standards that are probably more difficult to apply in individual circumstances but that take much more account of local variations.

A good example of the traditional form of library standards is the *Standards for Public Libraries* issued by the International Federation of Library Associations and Institutions (IFLA) in 1973. These were formulated to provide "guidance as to the levels of provision needed to maintain efficient library services . . . and should provide a basis for the formulation of national standards." They are expressed in terms of the various quantities of each input thought to be required to meet the needs of given levels of population. The standards were framed in the specific belief that "separate standards were not desirable, since the general objectives in all countries are the same."

In direct contrast to the IFLA Standards are those concerning the *Staffing of Public Libraries,* published by the United Kingdom Department of Education and Science in 1976. These standards were calculated on the basis of detailed work study exercises that examined the various tasks undertaken in a modern public library. The result is a series of formulas that can be applied to produce information on the number of staff needed to provide a given level of service in the light of particular local circumstances.

Another example of the new way of thinking about standards is the recently completed work sponsored by the American Library Association and carried out by King Research, Inc. The thinking behind the project is that to formulate national standards based on outputs rather than inputs it was necessary to work on information generated by a thorough review of goals, objectives, and performance in a number of systems. The process that was devised to facilitate this review suggests that nationally produced standards may be redundant, because standards in this process are set locally as an integral part of the review.

**Statistics.** Library standards and library statistics almost go hand in hand. More and more countries now collect detailed statistical information about the workings of their public library systems. In most cases the information is published for use within individual public libraries. This supply of basic data is essential for the effective planning of a national system and is recognized by many to be an important input to the management process at the local level. It can also provide an invaluable information source for research workers.

In 1970 Unesco published its *Recommendation concerning the International Standardisation of Library Statistics* in an attempt to introduce a degree of standardization and comparability into the provision of library statistics. As a result of the recommendation many countries have adopted the Unesco format as a basis for their compilations. While this has resulted in considerable improvements, much remains to be done. It is still difficult to compare the performance of public library systems in different countries, and the situation is further aggravated by the fact that not all countries collect statistics in any systematic way.

Two countries that have done much to produce full sets of public library statistics are the U.S. and Canada. In both countries central government agencies—the Library Surveys Branch of the National Center for Education Statistics, United States Office of Education (USOE), and Statistics Canada—have attempted to collect and publish statistics from libraries of all types, including public libraries.

The system developed for the U.S. demonstrates an interesting and profitable example of cooperation between the professional association and the government. A National Conference on Library Statistics was sponsored jointly by the USOE and the ALA in 1967. The Conference recommended that a national library data collection system be set up; this did in fact happen, and by the mid-1970's the results had begun to appear from the system. The whole operation is not without flaws, but it does represent a serious attempt to produce compatible statistics on a national basis.

A completely different situation is found in most other countries. For example, a review of library statistics in the United Kingdom claimed in 1976 that the provision was "uneven, uncoordinated, unsystematic and confusing." This was despite a serious attempt in the early 1970's to introduce a unified system based on the Unesco recommendation.

Much of the momentum of the early 1970's for the improvement of library statistics has been dissipated. However, much has been achieved, and the need for accurate and regular statistics should ensure that improvements continue to be made.

**Public Library Research.** Public library research is a rapidly growing activity. Research in one form or another has always been carried out in the larger, better organized authorities. In the postwar years library schools all over the world conducted research into the activities of local public libraries. The 1970's saw a noticeable increase in the involvement of central bodies—governments and professional associations. The implications of this are considerable, since the availability of support funds from these organizations can completely change the character of research.

Public libraries in the U.S. benefited from the general boom in federally funded social research that took place in the latter half of the 1960's. The benefits that accrued from this research are often hard to identify, and if the same resources were available today, they might well be used in a very different fashion.

In the United Kingdom funds for public library research first began to become available in 1974 when the British Library decided to include public libraries within the terms of reference of its Research and Development Department. The program began slowly, but later years show evidence that the demand for research funds, particularly from public librarians, is considerable.

In Canada there are signs that federal and provincial funds are becoming available for library research in general and for public library research in particular. There is a similar situation in Sweden, where the government decided to allocate substantial funds to support library research.

As research programs develop, there is a tendency for them to be dominated by academic researchers or, in some cases, by research consultants. While this trend is understandable, there are strong arguments for involving practitioners in the research process. Above all, there is a general move toward making the research relevant to the "real world" and oriented toward operational improvements. In the U.K. the public library research program has as its basic principle that the main thrust of the program should be toward research into particular problems rather than toward theoretical conceptualization.

It can generally be concluded that in public libraries there is a continuing trend toward systematic management. This implies full use of statistical information, the acceptance of research as an integral part of the management process, and, it would seem, the recognition that in the matter of standards local calculations are of more value than national pronouncements. The emphasis is on using nationally provided resources to arrive at local solutions to local problems.

Hennepin County Library

*Above, exterior of Southdale Hennepin Area Library. Left, display area for circulation, art prints, and special exhibits in the Edina Community Library.*

**REFERENCES**

*Planning for a Nationwide System of Library Statistics* (ALA, 1970).

Frank N. Withers, *Standards for Library Services: An International Survey* (1974), the standard work reviewing library standards throughout the world.

NICK MOORE

PUBLIC LIBRARY LEGISLATION IN THE U.S.

The earliest legislative measure in the United States dealing with public libraries was enacted in 1848 as a speical act of the General Court of Massachusetts, authorizing the establishment of the Boston Public Library. A year later a general act was adopted by the legislature of New Hampshire authorizing cities and towns to establish free tax-supported public libraries. This New Hampshire law was adopted by the other New England states between 1851 and 1869. In 1872 Illinois approved a public library act that for the first time provided for a separate board to govern public libraries; the Illinois law was more comprehensive than the New Hampshire act and served as a model for many of the western states to follow.

**Public Library Acts.** Today every state in the Union has a public library act on its statute books that provides the legal basis for the establishment, governance, administration, and tax support of public libraries. Although these enactments are all similar, no two of them are exactly alike. In some states the public library law is so framed that it covers all types of public libraries whether they are city, village, township, county, district, regional, or school district libraries. In other states there may be a separate law for each of these various governmental units.

One of the major provisions in a public library act is a grant of authority from the legislature to the municipality empowering it to establish a public library. There are three such types of grants. In most of the states the grant is extended to the corporate authority—that is, the city council, village board, or county board of commissioners. In other states the law provides for a referendum of the voters to decide whether a public library is to be established. Finally, in a few states the statute permits the establishment of a public library initiated by a petition addressed to a municipal body and containing the signatures of a requisite number or percentage of the legal residents.

Another vital provision in a public library act is the grant of power to levy taxes for library purposes. This authorization is made to the corporate body and not to the library board, except in the case of certain district libraries that are expressly granted such power. Funding is made available in one of two ways: (1) through a special library tax on property, usually expressed in terms of a millage rate as, for example, one mill or more on each dollar of the assessed valuation of property; or (2) through a lump sum appropriation from the general revenue of the municipality.

A third important provision in a public library act relates to the governmental structure of the library. The law usually provides for a board of directors of a specified number, appointed or elected for a given term of years, and enumerates the powers and duties of the board.

There are a variety of other provisions. Almost all public library acts provide that use of the library shall be forever free to the inhabitants of the municipality. A provision authorizing the corporate authorities to provide suitable penalties for persons committing injury to library property or for failure to return books belonging to the library is also included. An extremely significant provision is the requirement that the proceeds from the library tax shall be kept in a separate fund, designated as the "library fund," and must not be intermingled with other funds of the corporate authority. A very common provision requires the library board to submit an annual report to the corporate authority as well as to the state library agency. Finally, a large number of the laws provide for joint library service between two or more governmental units.

**Boards.** In general, public library boards are appointed by the mayor with the approval of the city council. In a few jurisdictions boards are elective, but the practice is chiefly in towns, villages, and townships. Library boards vary from three to nine members. At least 20 states provide for a board of five members. The term of office of board members varies, but most states provide for three-year terms.

Although for the most part library boards do not

Detroit Public Library

*Detroit Public Library's Rare Book Room supports research collections with historical materials and examples of fine printing.*

have the power to levy taxes, they do have exclusive control of the expenditure of library funds. The board has complete power over the management and care of library property, but with respect to real property there is some diversity of legal practice. Many boards enjoy the power in their own right to purchase land and erect buildings. In some states, however, it is necessary to proceed through the city council or county board to acquire land or buildings. Library boards do not have the power to issue bonds to finance construction. This must be done by the corporate authorities, and in most cases the floating of a bond issue is subject to a referendum of the voters. In most states it is possible to acquire property for library purposes through eminent domain.

The library board also has the power to make rules and regulations covering the operation and management of the library. Under this power, the board is permitted to determine the service hours of the library and fix the schedule of fines for failure to return books, nonresident fees, and similar matters. The board has the power to accept donations of money, personal property, and real estate by gift, will, or through a trust for the benefit of the library. In the area of personnel, the board has generally complete control over the library staff, including appointments, dismissals, salaries, hours of employment, and working conditions.

Since the public library is not a legal entity in itself but merely a division or department of the municipality, a large body of municipal law impinges on the powers of the library board. For example, a municipal civil service act may limit the power of the board over personnel. A central purchasing law, requiring that purchases for city departments be handled by a central purchasing agency, may interfere with the library board's exclusive power over purchasing. A state law mandating across-the-board limitations on tax levies by municipalities may reduce the amount of revenue available for library purposes. Thus to determine the actual legal authority of a library board, it is necessary not only to consult the public library act but also to examine a related body of municipal law.

**State and Federal Legislation.** To promote the extension and development of public libraries, states began to enact legislation providing for the establishment of state library agencies. Massachusetts was not only the first state to inaugurate tax-supported public library service but also the first to create a state library agency for the express purpose of promoting public libraries. In 1890 the General Court of Massachusetts passed a law establishing a State Board of Library Commissioners, whose duties were to render advice, encouragement, and a modicum of financial assistance to communities planning to organize a public library. Within a few years several other eastern states had adopted similar measures. In 1895 the idea was taken up vigorously by Wisconsin and transmitted to many of the western states, becoming popularly known as the free public library commission movement. By 1909, 34 states had provided legislation establishing state library commissions, boards, or similar bodies designed to extend and improve public libraries. Today every state has a state library agency that is responsible by law to plan a state program of public library development, render consultative services, distribute state aid, and assume leadership in making provision for adequate public library services on a statewide basis.

In approximately 30 states, this legal responsibility is vested in a commission, board, or committee, the members of which are appointed by the governor. There is considerable diversity in the functioning of these administrative bodies, but essentially they are endowed with the power and duties to promote public library development. Operationally they act through the appointment of a state librarian or an officer who holds a similar title. In about 15 states, the responsibility to extend public library service is lodged in the state department of education through the creation of a library extension agency. Here, too, there is considerable diversity in administrative practice. In most cases, however, the head of the extension agency is under the direction of the department of education. There are notable exceptions, as in California, where the state librarian is appointed by the Governor and serves at the pleasure of the Governor. But even in this instance the legal power to determine policy rests with the state board of education. In the remaining jurisdictions, the state library agency reports directly to the Governor or is under the office of the Secretary of State or some special department of state government.

State aid is one of the key elements today in providing for the improvement of public library service. The legal rationale for state aid is based on the constitutional principle that education is a primary function of state government, and since public libraries are part of the educational establishment, it follows that the state has a direct responsibility for their financial support. In this connection the Supreme Courts of no less than nine states have declared that a public library is an educational institution. In *State ex rel. Carpenter* v. *St. Louis,* 318 Mo. 870, for example, the Supreme Court of Missouri in 1928 ruled that a public library is an educational institution and that public library service is a state governmental function.

Although the origin of state aid for public libraries can be traced back to a New York act of 1838, it was not until a century later that this idea took firm root. Ohio in 1935 and Michigan in 1937 were successful in enacting state aid laws providing for the distribution of a sizable amount of state funds to public libraries. In the South a number of states adopted similar legislation at about the same time. The most ambitious state aid program arrived several decades later, however, when New York in 1958 adopted an act providing for the establishment of cooperative library systems blanketing the entire state. In support of the system concept, New York has continued to make substantial annual appropriations for this purpose, with the appropriation in 1978 totaling approximately $35,000,000. In the 1960's and 1970's Illinois, Pennsylvania, Massachusetts, New Jersey, Rhode Island, and Maryland have likewise enjoyed large-scale state-supported public library system development programs. Other states, such as Texas, California, Indiana, Michigan, and Wisconsin, have state aid measures for financing public library systems also.

Another form of state assistance is emerging that

provides direct aid to public libraries that meet certain statutory conditions. New York, Illinois, Georgia, and West Virginia are taking the lead in this type of legislation. There are other experimental attempts at state aid such as the Michigan act undertaking to fund the Detroit Public Library completely. Another innovative measure is the California Library Services Act adopted in 1977.

The federal government was a latecomer in the field of public library legislation. More than a century and a half elapsed before Congress took any legislative recognition of public libraries. In 1956 Congress passed the Library Services Act. Designed to promote the extension of library services to rural areas, it was in essence a library demonstration program for rural communities. To participate in the program a state was required to submit a plan for extension of library service that had to be approved by the U.S. Commissioner of Education. In 1964 the Library Services Act was amended, making it applicable to all public libraries, rural as well as urban, and became known as the Library Services and Construction Act (LSCA).

LSCA now consists of four titles: Title I—Services; Title II—Construction; Title III—Interlibrary Cooperation; Title IV—Older Readers Services. In 1977 Title I was amended to provide special assistance to urban public libraries located in cities with a population of 100,000 or more. Since 1974 Congress has appropriated funds only for Titles I and III; for fiscal 1979 Congress appropriated $62,500,000 for Title I and $5,000,000 for Title III.

At the state level a most erupting event affecting public libraries occurred in 1978 with the passage of the California initiative, referred to as Proposition 13, which placed a limitation on property tax levies. This law, adopted by the voters of the state, provides that the maximum amount of any ad valorem tax on real property shall not exceed 1 percent of the full cash value of such property based on the 1975–76 assessed valuation. The impact of this mandate is proving to be extremely severe on public libraries. Other states moved in the same direction, and it became clear that public libraries would be required to seek other sources of revenue.

**REFERENCES**


Carleton B. Joeckel, *The Government of the American Public Library* (1935).

Alex Ladenson, editor, *American Library Laws,* 4th ed. (ALA, 1972).

Alex Ladenson, editor, "State and Federal Legislation for Libraries," *Library Trends* (1970).


ALEX LADENSON

LIBRARY COOPERATION

Cooperation is as old as libraries themselves. A basic principle has been that there should be equity in the public sector and that every individual should have the opportunity to develop to his highest potential. This approach expresses an aspiration of public librarians worldwide. Typically, the purpose of cooperation has been the interlending of monographs and serials, and the largest libraries have borne a high proportion of the administrative costs as well as the costs of being heavy net lenders. Administrative centers, union catalogues, schemes for collective acquisition, storage, and relegation have arisen as interlending became formalized, and such cooperatives have often used the new technology to improve systems with computer output microform (COM) catalogues, international standard book number (ISBN) location lists, telex links, and other means. The best developed model of voluntary interlending between public libraries on a national scale is that established in Great Britain since the 1930's and still surviving in a modified form in cooperation with the British Library Lending Division.

Recent experience in a more cost-conscious age has shown the limitations of the older systems of voluntary cooperation. The small members tend to contribute little of significance; the administrative costs of maintaining union location lists are considerable. There is a tendency to abuse the facilities of the cooperative to compensate for basic weakness, ultimately hindering pressure for real improvement through consolidation of nonviable libraries and more adequate funding for units with a potential to be largely self-sufficient. Critics doubt whether such cooperatives really achieve a meaningful improvement in access to resources. There is a further problem in the metropolitan areas that are served by the greatest concentration of public libraries in that the new suburban systems of multibranch type, serving the prosperous communities, make no contribution to the major reference collections in the declining core cities.

*Paphos Municipal Library, Cyprus.*

Public Information Office, Nicosia, Cyprus

The growing interdependence of library units, revealed by an astonishing spread of networks in North America and by administrative restructuring in Great Britain, demonstrates that the public library sector needs cooperation more than ever. The reasons are

economic recession

growth and sophistication of demands on public libraries

advanced technology arising from the convergence of computers, telecommunications, and office mechanization, vastly improving the potential for data handling and transmission, and creating a need for much larger economic bases

the consequent arrival of on-line cataloguing systems

availability of federal and state funds to develop networks and agencies

population changes, especially a concentration into the metropolitan areas, in which over 70 percent of Americans now live and 85 percent will do so by the year 2000

within the vast conurbations, a tencency for the core city to decline at the expense of prosperous suburbs

administrative restructuring in order to achieve economies of scale for a range of public services, including libraries.

The new generation of cooperatives and networks (which term is generally taken to refer to a cooperative based on computers and telecommunications, and necessarily formal in its procedures) have to be cost-effective, not so much extending equity as offering a more economic trade-off between building up local resources and buying services or obtaining them at the expense of a higher level of government. This approach requires a wider definition of cooperation, perhaps as contractual services. The Rochester Regional Council markets a variety of services to 49 libraries of various types in which contracts are used as a convenient and formalized means for securing more services for any single library in a network of libraries. The new library networks are frequently multitype and perform brokerage for remote commercial or fee-charging public services providing bibliographic processing or information. Another characteristic, in the U.S. and Canada, is the use of cooperatives as a means of applying federal or state/provincial funds so as to reorganize and strengthen a group of autonomous public libraries, inherited from an earlier period, when the aim was for each town or city to provide itself with a general cultural facility, on a scale determined by local means and will to pay.

The complaint about "localism," i.e., jealous preservation of autonomy, so often heard from network planners, derives from a conflict between the traditional assumption that the local library, with its permanent collections, is largely self-sufficient, contrasted with the planners' view that local libraries should serve primarily as public service outlets, with technical services support coming from a central service elsewhere and distributed to libraries as needed. The planners are unlikely to prevail in isolated towns and small cities unless they can "buy themselves in" with funding from other sources. Here is the fundamental structural weakness that faces public libraries in the Anglo-American and Scandinavian countries that pioneered the type. In Canada public libraries outside the metropolitan areas are inadequately funded and organized and are too small. Similar problems affect countries such as the German Federal Republic, which are trying to build up a public library network side by side with outmoded types, and such socialist economies as China, where public libraries have been established as a widespread community service with fairly low standards and now have to be improved by central and provincial government support.

**Forms of Library Cooperation.** M. M. Reynolds's *Reader in Library Cooperation* includes a useful typology of cooperation:

| | |
|---|---|
| Corporate: | 1 board, 1 fund |
| Federated: | x boards, 1 fund |
| Cooperative: | x boards, x funds |

If we take the traditional mode already described as *cooperative networks,* a useful comparison can be made between the choice of *federated networks* in North America, with its vast distances and very fragmented administrative structure, and *corporate networks* in Great Britain since the reorganization of both national and local library services in the mid-1970's. In Canada, Saskatchewan and Metropolitan Toronto illustrate a restructuring approach. New York State and Illinois are notable examples of the federated approach; in Ohio the State Planning Committee, because of the legal, political, and attitudinal barriers to cooperation they encountered, required that cooperation be cost-effective and involve a minimum of administrative structuring and restructuring. The initiative does not always come from the top—witness Ontario's 14 regional library systems agreeing to pool their provincial grants in order to set up a network for cooperation. It is early to generalize about who is going to run the resource-sharing networks and what kind of an organization is needed. But in the U.S., where over 350 consortia are already in existence, the trend seems to be best illustrated by Illinois, where regional networks based on major public libraries are being merged into a multitype state and interstate network, which would limit the growth of the powers of the public library systems, and which will instead provide a highly efficient service delivery mechanism. A general prediction has been made that the future public library will serve primarily for face-to-face public services and as a switching point or broker between users and information regardless of location. Illinois shows the logical result of such thinking in a statement on collection management policy that envisages that every library unit will concentrate its local resources on satisfying expressed demand, without constraints of quality or literary merit—a qualification clearly aimed at the public library sector. Others have argued the dangers of systematic shedding of less-used material, among them a loss of browsing value and of demand derived from immediate availability. In other countries different methods for getting around administrative fragmentation are used, e.g., in West Germany the Ein Kauf Zentral in Reittlingen functions as a purchasing and servicing agency for public libraries and for two research and planning bodies. In developing countries such as Malaysia and Singapore public libraries are being built up on a planned basis with strong direction by the national library.

Great Britain provides the prime example of the corporate approach. The various libraries at the national level have been integrated under the British Library Board with its divisions for reference, lending and bibliographic services, and research and development. At the local level most people in England and Wales are now served by a county library for an average 600,000 population, with library authorities in the metropolitan areas serving populations between 250,000 and 350,000, or rather less in London. The British Library Board has a specific duty to provide support to the whole library and information community and is thus creating networks of service that are modifying existing cooperatives. The Lending Division (BLLD) serves as an example. It dominates the national interlibrary lending of serials through mass photocopying and is in the process of establishing similar preeminence in monograph loans. A recent development is the establishment of a national delivery service, achieving over 80 percent success in document delivery in 24 hours and almost complete success in 48 hours. The individual library is still able to borrow directly from others in the region using an ISBN list of holdings or can go directly to BLLD or indirectly through the regional bureau.

Cooperation between public and school libraries has left much to be desired in the past. In the U.S., where school libraries have been professionally staffed for generations, school and public library relations were still being defined as a problem in 1972 because of an unorganized ebb and flow of students, poor communications with teachers on study assignments, and a lack of role definition. The school-public library seems at first sight to have much promise for giving rural areas improved library services. Promising developments were reported from New Zealand, but Newfoundland abandoned the practice. In Great Britain dual-use libraries are growing in number after a slow start. In Adelaide, Australia, the experimental use of school audiovisual materials by the general community is one positive gain from such cooperation.

Jurisdictional boundaries between public libraries and other social agencies that have library and information needs, especially at the metropolitan and regional level, form a barrier to developing the full potential of the public library. Of 300 Regional Councils of Government (COG) in the U.S., only three had a library component; Denver is quoted as an admirable exception to the rule. In Great Britain the Department of Education and Science saw opportunities in the local government reorganization of 1974 for a corporate library and information service reaching out to schools, social service establishments, hospitals, and prisons, and also a special library service to local government. This is made simpler by the concurrency of powers of the new local authorities. The original British impetus in multitype cooperatives was to provide a serials interlending service, a declining need with the arrival of BLLD. Major British research-type public libraries do not have the advantages of Toronto in that they provide services to their region entirely at the cost of the local taxpayers in the core city.

**Cooperation with Cultural and Technical Services.** The literature of cooperation tends to ignore the role of the public library as a cultural agency. In Bulgaria public libraries are housed in cultural centers; in France a public library is an important function in the *Maisons de la Culture,* while in Britain most metropolitan public libraries are administered as part of a leisure or cultural directorate (although this is opposed by the Library Association).

Participation in automated networks is of two kinds: to support internal operations and to provide user services. The latter are easily assessed, as they provide additional resources at an established cost, but participation in joint cataloguing, processing, and collection management involves in addition a partial loss of control of standards and performance. Since public libraries are minor users in most bibliographic networks, the product is not always optimal for them; hence the complaint of public libraries using the MARC files—that the search for bibliographic authority and completeness results in an unwieldy record and a loss of currency. What the public librarian wants is a brief but authoritative record, available on, or preferably before, publication, for use in an integrated order, catalogue, circulation, and stock control system—a management record rather than a bibliographic record. The OCLC Mini Catalog project and British interest in a Mini-MARC record are responses to such complaints. Another reason for disappointment with centralized systems like OCLC is the poor response time.

Given a choice between centralized shared cataloguing and working with a regional consortium, public librarians prefer the latter because they normally have a place in policymaking. Critics of OCLC and similar systems argue that they are based on an obsolescent configuration of a remote mainframe computer, with heavy line costs, and that the new networks will be based on the chain of local minicomputers linked to one another to give a distributed national data base. One side effect of using automated cataloguing is the long-delayed abandonment by North American libraries of expensive card catalogues in favour of COM output. The real gains in public library applications of automation lie in an integrated approach to all internal operations. Public libraries that have already automated find it much more difficult to join in a network because of incompatibility of systems and probable loss of performance.

It should be advantageous for new users to adopt software already proved in a similar public library, and although there are many cautionary tales about the difficulty of doing this when the original program was not designed to be transportable, most of the British on-line cataloguing systems are based on the work of a handful of pioneers. Small public libraries should always find it better to delegate as much as possible of their internal systems to a remote agency, whose standards will be superior, and which will probably be cheaper owing to subsidy. There are cooperative examples of practically every library operation from preselection of stock to staff placement, which are often substitutes for consolidating small library units.

Turning to cooperation of a service nature, interlending has already been discussed. There is one great question: whether it is more cost-effective to establish a comprehensive national collection as a direct backup to local libraries of all types, as an alternative to the traditional interlending networks. BLLD in direct competition with long-established cooperatives has demonstrated a clear superiority in performance on serials; indeed it has a world market that is growing fast. The U.S. has a proposal to form a national periodicals center. What puts these serials networks in jeopardy is the concept of intellectual property, which may cramp the scope for mass photocopying in the future. Electronic mail is only on the horizon, but Columbus Public Library is using facsimile transmission as a means to supply local school and public libraries with documents that they have identified from on-line bibliographic services. It has been demonstrated theoretically that the optimal national network should be based upon a nodal system comparable to that already mentioned for minicomputers.

Sociotechnological phenomena of the late 20th century, vastly improved communications and metropolitan living, are being encountered by a public library sector still structured on a 19th-century model. The response of government to the general situation is to create larger units of administration and to fund coordinating mechanisms, of which the fast-growing library and information networks are an example. The involvement of librarians in policy development will determine the extent of their future participation in these developing networks.

Planners see a role for the public library as an outlet for network information. But little is said about its cultural and educational roles, while the trend toward contracts and direct charges threatens the goal of serving people disadvantaged in access to knowledge.

Multitype networks are helpful in providing a corporate library and information service to the community, but one might prefer a matrix network that would help to consolidate public libraries into multipurpose units of adequate size. The public library subsystems could thereby have the capability of achieving their cultural and educational goals while subscribing wholeheartedly to information networks in order to claim their share in the "distributed national library."

**REFERENCES**

H. C. Campbell, *Public Libraries in the Urban Metropolitan Setting* (1973).

Michael M. Reynolds, editor, *Reader in Library Cooperation* (1972).

W. L. Saunders, editor, *British Librarianship Today* (1976).

ALEX WILSON

# Public Relations

Public relations as a professional skill is a late-20th-century development, the outgrowth of mass communication, mass marketing, and the coupling of both to stimulate action. There are as many definitions of public relations as there are opinions about its stature and the validity of its role in marketing everything from political candidates to library services. Simply defined, public relations involves a planned and sustained effort to establish mutual understanding between an organization and its public.

The practice of public relations involves research of the attitudes and opinions of the many publics served by an organization, advising management on attitudes and responses, helping set policy that demonstrates responsiveness, communicating information about the organization, and constantly evaluating the effectiveness of all programs.

It is ironic that public relations has an image problem and is so frequently misunderstood. The term is often used interchangeably with publicity, which is just one of its tools. It is seen by some as little more than a nice attitude, smile, and "have a good day" that create friendly

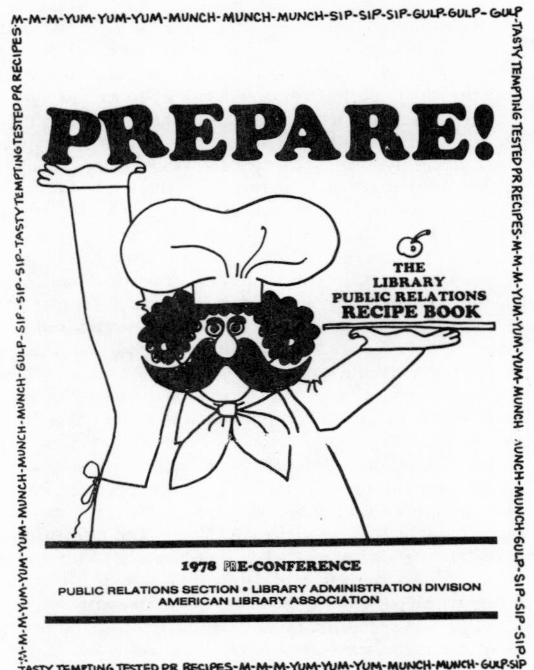


ALA

*"The Library Public Relations Recipe Book," edited by Irene Moran, covered a wide range of library public relations.*

Where do I go when I fall asleep?

That may sound like a child's question. It is.
Questions like that can be very important to a young mind, and the way they're answered can be very important, too.
That's why libraries hire people who like people. People who want to help.
If your children have questions, bring them to us. If you have questions, do the same. We have a special place in our hearts for adults, too.
By the way, the child's question doesn't fall strictly into the reference category, so we rather like: "Wherever your mind takes you."
Call the Library.
Produced by the Texas Library Association with funds from the Texas State Library and the U.S. Office of Education.

Texas Library Association

*Print ad produced by the Texas Library Association urged citizens to use the library.*

relations. There is also a tinge of suspicion and distrust that may be associated with aggressive press agentry that specializes in stunts and puffery. Yet in spite of these misconceptions, public relations has become a powerful and indispensable tool of management. And PR practitioners insist that they do not create images; a good reputation must be earned.

A public relations program may include marketing, merchandising, press agentry, promotion, publicity, public affairs, and even advertising; a good program is rarely just one of these. PR is notably different from advertising alone, which uses paid space and time, while public relations depends on free editorial space and news or public service time.

**History.** Public relations was "invented" in the early 20th century when big business was forced to abandon its "public be damned" attitude. The muckrakers were fighting corruption in business and government, and the public was reading, listening, and demanding reform. Ida M. Tarbell exposed the antisocial actions of Standard Oil in her history of the company, and Upton Sinclair unmasked the horrors of the meatpacking industry in *The Jungle*. In response to such attacks, business produced a whitewash of words, one-sided communication, and little action.

In 1906 Ivy L. Lee was hired as publicity adviser by a group of anthracite producers whose aloof attitude of secrecy had angered the press and public during a labor dispute. Lee's belief in public information for business organizations made him one of the pioneers of public relations. As adviser to the Pennsylvania Railroad, he ended their policy of secrecy by inviting reporters to the scene of a train wreck to see for themselves exactly what happened and even provided background information for their stories. His frankness generated "good press" for the railroad in reports of the wreck.

By the end of World War I, it was clear that words could be skillfully used to mold public opinion and that public understanding was necessary for the survival of institutions. One of Woodrow Wilson's first acts after the declaration of war was appointment of a Committee on Public Information, headed by journalist George Creel. Creel recruited magazine writers, advertising specialists, university professors, and a host of others for an "educational" campaign that sent American propaganda around the world; according to some historians, words won the war.

Another PR pioneer, Edward L. Bernays, who wrote the first book on the subject, *Crystallizing Public Opinion* (1922), developed the theory of specialized publics, stressing that messages should be targeted to a specific audience.

Although public relations was not defined in standard dictionaries until 1946, it has since become part of everyday vocabulary and is an accepted management function. Few business or government organizations are without a public relations department, and two of the largest public relations firms employ over 600 and have annual billings in excess of $22,000,000. While most PR practitioners entered the field through training or experience as journalists, there are currently over 300 colleges offering one or more courses in public relations.

**Library Use.** Libraries have made use of the philosophy and technique of public relations vigorously but inconsistently. As early as 1910 John Cotton Dana horrified some of his more staid library colleagues by using a billboard to advertise the library. He identified local interests and developed accordingly the libraries he directed in Denver, Colorado, Springfield, Massachusetts, and Newark, New Jersey, and he believed in telling the community what the library had and did. A major section of his practical guide, *Modern American Library Economy as Illustrated by the Newark, N.J. Free Public Library* (1910), was devoted to advertising and is still a useful tool. He asserts:

> Nothing is better for a public institution than publicity. The people who pay for its support are entitled to know—it is part of their education to know—all its ins and outs, its receipts, its expenditures, its methods, its plans and ambitions. Newspapers are almost invariably willing to print notes of these things. They feel that about the management of a public library there should not be, toward the public, the slightest intimation of a desire for secrecy.

His guide outlines numerous ways a library can involve

its community and communicate effectively, from stories for the newspaper to working with local schools.

Dana said that he came to his library every day with pleasure and left it with regret. His enthusiasm was contagious, and his tradition of public relations has been continued by a profession that gives an annual John Cotton Dana Library Public Relations Award. Excellence in public relations in all types of libraries is recognized by this award program, established in 1946 by the H. W. Wilson Company and the American Library Association.

Librarians appeared progressive in embracing PR when the Library Public Relations Council (LPRC) was founded in 1939. This group had a membership of 300 in 1979; it is devoted to investigation, discussion, and promotion of every phase of library public relations. Similar organizations focusing on college and school public relations were not founded until 1949 and 1950, respectively. "Public relations of libraries" first appeared as a subject heading in *Library Literature* in the 1943–45 volume, and the articles on the subject have been numerous.

Yet in spite of the early and enthusiastic interest in public relations, librarians are uneasy about PR and are still debating its merits. A January 1974 *Library Journal* editorial, for example, protested the "selling of the public library." The writer objected to aggressive PR messages, holding that people need and will use the public library just as they use hospitals, schools, and other essential services:

> This commerical pap, when applied to an institution like the public library, may be effective to a degree, if we want to pack 'em in, but beyond its lack of dignity, it overlooks the basic justification for all public services—that people need them. No other essential public service finds it necessary to peddle its wares as if they were new appliances for a consumer public that is tired of washing dishes, preparing food from scratch, or having hair with split ends.

The editorial inspired a flurry of letters and articles on both sides of the issue. Confusion between public relations and publicity continues, and both are seen by some as undignified hucksterism. Billboards advertising libraries are still just as shocking to many librarians as they were to Dana's colleagues. A basic text on administration of the college library prefers the term *interpretation* to *public relations* "for reasons less of logic than of sensibility." It was estimated that there were fewer than 250 full-time public relations specialists in U.S. public libraries and only three or four academic libraries with PR staff at the end of the 1970's.

Should libraries make use of "business" skills such as marketing and public relations? A business produces goods and services, and its bottom line is profit; a nonprofit organization such as the library provides services, and its bottom line is "quality of life." Such a concept is considerably more difficult to measure than profit. It is dangerous for a library to assume that the quality of the cause will generate public support. Many organizations with this attitude fail to develop a clear statement of their service and fail to develop marketing plans and delivery systems for the service.

In his keynote address to the combined 1978 conference of the Southeast and Southwest library associations, O. B. Hardison, Jr., Director of the prestigious Folger Shakespeare Library, stressed the "imperative of responsiveness" and described the funding realities that make research libraries "ivory towers in the arena":

> There *is* a public out there in the arena. It has legitimate needs, interests and demands. Since it pays the bills, the institutions that receive its support have a moral obligation to meet these needs, and demands in ways that are appropriate, and even at times, in ways that may seem odd when first seen from the barbican of the ivory tower. Lunch-time blue-grass at the Library of Congress? Well, why not if it makes the institution seem more open, less forbidding. . . . What I am saying is that every research library from the Library of Congress to the Folger is more in the arena today than it was even a decade ago. Libraries have entered the arena because most of them have no other choice. The problem is not whether to enter the arena but, having entered, to guide the institution along paths that are compatible with its long-range interests. This situation creates stress, but I think it is basically healthy. It is an adjustment to current realities. The alternative is—or seems to me to be—withdrawal and decline.

The question now should not be *whether* public relations is appropriate to libraries but rather *how* every public, school, academic, and special library can best use the techniques and skills of PR to assure that its services are well defined, understood, used, and supported.

**Four Basic Steps.** According to most public relations specialists, there are four basic steps involved in the public relations process: research, planning, communication, and evaluation. These are steps in a process that can be applied to any type and size of library. They are a function of good management.

*Research* involves identifying the library's publics and their attitudes toward the library. These publics may include the staff, governing board, volunteer or friends group, users, and nonusers, and booksellers or other suppliers. Research should begin inside the library to determine how the staff and trustees view the library, how well they understand its goals and policies, what they see as its major strengths and weaknesses, and how they feel about their relationship with the library administration. The evaluation of the library should also include an objective view of its physical appearance, from the cold realities of access, signage, and lighting to the warmer considerations of welcoming comfort and good cheer.

Beyond the library, research involves gathering all available demographic information about the community: age, income, ethnic background, occupations, religions, interests, community groups, and whatever other formal or informal data are available. Original research should also be undertaken to discern attitudes toward the library and information needs. Librarians have used numerous survey techniques to gather this information, among them mail questionnaires and telephone surveys of scientifically drawn population samples and personal contact and responses from clubs, churches, and other local institutions. The goal is constant sensitivity to public opinion.

*Planning*. The planning stage should make the PR process an integral part of the total library program. There should be a written PR plan with short- and long-range goals, a clear idea of the specific publics to be reached, a timetable and reporting schedule, lists of resources such as printing facilities, artists, and volunteers, a staffing plan, and a budget. Although most libraries are not in a position to afford the large public relations staff employed by major businesses, PR does require special expertise, and it cannot be done well without sufficient funding.

In 1975 the Council on Library Resources funded a study by Sue Fontaine of the managerial patterns in the implementation of public relations and publicity in 26 public libraries. Fontaine found that few of the libraries had public relations budgets; funds for PR were usually integrated into departmental budgets with only printing costs appearing as a separate line item. Of the 26 libraries, 19 had persons identified as public relations or community relations specialists. Of these, 12 had journalism or other communications degrees and experience, 3 had degrees in other fields with media experience, 2 were librarians, and 2 combined media and library degrees. While no attempt was made to evaluate the effectiveness of the various staffing patterns, the study showed that the most successful libraries have a definite staff assignment for public relations (on a par with department heads), support staff, graphic arts services, and a budget.

Percentages of the total library budget have been suggested to guide administrators on the cost of PR. The suggested percentages range from 1 to 10 percent and have little significance. Building a specific plan with a budget is a much more logical and convincing way to justify investment in a public relations program.

*Communication.* The communication phase of the public relations process comprises the outreach, programming, and publicity that the research and planning have prepared for. The possibilities are great, as is attested by the success stories reported by libraries in the literature.

One of the first steps toward communication for the library is building a media or press list of all available publications and broadcast channels, including daily and weekly newspapers, radio and television stations, community group newsletters, school newspapers, and any other media that may reach the particular target audience. Personal contact with the people on the press list is especially important. The Federal Communications Commission requires that a radio or television station broadcast information in the interest of the local community in order to retain its license. Libraries are eligible for free public service time but must compete with numerous other community agencies and services.

Beyond mass media, there are many other publicity tools that are regularly used by libraries, including newsletters (internal and external), annual reports, posters, booklists and bibliographies, displays, special programs, audiovisual presentations, speakers bureaus, and more. The Plainedge Public Library (Massapequa, New York) prepares special newsletters for expectant parents and senior citizens as well as its regular newsletter that goes by bulk mail to every household. The Library also has a written public relations policy approved by its board of directors. Several Portland (Oregon) school libraries act as career centers for teenagers. Once a month the library features a career display. Parents are invited to go to the library and discuss their occupations with teens. The University of Texas at Austin covered the opening of a new library in the football program. "Black History," a radio show, airs twice a week from the Dallas Public Library. The Clark County (Nevada) Library sponsors a Traveling Artist Series. An artist travels over the state in a mobile library demonstrating work for a two-week period.

*Evaluation.* The final step of the PR process, evaluation, requires that the public relations staff determine whether the communication program meets its stated objectives. One objective may have been media coverage, and a tally on how often radio or television stations carried the library messages along with a description of their audience is proof of achievement. Other means to evaluate a specific aspect of the PR program might include clips of newspaper coverage, use of evaluation forms at programs, or surveys in the library to determine how users found out about various services. It may be difficult to prove a direct cause and effect between a communications program and increased library usage, but an attempt should be made to measure the impact of the public relations investment.

**National Programs.** There is a growing national effort to increase citizen use and support of libraries. Since 1945 the Children's Book Council has created posters and other promotional materials for Children's Book Week, observed each year since 1919. In 1958 National Library Week (NLW) was initiated by publishers and librarians and remains the first and only national promotion program to increase use and support of libraries. The NLW program mobilized prominent citizens and librarians at the national and local levels to focus public and media attention on libraries. Workshops, handbooks, promotional materials, and national public relations support have made NLW a means to inform the public about library services, as well as an important public relations teaching tool for the profession.

*ALA.* In 1975 the American Library Association's Public Information Office assumed responsibility for National Library Week. Although long recognized as the national voice for librarians, the ALA had not previously been active in generating national media coverage. Both need and media interest were great, and the first full-fledged ALA effort—the 1975 NLW campaign—was awarded the Silver Anvil by the Public Relations Society of America and the Golden Trumpet by the Chicago Publicity Club.

ALA has continued to produce posters and other graphic materials that generate an income for support of a year-round PR effort. It places radio and television public service announcements with the networks, feature stories and print public service ads in national magazines, wire service stories, and other national publicity. In 1976 ALA also began producing a weekly syndicated book review column distributed by Newspaper Enterprise Association to over 700 subscribing newspapers nationwide. Attached to each column is a survey of "What Americans Are Reading," compiled from tabulations of most-requested books submitted by 150 participating libraries.

The ALA Public Information Office in 1978 generated news headlines by releasing results of a Gallup Organization study of attitudes toward libraries and reading. The study was sponsored by a special grant from Baker and Taylor and was planned to gather data on how Americans perceive libraries for the delegates participating in the 1979 White House Conference on Libraries and Information Services. Among many findings: although 51 percent of the American public had used the library in the past year, about one-fifth of the 1,515 respondents had no idea where the funding for the library comes from, and an additional 39 percent incorrectly stated the principal source of library funding. The ALA's National Library Week Committee also administers the $1,000 annual Grolier National Library Week Grant awarded to the state library association presenting the best proposal for a public relations program.

The Public Relations Section of the Library Administration and Management Association, a division of ALA, provides further national leadership in public relations. The 1,200-member section involves PR specialists from libraries across the country who work together to produce active and effective continuing education programs, workshops, and publications. Their annual "PR Swap 'n Shop" has become one of the best-attended ALA conference programs and offers librarians a chance to sample promotional materials from libraries across the country and get expert counseling on PR matters. The Public Relations Section is also the national home for the Friends of the Library groups and administers the John Cotton Dana Library Public Relations Awards.

*Other Activities.* Citizen support of libraries is the concern of another U.S. national group, the National Citizens Emergency Committee to Save Our Public Libraries. The independent committee was founded in 1976 by Whitney North Seymour, Jr., attorney and former New York Public Library Trustee. In fall 1978 the Committee launched a nationwide campaign to enlist grass roots support for library funding. Seymour notes that some Friends groups are already waging successful local campaigns, but he adds, "Many Friends are better cake-bakers than legislative arm-twisters."

At the grass roots, thousands of citizen delegates participating in the state pre-White House Conferences in 1978 and 1979 asked libraries to do a better job of informing the public of their services. Almost every state conference produced a resolution similar to this one from Ohio:

> Develop an aggressive, consistent, and better organized marketing, advertising, and public relations program using all available media and other agencies to increase public awareness of library and information services and their value to daily life, destroy stigmas, and improve the image of all libraries.

Although U.S. libraries are seen as pioneers in library public relations, some of the same techniques have been used very effectively elsewhere. National Library Weeks have been observed in the United Kingdom, Denmark, Australia, New Zealand, Canada, and elsewhere, but these are usually conducted on a more occasional basis than in the U.S. In the latter 1970's the Australian Library Promotion Council adapted the U.S. National Library Week graphics for its "week." Children's Book Week is a tradition known in England and Scandinavia. In Sweden the Bibliotekstänst, or Library Service Ltd., started in 1951, produces a great variety of public relations materials such as posters, pamphlets, and booklists. Dutch libraries have an outstanding array of well-designed graphic materials, including a national library logo available from the Nederlands Bibliotheek en Lektuur Centrum.

How will librarians be prepared to meet the growing demands for public relations programs? More and more library schools are offering seminars and short courses in public relations. At last count (1979), approximately 10 of the 67 graduate programs accredited by ALA offered full courses in library public relations. Many include PR in a general library management course, and there are many programs and workshops offered at ALA conferences and state and regional library association meetings.

A planned communication program is a necessity for passing a bond issue, competing effectively for funds, and generating the support needed to keep the library doors open and service flowing. In winter 1979, ALA's Public Information Office sent a questionnaire to state library agencies seeking information on library funding and the "taxpayer revolt." It asked for examples of libraries that are well funded and the reasons why. The responses provided another endorsement of effective public relations; for example, the Florida State Library said Broward County, Orlando Public, and Miami-Dade Library Systems succeeded in maintaining adequate support because:

> All have utilized excellent friends groups and each library has a community minded library director who works effectively with governmental leaders. Broward County recently passed a $32 million bond issue for public library construction after a masterful public relations effort.

Libraries will have a future as primary information resources if librarians use public relations principles and techniques to find political allies and build positive public opinion. It may well be a matter of survival. Abraham Lincoln said, "With public sentiment nothing can fail; without it nothing can succeed." Lee Brawner, Director of the Metropolitan Library System in Oklahoma City, observed, "People are usually down on what they ain't up on!"

**REFERENCES**

Allan Angoff, editor, *Public Relations for Libraries: Essays in Communications Techniques* (1973), essays on the general theory of public relations plus PR in different sizes and types of libraries.

Cosette Kies, *Problems in Library Public Relations* (1974), an interesting case study approach to library public relations, with emphasis on human relations.

Irene Moran, compiler, *Prepare: The Library Public Relations Recipe Book* (1978); just as the humble church cookbook often has the best recipes, this typescript, spiral-bound collection of articles by library PR specialists, compiled for ALA's Library Administration and Management Association, is a gold mine of practical information and includes a good bibliography.

Betty Rice, *Public Relations for Public Libraries* (1972), practical public relations advice including a chapter on how to win a bond issue.

PEGGY BARBER

# Puerto Rico

Puerto Rico Librarians Society 464

Puerto Rico, University of Graduate School of Librarianship 222

Puerto Rico, a self-governing commonwealth since 1952, associated with the U.S., lies in the Caribbean Sea and is bounded by the Lesser Antilles on the south, the Dominican Republic on the west, and the Atlantic Ocean on the north and east. Pop. (1977 est.) 3,303,000; area (including the islands of Culebra, Mona, and Vieques) 8,897 sq.km. The official language is Spanish.

**Early History.** The first library in Puerto Rico was founded by Bishop Alonso Manso in 1512 at Caparra. During the 1625 Dutch attack of San Juan, the two existing libraries of the Dominican Monastery and the private collection of Bishop Bernardo de Balbuena were destroyed. In the 1830's the San Juan Conciliar Seminary Library opened and later, in 1899, merged with the Bar Association Library. In 1843 La Real Sociedad Económica de Amigos del País (The Royal Society of Friends of the Island), with the donation of a book collection owned by Rufo Manuel Fernández, founded a public library; by 1885 that collection had increased to 13,000 volumes, and in 1876 the cultural group Ateneo Puertorriqueño took over the library. Between 1872 and 1894, the last years of Spanish rule, libraries were set up in several municipalities, including Ponce and Mayaguez. More public libraries were established following the United States military occupation in 1898, and in 1917 Governor Arthur Yager obtained a grant from Andrew Carnegie to establish the Carnegie Library. In that year the Department of Education was given full control of libraries, and in subsequent years more libraries, both public and private, were established.

**National Library.** The Biblioteca General de Puerto Rico (General Library of Puerto Rico), established in the 1970's in the General Archives building and operated by the Institute of Puerto Rican Culture, houses 75,000 books and is oriented toward book collection and preservation.

**Academic Libraries.** The University of Puerto Rico, consisting of ten campuses with their own libraries, serves as the public university. Most important is the José M. Lázaro Library, founded in 1905 and on the Río Piedras Campus. This library has about 2,200,000 books and printed documents, 3,400 periodicals, and 33,000 bound volumes of periodicals. Special sections are Maps and Documents, Music, the Puerto Rican Collection, the Zenobia and Juan Ramón Jiménez Room, and the Library for Blind Students. Departmental libraries in the graduate school include Library Science, Public Administration, Social Work, School of Planning, the Natural Sciences Library, the Reserve Rooms of the Colleges of Business Administration and Social Sciences, the College of Education, the Law School, and the Commerce Library. Because there is no large public library in the metropolitan area, the Lázaro Library serves the general public and the faculty and student bodies of private universities in the area in addition to its university community.

Holdings in the libraries of the other campuses of the University of Puerto Rico include the Mayaguez Campus Main Library, with 167,000 volumes; other libraries on

**Libraries in Puerto Rico (1976)**

| Type | Number | Volumes in collections | Annual expenditures (dollar) | Population served | Professional staff | All staff (total) |
|---|---|---|---|---|---|---|
| National | 1 | 75,000 | $ 81,840 | 900 | 7 | 17 |
| Academic | 21 | 4,194,180 | 8,670,390 | 175,007 | 192 | 645 |
| Public | 355 | 1,085,331 | 2,256,567 | 2,555,950 | 15 | 382 |
| School | 542 | N.A. | 3,401,053 | N.A. | N.A. | N.A. |
| Special | 20 | 121,450 | 209,370 | 2,876 | 4 | 26 |
| Totals | 979 | | $14,619,170 | | | |

Sources: Library Directors.



that campus include the Agricultural Experimental Library and the Center for Energy and Environmental Research. The School of Medicine Library in San Juan has 79,000 volumes and 700 current periodicals. The Cayey University College Library, in the center of the island, has 60,000 volumes, 3,500 government documents, 1,000 periodicals, and 2,400 microfilms. The Humacao University College Library in the east holds 41,078 volumes and 518 periodicals. Aguadilla Regional College Library in the northwest has 15,000 volumes. The collection of the Arecibo Regional College Library on the northwest coast is 33,000 volumes. The Bayamón Regional College Library, west of San Juan, has 26,900 volumes and 12,000 audiovisual items. The Carolina Regional College Library, east of San Juan, has 21,500 volumes, 275 periodicals, and 20,000 audiovisual items. The Ponce Regional College Library in the southeast holds 21,500 volumes.

The six private universities have extensive library holdings. The Inter-American University comprises 13 campuses (in San Juan, San Germán, Bayamón, Aguadilla, Arecibo, Barranquitas, Fajardo, Guayama, Ponce, and Fort Buchanan, with total library collections of 327,963 volumes). The Encarnación Valdés Library of the Catholic University in Ponce holds 155,000 books, periodicals, and other items. The World University Learning Resources Center in San Juan has 82,000 volumes; the Sacred Heart University Library Collection in San Juan contains 117,000 items; and the Puerto Rico Junior College Library and Turabo University College Library contain 38,736 volumes and 35,448 volumes, respectively.

**Public Libraries.** The Educational Extension Program of the Department of Education, responsible for public library programs, serves 78 municipalities, with a total population of 3,223,800. The program reaches 2,560,000 persons through public library services that include 60 public libraries in the various towns and municipalities, 9 bookmobiles, 19 housing project libraries, 16 correctional institution libraries, 250 rural traveling libraries, and a Regional Library for the Blind and Physically Handicapped. These collections total over 1,000,000 volumes.

**School Libraries.** While all high schools and 50 percent of the intermediate schools have libraries, only 7 percent of the elementary schools have libraries. Most of the existing 618 libraries were small in size and holdings at the end of the 1970's.

**Special Libraries.** The Caribbean Regional Library, covering the entire Caribbean region with emphasis on the English-speaking Antilles, has a collection of 116,000 books and periodical volumes housed at the José M. Lázaro Library. Other special libraries include the Legislative Reference Library at the Capitol, with 40,450 volumes of books and periodicals used by legislators of the House and Senate and by researchers, and the Supreme Court Library with holdings of 75,000 books and periodicals. There are several small libraries in government agencies and public and private corporations, including the libraries of the Budget Bureau, Development Bank, Planning Board, State Department, the Institute of Culture, and the Economic Development Administration. Collections range from 6,000 to 75,000 volumes. Most are open to the public and lend materials to public libraries through interlibrary loan.

**Association.** The Puerto Rico Librarians Society (Sociedad de Bibliotecarios de Puerto Rico), founded in 1961, maintains contact with mainland and foreign professional groups, is a member of the International Federation of Library Associations, and cooperates with the Association of Caribbean University, Research and Institutional Libraries. The Society publishes journals and newsletters encouraging library and bibliographical research.

**REFERENCE**


Puerto Rico, Departamento de Instrucción Pública, *Public Library Needs, Survey and Analysis . . . Final Report of the Results of a Survey Conducted by the Synectis for Management Decisions Inc.* . . . (Hato Rey, Puerto Rico, 1975).


RAFAEL R. DELGADO

# Putnam, (George) Herbert
(1861–1955)

Herbert Putnam, Librarian of the Minneapolis Athenaeum (1884–87), the Minneapolis Public Library (1887–91), the Boston Public Library (1895–99), and Librarian of Congress (1899–1939), was a leading figure in the American library movement—especially during the first half of his 40-year term as Librarian of Congress. He was the first experienced librarian to hold the post of Librarian of Congress. His major contribution to the Library of Congress came directly from this experience: he linked firmly the policies of the Library of Congress with the broader interests of American librarianship. To do so he sought and obtained the support of the Congress, professional librarians and especially the American Library Association and the American scholarly community. The result was that Herbert Putnam, more than any other Librarian of Congress, established and defined the Library's pattern of national library services to its major constituencies—the Congress, the nation's libraries, and the world of scholarship.

Putnam was born in New York City on September 20, 1861, the tenth child of Victorine Putnam and George Palmer Putnam, the founder of the Putnam publishing house. Herbert attended private schools and received his B.A. from Harvard in 1883, graduating magna cum laude. The next year he attended Columbia University Law School but soon was enticed by friends to Minneapolis as the head of the library at the Minneapolis Athenaeum. While successfully responding to the problems facing that institution, he pursued his legal studies and was admitted to the Minnesota bar. In 1887 he became

Librarian of the new Minneapolis Public Library, which had absorbed the Athenaeum. After vigorously leading the Minneapolis Public Library through its fledgling years, Putnam resigned in late 1891 and returned with his family to Massachusetts to be near his ailing mother. He practiced law until he was persuaded to return to librarianship—as Superintendent of the Boston Public Library, the nation's largest public library. He assumed those duties in February 1895, at the age of 33.

Putnam's leadership abilities and his new position quickly involved him in the American Library Association. From November 16 to December 7, 1896, the Congressional Joint Committee on the Library held hearings on the "condition" of the Library of Congress on the eve of its move into its new building, and Herbert Putnam was one of the ALA witnesses.

The Librarian of Congress at the time was Ainsworth Rand Spofford, who had been Librarian for over 30 years and was personally responsible for the rapid growth of the Library into an institution of national significance. The ALA sent six witnesses to the hearings. Putnam and Melvil Dewey dominated, each advocating an expanded national role for the Library of Congress—a role that extended far beyond Spofford's basic concept or his accomplishments. Many specific suggestions for national library service were offered by the two library leaders.

The 1896 hearings marked a turning point in the relations between the Library of Congress and the American library movement. For the first time ALA offered, albeit cautiously, its advice to Congress about the purpose and functions of the Library of Congress. Moreover, Congress listened; the testimony at the hearings, along with a report filed by Spofford on January 18, 1897, were major influences on the reorganization of the Library that was contained in the legislative appropriations act for fiscal year 1898, approved by President Grover Cleveland on February 19, 1897. The restructuring and expansion of the Library simply could not wait for the report on the hearings held by the Joint Committee on the Library. Because the changes were part of the appropriations act, they became effective on July 1, 1897, the beginning of the new fiscal year. On June 30, 1897, President William McKinley nominated his friend John Russell Young, a journalist and former diplomat, to be Librarian of Congress. The Senate confirmed the nomination on the same day, and Young was sworn in on July 1, the day the reorganization became effective.

Young did a remarkable job in the year and a half that he served as Librarian. After presiding over the move from the Capitol into the new building, which opened to great public acclaim on November 1, 1897, he concerned himself with organizational matters and the new appointments. The new law authorized an increase in the staff of the Library proper from 42 to 108; Young was flooded with applications, and he chose well. Never a healthy man, Young did not recover from two severe falls during the winter of 1898–99, and he died on January 17, 1899. The newspapers immediately were filled with speculation regarding his successor. This time the ALA, through Richard R. Bowker and William Coolidge Lane, ALA President and Librarian of Harvard University, took the lead. Two of Young's appointees, Solberg and Hanson, worked closely with the librarians. On January 23, less than a week after Young's death, Lane wrote a letter, printed in the *Library Journal,* to President McKinley urging the appointment of an experienced library administrator as the next Librarian of Congress since that library—as the national library—should "stand at the head of American libraries as the best organized and the best equipped of all."

Within the next few days, the ALA leaders settled on Herbert Putnam as their candidate. The story of how Putnam finally was nominated is complicated, but there is no doubt that without the intervention of the ALA he would not have become Librarian. William Coolidge Lane not only persuaded President McKinley; it appears that in the end he also persuaded Putnam. On March 13, 1899, during the congressional recess, McKinley appointed Herbert Putnam to be the eighth Librarian of Congress. He took the oath of office on April 5 and was confirmed by the U.S. Senate, somewhat after the fact, on December 12.

With Putnam's appointment, the relationship between the Library of Congress and the ALA truly entered a new era. Putnam not only was a librarian's librarian, he was also an association spokesman. Twice he served as ALA President: from January to August, 1898, when he completed the unexpired term of the late Justin Winsor, and again in 1903–1904. From 1900 to 1905, the critical years of his administration, he served on the ALA Council.

As Librarian of Congress Putnam moved quickly to expand the Library into the type of national library put forward in his 1896 testimony before the Joint Committee of the Library. He initiated a new classification scheme, the sale and distribution of printed catalogue cards, interlibrary loan, and a national union catalogue. In an appendix to his annual report of 1901, he described the organization and collection of the Library in a "manual" that came to be regarded as a model for libraries. Other Putnam actions during the first two decades of the 20th century included obtaining the support of President Theodore Roosevelt for the expansion of the Library's activities, perhaps most dramatically through an executive order transferring presidential and other state papers to the Library; revision of the 1870 copyright law, begun in 1905 and completed in 1909; the acquisition, in 1907, of collections of Russian and Japanese books, thereby establishing the foundation of the Library's Slavic and Oriental collections; and direction of the ALA's Library War Service Committee (1917–19), which was a model of efficiency and a triumph of American librarianship.

During the first half of Putnam's administration, lasting roughly from 1899 through World War I, the Librarian had, by and large, the full support of professional librarians and the ALA. The next 20 years were not so harmonious, and the Library of Congress and the American library movement drifted apart.

One reason was that Putnam gave increasing attention to matters that did not directly concern the American library community. A separate Legislative Reference Service was created in 1914. In 1921 the Declaration of Independence and the Constitution of the United States were transferred from the State Department to the Library, enhancing the image of the Library of Congress as a symbol of American democracy. In the mid-1920's, through Putnam's efforts, the Library became a national patron of the arts; a gift from Elizabeth Sprague Coolidge provided an auditorium for the performance of chamber music, and a generous endowment from Mrs. Coolidge shortly thereafter led to the creation in 1925 of the Library of Congress Trust Fund Board, an instrument that enabled the Library, for the first time, to accept, hold, and invest gifts and bequests.

Furthermore, Putnam's personal interest in library cooperation and related technical matters was replaced with an increasing concern for the "interpretation" of the collections. Putnam had always viewed the use of the Library's collections as the prime object of the administration; in the 1896 hearings, for example, he described the national library as, ideally, the library "which stands foremost as a model and example of assisting forward the work of scholarship in the United States." After the establishment of the Library of Congress Trust Fund Board, he began to obtain private funds to support "chairs" and consultantships for subject specialists who

ALA

*George Herbert Putnam, 8th Librarian of Congress.*

could aid scholars in their use of the collections.

In sum, as Putnam focused on other activities, his interest in the role of the Library of Congress as a leader among American libraries lessened. For example, in 1935, in a letter to ALA Secretary Carl H. Milam, the Librarian flatly rejected the notion of locating a federal library bureau in the Library of Congress, contending that the functions of such an agency "would tend to confuse and impede the service to learning which should be the primary duty of our National Library." In Putnam's opinion, the bureau instead "should be associated with one of the executive departments of the government."

Putnam's authoritarian style presented further difficulties. He was a stern administrator, both venerated and feared. Apparently no associate ever called him by his first name, and it appears that there was no one, either inside or outside the Library, who was able to influence him to any significant degree.

By the late 1930's the Library of Congress was suffering from administrative stagnation, intensified by low staff morale and operational problems such as a large cataloguing backlog. These problems were compounded by Putnam's refusal, or inability, to delegate responsibility. By 1939 there were 35 divisions, each reporting directly to the Librarian, compared to the 16 listed in his 1901 annual report. Even Herbert Putnam, with all his gifts, could not successfully oversee himself 35 diverse units and 1,100 employees. In the late 1930's there were many librarians and politicians who were waiting for Putnam to decide to retire. Apparently even President Franklin D. Roosevelt chose to wait.

Such difficulties aside, Putnam was enormously respected by scholars and librarians alike. When he did retire to become, on October 1, 1939, Librarian Emeritus of Congress, his friends in the American Library Association paid him tribute as "dean of our profession" who had led LC to "its present proud position as the world's largest bibliographical institution." He continued to contribute to the Library of Congress, keeping regular office hours, for the next 15 years. He died on August 14, 1955. Putnam wrote no memoirs; his 40 annual reports between 1899 and 1939 serve as the record of his achievements at the Library of Congress.

**REFERENCES**

J. Christian Bay, "Herbert Putnam, 1861–1955," *Libri* (1956).

John Y. Cole, "Herbert Putnam and the National Library," in *Milestones to the Present: Papers from Library History Seminar V,* edited by Harold Goldstein (1978).

JOHN Y. COLE

# Qatar

Qatar, an independent emirate, juts out from the Arabian Peninsula into the Persian Gulf. It is bordered by the Gulf on the north and west, and mostly by it on the east except for the land mass of the emirate of Bahrain. Saudi Arabia and the United Arab Emirates border on the south. Pop. (1978 est.) 200,000; area 11,400 sq.km. The official language is Arabic.

**National and Public Library.** There is a national library in the capital city of Doha; it also functions as a public library. All Qataris have access to the entire collection of the National Library. Supervised by the Ministry of Education, it was founded in 1963 as a merger of two former libraries: the Public Library (founded in 1956) and the Educational Library (1954). The Library preserves the Qatari heritage. Book production is small in Qatar; as of 1975 only 93 books were reported by the Arab League Educational, Cultural and Scientific Organization as published in Qatar.

The National Library of Qatar issues the annual *Bibliography of Books and Pamphlets Published in Qatar* (since 1970). The Library also has a center for exchange of publications. Its book collection totals some 42,000 volumes in Arabic, 17,000 volumes in English, and approximately 1,100 Arabic and Persian manuscripts. The Library subscribes to over 100 periodicals titles.

**Academic Libraries.** The only existing academic library in Qatar is that of the College of Education, founded in 1973. As of 1978 Qatar was in the process of establishing a new university, with aid from Unesco, which will have colleges of Maritime and Sea Services, Petroleum Engineering, Civil Aviation, as well as the already established College of Education. A modern university library was also being planned.

**School Libraries.** The Ministry of Education has embarked on a plan for establishing and developing school libraries. There are 69 libraries in Qatari schools, the largest among them being in the secondary schools, the Religious Institute, and the Institute of Administration. All school libraries in Qatar are staffed with librarians recruited from other Arab countries.

**Special Libraries.** Government departments and ministries are planning to introduce library services to their officials. The Ministry of Education has established an Educational Documentation Center to serve administrators, teachers, and students and to aid in planning and issuing local textbooks.

MOHAMED M. EL HADI

# Rajwade, Vishwanath Kashinath
(1863–1926)

Vishwanath Kashinath Rajwade is remembered principally for his monumental work in the collection, preservation, editing, and publication of primary historical source material on the history of the Marathas. He was born June 24, 1863, in a Chitpavan Brahmin family of Varsai, a village in the Kolaba district of Maharashtra State. He studied at Elphinstone College, Bombay, and Deccan College, Pune (B.A., 1890, in History). After three years of schoolteaching, he decided to devote himself entirely to the pursuit of knowledge. At college he had read widely in European history, economics, political science, ethics, theology, logic, metaphysics, botany, and other fields, and he was influenced by the writings of Plato, Hegel, and Comte. He mastered English, and he also acquired a working knowledge of French and Persian. But he remained a staunch protagonist of the Marathi language. He started a periodical called *Bhashantar* ("Translation") in 1894, and within a period of 37 months, Marathi translations of 23 classics, including some works of Plato and Montesquieu, had been published in the journal.

His interests were varied. He wrote on history, linguistics, grammar, etymology, philosophy, sociology, politics, anthropology, and Sanskrit and Marathi literature. His books number about 76 and his articles 343. His name, however, will ever be remembered for his work on the history of the Marathas, which embraced the source material published in 26 volumes (4 after his death) in a famous series, *Marathyanchya Itihasachi Sadhane*. The analytical introductions to volumes 1, 3, 4, 5, and 8 of this series could stand as independent monographs. His introductions to *Mahikavatichi Bakhar* and *Radha Madhav Vilas Champu* deserve special attention. A poor collector of source material, he was his own publisher. He sought no help from government or patron.

He helped revolutionize historical methodology. According to him history should encompass social, economic, political, and intellectual activities of man irrespective of time and space. Rajwade's broad concept of history, its scope, and arrangement was comparable to that of Leopold von Ranke (1795–1886), who has been called the father of modern historical methodology.

Rajwade founded the Bharat Itihas Samshodhak Mandal (1910) for promoting historical research.

He was the first to decipher the secret script of Mahanubhav literature. He was also the first to edit and publish the *Jnaneshwari,* a premier work in Marathi literature.

A contemporary historian of India, Sir Jadu Nath Sarkar, called Rajwade "the greatest discoverer, the lifelong searcher, the exclusive devotee without a second love, the most fruitful collector of the raw materials of Maratha history, and at the same time their most painstaking editor, and their most speedy and prolific publisher" *(House of Shivaji,* p. 276).

Rajwade died on December 31, 1926, at Dhule in Khandesh (Maharashtra). With a view to perpetuating his memory, the people of Dhule founded a historical research institute bearing his name—Rajwade Samshodhan Mandir.

**REFERENCES**

Jadunath Sarkar, "The Historian Rajwade," in *House of Shivaji,* 3rd ed. (Calcutta, 1955).

S. P. Sen, editor, "Vishwanath Kashinath Rajwade," *Historians and Historiography of Modern India* (Calcutta, 1973).

A. R. KULKARNI

# Ranganathan, Shiyali Ramamrita
(1892–1972)

The author of *Colon Classification* and of many books and papers on classification and of the Five Laws of Librarianship, Ranganathan stands as one of the immortals of library science. Ranganathan was born on August 9, 1892, into the Brahman community at Shiyali in the Tanjur District of Madras State. He was educated at Sabhanayaka Mudaliar's Hindu High School, Shiyali, from 1897 to 1908 and at Madras Christian College, where he majored in mathematics, from 1909 to 1916. He took a teaching diploma at the Teachers' College, Saidapet, Madras, in 1917 and became Assistant Lecturer in Mathematics at Government College (later Presidency College), Bangalore. In 1921 he was appointed Assistant Professor of Mathematics there.

In 1924 Ranganathan began a new career when he was appointed the first Librarian of the University of Madras. He was required to study for his new profession in Britain and went to University College, London, where he met and was considerably influenced by W. C. Berwick Sayers. During his two years in Britain (1924–25) he visited about 100 libraries and was confirmed in his new vocation. He received an Honours Certificate from the School of Librarianship at University College in 1925 and was elected a Fellow of the (British) Library Association in 1930.

He remained Librarian of the University of Madras until 1944, later becoming University Librarian and Professor of Library Science at Banaras Hindu University (1945–47), Professor of Library Science at the University of Delhi (1947–54), and Visiting Professor of Library Science at Vikram University, Ujjain (1957–59). He was appointed Honorary Professor and Head of the Documentation Research and Training Centre, Bangalore, which he had founded under the auspices of the Indian Statistical Institute, in 1962; in 1965 the Indian government appointed him National Research Professor in Library Science.

Ranganathan married in 1907, and his wife died 21 years later on the exact date prophesied by a former schoolfellow. In 1929 he married again; by all accounts this marriage was as happy as the first, and his second wife survived him. Ranganathan died on September 27, 1972, one month after his 80th birthday.

**Contributions.** Ranganathan will almost certainly be best remembered by librarians for his *Colon Classification*; had he achieved nothing else, this pioneer faceted classification would have been sufficient to place him among the giants of librarianship. The classification is hardly used outside India, though at least two quite different British libraries (at Metal Box Limited and Christ's College, Cambridge) use it, but its influence has been tremendous: on successive editions of the Dewey Decimal Classification, the Universal Decimal Classification, and, more recently, the Bliss Bibliographic Classification; on many specialist classifications; on various indexing methods; and on bibliographies like *The British National Bibliography*. Chain indexing, developed by Ranganathan as a demonstration of the "symbiosis" between classification and subject indexing and as a technique for ensuring that aspects of a subject separated by a classification scheme are collocated in the index, is a method of subject indexing widely used in British libraries.

Apart from the *Colon Classification*, Ranganathan wrote many books and papers on classification, ranging from the introductory *Elements of Library Classification* to the monumental *Prolegomena to Library Classification*. Douglas Foskett has said that "in his writings, Ranganathan sometimes gave the impression that he was difficult or abstruse." To some extent this is true, but the *Elements* is not difficult to master, and the *Prolegomena* will repay considerable effort on the part of the reader.

But classification was only one of Ranganathan's interests, if a major one. His other contributions to cataloguing include codes of rules for dictionary and classified catalogues, *Theory of Library Catalogue*, and a stimulating comparative study of catalogue codes, *Heading and Canons*, which K. G. B. Bakewell rates second only to Lubetzky's *Cataloging Rules and Principles* as the outstanding contribution to cataloguing thought in this century. As S. S. Agraval points out, Ranganathan's influence on the *Anglo-American Cataloging Rules* of 1967 was not inconsiderable; his canons of "sought heading" and "ascertainability" being particularly relevant.

Before any of these works came his analytical study of the purpose of libraries, resulting in the Five Laws of Library Science that formed the basis of his first published book on librarianship: books are for use; every book its reader; every reader his book; save the time of the reader; a library is a growing organism. Although many today would substitute "documents" or "library materials" for "books" (and say "every reader his/her document"), these laws are as valid today as they were when first enunciated. They seem—and are—simple, but they remain fundamental objectives of the library profession; Pauline Atherton said, "These words stir students to think of and believe in library *service* above library *work* as their life goal."

Some of Ranganathan's works were specifically concerned with the development of libraries in India. Following a request from the Punjab Library Association, he produced a pamphlet in 1944 on the postwar reconstruction of libraries in India, in which he proposed a national library network of national, state, university, public, and school libraries. This was followed in 1950 by a more detailed work, *Library Development Plan*, outlining a 30-year program. Library development in India was considerably influenced by these two publications, which were followed by library development plans and draft legislation for other Indian states.

There is scarcely an area of librarianship to which Ranganathan did not turn his attention: library management, school and college libraries, the broader aspects of libraries and education, book selection, reference service, and bibliography. In addition to his own writings, he edited many works and shared with others in the authorship of more books and papers. He founded *Annals of Library*

Courtesy of The Newberry Library

*Shiyali Ramamrita Ranganathan*

special libraries **536**
standards **39, 41**


*Science* in 1956 and *Library Science with a Slant to Documentation* in 1965 and edited both journals until they had become firmly established. Jesse Shera said, "That one cannot properly judge the work of S. R. Ranganathan without reference to the totality of librarianship is a tribute to the breadth and depth of his contribution to the profession."

**International Library Scene.** V. V. Giri, then Governor of Mysore and later President of India, described Ranganathan as "the father of library science in India" when presenting him with a copy of the Ranganathan Festschrift at Bangalore on December 18, 1965. This was an apt description, for Ranganathan had done more than anyone to further library development in India, but his work transcended national barriers. As Girja Kumar said, "He was universal because his work was not confined to any geographical boundary."

H. Coblans has written about Ranganathan's contributions to international librarianship: his influence on the development of the United Nations Library; his foundation of the International Federation for Documentation (FID) Committee on General Classification, and his work as Secretary and Chairman of this committee; and his work for Unesco, the International Federation of Library Associations, and the International Standards Organization. His fervent belief in international standardization is well known.

**Offices and Honors.** Ranganathan had been a librarian for only four years when he was elected the first Secretary of the Madras Library Association, which he had founded in 1928; he held that office for 25 years. Such was his energy that he managed also to hold the office of Treasurer of the Indian Mathematical Society for six of those years (1928–34). He was President of the Indian Library Association, 1944–53, and of the Madras Library Association, 1958–67.

His other offices included: Chairman of the Documentation Committee of the Indian Standards Institution (1947–66); Vice-President of the Madras Library Association (1948–57); Secretary of the Indian Adult Education Association (1949–53); Vice-President of FID (1953–56 and 1958–61); Secretary and Chairman of the FID Committee on General Classification (1954–64). He was an Honorary Fellow of FID and an Honorary Vice-President of the LA.

Among his many awards are two of special distinction that he received from the government of his country in recognition of his achievements: the title *Rao Sahib* and the distinction of *Padmashree*. He was given an Honorary Doctorate of Literature by the University of Delhi and the University of Pittsburgh. In 1970 he was awarded the Margaret Mann Citation in Cataloging and Classification by the American Library Association. His contributions to library science were recognized in 1965 by the publication of a Ranganathan Festschrift to mark his 71st birthday. After his death the FID Committee on Classification Research further recognized his achievements by establishing a Ranganathan Award for Classification Research.

**The Man.** What kind of man was this energetic genius who was so immersed in his work? Kaula tells us that Ranganathan never took a single day's leave during the 20 years he spent as University Librarian at Madras and even returned to the library soon after the conclusion of his wedding ceremony. The Ranganathan Memorial Number of *Herald of Library Science* contains many personal anecdotes about Ranganathan and 14 obituaries, with references not only to his analytical mind, consideration, and sense of humor but also to the fact that he could be frank, intolerant, uncompromising, and selfish. Girjar Kumar refers to his sense of humor as well as to his optimism and his interest in mysticism. V. V. Giri, when presenting the Ranganathan Festschrift to him, mentioned his humility and philanthropy but said that what struck him most about Ranganathan was "his enthusiasm and ebullient spirit which even many a youth in the country could envy."

Perhaps the most moving accounts of Ranganathan as a person have come from English Librarian Bernard Palmer, who tells how, inspired by reading the *Prolegomena* when he began to teach classification in 1940, he made a vow that if ever he had the money, he would go to Madras to meet the author. The opportunity came only a year later when, serving in the Royal Air Force, Palmer found himself at a camp on the outskirts of Madras. On his first free afternoon he went to the University Library and introduced himself to Ranganathan, thus laying the foundations of a friendship that lasted until Ranganathan's death. Like others, Palmer refers to Ranganathan's analytical mind, his enthusiasm, his good humor, his kindliness, and his genial personality (though admitting that he could be cold and offhand with those he believed to be fools or opponents). Palmer states that although conscious of his unique position in Indian librarianship, Ranganathan was modest and unassuming and welcomed him, then "a quite humble member of the profession," as though he were his intellectual and cultural equal.

In honor of his wife and at her suggestion, he endowed all his property to the Sarada Ranganathan Chair of Library Science in the University of Madras in 1957. He also established the Sarada Ranganathan Lectures on Library Science, the first of which was given by Palmer in 1965.

Ranganathan was passionately concerned about library science, which he saw as a vital tool for the development of mankind. As he wrote in *Heading and Canons:*

> Thus by the promotion of international co-operation in library science, the library profession will make its own contribution to the ultimate benefit of
> 1. the development of each of the nations of the world towards its own fulness at its own speed and along its own lines;
> 2. the development of an atmosphere of peaceful co-existence among nations; and
> 3. the evolution of One-World.
>
> May Every Human Group Become Happy!

**REFERENCES**

Edward Dudley, editor, *S. R. Ranganathan, 1892–1972: Papers Given at a Memorial Meeting on Thursday 25th January 1973* (1974).

P. N. Kaula, "Some Less Known Facts about Ranganathan," *Herald of Library Science* (1973).

*Ranganathan Festschrift*, volume 1: *Library Science Today: Papers Contributed on the 71st Birthday of Dr. S. R. Ranganathan (August 1962)*, edited by P. N. Kaula; and volume 2: *An Essay in Personal Bibliography: A Bibliography of the Writings on and by Dr. S. R. Ranganathan*, compiled by A. K. Das Gupta (1965–67).

K. G. B. BAKEWELL

## Reference Services

Reference service, sometimes referred to as "reference and information services" or "reader services," has been defined as personal assistance provided to users in the pursuit of information. As distinguished from other library activities or services, reference service is characterized by a high degree of personal interaction between library staff members and library users; the service is typically provided to individual users or specifically identified small groups of users, and the information needs of the users are known at the time of the interaction.

Reference service has three major aspects or service techniques: (1) information service, which consists of finding needed information for the user or assisting the user in finding such information; (2) instruction in library use, consisting of helping users learn the skills they need to find and use library materials; and (3) guidance, in which users are assisted in choosing library materials appropriate to their educational, informational, or recreational needs. In addition to these "direct" reference services, reference librarians provide "indirect" services. These include building and maintaining a collection of bibliographic tools and other information sources, participating in co-operative programs to provide users access to resources outside the library, and various administrative activities.

**Historical Development.** Reference service had its beginnings in American librarianship in the last quarter of the 19th century. By the time of World War II, most of its basic forms and techniques had been developed. Most historians of reference service find it convenient to begin with Samuel Swett Green's 1876 paper, "Personal Relations between Librarians and Readers." Until that time, the predominant view of the function of library service emphasized the acquisition and organization of library materials, and library clientele were expected to use the materials independently. Green, on the other hand, pointed out that library users were unskilled in using the catalogue to find materials and lacked the knowledge necessary to select the material appropriate to their needs. Personal assistance to such users, said Green, would benefit them and would result in their taking a more positive view of the library.

Green's ideas won widespread acceptance and support. By the 1890's the term *reference work* was replacing the earlier terms *aid to readers* and *assistance to readers*. This was particularly true in public libraries, where by the turn of the century most larger libraries were employing identified reference staffs. The early years of the 20th century saw the establishment of separate reference departments in public libraries, the acceptance of reference questions via telephone and correspondence, the extension of reference service to branches, and the differentiation of reference services by level of complexity and subject field. During the period between the two world wars, public libraries developed methods to deal with the greatly increased number of requests for assistance and began to apply specialized techniques to different types of requests. The "information desk" to deal with the multitude of directional and simple requests, "readers' advisory services" to assist readers in choosing materials for self-education and development, and the growth of subject specialist reference librarians and departments were all features of reference service that developed from 1918 to 1940.

The development of special libraries in the early 20th century, with their concept of amplified service, was fertile ground for the development of reference service concepts and techniques. Especially important in the period before World War I was the application of special librarianship to the field of legislative and municipal reference work. The basis of such work, and the example it held out to reference work elsewhere, was a detailed knowledge by the librarian of the information needs of the clientele, a thorough knowledge of information sources and a willingness to seek out needed information from any source, and an ability to synthesize or otherwise to prepare information for use by the client. During and following World War I, reference work in business, industrial, and research libraries assumed increasing importance. By the 1940's the special librarian frequently offered the following services: answering factual inquiries, preparing bibliographies, scanning and referring incoming literature, preparing abstracts and translations of literature, and doing literature searches.

Rothstein points out that the development of reference services was slower in college and university libraries than in public and special libraries. This was due, at least

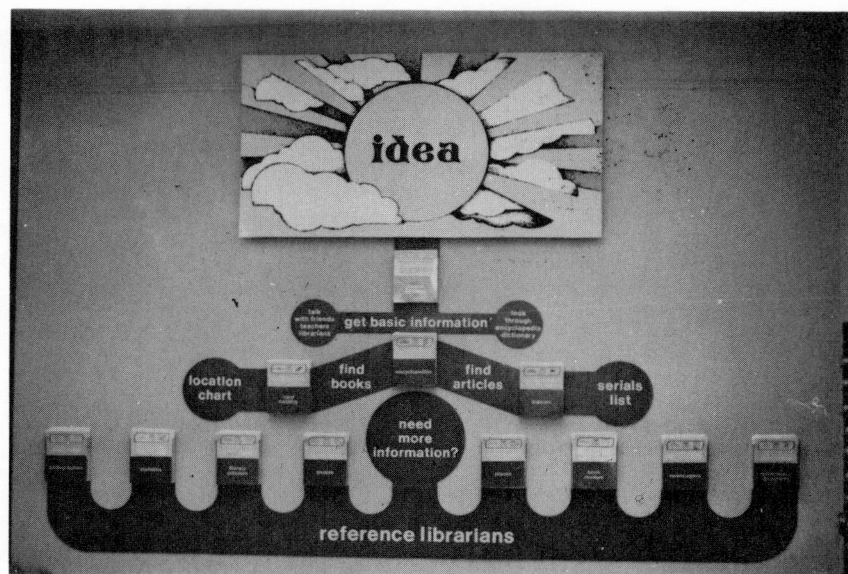


University of Texas at Austin

*Wall display, showing search strategy, is used in bibliographic instruction by librarians at the Undergraduate Library, University of Texas at Austin.*

in part, to the expectation that faculty members and students should be able to find their own materials and information and to the emphasis the scholarly community placed on collection development and subject access to materials through cataloguing. By the turn of the century, in spite of the example of a well-developed reference service established by Melvil Dewey at Columbia University, full-time reference staffs were not yet common in academic libraries. In the early decades of the century the relatively new state university libraries led the way in establishing reference services, and by World War I reference work was accepted as a necessary service in a university library. The years between the world wars saw a great increase in the number and variety of reference questions, the establishment of separate reference departments in many or most university libraries, and their assumption of such duties as special bibliographic and indexing projects and greatly expanded interlibrary loan work.

In the first half of the 20th century proponents of reference services reached wide agreement on the importance of such service and developed the basic concepts and methods of reference work. They also discussed the nature and extent of the assistance to be offered library users—a discussion that continues at the present time. On the one hand, many reference librarians and library administrators, especially in academic libraries, have argued that reference service exists to help inquirers to become independent users of library materials; i.e., to guide and instruct them so that they may find their own answers to their questions. Some authors have referred to this as the "conservative" philosophy of reference service.

Special librarians and others have argued that the function of reference service is the provision of information itself to inquirers–information located by the reference librarian and provided in the form needed by the user. This is frequently referred to as the "liberal" reference philosophy. Most public and academic libraries have adopted what can be called a "moderate" philosophy, which balances the desire to provide maximum assistance to each user with the capacity of the staff, in terms of time and training, to do so. In the 1970's there was less debate concerning the "conservative," "liberal," or "moderate" philosophies of service in favor of a recognition that users have different needs at different times and that reference programs should provide services–including instruction, guidance, and information–as appropriate to the needs of a particular user at a particular time.

**Instruction in Library Use.** From the time of Samuel Swett Green's groundbreaking paper to the present, instruction in the use of the library and library materials has been an important facet of reference service. Contemporaries of Green, both librarians and nonlibrarians such as university presidents, urged the importance of teaching library users about books and the bibliographic apparatus for their location and selection for use. Throughout the first half of the century, there were frequent references in the literature of librarianship to the need for such instruction and to the nature and content of the programs that were instituted. After a period of debate in the 1960's between those who emphasized "information" and those who emphasized "instruction" as the legitimate role of reference service, there was a resurgence of interest in library instruction in the 1970's, leading to the establishment in 1977 of the Library Instruction Round Table in the American Library Association.

Instruction in library use has had its fullest development in school libraries. For several decades most school librarians and teachers have agreed on the importance of teaching skills in the use of libraries and library materials to elementary and secondary school students. There is fairly broad agreement among school library media specialists on the aspects of library use and information finding skills that should be introduced and taught at various grade levels. Many states and individual school districts have adopted courses of study in library instruction to be integrated with other parts of the curriculum. Recent discussions and developments in the school library field have concentrated on teaching techniques and methods, strategies for obtaining the cooperation of classroom teachers, and the evaluation of instruction programs.

Public and special libraries have emphasized the information and guidance aspects of reference service so that, in the main, their library instruction programs have consisted of basic orientation to the library and to publicity regarding the library and its services. Over the years there has been considerable discussion of the need for more extensive efforts, and there have been specific programs related to individual subject areas, user groups, or projects. However, these have not had much cumulative impact on services in either public or special libraries.

The most important recent developments in library instruction have occurred in college and university libraries. These developments have been concentrated in the 1970's. They include the establishment in 1977 of the Bibliographic Instruction Section of the Association of College and Research Libraries and the issuance in 1977 by ACRL of "Guidelines for Bibliographic Instruction in Academic Libraries."

Several important aspects of instruction in library use have been clarified and developed in the last decade in college and university libraries. First, the philosophy has been enunciated that knowledge and skill in the use of information resources has importance beyond that attached to succeeding in one's college or university career. Indeed, the learning of such skill is important preparation for a lifetime of information use, especially in the postindustrial society, and such learning is an important objective for the curriculum of the college or university as a whole.

Library orientation, a term once used almost synonymously with library instruction, is now generally recognized as only the most basic aspect of library instruction, consisting of familiarizing users with the library's policies, procedures, and layout. Library instruction (frequently referred to as "bibliographic instruction") is of three major types: the separate course, course- or assignment-related instruction, and point-of-use or point-of-need instruction. The separate course or set of learning experiences has been a prominent feature in library instruction. Such a course usually has a combination of content about the use of information materials and biographic tools in general and the specific library resources on the campus where it is offered. In the 1960's and 1970's these courses employed such techniques as computer-assisted instruction, workbooks, media presentations, and other individualized and programmed approaches. The separate course allows a more sustained and in-depth coverage of bibliographic knowledge and skills than do other forms of instruction. Some campuses are reluctant, however, to give academic credit for such courses (almost a necessity if students are to be motivated to take them), and students often have difficulty relating course content to the rest of their academic life and to their general educational needs and goals.

Bibliographic instruction related to specific courses has been found to be an effective form of library instruction. Here the librarian and the classroom teacher cooperate so that the librarian helps students learn about bibliographic methods and library resources as a part of the course and at a time when the students have a need for the learning in order to complete other course requirements. Such instruction can be part of courses that are required of all students, of courses required of subject majors, or of graduate research methods courses. They can involve problem sets, programmed instruction, or other individualized methods. Librarians have found that integration of library instruction with college and university courses enhances student motivation because of its relationship with course requirements and increases retention of learning because of its immediate application to course assignments and projects. However, gaining the full cooperation of classroom faculty is a continuing problem in this instructional method.

Point-of-use library instruction involves the provision of instructional assistance at the time and place where a library user encounters a problem. Examples of this technique include media-based programs on catalogue or reference tool use situated at the catalogue or near the reference tool. Perhaps the most widely known recent development in this area has been the "library pathfinder," which was initiated as part of Project Intrex at the Massachusetts Institute of Technology and which has been widely adapted. The "pathfinder" or "roadmap" is a printed handout that is intended to help an individual develop and follow a search strategy in a specific subject area. Many libraries have developed such handouts to assist students in getting started finding and using library materials on topics that are popular for term papers and course projects. Similar in concept are handouts for library users on such topics as how to find biographical information, how to find book reviews, or how to locate plot summaries. Librarians have found that library users appreciate having assistance at the time they become aware of their need for it and that considerably more assistance and learning can be provided through the provision of point-of-use aids for frequently recurring problems than would be possible with individual user contacts. However, reference staffs have great difficulty finding sufficient time and expertise to prepare effective point-of-use programs and materials.

The concerns of the college and university instruction librarians in the late 1970's were similar to those of the school librarians. These include securing a commitment to the importance of library instruction from those who govern and administer colleges and universities, gaining the cooperation of individual classroom instructors, and developing effective planning strategies, from needs assessment through evaluation.

**Guidance.** Reading guidance, as a distinct method or function of reference service, includes stimulating reading, identifying and locating appropriate materials, and helping to interpret materials so that readers can choose among them according to their interests and needs. Many public libraries established "reader's advisory" services in the 1920's as a way of dealing with the increasing volume of requests for advice on "best" books and the need to separate such queries from those for specific information. The evolution of an administrative device into a specialized service technique was due to the public library's embracing the adult education movement from the mid-1920's onward.

The hallmarks of reading guidance are the unhurried interview, during which the reader's needs, goals, and reading habits are articulated; reading lists or reading courses, individually designed to meet the reader's need; and friendly follow-up, to see that the reader gets the materials when needed and to see if changes in the list or course are needed. These core aspects of reading guidance are supported and supplemented by annotated booklists and guides that can be used to choose and suggest appropriate materials, book talks and reviews, displays and exhibits to stimulate interest and suggest materials, and a reader-interest file that allows the library to notify readers of newly received books that will interest them.

In the 1940's and 1950's the public library's involvement in adult education activities moved from the era of planned reading programs and reader's advisory service into one of services to groups and finally to one of library-sponsored adult education groups. Separate reading guidance staffs generally began to be replaced by the provision of guidance service by the reference staff. While the literature of the 1950's through the 1970's continued to discuss reader's advisory services and to distinguish between information and guidance techniques (e.g., between the "reference interview" and the "advisory interview"), the separate reader's advisory service was not a prominent feature of reference service.

Recent developments in the guidance aspects of reference services have paralleled the growth of the philosophy "special publics." This philosophy finds inadequate the concept of the "general reader" and the characterization of library users by broad occupational, educational, and socioeconomic traits. Rather, librarians are recognizing that there are a very large number of distinctive user groups among a general library's clientele, each with special needs for specially adapted services. The development of effective reference services to such a special public is based on detailed study of the characteristics of the group that affect reading, learning, and information use; involvement of members of the group in planning the service and setting priorities; the development of collections of materials with particular relevance to the special group, which may involve the use of nontraditional and locally produced materials; and the use of a broad spectrum of stimulation and guidance techniques to assure that materials serve the goals of the program.

Special publics to which particular attention has been given in the 1960's and 1970's include the economically and educationally disadvantaged, the aging, persons with certain behavioral or psychological disfunctions, and those who wish to pursue further education (especially independently and outside the classroom context). Two special guidance strategies, bibliotherapy and learner's advising, illustrate the adaptations that are made to meet the needs of such special publics.

Bibliotherapy involves the use of selected reading materials to help the reader regain health or develop desirable behavior. Much of the literature on bibliotherapy is written within the context of service to persons in such institutions as hospitals or prisons. However, with the recent trend toward "mainstreaming" and returning persons with emotional and behavioral problems to their home communities, bibliotherapy outside the institutional context is gaining in emphasis. In bibliotherapy the guidance process of identifying needs, selecting and interpreting materials, and encouraging their use is often performed by the librarian as a part of an interdisciplinary team of helping professionals. Librarians, psychiatrists, social workers, corrections officials, and others continue to do research and develop principles and techniques to enhance the healthful effect of reading on the reader.

Hennepin County Library

*Telephone reference service, of special importance to the elderly and handicapped, is provided by most public libraries.*

The concept of the reference librarian as "learning adviser" almost brings the guidance function full circle to its early roots in adult education. In the past decade rapidly changing technology and an ever-increasing body of knowledge, coupled with the development of various formats of independent and nontraditional education, have brought to the library needs for assistance in identifying, choosing, and pursuing independent education programs. For example, in 1975 and 1976 nine major public libraries tested a planned learner's advisory program. This experiment and the interest it generated were part of a larger movement among libraries and other agencies to assist the many adults who study and learn at their own pace in their own personal style.

The learner's adviser strategy of guidance consists of the learner and the adviser working together to develop a shared understanding of the learner's goal (e.g., job advancement, academic or high school equivalency credit by examination, self-fulfillment) and the development of a learning plan. The learning plan outlines the approaches that match the goals and learning style of the learner and details the sequence of learning experiences. Implementing the learning plan frequently involves referral to other formal and informal educational agencies and organizations.

**Information Services.** Most libraries, whether or not they offer instructional or guidance services, provide information to users in response to identified needs. Usually, the provision of such information is made upon a request or query by the user. However, information is sometimes provided to users at the initiation of the library, in anticipation of an expressed need or in response to a need identified or even stimulated by the library.

The amount or type of assistance that a library will provide in response to a reference question varies from library to library and from one question to another, depending on the policy of the library, the staff available, the nature of the question, and other factors. Such assistance can range from merely pointing out materials or bibliographic tools that might be of help to the user to making an extensive search for the needed information and providing it in the form that is most appropriate to the user. The types of questions answered by library information services vary widely. A large proportion of questions asked at most reference desks are "directional" in nature; that is, they ask for information about the library, its facilities and services, and can usually be answered without using reference materials. Many other information needs can be served by the provision of bibliographic information; services provided in this category range from the simple verification or completion of a citation to extensive bibliography compilation and such current awareness services as selective dissemination of information programs. Questions that ask for information itself, rather than citations, can range from simple factual questions that can be answered from a single source to complex questions, whose answers require information from several sources, and requests for library-prepared state-of-the-art reports that require synthesis of information based on critical judgment.

The process through which a reference librarian provides the answer to a reference query has a number of highly interrelated parts. One of the most important of these is the clarification of the question itself, to make sure that it represents accurately the user's information need. This aspect of reference service, often referred to as "the reference interview" or "question negotiation," involves helping the user understand and articulate the information need, and making sure that the librarian understands the terms and meaning of the question.

When the reference librarian and the user have agreed upon the question in the user's terms, the librarian must analyze the question and translate it into the structure and terms of the information system and resources available to answer it. This involves such considerations as the type of information sought, the type of tool or source that is likely to provide the answer, and the index or catalogue headings under which the information might be sought. Using the results of this analysis and translation or question indexing, the librarian formulates a search strategy, considering such matters as the actual sources to be consulted, the order in which they will be used, the combination of terms to be searched, and the relationships among them.

The actual search for information, especially if the user is present during the search, often involves refinement of the search strategy and further analysis of the question as the librarian and the user learn more about the information that is available. Depending on the policies and practices of the library and the wishes of the user, the reference librarian either can perform the search for the user or can provide some suggestions regarding search strategy and potential sources and let the user conduct the search.

There is also wide variation regarding the delivery of the information found by librarians in response to questions. Some libraries or the users they serve prefer to receive only the documents or materials containing the information, with the process of extracting and interpreting it left to the user. Other libraries, particularly special libraries, will extract information and synthesize it into a state-of-the-art report as an answer to a question that requires judgment and interpretation.

While the major features of information services were developed by the mid-20th century, their particular concerns and activities are continually changing, as user needs and information resources change. Three examples will be used to illustrate these changes: cooperative reference services, computer-assisted reference service, and information and referral services.

The borrowing of specific materials by one library from another on behalf of users (interlibrary loan) is a long-standing practice. In recent years, libraries have begun to request assistance from each other in the form of answers to reference questions that have not been translated into specific author-title interlibrary loan requests. Referring reference questions from library to library is a very important aspect of the current trend toward library cooperation and resource sharing, and it introduces some fundamental changes into the question-answering process. For example, in a cooperative reference situation the reference interview is conducted by one librarian while the search is formulated and implemented by another. The search must be conducted in the absence of the user, and the information that is found is delivered to the user without the user-searcher interaction and evaluative feedback that can enhance search effectiveness. Reference librarians and administrators are exploring and developing various means for improving the quality of cooperative reference service, especially the full exploitation of modern communications technology to maintain as much as possible the interaction between users, librarians, and information resources that characterizes effective information service. For example, the format in which the reference question is transmitted from library to library (whether it be by mail, teletype, or telephone) should be designed so as to capture and transmit as much relevant and accurate information as possible about the user and the information need. At times it is appropriate to have the user in direct contact with the librarian to which the question has been referred. Policies and practices regarding such direct contact, as well as for other aspects of cooperative reference service, will continue to be developed and refined.

One of the most important developments in the information resources available to the reference librarian and the user has been the wide availability of computer searchable data bases, especially of bibliographic data, and the means for searching these data bases at any time and in an interactive mode. An increasing number of user needs can be met, either partially or in full, by conducting searches of data bases via computer. Originally concentrated in the natural sciences, indexing and abstracting coverage of data bases is extending into the social sciences and the humanities.

The role of the reference librarian in assisting users with computer readable data bases is basically the same as with more traditional information sources. The need to clarify the question is still there, as is the need for the identification of and choice between potential answering sources, the translation of the question into the terms of the information source, the formulation of a search strategy, and assistance in conducting the search. On the other hand, there are also some important differences. For various reasons—including the "peep hole" effect, whereby only a small portion of the computerized information source and its structure can be seen at one time, the high cost of "browsing" by computer, and the need to make explicit in a computer search what can be left implicit in a traditional search—the reference process is more formal in a computer search than is typically the case in the ordinary situation.

Often the user for whom a computerized search is to be made will be given an appointment to discuss the information need and the search with a librarian (as contrasted to the "first come, first served" immediate service for other users). The reference interview is usually considerably longer in this situation than for other users. The pre-search planning, including choice of potential answering sources (data bases), selection of indexing terms, and formulation of a search strategy (usually a matter of expressing algebraic relationships among the search terms), is done more formally and completely for a computerized search than for a traditional search. It is more common for the librarian actually to conduct the search (i.e., to operate the computer terminal) when working with a computer readable data base than is the case with manual searches in printed sources.

Just as the sheer number of information sources can be a barrier between a person who needs information and the resolution of that need, so can the number and complexity of service agencies be a barrier between a person with a problem and an agency that can help solve that problem. It has long been recognized that persons with needs for assistance (whether persons needing charity aid, persons whose lives are disrupted by war, or persons who could be served by government welfare agencies) fail to receive that assistance because they fail to find or use the agencies that exist. It has also been recognized that information and personal assistance provided by a referral service can effectively link persons who have needs or problems with agencies that can serve the needs or solve the problems. During the last few years an increasing number of libraries, especially urban public libraries, have been including such a service, now commonly called "information and referral service" (I&R) among their reference services.

While the reference function in information and referral services is basically the same as in other information services, there are some differences in particulars. The information provided is not in books or printed sources prepared by others and purchased by the library; rather, it is found in a resource file about community services and agencies that has been created by the library staff. This resource file, commonly in a card or loose-leaf format and with detailed subject indexing, can be supplemented with pamphlets and hand-out information on the agencies.

Another important difference between information and referral service and traditional question-answering service is that I&R service does not stop with the provision of a piece of information. There is usually some sort

John Crerar Library

*Science reference librarians at John Crerar Library, Chicago, provide special reference guidance for map and atlas users.*

University of South Carolina Library

*Instruction programs, like this videotape presentation on the card catalogue, are effective in orienting library users.*

of additional service to make sure that the link is actually made between the person and the service agency. Depending on the policies of the library and the needs of the user, this might include contacting the agency to make an appointment for the user or even escorting the user to the agency. Most writers on I&R services emphasize the importance of follow-up with the user to see if the service of the agency actually helped solve his or her problem. Such follow-up can help the I&R service evaluate its effectiveness, improve the accuracy of the resource file, help keep service agencies accountable and responsive, and lead to alternative referrals if the user was not helped by the initial one.

**Issues.** Information, instruction, and guidance services in libraries have had a somewhat short period of development, beginning in the last quarter of the 19th century. Their broad function of providing personal assistance to users in overcoming barriers between them and the information they need has remained the same over the years. Likewise, their essential process of identifying and clarifying the user's need, selecting information or learning resources to meet that need, and assisting the user in finding and using those resources remains unchanged. On the other hand, information, instruction, and guidance services are continually evolving as user needs change and become better known, as information resources change and develop, and as equipment and processes for bringing users and information together are developed and refined.

The key to any personal assistance service is, of course, the staff that provides it. Reference staff members will need to master fundamentals, such as a thorough knowledge of their users and skill in communicating with them and a thorough knowledge of information resources and skill in exploiting them on behalf of users. They will also need continually to be changing, as users change and as the nature and structure of information resources change.

In the immediate future two important concerns are likely to receive major attention from reference librarians and administrators. The first of these is the matter of direct user fees for information services. This has been brought into sharp focus by the financial problems associated with the addition of computer-based searching to reference services. Access to and interactive searching of computerized data bases is quite costly, and many libraries have not been able to increase their budgets to cover the costs of such service. On the other hand, it has seemed unwise to deny the service to those who would pay for it. Since computer-assisted searching is a special service, involving staff time and other service beyond that which is provided to all users and with costs that can easily be associated with specific users, administrators see some justification for direct user fees. Many reference librarians, however, are aware that such service is appropriate to a wide range of users, some of whom cannot pay for it, and find the inequitable access to information caused by fees contrary to their philosophy of reference service. This is a hard dilemma, exacerbated by uncertain economic conditions, which will receive much discussion as reference librarians attempt to minimize barriers between all their users and the information they need.

The other matter of major concern to information, instruction, and guidance librarians is the planning and evaluation of services. Increasingly, reference librarians are recognizing that effective services can be based only on careful identification of user needs. This involves the identification of special target publics and collaboration with members of these user groups to ascertain information needs and to translate these into service objectives and priorities. Likewise, reference librarians are increasingly aware of the need for accurate measurement and evaluation of their services. Most authors of the literature of reference service evaluation admit that the state of the art is fairly rudimentary; yet all agree that continued study and development will result in improvement and increased effectiveness in personal assistance to library users in the pursuit of information.

**REFERENCES**

Samuel Rothstein, *The Development of Reference Services,* ACRL Monograph 14 (ALA, 1955), is the standard history of reference services to the mid-20th century.

William A. Katz, *Introduction to Reference Work,* 3d ed. (1978). This two-volume work is the standard textbook in the field. Volume 2 is especially relevant to this article because of its good discussions and references to further reading regarding the trends, issues, and current status of the various aspects of reference service.

Marjorie E. Murfin and Lubomyr R. Wynar, *Reference Service: An Annotated Bibliographic Guide* (1977), a comprehensive bibliography of books and articles in English from 1876 to 1975, for further reading on almost any facet of reference service.

CHARLES A. BUNGE

# Renaissance Libraries

The history of the Renaissance is inseparable from the history of its books and libraries. The expansion of knowledge within the scholastic tradition, the secularization of society, and the rekindling of interest in ancient history, literature, and art, both in Italy and in Northern Europe, placed new demands on both books and libraries from 1400 to 1700. The intellectual achievements of the Renaissance were as complex and varied as the kinds of books and libraries that the Renaissance produced. Renaissance libraries included university libraries, since the universities founded in the Middle Ages greatly expanded during the Renaissance, and new universities with new libraries of scholastic texts were created. Other Renaissance libraries were religious libraries, established to serve the new reformed orders that spread during the period. These libraries also contained rich collections of scholastic literature. Still other Renaissance libraries were courtly libraries, assembled to preserve the new vernacular literature that expanded particularly in France under the patronage of King Charles V and great noblemen like Jean du Berry and in England under the patronage of Edward IV. Other Renaissance libraries were humanist libraries, assembled by Italian humanists and their lay and ecclesiastical patrons to preserve the manuscripts of newly recovered ancient texts. Finally, Renaissance libraries can be said to have included theological libraries formed chiefly from printed books to serve the Protestant Reformation and the Catholic Counter-Reformation

Despite their remarkable variety, Renaissance libraries reflected a single and common phenomenon: a rise in the rate of literacy that, when set in the context of a moderate increase in population, yielded a dramatic increase in the number of people who were able to read and write and therefore sought to use books and to avail themselves of libraries. In the 12th century only a small, chiefly monastic, elite were able to read and write, and literate people constituted a tiny fraction of the general population. By 1533 Thomas More estimated that over half the population of England was literate in the vernacular. The rate of increase in literacy accelerated at the end of the 14th and during the 15th century. During the Renaissance, Europe was transformed from an oral culture, with a population primarily of listeners, to a population that included significant numbers of readers.

**Manuscript Book Production.** Monasteries had been the major centers of book production in the Middle Ages, when they also served as the major libraries. Although monastic book production continued after 1300, book production generally became the domain of professional scribes, who served a varied clientele of schoolmen and lay aristocracy. Beginning in the mid-13th century Europe witnessed a growth in demand for scholastic textbooks, which stimulated a remarkable series of innovations in the way in which these books were produced. The first of these was the *pecia* system employed in the universities of Naples, Bologna, Padua, Paris, Oxford, Cambridge, and Upsala from the 13th through the 15th centuries. Fundamental to the operation of the pecia system was the creation of exemplars—model manuscripts certified for their textual accuracy which were subdivided into their component quires of six or eight folios and rented to licensed scribes. Whereas previously a given manuscript could be copied only by one scribe at a time, the pecia system allowed a number of scribes to make copies of the same text simultaneously. The result was an increase in manuscript production combined with greater control of the textual uniformity, for the quality of the exemplars was under the control of the university. The awareness of the need for accurate textual transmission reflected in the pecia system was to become a hallmark of Renaissance book production.

Succeeding centuries brought continued innovation, reflecting the desire to produce standardized manuscripts with great speed. In France, the Low Countries, and England in the 14th century, scribes developed the practice of imposition, the significance of which is still being assessed by manuscript scholars. Imposition meant that texts were written on uncut quires before folding and thus out of narrative sequence, in a manner similar to the uncut pages produced by later printing presses. Another innovation that began throughout Europe in the 14th century was the adaptation of cursive handwriting to book production. Cursive scripts could be written with fewer liftings of the pen, allowing books to be made swiftly and thus sold at lower prices. The use of paper was also a major development. It was first introduced to book production in the 14th century but took firm hold only in the course of the 15th century when paper played a more important role in lowering the cost of books than did the introduction of printing by movable type. Paper books, written in cursive scripts, became the first truly cheap books, easily within the means of townspeople, gentry, and poor students in Italy, England, and France. In the early 1400's ordinary school manuals were being produced by *scriptoria* in editions of 200 to 300 copies, numbers comparable to the runs of printed editions a century later.

While some changes in technical procedure allowed the production of cheap manuscript books, other changes increased the supply of deluxe books, which in the 15th century were becoming more standardized as they were produced in larger and larger quantities. The use of a form of tracing paper permitted the exact reproduction of miniatures and thus the standardization of iconography. Some miniatures intended for books of hours were mass produced separately from the text. Increasing division of labor separated the copying, illustration, and decoration of the manuscript. As a result, deluxe manuscript books of the 15th century showed increased uniformity in appearance, dimensions, and length.

**The Impact of Printing.** The invention of printing by movable type must be viewed in the light of the growing appetite in Western Europe for standardized books. The invention has traditionally been attributed to Johann Gutenberg of Mainz in 1444. Before Gutenberg, block printing was used in textile decoration, illustrations, and short texts. However, these processes did not play a major role in book production and are of importance only insofar as they may have stimulated printers to think of the possibility of using movable type cast in molds to produce books. It is important to note that the earliest printers came from outside the group of artisans directly concerned with manuscript book production. Gutenberg was a goldsmith, as were apparently early printers in Avignon and Basle, and the secret method of *artificliter scribere,* like other skills of goldsmiths, was initially meant to be applied to works of beauty and high cost. The first printed books were often printed on vellum, an indication of the luxury market to which early printers most often sought to cater. Early printed books were often illustrated with hand-painted miniatures and decorated with floral borders identical to those in contemporary manuscript codices.

Only after 1480 did printers, many of whom were former scribes, begin to produce cheap books. By 1500 printing had become an important source of cheap university textbooks, and most of the titles printed were works of proven value that had been previously disseminated in manuscript. However, in the first third of the 16th century there emerged a new kind of author who wrote with the press and its potentially wide audience in mind. Printing played an especially important role in spreading the new ideas of the Protestant Reformation and was probably a decisive factor in making Protestantism a different phenomenon from the 14th-century heresies of Wyclifism and Hussitism, which lacked a comparable means of mass communication. During the Wars of Religion in France (1562–98), printing became an important medium for the expression of political theory.

Printing had an enormous impact on the content of Renaissance libraries, since standardized and uniform books ultimately led to standardized collections. Before printing, Jerome's *De Viribus Illustribus* had on occasion been used as a model for library catalogues, but manuscript collections had remained incredibly diverse. Printing led to standardization of the texts and the definition of the corpus of ancient and medieval authors. Bibliographies like those prepared by Conrad Gesner were meant by their authors to serve as standardized catalogues of libraries of printed texts. By the mid-16th century the corpus of cited literature was increasingly defined by what had been printed. Works that for whatever reason had escaped the press fell from the tradition of learned discourse. Whereas printing standardized the bibliographical base of 16th-century culture, it did not immediately lead to libraries larger than those of the previous century, which had been composed exclusively of manuscripts. Many printed book libraries were in fact smaller than important manuscript collections; for example, under Louis XIII the royal library of France had only 400 more printed books than the library of Charles V had manuscript books two centuries earlier. Most printed books found their way into the increasing number of small personal libraries.

Scala

*The 16th-century Medici Library in Florence, Italy, was designed by Michelangelo.*

**The Renaissance Book.** In addition to changes in techniques and technology, intellectual and social changes played a major role in determining the physical appearance and content of Renaissance books and libraries. In Italy humanism was of enormous import. Humanism developed outside the universities, which had been responsible for the greater portion of Italian book production in the 13th and 14th centuries. In general, early humanists were not the university-trained doctors of theology, medicine, and law but laymen, often notaries, trained in the tradition of the *ars dictaminis.* The early humanists shared a common goal: the restoration of eloquence in Latin prose. To achieve this end Petrarch, Boccaccio, and Salutati assembled collections remarkable for their richness in ancient Latin literature. The humanists avidly collected the oldest possible manuscripts of classical authors and had them copied in order to build libraries of ancient texts in their original form, free from the corruptions in orthography and grammar introduced by medieval scribes. For the books that they themselves copied and for their libraries, the first humanists used the highly legible Gothic textual scripts favored in courtly and bourgeois Italian circles of the 14th century. In the first decade of the quattrocento, however, Florentine humanists began to produce books whose scripts and decoration were based on older manuscripts, particularly Tuscan manuscripts of the 10th to 12th centuries, which were characteristically written in Caroline script and decorated with white ivy stem motifs. Whether the humanists really believed these manuscripts to have resembled those of the age of Cicero is not clear; nevertheless, it is certain that the humanists believed that *littera antiqua* was the appropriate script for the classical texts. During the 15th century these scripts came to be used for other materials, including vernacular literature, and even for scholastic treatises and papal bulls. When printing was introduced into Italy in 1458, the dominant type fonts—Roman and Italic—were modeled on two varieties of humanistic script. In the second half of the 15th century, humanists exhibited an increasing interest in epigraphy, with particular emphasis on the inscriptions of the Roman Empire; capital letters of the Imperial period became the models for the capital letters of manuscript books and ultimately of printed books.

The link between humanism and the physical appearance of the book, so strong in Italy, was weak in Northern Europe. In 15th-century France humanistic script was not popular, and humanistic texts were frequently copied in scripts wholly unhumanistic in appearance. The major force in forming scripts and secular libraries in the early Northern Renaissance was the growth in vernacular and courtly literature under aristocratic patronage. Beginning with King Charles V of France, the French-speaking aristocracy in France, the Low Countries, and England began forming libraries of vernacular texts equal in size (roughly 400 to 1,000 volumes) to those of the bibliophilic Italian humanists. In earlier centuries Princes had been read to by professional readers, who were at ease with the Gothic textual script of the universities. As lay readership increased, however, a new and more legible script became popular in aristocratic circles. *Lettre batarde,* termed *hybrida* by some modern palaeographers, achieved a dominance for the vernacular literature of Northern Europe equal to that of the forms for humanistic texts in Italy. The vernacular chronicles, chivalric romances, and books of devotion so popular in aristocratic circles were written and printed in lettre batarde until the first third of the 16th century. In France humanistic type fonts then replaced lettre batarde, but in Germany lettre batarde prevailed and became the model for the *fractura* type font, which remained the standard German type font until the 20th century.

**Renaissance Libraries.** Throughout the Renaissance the largest libraries remained university libraries; the Sorbonne, for example, in 1338 already possessed over 1,700 volumes. The holdings of university libraries were divided into reference collections, which were chained to desks for consultation only in the library, and general collections, which circulated to both students and masters. The reference collections were often freely open for consultation, and the circulating collections were, in some cases, available to even the poorest students. The university libraries were therefore the early Renaissance forerunners of public libraries. In architecture they differed greatly from the smaller monastic libraries, which had been installed in cloisters. The university libraries were centralized in halls equipped with benches and tables. They became the models for the libraries of religious houses as well as for the great princely collections of the 14th and 15th centuries.

Pope Urban V in Avignon and King Charles V in Paris founded the first of the great princely libraries in the mid-14th century. Subsequently, other important libraries were formed by Gian Galeazzo Visconti, Jean Duke of Berry, Philip Duke of Burgundy, King Alfonso the Magnanimous of Naples, and King Matthias Corvinus of Hungary. Pope Nicolas V founded the Vatican Library in Rome to take the place of the Avignon library lost during the Great Schism. In contrast to university collections, princely libraries were considered private possessions, and admission was accorded only to the favorites of the prince. The books in princely libraries were more luxurious than those in university libraries, and new standards of cataloguing—with emphasis on description of decoration and script—were developed, in part, to prevent theft.

Princes did not always think only of themselves. Cosimo de Medici in the mid-15th century purchased volumes and donated them, along with selected items from his own collection, to the Dominican convent of San Marco to establish a public library for the use of the citizens of Florence. Cosimo's grandson, Lorenzo the Magnificent, established the Biblioteca Medicea-Laurentiana with similar intent. Sixtus IV in 1475 opened the Vatican Library to the public. During the reign of Charles IX, public access was permitted to the French Royal Library. By the 17th century many of the private libraries of the 14th and 15th centuries had become the possession, through inheritance and purchase, of the libraries of sovereign princes, who permitted consultation to the public.

In the mid-16th century Europe's largest and oldest libraries still were manuscript collections. Frederigo Duke of Urbino was said to have been proud that he had only handwritten books and no printed books. While Paul II and Sixtus IV were patrons of printing, the Vatican appears to have retained its preference for manuscripts until the middle of the 16th century. Under Louis XIII in 1645, the Royal Library still had twice as many manuscripts as printed books. By contrast, the new libraries of Protestant institutions were composed principally of printed volumes. Protestants, alienated from their society, built some of the first comprehensive collections of exclusively printed materials to compensate for their lack of access to the older royal and ecclesiastical collections with their great manuscript holdings. The destruction of monastic libraries during the Reformation added to the dependency of Protestants on printed sources. In Geneva the Academy of Calvin was composed entirely of printed works, as was the library of the Protestant University of Leiden at its foundation. Protestants, who used the printing press so effectively to communicate their ideas, frequently presented copies of their works to libraries. Gifts were not the only source, however; in Geneva the law of copyright deposit of 1530 was an important aid in building the library of the Academy of Calvin. Among Catholics the Jesuits, leaders in the Counter-Revolution, had no manuscript collection of their own and were particularly active in building large libraries of printed books and in increasing the level of bibliographic expertise. The Jesuit Library of Paris at the end of the 16th century is said to have numbered 20,000 volumes, an astounding figure when compared with libraries of the previous century.

**Librarians.** In the monasteries of the Middle Ages, the functions of Librarian were regularly performed by the *precentor,* who had general responsibility for liturgy, of which reading was seen as an extension. In the universities the formal office of Librarian was created, but it did not have great importance as a position of erudition, although some scholastics of note at times performed its functions. Similarly, Librarians of the Kings and Princes of France in the 14th and 15th centuries were not known as scholars. The first scholar-librarians in the modern sense appeared in Italy in the 15th century, when humanist scholars like Niccolò Niccoli built their own extensive collections. In the second half of the 15th century the Popes consistently placed scholars in charge of the Vatican Library. In the early 16th century Pope Julius II chose the renowned humanist Tommaso Inghirami as his second Librarian; Pope Leo X chose as his Librarian Filippo Beroaldo, who in 1515 prepared the first edition of the *Annales* of Tacitus. The custom of placing libraries in the charge of scholars was emulated in France under Francis I, who chose Guillaume Budé as *maitre de la librairie du Roy* and Jacques Lefevre d'Étaples as one of his librarians. The collection of Greek manuscripts flourished under their care, and both men were responsible for a significant revival of interest in the Greek language and literature. The modern connection between scholar-librarians and the editing of texts became clearly established in the 16th century. Marguerin de la Bigne, the first great editor of the Western Church Fathers, was Librarian of the Sorbonne and founded a tradition of entrusting the editing of patristic texts to librarians. This practice was maintained in the 17th century by Jean Mabillon and the Congrégation de Saint-Maur. Under the administration of eminent scholar-librarians, libraries at the end of the Renaissance also showed an increased interest in the preservation of books, with particular emphasis on binding, which with the support of their wealthy patrons evolved into an art form in its own right. With their interest in editions and textual problems, scholar-librarians also established the tradition—which endured until the 19th century—of maintaining a corps of scribes in the service of great libraries for the preparation of accurate copies for the library itself and for the benefit of scholars unable to make a personal consultation.

**REFERENCES**


Hanna H. Gray, "Renaissance Humanism: The Pursuit of Eloquence," *Journal of the History of Ideas* (1963), reprinted in Paul Oskar Kristeller and Philip P. Wiener, *Renaissance Essays* (1968).

Berthold L. Ollman, *The Origin and Development of Humanistic Script* (1960).

Paul Oskar Kristeller, *Renaissance Thought: The Classic, Scholastic and Humanist Strains* (1961).

———, *Renaissance Thought II: Papers on Humanism and the Arts* (1965).

Curt Ferdinand Bühler, *The Fifteenth Century Book* (1960).

John Willis Clark, *The Care of Books: An Essay on the Development of Libraries and Their Fittings, from Earliest Times to the End of the Eighteenth Century* (1909).

Lucian Febvre and Henri-Jean Martin, *The Impact of Printing, 1450–1860,* translated by David Gerard (1976).

Sandra Hindman and James Douglas Farquhar, *Pen to Press: Illustrated Manuscripts and Printed Books in the First Century of Printing* (1977).

Malcolm Parkes, "The Literacy of the Laity," in *Literature and Western Civilization,* edited by David Daiches and Anthony Thorlby (1972–76), volume II.

Sigfrid Heinrich Steinberg, *Five Hundred Years of Printing* (1955; revised ed. 1974).

Berthold L. Ullman and Philip A. Stadter, *The Public Library of Renaissance Florence* (1972).

Francis Wormald and C. E. Wright, *The English Library before 1700* (1958).


PAUL SAENGER

# Reprography

During the 1950's a new word, "reprography," came to be used to describe the technology of reproducing two-dimensional visual communication media in administrative, business, and institutional operations. The term appeared sporadically in the library literature of the 1960's and entered the working vocabulary of librarians in the mid-1970's, gradually replacing photoduplication, document copying, documentary reproduction and, to some extent, photocopying, although the latter term is still very much in use. Copying is uniquely important as a means of carrying out the library's mission of information transfer.

**Technology.** Reprographic processes are based on the differential chemical or physical changes effected in some materials by an exposure to radiant energy, which form an image that is visible, or can be made visible, and permanent. The currently used processes—photography, electrophotography, and thermography—depend on chemical systems (e.g., iron salts, silver halides, diazonium), or electrical phenomena, or on the action of heat.

The various copying processes and methods may be characterized by the tonal relationships of the copies to the original that was copied (the so-called polarity, whether positive or negative), the image orientation (right-reading, or reverse-reading), the size of copies, the method of image production (direct or transfer), the method of exposure (contact or optical), the color sensitivity (blue-sensitive, ortho, pan), speed (sensitivity to the radiant energy), and the resolving power and contrast of the sensitized materials used.

Black areas in the original image appear black, and white areas appear white in a *positive* copy: the tones correspond to those of the original. In a *negative* copy, the tone values are reversed. *Positive* and *negative* are also used in another sense, the former to describe an original image with dark letters on a light background; the latter, white letters on a dark background. When a negative-working process is used, the first copy made from a positive original will be a negative copy (tonal values reversed) and must be recopied to get a positive copy. Similarly, if a procedure yields reverse-reading copies, another step is required for getting right-reading copies.

A *direct* process produces a copy directly on a piece of material. A *transfer* process first produces an image on a piece of sensitized material that is used as an intermediate and that then transfers it to another piece of material that becomes the copy.

The sensitized material may be exposed to energy (e.g., light or heat, depending on the process) in contact with the original or through a lens (optic). Thus, the method of exposure may be called *contact* or *optical.*

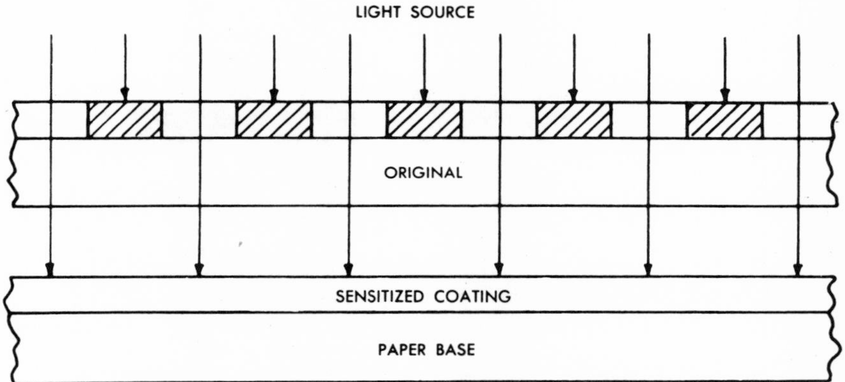


*Figure 1. Copying by the direct contact method*

Contact exposure can be either *direct* (the light passes through the original to expose the sensitized material) or *reflex* (the light passes through the sensitized material, to be absorbed by the dark and reflected by the white parts of the original). The *direct-contact* method can be used only for copying originals printed on one side of translucent paper or film, as the light must pass through it to create the image.

*Figure 2. Copying by the contact-reflex method*

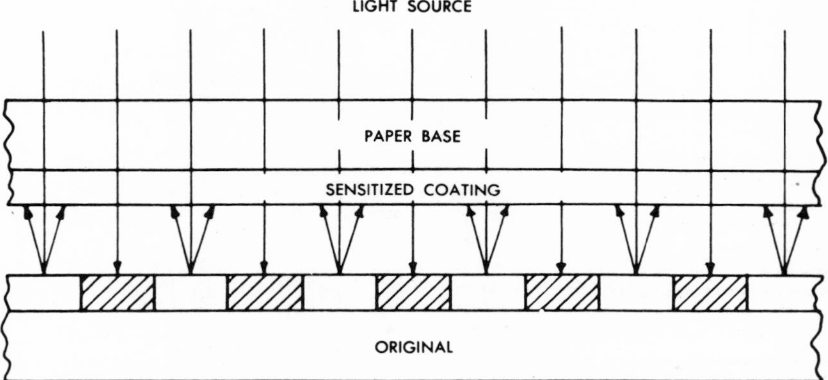

The copy will be right-reading or reverse-reading, depending on whether the translucent original is placed face up or face down on the sensitized material. Unless special (autopositive) material is used, the copy will be negative. Originals printed on both sides and on opaque materials can be copied with the *contact-reflex* method. Normally, the copy made by "reflexing" is negative and reverse-reading, and a right-reading copy is then made of it by the direct-contact method.

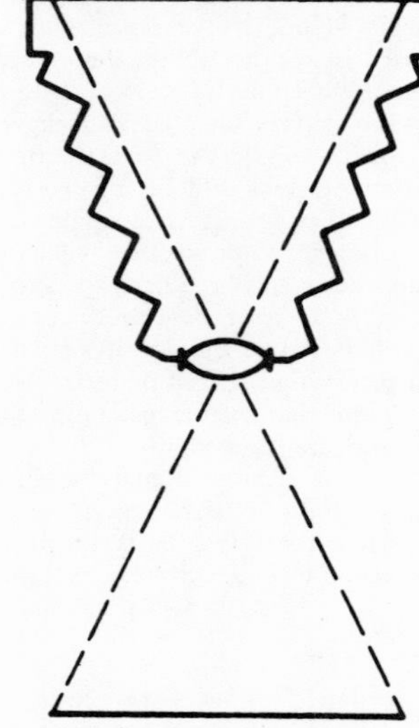

*Figure 3. Optical copying (full-size)*

Contact methods work quite well with loose sheet material, as it is usually possible to bring the original and the sensitized material into the near-perfect contact necessary for satisfactory imaging. The difficulties in using this method with bound volumes, however, are great. The size, thickness, and weight of the book, the variations in paper surface and condition, the stiffness of the binding (as in, for example, oversewn binding), insufficient margins, and other variables can pose problems that might be difficult or impossible to solve.

Although a variety of light-sensitive materials were used with success in the early days of photography in the 1840's, the predominant role in photographic (including reprographic) imaging was soon taken by silver halide systems. Silver halide materials can be fashioned to suit many purposes and processes and yield excellent results. Alternative systems, which have been developing during the past several decades, have so far found a place only in a few special, though important, applications, such as reprography.

At a Paris exhibition in 1900 a camera was shown that was designed to make copies from books on a roll of paper and was equipped with a reversing prism; it was awarded a prize. In 1910 a similar machine, the *Photostat* camera, entered the American market. The Photostat system (and similar apparatus made by other manufacturers) combines a copyboard, a prism-equipped camera capable of making prints up to 18 by 24 inches, a large capacity paper supply, and developing and fixing trays in one machine. There is no need for a darkroom. The first copy is negative, but right-reading, and copy size may be varied from 50 to 200 percent of the original. Various photographic controls may be exercised during exposure and processing; the quality of the product is potentially very high.

One of several important reprographic systems introduced in the 1950's was a new silver halide process: *diffusion-transfer-reversal* (DTR). Thanks to the speedy and simple processing and the one-step production of a positive copy, inexpensive equipment, and numerous fiercely competitive suppliers, DTR became the dominant copying method of the 1950's. Another innovation of the 1950's was Verifax (TM), a *gelatin-dye-transfer* process, which achieves the same result as the DTR process by different means, and which was also popular for a time.

Another important reprographic novelty of the 1950's was Thermo-Fax (TM)—the first practical imaging process operating by the action of heat rather than light. The process is simple, clean, convenient, and very fast. It has the disadvantage, however, that the text of the original must be written, typed, or printed with heat-absorbing (carbon content) ink (dyes do not absorb heat), and that the unexposed parts of the material retain their heat sensitivity and are subject to deterioration. The *dual spectrum* process is a combined photographic-thermographic process introduced a few years later. The original need not absorb heat and, like the Thermo-Fax process it largely replaced, does not need chemicals for processing.

Xerography was another new reprographic process introduced in the 1950's. After a relatively slow start, it has had a more far-reaching effect in the long run than either DTR or thermography. Xerography is based on the behavior of certain materials (photoconductors), which retain an electrostatic charge in the dark, but dissipate it upon exposure to light. If the photoconductor (e.g., a selenium-coated plate or cylinder) is given an electrostatic charge prior to exposure, the charge is retained or dissipated and a latent image formed according to the pattern of light reflected from the original. Pigment (toner) particles attracted by the retained charge make the latent image visible. The pigment is transferred from the plate or cylinder to some material (e.g., uncoated paper) and fused by heat or pressure. Xerography is an *electrophotographic transfer* process.

A *direct electrophotographic* process (Electrofax) became commercially available in 1954. In this process the latent image is formed on a thin photoconductive layer coated on the copy paper itself. The coating—zinc oxide—is readily available, inexpensive, nontoxic, and stable. The sensitivity of zinc-oxide paper can be modified and controlled by the addition of dyes to the coating, and with pigment suspended in liquid, very high resolution can be achieved.

By the end of the 1960's, the highly developed, self-contained, automated equipment manufactured for office copying with the electrophotographic method made almost all previous copying processes look obsolete and unquestionably dominated the marketplace.

**Applications.** Copying processes are used in libraries for (1) the acquisition, sharing, and preservation of library materials, (2) the assistance of patrons in using library materials, and (3) communication and record management purposes. In the last category, with the possible exception of catalogue card reproduction, the application requirements and procedures are essentially the same in the library as in other organizations. Copying for the purpose of adding something to the collection that is unavailable in the original, making facsimiles of highly prized or fragile items, sharing resources with other libraries without depriving the library's own constituency of potential use, replacing deteriorating items, missing issues, lost pages—these are the principal copying uses in the library, and they have requirements that are often different from and more difficult to meet than those in many other applications of copying technology.

The need for copying is as old as writing. Until the development of photography around the middle of the 19th century, an existing document had to be copied by hand. The new medium's potential for making facsimiles for the purpose of extending the use of literature in hitherto impossible ways was quickly recognized. Microphotocopying was demonstrated in 1839, and the idea of republishing by microphotographic means was first communicated by Sir John Herschel in 1853. During the second half of the century the materials and apparatus of general photography were used for copying. Some of the advantages of specially designed copying equipment were realized at the turn of the century. By then some libraries had installed photographic laboratories.

Photocopying for acquisition and preservation purposes, as well as for patrons' use, was greatly expanded by the introduction of the photostat-type camera, which is well suited to copying library materials. In 1912 photostat-type cameras were installed in the Library of Congress, Chicago's John Crerar Library, and the New York Public Library; by 1929, 42 libraries operated such machines. Until the mid-1930's, when microfilm took over such tasks, libraries used photostats for reprinting rare books in small editions and for the preservation of deteriorating newspaper collections. By 1946 the public demand for copies had increased so much that the New York Public Library produced almost half a million photostat copies in one year.

Photostat services proved valuable to libraries and library users. Yet they required relatively large investment and, in order to be economically efficient, consistently high production levels; thus only a few dozen libraries could afford them. The majority had to wait for simpler and cheaper copying methods. These came about when some major manufacturers decided to concentrate on one segment of the copying market that had the highest sales potential, i.e., office records.

The new processes of the 1950's were conceived as office systems, for an input (i.e., business letters and records) that was of standard size and of fairly uniform graphic quality, and for an output that satisfied rather modest functional requirements of appearance, legibility, and permanence. Since the machines were cheap and the process simple, any library could afford them. Most did acquire them, in spite of the serious shortcomings of the equipment and materials for library purposes. Copying from bound volumes was difficult and wasted much time and material. Books were subject to far more wear and tear than in photostating or microfilming. Larger books and other "difficult" items could not be handled at all, and the results from even routine materials were normally quite inferior to photostats. But copies were readily available and affordable; "convenience copying" had begun.

In 1959 with the Xerox 914 automated copying reached the market. Copying became easier and faster than at any time previously, and the copies, made on inexpensive plain paper, were usually better. The machine was complex and expensive; the 914, however, was not sold, just leased, with charges based on usage. Under these circumstances, many libraries were able to install these machines and offer a copying service that was faster, cheaper, and for the most part better than before.

Owing to the ease and speed of their operation, and to effective marketing plans, the Xerox and other electrostatic machines quickly and firmly established themselves in libraries. Very low prices and fast service led to such a great expansion in demand that not only were the staff-operated copy services kept busy but also the numerous coin-operated, self-service copiers, which became prevalent in libraries around the mid-1960's. With the advant of these machines, convenience copying increased significantly.

Convenience was also a factor in the use of electrostatic copiers for catalogue-card reproduction. The cards produced on office copiers do not match the appearance and durability of cards made by quality offset printing or from microfilm intermediates on continuous electrostatic printers, but they are instantly available and cheap. The method has therefore become popular in many libraries.

When the price of copies fell to a few cents, many library users quit taking notes and copied the entire text of their reading instead. Low-cost, instant copying has thus changed study habits and has been instrumental in the partial conversion of the circulating library into a duplicating library. For libraries there have been several consequences of this development. First, by the early 1970's self-service copying had lowered the volume of work in staff-operated services to the point that some were no longer economically justifiable. Second, electrostatic copiers add to the preservation problems in the library because of wear and tear. Third, a part of the public seems to have developed a sense of unquestionable right to uninterrupted copying in the library. The library user normally copies from relatively difficult-to-handle originals yet often lacks the elementary skills required for operating the copier and seems not to have an understanding of the frailties of the machine. Service interruptions and "bad copies" (often due to failure to use the machine correctly) tend to cause occasionally extreme adverse public reaction.

John Crerar Library

*Sophisticated printing equipment converts microfilm to hard copy.*

Legally, it may be argued, most copying in the library seems to constitute "fair use," and it does not appear that legitimate publisher interests are harmed by the practice. Nevertheless, the implications of the large expansion in copying, especially for interlibrary loan purposes, was one of the hotly argued issues in writing the U.S. Copyright Law of 1976.

**REFERENCES**

F. C. Crix, *Reprographic Management Handbook* (1975).

William R. Hawken, *Copying Methods Manual* (ALA, 1966).

Patrick Firpo, Lester Alexander, and Claudia Katayanagi, *Copyart: The First Complete Guide to the Copy Machine* (1979).

Charles LaHood and Robert C. Sullivan, *Reprographic Services in Libraries: Organization and Administration* (ALA, 1975).

*Library Technology Reports* (ALA, 1965– ) includes test reports and news about copying equipment.

Peter G. New, *Reprography for Librarians* (1975).

FRANCIS F. SPREITZER

## Resource Sharing

One of the critical issues facing libraries at the end of the 1970's was access to, versus ownership of, library materials. The issue has been brought into sharp focus by the following five factors, trends, and events:

## Resource Sharing



(1) Equal access: a nationally stated goal which has heightened expectations with the belief that access to information is a right of the individual and a responsibility of society. One of the *Goals for Action* of the U.S. National Commission on Libraries and Information Science is "to eventually provide every citizen in the United States with equal opportunity to access to that part of the total information resource which will satisfy the individual's education, working, cultural and leisure-time needs and interests, regardless of the individual's location, social or physical condition, or level of intellectual achievement."

(2) Fiscal realities: the economic environment created by rising costs and reduced government and institutional financial support for libraries. Librarians increasingly acknowledge the impossibility of building totally comprehensive collections and providing totally comprehensive services to their users.

(3) Network development: a phenomenon of the 1960's and 1970's enabling formerly independent libraries to develop interdependent relationships in order to provide access to the incredible accumulation of material upon which a vast range of library and information services depend. The most commonly stated objective of library network development is resource sharing.

(4) Pittsburgh Conference on Resource Sharing in Libraries: a 1976 conference which signaled a dramatic attitudinal change among library leaders toward accepting, perhaps reluctantly, resource sharing as a way of life.

(5) Great library tradition: a longstanding belief that there is no substitute for providing needed items locally, that great libraries have great collections, and that users measure a library by the probability that their information needs, perceived or actual, can be met immediately.

**Major Concerns.** Resource sharing is not new—there is a century-long tradition of interlibrary loan activity. In the late 1960's and early 1970's, however, it reached crisis proportions for research libraries. Research was sponsored by the Association of Research Libraries to investigate the magnitude, costs, and characteristics of interlibrary loans made by academic libraries; explore the feasibility of community-based communications, accounting, message switching, and referral interlibrary loan systems; pursue methods of financing interlibrary loans; and develop and evaluate three basic configurations for a national periodical system in the U.S. Three concerns ultimately emerged.

The unique purchasing and copyright problems posed by periodicals was one concern. As these problems were being grappled with, the development of on-line subject bibliographic searching greatly increased the demand for access to journal literature. Consequently, periodicals were singled out for priority treatment. The professional community recognized that the existing system of library access to journal literature was inadequate for the needs of their patrons. Costs of periodical subscriptions were unduly constraining library budgets. Interlibrary loan was costly and inefficient for both libraries and their users. In 1975 the National Commission for Libraries and Information Science appointed a National Periodical System Task Force to study the problem; it recommended a system that would include a National Periodicals Center, which is still being planned and discussed. The Commission on New Technological Uses of Copyrighted Works (CONTU) suggested the need for alternative periodical-purchasing options.

Another concern was that inadequate bibliographic access hampered the physical access possible through resource sharing. Lack of standardization created difficulty in identifying needed items. The National Union Catalog and the Union List of Serials developed and produced by the Library of Congress became increasingly difficult to maintain, and a limited number of holdings locations greatly constrained their usefulness. The magnitude of data simply required utilization of electronic data processing. The Library of Congress took the leadership in developing the essential prerequisite—a machine-readable cataloguing record with communication protocols—MARC. Simultaneously, increased awareness of the importance of standards was developing nationally and internationally. The work of American and international committees took on added importance as international systems for book and serial numberings and for bibliographic descriptions began to have significant impact. The various nationally developed versions of the MARC format were related through UNIMARC, a communications format designed to facilitate the international exchange of bibliographic data.

Several large library computer systems developed on-line cataloguing. RLIN, OCLC, Inc., and the Washington Library Network survived and were labeled bibliographic utilities. All of them were built on MARC and incorporate the concept of individual participating libraries contributing their cataloguing for non-MARC titles. OCLC was the first to make a significant impact and to demonstrate the possibility and potential of a large multilibrary on-line bibliographic data base. By mid-1979 this union catalogue included over 5,000,000 unique titles with over 50,000,000 locations held by 1,700 libraries. Numerous state or regional networks, such as AMIGOS, RLIN, BCR, CLASS, FEDLINK, ILLINET, INCOLSA, Michigan Library Consortium, MIDLNET, MINITEX, NELINET, OHIONET, PALINET, Pittsburgh Library Consortium, SOLINET, WLN, and Wisconsin Interlibrary Loan Service (WILS), Wisconsin Library Consortium, were established to facilitate resource sharing through utilization of one of the bibliographic utilities. Abroad, similar networks, to some extent following American patterns and using variations on the MARC format, developed in Britain, Canada, Australia, and several European countries.

The third concern was that, outside the American Library Association Interlibrary Loan Code, there were no national or international resource-sharing protocols. The Interlibrary Loan Committee of the ALA Reference and Adult Services Division addressed the problem, but neither the Committee nor the networks were able to resolve it adequately. In 1979 OCLC began testing its online interlibrary loan system; 1,700 libraries now have the potential to send an electronic interlibrary loan request with automatic referrals to selected holding libraries. Undoubtedly this new freedom to send requests anywhere without regard to existing geographic, jurisdictional, or subject relationships and responsibilities will create a need for protocols. Internationally, work on international interlibrary loan mechanisms is being conducted through IFLA.

Not everyone is convinced that resource sharing is the answer. This argument is interestingly made by E. F. Shumacher in his *Small Is Beautiful* (1973):

> From the point of view of Buddhist economics, therefore, production from local resources for local needs is the most rational way of economic life, while dependence on imports from afar and the consequent need to produce for export to unknown and distant people is highly uneconomic and justifiable only in exceptional cases and on a small scale. Just as the modern economist would admit that a high rate of consumption of transport services between a man's home and his place of work signifies a misfortune and not a high standard of life, so the Buddhist economist would hold that to satisfy human wants from faraway sources rather than from sources nearby signifies failure rather than success.

Richard De Gennaro, of the University of Pennsylvania, has written eloquently on this issue also:

> Resource sharing is essential but it is not a panacea. The library market is shrinking and hardening, and publishers—both commercial and scholarly—will have to accept that fact and make adjustments. Librarians will have to accept that the savings they make through networking, cooperation, and resource sharing in the next several years will be quickly absorbed by the continuing inflation in book and journal prices and rising personnel costs. Moreover, library budgetary support will continue to decline and the pressures to reduce expenditures will increase.
>
> . . . libraries can no longer afford to maintain the collections, staffs, and service levels that librarians and users have come to expect in the last two decades. Libraries are experiencing a substantial loss in their standard of living as a result of inflation, increasing energy costs, and changing priorities in our society. We can rail against it and search for scapegoats, but it would be better if we came to terms with this painful reality and began to reduce our excessive commitments and expectations to match our declining resources.
>
> The importance of resource sharing mechanisms, and particularly the most cost-effective ones—the centralized libraries' libraries, such as the Center for Research Libraries and the British Library Lending Division—is not so much that they will save us funds we can relocate to other purposes, but that they will permit us to continue to have access to a large universe of materials we can no longer afford, spending our diminishing funds on the materials we need and use most. In sum, effective resource sharing will help ease the pain that will accompany the scaling-down of commitments and expectations we face in the years ahead (*American Libraries,* September 1977).

By mid-1979 the library community was pushing for legislation to support a National Periodicals Center, and the Council on Library Resources assumed leadership in developing a National Bibliographic System. Meanwhile, library resource sharing was expanding exponentially. Geographic networks including municipal and multicountry, state, and regional as well as subject networks (e.g., National Library of Medicine) developed and began to facilitate resource sharing among libraries. In many cases federal funding supported this cooperative activity. Users liked it; funding agencies supported it; and libraries hoped for a rational, responsive system. In the absence of a national plan, many systems were built on local strength, molded by existing stake holders and responsive to local needs; however, this may not be the best way to build an integrated system or to be sensitive to the symbiotic relationship between various segments of the information community.

Under the leadership and subsidy of the National Library of Medicine, an extensive hierarchical resource-sharing system was developed to support the health sciences communities. Under state library leadership, New York and Illinois continued to strengthen already strong interlibrary loan programs. Minnesota offered another model. MINITEX (Minnesota Interlibrary Telecommunications Exchange) is a legislatively funded program of the Minnesota Higher Education Coordinating Board facilitating resource sharing with heavy reliance on the University of Minnesota collections. Prior to MINITEX in 1968 fewer than 20,000 ILL transactions were documented in the state; ten years later over 389,000 transactions were documented.

No single source for comprehensive data collected on resource sharing among American libraries existed in 1979. Many separate groups collect and tabulate data for their own groups, but frequently they duplicate those submitted by individual libraries.

**Impact on Local Libraries.** Resource sharing makes substantive changes in the local library, since ultimately it is the local library that will share its resources and become dependent upon the collections of other libraries. This change from independent to interdependent institutions is not simple for the institutions, the librarians, or the users.

The basic question is no longer whether there should be resource sharing but rather when, how, and under what constraints it will occur. Some of the critical questions a library must consider are: What are its responsibilities to its primary users, to secondary users, to future generations? Is it a research library and, therefore, has it a need to collect for future generations, or is its mission to support curriculum and current needs? How large a collection will it take to provide 95 percent of its needs locally? How can it best get access to the remaining 5 percent? How can it improve its selection of new materials? What criteria are useful in selection and evaluation of a responsive referral system? What are approximate and real costs of resource sharing? What are the short-term benefits and the long-term implications of interdependency?

Local libraries need to clarify their own objectives, responsibilities, and relationships in cooperative resource-sharing arrangements. A suggested beginning list of considerations follows:

(1) The principal objective of participation in resource-sharing programs is the improvement of the library's service performance. Network participation should assist the library in supporting its institutional, instructional, and/or research programs.

(2) A secondary objective for participation in resource-sharing networks is to contribute to the cost effectiveness of library service. Membership or participation in cooperative programs will ultimately affect bibliographic standards and the library's collection-development policies, including binding and retention policies.

(3) The library's participation in a resource-sharing network should help define its obligations to, and formalize its service agreements with, clientele outside the institutional or jurisdictional community.

(4) The library must resolve any conflicts between local autonomy and cooperative responsibility in a way that is acceptable to its parent institution and its client system. Cooperative agreements should have a positive, not adverse, impact on the libary's response to the needs of its primary users.

(5) The library should be prepared to fulfill its responsibilities in cooperative arrangements. The costs of cooperative programs need to be recognized and budgeted; provisions should be made to use the programs fully. The library should periodically analyze the costs and benefits of any cooperative resource-sharing program in which it participates.

(6) The library should be aware of and make appropriate use of its cooperative resources and services, including bibliographic, physical (documents), and human.

(7) The library should be conscious of the implications of the cessation of a resource-sharing program, assessing the impact it would have upon the library community and the region.

Daniel Boorstin, Librarian of Congress, stated succinctly, "The whole point of library work is to put the needed object—book, periodical, map or recording, or its intellectual substance into the hands of the user"

(1977). If libraries are to succeed in their mission and supply what is needed rather than offer only what they have, resource sharing is essential. Resource sharing provides the means to strengthen library services, aid in cost effectiveness, and provide the user with expanded access to library and information materials.

**REFERENCES**

Richard De Gennaro, "Copyright, Resource Sharing, and Hard Times: A View from the Field," *American Libraries* (1977).

Robert M. Hayes, *A System for Inter-Library Communications (SILC)* (1973).

Vernon E. Palmour et al., *Access to Periodical Resources: A National Plan* (1974).

———, *Methods of Financing Interlibrary Loan Services* (1974).

ALICE WILCOX



## Richardson, Ernest Cushing
(1860–1939)

Exemplar of the scholar-librarian tradition, Ernest C. Richardson made enduring contributions to American librarianship. Among his notable accomplishments may be counted the directorship of the Princeton University Library (1890–1920), the development of a classification scheme, the pursuit of cooperative bibliographic arrangements, and the publication of nearly 200 items covering an impressive range of library topics and other scholarly subjects.

Richardson was born on February 9, 1860, in Woburn, Massachusetts. His early years were devoted to school, athletic activities, and frequent use of the local public library. He entered Amherst College in 1876 at 16, the last year of Melvil Dewey's term as Assistant Librarian. Although Richardson became a library student assistant during his freshman year, it is not known if he was captivated by the charismatic Dewey. Richardson's apprenticeship under Dewey's brilliant successor, Walter S. Biscoe, was a decisive influence on the selection of a career in librarianship.

Deeply religious and committed to a life of scholarship, Richardson entered the Hartford Theological Seminary in 1880. He worked as a student assistant for several years, became Assistant Librarian in 1882, and accepted the position of Director in 1884. It was during 1884 that Richardson traveled to Europe, where he studied at various university libraries, a journey that he repeated many times in the ensuing years. The European visit marked the beginning of a lifetime concern with international library cooperation. At the Hartford Seminary, Richardson devised and implemented a classification scheme and completed many learned studies. In 1888 he was awarded an honorary doctorate from Washington and Jefferson College for preparation of the *Bibliographical Synopsis of the Ante-Nicene Fathers* (1887), a guide to the literature relating to early Christian leaders.

*Ernest Cushing Richardson*

Although Richardson enjoyed the congenial atmosphere at the Hartford Seminary, the need for salary improvement and the challenge of managing a distinguished research library convinced him to accept the Librarian's position at Princeton University in 1890. One year after his appointment, Richardson married Grace Duncan Ely, a woman of above-average financial means.

For 30 years Richardson struggled to provide the collections, facilities, and services that he believed Princeton needed. By 1900 Princeton had adopted a decimal classification scheme devised by Richardson, and in 1901 the Library became one of the early subscribers to the Library of Congress catalogue cards. That momentous decision was reached in a meeting which included such luminaries as Woodrow Wilson, Grover Cleveland, and John S. Billings. Richardson was perhaps most successful with the acquisitions program; the collection grew from 81,000 volumes in 1890 to approximately 450,000 volumes in 1920.

The reduction of bibliographic complexity was one of Richardson's many crusades that found application at Princeton. He believed in abbreviated cataloguing, an approach that provided the minimum information needed to identify and locate library materials. Richardson's "title-a-bar" theory involved the use of a Linotype machine to print one-line entries for each book in the form of a printed catalogue. That type of catalogue was not uniformly endorsed by the Princeton faculty. Beginning in 1913 the Princeton Library experienced reduced financial support, and salary levels declined. Faculty demands for more services and various complaints led to the appointment of an investigatory committee in 1920. An Associate Librarian, James Gerould, was employed with special authority to institute changes. He immediately abandoned the printed catalogues and began to reclassify portions of the collection. Administratively dethroned and elevated to figurehead status, Richardson argued bitterly with the university until 1925, when he accepted a position as honorary consultant in bibliography at the Library of Congress. Neither side was without fault, but Richardson was clearly stubborn, unwilling to compromise or concede shortcomings. This unfortunate propensity to pursue a collision course would occur again.

At the Library of Congress Richardson continued to teach as he had done at Princeton and initiated one of the most significant bibliographic projects of that era. For 20 years Richardson had been writing and speaking, primarily through the American Library Institute, a deliberative body affiliated with the American Library Association, about the paucity of resources in research libraries and the lack of systematic bibliographic organization. As Chairman of ALA's Committee on Bibliography, Richardson had laid the groundwork for "Project B," a cooperative cataloguing program to augment and revitalize the national union catalogue at the Library of Congress. Richardson and his staff succeeded in enlarging the union catalogue file from 1,500,000 titles in 1927 to approximately 7,000,000 titles in 1932. Unhappily, Richardson became enmeshed in a debate with the ALA Executive Board over the jurisdiction of another committee, the Cooperative Cataloging Committee. After a protracted controversy, which erupted in the professional journals, Richardson resigned in 1934 to pursue his many scholarly interests. His commitment to bibliographic control and cooperative arrangements exceeded that of most contemporaries, and "Project B" may be considered the unheralded predecessor of the more well-known Farmington Plan of the 1940's.

Foremost a scholar, Richardson published extensively in the fields of librarianship, history, and theology. Significant contributions to the library field included *Classification, Theoretical and Practical* (1901), which influenced such classificationists as England's W. C. Berwick Sayers, *Some Aspects of International Library Cooperation* (1928), *General Library Cooperation and American Research Books* (1930), and *Some Aspects of Cooperative Cataloging* (1934). His writings in library history reveal a serious as well as a whimsical side: *Some Old Egyptian Librarians* (1911), *Biblical Libraries* (1914), and *The Beginnings of Libraries* (1914). Historians remain indebted to his pioneering editorial work on the first volume of *Writings on American History* (1904).

Richardson was an active member and officer of many learned societies and professional groups: American Library Association (President, 1904–05); councillor of the Bibliographical Society of America (1917–37); Chairman of the Bibliography Committee of the American Historical Association (1902–15); and Chairman of the

ALA Committee on Bibliography (1922–34). Following World War I his service extended beyond the academy to participation on the United States House Inquiry Commission, a group designated to select and transport documents for the peace conference at Versailles.

After the death of his wife in 1933 and the confrontation with the Executive Board in 1934, Richardson withdrew from library affairs and moved to a cottage near Old Lyme, Connecticut. His scholarly work continued, especially in theology, and he remained actively associated with several institutions of higher education. He died on June 3, 1939, while engaged in a study of rare books. Although Richardson does not today enjoy the reputation accorded some early library leaders, his accomplishments were impressive. Few librarians have surpassed his scholarly attainments or pursued more vigorously the goal of bibliographic interdependence. Fittingly, Richardson defined and exemplified the object of library science as the need "to connect a reader, surely and promptly, with the book that he wants to use."

**REFERENCES**

Lewis C. Branscomb, *A Bio-Bibliographical Study of Ernest Cushing Richardson, 1960–1939,* the standard biography (Ph.D. dissertation, University of Chicago, 1954).

Primary sources are in the Princeton University Library, the Library of Congress, and the Hartford Seminary Foundation Library.

ARTHUR P. YOUNG

## Rider, Arthur Fremont

(1885–1962)

Arthur Fremont Rider, self-described as inquisitive, introverted, and principled, was one of the library profession's most versatile figures. He was an editor, publisher, and writer, associate of Dewey, university librarian, and early microform advocate. Blending the conceptual with the practical was his forte. Rider's bequest to library scholarship is confirmed by the frequent citations to his seminal writings. The son of George Arthur and Charlotte Elizabeth Meader Rider, he was born in Trenton, New Jersey, on May 25, 1885. His childhood years were spent in Middletown, Connecticut, where he first used the Wesleyan University Library, a library he would later direct. Rider graduated from Syracuse University in 1905 and enrolled in the New York State Library School (class of 1907). Before graduating he was invited by Melvil Dewey, a lifelong influence, to work on a revision of the Decimal Classification at the Lake Placid Club. Rider met his first wife, Grace Godfrey, a relative of Dewey, at Lake Placid, and they were married in 1908. Rider was married to Marie Gallup Ambrose in 1951.

Rider began in 1907 the first of many, often overlapping careers. Between 1907 and 1917 he served as Associate Editor of *The Delineator* and Editor of *Monthly Book Review, Publishers' Weekly,* and *Library Journal.* From 1914 to 1932 he was President of Rider Press, a periodical press that printed most of the R. R. Bowker publications. The press failed at the depth of the Depression following a debilitating struggle with a union and the withdrawal of Bowker's patronage. During that period he published a series of well-received guidebooks to New York City, Washington, Bermuda, and California. Still not content with those accomplishments, Rider wrote numerous short stories for popular magazines and dabbled in poetry, drama, and real estate.

Rider's early association with Dewey and library publishing together with business acumen and literary inclinations were valuable assets for the next phase of his career. He was invited to become Librarian of Wesleyan University's Olin Library in 1933, and for the next two decades Rider challenged tradition, experimented, and proselytized new concepts. The results of these reappraisals and other pertinent information about the Wesleyan Library were reported in the Rider-edited periodical, *About Books.* The collection more than doubled during his tenure, largely through *en bloc* purchases. New cost accounting procedures were introduced; catalogue cards for Wesleyan titles not listed in the Library of Congress catalogue were printed and distributed to many libraries; and cooperative relationships with neighboring libraries were pursued. Faced with limited shelving, Rider initiated a compact shelving program for seldom-used books. The books were shelved, after cropping, on their foreedges. His controversial ideas on compact shelving were published in *Compact Book Storage* (1949). Because of his provocative writings and practical adaptations at Wesleyan, Rider was in constant demand as a speaker and received innumerable requests for advice.

Of his numerous achievements, perhaps his enduring legacy remains his insightful analysis of research library growth and advocacy of microcards espoused in *The Scholar and the Future of the Research Library* (1944). By studying collection growth patterns Rider concluded that the collections of research libraries double approximately every 16 years. This observation, startling in its time, coupled with the infrequent use of research-level materials, led Rider to propose the microcard as a cost-effective, space-saving solution. Ingeniously, the catalogue card and the relevant document were combined to form a single card with bibliographic description on the front and microtext on the back. His book was reviewed extensively in the library literature and in such nonlibrary journals as the *Columbia Law Review* and the *New England Quarterly.* He invariably received high marks for his trenchant analysis and concise style, but many reviewers questioned the immediate practicability of the idea; however, all would have concurred with William Warner Bishop's remark that Rider had "given librarians much to think about and to think about furiously." Unselfish about the microcard, Rider never patented the concept. Years later, in 1961, he was awarded the annual medal of the National Microfilm Association for his distinguished contribution to microform technology.

Near the end of his library career, in 1951, Rider built the Godfrey Memorial Library, a noncirculating library for the study and promotion of genealogical research. Of major importance to historians and genealogists is the *American Genealogical-Biographical Index* (100+ volumes), issued by that research facility. In 1961, one year before his death, Rider published *Rider's International Classification for the Arrangement of Books on the Shelves of General Libraries.* Reviewers were impressed with the brave attempt but decidedly lukewarm over the results.

Rider's multidimensional career is flamboyantly reconstructed in an often vainglorious autobiography, *And Master of None* (1955), a mine of information, especially about his nonlibrary activities. His contribution to library history was *Melvil Dewey: A Biography* (ALA, 1944); although expectedly favorable toward Dewey, Rider's study was a refreshing corrective to Grosvenor Dawes's earlier deification of the great pioneer.

He died on October 26, 1962, in Middletown, Connecticut. His intellect, vision, and creative applications place him in the front rank of library forebears.

ARTHUR P. YOUNG

## Robinson, Joyce

(1925–   )

Joyce Lilieth Robinson became a leading figure in the development of library services in Jamaica and the Carib-

*Joyce Lilieth Robinson*



bean, heading a major program to promote literacy among the people of Jamaica.

One of the curious twists of history occurs when propitious forces combine to provide the right person functioning at the right time within the right political and economic milieu to effect social change. In 1972, upon learning that 50 percent of the country's adult population over 15 years old were illiterate, government officials of the West Indian country of Jamaica established its National Literacy Programme to eradicate illiteracy and to upgrade the literacy skills of adult Jamaicans. Knowledgeable, skillful, dedicated, and centralized leadership was seen as necessary for administering an effective national literacy effort. In 1973 Joyce Lilieth Robinson was selected as the Executive Director of the Programme, which was renamed JAMAL, the Jamaican Movement for the Advancement of Literacy.

Joyce Robinson was the choice to assume the directorship of such a program. Born in Saint James, Jamaica, July 2, 1925, and educated in Jamaica and in London, she had an impressive record of educational and professional achievement. As the first Jamaican director of the Jamaica Library Service, she effectively expanded island-wide public and school library services during the 19 years (1957–76) of her administration. A founding member of the Jamaican Library Association, Robinson held offices in JLA and wrote numerous articles and pamphlets on Jamaican library services published in international journals and by the Jamaican press. She participated as a committee member, delegate, or course director in several international library activities. As a volunteer committee member, she became part of many social, educational, and cultural organizations.

JAMAL is a community-centered basic literacy program for adults 15 years and older. Twelve thousand volunteer tutors across Jamaica instruct upward of 114,000 students in reading, writing, and numeracy skills. The curriculum is Jamaican-based with an emphasis on survival information and reading for pleasure. The program uses island-developed materials that have a strong appeal to both the rural and urban life style. Robinson noted that the curriculum is good because "it works" for Jamaicans. The JAMAL experience proved that an adult can be taught to read and write in 400 instruction hours, or six months at three hours daily. The instructional program is supplemented with pedagogical media programs in addition to the publication of leisure reading materials including books and newspapers.

As Executive Director, Joyce Robinson became responsible for 12,000 volunteer tutors, 2,000 additional voluntary committee members, and 850 JAMAL staff members. Her background as a librarian led her to a strong conviction that the adult new readers will not maintain their newly acquired skills without continuous access to reading-for-pleasure resources. Because newly literate persons can be encouraged to read for information only a small portion of their time, stimulating the adult new reader to read for pleasure is the key to preventing lapsing of skill achievement. "Follow-through" is Joyce Robinson's theme; she sees the public library as playing a major role in the "follow-through" that maintains the reading skills of the newly literate person.

The American Library Association invited Joyce Robinson to be its 1979 Carl Milam International Lecturer. She spoke about the role of libraries in the JAMAL effort at several library schools in the United States and Canada. She was awarded an honorary doctorate by Dalhousie University, another recognition of her vital role in the development of social change in Jamaica.

JEAN ELLEN COLEMAN

# Romania

Romania, a socialist republic of the Balkan Peninsula in southeastern Europe, is bounded by the Black Sea on the east, by the U.S.S.R. on the east and north, by Hungary on the west, by Yugoslavia on the southwest, and by Bulgaria on the south. Pop. (1977 est.) 21,559,400; area 237,500 sq.km. The official language is Romanian.

**National Libraries.** The Central State Library of the Socialist Republic of Romania was founded in 1955 as the national library that continues the traditions of the State Central Library in Bucharest created in the fourth decade of the 19th century and incorporated with the Library of the Romanian Academy in April 1901. The collections are encyclopedic in character, and at the end of 1978 they totaled about 7,290,000 bibliographic units, including, besides books and serials, 27,230 manuscripts, 155,880 archive documents, and thousands of rare and precious books, graphic works, maps, atlases and globes, photographs and illustrated postcards, records, and other items.

The Central State Library acts as the National Center of Bibliographic Information. It provides bibliographic control on the national level by publishing the national bibliography *(Bibliografia Republicii Socialiste România);* it prepares the cumulative indexes of the national production of printed works *(Anuarul Cărtii),* makes up the national union catalogue on cards, and publishes directories and union catalogues of foreign books and serials among other activities.

The Central State Library also functions as the Documentation Center in Librarianship and Book Restoration. It monitors current literature in the field, publishes some secondary publications, undertakes studies and documentary analyses on subjects regarding research in library science, book preservation and care, and library development in Romania, and makes translations.

The Library acts as the Documentation Center on Culture and produces secondary publications *(Buletin de informare documentară in cultură),* undertakes studies and documentary analyses, draws up syntheses, and makes translations.

In its capacity of Central Legal Deposit it receives and redistributes to the libraries having this right the legal deposit copies, provides the statistics regarding the national production of printed works, and controls the way in which the law concerning the legal deposit is brought into operation.

The Central State Library functions as the National Exchange Center of Romania; it receives and redistributes the publications sent on exchange by and to other Romanian institutions, compiles statistics on international exchange, and is concerned with international interlibrary loans, among other activities.

The Methodology Center of the Central State Library assures the specialized assistance needed by the public libraries and other libraries in the country, undertakes sociological studies in library activity and reading, prepares materials on the methodology of book-promotion activities, organizes pioneer libraries and study sessions for exchanges of experience, and assists in professional training of the library workers and in offering periodically professional refresher courses.

The Central State Library has several reading rooms specialized by fields of knowledge and by categories of publications and media (manuscripts and letters, Romanian bibliophilic books, foreign bibliophilic books, maps, loose sheets, newspapers); there is also a special department for official publications and offices for Unesco publications and publications of other international bodies. Educational activities include organizing exhibitions, meetings with writers and scholars, musical programs, and other events.

The Library of the Academy of the Socialist Republic of Romania is the second of the two national libraries of the country. It was founded in 1867. Its early growth owed much to private donations and to legal deposit privileges (since 1885). Until 1948 the Library covered almost exclusively humanities and social sciences, but after the reorganization of the Romanian Academy, the Library started collecting works in scientific and technical fields as well.

Holdings totaled 4,771,800 volumes; in addition there were thousands of manuscripts, rare books, engravings, maps, about 300,000 letters, different archives of important personalities, records, and other items (1979).

The Library is concerned with the publication of the Romanian national retrospective bibliography of books and periodicals from the 16th century. It provides various bibliographic tools and services for its collections. It also administers a major exchange program with publications issued by the Publishing House of the Academy, which are sent to about 10,000 exchange partners in over 100 countries and fulfill interlibrary loan requests.

**Academic Libraries.** In 1977 there were 43 academic libraries, namely, 3 central university libraries (with general holdings), 4 university libraries, and 36 libraries of the institutes of higher education. These libraries have a rich documentation basis (17,300,000 bibliographic units) and include in their holdings Romanian works of great cultural value and outstanding works of the world cultural heritage.

The three central university libraries have also in their collections works by Romanian personalities in manuscript form, private collections of books with dedications, and autographed books. The central university libraries in Bucharest (founded in 1891), Cluj-Napoca (founded in 1872), and Iași (founded in 1640) have a special status; they are directly subordinated to the Ministry of Education and serve the entire university community on the campus, providing, at the same time, support for the library activities and for refresher courses for librarians in the university libraries.

The Central University Library in Bucharest ensures the acquisition of foreign publications (books and periodicals) for all libraries in the academic network and the completion of holdings for the departments of Romanian language, literature, and civilization created abroad.

Academic libraries in Romania are expected to meet not only the requirements of education and research but also those of study and documentation of the specialists on the university campuses where they serve. To satisfy the information needs of their clients they issue information bulletins, bibliographies, indexes of journals, bibliographic studies on subjects, directories, and other information sources and instruments. They contribute—on the local and national level—to bibliographic and documentary information works and instruct students in library use methods.

Other libraries include the Library of the Medical and Pharmaceutical Institute (founded in 1857, 808,623 books and 8,664 periodicals in 1976), Library of the Polytechnic Institute Gheorghe Gheorghiu-Dej (founded in 1868, 1,250,000 books and periodicals in 1976), Central Library of the Academy of Economic Studies (founded in 1913, 724,000 volumes in 1976), and Central Library of the Nicolae Bălcescu Agronomic Institute (founded in 1948, 437,000 volumes in 1976).

**Public Libraries.** Romania recognizes three categories: state public libraries, libraries of the trade unions, and libraries of the craftsmen's cooperatives. During 1978 6,381 public libraries functioned with holdings that add up to 56,704,888 volumes, registering 3,741,923 readers and 37,739,309 consulted volumes.

*State Public Libraries.* Under a decree of the Council of Ministers of December 1951, public libraries were organized according to territorial and administrative criteria. From 1968 each state public library was sponsored by the local administration institutions (county, municipality, town, village), being at the same time placed under the guidance and control of the Council of Culture and Socialist Education.

County public libraries (40 in 1977) have encyclopedic holdings (9,037,885 volumes in 1978). They gather the printed works issued within the boundaries of the county and the works regarding the county issued outside its boundaries, draw up the local bibliography, prepare local union catalogues, edit orientation bibliographies to support the social and economic development of the county and the educational program, organize exhibitions and public meetings, undertake studies on reading, ensure the availability of library materials to the population in the county residentiary town in reading rooms and by means of lending facilities (558,842 readers and 12,298,743 volumes consulted in 1978), organize libraries for children that work as sections of the county public library, organize branch libraries and mobile lending centers, administer interlibrary loan to serve all the population in the area, and provide other services.

Municipal and town libraries function in urban settlements (185 in 1977), gather holdings of encyclopedic character (6,771,880 volumes in 1977), ensure the availability of library materials to the population in the municipality or town (483,252 readers and 7,135,315 volumes consulted in 1977), and participate in various educational programs.

Village libraries (2,704 libraries with 26,070,084 volumes in 1977) cooperate with the school libraries in providing the library materials to the population in the area and in supporting the educational programs.

*Libraries of the Trade Unions.* These libraries (3,306 with 12,758,045 volumes in 1977) belong either to the local trade union committees or to the trade union committees of the industrial or other economic units. They serve the members of the trade union organization and their families. They carry on—by themselves or in cooperation with the state public libraries and other cultural institutions—activities of an educational character.

*Libraries of the Craftsmen's Cooperatives.* These libraries (185 in 1977 with a total of 1,404,414 volumes) belong to the Union of the Craftsmen's Coöperatives and serve the members of the cooperatives and their families.

**School Libraries.** In Romania school libraries (10,782 in 1977) are organized within each elementary

Central State Library of Romania

*The Central State Library of Romania was created in 1955 and incorporated the State Central Library in Bucharest with the Library of the Romanian Academy.*

**Libraries in Romania (1977)**

| Type | Number | Volumes in collection | Population served |
|---|---|---|---|
| National | 2 | 12,520,843 | 1,948,611 |
| Academic | 43 | 17,301,178 | 182,337 |
| Public | 6,420 | 55,559,000 | 21,657,569 |
| School | 10,782 | 41,382,034 | 4,345,455 |
| Special | 4,189 | 18,278,592 | ——— |
| Total | 21,436 | 145,041,580 | |

school, gymnasium, secondary school, or vocational school, being sponsored by the local educational bodies or by the corresponding ministries (the technical and vocational schools). They are placed under the guidance and control of the Ministry of Education and Instruction; their holdings contain materials that cover the curriculum requirements and materials concerning problems of children and youth education (41,382,034 volumes in 1977).

School libraries organize activities with educational character on their own or cooperate with other cultural institutions in supporting other such activities. They organize special circles for children that aim to promote skills of intellectual activity and to instruct them in the techniques of bibliographic and documentary activities. They participate in the sociological studies concerned with the reading interests of school children and young people.

Methodological guidance for the school libraries is assured by the Central Pedagogical Library (see *Special Libraries*).

**Special Libraries.** Special libraries in Romania (4,189 in 1977) belong to research institutes, institutes of higher education, academies, scientific and cultural associations, cultural institutions, institutions of the state administration, industrial units, documentation centers, and offices. Their holdings reflect the more specialized character of the fields they serve (18,278,595 volumes in 1977); they serve research workers, engineers, and various specialists. According to the law, such a library may be constituted with no fewer than 3,000 bibliographical units.

The Central Pedagogical Library was founded in 1880 as the library of the Higher Normal School. Its collections are specialized in teaching and in 1978 numbered 322,500 volumes. Its holdings are available to school administrators, university professors, and teachers in all grades of the general obligatory schools or of secondary schools in its own reading rooms or on loan; it publishes educational news and information on methods and makes bibliographic and documentary studies on request; it acts as a forum for the 40 county pedagogical libraries and all school libraries in the country; it also informs other countries on the educational achievements and pedagogical research in Romania (it had 316 exchange relations in 39 countries in 1978).

Other libraries include the Library of the National Institute for Information and Documentation, founded in 1949 (holdings of 230,000 bibliographic units in 1976); the Central Medical Library founded in 1951 (holdings of 500,000 volumes); and the Central Library of the Academy of Agricultural and Forestry Sciences founded in 1928 (holdings of 91,550 books and 7,140 collections of periodicals).

**Association.** The Association of Librarians in the Socialist Republic of Romania was founded in 1957. It contributes to the development of library programs and the drafting of legal documents concerning libraries, participates in activities connected with training and refresher courses for those working in all categories of libraries, and organizes meetings for professional purposes. It became a member of IFLA in 1957 and always undertook an active part in the life of the international library community.

ANGELA POPESCU-BRĂDICENI

# Rome

There is considerable literary evidence of the private book collections assembled in the latter days of the Republic, thanks successively to Greek stimulation, Roman pride, and military conquest. Much less is known about libraries of a public sort because the archaeological testimony becomes more critical and very little has survived. It is possible that M. T. Varro, a leading Roman of the 1st century B.C., composed a treatise on libraries, but it is established only that Caesar asked him to take charge of a project to build a grand public library, Rome's first, and that nothing came of it directly after Caesar's assassination. Caesar's friend, C. Asinius Pollio, did found near the Forum ("Atrium Libertatis") in the 30's B.C. a library apparently of the sort Caesar had wanted. Reportedly it comprised mainly book booty from the Illyrian campaign of 39 B.C. Latin and Greek sister libraries were formed; the premises were decorated with likenesses of the outstanding writers, Varro being the only living author among the honorees. What became of it is not known.

Several libraries were organized in the imperial capital to memorialize past achievement and nourish national pride. When in 28 B.C. Augustus dedicated a temple of Apollo on the Palatine, Latin and Greek libraries were attached to it. This pairing, as well as the temple nexus, had precedent, but this occasion may have been the first time a practical advantage was manifest, inasmuch as the Latin division was strong in Roman law and the Senate met there occasionally. The Palatine library story is further marked by severe losses from fire, some rebuilding, and leadership by a number of learned men appointed by the emperor; the fire of 363 was apparently the end. The same career and fate seem to have been the lot of the paired libraries begun by Augustus about 25 B.C. on the Campus Martius, named in honor of his sister Octavia. Later emperors also founded libraries, some of which endured: 28 in Constantine's day, it is said (reasonably, although only ten names are known). Noteworthy is the Pantheon Library, founded by Emperor Alexander Severus around 230, perhaps the first public library in Rome to have held Eastern religious materials, especially Christian and Jewish writings. It is interesting, and possibly of critical significance, that Julius Africanus, appointed Director, was not only a career soldier and engineer but also a scholar in Christian church chronology and a man of sufficiently varied interests to compile an encyclopedia.

The royal example was followed almost from the start by individuals prominent in letters and well enough off to endow a library—or wealthy and desiring to be remembered as friendly to the world of intellect. We know of a library for the Musicians and Actors Association, and it seems likely that various other associations and institutions had book collections too, whether endowed or not. Were they, like the imperial gifts, placed at temples, public baths, or colonnades?

When chronicler Ammianus Marcellinus complained late in the 4th century that the libraries of Rome were shut up like tombs, he, a Syrian Greek defending Rome against the declining tone in upper-crust Roman life, may well have taken comfort from the vigor outside Rome. From the early 3rd century until the empire's collapse, public libraries were a fairly standard feature of Roman centers in western Europe and North Africa, scattered details being available in the literary records and occasionally from archaeology. Verified information about such institutions in the East is similarly fragmentary, but many of them played a part in the rise and 4th-century triumph of Christianity; of course they were often ecclesiastical rather than really "public." Also, the leading library at Constantinople is apparently the first to have drawn attention in public law, a decree of 372 incorporated in the Theodosian Code.

The first books in a Roman library were most likely to have arrived by arrangement with whoever had donated the building. Such a donation was one recognized means of winning honorable notice, perhaps even from the Emperor; it often led to the erection of a statue. The sovereign did not hesitate to ban from these libraries books he considered objectionable, but the general practice was reportedly rather generous, admitting Christian and non-Roman philosophy. Proscription first of Christian and then of anti-Christian materials did not begin until the struggles of the 4th century.

The book trade could be counted on only for ordinary current works, and the copies supplied by dealers were held in low esteem. Libraries tended to make their own, insofar as they could not fill gaps with the help of auctions or other special opportunities; besides, papyrus exposed to the air lasted no more than 200 years. Many libraries public and private, not just the very largest, operated copying rooms. Regulations sometimes called for annual fresh copies of certain works, and there must have been great dependence on a cadre of skilled copyists. We know that in late-4th-century Constantinople the copyists *(antiquarii)* were important individuals, reminiscent of the scribes 2,500 years earlier.

Extant catalogue information indicates beyond serious doubt that titles were listed in subject groups. It seems almost as clear that the shelving of rolls followed the same plan; at least the recorded placement of likenesses of writers also argues for that conclusion. In each closet *(armarium),* the rolls were arranged in author-alphabetical order, individually identified by a small stick projecting from the center of the roll *(titulus).* No location number has been found for an individual work. Closet doors were kept closed to protect the rolls from light.

For a book owner to allow friends to read on the premises was common, but to loan a book for use elsewhere called for unusual friendship. The public libraries were essentially limited to reading on the premises. Evidence has survived of an oath required of readers in an Athenian library that they would not walk off with the book entrusted to them. Now and then, of course, permission to borrow was granted to a person of known scholarship or exceptional influence.

The daylight hours were obviously of prime importance. Architect Vitruvius urged that a library be arranged so that its windows maximized the availability of sunlight. The Athenian library just mentioned was open, according to an inscription, from sunrise to 6 P.M.

The would-be reader in a public library went first to the catalogue, then applied to the staff for the desired item; only the latter were supposed to go to the book-closets. Literary testimony suggests that this procedure was reasonably satisfactory. Some moments were remembered because the catalogue generated either frustration or a pleasant surprise.

Some staff members were imperial slaves assigned to the leading libraries founded in the 1st century A.D.; these are noted, with their library relationship, in many tomb inscriptions. Anonymity absorbed their successors, perhaps in connection with the civil service reforms begun under Hadrian. Library direction was customarily in the hands of scholars: they were among the procurators in the 1st century, but the latter category gradually became transformed primarily into performer of fiscal and other external functions—by the 4th century part of the duties of the city prefect—and the scholars tended to be limited to internal affairs like book selection.

The division of library labor had by empire days reached the stage of establishing perhaps a dozen Latin verbs for specifically library functions. They included special meanings for terms used in other ways too, like *disponere* ("organize"), and terms peculiar to the library, for example, *commutare* ("replace a poor copy with a better one").

Librarianship as a set of skills attracted some thoughtful attention, but the extant records give greatly varying support on different issues. Least questioned is the tradition of scholarly management and purpose well established in Hellenistic days, especially at Alexandria; the testimony is almost entirely literary. That Varro could have said many useful things in his treatise on libraries, with known ideas and practices to back them up from Hellenistic data, is quite plausible. Unfortunately, not one scrap survives; we cannot be certain that he ever wrote that treatise. Widely accepted as likely, though impossible to prove with archaeological evidence, is the debt of Rome's noted library buildings to whatever the Ptolemaic architects devised at Alexandria. Indications are available from the physical remains at other sites like Pergamum. In any case, architect Vitruvius, writing in the late 1st century B.C., advised on library design as an expected topic. The same applies to library catalogues, for whose existence the literary testimony from at least the 1st century A.D. is noticeable though neither routine nor detailed. If the Alexandrian customs were known, they would apparently have been associated with Callimachus's *Pinakes.* The sole regular allusions to libraries surviving from Roman times are those in Suetonius, who names sponsoring emperors, librarians, and the writers of consequence represented in those libraries. The data are scientific materials only in the sense that they give us a proximate source for Aulus Gellius's and Isidor of Seville's passages on libraries.

The story of the Christians' book collections actually begins also during the Roman Empire but falls more naturally with the discussion of the Middle Ages.

SIDNEY L. JACKSON

# Rovira, Carmen
(1912- )

Carmen Rovira's long experience and pioneering scholarship in the bibliography, classification, and cataloguing of Spanish-language materials, together with many related and significant organizational activities, have made her a figure of central importance in Latin American librarianship.

Rovira was born in Santiago de Cuba on June 13, 1919, and her early life was spent in both Spain and Cuba. In 1946 she received a doctoral degree in Philosophy and Letters from the University of Havana and graduated from its Library School in 1952. In 1969 Rovira received a Masters degree in Library Science from the Graduate Library School of the Catholic University of America in Washington, D.C.

In 1942 Rovira began her professional career as Librarian of the Art History Department of the University of Havana. In 1952 she was appointed library cataloguer at the Catholic University of Saint Thomas of Villanova, and in 1953 she was made Head of the library, a post she held until she left Cuba in 1960 after the revolution. Between 1951 and 1960 she gave numerous courses in librarianship in both the summer school and regular sessions of the University of Havana's Library School, most frequently on the subjects of cataloguing and classification.

From 1960 Rovira worked in the Library Development Program of the Organization of American States, which she headed from 1978. Between 1961 and 1966 she compiled, together with Jorge Aguayo, the *Lista de Encabezamientos de Materia para Bibliotecas (Subject Heading List for Libraries),* a milestone work that has served the entire Spanish-speaking world since its publication in 1967 as the basic subject-heading list for library materials in Spanish. She also served as a consultant to Forest Press on the Spanish translation of the 18th edition of the Dewey Decimal Classification.

Carmen Rovira's other major publication is *Los Epígrafes en el Catálago Diccionario* (1953; 2nd edition, 1966), the first Spanish-language work on the theory of subject headings. She also served as Director of the professional journal *Cuba Bibliotecológica* in 1953 and again between 1955 and 1957.

MARTHA TOMÉ

## Rudomino, Margarita Ivanovna
(1900– )

Margarita Ivanovna Rudomino founded the All-Union State Library of Foreign Literature in Moscow in 1921, remained its Director for over 50 years, and had a broad international experience, mainly through the International Federation of Library Associations. She became the principal ambassador of Soviet librarianship abroad.

She was born July 3, 1900, in Bialystok, and although orphaned at an early age, she was able to finish secondary school in Saratov. She was Librarian in the school for foreign studies in the same city four years before being entrusted with the library of foreign literature—known at the time as the Neophilological Library.

The All-Union State Library of Foreign Literature had a modest start in 1921. Initially on the fifth floor of a 19th-century building in the center of Moscow, it moved four times and used several buildings before it finally occupied in 1967 a large modern building, designed as a library by the architect V. Sitnov. At the time of the dedication it had 700 staff members, 55,000 registered readers, and a collection of about 4,000,000 volumes in 128 languages. It became one of the important libraries in the world, while its objective gives it a unique character. It has quite a number of unusual features, foreign languages being fundamental to the entire operation: language courses in laboratories with sophisticated audiovisual equipment, readings by foreign authors, exhibitions of foreign books, bibliographic control of foreign literatures, and guidance to Soviet libraries with foreign language departments and departments of foreign library literature.

At the dedication ceremonies Margarita Ivanovna Rudomino said, "All about this building—both its exterior view and its light reading rooms—create that atmosphere of peace and joy which is so important for thoughtful, thorough study of a book or a manuscript." The architecture contributes to the urban landscape of Moscow both a local ponderousness and an imported elegance, Scandinavian influence being most obvious in the interior design and furniture.

The collections come mainly, but not exclusively, from the West. They are organized according to Western patterns, and an American or European librarian can easily understand its structure. Catalogues and other tools match familiar standards and traditions. Rudomino carefully studied European library techniques, particularly in Denmark.

The founder of the library was still in charge at the celebration of its 50th anniversary; that remarkable achievement was reached by Margarita Ivanovna Rudomino in 1972. She could look on a brilliant achievement both at home and abroad. She took most of her professional, political, and philological training after she had started the All-Union Library of Foreign Literature. In 1926 she graduated from Moscow University, Philological Department, Romanic-Germanic division, and in 1939 she finished the University of Marxism-Leninism. As late as 1955 she completed a postgraduate course at the Moscow State Library Institute. In the meantime she had married a physician, Vasili Moskalienko, and had two children. She retired in 1973.

The many publications that the Library issued over the years are linked to the overall purpose of the Institution: opening up foreign literature, classical and new in all fields, to the Soviet reader—whether expert or beginner—through indexes, reference tools, bio-bibliographic monographs, union catalogues, and so forth. Rudomino took responsibility for them all. The long list of her own writings shows an unfailing interest in Western librarianship. Her articles appeared in Russian and foreign professional journals. She is mainly responsible for introducing Western ideas into Soviet librarianship; now foreign library literature is acquired, analyzed, indexed, summarized, and, when needed, translated into Russian. For many years she edited the Russian version of the *Unesco Bulletin for Libraries*.

Rudomino always believed in two-way traffic, from abroad toward the Soviet Union but also from her home country to the rest of the world. She has often officially represented the U.S.S.R. abroad. From the early 1950's she was an active member of the International Federation of Library Associations and was elected Vice-President in 1967, First Vice-President in 1971, and Honorary Vice-President in 1973. She took part in all annual general council meetings of the Federation and was the key figure of the one organized in Moscow in 1970. Several times she was the Soviet representative at library meetings organized by Unesco—such as the Brussels meeting in 1958 on the exchange agreements of library materials and, at Unesco headquarters in Paris, of the International Advisory Committee on Libraries, Archives, and Documentation.

Her leadership position made her a member or chair of domestic professional committees, organizations, or editorial boards. She was close to the Lenin Library, the State Committee on Public Libraries, the Council for Library Service, and many other government agencies. Through her professional interest abroad she played an important role in the Council of Societies for Friendship with Foreign Countries, the U.S.S.R.-Denmark Society, the U.S.S.R.-France Society, and the National Unesco Commission.

Margarita Ivanovna Rudomino, interested in the contents of the books that she handled as a librarian, read widely, and although the choice of her authors—mainly foreign—reflected the social system to which she belonged, her critical sense always remained alert. She had friendly relations with many foreign writers, whom she always tried to meet during her numerous trips abroad. She traveled widely in the Communist world, Western Europe, the United States, Canada, and the East. Like many of her countrymen, she demonstrated an outspoken leaning toward a theoretical foundation of all professional and intellectual activities, favoring a view of major issues in a wide historical and methodological perspective. This did not, however, prevent her interest in human influences; biographies of leading figures, in professional and other fields, remained close to her heart. She would have been happy to be the editor of a Russian counterpart of a work like this *Encyclopedia*. In her "dacha," near Moscow, she worked in the late 1970's on a history of her own library and of the International Federation of Library Associations.

HERMAN LIEBAERS

# Rwanda

Rwanda, a republic in eastern Africa, is bordered by Uganda on the north, Tanzania on the east, Burundi on the south, and Zaire on the west and northwest. Pop. (1978 est.) 4,820,000; area 26,338 sq.km. The official languages are Kinyarwanda and French.

There was no national library in Rwanda at the end of the 1970's, although the government considered creating one. The Ministry of National Education was considering establishing a national archives.

**Academic Libraries.** The library of the National University of Rwanda in Butare is the most important academic library in the country. Founded in 1964, it contained 41,000 books in 1971, and the number grew to 78,000 books and 630 periodicals in 1977. It comprises a main library, law library, medical library, Centre for Documentation, binding department, and bibliographic center for information on Rwanda. The Library of the National Pedagogic Institute, established in 1966 in Butare, had an estimated 20,000 volumes in 1976. The Catholic Major Seminary of Nyakibanda has a library specializing in philosophy and theology. Also, two young institutions are developing their libraries in Kigali: the African and Mauritius Statistical and Applied Economy Institute, and the Higher Military School.

**Public Libraries.** Before Rwanda's independence in 1962, there were two categories of libraries; one for Europeans, and another for Africans. A library was set up in Kigali for Europeans before the 1940's; it contained 2,300 books in 1946. It remained the only library for Europeans in Rwanda until independence. Ten public libraries were established for indigenous persons between 1947 and 1954; the most important, at Kigali, had a collection of 2,623 books in 1960. By 1970 none of these libraries was still in existence. Since independence, there has been no governmental responsibility for libraries. The foundation of public libraries was taken in charge by the embassies, religious institutions, the National University of Rwanda, and others. The French Cultural Centre Library was founded in 1967 in Kigali and later extended its branch libraries in Gisenyi and in Butare. Also worthy of mention are the several libraries in Kigali, such as the American Cultural Centre Library, the Protestant Centre Library (CELTAR), the Club Rafiki Library, which was founded in 1975 by the Dominican Fathers in Nyamirambo, and the University Extension Library in Butare. The public libraries have few trained workers and, because of the shortage of the books in Kinyarwanda, the national language, are used almost exclusively by the minority able to read both French and English.

**School Libraries.** Secondary schools are generally supplied with small libraries, usually founded through the enthusiasm of one of the teachers or of the schoolmaster. Their collections are almost exclusively obtained from donation. Until 1976 the library of the "Groupe Scolaire" in Butare was the only one to have a professional librarian; it had 15,500 volumes. In order to serve the secondary school libraries, the National University of Rwanda set up, through its University Extension, a book van service. This service reached nearly 8,000 students in 30 schools in 1977.

**Special Libraries.** The National Institute for Scientific Research (INRS) in Butare is developing a collection in the natural sciences and a sound archives of historical and linguistic interest. The Agronomic Sciences Institute of Rwanda (ISAR) specializes in agriculture, animal husbandry, and botany. Most ministries and public establishments have either small special libraries or documentation services. The most important are the Ministry of National Education (with 12,500 volumes and 2,300 slides in 1977), the Ministry of Quarry and Natural Resources, the Ministry of Public Health, the Ministry of Foreign Affairs and Cooperation, the National Rwandese Office for Information, and the National Bank of Rwanda. There are several libraries in religious communities and Bishoprics; the best known are the Library of the Archbishopric of Kigali (with some 3,000 volumes in 1976), the Library of the Dominican Fathers in Kigali (15,000), and that of the monks of Gihindamuyaga (about 8,000).

The number of professionals is small, and there was no association for persons in information services in Rwanda at the end of the 1970's.

**REFERENCES**

Jean Brock, "Les bibliothèques en Afrique centrale," *Archives et Bibliothèques de Belgique* (1972), a summary of library development problems in Black Africa; five pages for Rwanda.

André Guitard, "Etre bibliothécaire au coeur de l'Afrique," *Argus* (1974); the working conditions of the librarian in Rwanda are presented by a Canadian librarian.

EMANUEL SERUGENDO

**SAA:** *see* Society of American Archivists

**Sabin, Joseph,** U.S. bibliographer and rare book dealer **169**

# Sabor, Josefa Emilia

(1916– )

*Josefa Emilia Sabor*

Josefa Emilia Sabor, Argentine library educator and administrator, attended numerous international congresses, lectured in and outside Argentina, and studied libraries, documentation centers, and schools for librarians in Europe and the three Americas. Born November 23, 1916, in Villanueva de Arosa, Spain, she became an Argentine citizen in 1937. She was a high school and normal school teacher, specializing in history in the Faculty of Philosophy and Letters of the University of Buenos Aires and a librarian in the same faculty. She was granted a scholarship by Unesco and the Office of Ibero-American Education to study documentation in Spain, France, Italy, West Germany, and Brazil and received another scholarship from the U.S. State Department's Bureau of Educational and Cultural Affairs to study the teaching of library techniques in ten U.S. universities.

In 1938 Josefa Sabor became a library assistant in the Teaching Institute of the Faculty of Philosophy and Letters of the University of Buenos Aires. She was Director of the Library and of Bibliography, Library Institute, University of Buenos Aires, 1943–46, and Director of the Library, Argentine Museum of Natural Sciences, from 1948 until 1952, when she was dismissed for political reasons. From 1955 to 1964 she served as Director of the Central Library of the Faculty of Philosophy and Letters, University of Buenos Aires.

Her teaching activities in Argentina included service from 1947 to 1951 as Professor of Reference in the School for Librarians of the Argentine Social Museum, from 1955 to 1970 as Director of the School for Librarians, Faculty of Philosophy and Letters, University of Buenos Aires, and from 1963 as Associate—later full—Professor of Bibliography, Reference Services, and Documentation in that faculty. From 1955 to 1957 she was Director, organizing the National School for Librarians for the Ministry of Justice and Education, and from 1963 to 1973 she was founding Director of the Center for Library Investigations of the Faculty of Philosophy and Letters in collaboration with Unesco.

Her international activities included contributions as Director of the Library and Publications Department of the Inter-American Living Center, Bogotá, for the Organization of American States (1952–53), Unesco expert, consultant, and Professor at the Central Library of the University of Costa Rica (1962), member of the International Consulting Committee for Librarians, Unesco, Paris (1965–69), OAS Visiting Professor at the Inter-American School for Librarians at Medellin, Colombia (1973–74), and Visiting Professor at the School for Librarians, University of Asuncion, Paraguay (1975). For the OAS she presented two programs for teachers in the School for Librarians of the University of Guanajato, Mexico, in 1977.

Her publications include *Manual of Information Sources* (1957; 3rd ed., 1979), *Manual of Library Science* (1951; rev. ed., 1969), *Methods of Teaching the Library Sciences* (Unesco, 1968), and many articles in library journals.

EMMA LINARES

## St. John, Francis R.

(1908–1971)

Francis R. St. John's life and career were centered in the East from his birth in Northampton, Massachusetts, on June 16, 1908, until his death in Manchester, New Hampshire, on July 19, 1971. He was Director of the Brooklyn Public Library, the position for which he is best known and remembered, from 1949 to 1963.

His association with libraries began as page and desk assistant at the Northampton Public Library when he was 11 years old and continued through his student years at Amherst (A.B., 1931). Professional education at Catholic University followed immediately (B.S., 1932).

His professional career began at the New York Public Library, where he held several professional positions, the last of which was Chief of the Circulation Department. In 1939 he became Assistant Librarian of the Enoch Pratt Free Library under Joseph L. Wheeler during Wheeler's famous tenure as Director.

During the World War II years, St. John organized the Army Medical Library (1943–45), which later became the National Library of Medicine. Following the war he was the first Director of Library Services for the Veterans Administration. In 1949 he left the VA for Brooklyn, where he was to earn his national reputation.

The St. John years at Brooklyn were a time of enormous change and growth for the system. Circulation of materials doubled from over 5,000,000 to more than 10,000,000 annually. The number of branches increased from 38 to 55. There were innovations in service programs as well. The District Library concept, which put strong subject collections and specialists closer to the people, was inaugurated, and the Community Coordinator program, which placed librarians on detached duty in the community to form linkages with agencies and organizations, was begun.

St. John quickly became identified as a manager. The introduction of assembly-line book processing and other management innovations held down operating costs, freeing funds for expanded service programs.

Personal professional activities were diverse and extensive. He was a founding member of the National Book Committee and initiator of the Franklin Books program. His *Survey of Library Service to the Blind, 1956* (1957) is a major document in the development of library services.

Following his retirement from Brooklyn in 1963, St. John opened a private consulting firm. Among the projects undertaken was a statewide library survey for the state of Oklahoma. In the years before his death he served as Consultant to the New Hampshire College and University Council and was also Librarian at Saint Anselm's College.

F. WILLIAM SUMMERS

## Samper Ortega, Daniel

(1895–1943)

Daniel Samper Ortega, educator, historian, and writer, was the leading promoter of library development in Colombia. He was born in Bogotá, Colombia, November 28, 1895. After graduation from the Military Academy, he wrote four novels, two plays, and several essays. Later he went to Spain to do research for a historical novel and to lecture at a Spanish university. He taught also in the Gimnasio Moderno, a progressive, independent, and private high school founded by his father, one of his uncles, and other businessmen with Agustín Nieto Caballero, an outstanding educator trained in Europe.

In 1930, during the Depression, the Liberal Party came to power after 50 years of Conservative rule in Colombia. There was a spirit of renewal in the country, and in February 1931 Samper Ortega was called by President Olaya Herrera and his Minister of Education to become the Director of the National Public Library in Bogotá, a position given traditionally to men of letters who took little serious interest in library development.

The state in which he received the Library was appalling. It was in a dilapidated old colonial house near Plaza de Bolívar, the main square. Books, magazines, and newspapers were thrown on the floors; the rest, unreachable, were piled on dusty shelves. Eighty-seven boxes of exchange publications, sent not only for the National Library but for other institutions in the country, remained unopened, some dated as far back as 1898. In the main room 52,000 volumes were uncatalogued except for a few private collections donated to the Library. Sixteen thousand valuable incunabula and parchment books were found, piled on shelves three volumes deep or on the floor. The final search yielded a total of 85,355 volumes, of which 60 percent were unreachable for lack of shelves.

He undertook a thorough reorganization of the National Library and despite the financial limitations turned it into one of the most modern and efficient public libraries of Latin America at that time. By 1934 a total of 192,914 additional reference cards had been made; the exchange system had been organized, and 15,898 volumes had been sent to other libraries; the National Archives were incorporated in the Library and 290,000 historical documents had been organized; and readers had increased to 9,362 a month, an increase of 358 percent from the time the reorganization was started.

Director Samper organized with Janeiro Brooks (later Schmidt) the first Library School of Colombia. Librarians were trained for the other ministries, the National University, the Central Bank (Banco de la República, which today has the best economic library in the country), and other institutions. By 1938 the National Library had in operation a children's library and theater, which was used as a model for the future satellite libraries.

He conceived the National Library as a dynamic center for the diffusion of education and culture, capable of breaking down the provincial and national boundaries. He did not want to wait for the readers to come to the Library; he went out to the readers. The books, to him, were only one of the means to serve the readers. Early in the reorganization he started the National Radio Station, as part of the Library, and a section to produce educational movies. He compiled a 100-volume selection of Colombian literature *(Selección Samper Ortega),* a titanic effort, unparalleled in Colombia and in the rest of Latin America. He started the *Biblioteca Aldeana de Cultura Popular,* a series of manuals prepared for farmers on subjects such as cultivation of different crops, health, care of children, and food, to take culture and education to the rural regions, through the National Library. Finally, in 1934 he started the publication of a monthly journal, *Senderos,* finely designed and printed, for the diffusion of ideas and knowledge as well as of information about the National Library. Later the Ministry of Education assumed these educational services.

The culmination of his seven years of service as Director of the National Library was the inauguration, in August 1938, of a magnificent, large, functional, and complete new building, in a corner of the Park of Independence, planned for a growth of at least a century. The inauguration of the new building was one of the main events with which Colombia celebrated the 400th anniversary of the founding of the city of Bogotá. Daniel Samper Ortega was at that time a Founding Member of the Academy of Arts, the Permanent Secretary of the Academy of Letters, and the President of the Academy of History. Samper Ortega resigned and became Cultural Counselor of the Colombian embassy in the United States. In Washington, D.C., he displayed his boundless energy for two years, making known the cultural achievements of Colombia, lecturing at the universities, and keeping in touch with educational and professional groups, among them the American Library Association.

He resigned his diplomatic post in 1941 to return to Colombia as Director of the Gimnasio Moderno, a school with which he had sentimental ties. There, with renewed energy, he undertook the task of turning it into a private university. With assistance from the Business School of Harvard University he opened the first College of Business Administration and Economics in Colombia, where the new business executives and economists of the country were trained.

He died in Bogotá on November 3, 1943.

**REFERENCE**

Guillermo Hernandez de Alba and Juan Carrasquilla Botero, *Historia de la Biblioteca Nacional de Colombia* (1977), a complete and concise history of the National Library of Colombia. Chapter 24 is dedicated to "Daniel Samper Ortega, the Restorer" and chapter 25 to "Daniel Samper and the new building of the Library."

ARMANDO SAMPER

## Sarmiento, Domingo Faustino
(1811–1888)

A man whose activities embraced many interests, including public education, politics, diplomacy, literature, and librarianship, Domingo Faustino Sarmiento has been termed a "universal man" and a "father of public education." He was President of the Argentine Republic, 1868–74. To his own passion for books and popular education he added lessons learned from years of travel and investigations abroad, and he took advantage of the opportunity to act offered by political office.

Born in San Juan City, province of San Juan, Argentina, February 14, 1811, Sarmiento rose quickly in local and national politics, serving in provincial and cabinet posts. In 1840, as a consequence of political events, he was forced to flee. He settled in Chile, involving himself in politics and devoting himself to putting his ideas on public education into practice.

Sarmiento was an indefatigable traveler and a born journalist. In 1845 the Chilean government commissioned him to study the organization of schooling in Europe and the United States. He visited France, Spain, Germany, Switzerland, Holland, Belgium, and Great Britain on the European leg of his tour. Before returning home by way of Cuba, Panama, and Peru, he conducted a survey of U.S. educational innovations. While in the United States he cultivated the friendship of Horace Mann. Sarmiento thereafter spread Mann's ideas on education throughout South America.

Sarmiento returned to Chile in February 1848. He founded a well-equipped printing house directed by Julio Belin, who later married Sarmiento's daughter, Faustina, in 1850. Throughout his exile, Sarmiento remained a prolific writer on matters of education, culture, and intellectual interests. His collected works would ultimately amount to 52 volumes. He played a significant role in the overthrow of the Rosas government in 1852, and in December 1863 the President of Argentina appointed Sarmiento Ambassador to the United States. He returned to the U.S. in May 1865. Sarmiento displayed remarkable energy, constantly traveling throughout the land in order to acquaint himself with subjects of practical interest to the development of Argentina. In 1866 he published a biography of his personal hero, Abraham Lincoln, and "Schools as the Basis of Prosperity in the U.S." He attended an international conference of teachers, and in June 1868 the University of Michigan awarded him an honorary doctorate. Horace Mann's widow, Mary, translated his *Reminiscences of a Province* and introduced Sarmiento in North America.

Sarmiento remained in the United States until July 1868, when he was elected President of the Argentine republic, a post he held until 1874. Under his leadership, the first nationally financed normal schools for the training of teachers were founded in Argentina. He arranged for 65 professional teachers from Mann's state of Massachusetts to establish and train personnel for both normal and primary schools in his country.

Sarmiento quickly acted to assure the parallel development of popular libraries. On September 23, 1870, he signed into law legislation creating the Protective Commission of Popular Libraries. Sarmiento later said in reference to this major cornerstone of his education program that "the need for libraries is everywhere felt. It is necessary to create the school library to complement the school and enliven it, serving as an aid to the teacher and an incentive to the child's curiosity." He also noted that it is "not without reason that we include schools and libraries within the same function. The latter complement the former; and as education becomes more generally available so will the number of libraries, occupying the position due them within the scheme of public instruction. Now the library is an integral part of the social organization, just like the free and compulsory schools—something not so before." He died in Asunción, Paraguay, on September 11, 1888. Though Sarmiento's goals were far from realization in the countries of South America in the latter 1970's, his ideal remains true.

REINALDO JOSÉ SUÁREZ

## Saudi Arabia

Saudi Arabia, a monarchy in southwest Asia, comprises most of the Arabian Peninsula. It is surrounded by Jordan on the northwest, Iraq on the north, Kuwait on the northeast, the Persian Gulf, Qatar, and the United Arab Emirates on the east, Oman on the southeast, Yemen (Aden) on the south, Yemen (Sana'a) on the southwest, and the Red Sea on the west. Pop. (1974 census) 7,012,600; area 2,240,000 sq.km. The official language is Arabic.

**National Library.** The National Library, established in the capital city of Riyadh in 1963, was placed in 1968 under the auspices of the Department of Public Libraries of the Ministry of Education. Its holdings total more than 20,000 volumes. A legal deposit law has not been issued because of the small quantity of published books in the country; only 57 published titles were reported by the Arab League Educational, Cultural and Scientific Organization for 1975.

The National Library issued a prospective national bibliography under the title *Mújam al-Matbu'at al-Sa'udiyah* in 1973. The bibliography claimed to include all commercial and official publications issued in Saudi Arabia up to 1973. It also publishes a bimonthly bibliography that includes the new additions as well as indexing of periodical articles.

**Academic Libraries.** Modern academic libraries have been established with the emergence of university education in Saudi Arabia. Those universities that have developed in the kingdom since the 1950's have shown special interest in developing their libraries as focal points in the teaching process. The University of Riyadh, which was established with only one college in 1957, by the end of the 1970's had eight colleges—Arts, Sciences, Commerce, Pharmacy, Agriculture, Education, Engineering, and Medicine, all of which established their own libraries. The Central Library of the University was established in 1964; all college libraries and the Central Library were placed under the administration and direction of the Dean of the University Library Affairs in 1974. The University libraries possess about 250,000 volumes and 1,600 periodical titles.

SAVAGE, ERNEST ALBERT 282

The King Abdul Aziz University, with its two campuses in Jeddah and Mecca, was established in 1967. The central library at Jeddah has more than 115,000 volumes and 2,000 periodical titles; the library at Mecca possesses about 50,000 volumes and subscribes to some 400 periodicals. The Islamic University in Medina, founded in 1961, has a central library and three college libraries for law, theology, and a secondary institute. The libraries of the Islamic University have more than 30,000 volumes. The libraries of the Islamic University of Imam Muhammad Ibn Saud in Riyadh, founded in 1950, and gaining university status in 1974, and the Petroleum and Minerals University in Dharan, founded in 1963 and achieving university status in 1975, both have growing collections of library materials.

**Public Libraries.** The Departments of Public Libraries at the Ministry of Education and at the Ministry of Hag and Awqaf are considered the custodians of about 28 public libraries throughout the country. Some of the noteworthy ones are housed in mosques, such as the Holy Mosque Al Harm, Mecca (7,000 volumes), and the Prophet's Mosque in Medina. The Saudi Library in Riyadh has over 15,000 volumes and 200 manuscripts. The Mahmoudia Library, which possesses about 5,000 volumes and 500 manuscripts, and the Arif Hikmat Library, with 2,000 volumes and 4,500 manuscripts, are in Medina. The Abbas Kattan Library in Mecca has over 8,000 volumes and 200 manuscripts. Other public libraries are found in Saudi towns, such as Taif, Ahsaa, Damman, Buraida, Onaiza, Shakra, Hawdit, and Sidair.

**School Libraries.** The development of modern school libraries is entrusted to the Department of School Libraries of the Ministry of Education. Vigorous efforts are being made to establish, organize, maintain, and staff school libraries for all types and levels of schools in the country. Acquisition and technical processing of library materials are done centrally and delivered to school libraries. Most of the school libraries are staffed with professionally trained librarians recruited from other Arab countries, mainly from Egypt.

**Special Libraries.** Saudi Arabian ministries, government agencies, organizations, companies, and research centers have shown interest in establishing special libraries to serve their officials. More than 24 special libraries have been founded in Saudi organizations since the mid-1950's. The following institutions maintain well-organized special libraries: the Ministry of Finance and National Economy, the Ministry of Petroleum and Mineral Resources, the Ministry of Labor, the Ministry of Planning, the General Statistics Directorate, Arab Saudi Organization for Specification and Measurement, Saudi Fund for Industrial Development, Industrial Research Development Center–Riyadh, General Organization of Petroleum and Minerals, Saudi Monetary Organization, Institute of Applied Geology–Jeddah, Institute of Public Administration–Riyadh, General Directorate of Broadcasting Press and Publicity, the Arab American Oil Company, the Saudi Airlines, and the Information Center of the Department of Educational Statistics, Research, and Documentation of the Ministry of Education. Many of these libraries have established documentation centers serving specialized needs, such as inquiry services, indexing, abstracting, bibliographical services, translation, and reprography.

MOHAMED M. EL HADI

## Savage, Ernest Albert
(1877–1966)

Ernest Albert Savage had one of the most original minds and was one of the most vigorous personalities in the history of the British public library service. He was born at Croydon, Surrey, March 30, 1877, and it was at the recently established Croydon public library that he began his library career at the age of 13. By a fortunate chance he rejoined the Croydon staff, after two years at Watford Public Library, just before the Croydon libraries came under the direction of Louis Stanley Jast. Jast was not only a bold experimenter; he was infectiously enthusiastic. Perceiving that Savage was of more than average ability, he made him his deputy. As Savage later realized, working closely with Jast was a better professional education than going to a library school.

In 1904 Savage became Librarian of Bromley, Kent, and in 1906 Librarian of Wallasey, Cheshire. At each of these towns he planned a Carnegie library, but it was not until he became Librarian of Coventry in 1915 that he had a major opportunity to prove his mettle. As a versatile industrial city of high repute, Coventry was then much concerned with war contracts. It seemed to Savage that its industrial efficiency would be all the greater if its factories had the benefit of a public technical information service. He therefore set about providing one at the central library. Following the success of this novel enterprise, Savage persuaded the Library Association to appoint a special committee to discuss means of improving the supply of technical information throughout the country. Although this committee, of which Savage was Secretary, failed to secure government support for its ambitious plan for a national technical information service (in suggesting the establishment of a National Lending Library of Science and Technology it was over 30 years ahead of its time), it did encourage the public libraries of several of the larger British industrial cities to provide out of their own resources special library and information services for local industrial and commercial firms.

Savage was also one of the first British librarians to recognize the value of local studies and perceive how public libraries might assist and stimulate them. The Coventry and Warwickshire Collection, which Savage organized and for which he devised a special classification scheme still in use today, was far ahead of the average local collection at that time.

In 1922 Savage was appointed Principal Librarian of Edinburgh city libraries. He took over a library system that, like too many others in the United Kingdom, was suffering from old-fashioned administration, unimaginative policies, and the unavoidable restrictions imposed by World War I.

Savage's career at Edinburgh spanned two decades. During the first he brought the city libraries up to the level of the best in the country; during the second he raised them above it, although not as far as he wished. Lack of resources prevented him from making Edinburgh Central Library the first completely subject departmentalized public library in Britain. The conversion of the city libraries to open access during the first decade was not in itself novel. The adoption of the Library of Congress

Classification, which Savage greatly admired, instead of the ubiquitous Decimal Classification, was.

The partial reorganization of the central library into subject departments, during the 1930's, was inspired by the pioneering divisional organization of the U. S. public libraries of Cleveland, Los Angeles, and Baltimore. While Jast was planning a new and unusually large central library at Manchester, which would have offered ample capacity for subject departmentalization had Jast favored it, Savage was struggling with the restrictions of an existing Carnegie library. His establishment of an Edinburgh Historical and Topographical Library, an Economics and Commercial Library, a Music Library, and a Fine Arts Library were steps in the right direction. Not until after World War II, when George Chandler reorganized the Liverpool Central Library, was a more sophisticated pattern of subject specialization established in any British public library.

Savage's 20 years at Edinburgh were notable also for his outside activities. Early in 1933, at the request of the Carnegie Corporation, Savage went to the West Indies to investigate and report on the various libraries available to the public. Most of the libraries Savage visited were subscription libraries; he recommended the establishment of a public library service modeled after English county libraries. Although Savage's recommendations could not be adopted in their entirety, a public library service was eventually inaugurated at Trinidad and Tobago with the help of the Carnegie Corporation.

Savage believed in the need for the Library Association; though he was always its most vehement critic, he was also its savior. In 1926 Savage attended the jubilee meeting of the American Library Association in Atlantic City. Impressed by the ALA's resources, activities, and status within the library profession, he felt that ALA was "the powerful driving force of the library movement in the States and Canada." He returned to Britain resolved to bring the Library Association out of the doldrums, where it had been becalmed for many years, with a small membership and negligible resources.

The essence of Savage's plan was to engineer amalgamation with the Association of Assistant Librarians and the other independent library associations and to obtain financial aid from the Carnegie United Kingdom Trust. When Savage became Honorary Secretary of the LA in 1928, he was in a good position to further his plan. With CUKT funds and the cooperation of the other library associations, the LA was transformed with a few years. By the early 1930's it had a paid secretary, its own headquarters building, and a library. Having piloted the LA through a crucial period in its history, Savage resigned from the honorary secretaryship in February 1934. In 1936 he served as President and for the rest of his life told the LA what it should do.

Savage's retirement in 1942 was purely nominal. Over the next 20 years he wrote several books and many articles, all of them written in his uniquely pungent, didactic, aphoristic style. Usually he was wise; often he was farsighted. Only in his opposition to the McColvin Report (*The Public Library System of Great Britain,* 1942), which advocated fewer and larger public library authorities, did Savage join forces with the reactionaries. For the most part, his contributions to the *Library Association Record,* the *Library World,* and the *Library Review* during the 1940's and 1950's rank high in the annals of library literature.

Among his books the most notable is *Special Librarianship in General Libraries and Other Papers* (1939). This collection of published and unpublished papers was the most original and stimulating book on librarianship published in Great Britain before World War II. Savage attacked the traditional pattern of public library organization in Britain, the common division of the stock into a general reference library and a general home reading library, and offered sound advice on how to replace them with subject departments. Even more striking, however, was the long essay on "The Training of Librarians," which foreshadowed the establishment of the postwar library schools in Great Britain and their eventual emancipation from the Library Association's unsatisfactory examination system.

*Special Librarianship* also included two of Savage's best contributions to library history, yet another area in which he excelled. When he was Librarian of Wallasey, he had somehow found time to write an impressive treatise called *Old English Libraries* (1911), which is still in use. In his retirement Savage wrote a fascinating professional autobiography, *A Librarian's Memories: Portraits and Reflections* (1952), which, despite its omissions and its occasional unfair judgments on some of his contemporaries, is likely to survive longer than any of his writings. When Savage published his last essay, in October 1963, he brought to a close a period of 73 years devoted almost entirely to librarianship.

In his day Savage was not appreciated as much as he deserved. His abiding and ill-concealed dissatisfaction with so many things in the library world gave him the reputation of a captious schoolmaster, which was not altogether fair. Savage's criticism was always constructive, and he never suggested anything should be done that he was incapable of doing himself. Jast was more endearing as a critic of library practice, and W. C. Berwick Sayers was a more patient mentor, but Savage was the most versatile and, in the end, the most influential public librarian of his day. He died at Edinburgh February 4, 1966.

ALA

*Ernest Albert Savage*

**REFERENCES**

The major sources of information on Savage are the detailed, fully documented biography *Ernest A. Savage: Librarian Extraordinary* by James G. Ollé, 2nd revised edition (1978), and Savage's own *A Librarian's Memories,* which provides a vivid picture of his professional life before he went to Coventry.

JAMES G. OLLÉ

## Sayers, W(illiam) C(harles) Berwick (1881–1960)

W. C. Berwick Sayers was one of the most prominent public librarians of his generation in Britain. Indeed, through his textbooks, he influenced the library education of at least two generations after him. His influence was not confined to the development of public librarianship, since as an editor and writer on such pervasive topics as classification he had an important hand in the progress of all types of librarianship during his life. Furthermore, he can be described as a Library Association man. He was a Council member for nearly 50 years, President in 1938, and one of the great figures in the Association's history.

Library Association

*William Charles Berwick Sayers*

Born on December 23, 1881, at Mitcham, England, he received his early education in Bournemouth, and it was at Bournemouth Public Libraries that he began his career. He was Sublibrarian there for four years from 1900, and then at the age of 23 he was appointed Deputy Librarian of Croydon under the great Louis Stanley Jast. It was Jast who helped most in the molding of Sayers as a professional librarian. From the viewpoint of his future career, Sayers could not have been at a better age, in a better place, or under a better guide.

Education for librarians was at that time in an embryonic stage in Britain, and aspirants had to enlarge their knowledge as best they could, since there were no library schools. Before going to Croydon, Sayers had already demonstrated his professional ambitions by winning the Greenwood prizes in librarianship, and with Jast's encouragement he widened his knowledge by attending lectures organized by the London School of Economics from 1905 to 1908.

It was about this time that Sayers became interested in the activities of the Library Assistants' Association, which had been formed in 1895. For ten years, until he became a chief librarian, he worked heart and soul for the LAA, being Honorary Secretary from 1905 to 1909, President from 1909 to 1912, and again Honorary Secretary from 1912 to 1915. At the same time his interest in the Library Association was growing. In 1908 he became a Fellow by honors diploma, and in 1912 he was elected to the Council and also became one of the Association's examiners.

In 1915 he was appointed Chief Librarian of Wallasey, where he succeeded Ernest A. Savage. But Sayers was destined to hold his new position for less than a year. Jast, his erstwhile chief at Croydon, was leaving to go to Manchester, and the Croydon authorities, no doubt on Jast's advice, invited Sayers to return to Croydon as chief.

Sayers remained Chief Librarian of Croydon until his retirement in 1947. Although his term of office was affected by two world wars, he instigated the provision of several new branch libraries for the rapidly expanding suburban population. Sayers also saw to it that Croydon remained the professional powerhouse of British librarianship created by Jast. Sayers in his time brought along such later notables as McColvin, Musgrave, Sharp, and Harrod.

But Sayers is remembered even more for his influential writings and for his work for the LA and for the National Central Library. In addition to writing hundreds of articles, he was the author of 12 books, as well as being editor of 4 editions of Brown's *Manual of Library Economy*. It was also an open secret that for many years he was the anonymous editor of *The Library World,* the monthly journal Brown had founded in 1898. His first book appeared in 1912; entitled *The Children's Library,* it was later described by Munford as a pioneer British book on the subject. Twenty years after, Sayers was to return to the same theme with a more mature book called *Children's Libraries*.

Sayers was not merely an author on library topics. He wrote books about Croydon and in 1913 published *Over Some Alpine Passes*. He was also a poet and musician. He composed many songs and wrote the definitive biography of the British composer Samuel Coleridge-Taylor. This appeared in 1915, with a later edition in 1927.

Classification was, however, the topic always associated with the name of Sayers. His earliest book on this subject was the *Canons of Classification,* issued in 1915, followed by *An Introduction to Library Classification* in 1918. This latter title achieved no fewer than nine editions in the ensuing 40 years. His magnum opus was undoubtedly the *Manual of Classification,* which appeared in 1926, with second and third editions in 1944 and 1955. Arthur Maltby produced a completely revised edition in 1967, and, with a new edition in the offing at the end of the 1970's, this too appears likely to have a long and influential life.

Sayers added much to our knowledge of the history of classification, and he was a judicious if sometimes biased assessor of modern bibliographical schemes. He favored the enumerative schemes of Dewey, Cutter, LC, and Brown but was much less at home with Bliss and with faceted schemes such as that of Ranganathan, his former pupil. Nevertheless, he was an inspiring writer on classification, and for no fewer than 32 years he lectured on the subject at the University of London School of Librarianship.

Although he retired from practicing librarianship in 1947, he remained active and influential until his death on October 7, 1960. He had been Chairman of the LA Executive Committee throughout World War II and received the accolade of the Honorary Fellowship in 1947. He continued to serve on the LA Council, being a particularly valuable member of the Education and the Publications Committees. For many years he was a member of the Executive Committee and later a Trustee of the National Central Library.

The profession was preparing to celebrate his 80th birthday with a *Festschrift* edited by D. J. Foskett and B. I. Palmer when Sayers died shortly before his 79th birthday. Work went ahead on the proposed tribute, which eventually appeared in 1961, published by the LA as the *Sayers Memorial Volume*. It contained 16 chapters by various writers, mainly on classification themes, and it proved a fitting tribute to a man who was a tower of strength to the libraries he served, to the Library Association, and to library education and library cooperation in his country. He is still remembered as a gentlemanly librarian, urbane of speech, and possessed of a Churchillian turn of phrase suitable for the big occasion.

K. C. HARRISON

## Scandinavian Federation of Research Librarians

The Nordiska Vetenskapliga Bibliotekarieförbundet (NVBF; Scandinavian Federation of Research Librarians), an umbrella body, was established on August 15, 1947, in Copenhagen to aid in the development of communications and cooperation among Scandinavian and Icelandic scientific libraries and librarians. Membership is open only to research associations and consists of members from the five following associations: Bibliotekarsammenslutningen for Danmarks Forskningsbibliotek (Denmark), Finlands Vetenskapliga Bibliotekssamfund (Finland), Deild bókvarda í íslenskum rannsóknarbókasöfnum (Ieeland), Norske Forskningsbibliotekarers Forening (Norway), and the Svenska Bibliotekariesamfundet (Sweden).

NVBF is governed by an Executive Council consisting of nine delegates elected by member associations for a three-year term; it is supported by fees from member associations, government aid, and grants from private bodies. Officers (Chairman, Vice-Chairman, Secretary-Treasurer) are elected for a two-year term. The chairmanship rotates in the following order: Norway, Finland, Sweden, and Denmark. At the end of the 1970's, important efforts have been made, in spite of the long distance to the other member countries, to fit Iceland into the work of the organization. The entire membership meets every two years; a general assembly met in Reykjavík, Iceland, in 1978. During the period 1978–80, NVBF established temporary headquarters at the Aalborg University Library in Aalborg, Denmark (also the residence of the chairman for the period). The permanent depository for the archives of the organization is the University library of Uppsala, Sweden. Staff consists of volunteers.

The association has no official journal. NVBF published a handbook on librarianship in Danish, and a handbook on library terminology in English, Danish, Finnish, Norwegian, and Swedish. In addition, NVBF issues proceedings of meetings, seminars, conferences, workshops, and Round Table Conferences, devoted to such topics as user education and library administration.

The association established a regular annual program of Round Table Conferences, each year on a different topic, and has been active in the Scandia Plan, a cooperative venture to coordinate acquisitions among Scandinavian libraries. Projects in the late 1970's included the development of summer school educational programs for librarians. Since the establishment in 1977 of NORDINFO, which obtains considerable grants from the government in the same countries whose organization for research libraries is a part of NVBF, the main tasks of NVBF have become conference and information activities which have nothing to do with the activities of NORDINFO. (NORDINFO took over the overall responsibility for the Scandia Plan.) NVBF relies principally on voluntary efforts and occasional grants from the government or other authorities.

WILHELM ODELBERG

# Schellenberg, Theodore R.
(1903–1970)

Theodore R. Schellenberg, archivist whose major influence was less as an archival administrator than as a theoretician, author, and teacher, was born February 24, 1903, in Harvey County, Kansas. He received his undergraduate degree from Kansas State University and earned a Ph.D. in History at the University of Pennsylvania. In 1934 he moved to Washington to serve as Secretary of the Joint Committee on Materials for Research of the American Council of Learned Societies and the Social Science Research Council, a position that involved him in the early application of microfilm to documentary materials. He then served briefly as Associate National Director of the Survey of Federal Archives before joining the staff of the recently established National Archives in 1935.

Schellenberg began his archival career as a Deputy Examiner, one of a small group of academically trained professionals who advised the Archivist of the United States on the appraisal and disposition of noncurrent government records, determining whether records no longer needed for conducting current business should be preserved in the Archives or destroyed. A concern with this most difficult responsibility of the Archivist became a central theme in Schellenberg's writings and teaching for the next 30 years, and one of his most important contributions to archival theory and practice was his elaboration of the "evidential" and "informational" criteria to be applied in the collective appraisal of institutional records. Within the National Archives Schellenberg rose rapidly to the position of Chief of the Agriculture Department Archives, where he contributed to the development of records disposition schedules for federal agencies, which identified and authorized, on a continuing basis, the destruction of those recurring record series without archival value.

After World War II Schellenberg became Records Officer of the Office of Price Administration, enabling him to participate directly in the development of the subdiscipline of records management. Emphasizing the life-cycle concept of records—from creation or receipt through maintainance and use to preservation as archives or destruction when noncurrent—records management attempts to reduce the quantity and improve the quality of records in their creation-receipt phase, to achieve greater economy and efficiency in the maintenance and use of current records, and to assure an orderly and timely retirement and disposition when records become semicurrent, including their intermediate storage in records centers. In 1948 Schellenberg returned to the National Archives as Program Adviser to the Archivist. He became Director of Archival Management the following year when the National Archives was reorganized as the National Archives and Records Service and in 1962 was appointed Assistant Archivist for a newly established Office of Records Appraisal, a position he held until his retirement from the federal service at the end of 1963.

He prepared the first comprehensive handbook of procedures for the National Archives—covering all professional activities—and wrote a number of staff information papers, bulletins, and journal articles on modern archival theory and practice. He organized and taught training courses for staff members of the National Archives; together with Ernst Posner of the American University, he taught credit courses and short intensive institutes on the preservation and administration of modern archives. In 1954 he was a Fulbright Lecturer in Australia and New Zealand; these lectures were the basis of the manual, published in 1956, *Modern Archives: Principles and Techniques*. The work became the most widely known and influential American publication in the field and formed the basis for Schellenberg's international reputation and influence with its eventual translation into Spanish, Portuguese, German, and Hebrew.

Having provided a theoretical and methodological foundation for the administration of modern public records and archives, Schellenberg then turned to bridging the gaps that had developed between archivists, manuscript curators, and librarians in their increasing specialization. After his retirement he lectured widely and taught courses at several universities. In 1965 he published his second major work, *Management of Archives*, which was based on the conviction that the principles and techniques of administering modern public records and archives are also applicable to those of private institutions and to accumulations of personal papers. He also proposed that chief responsibility for the training of archivists be placed with graduate library schools. Although the book did not have the widespread acceptance and impact of his earlier treatise, it has had a continuing influence on the relations between archivists, manuscript curators, and librarians.

Schellenberg continued to teach and write until shortly before his death on January 14, 1970. In addition to his travels throughout the United States, he was also active internationally, particularly in the Caribbean and Latin America. In 1961 he organized and directed the first Inter-American Archival Council and continued to serve as an adviser on the development of archival programs in this region. In recognition of his contributions to the archival profession worldwide, he was the first American to be elected to honorary membership in the International Council on Archives.

FRANK B. EVANS

# Scholarly and Research Services

In examining the scholarly services provided by libraries to the research community, we should first distinguish between the active role of research libraries in making their own direct contributions to knowledge and the more "passive" role of bibliographical or intellectual handmaiden, providing information that scholars and researchers use in their individual ways to make their own contributions to knowledge. Isaiah Thomas's Act of Incorporation for the American Antiquarian Society in 1812 already drew this connection, stating that the "collection and preservation of the antiquities of our country . . . have a tendency to enlarge the sphere of human knowledge, aid the progress of science, to perpetuate the history of moral and political events, and to improve and instruct posterity." Historically, the role of research libraries in "enlarging the sphere of human knowledge" has been the more limited function but one that deserves attention at the outset.

**Collection.** In a general way large research libraries often play an active role in shaping the direction of scholarship itself through their decisions about what is important to preserve for posterity and what is chaff to be discarded. By determining what is retained and made accessible from the human record, research librarians often have the power to determine new directions in scholarship, or at the least to affect the extent of those directions.

More specifically, libraries have made their own contributions to knowledge through their support of research, for example, in such fields as conservation and preservation (e.g., leaf-casting, paper deacidification, binding structures, encapsulation), the scholarship of cataloguing (e.g., attributions of authorship or date), and library history, a field that has assumed a scholarly life of its own as a subset of institutional history. In addition, many research libraries (notably the Library of Congress, the New York Public Library, the Folger Library, and the Huntington Library, to name a few) have supported active publication programs intended to enlarge the sphere of human knowledge and to make that knowledge more accessible to a wider public. Such massive projects as the *National Union Catalog,* the *Union List of Serials,* the *National Union Catalog of Manuscript Collections,* and the aspiration for a national bibliographical data base can be considered direct contributions to knowledge in their own right. Several research libraries, especially independent research libraries such as the Newberry Library, the Folger, and the Huntington, have sponsored series of seminars, lectures, and research-oriented symposia that have also made active contributions to the advancement of learning.

To most users, however, the primary functions of research libraries lie in the accumulation, organization, and preservation of vast amounts of information in various formats. Some of it may seem arcane, esoteric, and unimportant until synthesized by the inspired researcher. For example, the French anthropologist Claude Levi-Straus stated somewhat hyperbolically that everything he learned about anthropology he learned during long hours in the Main Reading Room of the New York Public Library during the early 1940's. Or consider the wide reading by Karl Marx in the British Museum a century earlier.

The habit of hoarding, often unrelated to imminent use, is predicated on the unpredictability of both the frontiers of knowledge and the demands that might develop for information. Although this assumption may be challenged, as it has been in recent studies at the University of Pittsburgh, and although the assumption may be more easily demonstrable for retrospective humanistic and historical research than for most scientific inquiry with its emphasis on currency of information, most large research libraries have traditionally accepted the necessity for comprehensive and vast collections sufficient to meet the unpredictable needs of the scholarly process.

While continuing to assume that necessity, however, research libraries are now faced with an insoluble dilemma created by finite resources. They operate in an arena where selectivity, for practical reasons, is an absolute necessity, even though selectivity in acquisition has been called "anathema to future research needs." Despite the continued growth in researchers' demands for comprehensive collections in their own institutions, economic forces are inevitably leading research libraries to coordinated distribution of collecting responsibility so that on a national scale the more harmful results of selectivity in the limitation of the scope of research may be minimized.

**Preservation.** An important component of the scholarly service known as collection development is the preservation of those collections for future use. Deterioration of physical materials has brought its own uncontrolled selectivity in most libraries. As noted above, libraries have already made impressive contributions to this field, and research and interest are continuing at an accelerated rate. Some large libraries and specialized collections have diverted considerable funds from other activities, including collecting, to preserve materials already in their collections. Like collecting, however, the task is too great for individual libraries to undertake alone. The most pressing present need, given the widespread deterioration of post-1850 papers, is a coordinated national program for nonduplicative micropreservation. In the U.S. a major tool toward that end has been the *National Register of Microform Masters,* produced at the Library of Congress since 1965 and cumulated in six volumes of almost 6,000 pages. As a record of past micropreservation activities and as an admittedly imperfect guide to the present availability of preserved materials, the *National Register* has proved to be an extremely valuable tool. What is now needed is on-line access to current bibliographic data concerning ongoing micropreservation activities. Such a system would allow research libraries to coordinate preservation activities along the lines of primary collecting responsibilities and to avoid duplication of the most costly step, the creation of a master negative. Although the Library of Congress has recently indicated its inability to undertake this development work because of other extensive commitments, there was hope at the end of the 1970's that the Research Libraries Group would assume the responsibility within its developing Research Libraries Information Network (RLIN).

No less crucial, though requiring even greater financial resources, are the conservation and preservation of records in their original formats. No libraries have yet made strides in this area commensurate to the scope of the problem. The task of restoring valuable materials is time consuming and expensive, and it requires highly skilled craftsmen and technicians. Research libraries have been able to deal with only a minuscule proportion of their problem collections. The most significant gains in recent years have been the growing awareness of the scope and importance of the problem and the development of both institutional and regional conservation centers. What is needed is a training program designed to produce a trained cadre of skilled conservators able to carry out pragmatic programs of conservation within the fiscal restraints necessitated by other institutional commitments. Again, coordination of such programs within the guidelines of primary collecting responsibilities is a *sine qua non* for success.

Recent research has made some progress toward an economically feasible system of mass deacidification that holds promise for protecting current acquisitions and reducing the rate of deterioration. Such a program is unlikely, however, to strengthen already embrittled papers, which will continue to disintegrate with any use.

*Research needs of scholars are met by special divisions within the New York Public Library. These include: the Oriental Division (above), the Map Division (p. 497), and the Local History and Genealogy Division (p. 498).*

Although the environmental conditions in which collections are kept generally improved during the 1960's and 1970's, greater preventive measures for protection of materials are needed. Few research libraries meet even minimal standards for proper storage, and energy problems of the 1980's are likely to make achievement of adequate environmental control even more difficult. Many libraries, including the New York Public Library, have invested large sums in conservation and micropreservation only to return preserved materials to a hostile environment. Much remains to be done in the entire field of preservation and environmental control.

Alexis de Tocqueville in *Democracy in America* complained about American carelessness in preserving the records of its past:

> The instability of administration has penetrated into the habits of the people; it even appears to suit the general taste, and no one cares for what happened before his time: no methodical system is pursued, no archives are formed, and no documents are brought together when it would be very easy to do so. Where they exist, little store is set upon them. I have among my papers several original public documents which were given to me in the public offices in answer to some of my inquiries.

While the collecting of books and archives has improved immeasurably since de Tocqueville wrote in 1834, care and custody of those in the U.S. collections has been almost irresponsible.

**Organization.** Inextricably connected to the primary scholarly service of research libraries in collecting and preserving comprehensively is the task of organizing those collections for use. Since this task is basically similar in all libraries, we need not dwell on the subject here except to note the greater importance of authority control in research library cataloguing practice. This importance is largely a factor of the greater size of research libraries, the retention of virtually all materials received, and the necessity of assuring the scholar that in consulting a library's catalogues he or she has access to all of the works available by a given author, on a given subject, or about a particular work. Authority control, by which a library maintains consistency in the bibliographical organization of its collections for use, is a major aid to the scholar and thus justifies its greater expense in research libraries. The collection of like works in catalogue listings to some extent makes up for the inability to house all like works together on the shelves.

Classification, the attempt to bring like works together physically, according to some organizational principle (e.g., subject or size), has often been seen as a scholarly aid to serendipitous discovery. As a result, so-called stack access has always been a valued privilege among scholars. However, several pressures will eventually lead many large academic research libraries to abandon or severely limit such access within the foreseeable future. Automated bibliographical systems, with their multiplicity of access points, already provide better means of access to materials than through classification and open access. As browsing through the computer develops, the importance of locating books through classification by subject is likely to diminish, at least as a part of the scholarly process. The open access tradition in U.S. academic libraries has been maintained at the very great but unquantifiable cost of widespread theft and mutilation, as well as the cost of poor service through the inability of many research libraries to provide access to substantial portions of their collections. Furthermore, classified open access collections require more space and room for growth than closed collections in various forms of compact housing. Despite the increased cost of retrieving materials for patrons, and despite the political problems of withdrawing stack privileges, the advantages of greater security, reduced space needs, greater control and accessibility, and better possibilities for optimum environmental control are likely to lead most research libraries to close their general collections from direct public access. Such a movement will also put a higher priority on development of alternate means of retrieval and remote access to stored optical images and other computerized information.

Other services traditionally offered to scholars by research libraries share a commonality with services in most other kinds of libraries. Direct reference services, reference correspondence, interlibrary loan, computerized literature services, and SDI services have become staples of the trade. In addition, research library photo service departments have greatly aided scholarly access to information, as has cooperation with publishers and commercial microfilmers in producing facsimiles in various formats of vast holdings of interest to researchers. Some libraries have even provided translation services to extend further access to materials in their care. And finally, the 1970's have seen an increasing preoccupation with educating users, both students and more advanced scholars, in the use of current information services available through research libraries.

Collecting and preservation should remain the most important functions of research libraries. The National Enquiry into Scholarly Communication (1979) points to inadequate library collections as a major concern to scholars in the humanities who wish to have comprehensive collections available locally. Nonetheless, the Enquiry's report goes on to state that "sheer growth of written and recorded materials coupled with inevitable limitations on library budgets suggests that the understandable desire of scholars for local self-sufficiency in library resources will increasingly fall short of attainment." These contradicting forces only seem to reemphasize the impossibility of single libraries "of last resort" and the absolute necessity for effective networking among research libraries based on efficient communications and delivery systems.

Despite recent predictions on the future of the information society and the marginal importance of libraries in that future, the need for the book and for comprehensive and coordinated repositories for the book seems secure. The codex remains the best medium for reflective learning and for access to the greatest and most creative works of the human mind. It is also the storehouse of that mind. Until its contents are captured in some other form or until

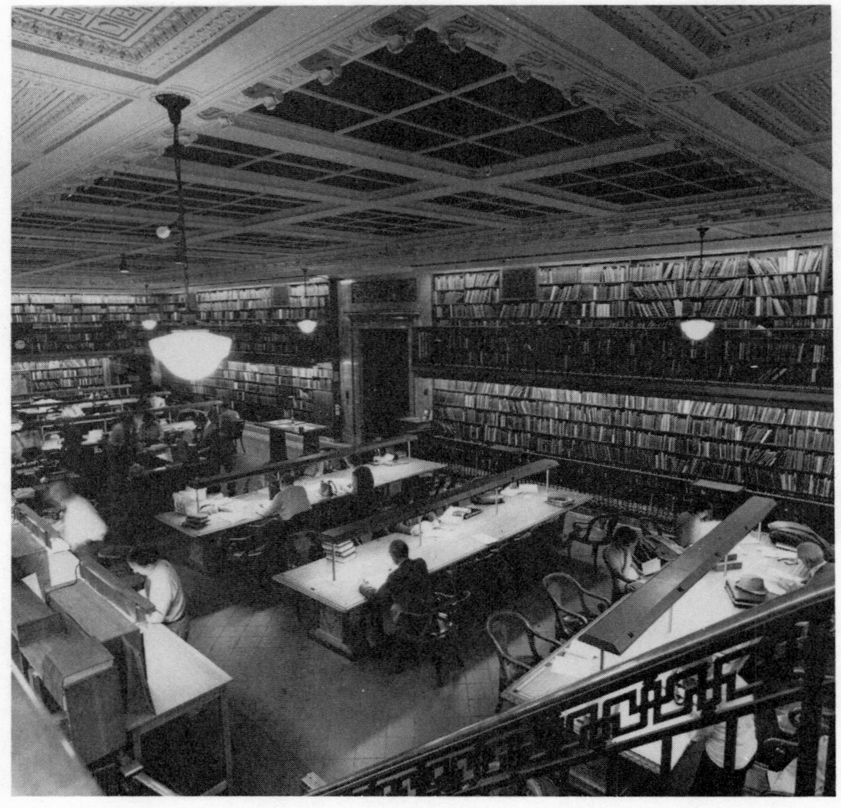

it is abandoned, there is compelling need for its retention.

REFERENCES
Albert H. Rubenstein et al., "Search versus Experiment: The Role of the Research Librarian," *College and Research Libraries* (1973).
*Scholarly Communication: The Report of the National Enquiry* (1979).
David H. Stam, "The Preservation of the Human Record in a Democratic Society: Who Is Responsible? The Role of Libraries," *New York Library Association Bulletin* (1978).

DAVID H. STAM



# School Libraries/Media Centers

PURPOSES AND OBJECTIVES

School Library development in the United States was first promoted in the late 1800's. Around 1895 farsighted high school principals and directors of public libraries in individual and isolated communities began to create school libraries, and by 1900 the first high school librarian, Mary Kingsbury, had been appointed in Brooklyn, New York. The National Education Association through its Library Department, the Library Section of the National Council of Teachers of English, and the American Library Association supported the development of this concept.

In 1915 the New York City District Superintendent of High Schools said, "It may confidently be asserted that the most potent single agency in the modern cosmopolitan high school is the library." The National Education Association Proceedings for 1912 stated that "the school library will be the proof of the educational value of the new curriculum . . . the library will be the open door to the opportunity of the present." Mary E. Hall, who was considered one of the outstanding early leaders in high school library development, said that the modern high school library could be depicted in this fashion:

> The room may fulfill all its pedagogical functions as a reference collection for obtaining information, a training school in the best methods of securing that information, a laboratory for special topic work and collateral reading in connection with the subjects in the curriculum and yet fail one of its highest functions if it fails to be a place of inspiration and recreation as well *(Selected Articles on School Library Experience,* 1925).

"The old high school library was static," said Hall, "but the new is dynamic. The old was largely for reference and required reading in History and English; the new is all things to all departments." These earliest statements by educators and librarians indicated a clear vision of what high school library service could become.

The high school library movement continued to expand, but elementary school libraries were slower in their development. The *Certain Standards for Elementary School Libraries* was published in 1925, and in 1933 the NEA, Department of Elementary School Principals, devoted its yearbook to supporting the concept. However, not until after World War II did elementary school libraries dramatically increase their visibility.

The increased birthrate necessitated the building of a large number of elementary schools, and these schools included libraries—often called library resource areas or media centers. Local, state, and federal funds helped to purchase books and nonprint materials, and the elementary schools flourished, as did their libraries. Professional staffs and experimental programs were considered an important part of reading programs as well as other aspects of the instructional curriculum.

Unfortunately, during this period specific legislation among the states that would require certified librarians in elementary schools similar to secondary school library requirements was not forthcoming. Hence, the economic pressures of the 1970's have produced serious cutbacks and threaten this aspect of school library service in many states. A reevaluation by librarians, teachers, school administrators, parents, and other citizens of the values of the elementary school library media center is a current necessity, so that these libraries not only will be resuscitated but also will actually expand into the vital force they could be as basic support for developing educational and leisure-time pursuits for all future adults. Strong state standards that insist on quality as well as quantity of materials and well-educated librarian media specialists, new efforts at multitype library cooperation, and specific legislation to guarantee support could do much to enhance and solidify the value of school libraries in tomorrow's education program.

**Education.** "The teacher librarian should meet the requirements for teachers plus training in the use of books and library methods. School librarians should have more training than the teachers in the schools wherein they serve. To create libraries without training librarians is futile." "One of the cardinal mistakes of the library movement has been to emphasize books more than service, and too often this can lead to a clerical type of library service." "School libraries activities are fundamentally educational: that they enrich the curriculum; that they stimulate initiative on the part of the pupils and develop healthy minds; that they socialize and democratize values and that they have an important part in character development." "[It is recommended that] every school that can employ a full time librarian, even if it must select its best teacher and send him at public expense to the best library school and into the best library system for instruction and inspiration." These quotations from a 1924 address by Joy Morgan before the Department of Elementary School Principals (NEA) epitomize the belief that has prevailed consistently in the library profession—the school librarian must be both teacher and librarian. There is a dichotomy of thought as to the minimum requirements for personnel, which are often influenced directly by state fiat. Nevertheless, certification codes also specify minimum standards in both education and librarianship at the secondary level and, in some states, at the elementary. The requirement of a Bachelor's degree with a teacher education emphasis plus a Master's degree in librarianship is the preferred level of education for school librarians today. Library schools emphasize courses in curriculum materials and methods, management, organization, instructional technology, child psychology, teaching of reading, and other matters, whereas in media centers services are coordinated with current educational trends.

**Professional Organization.** It was inevitable that with the increased visibility of school libraries a movement would develop within the ALA to recognize this group of libraries. In December 1914 at the ALA Midwinter Meeting, the American Library Association Council approved a petition from the Round Table of Normal and High School Librarians to form a school library section. The petition was supported on the grounds that there was "likely to be in the near future a rapid and extensive development of activity in this field of library work and the existence of a section . . . especially devoted to its study and discussion should be of material aid to those professionals concerned with it." Likewise, "The work and problems of school librarians are sufficiently different of those other library workers to justify their special organization as a section."

From 1915 to 1944 the School Libraries Section maintained a rather uneventful existence. However, in 1941 the section was reorganized as a part of the Division of Libraries for Children and Young People and became visible and active at the national level. In 1944 it was renamed the American Association of School Librarians, becoming an autonomous division within ALA in 1951. Patricia Pond noted that AASL reached three benchmarks in the development of a professional association: (1) forming an association that united members of the same occupation and/or those who wished to promote goals of an occupational group; (2) preparing a statement of goals and objectives most often incorporated in the association's contribution; and (3) structuring an organization that provided continuity of leadership, mechanisms for good achievement, and representation of the interests of members.

From 1951 AASL has had a full-time Executive Secretary, published a quarterly journal, set standards for the profession, and functioned as a liaison with state school library/media associations and associations with similar educational concerns and interests.

**Guidelines and Standards.** Influenced by changes in curriculum, technological developments, socioeconomic pressures, wars, and depressions, the basic principle that school libraries should participate effectively and completely in the school program has remained constant. This principle has been expressed in guidelines and standards published by the ALA school library section as it grew and expanded from 1915 to the present. The changes in interpreting this principle or role can best be seen by a review of the goals and objectives developed since the 1940's by the American Association of School Librarians.

Standards for school libraries had been constantly supported by both the American Library Association and the National Education Association, but the first significant statement issued by these two organizations was in 1941, in *Schools and Public Libraries Working Together in School Library Service*.

The school library is an essential element in the school program; the basic purpose of the school library is identical with the basic purpose of the school itself.

School library service, being an essential part of the school program, is basically a responsibility of the board of education.

The distinctive purpose of the school library within the total complex of the work of the school is that of helping children and young people to develop abilities and habits of purposefully using books and libraries in attaining their goals of living.

The school library program should carry out the purposes of sharing in the whole school program and of encouraging the effective use of books and libraries by providing individual service to individual children through reading guidance, ample reading materials, and library experience.

Three essential factors without which a school library does not exist are: (1) the librarian, (2) the book collection, and (3) the library quarters.

A school library does not become effective without the informed and constructive participation of many persons within the school system in addition to the librarian and the pupils, including especially: (1) the superintendent of schools and the central administrative staff, (2) principals of school buildings, and (3) classroom teachers.

School libraries and the public library should work together to provide a coordinated and complete library service to school children without unnecessary duplication of activities.

State leadership, operating under adequate state laws and regulations and working in cooperation with local groups, is essential in performing certain promotional, advisory, administrative, and coordinating services not otherwise available to local school libraries.

Josephine Riss Fang

*Nankai Middle School Library in Tianjing (Tientsin) China.*



*School Libraries for Today and Tomorrow: Functions and Standards,* published in 1945, was both a qualitative and quantitative effort, emphasizing services to pupils and teachers as well as specific standards for personnel, resources, housing and facilities, and budgets and administration. The purposes of the school library as stated in this first AASL document were to:

1. Participate effectively in the school program as it strives to meet the needs of pupils, teachers, parents, and other community members.

2. Provide boys and girls with the library materials and services most appropriate and most meaningful in their growth and development as individuals.
3. Stimulate and guide pupils in all phases of their reading so that they may find increasing enjoyment and satisfaction and may grow in critical judgment and appreciation.
4. Provide an opportunity through library experiences for boys and girls to develop helpful interests, to make satisfactory personal adjustments, and to acquire desirable social attitudes.
5. Help children and young people to become skillful and discriminating users of libraries and of printed and audio-visual materials.
6. Introduce pupils to community libraries as early as possible and cooperate with those libraries in their efforts to encourage continuing education and cultural growth.
7. Work with teachers in the selection and use of all types of library materials which contribute to the teaching program.
8. Participate with teachers and administrators in programs for continuing professional and cultural growth of the school staff.
9. Cooperate with other librarians and community leaders in planning and developing an overall library program for the community or area.

In 1956 AASL unanimously passed a statement, *School Libraries as Instructional Materials Centers,* the first official recognition that the flood of nonprint materials and equipment—beyond the traditional picture file or records and slides—had become an important part of the school's educational program and belonged in the library, where it would be shared by the entire school community. The statement reiterated the role of the school librarian and stressed teacher training requirements.

> The American Association of School Librarians believes that the school library, in addition to doing its vital work of individual reading guidance and development of the school curriculum, should serve the school as a center for instructional materials. Instructional materials include books—the literature of children, young people and adults—other printed materials, films, recordings, and newer media developed to aid learning. . . .
>
> The function of an instructional materials center is to locate, gather, provide and coordinate a school's materials for learning and the equipment required for use of these materials. Primary responsibility for administering such a center, producing new instructional materials, and supervising regular programs of in-service training for use of materials may be the province of librarians, or, it may be shared. In any case, trained school librarians must be ready to cooperate with others and themselves serve as coordinators, consultants, and supervisors of instructional materials service on each level of school administration in the individual school building, for the city or county unit, for the state.
>
> School librarians are normally educated as teachers and meet state requirements for regular teaching certificates. They must also receive special training in analysis, educational evaluation, selection, organization, systematic distribution and use of instructional materials. The professional education of school librarians should contribute this basic knowledge as well as provide understanding of fundamental learning processes, teaching methods, and the psychology of children and adolescents. Also, school librarians must be familiar with the history and current trends in development of school curricula.
>
> In summary, the well-trained professional school librarian should anticipate service as both a teacher and as an instructional materials specialist. Where adequate funds and staff are available, the school library can serve as an efficient and economical means of coordinating the instructional materials and equipment needed for a given school program. It should always stand ready to provide informed guidance concerning selection and use of both printed and newer media.

This declaration was soon followed by the 1960 *Standards for School Library Programs,* produced by a committee of school librarians in cooperation with representatives from 20 other related school groups and based on good school library practice as determined by a questionnaire sent to 1,400 schools. These standards expanded the concept of the school library as an educational force:

> The school library thus stands as a symbol for the truthful expression of man's knowledge and experiences. The extent to which many children and young people of today will be creative, informed, knowledgeable, and within their own years, wise, will be shaped by the boundaries of the content of the library resources available within their schools.

This represents an enhancement of the 1915 vision. The statement of (1) principles of policy and practice, (2) principles of administration and organization, and (3) specifications for staff, materials, and finances was intended to apply to all types of school libraries. Once again the basic guidelines from 1945 were restated and were interpreted in a way that could be significant to lay persons as well as school librarians. The qualitative standards were guidelines toward which all libraries should strive.

The general principles for planning were stated as follows:

1. The school library program reflects the philosophy of the School and enriches all parts of its educational program.
2. For the individual student, the library program offers valuable experiences and instruction that start with kindergarten and, expanding in breadth and depth, continue through the secondary school. This continuity of the library program provides for the student a cumulative growth in library skills and in the development of reading, listening, and viewing abilities and tastes.
3. The true concept of a school library program means instruction, service, and activity throughout the school rather than merely within the four walls of the library quarters. All phases of the school program are enriched by means of library materials and services. The degree to which teachers and pupils can and do depend on the services, materials, and staff of the library measures the extent to which the library program is successful.
4. Every boy and girl within the school is reached by the library program according to his individual needs.
5. Through varied types of materials, the collections of the library provide for the many kinds of interests that its users have, for the different levels of maturity and ability of the student population, and for the wide range of demands evoked by the curriculum and the services of the modern school.
6. The library is a laboratory for research and study where students learn to work alone and in groups under the guidance of librarians and teachers. Thus it contributes to the growth and development of youth in independent thinking, in abilities to study effectively, and in desirable attitudes toward reading, toward other media of communication, and toward all learning and research.
7. The library program forms one facet of an over-all

guidance program in the school by making important contributions through its teaching, materials, and services to the personal, social, and vocational guidance of students.

8. School library experiences serve as steppingstones to the use of other library resources in the community and to the formation of a lifetime habit of library usage, as well as to pride in the ownership of books.

By 1969 there were significant social, educational, and technological developments in society, and a new set of standards was published, *Standards for School Media Programs*. They constituted a unique cooperative effort by the AASL and the Department of Audiovisual Instruction of NEA and were designed to coordinate standards for both school library and audiovisual programs—a unified program.

> The philosophy of a unified program of audiovisual and printed services and resources in the individual school is one that has continuously grown and been strengthened in the last thirty years. This fusion of media resources and services provides optimum service for students and teachers. Many schools now have unified media programs. For those others that have separate audiovisual departments and school libraries, it is recommended that where ever possible, these services be combined, administratively and organizationally, to form a unified media program. New schools should start with a unified media center and program of services, which includes:
>
> Consultant services to improve learning, instruction, and the use of media resources and facilities.
>
> Instruction to improve learning through the use of printed and audiovisual resources.
>
> Information on new educational developments.
>
> New materials created and produced to suit special needs of students and teachers.
>
> Materials for class instruction and individual investigation and exploration.
>
> Efficient working areas for students, faculty, and media staff.
>
> Equipment to convey materials to the student and teacher.

Since the emphasis in this publication was on the building library, it soon became evident that directions were needed for districtwide centers as well. Four major assumptions form the basis for the most recent publication, *Media Programs: District and School* (1975), and further delineate the shift in emphasis within the school library programs: (1) full acceptance of a total media concept; (2) a greater participation in instructional decision making; (3) stress of programmatic activity focused on the "user"; and (4) utilization of pertinent principles of management theory. Here was an even stronger movement away from quantitative standards for resources and a more deliberate emphasis on how these resources would be used.

According to this document, published by ALA for AASL and the Association for Educational Communications and Technology (AECT), the media program is considered in light of four functions: design, consultation, information, and administration. The premise that there is an obligation to share implementation of goals as well as operation of programs with the community is strongly evident throughout this statement.

> In quality media programs users are observed in all of these activities and adaptations of them:
>
> Finding needed information on an appropriate level and in an acceptable format.
>
> Selecting and using appropriate means for retrieval of information in all media formats.
>
> Obtaining resources from the media center, district center, local agencies, and networks.
>
> Communicating in many modes, demonstrating an understanding of the structure and language of each mode.
>
> Utilizing instructional sequences of tested effectiveness to reach personal and program objectives.
>
> Designing and producing materials to achieve specific objectives, as well as using materials designed and produced for them by the media staff.
>
> Employing a variety of media to find, evaluate, use, and generate information.
>
> Enjoying the communication arts and gaining inspiration from them.
>
> Exchanging with school personnel pertinent information regarding students' progress and problems.
>
> Developing user understanding of the strengths and limitations of various presentation forms.
>
> Planning and providing instruction in the use of the media center and its resources.
>
> Helping students develop good study habits and techniques, acquire independence in learning, and gain skill in critical thinking.
>
> Helping students develop competencies in listening, viewing, reading, and other communication skills, attitudes, and appreciations.
>
> Assisting users in the techniques of finding, using, abstracting, translating, synthesizing, and evaluating information.
>
> Receiving assistance, both formally and informally, in the use and production of learning resources.
>
> Functioning in learning environments that reflect their developmental level as well as the tasks at hand.
>
> Locating space in which to accomplish a variety of activities responding to curricular and personal needs.
>
> Participating in the formulation and implementation of both general and specific media program policies.

**Program Trends.** As the evolution of the standards kept pace with a changing society, so too have new aspects of library service and programs. A survey of the topics covered from 1965 to 1975 by the official AASL publication *School Libraries* (later retitled *School Media Quarterly*) suggests the wide variety of interests and concerns that stimulated innovative and creative programs. The child's right to read, collection building, staff deploy-

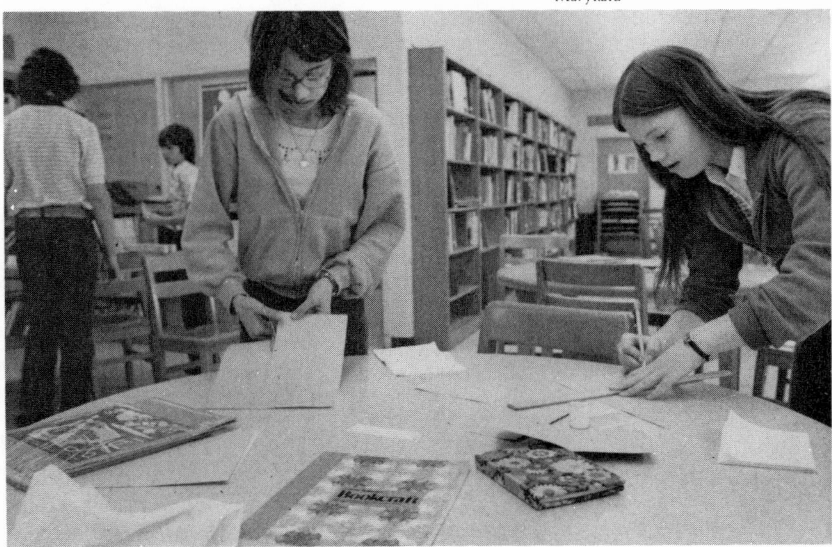


*Learning how to make books—in a Maryland junior high school library.*

Prince George's County Public Schools, Maryland

Media equipment holds the attention of users of school libraries in Madison, Wisconsin, (above) and in St. Paul, Minnesota (p. 505).

(This page): Bureau of School Library Media Programs, Madison, Wisconsin; (p. 505): St. Paul School District, St. Paul, Minnesota

ment and personnel needs, demonstration school libraries, and federal legislation dominated the scene in the early part of the 1970's. The influence of technology, computers, TV, photography, and more sophisticated audiovisual hardware and software became evident in the actively expanding media centers in which programmed or self-instruction, listening, and viewing as well as production were promoted. Exceptional children's needs, individualized instruction, intellectual freedom, and international understanding programs were topics of concern. In the latter part of the 1970's, research about school library media center programs, services, user needs, teacher involvement, and student attitudes was produced, and librarians became aware of the value of research as an aid in their own program justification. Socioeconomic changes, as well as technological ones, influenced the media center specialist, producing a need for articles that would educate librarians and help them to prepare to meet these changes in a competent fashion. Censorship, networking, children's rights, community education, copyright, access, selection and acquisition policies for print and nonprint media, nonsexist materials, media needs of special children from the gifted to the handicapped, and new approaches to school and public library cooperation currently occupy the attention of the profession.

As federal legislation shifted emphasis and financial support, so have school library programs. Services and materials for bilingual children, ethnic minority groups, disadvantaged persons, and literacy programs were produced, and AASL committees and staff endeavored to assist in these demands through publications of all types.

**International.** The burgeoning school library in the U.S. in the late 1940's and 1950's was followed by comparable growth and interest in other countries. The Canadian pattern developed along similar lines, and Canadian and American school librarians often share their endeavors through workshops, conferences, and standards. In Europe—particularly Denmark and to a somewhat lesser degree in Sweden and England—legislation that promoted school libraries was passed, and federal funds supported rapid expansion of school libraries in the early 1970's. Denmark now has a national mandate for a library in every school with professional teacher-librarians. Australian school librarians quickly followed, requesting legislative and financial support at federal and state levels. By the late 1960's an international interest was evident in the field of education, and it resulted in a movement to advance school library services in both developed and developing countries. New Zealand, Japan, Malaysia, Singapore, Indonesia, the Philippines, Nigeria, and Ghana are all examples of countries where specific efforts to promote such activity can be identified.

One of the interesting international developments is the growth of associations for school librarians, as either independent organizations or special divisions in national library associations. Some 30 such associations have been identified as having active programs, and most of them publish a journal or newsletter. They organize workshops and institutes for training personnel, promote legislation in support of libraries, and argue for indigenous publications relevant to their children's interests. A good example is Nigeria, where the Universal Primary Education Act has compelled authorities to state that libraries are a necessary part of this program, although the problem of providing personnel and materials remains serious and unmet. The new Nigerian School Library Association had as its objective publishing a journal to assist school librarians in becoming acquainted with programs in their different states and create a forum through which those concerned with school library development may promote their cause.

The Fiji Library Association helped develop school library programs and urged that pupils have an opportunity to develop language fluency and increase their vocabularies in a second language, encouraging teachers to read books to the children and urging school libraries to purchase materials relevant to their student needs.

In Ghana school library services are coordinated at the Central Library in Accra, and a bookmobile carries current materials to regional centers. This remarkable program of selecting, processing, and delivery is conducted by a small staff. The Ghana Library Association has focused on the development of school libraries and the future of library education.

These efforts highlight some of the basic problems facing school library development in third world countries. The competition for funds is far more intense than in the U.S.; education and libraries are often forced to take a second place behind such basic needs as food, clothing, and shelter. Where do books and libraries fit into a country's program when the population increases proportionately faster than the number of teachers, let alone librarians? The problem is further exacerbated by the difficulty of obtaining reading materials of any kind in sufficient quantity, especially in the language of the people, relevant to the culture, or written by indigenous authors. But the acceptance of the concept of school library service is evident. Ministries of education are promoting legislation that will begin to support types of library resource centers and are encouraging the development of a corps of professional librarians to serve as organizers and supervisors.

National, regional, and international organizations are promoting exchange of information, programs, research, and standards. The impact of school library media and services, and their role and function in education, will continue to grow in all countries. Services to all, good administration, effective legislation, and sound education are aspects that will support and promote systematic development.

**REFERENCES**

Mary E. Hall, "The Development of the Modern High School Library," in Martha Wilson, compiler, *Selected Articles on School Library Experience* (1925).

Joy E. Morgan, "Schools and Libraries," in Wilson, *Selected Articles.*

Patricia Pond, "Development of a Professional School Library Organization," *School Media Quarterly* (1976).

JEAN E. LOWRIE

COLLECTIONS

The changing trends in education that have resulted in the development of new teaching strategies and in a variety of organizational patterns in the school have directly affected the growth of the school library media center. The shift away from the single-textbook, self-contained classroom mode of teaching to the interdisciplinary, diversified curriculum approach aimed at individualized instruction has created the demand for a wide range of instructional materials available from a centralized source in the school. The book collection of the traditional library has given way to the multimedia collection of the school library media center. The collection, together with the center's program of service and instruction, plays a vital role in the attainment of the school's objective of providing a high-quality education for all children and young people.

**Collection Building.** The school library media center's program has become an integral part of the instructional program of the school, and its collection of materials is a key factor in the success of the school's program. The basic purpose of the collection is to support and supplement the curriculum and to provide quality recreational reading material for student enrichment. Each collection is unique in size and content and is developed, ideally, to meet the needs and objectives of the individual school program as well as the interests and abilities of the school population. The number of students in the various grade levels, the wide span of reading levels represented, the curriculum content, the socioeconomic backgrounds of the students, and the resources available in the community are among factors considered in developing a well-balanced, dynamic, useful collection.

In building such collections, standards of excellence will be applied to all forms of materials representing a broad coverage of subjects and varying levels of difficulty. Consideration is given to both the long-range goals of the instructional program and the immediate needs. To support a variety of learning experiences, the collection will include a diversity of media formats, including hardbound and paperback books, pamphlets, periodicals, newspapers, clippings, pictures, audiovisual materials, and other learning aids. *Media Programs: District and School* (ALA, AECT, 1975) provides a detailed listing of the types of media and necessary equipment that may be included in the media center.

By creating a collection of varied media, the library offers students and teachers the opportunity to use the medium that most effectively meets the needs of a particular learning situation. Appropriate reference tools are included for research work, and suitable materials for viewing and listening activities are available, as well as books for pleasure reading and a current, diverse collection of professional materials.

**Organization.** The effectiveness of the media center depends not only on the materials in the collection but also on the accessibility of those materials for the library users. It is essential that students and teachers be able to find readily and use the desired media as the need arises. The collection must be well organized according to those standard library procedures most suitable for the particular school. A current, viable collection is achieved through careful selection, constant maintenance, and good systems for organization and access.

An integrated approach in organizing materials results in a collection in which all materials, regardless of format, are catalogued and classified according to a single system. The complete index to the collection (whether in card or book form or on a computer terminal) indicates all book and nonbook materials in a single listing, enabling users to identify and locate the media center's holdings on a given subject. Whether the various types of media are placed together on the shelves or stored in separate areas in the center will depend upon the facilities available and the policy of the individual media center. Some materials may even be housed elsewhere in the school, but through a unified catalogue, users are provided with bibliographic information on all available materials.

Ephemeral materials such as pamphlets, clippings, and unmounted pictures, which do not warrant the time or cost involved in cataloguing, are housed in filing cabinets and are arranged according to subject headings that correspond to those used for other material in the collection. The media center's catalogue may indicate that information on a particular subject can be found in the pamphlet file, or there may be a separate listing of subjects represented in the file.

Current issues of periodicals and newspapers are usually displayed on special shelving or racks and a list of the titles made available. The policy regarding retention of back issues depends upon storage facilities in the media center. Microform copies require minimal space and with adequate equipment for viewing and copying can meet the need for periodical information.

The books and audiovisual materials may be catalogued and classified for the individual school collection by a centralized processing center in the school district, by commercial firms, or through arrangements with other agencies or school districts. Processing at the local level is least desirable in terms of cost effectiveness and staff time. However the cataloguing and physical processing are provided, they must be consistent and meet the specifications of the individual media center and should meet the standards of the field at large.

With the publication in 1978 of the second edition of the *Anglo-American Cataloguing Rules,* a standard for cataloguing nonbook materials was established. Book and nonbook materials can be processed with uniformity, with the result of increased potential for sharing resources through systems and networks, thus offering a greater wealth of material to students and teachers.

Continuous reevaluation of the collection for accuracy of information, current interests, and changing curriculum content is important if the collection is to be meaningful and useful.

Weeding is an ongoing process involving the removal from the collection of all forms of material, including books that contain out-of-date information; books that are defaced, dirty, worn, or have discolored or brittle pages; books for which new or revised editions are available; duplicate copies of books no longer needed in quantity; books no longer of interest or that are too easy or too difficult for a changing student body; periodicals, pamphlets, and other vertical file materials that are outdated or worn; audiovisual materials that are outdated, worn, or damaged. As these materials are discarded, procedures for replacement are established as part of the regular selection process.

**Collection Policy.** Today, with an abundance of library materials available for children and young people, selection of quality materials for the school library media center program is imperative. Each school district should have a written policy statement regarding selection. Professional library staff, administrators, teachers, parents, and school board members often participate in the development of this statement, which may include the philosophy of the school's educational program, the types of materials to be ordered, criteria for their evaluation, and procedures for handling problems that may arise when material selected is questioned.

Administrators, teachers, students, and parents may be encouraged to recommend materials to be included in the school library media collection. A school faculty consists of many subject area experts, and they are aware of materials that are needed to supplement the curriculum. Students and parents are aware of the needs, interests, and abilities of the students and are a great help in the selection process. School library media center budgets will affect the amount of materials that may be purchased. The final selection of materials is the responsibility of the principal, who usually delegates the leadership activity to the professionally trained staff of the media center.

With the great quantities of library materials produced each year, it is difficult to read or preview all materials before ordering them. Faculty members may be able to preview library materials while attending conferences. The library staff may also request audiovisual materials for review by a department or a teacher. Excellent selection aids are available for use in choosing materials, and special reference tools locate quality materials in particular subjects. Selection guides are used in establishing a new media center collection or in developing balance in an established collection. Reviews of books and audiovisual materials are found in major library periodicals, and discriminating reviews and recognized selection aids are considered more reliable in selecting materials than vendors' catalogues, which are ordinarily only descriptive announcements of materials.

In evaluating books the following general criteria may be considered:

The subject matter is appropriate, desirable, and significant.

The information is accurate, up-to-date, and unbiased.

The characters are not stereotyped.

The author is qualified to write about the particular subject.

The writing has literary quality and style.

The style is suitable for the content and for the reader for whom it is intended.

The illustrations reflect the subject matter with propriety, accuracy, clarity, and have artistic value.

The format relative to size, binding, paper, margins, type, and spacing is satisfactory.

A recognized list or reviewing tool has included this title.

The material challenges the student's thinking, and he is stimulated to search for further information.

The concepts and policies are in keeping with the philosophy and objectives of the educational program of the school.

In evaluating audiovisual materials, these general criteria may be applied:

The subject matter is appropriate, desirable, and significant to the student.

The information provided is accurate, up-to-date, and unbiased.

The material has been previewed, or included in a recognized list, or reviewed in a reliable selection aid.

The material challenges the student's thinking, and he is stimulated to search for further information.

The objectives of a particular lesson or problem-solving activity are met by the content and the type of material.

A guide is provided to assist the teacher in making the most effective use of the material.

The technical quality of the material is adequate.

The cost of the material will be justified by its use.

The concepts are in keeping with the philosophy and objectives of the educational program of the school.

Magazines have a tremendous appeal for children and young people. Local, national, and international newspapers may also be represented in the school library media center collection to provide supplementary information, serve special interests, and provide examples of a variety of viewpoints.

Another important consideration in the selection process, and an underlying principle of the selection policy, is the need for a balanced library collection. Balance must be maintained between print and nonprint collections, fiction and nonfiction, paperbacks and hardbound books. Different reading levels among students should be addressed, so books for poor readers, average readers, and superior readers can be provided to meet individual needs. An adequate reference collection for student research should be considered, while a well-rounded professional collection will serve teachers and parents. The professional staff must know the total collection so that gaps can be recognized, popular items needing duplicate copies identified, and replacements for lost items ordered.

Building the school library media center collection requires the participation of many interested people. The professional media center staff contributes its expertise in developing, organizing, and maintaining the collection. A collection rich in depth and breadth of content, containing a wide range of media formats, and meeting the needs of students and teachers is basic for the development of the media center program, which in turn determines the success of the educational program of the school.

WINIFRED E. DUNCAN;
MARIE A. McNAMARA

SERVICES TO USERS

The concept of the school library as an instructional resource center and laboratory for learning is derived from, but represents a distinct break from, the U.S. tradition of public library services to children that took form, beginning in the late 19th century, as separate library rooms for children, book loan services to schools, summer reading promotions, and the specialization of children's work as a branch of librarianship. Often established at the initiative of public libraries, book rooms and services in schools had a simple reason for being, by comparison with today's school media centers—to enrich textbook teaching with good books and to introduce children to the wonderful world of imaginative literature through storytelling, book talks, and reading guidance.

A noticeable break with these traditions occurred during the mid-1950's, in the series of public education reforms precipitated by an extraordinary increase in knowledge and the proliferation of communication technologies. These, in a few years' time, rendered the predominant textbook-based curriculum obsolete, raised doubts about the validity of the printed word as the exclusive communication medium of education, and highlighted the futility of attempting to teach children everything there is to know in 12 years of schooling.

Concurrently, educational researchers were advancing new insights on how children learn and why a substantial number do not. Their judgment that all children can learn, though not necessarily at the same rate of speed or in the same way, was an indictment of current practices in most American schools and induced educators to experiment with a variety of audiovisual equipment and teaching strategies that would allow the aberrent learner to be educated in his own way rather than by the methodologies predominant in the majority of classrooms of that period. Individualizing learning, motivation, and humanizing education became the buzzwords of school reform. The subsequent decades were characterized by revolutionary changes in curriculum content, the introduction of alternate patterns of instructional organization, e.g., the open classroom, and many innovative uses of technology borrowed from business and the military.

Libraries became important as places where students would learn from a range of information sources, using "discovery" and problem-solving learning procedures.

With the help of federal funds, school libraries were established where formerly there had been none, and existing collections were expanded. Motion pictures, recordings, audio tapes and videotapes, transparencies, filmstrips and slides, programmed instruction, computer programs, microforms—along with a bewildering array of projection, reception, recording, magnification, and production technologies—were introduced into library collections.

Libraries were enlarged, wired, and adapted to accept the strange shapes and sizes of nonbook information packages and their hardware. Photo darkrooms, television studios, microform libraries, projection and recording rooms, and AV production centers where students could work creatively with the new media were incorporated into the design of media facilities. Teachers, including librarians, were sent off to government-financed workshops to learn how to use the wonderful new educational tools. District and regional media resource centers were established.

The result of three decades of school and school library reform has been to move the library and the librarian from the periphery of the instructional program into the mainstream of educational effort. In the process, many schools and school systems have renamed their libraries "media centers" and those that administered them "media specialists"—recognizing both the expanded functions of the areas and the augmented competencies of those providing leadership within them. Hereafter in this account only the newer terms, *media center* and *media specialist,* will be used.

**Dimensions of Services.** The school media center serves two publics, teachers and students, both within the context of the school system's educational goals and objectives. The student users may range in age from 5 to 18 years—younger when prekindergarten programs exist, older if classes of mentally retarded students are housed within the school. Within each age group, students differ from one another in degrees of physical, mental, and emotional maturation, any of which may affect the students' progress through the educational system. They are, like all people, fast or slow, eager to learn, or stubbornly resistant to schooling. Some are emotionally impaired or learning disabled in ways that require the intervention of knowing adults, including librarians. The talented and gifted among them, along with those educationally handicapped by reason of cultural, emotional, physical, or economic circumstances, are singled out by law for supplementary, compensatory, or alternative services, many of them media-related.

The second public that the school media center serves is the teaching faculty. Like students, teachers also come with individual differences: in years from 21 to 65 and older, by experience from neophyte to experienced, with varying curriculum-area interests and responsibilities, teaching styles, and perceptions about what the school media specialist is supposed to be doing. Outside the school, they may be students enrolled in higher-degree or continuing-education programs. As classroom teachers they are isolated from other professions for most of their working hours, needing to keep up with current trends in education and better ways to deal with classroom and curriculum problems. The users of district media centers are teachers and media personnel in the dependent schools, school administrators, board of education members. The educational community consisting of parent-teacher and other organizations for protecting or promoting special educational interests and the taxpaying public are also potential users of the district media center.

**Factors Affecting Services.** There is frequently a gap between which services can be provided and those that should be. The extent to which media centers can provide services to their users depends on resources of personnel, physical facilities, and collections.

The scope of services offered and the number of users that can be accommodated depend primarily on the size and competence of the staff. The ratio of staff to users recommended by the 1975 AASL/AECT school media standards is one professional and two aides for each 250 students and their teachers. In many schools, however, the number of professionals and supporting staff is less than what is needed to assure a desired range and quality of services.

Similarly, the size of the facility within which the media program is housed and its suitability for the services that take place within or outside it also affect services to users, particularly since new communication media have moved into the media center. A facility that is not large enough to accommodate the number and variety of materials for its many categories of users, or that lacks space for all the people who want to or should use it, and that cannot house the instructional equipment it should have will not meet legitimate expectations for service, no matter how committed its leadership to a philosophy of comprehensive user services.

Finally, the media center's collections and budget must be large enough to support the information requirements of the school's instructional program and the diverse developmental needs of its total student population. The standards have defined a level of probable adequacy: from 16 to 24 books per student and a sufficient number of multisensory materials to bring the total of items to 40 per student.

**Traditional Services.** Despite the many changes school libraries have experienced, some services have changed very little.

*Reading.* School media specialists are advocates of books and reading. In this role they help students acquire an enduring love of books and learning. They tell stories and give book talks. They compile special reading lists, prepare bibliographies, create alluring displays, and promote reading clubs. They make the library a reading-guidance center to which students as individuals, or in groups with their teachers, come to find books for information or recreational reading.

*Reference.* The school media center is the information

Greenwich Public Schools

*Students at Julian Curtiss School, Greenwich, Connecticut, locate their town on a globe.*

center of the school. The media specialist maintains a collection of basic reference sources and offers help in locating information as needed. Where the available resources are inadequate, the media specialist calls upon resources outside the school—the public library, museums, historical societies, interlibrary loan, and whatever other information networks are accessible to the school.

*Teaching.* The school media specialist is a teacher as well as information expert, who knows not only how libraries are administered but also how children learn the process of purposeful inquiry. The media specialist helps students to become confident seekers and organizers of information and increasingly independent library users. Instruction is sequential and classroom-related. For younger students, an information skills lesson may focus on learning how to use the table of contents and index of a book—or threading a filmstrip viewer. For a college-bound high school senior it may be an introduction to the *New York Times Index* as a research tool—or how to use a microfilm reader. In the search for knowledge there is no primacy of print or nonprint; students learn to learn from all kinds of information sources and to use the technology they require.

**Administrative Services.** In a well-managed media center a user should be able to know what materials the media center has and, with reasonable effort, be able to locate them. Efficient procedures for cataloguing, processing, listing, storage, and circulation ensure ease of access and equitable availability of instructional materials for all users. Equipment is scheduled, distributed, and maintained in good operating order. Hours of opening are planned for the convenience of the users. Facilities are designed and furnished for comfort and suitability to the educational purposes intended. The atmosphere is hospitable, the staff friendly.

**Instructional Support Services.** *Curriculum.* Media specialists are instructional materials experts, contributing their professional expertise to the planning, design, and implementation of curricula. They identify, select, and locate educational materials through current bibliographies, publishers and producers catalogues, reviewing media, and other selection aids. They assemble, organize, acquire, and list materials, prepare bibliographies, assist in the design of activities, and make other contributions to the fulfillment of educational objectives. They provide alternative materials for the fast, slow, emotionally disturbed, learning disabled, and those with limited competencies in the English language.

*Supervision.* The media specialist manages the media center as a learning laboratory available to individuals and classes for exploring, investigating, and researching their intellectual interests and for becoming acquainted with the means available in the media center for so doing. It is open for self-directed learning or recreational reading, viewing, and listening throughout the school day and before and after school hours. All levels of student interest, ability, academic achievement, maturity, and motivation are matched within it.

*Planning.* Another instructional support service that the media specialist performs is the planning and implementation of curriculum-related activities that extend and enrich the classroom experiences of students. This might mean bringing into the school, or arranging a telephone conference with, persons of achievement in the arts, sciences, or public life. Book fairs, career awareness days, art exhibits, and other learning experiences come into the classroom by way of the media center, cutting across all levels and disciplines.

*Staff Development.* Another category of services contributes to the professional growth of teachers. Wherever possible, a portion of the media center budget is allocated for purchasing professional journals and books on current issues in education. For teachers working on advanced degrees, the media specialist helps locate research materials, drawing on interlibrary loan and information network resources. In coordination with district or regional centers, the media staff sponsors workshops to introduce to teachers new materials and equipment for improving teaching and learning and makes teachers aware of staff development opportunities both in and outside the school and community.

**New Technologies.** Much of the responsibility for integrating the new communication media into the fabric of instruction falls upon the school media specialist, who identifies, selects, organizes, and makes these resources available to faculty and students. Implicit in this responsibility is the care, maintenance, scheduling, and—as needed—repair of the presentation devices needed for their use. The media center staff provides assistance to teachers whose professional education has not included preparation for using audiovisual equipment and materials.

*Production.* Some of the new technologies are not only sources of information but also media of communication and vehicles for artistic expression. The fully equipped media center provides locations, equipment, and raw materials for creating in the new media formats and a staff with professional expertise for teaching the technology-related communication arts. Photography, film making, the operation of radio and video equipment, slide-sound techniques, and graphics are frequently taught under media center auspices.

*Learning Centers.* The supervision of skill development or "prescriptive" learning centers is yet another service of media centers at both elementary and secondary levels. Many school media centers also house, within or adjacent to their own areas, learning centers where supplementary teaching staff and instructional equipment may provide remedial experiences for the problem learner, principally in reading and mathematics. Using teaching machines and programmed instruction, media center staff work in a team relationship with the classroom teacher, identifying problems, testing, scheduling, monitoring, recording, and reporting progress back to the teacher. Students for whom English is a second language find in the media center a place where special language problems are dealt with in accordance with "prescriptions" supplied by the classroom or special teacher to help students. These same centers offer opportunities for the academically gifted or creative students to undertake projects that lead them into experiences beyond what is offered in the classroom.

**District Services.** The consolidation of school districts into larger units for administering educational services has expanded the range of school-level media services and created a new category of services from district or regional centers. The services most commonly provided on a systemwide basis are evaluation of materials, staff development, equipment maintenance and repair, film, television and computer services, and a professional reference library.

The district media center coordinates the review, evaluation, and purchase of instructional materials. The staff meets with publishers' representatives, arranges for the evaluation of materials by appropriate personnel, and distributes the results of evaluations in order to ensure that the best educational materials available will be purchased.

The district media center provides staff development opportunities for media personnel and teachers on media and media-related topics.

It maintains collections of the more expensive instructional materials, such as 16-mm films and videotapes for use in classrooms and media centers throughout the district. It also provides for the maintenance and repair of costly instructional equipment on a systemwide, cost-effective basis.

An educational reference library for teachers and the educational community is found in district media centers. The library will include current titles, journal literature, bibliographies and indexes, and basic reference materials needed for decision making in the management of school facilities and programs.

The district center provides coordination in the management of systemwide communication resources, specifically instructional television and computer systems. In addition, it supervises school-level media programs, ensuring that equitable fiscal support and services are available throughout the system.

**Services of the Future.** Some people would like to see the school media center of the future become more like the libraries of the past, before they were cluttered with the trappings of our electronic communications age. The probability of this happening is remote; the conditions that created today's school media center out of the post-Sputnik educational reform movement in the U.S. still pertain. Nor is it likely that education will abandon its ideal of educating *all* children, not just the academically able, in those essential skills required for survival in our technology-based and information-dependent world. The effort to reach all children in accordance with their particular needs will continue. It is possible that educational research will give educators more precision than they now have for diagnosing problem learners and dealing with their aberrations. Individualizing and enriching the educational fare for the talented and gifted students will also remain an important concern of educators.

The future will probably see a greater, not lesser, dependence on machines for individualizing instruction, reinforcing learning with sight and sound, remediating learning deficiencies, and programming instruction for the slow and unmotivated student. Machines will be more pervasive in the schools, and teachers will become more skilled in their use. There will be greater use of technology for meeting general information needs. Through their media centers, schools will be linked in educational networks supplying computerized information banks and computer-based, computer-managed curriculum materials of many kinds.

It is likely that there will be a continuing emphasis on teaching children how to learn, to enjoy learning, and to grow up with inquiring minds. In a world in which mastering the body of knowledge in even one field is beyond the capability of any one individual, simply learning facts in school, without learning how to go about learning, is futile.

Tomorrow's schools and school media centers, in recognition of the tremendous power of the mass communication media in our society, will pay more attention than is now given to "visual literacy," the ability of viewers to be perceptive and judgmental about what they see and hear on the screen and to know when they are being manipulated. More children will become active users of the communication technologies, learning to express ideas and to create art forms in visual and sound formats and becoming facile in the techniques employed in the communications technologies.

Media centers and the schools they serve probably will also share greater commonality of purpose. In the past the school library has been faulted for functioning as a separate agency within the school, its goals and objectives not always meshed with those that hold together the fabric of the educational enterprise. The reasons for this criticism are understandable from a historical perspective, but no longer tenable. School librarianship is a discrete branch of library services to children, with its locus in the schools and its allegiance to the educational program and the learner.

**REFERENCES**

American Association of School Librarians and Association for Educational Communications and Technology, *Media Programs: District and School* (ALA, 1975).

R. A. Davis, *The School Library Media Center: A Force for Educational Excellence,* 2nd ed. (1974).

J. T. Gillespie and D. L. Spirt, *Creating a School Media Program* (1973).

E. T. Prostano and J. S. Prostano, *The School Library Media Center* (1971).

ELFRIEDA McCAULEY

LIBRARY COOPERATION

The educational philosophy accepted by educators throughout the history of education in the U.S. has had a direct effect upon the type and scope of cooperation between school libraries and other libraries. In the early years secondary school libraries represented the majority of libraries serving students in the public schools, while the public library provided the services now performed by the elementary school library. In some communities the Board of Education, the governance unit for the school, and the public library jointly organized and controlled the school library materials. Minimal use of the school library was directed toward meeting the needs of the school's curriculum during this time period.

The National Education Association and the American Library Association were forerunners in encouraging the development and functional use of school libraries through jointly sponsored publications and documents. *School and Public Libraries Working Together in Library Service* (1941) asked that local boards of education establish school libraries in every school for the purpose of serving the educational objectives of the school. When the philosophy of education changed its emphasis from subject mastery to individualization for the learner, the curricular offerings for the nation's schools became more diversified, and the educational environment gave the school library its need for existence.

The realization of resource sharing among school library media centers was preceded by an era of rapid school library growth that began in the 1950's and accelerated in the 1960's. This growth was stimulated by the publication of the first national standards for school libraries, *School Libraries for Today and Tomorrow,* published by ALA in 1945. Cooperation among libraries for the purpose of encouraging continuing education and cultural growth was referred to in these standards and again identified in the 1960 *Standards for School Library Programs,* which were endorsed by 20 educational and professional organizations as a force for excellence in library programs.

Today school library media centers represent a vast bank of resources and information, including print, visual, auditory, and tactile materials and equipment that are selected and evaluated according to school policies that guarantee a balanced collection of instructional materials meeting curriculum goals. In 1974 the National Center for Education Statistics reported in its *Statistics of Public School Libraries Media Centers* that 507,000,000 library books and 68,000,000 titles of audiovisual materials were available to students with central library media centers. However, it is generally understood and accepted that no one school building or district can provide students with the necessary range of instructional materials and equipment to meet the goal of the National Commission on Libraries and Information Science. The goal of the Commission calls for every person in the United States to have equal opportunity of access to the total information resource that will satisfy the individual's educational, working, cultural, and leisure-time needs and interests. This goal can be achieved only when schools are involved as full participating members in a library network.

*Media Programs: District and School,* the 1975 standards of the American Association of School Librarians and the Association for Educational Communications and Technology, modified the singular, self-sufficient role of the school library media center. This was the first time that networks were mentioned in published, comprehensive standards for school media programs, referring to networks as avenues of access to information or knowledge not readily available to regional, district, and school programs. Such information is to be transmitted to the schools by such advanced communication techniques as telecommunications, computer systems, and high-speed, random-access retrieval systems.

It is apparent that the school library media center has been required to broaden its vision and responsibilities to include increased interaction and cooperation among personnel, processes, and information sources. In the decade of the 1970's, many school library media specialists became convinced that the sharing of resources would result in improved services and communication with other librarians to develop effective library cooperatives.

Cooperation in the school media area has been stimulated in large part by the desire of school media professionals to help users of library media programs make more effective use of library resources and services and by the realization that it is impossible to satisfy all user needs through one library program. Resulting cooperative efforts progressed through a series of stages in the 1970's toward an increased emphasis on promoting more sophisticated cooperative programs among different types of libraries.

**Single-Type Networks.** The single-type network is not new in school librarianship. The most common form of cooperation that occurs in school library media centers is the single-type library cooperative, in which a group of centers work together, generally on an informal basis, to achieve a mutual goal, such as continuing education or joint book evaluation. *Media Programs: District and School* identifies regional media programs that are cooperatively developed as another level of the single-type library cooperative. The chief reasons that this type of cooperative has been the preferred mode of operation among media professionals are that the school libraries involved share the same organizational pattern, funding base, governance, and service patterns and that the majority of participating media professionals are faced with similar problems with which they can closely identify.

Individual states have organized regional educational service centers that provide sophisticated collections of media program materials for local districts. Regional centers feature large film libraries, evaluation and selection centers, facilities for local production of audiovisual materials, and in-service training for personnel. Examples of intermediate units that contract with local boards of education are found in New York, Michigan, Iowa, Texas, and Oregon.

**Multitype Cooperation.** Multitype library cooperation became somewhat more accepted in the 1970's among school media personnel, although it did not gain nearly the degree of acceptance of the single-type library cooperative. Through this means, school library media centers share resources, personnel, facilities, and/or programs with a library or libraries of another type having a different legal base. According to G. Flint Purdy, in multitype library cooperatives the activities fall into two categories: (1) methods of sharing resources more generously, more systematically, and more expeditiously than they would otherwise be shared, and (2) strengthening the resources to be shared. Some specific examples of these types of activities engaged in by school and other types of libraries are union catalogues and lists, reciprocal borrowing and interlibrary loan, centralized processing, and cooperatively sponsored planning and surveys.

The legal basis for multitype library cooperation differs from state to state. The *ASLA Report on Interlibrary Cooperation 1978* identifies specific authorization in some states that allows all types of libraries to merge and provide more effective library service. In other states the authorization extends only to designating a state agency that will coordinate and promote cooperative activities. Another basis for authorization used in some states is a blanket law allowing two or more public agencies to enter into agreements with any other agency for joint or cooperative action. Even where specific authorization does not exist, few states have reported legal barriers to statewide participation in multitype library cooperatives.

Many people in the library profession have questioned the extent to which school libraries can be involved effectively in cooperative efforts. Anne Marie Falsone has identified five reasons why these programs fail to participate more fully in multitype library cooperation. They are that (1) schools are open only during the school day; (2) collections are chosen to support the curriculum; (3) interjurisdictional loan of school library materials or equipment is sometimes prohibited by school district policy; (4) in some cases there is a lack of basic communications tools such as a telephone; and (5) students and teachers have an "immediacy of need" for materials that inhibits interlibrary loan of materials. Other barriers to multitype library cooperation are inadequate funds and resources to be shared, lack of incentives, lack of time and staff, and negative attitudes of staff members and administrators toward cooperation. Esther Dyer points out the difficulty of overcoming some of these barriers in her study of library services to children. Her queries of selected school media supervisors, public library directors, superintendents, and other pertinent groups of professionals revealed that "the highest priorities for both (the school and public libraries) are self-preservation and protection of territory, and cooperation is an implicit threat to autonomy. . . . As regards network participation and other modes of cooperation which respect institutional territory of both (public and school libraries), the prospects are more favorable."

Those who advocate including school media programs in multitype library cooperatives enumerate a number of special contributions these programs can offer. Among them are strong audiovisual collections, broad collections of children and young adult materials, expertise in the selection, use, and evaluation of audiovisual materials and equipment, in-depth knowledge of local production of materials, and much experience and education in developing and implementing effective techniques of carrying out the library's instructional function. In order for these resources to be incorporated effectively into multitype library cooperatives, however, proponents of cooperative ventures point out that the barriers identified above must be eliminated through adequate planning, sufficient money, staff, time, reciprocal agreements, and attitudinal changes.

A form of multitype library cooperation that has recently received renewed attention is the combining of school and public library services in the same facility. The current interest in this concept is the result of such factors as broader acceptance of the community school concept, decreasing fiscal resources, increased public pressure for most cost-effective library operations, and a growing desire on the part of the public toward access to information regardless of format. *A Study of the Combined School Public Library,* conducted for the State Library of Florida by Shirley L. Aaron and Sue O. Smith, concluded that it is unlikely that a community able to support or now supporting separate types of libraries will offer better school and public library service through a combined program because the combination of factors required to promote a successful combined program seldom occurs. Further, when a community is unable to provide minimum library services through separate facilities, and no option for improved services through system membership exists, the combined program presents a possible alternative to limited or nonexistent services under certain conditions. However, communities searching for a cheaper way to provide better library service should be aware that the study revealed no documented evidence that economy results from this organizational pattern.

A study prepared by the Interdepartmental Liaison Group on Library Development, Alberta Education Culture (Edmonton), came to a similar conclusion. The 1979 *Statement on Community School Libraries* acknowledges that consolidated operations are unsuccessful in serving the public at large. There are 74 combined libraries in Alberta.

**Multitype Networks.** The informal agreements that characterize many multitype library cooperatives are becoming increasingly inadequate to cope with the complexities of present and projected efforts in this area. Consequently, the trend has been toward the development of multitype library networks. Multitype networks tend to incorporate public, academic, school, institutional, and special libraries into a state network, granting full shares in governance, responsibility, and participation to all types of libraries involved. Flexibility is essential in a multitype network where the requirements of the members will vary from one type of library to the other. School districts in Colorado, Washington, California, and Illinois have become a part of multitype networks, although in general, there is a paucity of networking plans that grant equal representation to the school library media center.

The Washington Library Network reports one-fourth of its 200 members are school districts at the local and regional level. These school districts have signed a written agreement that requires a willingness to participate in interlibrary loan and reference/referral services. Some districts circulate books to the public library for summer reading programs. One school district has established a delivery system between the school and the local public library. Two regional educational service centers are sharing their facilities with regional public libraries. In these facilities, coordination occurs in the sharing of pho-

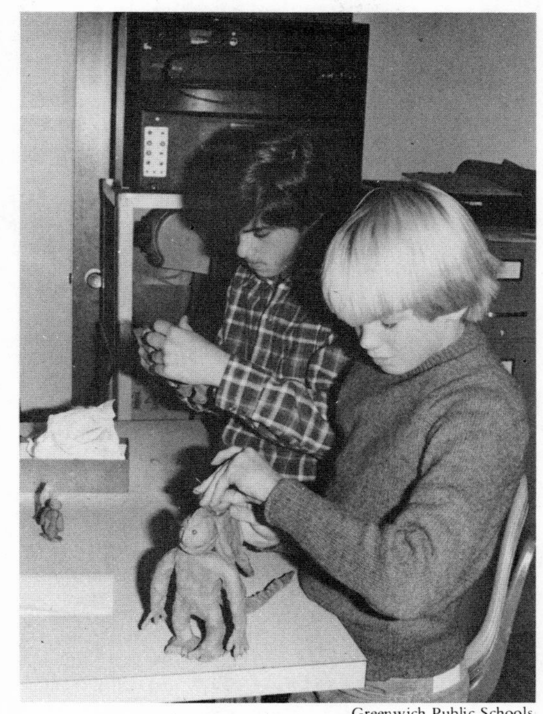

Greenwich Public Schools

*Making clay characters for animation movie (left), and constructing the set and preparing to film, at Western Junior High School, Greenwich, Connecticut (p. 510).*

tographic and graphic reproduction services. According to Audrey Kolb, the laws and regulations that have been established for the Washington Library Network have changed the roles of the Washington State Library and the State Library Commission. Interdependency has been reinforced, and increased attention given to cooperation and coordination among all types of libraries.

In 1975 the state of Colorado adopted legislation creating multitype regional library systems. School representatives had a voice in the planning stages and in the development of the rules and regulations governing the network. The boards governing Colorado's regional library systems have at least one representative from each type of library.

A national effort to clarify, delineate, and describe the role of the school library media program in networking was developed through a task force established by the National Commission on Libraries and Information Science in cooperation with the American Association of School Librarians. The 1978 *Report of the Task Force on the Role of the School Library Media Program in Networking* has identified immediate, intermediate, and long-range recommendations for the purpose of alleviating the psychological, political, funding, communication, and planning problems that have inhibited the full participation of schools in interlibrary networks.

The issue of cooperation among school libraries on the international scene was addressed at the seventh annual conference of the International Association of School Librarianship in Melbourne, Australia, in 1978. Over 150 librarians from ten countries reviewed alternative structures for support services for school libraries at local, regional, and national levels. Australian, Canadian, and Danish concepts were introduced to form a framework for the discussion. The fourth Congress of Southeast Asian Librarians met in Bangkok, Thailand, in June 1978 for the purpose of establishing national committees that would work toward the development of regional cooperation in information services. Children's materials and services were identified in projected surveys of user needs.

School library media professionals are becoming aware of the benefits that can be derived from involvement in a multitype network. Schools can make a substantial contribution to the services provided through the reciprocal arrangements that are part of the network concept, but it will require the changing of organizational relationships. Bernard Franckowiak, a member of the NCLIS Task Force, challenged school library media specialists to become knowledgeable about networks and data bases and to assume the responsibility for developing guidelines that will guarantee the participation of school media programs in networks.

**REFERENCES**

Esther R. Dyer, *Cooperation in Library Service to Children* (1978).

Anne Marie Falsone, "Participation of School Libraries," in Beth A. Hamilton and William B. Ernst, Jr., editors, *Multitype Library Cooperation* (1977).

Bernard Franckowiak, "Networks, Data Bases, and Media Programs: An Overview," *School Media Quarterly* (1977).

Audrey Kolb, "Development and Potential of a Multitype Library Network," *School Media Quarterly* (1977).

G. Flint Purdy, "Interrelations among Public, School, and Academic Libraries," *Library Quarterly* (1969).

SHIRLEY L. AARON;
ALICE E. FITE

FEDERAL AND STATE ADMINISTRATION GOVERNANCE AND FINANCE

The Tenth Amendment of the United States Constitution, passed in 1791, states that "The powers not delegated to the United States by the constitution, nor prohibited by it to the states, are reserved to the states respectively, or to the people." Since education is not specifically mentioned, such powers are thus the responsibility of state government. State legislatures elected by the people control the establishment and maintenance of the schools within the state through a State Board of Education and a State Department of Education. Most U.S. states employ professional school library/media staff to develop programs in the schools.

**Federal Leadership.** Although state governments have responsibility for education, the courts have ruled that under the "general welfare" clause of the Constitution, Congress may enact laws that affect public education. The United States Office of Education (USOE) was made responsible for administering federal efforts in relation to public and private schools.

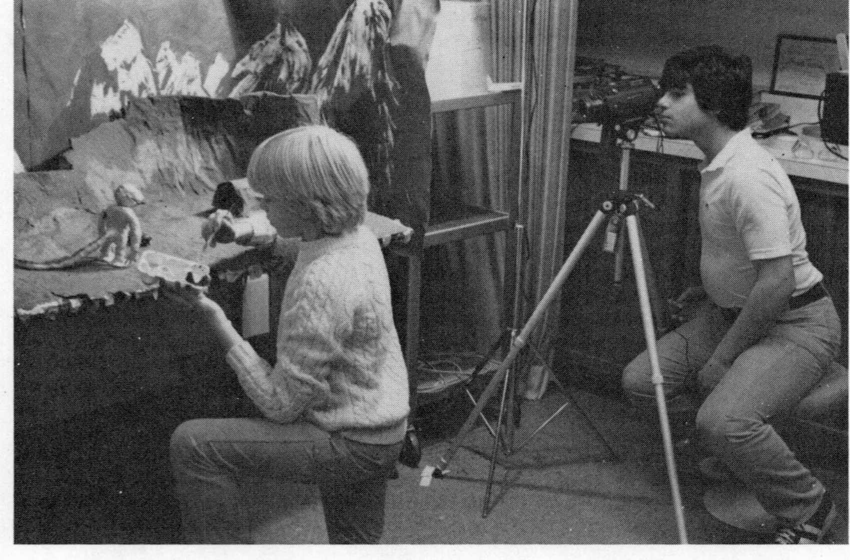

In January 1938 the first specialist in school and children's libraries in the Office of Education was employed to serve as consultant to USOE staff members, school superintendents, school board members, trustees of public libraries, library administrators, state departments of education, state library agencies, state and federal government officials, and professional organizations concerned with library services for children and young people. This person was responsible for serving both libraries in public and private schools and libraries and children's and young people's departments in public libraries. The charge of the first specialist in school and children's libraries was to promote and assist in the extension and improvement of library service for children and young people and was to include the following activities:

> To apply the results of original studies and investigations through the solution of current problems in the field of school and children's libraries; to apply and lead conferences and institutes on library problems including in-service training of school and children's library personnel; to establish and maintain cooperative working relationships within professional organizations in the field of library service for children and young people and the staff of the Office of Education and the governmental agencies and any other organizations interested in and affected by services of libraries for children and young people; to stimulate cooperative experimental study and demonstrations in the field of children's reading and the improved techniques, management, and news services in school and children's libraries; to inspect for the purpose of research and information the operations and services of individual libraries, and to evaluate their programs; to conduct or participate in conducting surveys of school and children's libraries; to address meetings and conventions of professional and lay organizations on the problems, the development, and the services of school and children's libraries.

The first person to hold the position of specialist in school libraries in the U.S. Office of Education was Nora E. Beust, who served until 1958, when she was succeeded by Mary Helen Mahar, who was then titled Coordinator of School Libraries. That office has been responsible for the compilation of school library statistics, booklists, bibliographies, and articles on elementary libraries and national trends in school and public libraries service for children and young adults. It has important national leadership responsibilities for developing and communicating and understanding the need for and the role of programs of library services for children and young adults.

In 1958 the U.S. Congress, spurred by Soviet advances in science and technology, passed the National Defense Education Act (NDEA). The Act was designed to provide federal resources to strengthen and improve various areas of the elementary and secondary education program. Title III of the National Defense Education Act was specifically designed to strengthen instruction in science, mathematics, and modern foreign languages and provided for the purchase of materials, equipment, and minor remodeling of facilities to accomplish this goal. Many schools and school libraries purchased materials and equipment related to the critical subject areas within this federal program. Gradually, those three areas were expanded to more than ten during the life of the NDEA program. Federal interest in aiding elementary and secondary education reached a high point in 1965 with the passage of the Elementary and Secondary Education Act (ESEA). Title II of the Act provided grants to states on a formula basis to aid local education agencies in acquiring school library resources, textbooks, and other instructional materials. Between 1966 and 1976 this program provided over $895,000,000 to public and private schools in the United States.

In addition to federal funds, a number of states such as North Carolina, Michigan, and Wisconsin also provide segregated funding from the state level for the purchase of school library/media materials. Most state-aid formulas for schools include salaries for library/media personnel and funds to purchase resources as part of the instructional costs that are matched by these formulas.

**State Supervision.** State school library supervision in North America traces its beginnings to the 1890's, when the New York State Education Department established a position for an inspector to "help schools improve their book collections and encourage people's reading." In 1891 the Wisconsin legislature authorized the state superintendent to appoint one clerk to aid in "promoting the establishment and maintenance and control of libraries as provided by the law." In 1904 the Division of School Libraries was established by the Regents of New York State, and a School Library Supervisor position was created. In 1911 Minnesota set up an Office of Supervisor of School Libraries in the Department of Public Instruction, and in 1915 Wisconsin changed the title of the Library Clerk to Supervisor of School Libraries. By 1952 there were 25 states and one Canadian province in which there were one or more persons specifically assigned responsibility for state supervision of school libraries; most of these positions were established after 1940. State school library supervision in the U.S. developed in the early 1960's as a result of a new set of national standards, an intensive implementation process, and several key publications concerning the need for and the role of professional personnel at the state level.

In the early 1960's Mahar indicated that the responsibilities of the State Departments of Education toward school libraries fell into six broad categories:

1. Certification of school librarians
2. Standards for school libraries
3. Supervision of school libraries
4. Cooperation for school libraries
5. Statistics and research on school libraries
6. Information on school libraries

In USOE the Elementary and Secondary Education Act Title II program was administered by the staff responsible for school library programs under a state plan submitted by each state. The state department of education administration of the ESEA Title II program often was developed and conducted by people who were school library/media supervisors. These new federal funds coming into the state resulted in the creation of a number of new positions of school library supervisor-consultants within state departments across the country. This was caused by the need for staff to administer the new federal program, coupled with a provision in the program for a certain amount of funding to support administration of the program. In 1969 Milbrey Jones indicated that there were about 120 state library school consultants in 48 states and the District of Columbia. The fluctuation in ESEA Title II appropriations during the 1969–70 year resulted in some change in the number of state school library consultants and supervisors.

Examination of a list of state school library/media supervisors dated March 1979 provided by Milbrey Jones shows 165 people as supervisors, consultants, and program administrators for the ESEA program and state programs related to the school library/media area in the 50 states, the Trust Territories of the Pacific, Guam, Puerto Rico, Virgin Islands, and the Bureau of Indian Affairs. A number of these people have other responsibilities besides those related to school library/media programs.

Irmo Middle School Complex, Irmo, South Carolina

*Library media centers provide equipment and guidance which enables middle-school students to produce a video news spot.*

In 1975 David R. Bender examined the state education agencies' roles and functions related to school library/media programs and identified 11 functions that illustrate one state's responsibility for program development. These areas are:

1. To formulate long-range plans for the development of school media programs, including cooperative planning for regional and state services
2. To provide advisory and consultative service to local school systems, particularly in areas of new media services and technology in school media facilities
3. To develop standards and guidelines for the improvement of media programs
4. To provide programs of in-service education on the concepts of the utilization of media to administrators, supervisors, media personnel, and teachers
5. To develop proposals for needed research in media services
6. To collect, analyze, and disseminate information on the scope and quality of media programs in the state
7. To assist in the determination of the qualifications for certification for media personnel
8. To administer federal funds available for media programs
9. To provide for the effective coordination of media services with the critical educational concerns of the state and local school systems
10. To develop coordinated plans and policies with other personnel agencies that will strengthen library/media services for all citizens
11. To act as a clearinghouse for information on library services in the state and foster interlibrary loans and cooperative arrangements with the school, public, academic, or other libraries

The 1974 National Center for Education Statistics (NCES) survey, *Library General Information Survey* (LIBGIS), showed that a tremendous amount of development had taken place in school library/media centers in the period 1964–74. The survey estimated that 74,725 public schools serving 43,900,000 pupils had central library/media centers in 1974, based on the responses of about 3,500 schools. Total number of public schools was 89,000, with an aggregate fall 1974 enrollment of 45,053,000. The survey showed that 84 percent of all schools in the nation serving 39,000,000 of 40,000,000 school children had centralized school libraries available to them; the other 14,000 schools serving more than 1,000,000 children did not have library/media centers. Library/media centers in 1974 were provided for 50 percent more school children—14,600,000 more—than was the case in 1964. The number of school library/media centers

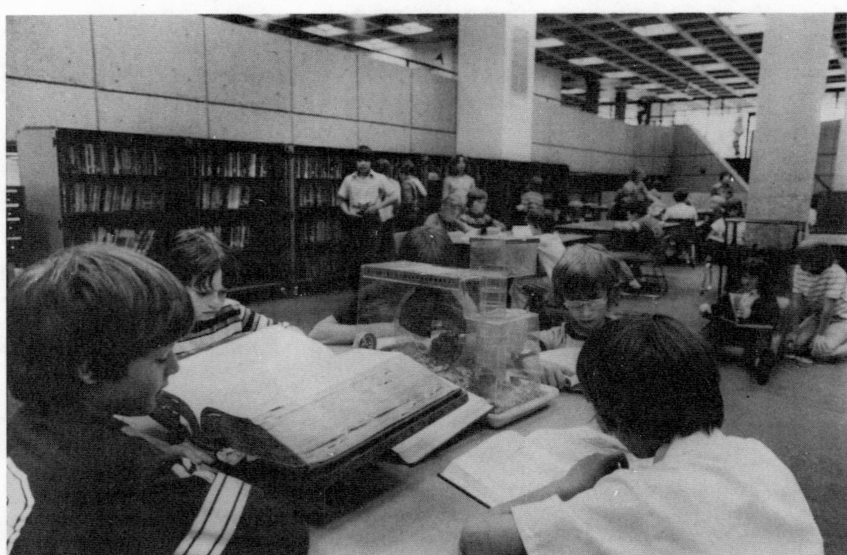

Highwood Hills Elementary School, St. Paul School District

*Hamsters and gerbils keep elementary school students company in the library.*

increased over the decade from 56,000 in schools of 150 pupils or more to an estimated total of 74,725. To a considerable extent this tremendous expansion in the availability of school library/media centers to children and young people in the public schools must be credited to the dedicated leadership provided by the U.S. Office of Education personnel and to state school library/media supervisors, along with federal funds provided mainly by the ESEA Title II program. Much work remains to be done, particularly in providing library/media centers and services to the elementary school children in U.S. areas where the greatest staff shortages still remain. Recent pressure on local property taxes has led a number of states to increase the amount of state level funding for public education programs. The result of this may be an increased state support for providing school library/media programs at the local level.

**REFERENCES**

Mary Helen Mahar, *State Department of Education Responsibilities for School Libraries* (1960).

Council of Chief State School Officers, *Responsibilities of State Departments of Education for School Library Services: A Policy Statement* (1961).

———, *Developing the Use of New Educational Media* (1964).

Milbrey Jones, "ESEA Title II, Contributions to State Department of Education Leadership of School Media Programs," in Norman D. Stevens, editor, *Essays for Ralph Shaw* (1975).

David R. Bender, "State Educational Agencies: Roles and Functions," *School Library Journal* (1975).

BERNARD FRANCKOWIAK

MEASUREMENT AND EVALUATION

"Any philosophy that can be put in a nutshell belongs there!" This "law" underscores the fact that there is no simple way to parse the topic of measurement and evaluation. Despite these difficulties, two fairly recent general surveys do exist—Evelyn Daniel's state-of-the-art review in the 1976 volume of *Advances in Librarianship* on performance measures for school librarians and the summer 1975 issue of *School Media Quarterly*, entitled "Evaluation for Accountability."

This account builds on these two earlier efforts with an overview, an update, and suggestions for further study. To do this, a definition of terms and a discussion of salient issues will first be presented, followed by a description of the ongoing process of standards development and acceptance, with addenda on the status of the national statistics collection effort. Next comes major research and development efforts, followed by a few paragraphs on some useful measurement techniques. The final part deals with the uses of measurement and evaluation.

**Terms and Issues.** Although there is some dissent on the shades of meaning in the terms *measurement* and *evaluation,* generally speaking, *evaluation* refers to the larger process of making a considered judgment as to the worth of an object, a person, or an event. It usually involves collecting evidence (formally or informally), analyzing it, and weighing it against one or more criteria (implicit or explicit) in order to make a value judgment. *Measurement,* more narrowly, is quantitative in approach, usually referring to the specific act of determining the number or extent of certain phenomena on the basis of which an evaluation, or appraisal of worth, can be made.

It is often pointed out that one can measure quantities precisely, but one can only *infer* quality for judgment of value; measurement is considered a science, evaluation an art. In the generally accepted "ideal" model of evaluation, some general goals and specific objectives are developed (or received as givens); some criteria are established as the basis for making judgments; indicators that are observable and can be measured are selected to serve as evidence that the criteria are being met; data are collected on the indicators in ways that are reliable and unbiased; the collected data are compared to some standard of acceptability or excellence; and judgment is passed.

In the statement above, *goals* are broad statements of philosophy or direction usually quite general in scope. *Objectives* describe the expectations and intended accomplishments of an organization or an individual within some specified time frame. *Criteria* can be either *normative,* that is, related to the average performance of some similar phenomena, or *absolute,* as, for example, embodied within a particular published standard.

Evaluation is often referred to as being either formative or summative in nature. *Formative* evaluation is ongoing; it occurs during the activity and is intended to guide decision making and to "form" or shape the future of the event or agency being evaluated. *Summative* evaluation is administered at a single point in time, usually at the end of a program or at the end of a cycle. The intent here is to "sum up," to grade, to make an overall judgment as to the worth of the phenomena. It relates to the process of accountability. *Confirmative* evaluation, another term less often seen, relates to a regularly recurring review process toward the end of "confirming" that the project or program should or should not continue.

Thus, evaluation involves one or more comparisons. A major political issue becomes who sets the criteria, or the standards of comparison. In one approach the professional association develops goals and objectives, criteria and indicators, and publishes standards. The individual professional operating as manager within a media center then uses the published standard to establish the criteria against which the performance of the center and that of the media specialist are to be measured. In a bureaucratic situation (as in a school), there may be standardized rules and procedures that govern behavior. In a more political milieu, groups may compete against each other to determine directions and criteria for performance. Where a strong central authority exists, standards for evaluation may be imposed.

A second major issue revolves around a difference of opinion as to whether evaluation should be based on quantitative measures, or whether it should be largely subjective and intuitive. Proponents of the latter view suggest that inferring quality from quantity may be dangerously misleading. While it is true, as Ernest DeProspo has observed, that "any measurement process that generates numbers must over-compensate for a built-in anticipation that larger numbers suggest directly or indirectly more effective and efficient service even if that is not the intended meaning," the current trend seems to be toward a more quantitative approach.

A third issue arises from the differing concerns of the researcher and the practitioner. Fritz Machlup, expressing the frustration he felt when attempting to collect quantitative data on how much libraries spend each year to acquire materials in different fields, says, "Alas, the librarians did not have the answers and the most I have learned from them is why the answers are not available and how enormously difficult, if not impossible, it would be to obtain them." The methodology that surrounds unbiased data collection and statistical analysis of results is highly sophisticated. The expenditure of time, money, staff, and energy on collecting clean assessment data will be considered by the practitioner from a managerial perspective, somewhat different from that of the researcher.

**Standards and Statistics Collection.** The typical standard or guideline used in the library profession is prescriptive in nature; it describes what ought to be. Publications like AASL/AECT *Media Programs: District and School,* the current standard for school media programs, are generated by committees made up primarily of professional librarians who attempt through this device to establish acceptable criteria for the elements of a good library program. Some qualities considered necessary for a library standard to be used as criteria for evaluation purposes are that each standard be measurable, clearly defined, appropriate, authoritative, and realistic. Some effort is now being expended to compile statistical norms for areas being measured.

Critics of library standards point out a number of shortcomings. Standards are more concerned with measuring inputs to the library rather than outputs, or benefits, to the user. The quantitative criteria, although measurable, are often set by arbitrary judgments. They tend to discourage progress, as the minimum set by the standard often becomes the maximum. On the positive side, standards can be useful to the practicing school library media specialist in the goal-setting, objective-stating process and also as a widely accepted authoritative source for persuading resource allocators to provide adequate support.

Of all the standards generated by the various types of libraries, the national school library standards are perhaps the most nearly complete and the most satisfactory when compared to the qualities of a good standard as set forth above. Still, it may be helpful for the school media specialist to examine and compare national standards from other types of libraries. In addition, virtually every state in the U.S. has its own standard for school media services, and many state and regional associations also publish standards for service. State and regional standards are usually lower (i.e., more "realistic") than the national standards.

School-accrediting agencies also employ published evaluative criteria for each area of the school program. The Committee on Evaluation of School Media Programs of the American Association of School Librarians, a division of the American Library Association, works to maintain contact with the five regional accrediting agencies to monitor the development of new standard criteria and to influence the process of criteria selection for the evaluation of school media programs.

A more quantitative effort to measure the national "health" of libraries is that undertaken by the U.S. government through the National Center for Education Statistics (NCES). Although school libraries are scheduled for collection and reporting of data every three years, there have, in fact, been only two publications of statistics for public school library media centers—one reporting data from 1962–63 published in 1964 and the other reporting data of 1974 published in 1977. A good summary of the latter is in the 1978 *Bowker Annual.* NCES has also commissioned two studies of interest to school media specialists, a handbook of standard terminology for reporting information about educational technology and another handbook with a similar title that attempts to unify the data collection techniques and categories for all libraries. The American National Standards Institute has recently reactivated a subcommittee to work with all interested parties to revise the existing standard for library statistics published in 1968.

These efforts may seem remote from the work of the individual school media practitioner, but because they are attempts to establish criteria and standards that will have an impact on resources received, it is important to be aware of these activities. The American Library Association, through the Statistics Section of the Library Administration and Management Association, has eight statistics committees, one of which is the Statistics for School Library Media Centers Committee, who discuss, critique, and offer suggestions for activities in this area.

**Major Research Efforts.** Educational evaluation is rapidly becoming a separate specialty within education. DeProspo and James W. Liesener provide a good overview of some of the major evaluation models in a 1975 report.

The public, academic, and school sectors of librarianship have each had a major research effort in the measurement and evaluation area. The Management Review and Analysis Program (MRAP), designed and operated by the Office of Management Studies of the Association of Research Libraries, is a set of guidelines for an academic library to use in conducting an internal assessment of its management practices. It was originally instituted for large research libraries but is now developing self-improvement techniques for use by small and medium-sized academic libraries. Many of the techniques used in this program are drawn from organizational development (OD) theories.

Ellen Altman, DeProspo, and others mounted the major public library research effort that focused on the development of performance measures that would be easy for practitioners to collect and that would employ good sampling techniques, thus keeping costs of data collection low. Many of the performance measures they have developed have application for the school library media program.

The major school library research effort shares with MRAP a consensus building approach. Liesener, the major researcher in this area, views evaluation as only one aspect of the larger problem of program planning and the development of overall goals and objectives. Some research has elaborated service statements useful for evaluating media center services, while other work has been directed to the problem of competency assessment, specifically within the context of media educational preparation programs.

**Measurement Techniques.** A number of published surveys exist that collectively provide a good overview of the array of measurement techniques. These techniques include catalogue use and other use studies, library surveys, and specific evaluation measures for reference, search and retrieval, collections, technical services, and document delivery. Quantitative measures may include measures for document exposure time, indexes of availability or capability, failure analyses, circulation predictors, a number of techniques for collection evaluation, and an attitudinal expectation rate measure in which users estimate their chances of successfully retrieving a given item.

A number of evaluation tools have been published to

assist in evaluating school library media centers; several of these tools have already been mentioned here. One more major document, *Evaluating Media Programs,* a publication of the Association for Educational Communications and Technology, uses the national standard, *Media Programs: District and School,* as its main source of criteria. Through a modular format, the instrument provides a series of checklists and scales for use in a formative evaluation procedure. Courses, workshops, and conferences on measurement and evaluation are now being offered on a fairly regular basis.

**Uses of Evaluation.** Evaluation can be used for improvement, for justification or attack, to delay action, or to exert control. Responses to evaluation information can be a change of behavior or opinion, a distortion, rejection, or ignoring of the data. Factors that affect the reception of evaluation information include the adequacy and appropriateness of the methodology used, the need for a value judgment, the timing of the delivery of results, the degree to which the information fits preconceived ideas or supports vested interests, the potential threat involved in acceptance of results, and the acceptability of the motive for undertaking the evaluation.

Before any measurement and evaluation process is undertaken, it is important to recognize that some prior decisions must be made: the purpose of the evaluation, the person or group for whom the evaluation is intended, the question(s) to be answered, the criteria and indicators to be used, what data are to be collected and how they are to be analyzed, and what form the final report will take.

Because of the variety of uses and users of evaluation information, it may be helpful for an evaluation team to be set up comprised of the major users of evaluation information about the media center. This team might be composed of administrators, peer teachers, media specialist and staff, and students. An examination of consensus and dissensus among these four components can be a useful by-product of this approach.

**REFERENCES**

Evelyn H. Daniel, "Performance Measures for School Librarians; Complexities and Potential," *Advances in Librarianship* (1976).

*Handbook of Standards Terminology and Guide to Recording Information about Libraries* (National Center for Higher Education Management Systems, 1979).

Ernest R. DeProspo, "Potential Limits and Abuses of Evaluation," *School Media Quarterly* (1975).

Ernest R. DeProspo, Ellen Altman, and Kenneth E. Beasley, *Performance Measures for Public Libraries* (ALA, 1973).

Ernest R. DeProspo and James W. Liesener, "Media Program Evaluation: A Working Framework," *School Media Quarterly* (1975).

Fritz Machlup, "Our Libraries: Can We Measure Their Holdings and Acquisitions?" *American Association of University Professors Bulletin* (1976).

EVELYN H. DANIEL

LAWS AND LEGISLATION

**History.** The earliest recorded legislation for school libraries in the U.S. was on the state level. In 1827 Governor DeWitt Clinton of New York began to urge that collections of books be placed in school districts. In 1835 he was able to get a law passed permitting the voters of any school district to levy a tax of $20 to start a library and $10 annually to maintain it. This did not prove successful for a number of reasons. Permissive legislation did not appeal to the rural taxpayer. There were no library quarters provided; books were kept in the homes of individuals, and many were lost. There were no trained librarians, nor were the individuals who held the collections accountable to any authority for the administration of the books. The books were purchased, for the most part, from peddlers and were unsuitable for their potential users. The school curriculum of that time was rigid and did not call for the general use of books. The library collections were more for the people of the community and only secondarily for the school children.

In the same year, 1835, Massachusetts followed the example of New York and passed a permissive school district law. Achieved through the efforts of Horace Mann, who had returned from Europe where he had gone to study the education of the young, this law set up $30 a year (thereafter) for books.

Other states soon began to follow suit. In 1837 Michigan and then Rhode Island passed laws allowing each school district to raise $10 for school libraries. In Rhode Island they were to receive the fines levied in cases of breach of peace laws. The Virginia constitution recommended in 1870 that school libraries be developed and by 1876, 19 states had some legislation providing for school district libraries. In 1894 North Carolina passed the first law permitting state funds for the establishment and maintenance of libraries in rural schools. Georgia enacted similar legislation that same year.

In 1892 New York made distinct advances in school library legislation. The state, profiting from past mistakes, again set up district school libraries but this time required that all books be housed in the school building. A school librarian had to be appointed who would be responsible for the books. Each school district was required to raise an equal amount of money as that provided by the state, and all books purchased had to be approved by the State Superintendent of Public Instruction. The 1890's also proved to be a period of marked effort on the part of public libraries to extend library services to schools.

In 1901 North Carolina appropriated $2,500 to aid in book purchase on a matching basis, $10 for $10. The matching idea caught on, and by 1909 Georgia, Texas, South Carolina, Virginia, Kentucky, Tennessee, Louisiana, and Alabama had begun the state matching for funds for books for schools. Alabama, for example, funded $6,700, or $100 per county. For every $1 of state money, $2 had to be raised locally.

It is not possible to detail the many pieces of legislation that exist today in the states and territories regarding school library services, finance, and staff certification. The remainder of this discussion concentrates on comparatively recent U.S. federal legislation that has had significant impact on school libraries in the country.

**National Defense Education Act of 1958.** The greatest leap in the growth of school library collections was to come when the federal government, shocked by the successful launching of Sputnik, passed the National Defense Education Act (NDEA), Public Law 85-864, in August 1958. The purpose of this federal legislation was stated in part, in Title I:

> The Congress hereby finds and declares that the security of the Nation requires the fullest development of the mental resources and technical skills of its young men and women. The present emergency demands that additional and more adequate educational opportunities be made available. The defense of this Nation depends upon the mastery of modern techniques developed from complex scientific principles. It depends as well upon the discovery and development of new principles, new techniques, and new knowledge.
>
> We must increase our efforts to identify and educate more of the talent of our Nation. This requires programs that will give assurance that no student of ability will be denied an opportunity for higher education because of financial need; will correct as rapidly as possible the existing imbalances in our educational programs which have led to an insufficient proportion of our

population educated in science, mathematics, and modern foreign languages and trained in technology.

Title II provided funds to institutions of higher education to lend to prospective school librarians, teachers of science, etc. These loans provided $1,000 per year and a total of $5,000 for all years of study. Provision was made to encourage teachers to be retrained. If a school librarian who received a loan served in a public elementary or secondary school in a state, 10 percent of the amount of the loan, plus interest thereon, was canceled for each year, up to five years' service.

Title III, Financial Assistance for Strengthening Science, Mathematics and Modern Foreign Language of the NDEA, became known as "the matching fund." It provided for the acquisition of audiovisual materials and equipment and printed materials (other than textbooks) suitable for use in providing education in science, mathematics, or modern foreign languages in public elementary or secondary schools, or both, and minor remodeling of laboratory or other space used for such materials or equipment. Funds under Title III as grants to individual public elementary and secondary schools or school systems were based on projects submitted by the local school systems to the State Department of Education. Funds under Title III for nonpublic schools were available as loans.

Title IV provided for the National Defense Fellowships. School librarians benefited especially through fellowships to individuals for study in graduate programs approved by the Commissioner of Education. The programs had to be new or expanded programs "for the graduate training of college or university level teachers." These fellowships provided a stipend of $2,000 for the first, $2,200 for the second, and $2,400 for the third year of study.

Under Title V provision was made for establishing, maintaining, and improving guidance, counseling, and testing in secondary schools. Under this title libraries were able to procúre printed and audiovisual materials necessary to teachers and students in such programs.

Title VII addressed research and experimentation in more effective utilization of television, radio, motion picture, and related media for educational purposes. It enabled library schools to design studies to train school librarians in the utilization of newer media. Projects for research and experimentation in more effective use of TV, radio, motion pictures, and related media in elementáry and secondary education were funded through Title VII.

Title VIII was an extension of the Smith-Hughes Vocational Education Act and the Vocational Education Act of 1946. The purchase of teaching aids, under this title, could include reference books, visual aids, instructional supplies, and instructional materials, which could be a part of the library collection.

Improvement of statistical services of state education agencies was the direction of Title X. State school library supervisors were able to use this title to strengthen supervision in education. Programs for the improvement of statistical services of state educational agencies were required to submit state plans to the Commissioner of Education. Each state was required to submit an overall basic plan to the U.S. Commissioner of Education including: priorities for projects, standards for equipment and materials, and expenditures solely for equipment, materials, and minor remodeling. By the end of June 1959, 48 states and territories had developed effective plans.

**The Library Services and Construction Act.** The Library Services Act of 1956, amended in 1964 and renamed the Library Services and Construction Act (LSCA), primarily supported public library development in the states. The intent of Title III was to establish and maintain local, regional, state, or interstate cooperative networks of libraries for the systematic and effective coordination of the resources of school, public, academic, and special libraries and special information centers. This was an early effort to bring school libraries into the developing network concept.

**Elementary and Secondary Education Act of 1965.** It had become apparent to the U.S. Congress by 1965 that there was a need for library legislation to "strengthen and improve educational quality and educational opportunities in the nation's schools." The law they enacted (Public Law 89-10) was a landmark in education legislation because its scope was broad and its possibilities infinite. The appropriations of federal funds for carrying out its provisions during the first year alone were $1,300,000,000; during the second year, a total of $1,464,610,000; and during the third, $1,588,577,000.

The Act provided for the following:

Title I: Strengthening educational programs for children of low-income families;

Title II: Provision of school library resources, textbooks, and other instructional materials for the use of children and teachers;

Title III: Provision of supplementary educational centers and services;

Title IV: Grants for educational research and training;

Title V: Strengthening state departments of education.

Title I provided financial assistance to local educational agencies for the education of children of low-income families. The number of children in the school district from 5 to 17 years of age in families with an annual income level below $2,000 formed the base for eligibility. It was estimated that a large majority of the school districts of the United States would qualify for this aid. In writing plans under Title I, local educational agencies were encouraged to develop new and varied approaches to the education of culturally deprived children. School libraries became involved where their services could be related to the approved plan. There was evidence that among the supposedly ineducable children from lower-income families some were actually highly gifted. Under this Title, special educational approaches and methods were developed to identify and encourage potential talent. Programs were developed for strengthening the educa-

Prince George's County Public Schools, Maryland

*Poetry readings hold a special appeal for young audiences.*

tion of the disadvantaged through instructional materials, books (including textbooks), periodicals, films, and recordings, as well as other types of materials.

Title I also provided for facilities, staff, equipment, and supplies to provide school library service where not previously available or to strengthen libraries already in operation. Varied kinds of support for school library programs serving the special needs of the disadvantaged were available.

Title II dealt most directly with the improvement of school libraries. Title II authorized $100,000,000 to the states for school library resources, textbooks, and other instructional materials for the use of children and teachers in public and private elementary and secondary schools. School library resources referred to printed and published instructional materials such as trade and textbooks, periodicals, documents, pamphlets, photographs, reproductions, pictorial or graphic works, musical scores, maps, charts, globes, recordings, slides, films, filmstrips, videotapes, etc.

During the first year of a program's operation under Title II, up to 5 percent of each state's grant could be used for administrative expenses. After the first year, up to 3 percent of the state grant was available for these costs. The funds for materials under Title II were not to be considered a substitute for state or local support but would encourage and supplement the state and local funds. The states submitted plans that took into account the relative need of all children and teachers in all the schools of the state and provided assurance that the children and teachers in private schools would receive materials on an equitable basis. State plans also indicated the criteria to be used for making determinations of the adequacy, quality, and quantity of school library resources, textbooks, and other instructional materials.

School library resources were immeasurably strengthened under Title II. The cost of the materials obtained for the use of children and teachers in the elementary and secondary schools could also include the necessary and essential cost of processing, cataloguing, and delivery. Schools with the greatest needs received materials to develop fully their library collections, while schools with strong existing collections were able to enrich their collections. Schools with special needs, such as those with a high proportion of gifted children or advanced placement programs, also improved their collections, and some schools were selected as models or pilot schools to demonstrate the use of various types of materials in new patterns of instruction.

Title II was enacted in response to testimony showing the overwhelming and well-documented need in schools for more and better instructional materials. Singled out for special attention were the number of elementary schools still without libraries and the inability of many schools with centralized libraries to meet ALA standards for materials without federal assistance. In its first year of operation, Title II stimulated the establishment of over 3,000 new public elementary school libraries serving 1,400,000 children and about 250 new school libraries in public secondary schools enrolling 145,000 children. The 62,000 existing public school library collections that were expanded in the first year served 1,500,000 children. The 17,700,000 volumes acquired with Title II funds, however, added only slightly more than one-third of one school library book per child in the elementary and secondary schools in the United States. A significant outcome of the inclusion of Title II in the Elementary and Secondary Education Act was indirect—it served to direct the focus of attention to the essential role that school libraries play in providing quality instruction.

Title III authorized funds for supplementary educational centers and services and sanctioned an unusually broad scope of educational activity. The purpose of these centers was to provide educational services not previously available to children in a particular area, to strengthen services already available, or to develop models of commendable educational programs. Model school libraries could be provided in these centers. Under Title III, special programs representing various subject fields or educational services, such as science or guidance and counseling, could be instituted. Instructional materials and staff to support such programs and to demonstrate model use of the materials could be secured and audiovisual equipment and materials purchased to enrich academic programs.

Title IV provided $100 million to be made available over a five-year period for regional educational research and training facilities. Institutions of higher education and other nonprofit organizations could receive grants for programs to benefit public schools. This title extended the Cooperative Research Act and provided for national and regional research and training laboratories to be located in areas of population concentration. Under this title, school library problems could be thoroughly explored. Each laboratory would come up with its own plan for research to benefit schools.

Title V authorized $25,000,000 to strengthen state departments of education. Two types of grants were available under the provisions of this title; funds for basic grants made up 85 percent of the authorized funds, while the remainder supported experimental projects or the establishment of services that might contribute to the solution of problems common to other states. In state education agencies 80 new supervisory positions were established in a single year after the passage of ESEA, most of them for school library consultants or media and instructional materials specialists.

**Higher Education Act of 1965.** The Higher Education Act of 1965 (HEA) authorized a program of federal financial assistance to institutions of higher education to assist in training persons in librarianship, under Title II-B, Library Education. Grants were used to assist institutions in covering the costs of courses of training or study and to upgrade or update the competencies of persons serving all types of libraries, information centers, or instructional material centers and those working as educators. Grants were made for fellowships at the master's, post-master's, and doctoral levels for training in librarianship and information science. This legislation was implemented through the institute and the fellowship program.

*Institute Program.* Institutes provided educational opportunities for librarians and information specialists to retrain, acquire special skills, or keep up to date. The institute has traditionally provided an opportunity for keeping up with educational principles and advances in various subject areas. The HEA institute program reflects a legislative change that amended that portion of the NDEA that specifically authorized institutes for school library personnel, expanding the base of educational opportunities for librarians and information scientists by offering them training in the principles and practices of the library and information sciences.

For fiscal year 1970, 124 proposals for institutes were received; of this total, 46 institutes were funded to train approximately 1,347 participants. The length of the institutes varied from 1 to 46 weeks; the average number of participants was 30. The subject matter of the institutes varied. One-third of the programs were concerned with school libraries or media centers; 12 programs dealt with services to the disadvantaged or handicapped; and the remaining programs were concerned with such subjects as management and administration, special libraries, academic librarianship, and public libraries.

**Other Legislation.** Additional legislation that has been of concern to school librarians includes the following:

*Educational Professions Development Act Parts C and D: Media Specialists.* The purpose of this act is to train specialized personnel for state and local instructional media support. Individuals who apply for this grant are prospective and/or experienced school media specialists, administrators, and educators.

*HEA Title II-B: Training for Library Service.* This legislation increased opportunities throughout the nation for training in librarianship, assisting prospective and/or experienced librarians and information specialists in school library service.

*School Aid to Federally Impacted and Major Disaster Areas (P.L. 815).* The purpose of this act is to aid school districts in providing minimum school facilities in federally impacted and disaster areas.

*Postal Reorganization Act Amendment of 1976, P.L. 94-421.* The two provisions of this law of special interest to school librarians/media specialists was the extension of the lower library rate to books sent to libraries and the addition of the new rate-setting criterion relating to the educational, cultural, scientific, and informational value of materials.

*Copyright Law of 1976.* On October 19, 1976, the bill for general revision of the copyright law (S. 22) was signed by the President and became Public Law 94–553; the new law became effective January 1, 1978. It preempts and abolishes any right under state common or statutory law that comes within the scope of the federal copyright law with a few exceptions, none of which deals directly with the use of materials in the school media center. The law allows copying of a limited amount of material without permission from, or payment to, the copyright owner where the use is reasonable and not harmful to the rights of the copyright owner (Sec. 107). It forbids excessive duplication of materials for instructional purposes. Copyright duration is extended to the life of the author plus 50 years, bringing U.S. law into conformity with international practice.

RUTH WALDROP

# Scoggin, Margaret Clara

(1905–1968)

Margaret C. Scoggin was a pioneer in the establishment of young adult services in public libraries. She designed, opened, and supervised the Nathan Straus Branch of the New York Public Library (NYPL), which was devoted exclusively to patrons 21 and under. As a result of her experience there, she was invited by ALA to help organize the International Youth Library in Munich, Germany, and she toured other European libraries in an advisory capacity for Unesco. As successor to Mabel Williams, Scoggin served as Superintendent of Work with Young People for the New York Public Library from 1952 until 1967. She was the recipient of many awards and honors, most notably the ALA Grolier Award for outstanding service to young people.

Born in Caruthersville, Missouri, April 14, 1905, Margaret Scoggin graduated as high school valedictorian with a record-setting average; she then finished Radcliffe magna cum laude and was elected to Phi Beta Kappa. Her interest in youth work may have started with the classes she taught in a local settlement house during college.

In July 1926 Scoggin worked as a summer replacement at the Mott Haven Branch of New York Public, moving around in various branches to gain experience, under the encouraging supervision of Mabel Williams, Supervisor of Work with Schools. Young people's opinions were very important to Scoggin, who believed that libraries would serve young people best through identifying their interests and through listening carefully to what they had to say. She wrote, "True reading guidance lies in discovering in each boy and girl the interests he has. . . . It calls for tolerance of young people's choices—listening instead of telling." She saw this communication process as one that enhanced the growth of critical judgment in young people through the testing of their ideas in a supportive environment. She created this environment at that time in two ways—through library-based clubs in which young adults discussed books and produced plays and puppet shows, and through skilled one-to-one reading guidance.

After completing a degree at the School of Librarianship at the University of London, Scoggin returned to NYPL to continue her YA work and introduced a teen book review booklet, called *Back Talk,* which included articles on topics of interest to young people as well as reviews. She said, "In school only the best is taken, but the public library takes everything." This attitude continues to distinguish public library YA work from school-related activities.

Although she started a Master's program at Columbia University, Scoggin never completed the degree because of pressures of time and money. In 1935 she was named systemwide Librarian in Charge of Vocational and Industrial Schools of NYPL. In this capacity she spoke at assemblies and arranged class visits and presentations all over the city. She also compiled bibliographies of simple technical books for the vocational school students, because she identified their great need for books on a level they could comprehend. NYPL published *Simple Technical Books* in 1939.

In April 1940, having completed her work with the vocational schools, Scoggin began work with designers on the Nathan Straus Branch Library for Children and Young People. She insisted upon good light, bright colors, a welcoming atmosphere, a collection built around youth interests, and a specially trained staff. The branch opened in 1941, and its success can be measured, in Scoggin's own terms, by comments from patrons of 1943:

> I can get the kind of books I want without wading through a mess of junk that's way over my head.
>
> The librarians LIKE to help you in any problem you have and they are all very nice.
>
> You feel as you come in that you are going into your own home.
>
> I guess I don't dislike anything or anyone in this library.

While supervising Nathan Straus, which quickly became a professional demonstration library in addition to its other mission of service to young people, Scoggin lectured at Saint John's University, served on local agency councils and ALA committees, and was consulted by innumerable literary, publishing, and youthwork groups. It was during her time at Nathan Straus that she also pioneered music library programs for young adults and was a leading advocate of recordings as part of YA collections. The Nathan Straus branch continued from 1941 until 1955, when the YA services and collection were moved to their present location at the Donnell Library Center on 53rd Street.

In 1945, after an interview on New York radio station WMCA, owned by Mrs. Nathan Straus, wife of the philanthropist who gave money for the branch bearing his name, Scoggin was invited to organize a young people's radio review program. The enormously successful program continues on WNYC today. The quality of "The Young Book Reviewers" program was recognized by awards from the Institute of Education by Radio and Television at Ohio State University. When the program moved to WNYC as the library-sponsored "Teen Age Book Talk," it won the George Foster Peabody Broadcasting Award of the Henry W. Grady School of Journalism at the University of Georgia. In 1965 the radio pro-

The New York Public Library

*Margaret Clara Scoggin*

gram was judged "Best Radio Program for Youth" as one of the Thomas Alva Edison Foundation's National Mass Media Award Winners.

With her good sense of what really interested young adults, Margaret Scoggin produced six anthologies of stories for young people taken primarily from adult books. Two featured humor—*Chucklebait* (1945) and *More Chucklebait* (1949); three adventure—*Lure of Danger* (1945), *Edge of Danger* (1951), and *Escapes and Rescues* (1960); and one true stories from World War II—*Battle Stations* (1953). Of *Chucklebait,* the *Saturday Review* said, "There are few people better qualified by experience and natural endowment to make a selection of stories for young people than Margaret Scoggin."

Scoggin left a rich body of professional writings. In 1947 she presented "The Library as a Center for Young People in the Community" at the University of Chicago's Symposium, *Youth, Communication and Libraries.* In 1948 she originated "Outlook Tower" in *Horn Book,* a review column of recommended adult books for YA's of which she was editor for almost 20 years. In 1952 Scoggin coedited *Gateways to Readable Books,* a graded, annotated list of books for slow readers in high school. Her articles were as eloquent as entertaining, as this 1952 quote from *ALA Bulletin* shows:

> Young readers need an adult mind to challenge their ideas of books and authors. Let us be sure that the minds we provide as the challenge are both adult and functioning.

Scoggin continued to be a "Renaissance Woman" as Superintendent of Work with Young People. Even in that demanding position, she still managed to find time to teach a weekly course at the Simmons library school. It was also during this period that she initiated annotations as Editor of *Books for the Teenage,* an annual list started in NYPL in 1929.

In postwar Germany the success of an International Book Exhibition organized by Jella Lepman under the American military government led to the idea of a permanent International Youth Library. Such a library would collect the best children's books of the world to help foster international understanding through books. With funds from the Rockefeller Foundation and the Bavarian government, ALA chose Margaret Scoggin as its representative because of her work at Nathan Straus. Scoggin spent six gruelling months weeding and classifying 8,000 books from 24 countries, and developing programs to lure and keep the young interested in the Library. In addition, she toured other European libraries for Unesco and persuaded authorities to include books in CARE packages. After much effort and encouragement, the International Youth Library opened in 1949, and Scoggin continued soliciting materials and equipment for it after she returned home. Because of her work with the Library, the Children's Book Council has established the Margaret Scoggin Memorial Collection there, which includes all the titles on the annual ALA Notable Children's Books and Best Books for Young Adults lists.

Scoggin was active in professional associations in many capacities. She was the first Chair of the newly formed Children's and Young Adult Services Division of the New York Library Association in 1951–52. In ALA she chaired the International Relations Committee and the Young People's Reading Round Table, was elected an ALA Councilor, and received the Grolier Award. From the Women's National Book Association she received the Constance Lindsay Skinner Award.

The full measure of Margaret Scoggin's outstanding contributions to librarianship may be best measured, and remembered, by two comments. The first is from "some of her grateful young book reviewers" on a scroll they presented to her:

> To Margaret Scoggin, who has opened the door to the wonderful world of books for many who might not have found the way themselves.

The second is a tribute written after her death July 11, 1968, by Dorothy L. Cromien, formerly her assistant at Nathan Straus:

> The professional world is served today in many places by those whom Miss Scoggin encouraged and inspired. The most lasting tribute we can give Margaret Scoggin is to turn with her generosity to the generations we may have scarcely noticed coming up behind us.

**REFERENCE**

Beverly Lowy, "Margaret C. Scoggin (1905–1968): Her Professional Life and Work in Young Adult Librarianship" (unpublished M.A. thesis, Palmer Graduate Library School, Long Island University, May 1970.)

MARY K. CHELTON

## Sears, Minnie Earl
(1873–1933)

Minnie Earl Sears, cataloguer, reference librarian, bibliographer, teacher, and editor of reference books, is best known for her *List of Subject Headings for Small Libraries.* She was born November 17, 1873, in Lafayette, Indiana, and at the age of 18, in 1891, she received the B.S. degree from Purdue University, the youngest member of her class. Two years later, in 1893, she received the M.S. degree from the same university, and in 1900 she received the B.L.S. degree from the University of Illinois.

Her particular interest was cataloguing, and she served as Head Cataloguer at Bryn Mawr College Library, 1903–07, Head Cataloguer at the University of Minnesota Library, 1909–14, and as First Assistant of the Reference-Catalogue Division of the New York Public Library, 1914–20.

Isadore Gilbert Mudge, colleague, friend, and co-editor of several works, described her in the January 1934 issue of *Wilson Bulletin for Librarians* as follows: "She had an unusual ability for research work of a high order and, had her tastes turned in that direction, would have made one of the great reference librarians of the country, but from the beginning she was interested especially in the scholarly side of cataloging and cataloging research, and in the problems of subject cataloging."

Along with her deep interest in cataloguing she also had a strong interest in bibliographic and literary research evident in the *Thackeray Dictionary* (1910) and the *George Eliot Dictionary* (1924), which were written with Isadore Gilbert Mudge.

In 1923 she joined the editorial staff of the H. W. Wilson Company, where she combined her cataloguing expertise with her research ability. In this capacity she was able to use her knowledge and understanding of libraries to assist not just one library but many libraries throughout the country. She edited the third edition of *Children's Catalog* in 1925 and the fourth edition in 1930. Because of Minnie Sears's interest and care, this selection tool for juvenile books became a cataloguing and reference tool and also a useful source for teaching in library schools. She edited other similar reference works: the second edition of the ALA *Standard Catalog for High School Libraries* (1932) and the ALA *Standard Catalog for Public Libraries* (1927–33).

One of the goals in compiling the *George Eliot Dictionary* was to identify the references to songs and musical compositions in George Eliot's works. This task required the use of the resources of the three largest music libraries in the country at that time as well as foreign correspondence. When Sears accepted the task of editing the *Song Index,* she did so with a practical knowledge of the problems involved and an appreciation of the need for such a tool. The *Song Index* was published in 1926.

The plan for *Essay and General Literature Index* (1931–33), which Sears edited with Marion Shaw, "was based on one of the points of her cataloguing creed upon which she always felt very strongly, that is, the economic waste of analyzing in individual card catalogs material which could be analyzed once for all in a printed catalog or index," according to Mudge *(Wilson Bulletin for Librarians,* January 1934*)*. Thus the basis for describing titles included in such works as *Essay and General Literature Index* and *Standard Catalog for Public Libraries* was careful cataloguing and the availability of cooperative cataloguing to libraries everywhere.

Her *List of Subject Headings for Small Libraries,* first published in 1923 and in its 11th edition under the editorship of Barbara M. Westby at the end of the 1970's, filled a long-felt need among smaller libraries and soon became a tool for teaching subject heading work in library schools. In the 3rd edition, published in 1933, the last one Sears edited, she added a chapter entitled "Practical Suggestions for the Beginner in Subject Heading Work." Also published as a separate pamphlet, it contained simple rules with logical explanations about how to assign subject headings, told how new subject headings are established, and gave advice on how to handle subject heading changes. From the start Sears used the Library of Congress form for subject headings. This made it possible for cataloguers to easily add Library of Congress headings when a subject was not included in the Sears *List.* One exception to this practice was the use of hyphens; in the *Wilson Bulletin* (vol. 2, 1922–26), Sears commented on her preference in the *Sears List* for the more modern usage of less hyphenation.

In a talk to the New York Regional Catalogers Group on "The Teaching of Cataloging" (*Library Journal,* June 1, 1927), she discussed several issues about elementary and advanced cataloguing courses and the continuation of learning about cataloguing that needs to follow library school graduation. One issue that she discussed seems to summarize the essence of her purpose as cataloguer and reference librarian: "Can not more be done to make them [cataloguers] realize that there is no difference between the research work often demanded in cataloging, especially in a large library, and the work that is done as pure reference work? . . . Could something more be done in reference courses to connect practical reference with cataloging and vice versa?"

In 1927 Sears joined the faculty of the Columbia University School of Library Service and served there until 1931. She organized the first graduate course in cataloguing for the Master's degree. She served as Chairman of the ALA Catalog Section, 1927–28, Chairman of the New York Regional Catalog Group, 1931–32, and from 1932 until her death in November 28, 1933, she was a member of the ALA committee advising on the revision of *ALA Catalog Rules.*

BARBARA GATES

## Seminar on the Acquisition of Latin American Library Materials

The Seminar on the Acquisition of Latin American Library Materials (SALALM) came into being as a result of a meeting, sponsored by the University of Florida Libraries and the Pan American Union, at Chinsegut Hill, Brooksville, Florida, on June 14 and 15, 1956, to consider the problems faced by U.S. research libraries in acquiring materials from Latin America. What was planned as a single, one-time effort led first to further meetings on a regular annual basis and eventually to an incorporated organization. Although the interests of SALALM have from the very first conference been broader than the acquisition of materials, the organization has retained its original name and the acronym (SALALM) derived from it. SALALM is basically an association of persons—librarians, scholars, book dealers, and others—whose interests embrace printing, publishing, and bookselling in Latin America; acquisition of publications from and about the area; the organization of libraries in Latin America and of Latin American collections in the U.S. and other countries; the education and training of librarians who work in and administer such collections; the history of libraries in Latin America and of Latin American collections elsewhere; and the stimulation of library development in Latin America.

An annual conference of four or five days' duration constitutes SALALM's most important way of addressing these concerns. Working papers prepared in advance form the main framework for the discussions, but round tables, informal workshops, and committee meetings are also utilized; the general conclusions take the form of a series of resolutions. The results of the meetings are disseminated through published proceedings.

**History.** SALALM's organizational history falls into two periods, pre- and post-1968. A Steering Committee and an Executive Secretary composed the only formal structure during the earlier period. The institution serving as host for the annual meeting secured meeting rooms, reproduced the working papers, and handled other local arrangements; a registration fee defrayed most of these out-of-pocket costs, thus making the seminars essentially self-supporting. There were no members, only participants in the annual conference. In December 1967 SALALM took steps to incorporate so that it would have a permanent organizational structure and the legal basis for accepting grants and contributions; thereafter it resembled other organizations in having a constitution and bylaws, executive board, officers, members, and dues. The Constitution gives the organization's main power to the Executive Board, which appoints both the Executive Secretary and the Treasurer. Consequently the members vote annually for one officer (Vice-President, who advances automatically the following year to President) and for two members of the Executive Board. There are four categories of membership: personal, institutional, special, and honorary. Reflecting steady growth, the combined total of personal and institutional members rose from 135 to nearly 400 by the end of the 1970's.

From 1956 through June 1973 the Organization of American States unofficially maintained SALALM's Secretariat within its Library Development Program (LDP); this was possible because the Executive Secretary of SALALM, Marietta Daniels Shepard, was Chief of the LDP. However, the workload of the Secretariat gradually increased; deciding that it would be desirable to place the Secretariat on a university campus, the Executive Board accepted the offer of the University of Massachusetts. The Secretariat remained in Amherst from July 1973 through June 1976 and then moved to the University of Texas at Austin for the next triennium (1976–79).

**Committees.** From the beginning of SALALM as an organization, the committee has probably been its chief working unit. Several changes and modifications of committee arrangements over the years led to the establishment of three committees (now called Substantive Committees) representing the organization's major interests: acquisitions, bibliography, and library operations and services. Each of them has, in addition, a number of subcommittees with specific charges. The Executive Board assumed most of the overall responsibilities formerly handled by the Steering Committee, then delegated them functionally to committees (mainly in the areas of organization and finance) that it set up. In order to utilize fully the diverse talents and interests of the membership, SALALM has long had a policy of allowing membership on committees to be open as widely as possible to those who wish to contribute and participate, but it finally became necessary to codify general practices in the bylaws. By 1977–78, including members of the Executive Board, 104 persons held committee appointments (approximately 40 percent of the membership). The *Resolutions and List of Committees,* issued annually, provides a current listing.

**Finance.** Prior to incorporation SALALM had no regular source of income as an organization. It survived because the Pan American Union maintained the Secretariat and published the *Final Report and Working Papers* and because the annual seminar itself operated on a self-sustaining basis. Finances after 1968, though still quite limited in amount, entered a period of relative stability; income came mainly from dues and was utilized in turn chiefly to provide for the Secretariat's operations. By general policy registration fees from the annual meeting and the expenditures for it are in balance over a period of several years, while publications require a net subsidy. SALALM received grants from the Tinker Foundation, including $5,000 toward the expenses of the 23rd meeting in London. Income and expenditures were kept in balance at approximately $16,000 a year in the late 1970's.

**Annual Meeting.** Without doubt, the annual meeting constitutes SALALM's most important activity. The first 13 Seminars (1956–68) took place with 11 different universities, the Library of Congress, and the New York Public Library serving as host institutions; the next 3 met for the first time outside the U.S. (the 14th in Puerto Rico, the 15th in Canada, and the 16th in Mexico); the next 4 alternated U.S. with foreign sites (the 17th and 19th in the U.S., the 18th in Trinidad and Tobago, the 20th in Colombia); after 2 more U.S. locations, the 23rd Seminar (1978) met for the first time outside the Western Hemisphere (London). Attendance at the first meeting came to 32 persons, but, although it increased gradually, it remained below 100 until the 11th Seminar (1966). By the 20th Seminar (1975) the average attendance was 226 per meeting.

While the 1st Seminar in 1956 considered the many dimensions of acquiring publications from Latin America, the decision to continue meeting annually brought adoption of a policy to study acquisition problems not for the entire area but for one or more countries. The Seminars thus dealt successively with acquiring materials from Mexico (2nd), Chile and Argentina (3rd), the Caribbean (5th), Colombia and Venezuela (6th), Central America and Panama (7th), Brazil (8th), and finally the remaining countries—Bolivia, Ecuador, Paraguay, Peru, and Uruguay (9th). As an exception the 4th Seminar, held in Washington in 1959, departed from the geographical approach and considered library support to Latin American area studies. Appropriately enough at the end of this series, the 10th Seminar reviewed progress in solving Latin American acquisition problems and the organization's general accomplishments; a similar review of SALALM's achievements after two decades formed the basis for the 21st meeting (1976).

Many members feel that the conference working papers stand as the organization's major contribution to Latin American bibliography. In the early years the Executive Secretary identified topics and potential authors and then invited these persons to prepare papers, but the President now has the responsibility for planning and soliciting papers for the program. There were 16 working papers for the 1st Seminar; in subsequent years the number has varied from 3 (2nd) to as many as 39 (20th). For the first 23 meetings of SALALM a total of nearly 400 working papers (exclusive of some special reports) were prepared, making an average of about 18 papers per conference.

From early years SALALM's annual meetings were useful both for their content and for the resolutions (many of which were recommendations for further action) resulting from the deliberations. The first 23 seminars (1956–78) passed 842 such resolutions, ranging from as few as 17 to a high of 99, or an average of 37 per meeting.

**Publications.** Although publications represent an important activity for SALALM, problems in financing them have led to inconsistencies in imprint and to varying patterns of distribution. The most important are the volumes resulting from the annual conference, entitled *Final Report and Working Papers* (this phrase, since 1975, appears as a subtitle, under a distinctive title taken from the theme of the conference). Because of financial limitations, there was no SALALM imprint in the early years. The host institutions published those for the 1st through 4th and the 6th meetings; the 5th and 7th through 16th were issued by the Pan American Union; and from the 17th Seminar (1972) SALALM itself was the publisher. Similarly the annual *Resolutions and List of Committees* fell within the Cuadernos Bibliotecológicos series of the Pan American Union from 1961 through 1972; thereafter the Secretariat compiled and issued them a few months after the annual conference. In January 1973 the first issue of the *SALALM Newsletter* came out, and it now appears quarterly; volume 6, number 1 (September 1978) contains a cumulative index for the first five volumes. A Bibliography Series reached three numbers by 1979.

**Relations with Other Organizations.** For nearly two decades SALALM enjoyed an informal association with the Pan American Union; relations were closest from 1956 until the transfer of the Secretariat to the University of Massachusetts in 1973. For the 13 years in which the Latin American Cooperative Acquisitions Program (LACAP) flourished, there were many close ties between SALALM and LACAP, the latter having come into being as an outgrowth of SALALM's attempts to grapple with the acquisition problem. Among the other organizations with which SALALM has had more than casual working relationships, although in varying degrees of closeness over the years, are the Hispanic Division of the Library of Congress; the Latin American Studies Association (LASA); the International Relations Committee (IRC) and the International Relations Round Table (IRRT) of the American Library Association; and the Association of Caribbean University, Research, and Institutional Libraries (ACURIL).

WILLIAM VERNON JACKSON

# Senegal

Senegal, a republic of West Africa, lies on the Atlantic Ocean and is bounded by Mauritania on the north, Mali on the east, and Guinea and Guinea-Bissau on the south. Pop. (1976 est.) 5,000,000; area 196,722 sq.km. The official language is French.

**National Library.** The National Library of Senegal exists as a legal entity only. There are three libraries, however, that together perform the functions of a national library: the Institut Fondamental d'Afrique Noire (IFAN), the Archives Nationales, and the Centre de recherche et do documentation du Sénégal (CRDS). The library of the Institut Fondamental d'Afrique Noire (Fundamental Institute of Black Africa) was established in 1938, when it inherited more than 6,000 works from the library of the government of French Occidental Africa. In the late 1970's its collection, specializing in Africana, consisted of approximately 60,000 volumes and 4,000 periodicals. The library owns manuscripts, rare books, and old newspapers dating back to colonial times. The Institute's library received copyrighting privilege on July 17, 1946. A new decree on legal deposit requirements was adopted on April 9, 1976. The library of the Archives Nationales du Sénégal was founded in 1913 and is housed in Dakar at the headquarters of the National Archives. The library collects materials on the history of Senegal and the

**Libraries in Senegal (1976)**

| Type | Number | Volumes in collections | Population served | Professional staff | All staff (total) |
|---|---|---|---|---|---|
| National | 3 | 96,000 | | 23 | 55 |
| University | 1 | 350,000 | 8,014 | 17 | 42 |
| School | 151 | 125,100 | 440,911 | 17 | 102 |
| Public | 73 | 91,631 | 1,677,729 | 9 | 26 |
| Special | 74 | 136,405 | 25,000 | 27 | 81 |
| National Archives | 1 | | 44,000 | 25 | 35 |
| Total | 303 | 799,136 | | 118 | 341 |

Source: Data courtesy Dominique Zidouemba, Institut Fondamental d'Afrique Noire à Dakar (IFAN).

territories that previously were part of French Occidental Africa, as well as publications on law and government. The number of volumes in its collection is approximately 20,000, and it receives 380 periodicals. From 1962 the Archives published a bibliographical bulletin entitled, as of issue 40 (1972), the *Bibliographie du Sénégal,* a compilation of bibliographical data on the library's acquisitions. This work can be considered a first draft of a national bibliography. In addition, the Archives has set up an exchange system for foreign correspondents as a national library would.

Since its founding in 1913, the Library has received every official ministerial and state service publication for deposit. The library of the Centre de Recherche et de Documentation du Sénégal (Center for Research and Documentation of Senegal) in Saint-Louis was founded in 1944 when it acquired the former IFAN center of Senegal. Its collection consists of more than 16,000 volumes and 660 periodicals. In the late 1970's the possibility of combining the collections of these libraries into one national library was under discussion.

The National Archives collects the official archives of every Senegalese institution dating back to the beginning of the 19th century. The Archives serves about 44,000 civil servants working for the administration and other public utilities, as well as other readers. Although the establishment of branches of the National Archives in the major town of every district was planned, only one branch, in Kaolack, had been opened by the end of the 1970's.

**Academic Libraries.** Senegal has one university, the Université de Dakar, which was founded in 1952. The University has four faculties (Humanities, Sciences, Law and Economics, and Medicine and Pharmacy) and several institutes. A program to Africanize the courses offered at the University has been successfully implemented. The University's central library houses nearly 350,000 volumes and 5,000 periodicals, including a special Africana collection. In addition to this central library, there are 59 other institutional, professional school, and pedagogical libraries.

**School Libraries.** More than 40 percent of all children of school age are enrolled in elementary and secondary schools. Particular emphasis has been placed upon increasing school enrollment in rural areas. In the late 1970s there were 92 school libraries, serving a total number of 432,897 elementary and secondary students.

**Public Libraries.** There are few public libraries in Senegal. Library facilities are provided primarily through cultural centers, social centers, district centers of physical education and sports (CDEPS), and youth centers.

Frequently the public libraries of the centers are supported through donations of embassies, particularly the French embassy. Public library budgets are either nonexistent or very minimal. The total book stock of these libraries, which are located mainly in towns and large villages, is 91,631. In the late 1970's, 1,677,729 readers were served.

There are 73 public libraries, including 22 social centers, 31 CDEPS's and youth centers, 8 cultural centers, and 12 private cultural centers. Staff at such libraries is usually very small, and many members work on a voluntary basis.

**Special Libraries.** There are 44 special libraries and 30 documentation centers, primarily in Dakar. Approximately 25,000 persons are served by these organizations, many of which have important libraries. Some of the more notable are those of foreign embassies in Dakar, particularly the Austrian, Canadian, Japanese, and Lebanese embassies, and those of the institutes of the university, such as the Institut de médecine tropicale appliquée, the Institut africain de lutte contre le cancer, and the Institut de pédiatrie sociale (IPS). Among research institutions, the Institut Pasteur is one of the oldest in West Africa; it was founded in 1924. Most of these specialized libraries have limited collections.

**Association.** The National Association of Librarians, Archivists and Documentalists of Senegal was founded in Dakar on March 18, 1975. It was established to advance the development of libraries, archives, and documentation centers in Senegal and to study concerns common to librarians in the country. The Association is affiliated with IFLA, FID, Council of International Archives, and the national FIAB. It issues proceedings of meetings.

MARIE GABRIELLE VEAUX

# Seychelles

Seychelles, a republic in the Indian Ocean off the east coast of Africa, comprises a group of islands of disputed number. The islands were a British colony until 1976; they had been a dependency of the Mauritius Islands until 1903. Pop. (1977) 61,950; area 443 sq.km. The official languages are English and French. Creole patois is spoken also.

On Mahé, the largest island of the country, is the National Library; of some major importance, it was inherited from the Carnegie Foundation Library. Also on Mahé the Museum Library offers a collection of the life sciences, and the National Archives preserves documents of importance concerning the history of the Indian Ocean.

The Association of the Institutions of Research and Development of the Indian Ocean (AIRDOI) set a goal in September 1976 to produce bibliographical works on the islands and archipelagoes of the Indian Ocean. In the late 1970's it was conducting inventories of available materials.

J. C. RODA

# Sharp, Katharine Lucinda

(1865–1914)

One of the outstanding library leaders of the late 19th and early 20th century, Katharine Sharp built the cornerstone of the University of Illinois research libraries and contrib-

*Katherine Lucinda Sharp* ALA

uted to the acceptance of graduate education for librarianship in the Midwest. She was born in Elgin, Illinois, on May 21, 1865. The details of Katharine Sharp's childhood years are largely unrecorded; her mother's death, when Katharine was seven, led to her being housed with relatives while she attained her basic education at the Elgin Academy from 1872 to 1880. She enrolled, in 1881, at Northwestern University, Evanston, Illinois, and graduated in 1885 with a Bachelor of Philosophy degree with honors. At the New York State Library School, Albany, she earned a Bachelor's degree in 1892 and a Master's degree in 1907. Sharp also, in 1899, received a Master of Philosophy degree from Northwestern.

She spent the years from 1888 until 1907 devoted to studying, practicing, and living the profession of librarianship. Until her accidental death in an automobile accident on June 1, 1914, she was closely associated with other 19th-century library pioneers, particularly her mentor and friend Melvil Dewey. Sharp studied with Dewey at Albany, and when she left the University of Illinois, in 1907, she found a close circle of friends at his Lake Placid Club in New York, where she served as Vice-President.

Three years after her graduation from Northwestern she accepted her first library position as Assistant Librarian at the public library at Oak Park, Illinois. During the intervening years she had taught at the Elgin Academy. Her first exposure to library work quickly led her to the conclusion that she should enroll in the country's first library school; Dewey later noted, she "was so easily first" there. His recommendation to Frank W. Gunsaulus, President of the newly established Armour Institute in Chicago, brought her appointment, in 1893, as Director of both the Library and the Department of Library Economy. Of special note was the establishment of the library training class, the fourth opened in the U.S. and the first in the Midwest.

In 1897 she moved to the Champaign/Urbana campus of the University of Illinois; the Armour library class was transferred with her. She was already recognized for her ability and leadership in the emerging library profession. Her students at Armour included other future leaders such as Margaret Mann, Cornelia Marvin Pierce, and Alice Tyler. Sharp also was perceived as a national figure through her activities in the American Library Association and her vibrant advocacy of state library organizations, extension work, and cooperative information systems. At Illinois she was named Head Librarian, Director of the Library School, and Professor of Library Economy.

In the ten years of her work at the University of Illinois, Katharine Sharp's life was dominated by three concerns: the Illinois State Library School, now the Graduate School of Library Science; the University library itself; and the development of a strong library organization and information network in Illinois. In each area she had extraordinary successes, but in each area she also had many disappointments.

The main interest of Sharp's professional career rested in her personal belief in education for librarianship that was housed in an academic setting. Dewey had broken the pattern of "learning by experience" in his prototype school; Katharine Sharp, his protegeé, accepted the philosophy that Dewey promulgated and carried it as far as she could at the University of Illinois. The classes at the Armour Institute and at the University of Illinois were founded to provide a specialization taught in an institution of higher education. At Illinois a combination of three elements, faculty, curriculum, and students, was brought together in such a way as to set a standard of achievement essential to the continuation of formal education for librarianship. The School, under her leadership, moved steadily from a B.L.S. based on a junior and senior year of college work toward acceptance of a graduate program. Although she did not completely achieve that objective, the curriculum evolved from routine "economy" courses in cataloguing, classification, and library "techniques" to administration, the study of different kinds of resources such as public documents, library extension, special services, research methods, and the newest technology of the era.

Katharine Sharp arrived at Illinois at a critical period in its history; the University Library was disorganized and lacked a professional perception. Sharp imposed her own distinctive conception of library service on the institution. A logical order and arrangement of the collection was basic; this was followed by an expansion of the services, including reference (which was directed by Isadore Gilbert Mudge) and a modernization of procedures. She enlarged the staff from 3 in 1897 to 15 in 1907, while the number of volumes increased from 37,000 to 96,000 volumes—all catalogued, classified, and accessible. She left a sound foundation for her successors.

Sharp's third, closely linked professional concern lay in the extension of the library into the community and the development of an effective political body that could work for the betterment of library services for all citizens. In this larger arena she did attain certain goals but also failed, since her efforts in Illinois to provide a strong authority for the promotion of library interests were not rewarded. An effective state library association was founded and set firmly on its way, but she and her colleagues did not initiate successful legislation to establish a state library commission. Her efforts to centralize library extension at the University also failed, although she did leave behind dedicated followers who continued to stress the Sharp philosophy and who mustered library supporters throughout the state.

Although she was not a prolific writer, she published nearly two dozen articles and a monumental compilation on the condition of libraries in Illinois, *Illinois Libraries* (1906–08), a multivolume survey of the current status of public, school, academic, and special libraries. It contained an exhaustive historical study.

Throughout her life Sharp was active in library and professional associations. In each organization she was a major officer, including ALA, for which she was active on many committees, served ten years on the Council, and was twice elected Vice-President.

**REFERENCES**

Laurel A. Grotzinger, *The Power and the Dignity: Librarianship and Katharine Sharp* (1966), the only book-length treatment of Katharine Sharp, contains detailed assessment of her educational preparation, Armour years, University of Illinois contributions, work at Lake Placid, and personal characteristics.

Harriet E. Howe, "Katharine Lucinda Sharp, 1865–1914," in *Pioneering Leaders in Librarianship,* edited by Emily Miller Danton (ALA, 1953), a memoir, prepared by a former student, which illustrates the strong influence of Sharp on her students and gives examples of her professional contributions.

LAUREL GROTZINGER

## Shaw, Ralph Robert

(1907–1972)

Ralph Robert Shaw, internationally known library administrator, researcher, educator, and inventor, was one of the most creative librarians to have worked in the United States. He was considered a radical in his early years and a conservative, by some of his colleagues, in his later years. His brilliant mind had the capacity to see a problem, create a solution, then turn it over frequently to colleagues to perfect and implement.

Shaw was born in Detroit, Michigan, May 18, 1907. He secured an A.B. degree from Western Reserve University in 1928, the B.S. and M.S. at Columbia in 1929 and 1931, respectively, and the Ph.D. at the University of Chicago in 1950. His early professional experience included the New York Public Library (1928–29), Engineering Societies Library (1929–36), and service as Chief Librarian, Gary (Indiana) Public Library (1936–40). In 1940 he became Director of Libraries, U.S. Department of Agriculture, a position that he held (with time out to serve in the U.S. armed forces) until 1954, when he went to Rutgers the State University of New Jersey. There he served as Professor in the newly established Graduate School of Library Service, becoming Dean for the period of 1959–61 and Distinguished Service Professor, 1961–64. Finally he became Professor, Dean of Library Activities, and Professor Emeritus at the University of Hawaii in Honolulu until his retirement in 1969, although he continued to lecture occasionally at Rutgers until 1968.

Everywhere Shaw worked, his keen mind attacked the problems of the institution and produced innovative solutions, showing especial interest in the scientific and efficient management of libraries. In Gary he instituted transaction charging, the use of photography in circulation control, and the use of truck cabs coupled with trailers as bookmobiles, which could be left on location for several days or longer. His invention of the rapid selector came during this period, as well as his translation of Schneider's work *Theory and History of Bibliography* (Columbia University Press, 1934). His dissertation at Chicago, revised and published as *Literary Property in the United States* (Scarecrow, 1950), marked the beginning of a continuing concern with copyright problems, evidenced again in one of his last works, "Williams and Wilkins v. the U.S.: A Review of the Commissioner's Report" (*American Libraries,* October 1972).

His work at the U.S. Department of Agriculture offered ample opportunity to continue his interest in the use of machines as tools of management. There he initiated the first study of scientific management as applied to libraries at the Graduate School of that department, and later he carried this to Rutgers, where one of the first courses on this subject was introduced in the regular library school curriculum. His concern with bibliography brought his attention to the development of the *Bibliography of Agriculture,* which became a major tool for the dissemination of agricultural information on a worldwide basis.

His interest in international problems was also shown at this time and continued throughout his career. He was active on numerous committees for ALA and Unesco and served as a consultant on major library studies for a variety of governmental agencies. He advised, for example, the Department of State, the National Science Foundation, and the U.S. Veterans Administration, to name only a few. He planned a network of agencies to distribute agricultural information in India (1957), developed the information component of the International Rice Research Institute at Los Baños, Philippines (1962), and worked as well in many Latin American countries through his membership on the advisory committee of the Inter-American Institute of Agricultural Science.

Shaw's continuing service to public libraries was shown through a survey for the Toronto Public Library (*Libraries of Metropolitan Toronto,* 1960); a feasibility study for the Boards of Trustees of the Brooklyn Public Library, New York Public Library, and Queens Borough Public Library (*A Study of the Advantages and Disadvantages of Consolidation,* January 1957); and work at the local level to establish new public libraries, such as the one in Woodbridge, New Jersey. To all of these projects, and many more, he brought enthusiastic commitment, positive support, and expertise seldom matched in an individual librarian.

Publishing, as the other side of the coin of library development, received his attention in 1950 when he established the Scarecrow Press, Inc., on the principle of producing scholarly works and bibliographies in librarianship for which only a small market could be anticipated at a reasonable price, usually printing by offset from plates made from typewritten copy, yet always paying a royalty to authors. Among other experiments he tried miniprint, published especially to meet the needs of scholars in developing countries. With the help of Viola Leff Shaw (deceased 1968), whom he had married in 1929, he worked from the basement of their homes in Alexandria, Virginia, and New Brunswick, New Jersey, and built a business until it became too large to manage at home and then sold a controlling interest in 1955 to Albert Daub, Senior; in 1968 it was sold outright to Grolier Educational Corporation. Other similar publishers have used Scarecrow as a model for their operations. In 1969 he was married to Mary McChesney Andrews in Honolulu.

Few who knew Shaw during his days in Washington would have thought of him as having potentiality as a university professor, and yet when he was interviewed at Rutgers by Mason Gross, the President phoned the Dean and said, "We *must* have that man." When Shaw joined the small group of faculty who established the school in 1954, he quickly made an impact as an excellent instructor, an effective colleague in the development of curriculum, and a person deeply sympathetic to students, even though he was tough-minded, frequently dogmatic, could seldom suffer fools gladly, and had a special gift for stirring controversy. He initiated courses new to the library field, was influential in developing the doctoral curriculum, was tireless in seeking support for students and generous to colleagues, but brooked no delay on the part of faculty in responding to deadlines for dissertations and other related responsibilities.

A major contribution to the School and to the profession at this time was his editorship of the State of the Library Art series (Rutgers University Press, 1960–61, 5

ALA

*Ralph Robert Shaw*

vol.), published under a grant from the Council on Library Resources. He also initiated the Shaw/Shoemaker project *American Bibliography: A Preliminary Checklist for 1801–1819* (Scarecrow, 1958–66, 22 vol.) in order to close a 20-year gap left by Evans's pioneering work. It was typical of a Shaw project that he conceived the idea of using the "WPA shoe boxes" of cards plus photocopying as a method of expediting the work; as a result he was successful in producing, from a variety of secondary sources, a tool that has a remarkably high record of accuracy. Another contribution to librarianship was his development, as adviser to doctoral students, of a number of related research studies in the field of management as a means of "growing the field," in his words.

In 1964 when he was invited to go to the University of Hawaii, he carried much of the Rutgers curriculum and some of the faculty and doctoral students to establish a new library school there and to breathe new life into its library system. True to form, he experimented there too, particularly using his "visiting professor" idea, begun at Rutgers when such luminaries as Ranganathan, Joseph Wheeler, and Keyes Metcalfe visited and lectured to library school students. At Honolulu he applied this idea to undergraduate students with some success, though limited by the economics of the situation.

Shaw was also always active in professional associations, although he questioned the effectiveness of library meetings. He was President of the Indiana Library Association (1938–39), the New Jersey Library Association (1962–63), and the American Library Association (1956–57), becoming an Honorary Member of that Association in 1971. He was active in committees related to all his many, varied interests but in the ALA especially in association reorganization. It is difficult to set priorities for a presidential year and equally difficult to assess the impact of an ALA President. In Shaw's case, his report to Council at the 1957 Midwinter Conference reflects both his expectations and his frustrations. He criticized ALA at that time for "not approaching its goals, . . . in fact, appearing to go in the opposite direction" ("The President's Report," *ALA Bulletin,* March 1957). In his year as President, however, Shaw could take satisfaction in having eliminated a considerable amount of work from membership reocrd keeping and in bringing about the consolidation of *Booklist* and *Subscription Books Bulletin.*

One of his colleagues at that time, looking back on his presidency, has stated that "Shaw maintained that A. L. A. was a sprawling, inefficient, wasteful, nonproductive organization, badly in need of effective business procedures and more democratic membership control," typical of Shaw's usual incisive analysis. Some of his criticisms are still true today; others have been ameliorated by recent activisits.

Shaw's printed publications make up a list of more than a hundred references from 1932 to 1972, with many more unpublished speeches, in-house reports, and the like remaining to be sorted and organized. In addition to those publications already mentioned, a few of his more significant contributions are worthy of special mention. As he was never averse to controversy, one of the more interesting examples arose as a result of Jesse Shera's article "Beyond 1984" (*ALA Bulletin,* January 1967), to which Shaw responded promptly (*ALA Bulletin,* March 1967). This exchange on the role of machines in libraries provided an opportunity for Shaw to reiterate once more his position that "it is just as stupid to hate machines as it is to love them. They are tools which may, used properly, help us to do the library and bibliographical jobs that we are supposed to do, and if used improperly can waste our resources." Shaw's *Pilot Study on the Use of Scientific Literature by Scientists* (Scarecrow Reprint Corp., 1971), originally published in 1956, was constantly referred to in his teaching as a model for services by librarians and information scientists. His "CATCALL: Completely Automated Technique [for] Cataloging [and] Acquisition [of] Literature [for] Libraries" (*College & Research Libraries,* March 1970), in addition to illustrating his addiction to acronyms, also illustrates his forward-looking ability to advocate new and more economic ways of carrying out library procedures, in this case through cooperation with publishers and the book trade; some of the recommendations he made have since been realized, but others still await fulfillment.

Finally, almost on his deathbed, Shaw completed the translation and editing of the monumental work by Richard Muther, *German Book Illustration of the Gothic Period and the Early Renaissance (1460–1530)* (Scarecrow, 1972). In his own words, Shaw's work on this book was intended to illustrate how such early works—"verbose, using various German languages, and tough even if you are a German scholar"—can be reorganized with integrity to the original. "My editing has tried to limit it to the critical changes in book illustration during this almost revolutionary period . . . which are half or more illustrations and could be half or less in price with English, and much more useable."

Shaw died in Honolulu on October 14, 1972. Until the end this amazing and unique scholar-librarian continued experimenting and breaking new ground. His greatest impact, however, will be felt through his students, especially those in his doctoral classes, who treasured his Shavian witticisms and aphorisms, crowded his classes to catch every word, and carry on his ideals of research and experimentation. A colleague, Lawrence Thompson, characterized him "as a globe-trotter, raconteur, wit, host, and in some dozens of other capacities . . . approaching the ideal of the Renaissance man" (*College & Research Libraries,* October 1954).

**REFERENCES**

Norman D. Stevens, editor, *Essays for Ralph Shaw* (1975), contains a tribute to Ralph Shaw (Lowell Martin), "Shaw and the Machine" (Theodore C. Hines), and an "Afterword: The Aphorisms of Ralph Shaw," as well as other more typical *Festschrift* articles by Rutgers doctoral graduates.

Mary V. Gaver, "Ralph Shaw at Rutgers," *Wilson Library Bulletin* (February 1973).

Stanley L. West, "Ralph R. Shaw: The Hawaiian Years," *Hawaii Library Association Journal* (December 1973).

MARY V. GAVER

## Shera, Jesse H.
(1903– )

Jesse H. Shera, educator, philosopher, and theoretician, considers that perhaps his most significant contribution to librarianship is not a "thing" but a concept—"the concept of librarianship as a totality, a unity in which all the facts are inter-related and interdependent." He consistently holds to the conviction that documentation and information science are an integral part of the totality of librarianship, that librarianship is the generic term, and information science contributes to the theoretical and intellectual base for the librarian's operations. The role of the librarian, he feels, is to act as mediator between man and his graphic records, and "the goal of the librarian is to maximize the social utility of graphic records for the benefit of humanity." Shera was born December 8, 1903, in Oxford, Ohio. He attended William McGuffey High School in Oxford and went on to Miami University, where he earned an A.B. with honors in English (1925). His graduate work at Yale culminated with an A.M. in English Literature (1927). He received a Ph.D. in Library Science from the University of Chicago in 1944.

Initially, Shera wanted to become a professor of English, but signs of the Depression were already visible when he completed his work at Yale. Opportunities to teach—especially English—were diminishing drastically; Shera felt even more restricted because of his somewhat impaired vision. Thus, when Librarian Edgar King offered him a job in Miami University's Library, he took it. Later King urged him to apply to library school. Shera was accepted at Columbia (King's school) in 1928 but instead decided to work as Bibliographer and Research Assistant of the Scripps Foundation for Population Research at Miami, a position he held until 1938.

Shera's glimmer of interest in the sociological aspects of librarianship—reflected in his master's thesis at Yale and subsequent doctoral work at the Graduate School of the University of Chicago from 1938 to 1940—grew more ardent through his association with Warren S. Thompson, Director of the Scripps Foundation, who held a Ph.D. in sociology from Columbia and had already made a name for himself in demography. So without professional training and education, Shera "backed into library work," as he put it.

At Chicago he encountered ideas about the breadth of librarianship that underscored and affirmed his own thinking. GLS offered a philosophical, theoretical, and interdisciplinary approach to library service. Louis Round Wilson, Douglas Waples, Carleton Joeckel, Ralph Beals, and Pierce Butler, to mention only a few, were among the library leaders he met there.

For several years after Shera completed his course work at GLS and before his degree was conferred, he worked in Washington: first as Chief of the Census Library Project at the Library of Congress, 1940–41, later as Deputy Chief, Central Information Division Research and Analysis Branch, Office of Strategic Services (OSS), November 1941–March 1944. His first year in Washington was frustrating because of the lack of a clear charge in his assignment, but the experience at OSS was significant. In addition to supervising a conventional library, picture collection, and "intelligence documents" (reports from various armed services), there was something called "censorship intercepts" (taken from the mail by the Office of Censorship). This amorphous mass of material had to be organized to provide easy access to it, necessitating experimenting with methods of retrieving information. Having had exposure at Scripps to tabulating machines, punched cards, and the like, Shera utilized these same devices for recording, storing, searching, and retrieving information through a system of assigning subject headings (or descriptors). Besides experimenting with these aspects of mechanization, Shera gained valuable experience in administration and an insight into government libraries.

While in Washington, Shera continued to work on his dissertation (which was later published) and solidified his friendship with Ralph Beals—a colleague from GLS who was Assistant Director of the Public Library in Washington, D.C., and who helped strengthen and widen Shera's grasp of librarianship. In March 1944 Beals became Director of the University of Chicago libraries and invited Shera to be Associate Director, first in charge of technical services, then of public services; when Beals was appointed Dean of GLS, he asked Shera to teach on a part-time basis. So Shera found his teaching career—though not in English literature—and in 1947 was appointed to the faculty of GLS on a full-time basis. There he taught courses on academic libraries, administration, cataloguing, American library history, and the theory of classification, the latter two being his chief interests.

With his colleagues at GLS, he pondered the implications of the new technology on library service but would wait a few years before he did anything more concrete with his ideas than to attend conferences, to organize with Margaret Egan in 1950 a conference on bibliographic organization, and to become a charter member of the revived American Documentation Institute (ADI) early in 1952. Later that year Shera was appointed Dean of Western Reserve's School of Library Science (SLS).

Shera's deanship was one of the most felicitous and fruitful of appointments, both for the individual and the institution. For Shera, Reserve provided a setting where he had strong moral support and had time to write and speak. For Reserve, especially the SLS, Shera initiated a new era. Probably Shera's greatest single contribution was the establishment of the Center for Documentation and Communication Research (CDCR), which developed a program of teaching and research in the emerging field of information retrieval. In November 1952 Shera and James Perry, then at Battelle Memorial Institute (BMI) in Columbus, agreed to work jointly in the new field and later proposed an international conference to be sponsored by BMI and WRU, held at the latter institution. When conditions soon changed at BMI and Perry left, Shera persuaded him and his associate, Allen Kent, to join WRU, and the CDCR was established in spring 1955.

The CDCR prospered. A three-day International Conference held in January 1956 and known as the PURK Conference (Practical Utilization of Recorded Knowledge) was a huge success, gathering some 700 attendees who represented business, industry, government, and academe, as well as the library world. This was the first in a series of significant conferences, international and interdisciplinary in their appeal, held in the following decade. Perry designed and constructed at WRU a "searching selector," and early in 1959 the University signed a contract with General Electric to build a high-speed electronic counterpart of it for the CDCR (delivered in 1961). Research contracts were made with various scientific societies and government agencies, notably the American Society for Metals to organize and abstract the literature of metallurgy. With all those successes in various operations, the original purpose of the CDCR to promote research in the development and evaluation of new and unconventional methods in information storage and retrieval was greatly diminished, although the educational program was enriched through new courses and seminars. Perry left WRU in 1960 and Kent in 1962. In 1963 Shera appointed A. J. Goldwyn, a senior member of the CDCR staff, Executive Director, and a reorganization of the work of the Center freed the staff from the burden of operations and made possible the creation of a Comparative Systems Laboratory.

In addition to guiding the work of the CDCR and participating actively in its conferences, Shera continued not only to carry the responsibilities of Dean and administrative head of the SLS but also to teach, to plan and execute the observances in connection with the 50th anniversary of the School in 1954, to participate in professional affairs, including holding important offices and making significant addresses, to serve as Editor of the official journal of ADI (1953–60) and of the WRU Press (1954–59), and to write a monthly column for the *Wilson Library Bulletin* (1961–68). Verner Clapp said, "Shera is too many for us." As Dean, Shera increased the number of full-time faculty and made it possible for graduates holding the Bachelor's in Library Science to earn the Master's through additional study and the writing of a master's paper. He also initiated a doctoral program that strengthened work in library and information science with emphasis on research.

Greatly concerned with the foundations of education for librarianship, he held a series of meetings with the faculty on the philosophy and theory of librarianship. He received from the Carnegie Corporation funding in February 1956 for a three-year study. In 1972 the book resulting from this study was published as *Foundations of Education for Librarianship*. It was delayed because of his

*Jesse Hauk Shera* ALA

many activities and other difficulties, but Shera said, "It is by the quality of the finished study that the wisdom of the original investment will be eventually judged." The book was awarded the Scarecrow Press Award in 1974.

Other activities in which Shera engaged during these years were many and varied. His contribution to the Ohio Library Association, for example, was substantial—helping to avert the closing of the State Library, establishing the Office of Executive Secretary for the Association, and initiating a Library Development Committee.

Shera retired as Dean of the CWRU School of Library Science in June 1970. His first year thereafter was spent teaching in the Graduate Library School of the University of Texas, and the next year he returned to Reserve to teach. He has continued to teach, both at Reserve and at a number of other schools, sometimes for a week or two, sometimes for a quarter or semester. He has continued to write—"It gets in your blood," he says—and to take an active part in professional affairs. [For this *Encyclopedia,* he contributed "Librarianship, Philosophy of"]. He continued to be in demand as speaker, editor, contributor, consultant.

Shera became known for his wide range of interests and for his ability to talk with all kinds of people, on all kinds of topics whether it be football, TV, social epistemology, or classical music. He won notice for his wit. When Alan Rees told Shera he had been asked to write a personality portrait of him for *Science Information News,* Shera replied, "It seems most appropriate that a publication known as SIN should take some notice of my retirement."

**REFERENCE**

The Shera Festschrift, *Toward a Theory of Librarianship: Papers in Honor of Jesse Hauk Shera,* edited by Conrad H. Rawski (1973), provides a bibliography of 381 of Shera's writings compiled through December 1971.

MARGARET KALTENBACH

## Sierra Leone

Sierra Leone, a republic in West Africa, is bounded by Guinea on the north and east, Liberia on the south, and the Atlantic Ocean on the west. Pop. (1978 est.) 3,220,000; area 71,740 sq.km. The official language is English.

**National Library.** In the absence of a national library, the Public Library System performs certain national library functions; for example, by the Publications Ordinance of 1962 the Public Library became one of two copyright libraries (the other is Fourah Bay College in Freetown) empowered to produce an *Annual List of Publications.* Though not a national bibliography, since it is not a comprehensive list of titles published in Sierra Leone, the list is useful in providing information mostly on titles published by the Government Printing Office. The Public Library also provides interlibrary loan service, which is used locally and internationally.

**Academic Libraries.** The principal academic library is Fourah Bay College of the University of Sierra Leone. Established in 1827, the College became affiliated with the University of Durham, England, in 1876. By 1968 the College had been granted full university status. A University Act of 1972 established a unified university system connecting it with Njala University College (1964), an agricultural college that also offers degree courses in education. Their combined bookstock totals approximately 160,000 volumes, with Fourah Bay housing just over 100,000. Four of the University's faculties are at Fourah Bay: Arts, Science, Economics and Social Science, and Engineering; two exist at Njala: Agriculture and Education.

Fourah Bay College's Documentation Centre consists of a UN Depository Collection and a Sierra Leone Collection, which includes materials on Sierra Leone, Liberia, Guinea, Guinea Bissau, and the Gambia. The Centre also conducts literature search for its readers. Njala University College's Sierra Leone Collection has notable agricultural and educational material.

Other institutions with libraries include teachers colleges and technical institutes. Teacher education began in 1926. Initially, male teachers were trained at Fourah Bay College and females at a separate women's college at Wilberforce Village, Freetown. The latter merged with the Department of Teacher Education, Fourah Bay College, in 1946–47 but later separated from it and became Milton Margai Teachers College in 1960, at Goderich Village, Freetown. Bunumbu Teachers College was established in the provinces early in the 1930's as recognition that a college for pastor/teachers was needed outside the Freetown area. It became the first provincial college to grant the Higher Teachers Certificate to primary school teachers for rural development, a program funded by the government and Unesco. Other teacher colleges include Bo Teachers College (1963), Port Loko Women's Teachers College (1966), and Makeni Teachers College (1972).

The first Technical Institute was established in Freetown in 1953. It offers courses in construction, civil engineering, and other areas of engineering for the Diploma of the City and Guilds of London Institute. It also offers certificate courses in business studies and secretarial practice. Other institutions include the Technical Institute in Kenema Eastern Province, established in 1956, the Trade Centre located in Magburaka (1962), and the Trade Centre in Kissy, Freetown (1964). Libraries in these institutes were not fully developed at the end of the 1970's.

**Public Libraries.** The Sierra Leone Library Board Ordinance of 1959 empowered the Board to establish, equip, manage, and maintain libraries in the country. The Minister of Education appoints the Chairman and 14 other members of the Board.

The Board's headquarters and Central Library in Freetown formally opened in 1964. Apart from the Central Library with its lending, reference, and children's departments, the Board has three regional libraries in Bo, Kenema, and Makeni, which were established in the 1960's; seven branch libraries; and a primary school service. Branch libraries are located in the provincial towns of Magburaka and Kambia (Northern Province); Kailahun, Koidu, and Pujehun (Eastern Province); and Bonthe and Mattru (Southern Province).

The primary school service, established in 1961, provides a bookmobile service to schools in towns without libraries. Books are processed centrally, and schools are visited once a year, thus providing an annual loan service to these schools. About 90,000 children and 4,000 teachers are served by this service.

**School Libraries.** Individual schools are responsible for school libraries. Many primary schools have book corners, and pupils are encouraged to join the children's section of the Sierra Leone Library Board's libraries. There are a little over 1,000 primary schools in Sierra Leone, many of which are in close proximity to a public library service or are serviced by the Board's bookmobile service. Many secondary schools have been provided with new library buildings and equipment under the International Development Agency project schemes. All Sixth Form schools and most of the Fifth Form secondary schools have library facilities. But in most of these libraries, books and periodicals are in short supply. The Ministry of Education library grant to secondary schools was discontinued under the military regime in 1967. Therefore, some secondary schools levy a library fee unofficially. These funds are largely used for the purchasing of books and other library materials.

**Table 1. Libraries in Sierra Leone (1976)**

| Type | Number | Volumes in collection | Annual expenditures (leone) | Population served | Professional staff | All staff (total) |
|---|---|---|---|---|---|---|
| Academic and vocational | 7 | 185,000 | Le 270,000 | 9,000 | 13 | 53 |
| Public | 11 | 347,932 | Le 139,000 | 3,500,000 | 10 | 40 |
| School | 13 | 4,000 | Le 18,000 | 10,000 | N.A. | 12 |
| Special | 12 | 34,440 | Le 178,000 | 10,000 | 6 | 31 |
| Total | 43 | 571,372 | Le 605,000 | | | 126 |

Source: Annual reports; interviews; *Directory of Libraries and Information Services,* 2nd edition (Sierra Leone Library Association, 1976).

**Table 2. Archives in Sierra Leone (1976)**

| | |
|---|---|
| Number | 5,383 |
| Holdings | 12,000 cu.ft. |
| Annual expenditures | Le24,000 |
| Professional staff | 3 |
| All staff (total) | 6 |

Source: Annual reports; interviews.

The British Council of the United Kingdom provided books and periodicals through its Book Presentation Programme for secondary schools. To ensure that materials provided under this program are maintained, the local British Council Office encourages the appointment of a Library Assistant who serves as the paraprofessional staff. The Ministry of Education provides the salary of a library assistant who has acquired educational qualification and has participated in one of the University's library training courses.

Many secondary schools have also appointed teacher/librarians to be in charge of their libraries. These are qualified teachers, often graduates, who are required to attend short library courses organized annually by the university.

The Sierra Leone School Library Association has produced minimum standards for secondary school libraries, which were endorsed and accepted by the National Conference of Principals of Secondary Schools; they awaited implementation by the Ministry of Education at the end of the 1970's.

**Special Libraries.** The establishment of special libraries is based on the provision of library facilities in government administrative departments and ministries. On the country's independence in 1961, foreign embassies and other parastatal institutions were established, many of which have their libraries or information centers serving their individual needs. There are about 20 special libraries in addition to libraries in ministries. Many suffer from lack of funds for the purchase of materials, but the collections are useful.

The National Museum Library's basic collection was formed by Captain Butt-Thompson's Library, donated to the museum. This Library serves as a research library for museum users.

**Associations.** There are two associations: the Sierra Leone Library Association, founded in June 1970, and the Sierra Leone School Library Association (1975).

The Sierra Leone Library Association holds workshops, seminars, and conferences to further the general development of libraries in Sierra Leone. It published *The Sierra Leone Library Journal* from 1974 (two issues a year) and a *Directory of Libraries and Information Service* in Sierra Leone.

The Sierra Leone Library Association

*The Central Library in Freetown opened in 1964 and serves as the National Library of Sierra Leone.*

The Sierra Leone School Library Association operates through four regional branches. It holds an annual conference.

GLADYS M. JUSU-SHERIFF

# Singapore

Singapore, a republic on the southern tip of the Malay Peninsula in Southeast Asia, includes the island of Singapore and 50 islets. Pop. (1978 est.) 2,334,400; area 616 sq.km. The official languages are Chinese, English, Malay, and Tamil.

**National Library.** The National Library of Singapore was formally established in 1957 by the Raffles Library Ordinance whereby the former Raffles Library, a subscription library, became a public and national library. It was called the Raffles National Library until December 1960, when the name "Raffles" was dropped. The National Library inherited the legal deposit functions that had been in force since 1886 as well as the archival functions that had been added in 1938. With the National Archives and Records Centre Act of 1967, the archives were separated from the Library and administered as a separate department but continued to be housed in the National Library until 1970 and concurrently headed by the same Director until February 1978. The National Library provides reference services, interlibrary loans and exchanges,

*The children's section in the National Library of Singapore was established in 1957.*

reprographic services, and bibliographic services, including the compilation of the national bibliography, periodicals index, and various union catalogues. Its research collection on Southeast Asia is open to local and overseas scholars and researchers.

The National Library's collection totaled 784,660 volumes in Malay, Chinese, Tamil, and English in 1974 and 1,080,102 in the fiscal year April 1977–March 1978, plus over 49,000 items of special materials, including sheet music and scores, microforms, films, slides, tapes, and recordings.

**Table 1. Archives in Singapore (1976)**

| | |
|---|---|
| Number | 1 |
| Holdings | 4,800 (linear meters) |
| Annual expenditures | S$ 220,000/- |
| Professional staff | 7 |
| All staff | 27 |

Source: National Archives and Records Centre of Singapore, *Annual Report 1976*.

**Academic Libraries.** There are two university libraries, the University of Singapore and Nanyang University; two technical colleges, the Singapore Polytechnic and the Ngee Ann Technical College; one teacher training institution, the Institute of Education; and a private theological college, Trinity College. The University of Singapore was founded in 1949 as the University of Malaya, which amalgamated the former King Edward VII Medical College, founded in 1905, and the Raffles College, founded in 1928. In 1959 the University was split into two autonomous divisions, the University of Malaya in Kuala Lumpur and the University of Malaya in Singapore. From January 1, 1962, the former became known as the University of Malaya and the latter the University of Singapore. The University of Singapore Library has over 600,000 volumes in six constituent libraries—the Main Library and Chinese Library at the Bukit Timah Campus; Architecture, Engineering, and Law Libraries at the new Kent Ridge Campus; and the Medical Library in the Faculty of Medicine building at College Road. Nanyang University, founded in 1956 as a Chinese-language institution, has adopted English as the medium of instruction. A policy of having its first-year students undergo courses jointly with University of Singapore students at Bukit Timah took effect in July 1978.

**Public Libraries.** The National Library operates the public library system, which includes a central library, two full-time branches, three part-time branches, and ten bookmobile points. A third full-time branch opened in November 1978. Loans of books and periodicals totaled over 2,700,000 in 1977, including bulk loans to social welfare homes, community centers, and other agencies. The total number of registered users in 1977–78 was estimated at 14.97 percent of the total population, including 58.28 percent of the primary school population and 40.9 percent of the secondary school population.

**School Libraries.** All 123 secondary schools, 7 junior colleges (which provide two years of preuniversity education), and 12 vocational and technical institutes have centralized libraries. Of the 336 primary schools, 70 percent also have centralized libraries, while the remainder have classroom libraries. There is one School Library Development Officer at the Ministry of Education. A Standing Committee on School Libraries set up in 1970 has drawn up recommended standards for secondary school libraries (1972) and for primary school libraries (1974); it organizes courses for teacher-librarians and places bulk orders of books for school libraries.

**Special Libraries.** There are 16 government libraries staffed by professionals and a few others with subprofessional staff. While most serve only the staff of their ministry-department, some are open to the public, including those of the Department of Statistics and the Department of Trade. In addition there are six libraries of statutory bodies also with professional staff and a number of libraries in such foreign and regional agencies as the American Resource Center, the British Council, the Regional Language Center, and the Colombo Plan Staff College for Technician Education.

HEDWIG ANUAR

**Table 2. Libraries in Singapore (1976)**

| Type | Number | Volumes in collections | Annual expenditures (dollar) | Population served | Professional staff | All staff (total) |
|---|---|---|---|---|---|---|
| National and Public | 1 | 988,824 | S$ 4,035,580/- | 2,278,000 | 84 | 281 |
| Academic | 6 | 1,173,207 | S$ 3,774,137[a] | 15,759 | 60 | 231 |
| School | 363 | 2,243,600 | S$ 867,897[b] | 311,169 | 5 (full-time)<br>8 (part-time) | 20 (full-time)<br>530 (part-time) |
| Special | 23 | 304,527 | S$ 1,516,436 | 155,762 | 27 | 103 |
| Total | 393 | 4,710,158 | S$ 10,194,050 | | 176 | 635 |

[a]Excluding salaries of one library. [b]Excluding salary.

Sources: National Library of Singapore, *Annual Report, April 1976–March 1977;* Unesco, *Statistics on Libraries, 1974;* and replies to questionnaires.

## Somalia

Somalia, a republic of northeastern Africa, on the Indian Ocean and the Gulf of Aden, is bounded by Kenya, Ethiopia, and Djibouti on the west. It lies on the Horn of Africa. Pop. (1978 est.) 3,446,000; area 638,000 sq.km. The official language is Somali.

Library development in Somalia is of a recent origin. The country has no old and well-established libraries, and hardly any tradition exists for library service. Education and literacy did not receive much attention in the colonial times and was of little interest to the vast majority of the people who are nomads; Somali became a written language only after 1971. However, by the 1970's progress had been made in education and mass literacy. The importance of library and information services for supporting national developmental programs is being recognized. Many government departments and agencies planned to set up library and documentation centers. Unesco and countries such as the United States and Italy provided assistance to the country for development of libraries.

**National Library.** There are no public libraries that meet any significant standards. At the most there may be a few reading rooms in some regions of the country. A National Library set up in June 1976 on the initiative provided by Unesco was still in a formative stage of development three years later. Its holdings comprise hardly a few thousand items. Under library legislation of 1976, the Ministry of Higher Education and Culture was given responsibility for library development. In spite of the enactment of library legislation and formulation of guidelines for evolving a national library system, there was no strong commitment on the part of the country to undertake development of libraries within the framework of an over-all plan as the 1980's began.

**Academic Libraries.** The Somali National University has a central library and a few faculty libraries. The Central Library was organized largely with Italian assistance. It has a collection of about 23,000 volumes.

In a proposed new campus of the University, there was provision for a separate library building. Among the faculty libraries, the Library of the College of Education has good facilities and resources, a result of U.S. AID assistance to the College.

The Library of the College of Education has 32,000 volumes, and it includes also textbooks in multiple copies. The libraries of the Faculty of Medicine and Agriculture are also fairly well equipped. Generally speaking, the University Library System is far from adequate for supporting the instructional and research programs.

School libraries do not seem to exist. The Library of the American School has excellent facilities, but it is not a Somali institution.

**Special Libraries.** Some of the ministries and government agencies have set up libraries. Among such special libraries particular mention should be made of the Documentation Center of the State Planning Commission, which was being developed as a Unesco project. It has a fairly comprehensive collection of Somali documents devoted to socioeconomic matters. It also has a good collection of documents of international organizations. It has about 8,000 items in its collection and receives about 200 periodicals. It has initiated a few documentation services. The Somali Institute for Development Administration and Management, another UN project, has a fairly well-established library. The Ministry of Foreign Affairs also established a library. It had good physical facilities, but its collection was yet to be developed by 1979. The Ministries of Agriculture and Livestock and the Somali Development Bank were in the process of organizing their libraries.

The Library of the United Nations Development Programme has a good collection of publications of international organizations. The libraries of foreign missions such as those of the United States, Italy, France, and India are used by the reading public.

The absence of sufficient staff for library and information work proved a serious handicap. Under Unesco projects a few short-term training courses were conducted, but there remained a pressing need for regular training, especially for middle-level staff.

T. S. RAJAGOPALAN

## South Africa

South Africa, a republic on the southern tip of Africa, is bounded on the west and east by the Atlantic and Indian oceans and is surrounded by Botswana, Namibia (South West Africa), Zimbabwe Rhodesia, Mozambique, and Swaziland. Pop. (1978 est.) 24,190,000; area 1,140,943 sq.km. The official languages are Afrikaans and English.

**National and Legal Deposit Libraries.** South Africa has three national libraries: the South African Library (Cape Town), the State Library (Pretoria), and the South African Library for the Blind (Grahamstown). The South African Library, established in 1818, is the oldest of the three; it has Africana and rare book collections and has concentrated on its functions as a national reference and research library in the humanities. The State Library, founded in 1887, serves as the national lending library, coordinates interlibrary loan activities, maintains the Joint Catalogue of Books (the country's union catalogue), and published the *South African National Bibliography* from 1959. The State Library also developed a major microfiche publishing program. The third national library, dedicated to serving the blind, was founded in 1919 and became a national library in 1968. It provides books in braille and on tape.

The country has five legal deposit libraries, which receive a copy of every work published in the country. In addition to the South African Library and State Library, the three other legal deposit libraries are the Library of Parliament (Cape Town), the Natal Society Library (Pietermaritzburg), and the Bloemfontein Public Library.

**Academic Libraries.** Library services to academic staff and students are provided at all 16 universities in



*The South African Library, Capetown, was established in 1818 and is one of three national libraries in the country.*

South African Library

South Africa: Cape Town, Durban-Westville, Fort Hare, Natal (Durban), Natal (Pietermaritzburg), the North, Orange Free State, Port Elizabeth, Potchefstroom, Pretoria, Rhodes, South Africa, Stellenbosch, Western Cape, Witwatersrand, Zululand.

The older university libraries are distinguished by important research and special collections; notable examples on Africana include the Killie Campbell Collection at the University of Natal Library, Durban; the Gubbins, Humphreys, and Jeffreys collections at the University of the Witwatersrand; the Hugh Solomon Collection at the University of Stellenbosch; and the Cory Library for Historical Research at Rhodes University. Because of their resources the university libraries are major links in the interlibrary loan system.

The university libraries led in technological development. The University of the Witwatersrand Library introduced, for example, a computer produced microfiche catalogue for its entire system and a nonprint media resource center. Other libraries strengthened their subject specialist approach to library service and offered sophisticated information systems, including access to on-line data bases.

Libraries also exist in the various colleges, including teacher training colleges, technical colleges, and colleges for advanced technical education.

**Public Libraries.** In the South African context public libraries are best considered in two distinct categories, municipal and provincial libraries.

*Municipal Libraries.* The libraries of all the larger cities have free, tax-supported public libraries. Some are quite highly developed, for example, the Johannesburg Public Library, with its central reference library, with some 24 suburban branch libraries, and with important subject libraries for Africana, Art, Music, and Local Government (one of the largest and most important public libraries, it opened its doors to all races).

*Provincial Libraries.* The majority of public libraries are affiliated to one of the four Provincial Library Services—Cape, Natal, Orange Free State, and Transvaal—established in 1945, 1950, 1948, and 1942, respectively. They provide for the flow of books through regional centers to libraries that are housed and staffed by urban local authorities. In 1975 some 516 public library service points were affiliated with the provincial libraries. Nonprint media, such as art prints, phonograph records, and films, are a feature of these provincial library services.

**School Libraries.** These have undergone major recent development in all three provinces of the country. Credit for their development in the Transvaal belongs to the Transvaal Education Department Library Service, which has a central teachers' library of over 100,000 books and which assists teachers with the choice, purchase, and binding of books in school libraries. The same service has a number of full-time school library advisers who tour the provinces offering advice and guidance in school library administration. The Transvaal is beginning to integrate school audiovisual centers and libraries to form media centers. Regular vacation courses are offered, and manuals are published from time to time. The Cape Provincial Education Department has a similar central school library organization, while in Natal Province the Education Department spearheaded the development of resource centers in schools; models were established in the larger cities. School library services to Coloureds, Indians, and Blacks (the South African official population designations) have also been developing rapidly in recent years.

**Special Libraries.** South Africa has over 350 special libraries of many different kinds. They are found in the public and private sector; in financial, industrial, and mining circles; in government and semigovernmental corporations; in museums and art galleries; and elsewhere. Some 160 libraries covering many subject fields are attached to government departments and form part of the Division of Library Services of the Department of National Education.

**Other Library Aspects.** South Africa has an enviable bibliographical record, with well-developed current and retrospective national and subject bibliographies. There are excellent union catalogues in microfiche of book and periodical holdings, and a computerized national register of manuscripts was in preparation at the end of the 1970's. The country also has a well-developed interlibrary loan and photocopying network, linking the resources found in all the major libraries and in many of the smaller libraries as well.

**Associations.** The South African Library Association was founded in 1930 and in 1978 had a membership of 1,588. The Association functions through seven geographical branches; its newest is a subject branch for law. The branches are coordinated through a central Administrative Council. The Association organizes a biennial conference and publishes a quarterly journal, *South African Libraries,* and a monthly newsletter.

Although segregated associations for Blacks, Indians, and Coloureds were formed in 1960, a decision was taken in September 1978 at a national conference of the Association to unify those associations, in a move toward one professional multiracial organization addressing the interests of the library and information profession in South Africa. The mood and spirit at that conference are perhaps best summarized in the words of a speaker: "The root of the public librarian's philosophy lies in the desire to create the opportunity for access to culture and information to all people, and I believe that restricted access on grounds of race is a professionally untenable attitude that will soon pass into history."

**REFERENCES**

N. Shillinglaw, "The Public Library in South Africa—

**Libraries in South Africa (1975)**

| Type | Number | Volumes in collections | Annual expenditures[a] (rand) | Population served | Professional staff | All staff (total) |
|---|---|---|---|---|---|---|
| National | 3 | 40,783[b] | R 760,488 | N.A. | 56 | 118 |
| Academic | 115[c] | 176,421[b] | R 6,217,004 | N.A. | 436 | 1,186 |
| Public[d] | 694[c] | 560,788[b] | R 14,361,112 | N.A. | 558 | 3,000 |
| School | N.A. | N.A. | N.A. | N.A. | N.A. | N.A. |
| Special[e] | 352[c] | 89,273[b] | R 3,489,269 | N.A. | 254 | 875 |

[a]Includes personnel and acquisition costs.
[b]Linear meters (not volumes).
[c]Library service points.
[d]Includes all public and provincial library services.
[e]Includes government libraries.

Source: *Directory of Southern African Libraries* (1975).

Today and Tomorrow" (South African Library Association, papers presented at conference, Johannesburg, 1978).

L. E. Taylor, *South African Libraries* (1967), is a readable, well-written, wide-ranging survey of the library scene in South Africa and the only comprehensive book. Includes useful background and historical information.

REUBEN MUSIKER

# Spain

Spain, a monarchy in southwestern Europe, is bordered by France, Andorra, and the Bay of Biscay on the north, the Mediterranean Sea on the east and southeast, the Atlantic Ocean on the northwest and southwest, and Portugal on the west. Its territory includes the Balearic Islands (off the east coast) and the Canary Islands (off the west). Pop. (1978 est.) 37,109,000; area 504,750 sq. km. The official language is Spanish.

**National Library.** The National Library of Spain was founded in Madrid in 1712 by King Philip V as a public library. In 1836 it was nationalized and became a governmental unit. In 1896 it was installed in a large and handsome central building. Of all Spanish libraries, it provides the greatest number of services and contains the largest and richest collection, specializing in the humanities—specifically in Spanish culture and language and in its important Hispanic-American Section. The Manuscript Section possesses more than 2,000 medieval codices, the oldest dating from the 10th century. There are many Latin and Spanish codices of greater importance, and there are also many excellent ones in Greek, Arabic, and Hebrew. A significant number of codices are adorned with miniature paintings. The collection of Spanish comedies of the Golden Age includes the manuscripts of such great dramatists as Lope de Vega and Calderón, while the Cervantes Collection contains 13,000 books and 3,000 pamphlets. The Incunabula and Rare Books Section holds 2,938 unique and valuable volumes that were produced before 1500. The Section of Prints and Beaux Arts holds 200,000 prints, engravings, and 14,000 drawings of interest for their themes or such names of Dürer, Velázquez, Rubens, Titian, and Goya. The Music Section contains 100,000 scores and 150,000 records and cassettes, while the Map Section has 100,000 maps and plans. In the Periodical Section there are 30,000 titles, of which 8,000 are current publications.

The Library holds more than 3,000,000 volumes, and in 1977 the collection increased by some 83,000 volumes. Every year it is visited by more than a half-million readers who use twice that number of works. More than 100,000 works are on outside loan, and its laboratories produce more than 300,000 photocopies and 150,000 microfilms upon request of its readers. A quarter of its new acquisitions come by direct purchase, the remainder through donations and exchanges. Half of the collection has developed through legal deposit, a privilege of the Library since its founding (but not always adhered to in the past with the same rigor as in later years), whereby two copies of all printed matter, including sound recordings, must be supplied.

The General Direction of Books and Libraries supervises the function of the nation's libraries, including the National Library, the National Reading Center, and other centers serving the libraries, such as the Center for International Exchange, the Center for Restoration of Books and Documents, and the Registry of Intellectual Property, whose names describe their functions. The National Center for the Documentary and Bibliographic Treasure of the Nation inventories the works that are part of that national heritage and ensures their acquisition when they first appear. The Hispanic Bibliographic Center prepares the national bibliography and enforces the legal deposit system.

**Academic Libraries.** There are great variations among academic libraries in their collections, yearly acquisitions, financial resources, personnel, and services. The libraries of the 22 universities are preeminent, with greater means and services than other centers such as the engineering schools. Although each university library is considered a central unit headed by an individual director, in reality it is divided into different faculty and departmental libraries; the latest items are exclusively for the use of the professors. The faculty libraries are oriented more toward the requirements of the teachers, rather than the study and reading needs of students, who lack places for study. The staff is limited in all of them, but better times may be ahead because of a law on university autonomy and an increase in the number of librarians approved in 1979. Worthy of note are the Madrid Library (the Complutense, at Alcalá de Henares), with 700,000 volumes, as well as Barcelona (Central), Valencia, Zaragoza, and Salamanca, as much for the number of new books acquired each year as for the wealth of their historical collections containing valuable medieval manuscripts and incunabula, these institutions having been established many centuries ago.

**Table 2. State Archives in Spain (1976)**

| | |
|---|---|
| Total | 145 |
| Volume | 550,593 meters |
| Professional staff | 193 |
| All staff (total) | 300 |

Sources: Inspección General de Archivos, *Guía de los Archivos Estatales Españoles; Guia del Investigador* (Madrid: Servicio de Publicaciones del Ministerio de Educación y Ciencia, 1977).

**Public Libraries.** The National Reading Center, under the General Direction of Books and Libraries, is responsible for the promotion of reading among the public through the creation of libraries. Its activities are realized through the Provincial Coordinating Library Cen-

**Table 1. Libraries in Spain (1976)**

| Type | Number | Volumes in collections | Annual expenditures (peseta) | Population served | Professional staff | All staff (total) |
|---|---|---|---|---|---|---|
| National | 2 | 3,242,613 | N.A. | N.A. | 60 | 229 |
| Academic | 306 | 5,462,854 | N.A. | 604,803 | 232 | 1,254 |
| Public | 1,465 | 10,134,372 | N.A. | 19,555,434 | 430 | 2,755 |
| School | 639 | 2,152,437 | N.A. | 627,964 | 87 | 1,411 |
| Special | 342 | 5,762,005 | N.A. | 1,540,656 | 259 | 974 |
| Total | 2,754 | 26,754,281 | | | 1,068 | 6,623 |

Sources: Instituto Nacional de Estadística, *Anuario Estadístico de España* (Madrid, 1978).

ters, a system maintaining a central library in a provincial capital with branches in other municipalities. These are regulated by boards of trustees and sustained by donations from three sources, the central government and the provincial and municipal governments. In 1977, 48 provinces had coordinating centers with 1,245 libraries and 6,554,414 volumes; 13,003,436 readers had used 18,348,814 books. The provincial governments of Navarra and Barcelona employ their own systems, Barcelona's, 50 years old, the most important. Its central library possesses more than a half-million books, and its network of 75 branches serves the neighborhoods of the capital and the provincial municipalities. Aside from a few independent municipal libraries, there are other networks in several provinces maintained by diverse savings banks. In number of libraries, the most important is the network sponsored by the Old Age and Savings Fund of Catalonia.

**School Libraries.** In reality, there are few school libraries that truly merit that designation, although some primary and secondary schools do have collections that are sufficient to constitute a library. Standards for staff, resources, and operations do not as yet exist. The books that make up these collections are in general occasional donations of the Ministry of Education.

**Special Libraries.** There are many special libraries of varying importance serving official and private research centers. First in importance is the Consejo Superior de Investigaciones Científicas (Superior Council of Scientific Research), which has approximately 1,500,000 volumes distributed among two general libraries and 50 other libraries serving specialized centers in science, technology, and the humanities.

In the humanities two royal foundations are distinctive: the libraries of the National Palace and the Monastery of el Escorial. The Palace preserves 300,000 volumes—including priceless manuscripts and incunabula—a collection of fine bindings, and an excellent collection of drawings. El Escorial was founded by King Philip II in the 16th century; although in the 17th century a fire destroyed a great part of its riches, it still may be the most outstanding library in Spain for its collection of rare codices and manuscripts, in such languages as Turkish and Persian, and other significant collections. Mention should also be made of the libraries of the Royal Academies, especially of History, which holds 200,000 books and an ample collection of historical manuscripts, and of Language, with 80,000 volumes. Finally, the Central Library of the Army contains 300,000 books in Spanish history.

**Association.** In 1978 the old professional association was renamed the Asociación de Archiverios, Bibliotecarios, Conservadores de Museos y Documentalistas (Association of Archivists, Librarians, Museum Curators and Documentalists) (ANABAD), to include a section for documentalists. The Association represents its members to Spanish authorities, with whom it collaborates in the improvement of services and in professional international organizations. It sponsors meetings provides scholarships and aid for study trips abroad, and conducts an efficient publishing program reflected in a series of books and particularly in the *Boletin (Bulletin)*. Its official quarters are in the National Library.

HIPÓLITO ESCOLAR-SOBRINO



# Special Libraries

*Undoubtedly one of the greatest problems of the time is to put the knowledge which we possess at work.*

John A. Lapp,
coining the motto of the
Special Libraries Association (1916).

PURPOSE AND OBJECTIVES

Information service is the raison d'être of the special library. While other types of libraries may encompass multiple objectives—education, recreation, aesthetic appreciation, and/or scholarly research—the major, and usually only, objective of the special library is the provision of information in support of the objectives of its parent organization.

The special library may have its own goals and objectives regarding the resources, services, and clientele needed or desired in order to provide such services, but these goals are usually internal to the special library. Indeed, the organization usually has little interest in library service as an end in itself; rather, it is interested in the library and will support it as the means of getting the information it needs. Thus, for the special library to exist it must provide information—it must provide information more efficiently and economically than could be provided by alternative methods, and it must continually demonstrate to the management of its parent organization that it is doing so. If the special library does not accomplish this, it will not thrive; it may even cease to exist. The ultimate decision as to the practicability, efficiency, and value of the special library and the resources that will be allocated to it is made by the parent organization. Such a decision is not based on how well the library is meeting its own goals; it is based on how well the library is providing information service.

Special libraries exist in a wide variety of organizational settings. They are units of larger organizations whose purposes are usually other than the provision of education or library service. Special libraries are found in private business and industrial organizations such as banks, insurance companies, advertising agencies, public utilities, publishers, chemical and pharmaceutical manufacturers, petroleum producers, engineering firms, and the aerospace and automotive industries, to name a few. Others serve federal, state, county, or municipal governments or quasi-governmental agencies. A number of special libraries are in nonprofit institutions such as hospitals and health agencies, social and welfare organizations, and museums or are part of trade and professional associations or societies.

Limited in scope, special libraries are often described (and usually associate or organize) along subject lines because they are oriented to a single subject or, more often, a group of related subjects that comprise a field of activity. This scope is determined by the interests of the parent organization. The library collects and organizes intensively in its primary subject areas, often at a depth impossible for other types of libraries. While the special library may collect some material peripheral to its primary interests, it depends on outside resources for material that is little used or out of scope.

Special libraries serve a limited and well-defined clientele. Most frequently, the special library's clientele is limited to its parent organization, and within this limitation the clientele may range from the personnel of a single department to employees throughout the organization and may or may not extend to the organization's employees in other geographic locations. Some special libraries, such as those maintained by societies and associations, may consider the group's membership or anyone with a serious interest in the subject as their clientele. When the clientele is limited to a particular organization, special libraries often develop close working relationships with their users and are able to identify, not only on an organizational basis, but also on an individual basis the type of information needed and how it should be delivered. Thus, within the special library, services can be closely tailored to fit the needs and working habits of the users. Most special libraries admit outsiders who have a need to use their resources, although such access is usually within the constraints of the parent organization's policy, the library's own staff, space, and time resources, and the confidentiality of unpublished or proprietary (internal) materials in the collection.

One point of view propounds the presence of the special librarian as the distinguishing characteristic of the special library. This view is based on the belief that the special librarian's active role in information service is the main working asset of the library. Without the special librarian's presence the organization might have a library, but it would not have information service. The special librarian serves as a specialist in the literature of the subject, bringing to the organization professional expertise in the identification, acquisition, organization, evaluation, and interpretation of materials. The special librarian's function is not to instruct users in the use of the library but to obtain information for the user, in response to requests and in anticipation of need.

Special libraries have another characteristic that adds to the frame of reference in discussing their nature—size. There are special libraries with scores of employees and hundreds of thousands of volumes in their collections, but surveys and studies of special libraries have found that a majority of them are small in staff, space occupied, and size of collection. Over half of all special libraries are estimated to be one-person (librarian) or two-person (librarian and assistant or clerk) operations.

**Problems of Definition.** The precise definition of *special library* is one of the larger, unresolved issues of librarianship. The literature is littered with definitions ranging from those based on the logic that the term fits all those that are specialized in some way (form, purpose, collection, ownership, or clientele) and therefore may include all libraries through definitions that are based on the presence of a combination of characteristics (special collection or special form and/or ownership) to those definitions that attempt a pragmatic, discrete delineation of a type of library. Even within this last, relatively narrow, type of definition of the special library as distinct from public, college and university, or school library, special libraries display such diversity and individuality that descriptions of characteristics and activities must be broad rather than specific.

*Special library* also still carries with it, as a carry-over from the 19th century, the connotation of a library that does not fit into other categories when, early in the 20th century, the term was adopted to describe an entirely new form of library—the modern special library or information center, located within business, industrial, professional, governmental, and other organizations and designed as a working collection to provide information service for the organization of which it is a part. The modern special librarians wanted to define the "miscellaneous" special libraries out of the term but did not entirely succeed in doing so, particularly in the view of those outside special librarianship.

Another problem in special librarianship arises in defining the difference between the special library and the information center. Most special libraries use the word "library" with a modifier to indicate the scope of the library or its primary clientele. Technical library, business library, corporate library, law library, and research library are common examples. Other styles are used to denote the unit's purpose more clearly or to indicate a greater range of services or to avoid what some regard as a passive connotation of "library." Such variations include information bureau, information center, or information service. These variations also may carry a modifier—technical information center, business information service, among others.

Although the terms library and information center are often used interchangeably, recent developments in the information systems of organizations have led to a greater distinction between the two in the nature and extent of their information service and the forms of material used. The information center often undertakes greater depth of analysis and control of the subject field and provides more advanced information services. It may make heavy use of computers and other advanced technology. Information centers may have a wider variety of materials, including such raw data as company sales and production figures, inventory records, or engineering information. The staff of the information center may include subject specialists, writers, and editors, as well as librarians. The information center may have responsibility for report writing, preparing papers, and other editorial activities, as well as for literature research and evaluation. In very large organizations, the library may be a component of the information center, and the information center itself may be a subsystem of the organization's total management information system.

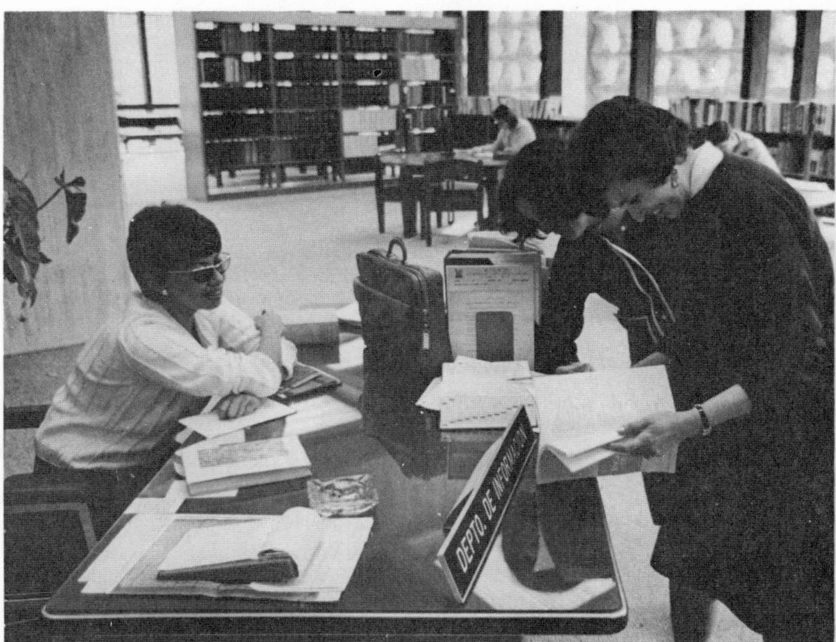


United Nations

*Information desk at the National Agricultural Institute's library, Chapingo, Mexico, one of Central America's largest special libraries.*

**U.S. Growth.** Special libraries first began to appear in significant numbers in the United States in the first decades of the 20th century. They were a new form of library, sharply differentiated from the mainstream of American librarianship at that time in their singleness of purpose and in their eschewal of traditional methods of collection and organization of materials. The early special libraries were largely isolated from each other and invisible to the library community until the founding of the Special Libraries Association in 1909 provided a focal point for the emerging special libraries and leadership for the modern special library movement as it gathered momentum.

Vast changes had begun to take place in American business and industry in the late 19th century. Organizations increased in size and complexity as business and industry moved from smaller entrepreneurial enterprises to larger corporations. Governmental units proliferated and increased in size and jurisdiction. In business and industry, interest in efficiency and scientific management developed. In government there was a strong move toward legislative and social reform. Professional and trade associations and societies with strong interests in standards and education were formed. All of these interests required information to support decision making and action. A whole new business and technical literature, often in nontraditional and ephemeral formats, began to develop with increases in the collection and publication of statistics, the issuance of government regulations, publication of financial reports, and dissemination of business records.

Legislative reference libraries serving state and local governments were among the earliest modern special libraries, becoming models for intensive or "amplified" reference service. Special libraries in business and financial organizations emerged next to "manage" business and financial materials. These libraries also developed high levels of information service for a clientele relatively unfamiliar with the use of print.

The exigencies of World Wars I and II and the information explosion of the post-World War II years contributed to the continuation of an environment hospitable to the establishment of special libraries. Following both wars there was an expansion in the need for scientific and technical research. Research and development became increasingly institutionalized, and the number and size of research departments and organizations grew as the research team supplanted the individual investigator. This growth was paralleled by the increase and expansion of scientific and technical libraries to support the research and to cope with the ever increasing flow of published results.

Although efforts have been under way since the late 1950's to develop census statistics for special libraries, there had not been an accurate count of the number of special libraries in existence by the end of the 1970's. The problem of definition, the great diversity of special libraries, and their poor visibility because of small size or nonparticipation in the library community are the barriers to statistics on special libraries. Although some segments of the field—medical, law, and government libraries—have been surveyed, a large segment of the special library universe remains unexplored.

Such figures as are available are derived as byproducts of directories. The *American Library Directory* (31st ed., 1978) reports 10,991 special libraries, including law, medical, and religious libraries not affiliated with colleges and universities in the United States and 825 special libraries in Canada. The other principal directory, Young, Young, and Kruzas's *Directory of Special Libraries and Information Centers* (3rd ed., 1976), reports 12,540 special libraries including those affiliated with public and university libraries in the United States and 1,459 in Canada.

Despite the inability to document an exact number of special libraries, growth has been one of their outstanding characteristics in the past, and all evidence points to continued growth. The factors that gave rise to the emergence of special libraries in the past have not disappeared; they are stronger than ever before and spreading in influence as new industries and new organizations evolve. The challenge of putting information to work continues to grow.

**Other Countries.** While the study of special libraries on an international scale is in its early days, the pattern of the U.S. special library movement has been repeated around the world as special libraries emerge in other nations as industrialization and increased research lead to a need for more information resources.

In Great Britain, France, Germany, and other industrialized nations, special libraries were being established in the first decades of the 20th century, and their rate of growth, particularly in the scientific and technical fields, increased to meet the demand for support of increased research activities in the postwar periods. As nations continue to industrialize and increase their research efforts, special libraries have been established in government ministries and agencies, research institutes, and private business and industry in nations around the world, including the developing countries. Many U.S. corporations with international facilities have libraries in their foreign subsidiaries and affiliates. The spread of special libraries around the world is illustrated by the action in 1976 of the International Federation of Library Associations to transform its Special Libraries Section into the Special Libraries Division. The Division includes six Sections—administrative libraries, geography and map libraries, social science libraries, astronomical and geophysical libraries, biological and medical science libraries, and science and technology libraries. Two Round Tables, for art and music libraries, have also been established within the Division.

SERVICES TO USERS

*The major advantage of an information function is that it can find the answers for the inquirer more rapidly than he could himself. To this might be added that it can also provide answers which the inquirer needs but has not thought to request.*

Herbert S. White,
"Organizational Placement
of the Special Library,"
*Special Libraries* (1973).

The special library provides two basic types of information service. The first is that provided in response to requests for information and encompasses reference and research services. The second is information service in anticipation of need and encompasses services designed to keep the library's clientele up to date on new and current information—usually described as current awareness services.

The major effort in the special library is devoted to the dissemination of information through these services; all other functions support such information services. All decisions concerning allocation of the library's resources, and particularly staff resources, between acquiring and organizing materials and information service must take this into account.

**Reference Services.** Reference and research services range from answering simple reference questions to undertaking complex research and literature searches. The special librarian may assist requesters who wish to pursue their own search, but more often the librarian, as the information expert whose function is to save the inquirer's time, is the primary user of the library, locating the information and transmitting it in the most useful form.

The special librarian's expertise in information handling may be applied to a reference question that requires a specific answer—a name, an address, a copy of an annual report, or an article. Most special libraries devote a good deal of time to literature searches, either comprehensive or limited by a time period, language, or other parameter; the result may be a bibliography, though more often the information is interpreted in a memorandum or report. The inquirer may request several "relevant" articles, and the librarian makes the decision on what is relevant. Unless the inquirer requests the information in a certain form, it is left to the librarian, on the basis of the results of the search and knowledge of the inquirer's preference and working habits, how best to present the information.

Some special libraries are involved in translations, either providing in-house translation service or obtaining them from outside sources. Many serve as the centralized source for ordering publications and subscriptions for the organization as well as for the library to eliminate unnecessary duplication of materials.

Special librarians, particularly those whose primary clientele is located within an organization, develop a close working relationship with their users. They learn their ongoing information needs and interests; they learn how to negotiate requests effectively; they learn how the inquirer wants the information delivered. The alert special librarian also tries to anticipate need so that information can be collected and, when desirable, disseminated in advance of need.

**Current Awareness Service.** Special libraries have developed a wide range of activities to keep their clientele informed of new and current developments. Such services may be directed to the organization as a whole or tailored to the individual client. Some also make their current awareness services available to a secondary clientele—to other offices or libraries in the organization, to special libraries in other organizations, or to individual subscribers.

Routing of current periodicals is one of the most common functions of the special library. The library periodically surveys its clientele as to which periodicals they wish to see on a regular basis, then circulates them to readers as they arrive. Acquisition bulletins are another common service. The bulletin may be a simple list of new material received or may include annotations or abstracts. Subject-oriented abstract bulletins that pull together information from various sources—books, articles, pamphlets, reports—and news summaries and digests are other current awareness services used by the special library. Some libraries prepare indexes to cover nonindexed periodicals, which may be used within the library or may be published to serve as combination bulletins and order forms for readers.

**SDI.** More sophisticated current awareness services have been developed. Such systems, usually known as Selective Dissemination of Information, or SDI, match the individual user's interests against incoming information, resulting in a personalized service for each user. In the special library with a relatively small clientele, the librarian may be well acquainted with individual interests; in larger special libraries, the SDI system may be card-file or computer based. Some special libraries now supplement, or substitute for, their own SDI services with other services offered by commercial abstract and index services.

The U.S. Copyright Law of 1976, which became effective in January 1978, has affected current awareness services. Many special libraries, after consultation with their organization's legal counsel, have altered such practices as honoring requests for photocopies or have ceased to publish some digests and news summaries. Some are substituting commercial services for in-house ones. There undoubtedly is some restrictive effect on the cost, efficiency, and availability of current awareness services in special libraries.

**Three Levels.** The nature and extent of information services offered by the individual special library varies according to the working habits and needs of its primary clientele and according to its own staff and collection resources. If the clientele is very large in proportion to the library staff or if the clientele is made up of users who, as part of their jobs, perform their own research, then the library staff is engaged more with general reference work, fact checking, advising on research problems, or performing research involving unfamiliar subjects or use of outside resources than in literature research. On the other hand, if the library is primarily responsible for the conduct of literature research and the provision of information, then the staff become the primary users of the library and function at a more intensive level of service.

Three functional levels are sometimes used to describe the range of services provided by the special librarian. At the minimum level of information service, the librarian disseminates information and materials, answers reference questions, directs users needing detailed or research information to possible sources, and handles such simple current awareness services as periodical routing. At the intermediate level, the special librarian adds literature searches, bibliography preparation, selection and transmittal of research materials, and additional current awareness services such as acquisition bulletins. At the maximum level of service, the special librarian becomes the primary user of the library and adds to or substitutes for the activities already described the synthesis and evaluation of information into written form, preparation of critical bibliographies, evaluative, comprehensive literature searches, and more complex current awareness services such as SDI systems. The information center concept is best exemplified at the maximum level of service.

Most special libraries do not function at a single level of service; rather, the individual library operates at various levels, depending on the needs of its clientele. Nevertheless, the ultimate goal of the special library may be to function at the maximum level of information service whenever given the opportunity to do so.

## COLLECTIONS

*The proper view of printed things is, that the stream thereof need not be anywhere completely stored behind the dykes and dams formed by the shelves of any library . . . but from that stream as it rushes by expert observers should select what is pertinent, hold it as long as it continues to have value to those for whom he selects it, make it easily accessible by some simple process, and then let it go.*

John Cotton Dana,
"The Evolution of the Special Library,"
*Libraries: Addresses and Essays* (1914).

Special library collections are working collections to provide support for information services. Their emphasis is on current and up-to-date information, with the extent of retrospective material determined by need and use patterns and available outside resources. Although some collections may concentrate on a single format, e.g., pictures, clippings, or maps, special library collections typically include a wide variety of formats. Some special libraries, particularly those in scientific and technical areas, will have collections that are largely in the traditional formats of books, journals, and technical reports. Other special libraries have collections whose significance lies in their vertical files of information found in business records and data and ephemeral material.

While its size may be physically small, the special library collects in great depth in its primary areas of interest and includes materials not found in other types of libraries. A union list of special library periodical holdings in a large metropolitan area showed that a substantial portion of the titles were not available in other types of libraries.

Some of the larger subject groupings of special library collections include: advertising and marketing, aerospace, biological sciences, business and finance, chemistry, education, engineering, environmental sciences, food and nutrition, insurance, law, metals/materials, nuclear science, petroleum, pharmaceuticals, physics, public utilities, legislative reference, social welfare, and transportation. Even within these broad groups, individual libraries display a wide diversity of subject interests. A transportation library may cover all forms of transportation, or it may focus on automotive, air, railroad, or urban transportation and further specialize by technical, business, or consumer aspects of transportation. Insurance libraries may specialize in one or more branches of insurance—life, property, health, casualty—and such related areas as actuarial science, insurance law, marketing, and insurance education for employees.

Libraries that serve such organizations as accounting firms, advertising agencies, banks and other financial institutions, law firms, and consultants in many fields will encompass not only accounting, advertising, banking, or law but also the subject areas represented by their present and prospective clients.

The subject scope of the collection is not static but

Cami L. Loucks, Trinity Lutheran Hospital, Kansas City

*The Midwest Research Institute's Library supports a wide variety of research projects.*

dynamic. As related subjects, new products or services, merger or acquisitions, or the extension of interdisciplinary methods affect the parent organization, they also affect the subject scope of the special library. The special librarian must be constantly alert to possible new areas and the changing interests of the organization in order to build the library's collection in anticipation of the demands for information.

Special library collections have three major components; the first is published information, the second internally generated information, and the third the information available from sources outside the organization.

**Published Information.** In most special libraries, periodicals provide the most current and up-to-date information; in some they provide the only information. Thus, although books are important in some special libraries, periodicals often form a large and important segment of the collection. Periodical collections include not only research journals but also the many business and trade magazines and newsletters published for specialized audiences.

Vertical file materials are another major resource in the special library. Such collections bring together large and small bits of information from such varied sources as clippings, pamphlets, speeches, statistical compilations, advertising brochures, sales literature and samples, trade catalogues, annual reports and financial statements, patents, and government documents.

Technical reports—the results of government-supported research and development and industry research—are an important and sometimes overwhelming part of the special library collection, especially in scientific and technical fields. Such reports figured largely in the information explosion of the post-World War II period. In the early years of this period, special libraries scrambled frantically to bring some sort of order to the acquisition and control of technical reports. Special indexing and cataloguing techniques were developed; many special librarians were able to use their organizations' computers to assist them in the compilation of catalogues and indexes. The situation has improved since the mid-1960's as various commissions studied the needs of producers, users, and governments for information control and transfer, and various public and private agencies were established to attack the problem. A notable development in the control of government reports was the creation in 1970 of the National Technical Information Service, an agency of the U.S. Department of Commerce.

Other formats are also found in special library collections. Many have files of maps, pictures, audiovisual materials, and realia. Microforms are used to add retrospective resources and/or to conserve space.

**Internal Information.** The second major component of the collection is internally generated information: company and department research reports, technical memoranda, laboratory notebooks, working papers, company correspondence, house organs and newsletters, sales literature, and company and competitive advertising. The library usually makes a conscious decision either to be responsible for collecting all or part of the company's internal material or to collect only such information as is germane to its primary clientele. A library in a research department may be responsible for the department's file of research reports and working papers but may collect only those reports issued by other departments that are useful to the research department. Some special libraries maintain the corporate archives, and some are responsible for records management and/or general files. These are usually separate functions and added to the library's primary function of information service.

The presence of internal material in the special library is sometimes a barrier to use of the collection by outsiders. In practice, however, such material usually is either removed before the outside user is given access to the file or is isolated from the general collection and is thus kept confidential.

**Outside Resources.** Use of outside resources is the third component of the special library collection. It is said that a special librarian's best friend is the local directory of special libraries and, indeed, one of the long-standing traditions of special librarianship is informal cooperation with other special libraries. Special libraries also use public, academic, and large research libraries through more formal interlibrary loan procedures, supporting such use by purchasing company library cards or memberships or by paying user fees. Special libraries have benefited, as have individual users, from multitype library cooperatives and networks which provide access to resources that might otherwise be closed to them. They also seek both unpublished and published information from research organizations, professional and trade associations, and subject experts.

The special library's use of outside resources has a practical basis in that it permits special librarians to extend their resources by relying on information available to them elsewhere. They can thereby concentrate on their primary subject areas, acquiring the most heavily used materials for their own collections. Use of outside resources also has a philosophical basis in the special librarian's intention and ability to tap all available resources.

**Organization.** In addition to acquisition of purchased and free materials through the usual channels, the special library often acquires the core of its collection by consolidating materials scattered in offices around the institution. This process of consolidation usually brings to light a vast amount of both published and internal material that may be used by a few but, because of its lack of organization, is unknown to the majority of the staff.

The decision as to what to process and keep is as important as what to acquire. Weeding of outdated, nonessential information goes on constantly, and retention policies are used to keep the size of the collection under some control. In spite of such rigid measures, however, collections do tend to grow rapidly. One estimate suggests a newly established special library will double in size and space requirements within five years.

Special libraries employ a wide spectrum of methods of organization, with an emphasis on flexibility and adaptability to changing needs. While simple methods of organization are used wherever possible, special libraries also develop specialized, detailed systems where needed. Organization, while the key to efficient use of the collection, must also be balanced against the higher priority of information service.

Special libraries with small collections and limited staff usually operate at a minimum level of organization. Material is arranged in a simple, logical order—books by author or subject, periodicals by title and date, vertical file materials under broad subject headings, and other materials similarly. The catalogue, if there is one, may be limited to one or two entries per item. As the collection increases in size and as the need is felt, more formal methods of organization are added or substituted.

Some special libraries adopt or adapt one of the larger classification systems—the Dewey Decimal or Library of Congress classification. Others use a classification designed for their subject area; although some special libraries develop their own classification systems, most find an existing system to be suitable, with adaptation and expansion, for their relatively small book collections.

In subject analysis, special libraries can select from one of the large, general subject heading lists, from the many specialized subject heading lists and thesauri, or, again, develop their own. However, even when a subject heading list or thesaurus is published in their subject field, individual special libraries generally need to adapt and supplement the list in order to achieve maximum effectiveness for their areas of interest and in order to coincide with the vocabulary of their own organization. The card or book catalogue will also become more complex with additional entries per item. Printed cards may be used, or cataloguing information may be provided through an online source such as OCLC.

As in information service, special libraries seldom function at a single level of organization, nor do they process each item to the same degree. Rather, the maximum organizational effort is devoted to the in-depth subject analysis of the most important information. Any one item, no matter what its form, will be given the amount of processing it needs to be retrieved most efficiently, according to the importance of the information it contains, its probable use, the length of time it will be retained, and the availability of published guides to it.

Another consideration that affects how the library is organized is who actually uses it. If most of the actual physical use is by the library staff itself, many organizational shortcuts can be taken. On the other hand, if a large number of users come to the library, then the organization must be made more clear to facilitate access. Although some adopt an overall organization for the entire collection, most special libraries consist of separate segments, each arranged according to the use and need factors described above.

**Retrieval.** Abstracting and indexing are of paramount importance in the special library. Special libraries have a long tradition of indexing, first because there were no indexes or abstracts that covered their areas of interest and later, as commercial indexes became available, to supplement such coverage. The purpose of indexing may be to provide in-depth analysis of important information. It may focus on a new subject of vital interest to the organization or on material, for example, trade magazines and newsletters, important to the field but not covered in commercial indexes. Internal material is frequently indexed in depth, and while reports are most often treated in this way, the library may also index memoranda, minutes, house organs, and other internal documents. Some special libraries make their indexes available outside their parent organization; a few offer them on a subscription basis.

Special librarians were among the early developers of the newer methods of information retrieval in both manual and computer-based applications. Today, with the increasing availability of commercial abstract and index services in both printed and machine-readable form, there is some degree of commercial coverage in most subject fields. Many special libraries continue their own indexing and abstracting, however, to meet their needs more specifically.

ADMINISTRATION

> *To be successful the business librarian must learn to speak and understand the language of business . . . not only to be able to serve his constituents, but also to function as an accepted member of the professional and managerial staff of a modern corporation.*
>
> Shirley Echelman,
> "Libraries Are Businesses, Too,
> *Special Librarires* (1974).

There are two key aspects to the consideration of special library administration. One is its administrative relationship to its parent organization; the other is its internal administration.

The place the special library occupies in the structure of its parent organization varies according to what part of the organization it serves and how the organization is structured. If it is established to serve the entire organization, its optimal location is one in which it is directly accessible to its clientele and from which it can build and maintain effective, direct communication with all departments. Personnel have direct access to the library and do not ordinarily have to go through administrative channels to use the library or request service. Similarly, the special librarian has direct access to and communication links with the clientele. The library whose primary clientele is a single department or division typically would be located with that department.

The special library may be directly under the cognizance of top management, with the librarian reporting directly to the chief executive officer or to an administrative assistant to the officer. More often, whether it is a separate department or a subunit of a department, the library will be part of research and development, administrative services, public relations or public information, editorial, or the information systems division, reporting to the senior executive in charge of that area. Many special librarians are on a middle management level, not more than two levels from the top.

In addition to the importance of organizational location for effective communication, the library's place in the hierarchy and, particularly, the reporting channel are important for facilitating general communication with the decision makers. The special library not only must provide an efficient and economic information service but also must be able to demonstrate to management that it is doing so and must educate management in the resources required to provide such service. Frequently, the library's users, while in the best position to appreciate and understand the library and its needs, are not among the decision makers who determine its support.

The special library within the research and development, editorial, or management information systems area operates in a close relationship with those who use information, appreciate its value, and recognize the library as a tool in their work; the executive in charge is likely to be in a better position to understand and endorse the library's needs. On the other hand, the library that is under administrative services (perhaps along with the mail room and the cafeteria), or reports to an administrative assistant, may have direct access to the decision-making level but may be reporting to an executive who has little direct experience with library service and only a vague idea of how it contributes to the organization.

Although the practice is not widespread, some special libraries have an advisory committee drawn from the organization's personnel or membership. The advisory committee may act on day-to-day operations or aid in selecting materials, or it may advise on such matters as goals and evaluating services.

While most organizations maintain one library, some large organizations have two or more separate libraries. When divisions of an organization are geographically separate, separate or branch libraries are often established in various locations. While some organizations consolidate business, technical, legal, and other subjects in one library, a more common pattern is to provide separate libraries, conveniently located near the appropriate departments. These intraorganizational libraries may operate autonomously, coordinating matters of common interest on an informal basis, or may be directed by one senior person. A survey of special libraries in large industrial corporations identified five corporations with more than 20 libraries, the largest having 32. One firm had 25 libraries, of which 23 were scientific and technical and 2 were business libraries. Of these libraries, 21 were in the United States, 2 in Canada, and 2 in other nations.

In a few cases, the parent organization may qualify for a grant or other outside assistance, and the special library may obtain some outside funding. In general and for the vast majority of libraries, however, funding comes from the library's parent organization, and its accounting and budgeting procedures are set by the organization. Although budgeting and costs are widely discussed by special librarians, concrete cost figures for establishing and maintaining special libraries have not been gathered on a regular basis. The great diversity of budgeting procedures and differing levels of service make standard reporting difficult, and many libraries do not have the prerogative of revealing such information. However, some generalizations have been made over the years.

It has been found that in certain fields from 2 to 3 percent up to 9 or 10 percent of the research budget is generally allocated for libraries in research and development; in other fields the expenditures are probably comparable for comparable levels of service. Some business and social science libraries with maximum service objectives may have higher budgets because the literature they cover is not as well indexed as scientific and technical literature. The library must therefore devote more professional time to organizing and indexing as well as searching, and the budget must cover the higher cost of doing so.

Since virtually all organizations classify the cost of the library as an overhead or indirect expense, the library budget is thus vulnerable to pressures within the organization to reduce overhead. The special library may allocate or charge some of its expenses directly; the library in a service organization, for example, may be able to charge project research time to a client, thus transforming part of the overhead to a direct cost. Such charges may include library overhead or may be limited to staff or computer time. While this practice results in a reduction of the cost of the library as an overhead expense, it also increases pressure on the library to bill as much of its time as possible and, correspondingly, to spend less time on nonbillable activities. A common method of distributing library costs indirectly is on a pro-rata basis to departments or budgetary units within an organization.

The special library operating budget includes the categories of personnel, materials and computer time, equipment and supplies, and professional dues and meetings. The library may or may not be responsible for such overhead allocated costs as space occupied, utilities, and other office services. Personnel has generally taken 60 to 80 percent of the special library budget; materials and computer time, the major part of the rest. However, several recent studies of scientific and technical libraries and information centers indicate that this proportion is changing toward 50 percent for personnel as materials and computer time figure larger in the budget.

Studies have found, as noted earlier, that about half of all special libraries fall into the categories of one- or two-person libraries; about 65 percent have three or fewer staff members. The special librarian is thus at once a manager, a librarian, and a subject specialist. The special librarian needs the same professional skills needed in other libraries and must also be able to respond to the library's special users and deal effectively as part of the organization. One of the continuing debates in special librarianship is whether the special librarian should be primarily a subject specialist, a librarian, or both. Ideally, the special librarian will have a library degree and some education or equivalent experience in the organization's areas of interest. Although the special librarian is equipped through a library education to obtain a working knowledge of a subject and its literature, organizations often feel more comfortable with a subject specialist. The organization understands what the subject specialist knows; it is less likely to understand what the librarian knows. Often experience makes the librarian a subject expert, for with a few exceptions (law and medical librarians, for example), there are few library school offerings designed to produce librarians in subject specialties germane to business and industry.

In addition to library and subject skills, the special librarian must have a strong motivation toward service, flexibility in procedures, and aggressiveness in promoting the library to the organization. Managerial skills are also needed since the librarian functions as a staff executive in the organization as well as a manager of the library staff.

In the small special library, the librarian must assume all professional responsibilities; as staff size increases, specialization becomes possible. Additional professional staff may include reference personnel, cataloguers, indexers, abstracters, literature specialists, or translators. The issue of professional staffing commonly arises in organizations seeking to establish a new library, in some smaller special libraries, and sometimes in larger libraries adding professional staff. This issue has been dubbed the "smart secretary syndrome." While the organization may perceive that it needs information service, it is unsure how this is accomplished and unfamiliar with the professional qualifications of the librarian. Management will attempt to staff the special library with a secretary or a junior staff member. Such a person eventually may be able to organize and maintain a library but is generally found to be unable to provide effective information service.

Another matter, also related to management's imperfect perception of the library's function and the requirements for provision of information service, is the problem of noninformation service responsibilities. Again, new and small special libraries are particularly vulnerable. In some instances, management expects the special librarian to handle records management, mail room, or other duties unrelated to the operation of the library with the result that only part-time attention is devoted to the library. While in larger special libraries the director may, as a secondary responsibility, supervise nonlibrary functions, the library has sufficient additional professional and clerical staff to provide full-time information service. In the small special library, information services suffer when the attention of the special librarian is diverted.

The minimum staffing level for a special library is considered to be one professional and one clerical person; in larger special libraries a ratio of one professional to two clerical assistants is often found. The small and new special library often has difficulty in obtaining a clerical assistant. The clerical assistant in the small special library works closely with the librarian and frequently gets considerable training in reference work, as well as performing clerical duties. As staff size increases, specialization at the clerical level may evolve into such positions as secretary, acquisitions clerk, file clerk, or typist.

The library's physical facilities should be designed in relation to its role, how it achieves its goals, how its staff operates, and what the future is likely to hold. The contents of the library have a direct bearing on space and furniture requirements, as does the amount of time devoted to administrative, bibliographic, information, and clerical functions. The library's space must also be physically contiguous and separate. While the small special library may occupy only a few thousand square feet of floor space, scattering shelving down hallways or in conference and storage rooms cuts down on efficiency, accessibility, and control. One major factor in space allocation is the nature of use; the library that is used primarily by the library staff will allocate less space for browsing and study areas than the library in which users frequently come in to do research or reading. Finally, space for growth must be provided. Although the special library weeds its collection of unused, outdated materials and may turn to microforms to conserve space, the collection still grows, and adequate space for expansion must be allowed.

Cami L. Louks

*The Kansas City Art Institute's Library provides books and graphic materials for students, curators, and researchers.*

MEASUREMENT AND EVALUATION

> *[Business] appreciates and at times is mildly grateful for the Library's service; but it has shown no great discernment when it came to an understanding of the means by which the service was rendered. It asks for and expects results, but has little appreciation of the price at which results must be bought.*
>
> Daniel N. Handy,
> "The Library as a Business Asset,"
> *Special Libraries* (1912).

The ultimate measure of the special library's value is its continued existence. In profit-making and nonprofit organizations, there are competitive pressures for the available resources. The library, along with other overhead services, is particularly vulnerable to such pressures, and the special library is continually challenged to demonstrate its contribution. This challenge is made even more difficult when it is taken into account that the lingua franca of many organizations is economic, while the economics of information are yet dimly understood.

The major concern of the special library and management has been to evaluate the library and its services according to its effectiveness in meeting its clientele's information needs. The traditional statistics that measure library activity are collected and used by some special libraries. While such statistics as collection size, processing volume, number of users, and reference and research activity are useful measures of certain library activities, they do not reflect the depth, quality, relevance, or effectiveness of information service. Further, such statistics are time-consuming to collect and so are of relatively low priority in the special library with limited staff time.

Special library collections do not lend themselves well to statistical description. Although some may have significant book collections, in many the journal is predominant, and the size of the periodical collection is far more significant. For many special libraries the number of vertical file drawers, technical reports, pictures, maps, or clippings may be more significant. In any case, size of the collection and growth rate are not as important as the relevance of the materials and the use made of them. Counts of books catalogued, material processed, or number of items indexed or abstracted may indicate that the library is busy but mean little to management. Similarly, circulation statistics (where there is a formal circulation system) do not reflect either use of materials in the library or the output of information in the form of verbal messages, written memoranda, or reports—both of which may be more significant.

Statistics on the number of users and of reference and research requests do relate more directly to information service and, to some extent, as indicators of who is using the library and what type of information is being sought. The special library usually can measure its potential user population as the total number of employees or members of the organization to whom services of the library are available. User statistics are somewhat more difficult to collect since few special libraries have any type of registration and the count of users must take into account on-site use, telephone or written requests, and those who are on routing or distribution lists. Reference and research statistics, to be at all meaningful, must be based on the relative levels of service provided—how much reference, how many bibliographies, how many memoranda or reports, and the like.

On an informal basis the special librarian is uniquely able to evaluate the effectiveness of information service. The librarian has constant feedback through day-to-day interaction with users and can evaluate how well the library is meeting the information needs of the users and adjust services to meet the organization's changing needs. Formal user surveys are undertaken from time to time to evaluate library services. The survey may be conducted by the library itself, management, or an outside consultant, and various methods, including personal interviews or questionnaires, may be used. A typical survey covers services used and users' satisfaction with the quality, relevance, and promptness of service.

The orientation of the user to the library and its information services—obtained either by statistics of use, user surveys, or informal response—is the most generally applied method of evaluating the special library's contribution to the goals of the organization on the theory that if the special library meets or exceeds the demands of its users, it is providing effective service.

There is current research and interest in the use of cost/effectiveness and cost/benefit analyses to evaluate information systems and special libraries. Cost/effectiveness centers on the relationship between level of performance and the costs of achieving that level; cost/benefit refers to the relationship between the benefits of a particular product or service and the costs of providing it. Research into cost/effectiveness measurement has emphasized the criteria of coverage, recall (the ability to retrieve wanted

Cami L. Louks

*Compact shelving systems can ease the space burden for special libraries.*

items), precision (the ability to avoid retrieval of unwanted items), response time, and amount of effort required from the user. These measures have been developed for single information systems and to compare alternative systems in system coverage, indexing policies and procedures, system vocabulary, searching procedures, and system/user interaction. However, they have not yet been widely adopted for use in special libraries and information centers.

The ideal measure of the special library or information center's worth would be cost/benefit analysis. Cost/benefit has been successfully applied to certain special library operations and to specific instances of information service. However, while the total costs of maintaining the special library can be identified, it has not yet been shown that it is possible to identify the total benefits of information service in economic terms.

While in some instances the special library may be able to say that the location of a specific bit of information was worth *x* dollars saved in research costs or that the expenditure of *y* dollars of library staff time saved a greater dollar value of the user's time, it is not so easy to put a dollar value on such benefits as the general contribution to the knowledge of the staff, improvement of productivity due to this knowledge, or time and resources freed for other activities—in other words, the general contribution to business efficiency.

## COOPERATION

> *Give me the . . . telephone book . . . a desk with a pad of paper, my present acquaintance with the Special Libraries Association . . . and I should not be afraid to offer myself as a special librarian to many a business house.*
>
> Guy E. Marion,
> "Résumé of the Association's Activities,"
> *Special Libraries* (1916).

Cooperation is one of the cornerstones of special librarianship. Pioneer special librarians at the turn of the century recognized that effective and efficient information service depended on extending the individual library's resources through cooperation with other libraries. The specialized library associations proved to be a strong force in facilitating cooperation, providing leadership in cooperative projects, and as a forum for communication. Within the U.S., Special Libraries Association and its geographic Chapters and subject-oriented Divisions, three activities have been commonly used to facilitate resource sharing: directories of special libraries, union lists of serials, and exchange of materials. Within six months of its founding, the SLA had published its first directory of special libraries (April 1910); over the next 40 years, four more editions were published. Although after the mid-1950's other directories began to serve as national inventories of special libraries, SLA issued the *SLA Directory: Institutions Where SLA Members Are Employed* (1977) in response to requests from its members. Local and regional directories of special libraries and their subject specializations have been an important part of Chapter activities. Boston special librarians produced the first regional directory in 1920, and since then most of the SLA Chapters have done likewise. A number of Chapters have similarly produced local and regional union lists of serial holdings in special libraries, and many coordinate exchange of materials through duplicate exchanges.

In the United Kingdom functions and activities similar to those of SLA are conducted by Aslib, founded in 1924 as the Association of Special Libraries and Information Bureaux. With over 2,000 individual and institutional members, Aslib publishes a research journal, *Aslib Proceedings,* a current awareness publication, *Aslib Information,* and a variety of monographic and reference works. It sponsors frequent seminars, workshops, and training courses.

The need for bibliographic access and control of technical, nontraditional, and specialized subject literature has also been the focus of cooperative efforts. The *Industrial Arts Index* and *Public Affairs Information Service* both had their genesis as cooperative efforts of special librarians. SLA's Engineering-Aeronautical Section began an index of translations in 1946 that evolved into the Translations Center at the John Crerar Library. SLA units also initiated such publications as *Unlisted Drugs, Technical Book Review Index, Scientific Meetings, Dictionary of Report Series Codes,* and countless bibliographies published in *Special Libraries* and as monographs.

Traditionally, informality has been the predominant characteristic of special library cooperation in resource sharing. Such informality has been possible because the local groups of special librarians have tended to be small and closely knit, forming "old boy networks" in which special librarians can operate, with some discretion, even when their parent organizations are competitive. Despite the development of more formal single and multitype cooperatives and networks, informality will probably continue to characterize the cooperative relationships special librarians maintain among themselves simply because informal cooperation works so well.

At the most basic level, cooperation in resource sharing among special libraries is on an ad hoc basis with no long-term commitments. However, in a number of instances, special libraries in physical proximity, ranging from a region of several counties to an area as small as a complex of office buildings, may develop more lasting relationships that are usually based on union lists, sharing of responsibility for long-term retention of journals, or, more recently, groups of users of bibliographic utilities.

Cooperative relationships also have been initiated by the special libraries within a single company. Although some very large organizations with multiple special libraries in various locations sometimes provide a centralized organizational structure for their library and information services, more often they do not. In such instances the special libraries serving the autonomous or decentralized units will develop cooperative relationships to share resources and coordinate activities. Such intraorganization systems may evolve into more formalized relationships as the advantages of coordination grow.

Modern special libraries, despite their contributions

to librarianship and access to specialized literature, have continued to be separated from the mainstream of librarianship. Special libraries are an information resource that is little known and poorly understood. In the 1970's significant moves were made on both sides to bring the resources of special library collections and expertise to bear on total information resources and to show the special library to be an effective part of the library community at large.

In the United States special libraries followed the proceedings of the various government committees and commissions concerned with scientific and technical communications and libraries. Nevertheless, until the establishment of the current National Commission on Libraries and Information Science (NCLIS), they were largely bypassed, except in the role of users, as active contributors to national information resources. As recently as 1967, when the National Advisory Commission on Libraries prepared its report, the focus of attention was on the barriers to special library participation in networks. As multitype library networks have emerged, however, special libraries have strongly supported and participated in them, demonstrating that some of these barriers are not insurmountable.

Underlying the development of the multitype cooperative has been the concept of the mobilization of total library resources to meet the needs of all users without regard to the type of library. This concept was the philosophical basis for the inclusion of special libraries in such networks. A survey showed that almost 90 percent of all multitype cooperatives include special libraries.

The role that special libraries will play in total library resources is still evolving, just as networks themselves are in the process of evolution. Networks have proved to be a valuable tool for special libraries in gaining access to additional resources that were otherwise closed to them—as was indeed expected by those who identified special libraries as potential network users. The special library's potential contribution to networking is also beginning to be recognized as network experience accumulates. While special library use of outside resources has revealed their limitations, it has not yet revealed their strengths in in-scope coverage or in the special librarian's subject expertise and experience in information service.

The Illinois Regional Library Council found that its special library members hold a considerable number of serial titles not represented elsewhere in the state. The special libraries are serving as specialized subject centers, with about 11 percent of user referrals going from public and academic libraries to special libraries. Special librarians are also committing a significant amount of time to the governance and projects of the network.

If other types of libraries have reservations about including special libraries in networks, then special librarians also have reservations about joining them. Most barriers to special library participation have proved largely psychological and include the problems of proprietary information, of convincing management of the benefits of resource sharing, and of the logistics of handling referrals in the small library. None of these has proved to be a serious problem for the majority of the special libraries who have joined networks; on the contrary, some special libraries feel they are and will continue to be underused until the network learns to refer down to smaller libraries, in addition to referring up to large libraries, public and academic. A more serious barrier is that special librarians are too comfortable with their long-term practice of informal cooperation among themselves and are reluctant to trade their comfortable relationships for the more complex or different methods required by formal cooperation. Another concern has been the possible exclusion of special libraries in profit-making organizations from certain networks or network activities, particularly when public funds are involved. This problem has been surmounted in some cases but is likely to surface more often as new and more intensive resource-sharing programs develop.

Another barrier may arise when networks move toward more coordination and common standards. Special libraries have long followed traditions based on individuality and unique methods of operation. From long experience with informal cooperation, they eschew the time-consuming red tape of formal procedures. Even simple network procedures are more complex than the relaxed practices special libraries currently enjoy. If the formalities of networks begin to require too much in the way of organization, standardization, and procedures, special libraries will become increasingly reluctant and unable to participate fully, viewing such governance as impinging on their independence.

## LAWS AND LEGISLATION

> *We suggest one small cheer for Section 108.*
>
> SLA Special Committee on Copyright Law Practice and Implementation, *Library Photocopying and the U.S. Copyright Law of 1976* (1977).

As a rule special libraries, nestled within larger organizations that provide their financial support, have seldom been directly involved in or affected by legislation. There are exceptions—there are always exceptions where special libraries are concerned. There are instances of involvement in government regulation and funding among groups of special libraries, most notably libraries in the public sector, medical libraries, and individual libraries in private organizations receiving grants and contracts. But on the whole special librarians have not been involved with laws and legislation to the same degree as have their colleagues in other types of libraries.

Recently, however, special libraries in the U.S. have become concerned with two major legislative areas that affect them directly, the Copyright Law of 1976 (PL 94-553, Title 17 U.S. Code) and legislation concerning multitype library cooperatives and networks.

As revision of copyright moved toward passage in Congress, special librarians became deeply involved in the legislative process as they, individually and through the Special Libraries Association, joined with five other major U.S. library associations (American Association of Law Libraries, American Library Association, Medical Library Association, Music Library Association, and Association of Research Libraries) in a unified effort to ensure equitable treatment for libraries. After enactment of the new law, which took effect January 1, 1978, SLA continued to respond to the concerns of special librarians as it disseminated information on copyright law practice and implementation in print and in conference sessions and continued to express the views of special libraries to the National Commission on New Technological Uses of Copyrighted Works (CONTU).

For all libraries the most significant part of the U.S. copyright law has been library reprography and photocopying, specifically Sections 107 governing fair use and 108 governing reproductions by libraries and archives. Special libraries—and particularly those in for-profit organizations that are singled out in Section 108—have also had some special problems with Section 108 and with the interpretation of "direct or indirect commercial advantage" and "systematic" reproduction.

In implementing provisions of the law, special librarians were faced with the same problems of interlibrary loan procedures, interpretation of fair use, and warning notices as were other types of libraries. However, the prohibitions against "multiple" and "systematic" photo-

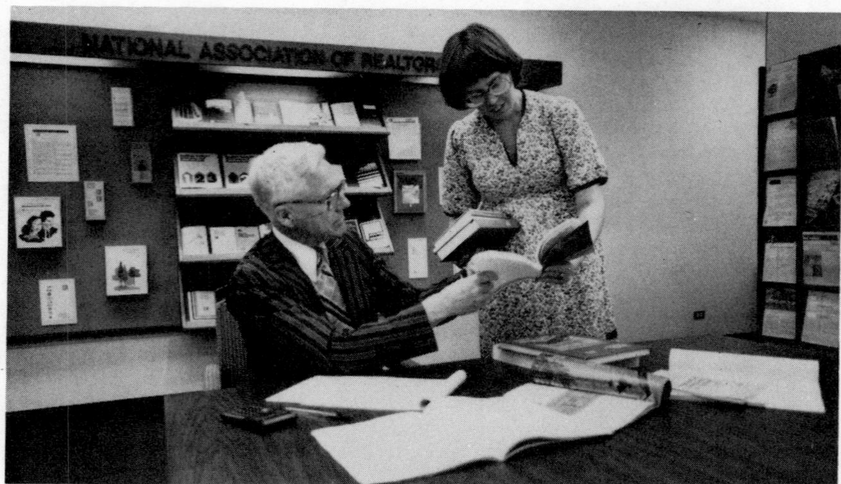

National Association of Realtors

Library of the National Association of Realtors, Chicago.



copying meant that special librarians would have to review carefully many of their current awareness, SDI, and abstracting services for possible infringements. Despite soothing messages to remain calm, many special librarians, naturally quite reluctant to embroil their parent organization in legal difficulties, beat a path to the offices of their firms' lawyers in an effort to obtain advice, with the result that each special library has developed its own policies, reflecting the opinions of their individual legal counsel. While in many cases alternative methods have been adopted for disseminating information, a good many services have simply been dropped, either because of possible infringement or because an efficient, effective alternative could not be found.

Special libraries also have had a strong interest in legislation concerning multitype library cooperatives and networks, although their involvement has been less direct. Possible legal problems in the inclusion of special libraries in for-profit organizations was identified very early in multitype network planning as a barrier to special library participation. At the same time, special libraries were increasingly being given at least lip-service recognition as a part of total library resources. It is from the philosophic base of mobilization of total library resources that federal and state legislation has by and large implicitly, if not explicitly, enabled special libraries to be included in multitype cooperatives and networks. The potential barrier remains at the individual cooperative/network level, where special libraries in profit-making organizations may be excluded from certain networks or network activities, particularly where public funding is involved. Although this has somehow been surmounted in the multitype networks when it has arisen, it seems likely that the problem will surface more often as networks multiply and new programs develop.

**REFERENCES**

Although it is brief and is intended for a management audience, Edward G. Strable, editor, *Special Libraries: A Guide for Management* (1975), is a comprehensive introduction to special libraries. Morton F. Meltzer, *The Information Center, Management's Hidden Asset* (1967), and Lucille J. Strauss, Irene M. Shreve, and Alberta Brown, *Scientific and Technical Libraries: Their Organization and Administration,* 2nd ed. (1972), are comprehensive treatments, although more specialized in the type of special library covered.

Historical treatments include Anthony T. Kruzas, *Business and Industrial Libraries in the United States, 1820–1940* (1965), and Samuel J. Rothstein, *The Development of Reference Services through Academic Tradition, Public Library Practice and Special Librarianship,* ACRL Monographs, no. 14 (ALA, 1955). Bill M. Woods, "The Special Library Concept of Service," *American Libraries* (1972), provides excellent coverage of the two decades following World War II.

Three recent studies are of particular interest for their explorations of special libraries. They are U.S. National Center for Education Statistics, *Survey of Federal Libraries, Fiscal Year 1972* (1975), and the articles by Eugene B. Jackson and Ruth L. Jackson, "The Industrial Special Library Universe—A Base Line Study of Its Extent and Characteristics," *Journal of the American Society for Information Science* (1977), and Joseph Talavage, "Financial Aspects of Industrial Information Centers: A Survey," *Journal of the American Society for Information Science* (1979).

*Special Libraries,* published by the Special Libraries Association from 1909 and the principal journal of the field, carries many articles on special libraries, their services and collections, and administration. In the area of administration, Shirley Echelman, "Libraries Are Businesses, Too!" *Special Libraries* (1974), and Herbert S. White, "Organizational Placement of the Industrial Special Library: Its Relationship to Success and Survival," *Special Libraries* (1973), are particularly articulate presentations.

*Special Libraries,* the *Journal of the American Society for Information Science* (1949– ), and the *Annual Review of Information Science and Technology* (1966– ) are the principal sources for reports of work on the measurement and evaluation of information systems and special libraries.

The role of the special library in multitype library cooperatives is presented in Beth A. Hamilton and William B. Ernst, Jr., editors, *Multitype Library Cooperation* (1977).

ELIN B. CHRISTIANSON

## Spofford, Ainsworth Rand
(1825–1908)

The modern history of the Library of Congress began when Ainsworth Rand Spofford became Librarian, for during his 32-year administration (1865–97) he transformed the Library of Congress into an institution of national significance. Spofford permanently joined the legislative and national functions of the Library, first in practice and then, through the 1897 reorganization of the Library, in law. He provided his successors as Librarian with four essential prerequisites for the development of an American national library: (1) firm congressional support for the notion of the Library of Congress as both a legislative and a national library; (2) the beginning of a comprehensive collection of Americana; (3) a magnificent new building, itself a national monument; and (4) a strong and independent office of Librarian of Congress. It was Spofford who had the interest, skill, and perseverance to capitalize on the Library of Congress's claim to a national role. Each Librarian of Congress since Spofford has shaped the institution in a different manner, but none has wavered from Spofford's fundamental assertion that the Library was both a legislative and a national institution.

Ainsworth Rand Spofford was born in Gilmanton, New Hampshire, on September 12, 1825. He was tutored at home and developed into an avid reader and student. In 1845 he migrated west to Cincinnati and found a job in a bookstore that soon became, due to his efforts, the city's leading importer of the books of the New England transcendentalists. From the book business he moved, in 1859, to a new career as Associate Editor of Cincinnati's leading newspaper, the *Daily Commercial;* his first editorial, titled "A Bibliologist," attacked the naive book-buying practices of the city librarian. Two years later the newspaper sent Spofford to Washington, D.C., to report on President Abraham Lincoln's inauguration, a trip that led to his acceptance, in the autumn of 1861, of the position of Assistant Librarian of Congress. On December 31, 1864, President Lincoln named the knowledgeable, industrious, and ambitious Spofford to the post of Librarian of Congress. Located in the west front of the U.S. Capitol, the Library had a staff of seven and a book collection of approximately 82,000 volumes.

Spofford soon proved to be a skilled politician as well as an energetic librarian. Congressmen liked him and the nonpartisan manner in which he administered the Library. As one result, between 1865 and 1870 he obtained support for several legislative acts that ensured the growth of the collections and made the Library of Congress the largest library in the United States. The most important new measure was the copyright law of 1870, which centralized all U.S. copyright registration and deposit activities at the Library. The new law brought books, pamphlets, maps, prints, photographs, and music into the institution without substantial cost, thus assuring the future growth of the Americana collections and providing the Library of Congress with an essential and unique national function.

In his annual reports to Congress, Spofford continually emphasized that a national library should be a permanent, comprehensive collection of national literature "representing the complete product of the American mind in every department of science and literature." The copyright law of 1870 enabled him to begin accumulating such a collection at the Library of Congress. Comprehensiveness was essential, for in his view the American national library should serve both the American citizenry and its elected representatives. Books and information were needed about all subjects and, as the library of the American government, the Library of Congress was the natural site for such a comprehensive collection.

In 1874, for the first time, the copyright law brought in more books than were obtained through purchase, and three years later Spofford's already cramped library was out of space and more than 70,000 books were "piled on the floor in all directions." The Librarian's struggle for a separate building, which began in 1871, was a crucial part of his national library effort. A separate structure would ensure, once and for all, the unique status of the Library of Congress among American libraries—and would give the United States a national library that would equal if not surpass the great national libraries of Europe. The latter argument was a particularly popular one with the Congress. Spofford personally wanted a national monument that would also serve as an efficient, well-functioning building. The new building, however, was not authorized until 1886 and not completed for another decade. Spofford's dream was fulfilled in 1897 when the doors to the ornate new structure across the east plaza from the Capitol, at the time the "largest, safest, and costliest" library building in the world, were finally opened to an admiring public.

For the most part Spofford operated quite independently of the American library movement and the American Library Association. By 1876, when ALA was founded, Spofford's Library of Congress was already the leading library in the United States, and he was completely absorbed in his struggle for a new building. His independence from other libraries and librarians was accentuated by his idea of a national library as well as by his personal temperament. The national library was a single, enormous accumulation of the nation's literature. He did not view it as a focal point for cooperative library activities and was not inclined to exert leadership in that direction.

From November 16 to December 7, 1896, the Joint Committee on the Library held hearings about the Library of Congress, its "condition," and its organization. Although Spofford was the principal witness, ALA sent six librarians to testify. The testimony of Melvil Dewey and Herbert Putnam on the desirable features of the Library of Congress was of special interest; both men avoided direct criticism of Spofford, but it was obvious that their view of the proper functions of the Library differed from that of the aging Librarian. Putnam wholeheartedly endorsed Dewey's description of the necessary role of a national library: "a center to which the libraries of the whole country can turn for inspiration, guidance, and practical help." Centralized cataloguing, interlibrary loan, and a national union catalogue were among the services described.

Immediately after the end of the hearings, Putnam supplemented his comments in a letter in which he summarized the testimony of the ALA witnesses and stated, tactfully, that not only was it time for the Library of Congress to modernize but also its services should be expanded far beyond those offered by the Library under Spofford.

The hearings resulted in a major reorganization and expansion, effective July 1, 1897. Spofford became Chief Assistant Librarian under a new Librarian of Congress, John Russell Young, and he continued as Chief Assistant under Herbert Putnam, who became the Librarian of Congress in April 1899. Spofford died on August 11, 1908.

Ainsworth Rand Spofford's professional and personal interests were perhaps most accurately described in the formidable title of his *A Book for All Readers, Designed as an Aid to the Collection, Use, and Preservation of Books and Formation of Public and Private Libraries* (1900). He was respected by librarians, politicians, and the general public, not only because of his accomplishments at the Library of Congress, but also because of his fair-mindedness and his continual delight in sharing his views about his favorite subjects—reading, bibliography, and collection-building.

**REFERENCE**

John Y. Cole, editor, *Ainsworth Rand Spofford: Bookman and Librarian* (1975).

JOHN Y. COLE

## Sri Lanka

Sri Lanka (Ceylon), an island republic in the Indian Ocean, lies off the southeastern coast of India. Pop. (1977 est.) 13,940,000; area 65,610 sq.km. The official language is Sinhalese.

Possessing an ancient civilization stretching back over 2,500 years of recorded history, the island of Sri Lanka has a longstanding intellectual tradition and a background of learning and scholarship. Temple libraries were widespread, but not until the development of Western-style institutions of education in the 19th century did a modern system of libraries begin to appear. Over a hundred years of state-sponsored education have provided the stimulus to a growing network of libraries of all kinds serving a population whose general literacy rates are in the region of 75–85 percent.

**National Library.** There was no National Library as of 1979, but the blueprint for its construction had been accepted, and the foundation stone was laid in 1977. In the absence of one, the principal state reference library is the National Museum Library, established in Colombo, the capital city, in 1877. Its collections number 400,000 volumes, including manuscripts, and it served as a legal deposit library as well from 1885.

The Sri Lanka National Library Services Board was

Library of Congress

*Ainsworth Rand Spofford*

Sri Lanka Library Association

*The Oriental Library in the Temple of the Tooth, Kandy, Sri Lanka, was built in the 17th century and houses ancient* ola *(palm) manuscripts.*

begun under an act of 1970. Its primary objectives are to formulate a national library policy, to promote and assist the development of all types of libraries, especially those maintained by state funds, and to set up a National Library. It is responsible for producing the Sri Lanka National Bibliography (begun in 1962) and has been accorded legal deposit privileges for this purpose from 1974.

The Department of National Archives is also a legal deposit library, and the Director of National Archives is the Registrar of Books, Periodicals, Newspapers, and Printing Presses.

**Academic Libraries.** At the apex of the higher (or tertiary) system of education established in 1870 with a Ceylon Medical College and in 1921 with the Ceylon University College are the six universities and their affiliated colleges and institutes. The oldest and largest of these are the two Universities of Peradeniya and Colombo. Peradeniya has much the larger library, amounting to 400,000 volumes, excluding its legal deposit materials since 1952. The collections in the six universities alone total nearly a million volumes covering all disciplines. There are special collections on Sri Lanka and Oriental subjects in the bigger universities. The libraries in technical colleges and institutes are much smaller and of more recent origin.

**Public Libraries.** Various sorts of subscription libraries existed from early British times, and two of them (the United Services Library and the Colombo Pettah Library) were amalgamated in 1925 to form the Colombo Public Library, which developed into the premier public library in the island. The organization and maintenance of public libraries is not obligatory for local government authorities but is only a permissive function. The scope and nature of such libraries differ widely from region to region. The Ministry of Local Government stepped up the provision of library services and elevated the resources of buildings, staff, and books; in 1979 it hoped to develop one library with minimum standards of service and adequacy as a resource center for each of the 24 districts. Out of about 675 local government bodies, about 496 maintained libraries in the late 1970's, and the total collections numbered 710,000.

**Table 2. Archives in Sri Lanka (1976)**

| | |
|---|---|
| Number | 1 |
| Holdings | 9 linear miles |
| Annual expenditures | Rs. 815,922 |
| Professional staff | 6 |
| All staff (total) | 32 |

Sources: Personal inquiries.

**School Libraries.** Despite considerable activity in public education since independence in 1948 and the high participation rate in the free educational stream, the provision of school libraries of sufficient quality lagged behind that of other educational facilities. The Ministry of Education took active steps to remedy this deficiency and to promote the concept of a school library as a center of learning. Most schools have libraries of sorts and, as in public libraries, literature is provided in all three languages—Sinhalese, Tamil, and English—used as media of education and administration.

**Special Libraries.** Special libraries and documentation centers are located in state corporations, government departments, and private organizations dealing with industry, commerce, scientific research, technology, agriculture, and allied fields. The clientele are select groups of users connected with the institutions, and this class of library service has grown rapidly. The National Science Council of Sri Lanka operates a Science and Technology Information Center.

**Association.** The Sri Lanka Library Association was established in 1960 and conducts part-time classes in librarianship and information studies at various levels. A Department of Library Studies in the University of Kelaniya was begun in 1973.

**REFERENCE**

I. Corea, editor, *Libraries and People* (Colombo Public Library, 1975), a valuable symposium of articles on all aspects of the library scene in Sri Lanka.

HENRY ALFRED IAN GOONETILEKE

**Table 1. Libraries in Sri Lanka (1976)**

| Type | Number | Volumes in collections | Annual expenditures (rupee) | Population served | Professional staff | All staff (total) |
|---|---|---|---|---|---|---|
| Academic | 21 | 1,225,000 | Rs. 3,600,000 | 20,000 | 136 | 454 |
| Public | 496 | 710,000 | Rs. 2,310,000 | 3,700,000 | 91 | 314 |
| School | 793 | 1,423,000 | Rs. 660,000 | 4,000,000 | 60 | 793[a] |
| Special | 51 | 435,000 | Rs. 2,100,000 | 3,000 | 37 | 185 |
| Total | 1,361 | 3,793,000 | Rs. 8,670,000 | | 324 | 1,746 |

[a]Includes part-time staff.

Sources: Annual reports and personal inquiries.

## Standing Conference of African University Libraries

The Standing Conference of African University Librarians was formed as a result of the discussions at the Leverhulme Inter-University Conference on the Needs and Problems of University Librarians in Tropical Africa, held in Salisbury, Rhodesia, September 14–23, 1964. At the end of the Conference, a Continuation Committee was appointed and charged with the responsibility of implementing the conference resolutions, one of which recommended that further conferences be held periodically.

Members of the Continuation Committee took the opportunity of the Conference of Librarians from Commonwealth Universities in Africa, sponsored by the Commonwealth Foundation and held in Lusaka, Zambia, August 24–29, 1969, to discuss further the organization of the Standing Conference of African University Librarians. At this conference, the non-Commonwealth Committee members, Ethiopia and Senegal, took part as observers. Some important recommendations concerning the organization of SCAUL were made, and a draft constitution was drawn up.

According to this constitution, full membership of SCAUL would be open to heads of Libraries of universities eligible for membership in the Association of African Universities, with associate membership open to university libraries in other parts of the world. SCAUL activities would be developed mainly within Area Organizations of SCAUL. A Central Committee, comprising the Convener/Secretary (Chairman), representatives of Area Organizations, and the Editor of the *Newsletter,* would meet periodically to coordinate the work of the Areas. Each member of SCAUL would be free to choose the Area that it would join and would be allowed to attend as an observer the conferences in the Areas to which it did not belong. Each Area would determine its own membership requirements and draft its own constitution based on that of SCAUL. The *Newsletter* was to be published as the official organ of SCAUL. The name of the organization was changed to Standing Conference of African University Libraries.

These recommendations were subsequently approved in a postal ballot, and the draft constitution was fully discussed at Area meetings in 1971 and 1972 and subsequently approved.

SCAUL now operates through two Area Organizations: the Eastern Area (SCAULEA), headquartered at the library of the University of Nairobi, Kenya, and the Western Area (SCAULWA), at the University of Liberia Library, Monrovia. Each of the Area Organizations has both anglophone and francophone countries as members. SCAULEA has held successful conferences in Addis Ababa (1971), Mauritius (1973), and Nairobi (1977). SCAULWA held conferences in Lagos (1972), Dakar (1974), Accra (1976), and Kinshasha (1978).

The aims of SCAUL are (1) to keep members informed of each other's activities and, whenever possible, to correlate such activities in the common interest; and (2) to support and develop university library services in Africa.

SCAUL seeks to advance the development of university libraries by organizing conferences as a forum for discussing the problems of university librarianship in Africa and of the programs of each member library. SCAUL sponsors individual research activities and projects and meetings of specialists on African bibliography, cataloguing, classification, and other library topics.

SCAUL publications include proceedings of the conferences of SCAULEA and SCAULWA; *SCAUL Newsletter.*

E. BEJIDE BANKOLE

SCAUL

*Delegates to the 1972 SCAUL conference in Lagos, Nigeria.*

## State Library Agencies in the United States

Each of the 50 states of the United States has developed a library agency (or sometimes several library agencies) to carry out appropriate statewide library services and library development activities; to a more modest degree, the extraterritorial possessions of the United States have developed similar agencies. The role and functions of state library agencies have evolved under different administrative arrangements and developed different patterns of organization and services.

A convenient listing of the more common functions and responsibilities of state library agencies divides them under five major headings: library services to state governments; statewide library services development; statewide development of library resources; statewide development of information networks; and financing library programs.

The first decades of the 19th century saw the establishment of the first state libraries. Characteristically, they were given responsibilities for the legal collections of the states and often for state documents and historical materials. As state governments grew in size and complexity, state libraries also were asked to provide materials and services to support the activities of the legislative and executive branches of government.

Toward the end of the 19th century, states saw the need to establish agencies to deal with statewide library development needs, particularly for public libraries. At least two organizational patterns emerged. In the older states with established state libraries, public library development responsibilities were often added to these existing agencies. In newer states, and in some of the older states, library commissions were created, with assistance in the establishment and development of public libraries as the chief function.

In more recent decades state library functions have been both broadened and strengthened as a result of administrative responsibilities connected with the federal Library Services Act, passed in 1956, and its successor, the Library Services and Construction Act (LSCA), extended, as of the end of the 1970's, through 1982. The entity in each state administering the state plan-based Library Services and Construction Act is the state library administrative agency indicated by the Governor as re-

George Holmes Bixby Memorial Library, Francestown

*Small library in Francestown, New Hampshire, uses state library extension services.*

sponsible for public library development within the state. A summary of the organizational placement of these agencies showed that 21 of them were independent, 19 within a department of education, and 10 within other departments or branches of state government. It must be realized that in many of the states there are separate libraries serving to support state government functions—law, legislative and executive departments, and reference and interlibrary loan responsibilities.

**Services to Government.** Among the broad categories of state library services to state government, a listing of common specific functions would include government documents, information and reference, legislative reference, law library, genealogy and state history, archives, and liaison with state institutional libraries. State libraries or state library administrative agencies are more likely to have primary or exclusive responsibility for liaison with institutional libraries, for information and reference services for state departments and employees, and for state documents. Primary responsibility for archives, law collections, legislative reference, and genealogy and state history is more likely to rest with other state agencies or specialized libraries, with the state library playing a supportive and coordinative role.

The information needs of state government are growing more diverse and more complex, as the size, complexity, and number of functions carried out by state governments have increased. In many states this has necessitated expansion and reorganization of the state library or libraries responsible for providing these information needs. There have been relatively few written reports in recent years on how state libraries have responded to these challenges. Among the state libraries with traditional strength in serving state government have been New York, New Jersey, Pennsylvania, North Carolina, Virginia, Ohio, Indiana, Illinois, Washington, Oregon, and California. The New York State Library completed a reorganization of its library services to state government. In a 1978 article Paulson, Greer, McDonough, and Minor listed essential elements in developing an effective program of state library services to state agencies. They include an aggressive outreach attitude, serving as the hub of library activity in state government (with assigned staff on liaison duties), involvement of all relevant agencies in planning and evaluating the service, shared activities and financing, and visibility and direct contact with the administration and the legislature. Also important, particularly in recent years, have been network linkages to a variety of specialized library collections and increasing use of new forms of media and equipment, especially microforms and computers.

**Statewide Services and Planning.** The broad function of statewide library services development has received the most emphasis from state libraries over the last 30 years. A convenient itemization of subfunctions in library services development includes coordination of academic libraries; coordination of public libraries; coordination of school libraries; coordination of institutional libraries; research; coordination of library systems; consulting services; interlibrary loan, reference, and bibliographic services; statistical gathering and analysis; library legislation review; interstate library compacts and other cooperative efforts; specialized resource centers; direct service to the public; annual reports; public relations; and continuing education.

Least often performed by state library agencies is coordination of academic libraries; relatively few such agencies are responsible for school library coordination. Among the most commonly performed are coordination of public libraries and library systems, the provision of consulting service, and statistical gathering and analysis. Although the number of full-time personnel is low, coordination of institutional libraries is attempted by most state libraries, and most state libraries give considerable attention to interlibrary loan and reference and bibliographic services.

Under the general heading of statewide development of library resources, state libraries are involved with long-range planning; determination of size and scope of collections in the state; mobilization of resources; subject and reference centers; resources of books, other printed materials, and multimedia; resources and materials for the blind and physically handicapped; coordination of resources; and the storage of little-used materials.

Broad-scale planning characterized the best efforts of certain state libraries from the last decade of the 19th century. The most effective state librarians were able to mobilize government and educational leaders, along with librarians, in creative approaches to planning the kinds of coordinated library services that met the needs of their states. They were also often leaders in the national plans and standards developed by the American Library Association.

The 1970 amendments to the federal Library Services and Construction Act, which placed considerable emphasis on the development by state libraries of long-range programs, had the greatest influence on strengthening the planning functions of these agencies. Built into the process was involvement of an advisory committee representing all types of libraries. Although the early efforts by most state libraries were relatively crude, the long-range programs did focus attention on such skills as the assessment of library needs, establishment of priorities, the tying of projects to long-range objectives, and—more tentatively— the evaluation of ongoing programs.

**Standards.** Playing a considerable part in the statewide development of library resources has been the development of state library standards. Most commonly, such state standards as were developed by state libraries, often with the assistance of representative committees, were basically concerned with public libraries and, in more recent years, with health and rehabilitative library services. For state libraries themselves there have been two editions of national standards developed for state library activities, in 1963 and 1970. A committee of the

ALA Association of Specialized and Cooperative Library Agencies was developing a third edition at the end of the 1970's.

The *Standards for Library Functions at the State Level* (1970) emphasized throughout the importance of leadership and coordination as keys to state library success. It was recognized that the state library must work in concert with library groups and individuals in their states in order to develop successfully the kinds of library resources needed. Because there are inherent difficulties in establishing national standards for state library resources—given the diversity of state needs, economic resources, and organizational patterns—these standards emphasize functions rather than quantitative measures of resources.

The first attempt of the National Center for Education Statistics to gather and publish statistics concerning state libraries was expected to be available before 1980. It prepared in tabular form consistent and detailed information on state library organization, collections of materials, services, income, and expenditures. Of particular interest are tables on state library materials resources, which illustrate that a very few state library collections can be called major resource libraries. Another 10 to 15 have substantial book collections of between 500,000 and 1,000,000 volumes, while a majority of the state libraries have smaller collections, and a few rely on contracts with other libraries for basic services. A survey of this type prepared and published at regular intervals would facilitate comparisons among the state libraries over a period of time.

Much remains to be done by state libraries in the area of statewide development of library services. Perhaps most progress has been made in resources and materials for the blind and physically handicapped. That can be attributed, however, mostly to vigorous leadership and growing budgets at the national level for provision of materials. LSCA and state funds have been used to strengthen and diversify public library collections, but much remains to be done. In a number of states, some progress has been made at improving the library resources of health and rehabilitative libraries. In those state libraries responsible for administering federal Elementary and Secondary Education Act instructional materials funds, great strides were made after 1965 in improving the materials resources of school media centers. Interconnecting the functions of library services development and library resources development have been state library activities directed at planning and establishing larger units for public library services, variously called regional libraries, federated library systems, and cooperative library systems. A general feature in most states was building on existing centers of library strength in the state. By these means, the coordination of library resources has been improved in virtually every state.

**Information Networks.** A relatively new but rapidly growing major function of state libraries is the statewide development of information networks. Chief components of this function include the planning of information networks, provision of centralized facilities, the exchange of information and materials, and interstate cooperation. A great stimulus for state library involvement in the development of information networks was the inclusion in the 1965 revisions to the Library Services and Construction Act of a new Title III, Interlibrary Cooperation. Even though appropriations for this Title have remained extremely small, it has given state libraries a tool for planning and experimentation in the establishment and maintenance of local, regional, state, or interstate cooperative library networks.

Other stimuli for the state library's recent emphasis on planning, funding, coordinating, and participating in multitype library networks include the explosion of knowledge and its publication in a multiplicity of forms, making it impossible for even the largest libraries to be self-sufficient; the revolutions in communications and computer technology, making it possible to organize, store, and transmit information in more rapid and efficient ways; and the feeling of funding agencies and taxpayers that library resource sharing is more economical than alternatives calling for larger expenditures for individual library materials collections.

New Hampshire State Library

*New Hampshire State Library, Concord.*

There is as yet no single pattern for multitype library networks within the states, and the great diversity of the states will assure that this will always be true. A variety of commonly used practices in multitype cooperative activities, not mutually exclusive, can be listed. In general, state libraries in the Rocky Mountain and Pacific Coast states, and in the Southeast and New England states, have helped plan and have been active partners in multistate networks and cooperative activities. Some of these efforts antedated the computer, but most current multistate programs rely on them to a great degree. Other states have established comprehensive state interloan networks or a combination of resource library contracts and interloan networks. Still others have utilized commercial or computer-utility contractual services to begin integrating state networks; the most familiar examples are OCLC consortia. In other states, metropolitan and area intertype library councils have been activated.

Finally, and perhaps the strongest, is the current trend in many states toward planning or experimenting with the organization of multitype library systems. In most cases these efforts are directed at broadening and restructuring public library systems. In other states that have not developed strong public library systems, the state libraries are attempting to initiate cooperation with state and federal funds on a multitype basis. In still other states multitype cooperatives are constituting or will constitute an extra layer of organization on top of single-type library systems.

A final functional aspect of state libraries is the financing of library programs. The administration of federal and state aid, and the financing of library systems, resource centers, and networks, permits state libraries to operate in the real world with their library development and library services activities. Although such funds are not the only measure of success for the state libraries, there is little doubt that their existence is a source of strength and that the stronger the financial resources, the more successful the state library program tends to be. State libraries played a key role in planning and lobbying for federal library program authorizations. Their efforts, along with those of other libraries and library groups, are necessary if appropriate and adequately funded federal programs for libraries are to continue. Again, the success of state librar-

Arthur Plotnik

The New York State Library's award-winning building.



ies in getting state aid programs established and funded is dependent on a spirit of cooperation with other libraries and library associations and on continual planning and hard work. It is recognized that success is also dependent on such external factors as the economy and political traditions of the various states and territories.

It is clear that state libraries are—and must remain—vital components of the emerging national network of library and information services. Even more important than their financial and library materials resources will be their attitude toward leadership responsibilities. If they attract competent leadership and professional personnel, and if they develop and use skills in working with other libraries, library organizations, government agencies, and citizen groups, they can build state networks as sound operational nodes of multistate and national networks.

At the national level state libraries continue to play an important role in the programs of the American Library Association and many of its units. The Association of Specialized and Cooperative Library Agencies, with its State Library Agency Section, attracts primary allegiance of many staff members of state libraries, but they are also active in a variety of other divisions and in the general activities of ALA. The Chief Officers of State Library Agencies, established early in the 1970's, is an organizational vehicle by which those responsible for state library administration can plan together, study and establish policies on national issues, and meet with and coordinate services with important national library agencies and services vital to their diverse functions.

**REFERENCES**

*Standards for Library Functions at the State Level,* revised edition (ALA, 1970), the most recent authorized guidelines for carrying out the library leadership, coordination, development, and service activities of state libraries.

Association of State Library Agencies, Interlibrary Cooperation Committee, *The ASLA Report on Interlibrary Cooperation,* 2nd edition (ALA/ASLA, 1978), basic information, arranged alphabetically by state, on cooperative, resource-sharing, and networking programs and activities.

John A. McCrossan, issue editor, "State Library Development Agencies," *Library Trends* (1978), a collection of articles on the organization and activities of state libraries, with strong emphasis on the library development functions. See especially the article by Peter J. Paulson, Roger C. Greer, Roger McDonough, and Barbara Minor, "Development and Coordination of Library Services to State Government."

National Center for Education Statistics, *Survey of State Library Agencies* (1979), a first attempt, carried out by the State Library of Florida, to collect in Library General Information Survey (LIBGIS) format basic tabular data on state libraries.

Donald B. Simpson, compiler, *The State Library Agencies A Survey Project Report* (ALA/ASCLA, 1979), descripti information on state library organization, staffing, legal authority, general services, and special projects, alphabetically by state.

W. LYLE EBERHART

## Sudan

The Democratic Republic of the Sudan, in northeast Africa, is bounded by the Red Sea and Ethiopia on the east, the Central African Republic and Chad on the west, Egypt on the north, Libya on the northwest, and Kenya, Uganda, and Zaire on the south. Pop. (1978 est.) 17,141,000; area 2,505,890 sq.km. The official language is Arabic.

**National Library.** There is no national library in the Sudan, but many of the functions of a national library are performed by the University of Khartoum Library, the largest library in the country. One of three legal deposit libraries for all works published in the Sudan, it is a depository for publications of the UN and its specialized agencies and of many U.S. publications. It also carries out many of the bibliographical activities usually associated with a national library, including the *Classified Catalogue of the Sudan Collection* with its annual supplements, which represents a retrospective national bibliography.

**Academic Libraries.** The University of Khartoum Library, founded in 1945 with a collection of 3,000 volumes, has five special branches, serving departments in agriculture, engineering, law, medicine, and education. The library also extends its services outside the University. Its collection now contains 328,000 volumes. Other academic libraries are at the Islamic University of Omdurman (25,000); Cairo University Khartoum Branch (holdings not available); Khartoum Polytechnic (11,000); Institute of Commerce (3,000); Shambat Agricultural Institute (5,000); the Institute of Public Administration (2,500); Bakht er Ruda (28,000); and the Juba University Library and Gezira University Library, both established in 1977–78 (holdings not available).

**Libraries in Sudan (1976)**

| Type | Number | Volumes in collections |
|---|---|---|
| Academic | 9 | 425,000 |
| Public | 83 | 114,000 |
| School | 4,676 | 89,000 |
| Special | 110 | 286,000 |
| Total | 4,878 | 828,000 |

**Public Libraries.** Omdurman Central Library is administered by the Ministry of Education. Its book stock deteriorated from 23,900 volumes in 1960 to 10,000 in 1972. There are six council public libraries with 14,000 volumes. Youth library services are provided through the Ministry of Youth and Sports, which has established a Central Public Library and 60 libraries attached to youth centers in different parts of the Sudan. Their total number of books is 15,000. Bakht er Ruda Institute of Education provides a postal lending library service of 6,000 volumes to approximately 600 schoolteachers. Sudan Railways also provides a limited mobile library service in a railway truck for members of its staff stationed in remote areas.

**School Libraries.** The total number of school libraries in the Sudan is about 4,676 with total book collections of 89,000.

**Special Libraries.** There are 110 special libraries and documentation centers with a total stock of 286,000 volumes. The Ministry of Religions and Wakf's established six religious libraries with total stock of 10,000 volumes. There are nine foreign mission libraries with total stock of 75,000 volumes. Other important foreign libraries include the UN Information Centre, the British Council Library, French and Soviet cultural centers, and the Goethe Institute.

**Association.** The Sudan Library Association, established in 1971, is the only professional library organization in the country.

**REFERENCE**

J. S. Parker, *Development of Library and Documention Services: Democratic Republic of the Sudan* (Unesco, 1972).

QASIM OSMAN NUR

## Suriname

Suriname, an independent republic in north central South America, is bounded by the Atlantic Ocean on the north, French Guiana on the east, Brazil on the south, and Guyana on the west. Pop. (1977 est.) 448,000; area 181,455 sq. km. The official language is Dutch.

Suriname has had a tradition of libraries since the 18th century, when the capital of Paramaribo already had a large scientific library comparable to similar libraries in Western Europe and the U.S. The library was destroyed in the 19th century by a fire set by the freedom fighters of the time, the Maroons. Various private libraries also date from this period, as do the personal libraries. The so-called Volksbibliotheek (People's Library) was set up at the end of the 18th century under the influence of the Maatschappij tot Nut van het Algemeen (Public Benefit Company) in the Netherlands, but that library was also destroyed by fire in 1821.

**National Library.** Between 1821 and 1856 some brief attempts were made to establish loan associations for books on a commercial basis, but it was not until 1856 that two medical doctors, F. A. G. Dumontier and C. Landré, proposed a plan to set up a library in Paramaribo. Their plan was successful, and on December 1, 1857, the Colonial Library was established under the jurisdiction of the Inspector of Education. This was the first attempt to found a national library, which had to serve as both public and a research library. A lack of expert personnel and poor facilities caused the National Library to close in 1957. The collection was distributed among a number of libraries in the Netherlands, including the library of the Royal Institute for the Tropics and the Royal Library. In 1950 the collections for adults and children had already been turned over to the Public Library of the Cultural Centre of Suriname (CCS), which had begun operating in 1949.

**Academic Libraries.** There are separate faculty libraries of the University of Suriname, which were to be united under the projected Central Scientific Library. The six libraries are at the Faculty of Law (with holdings of 10,000 publications), the Faculty of Medicine (10,000), the Faculty of Social and Economic Sciences (3,000), the Engineering Faculty (10,000), the Faculty of Natural Resource Studies (10,000), and the International Law library (2,000). These faculty libraries primarily serve the University's 1,000 students.

**Public Libraries.** The Public Library of the CCS was set up on the initiative of the Cultural Committee for Suriname. Pioneering work was performed by M. Nassy, the first Librarian of this institution. It quickly became apparent that an organization of the existing libraries was necessary. From 1950 to 1957 the National Library functioned as a center for reference works and scientific literature, while the CCS library covered belles-lettres and services to youth.

The CCS library now operates as a central public library and is trying to set up public libraries in different regions. Until 1975 it was subsidized by STICUSA (Foundation for Cultural Cooperation between the Netherlands, Suriname, and the Netherlands Antilles), but since Suriname's independence in 1975, it is supported by the state. The central library and its six branches and two bookmobiles make loans amounting to about 400,000, with a total collection of about 160,000.

**School Libraries.** The Ministry of Education and Community Development is largely responsible for school libraries; a special Library Affairs Section was attached to the Ministry in 1968. The first library it established was the General Educational Library (1969), a central library for all the school libraries, where expensive research material may be consulted. The Library also provides materials for evening school courses. The Library Affairs Section's impressive development includes the founding of 60 school libraries, with estimated total collections of about 60,000 items with a total number of 250,000 annual loans. The General Educational Library has about 35,000 publications, with some 75,000 annual loans and visitors.

It is planned to set up some 15 school libraries each year. Work at the school libraries is usually done by teachers who take a three-week in-service training course at the Library Affairs Section. The staff at the Library Affairs Section must have at least four years of practical experience and one year of professional training. There is also a two-year library course at the CCS.

**Special Libraries.** Most of the special libraries in Suriname are in ministries. Mention can be made of those in the Ministry of Agriculture, Animal Husbandry and Fisheries (30,000 publications), the Ministry of Justice and Police Affairs (5,000), the State Forest Administration (10,000), and the Central Bank (9,000). Others libraries that are open to a larger public are the library of the Suriname Museum Foundation, which has the largest collection of writings on Suriname (12,000 publications), the Institute for Advanced Teacher Training (3,000 publications), and the Scientific Institute Foundation (3,000).

**REFERENCE**

*Encyclopedie van Suriname* (1977).

R. CH. W. LONT

## Swaziland

Swaziland, a monarchy based on tribal tradition in southwestern Africa, is bounded on the east by Mozambique and on the north, west, and south by South Africa. Pop. (1977 est.) 496,000; area 17,364 sq.km. The official languages are English and siSwati.

**National Library.** Swaziland does not have a national library, but the country's copyright law implies that one might be established in the future. The functions of a national library are performed by the Swaziland National Library Service and the University College of Swaziland Library, which enjoy legal deposit status.

**Academic Library.** The only academic library is the University College of Swaziland Library, founded in 1971 at the devolution of the University of Botswana, Lesotho, and Swaziland and incorporating the Swaziland Agricultural College and University Centre. It consists of the Main Library at Kwaluseni and the Faculty of Agriculture Library at Luyengo. Besides the undergraduate material, the Library has a collection of Swaziana and compiles the *Swaziland National Bibliography* (1976– ). It also has deposit status for documents of the Food and Agriculture Organization and the World Bank.

**Table 1. Libraries in Swaziland (1976)**

| Type | Number | Volumes in collection | Annual expenditure (emalangeni) | Population served | Professional staff | All staff (total) |
|---|---|---|---|---|---|---|
| National | 0 | 0 | 0 | 0 | 0 | 0 |
| Academic | 1 | 34,652 | E 93,000 | 825 | 6 | 13 |
| Public | 10 | 337,274 | E 30,000 | 29,902 | 3 | 24 |
| School | 28 | 43,538 | E 8,000 | 109,273 | 3 | 77 |
| Special[a] | 7 | 17,865 | E 14,000 | 13,435 | N.A. | 3 |
| Total | 46 | 433,329 | E 145,000 | | | 117 |

[a]Includes other libraries.

Sources: *Directory of Swaziland Libraries; Fifth Annual Report of the Director of the Swaziland National Library Service* (1976); University College of Swaziland; *Recurrent Estimates of Revenue and Expenditure for 1976–77 . . .*; and replies to questionnaires.

**Public Libraries.** The Swaziland National Library Service provides public library services, operating a public library in Manzini with several branches, depots, and mobile unit stops. It has an annual circulation of around 120,000 and reaches over 20 percent of the country's literate population. There are plans for the establishment of another center in the administrative capital, Mbabane.

**School Libraries.** The Ministry of Education operates some 500 schools for about 110,000 pupils and distributes books among 48 school libraries, while the Swaziland National Library Service lends books to the schools. A number of secondary and high school libraries operate on their own budgets. The Swaziland College of Technology, the Swaziland Institute of Management and Public Administration, and two teacher training colleges have libraries with over 10,000 volumes.

**Table 2. Archives in Swaziland (1976)**

| | |
|---|---|
| Number | 1 |
| Holdings | 800 cubic meters |
| Annual expenditure | E 50,000 |
| Professional staff | 1 |
| All staff (total) | 13 |

Source: Office of Director of Archives.

**Special Libraries.** The Malkerns Research Station and the Lowveld Experimental Farm have libraries with a joint stock of over 6,000 volumes and over 200 agricultural journals. There is a library at the Mananga Agricultural Management Centre, run by the Commonwealth Development Corporation, which provides training for junior and middle level management and extension workers from the British Commonwealth developing countries. A few ministries of government have departmental libraries for their staff. The Attorney General's Chambers Library serves the Ministry of Justice, while the Central Statistical Office Library serves the Government Statistician. The Monetary Authority and the Ministry of Agriculture operate libraries, while the National Archives contains a library section devoted to Swaziana. The British High Commission Office and the United States of America Embassy run libraries with open membership, while the Mbabane Library Association is a subscription library.

**Association.** Plans were complete for the inauguration of the Swaziland Library Association in 1979, which would be affiliated with a regional library association of Botswana, Lesotho, and Swaziland.

**REFERENCES**

A. W. Z. Kuzwayo, *Information Systems and National Information Services in Swaziland* (University College of Swaziland Library, 1978), gives quantitative and qualitative assessment.

Wallace Van Jackson, "Library Development in Swaziland," *International Library Review* (1976).

A. W. Z. KUZWAYO

# Sweden

Sweden, a constitutional monarchy, lies on the eastern part of the Scandinavian Peninsula in northern Europe. It is bounded by Norway on the west, Finland on the northeast, the Gulf of Bothnia on the east, the Baltic Sea on the southwest, and the North Sea on the southwest. Pop. (1978 est.) 8,271,000; area 449,964 sq.km. The official language is Swedish.

**National Libraries.** By royal ordinances in the 17th century three libraries were entitled to become the depositories of copyrighted works: the Royal Library (Kungl. Biblioteket, 1661), the Uppsala University Library (1692). and the Lund University Library (1698). The universities newly established in the 20th century made claims to receive statutory copies, and in 1978 the government decided that the Royal Library should become the national library for the archival deposit copy, which could be consulted only in its reading rooms, and that Lund University Library should be the national library for the "spare copy" of copyrighted works, which could also be sent out on interlibrary loans; both are obliged to preserve deposits. The university libraries at Uppsala, Stockholm, Linköping, Göteborg, and Umeå are entitled to receive statutory copies (except newspapers) without any obligation to store them for the future. Deposit copies of films and sound and video recordings are handled by Arkivet för ljud och bild, Stockholm.

The Royal Library in Stockholm traces its origins to the 16th century. According to statute it must "collect, preserve and make available a national collection of printed documents produced and published in Sweden and printed documents published abroad in the Swedish language, by Swedish authors or relating to Sweden." As an old and large research library it collects foreign publications, especially in the humanities and the social sciences. Through its Bibliographic Institute it is responsible for the national bibliography and the union catalogue of foreign books and periodicals. Both activities are computerized and linked to LIBRIS (LIBRary Information System), for which operations it is responsible. LIBRIS started in the early 1970's as a communication and processing system for Swedish research libraries, linking 26 terminals in 14 libraries to a central computer. Through cooperative input the data base grew to 440,000 bibliographic records in 1978 and can be used for the production of catalogue cards or microfiche. An option to access

LIBRIS from dial-up terminals to a nearby connected terminal for just searching was initiated in 1978.

The Royal Library is a government agency directly under the Ministry of Education. Besides the Institute it has eight divisions, a newspaper film department, and a remote deposit library—Statens Biblioteksdepå, Bålsta. Its collections amount to 55,000 shelfmeters, corresponding to 2,000,000 volumes, and 10,000,000 other items. Its manuscript collection is 1,500 shelfmeters.

Lund University Library, founded in 1666, dates to medieval times, when it took over the books and manuscripts of the former Danish cathedral chapter. It is the largest Swedish library, with collections outnumbering the Royal Library and annual acquisitions of 25,000 volumes (1978). Its documentation center offers computerized SDI (Selective Dissemination of Information) service and on-line searches to both academic and industrial users.

The national bibliographies are *Svensk bokkatalog* and *Svensk bokförteckning;* the latter is also supplied on magnetic tape as SWEMARC, from which printed issues are set by photocomposition. The union catalogue of foreign acquisitions *(Accessionskatalogen)* was started in 1886, and the latest edition covers the period 1971–73; that catalogue is accessible through LIBRIS. Foreign acquisitions in public libraries form a data base in the BUMS-system, created by the public libraries' own cooperative service, Bibliotekstjänst, Lund.

**Academic Libraries.** The most renowned academic library is the Uppsala University Library, Carolina Rediviva, Uppsala, founded in 1620 but integrating earlier monastic libraries like that of the Saint Bridget's monastery, Vadstena. It has a fine collection of manuscripts (2,000 shelfmeters), including the *Codex Argenteus*. The total holdings are 55,600 shelfmeters.

The younger university libraries—Göteborg University Library (1861), Umeå University Library (1964), Linköping University Library (1969), and Stockholm University Library (1971)—have substantial collections. There are many technical libraries in Sweden. Two of the most important are those of the Royal Institute of Technology in Stockholm and the Chalmers University of Technology in Göteborg. The Library of the Royal Institute of Technology, founded in 1826, is a central technology center, providing computerized information and documentation services. Its collection includes major holdings on mining and surveying and 5,300 periodicals. The Library of the Chalmers University of Technology, founded in 1829, houses approximately 250,000 volumes, with special collections on ceramics, textiles, and shipbuilding, and 5,000 current periodicals. The Information and Documentation Centre (IDC) of the Royal Institute of Technology has pioneered in systems development work related to interactive information retrieval and provides SDI service and interactive searches from a score of data bases. The Medical Information Centre (MIC) at the Karolinska Institutet is the Nordic centre for MEDLARS; a great many terminals in Sweden and in other parts of northern Europe are linked to MEDLARS through MIC. The Agricultural University Library, Ultuna, is the central library for agriculture and responsible for input to AGRIS and the utilization of CAIN in Sweden. Chalmers University of Technology Library, Göteborg, is noted for its programs to educate library users.

Uppsala-Bild

*Founded in 1620, the Uppsala University Library is the most famous of Sweden's academic libraries, with collections dating from early monastic libraries.*

**Public Libraries.** The public library movement in Sweden began around 1800. The libraries are financed by the communities, but government funds support central services in each region. There are 24 county libraries and 253 public libraries. The Stockholm Public Library has 43 branches and 3 bookmobiles; Göteborg Public Library has 25 branches and 5 bookmobiles. Public libraries are spread throughout Sweden, and the number of loans per inhabitant averages around ten per year. The establishment of state university affiliates in many smaller towns recently put strains on the public libraries because government reimbursement for textbook acquisition and loans had not yet been implemented by the end of the 1970's. In Linköping, Skara, Västerås, and Växjö there are libraries combining the functions of public and research libraries. Their origin stems from the medieval diocesan libraries that also served secondary education.

**School Libraries.** In Sweden libraries are compulsory for the primary schools. There is a "bookroom" in each school that serves as the central library and store for books, and every classroom generally has a smaller collection of handbooks and supplementary reading material. Often there is close cooperation between the school library and the public library, and in some places a complete integration of functions.

**Table 1. Libraries in Sweden (1976)**

| Type | Number | Volumes in collections | Annual expenditures (krona) | Population served | Professional staff | All staff (total) |
|---|---|---|---|---|---|---|
| National | 2 | 4,510,000 | Kr 34,170,000 | 25,000 | 74 | 378 |
| Academic | 16 | 6,860,000 | Kr 63,550,000 | 107,700 | 175 | 816 |
| Public | 411 | 32,998,000 | Kr 540,715,000 | 8,236,000 | 2,330 | 6,900 |
| School | 1,693 | 2,028,000 | Kr 5,380,000 | 1,206,500 | 230 | 1,700 |
| Special | 520 | 390,000 | Kr 72,000,000 | N.A. | 340 | 1,300 |
| Total | 2,642 | 47,786,000 | Kr 715,815,000 | | 3,149 | 11,094 |

Sources: *Statistisk årsbok 1977* (Stockholm, 1977); *Bibliotekskalendern 1978* (Lund, 1977).

**Special Libraries.** The Parliamentary Library (Riksdagsbibliöteket) serves both the parliament and the central government. It is responsible for the current bibliography of government publications. A central library for technical report literature is Studsvik Energiteknik, Nyköping, responsible for input to INIS and ERDA. The Nobel Library of the Swedish Academy provides the members of the Academy and the Nobel committee for literature with the necessary background works for the preparations of the Nobel Prize for Literature. The Royal Academy of Sciences Library, Stockholm, holds manuscripts by Emanuel Swedenborg, Carl Linnaeus, Jöns Berzelius, and others. A fine example of a nobleman's library is the Skokloster Castle Library.

**Table 2. Archives in Sweden (1976)**

| | |
|---|---|
| Number | 9 |
| Holdings | 21,000 cubic meters |
| Annual expenditures | Kr 23,251,000 |
| Professional staff | 71 |
| All staff (total) | 258 |

Source: *Statistisk årsbok 1977* (Stockholm, 1977).

**Associations.** Sveriges Allmänna Biblioteksförening (SAB) was founded in 1915 and in 1978 had 1,800 individual members. It publishes *Biblioteksbladet* (BBL). The Swedish Association of Research Libraries (SVSF), founded in 1945, has around 200 members, primarily in Stockholm. Svenska Bibliotekariesamfundet (SBF) was founded in 1921 and has around 600 members. Its publication is *Bibliotekariesamfundet Meddelar.* These three associations are Swedish members of IFLA.

Special libraries belong to the Society for Technical Literature (TLS), with a membership of 1,300. Its publication is *The Scandinavian Documentation Journal* (TD).

Under the Ministry of Education was an advisory and cooperation committee, the Swedish Council of Research Libraries (FBR), which in 1979 was integrated with the funding agency, Statens råd för vetenskaplig information och dokumentation (SINFDOK), into a new agency, Delegationen för vetenskaplig och teknisk Informationsförsörjning (DFI). The new agency will act as a grant-giving research council for library and documentation activities. That delegation will also be responsible for the further development of LIBRIS.

**REFERENCE**

"Scientific and Technical Information Provision" in *Sweden: Proposal for New Organization,* report submitted by two Swedish government commissions, 1977 (Summary; Stockholm, 1978).

BJÖRN TELL

## Switzerland

Switzerland, a federal republic in central western Europe, is bounded by West Germany on the north, Austria and Liechtenstein on the east, Italy on the south and southeast, and France on the west, southwest, and northwest. Pop. (1978 est.) 6,292,000; area 41,293 sq.km. The official languages are French, German, and Italian. Twenty-six cantons and semi-cantons are responsible for matters of cultural and educational policy. Therefore the historical background and the structure of the public authorities have both exerted a strong influence on the development and organization of Swiss libraries.

**National Library.** Regarding the Swiss National Library, the influence of the above factors is manifested through several characteristics. It was not founded until 1895, and initially its role was limited to the acquisition of Helvetica (works concerning Switzerland and those of Swiss authorship, as well as works printed in Switzerland) after 1848. Since legal deposit had not been adopted, "free deposit" was established in 1915 between the Library and the two associations of Swiss booksellers and editors, under which the latter two submit one copy of each new publication to the Library. Any Swiss national or any person residing in Switzerland over 15 years of age can borrow books.

Over the years the Library's functions have been augmented. It now manages a bookstock of 1,500,000 items, including publications of official Swiss, as well as international, organizations. It administers the Swiss Union Catalogue, which indexes more than 4,000,000 foreign publications held in 300 libraries. In order to exploit these resources a series of publications have been edited: *Das Schweizer Buch; Das Schweizer Bücherverzeichnis,* the cumulative edition published quinquennially; *Das Schweizer Zeitschriftenverzeichnis; Bibliographie der Schweizergeschichte; Bibliographia scientiae naturalis Helvetica; Jahresverzeichnis der schweizerischen Hochschulschriften; Bibliographie der Schweizer Familiengeschichte."* The Library also houses an office responsible for publishing the *Statistische Quellenwerke der Schweiz.*

**Academic Libraries.** Most of the ten Swiss university libraries were founded between 1460 (Basel) and 1629 (Zurich). The Fribourg Library was founded in 1848 through the fusion of the old libraries of the dissolved

*The National Library of Switzerland, Bern, was founded in 1895.*

National Library of Switzerland

**Libraries in Switzerland (1976)**

| Type | Number | Volumes in collections | Annual expenditures (franc) | Population served | Professional staff | All staff (total) |
|---|---|---|---|---|---|---|
| National | 1 | 1,500,000 | SFr. 5,527,657 | 6,269,783 | 29 | 85 |
| Academic | 8 | 10,689,000 | SFr. 38,531,345 | 43,431 | 181 | 561 |
| Public | 1,948 | 6,902,090 | N.A. | 6,269,783 | N.A. | N.A. |
| School | 2,764 | 2,460,546 | N.A. | 976,304 | N.A. | N.A. |
| Special | 1,276 | 10,254,072 | N.A. | N.A. | N.A. | N.A. |
| Total | 5,998 | 29,345,162 | | | | |

convents—Collège Saint-Michel. The Zurich Federal Polytechnic, founded in 1855, has developed considerably; it now possesses a bookstock of over 2,000,000 items. Swiss academic libraries possess a total of 11,000,000 volumes and approximately 6,000 incunabula. Several of these libraries have a second function. As "canton" libraries they serve the local population's needs in scientific literature.

Since a central institution does not exist, it has not been possible to establish formal relations between Swiss university libraries. However, a certain amount of cooperation is assured through meetings of the Chief Librarians of these libraries. Three of these libraries (Bibliothèque Cantonale et Universitaire, Lausanne; Bibliothek der Eidgenössischen Technischen Hochschule, Zurich; Zentralbibliothek, Zurich) were in the process of computerization in the late 1970's; several others were planning to follow their example.

In addition to university libraries in the strict sense of the term, mention must be made of the existence of 189 university institute libraries, 84 of which are in Zurich.

**Public Libraries.** The earliest public libraries in Switzerland were originally theological libraries established during the 16th-century Reformation (Bern, 1528; Sankt Gallen, 1551). The first public libraries without theological antecedents were at Berthoud (1729) and Glaris (1758). The development of public libraries gained momentum, however, principally in the 19th century. From 1868 to 1911 the number of these libraries almost tripled.

There are approximately 2,000 public libraries. Those "canton" libraries not controlled by a university acquire scientific and bibliographic reference works and additionally conserve the local printed production, which is incorporated in its entirety.

Public library networks have been created, notably in Geneva, Zurich (Bibliothek der Pestalozzi-Gesellschaft), and Bern (Berner Volksbücherei). The Schweizerische Volksbibliothek, an organization founded in 1920, has seven regional branches housing 200,000 volumes, which may be lent either to organizations or to individuals.

**School Libraries.** There are approximately 3,000 school libraries of varying size and importance.

**Special Libraries.** Approximately 1,300 special libraries may be divided into four categories: (1) 15 libraries of international organizations, among them the United Nations Library (700,000 volumes, 12,000 periodicals), the International Bureau of Education Library/Unesco (60,000 volumes, 800 periodicals), and the International Labour Office Library (300,000 volumes, 10,000 periodicals); (2) 200 libraries belonging to public societies and associations; (3) approximately 100 libraries belonging to private enterprise (industry, banks, and insurance companies), with collections totaling more than 1,200,000 volumes; and (4) 118 archival libraries.

**Monastic Libraries.** Among numerous libraries meriting citation the following are especially important: the Stiftsbibliothek Sankt Gallen (100,000 volumes, 2,000 manuscripts, 1,650 incunabula), the libraries of Einsiedeln, and those of Engelberg.

**Associations.** There are three library associations in Switzerland: the Vereinigung Schweizerischer Bibliothekare (VSB) (200 corporate members, 800 individual members), the Schweizerische Vereinigung für Dokumentation (SVD) (425 individual members), and the Vereinigung Schweizerischer Archivare (VSA) (35 corporate members, 124 individual members).

JEAN-PIERRE CLAVEL;
J. MÉDIONI

# Syria

Syria, a republic in southwest Asia, is bounded by Turkey on the north, Iraq on the east and southeast, Jordan and Israel on the south, Lebanon on the southwest, and the Mediterranean Sea on the west. Pop. (1977 est.) 7,845,000; area 185,180 sq.km. The official language is Arabic.

**National Libraries.** The two national libraries in the Syrian Arab Republic function also as public libraries. The Al-Zahiriyah National Library in Damascus, founded in 1877, is attached to the Academy of Arabic Language, which is affiliated with the Ministry of Higher Education. The library has about 75,000 volumes of books, 45,000 volumes of periodicals, and 12,500 manuscripts and other materials. The main emphasis of the collections is on humanities and social sciences. A department of photography and microfilming has been instituted in the Library. The second National Library is the Al-Maktaba al-Wataniyah in Aleppo, which was founded in 1924. The Library possesses about 30,000 volumes and 50 periodical titles and is mainly directed toward public library services. The legal deposit law of 1963 requires printers to deliver five copies of literary works published in the republic, four copies of nonliterary works, and two copies of books printed in the republic but published abroad to the Ministry of Information, which for its part has to transmit one copy to Al-Zahiriyah National Library; only 235 books were reported by the Arab League as published in Syria in 1975. The Al-Zahiriyah National Library issued the Bulletin of Books Published in the Syrian Arab Republic from 1971 as an annual Syrian national bibliography.

**Academic Libraries.** The three main universities in the Syrian Arab Republic have established libraries to serve their teaching staff, students, and scholars at large. The oldest and the largest of these libraries is the Central Library of the University of Damascus, founded in 1919. The Central Library and the 16 college branch libraries have more than 150,000 volumes and subscribe to about 1,400 periodical titles. The other academic libraries are those of the University of Aleppo (founded in 1960), the Tichreen University in Latakia (1971), and the Damascus Institute of Technology (1963).

**Public Libraries.** The Syrian Arab Republic has a well-developed public library system. The Directorate of

Libraries of the Ministry of Culture, Tourism, and National Guidance administers and controls 43 libraries in the Arab Cultural Centers, which are spread throughout the country. The rural population have access to public library services through ten bookmobiles. The Directorate of Libraries supplies materials, technical guidance, and personnel and also publishes a monthly bulletin of ministry publications.

**School Libraries.** Schools of various types possess libraries, but their use is not incorporated into the teaching process. The majority of school libraries in Syria are administered by part-time teachers who are not professionally trained.

**Special Libraries.** Many Syrian government agencies, organizations, and research centers established special libraries to serve their officials and the research community. Special libraries are found in the Ministry of Information, the Ministry of Transport, the Directorate of Scientific and Technical Affairs of the Ministry of Industry, the Directorate of Scientific and Technical Affairs of the Ministry of Petroleum and Minerals, the Directorate of Scientific and Agricultural Research of the Ministry of Agriculture, the Higher Council of Sciences, which incorporates the Council Library and the Nuclear Energy Library, the Central Bureau of Statistics, the Organization of Industrial Projects, and the Planning Institute for Economic and Social Development.

Some of these special libraries offer bibliographical services, indexing, abstracting, photocopying, and publishing and inquiry services. Other organizations emphasize documentation and information services, such as the Department of Documentation and Technical Information, attached to the Center of Industrial Testing and Industries (founded in 1967); the Directorate of Scientific Documentation and Information, attached to the Center of Scientific Studies and Research of the Ministry of Defense (1972); and the Educational Documentation Center of the Ministry of Education (1961).

MOHAMED M. EL HADI

## Tanodi, Aurelio Zlatko

(1914–      )

Aurelio Zlatko Tanodi, a leading Argentine scholar associated with the development of various scholarly pursuits, including historical research, paleography, and archival studies, conducted many research projects. His work in the organization of archival materials, together with the training of high-level personnel in the discipline, won him special recognition.

*Aurelio Zlatko Tanodi*

Tanodi was born September 1, 1914, in Hum, district of Zagreb, the capital of Croatia, Yugoslavia. He studied at the National College of Varazdin and in 1937 received a degree in Universal History from the Faculty of Philosophy of Zagreb University.

His work at the Colegio Clasico de Varazdin (Classic College of Varazdin) began with historical research based on medieval documents deposited in the municipal archives of this city. He worked at the National Archive of Croatia in Zagreb and, commissioned by the government of his country, studied at the Secret Archive of the Vatican and the National Archive of Hungary in Budapest. During this period he worked at the National Academy of Arts and Sciences of Croatia, obtaining the title Doctor of History at the University of Zagreb; his thesis, "Bula de Oro de Zagreb" (The Golden Papal Bull of Zagreb), won highest honors.

In 1945 he moved to Austria, continuing studies at the University of Graz. During 1947–48 he worked at the Biblioteca Mayor of the Antonianum University in Rome, simultaneously studying archival management at the Vatican Archive and librarianship at the Vatican Library. Having established residence in Argentina in 1948, Tanodi began a teaching career at the National University of Córdoba in 1953.

He published the *Manual de Archivología Hispanoamericana: teorías y principios* ("Manual of Hispanoamerican Archives: Theories and Principles") in 1961, within the Collectanea Archivistica series. During 1972–73 he visited various Latin American countries under the auspices of the International Archival Council and the Department of Cultural Affairs of the OAS, demonstrating the urgent need for professional training in this area.

Tanodi's work in Argentina was centered at the Escuela de Archiveros (School of Archival Management), part of the National University of Córdoba, of which he became Director in 1959. He also directed the Centro Interamericano de Desarrollo de Archivos (Interamerican Center for the Development of Archives), part of the School of Archival Management, from 1972, under the auspices of the OAS. Aside from administrative and teaching activities, Tanodi also did advisory and consulting work in the area of archival management in various Latin American countries and edited the annual *Boletín Interamericano de Archivos.* He participated in a number of national and international congresses and conferences.

REINALDO J. SUAREZ

## Tanzania

Tanzania, a republic in southeast Africa, is comprised of two distinct areas. Tanganyika, bordering the Indian Ocean, is surrounded by Kenya, Uganda, Rwanda, Burundi, Zaire, Zambia, Malawi, and Mozambique. Zanzibar—including Pemba Island, Zanzibar Island, and various small islets—is off the coast. Pop. (1977 est.) 16,073,000; area 945,087 sq.km. The official languages are English and Swahili.

The genesis of a nationwide library system in Tanzania dates to 1960 when Sidney Hockey was invited by the East African governments of Uganda, Kenya, Tanganyika, and Zanzibar to carry out a survey of their existing library facilities and make recommendations on services to be offered. Tanganyika was the first country to adopt the Hockey report. In 1963 the Tanganyika Library Services Board Act was passed, empowering the Board to promote, establish, equip, manage, maintain, and develop libraries in mainland Tanzania. In 1975 a new Act was passed that repealed that of 1963. Enacted in the framework of Unesco's NATIS concept, the Act empowers the Board to coordinate library and documentation services, arrange facilities for library training, promote literacy campaigns and the development of indigenous literature, and supervise all types of libraries in Tanzania.

**National Library.** As of 1978 there was no separate national library. The National Central Library operates both as a national and a public library. Plans were under way to establish a separate national library in the new capital, Dodoma. The National Central Library was founded in 1965 as a pilot library in temporary premises with a collection of 30,000 books from the East African Literature Bureau and 20,000 from the British Council. The new building was opened by President Mwalimu Julius K. Nyerere on December 9, 1967, and is the headquarters of a nationwide library service. It has public reference and lending service for both adults and children, a central book processing and supply unit, and a central advisory service. Since 1969 Tanzania Library Service has compiled the national bibliography of Tanzania, and it enjoys legal deposit status.

The Service is responsible for the promotion, establishment, and management of all public libraries in the country in both urban and rural areas. By 1978, 14 branch (regional) libraries had been established in major towns in mainland Tanzania, and rural library services were being offered to several areas by bookmobiles and village libraries.

**Academic Libraries.** Although there are several libraries in teacher training colleges and other institutions of higher education, they are not well developed. The most important academic library is that of the University of Dar es Salaam. The University College, Dar es Salaam, was founded by Tanganyika African National Union (TANU) in October 1961. The college at first was downtown in the building that now houses the Institute of Adult Education. In 1963 it became a constituent College of the University of East Africa along with Makerere University College and, Nairobi University College. The University of East Africa was initially affiliated with the University of London. In 1964 the College moved to its present campus on Observation Hill overlooking the city of Dar es Salaam. On July 1, 1970, an act of Parliament revoked the 1962 Act of the East African Common Service Organization (EACSO), which linked the three constituent Colleges, and consequently the University College of Dar es Salaam ceased to exist. The University of East Africa also terminated activities, and on August 29, 1970, the University of Dar es Salaam was formally inaugurated as an independent university. The University Library was established downtown at the same time as its parent institution in 1961 and moved to its present impressive building in July 1965.

The main library stock by 1971 was about 120,000 volumes (compared with 9,304 in 1961), including some 8,000 serials. A large quantity of materials, particularly Tanzanian government documents, were acquired under the Library (Deposit of Books) Act of 1962. Also placed in the library are publications of major international organizations. There are other special collections on law and East Africana; of particular importance is the East African Bibliography on punched cards, which includes entries from libraries at Makerere and Nairobi universities. The library has also an excellent collection of maps, mainly of East African countries, and manuscripts. In addition to the main library, branch libraries serve the faculty of medicine at Muhimbili Hospital in Dar es Salaam and the faculty of agriculture and veterinary science at Morogoro.

**School Libraries.** The Education Libraries Department at the National Central Library provides services to schools and teacher training colleges, including advice on book selection, design and planning of library buildings, library seminars, and actual visits to schools and colleges. There is, in addition, a school mobile library service with a van especially designed for this purpose. Visits are made to secondary schools where books are distributed to libraries to supplement their educational needs.

**Special Libraries.** The Tanzania Library Service is also responsible for special libraries. Many requests are received from government ministries and from other organizations and institutions for assistance in the organization of their libraries. The Tanzania Library Service staff, therefore, are called upon from time to time to give professional advice and, wherever possible, librarians are seconded to these institutions.

Tanzania Library Service

*The National Central Library in Dar Es Salaam was founded in 1965. It serves as both a national library and as headquarters for Tanzania's nationwide library service.*

**The Tanzania Library Association.** The Tanzania Library Association (TLA) was formed in 1965 as a branch of the East African Library Association (EALA), established in 1956. In 1971–72 the Tanzania Library Association ceased as a branch of the East African Library Association and became an autonomous national association. Since 1968 the TLA has published *Someni* as its official journal. The Association's main functions are: (1) to unite all people working or interested in library work; (2) to encourage the promotion, establishment, and improvement of libraries and library services; (3) to improve the standard of librarianship.

**REFERENCE**

E. E. Kaungamno, "The Functions and Activities of Tanzania Library Services within the NATIS Concept," *Unesco Bulletin for Libraries* (1975).

E. E. KAUNGAMNO

# Taube, Mortimer
(1910–1965)

Mortimer Taube, information scientist and library consultant, was born in Jersey City, New Jersey, on December 6, 1910. He received an A.B. degree from the University of Chicago, and was elected to Phi Beta Kappa.

**Libraries in Tanzania (1976)**

| Type | Number | Volumes in collections | Annual expenditures (shilling) | Population served | Professional staff | All staff (total) |
|---|---|---|---|---|---|---|
| National and Public | 1 | 100,000 | T.Shs 7,000,000[a] | 600,000 | 20 | 20 |
| Academic | 65 | 380,000 | T.Shs 7,900,000 | 19,000 | 32 | 180 |
| Public | 19 | 400,000 | T.Shs 4,000,000 | 850,000[a] | 23 | 290 |
| School | 130 | 325,000 | T.Shs 200,000 | 78,000 | [b] | 75 |
| Special | 63 | 175,000 | T.Shs 3,270,000 | 18,000 | 10 | 146 |
| Totals | 278 | 1,330,000 | T.Shs 22,370,000 | | | 711 |

[a]Most services are centralized—hence, the National Central Library requires a large portion of expenditures and many staff members.
[b]All schools, as of 1978, were served by Library Assistants; there were no professionals.

He did graduate work at Harvard University in philosophy under Alfred North Whitehead, received a Ph.D. from the University of California at Berkeley in 1935, and followed with a certificate in librarianship at Berkeley in 1936. Starting in 1936 he held a variety of responsible academic library positions: circulation librarian at Mills College, cataloguer at Rutgers University, and Head of the Acquisitions Department at Duke University from 1940 to 1944. He joined the Library of Congress in 1944 and served for five years as Assistant Chief of the General Reference and Bibliography Division, Assistant Director of the Acquisitions Department, and Chief of the Science and Technology Project. He left LC to serve, from 1949 to 1952, as Deputy Chief of the Atomic Energy Commission's Technical Information Service.

In 1952 he founded Documentation, Inc., and served as its Board Chairman and leader until his death. Documentation, Inc., was the first (and for a long time only) information science corporation in existence. Starting with only a handful of associates, Taube built an organization that, by the time of his death in 1965, numbered over 500. Under his guidance the corporation engaged in a large number of innovative studies for government agencies—including the U.S. Air Force and the National Institutes of Health—and pioneered in the field of information facilities management. The organization administered the first contract-operated national information program, the NASA Scientific and Technical Information Facility, from 1962 to 1968. Persons who worked with and for Mortimer Taube in the pioneering days at Documentation, Inc. came to comprise a Who's Who of the information science profession.

An innovator and inventor, as well as scholar and business executive, Mortimer Taube is widely credited with the implementation of coordinate indexing through the application of "uniterms," a concept that, although initially applied to manual retrieval systems, forms the basis of a significant amount of computerized search strategy. Throughout his career Taube found the time to lecture and write. He taught at the University of Chicago and Columbia University and flew to New York weekly for seminars at Columbia until his death. He wrote numerous articles and several significant books, including *Studies in Coordinate Indexing,* volumes 1–6; *Information Storage and Retrieval: Theory, Systems, and Devices;* and *Computers and Common Sense: The Myth of Thinking Machines.* He was Editor of *American Documentation,* 1951–52. The Special Libraries Association presented him its Professional Award in 1952, and the American Society for Information Science presented its Award of Merit posthumously to him in 1966.

Taube was indefatigable in his search for truth and honesty. He was often controversial, usually because his ideas were well ahead of their time. A natural teacher and brilliant and witty lecturer, Taube had strong convictions and was not afraid to express them, but he had abiding respect for other opinions if he felt they were honestly and intelligently derived. He was the outspoken foe of shoddy scholarship, meaningless studies, and twisted logic to support predetermined conclusions. Up to his death, Taube was particularly concerned lest practices designed for manual library systems simply be moved to computers. He feared the library profession would miss the opportunity to reexamine its premises in light of the opportunities computer technology would offer in bibliographic control and analysis. A person of many talents and interests, Taube worked tirelessly on behalf of religious, political, and numerous charitable interests. He died on September 3, 1965, at the age of 54. At the time of his death he was engaged in one of the many activities all of which involved him passionately: he was sailing on Chesapeake Bay.

HERBERT S. WHITE

# Thailand

Thailand, an independent constitutional monarchy in southeastern Asia, is bounded by Burma on the West and northwest, Cambodia on the southeast, and the Gulf of Thailand (part of the China Sea) on the south; a section of Thailand extends along the Malay Peninsula on the southwest, bounded by the Andaman Sea (of the Indian Ocean) on the west, Malaysia on the south, and the Gulf of Thailand on the east. Pop. (1977 est.) 44,035,100; area 514,000 sq.km. The official language is Thai.

**National Library.** The National Library of Thailand is composed of three libraries, the Vajirayana Library, Vajiravudh Library, and the Damrongrajanupharb Library. Established in 1905, the National Library is a division in the Department of Fine Arts of the Ministry of Education.

The present National Library building was opened in May 1966. Its printed book collection is strong in the history and geography of Thailand and totals 1,089,347 volumes in Thai and foreign languages. The library is entitled by law to receive two copies of every book published in Thailand, but this has not been well enforced. There is no copyright registration in Thailand.

The Library has over 146,000 Thai manuscripts. Written on palm leaves and Thai paper folded in accordion pleats, they are mainly copies of the Buddhist sacred books and other Buddhist literature, literary compositions, and works on medicine, law, history, arts, and astrology. There are 87 stone inscriptions in various ancient languages and scripts of the Southeast Asian region. Audiovisual materials include a special collection of tapes of Thai folklore, important lectures and discussions, and parliamentary debates and speeches. The library compiles various bibliographies.

Two libraries in addition to the National Library are the Phya Anuman Rajadhon Memorial Library and the Library of King Rama VI. The National Archives was developed along with the National Library and has its own building, which was to be utilized as the office of the Royal Institute.

**Academic Libraries.** Thailand has 12 universities, 9 in Bangkok and 3 in the country areas. All have their own libraries, many with more than 100,000 books, most in foreign languages and inadequate in all subjects. Financial support for university libraries varies from one institution to another. In most faculties, lecturers act as librarians along with their teaching.

In 1967 the Thai and U.S. governments set up funds for each university to acquire more books on science, technology, and the social sciences, a project that had ended by the late 1970's. In 1968 the National Council formed the Committee on Development of University Libraries, comprising ten university librarians and an official of the Council. The Committee planned to compile a union list of serials from all university and some government libraries and a union catalogue of books in all universities. There are incomplete union catalogues at Chulalongkorn and Kasetsart University Central libraries.

The Committee also attempted to promote recognition of higher status for university libraries and librarians and solve other problems but with no definite results by the end of the 1970's. Cooperation among university libraries includes interlibrary loan and duplicate exchanges with hope for cooperative acquisition and cataloguing.

**Public Libraries.** Public library development has been slow. The government initiated services in 1949. In 1979 there were 334 public libraries, most with small reading rooms and an average of 300 volumes and with no professionally trained librarians. The governmental agencies operating public libraries are the Adult Education Division, Elementary and Adult Education Department, Ministry of Education; the Bangkok Municipality; the National Security Command Community Development Department; and the Ministry of Interior. While each government agency has its own policies, there is cooperation among them.

Public libraries of the Bangkok Municipality and the Dhonburi Municipality have trained librarians and adequate budgets. Public libraries under the supervision of the Adult Education Division lack trained librarians, and the status of librarians is at the lowest grade of the civil servants. Budgets are too small to bring the public libraries up to the standards set up by the Ministry of Education in 1968. Those standards grew out of a 1962 Unesco study.

**School Libraries.** The Ministry of Education supervises school libraries. Lack of suitable children's books, few professional librarians, and low status accorded the school librarian contributed to limited student use of libraries. Out of 28,160 schools of all levels, fewer than 10 percent have libraries rendering good services to students.

In 1979 school libraries were receiving more attention. A committee for library development appointed in 1963 helped improve salary scales for school librarians and led to the adoption of standards. There are also projects to provide all schools with libraries and in-service training for staff. The Comprehensive School Project aims to improve the quality of instruction, library quarters, and book collections of 20 schools throughout Thailand.

**Special Libraries.** Special libraries in Thailand are found in research institutes, government agencies, professional and trade associations, learned societies, and business firms. Among the libraries that have special resources in the field of science are the Division of Scientific and Technological Information Department of Science Service, Ministry of Science, Technology, and Energy, Faculty of Science Library (Chulalongkorn University), and Faculty of Science Library (Mahidol University). Several outstanding libraries in health sciences e.g., Siriraj Medical Library, Mahedol University, Chulalongkorn Medical Library, and Ramathibodhi Hospital Library, are part of the medical schools of major universities. A number have had assistance from the China Medical Board and the Rockefeller Foundation.

The Library of the National Institute for Developmental Administration has a collection of 24,000 volumes. The Thailand Information Center at the Faculty of Political Science, Chulalongkorn University, specializes in information on Thailand, with particular emphasis on the behavioral and social sciences and related disciplines. The Asian Institute of Technology has an engineering library that pioneered in introducing computerized systems to library work. Plans called for it to serve as a regional information center for science and technology in Southeast Asia.

Other special libraries include the Siam Society Library of Southeast Asian materials, the Bank of Thailand, the Highway Department, and the Department of Technical and Economic Cooperation.

The Thai National Documentation Center, which supplies scientific and technical information, is the subject of a proposed Unesco automation project. Other international organizations have libraries in Thailand.

**Association.** The Thai Library Association was founded in 1954. The Asia Foundation helped to set up the Association, which sponsors workshops, conferences and seminars, radio and television programs, publications, and other activities and has played a very important role in the library development of the country.

**REFERENCES**

Suthilak Ambhanwong, *Libraries and Librarianship in Thailand,* Chulalongkorn University Department of Library Science, paper no. 5 (1967).

David Kaser, Walter C. Stone, and Cecil K. Byrd, *Library Development in Eight Asian Countries* (1969).

UTHAI DHUTIYABHODI

Central Library, Chulalongkorn University

*The Central Library of Chulalongkorn University. Thailand's 12 university libraries were strengthened in the fields of science, technology, and the social sciences with funds from the U.S. and Thai governments in a 10-year program begun in 1967.*

## Thorpe, Frederick A.
(1914– )

Frederick A. Thorpe, founder of large-print book publishing in Britain, was born and brought up in Leicester, one of the major English provincial cities. His initial experience in publishing was interrupted by war service in the Royal Air Force from 1940 to 1946. On his return to Leicester he resumed his publishing interests, which developed and expanded to become a highly successful business. In it he gained the experience in every aspect of the book trade and publishing that, like the contacts he made with agents and distributors worldwide, was to prove an apprenticeship for his second career, that of pioneering the publication of books in large print.

In 1963, when he was about to retire from his business, Thorpe was approached by a committee set up in response to the concern expressed by the British Government for the cultural well-being of elderly people. There were books available in abundance, but many elderly people could not easily read normal-size print. The committee sought Thorpe's advice, and he applied his experience in printing and publishing to the problem. He discussed it with the Library Association and learned of the results of earlier investigations into this and similar problems, none of which had produced a solution. He decided that the technical difficulties of printing and producing books in print twice as large as that in a normal book, and with an ink density and paper quality that would ensure a sharp contrast, could be solved; he founded the nonprofit publishing house of Ulverscroft Large Print Books to produce them.

In selecting the first titles for publication Thorpe found publishers reluctant to allow their authors' work to appear in a new and untried format from an unknown publisher. His market for large-print books was mainly the elderly who looked for established authors and well-written books. After some initial disappointments he approached Dame Agatha Christie, who gave the project her full support and encouraged other well-known authors to allow their books to appear in the new series. Four thousand copies of each of the first four titles were published in September 1964: *Pocketful of Rye* by Agatha Christie, *I Bought a Mountain* by Thomas Firbank, *The Avenger* by Edgar Wallace, and *The Fettered Past* by Netta Muskett. They established a precedent both in the careful selection of titles that is a hallmark of the firm and in their format. They were printed by offset lithography from photographic enlargements of the normal-size book. Their size, eleven by eight inches, and their distinctive book jackets (blue for romances and historical and romantic suspense, orange for westerns, black for mystery, red for general fiction, adventure, and suspense, green for nonfiction, and, later, purple for specialist series and brown for individual specialist titles) made them immediately recognizable.

Thorpe decided that the books should be sold directly to libraries and other institutions, not through the book trade, which helped to keep the selling price low. The Library Association sent one book, with a letter supporting the venture, to each library. While orders from libraries reached the expected level, there were few from hospitals and welfare institutions, which had been expected to purchase half the copies. Thorpe therefore sought overseas markets. Through his own international contacts, and others made through the American and Canadian Library Associations, Rotary International, and a number of interested individuals, the sales of Ulverscroft Large Print Books spread throughout the English-speaking world. Thorpe's personal interest, his visits to libraries, and his presence at conference exhibitions have made him an internationally recognized figure in librarianship.

The development of large print books from 1963 to 1969 was one of technical experiment to improve quality and overcome the difficulties caused by the photographic enlargement of existing typesetting, especially the broken type and uneven inking that are much more noticeable when enlarged. The solution was to reset the books in large print; this decision, along with the production of a thinner but opaque paper, led in 1969 to a new nine-by-six-inch format, easier for the reader to enjoy and the library to shelve. The new format was greatly appreciated, and the use of newer, still thinner papers has enabled even longer books to be included in the series without their becoming uncomfortable to handle.

The 500th title appeared in 1971 and the 1,000th in 1976, an event marked by the publication of a five-volume edition of *War and Peace*. By 1978, 132 titles were being published each year, and Thorpe had plans to increase the number because of the substantial demand from readers and librarians for more titles.

The profits from Ulverscroft Large Print Books are covenanted to the Ulverscroft Foundation, a charity that also receives donations from individuals, including many readers of Ulverscroft Large Print Books. The Foundation is administered by trustees and assists hospitals, schools, and libraries.

The importance of Thorpe's work has been recognized in several ways. In 1969 he was awarded the Order of the British Empire (OBE) by the Queen, in 1972 the ALA's Francis Joseph Campbell Award, in 1973 the Queen's Award to Industry and the Grimshaw Memorial Award from the National Federation of the Blind, and in 1976 he was the recipient of an ALA Centennial Citation.

Thorpe's achievement is expressed in the title of the book he chose as the 500th Ulverscroft large-print title *A Many Splendoured Thing*. He has made reading possible for many people by bringing unbounded energy and business experience to the creation of a new and now essential part of the resources of libraries in meeting the needs of the disadvantaged. Well known to librarians throughout the English-speaking world, he has established a publishing house with a reputation for a well-selected list and high technical standards.

**REFERENCES**

F. A. Thorpe, "Large Print: An Assessment of its Development and Potential," *Library Association Record* (March 1972).

W. A. Munford, "Books for the Partially Sighted," *British Book News* (April 1976).

GEOFFREY SMITH

# Tibet

Also known as the Land of Snow, Tibet occupies an area of approximately 1,221,700 sq.km. on the Himalayan plateau and has within its borders some of the highest mountains in the world. The average elevation of its inhabited areas is 16,000 feet (4,876 meters). It is bordered by Chinese provinces and a region on the southeast, east, northeast, and north; Jammu and Kashmir on the west; and India, Nepal Sikkim, and Bhutan on the south. Its two principal cities—Lhasa, the capital and former seat of the Dalai Lama, and Shigatse, the former seat of the Panchen Lama—have an elevation of 12,000 and 9,000 feet, respectively. This vast area is but scantily populated; according to a 1970 estimate, the total population was less than 1,400,000, and the bulk of it was concentrated in the southern valleys. The chief languages are Tibetan and Chinese.

Religion constitutes the principal form of Tibetan cultural life. In the 8th century the native Bon religion was displaced by a tantric form of Buddhism, a form that flourished from the 10th through the 13th centuries and has become known as the *rÑin-ma-pa,* or Red Hat sect. In the 15th century, in reaction against the decadent practices of the Red Hat sect, a reform took place that led to the formation of the *dGe-lugs-pa,* or Yellow Hat sect. Quickly the Yellow Hat sect became Tibet's major Buddhist sect and transformed Tibet into a theocratic state under the leadership of the Dalai Lama and the Panchen Lama. Tibet was incorporated into the People's Republic of China in 1951.

No structured library system existed within Tibet prior to 1951. Each monastery had its own library, and some of the major ones, such as Drepung and Sera, also functioned as publishing houses. No information is available on how materials within these monastic libraries were stored and made accessible, nor is there any indication that any monastery functioned as a national library or that material circulated between different monasteries. The monasteries gradually disappeared after Tibet's incorporation into the People's Republic of China.

Tibet's monastic libraries, however, never played an important role in the country's cultural life, serving more frequently than not as mere storage areas. In spite of a large output of religious literature, Tibet's population was, by and large, illiterate. Most of the monks limited their reading activities to a few basic texts. The degree of change in the country's literacy rate after Chinese rule is difficult to assess because of lack of reliable data. If, however, the experience within China proper can be used as a guide, the situation could have improved considerably. There was some doubt by observers as to whether an increase in literacy means knowledge of Tibetan rather than knowledge of Chinese. Indeed, most material published in Tibet in the late 1970's was published in Chinese. The country's main newspaper, the *Hsi-tsang Jih-pao* (The Tibet Daily), is exclusively in Chinese. The impact of China on Tibetan libraries could not be determined with precision in the 1970's; any libraries in the Tibetan Autonomous Region were likely to be structured along the lines followed in the People's Republic of China.

In 1959 Tibet witnessed an uprising against the Chinese in Lhasa that forced many refugees, including the Dalai Lama, to go to India. The majority of them settled in Dharmsala, Himachal Pradesh, where they began a conscious effort to preserve their cultural heritage, encouraged by the Dalai Lama. Within this context the Library of Tibetan Works and Archives was founded in 1971, with the principal purpose of collecting all materials, in printed as well as in manuscript form, dealing directly or indirectly with Tibet. Only scant details about the Library's operation and holdings are readily available. It reported in 1976 in its occasional newsletter that 12,400 Tibetan books and manuscripts had been catalogued. The Library is also engaged in an oral history project and a retranslation project; the former covers the recording of Tibetan oral traditions, the latter the translation of Tibetan Buddhist texts into Sanskrit.

**REFERENCE**

H. Hoffman, *Tibet: A Handbook,* Indiana University Asian Studies Research Institute, Oriental Series (1977).

LUC KWANTEN

# Togo

Togo, a West African republic, on the Bight of Benin, is bounded on the west by Ghana, on the east by Benin, and on the north by Upper Volta. Pop. (1977 est.) 2,348,000; area 56,785 sq.km. The official language is French.

**National Library.** The Bibliothèque Nationale in Lomé was decreed a national library on October 1, 1969. Under the directorship of the Ministère de l'éducation nationale, the library originally was established in 1937 as the Service de la documentation générale, a documentation center to study documentation concerns in museums, archives, and libraries. In 1945 it was taken over by the local IFAN Centre (Institut fondamental de l'Afrique noire), and in 1960 that center became the Institut togolais des sciences humaines. The Institut has departments of anthropology, archaeology, history, ethnography, geography, linguistics, and sociology. In the late 1970's the library's collection housed approximately 15,000 volumes and 1,000 periodicals; 85 percent of all holdings are in French. Togo does not have a national bibliography.

There is no central depot for the deposit of archives. The functions of a national archives are performed by the Institut togolais des sciences humaines and the Archives de la Présidence de la République. Although Togo has some laws relating to legal deposit, they have never been systematically enforced. Plans have been proposed, with Unesco support, to restructure the library system. A general directorate of library documentation and archives was under consideration at the close of the 1970's.

**Academic Libraries.** Togo has one university, the Université du Bénin, which was founded as a college in Lomé in 1965 and attained university status in 1970. All higher education institutions throughout the country are part of the University. The language of instruction is French. The University's libraries are decentralized. Holdings include 26,000 volumes and pamphlets and 580 periodicals, 90 percent of which are in French. Another institution of higher education is the École nationale d'administration (ENA), founded in Lomé in 1958 to provide a training center for Togolese civil servants. The library has over 1,000 volumes; in the late 1970's there were approximately 50 students. There are government-sponsored technical colleges at Lomé and at Sokodé and an agricultural school in Kpalimé. The library of the latter holds nearly 3,500 volumes. The library of the teacher training college at Atakpamé holds 6,000 volumes.

**Other Libraries.** Togo does not have an organized public library system. It was thought that the National Library would play an important role in the development of such a system in the near future. Detailed information was not available on library facilities as of 1979.

Important collections of specialized research institutes include those of the Institut national de la recherche scientifique and the Office de la recherche scientifique et technique Outre-mer (ORSTOM). The Institut national de la recherche scientifique, Lomé, was founded in 1965 as a coordination center for scientific research. Its library currently holds 2,500 volumes; findings of research activity are published in its quarterly, *Études togolaises*. The library of ORSTOM, founded in 1948, has more than 2,000 volumes, 50 current periodicals, 1,000 documents, and 250 maps. The library has holdings on child development, geography, sociology, and geophysics.

The library of the Centre régional d'études et de documentation économiques, founded in 1972 in Lomé, houses more than 3,500 volumes and 100 current periodicals, specializing in economics, labor, and unionism. It publishes the *African Trade Union News,* in English and French editions.

There are two cultural center libraries in Lomé, the American Cultural Center Library and the library of the Centre culturel français. The former's collection consists of approximately 5,000 volumes and the latter's of more than 23,000 volumes.

The documentation center of the Institut pédagogique national houses more than 3,000 volumes and 30 periodicals, specializing in education and educational psychology.

**Association.** A Togo branch of the Association internationale pour le développement de la documentation, des bibliothèques et des archives en Afrique was established in 1959. Its headquarters at the library of the Université du Bénin in Lomé. It is affiliated with IFLA.

STAFF

# Trinidad and Tobago

The republic of Trinidad and Tobago comprises two islands off the coast of Venezuela. Pop. (1977 est.) 1,115,000; area 931,000 sq.km. The official language is English.

**National Library.** There is no officially designated national library in Trinidad and Tobago, but plans for the development of the national library service in the government's Draft Plan for Educational Development, published in 1968, included a national library. An allocation of funds for a national library building and a proposed site have also been established. The Headquarters of the Central Library of Trinidad and Tobago, the main government public library service, were expected to occupy the new building, and plans for a national library were expected to be developed along the lines proposed in the 1968 Education Plan. In 1978 a Library Task Force was appointed by the Cabinet to expedite the plans.

**Academic Libraries.** The chief academic library is the main library of the University of the West Indies. It was established in 1960 by a merger between the university (which formerly had a single campus in Jamaica) and the Imperial College of Tropical Agriculture at Saint Augustine in Trinidad. Emerging from a college library of 30,000 volumes in 1960, the main library held over 148,000 volumes by 1976. In addition, 380,000 unbound pamphlets, journal parts, and nonbook items were in stock. The collection is especially strong in agriculture and the natural sciences but has also developed strengths in the humanities and West Indiana. Other academic libraries on the same campus are those of the School of Education (10,000 volumes), the Council of Legal Education (4,600 volumes), and the Institute of International Relations (8,000 volumes).

**Public Libraries.** There are three independent public library services in the country, two of which work in close collaboration. These are the Central Library of Trinidad and Tobago, formally established in 1949, and the Carnegie Free Library, founded in 1918. The third service, the Trinidad Public Library, became free only in 1951 after serving as a subscription library for 100 years. The latter serves workers and residents of the capital city, Port-of-Spain, and operates three suburban branches in addition to the Headquarters.

Thirteen branch libraries were operated in 1979 by the Central Library in the largest towns; rural bookmo-

**Table 1. Libraries in Trinidad and Tobago (1976)**

| Type | Number | Volumes in collections | Annual expenditure (Trinidad and Tobago dollar) | Population served | Professional staff | All staff (total) |
|---|---|---|---|---|---|---|
| National | none | — | — | — | — | — |
| Academic | 5 | 186,500 | TT$ 1,324,299 | 3,500 | 21 | 81 |
| Public | 3 | 607,990 | TT$ 2,177,790 | 1,100,000 | 27 | 161 |
| School | N.A. | N.A. | N.A. | N.A. | N.A. | N.A. |
| Special | 24 | 138,400 | TT$ 1,560,238 | 23,128 | 23 | 71 |

Sources of information: CEPAL/CLADES "Inventory of Development Units in Latin America and the Caribbean"; local file containing information about 31 documentation services; questionnaire responses from special libraries—1978.

**Table 2. Archives in Trinidad and Tobago (1976)**

| | |
|---|---|
| Number | 1 |
| Holdings (in cubic meters) | 11,894.4 |
| Annual expenditures | TT$ 180,494.00 |
| Professional staff | 1 |
| All staff | 20 |

bile services have been offered only sporadically in recent years. Total service points, which numbered 133 in 1960, dropped to 55 in 1962 and rose again to 96 by mid-1977. There are substantial pockets of urban and rural population unserved by library outlets. Some 12.5 percent of the country's residents are registered with the three systems, which together provided approximately 600,000 volumes and employed 27 professional staff members in 1976.

**School Libraries.** Library service in schools is largely confined to the secondary level, at which 18 such libraries were identified in 1960. Special attention is currently being focused on developing suitable collections for senior pupils in the sixth form (ages 17 and 18), and all new government school buildings at that level are provided with library rooms. Proposals had also been made by the end of the 1970's for centrally administered services to be developed for primary schools.

**Special Libraries.** Special libraries have grown from 34 in 1960 to over 100 such collections in 1976; half of these are fully organized, and over 20 have professional staffing (see table). They serve a wide range of government and private institutions with notable strengths in socioeconomic fields; law, medicine, science, and technology are also well represented. Many of the special libraries offer reading and reference services to the population as a whole.

**Association.** The Library Association of Trinidad and Tobago, founded in 1960, provides a channel of communication and cooperation for approximately 70 librarians in the territory, and its membership includes other persons interested in promoting its objectives. The Association publishes a bulletin on an irregular basis.

**REFERENCES**

Lynette C. Hutchinson, *The State of Library and Documentation Networks in Trinidad and Tobago* [Paper presented to] Unesco/Jamaica Library Service Workshop on the Planning of NATIS—Library and Documentation networks for the Caribbean area, November 10–14, 1975. Pegasus Hotel, Kingston, Jamaica. A basic source including historical and background information, maps, and a comprehensive list of libraries and other collections for which some funds are provided. School libraries are not included in the list and only slightly covered otherwise.

Alma Jordan, *The Development of Library Service in the West Indies through Inter-library Cooperation* (1970). Based on an extensive survey in 1960 this work provides a useful point of comparison for all types of libraries; it is still the only full source for school library data for the country.

E. H. Morton, *Trinidad and Tobago: Development of Library Services,* October–December 1972 (Unesco, 1974). This report suggests the lines of future development of the nation's library services, concentrating on the public and school library systems. The review of existing services is based on random sampling and visits, but no questionnaires were used.

ALMA JORDAN

# Tropovsky, Lev Naumovich
(1885–1944)

Lev Tropovsky was a Soviet specialist in library science and bibliography noted especially for his work in library classification. He was born in Kremenchug on February 12 (old style; February 25, new style), 1885. On graduating from secondary school he entered the Warsaw University (Faculty of Natural Sciences). Later he was expelled for taking part in a students' meeting and strike. In 1904 he joined the Polish Socialist-Democratic Party, and in 1905 he became a member of the Warsaw Committee of the Military and Revolutionary Organization of the Socialist-Democrats. After his arrest he emigrated.

While living in Paris, L. N. Tropovsky graduated from the Faculty of Natural Sciences of the Sorbonne. In 1917 he returned to Russia, where in 1920 he became a member of the Communist Party of the Soviet Union (Bolsheviks). From 1923 he was chief of the Bibliographic Department of the Central Board of Political and Educational Activities (Glavpolitprosvet), where he worked under the direct guidance of N. K. Krupskaya. In that period he delivered a number of reports at important scientific conferences dealing with party spirit in bibliography and problems of development of advisory bibliography. From 1932 he was Director of the Research Institute of Library Science and Recommendatory Bibliography and Head of the Bibliographic Department of the Moscow State Library Institute. He wrote such educational works as *Library Classification* and *Bibliography of Natural History*. Tropovsky was a member of the editorial board of leading specialized journals and helped make possible collections of articles such as *Bibliography, Bibliography and Library Science,* and *Soviet Bibliography*. He was also a member of the Learned Councils of the State Lenin Library, the All-Union Book Chamber, and the Moscow Library Institute. He died in Moscow on October 26, 1944.

With other library specialists and bibliographers he worked at modifying the UDC in keeping with the needs of Soviet libraries. A version of the UDC was introduced by Glavpolitprosvet in 1921; the work was the responsibility of a special committee, headed by L. Tropovsky, of the Research Institute of Library Science and Recommendatory Bibliography.

He substantially revised the decimal classification and introduced a number of amendments and additions into some of its classes, particularly those dealing with questions of philosophy, ideology, and sociopolitical activities. He introduced a new class in the classification—"Marxism-Leninism," in which works by Marx, Engels, Lenin, and leaders of the Communist Party and government were reflected. He also worked out geographical subdivisions for the U.S.S.R. and edited all the classes and subdivisions.

The tables of library classification, worked out by Tropovsky, were very popular and widely used in scientific and public libraries of the Soviet Union. Shortly before his death he also took part in the preparation of a new Soviet classification for books. The work was carried out in the late 1930's and early 1940's under the guidance of the State Lenin Library. In postwar years this work was continued by L. Tropovsky's pupil, Z. N. Ambartsumian (1903–70). The most important editions of this classification are *Library Classification Tables for Public Libraries,* which ran into three editions (1959, 1961, and 1968), and *Library Classification Tables for Children's Libraries* (1960, 1964, 1974).

The activities of Tropovsky and other Soviet library specialists advanced the preparation of the original Soviet library classification (BBK), the publishing of separate issues of which was begun in 1960. The BBK is a universal classification that embraces all branches of knowledge and areas of human practical activity reflected in printed matter. The BBK was published in 25 issues (30 volumes), the abbreviated version in 5 issues (7 volumes). The version for small public libraries and tables for children's libraries were worked out and published on the basis of the abbreviated tables. The BBK tables are used by over 300 scientific and special libraries. Work toward the introduction of the BBK into public library practice was in full swing at the end of the 1970's.

In Tropovsky's working out of theoretical and practical problems of bibliography, "recommendatory" bibliography in particular was especially great. He emphasized the importance of giving an estimate of a book in the annotations of bibliographic indexes. Tropovsky showed a marked interest in recommendatory bibliography all his life, and he paid special attention to its political and social role in the Soviet Union.

K. I. ABRAMOV

# Tunisia

Tunisia, a republic of North Africa, is bounded on the east and north by the Mediterranean Sea, on the west and southwest by Algeria, and on the southeast by Libya. Pop. (1977 est.) 6,065,000; area 164,150 sq.km. The official language is Arabic; French is widely spoken.

**National Library.** The Bibliothèque Nationale in Tunis, founded in 1883, houses the largest library collection in the country, approximately 500,000 volumes, published in 12 languages. The collection is primarily in Arabic and French, but there are considerable holdings in English. The National Library is a depository for Tunisian publications and has an accession rate of about 8,000 volumes a year. The Library's Documentary Department is responsible for legal deposit, but it did not officially have copyright deposit privilege at the end of the 1970's.

The Library has a collection of manuscripts totaling about 30,000, including some that date from the 5th century, and an extensive collection of current periodicals, with more than half published in Arabic. The Library is open to scholars and to others with academic qualifications.

In 1956 the Library began publication of a national bibliography; from January 1977 it was issued every two months. Books and pamphlets published in or about the country are listed. In addition, periodicals, university theses and dissertations, maps and plans, and a catalogue of manuscripts are included. From January 1977 official publications and administrative documents were also listed. Cumulative volumes of the national bibliography have been published: *Bibliographie nationale, 1956–1968; Bibliographie nationale courante depuis 1968 jusqu'à 1975; Bibliographie nationale courante 1976, 1977.* The Library also compiles current bibliographies on special Tunisian subjects.

Tunisia is one of the few African countries to have an International Serials Data System (ISDS) national center.

There are three major publishing organizations in Tunisia, and all are located in Tunis: the Société nationale d'edition et de diffusion, Maison tunisienne d'edition, and Service des publications et echanges de l'Université de Tunis. In 1977 the Maison tunisienne d'edition listed 47 titles, the Service des publications et echanges 13 titles. All government purchases are made from the approved Société nationale d'edition et de diffusion.

**Academic Libraries.** The University of Tunis, founded in 1960, incorporated all existing higher education institutions, including the Zitouna, the Faculty of Theology, which dates from the 8th century and is important for its collection of Arabic literature and Islamic studies, and the Institut des hautes études de Tunis, founded in 1945. Most of the schools, institutes, and training centers of the University are in Tunis, although the University has professional schools in Gabès, Monastir, Sousse, and Sfax. The languages of instruction are Arabic and French.

Among the most important schools of the University, with libraries of varying size, are those of the Faculty of Letters and Humanities, with a collection of approximately 45,000 volumes and 900 periodicals; the Faculty of Law, Political Science, and Economics, with a library of nearly 120,000 volumes, two-thirds in French and the remainder evenly divided into Arabic and English, and 500 current periodicals; the Faculty of Medicine, with 6,000 volumes, 11,000 theses, and 260 periodicals; and the Faculty of Mathematics, Physics, and Natural Sciences, with a collection of 18,000 volumes and 210 periodicals. All of the university libraries are decentralized.

The École nationale d'administration (National School of Administration), founded in 1949 and reorganized in 1964, is run by the Prime Minister and has a collection of 38,000 volumes and 320 periodicals. The Institut Bourguiba des langues vivantes (Bourguiba Institute of Modern Languages), founded in 1961, has a library created in 1966 with aid from the Ford Foundation; it is essentially used for linguistics research. Its collection includes almost everything published on linguistics in Arabic, but it also has a good selection in English and French.

**Public Libraries.** Tunisia's public library system, the Bibliothèques publiques, founded in 1965, was placed under the directorship of the Ministère des affaires culturelles et de l'information in December of 1975. Its central library is in Tunis; approximately 40 branch libraries are operated throughout the country. In addition, in the late 1970's the library maintained 40 children's libraries, six bookmobiles, and more than 100 local and community libraries. The total circulating stock is nearly 600,000 volumes, 65 percent in Arabic and 35 percent in French.

**School Libraries.** In 1956, when the distinction between state schools and religious schools was eliminated, all of the Qu'rānic schools were nationalized. Free education was made available to all students in Tunisia. Enrollment increased dramatically in the years following independence: between 1956 and the early 1970's the number of students in primary schools increased from 225,000 to more than 935,000. By 1978 that figure was 957,107, with fewer than 24,000 teachers available. In secondary schools the number of students increased from 30,000 in 1956 to approximately 195,000 in 1977. In addition, in the late 1970's there were 34,352 students enrolled in vocational schools and 1,059 students in teacher training programs. The languages of instruction are Arabic and French. Tunisia at the end of the 1970's was reevaluating its educational policy to accommodate the tremendous growth in student enrollment.

**Special Libraries.** One of the most important special libraries in Tunisia is that of the Institut des belles lettres arabes, a cultural center founded in 1930 in Tunis. Its library, established in 1949, houses more than 22,000 volumes and nearly 300 current periodicals. In 1937 it began publication of the *IBLA,* a prestigious journal issued biannually, which deals with the study of various cultural aspects of the Arab-Muslim world.

The Centre de documentation nationale, founded in 1966, is under the Ministère des affaires culturelles et de l'information and houses a collection of over 10,000 volumes in Arabic, French, and English. Its publications include the *Tunisie actualités,* issued three times a year, and the monthly *Événements du mois en Tunisie.* It also published the *Bibliographie économique de la Tunisie, 1955–1969.*

The Institut national d'archéologie et d'art (INAA), founded in Tunis in 1957, comprises several departments that specialize in archaeology, history, historical sites, ethnography, and art. Its library consists of 10,000 volumes and 300 periodicals.

In addition, there are numerous libraries attached to research institutes, such as the Institut national de nutrition, the Institut national de la recherche agronomique, and the Institut Pasteur, founded in 1906 and housing a collection of 4,500 volumes; it publishes a quarterly *Archives.*

Several embassies also maintain libraries, most notably that of the British Council, with a collection of over 10,000 volumes and nearly 100 periodicals.

**Associations.** The Association tunisienne des documentalistes, bibliothécaires et archivistes (Tunisian Association of Documentalists, Librarians and Archivists) was established on June 10, 1965, at the Institut Ali Bach Hawba, its headquarters in Tunis. The Association has three divisions: bibliothèques specialistes et d'études, commission de catalogue, and the comité de *Bulletin de l'A.T.D.* The *Bulletin* (1966–    ) is its official journal and is issued approximately three times a year. The Association is a member of IFLA.

**REFERENCE**

Douglas W. Cooper, "Libraries of Tunisia," *Wilson Library Bulletin* (June 1979), a librarian's account of visits to several major libraries in Tunis.

STAFF

# Turkey

Turkey, a republic in southeastern Europe and Asia Minor, is bordered by the Black Sea on the north, Iran and the U.S.S.R. on the east, Iraq, Syria, the Mediterranean on the south, the Aegean Sea on the west, and Greece and Bulgaria on the northwest. Pop. (1978 est.) 43,144,000; area 779,452 sq.km. The official language is Turkish.

**National Libraries.** The National Library of Turkey, in the capital of Ankara, was unofficially founded on April 15, 1946, in a basement room in the Ministry of Education. Its collection consisted of two books. Later that year a government program included a provision for a larger, official national library. Finally, in August 1948, the National Library opened to the public. Under the law of March 23, 1950, its purpose is to preserve the national culture and to form a basis for cultural research. It is one of six legal depository libraries. The collection totals about 675,000 volumes. The Library planned to move to a new building by 1981; a reorganization of the Library including automation of activities was also planned.

The Turkish Bibliographic Institute was initiated within the National Library in 1952 and was established by law in 1955. It issues the *Turkish National Bibliography* (*Türkiye Bibliyografyasi,* 1928–    ) and the *Turkish Articles' Bibliography* (*Türkiye Makaleler Bibliyografyasi,* 1952–    ).

The library of the Turkish Grand National Assembly, born with the Turkish Republic in 1923, serves the legislature with its collections in law, economics, and politics.

TÜRDOK, the National Documentation Centre for Science and Technology, was established in 1966 to disseminate scientific and technical information and to promote and coordinate library and information systems. It issues several periodicals, bibliographies, and reference works.

**Academic Libraries.** The structure of academic libraries in Turkey differs from one university to the other. There are 18 universities in Turkey, 4 of which were founded in 1976. The older ones lack centrally organized library services, and each faculty (college), institute, and department has its own library. The oldest academic library is the Central Library of İstanbul University, established in 1924, with 250,000 volumes, including 18,600 manuscripts. Some of the newer universities have well-organized central library systems, such as the Middle East Technical University, Ankara; the two campuses of Hacettepe University, Ankara; and the Boğaziçi University (formerly Robert College) in İstanbul. The total number of academic libraries in 1976 was 228 with a total collection of about 2,210,000 books and 39,000 periodical titles. There is no central authority for securing cooperation and resource sharing among academic libraries.

**Public Libraries.** During the Ottoman Empire, before the foundation of the Turkish Republic in 1923, public libraries were developed and governed by individual foundations. After the foundation of the national government of Turkey in 1920, active commitment of the state in library matters was realized; and by the "Unity of Education" Law enacted in 1924, public library service was recognized as a state function. Since March 1978 both the National Library and the public libraries have come together under the General Directorate of Libraries in the Ministry of Culture. In 1945 there were 82 public libraries, and the number of volumes totaled about 660,000. As of February 1979 the public libraries numbered 606, with a total collection of 3,800,000 volumes.

There are also "manuscript libraries," which have public library status and which are unique in their holdings chiefly of manuscripts in Ottoman, Persian, and Arabic. The most famous of these is the Süleymaniye (Suleiman) Library in Istanbul, with 64,083 manuscripts; the Library has a book facility where 250 books or 20,000–25,000 pages are repaired annually. The total number of manuscripts held by the libraries under the control of the Ministry of Culture is about 162,000.

The General Director of Libraries identified unfair regional distribution of public library services, inadequate physical facilities, insufficient allocation of funds, and lack of professional staff as key problems facing Turkey's libraries. Plans were being developed in the later 1970's for such projects as establishment of Regional Public Libraries, increasing bookmobile services, centralization of technical processes, a union catalogue of manuscripts, and construction of prefabricated library buildings in rural areas.

**School Libraries.** Theoretically, there must be a library in all primary and secondary schools, but school libraries are far from being adequately developed. They are under the authority of the Ministry of Education, but their development has been limited to the individual efforts of school authorities. There were 1,747 school libraries in 1968 in secondary schools. Generally speaking, the educational system is indifferent to library services.

**Special Libraries.** There is no central authority for special libraries, which are established haphazardly. In most cases they are underdeveloped and lack professional staff. Examples of well-organized special libraries exist, however, including the libraries of the Turkish Historical Society, Turkish Linguistic Society, State Planning Organization, and Ankara Nuclear Research and Training Centre (which is also the liaison center for INIS, International Nuclear Information System) in Ankara; the Çekmece Nuclear Research and Training Centre in İstanbul; and the Marmara Scientific and Industrial Research Institute in Gebze, Kocaeli.

There were 250 special libraries, which reported in a 1976 survey as having a total of about 840,000 books and 165,000 periodical titles. These figures by no means reflect the real situation. Although 3,000 libraries were identified by TÜRDOK in 1974 for an inventory, the response rate to the questionnaire was very low. The State Planning Organization has included in its Annual Executive Plans enforcing measures for the establishment and development of special libraries in the public and private sectors.

**Associations.** Türk Kütüphanecilet Derneği—TKD—(Turkish Librarians' Association) was founded in 1949 in Ankara. It has 50 branches and 1,000 members. It publishes the quarterly *Türk Kütüphaneciler Derneği Bülteni* (Bulletin of the Turkish Librarians Association).

*Universite Kütüphanecilik Bölümü Mezunlari Derneī*—KÜT-DER—(Association of the Library School Graduates) was founded in 1970 and has 250 members. Membership is limited to graduates of library schools. It issues the monthly bibliographical bulletin *Yeni Yayinlar—Aylik Bibliyografya Dergisi* (New Publications—Monthly Bibliographical Journal).

**REFERENCES**

İrfan Çakin *The Analysis of the Structure and Function of University Libraries in Turkey,* Ph.D. dissertation, University College, University of London (1978).

İlhan Kum and Phyllis Lepon Erdoğan, "Spotlight on Turkey," *Unesco Bulletin for Libraries* (1979).

Lawrence S. Thompson, "The Libraries of Turkey," *Library Quarterly* (1952).

SÖNMEZ TANER

# Uganda

Uganda, a republic in eastern Africa, is bounded by Sudan on the north, Kenya on the east, Tanzania on the south, Rwanda on the southwest, and Zaire on the west. Pop. (1978 est.) 12,436,000; area 241,139 sq.km. The official language is English.

The structure of Uganda's library services differs from that in developed countries but is comparable to that in many developing countries. First, there is no national library. Second, most library services are funded by the central government. Consequently, very few libraries have developed as a result of local initiative. This partly explains the homogeneity of library development and the marked concentration of large libraries in the capital city of Kampala. Some of the conventional functions of a national library are performed by the large academic libraries.

**Academic Libraries.** The largest academic libraries are associated with Makerere University, the only university in the country. The origins of the university can be traced as far back as 1922, when it started as a technical school; it was affiliated with the University of London (1948–63) and became a full-fledged university in 1970. It has a British-style system of organization with nine faculties and six associated schools and institutes. The university library system is composed of the Main Library, six sublibraries, and small departmental collections. According to 1977 estimates, the system had a stock of 400,000 volumes. The Main Library has a special collection of African materials, with concentration on eastern Africa. The Albert Cook Medical Library serves the Mulago Hospital Medical School, with a strong concentration on tropical medicine and research literature on medical problems in eastern Africa.

Because of its comprehensive collections, the university library system extends its services to serious readers throughout the country. The Main Library is the Uganda depository for such major international organizations as the United Nations, the World Health Organization, and the International Labour Office. It is undoubtedly the de facto, though not de jure, national reference library for the country.

**Public Libraries.** The earliest attempts to provide a public library service were made in the late 1940's as part of the postwar efforts to improve conditions in the country. Under the ten-year development plan (1946–56) social services were emphasized; among such services were lending libraries. This project lasted a few years before it was abandoned. In 1948 the East African Literature Bureau, an interstate institution (serving the three countries of Kenya, Uganda, and Tanzania), started a public libraries program based at Kampala. It was composed of two services: circulating book-boxes, which were loaned to subscribing institutions, and a postal loan service to subscribing individuals.

A modern public library system was introduced with the 1964 Public Libraries Act, which provided for a national headquarters and regional libraries under a Public Libraries Board. The Board is responsible for the headquarters library in Kampala with over 100,000 volumes and 18 branches throughout the country. Its other functions include a postal lending service to individuals, a book-box loan scheme to institutions, and a mobile library service.

**School Libraries.** Since the mid-1960's the central government has gradually taken control of the large schools in the country, so that by 1976 all the major schools were either fully or partly financed by the government. As a result, more emphasis has been put on the development of school libraries. Inspectors of schools in charge of English became responsible for inspecting libraries. Capital funds from foreign loans were used in establishing or equipping libraries. With funds from the

National Library of Turkey

*The National Library of Turkey in Ankara was officially opened in 1948.*

Africana Publishing Corporation

*The Kampala Library is the headquarters for 18 branch libraries throughout Uganda and functions under a public library system introduced by a Public Libraries Act in 1964.*



World Bank, a number of new secondary schools have been built, and old ones have been improved under an Agency for International Development (AID) project; all AID project schools were planned to include libraries.

In a study conducted between 1975 and 1976, it was found that the average high school library contained about 2,000–3,000 books. However, because of a shortage of funds, many schools cannot buy new editions fast enough to have current collections. Primary schools have less funds, and some do not have libraries.

**Special Libraries.** The Uganda Technical College Library is the leading special library in the country. Whereas its basic role is to serve the Uganda Technical College, it is also an important technical information source for practicing engineers in the country. It houses the Uganda Technical Information Service (UTIS), to which several consulting firms subscribe. It has a stock of over 16,000 volumes, over 240 journals, and collections of standards. Other notable special libraries include those of the Bank of Uganda, the East African Development Bank, and Kawanda Agricultural Research Station.

**Association.** The Uganda Library Association (ULA) was formed in 1972. Earlier it had been the regional branch of the interstate East African Library Association (EALA), which was created in 1958. The Uganda Library Association holds national seminars and collaborates with such international organizations as the International Federation of Library Associations (IFLA) and the Commonwealth Library Association (COMLA). Its journal is *Uganda Libraries*.


**REFERENCES**

B. W. K. Matogo, "Leading Issues in Developing Public Libraries in Emergent Uganda 1960–1970," *Libri* (1975).

G. L. Sitzman, "Uganda's University Library," *College and Research Libaries* (1968).

Anna-Britta Wallenius, *Libraries in East Africa* (1971).


HARRY M. KIBIRIGE



# Unesco

The United Nations Educational, Scientific and Cultural Organization (Unesco) was founded in 1946 by representatives of 20 countries convinced that "wars begin in the minds of men"; therefore, "it is in the minds of men that the defences of peace must be constructed" (Article 1 of the Unesco Constitution).

Unesco is committed to the objectives defined by its Constitution: to encourage international intellectual co-operation; speed development; and promote peace, human rights, and international understanding. These activities, as defined by the medium-term plan of action for 1977–82, are carried out by six Sectors: Education, Science, Culture and Communication, Social Sciences, Co-operation for Development and External Relations, and Administration and Program Support.

The supreme body of Unesco is the General Conference, meeting every even-dated year to decide policy and determine the program and budget for the next two years. At the 19th General Conference in Nairobi in 1976 a budget of $224,413,000 was voted for 1977–78; it also approved Unesco's first medium-term plan of action, setting out ten main objectives and means for achieving them over six years. A budget of $275,500,000 was voted for 1979–80 at the 20th General Conference of Unesco in 1978.

Between General Conferences, the program, implemented by the Secretariat of the Organization, is supervised by the Executive Board, whose 45 members are elected by the General Conference from among regional groupings. The Director-General is elected by the General Conference for a period of six years; Amadou Mahtar M'Bow, formerly Senegal's Minister of Education, was appointed Director-General for the 1974–80 term.

The 3,200-member staff of Unesco's Secretariat come from a wide variety of member states. Some of them work at Headquarters in Paris, while others work on projects in the field. Others serve at Unesco regional offices such as the Asian Bureau of Education, Bangkok; the African Office for Science and Technology, Nairobi; the Karachi Regional Office for Culture and Communication; or the Regional Centre for Adult Education and Functional Literacy for Latin America, Mexico.

**General Information Programme (PGI).** Information has been considered an essential element in the rational utilization of natural and human resources since Unesco's inception. The Unesco Constitution stipulates that the Organization shall "maintain, increase and diffuse knowledge . . . by encouraging co-operation among the nations in all branches of intellectual activity . . . the exchange of publications . . . and other materials of information; and by initiating methods of international co-operation calculated to give the people of all countries access to the printed and published materials produced by any of them."

Within this context, the General Information Programme was established in November 1976 by the 19th General Conference. Activities previously assigned to those sections dealing with "Scientific and Technological Documentation and Information"—responsible for carrying out the UNISIST program—were combined with "Documentation, Libraries and Archives"—concerned with developing the national information systems concept (NATIS).

UNISIST was initiated in 1973 following a five-year joint study with the International Council of Scientific Unions (ICSU). The ultimate goal of UNISIST is a loosely connected world network of existing and future information systems, based on their voluntary cooperation. The concept of NATIS was adopted after the 1974 Intergovernmental Conference on the Planning of National Documentation, Library, and Archives Infrastructures, which recommended actions for the development of national information systems.

This single General Information Programme is carried out according to plans adopted by the General Con-

Theodore F. Welch

*The United Nations, through Unesco and other agencies, has made major contributions to library and information services around the world. The U.N. Library in New York has a major collection in international studies.*

ference, which also created a new Intergovernmental Council of 30 member states to guide PGI implementation. The General Conference instructed the Council to ensure continuity in the development of the activities undertaken in the context of the UNISIST program and to promote the concept of the overall planning of national information systems, paying special attention to increasing the special contributions of libraries to the development of education, science, and culture, and to promoting the development of archival services. The UNISIST program is recognized as the only information program within the United Nations system that is of a general nature and provides a conceptional framework for information system development.

The main emphasis of the General Information Programme is defined within the objective 10.1 of the Unesco Medium Term Plan (1977–82). Under this objective, activities are pursued for the development of international cooperation to facilitate equal access to information by strengthening each nation's capacity for handling information; special emphasis is placed on the needs of the developing countries.

*Information Policies and Plans.* At the international level, Unesco organizes and participates in consultations on existing and planned information systems, and contributes to study on information exchange and transfer both within and outside the United Nations framework. At the national level, liaison with the Unesco program is ensured by national information focal points and UNISIST National Committees already established in 59 member states. A national focal point is a governmental agency responsible for overall information policy and coordination of national activities; a UNISIST National Committee is a consultative body designated to advise on all aspects of information exchange and on liaison with the Unesco General Information Programme. Working contacts are maintained at the regional level with existing information networks and programs, such as those of the Council for Mutual Economic Assistance and the Commission of the European Communities. Where general regional cooperation in the field of information is not yet formally and effectively established, meetings of governmental experts on regional information policy development are being sponsored to foster conditions appropriate to the development of regional activities. Guidelines are prepared and assistance on information policy made available to member states upon request.

*Norms and Dissemination.* Normative action is continually required to ensure the capability for universal access to information. An essential role of Unesco is the proposal of norms relevant to information work, cooperating closely with the International Organization for Standardization, which is responsible for the ultimate adoption of international standards. Although such normative action is not generally linked to specific subject disciplines, assistance is available to specialized networks and services wishing to develop disciplinary or mission-oriented tools compatible with the overall UNISIST framework.

A series of international directories of specialized information services was gradually being developed in the late 1970's to foster their ultimate linkage into a voluntary world referral network. The world register of periodical titles is maintained through the International Serials Data System (ISDS) sponsored by Unesco.

Compatible communication formats are seen within UNISIST as a major prerequisite to international exchange of information and data. In view of the basic importance of bibliographic descriptions in this context, a format for machine-readable bibliographic descriptions has been developed and is maintained by the UNISIST International Centre for Bibliographic Descriptions (UNIBID) at the British Library.

In order to promote application of available bibliographic standards to the totality of the world's published information, Unesco pursues, in collaboration with the International Federation of Library Associations and Institutions (IFLA), a program to assist member states in achieving Universal Bibliographic Control (UBC).

Other tools were under development in the late 1970's for the standardization of documentary terminologies (including thesauri and indexing schemes) in conjunction with the International Federation for Documentation (FID) and the International Information Centre for Terminology (Infoterm). International UNISIST clearinghouses were established to collect all information on existing thesauri and to recommend the application of standardized terminology. Guidelines were published to facilitate mono- and multilingual thesauri construction. *The Broad System of Ordering* was published in 1978 with the FID to serve as a switching mechanism for the exchange of bulk information and data among information centers and data banks.

One of the most important products of the norms and standards program is to be the *UNISIST Guide to Standards for Information Handling,* which will identify and advise on the use of all existing standards and guidelines relevant to information handling. It will aim at providing "UNISIST recommended" standards so as to ensure a high degree of compatibility among information systems.

*Information Infrastructures and Specialized International Information Systems.* Direct support is provided through the General Information Programme to international information systems of an interdisciplinary nature. In the field of numerical data, a long-term program with ICSU includes establishment of the World Data Referral Centre, as one link in the ultimate UNISIST network of international referral services. ISDS is another example of such a system, as is the International Information System on

Research in Documentation (ISORID).

At the regional level, pilot projects are sponsored to promote the introduction of such modern information techniques as computerized information retrieval services and library automation. Regional programs for cooperation in information exchange and the development of national information systems are pursued, often with international funding bodies such as the United Nations Development Programme (UNDP).

At the national level, pilot projects are developed and advisory missions are made available to assist member states in assessing their resources and needs in information system development. In addition, extensive assistance is made available in the information field through UNDP projects. Guidelines are available to assist in surveys of existing information facilities and users' needs for information. Other guidelines bear on the design and development of national information systems, on development of specific institutions such as documentation centers, libraries, and archives, and on modern technologies such as computerization and reprography.

*Education.* The program on education and training of information professionals and users is meant to raise the level of preparation and performance of information personnel (broadly defined to include information specialists, documentalists, librarians, and archivists) and to stimulate the development of programs for the education of information users. The principal objectives are to foster the harmonization and coordination of education and training activities; to assist in the establishment and development of national and regional schools for training various kinds of information specialists; to prepare teaching staff for such schools and other training programs; to contribute to the preparation of appropriate teaching materials; to organize at different levels international and regional courses, addressed in particular to teachers, managers of information systems and services, and specialists in the various branches of the information fields; and to promote information users' education in member states. In these activities Unesco funds act as seed money, which, supplemented by contributions from other sponsors, is intended to have a multiplier effect.

Activities included a 1978 meeting of agencies and organizations that sponsor international training programs, to identify means of fostering the exchange of information and increasing harmonization of efforts among them. Experimental issues of a newsletter on education and training were also produced. An expert meeting was planned for 1979 to make recommendations on archival training programs and to consider their relationship to education for librarianship and information science.

The principal long-term goal is to assist in building up in Unesco's member states—or at least in small homogeneous regions—the basic facilities needed for the professional education and training of information personnel. Short-term consultants are sent to advise on the planning and establishment of national or regional training facilities, assist in forecasting personnel requirements, or advise on the development or revision of curricula for professional schools. Some 15 missions in these categories were sent to member states during 1977–78. Important financial assistance has been given by UNDP for development of national and regional institutions for professional education, including schools in Dakar, Kampala, Accra, and Kingston. A nine-month postgraduate training course in information science was started with UNDP assistance at the University of the Philippines.

Unesco contributes to filling the need for teachers in the developing countries through various fellowship programs and refresher training at such courses as the summer schools organized for Unesco at the University of Sheffield.

The publication of guidelines and instructional materials designed in particular to fill needs in the developing countries is a growing program; e.g., the *Handbook for Information Systems and Services* and a guide for teachers entitled *Education and Training of Users of Scientific and Technical Information*. A training package was being developed in 1978, in collaboration with FAO and IAEA, as a general orientation course on basic concepts in information work and was designed to be used individually or in workshops.

Many member states urgently need access to facilities outside national or even regional boundaries, either for basic professional courses or for continuing education. About 15 courses, seminars, and workshops—varied in level, content, duration, language of instruction, and location—are offered each year. These are organized in collaboration with appropriate international, regional, or national organizations or institutions. They usually deal with precisely defined subjects and are aimed at specific audiences.

Appropriate units of Unesco undertake additional training activities, in particular fellowships for training information specialists in special subject fields and the organization of seminars on such subject areas as educational or social science documentation.

**Other Information Activities.** Operational information services within Unesco are administratively separate from the General Information Programme. The principal Unesco information services, managed by the Documentation Systems Division, include the Computerized Documentation Services (CDS), the Unesco Library, and the Unesco Archives. CDS, and the Library and Archives to a lesser extent, provides service to outside users as well as internal support for the Unesco program.

The objectives of CDS are to achieve bibliographic control of the documents and publications of Unesco, its regional offices, and affiliated institutes; to provide information to the member states on the Unesco program as reflected in its documentation; to facilitate access to specialized information data bases for Unesco experts and professional staff; to develop information and documentation software, in cooperation with other United Nations agencies, for use in participating organizations and institutions of the United Nations system and its member states; and to act as a demonstration and training center for the application of advanced computerization techniques in information processing, storage, and retrieval.

Several specialized data bases or information systems that are not under the direct responsibility of the PGI have been developed in accordance with the conceptual framework of the UNISIST program. The Data Retrieval System for Documentation in the Social and Human Sciences (DARE), a data bank and service center for Unesco, provides a means for the development of social science reference works and fosters international cooperation through exchange of social science information. The International System for the Exchange of Information on the Application of Science and Technology for Development (SPINES) was set up as a pilot project in 1977 for developing information exchange between member states for the collection, analysis, processing, and dissemination of selected documents and data related to policymaking management and transfer and assessment in science and technology. A long-term project was launched in 1976 for the creation of an International Information System for Architecture (ARKISYST), aimed at improving communication between developed and developing countries in architecture and urban planning.

The International Bureau of Education, Geneva, established important programs on educational documentation. The International Bureau of Education Documentation and Information System (IBEDOC), begun in

1974, is a computerized bibliographic data base on comparative education, education policy, and educational reform. The International Bureau of Education International Educational Reporting Service (IERS), operational from 1975, provides information on innovation in curriculum development, methods, structures, and organization of both formal and nonformal education and theoretical aspects of the change process in education. A worldwide system for exchanging educational information was planned on the basis of a network of educational documentation and information.

JACQUES TOCATLIAN

## UNICEF

UNICEF (the United Nations International Children's Emergency Fund) came into being in December 1946 when the UNRRA (UN Relief and Rehabilitation Administration) was coming to an end. The council of UNRRA recommended that a fund be created out of its residual assets to continue aid to children through the UN. Voluntary contributions from governments and individuals were to be its continuing source of funding. UNICEF is governed by an Executive Board made up of nations representing major contributing and recipient countries. The Executive Director is appointed by the Secretary General of the United Nations, in consultation with the Executive Board of UNICEF, which meets annually. In 1953 the General Assembly voted to continue UNICEF indefinitely, changed the official name to United Nations Children's Fund (but keeping the old acronym UNICEF), and recommended a change from emergency aid only to long-range programs of benefit to children in developing countries.

Headquarters for UNICEF are in New York. An office is in Europe, and regional offices are in Abidjan, Bangkok, Beirut, Nairobi, New Delhi, and Santiago. In addition some 50 offices and suboffices are in major cities in developing countries, and a warehousing and shipping center is in Copenhagen. Total UNICEF staff (international and local) numbers almost 2,000.

In order to stimulate funds in the developed countries and to educate their populations about the needs of children in developing countries, national committees were set up, either as private, nonprofit organizations or as semigovernmental agencies. The first was the U.S. Committee for UNICEF, established as a private nonprofit corporation in the state of New York in 1947. There were 31 National Committees and 4 national liaison organizations at the end of the 1970's.

UNICEF maintains at its headquarters a small collection of informational books and reports related to children in the developing countries. There is also a small documents section for the staff, consisting of documents produced in connection with projects in the field, all UNICEF headquarters documents, and related material from other agencies and organizations.

The six regional offices also have book and document collections, of varying sizes, with the largest being in New Delhi. In some cases these are indexed and catalogued, in others not.

The only National Committee maintaining a library is the U.S. Committee for UNICEF, which supports the Information Center on Children's Cultures, established in 1967 and functioning since 1968. The main purpose of the Center is to inform the general public, and specialized segments of it, about the lives of children in developing countries. The Center offers a mail and telephone reference service; initiates or assists with books, products, television programs, and other media about children in developing countries; and compiles and publishes numerous bibliographies and information sheets.

ANNE PELLOWSKI

Information Center on Children's Cultures.

*Anne Pellowski shows a piñata to a student visitor at UNICEF's Information Center on Children's Cultures.*

## Union of Soviet Socialist Republics

The Union of Soviet Socialist Republics is a federal state in northern Eurasia, comprising 15 Union Republics. Pop. (1979 est.) 262,442,000; area 22,402,200 sq.km. There are 91 languages in the U.S.S.R.; Russian served as an international communicational language.

**Historical and Legal Foundations.** The contemporary Soviet library system had its beginnings in 1917 after the October Socialist Revolution. Though prerevolutionary Russia had a considerable number of libraries, with a total number of about 76,000, they were largely inaccessible to the majority of the people. Three-fourths of the entire population were illiterate; only 1 to 2 percent of the inhabitants of the national outlying districts could read, and several nationalities did not even have written languages of their own. With the exception of a few large research libraries, most existing libraries were attached to church schools. The country had about 14,000 "popular libraries" with collections averaging from 100 to 200 religious or popular printed books. In some regions there was only 0.2–0.3 book per 100 population; there was often only one library per 50,000–60,000 population, and the number of registered readers in such libraries was under 100. At the first All-Russia Library Congress in 1911 it was pointed out that for eight years, because of the lack of means, 25 percent of all popular libraries had been unable to acquire a single book. Moreover, special governmental regulations forbade popular libraries to have most of the works of noted Russian writers Pushkin, Lermontov, Turgenev, Tolstoy, Chekhov, and Dostoevsky. The books of A. I. Herzen, N. G. Chernyshevsky, Nikolay Dobrolyubov, and many other authors and social critics were not allowed in those libraries' collections at all.

The Socialist Revolution and subsequent social and cultural reorganizations in Russia radically changed the situation and the role of libraries in the country's life. V. I. Lenin, along with the Communist Party and the Soviet government led by him, paid significant attention to libraries; indeed, on the second day after the October Revolution, in his talk with the People's Commissar of Education, A. V. Lunacharsky, Lenin pointed out the necessity of reorganizing library work. "The book is a great power. The thirst for it will considerably increase as a result of the Revolution," he said. He urged that readers be

U.S.S.R. Ministry of Culture

*Saltykov-Schedrin State Public Library in Leningrad, opened in 1814, contains an extensive collection of 19th-century Russian books and periodicals.*

provided with both large reading rooms and a system of ready delivery of the book to the reader.

More than 270 documents on libraries written and signed by Lenin formed a program for constructing a socialist system of library and bibliographic service and established the basic principles of Soviet library practice: the state character and centralized management of librarianship; general use of libraries for citizens; a role for library work in the tasks of building a new society; planned organization of a library network; and wide participation of the working masses in library construction.

A number of decrees and decisions adopted during the Soviet years indicate consistent introduction of these principles. Documents such as "On Organization of Librarianship" (1918), "On Centralization of Librarianship in the R.S.F.S.R." (1920), "About Village Libraries and Popular Literature for Providing Libraries" (1925), "On Librarianship in the U.S.S.R." (1934), and "On Conditions and Ways of Improving Librarianship in the Country" (1959) determined the rate of libraries' development, the nature of their activities, and the principles of library management at each stage of the socialist society's construction.

The Decree of the Central Committee of the Communist Party of the Soviet Union "On Enhancement of the Role of Libraries in Communist Education of the Working People and in Scientific and Technological Progress" was adopted in 1974. That Decree reaffirmed the significance of libraries and outlined a program for their future development. The main idea is the necessity to increase libraries' effectiveness, to strengthen their influence and to consolidate their position within the daily life and social and economic development of Soviet society. The main approaches to improving libraries are centralization of the library network, formation and more rational use of public book stocks, coordination of the libraries belonging to different administrative departments, improvement of library service to children and youth, and strengthening the material and technological bases of libraries.

By the end of the 1970's, 350,000 libraries operated in the Soviet Union, with book collections totaling 4,200,000,000 volumes, and the collections of public libraries averaged over six books per capita. Library service embraces practically all enterprises and organizations, educational establishments, and settlements. More than 200,000,000 people are reported to be regular readers, borrowing annually over 4,000,000,000 books. The number of staff in Soviet libraries was approximately 380,000. Library education is provided in 28 higher and 130 secondary educational institutions in the all-union republics; the annual number of graduating specialist-librarians is 20,000.

The State plans and finances library development, providing support to up to 90 percent of all libraries. In the period 1965–75 alone over 40,000 libraries were opened. Book collections increased by more than 1,500,000,000 volumes, and library personnel grew by 140,000.

**National and State Republican Libraries.** The main library of the country is the Lenin State Library of the U.S.S.R. in Moscow. Founded in 1862, it has served as the U.S.S.R.'s National Library since 1925. The Library's collection totals over 29,400,000 units in 247 languages. It has collections of manuscripts from the 16th through the 20th centuries and an exceptionally rich collection of early Russian manuscript books. Over 250,000 books from the beginning of printing to the present and about 800,000 printed works of art are held in the Rare Books Department. The Library receives all the printed production of the country in two to three copies and possesses literature in the 91 languages of the peoples of the U.S.S.R.

More than 30 percent of the collection is devoted to foreign literature. A large number of foreign books and periodicals are acquired through a well-developed international exchange program that connects the Library to approximately 4,000 various organizations in more than 100 countries.

The Library's reading rooms have more than 2,500 seats for the 7,000 to 8,000 daily users; over 2,500,000 people from all Soviet Union Republics use over 12,000,000 printed works each year. The Library serves as an all-union scientific, research, and information center, supporting the development of science, industry, and culture. It also provides guidance in library methodology to all libraries of the country.

The Saltykov-Schedrin State Public Library in Leningrad was opened in 1814; from 1870 it received on legal deposit all Russian printed works and thus possesses a unique and complete collection of Russian books and periodicals of the 19th century. The Library's collection totals 23,000,000 units and includes the "Free Russian Printing" collection; the first editions of works of Marx, Engels, and Lenin; the library of Voltaire; 4,000 incunabula; and the "Rossika" collection of early manuscript books. The Library serves as a research institute in library science and theory of bibliography; it is a methodological center for libraries of the R.S.F.S.R. The Library serves about 2,000,000 users annually.

Under the Soviet administration large general libraries were formed in each of 14 Union Republics, known as State Republican Libraries. The book collections of these libraries total 56,700,000 units; some individual libraries have over 6,000,000 units. The State Republican Libraries receive legal deposits of all home printed production plus free local legal deposits. As repositories for the U.S.S.R.'s national literatures and cultures, they contribute to the mutual enrichment of the many cultures of the U.S.S.R.

These libraries carry on substantial and varied work providing library, bibliographical, and information services to scientists and specialists. They operate in close cooperation and coordination with special libraries and information services, jointly working out plans for research work in the fields of library science, bibliography, and information science, as well as plans for publishing various manuals. Common regulations have been adopted as the basis for serving agricultural specialists, teachers, medical workers, and other categories of readers. Many libraries (the Kazakh, Turkmenian, Tajik,

Azerbaijan, Kirghizian, Moldavian, and Lithuanian) moved to new buildings during recent years.

**Public Libraries.** The central place in the Soviet Union's system for library service is occupied by 131,000 public libraries with book collections totaling 1,600,000,000 volumes serving 120,000,000 readers, i.e., nearly half of the country's population. They have 220,000 librarians on their staffs, one librarian per 500 rural readers and one per 750 urban readers. As many as 2,000 buildings are annually put into the service of public libraries.

Public libraries are viewed as contributing to the people's political, moral, and aesthetic education and to the development of culture. They play a significant role in the organization of leisure time of working people as well as in disseminating technical and agricultural literature. Along with books, their collections present a variety of periodicals, printed music, art reproductions, and audiovisual materials. Since 1973 the central publishing houses of the country have issued special series of books for the public libraries in all fields of knowledge. Similar series are also published in the all-union republics.

The public libraries—urban, regional, rural—are widely distributed throughout the country's territory, based on the formula of one library for 750–1,000 inhabitants in the rural areas and one library for from 3,000 to 20,000 and more inhabitants in cities, depending on the density of population. Most libraries are open to readers for at least 35 hours a week.

In accordance with the 1974 Decree, public libraries are now being actively centralized on a basis whereby the central city and regional libraries form centralized library systems (CLS) with common staff, book collections, centralized acquisitions, and materials processing. This process was planned for completion by 1980; over 70 percent of all public libraries had been incorporated into the new system by 1978. The reorganization of the public library system on the basis of centralization was planned to introduce more economical and progressive methods of library administration, increase the quality of the library service through larger book stocks, and significantly expand information services. The regional and territorial libraries, like the libraries of the Union Autonomous Republics, are large, general libraries. They number 167, and in 1976 they served 3,200,000 readers and charged 81,300,000 volumes.

There are also library and bibliographical systems to serve children and youth. In addition to republic and regional libraries of this type, these systems include 8,000 children's libraries, special divisions in city, regional, and rural libraries, and many thousands of school libraries.

**School Libraries.** School libraries are viewed as important in that they contribute to the process of teaching and educating the growing generation and advancing the training of school workers. The total number of school libraries is 156,000, with collections surpassing 600,000,000 units. In 1975 their acquisition allocations were increased twofold. The libraries receive the special "School Library" series and have stocks of teaching manuals, providing the schoolchildren with books free of charge.

**Scientific and Technical, Research, and Special Libraries.** There are 65,000 research, scientific and technical, and special libraries in the U.S.S.R. Their collections total over 2,000,000,000 volumes, and they serve 42,000,000 readers.

*Scientific and Technical Libraries.* Scientific and technical libraries are considered to play an important role; as a major part of the state system of scientific and technical information they actively contribute to scientific and technological progress, to technological education, to increasing the workers' level of knowledge, and to the dissemination of advances in science and technology. There are over 23,000 of them, including libraries in industries, research institutes, and planning and designing organizations.

The most important of these libraries are the central scientific and technical libraries of various ministries, Union Republics, and some large regions. The State Public Scientific Technical Library of the U.S.S.R. is the main library of this group. It was founded in 1958 and now serves as the national state library and information body in the natural sciences and technology and as all-union scientific, research, methodological, and coordinating center for the network of special, scientific, and technical libraries. The library collection totals 10,000,000 units and contains many special unpublished materials and stocks of Soviet and foreign industrial catalogues.

The State Public Scientific Technical Library uses computer technology to help publish union catalogues of foreign books and periodicals. Computers are also widely used in the acquisitions processes, circulation services, and other activities. The Library serves 90,000 readers annually and has international exchange agreements with 2,285 foreign organizations. The All-Union Patent Technical Library is another interdepartmental central library of importance. It was begun in 1896. Its collection totaled nearly 50,000,000 volumes in 1975. The Central Polytechnical Library of the All-Union "Znaniye" (knowledge) Society was founded in 1864. With its over 3,000,000 volumes this Library also belongs to the central scientific technical libraries group.

*Research and Academic Libraries.* Among the libraries serving research workers the principal position belongs to the system of academic libraries—a whole complex of scientific libraries and information centers, including over 500 libraries of the U.S.S.R. Academy of Sciences, academies of the Union Republics, specialized academies, research bodies, and universities. The academic libraries network is centralized, and its collections number over 80,000,000 units. The acquisition of Soviet and foreign literature is centralized at the regional level, enlarging the collections every year by about 4,000,000 units, including 1,000,000 new foreign publications. The collections contain scientific literature in all fields of modern research and are sufficient to meet the needs of scientists and specialists.

A small philological library, containing a few hundred volumes in three languages, was begun in Moscow in 1922. It is now the All-Union State Library of Foreign Literature, the largest specialized collection of literature in all languages of the world. Its collection, totaling over 4,000,000 units, is the nation's most complete collection in philology, fiction, literature, and art. The Li-

U.S.S.R. Ministry of Culture

*Map collection in the Vilnius State Library, Lithuania.*

brary is also a research, bibliographical, and methodological center for other libraries dealing with foreign books and periodicals. In 1978 it provided over 90,000 readers with access to 2,900,000 volumes.

The system of academic libraries includes the Library of the Academy of Sciences of the U.S.S.R. (Leningrad), the Library of Natural Sciences of the U.S.S.R. Academy of Sciences (Moscow), the Institute of Scientific Information in Social Sciences created in 1969, and the State Public Scientific Technical Library of the Siberian Branch of the U.S.S.R. Academy of Sciences (Novosibirsk). Each Union Republic has its own central academic library.

The Library of the Academy of Sciences of the U.S.S.R. in Leningrad is the oldest Russian scientific library, created in 1714. The Library is the administrative center of the Leningrad network of academic libraries. It is a large, general scientific library with a 12,000,000-unit collection; it has complete stocks of material published throughout the Academy's existence. The collection of chronicles is of great value, and the manuscript collection includes the works belonging to Peter the Great as well as his correspondence and personal papers. The Library, together with its Leningrad branches, serves over 30,000 readers annually.

The Library of Natural Sciences of the U.S.S.R. Academy of Sciences in Moscow was founded in 1973. It provides leadership to the academic libraries in the natural sciences and technology in and beyond Moscow and Leningrad. Its collection numbers over 13,000,000 volumes.

A significant role in preparing specialists is played by the libraries of the 860 institutions of higher education with their 5,500,000 students. The collections of the university libraries surpass 400,000,000 units.

The Gorky Scientific Library at the Lomonosov Moscow State University is the center for university libraries in the country. Created with the University in 1755, the Library, with over 7,000,000 volumes, serves about 50,000 readers a year. The library complex consists of a central library and 14 faculty, reference, and educational libraries in all departments.

*Agricultural Libraries.* There is a network of special agricultural libraries in the U.S.S.R., and their development is directly related to the development of agricultural science itself. There are 1,500 agricultural libraries with collections of some 80,000,000 units. They serve more than 1,500,000 readers with an annual circulation of over 58,000,000 volumes.

Some Union Republics founded republican agricultural libraries as methodological and bibliographical centers for all Soviet libraries serving agricultural specialists. The largest of these is the Central Scientific Agricultural Library at the All-Union Lenin Academy of Agricultural Sciences of the U.S.S.R. Ministry of Agriculture in Moscow. The Library was founded in 1930 and now has collections numbering 2,500,000 storage units. It includes such rare publications as the works of the first Russian agronomists and the records of Soviet and foreign agricultural pilot stations. The Library serves some 24,000 readers with an annual circulation of over 1,600,000 volumes.

*Medical Libraries.* The country has a well-established network of medical libraries serving doctors, secondary medical personnel, and all workers in the field of public health. The network consists of libraries of hospitals and clinics, health research institutes, special institutions of higher education, advanced training institutes for doctors, and centers for sanitary education. Their total number is 4,500, with collections of 80,000,000 volumes and about 3,000,000 readers.

A significant role is also played by the territorial medical libraries, republican and regional. The library network of the public health system is headed by the State Central Scientific Medical Library in Moscow. It was founded in 1919 and has collections numbering 2,000,000 units. This Library is the all-union depository of medical literature and includes medical dissertations, rare 16th-century publications on medicine, and a complete collection of Soviet medical periodicals. The Library provides bibliographical information about the world's medical literature for all health science workers.

**Library Coordination and Cooperation.** The future development of librarianship in the Soviet Union envisages a transition toward a more rational organization of library collections and toward a balanced distribution of them among the major economic regions of the coun-

**Libraries in the U.S.S.R.**

| Type | Number | Volumes in collections | Population served[c] | All staff (total)[a] |
|---|---|---|---|---|
| The Lenin State Library of the U.S.S.R. | | 29,400,000[c] | 420,000[c] | |
| The Saltykov-Schedrin State Public Library | | 22,700,000[c] | 240,000[c] | 7,813 |
| State Libraries of Union Republics | 14 | 56,700,000[c] | 440,000[c] | |
| Public | 131,000 | 1,600,000,000 | 120,000,000 | 220,000 |
| School | 156,000 | 602,000,000 | 48,000,000 | 57,000 |
| Scientific, Technical, and other Special Libraries | 65,000 | 2,019,000,000 | 42,000,000 | 95,188 |
| Including: | | | | |
| Academic | 500 | 81,700,000[b] | 500,000[b] | 714 |
| Technical | 23,000 | 340,000,000[b] | 18,000,000[b] | N.A. |
| University | 860 | 411,000,000[b] | 8,400,000[b] | 24,000 |
| Medical | 4,500 | 83,000,000[b] | 2,300,000[b] | 7,000 |
| Agricultural | 1,300 | 89,000,000[b] | 1,800,000[b] | 5,299 |
| Total | 350,000 | 4,221,000,000 | | |

[a]These figures do not include technical personnel, mechanization, automation, reprography workers as well as the personnel of the auxiliary divisions.

[b]The numbers of book collections and readers in these libraries are included in the total sum of figures for scientific and special libraries.

[c]The given data include only registered readers; the number of population in the libraries service areas is not taken into consideration. There is a certain degree of duplication in the numbers of readers of the U.S.S.R. libraries, as some of them simultaneously use several libraries.

try. The basis for improvement and more active use of scientific library collections lies in the creation of a system of depository libraries. By a special decree, 214 of the largest general and specialized libraries were declared depository libraries. Together they collect, process, and store all types of literature, including materials rarely requested.

Readers' needs are met both by individual library collections and through the interlibrary loan system. The State Interlibrary Loan System in the U.S.S.R. enables each library to meet its users' needs for books. Participation in the loan system is obligatory for all libraries; it is organized on the basis that their coordination excludes any artificial obstacles in the way of mutual use of book collections. The major links in the loan system are the republic and regional general and specialized centers. The all-union and central specialized libraries function as the all-union interlibrary loan centers, with the Lenin State Library of the U.S.S.R. acting as the coordinator of the loan system.

Coordination of activities in all fields of library and information services, including coordination of management of libraries in the ministries, departments, and social organizations, is performed by the State Joint Interdepartmental Library Committee organized by the government at the U.S.S.R. Ministry of Culture. In the Soviet view, "the libraries of the Soviet Union actively contribute to the Communist education of the working people and to the plans for economic and cultural construction determined by the decisions of the 25th Congress of the Communist Party of the Soviet Union." V. V. SEROV

# United Arab Emirates

The United Arab Emirates—a union of seven former Trucial Sheikdoms (Abu Dhabi, Ajman, Dubai, Fujairah, Ras al-Khaimah, Sharjah, and Umm al-Qaiwain) lies on shore of the eastern Arabian Peninsula off the Persian Gulf. Pop. (1978 est.) 860,000; area 83,600 sq.km. The official language is Arabic.

**National Library.** There is no national library in the country. The book production is negligible, so that neither a depository law nor national bibliography had been established as of 1979. In 1968 the Center for Documentation and Research was founded. Attached to the Presidential Court, it collects manuscripts, documents, books, maps, and articles relevant to the Gulf States and Arabian Peninsula. The Center also conducts research on subjects related to those areas. Its library contains more than 5,000 volumes in Arabic and Foreign languages.

**Academic Library.** The University of the United Arab Emirates at Al Ain, founded in 1978 began to establish a central library with its Teachers College as its primary focus. The University established colleges of Art, Political and Administrative Sciences, Natural Sciences, and Law and Jurisprudence.

**Public Libraries.** There is a public library in each of the seven emirates. Noteworthy is the Dubai Public Library, with a collection of about 15,000 volumes, mostly in Arabic. The public libraries support adult education in the country.

**School Libraries.** The numbers of new schools and enrollment are increasing rapidly. The Ministry of Education is charged with providing modern library facilities in the educational system of the country.

**Special Libraries.** Four ministerial libraries contain small collections of books, periodicals, reports, and newspapers. Also the Gulf Communicational Documentation Center in Abu Dhabi is under the supervision of the Ministry of Information and Tourism. The Center collects, processes, and disseminates communications information for the Gulf States and the Arabian Peninsula.

MOHAMED M. EL HADI

# United Kingdom

The United Kingdom, a constitutional monarchy, comprises the island of Great Britain—England, Scotland, Wales—Northern Ireland, and various islands. Pop. (1978 est.) 55,870,000; area 244,785 sq.km. The official language is English.

The oldest libraries in Britain can trace their origins back a thousand years. These are ecclesiastical collections, some of which still exist. The next oldest are those of colleges at the universities of Oxford, Cambridge, and St. Andrews. From 1753 to 1973 the national library was the British Museum Library, but it is interesting to note that copyright deposit dates back to 1666 in England, though after the union with Scotland in 1707 a Copyright Act of 1709 became the first to extend the practice to Great Britain as a whole. This act required nine copies of every printed publication to be delivered to Stationers' Hall, these being destined for the Royal Library, the two English and four Scottish university libraries, Sion College Library, and the Advocates' Library in Edinburgh.

From the 17th century a few libraries were open to the public, examples being Chetham's Library in Manchester and Archbishop Tenison's Library in Westminster, but public libraries as we know them date only from an act of Parliament passed in 1850. For over 50 years the whole of Britain has enjoyed a comprehensive public library service, while libraries in other institutions, universities, colleges, polytechnics, schools, and hospitals have steadily expanded. Since 1877 the Library Association has had a great and continuing influence on library progress. Full-time education for librarianship may be said to have begun in Britain in 1919.

**The British Library.** Britain's national library until 1973 was the British Museum Library, which could trace its origins back to 1753 when Sir Hans Sloane bequeathed his outstanding collection of books and manuscripts to the nation. In 1969, however, the Dainton Committee Report drew attention to the need to rationalize the British Museum Library and other related collections. The Library Association strongly urged the Government to act on the Dainton Committee Report; in 1972 Parliament passed the British Library Act; and on July 2, 1973, the British Library (BL) came into being. It was formed from the British Museum Library, the Science Reference Library, the Patent Office Library, the National Lending Library for Science and Technology, the National Central Library, and the *British National Bibliography*. The lat-

**United Arab Republic:** *see* Egypt, Arab Republic of

Joel Lee

*Samuel Pepys's Library, dating from the 17th century, is preserved at Magdalene College, Cambridge.*

ter, known as BNB, was formed in 1950; the British Museum and the Library Association were among the partners that had initiated and supported it.

The British Library derives the bulk of its finances from Parliament, though it receives considerable income from various of its activities. It is governed by a Board consisting of a part-time Chairman, nine part-time Members, and the Chief Executive and the Directors General of the three Divisions of the Library. The Chief Executive also acts as Deputy Chairman of the Board.

The British Library includes three main divisions—for Reference, for Lending, and for Bibliographical Services. In addition there is a Central Administration and a Research and Development Department. The Central Administration on Store Street, London, is conveniently next door to the Library Association headquarters and not too far away from the Reference and Bibliographic Services divisions. The main Reference Division is, in fact, at the old British Museum Library in Great Russell Street. Other reference collections are housed in Holborn and in Bayswater; there is a Newspaper Library at Colindale in northwest London. The resources of the British Library Reference Division (BLRD) total more than 9,000,000 books, over 150,000 manuscripts, and rich collections of other materials.

The British Library Lending Division (BLLD) is housed at Boston Spa in Yorkshire, more than 200 miles north of London, the site of the former National Lending Library for Science and Technology. To those collections was added the stock of the former National Central Library. The BLLD has more than 1,750,000 volumes, over 1,000,000 microforms, and nearly 50,000 periodicals. It lends to other libraries, normally by photocopying, though volumes are lent as well. It handled over 2,500,000 requests annually in the late 1970's, of which more than 10 percent were from overseas. IFLA established an office for International Interlending at the BLLD.

The Bibliographic Services Division continues to produce, among other services, the *British National Bibliography,* while the Research and Development Department is involved in a steadily increasing number of research projects. It has made—and continues to make—a number of grants to individuals and institutions in varied areas of library research. The BL is also aware of the need for good public relations; it has an effective Press and Public Relations Section, which publishes the *Annual Report* and other material offering up-to-date information about the BL and its operations.

The great need is to gather together all the BL's London activities under one adequate and centrally located roof. The Government recognized the need and allocated a site at Somers Town in Euston Road, London. Plans continued in the late 1970's, but it will be some time before the building can be started, and it may be the end of the century before the building will be fully operative. Even then it will not contain the BLLD, which will continue at Boston Spa in Yorkshire, Fortunately, there is plenty of room for expansion there.

**Library Cooperation.** The BLLD is the hinge upon which library cooperation and interlending works, but it was not always so. The idea of library interlending was talked about in Britain in the 1890's and later, but its real genesis took place in 1916 with the start of the Central Library for Students. This followed a Carnegie United Kingdom Trust (CUKT) report written by W. G. S. Adams. The Central Library for Students, set up with CUKT money, was originally designed to help public libraries meet the demands of adult classes for multiple copies of textbooks for study purposes. In 1930 the Central Library of Students was reconstituted as the National Central Library, a result of a Government committee report of 1927 known as the Kenyon Report.

Meanwhile, during the 1920's, the country's public libraries had begun to set up schemes of mutual help based upon various regions. These have been very successful, and there are nine Regional Library systems—seven in England, one in Wales, and one in Scotland. Originally, only public libraries were members; now most of the Regions include academic and special libraries as well. The systems are financed by subscriptions from the member libraries themselves. The networks operate as follows. When a reader submits a request for material that is not in the stock of his library, the library passes on the request to its Regional headquarters, which tries to satisfy the request from other libraries in the region. If that attempt proves unsuccessful, the request then goes to the BLLD, which tries to meet it from its own stock or from other Regions or overseas libraries. The Regions generally satisfy about 80 percent of the requests, while the BLLD success rate is over 90 percent.

To coordinate the work of the Regional Library systems and to provide for closer liaison between the Regions and the BLLD, there is a National Committee on Regional Library Cooperation, formed in 1931, but now as important as ever it was. There are also a number of district systems of library cooperation, based in such industrial centers as Liverpool, Sheffield, Bradford, and a number of other cities and counties.

**Other National Libraries.** In addition to the British Library there are two other national libraries—the National Library of Scotland, which can trace its origins back to the 17th century, and the more recent National Library of Wales. The National Library of Scotland was founded in 1682 as the Advocates' Library, but it was not until 1925 that the Faculty of Advocates presented its collections to the nation and Parliament set them up as the National Library. Since 1709 it has been a copyright library; it contains a notable collection of Scottish books and manuscripts. Housed in a building on George IV Bridge, Edinburgh, it includes a fine Reading Room and imposing Exhibition Rooms; the printed accessions number about 100,000 annually. There is a card catalogue of printed books and a printed catalogue of manuscripts. A Board of Trustees directs the Library's activities.

The National Library of Wales is at Aberystwyth, where its building was begun in 1911 and finally completed in 1955. It has three departments: Manuscripts and Records; Printed Books; and Prints, Drawings, and Maps. Classification is by the Library of Congress system. The Library has benefited under the Copyright Act since 1911, but it may demand only certain material, mainly Welsh, under the legal deposit system. It now possesses over 2,000,000 printed books and large collections of other materials. It is the headquarters of the Regional Library System for Wales.

**University, College, and Polytechnic Libraries.** Britain is well equipped with academic libraries, headed by those of the older universities of Oxford and Cambridge. Oxford is served by the Bodleian Library, which was actually begun in the 14th century but reorganized by Sir Thomas Bodley in 1598. The building was expanded in 1946; it now houses well over 2,000,000 volumes and substantial other material. Like the Cambridge University Library, the Bodleian Library in Oxford has enjoyed copyright deposit privileges since the inception of legal deposit. Cambridge University Library also has collections dating from the 14th century and is of similar size. Its distinctive building was opened in 1934. Next in importance are the libraries of the University of London. In addition to the Central University of London Library in Malet Street, London, are some 44 other libraries in the group. As a whole, the University of London libraries possess over 6,000,000 volumes and seat over 10,000 readers. The main controlling body is the Library Resources Co-ordinating Committee of the University.

Many of the 44 degree-giving universities in Britain are of more recent origin. The "red-brick" universities, such as Nottingham and Southampton, emerged in the early part of the century, but many of the county universities—such as those of York, Lancaster, Kent, Sussex, and others—were formed more recently. A University Grants Committee exists; under its aegis libraries have been provided for these newer institutions.

Certain academic librarians have been disturbed, however, by the Atkinson Report (1976), the result of an inquiry instituted by the University Grants Committee. The Report suggested the principle of the "self-renewing library," implying that once a university library had attained a required size, it should be maintained at that level and not grow beyond it. In other words, once the maximum size has been reached, all new acquisitions should be matched by equal numbers of stock withdrawals. The Report led to great debate among British academic librarians.

College and institute libraries also add much luster and value to the British academic library scene, good examples being university college libraries at Oxford, Cambridge, London, Durham, Wales, Saint Andrews, and elsewhere. The many institute libraries in the University of London complex also are worthy of mention. Britain has numerous university extramural libraries, as well as libraries in colleges of education. In addition, there were 30 polytechnics in England and Wales at the end of the 1970's, all of which possess libraries of growing importance. Just as university and national librarians have formed themselves into a body known as the Standing Conference of National and University Libraries (SCONUL), so the polytechnic librarians have started the Council of Polytechnic Librarians (COPOL). The Library Association also has been active in producing and revising minimum standards for college and certain other types of academic libraries.

**Public Libraries.** In 1850 the first Public Libraries Act was passed by Parliament, a weak, tentative law, permissive and not mandatory. Almost everything was left to local initiative in cities and towns. Not until 1919 were the counties permitted to operate public library services; it was 1964 before the provision of public libraries became a duty imposed on city, town, and county councils, happily achieved except in one or two tiny areas. By that date, complete coverage of the country had been achieved, apart from one or two small and insignificant areas.

After 1850 public library progress at first was slow but began to accelerate from the 1880's, favorable factors being the grants offered by Andrew Carnegie and the increasing professional influence of the Library Association. Not until the 1930's did British public libraries really begin to burgeon. By that time financial limitations had been relaxed, county libraries had been set up, and the library cooperative networks based on the National Central Library and the Regional Library Systems were working satisfactorily. Attracted by the more efficient services, often operating from new, purpose-planned buildings, new readers began to flock to Britain's public libraries in the days before World War II.

During the war years, in spite of reduced staffs and resources and often in the face of enemy bombardments, the country's public libraries were used more than ever before; their role as purveyors of reference work and information was increasingly recognized. After the war the profession began to build upon this new-found confidence. As soon as conditions permitted, existing services were expanded and new ones, such as the provision of audiovisual materials and the establishment of services to the disadvantaged, were embarked upon.

Until the mid-1960's, however, public library development in Britain was hampered by the fact that there were too many local authorities. They varied greatly in size and financial resources, and too many unacceptable inequalities in the service resulted. Lionel R. McColvin had drawn attention to this problem in his 1942 *Report on Public Library Systems in Great Britain,* which had been endorsed by the Library Association. There were over 600 separate public library authorities in McColvin's time, but a succession of new laws—the London Government Act of 1963, the Public Libraries and Museums Act of 1964, and the Local Government Act of 1973, along with separate legislation for Scotland and Northern Ireland—have reduced the number of authorities to 167.

Inequalities still persist but are less noticeable than before; the new, larger authorities created by mergers and combinations are financially more viable and capable of making better all-round provision for ever widening public library services and responsibilities. From about 1958, until national economic conditions made themselves felt, there was also a welcome renaissance of public library building in the country. Hundreds of new branch library buildings were erected, in the cities and in the counties. Reflecting the influence of Scandinavian architecture and design, the attractive buildings appeared up and down the country. The public were not slow to use them.

New main libraries for the cities and larger towns and new headquarters for the county libraries were at first not as common as the smaller branches, but more major public library buildings emerged in the 1960's and 1970's. These include main libraries in cities such as Birmingham, Bradford, and Norwich; in larger towns such as Luton, Grimsby, and Worthing; in the London area at Camden, Bromley, and Sutton; and in county library headquarters at Kent, Montgomeryshire, and elsewhere. Imposing extensions to existing main libraries also have been a feature at Liverpool, Belfast, and Glasgow.

Public library services in Britain have been, and remain, free, both for the borrowing of books and for the consultation of reference material. A loophole in the 1964 Act, however, did permit library authorities to charge for the borrowing of phonograph records and cassettes, and many, though not all, do so. Certain libraries offer annual subscriptions; others charge a small fee for each borrowing transaction. There were no moves to charge for books borrowed or consulted at the end of the 1970's. The free principle still survives.

British public libraries are among the best used in the world. In 1978, 55,000,000 people borrowed more than 650,000,000 volumes. In addition to providing comprehensive lending departments for both adults and children, most lend records and cassettes. Reference and information work is particularly well developed, and there are special services for the housebound, immigrant com-

*The British Library Lending Division building at Boston Spa, Yorkshire, was formerly the site of the National Lending Library for Science and Technology. It also contains the collection of the former National Central Library and handles over 2,500,000 requests annually.*

Logan Photography

*The Reading Room of the British Library, inside the quadrangle of the British Museum, was completed in 1857. Since 1973, the British Library has been independent of the British Museum.*

munities, slow readers, and other special groups. Some, but not all, British public libraries also operate the school, hospital, and prison libraries in their areas. Where this is not done, school libraries are organized by the education authority, hospital libraries either by the Regional Hospital Boards or voluntary effort, and prison libraries by the Home Office. School, hospital, and prison libraries in Britain still need greater organization. An inquiry into prison libraries was under way in 1979.

The larger British public libraries, especially those of the big cities, often have more in common with research libraries than with smaller public libraries. Many own important special collections, such as the Shakespeare collection of Birmingham City Libraries, the City Business Library of Guildhall, London, and the Central Music Library of Westminster City Libraries.

Children's and youth library work is emphasized by most British public libraries. Branch and mobile libraries are generally well provided; computerized methods of cataloguing and charging systems are frequently used; and public relations programs—oral, visual, and printed—are developed as far as staff and finances permit.

**Special and Industrial Libraries.** Although it is possible to prove earlier examples, it is still fair to say that most British special and industrial libraries are phenomena of the post-1920's. Indeed, it was probably World War I that first drew attention to the need for libraries catering to the needs of those concerned with technology, industry, commerce, and statistics. Steady increases in the appearance of such libraries took place throughout the 1920's and 1930's. They were sponsored by Government departments; industrial, commercial, and professional concerns; public authorities; research associations; and other bodies. To aid their development, the Association of Special Libraries and Information Bureaux (Aslib) was formed in 1924, and the Library Association was later to form a Reference, Special, and Information Libraries Section as well as an Industrial Libraries Group.

World War II gave further impetus to the need for more special and industrial libraries in Britain, and another fillip was added in 1948 when the Royal Society sponsored a Scientific Information Conference, which proved very influential in Government circles. Aslib's *Handbook of Special Librarianship* has run into several editions and has fostered developments in this field.

Some of the biggest and most important special libraries are Government owned, examples being those of the Department of Trade and Industry and the Department of Education and Science. Important public authority libraries include those of the BBC, the National Coal Board, and the U.K. Atomic Energy Authority. Outstanding among industrial and commercial libraries are those belonging to the Metal Box Company, ICI Limited, and Boots Pure Drug Company. Professional libraries also abound; important ones include those of the British Medical Association and the Royal Institute of British Architects.

**Associations.** For many years only one organization was devoted to the development of British libraries and librarianship—the Library Association, founded in 1877, only a year after the formation of the American Library Association. Although the LA had been formed and was supported in its early years by academic and research librarians, its emphasis gradually changed; by the early 1920's it was concerned largely with public librarianship. In 1924 the Association of Special Libraries and Information Bureaux (Aslib) was formed. Since that time there have sprung up a variety of other associations, such as those for national and university librarians, for polytechnic libraries, and for art libraries, among others.

*The Library Association.* In spite of the proliferation of other organizations, the Library Association has advanced steadily into its second century. Celebrating its centenary in 1977, the LA had nearly 24,000 members—a record number. Its financial position is sound, its greatest asset being ownership of the headquarters building in London. Opened in 1965, it houses council and committee rooms, a members' lounge, library, offices, and other facilities.

The LA is governed by a 60-strong Council, elected by the membership, and advised by four main committees: Executive Coordinating, General Purposes, Library Services, and Professional Development and Education. The Association also is divided into 12 regional Branches and 18 Groups, the latter representing such specialist interests as library education, rare books, and youth libraries. For the first 90 years of its existence the LA was vir-

***England's oldest surviving college library building is at Oxford University's Merton College, which was founded in 1264.***

Theodore F. Welch

**Libraries in the United Kingdom (1976)**

| Type | Number | Volumes in collections | Annual expenditures (pound) | Population served | Professional staff | All staff (total) |
|---|---|---|---|---|---|---|
| National | 1 | c. 25,000,000 | £25,000,000 | 55,000,000 | N.A. | 2,500 |
| Academic | 668[a] | 20,642,704[b] | £44,922,418 | 2,583,049[c] | 1,654[c] | 4,363 |
| Public | 171 | 125,459,606 | £185,748,413 | 55,000,000 | 8,097 | 27,394 |
| School | N.A. | N.A. | N.A. | N.A. | N.A. | N.A. |
| Special | N.A. | N.A. | N.A. | N.A. | N.A. | N.A. |

[a]In 1975.
[b]For England, Wales, and Northern Ireland, excluding universities (1975–76).
[c]Includes universities (1974–75), and polytechnics and further education, excluding Scotland (1975–76).

Sources: *Education statistics for the United Kingdom* (1975); *University Grants Committee Statistics* (1975); Department of Education, *Statistics of Libraries in the United Kingdom* (1976); Chartered Institute of Public Finance and Accountancy public library statistics; and the British Library.

tually the only body in Britain to have a concern for education in librarianship. From its earliest years it organized courses for aspiring librarians, planned a syllabus, conducted examinations, and maintained, as it still does, a professional register. It also encouraged the formation of library schools, of which there were 17 in the country in 1979.

Although the LA's role as an examining body diminished considerably, since the library schools now award their own degrees and diplomas, the Association still plays an important part in continuing professional education and training. It maintains the professional register of Fellows and Associates, organizes an increasing number of short courses on up-to-date aspects of library and information science, and carries on a continuing dialogue with the heads of the library schools.

The LA is also actively concerned with conferences and publications. In addition to the Association's own annual conference, most of the Branches and Groups arrange their own conferences, meetings, and study schools. Printed proceedings frequently result. The LA issues the monthly *Library Association Record,* the quarterly *Journal of Librarianship* and *Library and Information Science Abstracts,* the annual *Students' Handbook* and the *LA Year Book,* as well as such serials as *British Technology Index.* The LA also publishes many books, one of its best sellers being Walford's *Guide to Reference Material.* During its centenary year in 1977, it issued a number of centenary volumes, one of which was a history of the Association by W. A. Munford.

Research and development are also given prominence by the LA. Although it sponsors numerous projects on its own initiative and resources, it often works with other bodies such as the British Library and Aslib in several areas of research.

*Aslib and Other Organizations.* Although Aslib was formed in 1924 as an association for special libraries and information bureaus, it is only from 1949 that it has been known as Aslib. Aslib has over 500 personal members, but it largely is a body for institutional members, of which there are over 2,500. Like the LA, it is organized into Branches and Groups; it arranges conferences, meetings, and study schools; and it has an active publishing program, including the monthly *Aslib Proceedings,* the quarterly *Journal of Documentation,* as well as the *Aslib Directory* and *Aslib Year Book.* Aslib also maintains a library and information service, as well as a consultancy service, for its members. It keeps registers of specialist translators and indexers and a staff employment register.

Among the numerous other bodies devoted to developing various aspects of British librarianship are such organizations as SCONUL, COPOL, Art Libraries Society (ARLIS), Association of British Library and Information Science Schools (ABLISS), to name just a few.

**Influence on International Librarianship.** This article cannot be concluded without a brief reference to Britain's considerable influence on world librarianship. British librarians have traditionally played important parts in developing IFLA, itself formed after a conference in Edinburgh in 1927. Both the British Council and the Library Association have helped to start library movements in the developing countries of the Commonwealth and have had particular successes in Jamaica, Ghana, Nigeria, Kenya, Singapore, Sri Lanka, and India. The LA also gave invaluable help in setting up the Commonwealth Library Association in 1972. Large amounts of money have been fed into many of the developing countries by the Ministry of Overseas Development and the British Council, while many British librarians have acted as consultants for Unesco, the British Council, and other bodies. Other members of the profession have given their services through Voluntary Service Overseas (VSO), the British equivalent of the U.S. Peace Corps.

Theodore F. Welch

*The Bodleian Library at Oxford University was begun in the 14th century and reorganized by Sir Thomas Bodley in 1598. The building was expanded in 1946 and now houses over 2,000,000 volumes.*

**REFERENCES**

S. P. L. Filon, *The National Central Library: An Experiment in Library Cooperation* (1977).

K. C. Harrison, editor, *Prospects for British Librarianship* (1976).

Thomas Kelly, *A History of Public Libraries in Great Britain, 1847–1975* (1977).

W. A. Munford, *A History of theLibrary Association, 1877–1977* (1976).

W. L. Saunders, editor, *British Librarianship Today* (1976).

K. C. HARRISON

# United States

The United States of America is a federal republic of 50 states; the 48 coterminous states are bordered by the Atlantic Ocean on the east, the Pacific Ocean on the west, Canada on the north, and Mexico on the south. Alaska is bordered by Canada on the east and the Pacific on the west; Hawaii is in the mid-Pacific. Pop. (1978 est.) 218,863,000; area 9,363,123 sq.km. The official language is English.

For several decades after their arrival in 1602, New World colonists had little time for books and reading. With homes to build, forests to clear, and crops to plant and harvest, the emigrants had to spend most of their energy surviving a new environment and adapting to its special demands. Any immediate, practical information needs they had were answered most often by the experience of trial and error, on occasion by native Americans, or perhaps not at all. Intellectual and cultural needs received second priority. The colonial population—though growing—was neither large nor wealthy enough to support a literary class. The New World lacked prominent aristocrats to patronize authors and artists, and although some members of the medical and theological professions possessed a score or more of books they needed to ply their trades, most colonists required little print information beyond their Bibles, hymnals, and prayer books.

Despite these restraints, however, literacy was more widely diffused among the New World populations than in Europe, and soon libraries began to take root and grow. At first most collections were private. Until the turn of the 18th century, personal libraries characteristically consisted of 50 to 100 volumes held by ministers or doctors. But several stood apart. By 1639 Connecticut's Governor John Winthrop, Jr., had accumulated over 1,000 volumes in his personal library; six decades later Cotton Mather of Massachusetts and William Byrd of Virginia each boasted collections of over 4,000 volumes.

Several attempts were made during the late 17th century to expand access to print materials beyond private libraries. In 1656 Captain Robert Keayne, a Massachusetts merchant, willed part of his personal collection to establish a public library in Boston provided the city construct a suitable building to house it. At the turn of the century the Reverend Thomas Bray, an Anglican clergyman, made more serious efforts to create literary centers for colonists. Operating out of England, Bray set up more than 70 libraries in the colonies between 1695 and 1704. Five were located in large cities to serve entire provinces; 40 were given for use by the parishioners of specific churches; and the remaining libraries were controlled by ministers of the Anglican church and designed to serve laymen. Several colonial legislatures passed laws to maintain and staff the Bray libraries, but they made little provision to add new volumes to the original collections. As a result, the Bray libraries fell into disuse shortly after their sponsor died in 1704.

By that time the New World was changing. Within a century of the Plymouth Rock landing, the brush had been cleared from the Eastern seaboard, the forests pushed back, and the threat of Indian raids minimized. Colonists began to find time to reflect upon their current situation. European intellectuals, among them Newton, Locke, and Rousseau, were asking significant questions and offering important observations about man's nature and his social and political environment. Colonists found themselves thinking less about their religious needs and more about their secular and vocational goals. They desired to expand their interests, and they hungered for access to more information sources that would help them answer questions unique to their New World environment.

**Precursors to the Public Library.** In 1728 an enterprising Pennsylvania printer named Benjamin Franklin joined in organizing the Philadelphia Junto, a group of 12 men seeking intellectual stimuli. Franklin suggested that members pool their book holdings and locate them in one place for the benefit of all. Although that scheme failed, the resourceful Franklin did not give up. In 1731 he organized the Library Company of Philadelphia, asking members to purchase shares of stock (which could be subsequently traded or sold) and promising to use the money they invested to acquire books of interest to all. The newly acquired collections demonstrated the continued trend away from religious reading interests. The Library Company eagerly accumulated volumes on such topics as biography, philosophy, and travel.

The Company's proprietary structure served as a prototype for other kinds of social libraries. Some expanded their holdings by inviting nonshareholders to pay a "subscription" price to utilize library services, thus introducing the "subscription library." Others acquired newspapers and magazines for their collections and, by charging large stock prices and fostering other cultural activities, became known as "athenaeums." Another type of social library—the "mechanics" or "mercantile" library—resulted from the philanthropic inclinations of prosperous businessmen and industrialists who wanted to provide clerks and mechanics with opportunities to advance themselves through self-education. For over 150 years social libraries enjoyed measurable support, but by the mid-19th century they had begun to lose ground steadily to tax-supported, free public libraries.

Other types of libraries existed coterminously with the social library but served different purposes. Collections in Sunday school libraries emphasized religious themes that were designed to provide inspirational messages. Some industries sponsored "apprentice" libraries to foster educational and recreational reading among their employees. The "circulating" library served those who sought recreational reading; for a small fee a patron could withdraw books from a library (usually in a printshop or bookstore) whose collection consisted mainly of fiction. In 1835 the New York State Legislature passed a law authorizing school districts to impose a tax on citizens to fund libraries. The Legislature approved matching funds three years later, and collections contained some 1,500,000 volumes by 1850. Although several other states passed similar legislation, the success of school district libraries was short-lived. Legislators usually neglected to provide additional funds for staff and quarters, and the book selection procedures were haphazard. Most school district libraries died for lack of interest and attention.

The changes experienced by libraries in the United States mirrored changes in America's rapidly diversifying socioeconomic structure. By 1850 the United States began to suffer new growing pains. As the nation neared its 100th birthday, it was becoming less dependent upon foreign manufactures to fulfill industrial needs. New industries which clustered in or near major urban areas struggled to meet demands created by growing populations. In the process they created jobs that attracted people from rural areas (farms were becoming increasingly mechanized and required fewer laborers) and held ever-growing numbers of immigrants who had fled the socially static and often depressing economic and social conditions of their native lands for the promise of a new life in the United States. Industrialization and urbanization also stimulated the growth of a professional middle class which sought to perpetuate the country's growth patterns and to remove those obstacles that threatened to alter radically the socioeconomic structure that supported middle class endeavors. By 1875, as the professional middle class looked upon the manifestations of these national growing pains with increasing anxiety, they began to search for solutions to perceived problems.

One response traces its roots to Thomas Jefferson's firm belief that a democratic government cannot function properly without an informed public. Professional people concerned about the country's future began to question whether information was being adequately diffused to citizens. Did all Americans have sufficient access to information so vital to properly carrying out their essential civic duties? If not, how could this be provided for? Some 19th-century leaders believed tax-supported free public libraries might be one answer, and it was in this milieu that the free public library enjoyed its most significant growth period.

**Public Libraries.** The transition from the social to the public library was not sudden. Social libraries continued to enjoy moderate success long after 1833, when Peterborough, New Hampshire, established the nation's first library supported by public taxes and open to all its citizens. Other small publicly funded libraries followed, but not until mid-century did several state legislatures pass laws giving local governments the authority to tax their citizens to support public libraries. New Hampshire was first in 1849, but Massachusetts's 1851 law led directly to the 1854 opening of the Boston Public Library, which became the model for most urban libraries (and many smaller ones) for the remainder of the 19th century.

While city after city established and funded urban public libraries that were developing innovative methods to serve the newer populations flocking to their cities, state after state established library commissions to ensure that similar information services were extended to rural areas by traveling libraries or through the fostering of small town public libraries. Much of this activity was fueled by the philanthropic benefactions of Andrew Carnegie, the retired steel magnate who perceived the public library as a self-help mechanism particularly well suited to nurturing American democratic ideals. After retiring from industry he accelerated his philanthropy and by 1920 had dispensed more than $50,000,000 in the construction of 2,500 library buildings. To merit consideration for a grant, municipalities had only to guarantee an annual appropriation of 10 percent of the sum given in order to support the library.

World War I and its effects significantly influenced the American public library. While the American Library Association directed efforts to provide a Library War Service for American troops at home and abroad, public libraries also assisted in obtaining gift books and donating staff services. In addition, they allowed patriotic organizations to use their facilities, reached out to the new arrivals to their towns who had come to work in war-related industries, and served as a channel for information that the federal government wished to pass along to citizens. By the end of the war in November 1918, the public library had matured into a bona fide social service institution.

The 1920's contrasted sharply with the previous two decades. Resolution of the social problems that seemed so important and received so much attention during the first two decades of the 20th century appeared to dissipate in an overriding desire to accumulate more personal and corporate wealth. Just as individuals turned more attention to personal concerns, so the public library focused more attention on its internal mechanisms. Some public libraries attempted to reach out to nonuser populations and to harness the inertia of the adult education movement, but the nation was not ripe for new social crusades.

The next decade brought significant change, however. First, the Great Depression threw millions of people out of work. Partly to relieve their boredom and partly to improve their chances at reentering the labor market through vocational self-education, Americans began to use libraries more frequently. Circulation increased, and librarians found themselves called upon to meet increasing demands with decreasing budgets for staff and materials. Then, as European and Asian totalitarian governments posed an apparent ever-increasing threat to world stability through a variety of aggressive endeavors (including such censorious activities as book burnings), American public libraries promoted themselves as "guardians of the people's right to know." This theme persisted through the World War II years, the McCarthy era of the early 1950's, and up to the present day.

By the mid-1950's, the public augmented its focus on wider service, especially by reaching out to traditional nonuser groups. Fed by the Great Society programs of the mid- and late 1960's, outreach and rural services once again received increased attention. Public libraries attached themselves to the adult education movement and used the influx of new federal dollars to spur more efforts at cooperation and new activities such as information and referral services. In addition, federal dollars contributed significantly to the construction of new libraries, many of which replaced old Carnegie buildings.

*The James Madison Building was added to the Library of Congress in 1979.*

Library of Congress

Theodore F. Welch

*The main building of the Library of Congress, Washington, D.C., was completed in 1897.*

The 1970's brought a shrinking of the federal financial support, and public libraries increasingly fell back upon local funding. Inflation wreaked havoc on budgets, programs were canceled, and services were either curtailed or cut off altogether. The growth patterns that were characteristic of the 1960's appeared to have been arrested.

**Academic Libraries.** When the Reverend John Harvard donated nearly 300 books (three-fourths of which dealt with theological topics) in 1638, he did not realize that his gift to the Massachusetts institution of higher education would reflect three problems that plagued academic libraries for two-and-a-half centuries. First, academic institutions struggling to survive were reluctant to commit money for books for their libraries, forcing college librarians to augment their collections largely through donations. Second, the gift books themselves badly skewed the collections; many donated texts were discards that their owners no longer wanted, and most were in the subject areas of theology and the classics. As long as the institution's curriculum demonstrated a theological-classical emphasis, the college library could at least render lip service to supporting it, but once college curricula began changing during the mid-19th century, the utility of academic library collections became even more marginal. Third, the attitude that characterized college library administrators augmented the libraries' inherent problems. Too often academic librarians were faculty members whose library duties were simply added to their regular classroom duties, and the institution's trustees and administrators normally looked to these "caretakers" for library security and careful record keeping. Librarians extended borrowing privileges mostly to faculty, infrequently to upperclassmen, and almost never to underclassmen. They opened their libraries as little as possible and often at inconvenient times. Understandably, students shied away from academic libraries and began to develop their own alternative—the literary society library. Between the American Revolution and 1850, for example, literary society libraries at Ivy League colleges were more accessible, contained more books, were broader in scope, and were much more comfortable than their institutional counterparts.

By the mid-19th century, the situation began to change. Charles W. Eliot, President of Harvard, endorsed an elective system designed to give students more options, and other institutions followed Harvard's lead. In addition, the numerous American scholars who had been trained in German universities which emphasized research were taking faculty positions in American colleges and universities, and they began to demand more of academic libraries to meet personal and student research needs. Finally, the ramifications of urbanization, immigration, and industrialization combined to foster the growth of a professional middle class which looked to colleges for imparting the knowledge base necessary to function in selected professions.

All of these factors served to convince college administrators that they needed to provide the necessary funds to alter the traditional patterns of academic library service. Academic librarians began to push for longer hours, services to all members of the academic community, and better catalogues. That most literary society libraries had been absorbed into regular academic library collections by the turn of the century suggests that academic libraries were responding more directly to student needs. The inauguration of seminars, graduate education, and honors and independent study programs all had significant impact on the patterns of academic library use, and librarians instituted closed reserve systems to address the problem of circulating heavily used class-related materials. In the 1930's several academic library directors began dividing their collections and services by subject divisions, and academia started to acknowledge that formats other than print stored intellectual content worthy of preservation.

The post-World War II years brought changes that, although not as significant for service as those of the late 19th century, were much more impressive in numbers. The G.I. Bill provided a tempting invitation to returning veterans to commence and complete a college education, and institutional enrollments expanded. As veterans and their offspring progressed through the American educational system in the 1950's and 1960's, academic libraries found their collection resources and service capacities sorely tested. The federal government supplied some help; the Higher Education Act of 1965 awarded acquisition grants directly to academic institutions, while other federal acts funded the construction of numerous new academic library buildings in the 1960's, and the standards created by various national, regional, and local accrediting agencies had significant impact on the development of modern academic library service.

Academic libraries have developed prototypical growth patterns. Harvard's library system represents the largest of the privately endowed institutions whose collections and interinstitutional responsibilities have grown geometrically. The University of Wisconsin library system demonstrates a pattern of support by an individual state that looked to the major publicly supported institution of higher education within its borders for leadership. Many land-grant institutions provided indifferently for the libraries in the state institutions until the press of increasing numbers of students and the demand for new services forced changes in the 1960's. Small college libraries at institutions like Earlham College in Richmond, Indiana, have been the most consistent performers in providing services over the past 50 years. Although their collections and services have grown to meet the varied needs of more students, these institutions continue to pride themselves on individualized service. The same characterization applies to the junior and community college libraries that have survived uncomfortable embryonic periods of growth in the last two decades to become significant contributors to their students' intellectual and vocational development.

The curious combination of shrinking budgets and prospects for better service sparked several cooperative ventures. In 1942 several Boston libraries pooled little-used materials into the New England Deposit Library. The Center for Research Libraries, founded in 1949 by ten Midwestern universities, holds numerous materials which its 165 member institutions can use through interlibrary loan. The Ohio College Library Center (OCLC) started in 1968 as a cooperative cataloguing effort among several Ohio academic libraries and within a decade blossomed into a national system serving more than 1,500 libraries in 46 states. The Research Libraries Group (consisting in 1979 of Stanford, Yale, Columbia, and the New York Public) was organized in 1974 to identify collection strengths and minimize wasteful duplication.

**Privately Endowed Research Libraries.** The late-19th-century growth of public libraries combined with bibliophilic propensities of a few wealthy men encouraged several individuals to donate vast sums for the construction and maintenance of private research libraries. Chicago received a major share of attention in the 1890's when money left by Walter L. Newberry and John Crerar created research libraries that now bear their names. The Lenox and John J. Astor Libraries performed similar functions for New York City until they were merged into the New York Public Library system during the same decade. The Henry Huntington Library in San Marino, California, was founded by Huntington; it devotes its attention to rare books. The Folger Shakespeare Library was opened to the public in 1933 in Washington, D.C., as a result of the Shakespeare collections and fortune of Henry Clay Folger. Other prominent endowed research libraries include the Pierpont Morgan Library in New York City, the Hoover Library on War, Revolution and Peace at Stanford University, and the Marshall Research Library in Lexington, Virginia.

**Government Libraries.** The United States sponsors numerous governmental library systems. The largest is the Library of Congress, created by law in 1800 to serve the Congress's information needs. The British destroyed the Library during the War of 1812, but Thomas Jefferson offered to revive it by selling his personal library in 1816. After some political haggling, Congress decided to accept Jefferson's offer, subsuming not only his collection but also his classification scheme. The Library of Congress limped along for several decades on minimal budgets and in inadequate quarters, but space needs accelerated when the Smithsonian Institution gave its scientific periodical collections to the Library in 1866, and Congress authorized the purchase of Peter Force's collection of Americana in 1867. Then, when Congress passed the Copyright Law of 1870, which mandated that two copies of any work copyrighted in the United States be deposited in the Library, the collection really began to swell. Ainsworth Rand Spofford, Librarian of Congress, argued that the Library needed a separate building, and after nearly two decades of constant pressure, he finally convinced Congress of the Library's critical situation. Workmen applied the finished touches to the new structure in 1897, and two major additions followed in the 20th century, the Thomas Jefferson Building (1939) and the James Madison Building (1979).

Herbert Putnam became Librarian of Congress in 1899, and under his direction LC began to flex its muscle as a national library by spearheading efforts to centralize cataloguing processes. What started in the first decade of the 20th century as a service to distribute catalogue cards grew to the printing of the *National Union Catalog* in the fourth decade and ultimately led to Machine Readable Cataloging (MARC) tapes in the sixth. LC also plays a role in other national library activities; it is actively involved in investigating better methods for preserving print materials, in sponsoring book exchanges, and in acting as the National Library Service for the Blind and Physically Handicapped. In addition, Congress authorized the Library in 1977 to establish a Center for the Book to focus attention on that medium's traditionally important role in the communications process.

The federal government also supports other important libraries. The National Library of Medicine emerged in midcentury directly from its predecessor, the Army Medical Library, and serves America's physicians and medical scientists through MEDLARS (Medical Literature Analysis and Retrieval System), an intricate and sophisticated computerized storage and retrieval system that is a direct outgrowth of *Index Medicus*, the Library's paper-copy index to current medical literature. Holdings of the NLM currently surpass 1,500,000 catalogued items. The National Agricultural Library, currently with over 1,500,000 volumes, grew out of the Department of Agriculture Library and has led to the development of computerized storage and retrieval of information in the agricultural sciences.

Theodore F. Welch

*The National Agricultural Library had 1,500,000 catalogued items in 1979.*

Other federal government agencies have acquired impressive collections. The Department of State began building its library when President George Washington created the cabinet post in 1789, and libraries at other cabinet-level agencies have followed State's lead. The National Archives established its own library in 1934 to facilitate use of the millions of documents it houses. Libraries serve both faculty and students at each of the nation's military academies, and the United States supports a presidential library for every Chief Executive since Herbert Hoover. Each is in the former President's home town and is designed to collect manuscript materials and memorabilia pertaining to his life and term in office.

Services and collections among state libraries vary greatly. Although some state libraries (often called agencies) were created in the early 1800's, most began to grow at the turn of the century. Services usually include a legislative reference division, provision for traveling library services, and a library promotional division; but from there, functions differ markedly. Some have developed into large research libraries (California and New York), while others act as the center of the state's public library system and serve city and county public libraries through interlibrary loans and traveling exhibits. Within the past two decades, state libraries have also acted as the conduit for federal library funds.

At the beginning of the 20th century, municipal and local library systems were manifested by branch libraries, book stations, bookmobiles, and books-by-mail programs. More recently emphasis has been placed upon the development of local consortia, designed to pool resources, distribute costs, and share in acquisition and cooperate in weeding.

**School Libraries.** Although some school libraries had early-18th-century beginnings, significant growth awaited the last two decades of the 19th century, when many public libraries attempted to serve school curricula and student information needs by utilizing the schools as branch public library stations. While these efforts proved helpful, many members of the National Education Association (NEA) looked for more direct control over the library collection within schools. They began advocating more autonomy and sought acceptance of the concept of separate school libraries that were acquired, staffed, and organized solely for the use of school faculty and students and designed to support the school curriculum. The NEA continued efforts in this area and in the 1920's developed standards for elementary and secondary school libraries. State and local governments encouraged this trend by funding school library supervisors, recommended booklists, and specially developed handbooks.

The Great Depression temporarily stayed school library development, but the post-World War II years restored the growth patterns and introduced several new trends. One was more use of nonprint media for information. Since someone had to acquire, store, maintain, and circulate media equipment and materials, the school library was gradually transformed into an instructional materials center. Another trend after World War II was the effort to establish more elementary school libraries. This movement received tremendous impetus with the passage of the Elementary and Secondary Education Act of 1965. School libraries used the influx of federal money to mime the successful demonstration projects that had been supported by the Knapp Foundation and a School Library Development Project organized by the ALA and funded by Council of Library Resources. The Higher Education Acts of 1965 and 1966 also helped train more school librarians. Although the school library/media center's rapid development was hindered in the late 1970's by the leveling off and, in some cases, decrease in funds, its place on the educational horizon seems firmly fixed.

**Special Libraries.** Special libraries exist to serve specific clienteles. Because they do not ordinarily concern themselves with the information needs of larger populations, their collections are usually smaller, they are frequently staffed by library and information science professionals with special training, they offer tailored hours of service, and they reflect different patterns of organization. Sometimes they are affiliated with a larger library system (e.g., medical libraries within university systems), but more often they are attached to a specific industry or service with a need for quick access to specific kinds of information. The special libraries at Bell Telephone Laboratories, Westinghouse Corporation, and General Electric serve as examples. Newspapers, advertising agencies, and other businesses need special libraries for research use by staff. For newspapers, they often take the form of a "morgue," a series of file clippings arranged and indexed by subject or topic for quick information retrieval. Ready reference materials are frequently available, especially in larger newspaper and magazine libraries. Special libraries also serve professional organizations and schools; the ALA Headquarters Library in Chicago and the Engineering Societies Library in New York City are examples.

Special libraries at federal, state, and locally owned and operated mental or correctional institutions receive most of their funding from existing tax structures; those at historical and philosophical societies, theological schools and law firms, and hospital, banking, and scientific institutions receive their support from private sources. Most of these special libraries have developed within the last 75 years.

**Library and Related Professional Associations.** *ALA.* One hundred three people sharing an interest in libraries met in Philadelphia in the fall of 1876 to coincide with the nation's centennial celebration in that city. Melvil Dewey moved near the end of the meeting to form the American Library Association and, after his motion was seconded and approved, signed himself "No. 1."

In the early years, the ALA concerned itself primarily with matters such as cooperative activities, standardization of library procedures and forms, and debates on the relative merits of stocking fiction. In 1886 the Association established a section to oversee the publication of bibliographical aids, and a $100,000 gift from Andrew Carnegie in 1904 permitted the Publishing Section to expand its program significantly. By the beginning of World War I the Association had become the national voice for library interests. The war provided the ALA with an opportunity it had never before experienced. In organizing the Library War Service under Herbert Putnam's direction, the ALA willingly sought to supply the reading needs of U.S. soldiers and sailors at home and abroad. Association members helped to set up camp libraries and to collect books for shipment overseas. After the armistice in November 1918, some members of the ALA sought to capitalize on the Association's wartime experience and to push for an enlarged program designed to expand its program of activities. But funding agencies and the membership failed to support it, and the proposed program died for lack of interest.

Carl Milam served as ALA Executive Secretary from 1920 to 1948, and during that time he consolidated ALA programs and activities at ALA's Chicago Headquarters, where it continues to reside despite periodic efforts to move it elsewhere. Milam saw the ALA through the 1920's, when the Association concerned itself with the adult education movement, the status of library education, and librarians' welfare, through the 1930's, when many ALA members questioned its management as "undemocratic," and into the 1940's, when the ALA took up the banner of "intellectual freedom." Milam's successor, David Clift, carried that banner through the McCarthy era and into the late 1950's, when the federal government

**Libraries in the United States (1976)**

| Type | Number | Volumes in collections | Annual expenditures (dollar) | Population served | Professional staff | All staff (total) |
|---|---|---|---|---|---|---|
| National[a] | 3 | 21,738,633 | $193,657,585 | N.A. | 1,770 | 5,657 |
| Academic[b] | 3,000 | 468,000,000 | $1,180,000,000 | 11,500,000 | 23,700 | 56,700 |
| Public[c] | 8,307 | 387,564,798 | $1,113,544,833 | N.A. | 36,135 (FTE) | 86,003 (FTE) |
| School[d] | 74,625 | 506,964,551 | $1,182,284,107 | 43,929,114 | 78,219 | N.A. |
| Special | 5,287 | N.A. | N.A. | N.A. | N.A. | N.A. |

Sources: [a]Library of Congress, National Library of Medicine, National Agricultural Library.
[b]*Bowker Annual of Library and Book Trade Information* (1978). Statistics are estimated for fall 1976.
[c]U.S. National Center for Education Statistics, *Survey of Public Libraries, LIBGIS I, 1974,* by Helen M. Eckard (1977).
[d]U.S. National Center for Education Statistics, *Statistics of Public School Libraries Media Centers, Fall 1974,* by Nicholas Osso (1977).

began to provide funds for library service. Robert Wedgeworth, Executive Director of the ALA from 1972, directed his attention to implementing a change in the dues structure, controlling budget deficits, and rebuilding staff morale at Headquarters. The Association grew significantly from a membership of 69 in 1876 to 1,152 in 1902, 8,848 in 1926, 19,701 in 1951, and over 33,000 in 1976. By 1979 there were more than 35,000 members.

*Other Associations.* Other library associations serve members with more specific interests. The American Association of Law Libraries (AALL), established in 1906, has nearly 3,000 members and publishes the *Law Library Journal* quarterly. The American Theological Library Association was organized in 1947 to foster cooperation and understanding of the theological library's function within schools of theology; membership was near 600 in 1979. The Art Libraries Society of North America, begun in 1972, provides an information exchange forum for art librarians. ARLIS/NA institutional and personal members numbered over 1,000. The Theatre Library Association, established in 1937, had nearly 500 institutional and personal members in 1979; the Catholic Library Association, organized in 1921, had over 3,000 members; and the Music Library Association, founded in 1931, nearly 2,000 members. The Medical Library Association, begun in 1898, served over 4,000 members in 1979, and the membership of the Special Libraries Association, established in 1909, exceeded 10,000.

The Association of Research Libraries, organized in 1932, represents a different type of library association. It consists of over 100 member institutions that seek to address problems common to their needs.

U.S. librarians are also served by regional, state, and local library associations. The Mountain Plains Library Association was organized in 1948 (membership in 1979 over 500). The Pacific Northwest Library Association began in 1909 (over 1,000 members). The Southeastern Library Association began in 1920 (nearly 2,750 members); the Southwestern Library Association was organized two years later (2,500 members). Nearly every state in the Union has its own separate library association, ranging from the largest in New York (4,500 members) to the smallest in Nevada (175 members).

Other associations and agencies heavily involved in library and information activities include the American Society for Information Science (ASIS), born of the American Documentation Institute (founded in 1937; 4,000 members), and the Society for American Archivists, established in 1936 (membership of over 3,000). Beta Phi Mu, the international library science honor society, founded in 1948, has over 15,000 members in more than 40 chapters in library schools. The Freedom to Read Foundation dispenses legal aid to defendants implicated in First Amendment cases that involve libraries, librarians, and those who use them. The Continuing Library Education Network and Exchange (CLENE) was organized in 1975 to provide a forum for the discussion of the continuing education needs of library personnel. The National Commission on Library and Information Science (NCLIS), the Council on Library Resources, and the Urban Libraries Council are among organizations that deserve special recognition for their contributions and efforts to facilitate and improve library services.

**The Library Press.** Members of the library community in the United States enjoy numerous avenues of communication with their professional colleagues. The library press in the United States can trace its roots to 1876, when the *American Library Journal* published its first issue. Shortly thereafter, it dropped "American" from its title to become the *Library Journal,* and it acts as an independent voice in library affairs. The *Wilson Library Bulletin* is in the same category, and the *Journal of Academic Librarianship* serves an audience with more specific interests. The ALA and its divisions publish important communication organs, including *American Libraries,* the ALA's principal publication for communicating with its members and the public, *College and Research Libraries,* published by the Association of College and Research Libraries, and *RQ,* the quarterly sponsored by the Reference and Adult Services Division, and other journals and newsletters important to the profession. Most regional, state, and national library associations also issue journals that usually commenced publication with the founding of the organization sponsoring them. Periodicals such as *Library Quarterly* (University of Chicago) and the *Journal of Library History* (University of Texas) provide a forum for professionals of scholarly bent. In addition, commercial publishers, among them R. R. Bowker Company, the H. W. Wilson Company, Scarecrow Press, and Libraries Unlimited, regularly issue important monographs and reference tools considered essential to library service. Academic Press's *Advances in Librarianship* offers an annual review of topics of interest to the library and information science profession, and individual issues of *Library Trends* (University of Illinois) and the *Drexel Library Quarterly* (Drexel University) concentrate on specific topics of current interest.

Theodore F. Welch

*The National Technical Information Service is the nation's leading distributor of technical report literature.*

**REFERENCES**


Useful surveys include Elmer Johnson and Michael Harris, *History of Libraries in the Western World* (1976), and Howard Winger, editor, "American Library History: 1876–1976," *Library Trends* (1976).

Jesse Shera, *Foundations of the Public Library* (1949), and Sidney Ditzion, *Arsenals of a Democratic Culture* (ALA, 1947), remain standard.

Richard D. Johnson, editor, *Libraries for Teaching, Libraries for Research: Essays for a Century* (ALA, 1977), provides coverage of academic library activities from 1876 to 1976.

A. W. Johns, *Special Libraries: Development of the Concept, Their Organization, and Their Services* (1968), renders a general overview of special librarianship.

Edward Holley, "ALA at 100," *The ALA Yearbook* (ALA, 1976), is a useful, brief survey. Annual editions of the *Yearbook* provide statistics, reports, and names of officers for library state associations as well as summaries of activities each year under general titles—"Academic Libraries," "Special Libraries," "Public Libraries," and others.

Bohdan S. Wynar, editor. *Dictionary of American Library Biography* (1978), and Michael H. Harris and Donald G. Davis, Jr., *American Library History: A Bibliography* (1978), are also valuable as tools to identify sources for further information.


WAYNE A. WIEGAND;
MICHAEL H. HARRIS

# Upper Volta

Upper Volta, a republic of West Africa, is bounded on the north and west by Mali, on the south by the Ivory Coast, Ghana, and Togo, and on the east by Benin and Niger. Pop. (1978 est.) 6,464,000; area 274,200 sq.km. The official language is French; the dialect More is widely spoken.

Upper Volta does not have a national library, although a National Commission for Libraries, Archives and Documentation was established in 1969. To date little has been accomplished. The Centre National de la Recerche Scientifique et Technologique (CNRST), founded in 1950, receives copies of all Upper Volta publications, including those published outside of Upper Volta. Its library specializes in research in the humanities and its library specializes in research in the humanities and natural sciences and holds more than 6,000 volumes. The Centre publishes the quarterly *Notes et Documents Voltaïques,* on an irregular basis, the *Recherches Voltaïques,* and is responsible for the compilation of a current national bibliography. Volume one was issued in 1967, the *Bibliographie générale de la Haute-Volta,* covering the years 1956 through 1965. Volumes covering earlier years were planned but had not been published by 1979. An ongoing national bibliography that would be issued from 1966 onward was also still in the planning stage.

A National Center for Archives was organized in 1973. Its one major accomplishment has been to conduct a survey of the archives of all administrative districts of the country and to draw plans for a central depository at Ouagadougou. Construction of this central depository was not begun.

Upper Volta has one university, the Université de Ouagadougou, which was founded in 1970 and attained university status in 1974. The university's library holds approximately 30,000 volumes, 100 periodicals, and 1,400 maps. There are many smaller libraries affiliated with colleges in Ouagadougou. The academic library of the Lycée Philippe Zinda Kabore de Ouagadougou houses 224 volumes and 142 periodicals and is intended primarily for the use of teachers and secondary students.

There is no public library system in Upper Volta. Library facilities are available to the public primarily through the cultural centers in Ouagadougou, most notably those of Germany, the United States, France, Libya, and the Soviet Union.

The Documentation and Information Center of the Interafrican Committee for Hydraulic Studies (CIEH) in Ouagadougou houses 10,000 documents, including books, technical reports, proceedings of conferences, maps, aerial and satellite photographs, and periodical articles. The Center receives approximately 100 journals and compiles bibliographical bulletins, which are sent to more than a thousand recipients over five continents. The Center published two catalogues in 1977: *An Index of Authors* and a *Geographical Index* representing a total of 6,000 documents. The bulletins deal with documents selected and analyzed after the 1977 publication date.

Other documentation centers include those of the OCCGE in Bobo-Dioulasso, which specializes in public health and tropical medicine, with a collection of 8,200 volumes, 135 periodicals, and 300 maps; the Institut national de la statistique et de la démographie in Ouagadougou, with 2,582 volumes, primarily in the field of economics, four periodicals, and statistical bulletins from different countries; and the Institut national d'education in Ouagadougou, with approximately 6,000 volumes and 95 periodicals on educational theory and psychology.

The Association Voltaïque pour le développement des bibliothèques, des archives et de la documentation (AVDBAD) was founded in January 1972 at Ouagadougou. Its primary purpose is to aid in the development of libraries, archives, and documentation centers in Upper Volta. The Association is governed by an executive committee elected by its members and is affiliated with IFLA. There is no official publication.

KRISSIAMBA LARBA ALI

*Donald John Urquhart*

Library Association

# Urquhart, Donald John
(1909– )

Donald John Urquhart, British librarian and information expert, was born November 27, 1909, and reared in the northeast of England, brought up in Whitley Bay, and educated at Barnard Castle School and Sheffield University. He showed the qualities of determination, directness, and independence of mind that characterize the sons of that part of England and that in his case have marked his approach to librarianship and the work of the librarian.

After taking his B.Sc. and Ph.D. degrees at Sheffield, Urquhart worked from 1934 to 1937 in the Research Department of the English Steel Corporation. In 1938 he joined the library staff of the Science Museum, then under the directorship of Samuel Clement Bradford, the active supporter of the Universal Decimal Classification and one of the founders of the British Society for International Bibliography. Bradford's work and that of his successor, Lancaster-Jones, was of great significance in the library field and in the then new field of "documentation." During World War II Urquhart worked in several Government departments, most importantly in the Ministry of Supply, all of which were crucially concerned with the supply of scientific and industrial information and were grievously embarrassed by the consequences of past neglect of this vital aspect of library information work. The War had brought home to scientists and industrialists the significance of information in the day-to-day activities of an industrial society, and it was becoming clear that the speed at which new knowledge and ideas were made available was governed by the effectiveness of information services. Management also needed up-to-date assessments of raw materials, supply and production processes, and equipment design.

These problems prompted several conferences at which scientific information services were discussed in considerable detail, notably the Royal Society Empire Scientific Conference (1946), the Royal Society Scientific Information Conference (1948), and the 27th annual conference of the Association of Special Libraries and Information Bureaux (Aslib, 1952). At this last meeting Urquhart, who by this time had become attached to the Department of Scientific and Industrial Research (DSIR) and thereby much concerned with the results of the Scientific Information Conference, reviewed the results of the conference with special reference to the part played by DSIR in implementing them. He was able to point to the publication of a number of guides to sources of information, but the most important question to be resolved was how to ensure that the United Kingdom would have an adequate system of scientific libraries. The first attempt at solving this problem centered on the possibility of extending the Patent Office Library and the Science Museum Library to include every publication containing material of value to science and technology.

The final answer, however, was to establish and develop in DSIR itself, under Urquhart's direction, a so-called Lending Library Unit, which afterward became the National Lending Library for Science and Technology, a division of the British Library.

The National Lending Library embodies many of the ideas that Urquhart had strenuously advocated during the years of discussion after the Royal Society Conference in 1948. For example, the location of the Library in Boston Spa in Yorkshire was to a considerable extent conditioned by his belief that such a library should be a purely practical institution without elaborate architectural features or adornment, that it should be within easy postal reach of all parts of the country, and that it should have space to enable it to respond to all requests by return mail.

Urquhart's uncompromising ideas were slow to win acceptance, but the practical success of the National Lending Library has rapidly brought him worldwide acclaim and acknowledgment.

SIR FRANK FRANCIS

# Uruguay

Uruguay, a republic in southwestern South America, is bounded by Brazil on the north and east, the Atlantic Ocean on the southeast, the Rio de la Plata on the south, and the Uruguay River on the west, which separates Uruguay from Argentina. Pop. (1977 est.) 2,814,000; area 176,215 sq.km. The official language is Spanish.

**National Library.** The National Library was founded in Montevideo on May 26, 1816, by decree of General José Artigas. Eight months later invading Portuguese forces destroyed its collections. The Library reopened on July 18, 1838, and has served as the repository of the national documentary and bibliographic production; it maintains legal deposit and is responsible for bibliographical and information services through its Information and Consultative Section and the Center of Scientific, Technical, and Economic Documentation. It compiles the national bibliography, *Uruguayan Bibliographical Annual*.

The collection consists of 600,000 books, 800,000 manuscripts and related items, 35,000 pamphlets, and other special material. Inaugurated May 26, 1978, its Children's Section caters to the particular needs of children aged 3 to 12.

**Academic Libraries.** Each of the ten faculties of the University of the Republic has its own departmental library in the field of its specialty. They function under the direction of a librarian and are the best organized libraries in the country, conducting cooperative programs with related divisions. Holdings are estimated at approximately 900,000.

**Public Libraries.** The principal network of public libraries consists of 18 branches in the municipality of Montevideo, distributed by city wards. There are also public libraries in the capitals of departments. Rarely are they staffed by professional librarians, and in general, the collections are inadequate.

**School Libraries.** Libraries are not a part of the national school system, and such services have not been included in the educational structure of the country. Collections are inadequate in size and quality and are composed largely of donations.

**Special Libraries.** As a rule, special libraries in Uruguay are quite well organized, with adequate financial resources. They are found in branches of official agencies and in polytechnic and other schools of higher education. Others are maintained by banks and similar private businesses, by embassies, and by regional and international organizations.

The Uruguayan Institute of Conservation, founded in June 1977, is dedicated to the study and development of natural resources and the restoration of national roots through the exchange of techniques at national and international levels.

**Associations.** The Association of Librarians of Uruguay, active in the years 1945–73, contributed to the status of librarians. The Uruguayan Institute of Library Research, founded in 1977, addresses the study and investigation of the many branches of librarianship and promotes technical standards and cooperation.

ERMELINDA ACERENZA

**Libraries in Uruguay (1976)**

| Type | Number | Volumes in collections[a] | Annual expenditures (peso) | Population served | Professional staff | All staff (total) |
|---|---|---|---|---|---|---|
| National | 1 | 600,000 | N.A. | 93,000 | 50 | N.A. |
| Academic | 55 | 900,000 | N.A. | 400,000 | 150 | N.A. |
| Public | 72 | 166,000 | N.A. | 87,500 | N.A. | N.A. |
| School | 51 | 39,000 | N.A. | 10,000 | N.A. | N.A. |
| Special | 40 | N.A. | N.A. | N.A. | N.A. | N.A. |
| Others | 107 | 760,000 | N.A. | 270,000 | N.A. | N.A. |
| Total | 326 | | | | | |

[a]Books only.
Source: Biblioteca Palacio Legislativo, *Bibliotecas del Uruguay* (Montevideo, 1978).

# Utley, George Burwell
(1876–1946)

George Burwell Utley, Secretary of the American Library Association and Director of the Newberry Library, whose pioneering work in librarianship, managerial legacy to ALA, and pursuit of scholarly excellence for the Newberry attest to a significant career in librarianship, was born during the U.S. centennial year on December 3, 1876, in Hartford, Connecticut. His parents were George Tyler Utley and Harriet Ella Burwell Utley. His father, whose English forebears settled in the Connecticut valley in the 17th century, was a businessman and longtime Secretary of the Connecticut Railroad Commission. His mother died before George was three, and he was raised by maternal aunts in Pleasant Valley, about 25 miles from Hartford. Utley was deeply attached to his

ALA

*George Burwell Utley*

childhood home, and in retirement he returned to "Burwell Heights" for the remainder of his years.

He prepared for college at Vermont Academy, near Brattleboro, and after a year at Colgate transferred to Brown, where he majored in English literature and received a Ph.B. in 1899. Unable to secure a teaching position after graduation, he worked briefly for a Hartford insurance firm. He was soon persuaded by Librarian Frank B. Gay of the Watkinson Library in Hartford to join the staff. His apprenticeship enabled him to satisfy his scholarly inclinations in a congenial setting. It was the beginning of a significant and enormously productive career in librarianship.

In 1901 Utley married Lou Mabel Gilbert, who remained his close companion for the next 45 years. That same year he accepted an offer to head the Maryland Diocesan Library of the Protestant Episcopal Church in Baltimore. Utley, a Baptist, stayed in Baltimore for four years and while there began to research and write the first of many contributions to the professional and historical literature. Perhaps his earliest publication was a biographical sketch of genealogist Edmund J. Cleveland in the proceedings of the *New England Historical and Genealogical Society* (1903). Research for his first book, *The Life and Times of Thomas John Claggett, First Bishop of Maryland* (1913), was completed at the Maryland Library.

To enlarge his sphere of experience, Utley became Director of the Jacksonville Public Library (Florida) in 1905. Awarded a Carnegie building grant in 1902, the Jacksonville Public Library became the state's first tax-supported public library. With limited resources Utley organized the new library, upgraded its resources, and expanded services. His receptive manner, scholarly approach, and administrative finesse all contributed to a successful tenure at Jacksonville. Evidence of his social conscience may be gleaned from an article he wrote on black library patrons for *The Critic* in 1906. Long before most white librarians became sensitive to the needs of black citizens, Utley related the positive accomplishments of Jacksonville's "colored department" and emphasized the serious literature read by the black community.

Utley's achievements were noted outside Florida, and in 1911 he was invited to become Secretary of the American Library Association, a post he filled with distinction until 1920. He moved to Chicago to work in the Association's quarters in the Chicago Public Library, and he was soon immersed in the work of answering correspondence, traveling to state association meetings, speaking at library schools, expanding the membership, and improving the publicity and publication programs. The membership doubled during his term of office. Recognition of Utley's accomplishments and the Association's emerging status as the national voice for library affairs came in 1917 when he was appointed by the U.S. Commissioner of Education to a national committee to study Americanization.

From 1917 to 1920, ALA was engaged in a global book crusade, a program to furnish library materials and services to several million American soldiers. Designated the Library War Service, the project was headquartered at the Library of Congress and directed by Herbert Putnam and later by Carl H. Milam. Utley also served ably as Secretary of the wartime program and spent much of this period in Washington, D.C. Utley's personal qualities were succinctly captured in the Association's farewell resolution that referred to his "agreeable manner, abounding good nature, unfailing patience and clear voice."

After the war Utley was a supporter of the Enlarged Program, an unsuccessful ALA postwar attempt to extend its services and influence. He was recognized for his contributions to ALA by election as President in 1922. In his presidential address Utley urged the Association to press for library extension at all levels and, sensing the evolving bureaucratization of the profession, admonished the members never to forget their primary clients, the public. He continued to serve on various ALA committees for the next 20 years.

Another job offer, this one from the Newberry Library, enticed Utley to leave ALA in 1920. For the next 22 years Utley directed the Newberry in Chicago, a premier private library specializing in history, literature, genealogy, music, and the typographic arts. Under his direction the Library's staff, resources, and services to readers made impressive gains. To extend the Library's usefulness, checklists of its holdings were issued, and services to the scholarly community were revitalized. For his sponsorship of the Library's Dante exhibition, Utley was decorated by the Italian Monarch with the Order of the Crown of Italy in 1922. Eight years later he was appointed by the American Booksellers Association to a blue ribbon committee that selected books for the White House Library. His wish to serve the Newberry for a quarter of a century was not realized; retirement at 65 was mandatory, and so he returned to his beloved Pleasant Valley in 1942.

Befitting his long career in prominent positions, Utley was a member and officer of many organizations. His library affiliations included the Illinois Library Association (President, 1924–25) and the American Library Institute (President, 1937–39). Deeply committed to his adopted Chicago, Utley served as President of Chicago's Geographic Society (1929–31), Literary Club (1935–36), and Writers' Guild (1935–36). He was the author of over 60 publications, his writings appearing in such diverse periodicals as *Library Journal, The Touchstone,* the *Mississippi Valley Historical Review,* and *Survey.* Among his ten biographical sketches for the *Dictionary of American Biography* were vignettes of Katharine Lucinda Sharp, Walter Loomis Newberry, and Obadiah Rich. Utley's *Fifty Years of the American Library Association* (ALA, 1926) is a non-interpretive but informative reconstruction of ALA's first half-century. Retirement in Pleasant Valley afforded Utley the opportunity for gardening, stamp collecting, and resumption of a project that had been deferred for over two decades. When he died on October 4, 1946, he had nearly finished *The Librarians' Conference of 1853;* published in 1951 by ALA, this study remains the definitive history of America's first library convention.

Utley was an effective administrator and esteemed by his contemporaries. William Warner Bishop, an ALA President (1918–19) and ardent internationalist, lauded Utley in his reminiscences: "There are not so very many men who improve on closer acquaintance, but Utley was one of them." Utley's characterization of the purpose of libraries—"to induce people to read and to furnish ample and generous facilities for independent study and unrestrained mental activity"—was a goal measurably advanced by his achievements.

**REFERENCES**

Materials covering the Florida years are available in the Jacksonville Public Library. His ALA correspondence, especially for the World War I period, is in the ALA Archives, University of Illinois Library, Urbana, Illinois. Utley's Newberry papers are held by that library.

ARTHUR P. YOUNG

# Venezuela

Venezuela, a republic of northern South America, is bounded on the north by the Caribbean Sea and the Atlantic Ocean, on the south by Brazil, on the southwest and west by Colombia, and on the east by Guyana. Pop. (1978 est.) 13,122,000; area 899,180 sq.km. The official language is Spanish.

**National Library.** A Study Commission for the establishment of a National Library and Information System was formed by presidential decree in 1974, following the general NATIS (Unesco) program adopted by Venezuela in that same year. That Commission carried out a nationwide survey and in November 1975 presented a report covering all aspects of library, archival, and information services. In 1976 and 1978 a commission to organize the National Library and Information System (SINASBI) was created by presidential decree.

The Biblioteca Nacional de Venezuela was originally organized by decree in 1833. Its scope of responsibilities was expanded by law on July 27, 1977, changing its legal standing to that of an autonomous institute. Its full name is the Instituto Autónomo Biblioteca Nacional y de Servicios de Bibliotecas and is the coordinating body for the Library and Humanistic Information System. It is responsible for school libraries, public libraries, university libraries, and libraries specializing in humanistic information. The National Library houses 244,161 volumes, mostly on Venezuelan topics, 19,260 other items, such as musical scores, maps, graphic designs, and tapes. Publications of the National Library include the *Anuario Bibliográfico Venezolano,* which lists all books and pamphlets published in the country, official publications, academic theses and dissertations, musical scores, and standards; the *Catálogo General;* the *Indice Bibliográfico; and the Boletín de la Biblioteca Nacional.* The Centro Bibliográfico Venezolano compiles the national bibliography. There is a legal deposit law in Venezuela that requires two copies of every work published to be submitted to the National Library. A draft law on legal deposit for nonbook materials had not been approved by the National Congress by the close of the 1970's. Venezuela did not have a national union catalogue, although efforts were under way to establish one.

The Archivo General de la Nación (National Archives), founded in 1888, collects historical archives, religious archives, and public administration archives. Its collection is divided into three sections: La Colonia (1498–1810), La Revolución (1810–21), and La República (from 1830 to present). The National Archives publishes a biannual *Boletín.*

**Academic Libraries.** Nine central university libraries, which serve more than 1,300,000 users, form part of the Library and Humanistic Information System and are represented on a permanent working committee that carries out studies and evaluates university library services. Two of the more important central libraries, both in Caracas, are the Biblioteca Central de la Universidad Católica "Andrés Bello" (Central Library of the "Andrés Bello" Catholic University), founded in 1953, currently holding 180,000 volumes; and the Biblioteca Central de la Universidad Central de Venezuela (Central University Library), founded in 1874 and housing 328,500 volumes in the social sciences, humanities, pure sciences, and technology. There are many other fine central university libraries as well as libraries of university research institutes.

Theodore F. Welch

*The National Library of Venezuela in Caracas, organized in 1833, was expanded in 1977 to become an autonomous institution responsible for school, public, and university libraries.*

**Table 2. Archives in Venezuela (1977)**

| | |
|---|---|
| Number | 109 |
| Professional staff | 3 |
| All staff (total) | 206 |

Source: The Coordinating Nuclei of SINASBI.

**Public Libraries.** The public library system in Venezuela is composed of 14 libraries in the metropolitan area (Caracas and its suburbs) and 203 reading rooms and libraries distributed throughout the rest of the country. The Book Bank, a private research organization dealing primarily with the promotion of reading, also maintains two public libraries and a bookmobile service in the metropolitan area.

**School Libraries.** In the school library system are 47 school libraries that serve about 63,000 users in secondary and primary schools. The Ministry of Education, in close cooperation with the Book Bank, administers the Guayana Project, a major program in the southeast region of the country; 16 school libraries and library services in 31 public schools have been established. These facilities

**Table 1. Libraries in Venezuela (1977)**

| Type | Number | Volumes in collections | Annual expenditures (bolívar) | Population served | Professional staff | All staff (total) |
|---|---|---|---|---|---|---|
| National | 1 | 244,161 | 10,680,905 | 39,821[a] | 27 | 237 |
| Academic | 9 | 1,367,477 | 16,117,100 | 1,319,412 | 131 | 692 |
| Public | 219 | 196,014 | 7,571,810 | 2,184,184 | 28 | 526 |
| School | 47 | | 2,000,000 | 62,976 | 6 | 61 |
| Special[b] | 35 | 224,072 | 3,442,769 | 59,744[a] | 48 | 222 |
| Totals | 311 | 2,031,724 | 39,812,584 | 3,666,137 | 240 | 1,738 |

Source: The Coordinating Nuclei of SINASBI.

[a]Requests attended.
[b]Only the Social and Economical Information Network "REDINSE."

are used by 36,000 students in primary and secondary schools. The Ministry of Education has also organized two other school library networks, one in Caracas (Valle-Coche) and another in Maracaibo (Zulia).

**Special Libraries.** The Consejo Nacional de Investicaciones Cientificas y Tecnologicas (CONICIT), the National Scientific and Technological Research Council, created in 1967, is the coordinating center for scientific and technological networks. This central system includes many specialized libraries and documentation centers, comprising the following cooperative information networks: the Technological and Industrial Information network, the Biomedical Information network, the Engineering and Architecture Information network (REDINARA), the Social and Economical Information network (REDINSE), the Housing and Regional Urban Planning Information network, and the Agricultural Sciences Information network (REDIAGRO). The REDINSE network alone serves 35 libraries.

The Technological Institue for Petroleum Research runs a Technical Information Center (CIT) housing information on petroleum, petrochemical, and earth science fields. Additionally it is the only information facility in Venezuela connected to international information data banks.

In addition, there are many special libraries holding works in the sciences and technology. CONICIT distributes the *Catálogo colectivo de publicaciónes periódicas en ciencias y tecnología de Venezuela,* which includes more than 15,000 entries and identifies libraries holding such publications.

**Associations.** The Colegio de Bibliotecólogos y Archivólogos de Venezuela is the major national organization for professional librarians and archivists working in Venezuela. It was founded in 1952 to promote the welfare and professional competency of its members, which numbered nearly 700 by 1977. SINASBI, through the institutions integrated within it, is represented in many international organizations, including the FID, IFLA, ACURIL, ALA, and others.

MORRIS MATZA

# Vietnam

Vietnam, a socialist republic of southeast Asia, is bounded by China on the north, the South China Sea on the east, and Cambodia and Laos on the west. Pop. (1977 est.) 51,152,000; area 338,392 sq.km. Vietnamese is the official language; French and English are also spoken. The former North Vietnam and South Vietnam were merged after the resolution of the conflict in 1975.

**National Library.** The National Library of the Socialist Republic of Vietnam (SRV) in the capital city of Hanoi was first established by the French in 1919 as the Bibliothèque Centrale of Indochina. From 1921 until about 1941 it was the legal deposit library and officially received one copy of each publication produced in Indochina. By the 1950's its collections included 150,000 books and 2,300 periodicals. In 1954 the French took a portion of the collection to Saigon and Paris (approximately 50,000 books and 400 periodicals).

The Democratic Republic of Vietnam (DRV) quickly began to rebuild the central collections, adding over 20,000 items accumulated in the hills and filling out the missing items. A decree required that ten copies of all new publications go into the Library. By the 1970's the Library possessed over a million books and 4,000 periodicals. Besides the growing Vietnamese collection, it has good French, Russian, Chinese, English, and German collections. Special collections include Asian languages, ethnic minority material, maps, engravings, phonograph records, and children's books. It produces a national bibliography and lists of recommended reading.

The National and General Libraries of the Republic in the former Saigon (Ho Chi Minh City) with their collections of southern works and materials brought south in 1954 (respectively) undoubtedly serve as regional centers of the new system.

**Academic Libraries.** The main research library is the Central Scientific Library in Hanoi, founded in 1959 and based on and located in the old library of the Ecole Française d'Extreme Orient (1898). It too is a legal deposit for all Vietnamese publications and has two sections, natural and social sciences, which have a number of research institutes under them (as those of Archaeology, History, Literature, and Philosophy). Each Institute possesses its own collection.

**Public Libraries.** These are state libraries rather than "public" in the usual Western sense. From 1956 the DRV set up a series of provincial and municipal libraries. The provincial libraries, the largest being in Hanoi, Haiphong, and Nam Dinh, were meant to coordinate the use of written materials in their areas. By the 1970's there were 34 libraries in cities and provinces, 102 city or town reading rooms, and more than 20,000 libraries across the countryside. Their books totaled over 6,000,000. Over 4,000 trade union libraries were established in work locations to provide both technical detail and recreational reading. The general public has access to books through factory, union, or village. All this helped push the major DRV literacy campaign.

In addition, collections of over 500,000 items were made before 1975 to add to southern libraries upon unification. The latter thus joined the already existing network.

**School Libraries.** School libraries are apparently little developed. College libraries exist, and the collections in the southern schools and universities (particularly the Law, Medical, and Pedagogy Faculties of the old University of Saigon) probably remain in their locations, though reliable information was sketchy in the West at the end of the 1970's.

**Special Libraries.** Various units of the government, as the Ministries of Defense (32,000 items) and Agriculture (15,000 items), have their own libraries. In the South before 1975 there were the collections of the National Institutes of Administration and of Statistics, the Industrial Development Center, and the Ministry of Information, all in Saigon. In Dalat existed an irreplaceable collection of 19th-century imperial and land records. Where these collections were later located was not known in the West at the end of the 1970's.

**Association.** There is an Association of Vietnamese Library Workers.

**REFERENCES**

J. Rowlands, *Libraries in Indochina: A Brief Survey of Libraries in Laos, North Vietnam, South Vietnam* (1973), good summary of existing information.

J. K. Whitmore, "Vietnamese Retrospective Materials," *Foreign Acquisitions Newsletter* (Fall 1973), an examination of historical materials.

D. Kaser et al., *Library Development in Eight Asian Countries* (1969), a detailed, but early, description of the south.

JOHN K. WHITMORE

# Waples, Douglas
(1893–1978)

Douglas Waples was a man whose roots were in literature, culture, research, and educational psychology, and who grew with and contributed to the growth of theory in the field of communications, the central core of his professional attention. His work in army intelligence and psychological warfare was tied closely to his interest in international communications while serving in the U.S. Army during two world wars and as a consultant to the U.S. Department of State. Recruited to library education as a specialist in educational method and in research, Waples studied librarianship and library education with a fine glass and saw librarianship as having high potential but never thought of himself as a librarian. Critical and stimulating in his objective clarity, Waples was always an outsider in relation to the field he served so well. He was not only an interdisciplinary scholar but also an exemplar of the post-World War II international perspective.

Born on March 3, 1893, in Philadelphia, Douglas Waples was the only child of Rufus Waples and Christine Beach Isham Waples; his mother's battle with tuberculosis took him with her to Colorado Springs, Mexico City, and El Paso for the first five years of his life. Upon his mother's death in 1898, he returned to Pennsylvania, living in Wayne on Walnut Street and attending Miss Miel's school. With his father's marriage in 1901, Douglas entered Radnor public school, played with the North Wayne gang, and sang in the Saint Mary's Protestant Episcopal Church boys' choir. In 1904 he entered Haverford School and became enamored of athletics, English, Latin, and Greek. Vacationing in New England and Michigan meant sports and the out-of-doors over the years, with a three-week canoe trip on the French River in Canada a memorable highlight. Thus early in life, Waples's devotion to music, sports, and literature was well established. A bassoonist, Waples later played with equal pleasure in the University Orchestra and in a woodwind quartet in Chicago. Former students recall his familiar form jogging regularly around the Midway in his later years on the Chicago campus.

Four years at Haverford College culminated in 1914 with election to Phi Beta Kappa, some literary prizes, and a bid to the 1914 Olympics. Teaching English and athletics in the Gilman School in Baltimore led him back to study, this time at Harvard, from which he earned an M.A. in June 1917, the same month he married Eleanor Cary. His doctorate came three years and a world war later, a Ph.D. degree in Educational Psychology from the University of Pennsylvania in 1920, the same spring as the birth of his first child. His family and his career were launched with a position as Assistant Professor of Psychology and Education at Tufts in Boston, from which he continued studies at Harvard. In 1923 Waples moved to the University of Pittsburgh, where colleagueship with W. W. Charters was a highlight. When Charters moved to the University of Chicago in 1925, he saw that Waples also was added to that faculty, and the then five Wapleses—there now being three daughters—moved to the Hyde Park area of Chicago, which remained their home for many years. Only on his retirement in 1957 did Washington Island, Wisconsin, become home base for him and Dorothy (Blake) Waples, his wife since 1947. Their Fulbright research trips to India and Peru sustained Waples's activity in public communication research until a debilitating stroke in 1960 severely limited his activity until his death on April 25, 1978.

Douglas Waples's 15 years (1928–42) on the faculty of the Graduate Library School of the University of Chicago spread his influence among his students and brought three of his major interests to bear on librarianship: scholarship, research, and reading behavior—all related to his central focus on public communication.

Waples's writings in the area of scholarship dealt often with the international exchange of ideas. *National Libraries and Foreign Scholarship,* written with Harold D. Lasswell (1936), and his later article "Belgian Scholars and Their Libraries," *Library Quarterly* (1940), described the interaction between political nationalism and the importation of foreign social science literature and detailed the significance of broad general research collections in the development of scholarship.

Research was central to Waples's professional life. Each of his five important contributions to secondary education published between 1924 and 1930 made the research orientation central to curriculum evaluation, teaching methods, or supervision. Waples wrote with Ralph W. Tyler (1930) a textbook for teachers on the use of research methods that was precursor to Waples's later volume on research methods applied to librarianship, *Investigating Library Problems* (1939), which stressed the importance of building a research-based body of knowledge for librarianship. This emphasis made Waples, equally with Pierce Butler (*Introduction to Library Science,* 1934), spokesman for the unique research orientation of the Graduate Library School from 1928 to 1942.

Waples's studies of reading behavior, however, were then and remain his most substantive contribution to librarianship. He provided insight into the "hierarchy" of choices of reading materials: accessibility, readability, and subject interest in "The Relation of Subject Interests to Actual Reading," *Library Quarterly* (1932). "People versus Print," in L. R. Wilson's *Library Trends* (1936), with its corollary perspective on the library's role in making accessible the socially significant materials of an era, has had strong impact on American librarianship. Waples's sheer intellectual power in grouping and analyzing data, in generating hypotheses, and in giving order to the chaos of perceived significance in reading studies is demonstrated in the unmatched series of publications that use sociological research strategies to explore his psychological hypotheses in the area of adult reading. *What People Want to Read About,* written with Ralph W. Tyler (1931), was even more significant for its methodology and its analysis of the field of reading research problems than it was for the findings on subject interests of a wide diversity of adult groups. Similarly, his monograph *People and Print* (1936) studied the "social aspects of reading in the depression," opening research into the relationship of the larger trends and critical events in society and the use of library resources. Market analysis, special publics, advertising, and cost efficiency in various types of book service were explored. But the compelling problem was still seen as that of effective description of readers "to present why they read as they do." Methods of investigation that would allow penetration of this problem below the superficial level was always Waples's struggle and contribution. *Libraries and Readers in the State of New York,* which he wrote with Leon Carnovsky (1939), was the first study of research in total communities in an experimental design. His culminating research report in this area, with Bernard Berelson and Franklyn R. Bradshaw, was *What Reading Does to People* (1940). Notable not only for his full statement of "the five effects of reading," the record of reading as social history, it was also notable for a summation of the field of research in the social effects of reading and for recommendations on methodology of content analysis and case studies. A brilliant conceptualizer, a skilled practitioner in research design, Douglas Waples has not had his equal in the area of adult reading studies.

Following World War II and his return to the University of Chicago campus, Waples devoted himself to his public-communications studies, outside the context of the University's Committee in Communication from 1951 to his retirement in 1957. Waples was one of that small group of major figures at "GLS" who shared in establishing a base for library science and a research orientation to library education.

MARGARET E. MONROE

## Wheeler, Joseph Lewis
(1884–1970)

When the Enoch Pratt Free Library celebrated the 30th anniversary of the famous central building on February 15, 1963, the man responsible for making it a model of its

The Baltimore Sunpapers

*Joseph Lewis Wheeler*

ALA

*H(alsey) W(illiam) Wilson*

kind was present. He saw carved on the marble entrance to the auditorium named in his honor, *"Joseph L. Wheeler, 1926–1945. Under His Leadership the Enoch Pratt Free Library Became One of the Notable Libraries of the World."* A skilled publicist, he had an eye for potential talent and the ability to inspire his staff, many of whom went on to major positions.

Wheeler was born March 16, 1884, in Dorchester, Massachussetts. After public schooling in Bridgewater and frequent visits to the local library, he studied engineering at Brown University and worked at the Providence Public Library. He switched courses, taking a Bachelor of Philosophy degree and a Master's in Social and Political Science from Brown. Later he completed the course at the New York State Library School in Albany.

Wheeler's professional progress was rapid and steady. Beginning at the Washington, D.C., Public Library, he held positions of increasing responsibility in public libraries of Jacksonville, Florida; Los Angeles; and Youngstown, Ohio.

He was 42 years old, energetic, seasoned, and boiling with ideas when he took over as Librarian of Baltimore's unexciting public library in 1926. Wheeler breathed life into the institution, using his skills in publicity and personnel development. He motivated and prodded officials of the city, trustees, and staff. The Pratt quickly earned a reputation for being in the van of public library organization and service.

Service to the public was Wheeler's obsession, as shown in the Pratt building design. It was the first large public library with a street-level entrance, big display windows, and collections easily accessible to the public. Staff stations were strategically placed for assistance to readers.

Recognition of the Pratt Library for excellence and the proved efficiency of the central library created a nationwide demand for Wheeler's services as a consultant. After leaving Baltimore in 1944, he advised numerous libraries. He had completed more than 225 studies and surveys by the time of his death on December 3, 1970.

EDWIN CASTAGNA

## Wilson, H(alsey) W(illiam)

(1868–1954)

H. W. Wilson's contributions to librarianship cannot easily be overstated. It is hardly possible to imagine American libraries without the indexes and bibliographies of Halsey William Wilson, bookseller, publisher, and founder of the company that bears his name. Son of Althea Dunnell Wilson and John Thompson Wilson, a stonecutter, H. W. Wilson was born in Wilmington, Vermont, on May 12, 1868. He was a descendant of Roger Williams, Anne Hutchinson, and Mary Dyer, the Quaker martyr. Orphaned before the age of three, Wilson was brought up by his maternal grandparents in rural Massachusetts and later by an aunt and uncle in Iowa. He soon developed his legendary capacity for work and began to exercise his talent for simultaneous activity. Wilson's formal education was gained at a Beloit, Wisconsin, boarding school and the University of Minnesota. While attending the University intermittently between 1885 and 1892, he delivered newspapers, worked as a church custodian, ran a small job printing business, studied music in hope of becoming an organist, worked weekends at the Minneapolis Public Library, and, with his roommate, Henry S. Morris, acted as book agent for faculty and students.

In December 1889 the two young men pooled their modest resources, $200, and opened a campus bookstore in the main university building. The firm of Morris and Wilson began on a small scale, furnishing textbooks and supplies and printing syllabuses. After Morris's graduation in 1891, Wilson continued the business, bought out his partner, and soon built it up into the best bookstore in Minneapolis. At one period the store had a bicycle section and was in charge of the university post office. This latter ensured that everyone on campus made a daily visit to the bookstore. The success of the business enabled Wilson to marry, on August 12, 1895, Justina Leavitt, a graduate student. She was closely associated with the bookstore and the publishing firm until about 1913, when she turned her full attention to civic matters, especially the women's suffrage movement.

As a bookseller, Wilson became aware of the need for an accurate, up-to-date source for locating books in print. *Publishers' Weekly* had published semiannual cumulations of its weekly lists, but discontinued them in 1897 because of rising costs. Wilson, spurred on by what he later called the "bibliographic urge," conceived the idea of a monthly listing of new books, to be cumulated into a permanent record of American book publishing. Thus was born *Cumulative Book Index* (CBI), which first appeared in February 1898. CBI embodied the now familiar Wilson bibliographical features: author, title, and subject entries arranged in one alphabet. The success, limited at first, of CBI led Wilson to produce the first *United States Catalog, Books in Print,* in 1899. Hard on the heels of this came the most familiar of all the Wilson publications, *Readers' Guide to Periodical Literature,* which first appeared in 1901, indexing the contents of 20 general periodicals. These early publications were cumulated by another Wilson innovation: bibliographic entries on Linotype slugs that could be kept and rearranged at will before each printing.

In 1903 Wilson incorporated his bookstore-publishing firm, offering stock in the H. W. Wilson Company to friends in the academic, bookselling, and library communities. Thus began the company's continuing association with librarians. The first product of the new firm was the *Book Review Digest* (1905), edited by Mrs. Wilson. Over the next several years, some half-dozen periodical indexes, forerunners of now standard titles, appeared under the Wilson imprint, as well as two cumulative editions of *Readers' Guide,* two revisions of the *United States Catalog,* and a number of other library-oriented publications. The firm also issued dozens of titles as the unofficial University of Minnesota Press.

Early in his career, Wilson evolved a method of pricing *Readers' Guide* on a sliding scale, the "service basis," which made it possible for almost all libraries to afford this valuable reference source. He conceived the index as a *service:* the price depended upon a library's periodical holdings and thus the index's usefulness to that library.

The more titles indexed for a library, the more useful *Readers' Guide* was; and each library was charged accordingly. Similar but more complex scales were developed for the specialized Wilson indexes, involving not only the number of periodical titles held but also the number of indexing entries per title. The service basis, though criticized from time to time, has served both the company and the subscriber well.

As the firm flourished, Wilson recognized the need to be located on the East Coast, nearer to the publishing world and the majority of his subscribers. In 1913 he moved the firm to White Plains, New York. From White Plains came *Industrial Arts Index* (1913), *Agricultural Index* (1916), and still more library-oriented reference books. A house organ begun in this period evolved into *Wilson Library Bulletin*. After four years in White Plains, Wilson moved the firm even closer to New York City. On a site in the Bronx overlooking the Hudson River, he built in 1917 the first building of a complex that ultimately was to encompass four large structures. There also was erected the 30-foot lighthouse that was the company's colophon.

From the familiar 950 University Avenue address, the Wilson Company developed additional specialized periodical indexes, among them *Art Index* (1929), *Education Index* (1929), *Library Literature* (1936), and *Bibliographic Index* (1938). Other specialized reference guides from this period are *Essay and General Literature Index* (1934), *Vertical File Index* (1932), *Current Biography* (1940), and *Biography Index* (1946). The Standard Catalog series was developed fully in this period. The first *Union List of Serials in Libraries of the United States and Canada* (1928) was the result of cooperation between the Wilson Company, the American Library Association, and the participating libraries. Wilson later provided a feasibility study for the continuation of the Library of Congress's *Catalog of Books Represented by Library of Congress Printed Cards, issue to July 31, 1942,* which contributed in large measure to its continuation as the *National Union Catalog*.

Wilson realized quite early that the success of his firm, with its market limited mostly to libraries, depended upon close cooperation with librarians. The firm employed many librarians in its indexing operations. Practicing librarians were consulted at every step about the company's services and activities, even to the point of making decisions about the scope and content of many Wilson publications. To facilitate cooperation, Wilson attended more than 40 American Library Association national meetings, as many Midwinter meetings, and hundreds of regional, state, and local meetings of librarians. He also participated in and sponsored national and international bibliographical projects, created library awards, and placed librarians on his board of directors. The Wilson staff was encouraged to participate in library association activities and allowed generous time for committee work. Over the years the associations led to a steady stream of Wilson publications, each geared to some need in the library community.

In 1948 Wilson summed up his method of creating new publications, emphasizing the importance of listening to and talking with librarians.

> First, listen to the advice of prospective supporters of a project. If the project is important it will be discussed in librarians' meetings and journals. Then scan the field and study what has been done and why there may have been successes and failures. Consult and secure advice from librarians who may be expected to have an interest in the project. Then the final question: "If this is a good plan and if we proceed with it, will you plan to subscribe for it?"

While Wilson's business methods and bibliographical innovations were quite modern, his managerial approach was that of the paternalistic Yankee individualist. Though he grew to manhood in the age of Rockefeller, Carnegie, Gould, and Fisk, he became a Wilsonian Democrat in his middle years. An admirer of Henry Ford, he disliked the income tax, loathed Franklin D. Roosevelt and the New Deal, and unsuccessfully resisted unions in the firm. From the beginning, the staff of the Wilson Company was like a family, and this feeling never entirely disappeared as the firm grew. Though salaries were skimpy, Wilson provided such fringe benefits as stock sharing, pensions for older employees, cumulative sick leave, and hospitalization at a time when few American business firms did so. He encouraged vacations, though rarely taking them himself; employed women and placed them in positions of responsibility; and pioneered in the hiring of the physically handicapped.

Wilson began developing his publications at a time when the need for bibliographical control of an expanding world of print was becoming acute. Extension of secondary and higher education, growth of the book and periodical publishing industry, the Carnegie-inspired revolution in library expansion, the rise of scholarly and scientific publication and research, all had created a flood of information and generated a need for indexes to make this same information easily accessible. Wilson's knowledge of the needs of libraries, his high standards of indexing, his pricing systems to make his indexes widely available, his publication of a broad range of indexes and services, and his continuing modernization of his publications ultimately made for a unique, satisfying, and profitable bibliographical publishing career.

In person Wilson was a stocky, robust figure, balding, with a neatly trimmed moustache and fringe of hair that turned from dark to silver over the years. His round features and a twinkle in the eye relieved an otherwise stolid but not forbidding appearance. Though personally abstemious (he neither smoked nor drank alcohol), he did indulge a stupendous sweet tooth and a wry sense of humor. He was addicted to puns, and the wary soon learned to spot the signs that a particularly horrendous one was on the way. Fond of afterdinner stories, he published, under the transparent pseudonym Harold Workman Williams, three collections of jokes, stories, and quotations for all occasions.

Wilson was much honored in his lifetime. Brown University presented him an honorary Doctor of Letters degree in 1939; in 1948 the University of Minnesota honored him with its first Outstanding Achievement award. The American Library Association and the Special Libraries Association made special presentations on the 50th anniversary of the Wilson Company in 1948. In 1950 he received the American Library Association's Joseph W. Lippincott Award. In his turn, Wilson honored the library community. In 1946 the firm began to sponsor library awards, the most prestigious of which is the annual John Cotton Dana Library Publicity Award. After Mrs. Wilson's death in 1955, their estate was turned over to the H. W. Wilson Foundation, to be used primarily for the benefit of former employees. Grants were made for such purposes as library school scholarships, National Library Week, the activities of several library associations, and programs for the blind and physically handicapped.

Wilson resigned as President of the firm in December 1952 but continued as Chairman of the Board until his death at his home in Yorktown Heights, New York, on March 1, 1954. He died exactly 60 years to the day after the death of an earlier bibliographer and periodical indexer, William Frederick Poole.

A. E. SKINNER



## Wilson, Louis Round

(1876–1979)

Louis Round Wilson was Librarian of the University of

ALA

*Louis Round Wilson*

North Carolina at Chapel Hill, 1901–32, and Dean of the Graduate Library School of the University of Chicago, 1932–42. His career as librarian, teacher, writer, and editor and his active and influential participation in library associations exemplify the emergence of the professional university library administrator in the United States.

Born in Lenoir, North Carolina, December 27, 1876, Wilson was educated in Lenoir schools, attended Haverford College, and graduated from the University of North Carolina at Chapel Hill in 1899. He taught in private academies in North Carolina for two years before returning to Chapel Hill as University Librarian in 1901. He also pursued graduate study and received a Master's degree in English in 1902 and Ph.D. in 1905. Though Wilson had expected to become a professor of English, he decided instead to remain with the University of North Carolina as its Librarian, a decision that influenced his own life and made an indelible impact on the library profession.

Wilson foresaw the growth and development of the University of North Carolina into one of the major universities in the United States and endeavored to build a library collection that would support graduate study and research. Working with the university's academic departments he acquired books, periodicals, and bibliographic materials that greatly expanded the holdings of the main library. Wilson was especially interested in the special collections of the library; acknowledging the regional quality of the University, he envisioned a manuscript collection that would serve historians of the South. He lived to see the Southern Historical Collection take its place among the major manuscript repositories in the United States. He encouraged the development of a collection of North Caroliniana and sought and gained financial support from friends and alumni of the University for the purchase and preservation of rare books and incunabula.

Wilson supervised the construction of two library buildings. A Carnegie building was completed in 1907, and the present main university library, which bears his name, was dedicated in 1929. With the growth of the collections and the expanded physical facilities was an increase in the number of trained librarians on Wilson's staff. In 1907 when the Carnegie library was opened, Wilson ran the library with the aid of only one trained librarian and a few student assistants; by 1932 there were 23 librarians on the staff.

Wilson taught his first course in librarianship in the summer session of 1904. In 1907 courses in library administration were offered in the regular session, and Wilson was made an Assistant Professor of Library Administration. In 1920 Wilson was made a Kenan Professor of Library Science; the Kenan professorships are the University of North Carolina's oldest and most distinguished endowed professorships. Wilson taught courses in library science until he left the University and was vigorous and successful in campaigning for a School of Library Science, which opened in 1931 with Wilson as its first Dean.

As a member of the faculty of the University, Wilson assumed many additional duties. As Chairman of the Committee on Extension from 1912 to 1920, he drew the library heavily into extension work; through the Library Extension Department books were circulated to the people of North Carolina for more than 40 years. Wilson was Editor of the *Alumni Review*, 1912–24, and Co-founder and Director of the University Press, 1922–32.

In 1932 Wilson accepted the position of Dean of the Graduate Library School of the University of Chicago. As Dean of the seven-year-old school he led the faculty in developing a curriculum designed to produce librarians who would be specialists in administration of different types of libraries. Wilson taught courses in university library administration and library trends. He organized teams of students and faculty members to study current problems in librarianship and began institutes that explored new directions for the profession. Many of these studies resulted in books that were published as part of the University of Chicago Studies in Library Science series, of which Wilson was General Editor.

Wilson's own volume in the series, *The Geography of Reading* (1938), reflects his long-standing interest in the phenomenon of reading. As early as 1922 he was studying the reading habits of North Carolinians, and in the 1930's he extended this interest in reading and public libraries to the entire United States.

In 1942 Wilson returned to North Carolina, where he rejoined the faculty of the School of Library Science, from which he retired in 1959 at the age of 83. In 1945 he and Maurice F. Tauber published *The University Library*, a significant addition to the literature of library administration. After retiring from the faculty Wilson continued in service to the University as a consultant to the President of the university system until 1969.

Throughout his career Wilson served as a library consultant and surveyor. His opinions on academic libraries, library buildings, and possible sites for library schools were sought by the Carnegie Corporation, the General Education Board, and the Board of Education for Librarianship of the American Library Association. In the mid-1930's Wilson and Edgar A. Wight surveyed county libraries in the Southeast, and in 1941 and 1946 Wilson conducted surveys for the Tennessee Valley Authority and the Tennessee Valley Library Council, with a view to increasing library service to the Tennessee Valley region under the aegis of the Tennessee Valley Authority.

Wilson's participation in professional associations began when he joined ALA in 1904. As President of ALA in 1935–36 he led a successful campaign for adoption of a statement in support of federal aid to libraries. He helped to found the North Carolina Library Association in 1904 and was its President in 1910 and again in 1930–31. Wilson was President of the Southeast Library Association (SELA), 1924–26, and endeavored to join the efforts of SELA and the Southern Association of Colleges and Secondary Schools in providing standards for school and college libraries. Always mindful of the needs of the people of the state, Wilson helped to draft the legislation that created the North Carolina Library Commission in 1909 and served as Chairman of the Commission from 1909 until 1916. He was active in the Citizen's Library Movement in 1927.

Wilson's career demonstrates his belief in the role of the library as a service organization. He saw the library as an active force in American society and never ceased in his efforts to bring the library into active service to the people. He knew that the library was a vital and necessary adjunct to the school and college, but he also believed that the librarian must reach out beyond the walls of the library in bringing the materials of the library to the people.

Wilson was married in 1909 to Penelope Bryan Wright. They had four children. His oldest two daughters survive and lived with him in the house he built in Chapel Hill in 1911 until his death in Chapel Hill, Dec. 10, 1979, at the age of 102.

**REFERENCES**

*Louis Round Wilson Bibliography: A Chronological List of Works and Editorial Activities* (1976).

Maurice F. Tauber, *Louis Round Wilson: Librarian and Administrator* (1967).

Frances A. Weaver, *Louis Round Wilson, The Years since 1955* (1976).

Edward G. Holley, "The Centenary of a Giant of Librarianship: Louis Round Wilson" (illustrated), *The ALA Yearbook* (1977).

FRANCES A. WEAVER

*Constance Mabel Winchell*

ALA

WINCHELL, CONSTANCE MABEL 384

## Winchell, Constance Mabel

(1896– )

Constance M. Winchell, a member of the reference staff at Columbia University Library for 38 years, was responsible for the seventh and eighth editions of *A Guide to Reference Books*. She was born on November 2, 1896, in Northampton, Massachusetts, where her aunt was a librarian in the historic Forbes Library directed by Charles A. Cutter. Winchell earned a Bachelor of Arts from the University of Michigan, where she "filed her way through college" with a job in the university library. Upon graduation Winchell began her career as a librarian at the Central High School in Duluth, Minnesota. She had prepared for such a post by attending the "library summer school" sessions conducted at Michigan by the Director of the University Library, William Warner Bishop, following her junior and senior years. Unlike many who become librarians after trying some other profession, Winchell wanted that career from the beginning. In an interview she once remarked: "It never entered my mind that I was not going to be a librarian. I had always intended to be a librarian, always."

On Bishop's advice, she attended the Library School at New York Public Library and received a certificate in 1920. She then worked for the U.S. Merchant Marine in New York City and was responsible for libraries in lighthouses. Five months later Winchell returned to Ann Arbor, where she worked first as a reviser in the catalogue department of the university library and then as a reference assistant. She wanted to do reference work immediately, but Bishop advised that any reference librarian should have cataloguing experience.

In 1924 Winchell went to the American Library in Paris as Head Cataloguer. Bishop disapproved, but Winchell wanted the experience of life in another country. She returned to the U.S. in 1925 and joined the reference staff of the Columbia University Library. Winchell stayed there for 38 years, rising from Reference Assistant to Assistant Reference Librarian to Reference Librarian—the latter post assumed when Isadore Gilbert Mudge retired in 1941.

Mudge was Head of the Reference Department during Winchell's early years at Columbia and was also Winchell's teacher in the Columbia School of Library Service, where Winchell earned an M.S. in 1930. Mudge suggested and then supervised the preparation of Winchell's Master's essay, published as *Locating Books for Interlibrary Loan* (H. W. Wilson, 1930). The work incorporates many of the techniques and concepts Mudge had developed through 20 years of work with interlibrary loan problems. Winchell's lucid explication of practices at Columbia stood for many years as the standard guide for interlibrary loan operations, which were then expanding all over the country.

The value of this work was noted when Winchell received the Isadore Gilbert Mudge Citation for distinguished contributions to reference librarianship in 1960. Winchell was the second person to receive this award, established by the Reference Services Division of ALA in 1959. Winchell received it for: "her constructive service to the Library of Columbia University in building its reference collection and . . . her trail blazing book, *Locating Books for Interlibrary Loan,* which has been an effective aid to the development of interlibrary loan in this country and which continues to be useful as a systematic guide to finding the location of a needed book [and for] . . . that bible of the librarian, *A Guide to Reference Books.*"

*A Guide to Reference Books* was started by Alice Bertha Kroeger, who was responsible for the first edition in 1902, the five annual supplements that were published in *Library Journal,* and the second edition published in 1908. Isadore Gilbert Mudge prepared supplements to the second edition and was responsible for the third, fourth, fifth, and sixth editions and all the supplements in between. When Mudge retired in 1941, she turned over the *Guide,* as well as the Columbia Reference Department, to Constance Winchell. Winchell had been involved in the *Guide* ever since she helped with *Reference Books of 1929,* a supplement to the fifth edition. After Mudge's retirement, Winchell produced supplements to the sixth edition and both the seventh and eighth editions—the last published five years after her own retirement from Columbia. Reviewers of these volumes have praised Winchell's skill in making good use of the work of her predecessors while introducing significant and useful changes in the *Guide.*

Winchell not only knew the contents of reference books; she also understood what good reference service should be. When she retired in 1962, the Director of Libraries at Columbia, Richard Logdson, wrote a brief tribute in *College and Research Libraries:*

> Miss Winchell's standards of excellence, her almost uncanny skill in unraveling bibliographic snarls, her zeal in learning new tools to improve existing techniques, and her thorough training of younger assistants have characterized her work through the years. She possessed these qualities, desired in all good reference chiefs, to the highest degree, but beyond these were two deserving special mention. The first is Miss Winchell's concept of a university library as part of the university, not as an island alone. . . . Finally there is Miss Winchell's devotion to duty nurtured by such a profoundly kind heart that she has found it impossible to appear impatient, or bored, or irritated with a reader. . . .

Before she retired, Winchell took a four-month leave of absence for an extensive tour of Asia. Her interest in faraway places was reflected in the many post cards that decorated the home in upstate New York (New Paltz) where she moved after completion of the eighth edition of the *Guide.*

**REFERENCES**

Mary Jo Lynch, "Women in Reference Service," in *Women in the Library Profession: Leadership Roles and Contributions* (1971).

Constance M. Winchell, "The Reminiscences of Constance Mabel Winchell," transcript of an interview with Elizabeth Rumics in 1963, on file in the Oral History Collection, Columbia University Library.

MARY JO LYNCH

# Wing, Donald Goddard
(1904–1972)

Donald Goddard Wing, compiler of the *Short-Title Catalogue* of early printed English books and Associate Librarian at Yale University, was born in Athol, Massachusetts, on August 18, 1904. His interest in literature and books developed early; while in school in Athol he read and collected the *Smart Set* and other "Little Magazines." From Athol he went to Yale, where he studied English, added a book a day to his collection, and was elected to the Elizabethan Club. After graduating in 1926, he spent a year at Trinity College, Cambridge, tutored by George Rylands. A member of the Bloomsbury group, Rylands confirmed Wing's passion for contemporary poetry and literature. Wing traveled widely during his year abroad, and when he returned to the U.S. he had his copy of the still-banned *Ulysses* hidden in his laundry bag. After a year at Harvard to earn his M.A., Wing returned to Yale, remaining there until the end of his life. He received his Ph.D. in English from Yale in 1932 for his dissertation on "Origins of the Comedy of Humours."

Wing was associated for over 40 years with the Yale Library; he served as Head of Accessions (1939–45), Associate Librarian (1945–65), and Associate Librarian for Collections of the Libraries (1966–70). The Yale Library grew tremendously during these years and gained international prominence. Wing's remarkable memory and intimate knowledge of the Yale collections, combined with his diverse intellectual interests, significantly contributed to the Library's expansion. He loved books and delighted in American libraries' "delirious, exhilarating race toward adequacy."

Wing's great and enduring contribution to bibliography is his *Short-Title Catalogue of Books Printed in England, Scotland, Ireland, Wales and British America and of English Books Printed in Other Countries, 1641–1700.* It was issued in three volumes by the Index Society from 1945 to 1951. His work served as a continuation of Pollard and Redgrave's *Short-Title Catalogue of Books . . . 1475–1640.* Wing surveyed a greater range of libraries than Pollard and Redgrave had; he provided more cross references, gave longer imprints, and indicated by ellipsis the shortening of titles. In addition, he dealt with about 90,000 titles, about three times as many as the earlier STC. Remarkably, Wing compiled his STC during his spare time, except for a year in England in 1936 on a Guggenheim Fellowship.

Yale's acquisition of Falconer Madan's personal collection of Oxford books, and the need to make sense of Yale's holdings of early English books, provided Wing with reason to begin collecting notes while still in his 20's. He wrote out a slip for each title; on it he noted author, short-title, imprint, format, edition, and number of pages. He listed the location of copies, giving the British Museum and Yale shelf numbers and noting unusual provenance. He examined bibliographical reference works and added specific citations for each book. He searched sale catalogues from the 19th century for rare titles and noted the appearance of uncommon items at auction or in booksellers' catalogues in his own day. He not only looked at each tract in the Thomason Collection at the British Museum but also examined at least one copy of the great majority of the titles he listed. To fill in details, he corresponded with librarians and scholars.

Wing's achievement was astonishing. In little over a decade, he produced what quickly became an indispensable tool. Soon librarians and booksellers spoke of "Wing books," and many used "Wing numbers" for identifying, selling, cataloguing, and shelving "Wing period" titles. Librarians were able to measure the strength of their collections and to plot acquisition policy; booksellers could determine at a glance relative rarity and set prices accordingly; and scholars could refer to lists of an author's work or search for pamphlets on a similar theme or subject.

During the remainder of his career, Wing kept his slips up to date with the goal of preparing a revised edition. His *A Gallery of Ghosts* (1967) was based on his search list for 5,000 titles or editions that had appeared at auction or in a bookseller's catalogue or were listed in a previous bibliographer's work but for which no copy was found. Wing received a gratifying response; over half of his ghosts were quickly identified or laid to rest. With the benefit of a sabbatical year, the first granted to a Yale librarian, Wing prepared his revision of the first volume for publication in September 1972.

The period 1641 to 1700 comprised only part of Wing's interests. Although he put together an excellent collection of the works of James Howell, a prolific Wing period author, he also collected and read Henry James, Ronald Firbank, Marcel Proust, Edith Wharton, Ezra Pound (whom he first met, appropriately, in the Laurentian library in Florence), Ellen Glasgow, Wyndham Lewis, E. M. Forster, Andre Gide, all the Sitwells, and Virginia Woolf.

Wing was a member of the Grolier Club and of the Bibliographical Societies of America, London, Cambridge, Oxford, and Edinburgh. He wrote articles and reviews for the *Yale University Library Gazette,* the *Yale Review,* the *Saturday Review of Literature,* and the *William and Mary Quarterly.* He died on October 8, 1972. His research notes are available to scholars in the Yale Library; they form the basis of the revision of his STC, sponsored by the Modern Language Association of America.

TIMOTHY J. CRIST

# Winsor, Justin
(1831–1897)

Justin Winsor, U.S. librarian and historian, is probably best remembered for his efforts to make libraries more accessible to their users. He was born in Boston, Massachusetts, on January 2, 1831, one of five children of Nathaniel Winsor, a prosperous merchant. Descendents of English settlers, the Winsor family had lived in the Boston area since the early 1700's.

As a child Justin was somewhat introverted and very fond of reading; he was also quite independent and inclined to rebel against authority. As a result, he was often in difficulty at school and was sent to a boarding school at the age of ten with the hope that a more structured situation would benefit him.

Winsor, however, intensely disliked the uniformity that prevailed there and enjoyed neither his boarding school days nor his later studies at the Boston Latin School. Although intelligent, he was judged a poor student since he preferred to concentrate on his own projects rather than school assignments. He developed an aversion to memorization from textbooks that lasted throughout his life. Similarly, Winsor's student days at Harvard College were not distinguished. His rejection of the prescribed curriculum led to his leaving in January 1852 without graduating, though 15 years later he was awarded a degree in recognition of his scholarly writings.

His career as a historian began in 1849 with the publication, during his freshman year at Harvard, of *A History of the Town of Duxbury, Massachusetts. . . .* The material for this work had been collected on family trips to Duxbury while visiting relatives. On those visits young Winsor not only gathered information but also drew maps of the town to scale. He showed an early interest in cartography, a field in which he later became a recognized authority.

After leaving Harvard, Winsor traveled and studied in Europe for almost a year. He settled in Boston, devoting his time to writing poetry, short pieces of fiction, and literary criticism. Upon his return from Europe, Winsor became engaged to Caroline Tufts Barker, of his Harvard class of 1853; they were married on December 18, 1855. Marriage tended to expand his somewhat limited social contacts, and although he had never enjoyed churchgoing in his youth, he began to attend the Church of the Unity (Unitarian) in Boston and even compiled a small volume of hymns to be used by the congregation.

Rejected for military service during the Civil War because of poor eyesight, Winsor continued to spend most of his time in literary pursuits, becoming well known in Boston and New York for his critical writing, which appeared regularly in leading newspapers and periodicals. In large part due to this prominence he was appointed to the Board of Trustees of the Boston Public Library, and at 36, he was its youngest member in 1867.

The Boston Public Library, founded 12 years earlier, was the first large American library wholly supported by city taxes. It was then the yearly practice of the Board to appoint an Examining Committee of five city residents, chaired by a Trustee, to analyze and make recommendations on the operations of the library. Winsor was chosen to head the 1867 Committee.

Always a forthright person, Winsor presented clearly and concisely what he felt were the positive and negative aspects of the library operations. He commended the staff on the size of the collection and rate of accessions but noted the crowded conditions in the building, the lack of proper workrooms, and poor ventilation and insufficient lighting. Winsor also was greatly concerned over the circulation of books, which he felt was too low, and over the nature of the collection as compared with the nature of the reading public. Whereas fiction constituted only one-fourth of the collection, it accounted for two-thirds of the circulation at the time. He recommended setting up branch libraries to increase circulation and purchasing more and better fiction titles to satisfy patron needs.

Charles Coffin Jewett, then Superintendent of the Library, died suddenly in January 1868; since the Assistant Superintendent was in poor health and could not assume control, the Trustees appointed Winsor as Temporary Superintendent. He proceeded to take over the library administration so energetically and effectively, however, that they confirmed a regular appointment in February.

Winsor was by education a historian, with no experience or training as a librarian, but he had learned much in his few months as a Trustee. Always a humble person, he realized that he had risen rapidly considering his lack of training. The Trustees, however, had obtained a man with great administrative and executive talents, and the Boston Public Library expanded its services extensively during his leadership.

Among the innovations he brought to the library were the initiation of studies to identify the readers and what they read, in order better to serve their needs. Interlibrary loan procedures were instituted to obtain additional materials. He also supervised the repair and renovation of the existing building and established six branches.

Winsor's creation of a "shelf list" in card form in place of an accession ledger was widely adopted by other libraries, as was his system of "continuous inventory," which made unnecessary the closing of the library for a one-month inventory, as had been the earlier practice. He also opened the library on Sundays and reduced the age limit for borrowers. His guiding principle was always more and better service for the readers.

Winsor's career as Superintendent came to an abrupt end when the City Council, exceeding its authority, reduced the salaries of all library staff members, including Winsor's. Winsor had received an offer of the post of Librarian at Harvard to replace the retiring John Langdon Sibley, and when some of the Boston City Council members reneged on the terms of a proposed salary designed to keep him at the Public Library, he resigned, annoyed, and accepted the Harvard position on July 11, 1887.

In his first annual report at Harvard, Winsor stated the principle that was to guide his work for the next 20 years: "I consider nothing more important than the provision of large classes of books to which unrestricted access can be had." Accordingly, he opened the stacks to students, an unusual practice at the time, and greatly extended the reserved-book system begun by Sibley.

He began to keep precise records of circulation, including them in his annual reports to the President. He had studies made of book use by the students and in 1887, ten years after he had become Librarian, could report that nine out of ten students were using the library, in contrast to five out of ten in 1876. Winsor pioneered in that kind of statistical analysis in library administration.

Other notable accomplishments at Harvard included designing call slips to be filled out by borrowers, thus speeding up circulation; initiating instruction in library use; devising a compact metal stack storage plan for the collections; promoting more effective participation of the faculty in book selection; exchanging serials holdings lists with other libraries; and reorganizing the administrative structure of the library to delegate more responsibility to each staff member.

An early advocate of the employment of women in libraries, Winsor, at a conference in 1877, urged his British colleagues to train more women for library work. He stated that graduates of Vassar and Wellesley, skilled in languages, were finding challenging positions within the U.S. library system.

Winsor believed a university librarian should be both an administrator and a scholar, and his own career illustrated his philosophy. He continued to do historical research and to write and was considered a leading cartographer. While at Harvard he edited two important historical works: *The Memorial History of Boston* (four volumes, 1880–81) and *A Narrative and Critical History of America* (eight volumes, 1889). The more important of his own works include *Reader's Handbook of the American Revolution* (1879); *Christopher Columbus and How He Received and Imparted the Spirit of Discovery* (1891); *Cartier to Frontenac—Geographical Discovery in the Interior of North America in Its Historical Relations, 1534–1700* (1894); *The Mississippi Basin* (1895); and *The Westward Movement* (1897).

Always active in professional organizations, Winsor was one of the founders of the American Library Association and its first President, from 1876 to 1885, and President again in 1897, the year he died. He also helped found the *Library Journal*. Winsor foresaw a future in which librarians would be purveyors as well as preservers of knowledge, and his work in the profession was always directed toward that end.

Winsor died on October 22, 1897, at the age of 66.

**REFERENCES**


Joseph A. Borome, "The Life and Letters of Justin Winsor" (Ph.D. dissertation, Columbia University, 1950). The most complete study of Winsor available, it presents Winsor's life history, treating in some detail his library career, and contains an extensive bibliography of periodical articles by and about Winsor.

Kenneth J. Brough, *Scholar's Workshop: Evolving Conceptions of Library Service* (1953). Details the history of the four university libraries, covering the period of Winsor's tenure as Librarian at Harvard.

Walter Muir Whitehill, *Boston Public Library: A Centennial History* (1956). Contains a 29-page chapter dealing with the decade of Winsor's superintendency of the Library.


ROBERT E. BRUNDIN

ALA

*Justin Winsor*

# Yemen (Aden)

Yemen (Aden), a republic in the Arabian Peninsula (southwestern coastal area), is bounded by Yeman (Sana'a) on the west and northwest, Saudi Arabia on the north, Oman on the east, and the Gulf of Aden and the Arabian Sea on the south. Pop. (1977 est.) 1,797,000; area 287,680 sq.km. The official language is Arabic.

**National Library.** Although the People's Democratic Republic of Yemen does not possess a national library, a law of 1976 established the Yemeni Center for Cultural Research, which aims at offering some functions of a national library. Among the objectives of the Center are the collection and publication of the Yemeni national heritage; the gathering and preservation of manuscripts, documents, periodicals, and other materials relating to Yemeni culture and history; and administering a central library. The Center is organized into sections for manuscripts, microfilming, publishing, printing, museums, and the library. The Center's Library possesses about 2,000 volumes on Yemeni affairs. By the late 1970's there was no provision for legal deposit or a national bibliography.

**Academic Libraries.** The only academic libraries in Southern Yemen are those of Aden University, which has five college libraries and a central library in an early stage of development. The Central Library has a collection of about 2,000 volumes. The Library of the Higher College of Education, founded in 1970, possesses 15,000 volumes of which 10,000 are in Arabic. The new library of the College of Medicine, established in 1975, has 5,000 volumes, mostly in Spanish, a language not spoken in the country. The Library of the Higher Technical Institute, established in 1952, maintains a collection of some 10,000 volumes that are mostly duplicate copies. The Library of Nasser College for Agricultural Sciences, founded in 1972, possesses about 6,000 volumes. The Library of the College of Economics and Administration contains 2,000 volumes. All the academic libraries in Aden University are staffed by nonprofessional personnel. Most of the library holdings are not processed; its collections are not catalogued but only registered. The libraries have started recently to reclassify their collections according to the Dewey Decimal Classification.

**Public Libraries.** The public library system is not well developed enough to support the adult education campaign in the country. The Miswat Public Library in Aden and the People's Library at Al-Mukalla, Hadramawt, are the largest public libraries. The Miswat Public Library, with a collection of about 30,000 volumes, was established in 1953 and is administered by Aden Municipality. The People's Library of Hadramawt, established in 1930, is administered by the Ministry of Culture.

**School Libraries.** Although some secondary schools possess sizable collections of books, they are not well organized because of the lack of qualified school librarians in the country.

**Special Libraries.** There are no records available for the special libraries in Southern Yemen. But the Educational Research Center of the Ministry of Education has established a Section for Documentation and Libraries that collects and exchanges educational documents. The Teachers' Club has a library of over 2,000 volumes.

MOHAMED M. EL HADI

# Yemen (Sana'a)

Yemen (Sana'a), a republic in the Arabian Peninsula (southwest costal area), is surrounded by Yemen (Aden) on the south, Saudi Arabia on the north, and the Red Sea on the west. Pop. (1975 est.) 5,237,900; area 200,000 sq.km. The official language is Arabic.

**National Library.** The National Library in Sana'a was founded in 1968 with the establishment of the General Organization for Antiquities and National Library and is under the auspices of the presidency of the Yemen Arab Republic. All printed books that were found in the palaces of the deposed kingdom were transferred to this library, while the Arabic manuscripts remained in the Library of the Great Mosque in Sana'a. The country lacks a deposit law and a national bibliography; the publishing industry is almost nonexistent.

**Academic Library.** The only academic library is that of the Sana'a University, established in 1971 with financial aid from the Kuwaiti government. As of 1978 the Central Library and the college libraries of the University were being developed. A few recruited personnel from other Arab countries are directing and organizing the book collections in these libraries. The Dewey Decimal classification is in use.

**Public Libraries.** The General Organization of Antiquities and National Library is responsible for and supervises all public libraries in the country. The Library of the Great Mosque, founded by Iman Ahmed in 1925, was the first public library and was known as Al-Awqaf Library. After the Yemeni Revolution of 1962, the private library of Iman Yehia and all manuscripts in the libraries housed in the palaces of deposed Princes were transferred and preserved in the Library of the Great Mosque. The Library's manuscript collection totals about 10,000 volumes and is microfilmed by the Arab League with the aid of Unesco. Other public libraries are to be found in such major cities as Taiz, Hijah, and Al-Hudayduh.

**School Libraries.** Few secondary schools have book collections for their students. School librarianship has not yet developed because of the lack of adequate funding and professional library education.

**Special Libraries.** The Central Library of the Ministry of Education, the Library of the Central Planning Agency, founded in 1976, and the Library of the National Institute of Public Administration, founded in 1973, offer special library services to their employees and to all those interested in their collections.

MOHAMED M. EL HADI

# Young Adult Services

Since one of the main purposes of young adult services must be to enable young people to cross the bridge between children's library services and the adult library, these services must cater to some young people who begin to feel uneasy or dissatisfied with the service offered by the children's library at the age of 11 or 12 and to others who still need this support at the age of 17 or 18.

At some point between 11 and 18, young people move from childhood to adulthood. The physiological changes of puberty are accompanied by changes in attitudes, in interests, and in relations to others. Young people begin to question the opinions of their parents and teachers that they have hitherto taken for granted; they are likely to become more involved with the community and with society at large. Their interests, both intellectual and social, develop and widen. They have more freedom and more money to make use of that freedom. Their relationship to the adults in their lives changes as a consequence of all these things, but even more important in the case of most young adults is their growing awareness of sexuality and the development of special relationships. Both library needs and reading needs are likely to change in this period. Services to young adults must take account of these changes, as well as serve to encourage young people to go on using library services at a period when they might otherwise drift away from the library, perhaps because they feel they are too old for the children's library but at the same time are overwhelmed by the resources of the adult collection.

**Young Adult Fiction.** It is appropriate first to consider the literature that has been produced especially for young adults. The response of publishers to the request for novels for this group of readers has been great, particularly in the 1960's and 1970's, and has caused those librarians who might otherwise have questioned the need for young adult collections to establish them in order to exploit these books effectively.

Books read by the young have always shown young people growing to adulthood, but books by such authors as Julius Lester, S. E. Hinton, Judy Blume, and Paul Zindel are a far cry from the work of Louisa May Alcott, Susan Coolidge, and L. M. Montgomery. The United States may be said to be the home of the teenage novel; books by American authors are available in young adult libraries worldwide. An early "landmark" book, to which reference is frequently made, is Maureen Daly's *Seventeenth Summer* (1942), but M. Rankin, in research published in 1940, commented on the great popularity among girls in their early teens of Helen Dore Boylston's books about Sue Barton, which were first published in the 1930's and marked the first appearance of reasonably realistic career novels. These were a first attempt to provide young people with a fictional handbook to growing up; since then few relevant topics have escaped the attention of at least a handful of writers for young adults.

A young adult novel has certain basic characteristics. It usually tells a good story in an interesting way, and the central characters are likely to be adolescents with whom the reader can easily identify. The style must be straightforward, relying heavily on dialogue (unless the story is told, as is often the case, in the first person) but avoiding too much use of current teenage vocabulary, which may date very quickly. The author who tells the story in a way that involves the readers and helps them to identify with the problems and experiences of the central character is likely to be well received. As well as reading for enjoyment and entertainment, young adults use fiction to explore experiences that lie ahead and to come to terms with their own situations. The fiction, therefore, tends to reflect the problems and concerns of its readers; it is dominated by stories that deal with relationships between young adults, reflecting the development of interest in the opposite sex (since in the young adult novel little attention has so far been paid to the existence of homosexual relationships), and few books are without this interest, even if it is not central to the plot.

Beverly Cleary's *Fifteen* (1956) has remained one of the most popular titles, although it probably appeals at an earlier age than when it was first published; it still regularly finds a new audience as girls come across it at an appropriate moment in their development, able to identify with Jane Purdy's wish to appear grown-up and sophisticated but having to cope with the realities of life, such as parents who continue to regard her as a child and finding a boyfriend. A comparison of this book with Paul Zindel's *My Darling, My Hamburger* (1969) and the much discussed *Forever* by Judy Blume (1975) shows just how much young adult fiction has changed in the intervening period.

Writers for young adults also deal with such relevant themes as the search for identity (John Rowe Townsend's *The Intruder*), relationships between the young and the old (Paul Zindel's *The Pigman*), drugs (S. E. Hinton's *That Was Then, This Is Now*), homosexuality (John Donovan's *I'll Get There, It Better Be Worth the Trip*), and race

*Above, ninth-grade students prepare social studies report using microfilmed resources from school library media center.*
*Middle, Irving (Texas) Public librarian helps student use a periodical index.*
*Below, as a student videotapes, a parent volunteer at West Frederick Junior High (Maryland) leads a book talk to motivate students.*

(Kristin Hunter's *The Soul Brothers and Sister Lou* and Julius Lester's *Basketball Game*). These are good examples of books in which the "problem" is absorbed naturally into the story; there are others, less satisfactory, that give the impression that the author chose the problem first and then set about writing the story around it.

**Collections.** In any young adult collection, the specially published young adult fiction is likely to predominate. Depending on the amount of space allocated to it and the local conception of its purpose and use, it may also duplicate fiction titles held in the children's collection, but almost certainly, it should include adult titles such as J. D. Salinger's *Catcher in the Rye,* Harper Lee's *To Kill a Mockingbird,* or Jack Schaeffer's *Shane.* Too much reliance should not, however, be placed on the well-tried classics.

The young adult collection normally includes magazines and posters, tapes and records of music (e.g., rock), and other media of types that appeal mainly to this age group. It also includes nonfiction materials on topics of special interest to and reflecting the special needs of young adults. Materials on sex education, biography—particularly relating to such personal experiences as love, death and dying, or adolescence, sports, and other relevant topics—are appropriate components of the nonfiction collection. (It is considered wasteful to duplicate material available elsewhere in the library in order to cater to students doing school assignments. If young people have found their way to the public library in search of materials for this purpose, then use can be made of their motivation to introduce them to the whole range of public library resources.) What does have a special place in the young adult collection is ephemeral material (pamphlets, newspaper cuttings, periodical articles) on such topics as the civil rights movement, youth rights, sexuality, consumer education, the environment, the occult, women's rights, and black studies. These topics are often inadequately covered by books, and in any case the information provided needs to be up-to-date and immediately relevant.

In developing the selection policy for the young adult collection, consideration is given to encouraging reluctant readers by providing materials that look attractive and for catering to poor or unskilled readers by having plenty of material of high interest, low reading level. For most young adults, the paperback format has a special appeal. The establishment of a young adult collection in itself solves one of the problems likely to face the selector, since it automatically reserves as separate from a children's collection those books likely to meet with parental criticism on account of their themes or vocabulary, for the use of older children or early adolescents. Selection is complicated, however, by the fact that publishers do not have separate young adult departments. Little nonfiction of quality is written directly for YA's, so selections must be made from publishers' children's or adults' catalogues.

What physical form does young adult service take within the public library? In some cases there is a collection of relevant materials in the children's library or in the adult library; elsewhere there is a special young adult collection between the two. In some otherwise open-plan libraries it is not unusual to find an enclosed young adult area, since one of the special attractions for this age group is a place where they can meet friends and talk and perhaps have music playing in the background. In the clearly defined or enclosed young adult library, some are decorated with appropriate posters or artwork, where the patrons are encouraged to participate in displays, and have a bulletin board advertising events and services of interest to them. The young adult collection is a positive way of bringing together young people and those materials that have a proven appeal for them. Some of the group, however, may well resent being expected to use a special section of the library and will prefer to move from the children's library straight to the adult library.

The specialist study needs of many young adults are ordinarily met by their school library, where the materials are selected according to the teaching program of the school and the interests and abilities of the student body.

**Staff.** The public library staff must often take the initiative in making contact with other institutions that serve young adults, and this is particularly true in the case of youth organizations and other groups that may find it useful to borrow collections of materials to support special activities or projects or would like to send groups of young people to visit the library or would welcome a visit from the librarian but are not aware that such things are possible. Appropriate agencies differ from one community to another, but drug centers, runaway centers, juvenile detention facilities, and others may welcome such contacts.

An effective young adult program usually involves the special appointment of a young adult librarian. Too often such a program is seen merely as an extra job for the children's librarian or as one responsibility of the librarians working with adults. Many library schools offer special courses in young adult literature and/or library services, but astute employers also look for the right kind of personality. Responsibility for service to young adults requires sympathy with young people, an outgoing personality, ability to communicate well, and an understanding of young adults' developmental needs. Most public library staff, however, are involved in helping or serving young adults and therefore share the need for in-service training in the special needs of young adults. Some librarians are rather frightened of young adults, especially when they appear in the library in groups. An understanding that their apparent boisterousness, sudden movements, and loud voices are due to their period of growth may lessen the fears of those who have forgotten or choose to ignore their own period of teenage turbulence. Staff working in reference collections have found it helpful to meet with teachers from time to time so that they gain a better understanding of the demands likely to be made by students in search of materials for assignments.

**Publicity.** The young adult service thrives on good publicity material, which is designed, worded, and illustrated to reflect young adult culture. Audiovisual programs designed to be taken out to advertise the public library in places where young people gather are increasingly market tested to ensure that they are hitting the right target and that intentional humor is humorous to the intended audience. Imaginative booklists relating to appropriate topics or listing relevant and lively recreational reading are quite common.

**Activities.** Activity programs depend on facilities and the local conception of what libraries are about. Some libraries feature talks either by authors or by people who have expertise in subjects of interest to young adults, including book talks by library staff, films, poetry readings, and music sessions. Some young adults are interested in hearing authors talk about their craft or how to get published, but more are likely to be involved if the author writes about a subject of current concern. Young adults who are "hooked" on books and libraries tend to make use of the full range of library services as their needs dictate. Others seem to need a young adult program that involves a break from traditional library patterns and a less rigid approach to what is suitable library material or an appropriate library function.

**REFERENCES**

Melvyn Barnes and Sheila G. Ray, *Youth Library Work: Exploratory Essays,* 2nd ed. (1976).

Robert G. Carlsen, *Books and the Teenage Reader: A Guide for Teachers, Librarians and Parents,* rev. ed. (1972).

Mary Kingsbury, "Ostriches and Adolescents," *Journal of Education for Librarianship* (1971).

Margaret Marshall, *Libraries and Literature for Teenagers* (1975).

*Top of the News,* quarterly journal of the Association for Library Service to Children and the Young Adult Services Division of ALA, regularly contains articles on materials and services for young adults.

SHEILA G. RAY

## Yuan T'ung-li

(1895–1965)

Yuan T'ung-li, Chinese librarian, educator, and library administrator, was a pioneer in the modern library movement and was an exponent of closer cultural ties between East and West. He proposed large-scale exchange programs not only for librarians but also for students.

Yuan T'ung-li was born in 1895, the second son of a government official in Hsushui, Chihli (Hopei), China. At an early age Yuan showed an avid interest in books and scholarship. He graduated from National Peking University in 1916 and immediately began work as Assistant Librarian at Tsinghua College. He became Acting Librarian the following year, in which position he was largely responsible for construction of the College's new library building.

In 1920 Yuan went to the United States for advanced studies; he received the A.B. degree from Columbia University in 1922 and the B.L.S. degree in 1923 from New York State Library School in Albany. He also spent a year doing postgraduate work at the University of London's Institute of Historical Research. During this period he spent three summers at the Library of Congress helping to catalogue its Chinese collections. In 1924 he returned to China to become Librarian of Kwangtung University. He became Librarian and Professor of Bibliography at Peking University in 1925, and when the Peking National Library was organized in 1926, he became its Librarian, with Liang Ch'i-ch'ao as Director. In 1929 the Metropolitan Library and the old National Library were merged to form the National Library of Peiping, and Ts'ai Yuan-p'ei was made its Director, with Yuan as Associate Director. Later Yuan served successively as Acting Director and Director, helping to build it into the largest library in China and one of the largest in the world.

Many library activities in China were disrupted by the Sino-Japanese War, and in 1942 Yuan T'ung-li moved to China's wartime capital, Chungking, where he set up an office of the National Library of Peiping. There he also engaged in numerous cultural cooperation projects on behalf of the Chinese government with Great Britain and the United States. In 1945 he was an adviser to the Chinese delegation to the United Nations Conference on International Organization in San Francisco, and in May of that year he received an honorary degree from the University of Pittsburgh.

During the 1920's and 1930's he was credited with the discovery of rare works and manuscripts of Chinese literature, including the remains of a vast encyclopedia from the Ming Dynasty (the *Yung lo ta tien*), long thought to have been destroyed, but of which he compiled successive censuses of surviving extant volumes. Among his most important contributions to the library profession was his introduction to China of such Western practices as interlibrary loan, a photostat service, exchange of materials with foreign countries, and the compilation of union catalogues and serial lists.

In 1949 Yuan went to the United States, and from 1951 to 1953 he served as Chief Bibliographer of Stanford Research Institute. He rejoined the Library of Congress in 1957 in the Descriptive Cataloging Division and served in the Subject Cataloging Division from 1958 to the time of his retirement on January 15, 1965. His service with the Library of Congress totaled 8½ years but spanned more than 43 years. He died on February 6, 1965.

Among his more significant publications are *China in Western Literature* (1958), *Russian Works on China, 1918–1960, in American Libraries* (1961), and various guides to doctoral dissertations by Chinese students.

CHI WANG

## Yugoslavia

Yugoslavia, a socialist federal republic in eastern Europe, is bordered by Austria and Hungary on the north, Romania on the northeast, Bulgaria on the east, Greece on the south, Albania on the Adriatic Sea on the southwest, and Italy on the west. Pop. (1978 est.) 21,912,000; area 255,804 sq.km. The official languages are Serbo-Croatian, Slovenian, and Macedonian.

**National Libraries.** The Socialist Federal Republic of Yugoslavia consists of six republics and two autonomous provinces. Each republic and province has its national library. These are: SR Serbia, the National Library of Serbia; AP Vojvodina, the Library of Matica Srpska; AP Kosovo, the National and University Library of Kosovo; SR Slovenia, the National and University Library; SR Bosnia and Hercegovina, the National and University Library of Bosnia and Hercegovina; SR Croatia, the National and University Library, Zagreb; SR Montenegro, the Central National Library "Djordje Crnojević," Cetinje; and SR Macedonia, the National and University Library Kliment Ohridski. All national libraries of republics and provinces build up their collections by legal deposits of all published works throughout the whole country. National libraries of each republic and province take special care about the completeness of issues from their own territory as well as about materials referring to their territory that are found in libraries of other republics and abroad. National libraries also purchase the most outstanding works of world literature and sources in all branches of science.

The Yugoslav Bibliographical Institute develops the Bibliography of Yugoslavia: The Bibliography of Yugoslavia (from 1950), books, pamphlets and music; The Bibliography of Yugoslavia (from 1956), serial publications; The Bibliography of Yugoslavia (from 1950), Series A, articles from the social sciences, Series B, natural, applied, medical, and technical sciences, Series C. arts, philology and literature. The national libraries of all republics and provinces deal with bibliography, producing mainly national retrospective bibliographies. The National and University Library in Ljubljana, SR Slovenia, issues the "Slovenian Bibliography of Journals and Books." Also, the National and University Library in Zagreb (SR Croatia) maintains its national bibliography as well as the National and University Library Kliment Ohridski in Skopje (SR Macedonia).

**Academic Libraries.** National libraries are at the same time central university libraries except in Serbia, Vojvodina, and Montenegro. In all republics and provinces are large numbers of academic libraries—central faculty libraries, seminar libraries, and libraries at research institutions with extensive book holdings of domestic and foreign scientific literature. General scientific libraries that should be mentioned include those under the scope of republican academies of sciences such as the Library of the Serbian Academy of Sciences and Arts in Belgrade, Library of the Yugoslav Academy of Sciences and Arts in Zagreb, Library of the Academy of Sciences and Arts of SR Slovenia in Ljubljana, Library of the Macedonian Academy of Sciences and Arts in Skopje, Library of the Association of Science and Arts of SR Montenegro in Titograd, and Library of the Academy of Sciences and Arts of SR Bosnia and Hercegovina in Sarajevo. These libraries collect publications issued by academies of sciences, universities, and scientific and professional associations all over the world.

**Libraries in Yugoslavia (1976)**

| Type | Number | Volumes in collections | Annual expenditures (dinar) | Population served | Professional staff | All staff (total) |
|---|---|---|---|---|---|---|
| National | 8 | 4,873,691 | N.A. | 935,852 | N.A. | N.A. |
| Academic | 435 | 10,835,461 | N.A. | 3,044,186 | 2,079 | 3,074 |
| Special | 983 | 9,160,253 | N.A. | 1,609,759 | N.A. | N.A. |
| Public | 1,826 | 17,263,421 | N.A. | 22,349,393 | 2,252 | 3,552 |
| School | 9,982 | 24,004,000 | N.A. | 4,127,768 | N.A. | N.A. |

Source: *Statistical Bulletin of the Yugoslav Federal Institute of Statistics* (1976).

**Public Libraries.** Public libraries provide the basic library service in the area that they serve; i.e., in regions, communities, and local communities. These libraries provide at the same time the institutional support for educational and cultural activities. An organized network of public libraries makes books available to all living in an area.

In Yugoslavia there were 444 community public libraries with 3,482 smaller libraries in local communities and settlements (1976). Their stocks consisted of 15,950,436 books, 170,931 volumes of journals, and 66,224 volumes of newspapers.

**School Libraries.** School libraries on all levels of education provide educational-instructional services together with teaching programs. They represent one of the essential factors in formation of a complete personality of the citizen. In Yugoslavia there were 9,982 school libraries with about 24,004,000 books in the latter 1970's.

**Special Libraries.** These libraries are attached to industrial, social, scientific, and cultural institutions, agencies, and other organizations. In Yugoslavia there were in the latter 1970's more than 1,500 special, university, and scientific libraries collecting scientific and technical literature from all branches of science.

**Associations.** Librarians from all republic and provincial libraries are through their associations the members of the League of the Librarians Association of Yugoslavia. The seat of the League is changed every two years. National libraries of all republics and provinces together with the Yugoslav Bibliographical Institute are associated in the League of Yugoslav National Libraries. The seat is changed every two years also. In the Association are joined forces active in establishing a library-information network at the Yugoslav level. National libraries provide a complete coverage of the network in their territory. In building the network, consideration is given to recommendations of international organizations of which Yugoslavia is a member-country (Unesco, ISO, IFLA, FID, and others), and they are modified according to the Yugoslav social, economical, cultural, and other local conditions. The National Library of Serbia, for instance, from 1974 maintained a computerized union catalogue of foreign periodicals in the libraries of Serbia.

INES WESLEY-TANASKOVIC

# Zaire

Zaire, a republic of equatorial Africa (formerly the Democratic Republic of the Congo, which was a Belgian colony until 1960), is bordered on the east by Uganda, Rwanda, Burundi, and Tanzania, on the west by the Congo, the Cabinda enclave of Angola, and the Atlantic Ocean, on the north by the Central African Republic and the Sudan, on the south by Angola, and on the southeast by Zambia. Pop. (1978 est.) 26,478,000; area 2,344,885 sq.km. Although the official language is French, four national languages are recognized: Swahili, Tshiluba, Lingala, and Kikongo. More than 200 Pygmy, Bantu, and Nilo-Saharan languages and dialects are spoken throughout the country.

**National Library.** The Bibliothèque centrale du Congo, founded in 1949, became the Bibliothèque Nationale after independence in 1960. The national library, in Kinshasa-Gombe, is both a governmental library and a public library. Works published in or about Zaire are required by law to be deposited there. In addition, as of February 1950, two copies of all government publications had to be deposited. Although government publications comprise a large share of the total number of volumes, the library also has an important Africana collection and extensive holdings in economics, social sciences, and law. Because of continued fighting in the area, many libraries have lost much of their stock. Up-to-date statistics were not available for the national library at the end of the 1970's. The Archives Nationales, a section connected to the national library, attempts to acquire all administrative and historical archives relating to Zaire. In 1955 the library began a monthly accessions list, which later became the *Bibliographie nationale.* The library also issued a retrospective national bibliography of its acquisitions that had been published between 1871 and 1960. Efforts had been under way to establish a union catalogue of all of the libraries of Zaire, but the political turmoil curtailed such library activities. Book publishing in Zaire is limited; in both 1976 and 1977 the Presses universitaires du Zaire et l'office du livre (PUZ) in Kinshasa listed 30 titles. About 11 other publishers were in operation at that time.

**Academic Libraries.** In 1971 the three universities of Zaire were incorporated into the Université Nationale du Zaire (UNAZA): the Université Lovanium in Kinshasa, founded in 1949; the Université libre du Congo in Kisangani (1963); and the Université officielle du Congo in Lubumbashi (1956). Each campus has a central library; those at Kinshasa and Lubumbashi also have many departmental libraries. The library at Kisangani has, in addition to its central library, two faculty libraries of Science and Education. The Bibliothèque centrale, Kinshasa, holds approximately 280,000 volumes; the Bibliothèque centrale, Kisangani, 7,000 volumes; and the Bibliothèque centrale, Lubumbashi, 35,000 volumes. Holdings are primarily in French, with a considerably smaller number of volumes in English and in African and Arabic languages. The numerous departmental libraries are of varying size and are all catalogued at the central libraries. Interlibrary loans are available among the university libraries, research centers, and specialized libraries.

**Public Libraries.** There is no centralized public library system in Zaire. Individual public libraries throughout the provinces are administered through the local offices of the Ministry of Fine Arts and Cultural Affairs, which is actually a division of the Bibliothèque Nationale. Most of these libraries are subscription libraries, which require a fee for use of the library. Holdings are very limited and, for the most part, are not widely used. The illiteracy rate is high, and programs to promote reading are needed. In the late 1970's the public system consisted of 71 libraries, including the Bibliothèque Nationale, 7 academic libraries, and a library at the Prison centrale de Makala in Kinshasha. A list of public libraries was published by Ministry: *Liste des bibliothèques publiques* (1971). The size of the country and limited communication systems, as well as political unrest, worked against the establishment of effective public library service.

Most schools in Zaire have been established through the missions, particularly the Catholic missions. Statistical and detailed information concerning existing libraries for school students was not available in the late 1970's.

**Special Libraries.** Most special libraries were established prior to independence in 1960. Many of the governmental ministries have their own libraries, with collections of works on Africa and on Zaire in particular. These libraries are especially important to researchers, as are those attached to major research centers, such as the Institut national pour l'étude et la recherche agronomique (INERA) at Yangambi, founded in 1933. The library's holdings consist of approximately 44,000 technical and scientific volumes, plus about 3,000 maps and photographs. That library serves the agriculture department at the Kisangani campus. The Institut maintains several regional libraries. Also of importance are the libraries of the Institut de recherche scientifique (IRS) in Kinshasa, Lubumbashi, and Lwiro. The Institut's findings are published in its *Revue de recherche scientifique*. The Library, Documentation, and Publications section of the Institut Makanda Kabobi (IMK), established in 1974 in Kinshasa, houses approximately 10,000 volumes and has extensive newspaper clippings that relate to the institute's work. The IMK was founded to train executive personnel, but its library is open to the public. Its collection is particularly strong in the humanities. Many of the institutes connected with the universities have extensive libraries. The central library of the Institut pédagogique national (IPN), founded in Kinshasa in 1961, houses approximately 20,600 volumes and 369 periodicals, primarily in French and English. The Instituts supérieurs pédagogiques (ISP) have libraries in at least ten provinces, many of which were established in the late 1960's. In addition, numerous libraries are affiliated with private companies, independent research institutes, and cultural centers of embassies and consulates.

**Association.** The Zairian Association of Archivists, Librarians, and Documentalists was established in Kinshasa on October 5, 1968. Its purpose is to promote library and documentation centers throughout the country and to establish technology and information science centers in Zaire. It is affiliated with the IFLA, AIDBA, and the FID. Meetings are held every three years. The Association publishes an official journal, *Mukanda: Bulletin des archives, bibliothèques et documentation du Zaire* (1975– ) and issues proceedings of seminars and conferences.

STAFF

## Zambia

Zambia (formerly Northern Rhodesia), a republic in south central Africa, is bounded on the west by Angola, on the northwest by Zaire, on the northeast by Tanzania, on the east by Malawi, on the southeast by Mozambique, and on the south by Rhodesia, Botswana, and Namibia. Pop. (1978 est.) 5,514,000; area 752,614 sq.km. Many Bantu languages are spoken. Four major languages are Tonga, Bemba, Nyanja, and Lozi. The language of the administration is English.

**National Reference Library.** Zambia does not have a national library, although the library of the University of Zambia (UNZA) in Lusaka, founded in 1965, functions as a national reference library. The university library has not established rights to legal deposit; the Special Collections division, however, serves as a depository for governmental and international publications. The library's holdings in the late 1970's consisted of more than 300,000 volumes, 4,000 periodicals, and an extensive collection of UN documents and of governmental publications of countries of east, central, and southern Africa. Ninety percent of all holdings are in English.

The National Archives Library in Lusaka, founded in 1947, is a legal deposit library. A copy of every book, newspaper, or periodical published in Zambia is deposited there. It is also a lending library. Its collection consists of 12,000 volumes and approximately 1,000 periodicals, newspapers, and reports.

The National Archives is responsible for compilation of the annual *National Bibliography of Zambia*, which covers books, pamphlets, official publications, and first issues of new serials. The National Archives also publishes the *Calendars of the Districts Notebooks* and conducts an international exchange system.

Zambia does not have a union catalogue, although work was begun on such a project. In 1979 the cards of the University of Zambia library were given to the Zambia Library Service headquarters for that purpose.

Publishing is in its infancy in Zambia. In the early 1970's approximately 70 titles were published annually.

**Academic Libraries.** The University of Zambia is the only university; a Ndola campus of the university was established at the Zambia Institute of Technology (ZIT) campus in Kitwe. The ZIT library, founded in 1970, houses 20,000 volumes and 150 periodicals. There are also a few college libraries. The Evelyn Hone College of Applied Arts and Commerce, established in Lusaka in 1963, holds 16,000 volumes and 300 periodicals. Also in Lusaka is the Natural Resources Development College, founded in 1964, which holds approximately 15,000 volumes and 220 periodicals. The Northern Technical College, established in Ndola in 1964, houses about 11,000 volumes and 105 periodicals, as well as some films, maps, British Standards, and BS codes of practice.

One of the finest general educational libraries in Zambia is that of the Hammarskjöld Memorial Library in Kitwe, built by the churches of Sweden in 1963 as a memorial to the late Secretary General of the UN Dag Hammarskjöld (whose plane had crashed there in 1961). The Library is at the Mindolo Ecumenical Foundation, the largest lay training center in Africa; it holds almost 20,000 volumes, including 700 in French, and about 200 current periodicals. The Library serves the general public and elementary and secondary school students, as well as journalism students of the African Literature Center, students from the YWCA, the Kitwe Teachers' Training College, the Kitwe Police Training Camp, the Central Hospital Nurse Training program, Barclay Bank staff, the United Church of Zambia Ministerial Training College, and students taking courses through the Extramural Department of the University of Zambia.

**Public Libraries.** There is no single authority responsible for library service in Zambia. The Zambia Library Service (ZLS) under the Ministry of Education was founded in 1962 as the Northern Rhodesia Library Service through a grant from the Ford Foundation. It provides nationwide, although limited, lending service. The Zambia Library Service serves rural areas through mobile libraries and maintains 904 library centers, 6 regional libraries, 3 branch libraries, and a central library. Its total holdings consist of nearly 400,000 volumes, 90 percent in English and 10 percent in African languages. Periodicals, Reference, and Zambiana sections have been established. Library centers throughout the provinces are usually in primary schools, but some are in community development centers, one in a hospital, one in a prison, and another in a village shop. Some centers operate adult literacy programs. Rural library centers usually have small collections of 100 to 250 books.

Public libraries in urban areas are under local governmental authorities. These include the Kitwe Public Library (22,000 volumes), the Lusaka City Library (70,000 volumes), and the Ndola Public Library (50,000 volumes).

**School Libraries.** The library centers operated by the Zambia Library Service provide library services to elementary and secondary schools. The importance of library service for adult new-literates, as well as for students, was recognized by the Ministry of Education in proposals for the development of a national educational system.

**Special Libraries.** The NCCM/RCM (Nchanga Consolidated Copper Mines/Roan Consolidated Mines) copper mining companies at Kitwe have fine technical libraries, which hold more than 600 current scientific and technical periodicals. In addition, the NCCM/RCM Technical Library Service publishes a monthly *Survey of Technical Literature* for the copper industry—approximately 300 abstracts per month. There are other smaller mining libraries in the Copperbelt that are operated by mine township management boards.

The National Documentation and Scientific Information Center (NDSIC) of the National Council for Scientific Research was established in 1969. It currently holds 4,150 volumes and 350 periodicals and publishes the quarterly *Zambia Journal of Science and Technology*.

The Bank of Zambia Library houses approximately 2,000 volumes, mainly books on economics and related subjects, periodicals from banks and international financial institutions, such as the World Bank, and reports of governmental agencies and ministerial bodies.

The United National Independence Party Library, at Freedom House in Lusaka, holds 4,000 volumes and more than 100 current periodicals, primarily in the social sciences. The Party Archives holds public documents concerning party and governmental policies.

The ZBS Record and Reference Library holds a 75,000-disc collection and approximately 2,000 archival tapes. About 25 percent of this collection is Zambian. The reference section of the Library has mainly books on broadcasting and television engineering. There is also a Television Zambia Film Library (known as the TVZ Film Library), which circulates local documentaries as well as foreign films.

There are also British Council libraries at Lusaka (6,000 volumes) and at Ndola (11,800 volumes).

**Associations.** The Zambia Library Association (ZLA) was established in 1967 at the headquarters of the Zambia Library Service in Lusaka to improve training programs for librarians and to further the development of libraries throughout the country. Membership is open to all individuals and institutions interested in their aims. The *Zambia Library Association Journal* was issued quarterly from 1968. Its quarterly schedule was changed to biannual in 1979 (June and December). The bimonthly *Zambia Library Association Newsletter* was inaugurated in April 1979.

**REFERENCE**

H. C. Woakes, *Directory of Libraries in Zambia* (Lusaka, 1975).

STAFF

## Zimbabwe Rhodesia

Zimbabwe Rhodesia, a republic in southwestern Africa, is bordered by Zambia on the north, Mozambique on the northeast and east, South Africa on the south, and Botswana on the southwest and west. Pop. (1978 est.) 6,930,000; area 390,272 sq.km. The official language is English.

**National Libraries.** The Library of the National Archives, founded in the capital of Salisbury in 1935 as a department of the Central African Archives, is the principal legal deposit library, the foremost center for research on South Central Africa and its history, and the chief bibliographical services center. Its collections, which comprise all works published in Zimbabwe Rhodesia, works by Zimbabwe/Rhodesian authors, and works on Zimbabwe Rhodesia published elsewhere with wide coverage of southern, central, and eastern African subjects, totaled 26,250 monographs, 22,500 audiovisual materials, and 4,700 current serials in 1976. The Library publishes the *Zimbabwe Rhodesia National Bibliography,* maintains a *Directory of Zimbabwe Rhodesian Libraries,* and administers the allocation of international standard book numbers.

The national lending library and national center for interlibrary loans is the National Free Library Service, founded at Bulawayo in 1944. It maintained the Rhodesian union catalogue of books between 1956 and 1972 and coordinates the incorporation of the record of Zimbabwe/Rhodesian library holdings in more recent southern African union catalogues published on microfiche. Collections that in 1976–77 totaled 64,000 monographs, 15,000 bulletins and specifications, and 500 current periodicals supplement the public library service in academic, scientific, technical, and cultural books and information. There were plans to make it the headquarters of a national public library service as of the late 1970's.

Both libraries served the area of the Federation of Rhodesia and Nyasaland (1953–63) before and during Federation.

**Academic Libraries.** The principal academic library is at the University of Rhodesia (founded in 1957 as the library of the University College of Rhodesia and Nyasaland and to be known as the University of Zimbabwe or the University of Zimbabwe Rhodesia). The library quickly developed into the largest library in the country, lending generously from its stock through interlibrary loans. Its collections, comprising a main library and law, medical, education, and map libraries, totaled 250,000 volumes and 4,000 current periodicals in 1976. There are special collections on Rhodesiana and African languages.

**Public Libraries.** Public subscription libraries were established within a few years of the commencement of British South Africa Company rule (1890). The first major public library was established at Bulawayo in 1896 with a gift of books from Cecil John Rhodes, and the Queen Victoria Memorial Library was founded at Salisbury in 1902. Similar but smaller libraries, operating as private, grant-aided subscription libraries, were set up wherever there was a settled literate population. Financial assistance, which was never sufficient to permit their transformation into free public libraries, came primarily from local authorities in the two major cities and from the government in smaller centers. Municipal libraries requiring only a token annual subscription were set up in the African suburbs of major cities and towns from 1959, commencing with Bulawayo. Complexes of suburban branch libraries were limited almost entirely to Salisbury and Bulawayo.

Moves sponsored by the Carnegie Corporation of New York to foster a free public library system failed in 1929 for want of finance, although the pattern of uncoordinated and mainly small subscription libraries was improved by the establishment, with Corporation aid, of the National Free Library Service in 1944. A specially appointed Rhodesia Library Commission reported in 1971 serious deficiencies in the public library system, recommended the establishment of a National Library Council, and proposed a nationwide free public library system comprising municipal libraries for Salisbury and Bulawayo and a coordinated national public library service in all other areas with headquarters at the National Free Library Service. The first steps to implement the report were adopted by the government in 1975.

**School Libraries.** There is no coordinated system of school libraries. School library services are almost entirely limited to secondary schools and left to local initiative drawing on grants from the Ministry of Education, with the result that quality varies considerably. Part-time

**Table 1. Libraries in Zimbabwe Rhodesia (1976)**

| Type | Number | Volumes in collections | Annual expenditures (dollars) | Population served | Professional staff | All staff (total) |
|---|---|---|---|---|---|---|
| National | 2 | 92,000 | Rh.$122,000 | 6,310,000 | 8 | 16 |
| University | N.A. | N.A. | Rh.$350,000 | N.A. | 17 | 56 |
| Public | 70 | 500,000 | Rh.$300,000 | N.A. | N.A. | N.A. |

Sources: Library annual reports, libraries, and Directory of Rhodesian Libraries.

library assistants are employed at the majority of high schools.

**Special Libraries.** Most special libraries are in government departments and statutory (parastatal) bodies, which are coordinated by the Government Library Service based at the National Archives. Foremost is the Library of Parliament, Salisbury, founded in 1897 as the library of the Legislative Council, which is used by senators, members of Parliament, civil servants, and university lecturers. Its collections totaled 85,000 volumes and 500 current periodicals in 1976–77. Notable libraries of international standing are those of the National Museums and Monuments of Rhodesia and the Tobacco Research Board.

**Table 2. Archives in Zimbabwe Rhodesia (1976)**

| | |
|---|---|
| Number | N.A. |
| Holdings | 2,500 cubic meters |
| Annual expenditures | Rh.$93,000 |
| Professional staff | 10 |
| All staff (total) | 40 |

Source: National Archives.

**Association.** The Zimbabwe Rhodesia Library Association was founded in 1959 as the Library Association of Rhodesia and Nyasaland. It publishes the *Zimbabwe Librarian,* and its membership in 1976 was 111 institutional and 83 personal members.

**REFERENCES**

Norman Johnson, "Library Development in Rhodesia," *Give the People Light: Essays in Honour of Matthew Miller Stirling* (1972).

Douglas Harold Varley, *Library Services in the Rhodesias and Nyasaland* (1951).

N. JOHNSON

*The National Free Library in Rhodesia was founded at Bulawayo in 1944.*

Robel Studios, Ltd.

Composed by The Clarinda Company and by the
University of Chicago Printing Department in
VIP Bembo with Perpetua display. Parallel Index
composed by J. and J. Graphics in Comp Edit
Megaron. Film made by J. and J. Graphics.
Printed on 60# Forest Book, Natural English Finish
paper by Chicago Press Corporation and bound
by Brock and Rankin.